MILITARY AIRCRAFT MARKINGS 2017

MILITARY AIRCRAFT MARKINGS 2017

Howard J Curtis

Crécy Publishing Ltd

This 38th edition published by Crécy Publishing Ltd 2017

ISBN 978 1 85780 377 8

Print managed in the UK by Jellyfish

Crecy Publishing Ltd
1a Ringway Trading Est
Shadowmoss Rd
Manchester
M22 5LH
Tel +44 (0)161 499 0024
www.crecy.co.uk

Front cover:
Lockheed Martin F-35 Lightning II
ZM137, seen here at the 2016
Farnborough Air Show.
(c) Air Team Images/Oleg Belyakov

CONTENTS

This 38th annual edition of *abc Military Aircraft Markings*, follows the pattern of previous years and lists in alphabetical and numerical order the aircraft that carry a United Kingdom military registration and which are normally based, or might be seen, in the UK. It also includes airworthy and current RAF/RN/Army aircraft that are based permanently or temporarily overseas. Aircraft used as targets on MoD ranges to which access is restricted, and UK military aircraft that have been permanently grounded overseas and unlikely to return to Britain have generally been omitted.

Aircraft in UK military service which carry civil registrations are listed, as are historic aircraft wearing overseas markings which are based in the UK or likely to be seen in the UK. All aircraft carrying Irish military markings are listed in a separate section. Similarly, aircraft belonging to the armed forces or governments of foreign countries are listed, including American military aircraft based in the UK and Europe.

In the main, the registrations listed are those markings presently displayed on the aircraft. Where an aircraft carries a false registration it is quoted in *italic type*. Very often these registrations are carried by replicas, which are denoted by <R> after the type. The manufacturer and aircraft type are given, together with recent alternative, previous, secondary or civil identity shown in round brackets. The operating unit and its based location, along with any known unit and code markings, in square brackets, are given as accurately as possible. Where aircraft carry special or commemorative markings, a $ indicates this. To help identification of RN bases and landing platforms on ships, a list of tail-letter codes with their appropriate name, helicopter code number, ship pennant number and type of vessel, is included; as is a helicopter code number/ship's tail-letter code grid cross-reference.

Up-to-date code changes, for example when aircraft move between units, might not be as printed here because of subsequent events, but code lists are regularly updated and uploaded to the 'Military Aircraft Markings' web site, www.militaryaircraftmarkings.co.uk, from which monthly UK updates can also be accessed. Airframes which will not appear in the next edition because of sale, accident, etc., have their fates, where known, shown in italic type in the *locations* column.

Following the significant changes made to the 2016 edition, in this publication it is now possible to include fates for all aircraft listed and so the 38th edition includes details of, for example, American aircraft going to storage at AMARG at Davis-Monthan Air Force Base. Additionally, the extra space has enabled the inclusion of previous identities and these will be extended across the whole publication where space permits.

2016 saw yet more change in UK military aviation. As regards front line aircraft, the Tornado fleet continues to slowly diminish, mainly through being reduced to produce at Leeming while the delivery of Typhoons continues with Tranche 3 aircraft now coming into service and indeed the first few early models being retired to storage. In early 2017 it was also decided to recode the whole Typhoon fleet using the 'last three' of the registration and, at the time of going to press, this process had only just started. The RAF's last Sea King was retired in the Falklands on 1st April 2016, preceded a few days before by the Navy saying goodbye to its Sea King HC4 fleet and indeed 848 NAS in the process. Search and Rescue operations with the Navy came to an end also when 771 NAS decommissioned at Culdrose on 23 March. This now leaves the Sea King ASaC7 as the only remaining variant of the type still in service. While SAR operations around the UK are now fully in the hands of civilian contractors, at least there was good news for the Navy in that the first Merlin HC4 took to the skies on 21 November 2016. The final Wildcats for the Army and Navy have been delivered, with the consequence that the Navy Lynx HMA8 fleet now numbers around half a dozen aircraft; with the Army the Gazelle AH1 also is becoming a rarity. On the subject of helicopters, Westlands became Leonardo-Finmeccanica in late April 2016, with the company to be retitled just Leonardo from 2017. As the year ends, the training fleet is beginning to change considerably with the first Juno and Jupiter helicopters now in the UK, the first two Grob Prefects having been delivered and Texan and Phenom serials allocated. Going the other way, the Tutor fleet is beginning to be reduced with 28 aircraft being sold to Finland and flying at Colerne ending. Perhaps the most major change is in the gliding fleets with a large number of Volunteer Gliding Schools closing and many of their aircraft being withdrawn – hopefully 2017 will see some of these aircraft repaired and back into the air.

For overseas air arms, similar changes took place with types such as the Bo.105 and Super Etendard retiring completely – both will be sadly missed on the UK air show circuit. The US Air Force continues to receive the C-130J Hercules II, replacing earlier models, and the Navy continues to increase its P-8A Poseidon fleet as the P-3 Orion joins the Air Force's discarded Hercules at AMARG.

In 2016 at least there was no horrendous air show accident to report and indeed while no fewer than six F-35s of various sorts were (at last) showing off their capabilities in UK skies in the summer, there was, perhaps a feeling of exciting times ahead.

You can find 'MAM' on Facebook at www.facebook.com/MilitaryAircraftMarkings.

ACKNOWLEDGEMENTS

The compiler wishes to thank the many people who have taken the trouble to send comments, additions, deletions and other useful information since the publication of the previous edition of Military Aircraft Markings. In particular the following individuals: Phil Adkin, Dean Bartram, Derek Bower, Peter Budden, John Chalmers, Glyn Coney, Martin Coombes, Ben Dunnell, Paul Emery, Graham Gaff, Lewis Gaylard, Hugh Gibson, Norman Hibberd, Peter R March, Doug MacDonald, Tony McCarthy, Stuart McDiarmid, Phil Merry, Mark Ray, Graeme Robertson, Lloyd P Robinson, Mark Rourke, Ben Sadler, Paul Saxby, Kev Slade, Bill Tattum, David Thompson, Mike Tighe, Bob Turner and Tony Wood.

The 2017 edition has also relied upon the printed publications and/or associated internet web-sites as follows: Aerodata Quantum+, 'Aeroplane' magazine, Airfields Yahoo! Group, 'Air Forces Monthly' magazine, BAEG Yahoo! Group, CAA G-INFO Web Site, Delta Reflex, Fighter Control, 'FlyPast' magazine, Joe Baugher's Home Page, Mildenhall and Lakenheath Movements Group (SMAS), Brian Pickering/'Military Aviation Review', Mil Spotters' Forum, NAMAR Yahoo! Group, Planebase NG, RAF Leeming Yahoo! Group, RAF Shawbury Yahoo! Group, 'Scramble' magazine, Souairport Yahoo! group, Tom McGhee/UK Serials Resource Centre, USMil Googlegroup, Mick Boulanger/Wolverhampton Aviation Group and 'Wrecks & Relics'.

Information shown is believed to be correct at 24 February 2017.

HJC February 2017

Note: The compiler will be pleased to receive comments, corrections and further information for inclusion in subsequent editions of *Military Aircraft Markings* and the monthly up-date of additions and amendments. Please send your information to Military Aircraft Markings, Crécy Publishing Ltd, 1a Ringway trading Estate, Shadowmoss Road, Manchester M22 5LH or by e-mail to admin@aviation-links.co.uk.

$	Aircraft in special markings
AAC	Army Air Corps
AACS	Airborne Air Control Squadron
AC	Air Cadets
ACCGS	Air Cadets Central Gliding School
ACCS	Airborne Command & Control Squadron
ACS	Air Control Squadron
ACW	Air Control Wing
ADF	Air Defence Force
AEF	Air Experience Flight
AESS	Air Engineering & Survival School
AEW	Airborne Early Warning
AFB	Air Force Base
AFD	Air Fleet Department
AFRC	Air Force Reserve Command
AG	Airlift Group
AGA	Academia General del Aire (General Air Academy)
AGS	Air Ground Surveillance
AK	Alaska
AL	Alabama
AMD-BA	Avions Marcel Dassault-Breguet Aviation
AMG	Aircraft Maintenance Group
AM&SU	Aircraft Maintenance & Storage Unit
AMW	Air Mobility Wing
ANG	Air National Guard
AR	Arkansas
ARS	Air Refueling Squadron
ARW	Air Refueling Wing
AS	Airlift Squadron/Air Squadron
ATC	Air Training Corps
ATCC	Air Traffic Control Centre
AVDEF	Aviation Defence Service
Avn	Aviation
AW	AgustaWestland/Airlift Wing/Armstrong Whitworth Aircraft
AWC	Air Warfare Centre
BAC	British Aircraft Corporation
BAe	British Aerospace
BAPC	British Aviation Preservation Council
BATUK	British Army Training Unit Kenya
BATUS	British Army Training Unit Suffield
BBMF	Battle of Britain Memorial Flight
BDRF	Battle Damage Repair Flight
BDRT	Battle Damage Repair Training
Be	Beech
Bf	Bayerische Flugzeugwerke
BG	Bomber Group
BGA	British Gliding & Soaring Association
bk	black (squadron colours and markings)
bl	blue (squadron colours and markings)
Blt	Bojová letka (attack squadron)
BP	Boulton & Paul/Boulton Paul
br	brown (squadron colours and markings)
BS	Bomber Squadron
B-V	Boeing-Vertol
BW	Bomber Wing
CA	California
CAARP	Co-operative des Ateliers Air de la Région Parisienne
CAC	Commonwealth Aircraft Corporation
CACG	Command and Control Group
CAE	Centro Addestramento Equipaggi (Crew Training Centre)
CASA	Construcciones Aeronautics SA
CATS	Cassidian Aviation Training Services
CC	County Council
CC Air	Competence Centre Air
CCF	Combined Cadet Force/Canadian Car & Foundry Company
CEAM	Centre d'Expertise Aérienne Militaire (Centre of Military Air Expertise)

CEMAST	Centre of Excellence in Engineering & Manufacturing Advanced Skills Training
CEPA	Centre d'Expérimentation Pratique de l'Aéronautique Navale
CFAMI	Centre de Formation Aérienne Militaire Initiale de Salon
CFIA	Centre de Formation Interarmées NH.90
CFS	Central Flying School
CGMF	Central Glider Maintenance Flight
CIEH	Centre d'Instruction des Equipages d'Hélicoptères
CHFMU	Commando Helicopter Force Maintenance Unit
CinC	Commander in Chief
CinCLANT	Commander in Chief Atlantic
CLV	Centrum Leteckeho Vycviku (Air Training Centre)
CMU	Central Maintenance Unit
Co	Company
CO	Colorado
COMALAT	Commandement de l'Aviation Légère de l'Armée de Terre
Comp	Composite with
CT	Connecticut
CV	Chance-Vought
D-BA	Daimler-Benz Aerospace
D-BD	Dassault-Breguet Dornier
D&G	Dumfries and Galloway
DCTT	Defence College of Technical Training
DE	Delaware
DE&S	Defence Equipment and Support
DEFTS	Defence Elementary Flying Training School
DEODS	Defence Explosives Ordnance Disposal School
Det	Detachment
DFTDC	Defence Fire Training and Development Centre
DGA	Délégation Générale de l'Armement
DH	de Havilland
DHC	de Havilland Canada
DHFS	Defence Helicopter Flying School
DMS	Defence Movements School
DS&TL	Defence Science & Technology Laboratory
DSAE	Defence School of Aeronautical Engineering
DSEME	Defence School of Electro-Mechanical Engineering
DSG	Defence Support Group
DSMarE	Defence School of Marine Engineering
Dvlt	Dopravná vrtuľníková letka (Helicopter Transport Squadron)
EA	Escadron Aérien (Air Squadron)
EAAT	Escadrille Avions de l'Armée de Terre
EAC	Ecole de l'Aviation de Chasse (Fighter Aviation School)
EALAT	Ecole de l'Aviation Légère de l'Armée de Terre
EAP	European Aircraft Project
EAT	Ecole de l'Aviation de Transport (Transport Aviation School)
EC	Escadre de Chasse (Fighter Wing)
E-CATS	EADS Cognac Aviation Training Services
ECG	Electronic Combat Group
ECM	Electronic Counter Measures
ECS	Electronic Countermeasures Squadron
EdC	Escadron de Convoyage
EDCA	Escadron de Détection et de Control Aéroportée (Airborne Detection & Control Sqn)
EE	English Electric/Escadrille Electronique
EEA	Escadron Electronique Aéroporté
EFA	Ecole Franco Allemande
EFTS	Elementary Flying Training School
EH	Escadron d'Helicoptères (Helicopter Flight)
EHADT	Escadrille Helicoptères de l'Armée de Terre
EHI	European Helicopter Industries
EKW	Eidgenössiches Konstruktionswerkstätte
el	Eskadra Lotnicza (Air Sqn)
EL	Escadre de Liaison (Liaison Wing)
elt	Eskadra Lotnictwa Taktycznego (Tactical Air Squadron)
eltr	Eskadra Lotnictwa Transportowego (Air Transport Squadron)
EMA	East Midlands Airport
EMB	Ecoles Militaires de Bourges

EMVO	Elementaire Militaire Vlieg Opleiding (Elementary Flying Training)
EoN	Elliot's of Newbury
EPAA	Ecole de Pilotage Elementaire de l'Armée de l'Air (Air Force Elementary Flying School)
EPNER	Ecole du Personnel Navigant d'Essais et de Reception
ER	Escadre de Reconnaissance (Reconnaissance Wing)
ERV	Escadron de Ravitaillement en Vol
ES	Escadrille de Servitude
ESAM	Ecole Supérieur d'Application du Matériel
Esc	Escuadron (Squadron)
Esk	Eskadrile/Eskadrille (Squadron)
Esq	Esquadra (Squadron)
ET	Escadre de Transport (Transport Squadron)
ETED	Escadron de Transformation des Equipages Mirage 2000D
ETO	Escadron de Transition Operationnelle
ETPS	Empire Test Pilots' School
ETR	Escadron de Tranformation Rafale
ETS	Engineering Training School/Escadron de Transport Stratégique
ETTL	Escadre de Transport Tactique et Logistique
EVAA	Ecole de Voltige de l'Armée de l'Air (French Air Force Aerobatics School)
FAA	Fleet Air Arm/Federal Aviation Administration
FBS	Flugbereitschaftstaffel (Flight Readiness Squadron)
FBW	Fly-by-wire
FC	Forskokcentralen (Flight Centre)
FE	Further Education
FETC	Fire and Emergency Training Centre
ff	Front fuselage
FG	Fighter Group
FH	Fairchild-Hiller
FI	Falkland Islands
FJWOEU	Fast Jet & Weapons Operational Evaluation Unit
FL	Florida
FLO	Forsvarets Logistikk Organisasjon (Defence Logistics Organisation)
FlSt	Fliegerstaffel (Flight Squadron)
Flt	Flight
FMA	Fabrica Militar de Aviones
FMV	Forsvarets Materielwerk
FS	Fighter Squadron
FTS	Flying Training School
FTW	Flying Training Wing
Fw	Focke Wulf
FW	Fighter Wing/FlugWerk/Foster Wickner
FY	Fiscal Year
GA	Georgia
GAF	Government Aircraft Factory
GAFFTC	German Air Force Flight Training Centre
GAL	General Aircraft Ltd
GAM	Groupe Aerien Mixte (Composite Air Group)
GAM/STAT	Groupement Aéromobile/Section Technique de l'Armée de Terre
gd	gold (squadron colours and markings)
GD	General Dynamics
GEA	Gruppo Efficienza Aeromobili (Italian AF)/Gruppo Esplorazione Aeromarittima (GdiF)
GEM	Grupo de Escuelas de Matacán (Matacán Group of Schools)
GI	Ground Instruction/Groupement d'Instruction (Instructional Group)
gn	green (squadron colours and markings)
GRD	Gruppe fur Rustunggdienste (Group for Service Preparation)
GRV	Groupe de Ravitaillement en Vol (Air Refuelling Group)
GT	Grupo de Transporte (Transport Wing)
GTT	Grupo de Transporte de Tropos (Troop Carrier Wing)
gy	grey (squadron colours and markings)
HAF	Historic Aircraft Flight
HAPS	High Altitude Pseudo-Satellite
HavLLv	Hävittäjälentolaivue
HC	Helicopter Combat Support Squadron
HekoP	Helikopteripataljoona (Helicopter Battalion)
HF	Historic Flying Ltd
HI	Hawaii

HK	Helikopterikomppannia (Helicopter Company)
Hkp.Bat	Helikopter Bataljon (Helicopter Battalion)
HMA	Helicopter Maritime Attack
HMS	Her Majesty's Ship
HP	Handley-Page
HQ	Headquarters
HS	Hawker Siddeley
HSG	Hubschraubergeschwader (Helicopter Squadron)
IA	Iowa
IAF	Israeli Air Force
IAP	International Airport
IL	Illinois
IlmaStk	IlmataiStelukeskus
IN	Indiana
IntHubschr-	Internationales Hubschrauberausbildungszentrum
AusbZ	(International Helicopter Training Centre)
IOW	Isle Of Wight
IWM	Imperial War Museums
JADTEU	Joint Air Delivery Test and Evaluation Unit
JARTS	Joint Aircraft Recovery & Transportation Sqn
JFACTSU	Joint Forward Air Control Training & Standards Unit
JHC	Joint Helicopter Command
JMRC	Joint Multinational Readiness Centre
KHR	Kampfhubschrauberregiment (Combat Helicopter Regiment)
Kridlo	Wing
KS	Kansas
LA	Louisiana
lbvr	letka Bitevnich Vrtulníkú (Attack Helicopter Squadron)
Letka	Squadron
LTDB	Lufttransportdienst des Bundes (Federal Air Transport Services)
LTG	Lufttransportgeschwader (Air Transport Wing)
lTHSSta	leichte Transporthubschraberstaffel
LTO	Letalska Transportni Oddelek (Air Transport Department)
LtSt	Lufttransport Staffel
LTV	Ling-Temco-Vought
LVG	Luftwaffen Versorgungs Geschwader (Air Force Maintenance Wing)/Luft Verkehrs Gesellschaft
LZO	Letecky Zku ební Odbor (Aviation Test Department)
m	multi-coloured (squadron colours and markings)
MA	Massachusetts
MADG	Marshall Aerospace & Defence Group
MAPK	Mira Anachestisis Pantos Kerou (All Weather Interception Sqn)
MBB	Messerschmitt Bolkow-Blohm
MCAS	Marine Corps Air Station
McD	McDonnell Douglas
MD	Maryland
MDMF	Merlin Depth Maintenance Facility
Med	Medical
MFG	Marine Flieger Geschwader (Naval Air Wing)
MFSU	Merlin Depth Forward Support Unit
MH	Max Holste
MI	Maritime Interdiction/Michigan
MIB	Military Intelligence Battalion
MiG	Mikoyan — Gurevich
MN	Minnesota
MO	Missouri
Mod	Modified
MoD	Ministry of Defence
MPSU	Multi-Platform Support Unit
MR	Maritime Reconnaissance
MRH	Multi-role Helikopters
M&RU	Marketing & Recruitment Unit
MS	Mississippi/Morane-Saulnier
MT	Montana
MTHR	Mittlerer Transporthubschrauber Regiment (Medium Transport Helicopter Regiment)
MTM	Mira Taktikis Metaforon (Tactical Transport Sqn)

NA	North American
NACDS	Naval Air Command Driving School
NAEW&CF	NATO Airborne Early Warning & Control Force
NAF	Naval Air Facility
NAS	Naval Air Squadron (UK)/Naval Air Station (US)
NATO	North Atlantic Treaty Organisation
NAWC	Naval Air Warfare Center
NAWC-AD	Naval Air Warfare Center Aircraft Division
NBC	Nuclear, Biological and Chemical
ND	North Dakota
NE	North-East/Nebraska
NFH	NATO Frigate Helicopter
NH	New Hampshire
NI	Northern Ireland
NJ	New Jersey
NM	New Mexico
NV	Nevada
NY	New York
NYARC	North Yorks Aircraft Restoration Centre
OEU	Operational Evaluation Unit
OFMC	Old Flying Machine Company
OGMA	Oficinas Gerais de Material Aeronautico
OH	Ohio
OK	Oklahoma
or	orange (squadron colours and markings)
OSAC	Operational Support Airlift Command
OSBL	Oddelek Sholskih Bojni Letal (Training & Combat School)
P2MF	Puma 2 Maintenance Flight
PA	Pennsylvania
PAS	Presidential Airlift Squadron
PAT	Priority Air Transport Detachment
PBN	Pilatus Britten-Norman
PDSH	Puma Depth Support Hub
PLM	Pulk Lotnictwa Mysliwskiego (Fighter Regiment)
pr	purple (squadron colours and markings)
PR	Puerto Rico
r	red (squadron colours and markings)
R	Replica
RAeS	Royal Aeronautical Society
RAF	Royal Aircraft Factory/Royal Air Force
RAFC	Royal Air Force College
RAFM	Royal Air Force Museum
RAFGSA	Royal Air Force Gliding and Soaring Association
RE	Royal Engineers
Regt	Regiment
REME	Royal Electrical & Mechanical Engineers
rf	Rear fuselage
RFA	Royal Fleet Auxiliary
RHC	Régiment d'Helicoptères de Combat (Combat Helicopter Regiment)
RHFS	Régiment d'Helicoptères des Forces Spéciales (Special Forces Helicopter Regiment)
RI	Rhode Island
RJAF	Royal Jordanian Air Force
RM	Royal Marines
RMB	Royal Marines Base
RN	Royal Navy
RNAS	Royal Naval Air Station
RNGSA	Royal Navy Gliding and Soaring Association
RPAS	Remotely Piloted Air System
RQS	Rescue Squadron
R-R	Rolls-Royce
RS	Reid & Sigrist/Reconnaissance Squadron
RSV	Reparto Sperimentale Volo (Experimental Flight School)
RTP	Reduction To Produce
RW	Reconnaissance Wing
SA	Scottish Aviation
SAAB	Svenska Aeroplan Aktieboleg

SAAE	School of Army Aeronautical Engineering
SAC	Strategic Airlift Capability
SAL	Scottish Aviation Limited
SAR	Search and Rescue
Saro	Saunders-Roe
SARTU	Search and Rescue Training Unit
SC	South Carolina
SCW	Strategic Communications Wing
SD	South Dakota
SEPECAT	Société Européenne de Production de l'avion Ecole de Combat et d'Appui Tactique
SFDO	School of Flight Deck Operations
SHAPE	Supreme Headquarters Allied Powers Europe
si	silver (squadron colours and markings)
SKAMG	Sea King Aircraft Maintenance Group
Skv	Skvadron (Squadron)
SLK	Stíhacie Letecké Kridlo (Fighter Air Wing)
slt	stíhací letka (Fighter Squadron)
SLV	School Licht Vliegwezen (Flying School)
Sm	Smaldeel (Squadron)
SNCAN	Société Nationale de Constructions Aéronautiques du Nord
SOG	Special Operations Group
SOS	Special Operations Squadron
SoTT	School of Technical Training
SOW	Special Operations Wing
SPAD	Société Pour les Appareils Deperdussin
SPP	Strojirny Prvni Petilesky
Sqn	Squadron
Sz.D.REB	'Szentgyörgyi Deszö' Harcászati Repülö Bázis
TA	Territorial Army
TAP	Transporten Avio Polk (Air Transport Regiment)
TASF(N)	Tornado Aircraft Servicing Flight (North)
TAZLS	Technische Ausbildungs Zentrum Luftwaffe Süd (TAubZLwSüd, Technical Training Centre South)
TES	Test and Evaluation Squadron
TFC	The Fighter Collection
TGp	Test Groep
TH	Transporthelikopter
TIARA	Tornado Integrated Avionics Research Aircraft
tl	taktická tetka (Tactical Squadron)
TLG	Taktisches Luftwaffegeschwader (Air Force Tactical Squadron)
TMU	Typhoon Maintenance Unit
TN	Tennessee
Tr AB	Transport Aviation Brigade
TS	Test Squadron
ts	transportnia speciálni letka (special transport squadron)
TsAGI	Tsentral'ny Aerogidrodinamicheski Instut (Central Aero & Hydrodynamics Institute)
TsLw	Technische Schule der Luftwaffe (Luftwaffe Technical School)
TTH	Tactical Transport Helicopter
TukiLLv	Tukilentolaivue
TW	Test Wing
TX	Texas
UAS	University Air Squadron
UAV	Unmanned Air Vehicle
Überwg	Überwachungsgeschwader
UK	United Kingdom
US	United States
USAF	United States Air Force
USAFE	United States Air Forces in Europe
USAREUR	US Army Europe
USCGS	US Coast Guard Station
USEUCOM	United States European Command
USMC	United States Marine Corps
USN	United States Navy
USNWTSPM	United States Navy Test Pilots School
USW	University of South Wales
UT	Utah

VA	Virginia
VAAC	Vectored thrust Advanced Aircraft flight Control
VFW	Vereinigte Flugtechnische Werke
VGS	Volunteer Gliding Squadron
vlt	výcviková letka (training squadron)
VMGR	Marine Aerial Refuelling/Transport Squadron
VMGRT	Marine Aerial Refuelling/Transport Training Squadron
VQ	Fleet Air Reconnaissance Squadron
VR	Fleet Logistic Support Squadron
vrl	vrtulníková letka (helicopter squadron)
VS	Vickers-Supermarine
w	white (squadron colours and markings)
WA	Washington
Wg	Wing
WHL	Westland Helicopters Ltd
WI	Wisconsin
WLT	Weapons Loading Training
WMF	Wildcat Maintenance Facility
WR-ALC	Warner Robins Air Logistics Complex
WRS	Weather Reconnaissance Squadron
WS	Westland
WSK	Wytwornia Sprzetu Komikacyjnego
WST	Wildcat Support Team
WTD	Wehrtechnische Dienstelle (Technical Support Unit)
WV	West Virginia
WW2	World War II
WY	Wyoming
y	yellow (squadron colours and markings)
zDL	základna Dopravního Letectva (Air Transport Base)
zL	základna Letectva (Air Force Base)
zSL	základna Speciálního Letectva (Training Air Base)
zTL	základna Taktického Letectva (Tactical Air Base)
zVrL	základna Vrtulníkového Letectva (Helicopter Air Base)

A Guide to the Location of Operational Military Bases in the UK

This section is to assist the reader to locate the places in the United Kingdom where operational military aircraft (including helicopters and gliders) are based.

The alphabetical order listing gives each location in relation to its county and to its nearest classified road(s) (*by* means adjoining; *of* means close to), together with its approximate direction and mileage from the centre of a nearby major town or city. Some civil airports are included where active military units are also based, but **excluded** are MoD sites with non-operational aircraft (e.g. *gate guardians*), the bases of privately-owned civil aircraft that wear military markings and museums. For GPS users, Latitude and Longitude are also listed.

User	Base name	County/Region	Location [Lat./long.]	Distance/direction from (town)
Army	Abingdon	Oxfordshire	W by B4017, W of A34 [N51°41'16" W001°18'58"]	5m SSW of Oxford
Army	Aldergrove/Belfast Airport	Co Antrim	W by A26 [N54°39'27" W006°12'578"]	13m W of Belfast
RAF	Barkston Heath	Lincolnshire	W by B6404, S of A153 [N52°57'46" W000°33'38"]	5m NNE of Grantham
RAF	Benson	Oxfordshire	E by A423 [N51°36'55" W001°05'45"]	1m NE of Wallingford
QinetiQ/ RAF	Boscombe Down	Wiltshire	S by A303, W of A338 [N51°09'12" W001°45'04"]	6m N of Salisbury
RAF	Brize Norton	Oxfordshire	W of A4095 [N51°45'00" W001°35'01"]	5m SW of Witney

User	Base name	County/Region	Location [Lat./long.]	Distance/direction from (town)
Marshall	Cambridge Airport/ Teversham	Cambridgeshire	S by A1303 [N52°12'18" E000°10'30"]	2m E of Cambridge
RAF	Coningsby	Lincolnshire	S of A153, W by B1192 [N53°05'35" W000°10'00"]	10m NW of Boston
DCAE	Cosford	Shropshire	W of A41, N of A464 [N52°38'25" W002°18'20"]	9m WNW of Wolverhampton
RAF	Cranwell	Lincolnshire	N by A17, S by B1429 [N53°01'49" W000°29'00"]	5m WNW of Sleaford
RN	Culdrose	Cornwall	E by A3083 [N50°05'08" W005°15'17"]	1m SE of Helston
USAF	Fairford	Gloucestershire	S of A417 [N51°41'01" W001°47'24"]	9m ESE of Cirencester
Vector Aerospace	Fleetlands	Hampshire	E by A32 [N50°50'06" W001°10'07"]	2m SE of Fareham
RAF	Halton	Buckinghamshire	N of A4011, S of B4544 [N51°47'28" W000°44'11"]	4m ESE of Aylesbury
RAF	Kenley	Greater London	W of A22 [N51°18'20" W000°05'37"]	1m W of Warlingham
RAF	Kirknewton	Lothian	E by B7031, N by A70 [N55°52'32" W003°24'04"]	8m SW of Edinburgh
USAF	Lakenheath	Suffolk	W by A1065 [N52°24'33" E000°33'40"]	8m W of Thetford
RAF/Army	Leconfield (Normandy Barracks)	East Riding of Yorkshire	E by A164 [N53°52'39" W000°26'08"]	2m N of Beverley
RAF	Leeming	North Yorkshire	E by A1 [N54°17'33" W001°32'07"]	5m SW of Northallerton
RAF	Leuchars	Fife	E of A919 [N56°22'28" W002°51'50"]	7m SE of Dundee
RAF	Lossiemouth	Grampian	W of B9135, S of B9040 [N57°42'22" W003°20'20"]	4m N of Elgin
RAF	Marham	Norfolk	N by A1122 [N52°38'54" E000°33'02"]	6m W of Swaffham
Army	Middle Wallop	Hampshire	S by A343 [N51°08'35" W001°34'14"]	6m SW of Andover
USAF	Mildenhall	Suffolk	S by A1101 [N52°21'42" E000°29'12"]	9m NNE of Newmarket
RAF	Northolt	Greater London	N by A40 [N51°33'11" W000°25'06"]	3m E of M40 jn 1
RAF	Odiham	Hampshire	E of A32 [N51°14'03" W000°56'34"]	2m S of M3 jn 5
RN	Predannack	Cornwall	W by A3083 [N50°00'07" W005°13'54"]	7m S of Helston
RAF	Scampton	Lincolnshire	W by A15 [N53°18'28" W000°33'04"]	6m N of Lincoln
RAF	Shawbury	Shropshire	W of B5063 [N52°47'53" W002°40'05"]	7m NNE of Shrewsbury
RAF	Syerston	Nottinghamshire	W by A46 [N53°01'22" W000°54'47"]	5m SW of Newark
RAF	Ternhill	Shropshire	SW by A41 [N52°52'24" W002°31'54"]	3m SW of Market Drayton
RAF/Army	Topcliffe	North Yorkshire	E of A167, W of A168 [N54°12'20" W001°22'55"]	3m SW of Thirsk
RAF	Valley	Gwynedd	S of A5 on Anglesey [N53°14'53" W004°32'06"]	5m SE of Holyhead
RAF	Waddington	Lincolnshire	E by A607, W by A15 [N53°09'58" W000°31'26"]	5m S of Lincoln
Army	Wattisham	Suffolk	N of B1078 [N52°07'38" E000°57'21"]	5m SSW of Stowmarket
RAF	Woodvale	Merseyside	W by A565 [N53°34'56" W003°03'24"]	5m SSW of Southport
RAF	Wittering	Cambridgeshire	W by A1, N of A47 [N52°36'52" W000°27'01"]	3m S of Stamford
RN	Yeovilton	Somerset	S by B3151, S of A303 [N51°00'30" W002°38'43"]	5m N of Yeovil

The Committee of Imperial Defence through its Air Committee introduced a standardised system of numbering aircraft in November 1912. The Air Department of the Admiralty was allocated the first batch 1-200 and used these to cover aircraft already in use and those on order. The Army was issued with the next block from 201-800, which included the number 304 which was given to the Cody Biplane now preserved in the Science Museum. By the outbreak of World War I, the Royal Navy was on its second batch of registrations 801-1600 and this system continued with alternating allocations between the Army and Navy until 1916 when number 10000, a Royal Flying Corps BE2C, was reached.

It was decided not to continue with five digit numbers but instead to start again from 1, prefixing RFC aircraft with the letter A and RNAS aircraft with the prefix N. The RFC allocations commenced with A1 an FE2D and before the end of the year had reached A9999 an Armstrong Whitworth FK8. The next group commenced with B1 and continued in logical sequence through the C, D, E and F prefixes. G was used on a limited basis to identify captured German aircraft, while H was the last block of wartime-ordered aircraft. To avoid confusion letter I was not used, so the new post-war machines were allocated registrations in the J range. A further minor change was made in the numbering system in August 1929 when it was decided to maintain four numerals after the prefix letter, thus omitting numbers 1 to 999. The new K series therefore commenced at K1000, which was allocated to an AW Atlas.

The Naval N prefix was not used in such a logical way. Blocks of numbers were allocated for specific types of aircraft such as seaplanes or flying-boats. By the late 1920s the sequence had largely been used up and a new series using the prefix S was commenced. In 1930 separate naval allocations were stopped and subsequent registrations were issued in the 'military' range which had by this time reached the K series. A further change in the pattern of allocations came in the L range. Commencing with L7272 numbers were issued in blocks with smaller blocks of registrations between not used. These were known as 'broken blocks'. As M had already been used as a suffix for Maintenance Command instructional airframes it was not used as a prefix. Although N had previously been used for naval aircraft it was used again for registrations allocated from 1937.

With the build-up to World War II, the rate of allocations quickly accelerated and the prefix R was being used when war was declared. The letters O and Q were not allotted, nor was S, which had been used up to S1865 for naval aircraft before integration into the RAF series. By 1940 the registration Z9999 had been reached, as part of a broken block, with the letters U and Y not used to avoid confusion.

The option to recommence registration allocation at A1000 was not taken up; instead it was decided to use an alphabetical two-letter prefix with three numerals running from 100 to 999. Thus, AA100 was allocated to a Blenheim IV and this two-letter, three-numeral registration system which started in 1940 continues today. The letters C, I, O, Q, U and Y were, with the exception of NC, not used. For various reasons the following letter combinations were not issued: DA, DB, DH, EA, GA to GZ, HA, HT, JE, JH, JJ, KR to KT, MR, NW, NZ, SA to SK, SV, TN, TR and VE. The first post-war registrations issued were in the VP range while the end of the WZs had been reached by the Korean War.

In January 1952 a civil servant at the then Air Ministry penned a memo to his superiors alerting them to the fact that a new military aircraft registration system would soon have to be devised. With allocations accelerating to accommodate a NATO response to the Korean War and a perceived Soviet threat building, he estimated that the end of the ZZs would quickly be reached. However, more than six decades later the allocations are only in the ZKs and at the present rate are unlikely to reach ZZ999 until the end of this century!

Military aircraft registrations are allocated by MoD Head Office and Corporate Services, where the Military Aircraft Register is maintained by the Military Aviation Authority. It should be pointed out that strictly the register places a space before the last three digits of the registration and, contrary to popular opinion, refers to them as 'registrations', not serials.

A change in policy in 2003 resulted in the use of the first 99 digits in the ZK sequence (ZK001 to ZK099), following on from ZJ999. The first of these, ZK001 to ZK004, were allocated to AgustaWestland Merlins. There is also a growing trend for 'out-of-sequence' registration numbers to be issued. At first this was to a manufacturer's prototype or development aircraft. However, following the Boeing C-17 Globemasters leased and subsequently purchased from Boeing (ZZ171-ZZ178), more allocations have been noted.

Since 2002 there has also been a new official policy concerning the use of military registration numbers on some types of UAV. 'Where a UAV is of modular construction the nationality and registration mark shall be applied to the fuselage of the vehicle or on the assembly forming the main part of the fuselage. To prevent the high usage of numbers for target drones which are eventually destroyed, a single registration mark (prefix) should be issued relating to the UAV type. The agency or service operating the target drone will be responsible for the identification of each individual UAV covered by that registration mark by adding a suffix.' This has resulted in the use of the same registration on a number of UAVs (or RPASs as they are now referred to) and drones with numbers following it – hence the appearance of ZZ420/001 etc. on Banshee drones. Aircraft using this system are denoted in the text by an asterisk (*).

A serial in *italics* denotes that it is not the genuine marking for that airframe.

Serial	Type (code/other identity)	Owner/operator, location or fate	Notes
46	VS361 Spitfire LF IX <R> (*MH486*/BAPC 206) [FT-E]	Michael Beetham Conservation Centre, RAFM Cosford	
168	Sopwith Tabloid Scout <R> (G-BFDE)	RAF Museum Reserve Collection, Stafford	
304	Cody Biplane (BAPC 62)	Science Museum, South Kensington	
471	RAF BE2a <R> (BAPC 321)	Montrose Air Station Heritage Centre	
687	RAF BE2c <R> (G-AWYI/*471*)	Privately owned, Sywell	
687	RAF BE2b <R> (BAPC 181)	RAF Museum, Hendon	
1264	Bristol Scout C <R> (G-FDHB)	Privately owned, Bicester	
2345	Vickers FB5 Gunbus <R> (G-ATVP)	RAF Museum, Hendon	
2699	RAF BE2c	IWM Duxford	
2783	RAF BE2b <R> (BAPC 332)	Boscombe Down Aviation Collection, Old Sarum	
3066	Caudron GIII (G-AETA/9203M)	RAF Museum, Hendon	
5964	DH2 <R> (BAPC 112)	Privately owned, Stretton on Dunsmore	
5964	DH2 <R> (G-BFVH)	Privately owned, Wickenby	
6232	RAF BE2c <R> (BAPC 41)	Yorkshire Air Museum, stored Elvington	
8359	Short 184 <ff>	FAA Museum, RNAS Yeovilton	
9828	Avro 504K <R> (*H1968*/BAPC 42)	Yorkshire Air Museum, stored Elvington	
9917	Sopwith Pup (G-EBKY/N5180)	The Shuttleworth Collection, Old Warden	
A126	Nieuport 11 <R> (G-CILI)	Privately owned,	
A301	Morane BB (frame)	RAF Museum Reserve Collection, Stafford	
A653	Sopwith Pup <R> (*A7317*/BAPC 179)	Privately owned, Stow Maries, Essex	
A1452	Vickers FB5 Gunbus <R>	Spitfire Spares, Taunton, Somerset	
A1742	Bristol Scout D <R> (BAPC 38)	Privately owned, Old Warden	
A2767	RAF BE2e-1 <R> (G-CJZP)	WW1 Aviation Heritage Trust, Stow Maries	
A2943	RAF BE2e-1 <R> (ZK-TFZ)	WW1 Aviation Heritage Trust, Bicester	
A3930	RAF RE8 <R> (ZK-TVC)	RAF Museum, Hendon	
A4850	RAF SE5a <R> (BAPC 176)	Bygone Times Antique Warehouse, Eccleston, Lancs	
A6526	RAF FE2c <R> (BAPC 400)	RAF Museum, Hendon	
A7288	Bristol F2b Fighter <R> (BAPC 386)	Bristol Aero Collection, Filton	
A8226	Sopwith 1½ Strutter <R> (G-BIDW)	RAF Museum, Cosford	
A8274	Sopwith 1½ Strutter <R> (BAPC 413)	WW1 Aviation Heritage Trust, Stow Maries	
B595	RAF SE5a <R> (G-BUOD) [W]	Privately owned, Defford	
B619	Sopwith 1½ Strutter <R>	RAF Manston History Museum	
B1474	Henry Farman F.20 <R>	WW1 Aviation Heritage Trust, Stow Maries	
B2458	Sopwith 1F.1 Camel <R> (G-BPOB/*F542*) [R]	*Repainted as N6377 by February 2016*	
B5539	Sopwith 1F.1 Camel <R>	Privately owned, Booker	
B5577	Sopwith 1F.1 Camel <R> (*D3419*/BAPC 59) [W]	Montrose Air Station Heritage Centre	
B6401	Sopwith 1F.1 Camel <R> (G-AWYY/C1701)	FAA Museum, stored Cobham Hall, RNAS Yeovilton	
B7270	Sopwith 1F.1 Camel <R> (G-BFCZ)	Brooklands Museum, Weybridge	
C1096	Replica Plans SE5a <R> (G-ERFC) [W]	Privately owned, Egginton	
C1904	RAF SE5a <R> (G-PFAP) [Z]	Privately owned, Castle Bytham, Lincs	
C3009	Currie Wot (G-BFWD) [B]	Privately owned, Dunkeswell	
C3011	Phoenix Currie Super Wot (G-SWOT) [S]	Privately owned, Otherton, Staffs	
C3988	Sopwith 5F.1 Dolphin (BAPC 353) (comp D5329)	RAF Museum, Hendon	
C4451	Avro 504J <R> (BAPC 210)	Solent Sky, Southampton	
C4918	Bristol M1C <R> (G-BWJM)	The Shuttleworth Collection, Old Warden	
C4994	Bristol M1C <R> (G-BLWM)	RAF Museum, Cosford	
C5430	RAF SE5a <R> (G-CCXG) [V]	Privately owned, Wrexham	
C6468	RAF SE5a <R> (G-CEKL) [A]	*Sold to the USA as N17SE, 2010*	
C8996	RAF SE5a (G-ECAE/A2-25)	Privately owned, Milden	
C9533	RAF SE5a <R> (G-BUWE) [M]	Privately owned, Boscombe Down	
D276	RAF SE5a <R> (BAPC 208) [A]	Prince's Mead Shopping Centre, Farnborough	
D1851	Sopwith 1F.1 Camel <R> (G-BZSC) [X]	The Shuttleworth Collection, Old Warden	
D3540	RAF SE5a <R> (N125QB) [K]	WW1 Aviation Heritage Trust, Old Warden	

Notes	Serial	Type (code/other identity)	Owner/operator, location or fate
	D5649	Airco DH9	IWM Duxford
	D6447	Sopwith 1F.1 Camel <R> (BAPC 385)	Privately owned, Knutsford, Cheshire
	D7560	Avro 504K	Science Museum, South Kensington
	D8096	Bristol F2b Fighter (G-AEPH) [D]	The Shuttleworth Collection, Old Warden
	E449	Avro 504K (G-EBJE/9205M)	RAF Museum, Hendon
	E2466	Bristol F2b Fighter (BAPC 165) [I]	RAF Museum, Hendon
	E2581	Bristol F2b Fighter [13]	IWM Duxford
	E2977	Avro 504K (G-EBHB)	Privately owned, Henlow
	E3273	Avro 504K (H5199/BK892/ G-ACNB/G-ADEV/3118M)	The Shuttleworth Collection, Old Warden
	E6655	Sopwith 7F.1 Snipe <R> (BAPC 348) [B]	RAF Museum, Hendon
	E8894	Airco DH9 (G-CDLI)	Aero Vintage, Westfield, Sussex
	F141	RAF SE5a <R> (G-SEVA) [G]	Privately owned, Boscombe Down
	F235	RAF SE5a <R> (G-BMDB) [B]	Privately owned, Stow Maries, Essex
	F904	RAF SE5a (G-EBIA)	The Shuttleworth Collection, Old Warden
	F904	RAF SE5a <R>	South Yorkshire Aircraft Museum, Doncaster
	F938	RAF SE5a (G-EBIC/9208M)	RAF Museum, Hendon
	F943	RAF SE5a <R> (G-BIHF) [S]	Privately owned, White Waltham
	F943	RAF SE5a <R> (G-BKDT) [S]	Yorkshire Air Museum, Elvington
	F1010	Airco DH9A [C]	RAF Museum, Hendon
	F2367	Sopwith 7F.1 Snipe <R> (ZK-SNI)	WW1 Aviation Heritage Trust, Stow Maries
	F3556	RAF RE8	IWM Duxford
	F5447	RAF SE5a <R> (G-BKER) [N]	Privately owned, Bridge of Weir
	F5459	RAF SE5a <R> (G-INNY) [Y]	Privately owned, Temple Bruer, Lincs
	F5475	RAF SE5a <R> (BAPC 250)	Brooklands Museum, Weybridge
	F6314	Sopwith 1F.1 Camel (9206M) [B]	RAF Museum, Hendon
	F8010	RAF SE5a <R> (G-BDWJ) [Z]	Privately owned, Langport, Somerset
	F8614	Vickers FB27A Vimy IV <R> (G-AWAU)	RAF Museum, Hendon
	H1968	Avro 504K <R> (BAPC 42)	Repainted as 9828 by July 2016
	J7326	DH53 Humming Bird (G-EBQP)	de Havilland Aircraft Museum, London Colney
	J7904	Gloster Gamecock (BAPC 259) <R>	Jet Age Museum, Gloucester
	J8067	Westland Pterodactyl 1a	Science Museum, South Kensington
	J9941	Hawker Hart 2 (G-ABMR)	RAF Museum, Hendon
	K1786	Hawker Tomtit (G-AFTA)	The Shuttleworth Collection, Old Warden
	K1926	Hawker Fury I	Cambs Fighter & Bomber Society, Little Gransden
	K2048	Isaacs Fury II (G-BZNW)	Privately owned, Linton-on-Ouse
	K2050	Isaacs Fury II (G-ASCM)	Privately owned, Enstone
	K2059	Isaacs Fury II (G-PFAR)	Privately owned, Netherthorpe
	K2060	Isaacs Fury II (G-BKZM)	Privately owned stored, Limetree, Ireland
	K2065	Isaacs Fury II (G-AYJY/K2046)	Privately owned, Henstridge
	K2075	Isaacs Fury II (G-BEER)	Privately owned, Combrook, Warks
	K2227	Bristol 105 Bulldog IIA (G-ABBB)	RAF Museum, Hendon
	K2567	DH82A Tiger Moth (DE306/G-MOTH/7035M)	Privately owned, Tadlow
	K2572	DH82A Tiger Moth (NM129/G-AOZH)	Privately owned, Wanborough, Wilts
	K2585	DH82A Tiger Moth II (T6818/G-ANKT)	The Shuttleworth Collection, Old Warden
	K2587	DH82A Tiger Moth <R> (G-BJAP)	Privately owned, Shobdon
	K3241	Avro 621 Tutor (K3215/G-AHSA)	The Shuttleworth Collection, Old Warden
	K3661	Hawker Nimrod II (G-BURZ) [562]	Aero Vintage, Duxford
	K3731	Isaacs Fury (G-RODI)	Privately owned, Barkston Heath
	K4232	Avro 671 Rota I (SE-AZB)	RAF Museum, Hendon
	K4259	DH82A Tiger Moth (G-ANMO) [71]	Privately owned, Headcorn
	K4556	Boulton & Paul Overstrand <R> (BAPC 358)	Norfolk & Suffolk Avn Museum, Flixton
	K4972	Hawker Hart Trainer IIA (1764M)	RAF Museum, Hendon
	K5054	Supermarine Spitfire <R> (EN398/BAPC 190)	Privately owned, Hawkinge
	K5054	Supermarine Spitfire <R> (BAPC 214)	Tangmere Military Aviation Museum
	K5054	Supermarine Spitfire <R> (G-BRDV)	Privately owned, Kent
	K5054	Supermarine Spitfire <R> (BAPC 297)	Kent Battle of Britain Museum, Hawkinge

Serial	Type (code/other identity)	Owner/operator, location or fate	Notes
K5054	Supermarine Spitfire <R>	Southampton Airport, on display	
K5409	Hawker Hind	*Currently not known*	
K5414	Hawker Hind (G-AENP/BAPC 78) [XV]	The Shuttleworth Collection, Old Warden	
K5462	Hawker Hind	*Currently not known*	
K5554	Hawker Hind	*Currently not known*	
K5600	Hawker Audax I (G-BVVI/2015M)	Aero Vintage, Westfield, Sussex	
K5673	Isaacs Fury II (G-BZAS)	Privately owned, Morpeth	
K5673	Hawker Fury I <R> (BAPC 249)	Brooklands Museum, Weybridge	
K5674	Hawker Fury I (G-CBZP)	Historic Aircraft Collection Ltd, Duxford	
K5682	Isaacs Fury II (S1579/G-BBVO) [6]	Privately owned, Felthorpe	
K6035	Westland Wallace II (2361M)	RAF Museum Reserve Collection, Stafford	
K6618	Hawker Hind	*Currently not known*	
K6833	Hawker Hind	*Currently not known*	
K7271	Hawker Fury II <R> (BAPC 148)	Shropshire Wartime Aircraft Recovery Grp Mus, Sleap	
K7271	Isaacs Fury II <R> (G-CCKV)	Privately owned, Dunkeswell	
K7985	Gloster Gladiator I (L8032/G-AMRK)	The Shuttleworth Collection, Old Warden	
K8042	Gloster Gladiator II (8372M)	RAF Museum, Cosford	
K8203	Hawker Demon I (G-BTVE/2292M)	Demon Displays, Old Warden	
K8303	Isaacs Fury II (G-BWWN) [D]	Privately owned, RAF Henlow	
K9926	VS300 Spitfire I <R> (BAPC 217) [JH-C]	Privately owned, Newquay	
K9942	VS300 Spitfire I (8383M) [SD-D]	RAF Museum, Cosford	
K9998	VS300 Spitfire I (BAPC 431) <R> [QJ-K]	RAF Biggin Hill, on display	
L1019	VS300 Spitfire I <R> (BAPC 308) [LO-S]	Privately owned, Currie, Lothian	
L1067	VS300 Spitfire I <R> (BAPC 227) [XT-D]	Edinburgh Airport, on display	
L1592	Hawker Hurricane I [KW-Z]	Science Museum, South Kensington	
L1639	Hawker Hurricane I (BAPC 362)	Cambridge Fighter & Bomber Society, Little Gransden	
L1679	Hawker Hurricane I <R> (BAPC 241) [JX-G]	Tangmere Military Aviation Museum	
L1684	Hawker Hurricane I <R> (BAPC 219)	RAF Northolt, on display	
L2005	Hawker Hurricane I	Hawker Restorations, Milden	
L2301	VS Walrus I (G-AIZG)	FAA Museum, RNAS Yeovilton	
L2940	Blackburn Skua I	FAA Museum, RNAS Yeovilton	
L5343	Fairey Battle I	RAF Museum, Hendon	
L6739	Bristol 149 Bolingbroke IVT (G-BPIV/R3821) [YP-Q]	Blenheim(Duxford) Ltd, Duxford	
L6906	Miles M14A Magister I (G-AKKY/T9841/BAPC 44)	Museum of Berkshire Aviation, Woodley	
L7005	Boulton Paul P82 Defiant I <R> [PS-B]	Kent Battle of Britain Museum, Hawkinge	
L7181	Hawker Hind (G-CBLK)	Aero Vintage, Duxford	
L7191	Hawker Hind	*Currently not known*	
L7775	Vickers Wellington B IC <ff>	Lincolnshire Avn Heritage Centre, E Kirkby	
L8756	Bristol 149 Bolingbroke IVT (RCAF 10001) [XD-E]	RAF Museum, Hendon	
N248	Supermarine S6A (S1596)	Solent Sky, Southampton	
N500	Sopwith LC-1T Triplane <R> (G-PENY/G-BWRA)	Privately owned, Yarcombe, Devon/RNAS Yeovilton	
N540	Port Victoria PV8 Eastchurch Kitten <R>	Yorkshire Air Museum, Elvington	
N546	Wright Quadruplane 1 <R> (BAPC 164)	Solent Sky, Southampton	
N1671	Boulton Paul P82 Defiant I (8370M) [EW-D]	RAF Museum, Cosford	
N1854	Fairey Fulmar II (G-AIBE)	FAA Museum, RNAS Yeovilton	
N2078	Sopwith Baby (8214/8215/BAPC 442)	FAA Museum, RNAS Yeovilton	
N2532	Hawker Hurricane I <R> (BAPC 272) [GZ-H]	Kent Battle of Britain Museum, Hawkinge	
N2980	Vickers Wellington IA [R]	Brooklands Museum, Weybridge	
N3200	VS300 Spitfire IA (G-CFGJ) [QV]	IWM Duxford	
N3289	VS300 Spitfire I <R> (BAPC 65) [DW-K]	Kent Battle of Britain Museum, Hawkinge	
N3290	VS300 Spitfire I <R> [AI-H]	Privately owned, St Mawgan	
N3310	VS361 Spitfire IX <R> (BAPC 393) [A]	Privately owned, Abingdon	
N3313	VS300 Spitfire I <R> (MH314/BAPC 69) [KL-B]	Kent Battle of Britain Museum, Hawkinge	
N3317	VS329 Spitfire II <R> (P8140/BAPC 71) [BO-U]	Norfolk & Suffolk Avn Museum, Flixton	
N3378	Boulton Paul P82 Defiant I (wreck)	RAF Museum, Cosford	
N3549	DH82A Tiger Moth II (PG645/N3549)	Privately owned, Netherthorpe	
N3788	Miles M14A Magister I (V1075/G-AKPF)	Privately owned, Old Warden	
N4389	Fairey Albacore (N4172) [4M]	FAA Museum, stored Cobham Hall, RNAS Yeovilton	
N4877	Avro 652A Anson I (G-AMDA) [MK-V]	IWM Duxford	
N5137	DH82A Tiger Moth (N6638/G-BNDW)	Caernarfon Air World	

Notes	Serial	Type (code/other identity)	Owner/operator, location or fate
	N5177	Sopwith 1½ Strutter (BAPC 452) <R>	Privately owned, stored Mersham, Surrey
	N5182	Sopwith Pup <R> (G-APUP/9213M)	RAF Museum, Cosford
	N5195	Sopwith Pup (G-ABOX)	Museum of Army Flying, Middle Wallop
	N5199	Sopwith Pup <R> (G-BZND)	Privately owned, Yarcombe, Devon
	N5459	Sopwith Triplane <R> (BAPC 111)	FAA Museum, stored Cobham Hall, RNAS Yeovilton
	N5518	Gloster Sea Gladiator	FAA Museum, RNAS Yeovilton
	N5628	Gloster Gladiator II	RAF Museum, Cosford
	N5719	Gloster Gladiator II (G-CBHO)	Privately owned, Dursley, Glos
	N5903	Gloster Gladiator II (N2276/G-GLAD)	The Fighter Collection, Duxford
	N5912	Sopwith Triplane (8385M)	RAF Museum, Hendon
	N5914	Gloster Gladiator II (frame)	Jet Age Museum, Gloucester
	N6161	Sopwith Pup (G-ELRT)	Privately owned, Duxford
	N6290	Sopwith Triplane <R> (G-BOCK)	The Shuttleworth Collection, Old Warden
	N6377	Sopwith 1F.1 Camel <R> (G-BPOB/B2458)	Privately owned, Stow Maries
	N6452	Sopwith Pup <R> (G-BIAU)	FAA Museum, stored Cobham Hall, RNAS Yeovilton
	N6466	DH82A Tiger Moth (G-ANKZ)	Privately owned, Compton Abbas
	N6473	DH82A Tiger Moth (F-GTBO)	Privately owned, Orbigny, France
	N6537	DH82A Tiger Moth (G-AOHY)	Privately owned, Wickenby
	N6635	DH82A Tiger Moth (comp G-APAO & G-APAP) [25]	IWM Duxford
	N6720	DH82A Tiger Moth (G-BYTN/7014M) [VX]	Privately owned, stored Darley Moor, Derbyshire
	N6797	DH82A Tiger Moth (G-ANEH)	Privately owned, Swyncombe
	N6812	Sopwith 2F.1 Camel	IWM London, Lambeth
	N6847	DH82A Tiger Moth (G-APAL)	Privately owned, Braceborough, Lincs
	N6965	DH82A Tiger Moth (G-AJTW) [FL-J]	Privately owned, Tibenham
	N7033	Noorduyn AT-16 Harvard IIB (FX442)	Kent Battle of Britain Museum, Hawkinge
	N9191	DH82A Tiger Moth (G-ALND)	Privately owned, Pontypool
	N9192	DH82A Tiger Moth (G-DHZF) [RCO-N]	Privately owned, Sywell
	N9328	DH82A Tiger Moth (G-ALWS) [69]	Privately owned, Henstridge
	N9389	DH82A Tiger Moth (G-ANJA)	Privately owned, Thruxton
	N9503	DH82A Tiger Moth (G-ANFP) [39]	Sold to the Czech Republic, December 2016
	N9899	Supermarine Southampton I (fuselage)	RAF Museum, Hendon
	P1344	HP52 Hampden I (9175M) [PL-K]	Michael Beetham Conservation Centre, RAFM Cosford
	P2617	Hawker Hurricane I (8373M) [AF-F]	RAF Museum, Hendon
	P2725	Hawker Hurricane I (wreck)	IWM London, Lambeth
	P2725	Hawker Hurricane I <R> (BAPC 68) [TM-B]	Privately owned, Delabole, Cornwall
	P2793	Hawker Hurricane I <R> (BAPC 236) [SD-M]	Eden Camp Theme Park, Malton, North Yorkshire
	P2902	Hawker Hurricane I (G-ROBT) [DX-R]	Privately owned, Milden
	P2921	Hawker Hurricane I <R> (BAPC 273) [GZ-L]	Kent Battle of Britain Museum, Hawkinge
	P2921	Hawker Hurricane I <R> [GZ-L]	RAF Biggin Hill, on display
	P2921	Hawker Sea Hurricane X (AE977/G-CHTK) [GZ-L]	Privately owned, Biggin Hill
	P2954	Hawker Hurricane I <R> (BAPC 267) [WX-E]	IWM Duxford
	P2970	Hawker Hurricane I <R> (BAPC 291) [US-X]	Battle of Britain Memorial, Capel le Ferne, Kent
	P3059	Hawker Hurricane I <R> (BAPC 64) [SD-N]	Kent Battle of Britain Museum, Hawkinge
	P3175	Hawker Hurricane I (wreck)	RAF Museum, Hendon
	P3179	Hawker Hurricane I <ff>	Tangmere Military Aviation Museum
	P3208	Hawker Hurricane I <R> (BAPC 63/L1592) [SD-T]	Kent Battle of Britain Museum, Hawkinge
	P3351	Hawker Hurricane IIA (DR393/F-AZXR) [K]	Privately owned, Cannes, France
	P3386	Hawker Hurricane I <R> (BAPC 218) [FT-A]	RAF Bentley Priory, on display
	P3395	Hawker Hurricane IV (KX829)[JX-B]	Thinktank, Birmingham
	P3554	Hawker Hurricane I (composite)	The Air Defence Collection, Salisbury
	P3679	Hawker Hurricane I <R> (BAPC 278) [GZ-K]	Kent Battle of Britain Museum, Hawkinge
	P3700	Hawker Hurricane XIIA (Z5140/G-HURI) [RF-E]	Historic Aircraft Collection, Duxford
	P3708	Hawker Hurricane I	Norfolk & Suffolk Avn Museum, Flixton (on rebuild)
	P3717	Hawker Hurricane I (composite) (DR348/G-HITT) [SW-P]	Privately owned, Turweston
	P3873	Hawker Hurricane I <R> (BAPC 265) [YO-H]	Yorkshire Air Museum, Elvington
	P3901	Hawker Hurricane I <R> [RF-E]	Battle of Britain Bunker, Uxbridge
	P4139	Fairey Swordfish II (HS618) [5H]	FAA Museum, RNAS Yeovilton
	P6382	Miles M14A Hawk Trainer 3 (G-AJRS) [C]	The Shuttleworth Collection, Old Warden
	P7308	VS300 Spitfire IA (AR213/R9632/G-AIST) [XR-D]	Privately owned, Duxford
	P7350	VS329 Spitfire IIA (G-AWIJ) [EB-G]	RAF BBMF, Coningsby

Serial	Type (code/other identity)	Owner/operator, location or fate	Notes
P7370	VS329 Spitfire II <R> (BAPC 410) [ZP-A]	Battle of Britain Experience, Canterbury	
P7540	VS329 Spitfire IIA [DU-W]	Dumfries & Galloway Avn Mus, Dumfries	
P7666	VS329 Spitfire II <R> (BAPC 335) [EB-Z]	RAF High Wycombe, on display	
P7819	VS329 Spitfire IIA (G-TCHZ)	Privately owned, Exeter	
P7895	VS329 Spitfire IIA <R> [RN-N]	Repainted as P7923	
P7923	VS329 Spitfire IIA <R> (BAPC 369) [TM-F]	Ulster Aviation Society, Long Kesh	
P7966	VS329 Spitfire II <R> [D-B]	Manx Aviation & Military Museum, Ronaldsway	
P8088	VS329 Spitfire IIA (G-CGRM) [NK-K]	Privately owned, Knutsford, Cheshire	
P8140	VS329 Spitfire II <R> (P9390/BAPC 71) [ZF-K]	Repainted as N3317	
P8208	VS329 Spitfire IIB (G-RRFF)	Privately owned, Oxon	
P8448	VS329 Spitfire II <R> (BAPC 225) [UM-D]	RAF Cranwell, on display	
P9374	VS300 Spitfire IA (G-MKIA) [J]	Privately owned, Duxford	
P9398	Supermarine Aircraft Spitfire 26 (G-CEPL) [KL-B]	Privately owned, Damyns Hall, Essex	
P9444	VS300 Spitfire IA [RN-D]	Science Museum, South Kensington	
P9637	Supermarine Aircraft Spitfire 26 (G-RORB) [GR-B]	Privately owned, Perth	
R1914	Miles M14A Magister (G-AHUJ)	Privately owned, Rendcomb	
R4118	Hawker Hurricane I (G-HUPW) [UP-W]	Privately owned, Old Warden	
R4229	Hawker Hurricane I <R> (BAPC 334) [GN-J]	Alexandra Park, Windsor	
R4922	DH82A Tiger Moth II (G-APAO)	Privately owned, Henlow	
R4959	DH82A Tiger Moth II (G-ARAZ) [59]	Privately owned, Temple Bruer, Lincs	
R5136	DH82A Tiger Moth II (G-APAP)	Privately owned, Darley Moor, Derbyshire	
R5172	DH82A Tiger Moth II (G-AOIS) [FIJE]	Privately owned, Sywell	
R5246	DH82A Tiger Moth II (D-EDHA) [40]	Privately owned, Heringsdorf, Germany	
R5868	Avro 683 Lancaster I (7325M) [PO-S]	RAF Museum, Hendon	
R6690	VS300 Spitfire I <R> (BAPC 254) [PR-A]	Yorkshire Air Museum, Elvington	
R6775	VS300 Spitfire I <R> (BAPC 299) [YT-J]	Battle of Britain Memorial, Capel le Ferne, Kent	
R6904	VS300 Spitfire I <R> [BT-K]	Privately owned, Cornwall	
R6915	VS300 Spitfire I	IWM London, Lambeth	
R9125	Westland Lysander III (8377M)[LX-L]	Michael Beetham Conservation Centre, RAFM Cosford	
R9612	VS300 Spitfire I (X4650/G-CGUK) [LC]	Repainted as X4650 by September 2016	
R9612	Yakovlev Yak-52TW(mod) (N699DP)	Returned to the USA, September 2016	
R9632	VS300 Spitfire IA (AR213/P7308/G-AIST) [LC]	Repainted as P7308 by September 2016	
R9649	VS349 Spitfire F VB (EP122/G-CISV) [LC]	Repainted as EP122 by September 2016	
S1287	Fairey Flycatcher <R> (G-BEYB) [5]	FAA Museum, stored Cobham Hall, RNAS Yeovilton	
S1581	Hawker Nimrod I (G-BWWK) [573]	The Fighter Collection, Duxford	
S1595	Supermarine S6B [1]	Science Museum, South Kensington	
S1615	Isaacs Fury II (G-BMEU)	Privately owned, stored Netherthorpe	
T5298	Bristol 156 Beaufighter I (4552M) <ff>	Midland Air Museum, Coventry	
T5424	DH82A Tiger Moth II (G-AJOA)	Privately owned, Swindon	
T5854	DH82A Tiger Moth II (G-ANKK)	Privately owned, Baxterley	
T5879	DH82A Tiger Moth II (G-AXBW) [RUC-W]	Privately owned, Frensham	
T6296	DH82A Tiger Moth II (8387M)	RAF Museum, Cosford	
T6562	DH82A Tiger Moth II (G-ANTE)	Repainted as G-ANTE	
T6953	DH82A Tiger Moth II (G-ANNI)	Privately owned, Tisted, Hants	
T6991	DH82A Tiger Moth II (DE694/HB-UPY)	Privately owned, Lausanne, Switzerland	
T7109	DH82A Tiger Moth II (G-AOIM)	Privately owned, Bicester	
T7230	DH82A Tiger Moth II (G-AFVE)	Privately owned, Mazowiecke, Poland	
T7281	DH82A Tiger Moth II (G-ARTL)	Privately owned, Egton, nr Whitby	
T7290	DH82A Tiger Moth II (G-ANNK) [14]	Privately owned, Sywell	
T7793	DH82A Tiger Moth II (G-ANKV)	Privately owned, Wickenby	
T7794	DH82A Tiger Moth II (G-ASPV)	Privately owned, Breighton	
T7842	DH82A Tiger Moth II (G-AMTF)	Privately owned, Westfield, Surrey	
T7909	DH82A Tiger Moth II (G-ANON)	Privately owned, Sherburn-in-Elmet	
T7997	DH82A Tiger Moth II (NL750/G-AHUF)	Privately owned, Breighton	
T8191	DH82A Tiger Moth II (G-BWMK)	Privately owned, Henstridge	
T9707	Miles M14A Magister I (G-AKKR/8378M/T9708)	Museum of Army Flying, Middle Wallop	
T9738	Miles M14A Magister I (G-AKAT)	Privately owned, Breighton	
V3388	Airspeed AS10 Oxford I (G-AHTW)	IWM Duxford	

Notes	Serial	Type (code/other identity)	Owner/operator, location or fate
	V6028	Bristol 149 Bolingbroke IVT (G-MKIV) [GB-D] <rf>	The Aircraft Restoration Co, stored Duxford
	V6555	Hawker Hurricane I (BAPC 411/*P3144*) <R> [DT-A]	Battle of Britain Experience, Canterbury
	V6799	Hawker Hurricane I <R> (BAPC 72/*V7767*) [SD-X]	Jet Age Museum, Gloucester
	V7313	Hawker Hurricane I <R> (BAPC 346) [US-F]	Privately owned, North Weald, on display
	V7350	Hawker Hurricane I <ff>	Romney Marsh Wartime Collection
	V7467	Hawker Hurricane I <R> (BAPC 378) [LE-D]	RAF High Wycombe, on display
	V7467	Hawker Hurricane I <R> (BAPC 223) [LE-D]	Privately owned, Lytham St Annes
	V7467	Hawker Hurricane I <R> (BAPC 288) [LE-D]	Wonderland Pleasure Park, Farnsfield, Notts
	V7497	Hawker Hurricane I (G-HRLI)	Hawker Restorations, Milden
	V9312	Westland Lysander IIIA (G-CCOM)	The Aircraft Restoration Co, Duxford
	V9367	Westland Lysander IIIA (G-AZWT) [MA-B]	The Shuttleworth Collection, Old Warden
	V9673	Westland Lysander IIIA (V9300/G-LIZY) [MA-J]	IWM Duxford
	V9723	Westland Lysander IIIA (V9546/OO-SOT) [MA-D]	SABENA Old Timers, Brussels, Belgium
	V9875	Westland Lysander IIIA <R> [MA-J]	Gateguards (UK), St Mawgan
	W1048	HP59 Halifax II (8465M) [TL-S]	RAF Museum, Hendon
	W2068	Avro 652A Anson I (9261M/VH-ASM) [68]	RAF Museum, Hendon
	W2718	VS Walrus I (G-RNLI)	Privately owned, Audley End
	W3257	Supermarine Aircraft Spitfire 26 (G-CENI) [FY-E]	Privately owned, Sibson
	W3632	VS509 Spitfire T9 (PV202/*H-98*/G-CCCA)	*Repainted as PV202*
	W3644	VS349 Spitfire V <R> (BAPC 323) [QV-J]	Privately owned, Lake Fairhaven, Lancs
	W3850	VS349 Spitfire V <R> (BAPC 304) [PR-A]	Privately owned, Knutsford, Cheshire
	W4041	Gloster E28/39	Science Museum, South Kensington
	W4041	Gloster E28/39 <R>	Jet Age Museum, Gloucester
	W4050	DH98 Mosquito	de Havilland Aircraft Museum, London Colney
	W5856	Fairey Swordfish I (G-BMGC) [4A]	RN Historic Flight, Yeovilton
	W9385	DH87B Hornet Moth (G-ADND) [YG-L,3]	Privately owned, Oaksey Park
	X4178	VS300 Spitfire I <R> (BAPC 394) [EB-K]	IWM Duxford
	X4253	VS300 Spitfire I <R> (BAPC 326)	Lytham St Annes Spitfire Display Team
	X4276	VS300 Spitfire I (G-CDGU)	Privately owned, Sandown
	X4590	VS300 Spitfire I (8384M) [PR-F]	RAF Museum, Hendon
	X4650	VS300 Spitfire I (*R9612*/G-CGUK) [KL-A]	Privately owned, Biggin Hill
	X4683	Jurca MJ10 Spitfire (G-MUTS) [EB-N]	Privately owned, Fishburn
	X4859	VS300 Spitfire I <R> (BAPC 319) [PQ-N]	Grangemouth Spitfire Memorial Trust
	X7688	Bristol 156 Beaufighter I (3858M/G-DINT)	Privately owned, Hatch
	X9407	Percival P.16A Q6 (G-AFFD)	Privately owned, Seething (on rebuild)
	Z1206	Vickers Wellington IV (fuselage)	Privately owned, Kenilworth
	Z2033	Fairey Firefly I (G-ASTL) [275/N]	FAA Museum, RNAS Yeovilton
	Z2315	Hawker Hurricane IIA [JU-E]	IWM Duxford
	Z2389	Hawker Hurricane IIA [XR-T]	Brooklands Museum, Weybridge
	Z3427	Hawker Hurricane IIC <R> (BAPC 205) [AV-R]	Michael Beetham Conservation Centre, RAFM Cosford
	Z5207	Hawker Hurricane IIB (G-BYDL)	Privately owned, Thruxton
	Z5252	Hawker Hurricane IIB (G-BWHA/Z5053) [GO-B]	Privately owned, stored Milden
	Z7015	Hawker Sea Hurricane IB (G-BKTH) [7-L]	The Shuttleworth Collection, Old Warden
	Z7197	Percival P30 Proctor III (G-AKZN/8380M)	RAF Museum Reserve Collection, Stafford
	Z7258	DH89A Dragon Rapide (NR786/G-AHGD)	Privately owned, Membury (wreck)
	AB196	Supermarine Aircraft Spitfire 26 (G-CCGH)	Privately owned, Enstone
	AB910	VS349 Spitfire VB (G-AISU) [SH-F]	RAF BBMF, Coningsby
	AD189	VS349 Spitfire VB (G-CHVJ)	Privately owned, Raglan, Monmouthshire
	AD370	Jurca Spitfire (G-CHBW) [PJ-C]	Privately owned, Perranporth
	AD540	VS349 Spitfire VB (wreck)	Kennet Aviation, Tollerton (on rebuild)
	AE436	HP52 Hampden I [PL-J] (parts)	Lincolnshire Avn Heritage Centre, E Kirkby
	AG244	Hawker Hurricane XII (RCAF 5487/G-CBOE)	Privately owned, Aalen, Germany
	AJ841	CCF T-6J Texan (MM53795/G-BJST/*KF729*)	Privately owned, Duxford
	AL246	Grumman Martlet I	FAA Museum, RNAS Yeovilton
	AP506	Cierva C30A (G-ACWM) (wreck)	The Helicopter Museum, Weston-super-Mare
	AP507	Cierva C30A (G-ACWP) [KX-P]	Science Museum, South Kensington
	AR501	VS349 Spitfire LF VC (G-AWII/*AR4474*)	The Shuttleworth Collection, Old Warden

Serial	Type (code/other identity)	Owner/operator, location or fate	Notes
AV511	EHI-101 Merlin <R> [511]	SFDO, RNAS Culdrose	
AW101	AgustaWestland AW101 Mk.510 (G-17-510)	AgustaWestland, Yeovil	
BB803	DH82A Tiger Moth (G-ADWJ) [75]	Privately owned, Henstridge	
BB807	DH82A Tiger Moth (G-ADWO)	Solent Sky, Southampton	
BD713	Hawker Hurricane IIB	Currently not known	
BE505	Hawker Hurricane IIB (RCAF 5403/G-HHII) [XP-L]	Hangar 11 Collection, North Weald	
BH238	Hawker Hurricane IIB	Airframe Assemblies, stored Sandown	
BL614	VS349 Spitfire VB (4354M) [ZD-F]	RAF Museum, Hendon	
BL655	VS349 Spitfire VB (wreck)	Lincolnshire Avn Heritage Centre, East Kirkby	
BL688	VS349 Spitfire LF VB (G-CJWO)	Privately owned, Launceston	
BL735	Supermarine Aircraft Spitfire 26 (G-HABT) [BT-A]	Privately owned, North Coates	
BL924	VS349 Spitfire VB <R> (BAPC 242) [AZ-G]	Beale Park, Pangbourne, Berks	
BL927	Supermarine Aircraft Spitfire 26 (G-CGWI) [JH-I]	Privately owned, Perth	
BM361	VS349 Spitfire VB <R> (BAPC 269) [XR-C]	RAF Lakenheath, on display	
BM481	VS349 Spitfire VB <R> (BAPC 301) [YO-T] (also wears PK651/RAO-B)	Thornaby Aerodrome Memorial	
BM539	VS349 Spitfire LF VB (G-SSVB)	Privately owned, Hastings	
BM597	VS349 Spitfire LF VB (G-MKVB/5718M) [JH-C]	Historic Aircraft Collection, Duxford	
BN230	Hawker Hurricane IIC (LF751/5466M) [FT-A]	RAF Manston, Memorial Pavilion	
BP926	VS353 Spitfire PR IV (G-PRIV)	Privately owned, Newport Pagnell	
BR601	VS361 Spitfire IX (G-CIYF) [SH-F]	Privately owned, Biggin Hill	
BR954	VS353 Spitfire PR IV <R> (N3194/BAPC 220) [JP-A]	Fishburn Historic Aviation Centre	
BS239	VS361 Spitfire IX <R> (BAPC 222) [5R-E]	Battle of Britain Bunker, Uxbridge	
BS410	VS361 Spitfire IXC (G-TCHI)	Privately owned, Biggin Hill	
BS435	VS361 Spitfire IX <R> (BAPC 324) [FY-F]	Privately owned, Lytham St Annes	
BW853	Hawker Hurricane XIIA (G-BRKE) (fuselage)	Currently not known	
DD931	Bristol 152 Beaufort VIII (9131M/BAPC 436) [L]	RAF Museum, Hendon	
DE208	DH82A Tiger Moth II (G-AGYU)	Privately owned, Treswell, Notts	
DE470	DH82A Tiger Moth II (G-ANMY) [16]	Privately owned, Garford, Oxon (rebuild)	
DE623	DH82A Tiger Moth II (G-ANFI)	Privately owned, Cardiff	
DE673	DH82A Tiger Moth II (G-ADNZ/6948M)	Privately owned, Tibenham	
DE971	DH82A Tiger Moth II (G-OOSY)	Privately owned, Damyns Hall, Essex	
DE974	DH82A Tiger Moth II (G-ANZZ)	Privately owned, Clacton	
DE992	DH82A Tiger Moth II (G-AXXV)	Privately owned, Membury, Berks	
DF112	DH82A Tiger Moth II (G-ANRM)	Privately owned, Clacton/Duxford	
DF128	DH82A Tiger Moth II (G-AOJJ) [RCO-U]	Privately owned, White Waltham	
DF198	DH82A Tiger Moth II (G-BBRB)	Privately owned, stored West Wickham, Kent	
DG202	Gloster F9/40 (5758M)	RAF Museum, Hendon	
DG590	Miles M2H Hawk Major (G-ADMW/8379M)	Montrose Air Station Heritage Centre	
DP872	Fairey Barracuda II <ff>	FAA Museum, stored Cobham Hall, RNAS Yeovilton	
DP872	Fairey Barracuda II <rf>	FAA Museum, RNAS Yeovilton	
DV372	Avro 683 Lancaster I <ff>	IWM London, Lambeth	
DZ313	DH98 Mosquito B IV <R>	Privately owned, Little Rissington	
EB518	Airspeed AS10 Oxford V	Privately owned, Kenilworth	
EE416	Gloster Meteor F3 <ff>	Martin Baker Aircraft, Chalgrove, fire section	
EE425	Gloster Meteor F3 <ff>	Jet Age Museum, Gloucester	
EE531	Gloster Meteor F4 (7090M)	Midland Air Museum, Coventry	
EE549	Gloster Meteor F4 (7008M) [A]	Tangmere Military Aviation Museum	
EE602	VS349 Spitfire LF VC (G-IBSY) [DV-V]	Privately owned, Biggin Hill	
EF545	VS349 Spitfire LF VC (G-CDGY)	Aero Vintage, Rye	
EJ693	Hawker Tempest V (N7027E) [SA-J]	To the US, 2015	
EJ922	Hawker Typhoon IB <ff>	Privately owned, Booker	
EM720	DH82A Tiger Moth II (G-AXAN)	Privately owned, Darley Moor, Derbyshire	
EM726	DH82A Tiger Moth II (G-ANDE) [FY]	Privately owned, Headcorn	
EM840	DH82A Tiger Moth II (G-ANBY)	Privately owned, Middle Wallop	
EN130	Supermarine Aircraft Spitfire 26B (G-ENAA) [FN-A]	Privately owned, Enstone	
EN179	VS361 Spitfire F IX (G-TCHO)	Privately owned, Exeter	
EN224	VS366 Spitfire F XII (G-FXII)	Privately owned, Sywell	

Notes	Serial	Type (code/other identity)	Owner/operator, location or fate
	EN398	VS361 Spitfire F IX <R> [JE-J]	AMSS, Pyle, Bridgend
	EN398	VS361 Spitfire F IX <R> [JE-J]	RAF Coningsby, on display
	EN398	VS361 Spitfire F IX <R> (BAPC 184) [JE-J]	Northern 40s Re-enactment Group, Belper
	EN398	VS361 Spitfire F IX <R> [JE-J]	Spitfire Spares, Taunton, Somerset
	EN570	VS361 Spitfire F IX (G-CISP)	*Sold to Norway, April 2016*
	EN961	Isaacs Spitfire <R> (G-CGIK) [SD-X]	Privately owned,
	EP120	VS349 Spitfire LF VB (G-LFVB/5377M/8070M) [AE-A]	The Fighter Collection, Duxford
	EP121	VS349 Spitfire LF VB <R> (BAPC 320) [LO-D]	Montrose Air Station Heritage Centre
	EP122	VS349 Spitfire F VB (R9649/G-CISV) [GL-B]	Privately owned, Biggin Hill
	EV771	Fairchild UC-61 Argus <R> (BAPC 294)	Thorpe Camp Preservation Group, Lincs
	EX976	NA AT-6D Harvard III (FAP 1657)	FAA Museum, RNAS Yeovilton
	FE695	Noorduyn AT-16 Harvard IIB (G-BTXI) [94]	The Fighter Collection, Duxford
	FE788	CCF Harvard IV (MM54137/G-CTKL)	Privately owned, Biggin Hill
	FE905	Noorduyn AT-16 Harvard IIB (LN-BNM)	RAF Museum, Hendon
	FJ801	Boeing-Stearman PT-27 Kaydet (N62842/BAPC 375)	Norfolk & Suffolk Avn Museum, Flixton
	FJ992	Boeing-Stearman PT-17 Kaydet (OO-JEH) [44]	Privately owned, Wevelgem, Belgium
	FK338	Fairchild 24W-41 Argus I (G-AJOZ)	Yorkshire Air Museum, Elvington
	FL586	Douglas C-47B Dakota (OO-SMA) [AI-N] (fuselage)	WWII Remembrance Museum, Handcross, W Sussex
	FR886	Piper L-4J Grasshopper (G-BDMS)	Privately owned, Old Sarum
	FS628	Fairchild Argus 2 (43-14601/G-AIZE)	RAF Museum, Cosford
	FS728	Noorduyn AT-16 Harvard IIB (D-FRCP)	Privately owned, Gelnhausen, Germany
	FT118	Noorduyn AT-16 Harvard IIB (G-BZHL)	Privately owned, Wickenby
	FT323	NA AT-6D Harvard III (FAP 1513/G-CCOY)	Privately owned, Bruntingthorpe
	FT391	Noorduyn AT-16 Harvard IIB (G-AZBN)	Privately owned, Goodwood
	FX322	Noorduyn AT-16 Harvard IIB <ff>	Privately owned, Doncaster
	FX760	Curtiss P-40N Kittyhawk IV (A29-556/9150M) [GA-?]	RAF Museum, Hendon
	FZ626	Douglas Dakota III (KN566/G-AMPO) [YS-DH]	RAF Brize Norton, for display
	GZ100	AgustaWestland AW109SP Grand New (G-ZIOO)	RAF No 32(The Royal) Sqn, Northolt
	HB737	Fairchild Argus III (G-BCBH)	Privately owned, Paddock Wood, Kent
	HB751	Fairchild Argus III (G-BCBL)	Privately owned, Woolsery, Devon
	HG691	DH89A Dragon Rapide (G-AIYR)	Privately owned, Clacton/Duxford
	HH268	GAL48 Hotspur II (HH379/BAPC 261) [H]	Museum of Army Flying, Middle Wallop
	HJ711	DH98 Mosquito NF II (BAPC 434) [VI-C]	Night-Fighter Preservation Tm, Elvington
	HM580	Cierva C-30A (G-ACUU) [KX-K]	IWM Duxford
	HS503	Fairey Swordfish IV (BAPC 108)	RAF Museum Reserve Collection, Stafford
	IR206	Eurofighter Typhoon F2 <R> (BAPC 360) [IR]	RAF M&RU, Bottesford
	IR808	B-V Chinook HC2 <R> (BAPC 361)	RAF M&RU, Bottesford
	JG241	Supermarine Aircraft Spitfire 26B (G-SMSP) [ZX-J]	Privately owned, Blackbushe
	JG668	VS359 Spitfire T8 (A58-441/G-CFGA)	Privately owned, Haverfordwest
	JN768	Hawker Tempest V (4887M/G-TMPV)	Privately owned, Bentwaters
	JP843	Hawker Typhoon IB [Y]	Privately owned, Shrewsbury
	JR505	Hawker Typhoon IB <ff>	Midland Air Museum, Coventry
	JV482	Grumman Wildcat V	Ulster Aviation Society, Long Kesh
	JV579	Grumman FM-2 Wildcat (N4845V/G-RUMW) [F]	The Fighter Collection, Duxford
	KB889	Avro 683 Lancaster B X (G-LANC) [NA-I]	IWM Duxford
	KB976	Avro 683 Lancaster B X <ff>	Lincolnshire Avn Heritage Centre, E Kirkby
	KB976	Avro 683 Lancaster B X (G-BCOH) <rf>	South Yorkshire Aircraft Museum, Doncaster
	KD345	Goodyear FG-1D Corsair (88297/G-FGID) [130-A]	The Fighter Collection, Duxford
	KD431	CV Corsair IV [E2-M]	FAA Museum, RNAS Yeovilton
	KE209	Grumman Hellcat II	FAA Museum, RNAS Yeovilton
	KE418	Hawker Tempest <rf>	*Currently not known*
	KF183	Noorduyn AT-16 Harvard IIB (G-CORS) [3]	Privately owned, Duxford
	KF388	Noorduyn AT-16 Harvard IIB (composite)	Bournemouth Aviation Museum

Serial	Type (code/other identity)	Owner/operator, location or fate	Notes
KF435	Noorduyn AT-16 Harvard IIB	Maidenhead Heritage Centre	
KF532	Noorduyn AT-16 Harvard IIB <ff>	Privately owned, Bruntingthorpe	
KF584	CCF T-6J Texan (G-RAIX) [RAI-X]	Privately owned, Lee-on-Solent	
KF650	Noorduyn AT-16 Harvard IIB <ff>	Sywell Aviation Museum	
KF741	Noorduyn AT-16 Harvard IIB <ff>	Privately owned, Kenilworth	
KG374	Douglas Dakota IV (KP208) [YS-DM]	Merville Barracks, Colchester, on display	
KG651	Douglas Dakota III (G-AMHJ)	Metheringham Airfield Visitor Centre, Lincs	
KH570	Titan T-51B Mustang (G-CIXK) [5J-X]	Privately owned, Sywell	
KH774	NA P-51D Mustang IV (44-73877/G-SHWN) [GA-S]	Privately owned, Goodwood	
KJ351	Airspeed AS58 Horsa II (TL659/BAPC 80) [23]	Museum of Army Flying, Middle Wallop	
KJ994	Douglas Dakota III (F-AZTE)	Dakota et Cie, La Ferté Alais, France	
KK116	Douglas Dakota IV (G-AMPY)	Privately owned, Coventry	
KK527	Fairchild 24R Argus III (44-83184/G-RGUS)	Privately owned, Sibson	
KK995	Sikorsky Hoverfly I [E]	RAF Museum, Hendon	
KL216	Republic P-47D Thunderbolt (45-49295/9212M) [RS-L]	RAF Museum, Hendon	
KN353	Douglas Dakota IV (G-AMYJ)	Yorkshire Air Museum, Elvington	
KN645	Douglas Dakota IV (KG374/8355M)	RAF Museum, Cosford	
KN751	Consolidated Liberator C VI (IAF HE807) [F]	RAF Museum, Hendon	
KZ191	Hawker Hurricane IV (frame only)	Privately owned, East Garston, Bucks	
LA198	VS356 Spitfire F21 (7118M) [RAI-G]	Kelvingrove Art Gallery & Museum, Glasgow	
LA226	VS356 Spitfire F21 (7119M)	RAF Museum Reserve Collection, Stafford	
LA255	VS356 Spitfire F21 (6490M)	RAF Lossiemouth, preserved	
LA543	VS474 Seafire F46 <ff>	The Air Defence Collection, Salisbury	
LA546	VS474 Seafire F46 (G-CFZJ)	Privately owned, Colchester	
LA564	VS474 Seafire F46 (G-FRSX)	Kennet Aviation, North Weald	
LB264	Taylorcraft Plus D (G-AIXA)	RAF Museum, Hendon	
LB294	Taylorcraft Plus D (G-AHWJ)	Saywell Heritage Centre, Worthing	
LB312	Taylorcraft Plus D (HH982/G-AHXE)	Privately owned, Netheravon	
LB323	Taylorcraft Plus D (G-AHSD)	Privately owned, Tibenham (rebuild)	
LB367	Taylorcraft Plus D (G-AHGZ)	Privately owned, Melksham	
LB375	Taylorcraft Plus D (G-AHGW)	Privately owned, Coventry	
LF363	Hawker Hurricane IIC [JX-B]	RAF BBMF, Coningsby	
LF738	Hawker Hurricane IIC (5405M) [UH-A]	RAF Museum, Cosford	
LF789	DH82 Queen Bee (K3584/BAPC 186) [R2-K]	de Havilland Aircraft Museum, London Colney	
LF858	DH82 Queen Bee (G-BLUZ)	Privately owned, Henlow	
LH291	Airspeed AS51 Horsa I <R> (BAPC 279)	RAF Museum, stored Cosford	
LS326	Fairey Swordfish II (G-AJVH) [L2]	RN Historic Flight, Yeovilton	
LV907	HP59 Halifax III (HR792/BAPC 449) [NP-F] (marked NP763 [H7-N] on port side)	Yorkshire Air Museum, Elvington	
LZ551	DH100 Vampire	FAA Museum, RNAS Yeovilton	
LZ766	Percival P34 Proctor III (G-ALCK)	IWM Duxford	
LZ842	VS361 Spitfire F IX (G-CGZU) [EF-D]	Privately owned, Biggin Hill	
LZ844	VS349 Spitfire F VC [UP-X]	Currently not known	
MA764	VS361 Spitfire F IX (G-MCDB)	Privately owned, Biggin Hill	
MD338	VS359 Spitfire LF VIII	Privately owned, Sandown	
MF628	Vickers Wellington T10 (9210M)	Michael Beetham Conservation Centre, RAFM Cosford	
MH314	VS361 Spitfire IX <R> (EN526/BAPC 221) [SZ-G]	RAF Northolt, on display	
MH415	VS361 Spitfire IX <R> (MJ751/BAPC 209) [DU-V]	The Aircraft Restoration Co, Duxford	
MH434	VS361 Spitfire LF IXB (G-ASJV) [ZD-B]	The Old Flying Machine Company, Duxford	
MJ627	VS509 Spitfire T9 (G-BMSB) [9G-P]	Privately owned, Biggin Hill	
MJ772	VS509 Spitfire T9 (G-AVAV) [NL-R]	Privately owned, Biggin Hill	
MJ832	VS361 Spitfire IX <R> (L1096/BAPC 229) [DN-Y]	RAF Digby, on display	
MK356	VS361 Spitfire LF IXC (5690M) [5J-K]	RAF BBMF, Coningsby	
MK356	VS361 Spitfire LF IXC <R> [2I-V]	Kent Battle of Britain Museum, Hawkinge	
MK356	VS361 Spitfire LF IXC (BAPC 298) <R>	RAF Cosford, on display	
MK805	VS361 Spitfire IX (BAPC 426) <R> [SH-B]	Simply Spitfire, Oulton Broad, Suffolk	
MK912	VS361 Spitfire LF IXC (G-BRRA) [SH-L]	Privately owned, Biggin Hill	
ML295	VS361 Spitfire LF IXE (NH341/G-CICK)	Privately owned, Duxford	
ML407	VS509 Spitfire T9 (G-LFIX) [OU-V]	Privately owned, Sywell	

Notes	Serial	Type (code/other identity)	Owner/operator, location or fate
	ML411	VS361 Spitfire LF IXE (G-CBNU)	Privately owned, Ashford, Kent
	ML427	VS361 Spitfire IX (6457M) [HK-A]	Thinktank, Birmingham
	ML796	Short S25 Sunderland V [NS-F]	IWM Duxford
	ML824	Short S25 Sunderland V [NS-Z]	RAF Museum, Hendon
	MP425	Airspeed AS10 Oxford I (G-AITB) [G]	RAF Museum, Hendon
	MS902	Miles M25 Martinet TT1 (TF-SHC)	Museum of Berkshire Aviation, Woodley
	MT182	Auster J/1 Autocrat (G-AJDY)	Privately owned, Spanhoe
	MT197	Auster IV (G-ANHS)	Privately owned, Spanhoe
	MT438	Auster III (G-AREI)	Privately owned, Eggesford
	MT818	VS502 Spitfire T8 (G-AIDN)	Privately owned, Biggin Hill
	MT847	VS379 Spitfire FR XIVE (6960M) [AX-H]	RAF Museum, Hendon
	MT928	VS359 Spitfire HF VIIIC (D-FEUR/MV154/AR654) [ZX-M]	Privately owned, Bremgarten, Germany
	MV268	VS379 Spitfire FR XIVE (MV293/G-SPIT) [JE-J]	North Weald Heritage Aviation, North Weald
	MW401	Hawker Tempest II (IAF HA604/G-PEST)	Privately owned, Wickenby
	MW763	Hawker Tempest II (IAF HA586/G-TEMT) [HF-A]	North Weald Heritage Aviation, North Weald
	MW810	Hawker Tempest II (IAF HA591) <ff>	Privately owned, Bentwaters
	NF314	GEC Phoenix (BAPC 408)	Army, Larkhill, on display
	NF370	Fairey Swordfish III [NH-L]	IWM Duxford
	NF389	Fairey Swordfish III [D]	RN Historic Flight, Yeovilton
	NH238	VS361 Spitfire LF IXE (G-MKIX) [D-A]	Privately owned, stored Greenham Common
	NH341	VS509 Spitfire T9 (G-CICK) [DB-E]	Privately owned, Duxford
	NJ633	Auster 5D (G-AKXP)	Privately owned, Old Sarum
	NJ673	Auster 5D (G-AOCR)	Privately owned, Shenington, Oxon
	NJ689	Auster AOP5 (G-ALXZ)	Privately owned, Breighton
	NJ695	Auster AOP5 (G-AJXV)	Privately owned, Newark
	NJ719	Auster AOP5 (TW385/G-ANFU)	North-East Aircraft Museum, Usworth
	NJ728	Auster AOP5 (G-AIKE)	Privately owned, Yarcombe, Devon
	NJ889	Auster AOP3 (G-AHLK)	Privately owned, Ledbury, Herefordshire
	NL750	DH82A Tiger Moth II (T7997/G-AOBH)	Privately owned, Eaglescott
	NL985	DH82A Tiger Moth I (G-BWIK/7015M)	Privately owned, Sywell
	NM138	DH82A Tiger Moth I (G-ANEW) [41]	Privately owned, Henstridge
	NM181	DH82A Tiger Moth I (G-AZGZ)	Privately owned, Rush Green
	NP294	Percival P31 Proctor IV [TB-M]	Lincolnshire Avn Heritage Centre, E Kirkby
	NV778	Hawker Tempest TT5 (8386M)	RAF Museum, Hendon
	NX534	Auster III (G-BUDL)	Privately owned, Spanhoe
	NX611	Avro 683 Lancaster B VII (G-ASXX/8375M) [DX-F,LE-H]	Lincolnshire Avn Heritage Centre, E Kirkby
	PA474	Avro 683 Lancaster B I [KC-A]	RAF BBMF, Coningsby
	PD685	Slingsby T7 Cadet TX1 (BAPC 355)	Tettenhall Transport Heritage Centre
	PF179	HS Gnat T1 (XR541/8602M)	Privately owned, North Weald
	PG657	DH82A Tiger Moth II (G-AGPK)	Privately owned, Clacton
	PG712	DH82A Tiger Moth II (PH-CSL) [2]	Privately owned, Hilversum, The Netherlands
	PK519	VS356 Spitfire F22 [G-SPXX]	Privately owned, Newport Pagnell
	PK624	VS356 Spitfire F22 (8072M)	The Fighter Collection, Duxford
	PK664	VS356 Spitfire F22 (7759M) [V6-B]	Kennet Aviation, North Weald
	PK683	VS356 Spitfire F24 (7150M)	Solent Sky, Southampton
	PK724	VS356 Spitfire F24 (7288M)	RAF Museum, Hendon
	PL256	VS361 Spitfire IX <R> (BAPC 325) [AI-L]	Privately owned, Leicester
	PL279	VS361 Spitfire IX <R> (N3317/BAPC 268) [ZF-Z]	Privately owned, St Mawgan
	PL788	Supermarine Aircraft Spitfire 26 (G-CIEN)	Privately owned, Perth
	PL793	Supermarine Aircraft Spitfire 26 (G-CIXM)	Privately owned, Odiham
	PL904	VS365 Spitfire PR XI <R> (EN343/BAPC 226)	RAF Benson, on display
	PL965	VS365 Spitfire PR XI (G-MKXI) [R]	Hangar 11 Collection, North Weald
	PL983	VS365 Spitfire PR XI (G-PRXI)	Privately owned, Duxford (on rebuild)
	PM631	VS390 Spitfire PR XIX	RAF BBMF, Coningsby
	PN323	HP Halifax VII <ff>	IWM Duxford
	PP566	Fairey Firefly I <rf>	Privately owned, Newton Abbott, Devon
	PP972	VS358 Seafire LF IIIC (G-BUAR) [11-5/N]	Privately owned, Sywell
	PR536	Hawker Tempest II (IAF HA457)[OQ-H]	RAF Museum, Hendon

Serial	Type (code/other identity)	Owner/operator, location or fate	Notes
PS853	VS390 Spitfire PR XIX (G-RRGN) [C]	Rolls-Royce, East Midlands	
PS890	VS390 Spitfire PR XIX (F-AZJS) [UM-E]	Privately owned, Dijon, France	
PS915	VS390 Spitfire PR XIX (7548M/7711M)	RAF BBMF, Coningsby	
PT462	VS509 Spitfire T9 (G-CTIX/N462JC) [SW-A]	Privately owned, Caernarfon/Duxford	
PT462	VS509 Spitfire IX <R> (BAPC 318) [SW-A]	Privately owned, Moffat, Dumfries & Galloway	
PT879	VS361 Spitfire F IX (G-BYDE)	Hangar 11 Collection, North Weald	
PV202	VS509 Spitfire T9 (H-98/W3632/G-CCCA) [5R-H]	Historic Flying Ltd, Duxford	
PV303	Supermarine Aircraft Spitfire 26 (G-CCJL) [ON-B]	Privately owned, Barton	
PZ460	BBC Mosquito (F-PMOZ) [NE-K]	Privately owned, Fontenay-le-Comte, France	
PZ865	Hawker Hurricane IIC (G-AMAU) [EG-S]	RAF BBMF, Coningsby	
QQ100	Agusta A109E Power Elite (G-CFVB)	MoD/AFD/QinetiQ, Boscombe Down	
QQ101	BAe RJ.100 (G-BZAY)	MoD/ETPS, Boscombe Down	
QQ103	Diamond DA.42M-NG Twin Star (G-LTPA)	MoD/ETPS, Boscombe Down	
RA848	Slingsby T7 Cadet TX1	Privately owned, Leeds	
RA854	Slingsby T7 Cadet TX1	Yorkshire Air Museum, Elvington	
RA897	Slingsby T7 Cadet TX1	Newark Air Museum, Winthorpe	
RA905	Slingsby T7 Cadet TX1 (BGA1143)	Trenchard Museum, RAF Halton	
RB142	Supermarine Aircraft Spitfire 26 (G-CEFC) [DW-B]	Privately owned, Basingstoke, Hants	
RB159	VS379 Spitfire F XIV <R> [DW-D]	Privately owned, Delabole, Cornwall	
RB396	Hawker Typhoon IB (fuselage)	Privately owned, Goodwood	
RD220	Bristol 156 Beaufighter TF X	National Museum of Flight, stored E Fortune	
RD253	Bristol 156 Beaufighter TF X (7931M)	RAF Museum, Hendon	
RF398	Avro 694 Lincoln B II (8376M)	RAF Museum, Cosford	
RG333	Miles M38 Messenger IIA (G-AIEK)	Privately owned, Middle Wallop	
RG904	VS Spitfire <R> (BAPC 333) [BT-K]	RAF Museum, Cosford	
RH746	Bristol 164 Brigand TF1 (fuselage)	RAF Museum, stored Cosford	
RK838	VS349 Spitfire VB <R> (BAPC 230/AB550) [GE-P]	Eden Camp Theme Park, Malton, North Yorkshire	
RK855	Supermarine Aircraft Spitfire 26 (G-PIXY) [FT-C]	Privately owned, Henstridge	
RL962	DH89A Dominie II (G-AHED)	RAF Museum Reserve Collection, Stafford	
RM169	Percival P31 Proctor IV (G-ANVY) [4-47]	Privately owned, Great Oakley, Essex	
RM221	Percival P31 Proctor IV (G-ANXR)	Privately owned, Headcorn	
RM689	VS379 Spitfire F XIV (G-ALGT)	Rolls-Royce, stored East Midlands Airport	
RM694	VS379 Spitfire F XIV (G-DBKL/6640M)	Privately owned, Booker	
RM927	VS379 Spitfire F XIV (G-JNMA)	Privately owned, Biggin Hill	
RN218	Isaacs Spitfire <R> (G-BBJI) [N]	Privately owned, Builth Wells	
RP001	AeroVironment Puma AE Micro UAV	MoD	
RP002	AeroVironment Wasp AE Micro UAV	MoD	
RP003	AeroVironment Shrike Mk1 Micro UAV	MoD	
RR232	VS361 Spitfire HF IXC (G-BRSF)	Privately owned, Goodwood	
RT486	Auster 5 (G-AJGJ)	Privately owned, Old Sarum	
RT520	Auster 5 (G-ALYB)	South Yorkshire Aircraft Museum, Doncaster	
RT610	Auster 5A-160 (G-AKWS)	Privately owned, Shobdon	
RW382	VS361 Spitfire LF XVIE (G-PBIX/7245M/8075M) [3W-P]	Privately owned, Biggin Hill	
RW386	VS361 Spitfire LF XVIE (SE-BIR/6944M) [NG-D]	Privately owned, Angelholm, Sweden	
RW388	VS361 Spitfire LF XVIE (6946M) [U4-U]	Stoke-on-Trent City Museum, Hanley	
RX168	VS358 Seafire L IIIC (IAC 157/G-BWEM)	Privately owned, Exeter	
SE001*	Boeing Scan Eagle RM1 RPAS	QinetiQ, Cardigan Bay	
SL611	VS361 Spitfire LF XVIE (G-SAEA)	Supermarine Aero Engineering, Stoke-on-Trent	
SL674	VS361 Spitfire LF IX (8392M) [RAS-H]	RAF Museum Reserve Collection, Stafford	
SM520	VS509 Spitfire T9 (H-99/G-ILDA) [KJ-I]	Boultbee Flight Academy, Goodwood	
SM845	VS394 Spitfire FR XVIII (G-BUOS) [R]	Spitfire Ltd, Humberside	
SN280	Hawker Tempest V <ff>	South Yorkshire Aircraft Museum, Doncaster	
SR462	VS377 Seafire F XV (UB415/G-TGVP)	Privately owned, Sandown, Isle of Wight	
SR661	Hawker Fury ISS (G-CBEL)	North Weald Heritage Aviation, North Weald	
SX137	VS384 Seafire F XVII	FAA Museum, RNAS Yeovilton	
SX300	VS384 Seafire F XVII (G-RIPH)	Kennet Aviation, North Weald	
SX336	VS384 Seafire F XVII (G-KASX) [105/VL]	Kennet Aviation, North Weald	

Notes	Serial	Type (code/other identity)	Owner/operator, location or fate
	TA122	DH98 Mosquito FB VI [UP-G]	de Havilland Aircraft Museum, London Colney
	TA634	DH98 Mosquito TT35 (G-AWJV) [8K-K]	de Havilland Aircraft Museum, London Colney
	TA639	DH98 Mosquito TT35 (7806M) [AZ-E]	RAF Museum, Cosford
	TA719	DH98 Mosquito TT35 (G-ASKC)	IWM Duxford
	TA805	VS361 Spitfire HF IX (G-PMNF) [FX-M]	Privately owned, Biggin Hill
	TB382	VS361 Spitfire LF XVIE (X4277/MK673)	RAF BBMF, stored Coningsby
	TB675	VS361 Spitfire LF XVIE (RW393/7293M) [4D-V]	RAF Museum, Hendon
	TB752	VS361 Spitfire LF XVIE (8086M) [KH-Z]	RAF Manston, Memorial Pavilion
	TB885	VS361 Spitfire LF XVIE	Privately owned, Biggin Hill
	TD248	VS361 Spitfire LF XVIE (G-OXVI/7246M) [CR-S]	Spitfire Ltd, Humberside
	TD248	VS361 Spitfire LF XVIE (BAPC 368) [8Q-T] (fuselage)	Norfolk & Suffolk Avn Mus'm, Flixton
	TD314	VS361 Spitfire LF IX (G-CGYJ) [FX-P]	Privately owned, Duxford
	TE184	VS361 Spitfire LF XVIE (G-MXVI/6850M) [DU-N]	Privately owned, Biggin Hill
	TE311	VS361 Spitfire LF XVIE (MK178/7241M) [4D-V]	RAF BBMF, Coningsby
	TE462	VS361 Spitfire LF XVIE (7243M)	National Museum of Flight, E Fortune
	TE517	VS361 Spitfire LF IXE (G-JGCA) [HL-K]	Privately owned, Biggin Hill
	TE566	VS509 Spitfire T9 (VH-IXT)	Vintage Flyers, Cotswold Airport (rebuild)
	TG263	Saro SR A1 (G-12-1)	Solent Sky, Southampton
	TG511	HP67 Hastings T5 (8554M) [511]	RAF Museum, Cosford
	TG517	HP67 Hastings T5 [517]	Newark Air Museum, Winthorpe
	TG528	HP67 Hastings C1A [528,T]	IWM Duxford
	TJ118	DH98 Mosquito TT35 <ff>	de Havilland Aircraft Museum, stored London Colney
	TJ138	DH98 Mosquito B35 (7607M) [VO-L]	RAF Museum, Hendon
	TJ207	Auster AOP5 (NJ703/G-AKPI) [P]	Privately owned, Spanhoe
	TJ343	Auster AOP5 (G-AJXC)	Privately owned, White Waltham
	TJ518	Auster J/1 Autocrat (G-AJIH)	Privately owned, Bidford
	TJ534	Auster AOP5 (G-AKSY)	Privately owned, Dunsfold
	TJ569	Auster AOP5 (G-AKOW)	Museum of Army Flying, Middle Wallop
	TJ652	Auster AOP5 (TJ565/G-AMVD)	Privately owned, Hardwick, Norfolk
	TJ672	Auster 5D (G-ANIJ) [TS-D]	Privately owned, Netheravon
	TK718	GAL59 Hamilcar I (fuselage)	The Tank Museum, Bovington
	TK777	GAL59 Hamilcar I (fuselage)	Museum of Army Flying, Middle Wallop
	TP280	VS394 Spitfire FR XVIIIE (D-FSPT)	Hangar 10 Collection, Heringsdorf, Germany
	TP298	VS394 Spitfire FR XVIII [UM-T]	Privately owned, Sandown
	TS291	Slingsby T7 Cadet TX1 (BGA852)	Royal Scottish Mus'm of Flight, stored Granton
	TS798	Avro 685 York C1 (G-AGNV/MW100)	RAF Museum, Cosford
	TW439	Auster AOP5 (G-ANRP)	Privately owned, Strubby
	TW467	Auster AOP5 (G-ANIE)	Privately owned, Elmsett
	TW477	Auster AOP5 (OY-EFI)	Privately owned, Ringsted, Denmark
	TW501	Auster AOP5 (G-ALBJ)	Privately owned, Dunkeswell
	TW511	Auster AOP5 (G-APAF)	Privately owned, Chiseldon, Wilts
	TW519	Auster AOP5 (G-ANHX) [ROA-V]	Privately owned, Newark
	TW536	Auster AOP6 (G-BNGE/7704M)	Privately owned, Netheravon
	TW591	Auster 6A (G-ARIH)	Privately owned, Eggesford
	TW641	Beagle A61 Terrier 2 (G-ATDN)	Privately owned, Biggin Hill
	TX213	Avro 652A Anson C19 (G-AWRS)	North-East Aircraft Museum, Usworth
	TX214	Avro 652A Anson C19 (7817M)	RAF Museum, Cosford
	TX226	Avro 652A Anson C19 (7865M)	Privately owned, stored Compton Verney
	TX235	Avro 652A Anson C19	Privately owned, stored Compton Verney
	TX310	DH89A Dragon Rapide 6 (G-AIDL)	Privately owned, Duxford
	TZ164	Isaacs Spitfire (G-ISAC) [01-A]	Privately owned, Hampstead Norreys, Berks
	VF301	DH100 Vampire F1 (7060M) [RAL-G]	Midland Air Museum, Coventry
	VF512	Auster 6A (G-ARRX) [PF-M]	Privately owned, Popham
	VF516	Beagle A61 Terrier 2 (G-ASMZ)	Privately owned, Eggesford
	VF519	Auster AOP6 (G-ASYN)	Privately owned, Doncaster
	VF526	Auster 6A (G-ARXU) [T]	Privately owned, Netheravon
	VF557	Auster 6A (G-ARHM) [H]	Privately owned, Headcorn
	VF560	Auster 6A (frame)	South Yorkshire Aircraft Museum, Doncaster
	VF581	Beagle A61 Terrier 1 (G-ARSL) [G]	National Museum of Scotland, Edinburgh
	VF631	Auster AOP6 (G-ASDK)	Privately owned, Hibaldstow

Serial	Type (code/other identity)	Owner/operator, location or fate	Notes
VH127	Fairey Firefly TT4 [200/R]	FAA Museum, stored Cobham Hall, RNAS Yeovilton	
VL348	Avro 652A Anson C19 (G-AVVO)	Newark Air Museum, Winthorpe	
VL349	Avro 652A Anson C19 (G-AWSA) [V7-Q]	Norfolk & Suffolk Avn Museum, Flixton	
VM325	Avro 652A Anson C19	Privately owned, Carew Cheriton, Pembrokeshire	
VM360	Avro 652A Anson C19 (G-APHV)	National Museum of Flight, E Fortune	
VM657	Slingsby T8 Tutor TX2 (IGA-6)	Privately owned, stored Ashbridge, Eire	
VM687	Slingsby T8 Tutor (BGA794)	Privately owned, Lee-on-Solent	
VM791	Slingsby Cadet TX3 (XA312/8876M)	RAF Manston History Museum	
VN485	VS356 Spitfire F24 (7326M)	IWM Duxford	
VN799	EE Canberra T4 (WJ874/G-CDSX)	Cornwall Aviation Heritage Centre, Newquay	
VP293	Avro 696 Shackleton T4 [X] <ff>	Shackleton Preservation Trust, Coventry	
VP519	Avro 652A Anson C19 (G-AVVR) <ff>	South Yorkshire Aircraft Museum, Doncaster	
VP952	DH104 Devon C2 (8820M)	RAF Museum, Cosford	
VP955	DH104 Devon C2 (G-DVON)	Privately owned, Cricklade, Wilts	
VP957	DH104 Devon C2 (8822M) <ff>	No 1137 Sqn ATC, Long Kesh	
VP967	DH104 Devon C2 (G-KOOL)	Yorkshire Air Museum, Elvington	
VP975	DH104 Devon C2 [M]	Science Museum, stored Wroughton	
VP981	DH104 Devon C2 (G-DHDV)	Aero Legends, Headcorn/Duxford	
VR137	Westland Wyvern TF1	FAA Museum, RNAS Yeovilton	
VR192	Percival P40 Prentice T1 (G-APIT)	Privately owned, Cambs	
VR249	Percival P40 Prentice T1 (G-APIY) [FA-EL]	Newark Air Museum, Winthorpe	
VR259	Percival P40 Prentice T1 (G-APJB) [M]	Aero Legends, Sywell	
VR930	Hawker Sea Fury FB11 (8382M) [110/Q]	RN Historic Flight, Yeovilton	
VS356	Percival P40 Prentice T1 (G-AOLU)	Privately owned, Montrose	
VS562	Avro 652A Anson T21 (8012M) <ff>	Shannon Aviation Museum, Eire	
VS610	Percival P40 Prentice T1 (G-AOKL)[K-L]	The Shuttleworth Collection, Old Warden	
VS618	Percival P40 Prentice T1 (G-AOLK)	RAF Museum Reserve Collection, Stafford	
VS623	Percival P40 Prentice T1 (G-AOKZ)[KQ-F]	Midland Air Museum, Coventry	
VT812	DH100 Vampire F3 (7200M) [N]	RAF Museum, Hendon	
VT935	Boulton Paul P111A (VT769)	Midland Air Museum, Coventry	
VT987	Auster AOP6 (G-BKXP)	Privately owned, Thruxton	
VV106	Supermarine 510 (7175M)	FAA Museum, stored Cobham Hall, RNAS Yeovilton	
VV217	DH100 Vampire FB5 (7323M)	de Havilland Aircraft Museum, stored London Colney	
VV400	EoN Olympia 2 (BGA1697)	Privately owned, Rivar Hill, Wilts	
VV401	EoN Olympia 2 (BGA1125) [99]	Privately owned, Ringmer, E Sussex	
VV901	Avro 652A Anson T21	Yorkshire Air Museum, Elvington	
VW453	Gloster Meteor T7 (8703M)	Jet Age Museum, Gloucester	
VW957	DH103 Sea Hornet NF21 <rf>	Privately owned, Chelmsford	
VW993	Beagle A61 Terrier 2 (G-ASCD)	Yorkshire Air Museum, Elvington	
VX113	Auster AOP6 (G-ARNO) [36]	Privately owned, Stow Maries, Essex	
VX185	EE Canberra B(I)8 (7631M) <ff>	National Museum of Flight, E Fortune	
VX250	DH103 Sea Hornet NF21 [48] <rf>	de Havilland Aircraft Museum, London Colney	
VX272	Hawker P.1052 (7174M)	FAA Museum, stored RNAS Yeovilton	
VX275	Slingsby T21B Sedbergh TX1 (BGA572/8884M)	RAF Museum Reserve Collection, Stafford	
VX281	Hawker Sea Fury T20S (G-RNHF) [120/VL]	Naval Aviation Ltd, North Weald (on repair)	
VX573	Vickers Valetta C2 (8389M)	RAF Museum, stored Cosford	
VX580	Vickers Valetta C2 [580]	Norfolk & Suffolk Avn Museum, Flixton	
VX595	WS51 Dragonfly HR1	FAA Museum, RNAS Yeovilton	
VX665	Hawker Sea Fury FB11 <rf>	RN Historic Flight, at BAE Systems Brough	
VX926	Auster T7 (G-ASKJ)	Privately owned, Gamlingay, Cambs	
VX927	Auster T7 (G-ASYG)	Privately owned, RAF Scampton	
VZ193	DH100 Vampire FB5 <ff>	Privately owned, Warrington	
VZ440	Gloster Meteor F8 (WA984) [X]	Tangmere Military Aviation Museum	
VZ477	Gloster Meteor F8 (7741M) <ff>	Midland Air Museum, Coventry	
VZ608	Gloster Meteor FR9	Newark Air Museum, Winthorpe	
VZ634	Gloster Meteor T7 (8657M)	Newark Air Museum, Winthorpe	
VZ638	Gloster Meteor T7 (G-JETM) [HF]	Gatwick Aviation Museum, Charlwood, Surrey	
VZ728	RS4 Desford Trainer (G-AGOS)	Privately owned, Spanhoe	
WA346	DH100 Vampire FB5	RAF Museum, stored Cosford	
WA473	VS Attacker F1 [102/J]	FAA Museum, RNAS Yeovilton	
WA576	Bristol 171 Sycamore 3 (G-ALSS/7900M)	Dumfries & Galloway Avn Mus, Dumfries	

Notes	Serial	Type (code/other identity)	Owner/operator, location or fate
	WA577	Bristol 171 Sycamore 3 (G-ALST/7718M)	North-East Aircraft Museum, Usworth
	WA591	Gloster Meteor T7 (G-BWMF/7917M) [FMK-Q]	*Sold to the USA, March 2017*
	WA630	Gloster Meteor T7 [69] <ff>	Robertsbridge Aviation Society, Newhaven
	WA634	Gloster Meteor T7/8	RAF Museum, stored Cosford
	WA638	Gloster Meteor T7(mod) (G-JWMA)	Martin Baker Aircraft, Chalgrove
	WA662	Gloster Meteor T7	South Yorkshire Aircraft Museum, Doncaster
	WB188	Hawker Hunter F3 (7154M)	Tangmere Military Aviation Museum
	WB188	Hawker Hunter GA11 (XF300/G-BZPC)	Privately owned, Melksham, Wilts
	WB440	Fairey Firefly AS6 <ff>	Privately owned, Newton Abbot, Devon
	WB491	Avro 706 Ashton 2 (TS897/G-AJJW) <ff>	Newark Air Museum, Winthorpe
	WB555	DHC1 Chipmunk T10 <ff>	Privately owned, Ellerton
	WB560	DHC1 Chipmunk T10 (comp WG403)	Privately owned, South Molton, Devon
	WB565	DHC1 Chipmunk T10 (G-PVET) [X]	Privately owned, Rendcomb
	WB569	DHC1 Chipmunk T10 (G-BYSJ)	Privately owned, Duxford
	WB571	DHC1 Chipmunk T10 (D-EOSR) [34]	Privately owned, Porta Westfalica, Germany
	WB584	DHC1 Chipmunk T10 (comp WG303/7706M)	Solway Aviation Society, stored Carlisle
	WB585	DHC1 Chipmunk T10 (G-AOSY) [28]	Privately owned, Audley End
	WB588	DHC1 Chipmunk T10 (G-AOTD) [D]	Privately owned, Old Sarum
	WB615	DHC1 Chipmunk T10 (G-BXIA) [E]	Privately owned, Blackpool
	WB624	DHC1 Chipmunk T10	Newark Air Museum, Winthorpe
	WB626	DHC1 Chipmunk T10 [19] <ff>	Trenchard Museum, RAF Halton
	WB627	DHC1 Chipmunk T10 (9248M) (fuselage) [N]	Dulwich College CCF
	WB645	DHC1 Chipmunk T10 (8218M) <rf>	Privately owned, Halton
	WB654	DHC1 Chipmunk T10 (G-BXGO) [U]	Privately owned, Finmere
	WB657	DHC1 Chipmunk T10 [908]	RN Historic Flight, Yeovilton
	WB670	DHC1 Chipmunk T10 (comp WG303)(8361M)	Privately owned, Carlisle
	WB671	DHC1 Chipmunk T10 (G-BWTG) [910]	Privately owned, Teuge, The Netherlands
	WB685	DHC1 Chipmunk T10 (comp WP969/G-ATHC)	de Havilland Aircraft Museum, London Colney
	WB685	DHC1 Chipmunk T10 <rf>	North-East Aircraft Museum, stored Usworth
	WB697	DHC1 Chipmunk T10 (G-BXCT) [95]	Privately owned, Wickenby
	WB702	DHC1 Chipmunk T10 (G-AOFE)	Privately owned, Goodwood
	WB703	DHC1 Chipmunk T10 (G-ARMC)	Privately owned, Compton Abbas
	WB711	DHC1 Chipmunk T10 (G-APPM)	Privately owned, Sywell
	WB726	DHC1 Chipmunk T10 (G-AOSK) [E]	Privately owned, Turweston
	WB733	DHC1 Chipmunk T10 (comp WG422)	South Yorkshire Aircraft Museum, Doncaster
	WB922	Slingsby T21B Sedbergh TX1 (BGA4366)	Privately owned, Little Rissington
	WB924	Slingsby T21B Sedbergh TX1 (BGA3901)	Privately owned, Dunstable
	WB944	Slingsby T21B Sedbergh TX1 (BGA3160)	Privately owned, Bicester
	WB945	Slingsby T21B Sedbergh TX1 (BGA1254)	Privately owned, stored RAF Halton
	WB971	Slingsby T21B Sedbergh TX1 (BGA3324)	Privately owned, Felthorpe
	WB975	Slingsby T21B Sedbergh TX1 (BGA3288) [FJB]	Privately owned, Shipdham
	WB980	Slingsby T21B Sedbergh TX1 (BGA3290)	Privately owned, Husbands Bosworth
	WB981	Slingsby T21B Sedbergh TX1 (BGA3238)	Privately owned, Eaglescott
	WD286	DHC1 Chipmunk T10 (G-BBND)	Privately owned, Old Warden
	WD292	DHC1 Chipmunk T10 (G-BCRX)	Privately owned, White Waltham
	WD293	DHC1 Chipmunk T10 (7645M) <ff>	Privately owned, St Athan
	WD310	DHC1 Chipmunk T10 (G-BWUN) [B]	Privately owned, Deanland
	WD319	DHC1 Chipmunk T10 (OY-ATF)	Privately owned, Stauning, Denmark
	WD321	DHC1 Chipmunk T10 (G-BDCC)	Boscombe Down Aviation Collection, Old Sarum
	WD325	DHC1 Chipmunk T10 [N]	AAC, stored Middle Wallop
	WD331	DHC1 Chipmunk T10 (G-BXDH)	Privately owned, Farnborough
	WD355	DHC1 Chipmunk T10 (WD335/G-CBAJ)	Privately owned, Eastleigh
	WD363	DHC1 Chipmunk T10 (G-BCIH) [5]	Privately owned, Netheravon
	WD370	DHC1 Chipmunk T10 <ff>	No 225 Sqn ATC, Brighton
	WD373	DHC1 Chipmunk T10 (G-BXDI) [12]	Privately owned, Turweston
	WD377	DHC1 Chipmunk T10 <ff>	Wings Museum, Balcombe, W Sussex
	WD386	DHC1 Chipmunk T10 (comp WD377)	Ulster Aviation Soc, stored Upper Ballinderry, NI
	WD388	DHC1 Chipmunk T10 (D-EPAK) [68]	Quax Flieger, Hamm, Germany
	WD390	DHC1 Chipmunk T10 (G-BWNK) [68]	Privately owned, Compton Abbas

Serial	Type (code/other identity)	Owner/operator, location or fate	Notes
WD413	Avro 652A Anson T21 (7881M/G-VROE)	Privately owned, Coventry	
WD615	Gloster Meteor TT20 (WD646/8189M) [R]	RAF Manston History Museum	
WD686	Gloster Meteor NF11 [S]	Muckleburgh Collection, Weybourne, Norfolk	
WD790	Gloster Meteor NF11 (8743M) <ff>	North-East Aircraft Museum, Usworth	
WD889	Fairey Firefly AS5 (comp VT809)	Privately owned, Newton Abbot, Devon	
WD935	EE Canberra B2 (8440M) <ff>	South Yorkshire Aircraft Museum, Doncaster	
WD954	EE Canberra B2 <ff>	Privately owned, St Mawgan	
WD956	EE Canberra B2 <ff>	RAF Defford Museum, Croome Park	
WE113	EE Canberra B2 <ff>	Privately owned, Tangmere	
WE122	EE Canberra TT18 [845] <ff>	Blyth Valley Aviation Collection, Walpole, Suffolk	
WE139	EE Canberra PR3 (8369M)	RAF Museum, Hendon	
WE168	EE Canberra PR3 (8049M)	Norfolk & Suffolk Avn Museum, Flixton	
WE173	EE Canberra PR3 (8740M) <ff>	Robertsbridge Aviation Society, Mayfield	
WE188	EE Canberra T4	Solway Aviation Society, Carlisle	
WE192	EE Canberra T4 <ff>	Blyth Valley Aviation Collection, Walpole, Suffolk	
WE275	DH112 Venom FB50 (J-1601/G-VIDI)	BAE Systems Hawarden, Fire Section	
WE558	Auster T7 (frame)	East Midlands Airport Aeropark	
WE569	Auster T7 (G-ASAJ)	Privately owned, Coventry	
WE570	Auster T7 (G-ASBU)	Privately owned, Stonehaven	
WE591	Auster T7 (F-AZTJ)	Privately owned, Toussus-le-Noble, France	
WE600	Auster T7 Antarctic (7602M)	RAF Museum, Cosford	
WE724	Hawker Sea Fury FB11 (VX653/G-BUCM) [062]	The Fighter Collection, Duxford	
WE982	Slingsby T30B Prefect TX1 (8781M)	RAF Museum, stored Cosford	
WE987	Slingsby T30B Prefect TX1 (BGA2517)	South Yorkshire Aircraft Museum, Doncaster	
WE990	Slingsby T30B Prefect TX1 (BGA2583)	Privately owned, Tibenham	
WE992	Slingsby T30B Prefect TX1 (BGA2692)	Privately owned, Little Rissington	
WF118	Percival P57 Sea Prince T1 (G-DACA) [569/CU]	Gatwick Aviation Museum, Charlwood, Surrey	
WF122	Percival P57 Sea Prince T1 [575/CU]	South Yorkshire Aircraft Museum, Doncaster	
WF128	Percival P57 Sea Prince T1 (8611M)	Norfolk & Suffolk Avn Museum, Flixton	
WF145	Hawker Sea Hawk F1 <ff>	Privately owned, Newton Abbot, Devon	
WF219	Hawker Sea Hawk F1 <ff>	FAA Museum, stored Cobham Hall, RNAS Yeovilton	
WF225	Hawker Sea Hawk F1 [CU]	RNAS Culdrose, at main gate	
WF259	Hawker Sea Hawk F2 [171/A]	National Museum of Flight, E Fortune	
WF369	Vickers Varsity T1 [F]	Newark Air Museum, Winthorpe	
WF372	Vickers Varsity T1	Brooklands Museum, Weybridge	
WF408	Vickers Varsity T1 (8395M) <ff>	Privately owned, Ashford, Kent	
WF643	Gloster Meteor F8 [F]	Norfolk & Suffolk Avn Museum, Flixton	
WF784	Gloster Meteor T7 (7895M)	Jet Age Museum, Gloucester	
WF825	Gloster Meteor T7 (8359M) [A]	Montrose Air Station Heritage Centre	
WF877	Gloster Meteor T7 (G-BPOA)	Privately owned, stored Duxford (dismantled)	
WF911	EE Canberra B2 [CO] <ff>	Ulster Aviation Society, Long Kesh	
WF922	EE Canberra PR3	Midland Air Museum, Coventry	
WG303	DHC1 Chipmunk T10 (8208M) <ff>	Privately owned, Hooton Park	
WG308	DHC1 Chipmunk T10 (G-BYHL) [8]	Privately owned, Averham, Notts	
WG316	DHC1 Chipmunk T10 (G-BCAH)	Privately owned, Gamston	
WG319	DHC1 Chipmunk T10 <ff>	Privately owned, Blandford Forum, Dorset	
WG321	DHC1 Chipmunk T10 (G-DHCC)	Privately owned, Wevelgem, Belgium	
WG348	DHC1 Chipmunk T10 (G-BBMV)	Privately owned, Goodwood	
WG350	DHC1 Chipmunk T10 (G-BPAL)	Privately owned, Cascais, Portugal	
WG362	DHC1 Chipmunk T10 (8437M/8630M/WX643) <ff>	No 1094 Sqn ATC, Ely	
WG407	DHC1 Chipmunk T10 (G-BWMX) [67]	Privately owned, Croydon, Cambs	
WG418	DHC1 Chipmunk T10 (8209M/G-ATDY) <ff>	No 1940 Sqn ATC, Levenshulme, Gr Manchester	
WG419	DHC1 Chipmunk T10 (8206M) <ff>	Sywell Aviation Museum	
WG422	DHC1 Chipmunk T10 (8394M/G-BFAX) [16]	Privately owned, Eggesford	
WG432	DHC1 Chipmunk T10 [L]	Museum of Army Flying, Middle Wallop	
WG458	DHC1 Chipmunk T10 (N458BG) [2]	Privately owned, Breighton	
WG465	DHC1 Chipmunk T10 (G-BCEY)	Privately owned, White Waltham	
WG469	DHC1 Chipmunk T10 (G-BWJY) [72]	Privately owned, Sligo, Eire	
WG471	DHC1 Chipmunk T10 (8210M) <ff>	Privately owned,	

Notes	Serial	Type (code/other identity)	Owner/operator, location or fate
	WG472	DHC1 Chipmunk T10 (G-AOTY)	Privately owned, Bryngwyn Bach, Clwyd
	WG477	DHC1 Chipmunk T10 (8362M/G-ATDP) <ff>	RAF Scampton Heritage Centre
	WG486	DHC1 Chipmunk T10 [G]	RAF BBMF, Coningsby
	WG498	Slingsby T21B Sedbergh TX1 (BGA3245)	Privately owned, Aston Down
	WG511	Avro 696 Shackleton T4 (fuselage)	Flambards Village Theme Park, Helston
	WG655	Hawker Sea Fury T20 (G-CHFP) [910/GN]	The Fighter Collection, Duxford
	WG719	WS51 Dragonfly HR5 (G-BRMA)	The Helicopter Museum, Weston-super-Mare
	WG724	WS51 Dragonfly HR5 [932]	North-East Aircraft Museum, Usworth
	WG751	WS51 Dragonfly HR5 [710/GJ]	World Naval Base, Chatham
	WG760	EE P1A (7755M)	RAF Museum, Cosford
	WG763	EE P1A (7816M)	Museum of Science & Industry, Manchester
	WG768	Short SB5 (8005M)	RAF Museum, Cosford
	WG774	BAC 221	Science Museum, at FAA Museum, RNAS Yeovilton
	WG777	Fairey FD2 (7986M)	RAF Museum, Cosford
	WG789	EE Canberra B2/6 <ff>	Norfolk & Suffolk Avn Museum, Flixton
	WH132	Gloster Meteor T7 (7906M) [J]	RAF Leconfield, for display
	WH166	Gloster Meteor T7 (8052M) [A]	Privately owned, Birlingham, Worcs
	WH291	Gloster Meteor F8	Privately owned, Liverpool Airport
	WH301	Gloster Meteor F8 (7930M) [T]	RAF Museum, Hendon
	WH364	Gloster Meteor F8 (8169M)	Jet Age Museum, Gloucester
	WH453	Gloster Meteor F8	Bentwaters Cold War Air Museum
	WH646	EE Canberra T17A <ff>	Midland Air Museum, Coventry
	WH657	EE Canberra B2 <ff>	Romney Marsh Wartime Collection
	WH725	EE Canberra B2	IWM Duxford
	WH734	EE Canberra B2(mod) <ff>	Privately owned, Pershore
	WH739	EE Canberra B2 <ff>	No 2475 Sqn ATC, Ammanford, Dyfed
	WH740	EE Canberra T17 (8762M) [K]	East Midlands Airport Aeropark
	WH775	EE Canberra PR7 (8128M/8868M) <ff>	Privately owned, Welshpool
	WH779	EE Canberra PR7 <ff>	South Yorkshire Aircraft Museum, Doncaster
	WH779	EE Canberra PR7 [BP] <rf>	RAF AM&SU, stored Shawbury
	WH792	EE Canberra PR7 (WH791/8165M/8176M/8187M)	Newark Air Museum, Winthorpe
	WH798	EE Canberra PR7 (8130M) <ff>	Suffolk Aviation Heritage Centre, Foxhall Heath
	WH840	EE Canberra T4 (8350M)	Privately owned, Flixton
	WH846	EE Canberra T4	Yorkshire Air Museum, Elvington
	WH850	EE Canberra T4 <ff>	Privately owned, Marham
	WH863	EE Canberra T17 (8693M) <ff>	Newark Air Museum, Winthorpe
	WH876	EE Canberra B2(mod) <ff>	Boscombe Down Aviation Collection, Old Sarum
	WH887	EE Canberra TT18 [847] <ff>	Sywell Aviation Museum
	WH903	EE Canberra B2 <ff>	Yorkshire Air Museum, Elvington
	WH904	EE Canberra T19	Newark Air Museum, Winthorpe
	WH953	EE Canberra B6(mod) <ff>	Blyth Valley Aviation Collection, Walpole, Suffolk
	WH957	EE Canberra E15 (8869M) <ff>	Lincolnshire Avn Heritage Centre, East Kirkby
	WH960	EE Canberra B15 (8344M) <ff>	Rolls-Royce Heritage Trust, Derby
	WH964	EE Canberra E15 (8870M) <ff>	Privately owned, Lewes
	WH984	EE Canberra B15 (8101M) <ff>	City of Norwich Aviation Museum
	WH991	WS51 Dragonfly HR3	Yorkshire Helicopter Preservation Group, Elvington
	WJ231	Hawker Sea Fury FB11 (*WE726*) [115/O]	FAA Museum, RNAS Yeovilton
	WJ306	Slingsby T21B Sedbergh TX1 (BGA3240)	Privately owned, Weston-on-the-Green
	WJ306	Slingsby T21B Sedbergh TX1 (WB957/BGA2720)	Privately owned, Parham Park, Sussex
	WJ358	Auster AOP6 (G-ARYD)	Museum of Army Flying, Middle Wallop
	WJ368	Auster AOP6 (G-ASZX)	Privately owned, Eggesford
	WJ404	Auster AOP6 (G-ASOI)	Privately owned, Bidford-on-Avon, Warks
	WJ476	Vickers Valetta T3 <ff>	South Yorkshire Aircraft Museum, Doncaster
	WJ565	EE Canberra T17 (8871M) <ff>	South Yorkshire Aircraft Museum, Doncaster
	WJ567	EE Canberra B2 <ff>	Privately owned, Houghton, Cambs
	WJ576	EE Canberra T17 <ff>	Tettenhall Transport Heritage Centre
	WJ633	EE Canberra T17 <ff>	City of Norwich Aviation Museum
	WJ639	EE Canberra TT18 [39]	North-East Aircraft Museum, Usworth
	WJ677	EE Canberra B2 <ff>	Privately owned, Redruth
	WJ717	EE Canberra TT18 (9052M) <ff>	Privately owned, Crewe, Cheshire

Serial	Type (code/other identity)	Owner/operator, location or fate	Notes
WJ721	EE Canberra TT18 [21] <ff>	Morayvia, Kinloss	
WJ731	EE Canberra B2T [BK] <ff>	Privately owned, Golders Green	
WJ775	EE Canberra B6 (8581M) <ff>	Privately owned, stored Farnborough	
WJ865	EE Canberra T4 <ff>	Boscombe Down Aviation Collection, Old Sarum	
WJ880	EE Canberra T4 (8491M) <ff>	Dumfries & Galloway Avn Mus, Dumfries	
WJ903	Vickers Varsity T1 <ff>	South Yorkshire Aircraft Museum, Doncaster	
WJ945	Vickers Varsity T1 (G-BEDV) [21]	Cornwall Aviation Heritage Centre, Newquay	
WJ975	EE Canberra T19 <ff>	South Yorkshire Aircraft Museum, Doncaster	
WJ992	EE Canberra T4	Bournemouth Airport (derelict)	
WK001	Thales Watchkeeper 450 RPAS (4X-USC)	Army 43 Battery Royal Artillery, Boscombe Down	
WK002	Thales Watchkeeper 450 RPAS (4X-USD)	Army	
WK003	Thales Watchkeeper 450 RPAS	Army	
WK004	Thales Watchkeeper 450 RPAS	Army	
WK005	Thales Watchkeeper 450 RPAS	Army 43 Battery Royal Artillery, Boscombe Down	
WK007	Thales Watchkeeper 450 RPAS	Army	
WK008	Thales Watchkeeper 450 RPAS	Army 47 Regt Royal Artillery, Boscombe Down	
WK009	Thales Watchkeeper 450 RPAS	Army	
WK010	Thales Watchkeeper 450 RPAS	Army 43 Battery Royal Artillery, Boscombe Down	
WK011	Thales Watchkeeper 450 RPAS	Army	
WK012	Thales Watchkeeper 450 RPAS	Army	
WK013	Thales Watchkeeper 450 RPAS	Army	
WK014	Thales Watchkeeper 450 RPAS	Army	
WK015	Thales Watchkeeper 450 RPAS	Army	
WK016	Thales Watchkeeper 450 RPAS	Army	
WK017	Thales Watchkeeper 450 RPAS	Army	
WK018	Thales Watchkeeper 450 RPAS	Army	
WK019	Thales Watchkeeper 450 RPAS	Army	
WK020	Thales Watchkeeper 450 RPAS	Army	
WK021	Thales Watchkeeper 450 RPAS	Army	
WK022	Thales Watchkeeper 450 RPAS	Army	
WK023	Thales Watchkeeper 450 RPAS	Army	
WK024	Thales Watchkeeper 450 RPAS	Army	
WK025	Thales Watchkeeper 450 RPAS	Army	
WK026	Thales Watchkeeper 450 RPAS	Army	
WK027	Thales Watchkeeper 450 RPAS	Army	
WK028	Thales Watchkeeper 450 RPAS	Army	
WK029	Thales Watchkeeper 450 RPAS	Army 43 Battery Royal Artillery, Boscombe Down	
WK030	Thales Watchkeeper 450 RPAS	Army 43 Battery Royal Artillery, Boscombe Down	
WK032	Thales Watchkeeper 450 RPAS	Thales, for Army	
WK033	Thales Watchkeeper 450 RPAS	Thales, for Army	
WK034	Thales Watchkeeper 450 RPAS	Thales, for Army	
WK035	Thales Watchkeeper 450 RPAS	Thales, for Army	
WK036	Thales Watchkeeper 450 RPAS	Thales, for Army	
WK037	Thales Watchkeeper 450 RPAS	Thales, for Army	
WK038	Thales Watchkeeper 450 RPAS	Thales, for Army	
WK039	Thales Watchkeeper 450 RPAS	Thales, for Army	
WK040	Thales Watchkeeper 450 RPAS	Thales, for Army	
WK041	Thales Watchkeeper 450 RPAS	Thales, for Army	
WK042	Thales Watchkeeper 450 RPAS	Thales, for Army	
WK043	Thales Watchkeeper 450 RPAS	Thales, for Army	
WK044	Thales Watchkeeper 450 RPAS	Thales, for Army	
WK045	Thales Watchkeeper 450 RPAS	Thales, for Army	
WK046	Thales Watchkeeper 450 RPAS	Thales, for Army	
WK047	Thales Watchkeeper 450 RPAS	Thales, for Army	
WK048	Thales Watchkeeper 450 RPAS	Thales, for Army	
WK049	Thales Watchkeeper 450 RPAS	Thales, for Army	
WK050	Thales Watchkeeper 450 RPAS	Thales, for Army	
WK051	Thales Watchkeeper 450 RPAS	Thales, for Army	
WK052	Thales Watchkeeper 450 RPAS	Thales, for Army	
WK053	Thales Watchkeeper 450 RPAS	Thales, for Army	
WK054	Thales Watchkeeper 450 RPAS	Thales, for Army	

Notes	Serial	Type (code/other identity)	Owner/operator, location or fate
	WK060	Thales Watchkeeper 450 RPAS	MoD/Thales, Aberporth
	WK102	EE Canberra T17 (8780M) <ff>	Privately owned, Welshpool
	WK118	EE Canberra TT18 [CQ] <ff>	Avro Heritage Museum, Woodford
	WK122	EE Canberra TT18 <ff>	Privately owned, Wesham, Lancs
	WK124	EE Canberra TT18 (9093M) [CR]	Privately owned, South Clifton, Notts
	WK126	EE Canberra TT18 (N2138J) [843]	Jet Age Museum, stored Gloucester
	WK127	EE Canberra TT18 (8985M) <ff>	Privately owned, Peterborough
	WK146	EE Canberra B2 <ff>	Gatwick Aviation Museum, Charlwood, Surrey
	WK163	EE Canberra B2/6 (G-BVWC/G-CTTS)	Vulcan To The Sky Trust, Doncaster Sheffield Airport
	WK198	VS Swift F4 (7428M) (fuselage)	Brooklands Museum, Weybridge
	WK275	VS Swift F4	Privately owned, Doncaster Sheffield Airport
	WK277	VS Swift FR5 (7719M) [N]	Newark Air Museum, Winthorpe
	WK281	VS Swift FR5 (7712M) [S]	Tangmere Military Aviation Museum
	WK393	DH112 Venom FB1 <ff>	South Yorkshire Aircraft Museum, stored Doncaster
WK436	DH112 Venom FB50 (J-1614/G-VENM)	Privately owned, Coventry
	WK512	DHC1 Chipmunk T10 (G-BXIM) [A]	Privately owned, RAF Halton
	WK514	DHC1 Chipmunk T10 (G-BBMO)	Privately owned, Wellesbourne Mountford
	WK517	DHC1 Chipmunk T10 (G-ULAS)	Privately owned, Turweston
	WK518	DHC1 Chipmunk T10 [C]	RAF BBMF, Coningsby
WK518	DHC1 Chipmunk T10 (WP772)	*Repainted as WP772*
	WK522	DHC1 Chipmunk T10 (G-BCOU)	Privately owned, Duxford
	WK549	DHC1 Chipmunk T10 (G-BTWF)	Privately owned, Breighton
	WK558	DHC1 Chipmunk T10 (G-ARMG) [DH]	Privately owned, Shenington, Oxon
	WK562	DHC1 Chipmunk T10 (F-AZUR) [91]	Privately owned, La Baule, France
	WK570	DHC1 Chipmunk T10 (8211M) <ff>	No 424 Sqn ATC, Solent Sky, Southampton
	WK576	DHC1 Chipmunk T10 (8357M) <ff>	Tettenhall Transport Heritage Centre
	WK577	DHC1 Chipmunk T10 (G-BCYM)	Privately owned, Oaksey Park
	WK584	DHC1 Chipmunk T10 (7556M) <ff>	No 511 Sqn ATC, Ramsey, Cambs
	WK585	DHC1 Chipmunk T10 (9265M/G-BZGA)	Privately owned, Shoreham
	WK586	DHC1 Chipmunk T10 (G-BXGX) [V]	Privately owned, Shoreham
	WK590	DHC1 Chipmunk T10 (G-BWVZ) [69]	Privately owned, Grimbergen, Belgium
	WK608	DHC1 Chipmunk T10 [906,Y]	RN Historic Flight, Yeovilton
	WK609	DHC1 Chipmunk T10 (G-BXDN) [93]	Privately owned, Booker
	WK611	DHC1 Chipmunk T10 (G-ARWB)	Privately owned, Thruxton
	WK620	DHC1 Chipmunk T10 [T] (fuselage)	Privately owned, Enstone
	WK622	DHC1 Chipmunk T10 (G-BCZH)	Privately owned, Horsford
	WK624	DHC1 Chipmunk T10 (G-BWHI)	Privately owned, Blackpool
	WK626	DHC1 Chipmunk T10 (8213M) <ff>	South Yorkshire Aircraft Museum, stored Doncaster
	WK628	DHC1 Chipmunk T10 (G-BBMW)	Privately owned, Goodwood
	WK630	DHC1 Chipmunk T10 (G-BXDG)	Privately owned, Felthorpe
	WK633	DHC1 Chipmunk T10 (G-BXEC) [A]	Privately owned, Duxford
	WK634	DHC1 Chipmunk T10 (G-CIGE) [902]	Privately owned, Dunkeswell
	WK635	DHC1 Chipmunk T10 (G-HFRH)	Privately owned, Hawarden
	WK638	DHC1 Chipmunk T10 (G-BWJZ) (fuselage)	Privately owned, South Marston, Swindon
	WK640	DHC1 Chipmunk T10 (G-BWUV) [C]	Privately owned, Hooton Park (wreck)
WK640	OGMA/DHC1 Chipmunk T20 (G-CERD)	Privately owned, Spanhoe
	WK642	DHC1 Chipmunk T10 (G-BXDP) [94]	Privately owned, Kilrush, Eire
	WK654	Gloster Meteor F8 (8092M)	City of Norwich Aviation Museum
	WK800	Gloster Meteor D16 [Z]	Boscombe Down Aviation Collection, Old Sarum
WK864	Gloster Meteor F8 (WL168/7750M) [C]	Yorkshire Air Museum, Elvington
	WK935	Gloster Meteor Prone Pilot (7869M)	RAF Museum, Cosford
	WK991	Gloster Meteor F8 (7825M)	IWM Duxford
	WL131	Gloster Meteor F8 (7751M) <ff>	South Yorkshire Aircraft Museum, Doncaster
	WL181	Gloster Meteor F8 [X]	North-East Aircraft Museum, Usworth
	WL332	Gloster Meteor T7 [888]	Privately owned, Long Marston
	WL345	Gloster Meteor T7 (comp WL360)	Privately owned, Booker
	WL349	Gloster Meteor T7	Jet Age Museum, Gloucester
	WL375	Gloster Meteor T7(mod)	Dumfries & Galloway Avn Mus, Dumfries
	WL405	Gloster Meteor T7 <ff>	Privately owned, Parbold, Lancs
	WL419	Gloster Meteor T7(mod) (G-JSMA)	Martin Baker Aircraft, Chalgrove
	WL505	DH100 Vampire FB9 (7705M/G-FBIX)	Privately owned, Mendlesham

Serial	Type (code/other identity)	Owner/operator, location or fate	Notes
WL626	Vickers Varsity T1 (G-BHDD) [P]	East Midlands Airport Aeropark	
WL627	Vickers Varsity T1 (8488M) [D] <ff>	Privately owned, Preston, E Yorkshire	
WL679	Vickers Varsity T1 (9155M)	RAF Museum, Cosford	
WL732	BP P108 Sea Balliol T21	RAF Museum, Cosford	
WL795	Avro 696 Shackleton MR2C (8753M) [T]	Privately owned, Newquay	
WL798	Avro 696 Shackleton MR2C (8114M) <ff>	Privately owned, Elgin	
WM145	AW Meteor NF11 <ff>	Privately owned, Over Dinsdale, N Yorks	
WM167	AW Meteor NF11 (G-LOSM)	Privately owned, Coventry	
WM224	AW Meteor TT20 (WM311/8177M) [X]	East Midlands Airport Aeropark	
WM267	AW Meteor NF11 <ff>	City of Norwich Aviation Museum	
WM292	AW Meteor TT20 [841]	FAA Museum, stored Cobham Hall, RNAS Yeovilton	
WM366	AW Meteor NF13 (4X-FNA) (comp VZ462)	Jet Age Museum, Gloucester	
WM367	AW Meteor NF13 <ff>	East Midlands Airport Aeropark	
WM571	DH112 Sea Venom FAW21 [VL]	Solent Sky, stored Romsey	
WM729	DH113 Vampire NF10 <ff>	de Havilland Aircraft Musm, stored London Colney	
WM913	Hawker Sea Hawk FB5 (8162M) [456/J]	Newark Air Museum, Winthorpe	
WM961	Hawker Sea Hawk FB5 [J]	Caernarfon Air World	
WM969	Hawker Sea Hawk FB5 [10/Z]	IWM Duxford	
WN105	Hawker Sea Hawk FB3 (WF299/8164M)	Privately owned, Birlingham, Worcs	
WN108	Hawker Sea Hawk FB5 [033]	Ulster Aviation Society, Long Kesh	
WN149	BP P108 Balliol T2 [AT]	RAF Museum, stored Cosford	
WN411	Fairey Gannet AS1 (fuselage)	Privately owned, Sholing, Hants	
WN493	WS51 Dragonfly HR5	FAA Museum, RNAS Yeovilton	
WN499	WS51 Dragonfly HR5	South Yorkshire Aircraft Museum, Doncaster	
WN516	BP P108 Balliol T2 <ff>	Tettenhall Transport Heritage Centre	
WN534	BP P108 Balliol T2 <ff>	Tettenhall Transport Heritage Centre	
WN890	Hawker Hunter F2 <ff>	Boscombe Down Aviation Collection, Old Sarum	
WN904	Hawker Hunter F2 (7544M)	Sywell Aviation Museum	
WN907	Hawker Hunter F2 (7416M) <ff>	Robertsbridge Aviation Society, Newhaven	
WN957	Hawker Hunter F5 <ff>	Morayvia, Kinloss	
WP185	Hawker Hunter F5 (7583M)	Privately owned, Great Dunmow, Essex	
WP190	Hawker Hunter F5 (7582M/8473M/WP180) [K]	Tangmere Military Aviation Museum	
WP255	DH113 Vampire NF10 <ff>	South Yorkshire Aircraft Museum, stored Doncaster	
WP269	EoN Eton TX1 (BGA3214)	Privately owned, Little Rissington	
WP270	EoN Eton TX1 (8598M)	Gliding Heritage Centre, Lasham	
WP308	Percival P57 Sea Prince T1 (G-GACA) [572/CU]	Gatwick Aviation Museum, Charlwood, Surrey	
WP313	Percival P57 Sea Prince T1 [568/CU]	FAA Museum, stored Cobham Hall, RNAS Yeovilton	
WP314	Percival P57 Sea Prince T1 (8634M) [573/CU]	Privately owned, Carlisle Airport	
WP321	Percival P57 Sea Prince T1 (G-BRFC) [750/CU]	Privately owned, St Athan	
WP772	DHC1 Chipmunk T10 (WK518) [4]	RAF Manston History Museum	
WP784	DHC1 Chipmunk T10 (comp WZ876) [RCY-E]	East Midlands Airport Aeropark	
WP788	DHC1 Chipmunk T10 (G-BCHL)	Privately owned, Sleap	
WP790	DHC1 Chipmunk T10 (G-BBNC) [T]	de Havilland Aircraft Museum, London Colney	
WP795	DHC1 Chipmunk T10 (G-BVZZ) [901]	Privately owned, Lee-on-Solent	
WP800	DHC1 Chipmunk T10 (G-BCXN) [2]	Privately owned, RAF Halton	
WP803	DHC1 Chipmunk T10 (G-HAPY) [G]	Privately owned, Booker	
WP805	DHC1 Chipmunk T10 (G-MAJR) [D]	Privately owned, Lee-on-Solent	
WP809	DHC1 Chipmunk T10 (G-BVTX) [78]	Privately owned, Husbands Bosworth	
WP835	DHC1 Chipmunk T10 (D-ERTY)	Privately owned, Porta Westfalica, Germany	
WP840	DHC1 Chipmunk T10 (F-AZQM) [9]	Privately owned, Reims, France	
WP844	DHC1 Chipmunk T10 (G-BWOX) [85]	Privately owned, Adriers, France	
WP848	DHC1 Chipmunk T10 (8342M/G-BFAW)	Privately owned, Old Buckenham	
WP859	DHC1 Chipmunk T10 (G-BXCP) [E] (wreck)	Privately owned, Fishburn	
WP860	DHC1 Chipmunk T10 (G-BXDA) [6]	Privately owned, Kirknewton	
WP863	DHC1 Chipmunk T10 (8360M/G-ATJI) <ff>	No 1011 Sqn ATC, Boscombe Down	
WP869	DHC1 Chipmunk T10 (8215M) <ff>	de Havilland Aircraft Museum, London Colney	
WP870	DHC1 Chipmunk T10 (G-BCOI) [12]	Privately owned, Rayne Hall Farm, Essex	
WP896	DHC1 Chipmunk T10 (G-BWVY)	Privately owned, RAF Halton	
WP901	DHC1 Chipmunk T10 (G-BWNT) [B]	Privately owned, Carlisle	

Notes	Serial	Type (code/other identity)	Owner/operator, location or fate
	WP903	DHC1 Chipmunk T10 (G-BCGC)	Privately owned, Henlow
	WP912	DHC1 Chipmunk T10 (8467M)	RAF Museum, Cosford
	WP921	DHC1 Chipmunk T10 (G-ATJJ) <ff>	Privately owned, Brooklands
	WP925	DHC1 Chipmunk T10 (G-BXHA) [C]	Privately owned, Meppershall
	WP927	DHC1 Chipmunk T10 (8216M/G-ATJK) <ff>	Privately owned, St Neots, Cambs
	WP928	DHC1 Chipmunk T10 (G-BXGM) [D]	Privately owned, Shoreham
	WP929	DHC1 Chipmunk T10 (G-BXCV) [F]	Privately owned, Duxford
	WP930	DHC1 Chipmunk T10 (G-BXHF) [J]	Privately owned, Redhill
	WP962	DHC1 Chipmunk T10 (9287M) [C]	RAF Museum, Hendon
	WP964	DHC1 Chipmunk T20 (G-HDAE)	Privately owned, Wellesbourne Mountford
	WP971	DHC1 Chipmunk T10 (G-ATHD)	Privately owned, Denham
	WP973	DHC1 Chipmunk T10 (G-BCPU)	Privately owned, Turweston
	WP977	DHC1 Chipmunk T10 (G-BHRD) <ff>	Privately owned, South Molton, Devon
	WP983	DHC1 Chipmunk T10 (G-BXNN) [B]	Privately owned, Eggesford
	WP984	DHC1 Chipmunk T10 (G-BWTO) [H]	Privately owned, Little Gransden
	WR410	DH112 Venom FB50 (J-1539/G-DHUU)	Shannon Aviation Museum, Eire
	WR410	DH112 Venom FB54 (J-1790/G-BLKA) [N]	*To Swiss marks as J-1790, 2015*
	WR470	DH112 Venom FB50 (J-1542/G-DHVM)	Privately owned, Coventry
	WR539	DH112 Venom FB4 (8399M) <ff>	Privately owned, Cantley, Norfolk
	WR960	Avro 696 Shackleton AEW2 (8772M)	Museum of Science & Industry, Manchester
	WR963	Avro 696 Shackleton AEW2 (G-SKTN) [B-M]	Shackleton Preservation Trust, Coventry
	WR971	Avro 696 Shackleton MR3 (8119M) [Q] (fuselage)	Fenland & W Norfolk Aviation Museum, Wisbech
	WR974	Avro 696 Shackleton MR3 (8117M) [K]	Privately owned, Bruntingthorpe
	WR977	Avro 696 Shackleton MR3 (8186M) [B]	Newark Air Museum, Winthorpe
	WR982	Avro 696 Shackleton MR3 (8106M) [J]	Gatwick Aviation Museum, Charlwood, Surrey
	WR985	Avro 696 Shackleton MR3 (8103M) [H]	Privately owned, Long Marston
	WS103	Gloster Meteor T7 [709]	FAA Museum, stored Cobham Hall, RNAS Yeovilton
	WS692	Gloster Meteor NF12 (7605M) [C]	Newark Air Museum, Winthorpe
	WS726	Gloster Meteor NF14 (7960M) [H]	No 1855 Sqn ATC, Royton, Gr Manchester
	WS739	Gloster Meteor NF14 (7961M)	Newark Air Museum, Winthorpe
	WS760	Gloster Meteor NF14 (7964M)	East Midlands Airport Aeropark, stored
	WS776	Gloster Meteor NF14 (7716M) [K]	Bournemouth Aviation Museum
	WS788	Gloster Meteor NF14 (7967M) [Z]	Yorkshire Air Museum, Elvington
	WS792	Gloster Meteor NF14 (7965M) [K]	Brighouse Bay Caravan Park, Borgue, D&G
	WS807	Gloster Meteor NF14 (7973M) [N]	Jet Age Museum, Gloucester
	WS832	Gloster Meteor NF14 [W]	Solway Aviation Society, Carlisle
	WS838	Gloster Meteor NF14 [D]	Midland Air Museum, Coventry
	WS840	Gloster Meteor NF14 (7969M) [N] <rf>	Privately owned, Upper Ballinderry, NI
	WS843	Gloster Meteor NF14 (7937M) [J]	RAF Museum, Cosford
	WT121	Douglas Skyraider AEW1 [415/CU]	FAA Museum, stored Cobham Hall, RNAS Yeovilton
	WT205	EE Canberra B15 <ff>	RAF Manston History Museum
	WT308	EE Canberra B(I)6	RN, Predannack Fire School
	WT309	EE Canberra B(I)6 <ff>	Farnborough Air Sciences Trust, Farnborough
	WT319	EE Canberra B(I)6 <ff>	Privately owned, Lavendon, Bucks
	WT333	EE Canberra B6(mod) (G-BVXC)	Privately owned, Bruntingthorpe
	WT339	EE Canberra B(I)8 (8198M)	RAF Barkston Heath Fire Section
	WT482	EE Canberra T4 <ff>	Privately owned, Marske by the Sea, Durham
	WT486	EE Canberra T4 (8102M) <ff>	Privately owned, Newtownards
	WT507	EE Canberra PR7 (8131M/8548M) [44] <ff>	No 384 Sqn ATC, Mansfield
	WT520	EE Canberra PR7 (8094M/8184M) <ff>	Rays-Tek Surplus Ltd, Biddulph, Staffs
	WT525	EE Canberra T22 [855] <ff>	Privately owned, Camborne, Cornwall
	WT532	EE Canberra PR7 (8728M/8890M) <ff>	Bournemouth Aviation Museum
	WT534	EE Canberra PR7 (8549M) [43] <ff>	Privately owned, South Clifton, Notts
	WT536	EE Canberra PR7 (8063M) <ff>	Privately owned, Shirrell Heath, Hants
	WT555	Hawker Hunter F1 (7499M)	Vanguard Haulage, Greenford, London
	WT569	Hawker Hunter F1 (7491M)	No 2117 Sqn ATC, Kenfig Hill, Mid-Glamorgan
	WT612	Hawker Hunter F1 (7496M)	RAF Henlow, on display
	WT619	Hawker Hunter F1 (7525M)	RAF Museum Reserve Collection, Stafford
	WT648	Hawker Hunter F1 (7530M) <ff>	Boscombe Down Aviation Collection, Old Sarum

Serial	Type (code/other identity)	Owner/operator, location or fate	Notes
WT651	Hawker Hunter F1 (7532M) [C]	Newark Air Museum, Winthorpe	
WT660	Hawker Hunter F1 (7421M) [C]	Highland Aviation Museum, Inverness	
WT680	Hawker Hunter F1 (7533M) [J]	Privately owned, Holbeach, Lincs	
WT684	Hawker Hunter F1 (7422M) <ff>	Privately owned, Lavendon, Bucks	
WT694	Hawker Hunter F1 (7510M)	Caernarfon Air World	
WT711	Hawker Hunter GA11 [833/DD]	Lakes Lightnings, Spark Bridge, Cumbria	
WT720	Hawker Hunter F51 (RDAF E-408/8565M) [B]	Privately owned, Manmoel, Gwent	
WT722	Hawker Hunter T8C (G-BWGN) [873]	Cornwall Aviation Heritage Centre, Newquay	
WT723	Hawker Hunter PR11 (XG194/G-PRII) [692/LM]	Hunter Flight Academy, St Athan	
WT741	Hawker Hunter GA11 [791] <ff>	Privately owned, Doncaster	
WT744	Hawker Hunter GA11 [868/VL]	Privately owned, Braunton, Devon	
WT746	Hawker Hunter F4 (XF506/7770M) [A]	Dumfries & Galloway Avn Mus, Dumfries	
WT799	Hawker Hunter T8C [879]	Blue Lagoon Diving Centre, Womersley, N Yorks	
WT804	Hawker Hunter GA11 [831/DD]	FETC, Moreton-in-Marsh, Glos	
WT806	Hawker Hunter GA11	Privately owned, Bruntingthorpe	
WT859	Supermarine 544 <ff>	Boscombe Down Aviation Collection, Old Sarum	
WT867	Slingsby T31B Cadet TX3	Privately owned, Eaglescott	
WT874	Slingsby T31B Cadet TX3 (BGA1255)	Privately owned, Lasham	
WT877	Slingsby T31B Cadet TX3	Tettenhall Transport Heritage Centre	
WT905	Slingsby T31B Cadet TX3	Privately owned, Keevil	
WT908	Slingsby T31B Cadet TX3 (BGA3487)	Privately owned, Dunstable	
WT910	Slingsby T31B Cadet TX3 (BGA3953)	Privately owned, Llandegla, Denbighshire	
WT914	Slingsby T31B Cadet TX3 (BGA3194) (fuselage)	East Midlands Airport Aeropark	
WT933	Bristol 171 Sycamore 3 (G-ALSW/7709M)	Newark Air Museum, Winthorpe	
WV106	Douglas Skyraider AEW1 [427/C]	FAA Museum, stored Cobham Hall, RNAS Yeovilton	
WV198	Sikorsky S55 Whirlwind HAR21 (G-BJWY) [K]	Solway Aviation Society, Carlisle	
WV256	Hawker Hunter GA11 (WB188/G-BZPB)	Cornwall Aviation Heritage Centre, Newquay	
WV318	Hawker Hunter T7A (9236M/G-FFOX)	Hunter Flight Academy, Cranfield	
WV322	Hawker Hunter T8C (G-BZSE/9096M) [22/VL]	Privately owned, North Weald	
WV332	Hawker Hunter F4 (7673M) <ff>	Tangmere Military Aircraft Museum	
WV381	Hawker Hunter GA11 [732] <ff>	Privately owned, Chiltern Park, Wallingford	
WV382	Hawker Hunter GA11 [830/VL]	East Midlands Airport Aeropark	
WV383	Hawker Hunter T7	Farnborough Air Sciences Trust, Farnborough	
WV396	Hawker Hunter T8C (9249M) [91]	RAF Valley, at main gate	
WV493	Percival P56 Provost T1 (G-BDYG/7696M) [29]	National Museum of Flight, stored E Fortune	
WV499	Percival P56 Provost T1 (G-BZRF/7698M) [P-G]	Privately owned, Westonzoyland, Somerset	
WV514	Percival P56 Provost T51 (G-BLIW) [N-C]	Privately owned, Shoreham	
WV605	Percival P56 Provost T1 [T-B]	Norfolk & Suffolk Avn Museum, Flixton	
WV606	Percival P56 Provost T1 (7622M)[P-B]	Newark Air Museum, Winthorpe	
WV679	Percival P56 Provost T1 (7615M) [O-J]	Wellesbourne Wartime Museum	
WV705	Percival P66 Pembroke C1 <ff>	Privately owned, Awbridge, Hants	
WV740	Percival P66 Pembroke C1 (G-BNPH)	Privately owned, St Athan	
WV746	Percival P66 Pembroke C1 (8938M)	RAF Museum, Cosford	
WV781	Bristol 171 Sycamore HR12 (G-ALTD/7839M) <ff>	Caernarfon Air World	
WV783	Bristol 171 Sycamore HR12 (G-ALSP/7841M)	RAF Museum, Hendon	
WV787	EE Canberra B2/8 (8799M)	Newark Air Museum, Winthorpe	
WV795	Hawker Sea Hawk FGA6 (8151M)	Privately owned, Dunsfold	
WV797	Hawker Sea Hawk FGA6 (8155M) [491/J]	Midland Air Museum, Coventry	
WV798	Hawker Sea Hawk FGA6 [026/CU]	Privately owned, Newquay	
WV838	Hawker Sea Hawk FGA4 [182] <ff>	Norfolk & Suffolk Avn Museum, Flixton	
WV856	Hawker Sea Hawk FGA6 [163]	FAA Museum, RNAS Yeovilton	
WV903	Hawker Sea Hawk FGA6 (8153M) [128] <ff>	Privately owned, Stranraer	
WV908	Hawker Sea Hawk FGA6 (8154M) [188/A]	RN Historic Flight, stored Shawbury	
WV910	Hawker Sea Hawk FGA6 <ff>	Boscombe Down Aviation Collection, Old Sarum	
WV911	Hawker Sea Hawk FGA4 [115/C]	RNAS Yeovilton, Fire Section	
WW138	DH112 Sea Venom FAW22 [227/Z]	FAA Museum, stored Cobham Hall, RNAS Yeovilton	
WW145	DH112 Sea Venom FAW22 [680/LM]	National Museum of Flight, E Fortune	
WW217	DH112 Sea Venom FAW22 [351]	Newark Air Museum, Winthorpe	
WW388	Percival P56 Provost T1 (7616M) [O-F]	Privately owned, stored Hinstock, Shrops	

Notes	Serial	Type (code/other identity)	Owner/operator, location or fate
	WW421	Percival P56 Provost T1 (WW450/G-BZRE/7689M) [P-B]	Bournemouth Aviation Museum
	WW442	Percival P56 Provost T1 (7618M) [N]	East Midlands Airport Aeropark
	WW444	Percival P56 Provost T1 [D]	Privately owned, Brownhills, Staffs
	WW447	Percival P56 Provost T1 [F]	Privately owned, Shoreham
	WW453	Percival P56 Provost T1 (G-TMKI) [W-S]	Privately owned, Westonzoyland, Somerset
	WW654	Hawker Hunter GA11 [834/DD]	Privately owned, Ford, W Sussex
	WW664	Hawker Hunter F4 <ff>	Privately owned, Norfolk
	WX788	DH112 Venom NF3 <ff>	South Yorkshire Aircraft Museum, stored Doncaster
	WX853	DH112 Venom NF3 (7443M)	de Havilland Aircraft Musm, stored London Colney
	WX905	DH112 Venom NF3 (7458M)	Newark Air Museum, Winthorpe
	WZ425	DH115 Vampire T11	Privately owned, Birlingham, Worcs
	WZ450	DH115 Vampire T11 <ff>	Privately owned, Corscombe, Dorset
	WZ507	DH115 Vampire T11 (G-VTII) [74]	Privately owned, North Weald
	WZ515	DH115 Vampire T11 [60]	Solway Aviation Society, Carlisle
	WZ518	DH115 Vampire T11 [B]	North-East Aircraft Museum, Usworth
	WZ549	DH115 Vampire T11 (8118M) [F]	Ulster Aviation Society, Long Kesh
	WZ553	DH115 Vampire T11 (G-DHYY) <ff>	Privately owned, Stockton, Warks
	WZ557	DH115 Vampire T11	Privately owned, Over Dinsdale, N Yorks
	WZ572	DH115 Vampire T11 (8124M) [65] <ff>	Privately owned, Sholing, Hants
	WZ581	DH115 Vampire T11 <ff>	The Vampire Collection, Hemel Hempstead
	WZ584	DH115 Vampire T11 (G-BZRC) [K]	Privately owned, Binbrook
	WZ589	DH115 Vampire T11 [19]	Privately owned, Wigmore, Kent
	WZ589	DH115 Vampire T55 (U-1230/LN-DHZ)	*Repainted in Norwegian markings as PX-M*
	WZ590	DH115 Vampire T11 [49]	IWM Duxford
	WZ662	Auster AOP9 (G-BKVK)	Privately owned, Eggesford
	WZ679	Auster AOP9 (7863M/*XP248*/G-CIUX)	Privately owned, Cambs
	WZ706	Auster AOP9 (7851M/G-BURR)	Privately owned, Eggesford
	WZ711	Auster AOP9/Beagle E3 (G-AVHT)	South Yorkshire Aircraft Museum, stored Doncaster
	WZ721	Auster AOP9	Museum of Army Flying, Middle Wallop
	WZ724	Auster AOP9 (7432M)	AAC Middle Wallop, at main gate
	WZ729	Auster AOP9 (G-BXON)	Privately owned, Spanhoe
	WZ736	Avro 707A (7868M)	Museum of Science & Industry, Manchester
	WZ744	Avro 707C (7932M)	RAF Museum, stored Cosford
	WZ753	Slingsby T38 Grasshopper TX1	Solent Sky, Southampton
	WZ755	Slingsby T38 Grasshopper TX1 (BGA3481)	Tettenhall Transport Heritage Centre
	WZ757	Slingsby T38 Grasshopper TX1 (comp XK820)	Privately owned, Kirton-in-Lindsey, Lincs
	WZ767	Slingsby T38 Grasshopper TX1	North-East Aircraft Museum, stored Usworth
	WZ772	Slingsby T38 Grasshopper TX1	Trenchard Museum, RAF Halton
	WZ773	Slingsby T38 Grasshopper TX1	Edinburgh Academy
	WZ784	Slingsby T38 Grasshopper TX1 (comp WZ824)	Solway Aviation Society, stored Carlisle
	WZ784	Slingsby T38 Grasshopper TX1	*Privately owned, stored Felixstowe*
	WZ791	Slingsby T38 Grasshopper TX1 (8944M)	RAF Museum, Hendon
	WZ793	Slingsby T38 Grasshopper TX1	Privately owned, Keevil
	WZ796	Slingsby T38 Grasshopper TX1	Privately owned, stored Aston Down
	WZ798	Slingsby T38 Grasshopper TX1	Privately owned, Eaglescott
	WZ816	Slingsby T38 Grasshopper TX1 (BGA3979)	Privately owned, Redhill
	WZ818	Slingsby T38 Grasshopper TX1 (BGA4361)	Privately owned, Nympsfield
	WZ819	Slingsby T38 Grasshopper TX1 (BGA3498)	Privately owned, Halton
	WZ820	Slingsby T38 Grasshopper TX1 <ff>	Sywell Aviation Museum, stored
	WZ822	Slingsby T38 Grasshopper TX1	South Yorkshire Aircraft Museum, stored Doncaster
	WZ824	Slingsby T38 Grasshopper TX1	Privately owned, Bridge of Weir, Renfrewshire
	WZ826	Vickers Valiant B(K)1 (XD826/7872M) <ff>	*Privately owned, Rayleigh, Essex*
	WZ828	Slingsby T38 Grasshopper TX1 (BGA4421)	Privately owned, Little Rissington
	WZ831	Slingsby T38 Grasshopper TX1	Privately owned, stored Nympsfield, Glos
	WZ846	DHC1 Chipmunk T10 (G-BCSC/8439M)	No 2427 Sqn ATC, Biggin Hill
	WZ847	DHC1 Chipmunk T10 (G-CPMK) [F]	Privately owned, Sleap
	WZ868	DHC1 Chipmunk T10 (WG322/G-ARMF)	*Privately owned, stored St Athan*
	WZ869	DHC1 Chipmunk T10 (8019M) <ff>	Privately owned, Leicester
	WZ872	DHC1 Chipmunk T10 (G-BZGB) [E]	Privately owned, Blackpool

Serial	Type (code/other identity)	Owner/operator, location or fate	Notes
WZ876	DHC1 Chipmunk T10 (G-BBWN) <ff>	Tangmere Military Aviation Museum	
WZ879	DHC1 Chipmunk T10 (G-BWUT) [X]	Privately owned, Duxford	
WZ882	DHC1 Chipmunk T10 (G-BXGP) [K]	Privately owned, Eaglescott	
XA109	DH115 Sea Vampire T22	Montrose Air Station Heritage Centre	
XA127	DH115 Sea Vampire T22 <ff>	FAA Museum, RNAS Yeovilton	
XA129	DH115 Sea Vampire T22	FAA Museum, stored Cobham Hall, RNAS Yeovilton	
XA225	Slingsby T38 Grasshopper TX1	Privately owned, RAF Odiham	
XA226	Slingsby T38 Grasshopper TX1	Norfolk & Suffolk Avn Museum, Flixton	
XA228	Slingsby T38 Grasshopper TX1	National Museum of Flight, East Fortune	
XA230	Slingsby T38 Grasshopper TX1 (BGA4098)	Privately owned, Henlow	
XA231	Slingsby T38 Grasshopper TX1 (8888M)	RAF Manston History Museum	
XA240	Slingsby T38 Grasshopper TX1 (BGA4556)	Privately owned, Portmoak, Perth & Kinross	
XA241	Slingsby T38 Grasshopper TX1	Shuttleworth Collection, stored Old Warden	
XA243	Slingsby T38 Grasshopper TX1 (8886M)	Privately owned, Gransden Lodge, Cambs	
XA244	Slingsby T38 Grasshopper TX1	Privately owned, Brent Tor, Devon	
XA282	Slingsby T31B Cadet TX3	Caernarfon Air World	
XA289	Slingsby T31B Cadet TX3	Privately owned, Eaglescott	
XA290	Slingsby T31B Cadet TX3	Privately owned, Portmoak, Perth & Kinross	
XA293	Slingsby T31B Cadet TX3 <ff>	Privately owned, Breighton	
XA295	Slingsby T31B Cadet TX3 (BGA3336)	Privately owned, Eaglescott	
XA302	Slingsby T31B Cadet TX3 (BGA3786)	RAF Museum, Hendon	
XA310	Slingsby T31B Cadet TX3 (BGA4963)	Privately owned, Little Rissington	
XA459	Fairey Gannet ECM6 [E]	Privately owned, White Waltham	
XA460	Fairey Gannet ECM6 [768/BY]	Ulster Aviation Society, Long Kesh	
XA466	Fairey Gannet COD4 [777/LM]	FAA Museum, RNAS Yeovilton	
XA508	Fairey Gannet T2 [627/GN]	FAA Museum, at Midland Air Museum, Coventry	
XA564	Gloster Javelin FAW1 (7464M)	RAF Museum, Cosford	
XA634	Gloster Javelin FAW4 (7641M)	Jet Age Museum, stored Gloucester	
XA699	Gloster Javelin FAW5 (7809M)	Midland Air Museum, Coventry	
XA847	EE P1B (8371M)	Privately owned, Stowmarket, Suffolk	
XA862	WS55 Whirlwind HAR1 (G-AMJT) <ff>	South Yorkshire Aircraft Museum, Doncaster	
XA864	WS55 Whirlwind HAR1	FAA Museum, stored Cobham Hall, RNAS Yeovilton	
XA870	WS55 Whirlwind HAR1 [911]	South Yorkshire Aircraft Museum, Doncaster	
XA880	DH104 Devon C2 (G-BVXR)	Privately owned, Little Rissington	
XA893	Avro 698 Vulcan B1 (8591M) <ff>	RAF Museum, Cosford	
XA903	Avro 698 Vulcan B1 <ff>	Privately owned, Stoneykirk, D&G	
XA917	HP80 Victor B1 (7827M) <ff>	Privately owned, Cupar, Fife	
XB259	Blackburn B101 Beverley C1 (G-AOAI)	Fort Paull Armoury	
XB261	Blackburn B101 Beverley C1 <ff>	Newark Air Museum, Winthorpe	
XB446	Grumman TBM-3 Avenger ECM6B	FAA Museum, Yeovilton	
XB480	Hiller HT1 [537]	FAA Museum, stored Cobham Hall, RNAS Yeovilton	
XB812	Canadair CL-13 Sabre F4 (9227M) [U]	RAF Museum, Cosford	
XD145	Saro SR53	RAF Museum, Cosford	
XD163	WS55 Whirlwind HAR10 (8645M) [X]	The Helicopter Museum, Weston-super-Mare	
XD165	WS55 Whirlwind HAR10 (8673M)	Caernarfon Airfield Fire Section	
XD215	VS Scimitar F1 <ff>	Privately owned, Cheltenham	
XD235	VS Scimitar F1 <ff>	Privately owned, Lavendon, Bucks	
XD317	VS Scimitar F1 [112/R]	FAA Museum, RNAS Yeovilton	
XD332	VS Scimitar F1 [194/C]	Solent Sky, stored Romsey	
XD375	DH115 Vampire T11 (7887M)	Privately owned, Elland, W Yorks	
XD377	DH115 Vampire T11 (8203M) <ff>	South Yorkshire Aircraft Museum, stored Doncaster	
XD382	DH115 Vampire T11 (comp XD534) [41]	East Midlands Airport Aeropark	
XD425	DH115 Vampire T11 <ff>	Morayvia, Kinloss	
XD434	DH115 Vampire T11 [25]	Fenland & W Norfolk Aviation Museum, Wisbech	
XD445	DH115 Vampire T11 [51]	Tettenhall Transport Heritage Centre	
XD447	DH115 Vampire T11 [50]	East Midlands Airport Aeropark	
XD452	DH115 Vampire T11 (7990M) [66] <ff>	Privately owned, Dursley, Glos	
XD459	DH115 Vampire T11 [57] <ff>	Privately owned, Hanningfield, Essex	
XD506	DH115 Vampire T11 (7983M)	Jet Age Museum, stored Gloucester	

Notes	Serial	Type (code/other identity)	Owner/operator, location or fate
	XD515	DH115 Vampire T11 (7998M/*XM515*)	RAF Museum, stored Cosford
	XD525	DH115 Vampire T11 (7882M) <ff>	Privately owned, Templepatrick, NI
	XD542	DH115 Vampire T11 (7604M) [N]	Montrose Air Station Heritage Centre
	XD547	DH115 Vampire T11 [Z] (composite)	Privately owned, Cantley, Norfolk
	XD593	DH115 Vampire T11	Newark Air Museum, Winthorpe
	XD595	DH115 Vampire T11 <ff>	Privately owned, Glentham, Lincs
	XD596	DH115 Vampire T11 (7939M)	Solent Sky, stored Timsbury, Hants
	XD599	DH115 Vampire T11 [A] <ff>	Sywell Aviation Museum
	XD616	DH115 Vampire T11 [56]	Mosquito Aircraft Museum, stored Gloucester
	XD622	DH115 Vampire T11 (8160M)	*Sold to Germany*
	XD624	DH115 Vampire T11	Privately owned, Hooton Park
	XD626	DH115 Vampire T11 [Q]	Midland Air Museum, stored Coventry
	XD674	Hunting Jet Provost T1 (7570M)	RAF Museum, Cosford
	XD693	Hunting Jet Provost T1 (XM129/G-AOBU) [Z-Q]	Kennet Aviation, North Weald
	XD816	Vickers Valiant B(K)1 <ff>	Brooklands Museum, Weybridge
	XD818	Vickers Valiant B(K)1 (7894M)	RAF Museum, Cosford
	XD857	Vickers Valiant B(K)1 <ff>	Norfolk & Suffolk Aviation Museum, Flixton
	XD875	Vickers Valiant B(K)1 <ff>	Highland Aviation Museum, Inverness
	XE317	Bristol 171 Sycamore HR14 (G-AMWO) [S-N]	South Yorkshire Aircraft Museum, stored Doncaster
	XE339	Hawker Sea Hawk FGA6 (8156M) [149] <ff>	Privately owned, Glos
	XE339	Hawker Sea Hawk FGA6 (8156M) [E] <rf>	Privately owned, Booker
	XE340	Hawker Sea Hawk FGA6 [131/Z]	FAA Museum, stored Cobham Hall, RNAS Yeovilton
	XE364	Hawker Sea Hawk FGA6 (G-JETH) (comp WM983) [485/J]	Gatwick Aviation Museum, Charlwood, Surrey
	XE368	Hawker Sea Hawk FGA6 [200/J]	Privately owned, Barrow-in-Furness
	XE521	Fairey Rotodyne Y (parts)	The Helicopter Museum, Weston-super-Mare
	XE584	Hawker Hunter FGA9 <ff>	Privately owned, Hooton Park
	XE597	Hawker Hunter FGA9 (8874M) <ff>	Privately owned, Bromsgrove
	XE620	Hawker Hunter F6A (XE606/8841M) [B]	RAF Waddington, on display
	XE624	Hawker Hunter FGA9 (8875M) [G]	Privately owned, Wickenby
	XE627	Hawker Hunter F6A [T]	IWM Duxford
	XE643	Hawker Hunter FGA9 (8586M) <ff>	No 1137 Sqn ATC, Aldergrove
	XE650	Hawker Hunter FGA9 (G-9-449) <ff>	Farnborough Air Sciences Trust, Farnborough
	XE664	Hawker Hunter F4 <ff>	Jet Age Museum, Gloucester
	XE665	Hawker Hunter T8C (G-BWGM)	Privately owned, stored Cotswold Airport
	XE668	Hawker Hunter GA11 [832/DD]	Hamburger Hill Paintball, Marksbury, Somerset
	XE670	Hawker Hunter F4 (7762M/8585M) <ff>	RAF Museum, Cosford
	XE683	Hawker Hunter F51 (RDAF E-409) [G]	City of Norwich Aviation Museum
	XE685	Hawker Hunter GA11 (G-GAII) [861/VL]	RAF Scampton Heritage Centre
	XE689	Hawker Hunter GA11 (G-BWGK) <ff>	Privately owned, Cotswold Airport
	XE707	Hawker Hunter GA11 (N707XE) [865]	Bentwaters Cold War Museum
	XE786	Slingsby T31B Cadet TX3 (BGA4033)	Privately owned, Arbroath
	XE793	Slingsby T31B Cadet TX3 (8666M)	Privately owned, Tamworth
	XE797	Slingsby T31B Cadet TX3	South Yorkshire Aviation Museum, Doncaster
	XE799	Slingsby T31B Cadet TX3 (8943M) [R]	Privately owned, stored Lasham
	XE802	Slingsby T31B Cadet TX3 (BGA5283)	Privately owned, North Hill, Devon
	XE852	DH115 Vampire T11 [58]	No 2247 Sqn ATC, Hawarden
	XE855	DH115 Vampire T11	Midland Air Museum, stored Coventry
	XE856	DH115 Vampire T11 (G-DUSK) [V]	Bournemouth Aviation Museum
	XE864	DH115 Vampire T11(comp XD435) <ff>	Privately owned, Ingatstone, Essex
	XE872	DH115 Vampire T11 [62]	Midland Air Museum, Coventry
	XE874	DH115 Vampire T11 (8582M)	Paintball Commando, Birkin, W Yorks
	XE897	DH115 Vampire T11 (XD403)	Privately owned, Errol, Tayside
	XE921	DH115 Vampire T11 [64] <ff>	Privately owned, St Mawgan
	XE935	DH115 Vampire T11	South Yorkshire Aircraft Museum, Doncaster
	XE946	DH115 Vampire T11 (7473M) <ff>	RAF Cranwell Aviation Heritage Centre
	XE956	DH115 Vampire T11 (G-OBLN)	De Havilland Aviation, stored Rochester
	XE979	DH115 Vampire T11 [54]	Privately owned, Cantley, Norfolk
	XE982	DH115 Vampire T11 (7564M) (fuselage)	Privately owned, Saggart, Eire
	XE985	DH115 Vampire T11 (*WZ476*)	Privately owned, New Inn, Torfaen

Serial	Type (code/other identity)	Owner/operator, location or fate	Notes
XF113	VS Swift F7 [19] <ff>	Boscombe Down Aviation Collection, Old Sarum	
XF114	VS Swift F7 (G-SWIF)	Solent Sky, stored Romsey	
XF314	Hawker Hunter F51 (RDAF E-412) [N]	Brooklands Museum, Weybridge	
XF321	Hawker Hunter T7 <ff>	Privately owned, Welshpool	
XF321	Hawker Hunter T7 <rf>	Phoenix Aviation, Bruntingthorpe	
XF375	Hawker Hunter F6A (8736M/G-BUEZ) [6]	Boscombe Down Aviation Collection, Old Sarum	
XF382	Hawker Hunter F6A [15]	Midland Air Museum, Coventry	
XF383	Hawker Hunter F6 (8706M) <ff>	Gloster Aviation Club, Gloucester	
XF418	Hawker Hunter F51 (RDAF E-430)	Gatwick Aviation Museum, Charlwood, Surrey	
XF509	Hawker Hunter F6 (8708M)	Fort Paull Armoury	
XF522	Hawker Hunter F6 <ff>	Herts & Bucks ATC Wing, RAF Halton	
XF526	Hawker Hunter F6 (8679M) [78/E]	Privately owned, Birlingham, Worcs	
XF527	Hawker Hunter F6 (8680M)	RAF Halton, on display	
XF545	Percival P56 Provost T1 (7957M) [O-K]	Privately owned, Bucklebury, Berks	
XF597	Percival P56 Provost T1 (G-BKFW) [AH]	Privately owned, Brimpton, Berks	
XF603	Percival P56 Provost T1 (G-KAPW)	Shuttleworth Collection, Old Warden	
XF690	Percival P56 Provost T1 (8041M/G-MOOS)	Kennet Aviation, Yeovilton	
XF708	Avro 716 Shackleton MR3 [C]	IWM Duxford	
XF785	Bristol 173 (7648M/G-ALBN)	Bristol Aero Collection, stored Filton	
XF836	Percival P56 Provost T1 (8043M/G-AWRY) [JG]	Privately owned stored, Newbury	
XF840	Percival P56 Provost T1 <ff>	Tangmere Military Aviation Museum	
XF926	Bristol 188 (8368M)	RAF Museum, Cosford	
XF940	Hawker Hunter F4 <ff>	Privately owned, Kew Stoke, Somerset	
XF994	Hawker Hunter T8C (G-CGHU) [873/VL]	HHA, Scampton	
XF995	Hawker Hunter T8B (G-BZSF/9237M) [K]	HHA, Scampton	
XG154	Hawker Hunter FGA9 (8863M)	RAF Museum, Hendon	
XG160	Hawker Hunter F6A (8831M/G-BWAF) [U]	Bournemouth Aviation Museum	
XG164	Hawker Hunter F6 (8681M)	Davidstow Airfield & Cornwall At War Museum	
XG168	Hawker Hunter F6A (XG172/8832M) [10]	City of Norwich Aviation Museum	
XG190	Hawker Hunter F51 (RDAF E-425) [C]	Solway Aviation Society, Carlisle	
XG193	Hawker Hunter FGA9 (XG297) (comp with WT741) <ff>	South Yorkshire Aircraft Museum, Doncaster	
XG194	Hawker Hunter FGA9 (8839M)	Wattisham Station Heritage Museum	
XG195	Hawker Hunter FGA9 <ff>	Privately owned, Lewes	
XG196	Hawker Hunter F6A (8702M) [31]	Privately owned, Bentwaters	
XG209	Hawker Hunter F6 (8709M) <ff>	Privately owned, Kingston-on-Thames	
XG210	Hawker Hunter F6	Privately owned, Beck Row, Suffolk	
XG225	Hawker Hunter F6A (8713M)	DSAE Cosford, at main gate	
XG226	Hawker Hunter F6A (8800M) <ff>	RAF Manston History Museum	
XG254	Hawker Hunter FGA9 (8881M) [A]	Norfolk & Suffolk Avn Museum, Flixton	
XG274	Hawker Hunter F6 (8710M) [71]	Privately owned, Newmarket	
XG290	Hawker Hunter F6 (8711M) <ff>	Boscombe Down Aviation Collection, Old Sarum	
XG290	Hawker Hunter T7 (comp XL578 & XL586)	Privately owned, Burton-in-Kendal, Cumbria	
XG297	Hawker Hunter FGA9 <ff>	South Yorkshire Aircraft Museum, Doncaster	
XG325	EE Lightning F1 <ff>	Privately owned, Norfolk	
XG329	EE Lightning F1 (8050M)	Privately owned, Flixton	
XG331	EE Lightning F1 <ff>	Privately owned, Glos	
XG337	EE Lightning F1 (8056M) [M]	RAF Museum, Cosford	
XG452	Bristol 192 Belvedere HC1 (7997M/G-BRMB)	The Helicopter Museum, Weston-super-Mare	
XG454	Bristol 192 Belvedere HC1 (8366M)	Museum of Science & Industry, Manchester	
XG462	Bristol 192 Belvedere HC1 <ff>	The Helicopter Museum, Weston-super-Mare	
XG474	Bristol 192 Belvedere HC1 (8367M) [O]	RAF Museum, Hendon	
XG502	Bristol 171 Sycamore HR14	Museum of Army Flying, Middle Wallop	
XG518	Bristol 171 Sycamore HR14 (8009M) [S-E]	Norfolk & Suffolk Avn Museum, Flixton	
XG523	Bristol 171 Sycamore HR14 <ff> [V]	Norfolk & Suffolk Avn Museum, Flixton	
XG574	WS55 Whirlwind HAR3 [752/PO]	FAA Museum, RNAS Yeovilton	
XG588	WS55 Whirlwind HAR3 (G-BAMH/VR-BEP)	East Midlands Airport Aeropark	
XG592	WS55 Whirlwind HAS7 [54]	Task Force Adventure Park, Cowbridge, S Glam	
XG594	WS55 Whirlwind HAS7 [517]	FAA Museum, stored Cobham Hall, RNAS Yeovilton	
XG596	WS55 Whirlwind HAS7 [66]	The Helicopter Museum, stored Weston-super-Mare	

43

Notes	Serial	Type (code/other identity)	Owner/operator, location or fate
	XG629	DH112 Sea Venom FAW22	Privately owned, Stone, Staffs
	XG680	DH112 Sea Venom FAW22 [438]	North-East Aircraft Museum, Usworth
	XG692	DH112 Sea Venom FAW22 [668/LM]	Privately owned, Stockport
	XG730	DH112 Sea Venom FAW22	de Havilland Aircraft Museum, London Colney
	XG736	DH112 Sea Venom FAW22	Privately owned, East Midlands
	XG737	DH112 Sea Venom FAW22 [220/Z]	East Midlands Airport Aeropark
	XG743	DH115 Sea Vampire T22 [597/LM]	Fishburn Historic Aviation Centre
	XG797	Fairey Gannet ECM6 [277]	IWM Duxford
	XG831	Fairey Gannet ECM6 [396]	Davidstow Airfield & Cornwall At War Museum
	XG882	Fairey Gannet T5 (8754M) [771/LM]	Privately owned, Errol, Tayside
	XG883	Fairey Gannet T5 [773/BY]	FAA Museum, at Museum of Berkshire Aviation, Woodley
	XG900	Short SC1	Science Museum, South Kensington
	XG905	Short SC1	Ulster Folk & Transport Mus, Holywood, Co Down
	XH131	EE Canberra PR9	Ulster Aviation Society, Long Kesh
	XH134	EE Canberra PR9 (G-OMHD)	Privately owned, stored Cotswold Airport
	XH135	EE Canberra PR9	Privately owned, Cotswold Airport
	XH136	EE Canberra PR9 (8782M) [W] <ff>	Romney Marsh Wartime Collection
	XH165	EE Canberra PR9 <ff>	Blyth Valley Aviation Collection, Walpole
	XH168	EE Canberra PR9	RAF Marham Fire Section
	XH169	EE Canberra PR9	RAF Marham, on display
	XH170	EE Canberra PR9 (8739M)	RAF Wyton, on display
	XH171	EE Canberra PR9 (8746M) [U]	RAF Museum, Cosford
	XH174	EE Canberra PR9 <ff>	Privately owned, Leicester
	XH175	EE Canberra PR9 <ff>	Privately owned, Bewdley, Worcs
	XH177	EE Canberra PR9 <ff>	Newark Air Museum, Winthorpe
	XH278	DH115 Vampire T11 (8595M/7866M) [42]	Yorkshire Air Museum, Elvington
	XH312	DH115 Vampire T11	Privately owned, Dodleston, Cheshire
	XH313	DH115 Vampire T11 (G-BZRD) [E]	Tangmere Military Aviation Museum
	XH318	DH115 Vampire T11 (7761M) [64]	Privately owned, Sholing, Hants
	XH328	DH115 Vampire T11 <ff>	Privately owned, Cantley, Norfolk
	XH330	DH115 Vampire T11 [73]	Privately owned, Milton Keynes
	XH537	Avro 698 Vulcan B2MRR (8749M) <ff>	Bournemouth Aviation Museum
	XH558	Avro 698 Vulcan B2 (G-VLCN)	Vulcan To The Sky Trust, Doncaster Sheffield Airport
	XH560	Avro 698 Vulcan K2 <ff>	Privately owned, Foulness
	XH563	Avro 698 Vulcan B2MRR <ff>	Privately owned, Over Dinsdale, N Yorks
	XH584	EE Canberra T4 (G-27-374) <ff>	South Yorkshire Aircraft Museum, Doncaster
	XH592	HP80 Victor B1A (8429M) <ff>	Midland Air Museum, Coventry
	XH648	HP80 Victor K1A	IWM Duxford
	XH669	HP80 Victor K2 (9092M) <ff>	Privately owned, Foulness
	XH670	HP80 Victor SR2 <ff>	Privately owned, Foulness
	XH672	HP80 Victor K2 (9242M)	RAF Museum, Cosford
	XH673	HP80 Victor K2 (8911M)	RAF Marham, on display
	XH767	Gloster Javelin FAW9 (7955M) [L]	Yorkshire Air Museum, Elvington
	XH783	Gloster Javelin FAW7 (7798M) <ff>	Privately owned, Catford
	XH837	Gloster Javelin FAW7 (8032M) <ff>	Caernarfon Air World
	XH892	Gloster Javelin FAW9R (7982M) [J]	Norfolk & Suffolk Avn Museum, Flixton
	XH897	Gloster Javelin FAW9	IWM Duxford
	XH903	Gloster Javelin FAW9 (7938M) [G]	Jet Age Museum, Gloucester
	XH992	Gloster Javelin FAW8 (7829M) [P]	Newark Air Museum, Winthorpe
	XJ314	RR Thrust Measuring Rig	Science Museum, South Kensington
	XJ380	Bristol 171 Sycamore HR14 (8628M)	Boscombe Down Aviation Collection, Old Sarum
	XJ389	Fairey Jet Gyrodyne (XD759/G-AJJP)	Museum of Berkshire Aviation, Woodley
	XJ398	WS55 Whirlwind HAR10 (XD768/G-BDBZ)	South Yorkshire Aircraft Museum, Doncaster
	XJ407	WS55 Whirlwind HAR10 (N7013H)	Privately owned, Tattershall Thorpe
	XJ435	WS55 Whirlwind HAR10 (XD804/8671M) [V]	RAF Manston History Museum, spares use
	XJ476	DH110 Sea Vixen FAW1 <ff>	Boscombe Down Aviation Collection, Old Sarum
	XJ481	DH110 Sea Vixen FAW1 [VL]	FAA Museum, stored Cobham Hall, RNAS Yeovilton
	XJ482	DH110 Sea Vixen FAW1 [713/VL]	Norfolk & Suffolk Avn Museum, Flixton
	XJ488	DH110 Sea Vixen FAW1 <ff>	Robertsbridge Aviation Society, Mayfield

Serial	Type (code/other identity)	Owner/operator, location or fate	Notes
XJ494	DH110 Sea Vixen FAW2 [121/E]	Privately owned, Bruntingthorpe	
XJ560	DH110 Sea Vixen FAW2 (8142M) [243/H]	Newark Air Museum, Winthorpe	
XJ565	DH110 Sea Vixen FAW2 [127/E]	de Havilland Aircraft Museum, London Colney	
XJ571	DH110 Sea Vixen FAW2 (8140M) [242/R]	Solent Sky, Southampton	
XJ575	DH110 Sea Vixen FAW2 <ff> [SAH-13]	Wellesbourne Wartime Museum	
XJ579	DH110 Sea Vixen FAW2 <ff>	Midland Air Museum, Coventry	
XJ580	DH110 Sea Vixen FAW2 [131/E]	Tangmere Military Aviation Museum	
XJ714	Hawker Hunter FR10 (comp XG226)	East Midlands Airport Aeropark	
XJ723	WS55 Whirlwind HAR10	Privately owned, Newcastle upon Tyne	
XJ726	WS55 Whirlwind HAR10	Caernarfon Air World	
XJ727	WS55 Whirlwind HAR10 (8661M) [L]	Privately owned, Ramsgate	
XJ729	WS55 Whirlwind HAR10 (8732M/G-BVGE)	Privately owned, Crewkerne, Somerset	
XJ758	WS55 Whirlwind HAR10 (8464M) <ff>	Privately owned, Welshpool	
XJ771	DH115 Vampire T55 (U-1215/G-HELV)	Sold to Jordan as 711, 25 April 2016	
XJ772	DH115 Vampire T11 [H]	de Havilland Aircraft Museum, London Colney	
XJ823	Avro 698 Vulcan B2A	Solway Aviation Society, Carlisle	
XJ824	Avro 698 Vulcan B2A	IWM Duxford	
XJ917	Bristol 171 Sycamore HR14 [H-S]	Bristol Sycamore Group, stored Filton	
XJ918	Bristol 171 Sycamore HR14 (8190M)	RAF Museum, Cosford	
XK416	Auster AOP9 (7855M/G-AYUA)	Privately owned, Widmerpool	
XK417	Auster AOP9 (G-AVXY)	Privately owned, Messingham, Lincs	
XK418	Auster AOP9 (7976M)	93rd Bomb Group Museum, Hardwick, Norfolk	
XK421	Auster AOP9 (8365M) (frame)	Privately owned, Lincs	
XK488	Blackburn NA39 Buccaneer S1	FAA Museum, stored Cobham Hall, RNAS Yeovilton	
XK526	Blackburn NA39 Buccaneer S2 (8648M)	RAF Honington, at main gate	
XK527	Blackburn NA39 Buccaneer S2D (8818M) <ff>	Privately owned, North Wales	
XK532	Blackburn NA39 Buccaneer S1 (8867M) [632/LM]	Highland Aviation Museum, Inverness	
XK533	Blackburn NA39 Buccaneer S1 <ff>	Royal Scottish Mus'm of Flight, stored Granton	
XK590	DH115 Vampire T11 [V]	Wellesbourne Wartime Museum	
XK623	DH115 Vampire T11 (G-VAMP) [56]	Caernarfon Air World	
XK624	DH115 Vampire T11 [32]	Norfolk & Suffolk Avn Museum, Flixton	
XK625	DH115 Vampire T11 [14]	Romney Marsh Wartime Collection	
XK627	DH115 Vampire T11 <ff>	Davidstow Airfield & Cornwall At War Museum	
XK632	DH115 Vampire T11 <ff>	Privately owned, Greenford, London	
XK637	DH115 Vampire T11 [56]	Top Gun Flight Simulation Centre, Stalybridge	
XK695	DH106 Comet C2(RC) (G-AMXH/9164M) <ff>	de Havilland Aircraft Museum, London Colney	
XK699	DH106 Comet C2 (7971M) <ff>	Boscombe Down Aviation Collection, Old Sarum	
XK724	Folland Gnat F1 (7715M)	RAF Museum, stored Cosford	
XK740	Folland Gnat F1 (8396M)	Solent Sky, Southampton	
XK776	ML Utility 1	Museum of Army Flying, Middle Wallop	
XK789	Slingsby T38 Grasshopper TX1	Midland Air Museum, Coventry	
XK790	Slingsby T38 Grasshopper TX1	Privately owned, stored Husbands Bosworth	
XK819	Slingsby T38 Grasshopper TX1	Privately owned, stored Rufforth	
XK822	Slingsby T38 Grasshopper TX1	Privately owned, Partridge Green, W Sussex	
XK885	Percival P66 Pembroke C1 (8452M/N46EA)	Privately owned, St Athan	
XK895	DH104 Sea Devon C20 (G-SDEV) [19/CU]	Cornwall Aviation Heritage Centre, Newquay	
XK907	WS55 Whirlwind HAS7	Midland Air Museum, stored Coventry	
XK911	WS55 Whirlwind HAS7 [519/PO]	Privately owned, stored Dagenham	
XK936	WS55 Whirlwind HAS7 [62]	IWM Duxford	
XK940	WS55 Whirlwind HAS7 (G-AYXT) [911]	The Helicopter Museum, Weston-super-Mare	
XK970	WS55 Whirlwind HAR10 (8789M)	Army, Bramley, Hants (for disposal)	
XL149	Blackburn B101 Beverley C1 (7988M) <ff>	South Yorkshire Aircraft Museum, Doncaster	
XL160	HP80 Victor K2 (8910M) <ff>	Norfolk & Suffolk Avn Museum, Flixton	
XL164	HP80 Victor K2 (9215M) <ff>	Bournemouth Aviation Museum	
XL190	HP80 Victor K2 (9216M) <ff>	RAF Manston History Museum	
XL231	HP80 Victor K2	Yorkshire Air Museum, Elvington	
XL318	Avro 698 Vulcan B2 (8733M)	RAF Museum, Hendon	
XL319	Avro 698 Vulcan B2	North-East Aircraft Museum, Usworth	
XL360	Avro 698 Vulcan B2A	Midland Air Museum, Coventry	
XL388	Avro 698 Vulcan B2 <ff>	South Yorkshire Aircraft Museum, Doncaster	

Notes	Serial	Type (code/other identity)	Owner/operator, location or fate
	XL426	Avro 698 Vulcan B2 (G-VJET)	Vulcan Restoration Trust, Southend
	XL445	Avro 698 Vulcan K2 (8811M) <ff>	Norfolk & Suffolk Avn Museum, Flixton
	XL449	Fairey Gannet AEW3 <ff>	Privately owned, Steventon, Oxon
	XL472	Fairey Gannet AEW3 [044/R]	Hunter Flying Ltd, St Athan (spares use)
	XL497	Fairey Gannet AEW3 [041/R]	Dumfries & Galloway Avn Mus, Dumfries
	XL500	Fairey Gannet AEW3 (G-KAEW) [CU]	Privately owned, St Athan
	XL502	Fairey Gannet AEW3 (8610M/G-BMYP)	Yorkshire Air Museum, Elvington
	XL503	Fairey Gannet AEW3 [070/E]	FAA Museum, stored Cobham Hall, RNAS Yeovilton
	XL563	Hawker Hunter T7 (9218M)	Farnborough Air Sciences Trust, stored Farnborough
	XL564	Hawker Hunter T7 <ff>	Privately owned, Tilehurst, Berks
	XL565	Hawker Hunter T7 (parts of WT745) [Y]	Privately owned, Bruntingthorpe
	XL568	Hawker Hunter T7A (9224M) [X]	RAF Museum, Cosford
	XL569	Hawker Hunter T7 (8833M)	East Midlands Airport Aeropark
	XL571	Hawker Hunter T7 (XL572/8834M/G-HNTR) [V]	Yorkshire Air Museum, Elvington
	XL573	Hawker Hunter T7 (G-BVGH)	Hunter Flying Ltd, St Athan
	XL577	Hawker Hunter T7 (8676M/G-XMHD)	Sold to Jordan, February 2016
	XL580	Hawker Hunter T8M [723]	FAA Museum, RNAS Yeovilton
	XL586	Hawker Hunter T7 (comp XL578)	Action Park, Wickford, Essex
	XL587	Hawker Hunter T7 (8807M/G-HPUX)	HHA, stored Scampton
	XL591	Hawker Hunter T7	Gatwick Aviation Museum, Charlwood, Surrey
	XL592	Hawker Hunter T7 (8836M) [Y]	Maidenhead Heritage Centre
	XL600	Hawker Hunter T7 (G-RAXA)	Sold to Canada, March 2016
	XL601	Hawker Hunter T7 (G-BZSR) [874/VL]	Classic Fighters, Brustem, Belgium
	XL602	Hawker Hunter T8M (G-BWFT)	Hunter Flying Ltd, St Athan
	XL609	Hawker Hunter T7 <ff>	Privately owned, South Molton, Devon
	XL612	Hawker Hunter T7 [2]	Privately owned, Swansea
	XL618	Hawker Hunter T7 (8892M)	Sold to Germany, May 2016
	XL621	Hawker Hunter T7 (G-BNCX)	Privately owned, Dunsfold
	XL623	Hawker Hunter T7 (8770M)	The Planets Leisure Centre, Woking
	XL629	EE Lightning T4	MoD/QinetiQ Boscombe Down, at main gate
	XL714	DH82A Tiger Moth II (T6099/G-AOGR)	Privately owned, Boughton, Lincs
	XL736	Saro Skeeter AOP12	The Helicopter Museum stored, Weston-super-Mare
	XL738	Saro Skeeter AOP12 (XM565/7861M)	Privately owned, Storwood, Yorkshire
	XL739	Saro Skeeter AOP12	Privately owned, Forncett St Peter, Norfolk
	XL762	Saro Skeeter AOP12 (8017M)	National Museum of Flight, E Fortune
	XL763	Saro Skeeter AOP12	Privately owned, Storwood, Yorkshire
	XL764	Saro Skeeter AOP12 (7940M) [J]	Newark Air Museum, Winthorpe
	XL765	Saro Skeeter AOP12	Privately owned, Melksham, Wilts
	XL770	Saro Skeeter AOP12 (8046M)	Solent Sky, Southampton
	XL809	Saro Skeeter AOP12 (G-BLIX)	Privately owned, Wilden, Beds
	XL811	Saro Skeeter AOP12	The Helicopter Museum, Weston-super-Mare
	XL812	Saro Skeeter AOP12 (G-SARO)	AAC Historic Aircraft Flight, stored Middle Wallop
	XL813	Saro Skeeter AOP12	Museum of Army Flying, Middle Wallop
	XL814	Saro Skeeter AOP12	AAC Historic Aircraft Flight, Middle Wallop
	XL824	Bristol 171 Sycamore HR14 (8021M)	Bristol Aerospace Centre, Filton
	XL829	Bristol 171 Sycamore HR14	The Helicopter Museum, Weston-super-Mare
	XL840	WS55 Whirlwind HAS7	Privately owned, Bawtry
	XL853	WS55 Whirlwind HAS7 [PO]	FAA Museum, stored Cobham Hall, RNAS Yeovilton
	XL875	WS55 Whirlwind HAR9	Perth Technical College
	XL929	Percival P66 Pembroke C1 (G-BNPU)	Privately owned, stored Compton Verney
	XL954	Percival P66 Pembroke C1 (9042M/N4234C/G-BXES)	Privately owned, Weston, Ireland
	XL993	SAL Twin Pioneer CC2 (8388M)	RAF Museum, Cosford
	XM135	BAC Lightning F1 [B]	IWM Duxford
	XM144	BAC Lightning F1 (8417M) <ff>	Shannon Aviation Museum, Eire
	XM169	BAC Lightning F1A (8422M) <ff>	Highland Aviation Museum, Inverness
	XM172	BAC Lightning F1A (8427M)	Lakes Lightnings, Spark Bridge, Cumbria
	XM173	BAC Lightning F1A (8414M) [A]	Privately owned, Malmesbury, Glos
	XM191	BAC Lightning F1A (7854M/8590M) <ff>	Privately owned, Thorpe Wood, N Yorks
	XM192	BAC Lightning F1A (8413M) [K]	Thorpe Camp Preservation Group, Lincs
	XM223	DH104 Devon C2 (G-BWWC) [J]	Privately owned, stored Compton Verney

Serial	Type (code/other identity)	Owner/operator, location or fate	Notes
XM279	EE Canberra B(I)8 <ff>	Privately owned, Flixton	
XM300	WS58 Wessex HAS1	Privately owned, Nantgarw, Rhondda	
XM328	WS58 Wessex HAS3 [653/PO]	The Helicopter Museum, Weston-super-Mare	
XM330	WS58 Wessex HAS1	The Helicopter Museum, Weston-super-Mare	
XM350	Hunting Jet Provost T3A (9036M) [89]	South Yorkshire Aircraft Museum, Doncaster	
XM351	Hunting Jet Provost T3 (8078M) [Y]	RAF Museum, Cosford	
XM355	Hunting Jet Provost T3 (8229M)	Newcastle Aviation Academy	
XM358	Hunting Jet Provost T3A (8987M) [53]	Privately owned, Newbridge, Powys	
XM362	Hunting Jet Provost T3 (8230M)	DSAE No 1 SoTT, Cosford	
XM365	Hunting Jet Provost T3A (G-BXBH)	Privately owned, Bruntingthorpe	
XM373	Hunting Jet Provost T3 (7726M) [2] <ff>	Yorkshire Air Museum, Elvington	
XM383	Hunting Jet Provost T3A [90]	Newark Air Museum, Winthorpe	
XM402	Hunting Jet Provost T3 (8055AM) [18]	Fenland & W Norfolk Aviation Museum, Wisbech	
XM404	Hunting Jet Provost T3 (8055BM) <ff>	South Yorkshire Aircraft Museum, Doncaster	
XM409	Hunting Jet Provost T3 (8082M) <ff>	Air Scouts, Guernsey Airport	
XM410	Hunting Jet Provost T3 (8054AM) [B]	Privately owned, Gillingham, Kent	
XM411	Hunting Jet Provost T3 (8434M) <ff>	South Yorkshire Aircraft Museum, Doncaster	
XM412	Hunting Jet Provost T3A (9011M) [41]	Privately owned, Balado Bridge, Scotland	
XM414	Hunting Jet Provost T3A (8996M)	Ulster Aviation Society, Long Kesh	
XM417	Hunting Jet Provost T3A (8054BM) [D] <ff>	Privately owned, Cannock	
XM419	Hunting Jet Provost T3A (8990M) [102]	Newcastle Aviation Academy	
XM424	Hunting Jet Provost T3 (G-BWDS)	Privately owned, Coventry	
XM425	Hunting Jet Provost T3A (8995M) [88]	Privately owned, Longton, Staffs	
XM463	Hunting Jet Provost T3 [38] (fuselage)	RAF Museum, Hendon	
XM468	Hunting Jet Provost T3 (8081M) <ff>	Wings Museum, Balcombe, W Sussex	
XM473	Hunting Jet Provost T3A (8974M/G-TINY)	Privately owned, Wethersfield	
XM474	Hunting Jet Provost T3 (8121M) <ff>	Privately owned, South Reddish, Stockport	
XM479	Hunting Jet Provost T3A (G-BVEZ) [U]	Privately owned, Newcastle	
XM480	Hunting Jet Provost T3 (8080M)	4x4 Car Centre, Chesterfield	
XM496	Bristol 253 Britannia C1 (EL-WXA) [496]	Britannia Preservation Society, Cotswold Airport	
XM497	Bristol 175 Britannia 312F (G-AOVF) [497]	RAF Museum, Cosford	
XM529	Saro Skeeter AOP12 (7979M/G-BDNS)	Privately owned, Handforth	
XM553	Saro Skeeter AOP12 (G-AWSV)	Yorkshire Air Museum, Elvington	
XM555	Saro Skeeter AOP12 (8027M)	North-East Aircraft Museum, Usworth	
XM557	Saro Skeeter AOP12 <ff>	The Helicopter Museum, stored Weston-super-Mare	
XM564	Saro Skeeter AOP12	The Tank Museum, Bovington	
XM569	Avro 698 Vulcan B2 <ff>	Jet Age Museum, Gloucester	
XM575	Avro 698 Vulcan B2A (G-BLMC)	East Midlands Airport Aeropark	
XM594	Avro 698 Vulcan B2	Newark Air Museum, Winthorpe	
XM597	Avro 698 Vulcan B2	National Museum of Flight, E Fortune	
XM598	Avro 698 Vulcan B2 (8778M)	RAF Museum, Cosford	
XM602	Avro 698 Vulcan B2 (8771M) <ff>	Avro Heritage Museum, Woodford	
XM603	Avro 698 Vulcan B2	Avro Heritage Museum, Woodford	
XM607	Avro 698 Vulcan B2 (8779M)	RAF Waddington, on display	
XM612	Avro 698 Vulcan B2	City of Norwich Aviation Museum	
XM651	Saro Skeeter AOP12 (XM561/7980M)	South Yorkshire Aircraft Museum, Doncaster	
XM652	Avro 698 Vulcan B2 <ff>	Privately owned, Welshpool	
XM655	Avro 698 Vulcan B2 (G-VULC)	Privately owned, Wellesbourne Mountford	
XM685	WS55 Whirlwind HAS7 (G-AYZJ) [513/PO]	Newark Air Museum, Winthorpe	
XM692	HS Gnat T1 <ff>	Privately owned, Welshpool	
XM693	HS Gnat T1 (7891M)	BAE Systems Hamble, on display	
XM697	HS Gnat T1 (G-NAAT)	Reynard Garden Centre, Carluke, S Lanarkshire	
XM708	HS Gnat T1 (8573M)	Privately owned, Lytham St Annes	
XM715	HP80 Victor K2	Cold War Jets Collection, Bruntingthorpe	
XM717	HP80 Victor K2 <ff>	RAF Museum, Hendon	
XM819	Lancashire EP9 Prospector (G-APXW)	Museum of Army Flying, Middle Wallop	
XM833	WS58 Wessex HAS3	North-East Aircraft Museum, Usworth	
XN126	WS55 Whirlwind HAR10 (8655M) [S]	Pinewood Studios, Elstree	
XN137	Hunting Jet Provost T3 <ff>	Privately owned, Little Addington, Northants	
XN156	Slingsby T21B Sedbergh TX1 (BGA3250)	Privately owned, Portmoak, Perth & Kinross	
XN157	Slingsby T21B Sedbergh TX1 (BGA3255)	Privately owned, Long Mynd	

Notes	Serial	Type (code/other identity)	Owner/operator, location or fate
	XN185	Slingsby T21B Sedbergh TX1 (8942M/BGA4077)	Privately owned, Scampton
	XN186	Slingsby T21B Sedbergh TX1 (BGA3905) [HFG]	Privately owned, Wethersfield
	XN187	Slingsby T21B Sedbergh TX1 (BGA3903)	Privately owned, RAF Halton
	XN198	Slingsby T31B Cadet TX3	Privately owned, Bodmin
	XN238	Slingsby T31B Cadet TX3 <ff>	South Yorkshire Aircraft Museum, Doncaster
	XN239	Slingsby T31B Cadet TX3 (8889M) [G]	IWM Duxford, stored
	XN246	Slingsby T31B Cadet TX3	Solent Sky, Southampton
	XN258	WS55 Whirlwind HAR9 [589/CU]	North-East Aircraft Museum, Usworth
	XN297	WS55 Whirlwind HAR9 (XN311) [12]	Privately owned, Hull
	XN298	WS55 Whirlwind HAR9 [810/LS]	Privately owned
	XN304	WS55 Whirlwind HAS7 [WW/B]	Norfolk & Suffolk Avn Museum, Flixton
	XN332	Saro P531 (G-APNV) [759]	FAA Museum, stored Cobham Hall, RNAS Yeovilton
	XN334	Saro P531	FAA Museum, stored Cobham Hall, RNAS Yeovilton
	XN344	Saro Skeeter AOP12 (8018M)	Science Museum, South Kensington
	XN345	Saro Skeeter AOP12 <ff>	The Helicopter Museum, stored Weston-super-Mare
	XN351	Saro Skeeter AOP12 (G-BKSC)	Privately owned, Norwich
	XN380	WS55 Whirlwind HAS7	RAF Manston History Museum
	XN385	WS55 Whirlwind HAS7	Battleground Paintball, Yarm, Cleveland
	XN386	WS55 Whirlwind HAR9 [435/ED]	South Yorkshire Aircraft Museum, Doncaster
	XN412	Auster AOP9	Auster 9 Group, Melton Mowbray
	XN437	Auster AOP9 (G-AXWA)	Privately owned, North Weald
	XN441	Auster AOP9 (G-BGKT)	Privately owned, Exeter
	XN458	Hunting Jet Provost T3 (8234M/*XN594*) [19]	Privately owned, Northallerton
	XN459	Hunting Jet Provost T3A (G-BWOT)	Kennet Aviation, North Weald
	XN462	Hunting Jet Provost T3A [17]	FAA Museum, stored Cobham Hall, RNAS Yeovilton
	XN466	Hunting Jet Provost T3A [29] <ff>	No 184 Sqn ATC, Gr Manchester
	XN492	Hunting Jet Provost T3A (8079M) <ff>	East Midlands Airport Aeropark
	XN494	Hunting Jet Provost T3A (9012M) [43]	Privately owned, Camborne, Cornwall
	XN500	Hunting Jet Provost T3A	Norfolk & Suffolk Avn Museum, Flixton
	XN503	Hunting Jet Provost T3 <ff>	Boscombe Down Aviation Collection, Old Sarum
	XN511	Hunting Jet Provost T3 [64] <ff>	South Yorkshire Aircraft Museum, Doncaster
	XN549	Hunting Jet Provost T3 (8235M) <ff>	Privately owned, Warrington
	XN551	Hunting Jet Provost T3A (8984M)	Privately owned, Felton Common, Bristol
	XN554	Hunting Jet Provost T3 (8436M) [K]	Gunsmoke Paintball, Colchester, Essex
	XN573	Hunting Jet Provost T3 [E] <ff>	Newark Air Museum, Winthorpe
	XN579	Hunting Jet Provost T3A (9137M) [14]	Gunsmoke Paintball, Colchester, Essex
	XN582	Hunting Jet Provost T3A (8957M) [95,H]	Privately owned, Bruntingthorpe
	XN584	Hunting Jet Provost T3A (9014M) [E]	USW Aerospace Centre, Treforest, Glamorgan
	XN586	Hunting Jet Provost T3A (9039M) [91]	Brooklands Museum, Weybridge
	XN589	Hunting Jet Provost T3A (9143M) [46]	RAF Linton-on-Ouse, on display
	XN597	Hunting Jet Provost T3 (7984M) <ff>	Privately owned, Market Drayton, Shrops
	XN607	Hunting Jet Provost T3 <ff>	Highland Aviation Museum, Inverness
	XN623	Hunting Jet Provost T3 (XN632/8352M)	Privately owned, Birlingham, Worcs
	XN629	Hunting Jet Provost T3A (G-BVEG/G-KNOT) [49]	Privately owned, stored Bentwaters
	XN634	Hunting Jet Provost T3A <ff>	Privately owned, Blackpool
	XN634	Hunting Jet Provost T3A [53] <rf>	BAE Systems Warton Fire Section
	XN637	Hunting Jet Provost T3 (G-BKOU) [03]	Privately owned, North Weald
	XN647	DH110 Sea Vixen FAW2 <ff>	Privately owned, Steventon, Oxon
	XN650	DH110 Sea Vixen FAW2 [456] <ff>	Privately owned, Norfolk
	XN651	DH110 Sea Vixen FAW2 <ff>	Privately owned, Lavendon, Bucks
	XN685	DH110 Sea Vixen FAW2 (8173M) [703/VL]	Midland Air Museum, Coventry
	XN696	DH110 Sea Vixen FAW2 [751] <ff>	North-East Aircraft Museum, Usworth
	XN714	Hunting H126	RAF Museum, Cosford
	XN726	EE Lightning F2A (8545M) <ff>	Boscombe Down Aviation Collection, Old Sarum
	XN728	EE Lightning F2A (8546M) <ff>	Privately owned, Binbrook
	XN774	EE Lightning F2A (8551M) <ff>	Privately owned, Boston
	XN776	EE Lightning F2A (8535M) [C]	National Museum of Flight, E Fortune
	XN795	EE Lightning F2A <ff>	Privately owned, Rayleigh, Essex
	XN819	AW660 Argosy C1 (8205M) <ff>	Newark Air Museum, Winthorpe
	XN923	HS Buccaneer S1 [13]	Gatwick Aviation Museum, Charlwood, Surrey
	XN928	HS Buccaneer S1 (8179M) <ff>	Privately owned, Gravesend
	XN957	HS Buccaneer S1 [630/LM]	FAA Museum, RNAS Yeovilton

Serial	Type (code/other identity)	Owner/operator, location or fate	Notes
XN964	HS Buccaneer S1 [118/V]	Newark Air Museum, Winthorpe	
XN967	HS Buccaneer S1 [233] <ff>	City of Norwich Aviation Museum	
XN972	HS Buccaneer S1 (8183M/XN962) <ff>	RAF Museum, Cosford	
XN974	HS Buccaneer S2A	Yorkshire Air Museum, Elvington	
XN981	HS Buccaneer S2B (fuselage)	Privately owned, Errol	
XN983	HS Buccaneer S2B <ff>	Fenland & W Norfolk Aviation Museum, Wisbech	
XP110	WS58 Wessex HAS3 (A2636)	DSAE RNAESS, HMS Sultan, Gosport	
XP137	WS58 Wessex HAS3 [11/DD]	RN, Predannack Fire School	
XP142	WS58 Wessex HAS3	FAA Museum, stored Cobham Hall, RNAS Yeovilton	
XP150	WS58 Wessex HAS3 [LS]	FETC, Moreton-in-Marsh, Glos	
XP165	WS Scout AH1	The Helicopter Museum, Weston-super-Mare	
XP190	WS Scout AH1	South Yorkshire Aircraft Museum, Doncaster	
XP191	WS Scout AH1	Privately owned, Prenton, The Wirral	
XP226	Fairey Gannet AEW3	Newark Air Museum, Winthorpe	
XP241	Auster AOP9 (G-CEHR)	Privately owned, Spanhoe	
XP242	Auster AOP9 (G-BUCI)	AAC Historic Aircraft Flight, Middle Wallop	
XP244	Auster AOP9 (7864M/M7922)	Privately owned, Stretton on Dunsmore	
XP248	Auster AOP9 (7863M/WZ679/G-CIUX)	Repainted as WZ679, 2015	
XP254	Auster AOP11 (G-ASCC)	Privately owned, Cambs	
XP279	Auster AOP9 (G-BWKK)	Privately owned, stored Winchester	
XP280	Auster AOP9	Snibston Discovery Park, Coalville	
XP281	Auster AOP9	IWM Duxford	
XP282	Auster AOP9 (G-BGTC)	Privately owned, Scampton	
XP286	Auster AOP9	Privately owned, South Molton, Devon	
XP299	WS55 Whirlwind HAR10 (8726M)	RAF Museum, Hendon	
XP328	WS55 Whirlwind HAR10 (G-BKHC)	Privately owned, Tattershall Thorpe (wreck)	
XP329	WS55 Whirlwind HAR10 (8791M) [V]	Privately owned, Tattershall Thorpe (wreck)	
XP330	WS55 Whirlwind HAR10	CAA Fire School, Durham/Tees Valley	
XP344	WS55 Whirlwind HAR10 (8764M) [H723]	RAF North Luffenham Training Area	
XP345	WS55 Whirlwind HAR10 (8792M) [N]	Yorkshire Helicopter Preservation Group, Doncaster	
XP346	WS55 Whirlwind HAR10 (8793M)	Privately owned, Honeybourne, Worcs	
XP350	WS55 Whirlwind HAR10	Privately owned, Bassetts Pole, Staffs	
XP351	WS55 Whirlwind HAR10 (8672M) [Z]	Currently not known	
XP354	WS55 Whirlwind HAR10 (8721M)	Privately owned, Mullingar, Eire	
XP355	WS55 Whirlwind HAR10 (8463M/G-BEBC)	City of Norwich Aviation Museum	
XP360	WS55 Whirlwind HAR10 [V]	Privately owned, Bicton, nr Leominster	
XP398	WS55 Whirlwind HAR10 (8794M)	Currently not known	
XP404	WS55 Whirlwind HAR10 (8682M)	The Helicopter Museum, stored Weston-super-Mare	
XP411	AW660 Argosy C1 (8442M) [C]	RAF Museum, Cosford	
XP454	Slingsby T38 Grasshopper TX1	Privately owned, Sywell	
XP459	Slingsby T38 Grasshopper TX1	Privately owned, stored Nayland, Suffolk	
XP463	Slingsby T38 Grasshopper TX1 (frame)	Privately owned, Rufforth	
XP463	Slingsby T38 Grasshopper TX1 (BGA4372)	Privately owned, Lasham	
XP488	Slingsby T38 Grasshopper TX1	Privately owned, Keevil	
XP490	Slingsby T38 Grasshopper TX1 (BGA4552)	Privately owned, stored Watton	
XP492	Slingsby T38 Grasshopper TX1 (BGA3480)	Privately owned, Gallows Hill, Dorset	
XP493	Slingsby T38 Grasshopper TX1	Privately owned, stored Aston Down	
XP494	Slingsby T38 Grasshopper TX1	Privately owned, stored Baxterley	
XP505	HS Gnat T1	Science Museum, stored Wroughton	
XP513	HS Gnat T1 (N513X)	Privately owned, North Weald	
XP516	HS Gnat T1 (8580M) [16]	Farnborough Air Sciences Trust, Farnborough	
XP540	HS Gnat T1 (8608M) [62]	Privately owned, North Weald	
XP542	HS Gnat T1 (8575M)	No 424 Sqn ATC, Southampton	
XP556	Hunting Jet Provost T4 (9027M) [B]	RAF Cranwell Aviation Heritage Centre	
XP557	Hunting Jet Provost T4 (8494M) [72]	Dumfries & Galloway Avn Mus, Dumfries	
XP558	Hunting Jet Provost T4 (8627M) <ff>	Privately owned, Stoneykirk, D&G	
XP558	Hunting Jet Provost T4 (8627M)[20] <rf>	Privately owned, Sproughton	
XP563	Hunting Jet Provost T4 (9028M) [C]	Sold to South Korea, January 2008	
XP568	Hunting Jet Provost T4	East Midlands Airport Aeropark	
XP573	Hunting Jet Provost T4 (8236M) [19]	Jersey Airport Fire Section	
XP585	Hunting Jet Provost T4 (8407M) [24]	NE Wales Institute, Wrexham	

Notes	Serial	Type (code/other identity)	Owner/operator, location or fate
	XP627	Hunting Jet Provost T4	North-East Aircraft Museum, stored Usworth
	XP629	Hunting Jet Provost T4 (9026M) [P]	Gunsmoke Paintball, Colchester, Essex
	XP640	Hunting Jet Provost T4 (8501M) [M]	Yorkshire Air Museum, Elvington
	XP642	Hunting Jet Provost T4 <ff>	Cornwall Aviation Heritage Centre, Newquay
	XP672	Hunting Jet Provost T4 (8458M/G-RAFI) [03]	Privately owned, Bruntingthorpe
	XP680	Hunting Jet Provost T4 (8460M)	FETC, Moreton-in-Marsh, Glos
	XP686	Hunting Jet Provost T4 (8401M/8502M) [G]	Gunsmoke Paintball, Colchester, Essex
	XP701	BAC Lightning F3 (8924M) <ff>	Robertsbridge Aviation Society, Mayfield
	XP703	BAC Lightning F3 <ff>	Lightning Preservation Group, Bruntingthorpe
	XP706	BAC Lightning F3 (8925M)	South Yorkshire Aircraft Museum, Doncaster
	XP743	BAC Lightning F3 <ff>	Wattisham Station Heritage Museum
	XP745	BAC Lightning F3 (8453M) <ff>	Vanguard Haulage, Greenford, London
	XP757	BAC Lightning F3 <ff>	Privately owned, Boston, Lincs
	XP765	BAC Lightning F6 (XS897) [A]	Lakes Lightnings, RAF Coningsby
	XP820	DHC2 Beaver AL1 (G-CICP)	Army Historic Aircraft Flight, Middle Wallop
	XP821	DHC2 Beaver AL1 [MCO]	Museum of Army Flying, Middle Wallop
	XP822	DHC2 Beaver AL1	Museum of Army Flying, Middle Wallop
	XP831	Hawker P.1127 (8406M)	Science Museum, South Kensington
	XP841	Handley-Page HP115	FAA Museum, RNAS Yeovilton
	XP847	WS Scout AH1	Museum of Army Flying, Middle Wallop
	XP848	WS Scout AH1	Farnborough Air Sciences Trust, Farnborough
	XP849	WS Scout AH1 (XP895)	Privately owned, Woodley, Berks
	XP853	WS Scout AH1	Privately owned, Sutton, Surrey
	XP854	WS Scout AH1 (7898M/TAD 043)	Mayhem Paintball, Abridge, Essex
	XP855	WS Scout AH1	Currently not known
	XP883	WS Scout AH1	Currently not known
	XP883	WS Scout AH1 (XW281/G-BYNZ) [T]	Privately owned, Dungannon, NI
	XP884	WS Scout AH1	AAC, stored Middle Wallop
	XP885	WS Scout AH1	AAC Wattisham, instructional use
	XP886	WS Scout AH1	The Helicopter Museum, stored Weston-super-Mare
	XP888	WS Scout AH1	Privately owned, Sproughton
	XP890	WS Scout AH1 [G] (fuselage)	Privately owned, Ipswich
	XP893	WS Scout AH1	Destroyed by fire at Middle Wallop, 2001
	XP899	WS Scout AH1	Boscombe Down Aviation Collection, Old Sarum
	XP900	WS Scout AH1	AAC Wattisham, instructional use
	XP902	WS Scout AH1 <ff>	South Yorkshire Aircraft Museum, Doncaster
	XP905	WS Scout AH1	Privately owned, stored Sproughton
	XP907	WS Scout AH1 (G-SROE)	Privately owned, Wattisham
	XP910	WS Scout AH1	Museum of Army Flying, Middle Wallop
	XP924	DH110 Sea Vixen D3 (G-CVIX) [134/E]	Fly Navy Heritage Trust, Yeovilton
	XP925	DH110 Sea Vixen FAW2 [752] <ff>	Privately owned, Chorley, Lancs
	XP980	Hawker P.1127	FAA Museum, RNAS Yeovilton
	XP984	Hawker P.1127	Brooklands Museum, Weybridge
	XR220	BAC TSR2 (7933M)	RAF Museum, Cosford
	XR222	BAC TSR2	IWM Duxford
	XR232	Sud Alouette AH2 (F-WEIP)	Museum of Army Flying, Middle Wallop
	XR239	Auster AOP9	Privately owned, Stretton on Dunsmore
	XR240	Auster AOP9 (G-BDFH)	Privately owned, Eggesford
	XR241	Auster AOP9 (G-AXRR)	Privately owned, Eggesford
	XR244	Auster AOP9 (G-CICR)	Army Historic Aircraft Flight, Middle Wallop
	XR246	Auster AOP9 (7862M/G-AZBU)	Privately owned, Melton Mowbray
	XR267	Auster AOP9 (G-BJXR)	Privately owned, Hucknall
	XR271	Auster AOP9	Privately owned, stored Wroughton
	XR346	Northrop Shelduck D1 (comp XW578)	Bournemouth Aviation Museum
	XR371	SC5 Belfast C1	RAF Museum, Cosford
	XR379	Sud Alouette AH2 (G-CICS)	Army Historic Aircraft Flight, Middle Wallop
	XR453	WS55 Whirlwind HAR10 (8873M) [A]	RAF Odiham, on gate
	XR458	WS55 Whirlwind HAR10 (8662M) [H]	Privately owned, Irthlingborough, Northants
	XR485	WS55 Whirlwind HAR10 [Q]	Norfolk & Suffolk Avn Museum, Flixton
	XR486	WS55 Whirlwind HCC12 (8727M/G-RWWW)	The Helicopter Museum, Weston-super-Mare
	XR498	WS58 Wessex HC2 (9342M)	RAF St Mawgan, for display

Serial	Type (code/other identity)	Owner/operator, location or fate	Notes
XR503	WS58 Wessex HC2	MoD DFTDC, Manston	
XR506	WS58 Wessex HC2 (9343M) [V]	Privately owned, Corley Moor, Warks	
XR516	WS58 Wessex HC2 (9319M) [V]	RAF Shawbury, on display	
XR517	WS58 Wessex HC2 [N]	Ulster Aviation Society, Long Kesh	
XR523	WS58 Wessex HC2 [M]	MoD Pembrey Sands Air Weapons Range, GI use	
XR525	WS58 Wessex HC2 [G]	RAF Museum, Cosford	
XR526	WS58 Wessex HC2 (8147M)	The Helicopter Museum, stored Weston-super-Mare	
XR528	WS58 Wessex HC2	Privately owned, Little Rissington (GI use)	
XR529	WS58 Wessex HC2 (9268M) [E]	RAF Aldergrove, on display	
XR534	HS Gnat T1 (8578M) [65]	Newark Air Museum, Winthorpe	
XR537	HS Gnat T1 (8642M/G-NATY)	Privately owned, Bournemouth	
XR538	HS Gnat T1 (8621M/G-RORI) [01]	Heritage Aircraft Trust, North Weald	
XR540	HS Gnat T1 (XP502/8576M) [2]	Privately owned, Cotswold Airport	
XR571	HS Gnat T1 (8493M)	RAF Scampton Heritage Centre	
XR574	HS Gnat T1 (8631M) [72]	Trenchard Museum, Halton	
XR595	WS Scout AH1 (G-BWHU) [M]	Privately owned, North Weald	
XR601	WS Scout AH1	Privately owned, Sproughton	
XR627	WS Scout AH1 [X]	Privately owned, Storwood, Yorkshire	
XR628	WS Scout AH1	Privately owned, Ipswich	
XR629	WS Scout AH1 (fuselage)	Privately owned, Ipswich	
XR635	WS Scout AH1	Midland Air Museum, Coventry	
XR650	Hunting Jet Provost T4 (8459M) [28,66]	Boscombe Down Aviation Collection, Old Sarum	
XR654	Hunting Jet Provost T4 <ff>	Privately owned, Chester	
XR658	Hunting Jet Provost T4 (8192M)	RAF Manston History Museum	
XR662	Hunting Jet Provost T4 (8410M) [25]	Privately owned, stored Otherton	
XR673	Hunting Jet Provost T4 (G-BXLO/9032M) [L]	Privately owned, Gamston	
XR681	Hunting Jet Provost T4 (8588M) <ff>	Robertsbridge Aviation Society, Mayfield	
XR700	Hunting Jet Provost T4 (8589M) <ff>	No 1137 Sqn ATC, Aldergrove	
XR713	BAC Lightning F3 (8935M) [C]	Lightning Preservation Grp, Bruntingthorpe	
XR718	BAC Lightning F6 (8932M) [DA]	Privately owned, Over Dinsdale, N Yorks	
XR724	BAC Lightning F6 (G-BTSY)	The Lightning Association, Binbrook	
XR725	BAC Lightning F6	Privately owned, Binbrook	
XR726	BAC Lightning F6 <ff>	Privately owned, Harrogate	
XR728	BAC Lightning F6 [JS]	Lightning Preservation Grp, Bruntingthorpe	
XR747	BAC Lightning F6 <ff>	No 20 Sqn ATC, Bideford, Devon	
XR749	BAC Lightning F3 (8934M) [DA]	Privately owned, Peterhead	
XR751	BAC Lightning F3 <ff>	Privately owned, Thorpe Wood, N Yorks	
XR753	BAC Lightning F6 (8969M) [XI]	RAF Coningsby on display	
XR753	BAC Lightning F53 (ZF578) [A]	Tangmere Military Aviation Museum	
XR754	BAC Lightning F6 (8972M) <ff>	Privately owned, Upwood, Cambs	
XR755	BAC Lightning F6	Privately owned, Callington, Cornwall	
XR757	BAC Lightning F6 <ff>	Newark Air Museum, Winthorpe	
XR759	BAC Lightning F6 <ff>	Privately owned, Haxey, Lincs	
XR770	BAC Lightning F6 [AA]	RAF Manston History Museum	
XR771	BAC Lightning F6 [BF]	Midland Air Museum, Coventry	
XR806	BAC VC10 C1K (9285M) <ff>	RAF Brize Norton, BDRT	
XR808	BAC VC10 C1K [R] $	RAF Museum, Cosford	
XR810	BAC VC10 C1K <ff>	Privately owned, Crondall, Hants	
XR944	Wallis WA116 (G-ATTB)	Privately owned, Old Buckenham	
XR977	HS Gnat T1 (8640M)	RAF Museum, Cosford	
XR992	HS Gnat T1 (8624M/XS102/G-MOUR)	Heritage Aircraft Trust, North Weald	
XR993	HS Gnat T1 (8620M/XP534/G-BVPP)	Privately owned, Bruntingthorpe	
XS100	HS Gnat T1 (8561M) <ff>	Privately owned, London SW3	
XS100	HS Gnat T1 (8561M) <rf>	Privately owned, North Weald	
XS104	HS Gnat T1 (8604M/G-FRCE)	Privately owned, North Weald	
XS149	WS58 Wessex HAS3 [661/GL]	The Helicopter Museum, Weston-super-Mare	
XS176	Hunting Jet Provost T4 (8514M) <ff>	Privately owned, Kinloss	
XS177	Hunting Jet Provost T4 (9044M) [N]	Privately owned, Hexham, Northumberland	
XS179	Hunting Jet Provost T4 (8237M) [20]	Secret Nuclear Bunker, Hack Green, Cheshire	
XS180	Hunting Jet Provost T4 (8238M/8338M) [21]	MoD, Boscombe Down	
XS181	Hunting Jet Provost T4 (9033M) <ff>	Lakes Lightnings, Spark Bridge, Cumbria	

Notes	Serial	Type (code/other identity)	Owner/operator, location or fate
	XS183	Hunting Jet Provost T4 <ff>	Privately owned, Plymouth
	XS186	Hunting Jet Provost T4 (8408M) [M]	Metheringham Airfield Visitors Centre
	XS209	Hunting Jet Provost T4 (8409M)	Solway Aviation Society, Carlisle
	XS216	Hunting Jet Provost T4 <ff>	South Yorkshire Aircraft Museum, Doncaster
	XS218	Hunting Jet Provost T4 (8508M) <ff>	No 447 Sqn ATC, Henley-on-Thames, Berks
	XS231	BAC Jet Provost T5 (G-ATAJ)	Boscombe Down Aviation Collection, Old Sarum
	XS235	DH106 Comet 4C (G-CPDA)	Cold War Jets Collection, Bruntingthorpe
	XS238	Auster AOP9 (TAD 200)	Newark Air Museum, Winthorpe
	XS416	BAC Lightning T5	Privately owned, New York, Lincs
	XS417	BAC Lightning T5 [DZ]	Newark Air Museum, Winthorpe
	XS420	BAC Lightning T5	Lakes Lightnings, FAST, Farnborough
	XS421	BAC Lightning T5 <ff>	Privately owned, Foulness
	XS456	BAC Lightning T5 [DX]	Skegness Water Leisure Park
	XS457	BAC Lightning T5 <ff>	Privately owned, Binbrook
	XS458	BAC Lightning T5 [T]	T5 Projects, Cranfield
	XS459	BAC Lightning T5 [AW]	Fenland & W Norfolk Aviation Museum, Wisbech
	XS481	WS58 Wessex HU5	South Yorkshire Aircraft Museum, Doncaster
	XS482	WS58 Wessex HU5	RAF Manston History Museum
	XS486	WS58 Wessex HU5 (9272M) [524/CU,F]	The Helicopter Museum, Weston-super-Mare
	XS488	WS58 Wessex HU5 (9056M) [F]	Privately owned, Tiptree, Essex
	XS489	WS58 Wessex HU5 [R]	Privately owned, Westerham, Kent
	XS493	WS58 Wessex HU5	Vector Aerospace, stored Fleetlands
	XS507	WS58 Wessex HU5	RAF Benson, for display
	XS508	WS58 Wessex HU5	FAA Museum, RNAS Yeovilton
	XS510	WS58 Wessex HU5 [626/PO]	No 1414 Sqn ATC, Crowborough, Sussex
	XS511	WS58 Wessex HU5 [M]	Tangmere Military Aircraft Museum
	XS513	WS58 Wessex HU5	RNAS Yeovilton Fire Section
	XS515	WS58 Wessex HU5 [N]	Army, Keogh Barracks, Aldershot, instructional use
	XS516	WS58 Wessex HU5 [Q]	Privately owned, Redruth, Cornwall
	XS520	WS58 Wessex HU5 [F]	RN, Predannack Fire School
	XS522	WS58 Wessex HU5 [ZL]	Blackball Paintball, Truro, Cornwall
	XS527	WS Wasp HAS1	FAA Museum, stored Cobham Hall, RNAS Yeovilton
	XS529	WS Wasp HAS1	Privately owned, Redruth, Cornwall
	XS539	WS Wasp HAS1 [435]	Vector Aerospace Fleetlands Apprentice School
	XS567	WS Wasp HAS1 [434/E]	IWM Duxford
	XS568	WS Wasp HAS1 (A2715) [441]	DSAE RNAESS, HMS Sultan, Gosport
	XS574	Northrop Shelduck D1 <R>	FAA Museum, stored Cobham Hall, RNAS Yeovilton
	XS576	DH110 Sea Vixen FAW2 [125/E]	IWM Duxford
	XS587	DH110 Sea Vixen FAW(TT)2 (8828M/G-VIXN)	Gatwick Aviation Museum, Charlwood, Surrey
	XS590	DH110 Sea Vixen FAW2 [131/E]	FAA Museum, RNAS Yeovilton
	XS598	HS Andover C1 (fuselage)	Scrapped at Moreton-in-Marsh, Glos
	XS639	HS Andover E3A (9241M)	RAF Museum, Cosford
	XS641	HS Andover C1PR (9198M) (fuselage)	Privately owned, Sandbach, Cheshire
	XS643	HS Andover E3A (9278M) <ff>	Privately owned, Dudley, W Mids
	XS646	HS Andover C1(mod)	Currently not known
	XS651	Slingsby T45 Swallow TX1 (BGA1211)	Privately owned, Little Rissington
	XS652	Slingsby T45 Swallow TX1 (BGA1107)	Privately owned, Chipping, Lancs
	XS674	WS58 Wessex HC2 [R]	Privately owned, Biggin Hill
	XS695	HS Kestrel FGA1 [5]	RAF Museum, Cosford
	XS709	HS125 Dominie T1 [M]	RAF Museum, Cosford
	XS710	HS125 Dominie T1 (9259M) [O]	RAF Cranwell Fire Section
	XS713	HS125 Dominie T1 [C]	RAF Shawbury Fire Section
	XS714	HS125 Dominie T1 (9246M) [P]	MoD DFTDC, Manston
	XS726	HS125 Dominie T1 (9273M) [T]	Newark Air Museum, Winthorpe
	XS727	HS125 Dominie T1 [D]	RAF Cranwell, on display
	XS731	HS125 Dominie T1 (N19XY) (fuselage)	Privately owned, Marlborough, Wilts
	XS733	HS125 Dominie T1 (9276M) [Q]	Privately owned, Sproughton
	XS734	HS125 Dominie T1 (9260M) [N]	Privately owned, Sproughton
	XS735	HS125 Dominie T1 (9264M) [R]	Privately owned, Walcott, Lincs
	XS736	HS125 Dominie T1 [S]	MoD Winterbourne Gunner, Wilts
	XS738	HS125 Dominie T1 (9274M) [U]	RN, Predannack Fire School
	XS743	Beagle B206Z	QinetiQ Boscombe Down, Apprentice School

Serial	Type (code/other identity)	Owner/operator, location or fate	Notes
XS765	Beagle B206 Basset CC1 (G-BSET)	QinetiQ Boscombe Down, Apprentice School	
XS770	Beagle B206 Basset CC1 (G-HRHI)	Currently not known	
XS790	HS748 Andover CC2 <ff>	Boscombe Down Aviation Collection, Old Sarum	
XS791	HS748 Andover CC2 (fuselage)	Privately owned, Stock, Essex	
XS859	Slingsby T45 Swallow TX1 (BGA1136) [859]	Privately owned, stored Felthorpe	
XS863	WS58 Wessex HAS1 [304/R]	IWM Duxford	
XS865	WS58 Wessex HAS1 (A2694)	Privately owned, Ballygowan, NI	
XS885	WS58 Wessex HAS1 [512/DD]	SFDO, RNAS Culdrose	
XS886	WS58 Wessex HAS1 [527/CU]	Privately owned, Ditchling, E Sussex	
XS887	WS58 Wessex HAS1 [403/FI]	South Yorkshire Aircraft Museum, Doncaster	
XS888	WS58 Wessex HAS1 [521]	Guernsey Airport Fire Section	
XS898	BAC Lightning F6 <ff>	Privately owned, Lavendon, Bucks	
XS899	BAC Lightning F6 <ff>	Privately owned, Binbrook	
XS903	BAC Lightning F6 [BA]	Yorkshire Air Museum, Elvington	
XS904	BAC Lightning F6 [BQ]	Lightning Preservation Grp, Bruntingthorpe	
XS919	BAC Lightning F6	Privately owned,	
XS921	BAC Lightning F6 <R> [BA]	BAE Systems, Samlesbury, on display	
XS922	BAC Lightning F6 (8973M) <ff>	Lakes Lightnings, Spark Bridge, Cumbria	
XS923	BAC Lightning F6 <ff>	Privately owned, Welshpool	
XS925	BAC Lightning F6 (8961M) [BA]	RAF Museum, Hendon	
XS928	BAC Lightning F6 [AD]	BAE Systems Warton, on display	
XS932	BAC Lightning F6 <ff>	Privately owned, Walcott, Lincs	
XS933	BAC Lightning F6 <ff>	Privately owned, Farnham	
XS933	BAC Lightning F53 (ZF594) [BF]	North-East Aircraft Museum, Usworth	
XS936	BAC Lightning F6	Castle Motors, Liskeard, Cornwall	
XT108	Agusta-Bell 47G-3 Sioux AH1 [U]	Museum of Army Flying, Middle Wallop	
XT123	WS Sioux AH1 (XT827) [D]	AAC Middle Wallop, at main gate	
XT131	Agusta-Bell 47G-3 Sioux AH1 (G-CICN) [B]	Army Historic Aircraft Flight, Middle Wallop	
XT140	Agusta-Bell 47G-3 Sioux AH1	Privately owned, Malmesbury	
XT150	Agusta-Bell 47G-3 Sioux AH1 (7883M) [R]	South Yorkshire Aircraft Museum, Doncaster	
XT151	WS Sioux AH1	Museum of Army Flying, stored Middle Wallop	
XT176	WS Sioux AH1 [U]	FAA Museum, stored Cobham Hall, RNAS Yeovilton	
XT190	WS Sioux AH1	The Helicopter Museum, Weston-super-Mare	
XT200	WS Sioux AH1 [F]	Newark Air Museum, Winthorpe	
XT208	WS Sioux AH1 (wreck)	Blessingbourne Museum, Fivemiletown, Co Tyrone, NI	
XT223	WS Sioux AH1 (G-XTUN)	Sold to the USA	
XT236	WS Sioux AH1 (frame only)	South Yorkshire Aircraft Museum, Doncaster	
XT242	WS Sioux AH1 (composite) [12]	South Yorkshire Aircraft Museum, Doncaster	
XT257	WS58 Wessex HAS3 (8719M)	Bournemouth Aviation Museum	
XT277	HS Buccaneer S2A (8853M) <ff>	Privately owned, Welshpool	
XT280	HS Buccaneer S2A <ff>	Dumfries & Galloway Avn Mus, Dumfries	
XT284	HS Buccaneer S2A (8855M) <ff>	Privately owned, Felixstowe	
XT288	HS Buccaneer S2B (9134M)	National Museum of Flight, E Fortune	
XT420	WS Wasp HAS1 (G-CBUI) [606]	Privately owned, Thruxton	
XT427	WS Wasp HAS1 [606]	FAA Museum, stored RNAS Yeovilton	
XT431	WS Wasp HAS1 (comp XS463)	Bournemouth Aviation Museum	
XT434	WS Wasp HAS1 (G-CGGK) [455]	Privately owned, Breighton	
XT435	WS Wasp HAS1 (NZ3907/G-RIMM) [430]	Privately owned, Badwell Green, Suffolk	
XT437	WS Wasp HAS1 [423]	Boscombe Down Aviation Collection, Old Sarum	
XT439	WS Wasp HAS1 [605]	Privately owned, Hemel Hempstead	
XT443	WS Wasp HAS1 [422/AU]	The Helicopter Museum, Weston-super-Mare	
XT453	WS58 Wessex HU5 (A2756) [B/PO]	DSAE, stored HMS Sultan, Gosport	
XT455	WS58 Wessex HU5 (A2654) [U]	Mayhem Paintball, Abridge, Essex	
XT456	WS58 Wessex HU5 (8941M) [XZ]	Belfast Airport Fire Section	
XT466	WS58 Wessex HU5 (A2617/8921M) [XV]	Privately owned, Cotswold Airport	
XT467	WS58 Wessex HU5 (8922M) [BF]	Gunsmoke Paintball, Hadleigh, Suffolk	
XT469	WS58 Wessex HU5 (8920M)	Privately owned, Clatterford, Isle of Wight	
XT472	WS58 Wessex HU5 [XC]	The Helicopter Museum, stored Weston-super-Mare	
XT480	WS58 Wessex HU5 [468/RG]	Rednal Paintball, Shropshire	
XT482	WS58 Wessex HU5 [ZM/VL]	FAA Museum, RNAS Yeovilton	
XT486	WS58 Wessex HU5 (8919M)	Dumfries & Galloway Avn Mus, Dumfries	

Notes	Serial	Type (code/other identity)	Owner/operator, location or fate
	XT575	Vickers Viscount 837 <ff>	Brooklands Museum, Weybridge
	XT581	Northrop Shelduck D1	Muckleburgh Collection, Weybourne, Norfolk
	XT583	Northrop Shelduck D1	Privately owned, stored Wroughton
	XT596	McD F-4K Phantom FG1	FAA Museum, RNAS Yeovilton
	XT597	McD F-4K Phantom FG1	Privately owned, Bentwaters
	XT601	WS58 Wessex HC2 (9277M) (composite)	RAF Odiham, BDRT
	XT604	WS58 Wessex HC2	East Midlands Airport Aeropark
	XT617	WS Scout AH1	Wattisham Station Heritage Museum
	XT621	WS Scout AH1	Defence Academy of the UK, Shrivenham
	XT623	WS Scout AH1	DSAE SAAE, Lyneham
	XT626	WS Scout AH1 (G-CIBW) [Q]	Army Historic Aircraft Flt, Middle Wallop
	XT630	WS Scout AH1 (G-BXRL) [X]	Currently not known
	XT631	WS Scout AH1 [D]	Privately owned, Ipswich
	XT633	WS Scout AH1	Farnborough Air Sciences Trust, Farnborough
	XT634	WS Scout AH1 (G-BYRX) [T]	MoD Air Accidents Investigation Branch, Farnborough
	XT638	WS Scout AH1 [N]	AAC Middle Wallop, at main gate
	XT640	WS Scout AH1	Privately owned, Sproughton
	XT643	WS Scout AH1	Army, Thorpe Camp, East Wretham (wreck)
	XT653	Slingsby T45 Swallow TX1 (BGA3469)	Privately owned, Oakhill, Somerset
	XT672	WS58 Wessex HC2 [WE]	RAF Stafford, on display
	XT681	WS58 Wessex HC2 (9279M) [U] <ff>	Privately owned, Wallingford, Oxon
	XT761	WS58 Wessex HU5	RNAS Culdrose
	XT762	WS58 Wessex HU5	Hamburger Hill Paintball, Marksbury, Somerset
	XT765	WS58 Wessex HU5 [J]	FAA Museum, RNAS Yeovilton
	XT765	WS58 Wessex HU5 (XT458/A2768) [P/VL]	RNAS Yeovilton, on display
	XT769	WS58 Wessex HU5 [823]	FAA Museum, RNAS Yeovilton
	XT771	WS58 Wessex HU5 [620/PO]	RNAS Culdrose, stored
	XT773	WS58 Wessex HU5 (9123M)	RAF Shawbury Fire Section
	XT778	WS Wasp HAS1 [430]	FAA Museum, stored Cobham Hall, RNAS Yeovilton
	XT780	WS Wasp HAS1 [636]	CEMAST, Fareham College, Lee-on-Solent
	XT787	WS Wasp HAS1 (NZ3905/G-KAXT)	Westland Wasp Historic Flt, Barton Ashes, Hants
	XT788	WS Wasp HAS1 (G-BMIR) [474]	Privately owned, Storwood, Yorkshire
	XT793	WS Wasp HAS1 (G-BZPP) [456] <ff>	Privately owned, stored Thruxton
	XT863	McD F-4K Phantom FG1 <ff>	Privately owned, Cowes, IOW
	XT864	McD F-4K Phantom FG1 (8998M/XT684) [A]	Ulster Aviation Society, Long Kesh
	XT891	McD F-4M Phantom FGR2 (9136M)	RAF Coningsby, at main gate
	XT903	McD F-4M Phantom FGR2 <ff>	Michael Beetham Conservation Centre, RAFM Cosford
	XT905	McD F-4M Phantom FGR2 (9286M) [P]	Privately owned, Bentwaters
	XT907	McD F-4M Phantom FGR2 (9151M) [W]	Privately owned, Bentwaters
	XT914	McD F-4M Phantom FGR2 (9269M) [Z]	Wattisham Station Heritage Museum
	XV106	BAC VC10 C1K <ff>	Avro Heritage Museum, Woodford
	XV108	BAC VC10 C1K <ff>	East Midlands Airport Aeropark
	XV109	BAC VC10 C1K <ff>	Privately owned, Bruntingthorpe
	XV118	WS Scout AH1 (9141M) <ff>	Kennet Aviation, North Weald
	XV122	WS Scout AH1 [D]	Defence Academy of the UK, Shrivenham
	XV123	WS Scout AH1	RAF Shawbury, on display
	XV124	WS Scout AH1 [W]	Privately owned, Godstone, Surrey
	XV127	WS Scout AH1	Museum of Army Flying, Middle Wallop
	XV130	WS Scout AH1 (G-BWJW) [R]	Privately owned, stored Thruxton
	XV131	WS Scout AH1 [Y]	Destroyed by fire at Middle Wallop, 2001
	XV136	WS Scout AH1 [X]	Ulster Aviation Society, Long Kesh
	XV137	WS Scout AH1 (G-CRUM)	Privately owned, Chiseldon, Wilts
	XV137	WS Scout AH1 (XV139)	South Yorkshire Aircraft Museum, stored Doncaster
	XV138	WS Scout AH1 (G-SASM) [S]	Privately owned, Thruxton
	XV141	WS Scout AH1	REME Museum, Lyneham
	XV148	HS Nimrod MR1(mod) <ff>	Privately owned, Malmesbury
	XV161	HS Buccaneer S2B (9117M) <ff>	Dundonald Aviation Centre
	XV165	HS Buccaneer S2B <ff>	Privately owned, Ashford, Kent
	XV168	HS Buccaneer S2B [AF]	Yorkshire Air Museum, Elvington
	XV177	Lockheed C-130K Hercules C3A [177]	RAF, St Athan (wfu)
	XV188	Lockheed C-130K Hercules C3A [188]	RAF, St Athan (wfu)

Serial	Type (code/other identity)	Owner/operator, location or fate	Notes
XV196	Lockheed C-130K Hercules C1 [196]	RAF, St Athan (wfu)	
XV200	Lockheed C-130K Hercules C1 [200]	RAF, St Athan (wfu)	
XV201	Lockheed C-130K Hercules C1K <ff>	Marshalls, Cambridge	
XV202	Lockheed C-130K Hercules C3 [202]	RAF Museum, Cosford	
XV208	Lockheed C-130K Hercules W2 <ff>	Marshalls, Cambridge	
XV209	Lockheed C-130K Hercules C3A [209]	RAF, St Athan (wfu)	
XV221	Lockheed C-130K Hercules C3 <ff>	Privately owned, White Waltham	
XV226	HS Nimrod MR2 $	Cold War Jets Collection, Bruntingthorpe	
XV229	HS Nimrod MR2 [29]	MoD DFTDC, Manston	
XV231	HS Nimrod MR2 [31]	Aviation Viewing Park, Manchester	
XV232	HS Nimrod MR2 [32]	Privately owned, Coventry	
XV235	HS Nimrod MR2 [35] <ff>	Avro Heritage Museum, Woodford	
XV240	HS Nimrod MR2 [40] <ff>	Morayvia, Kinloss	
XV241	HS Nimrod MR2 [41] <ff>	National Museum of Flight, E Fortune	
XV244	HS Nimrod MR2 [44]	Morayavia, RAF Kinloss	
XV249	HS Nimrod R1 $	RAF Museum, Cosford	
XV250	HS Nimrod MR2 [50]	Yorkshire Air Museum, Elvington	
XV252	HS Nimrod MR2 [52] <ff>	Privately owned, Cullen, Moray	
XV254	HS Nimrod MR2 [54] <ff>	Highland Aviation Museum, Inverness	
XV255	HS Nimrod MR2 [55]	City of Norwich Aviation Museum	
XV259	BAe Nimrod AEW3 <ff>	Privately owned, Wales	
XV263	BAe Nimrod AEW3P (8967M) <ff>	BAE Systems, Brough	
XV263	BAe Nimrod AEW3P (8967M) <rf>	MoD/BAE Systems, Woodford	
XV268	DHC2 Beaver AL1 (G-BVER)	Privately owned, Cumbernauld	
XV277	HS P.1127(RAF)	National Museum of Flight, E Fortune	
XV279	HS P.1127(RAF) (8566M)	Harrier Heritage Centre, RAF Wittering	
XV280	HS P.1127(RAF) <ff>	South Yorkshire Aviation Museum, Doncaster	
XV302	Lockheed C-130K Hercules C3 [302]	Marshalls, Cambridge, fatigue test airframe	
XV304	Lockheed C-130K Hercules C3A	RAF JADTEU, Brize Norton, instructional use	
XV328	BAC Lightning T5 <ff>	Lightning Preservation Group, Bruntingthorpe	
XV333	HS Buccaneer S2B [234/H]	FAA Museum, RNAS Yeovilton	
XV344	HS Buccaneer S2C	QinetiQ Farnborough, on display	
XV350	HS Buccaneer S2B	East Midlands Airport Aeropark	
XV352	HS Buccaneer S2B <ff>	RAF Manston History Museum	
XV359	HS Buccaneer S2B [035/R]	Privately owned, Topsham, Devon	
XV361	HS Buccaneer S2B	Ulster Aviation Society, Long Kesh	
XV370	Sikorsky SH-3D (A2682) [260]	DSAE RNAESS, HMS Sultan, Gosport	
XV371	WS61 Sea King HAS1(DB) [61/DD]	SFDO, RNAS Culdrose	
XV372	WS61 Sea King HAS1	MoD Pembrey Sands Air Weapons Range, GI use	
XV383	Northrop MQM-57A/3 (fuselage)	Privately owned, Wimborne, Dorset	
XV401	McD F-4M Phantom FGR2 [I]	Privately owned, Bentwaters	
XV402	McD F-4M Phantom FGR2 <ff>	Privately owned, Kent	
XV406	McD F-4M Phantom FGR2 (9098M) [CK]	Solway Aviation Society, Carlisle	
XV408	McD F-4M Phantom FGR2 (9165M) [Z]	Tangmere Military Aviation Museum	
XV411	McD F-4M Phantom FGR2 (9103M) [L]	MoD DFTDC, Manston	
XV415	McD F-4M Phantom FGR2 (9163M) [E]	RAF Boulmer, on display	
XV424	McD F-4M Phantom FGR2 (9152M) [I]	RAF Museum, Hendon	
XV426	McD F-4M Phantom FGR2 <ff>	City of Norwich Aviation Museum	
XV426	McD F-4M Phantom FGR2 [P] <rf>	RAF Coningsby, BDRT	
XV460	McD F-4M Phantom FGR2 <ff>	Privately owned, Bentwaters	
XV474	McD F-4M Phantom FGR2 [T]	The Old Flying Machine Company, Duxford	
XV490	McD F-4M Phantom FGR2 [R] <ff>	Newark Air Museum, Winthorpe	
XV497	McD F-4M Phantom FGR2 (9295M) [D]	Privately owned, Bentwaters	
XV499	McD F-4M Phantom FGR2 <ff>	Privately owned, Bruntingthorpe	
XV581	McD F-4K Phantom FG1 (9070M) <ff>	No 2481 Sqn ATC, Bridge of Don	
XV582	McD F-4K Phantom FG1 (9066M) [M]	Privately owned, Bruntingthorpe	
XV586	McD F-4K Phantom FG1 (9067M) [010-R]	Privately owned, RNAS Yeovilton	
XV591	McD F-4K Phantom FG1 [013] <ff>	RAF Museum, Cosford	
XV625	WS Wasp HAS1 (A2649) [471]	Privately owned,	
XV631	WS Wasp HAS1 (fuselage)	Farnborough Air Sciences Trust, stored Farnborough	
XV642	WS61 Sea King HAS2A (A2614) [259]	DSAE RNAESS, HMS Sultan, Gosport	
XV643	WS61 Sea King HAS6 [262]	DSAE No 1 SoTT, Cosford	

Notes	Serial	Type (code/other identity)	Owner/operator, location or fate
	XV647	WS61 Sea King HU5 [28]	DSAE RNAESS, *HMS Sultan*, Gosport
	XV648	WS61 Sea King HU5 [18/CU]	Privately owned, stored Colsterworth
	XV649	WS61 Sea King ASaC7 [180]	DSAE, stored *HMS Sultan*, Gosport
	XV651	WS61 Sea King HU5	Mini Moos Farm, Edmondsley, Durham
	XV653	WS61 Sea King HAS6 (9326M) [63/CU]	DSAE No 1 SoTT, Cosford
	XV654	WS61 Sea King HAS6 [705/DD] (wreck)	RN, Predannack Fire School
	XV655	WS61 Sea King HAS6 [270/N]	DSAE RNAESS, *HMS Sultan*, Gosport
	XV656	WS61 Sea King ASaC7 [185]	RN No 849 NAS, Culdrose
	XV657	WS61 Sea King HAS5 (*ZA135*) [32/DD]	SFDO, RNAS Culdrose
	XV659	WS61 Sea King HAS6 (9324M) [62/CU]	DSAE No 1 SoTT, Cosford
	XV660	WS61 Sea King HAS6 [269/N]	DSAE RNAESS, *HMS Sultan*, Gosport
	XV661	WS61 Sea King HU5 [26]	*Currently not known*
	XV663	WS61 Sea King HAS6 [18]	FAA Museum, RNAS Yeovilton
	XV664	WS61 Sea King ASaC7 [190]	RN No 849 NAS, Culdrose
	XV665	WS61 Sea King HAS6 [507/CU]	DSAE RNAESS, *HMS Sultan*, Gosport
	XV666	WS61 Sea King HU5 [21]	RN MDMF, Culdrose
	XV670	WS61 Sea King HU5 [17]	DSAE, stored *HMS Sultan*, Gosport
	XV671	WS61 Sea King ASaC7 [183/CU]	RN No 849 NAS, Culdrose
	XV672	WS61 Sea King ASaC7 [187]	DSAE, stored *HMS Sultan*, Gosport
	XV673	WS61 Sea King HU5 [827/CU]	RN Culdrose, on display
	XV674	WS61 Sea King HAS6	Privately owned, Horsham
	XV675	WS61 Sea King HAS6 [701/PW]	DSAE RNAESS, *HMS Sultan*, Gosport
	XV676	WS61 Sea King HC6 [ZE]	DSAE RNAESS, *HMS Sultan*, Gosport
	XV677	WS61 Sea King HAS6 [269]	South Yorkshire Aircraft Museum, Doncaster
	XV696	WS61 Sea King HAS6 [267/L]	DSAE RNAESS, *HMS Sultan*, Gosport
	XV697	WS61 Sea King ASaC7 [181/CU]	RN No 849 NAS, Culdrose
	XV699	WS61 Sea King HU5 [823/PW]	DSAE RNAESS, *HMS Sultan*, Gosport
	XV700	WS61 Sea King HC6 [ZC]	RAF St Mawgan, instructional use
	XV701	WS61 Sea King HAS6 [268/N,64]	DSAE RNAESS, *HMS Sultan*, Gosport
	XV703	WS61 Sea King HC6 [ZD]	DSAE RNAESS, *HMS Sultan*, Gosport
	XV705	WS61 Sea King HU5 [29]	*Currently not known*
	XV706	WS61 Sea King HAS6 (9344M) [017/L]	RN ETS, Culdrose
	XV707	WS61 Sea King ASaC7 [184]	DSAE, stored *HMS Sultan*, Gosport
	XV708	WS61 Sea King HAS6 [501/CU]	DSAE RNAESS, *HMS Sultan*, Gosport
	XV709	WS61 Sea King HAS6 (9303M) [263]	MoD/QinetiQ, Boscombe Down
	XV711	WS61 Sea King HAS6 [15/CW]	DSAE RNAESS, *HMS Sultan*, Gosport
	XV712	WS61 Sea King HAS6 [66]	IWM Duxford
	XV713	WS61 Sea King HAS6 (A2646) [018/L]	DSAE RNAESS, *HMS Sultan*, Gosport
	XV714	WS61 Sea King ASaC7 [188]	RN No 849 NAS, Culdrose
	XV720	WS58 Wessex HC2 (A2701)	Privately owned, Hixon, Staffs
	XV722	WS58 Wessex HC2 (8805M) [WH]	Privately owned, Badgers Mount, Kent
	XV724	WS58 Wessex HC2	DSAE RNAESS, *HMS Sultan*, Gosport
	XV725	WS58 Wessex HC2 [C]	MoD DFTDC, Manston
	XV726	WS58 Wessex HC2 [J]	Privately owned, Biggin Hill
	XV728	WS58 Wessex HC2 [A]	Newark Air Museum, Winthorpe
	XV731	WS58 Wessex HC2 [Y]	Privately owned, Badgers Mount, Kent
	XV732	WS58 Wessex HCC4	RAF Museum, Hendon
	XV733	WS58 Wessex HCC4	The Helicopter Museum, Weston-super-Mare
	XV741	HS Harrier GR3 (A2608) [41/DD]	Privately owned, Thorpe Wood, N Yorks
	XV744	HS Harrier GR3 (9167M) [3K]	Tangmere Military Aviation Museum
	XV748	HS Harrier GR3 [3D]	Yorkshire Air Museum, Elvington
	XV751	HS Harrier GR3 [AU]	Gatwick Aviation Museum, Charlwood, Surrey
	XV752	HS Harrier GR3 (9075M) [B]	South Yorkshire Aircraft Museum, Doncaster
	XV753	HS Harrier GR3 (9078M) [53/DD]	Cornwall Aviation Heritage Centre, Newquay
	XV755	HS Harrier GR3 [M]	Privately owned, Selby, N Yorks
	XV759	HS Harrier GR3 [O] <ff>	Privately owned, Hitchin, Herts
	XV760	HS Harrier GR3 <ff>	Solent Sky, Southampton
	XV779	HS Harrier GR3 (8931M)	Harrier Heritage Centre, RAF Wittering
	XV783	HS Harrier GR3 [83/DD]	Privately owned, Corley Moor, Warks
	XV784	HS Harrier GR3 (8909M) <ff>	Boscombe Down Aviation Collection, Old Sarum
	XV786	HS Harrier GR3 [123] <ff>	RNAS Culdrose Fire Section
	XV786	HS Harrier GR3 [S] <rf>	RN, Predannack Fire School

Serial	Type (code/other identity)	Owner/operator, location or fate	Notes
XV798	HS Harrier GR1(mod) (BAPC 450)	The Helicopter Museum, Weston-super-Mare	
XV806	HS Harrier GR3 <ff>	Privately owned, Worksop	
XV808	HS Harrier GR3 (9076M/A2687) [08/DD]	Privately owned, Chetton, Shrops	
XV810	HS Harrier GR3 (9038M) [K]	Privately owned, Walcott, Lincs	
XV814	DH106 Comet 4 (G-APDF) <ff>	Privately owned, Chipping Campden	
XV863	HS Buccaneer S2B (9115M/9139M/9145M) [S]	Privately owned, Weston, Eire	
XV864	HS Buccaneer S2B (9234M)	MoD DFTDC, Manston	
XV865	HS Buccaneer S2B (9226M)	IWM Duxford	
XV867	HS Buccaneer S2B <ff>	Highland Aviation Museum, Inverness	
XW175	HS Harrier T4(VAAC)	DSAE No 1 SoTT, Cosford	
XW198	WS Puma HC1	RAF Benson (wfu)	
XW199	WS Puma HC2	RAF No 28(R) Sqn/No 33 Sqn/No 230 Sqn, Benson	
XW202	WS Puma HC1	Army, Stensall Barracks, York	
XW204	WS Puma HC2	RAF No 28(R) Sqn/No 33 Sqn/No 230 Sqn, Benson	
XW208	WS Puma HC1	RAFC Cranwell, GI use	
XW209	WS Puma HC2	RAF No 28(R) Sqn/No 33 Sqn/No 230 Sqn, Benson	
XW210	WS Puma HC1 (comp XW215)	RAF AM&SU, stored Shawbury	
XW212	WS Puma HC2	RAF No 28(R) Sqn/No 33 Sqn/No 230 Sqn, Benson	
XW213	WS Puma HC2	RAF No 28(R) Sqn/No 33 Sqn/No 230 Sqn, Benson	
XW214	WS Puma HC2	RAF No 28(R) Sqn/No 33 Sqn/No 230 Sqn, Benson	
XW216	WS Puma HC2 (F-ZWDD)	RAF No 28(R) Sqn/No 33 Sqn/No 230 Sqn, Benson	
XW217	WS Puma HC2	RAF No 28(R) Sqn/No 33 Sqn/No 230 Sqn, Benson	
XW219	WS Puma HC2	RAF No 28(R) Sqn/No 33 Sqn/No 230 Sqn, Benson	
XW220	WS Puma HC2	RAF No 28(R) Sqn/No 33 Sqn/No 230 Sqn, Benson	
XW222	WS Puma HC1	Ulster Aviation Society, Long Kesh	
XW223	WS Puma HC1	RAF AM&SU, stored Shawbury	
XW224	WS Puma HC2	MoD/AFD/QinetiQ, Boscombe Down	
XW226	WS Puma HC1	RAF AM&SU, stored Shawbury	
XW231	WS Puma HC2	RAF No 28(R) Sqn/No 33 Sqn/No 230 Sqn, Benson	
XW232	WS Puma HC2 (F-ZWDE)	RAF/Airbus, Romania	
XW235	WS Puma HC2 (F-ZWBI)	RAF No 28(R) Sqn/No 33 Sqn/No 230 Sqn, Benson	
XW236	WS Puma HC1	RAF Defence Movements School, Brize Norton	
XW237	WS Puma HC2	RAF No 28(R) Sqn/No 33 Sqn/No 230 Sqn, Benson	
XW241	Sud SA330E Puma	Farnborough Air Sciences Trust, Farnborough	
XW264	HS Harrier T2 <ff>	Jet Age Museum, Gloucester	
XW265	HS Harrier T4A (9258M) <ff>	No 2345 Sqn ATC, RAF Leuchars	
XW267	HS Harrier T4 (9263M)	Privately owned, Bentwaters	
XW268	HS Harrier T4N	City of Norwich Aviation Museum	
XW269	HS Harrier T4 [TB]	Caernarfon Air World	
XW270	HS Harrier T4 [T]	Coventry University, instructional use	
XW272	HS Harrier T4 (8783M) (fuselage) (comp XV281)	Privately owned, Welshpool	
XW276	Aérospatiale SA341 Gazelle (F-ZWRI)	Newark Air Museum, Winthorpe	
XW283	WS Scout AH1 (G-CIMX) [U]	Kennet Aviation, North Weald	
XW289	BAC Jet Provost T5A (G-BVXT/G-JPVA) [73]	Kennet Aviation, Yeovilton	
XW290	BAC Jet Provost T5A (9199M) [41,MA]	Privately owned, Bruntingthorpe	
XW293	BAC Jet Provost T5 (G-BWCS) [Z]	Privately owned, Bournemouth	
XW299	BAC Jet Provost T5A (9146M) [60,MB]	QinetiQ Boscombe Down, Apprentice School	
XW303	BAC Jet Provost T5A (9119M) [127]	RAF Halton	
XW304	BAC Jet Provost T5A (9172M) [MD]	Privately owned, Eye, Suffolk	
XW309	BAC Jet Provost T5 (9179M) [V,ME]	Hartlepool College of Further Education	
XW311	BAC Jet Provost T5 (9180M) [W,MF]	Privately owned, North Weald	
XW315	BAC Jet Provost T5A <ff>	Privately owned, Preston	
XW320	BAC Jet Provost T5A (9015M) [71]	DSAE No 1 SoTT, Cosford	
XW321	BAC Jet Provost T5A (9154M) [62,MH]	Privately owned, Bentwaters	
XW323	BAC Jet Provost T5A (9166M) [86]	RAF Museum, Hendon	
XW324	BAC Jet Provost T5 (G-BWSG) [U]	Privately owned, East Midlands	
XW325	BAC Jet Provost T5B (G-BWGF) [E]	Privately owned, North Weald	
XW327	BAC Jet Provost T5A (9130M) [62]	DSAE No 1 SoTT, Cosford	
XW330	BAC Jet Provost T5A (9195M) [82,MJ]	Privately owned, Knutsford, Cheshire	
XW333	BAC Jet Provost T5A (G-BVTC)	Global Aviation, Humberside	
XW353	BAC Jet Provost T5A (9090M) [3]	RAF Cranwell, on display	

Notes	Serial	Type (code/other identity)	Owner/operator, location or fate
	XW354	BAC Jet Provost T5A (XW355/G-JPTV)	Privately owned, Gamston
	XW358	BAC Jet Provost T5A (9181M) [59,MK]	CEMAST, Fareham College, Lee-on-Solent
	XW360	BAC Jet Provost T5A (9153M) [61,ML]	Privately owned, Thorpe Wood, N Yorks
	XW363	BAC Jet Provost T5A [36]	Dumfries & Galloway Avn Mus, stored Dumfries
	XW364	BAC Jet Provost T5A (9188M) [35,MN]	RAF Halton
	XW370	BAC Jet Provost T5A (9196M) [72,MP]	Privately owned, Sproughton
	XW375	BAC Jet Provost T5A [52]	DSAE No 1 SoTT, Cosford
	XW404	BAC Jet Provost T5A (9049M) [77]	Hartlepool FE College
	XW405	BAC Jet Provost T5A (9187M)	Hartlepool FE College, on display
	XW409	BAC Jet Provost T5A (9047M)	Privately owned, Hawarden
	XW410	BAC Jet Provost T5A (9125M) [80] <ff>	Privately owned, Norwich
	XW416	BAC Jet Provost T5A (9191M) [84,MS]	Privately owned, Bentwaters
	XW418	BAC Jet Provost T5A (9173M) [MT]	RAF Museum, Cosford
	XW419	BAC Jet Provost T5A (9120M) [125]	Highland Aviation Museum, Inverness
	XW420	BAC Jet Provost T5A (9194M) [83,MU]	RAF Woodvale, on display
	XW422	BAC Jet Provost T5A (G-BWEB) [3]	Privately owned, Cotswold Airport
	XW423	BAC Jet Provost T5A (G-BWUW) [14]	Deeside College, Connah's Quay, Clwyd
	XW430	BAC Jet Provost T5A (9176M) [77,MW]	Currently not known
	XW432	BAC Jet Provost T5A (9127M) [76,MX]	Privately owned, Thame
	XW433	BAC Jet Provost T5A (G-JPRO)	Privately owned, Coventry
	XW434	BAC Jet Provost T5A (9091M) [78,MY]	Halfpenny Green Airport, on display
	XW436	BAC Jet Provost T5A (9148M) [68]	DSAE No 1 SoTT, Cosford
	XW530	HS Buccaneer S2B [530]	Buccaneer Service Station, Elgin
	XW541	HS Buccaneer S2B (8858M) <ff>	Privately owned, Lavendon, Bucks
	XW544	HS Buccaneer S2B (8857M) [O]	The Buccaneer Aviation Group, Bruntingthorpe
	XW547	HS Buccaneer S2B (9095M/9169M) [R]	RAF Museum, Hendon
	XW550	HS Buccaneer S2B <ff>	Privately owned, Bruntingthorpe
	XW560	SEPECAT Jaguar S <ff>	Boscombe Down Aviation Collection, Old Sarum
	XW563	SEPECAT Jaguar S (XX822/8563M)	County Hall, Norwich, on display
	XW566	SEPECAT Jaguar B	Farnborough Air Sciences Trust, Farnborough
	XW612	WS Scout AH1 (G-KAXW)	Privately owned, Old Warden
	XW613	WS Scout AH1 (G-BXRS)	Privately owned, Thruxton
	XW616	WS Scout AH1	AAC Dishforth, instructional use
	XW630	HS Harrier GR3	RNAS Yeovilton, Fire Section
	XW635	Beagle D5/180 (G-AWSW)	Privately owned, Spanhoe
	XW664	HS Nimrod R1	East Midlands Airport Aeropark
	XW666	HS Nimrod R1 <ff>	South Yorkshire Aircraft Museum, Doncaster
	XW763	HS Harrier GR3 (9002M/9041M) <ff>	Privately owned, Wigston, Leics
	XW768	HS Harrier GR3 (9072M) [N]	MoD DFTDC, Manston
	XW784	Mitchell-Procter Kittiwake I (G-BBRN) [VL]	Privately owned, RNAS Yeovilton
	XW795	WS Scout AH1	Blessingbourne Museum, Fivemiletown, Co Tyrone, NI
	XW796	WS Scout AH1	Gunsmoke Paintball, Colchester, Essex
	XW838	WS Lynx (TAD009)	DSAE SAAE, Lyneham
	XW839	WS Lynx	The Helicopter Museum, Weston-super-Mare
	XW844	WS Gazelle AH1	Vector Aerospace Fleetlands, preserved
	XW846	WS Gazelle AH1	AAC No 665 Sqn/5 Regt, Aldergrove
	XW847	WS Gazelle AH1	AAC No 665 Sqn/5 Regt, Aldergrove
	XW848	WS Gazelle AH1 [D]	Privately owned, Stapleford Tawney
	XW849	WS Gazelle AH1	Privately owned, Hurstbourne Tarrant, Hants
	XW852	WS Gazelle HCC4 (9331M)	DSAE RNAESS, HMS Sultan, Gosport
	XW855	WS Gazelle HCC4	RAF Museum, Hendon
	XW858	WS Gazelle HT3 (G-ONNE) [C]	Privately owned, Steeple Bumstead, Cambs
	XW860	WS Gazelle HT2 (TAD 021)	DSAE SAAE, Lyneham
	XW862	WS Gazelle HT3 (G-CBKC) [D]	Sold as G-EZZL, 2010
	XW863	WS Gazelle HT2 (TAD 022)	Farnborough Air Sciences Trust, Farnborough
	XW864	WS Gazelle HT2 [54/CU]	FAA Museum, stored Cobham Hall, RNAS Yeovilton
	XW865	WS Gazelle AH1	AAC No 29 Flt, BATUS, Suffield, Canada
	XW870	WS Gazelle HT3 (9299M) [F]	MoD DFTDC, Manston
	XW888	WS Gazelle AH1 (TAD 017)	DSAE SAAE, Lyneham
	XW889	WS Gazelle AH1 (TAD 018)	Currently not known
	XW890	WS Gazelle HT2	RNAS Yeovilton, on display
	XW892	WS Gazelle AH1 (G-CGJX/9292M)	Privately owned, Hurstbourne Tarrant, Hants

Serial	Type (code/other identity)	Owner/operator, location or fate	Notes
XW897	WS Gazelle AH1	DSAE No 1 SoTT, Cosford	
XW899	WS Gazelle AH1 [Z]	DSAE No 1 SoTT, Cosford	
XW900	WS Gazelle AH1 (TAD 900)	Army, Bramley, Hants	
XW904	WS Gazelle AH1 [H]	AAC MPSU, Middle Wallop	
XW906	WS Gazelle HT3 [J]	QinetiQ Boscombe Down, Apprentice School	
XW908	WS Gazelle AH1 [A]	QinetiQ, Boscombe Down (spares use)	
XW909	WS Gazelle AH1	Privately owned, Stapleford Tawney	
XW912	WS Gazelle AH1 (TAD 019)	DSAE SAAE, Lyneham	
XW913	WS Gazelle AH1	Privately owned, Stapleford Tawney	
XW917	HS Harrier GR3 (8975M)	NATS Air Traffic Control Centre, Swanwick	
XW922	HS Harrier GR3 (8885M)	MoD DFTDC, Manston	
XW923	HS Harrier GR3 (8724M) <ff>	Harrier Heritage Centre, RAF Wittering	
XW924	HS Harrier GR3 (9073M) [G]	RAF Coningsby, preserved	
XW927	HS Harrier T4 <ff>	Privately owned, South Molton, Devon	
XW934	HS Harrier T4 [Y]	Farnborough Air Sciences Trust, Farnborough	
XW994	Northrop Chukar D1	FAA Museum, stored Cobham Hall, RNAS Yeovilton	
XW999	Northrop Chukar D1	Davidstow Airfield & Cornwall At War Museum	
XX108	SEPECAT Jaguar GR1(mod)	IWM Duxford	
XX109	SEPECAT Jaguar GR1 (8918M) [GH]	City of Norwich Aviation Museum	
XX110	SEPECAT Jaguar GR1 (8955M) [EP]	DSAE No 1 SoTT, Cosford	
XX110	SEPECAT Jaguar GR1 <R> (BAPC 169)	DSAE No 1 SoTT, Cosford	
XX112	SEPECAT Jaguar GR3A [EA]	DSAE No 1 SoTT, Cosford	
XX115	SEPECAT Jaguar GR1 (8821M) (fuselage)	DSAE No 1 SoTT, Cosford	
XX116	SEPECAT Jaguar GR3A [EO]	MoD DFTDC, Manston	
XX117	SEPECAT Jaguar GR3A [ES]	DSAE No 1 SoTT, Cosford	
XX119	SEPECAT Jaguar GR3A (8898M) [AI]$	DSAE No 1 SoTT, Cosford	
XX121	SEPECAT Jaguar GR1 [EQ]	Privately owned, Selby, N Yorks	
XX139	SEPECAT Jaguar T4 [PT]	Privately owned, Sproughton	
XX140	SEPECAT Jaguar T2 (9008M) <ff>	Privately owned, Selby, N Yorks	
XX141	SEPECAT Jaguar T2A (9297M) [T]	DSAE No 1 SoTT, Cosford	
XX144	SEPECAT Jaguar T2A [U]	Privately owned, Sproughton	
XX145	SEPECAT Jaguar T2A	Privately owned, Bruntingthorpe	
XX146	SEPECAT Jaguar T4 [GT]	Privately owned, Sproughton	
XX153	WS Lynx AH1 (9320M)	Museum of Army Flying, Middle Wallop	
XX154	HS Hawk T1	MoD/ETPS, Boscombe Down	
XX156	HS Hawk T1 [156]	RAF Valley, on display	
XX157	HS Hawk T1A [157]	RAF HSF, Valley	
XX158	HS Hawk T1A [158]	RAF AM&SU, stored Shawbury	
XX159	HS Hawk T1A [159]	RN No 736 NAS, Culdrose	
XX160	HS Hawk T1 [160]	RAF AM&SU, stored Shawbury	
XX161	HS Hawk T1 [161]	RN No 736 NAS, Culdrose	
XX162	HS Hawk T1	RAF Centre of Aviation Medicine, Boscombe Down	
XX165	HS Hawk T1 [165] (fuselage)	RAF No 71(IR) Sqn, Wittering, GI use	
XX167	HS Hawk T1 [167]	RAF AM&SU, stored Shawbury	
XX168	HS Hawk T1 [168]	RAF AM&SU, stored Shawbury	
XX169	HS Hawk T1W [169]	RAF AM&SU, stored Shawbury	
XX170	HS Hawk T1 [CH]	RAF AM&SU, stored Shawbury	
XX171	HS Hawk T1 [171]	RAF AM&SU, stored Shawbury	
XX172	HS Hawk T1 [172] (fuselage)	QinetiQ Boscombe Down, GI use	
XX173	HS Hawk T1	RAF AM&SU, stored Shawbury	
XX174	HS Hawk T1 [174]	RAF AM&SU, stored Shawbury	
XX175	HS Hawk T1 [175]	RAF AM&SU, stored Shawbury	
XX176	HS Hawk T1W [176]	RAF AM&SU, stored Shawbury	
XX177	HS Hawk T1	RAF Red Arrows, Scampton	
XX178	HS Hawk T1W [178]	RAF AM&SU, stored Shawbury	
XX181	HS Hawk T1 [181]	RAF AM&SU, stored Shawbury	
XX184	HS Hawk T1 [CQ]	QinetiQ, Boscombe Down, spares use	
XX185	HS Hawk T1 [185]	RAF AM&SU, stored Shawbury	
XX187	HS Hawk T1A [187]	RN No 736 NAS, Culdrose	
XX188	HS Hawk T1A	RAF Red Arrows, Scampton	
XX189	HS Hawk T1A [CR]	RAF No 100 Sqn, Leeming	

Notes	Serial	Type (code/other identity)	Owner/operator, location or fate
	XX190	HS Hawk T1A [CN]	RAF AM&SU, stored Shawbury
	XX191	HS Hawk T1A [CC]	RAF No 100 Sqn, Leeming
	XX194	HS Hawk T1A [CP]	RAF AM&SU, stored Shawbury
	XX195	HS Hawk T1W [195]	RAF AM&SU, stored Shawbury
	XX198	HS Hawk T1A [CG]	RAF No 100 Sqn, Leeming
	XX199	HS Hawk T1A [199]	RAF AM&SU, stored Shawbury
	XX200	HS Hawk T1A [CO]	RAF No 100 Sqn, Leeming
	XX201	HS Hawk T1A [CQ]	RAF AM&SU, stored Shawbury
	XX202	HS Hawk T1A [CF]	RAF AM&SU, stored Shawbury
	XX203	HS Hawk T1A [CF]	RAF No 100 Sqn, Leeming
	XX204	HS Hawk T1A	RAF *Red Arrows*, Scampton
	XX205	HS Hawk T1A [842/CU]	RN No 736 NAS, Culdrose
	XX217	HS Hawk T1A [217]	RAF AM&SU, stored Shawbury
	XX218	HS Hawk T1A [218]	RAF AM&SU, stored Shawbury
	XX219	HS Hawk T1A	RAF *Red Arrows*, Scampton
	XX220	HS Hawk T1A [220]	RAF AM&SU, stored Shawbury
	XX221	HS Hawk T1A [221]	RN No 736 NAS, Culdrose
	XX222	HS Hawk T1A [CI]	RAF AM&SU, stored Shawbury
	XX223	HS Hawk T1 <ff>	*Currently not known*
	XX224	HS Hawk T1 [224]	RAF AM&SU, stored Shawbury
	XX225	HS Hawk T1 [322]	RAF AM&SU, stored Shawbury
	XX226	HS Hawk T1 [226]	RAF AM&SU, stored Shawbury
	XX227	HS Hawk T1 <R> (*XX226*/BAPC 152)	RAF Scampton Heritage Centre
	XX227	HS Hawk T1A	RAF *Red Arrows*, Scampton
	XX228	HS Hawk T1 [CG]	RAF AM&SU, stored Shawbury
	XX230	HS Hawk T1A [CM]	RAF No 100 Sqn, Leeming
	XX231	HS Hawk T1W [213]	RAF AM&SU, stored Shawbury
	XX232	HS Hawk T1	RAF *Red Arrows*, Scampton
	XX234	HS Hawk T1 [234]	RAF AM&SU, stored Shawbury
	XX235	HS Hawk T1 [235]	RAF AM&SU, stored Shawbury
	XX236	HS Hawk T1W [236]	RAF AM&SU, stored Shawbury
	XX237	HS Hawk T1	RAF AM&SU, stored Shawbury
	XX238	HS Hawk T1 [238]	RAF AM&SU, stored Shawbury
	XX239	HS Hawk T1W [239]	RAF No 100 Sqn, Leeming
	XX240	HS Hawk T1 [840/CU]	RN No 736 NAS, Culdrose
	XX242	HS Hawk T1	RAF *Red Arrows*, Scampton
	XX244	HS Hawk T1	RAF *Red Arrows*, Scampton
	XX245	HS Hawk T1	RAF *Red Arrows*, Scampton
	XX246	HS Hawk T1A [CA]	RAF No 100 Sqn, Leeming
	XX247	HS Hawk T1A [247]	RAF AM&SU, stored Shawbury
	XX248	HS Hawk T1A [CJ]	RAF AM&SU, stored Shawbury
	XX250	HS Hawk T1W [250]	RN No 736 NAS, Culdrose
	XX253	HS Hawk T1A	RAF Scampton, on display
	XX254	HS Hawk T1A <R>	Privately owned, Marlow, Bucks
	XX255	HS Hawk T1A [CL]	RAF HSF, Valley
	XX256	HS Hawk T1A [256]	RAF No 100 Sqn, Leeming
	XX257	HS Hawk T1A (fuselage)	*Currently not known*
	XX258	HS Hawk T1A [CE]	RAF No 100 Sqn, Leeming
	XX260	HS Hawk T1A	RAF AM&SU, stored Shawbury
	XX261	HS Hawk T1A $	RN No 736 NAS, Culdrose
	XX263	HS Hawk T1A	RAF AM&SU, stored Shawbury
	XX264	HS Hawk T1A $	RAF AM&SU, stored Shawbury
	XX265	HS Hawk T1A [CP]	RAF No 100 Sqn, Leeming
	XX266	HS Hawk T1A	RAF Scampton, instructional use
	XX278	HS Hawk T1A	RAF *Red Arrows*, Scampton
	XX280	HS Hawk T1A [CM]	RAF/QinetiQ, Boscombe Down
	XX281	HS Hawk T1A	RAF/QinetiQ, Boscombe Down
	XX283	HS Hawk T1W [283]	RAF AM&SU, stored Shawbury
	XX284	HS Hawk T1A [CN]	RAF No 100 Sqn, Leeming
	XX285	HS Hawk T1A [CK] $	RAF No 100 Sqn, Leeming
	XX286	HS Hawk T1A [286]	RAF AM&SU, stored Shawbury
	XX287	HS Hawk T1A [287]	RAF AM&SU, stored Shawbury

Serial	Type (code/other identity)	Owner/operator, location or fate	Notes
XX289	HS Hawk T1A [CO]	RAF AM&SU, stored Shawbury	
XX290	HS Hawk T1W	RAF AM&SU, stored Shawbury	
XX292	HS Hawk T1	RAF AM&SU, stored Shawbury	
XX294	HS Hawk T1	RAF AM&SU, stored Shawbury	
XX295	HS Hawk T1 [295]	RAF AM&SU, stored Shawbury	
XX296	HS Hawk T1 [296]	RAF AM&SU, stored Shawbury	
XX299	HS Hawk T1W [299]	RAF AM&SU, stored Shawbury	
XX301	HS Hawk T1A $	RN No 736 NAS, Culdrose	
XX303	HS Hawk T1A [303]	RAF AM&SU, stored Shawbury	
XX304	HS Hawk T1A <rf>	Cardiff International Airport Fire Section	
XX306	HS Hawk T1A	RAF Scampton, on display	
XX307	HS Hawk T1 [307]	RAF AM&SU, stored Shawbury	
XX308	HS Hawk T1	RAF AM&SU, stored Shawbury	
XX308	HS Hawk T1 <R> (XX263/BAPC 171)	RAF M&RU, Bottesford	
XX309	HS Hawk T1	RAF AM&SU, stored Shawbury	
XX310	HS Hawk T1	RAF Red Arrows, Scampton	
XX311	HS Hawk T1	RAF Red Arrows, Scampton	
XX312	HS Hawk T1W	RAF AM&SU, stored Shawbury	
XX313	HS Hawk T1W [313]	RAF AM&SU, stored Shawbury	
XX314	HS Hawk T1W [314]	RAF AM&SU, stored Shawbury	
XX315	HS Hawk T1A [315]	RAF AM&SU, stored Shawbury	
XX316	HG I Iawk T1A [849/CU]	RN No 736 NAS, Culdrose	
XX317	HS Hawk T1A [317]	RAF/QinetiQ, Boscombe Down	
XX318	HS Hawk T1A [95-Y] $	RAF HSF, Valley	
XX319	HS Hawk T1A	RAF/QinetiQ, Boscombe Down	
XX320	HS Hawk T1A <ff>	RAF Scampton Heritage Centre	
XX321	HS Hawk T1A [CI]	RAF AM&SU, stored Shawbury	
XX322	HS Hawk T1A	RAF Red Arrows, Scampton	
XX323	HS Hawk T1A	RAF Red Arrows, Scampton	
XX324	HS Hawk T1A	RAF HSF, Valley	
XX325	HS Hawk T1	RAF Red Arrows, Scampton	
XX326	HS Hawk T1A	Currently not known	
XX327	HS Hawk T1	RAF Centre of Aviation Medicine, Boscombe Down	
XX329	HS Hawk T1A [CJ]	RAF No 100 Sqn, Leeming	
XX330	HS Hawk T1A [330]	RN No 736 NAS, Culdrose	
XX331	HS Hawk T1A [331]	RAF AM&SU, stored Shawbury	
XX332	HS Hawk T1A [CD]	RAF No 100 Sqn, Leeming	
XX335	HS Hawk T1A [335]	RAF AM&SU, stored Shawbury	
XX337	HS Hawk T1A	RAF HSF, Valley	
XX338	HS Hawk T1W	RAF AM&SU, stored Shawbury	
XX339	HS Hawk T1A	RAF No 100 Sqn, Leeming	
XX341	HS Hawk T1 ASTRA	MoD/ETPS, Boscombe Down	
XX342	HS Hawk T1 [2]	MoD/ETPS, Boscombe Down	
XX343	HS Hawk T1 [3] (fuselage)	Boscombe Down Aviation Collection, Old Sarum	
XX345	HS Hawk T1A [CB]	RAF No 100 Sqn, Leeming	
XX346	HS Hawk T1A [CH]	RAF/QinetiQ, Boscombe Down	
XX348	HS Hawk T1A [348]	RAF No 100 Sqn, Leeming	
XX349	HS Hawk T1W <ff>	RAF Scampton Fire Section	
XX350	HS Hawk T1A [D] $	RAF No 100 Sqn, Leeming	
XX351	HS Hawk T1A	RAF No 71(IR) Sqn, Wittering, GI use	
XX372	WS Gazelle AH1 <ff>	Privately owned, Hurstbourne Tarrant, Hants	
XX375	WS Gazelle AH1	Privately owned,	
XX378	WS Gazelle AH1 [Q]	AAC MPSU, stored Middle Wallop	
XX379	WS Gazelle AH1 [Y]	MoD/QinetiQ, stored Boscombe Down	
XX380	WS Gazelle AH1 [A]	AAC Wattisham, on display	
XX381	WS Gazelle AH1	Privately owned, Welbeck	
XX383	WS Gazelle AH1 [D]	Privately owned, Stapleford Tawney	
XX384	WS Gazelle AH1	Sold to The USA	
XX386	WS Gazelle AH1	Privately owned, Stapleford Tawney	
XX387	WS Gazelle AH1 (TAD 014)	Privately owned, stored Cranfield	
XX392	WS Gazelle AH1	Army, Middle Wallop, preserved	
XX394	WS Gazelle AH1 [X]	Privately owned, Stapleford Tawney	

Notes	Serial	Type (code/other identity)	Owner/operator, location or fate
	XX396	WS Gazelle HT3 (8718M) [N]	Privately owned,
	XX398	WS Gazelle AH1	Privately owned, Stapleford Tawney
	XX399	WS Gazelle AH1 <ff>	Privately owned, Hurstbourne Tarrant, Hants
	XX403	WS Gazelle AH1 [U]	AAC MPSU, stored Middle Wallop
	XX405	WS Gazelle AH1	AAC 7 Regt Conversion Flt, Middle Wallop
	XX406	WS Gazelle HT3 (G-CBSH) [P]	Privately owned, Hurstbourne Tarrant, Hants
	XX409	WS Gazelle AH1 (G-CHYV)	Sold to Malawi, 2015
	XX411	WS Gazelle AH1 [X]	South Yorkshire Aircraft Museum, Doncaster
	XX411	WS Gazelle AH1 <rf>	FAA Museum, RNAS Yeovilton
	XX412	WS Gazelle AH1 [B]	DSAE No 1 SoTT, Cosford
	XX414	WS Gazelle AH1 [V]	Privately owned, Biggin Hill
	XX416	WS Gazelle AH1	Privately owned, Stapleford Tawney
	XX418	WS Gazelle AH1 <ff>	Privately owned, Hurstbourne Tarrant, Hants
	XX419	WS Gazelle AH1	AAC MPSU, Middle Wallop
	XX431	WS Gazelle HT2 (9300M) [43/CU]	DSAE RNAESS, HMS Sultan, Gosport
	XX433	WS Gazelle AH1 <ff>	Privately owned, Hurstbourne Tarrant, Hants
	XX435	WS Gazelle AH1 (fuselage)	QinetiQ, Boscombe Down (spares use)
	XX436	WS Gazelle HT2 (G-ZZLE) [39/CU]	Privately owned, Hurstbourne Tarrant, Hants
	XX437	WS Gazelle AH1	Privately owned, Stapleford Tawney
	XX438	WS Gazelle AH1 [F]	Privately owned, Stapleford Tawney
	XX442	WS Gazelle AH1 [E]	AAC MPSU, stored Middle Wallop
	XX443	WS Gazelle AH1 [Y]	AAC MPSU, Middle Wallop
	XX444	WS Gazelle AH1	Wattisham Station Heritage Museum
	XX445	WS Gazelle AH1 [T]	Privately owned, Stapleford Tawney
	XX447	WS Gazelle AH1 [D1]	AAC MPSU, stored Middle Wallop
	XX449	WS Gazelle AH1	MoD/QinetiQ, Boscombe Down
	XX450	WS Gazelle AH1 [D]	Privately owned, Hurstbourne Tarrant, Hants
	XX453	WS Gazelle AH1	MoD/QinetiQ, Boscombe Down
	XX454	WS Gazelle AH1 (TAD 023)	DSAE SAAE, Lyneham
	XX455	WS Gazelle AH1	Privately owned, Stapleford Tawney
	XX456	WS Gazelle AH1	Privately owned, Stapleford Tawney
	XX457	WS Gazelle AH1 (TAD 001)	East Midlands Airport Aeropark
	XX460	WS Gazelle AH1	AAC AM&SU, stored Shawbury
	XX462	WS Gazelle AH1 [W]	Privately owned, Stapleford Tawney
	XX466	HS Hunter T66B/T7 [830] <ff>	Privately owned, Glos
	XX467	HS Hunter T66B/T7 (XL605/G-TVII) [86]	Privately owned, Bruntingthorpe
	XX477	HP137 Jetstream T1 (G-AXXS/8462M) <ff>	South Yorkshire Aircraft Museum, Doncaster
	XX478	HP137 Jetstream T2 (G-AXXT) [564/CU]	Solihull College, Woodlands Campus
	XX479	HP137 Jetstream T2 (G-AXUR)	RN, Predannack Fire School
	XX482	SA Jetstream T1 [J]	Privately owned, Hixon, Staffs
	XX483	SA Jetstream T2 [562] <ff>	Dumfries & Galloway Avn Mus, Dumfries
	XX486	SA Jetstream T2 [567/CU]	Privately owned, Bentwaters
	XX487	SA Jetstream T2 [568/CU]	Barry Technical College, instructional use
	XX491	SA Jetstream T1 [K]	Northbrook College, Shoreham, instructional use
	XX492	SA Jetstream T1 [A]	Newark Air Museum, Winthorpe
	XX494	SA Jetstream T1 [B]	Privately owned, Bruntingthorpe
	XX495	SA Jetstream T1 [C]	Bedford College, instructional use
	XX496	SA Jetstream T1 [D]	RAF Museum, Cosford
	XX499	SA Jetstream T1 [G]	Brooklands Museum, Weybridge
	XX500	SA Jetstream T1 [H]	Privately owned, Pinewood Studios
	XX510	WS Lynx HAS2 [69/DD]	SFDO, RNAS Culdrose
	XX513	SA Bulldog T1 (G-KKKK) [10]	Privately owned, Bagby
	XX515	SA Bulldog T1 (G-CBBC) [4]	Privately owned, Blackbushe
	XX518	SA Bulldog T1 (G-UDOG) [S]	Privately owned, Ursel, Belgium
	XX520	SA Bulldog T1 (9288M) [A]	No 172 Sqn ATC, Haywards Heath
	XX521	SA Bulldog T1 (G-CBEH) [H]	Privately owned, Charney Bassett, Oxon
	XX522	SA Bulldog T1 (G-DAWG) [06]	Privately owned, Blackpool
	XX524	SA Bulldog T1 (G-DDOG) [04]	Privately owned, Malaga, Spain
	XX528	SA Bulldog T1 (G-BZON) [D]	Privately owned, North Weald
	XX530	SA Bulldog T1 (XX637/9197M) [F]	No 2175 Sqn ATC, RAF Kinloss
	XX534	SA Bulldog T1 (G-EDAV) [B]	Privately owned, Tollerton
	XX537	SA Bulldog T1 (G-CBCB) [C]	Privately owned, RAF Halton

Serial	Type (code/other identity)	Owner/operator, location or fate	Notes
XX538	SA Bulldog T1 (G-TDOG) [O]	Privately owned, Shobdon	
XX539	SA Bulldog T1 [L]	Privately owned, Derbyshire	
XX543	SA Bulldog T1 (G-CBAB) [U]	Privately owned, Duxford	
XX546	SA Bulldog T1 (G-WINI) [03]	Privately owned, Conington	
XX549	SA Bulldog T1 (G-CBID) [6]	Privately owned, White Waltham	
XX550	SA Bulldog T1 (G-CBBL) [Z]	Privately owned, Abbeyshrule, Eire	
XX551	SA Bulldog T1 (G-BZDP) [E]	Privately owned, Boscombe Down	
XX554	SA Bulldog T1 (G-BZMD) [09]	Privately owned, Wellesbourne Mountford	
XX557	SA Bulldog T1	Privately owned, stored Fort Paull, Yorks	
XX561	SA Bulldog T1 (G-BZEP) [7]	Privately owned, Eggesford	
XX611	SA Bulldog T1 (G-CBDK) [7]	Privately owned, Coventry	
XX612	SA Bulldog T1 (G-BZXC) [A,03]	Ayr College, instructional use	
XX614	SA Bulldog T1 (G-GGRR) [1]	Privately owned, Cotswold Airport	
XX619	SA Bulldog T1 (G-CBBW) [T]	Privately owned, Coventry	
XX621	SA Bulldog T1 (G-CBEF) [H]	Privately owned, Leicester	
XX622	SA Bulldog T1 (G-CBGX) [B]	Privately owned, Shoreham	
XX623	SA Bulldog T1 [M]	Privately owned, Hurstbourne Tarrant, Hants	
XX624	SA Bulldog T1 (G-KDOG) [E]	Privately owned, Hurstbourne Tarrant, Hants	
XX625	SA120 Bulldog (G-AZHX) [45]	Privately owned,	
XX626	SA Bulldog T1 (G-CDVV/9290M) [W,02]	Privately owned, Abbots Bromley, Staffs	
XX628	SA Bulldog T1 (G-CBFU) [9]	Privately owned, Faversham	
XX629	SA Bulldog T1 (G-BZXZ)	Privately owned, Wellesbourne Mountford	
XX630	SA Bulldog T1 (G-SIJW) [5]	Privately owned, Audley End	
XX631	SA Bulldog T1 (G-BZXS) [W]	Privately owned, Sligo, Eire	
XX633	SA Bulldog T1 [X]	Sold to Sweden, 2016	
XX634	SA Bulldog T1 [T]	Newark Air Museum, Winthorpe	
XX636	SA Bulldog T1 (G-CBFP) [Y]	Privately owned, Empingham, Rutland	
XX638	SA Bulldog T1 (G-DOGG)	Privately owned, Hurstbourne Tarrant, Hants	
XX639	SA Bulldog T1 (F-AZTF) [D]	Privately owned, La Baule, France	
XX654	SA Bulldog T1 [3]	RAF Museum, Cosford	
XX655	SA Bulldog T1 (9294M) [V] <ff>	Privately owned, Stockport	
XX656	SA Bulldog T1 [C]	Privately owned, Derbyshire	
XX658	SA Bulldog T1 (G-BZPS) [07]	Privately owned, Wellesbourne Mountford	
XX659	SA Bulldog T1 [E]	Privately owned, Derbyshire	
XX664	SA Bulldog T1 (F-AZTV) [04]	Privately owned, Pontoise, France	
XX665	SA Bulldog T1 (9289M) [V]	Privately owned, stored Wellesbourne Mountford	
XX667	SA Bulldog T1 (G-BZFN) [16]	Privately owned, Ronaldsway, IoM	
XX668	SA Bulldog T1 (G-CBAN) [1]	Privately owned, St Athan	
XX669	SA Bulldog T1 (8997M) [B]	South Yorkshire Aircraft Museum, Doncaster	
XX671	SA Bulldog T1 [D]	Sold to Sweden, 2016	
XX687	SA Bulldog T1 [F]	Barry Technical College, Cardiff Airport	
XX690	SA Bulldog T1 [A]	Privately owned, Strathaven, S Lanarks	
XX692	SA Bulldog T1 (G-BZMH) [A]	Privately owned, Wellesbourne Mountford	
XX693	SA Bulldog T1 (G-BZML) [07]	Privately owned, Elmsett	
XX694	SA Bulldog T1 (G-CBBS) [E]	Privately owned, Newcastle	
XX695	SA Bulldog T1 (G-CBBT)	Privately owned, Perth	
XX698	SA Bulldog T1 (G-BZME) [9]	Privately owned, Sleap	
XX700	SA Bulldog T1 (G-CBEK) [17]	Privately owned, Popham	
XX702	SA Bulldog T1 (G-CBCR) [π]	Privately owned, Egginton	
XX704	SA122 Bulldog (G-BCUV/G-112)	Privately owned, Bournemouth	
XX705	SA Bulldog T1 [5]	Privately owned, Norfolk	
XX707	SA Bulldog T1 (G-CBDS) [4]	Privately owned, stored Caernarfon	
XX711	SA Bulldog T1 (G-CBBU) [X]	Privately owned, stored Perth	
XX720	SEPECAT Jaguar GR3A [FL]	Privately owned, Sproughton	
XX722	SEPECAT Jaguar GR1 (9252M) <ff>	Currently not known	
XX723	SEPECAT Jaguar GR3A [EU]	DSAE No 1 SoTT, Cosford	
XX724	SEPECAT Jaguar GR3A [C]	DSAE No 1 SoTT, Cosford	
XX725	SEPECAT Jaguar GR3A [KC-F,T]	DSAE No 1 SoTT, Cosford	
XX726	SEPECAT Jaguar GR1 (8947M) [EB]	DSAE No 1 SoTT, Cosford	
XX727	SEPECAT Jaguar GR1 (8951M) [ER]	DSAE No 1 SoTT, Cosford	
XX729	SEPECAT Jaguar GR3A [EL]	DSAE No 1 SoTT, Cosford	
XX734	SEPECAT Jaguar GR1 (8816M)	Boscombe Down Aviation Collection, Old Sarum	

BRITISH MILITARY AIRCRAFT MARKINGS

Notes	Serial	Type (code/other identity)	Owner/operator, location or fate
	XX736	SEPECAT Jaguar GR1 (9110M) <ff>	South Yorkshire Aircraft Museum, Doncaster
	XX738	SEPECAT Jaguar GR3A [ED]	DSAE No 1 SoTT, Cosford
	XX739	SEPECAT Jaguar GR1 (8902M) [I]	Delta Force, stored Upminster
	XX741	SEPECAT Jaguar GR1A [EJ]	Bentwaters Cold War Museum
	XX743	SEPECAT Jaguar GR1 (8949M) [EG]	DSAE No 1 SoTT, Cosford
	XX744	SEPECAT Jaguar GR1 (9251M)	Mayhem Paintball, Abridge, Essex
	XX745	SEPECAT Jaguar GR1A <ff>	No 1350 Sqn ATC, Fareham
	XX746	SEPECAT Jaguar GR1 (8895M) [S]	DSAE No 1 SoTT, Cosford
	XX747	SEPECAT Jaguar GR1 (8903M)	QinetiQ Boscombe Down, GI use
	XX748	SEPECAT Jaguar GR3A [L]	DSAE No 1 SoTT, Cosford
	XX751	SEPECAT Jaguar GR1 (8937M) [10]	Privately owned, Bentwaters
	XX752	SEPECAT Jaguar GR3A [EK]	DSAE No 1 SoTT, Cosford
	XX753	SEPECAT Jaguar GR1 (9087M) <ff>	Newark Air Museum, Winthorpe
	XX756	SEPECAT Jaguar GR1 (8899M) [W]	DSAE No 1 SoTT, Cosford
	XX761	SEPECAT Jaguar GR1 (8600M) <ff>	Boscombe Down Aviation Collection, Old Sarum
	XX763	SEPECAT Jaguar GR1 (9009M) [24]	Bournemouth Aviation Museum
	XX764	SEPECAT Jaguar GR1 (9010M)	Privately owned, Woodmancote, W Sussex
	XX765	SEPECAT Jaguar ACT	RAF Museum, Cosford
	XX766	SEPECAT Jaguar GR3A [EF]	DSAE No 1 SoTT, Cosford
	XX767	SEPECAT Jaguar GR3A [Z]	DSAE No 1 SoTT, Cosford
	XX818	SEPECAT Jaguar GR1 (8945M) [DE]	DSAE No 1 SoTT, Cosford
	XX819	SEPECAT Jaguar GR1 (8923M) [CE]	DSAE No 1 SoTT, Cosford
	XX821	SEPECAT Jaguar GR1 (8896M) [P]	DSAE No 1 SoTT, Cosford
	XX824	SEPECAT Jaguar GR1 (9019M) [AD]	DSAE No 1 SoTT, Cosford
	XX825	SEPECAT Jaguar GR1 (9020M) [BN]	DSAE No 1 SoTT, Cosford
	XX826	SEPECAT Jaguar GR1 (9021M) [34] <ff>	Shannon Aviation Museum, Eire
	XX829	SEPECAT Jaguar T2A [GZ]	Newark Air Museum, Winthorpe
	XX830	SEPECAT Jaguar T2 <ff>	City of Norwich Aviation Museum
	XX833	SEPECAT Jaguar T2B	DSAE No 1 SoTT, Cosford
	XX835	SEPECAT Jaguar T4 [EX]	DSAE No 1 SoTT, Cosford
	XX836	SEPECAT Jaguar T2A [X]	Privately owned, Sproughton
	XX837	SEPECAT Jaguar T2 (8978M) [Z]	DSAE No 1 SoTT, Cosford
	XX838	SEPECAT Jaguar T4 [FZ]	Privately owned, Bentwaters
	XX840	SEPECAT Jaguar T4 [T]	DSAE No 1 SoTT, Cosford
	XX841	SEPECAT Jaguar T4	Privately owned, Tunbridge Wells
	XX842	SEPECAT Jaguar T2A [FX]	Privately owned, Bentwaters
	XX845	SEPECAT Jaguar T4 [EV]	RN, Predannack Fire School
	XX847	SEPECAT Jaguar T4 [EZ]	DSAE No 1 SoTT, Cosford
	XX885	HS Buccaneer S2B (9225M/G-HHAA)	HHA, Scampton
	XX888	HS Buccaneer S2B <ff>	Privately owned, Barnstaple
	XX889	HS Buccaneer S2B [T]	Privately owned, Bruntingthorpe
	XX892	HS Buccaneer S2B <ff>	Blue Sky Experiences, Methven, Perth & Kinross
	XX894	HS Buccaneer S2B [020/R]	The Buccaneer Aviation Group, Bruntingthorpe
	XX895	HS Buccaneer S2B <ff>	Privately owned, Tattershall Thorpe
	XX897	HS Buccaneer S2B(mod)	Shannon Aviation Museum, Eire
	XX899	HS Buccaneer S2B <ff>	Midland Air Museum, Coventry
	XX900	HS Buccaneer S2B [900]	Cold War Jets Collection, Bruntingthorpe
	XX901	HS Buccaneer S2B	Yorkshire Air Museum, Elvington
	XX910	WS Lynx HAS2	The Helicopter Museum, Weston-super-Mare
	XX919	BAC 1-11/402AP (PI-C1121) <ff>	Boscombe Down Aviation Collection, Old Sarum
	XX946	Panavia Tornado (P02) (8883M)	RAF Museum, stored Cosford
	XX947	Panavia Tornado (P03) (8797M)	*Sold to The Netherlands, 2016*
	XX958	SEPECAT Jaguar GR1 (9022M) [BK]	DSAE No 1 SoTT, Cosford
	XX959	SEPECAT Jaguar GR1 (8953M) [CJ]	DSAE No 1 SoTT, Cosford
	XX965	SEPECAT Jaguar GR1A (9254M) [C]	DSAE No 1 SoTT, Cosford
	XX967	SEPECAT Jaguar GR1 (9006M) [AC]	DSAE No 1 SoTT, Cosford
	XX968	SEPECAT Jaguar GR1 (9007M) [AJ]	DSAE No 1 SoTT, Cosford
	XX969	SEPECAT Jaguar GR1 (8897M) [01]	DSAE No 1 SoTT, Cosford
	XX970	SEPECAT Jaguar GR3A [EH]	DSAE No 1 SoTT, Cosford
	XX975	SEPECAT Jaguar GR1 (8905M) [07]	DSAE No 1 SoTT, Cosford
	XX976	SEPECAT Jaguar GR1 (8906M) [BD]	DSAE No 1 SoTT, Cosford
	XX977	SEPECAT Jaguar GR1 (9132M) [DL,05] <rf>	Privately owned, Sproughton

Serial	Type (code/other identity)	Owner/operator, location or fate	Notes
XX979	SEPECAT Jaguar GR1A (9306M) <ff>	Air Defence Radar Museum, Neatishead	
XZ103	SEPECAT Jaguar GR3A [EF]	DSAE No 1 SoTT, Cosford	
XZ104	SEPECAT Jaguar GR3A [FM]	DSAE No 1 SoTT, Cosford	
XZ106	SEPECAT Jaguar GR3A [FR]	RAF Manston History Museum	
XZ107	SEPECAT Jaguar GR3A [FH]	Privately owned, Bentwaters	
XZ109	SEPECAT Jaguar GR3A [EN]	DSAE No 1 SoTT, Cosford	
XZ112	SEPECAT Jaguar GR3A [GW]	DSAE No 1 SoTT, Cosford	
XZ113	SEPECAT Jaguar GR3 [FD,FG]	Privately owned, Wallyford, Edinburgh	
XZ114	SEPECAT Jaguar GR3 [EO]	DSAE No 1 SoTT, Cosford	
XZ115	SEPECAT Jaguar GR3 [ER]	DSAE No 1 SoTT, Cosford	
XZ117	SEPECAT Jaguar GR3 [ES]	DSAE No 1 SoTT, Cosford	
XZ119	SEPECAT Jaguar GR1A (9266M) [FG]	National Museum of Flight, E Fortune	
XZ130	HS Harrier GR3 (9079M) [A]	Privately owned, Thorpe Wood, N Yorks	
XZ131	HS Harrier GR3 (9174M) <ff>	Privately owned, Spark Bridge, Cumbria	
XZ132	HS Harrier GR3 (9168M) [C]	Privately owned, Thorpe Wood, N Yorks	
XZ133	HS Harrier GR3 [10]	IWM Duxford	
XZ138	HS Harrier GR3 (9040M) <ff>	RAFC Cranwell, Trenchard Hall	
XZ146	HS Harrier T4 (9281M) [S]	Harrier Heritage Centre, RAF Wittering	
XZ166	WS Lynx HAS2 <ff>	Farnborough Air Sciences Trust, stored Farnborough	
XZ170	WS Lynx AH9	DSAE SAAE, Lyneham	
XZ171	WS Lynx AH7	Army, Salisbury Plain	
XZ172	WS Lynx AH7	*Currently not known*	
XZ173	WS Lynx AH7 <ff>	Privately owned, Weeton, Lancs	
XZ174	WS Lynx AH7 <ff>	Defence Coll of Policing, Gosport, instructional use	
XZ175	WS Lynx AH7	Privately owned, Barby, Northants	
XZ177	*Aérospatiale SA341G Gazelle (G-SFTA/XZ345) [T]*	North-East Aircraft Museum, Usworth	
XZ177	WS Lynx AH7	Delta Force, stored Upminster	
XZ178	WS Lynx AH7 <ff>	Privately owned, Hixon, Staffs	
XZ179	WS Lynx AH7 <ff>	Privately owned, Sproughton	
XZ180	WS Lynx AH7 [C]	DSAE SAAE, Lyneham	
XZ181	WS Lynx AH1	*Currently not known*	
XZ182	WS Lynx AH7 <ff>	*Sold to The Netherlands, 2016*	
XZ183	WS Lynx AH7 <ff>	MoD St Athan, instructional use	
XZ184	WS Lynx AH7 [B]	AAC Middle Wallop, at main gate	
XZ187	WS Lynx AH7	DSAE SAAE, Lyneham	
XZ188	WS Lynx AH7	DSAE SAAE, Lyneham	
XZ190	WS Lynx AH7 <ff>	Army, Longmoor Camp, Hants, GI use	
XZ191	WS Lynx AH7 [R]	DSAE SAAE, Lyneham	
XZ192	WS Lynx AH7 [H]	AAC, stored St Athan	
XZ193	WS Lynx AH7 <ff>	Privately owned, Weeton, Lancs	
XZ194	WS Lynx AH7 [V]	IWM Duxford	
XZ195	WS Lynx AH7 <ff>	Privately owned, Hixon, Staffs	
XZ198	WS Lynx AH7 <ff>	*Currently not known*	
XZ203	WS Lynx AH7 [F]	Army, Salisbury Plain	
XZ206	WS Lynx AH7 <ff>	Privately owned, Hixon, Staffs	
XZ207	WS Lynx AH7 <rf>	DSAE SAAE, Lyneham	
XZ208	WS Lynx AH7	Privately owned, Sproughton	
XZ209	WS Lynx AH7 <ff>	MoD JARTS, Boscombe Down	
XZ211	WS Lynx AH7	Bawtry Paintball Park, S Yorks	
XZ212	WS Lynx AH7 [X]	AAC Middle Wallop, GI use	
XZ213	WS Lynx AH1 (TAD 213)	Vector Aerospace Fleetlands Apprentice School	
XZ214	WS Lynx AH7 <ff>	DSAE SAAE, Lyneham	
XZ216	WS Lynx AH7 <ff>	MoD DFTDC, Manston	
XZ217	WS Lynx AH7	Privately owned, Hixon, Staffs	
XZ218	WS Lynx AH7	Warfighters R6 Centre, Barby, Northants	
XZ219	WS Lynx AH7 <ff>	Army, Bramley, Hants	
XZ220	WS Lynx AH7 <ff>	Privately owned, Weeton, Lancs	
XZ222	WS Lynx AH7	DSAE SAAE, Lyneham	
XZ228	WS Lynx HAS3GMS [313]	RN Historic Flight, stored Culdrose	
XZ229	WS Lynx HAS3GMS [360/MC]	Privately owned, Hixon, Staffs	
XZ230	WS Lynx HAS3GMS	RN Yeovilton, GI use (Wildcat ground trainer)	

Notes	Serial	Type (code/other identity)	Owner/operator, location or fate
	XZ232	WS Lynx HAS3GMS	Falck Nutec UK, Aberdeen, GI use
	XZ233	WS Lynx HAS3S [635] $	RN, stored Culdrose
	XZ234	WS Lynx HAS3S [630]	RN MPSU, Middle Wallop
	XZ235	WS Lynx HAS3S(ICE) [630]	Privately owned, Hixon, Staffs
	XZ236	WS Lynx HMA8 [LST-1]	RN ETS, Yeovilton, GI use
	XZ237	WS Lynx HAS3S [631]	Privately owned, Wild Park, Derbyshire
	XZ238	WS Lynx HAS3S(ICE) [633]	Repainted as ZF355, 2016
	XZ239	WS Lynx HAS3GMS [633]	Privately owned, Hixon, Staffs
	XZ245	WS Lynx HAS3GMS	Privately owned, Sproughton
	XZ246	WS Lynx HAS3S(ICE) [434/EE]	South Yorkshire Aircraft Museum, Doncaster
	XZ248	WS Lynx HAS3S	SFDO, RNAS Culdrose
	XZ250	WS Lynx HAS3S [426/PO] $	RN, Portland, on display
	XZ252	WS Lynx HAS3S	Privately owned, Hixon, Staffs
	XZ254	WS Lynx HAS3S	Privately owned, Hixon, Staffs
	XZ255	WS Lynx HMA8SRU [454/DF]	RN, stored St Athan
	XZ257	WS Lynx HAS3S	Currently not known
	XZ287	BAe Nimrod AEW3 (9140M) (fuselage)	RAF TSW, Stafford
	XZ290	WS Gazelle AH1	AAC No 665 Sqn/5 Regt, Aldergrove
	XZ291	WS Gazelle AH1	Sold to South Africa by 2016
	XZ292	WS Gazelle AH1	Privately owned, Stapleford Tawney
	XZ294	WS Gazelle AH1 [X]	AAC AM&SU, stored Shawbury
	XZ295	WS Gazelle AH1	MoD/ETPS, Boscombe Down
	XZ296	WS Gazelle AH1 [V]	Privately owned, Stapleford Tawney
	XZ298	WS Gazelle AH1 <ff>	AAC Middle Wallop, GI use
	XZ300	WS Gazelle AH1	Army, Bramley, Hants
	XZ303	WS Gazelle AH1	AAC MPSU, stored Middle Wallop
	XZ304	WS Gazelle AH1	Privately owned, Stapleford Tawney
	XZ305	WS Gazelle AH1 (TAD 020)	DSAE RNAESS HMS Sultan, Gosport
	XZ308	WS Gazelle AH1	QinetiQ, Boscombe Down (spares use)
	XZ311	WS Gazelle AH1 [U]	AAC MPSU, Middle Wallop
	XZ312	WS Gazelle AH1	RAF Henlow, instructional use
	XZ313	WS Gazelle AH1 <ff>	Privately owned, Shotton, Durham
	XZ314	WS Gazelle AH1 [A]	Privately owned, Stapleford Tawney
	XZ315	WS Gazelle AH1 <ff>	Privately owned, Babcary, Somerset
	XZ316	WS Gazelle AH1 [B]	DSAE SAAE, Lyneham
	XZ318	WS Gazelle AH1 (fuselage)	Tong Paintball Park, Shropshire
	XZ320	WS Gazelle AH1	AAC No 665 Sqn/5 Regt, Aldergrove
	XZ321	WS Gazelle AH1 (G-CDNS) [D]	Privately owned, Hurstbourne Tarrant, Hants
	XZ322	WS Gazelle AH1 (9283M) [N]	DSAE SAAE, Lyneham
	XZ323	WS Gazelle AH1	Currently not known
	XZ324	WS Gazelle AH1	Privately owned, Stapleford Tawney
	XZ325	WS Gazelle AH1	Currently not known
	XZ326	WS Gazelle AH1	AAC No 665 Sqn/5 Regt, Aldergrove
	XZ327	WS Gazelle AH1	AAC Middle Wallop (recruiting aid)
	XZ328	WS Gazelle AH1 [C]	AAC AM&SU, stored Shawbury
	XZ329	WS Gazelle AH1 (G-BZYD) [J]	Privately owned, East Garston, Bucks
	XZ330	WS Gazelle AH1 [Y]	AAC Wattisham, instructional use
	XZ331	WS Gazelle AH1 [D]	Currently not known
	XZ332	WS Gazelle AH1	DSAE SAAE, Lyneham
	XZ333	WS Gazelle AH1	DSAE SAAE, Lyneham
	XZ334	WS Gazelle AH1	AAC No 667 Sqn/7 Regt, Middle Wallop
	XZ335	WS Gazelle AH1	North-East Aircraft Museum, stored Usworth
	XZ337	WS Gazelle AH1 [Z]	MoD Abbey Wood, Bristol, on display
	XZ338	WS Gazelle AH1 (G-CHZF) [Y]	Sold to Malawi, 2015
	XZ340	WS Gazelle AH1	AAC No 29 Flt, BATUS, Suffield, Canada
	XZ341	WS Gazelle AH1	AAC AM&SU, stored Shawbury
	XZ342	WS Gazelle AH1	Currently not known
	XZ343	WS Gazelle AH1	AAC AM&SU, stored Shawbury
	XZ344	WS Gazelle AH1 [Y]	Privately owned, Stapleford Tawney
	XZ345	Aérospatiale SA341G Gazelle (G-SFTA) [T]	Repainted as XZ177
	XZ345	WS Gazelle AH1 [M]	AAC 7 Regt Conversion Flt, Middle Wallop
	XZ346	WS Gazelle AH1	AAC Middle Wallop, at main gate

Serial	Type (code/other identity)	Owner/operator, location or fate	Notes
XZ349	WS Gazelle AH1 <ff>	*Scrapped at Hurstbourne Tarrant, February 2016*	
XZ356	SEPECAT Jaguar GR3A [FU]	Privately owned, Welshpool	
XZ358	SEPECAT Jaguar GR1A (9262M) [L]	DSAE No 1 SoTT, Cosford	
XZ360	SEPECAT Jaguar GR3 [FN]	Privately owned, Bentwaters	
XZ363	SEPECAT Jaguar GR1A <R> (XX824/BAPC 151) [A]	RAF M&RU, Bottesford	
XZ364	SEPECAT Jaguar GR3A <ff>	Privately owned, Tunbridge Wells	
XZ366	SEPECAT Jaguar GR3A [FC]	Privately owned, Bentwaters	
XZ367	SEPECAT Jaguar GR3 [GP]	DSAE No 1 SoTT, Cosford	
XZ368	SEPECAT Jaguar GR1 [8900M] [E]	DSAE No 1 SoTT, Cosford	
XZ369	SEPECAT Jaguar GR3A [EU]	Delta Force, stored Upminster	
XZ370	SEPECAT Jaguar GR1 (9004M) [JB]	DSAE No 1 SoTT, Cosford	
XZ371	SEPECAT Jaguar GR1 (8907M) [AP]	DSAE No 1 SoTT, Cosford	
XZ372	SEPECAT Jaguar GR3 [FV]	Aberdeen Airport, on display	
XZ374	SEPECAT Jaguar GR1 (9005M) [JC]	DSAE, stored Cosford	
XZ375	SEPECAT Jaguar GR1A (9255M) <ff>	City of Norwich Aviation Museum	
XZ377	SEPECAT Jaguar GR3A [P]	DSAE No 1 SoTT, Cosford	
XZ378	SEPECAT Jaguar GR1A [EP]	Privately owned, Topsham, Devon	
XZ382	SEPECAT Jaguar GR1 (8908M)	Cold War Jets Collection, Bruntingthorpe	
XZ383	SEPECAT Jaguar GR1 (8901M) [AF]	DSAE No 1 SoTT, Cosford	
XZ384	SEPECAT Jaguar GR1 (8954M) [BC]	DSAE No 1 SoTT, Cosford	
XZ385	SEPECAT Jaguar GR3A [FT]	Privately owned, Bentwaters	
XZ389	SEPECAT Jaguar GR1 (8946M) [BL]	DSAE No 1 SoTT, Cosford	
XZ390	SEPECAT Jaguar GR1 (9003M) [DM]	DSAE No 1 SoTT, Cosford	
XZ391	SEPECAT Jaguar GR3A [ET]	DSAE No 1 SoTT, Cosford	
XZ392	SEPECAT Jaguar GR3A [EM]	DSAE No 1 SoTT, Cosford	
XZ394	SEPECAT Jaguar GR3 [FG]	Shoreham Airport, on display	
XZ398	SEPECAT Jaguar GR3A [EQ]	DSAE No 1 SoTT, Cosford	
XZ399	SEPECAT Jaguar GR3A [EJ]	DSAE No 1 SoTT, Cosford	
XZ400	SEPECAT Jaguar GR3A [FQ]	Privately owned, Bentwaters	
XZ431	HS Buccaneer S2B (9233M) <ff>	South Yorkshire Aviation Museum, Doncaster	
XZ440	BAe Sea Harrier FA2 [40/DD]	SFDO, RNAS Culdrose	
XZ455	BAe Sea Harrier FA2 [001] (wreck)	Privately owned, Thorpe Wood, N Yorks	
XZ457	BAe Sea Harrier FA2 [104/VL]	Boscombe Down Aviation Collection, Old Sarum	
XZ459	BAe Sea Harrier FA2 [126]	Privately owned, Sussex	
XZ493	BAe Sea Harrier FRS1 (comp XV760) [001/N]	FAA Museum, RNAS Yeovilton	
XZ493	BAe Sea Harrier FRS1 <ff>	RN Yeovilton, Fire Section	
XZ494	BAe Sea Harrier FA2 [128]	Privately owned, Wedmore, Somerset	
XZ497	BAe Sea Harrier FA2 [126]	Privately owned, Charlwood	
XZ499	BAe Sea Harrier FA2 [003]	FAA Museum, stored Cobham Hall, RNAS Yeovilton	
XZ559	Slingsby T61F Venture T2 (G-BUEK)	Privately owned, Tibenham	
XZ570	WS61 Sea King HAS5(mod)	RN, Predannack Fire School	
XZ574	WS61 Sea King HAS6	FAA Museum, stored Cobham Hall, RNAS Yeovilton	
XZ575	WS61 Sea King HU5	Privately owned, Horsham	
XZ576	WS61 Sea King HAS6	DSAE RNAESS, *HMS Sultan*, Gosport	
XZ578	WS61 Sea King HU5 [30]	Privately owned, Caernarfon	
XZ579	WS61 Sea King HAS6 [707/PW]	DSAE RNAESS, *HMS Sultan*, Gosport	
XZ580	WS61 Sea King HC6 [ZB]	DSAE RNAESS, *HMS Sultan*, Gosport	
XZ581	WS61 Sea King HAS6 [69/CU]	Mini Moos Farm, Edmondsley, Durham	
XZ585	WS61 Sea King HAR3 [A]	DSAE, stored *HMS Sultan*, Gosport	
XZ586	WS61 Sea King HAR3 [B]	DSAE, stored *HMS Sultan*, Gosport	
XZ587	WS61 Sea King HAR3 [C]	RAF St Mawgan, on display	
XZ588	WS61 Sea King HAR3 [D]	Vector Aerospace Fleetlands Apprentice School	
XZ589	WS61 Sea King HAR3 [E] $	DSAE RNAESS, *HMS Sultan*, Gosport	
XZ590	WS61 Sea King HAR3 [F]	DSAE, stored *HMS Sultan*, Gosport	
XZ591	WS61 Sea King HAR3 (fuselage)	Vector Aerospace, Fleetlands (dumped)	
XZ592	WS61 Sea King HAR3 [H]	Morayvia, Forres, Moray	
XZ593	WS61 Sea King HAR3 [I]	*Donated to The Falklands Museum, May 2016*	
XZ594	WS61 Sea King HAR3	DSAE, stored *HMS Sultan*, Gosport	
XZ595	WS61 Sea King HAR3 [K]	*Currently not known*	
XZ596	WS61 Sea King HAR3	DSAE, stored *HMS Sultan*, Gosport	
XZ597	WS61 Sea King HAR3 [M]	Privately owned, Colsterworth, Leics	

Notes	Serial	Type (code/other identity)	Owner/operator, location or fate
	XZ598	WS61 Sea King HAR3 [N]	Privately owned, Scarborough
	XZ599	WS61 Sea King HAR3 (fuselage)	Vector Aerospace, Fleetlands (dumped)
	XZ605	WS Lynx AH7	Wattisham Station Heritage Museum
	XZ606	WS Lynx AH7 [O]	Delta Force, stored Upminster
	XZ607	WS Lynx AH7 <ff>	MoD DFTDC, Manston
	XZ607	WS Lynx AH7 (comp XZ215)	MoD DFTDC, Manston
	XZ608	WS Lynx AH7 (fuselage)	Army Bury St Edmunds, GI use
	XZ608	WS Lynx AH7 (ZD272)[W]	Privately owned, Weeton, Lancs
	XZ609	WS Lynx AH7	AAC MPSU, Middle Wallop
	XZ611	WS Lynx AH7 <ff>	Privately owned, Hixon, Staffs
	XZ612	WS Lynx AH7	Delta Force, stored Upminster
	XZ613	WS Lynx AH7 [F]	DSAE RNAESS, HMS Sultan, Gosport
	XZ615	WS Lynx AH7 <ff>	Privately owned, Hixon, Staffs
	XZ616	WS Lynx AH7	MoD/Vector Aerospace, stored Fleetlands
	XZ617	WS Lynx AH7 <ff>)	DSAE SAAE, Lyneham
	XZ630	Panavia Tornado (P12) (8976M)	RAF Halton, on display
	XZ631	Panavia Tornado GR4	Yorkshire Air Museum, Elvington
	XZ642	WS Lynx AH7	DSAE SAAE, Lyneham
	XZ643	WS Lynx AH7 [C]	Currently not known
	XZ645	WS Lynx AH7	Delta Force, stored Upminster
	XZ646	WS Lynx AH7 <ff>	MoD JARTS, Boscombe Down
	XZ646	WS Lynx AH7 (really XZ649)	Bristol University, instructional use
	XZ647	WS Lynx AH7 <ff>	Aberdeen Airport Fire Section
	XZ648	WS Lynx AH7 <ff>	Privately owned, Weeton, Lancs
	XZ651	WS Lynx AH7 [O]	AAC MPSU, Middle Wallop
	XZ652	WS Lynx AH7	IFTC, Durham/Tees Valley
	XZ653	WS Lynx AH7	DSAE SAAE, Lyneham
	XZ654	WS Lynx AH7	Shannon Aviation Museum, Eire
	XZ655	WS Lynx AH7 <ff>	Privately owned, Weeton, Lancs
	XZ661	WS Lynx AH7 [V]	Army, Bramley, Hants
	XZ663	WS Lynx AH7 <ff>	Privately owned, Hixon, Staffs
	XZ664	WS Lynx AH7	Warfighters R6 Centre, Barby, Northants
	XZ665	WS Lynx AH7	Privately owned, Barby, Northants
	XZ666	WS Lynx AH7	Currently not known
	XZ668	WS Lynx AH7 [UN] <ff>	Privately owned, stored Cranfield
	XZ669	WS Lynx AH7 [I]	Sold to The Netherlands, 2016
	XZ670	WS Lynx AH7 [A]	RNAS Yeovilton, for display
	XZ671	WS Lynx AH7 <ff>	Leonardo, Yeovil, instructional use
	XZ672	WS Lynx AH7 <ff>	AAC Middle Wallop Fire Section
	XZ673	WS Lynx AH7	Privately owned, Weeton, Lancs
	XZ674	WS Lynx AH7 [T]	RNAS Yeovilton Fire Section
	XZ675	WS Lynx AH7 [H]	Museum of Army Flying, Middle Wallop
	XZ676	WS Lynx AH7 [N]	Privately owned, Weeton, Lancs
	XZ677	WS Lynx AH7 <ff>	Army, Longmoor Camp, Hants, GI use
	XZ678	WS Lynx AH7 <ff>	Privately owned, Sproughton
	XZ679	WS Lynx AH7 [W]	DSAE SAAE, Lyneham
	XZ680	WS Lynx AH7 <ff>	Privately owned, Weeton, Lancs
	XZ689	WS Lynx HMA8SRU [314]	RN No 815 NAS, MI Flt, Yeovilton
	XZ690	WS Lynx HMA8SRU [640]	Delta Force, stored Upminster
	XZ691	WS Lynx HMA8SRU [310]	RN No 815 NAS, MI Flt, Yeovilton
	XZ692	WS Lynx HMA8SRU [764/SN] $	DSAE RNAESS, HMS Sultan, Gosport
	XZ693	WS Lynx HAS3S [311]	Privately owned, Hixon, Staffs
	XZ696	WS Lynx HAS3GMS [633]	Privately owned, Hixon, Staffs
	XZ697	WS Lynx HMA8SRU [313]	MoD/Vector Aerospace, Fleetlands
	XZ698	WS Lynx HMA8SRU [316]	Delta Force, stored Upminster
	XZ699	WS Lynx HAS2	FAA Museum, stored Cobham Hall, RNAS Yeovilton
	XZ719	WS Lynx HMA8SRU [64]	RNAS Yeovilton Fire Section
	XZ720	WS Lynx HAS3GMS [410/GC]	FAA Museum, stored Cobham Hall, RNAS Yeovilton
	XZ721	WS Lynx HAS3GMS [322]	East Midlands Airport Aeropark
	XZ722	WS Lynx HMA8SRU [671]	AAC MPSU, Middle Wallop, RTP
	XZ723	WS Lynx HMA8SRU [672]	Delta Force, stored Upminster
	XZ725	WS Lynx HMA8SRU [415/MM]	RN, stored St Athan

Serial	Type (code/other identity)	Owner/operator, location or fate	Notes
XZ726	WS Lynx HMA8SRU [316]	School of Maritime Survival *HMS Raleigh*, Plymouth	
XZ727	WS Lynx HAS3S [634]	*Currently not known*	
XZ728	WS Lynx HMA8 [326/AW]	RNAS Yeovilton, on display	
XZ729	WS Lynx HMA8SRU [425/DT]	RN, stored St Athan	
XZ730	WS Lynx HAS3S	Privately owned, Hixon, Staffs	
XZ731	WS Lynx HMA8SRU [311/VL]	MoD, Boscombe Down	
XZ732	WS Lynx HMA8SRU [315/VL]	RN, stored St Athan	
XZ733	WS Lynx HAS3GMS [305]	*Scrapped*	
XZ735	WS Lynx HAS3GMS <ff>	Privately owned, Sproughton	
XZ736	WS Lynx HMA8SRU [307]	AAC MPSU, Middle Wallop	
XZ791	Northrop Shelduck D1	Davidstow Airfield & Cornwall at War Museum	
XZ795	Northrop Shelduck D1	Museum of Army Flying, Middle Wallop	
XZ920	WS61 Sea King HU5 [24]	DSAE, stored *HMS Sultan*, Gosport	
XZ921	WS61 Sea King HAS6 [269/N]	Mini Moos Farm, Edmondsley, Durham	
XZ922	WS61 Sea King HC6 [ZA]	DSAE RNAESS, *HMS Sultan*, Gosport	
XZ930	WS Gazelle HT3 (A2713)	DSAE RNAESS, *HMS Sultan*, Gosport	
XZ933	WS Gazelle HT3 (XZ936/G-CGJZ)	Privately owned, Hurstbourne Tarrant, Hants	
XZ934	WS Gazelle HT3 (G-CBSI)	Privately owned, Redhill	
XZ935	WS Gazelle HCC4 (9332M)	DSAE SAAE, Lyneham	
XZ936	WS Gazelle HT3 [6]	MoD, stored Boscombe Down (damaged)	
XZ939	WS Gazelle HT3 [9]	MoD/ETPS, Boscombe Down	
XZ941	WS Gazelle HT3 (9301M) [B]	*Currently not known*	
XZ964	BAe Harrier GR3 [D]	Royal Engineers Museum, Chatham	
XZ966	BAe Harrier GR3 (9221M) [G]	MoD DFTDC, Manston	
XZ968	BAe Harrier GR3 (9222M) [3G]	Muckleborough Collection, Weybourne	
XZ969	BAe Harrier GR3 [69/DD]	RN, Predannack Fire School	
XZ971	BAe Harrier GR3 (9219M)	HQ DSDA, Donnington, Shropshire, on display	
XZ987	BAe Harrier GR3 (9185M) [C]	RAF Stafford, at main gate	
XZ990	BAe Harrier GR3 <ff>	*Currently not known*	
XZ990	BAe Harrier GR3 <rf>	RAF Wittering, derelict	
XZ991	BAe Harrier GR3 (9162M) [AD]	DSAE Cosford, on display	
XZ993	BAe Harrier GR3 (9240M) <ff>	Privately owned, Upwood, Cambs	
XZ994	BAe Harrier GR3 (9170M) [U]	MoD JARTS, Boscombe Down	
XZ995	BAe Harrier GR3 (9220M/G-CBGK) [3G]	Privately owned, Dolly's Grove, Co Dublin, Eire	
XZ996	BAe Harrier GR3 [96/DD]	Privately owned, Bentwaters	
XZ997	BAe Harrier GR3 (9122M) [V]	RAF Museum, Hendon	
ZA101	BAe Hawk 100 (G-HAWK)	BAE Systems Warton, Overseas Customer Training Centre	
ZA105	WS61 Sea King HAR3 [Q]	DSAE, stored *HMS Sultan*, Gosport	
ZA110	BAe Jetstream T2 (F-BTMI) [563/CU]	Aberdeen Airport	
ZA111	BAe Jetstream T2 (9Q-CTC) [565/CU]	SFDO, RNAS Culdrose	
ZA126	WS61 Sea King ASaC7 [191]	RN No 849 NAS, Culdrose	
ZA127	WS61 Sea King HAS6 [509/CU]	Privately owned, Thornhill, Stirlingshire	
ZA128	WS61 Sea King HAS6 [010]	DSAE No 1 SoTT, Cosford	
ZA130	WS61 Sea King HU5 [19]	*Currently not known*	
ZA131	WS61 Sea King HAS6 [271/N]	DSAE RNAESS, *HMS Sultan*, Gosport	
ZA133	WS61 Sea King HAS6 [831/CU]	DSAE RNAESS, *HMS Sultan*, Gosport	
ZA134	WS61 Sea King HU5 [25]	DSAE, stored *HMS Sultan*, Gosport	
ZA135	WS61 Sea King HAS6	Privately owned, Woodperry, Oxon	
ZA136	WS61 Sea King HAS6 [018]	Privately owned, Hixon, Staffs	
ZA137	WS61 Sea King HU5 [20]	DSAE, stored *HMS Sultan*, Gosport	
ZA144	BAe VC10 K2 (G-ARVC) <ff>	MoD JARTS, Boscombe Down	
ZA147	BAe VC10 K3 (5H-MMT) [F]	Privately owned, Bruntingthorpe	
ZA148	BAe VC10 K3 (5Y-ADA) [G]	Cornwall Aviation Heritage Centre, Newquay	
ZA149	BAe VC10 K3 (5X-UVJ) [H]	*To the UAE, March 2016*	
ZA150	BAe VC10 K3 (5H-MOG) [J]	Brooklands Museum, Dunsfold	
ZA166	WS61 Sea King HU5 [16/CU]	DSAE, stored *HMS Sultan*, Gosport	
ZA167	WS61 Sea King HU5 [22/CU]	DSAE RNAESS, *HMS Sultan*, Gosport	
ZA168	WS61 Sea King HAS6 [830/CU]	DSAE RNAESS, *HMS Sultan*, Gosport	
ZA169	WS61 Sea King HAS6 [515/CW]	DSAE No 1 SoTT, Cosford	
ZA170	WS61 Sea King HAS5	*Currently not known*	

Notes	Serial	Type (code/other identity)	Owner/operator, location or fate
	ZA175	BAe Sea Harrier FA2	Norfolk & Suffolk Avn Museum, Flixton
	ZA176	BAe Sea Harrier FA2 [126/R]	Newark Air Museum, Winthorpe
	ZA195	BAe Sea Harrier FA2	Tangmere Military Aviation Museum
	ZA209	Short MATS-B	Museum of Army Flying, Middle Wallop
	ZA220	Short MATS-B	Privately owned, Awbridge, Hants
	ZA242	Short MATS-B	Boscombe Down Aviation Collection, Old Sarum
	ZA250	BAe Harrier T52 (G-VTOL)	Brooklands Museum, Weybridge
	ZA267	Panavia Tornado F2 (9284M)	RAF Marham, instructional use
	ZA291	WS61 Sea King HC4 [N]	Mini Moos Farm, Edmondsley, Durham
	ZA292	WS61 Sea King HC4 (fuselage)	Vector Aerospace, Fleetlands (dumped)
	ZA293	WS61 Sea King HC4 (fuselage)	Vector Aerospace, Fleetlands (dumped)
	ZA295	WS61 Sea King HC4 [U]	MoD/Vector Aerospace, Fleetlands
	ZA296	WS61 Sea King HC4 [Q]	MoD/Vector Aerospace, Fleetlands
	ZA297	WS61 Sea King HC4 (fuselage)	Vector Aerospace, Fleetlands (dumped)
	ZA298	WS61 Sea King HC4 (G-BJNM) [Y]	FAA Museum, RNAS Yeovilton
	ZA299	WS61 Sea King HC4 [D]	MoD/Vector Aerospace, Fleetlands
	ZA312	WS61 Sea King HC4 [E]	Privately owned, Colsterworth, Leics
	ZA313	WS61 Sea King HC4 [M]	*Currently not known*
	ZA314	WS61 Sea King HC4 [WT]	DSAE, stored *HMS Sultan*, Gosport
	ZA319	Panavia Tornado GR1 (9315M)	DSDA, Arncott, Oxon, on display
	ZA320	Panavia Tornado GR1 (9314M) [TAW]	DSAE No 1 SoTT, Cosford
	ZA323	Panavia Tornado GR1 [TAZ]	DSAE No 1 SoTT, Cosford
	ZA325	Panavia Tornado GR1 <ff>	RAF Manston History Museum
	ZA325	Panavia Tornado GR1 [TAX] <rf>	RAF AM&SU, stored Shawbury
	ZA326	Panavia Tornado GR1P	Privately owned, Bruntingthorpe
	ZA327	Panavia Tornado GR1 <ff>	BAE Systems, Warton
	ZA328	Panavia Tornado GR1	BAE Systems, Samlesbury
	ZA353	Panavia Tornado GR1 [B-53]	Privately owned, Thorpe Wood, N Yorks
	ZA354	Panavia Tornado GR1	Yorkshire Air Museum, Elvington
	ZA355	Panavia Tornado GR1 (9310M) [TAA]	Privately owned, Thorpe Wood, N Yorks
	ZA356	Panavia Tornado GR1 <ff>	RAF Tornado Maintenance School, Marham
	ZA357	Panavia Tornado GR1 [TTV]	DSAE No 1 SoTT, Cosford
	ZA359	Panavia Tornado GR1	Privately owned, Thorpe Wood, N Yorks
	ZA360	Panavia Tornado GR1 (9318M) <ff>	RAF Marham, instructional use
	ZA362	Panavia Tornado GR1 [TR]	Highland Aviation Museum, Inverness
	ZA369	Panavia Tornado GR4A [003]	RAF No 31 Sqn, Marham
	ZA370	Panavia Tornado GR4A [004]	RAF TASF(S), Marham
	ZA372	Panavia Tornado GR4A [006]	RAF Leeming, RTP
	ZA373	Panavia Tornado GR4A [007]	*Scrapped at Leeming, 2016*
	ZA375	Panavia Tornado GR1 (9335M) [AJ-W]	RAF Marham, Fire Section
	ZA393	Panavia Tornado GR4 [008] $	*Scrapped at Leeming, 2016*
	ZA398	Panavia Tornado GR4A $	RAF DFTDC, Marston
	ZA399	Panavia Tornado GR1 (9316M) [AJ-C]	Privately owned, Knutsford, Cheshire
	ZA400	Panavia Tornado GR4A [011]	*Scrapped at Leeming, 2016*
	ZA405	Panavia Tornado GR4A $	*Scrapped at Leeming, 2016*
	ZA406	Panavia Tornado GR4 [015]	RAF TASF(N), Lossiemouth
	ZA407	Panavia Tornado GR1 (9336M) [AJ-N]	RAF Marham, on display
	ZA409	Panavia Tornado GR1 [VII]	RAF Lossiemouth (wfu)
	ZA410	Panavia Tornado GR4 [016]	*Scrapped at Leeming, 2016*
	ZA411	Panavia Tornado GR1	BAE Systems stored, Warton
	ZA447	Panavia Tornado GR4 [019]	RAF No 31 Sqn, Marham
	ZA449	Panavia Tornado GR4 [020]	RAF No 12 Sqn, Marham
	ZA450	Panavia Tornado GR1 (9317M) [TH]	DSAE No 1 SoTT, Cosford
	ZA452	Panavia Tornado GR4 [021]	Midland Air Museum, Coventry
	ZA453	Panavia Tornado GR4 [022]	RAF No 15(R) Sqn, Lossiemouth
	ZA457	Panavia Tornado GR1 [AJ-J]	RAF Museum, Hendon
	ZA458	Panavia Tornado GR4 [024]	RAF No 9 Sqn, Marham
	ZA459	Panavia Tornado GR4 [025]	RAF No 31 Sqn, Marham
	ZA461	Panavia Tornado GR4 $	*Scrapped at Leeming, 2016*
	ZA462	Panavia Tornado GR4 [027]	RAF No 31 Sqn, Marham
	ZA463	Panavia Tornado GR4 [028]	RAF CMU, Marham
	ZA465	Panavia Tornado GR1 [FF]	IWM Duxford

Serial	Type (code/other identity)	Owner/operator, location or fate	Notes
ZA469	Panavia Tornado GR4 [029] $	RAF Marham, WLT	
ZA472	Panavia Tornado GR4 [031]	RAF No 31 Sqn, Marham	
ZA473	Panavia Tornado GR4 [032]	RAF TASF(S), Marham	
ZA474	Panavia Tornado GR1 (9312M)	RAF, stored Lossiemouth	
ZA475	Panavia Tornado GR1 (9311M) [AJ-G]	RAF Lossiemouth, on display	
ZA492	Panavia Tornado GR4 $	Scrapped at Leeming, 2016	
ZA541	Panavia Tornado GR4 [034]	RAF Leeming, RTP	
ZA542	Panavia Tornado GR4 [035]	RAF CMU, Marham	
ZA543	Panavia Tornado GR4 [036]	RAF No 12 Sqn, Marham	
ZA546	Panavia Tornado GR4 [038]	RAF No 12 Sqn, Marham	
ZA548	Panavia Tornado GR4 [040] $	RAF No 31 Sqn, Marham	
ZA549	Panavia Tornado GR4 [041]	RAF Tornado Maintenance School, Marham	
ZA550	Panavia Tornado GR4 [042]	RAF No 12 Sqn, Marham	
ZA551	Panavia Tornado GR4 [043]	RAF, stored Leeming	
ZA553	Panavia Tornado GR4 [045]	RAF No 9 Sqn, Marham	
ZA554	Panavia Tornado GR4 [046]	RAF No 31 Sqn, Marham	
ZA556	Panavia Tornado GR4 [047]	RAF CMU, Marham	
ZA556	Panavia Tornado GR1 <R> (ZA368/BAPC 155) [Z]	RAF M&RU, Bottesford	
ZA557	Panavia Tornado GR4 [048]	Scrapped at Leeming, 2016	
ZA559	Panavia Tornado GR4 [049]	RAF AWC/FJWOEU/No 41(R) Sqn, Coningsby	
ZA560	Panavia Tornado GR4 [EB-Q]	RAF AWC/FJWOEU/No 41(R) Sqn, Coningsby	
ZA562	Panavia Tornado GR4 [051]	Scrapped at Leeming, 2016	
ZA564	Panavia Tornado GR4 $	Scrapped at Leeming, 2016	
ZA585	Panavia Tornado GR4 [054]	RAF No 12 Sqn, Marham	
ZA587	Panavia Tornado GR4 [055]	RAF CMU, Marham	
ZA588	Panavia Tornado GR4 [056]	RAF No 15(R) Sqn, Lossiemouth	
ZA589	Panavia Tornado GR4 [057]	Scrapped at Leeming, 2016	
ZA591	Panavia Tornado GR4 [058]	RAF CMU, Marham	
ZA592	Panavia Tornado GR4 [059]	RAF Leeming, RTP	
ZA594	Panavia Tornado GR4 [060]	RAF No 9 Sqn, Marham	
ZA597	Panavia Tornado GR4 [063]	RAF No 12 Sqn, Marham	
ZA598	Panavia Tornado GR4 [064]	Scrapped at Leeming, 2016	
ZA600	Panavia Tornado GR4 [EB-G] $	Scrapped at Leeming, 2016	
ZA601	Panavia Tornado GR4 [066]	RAF CMU, Marham	
ZA602	Panavia Tornado GR4 [F] $	RAF Leeming, RTP	
ZA604	Panavia Tornado GR4 [068]	Scrapped at Leeming, 2016	
ZA607	Panavia Tornado GR4 [EB-X]	RAF AWC/FJWOEU/No 41(R) Sqn, Coningsby	
ZA609	Panavia Tornado GR4 [072]	Scrapped at Leeming, 2016	
ZA611	Panavia Tornado GR4 [073]	RAF CMU, Marham	
ZA612	Panavia Tornado GR4 [074]	RAF No 15(R) Sqn, Lossiemouth	
ZA613	Panavia Tornado GR4 [075]	RAF No 15(R) Sqn, Lossiemouth	
ZA614	Panavia Tornado GR4 [076]	RAF No 12 Sqn, Marham	
ZA630	Slingsby T61F Venture T2 (G-BUGL)	Privately owned, Tibenham	
ZA634	Slingsby T61F Venture T2 (G-BUHA) [C]	Privately owned, Saltby, Leics	
ZA652	Slingsby T61F Venture T2 (G-BUDC)	Privately owned, Enstone	
ZA656	Slingsby T61F Venture T2 (G-BTWC)	Privately owned, Hullavington	
ZA670	B-V Chinook HC4 (N37010) [AA]	RAF No 18 Sqn/No 27 Sqn, Odiham	
ZA671	B-V Chinook HC4 (N37011) [AB]	RAF No 18 Sqn/No 27 Sqn, Odiham	
ZA674	B-V Chinook HC4 (N37019)	RAF No 28(R) Sqn, Benson	
ZA675	B-V Chinook HC4 (N37020) [AE]	RAF No 18 Sqn/No 27 Sqn, Odiham	
ZA677	B-V Chinook HC4 (N37022) [AF]	RAF No 18 Sqn/No 27 Sqn, Odiham	
ZA678	B-V Chinook HC1 (N37023/9229M) [EZ] (wreck)	RAF Odiham, BDRT	
ZA679	B-V Chinook HC4 (N37025) [AG]	RAF No 28(R) Sqn, Benson	
ZA680	B-V Chinook HC4 (N37026) [AH]	RAF No 18 Sqn/No 27 Sqn, Odiham	
ZA681	B-V Chinook HC4 (N37027) [AI]	RAF No 18 Sqn/No 27 Sqn, Odiham	
ZA682	B-V Chinook HC4 (N37029) [AJ]	RAF No 28(R) Sqn, Benson	
ZA683	B-V Chinook HC4 (N37030) $	MoD/Vector Aerospace, Fleetlands	
ZA684	B-V Chinook HC4 (N37031) [AL]	MoD/Vector Aerospace, Fleetlands	
ZA704	B-V Chinook HC4 (N37033)	RAF No 1310 Flt, Mount Pleasant, FI	
ZA705	B-V Chinook HC4 (N37035) [AN]	RAF No 18 Sqn/No 27 Sqn, Odiham	
ZA707	B-V Chinook HC4 (N37040) [AO]	RAF No 18 Sqn/No 27 Sqn, Odiham	
ZA708	B-V Chinook HC4 (N37042) [AP]	MoD/Vector Aerospace, Fleetlands	

Notes	Serial	Type (code/other identity)	Owner/operator, location or fate
	ZA710	B-V Chinook HC4 (N37044) [AR]	RAF No 18 Sqn/No 27 Sqn, Odiham
	ZA711	B-V Chinook HC4 (N37046) $	RAF No 18 Sqn/No 27 Sqn, Odiham
	ZA712	B-V Chinook HC4 (N37047) [W] $	MoD/Vector Aerospace, Fleetlands
	ZA713	B-V Chinook HC4 (N37048)	RAF No 18 Sqn/No 27 Sqn, Odiham
	ZA714	B-V Chinook HC4 (N37051) [AV]	RAF No 28(R) Sqn, Benson
	ZA717	B-V Chinook HC1 (N37056/9238M) (wreck)	RAFC Cranwell, instructional use
	ZA718	B-V Chinook HC4 (N37058) [BN]	RAF No 1310 Flt, Mount Pleasant, FI
	ZA720	B-V Chinook HC4 (N37060) [AW]	MoD/Vector Aerospace, Fleetlands
	ZA726	WS Gazelle AH1 [F1]	Privately owned, Stapleford Tawney
	ZA726	WS Gazelle AH1 (XW851/G-CIEY)	Privately owned, Breighton
	ZA728	WS Gazelle AH1 [E]	Privately owned, Stapleford Tawney
	ZA729	WS Gazelle AH1	AAC Wattisham, BDRT
	ZA730	WS Gazelle AH1 (G-FUKM) <ff>	Privately owned, Hurstbourne Tarrant, Hants
	ZA731	WS Gazelle AH1	AAC No 29 Flt, BATUS, Suffield, Canada
	ZA735	WS Gazelle AH1	DSAE SAAE, Lyneham
	ZA736	WS Gazelle AH1	AAC No 29 Flt, BATUS, Suffield, Canada
	ZA737	WS Gazelle AH1	Museum of Army Flying, Middle Wallop
	ZA766	WS Gazelle AH1	AAC No 665 Sqn/5 Regt, Aldergrove
	ZA768	WS Gazelle AH1 [F] (wreck)	MoD/Vector Aerospace, stored Fleetlands
	ZA769	WS Gazelle AH1 [K]	*Currently not known*
	ZA771	WS Gazelle AH1	DSAE No 1 SoTT, Cosford
	ZA772	WS Gazelle AH1	AAC No 665 Sqn/5 Regt, Aldergrove
	ZA773	WS Gazelle AH1 [F]	AAC AM&SU, stored Shawbury
	ZA774	WS Gazelle AH1	Privately owned, Babcary, Somerset
	ZA775	WS Gazelle AH1	AAC AM&SU, stored Shawbury
	ZA776	WS Gazelle AH1 [F]	Privately owned, Stapleford Tawney
	ZA804	WS Gazelle HT3	Privately owned, Solstice Park, Amesbury, Wilts
	ZA935	WS Puma HC2	RAF No 28(R) Sqn/No 33 Sqn/No 230 Sqn, Benson
	ZA936	WS Puma HC2	RAF No 28(R) Sqn/No 33 Sqn/No 230 Sqn, Benson
	ZA937	WS Puma HC1	RAF Benson (wfu)
	ZA939	WS Puma HC2	RAF No 28(R) Sqn/No 33 Sqn/No 230 Sqn, Benson
	ZA940	WS Puma HC2 (F-ZWBZ)	RAF/Airbus, Romania
	ZA947	Douglas Dakota C3	RAF BBMF, Coningsby
	ZB101	BAE Systems Hawk Mk.165	*To Saudi Arabia as 2101, 1 April 2016*
	ZB102	BAE Systems Hawk Mk.165	*To Saudi Arabia as 2102, 1 April 2016*
	ZB103	BAE Systems Hawk Mk.165	*To Saudi Arabia as 2103, 8 June 2016*
	ZB104	BAE Systems Hawk Mk.165	*To Saudi Arabia as 2104, 9 May 2016*
	ZB105	BAE Systems Hawk Mk.165	*To Saudi Arabia as 2105, 8 June 2016*
	ZB106	BAE Systems Hawk Mk.165	*To Saudi Arabia as 2106, 21 November 2016*
	ZB107	BAE Systems Hawk Mk.165	*To Saudi Arabia as 2107, 9 August 2016*
	ZB108	BAE Systems Hawk Mk.165	*To Saudi Arabia as 2108, 13 December 2016*
	ZB109	BAE Systems Hawk Mk.165	*To Saudi Arabia as 2109, 9 August 2016*
	ZB110	BAE Systems Hawk Mk.165	*To Saudi Arabia as 7901, 24 October 2016*
	ZB111	BAE Systems Hawk Mk.165	*To Saudi Arabia as 7902, 24 October 2016*
	ZB112	BAE Systems Hawk Mk.165	*To Saudi Arabia as 7903, 21 November 2016*
	ZB113	BAE Systems Hawk Mk.165	*To Saudi Arabia as 7904, 21 November 2016*
	ZB114	BAE Systems Hawk Mk.165	*To Saudi Arabia as 7905, 13 December 2016*
	ZB115	BAE Systems Hawk Mk.165	*To Saudi Arabia as 7906, 20 February 2017*
	ZB116	BAE Systems Hawk Mk.165	BAE Systems, Warton, for Saudi Arabia as 7907
	ZB117	BAE Systems Hawk Mk.165	*To Saudi Arabia as 7908, 20 February 2017*
	ZB118	BAE Systems Hawk Mk.165	BAE Systems, Warton, for Saudi Arabia
	ZB119	BAE Systems Hawk Mk.165	BAE Systems, Warton, for Saudi Arabia
	ZB120	BAE Systems Hawk Mk.165	BAE Systems, Warton, for Saudi Arabia
	ZB121	BAE Systems Hawk Mk.165	BAE Systems, Warton, for Saudi Arabia
	ZB122	BAE Systems Hawk Mk.165	BAE Systems, Warton, for Saudi Arabia
	ZB123	BAE Systems Hawk Mk.166	BAE Systems, Warton, for RAFO
	ZB124	BAE Systems Hawk Mk.166	BAE Systems, Warton, for RAFO
	ZB125	BAE Systems Hawk Mk.166	BAE Systems, Warton, for RAFO
	ZB126	BAE Systems Hawk Mk.166	BAE Systems, Warton, for RAFO
	ZB127	BAE Systems Hawk Mk.166	BAE Systems, Warton, for RAFO
	ZB128	BAE Systems Hawk Mk.166	BAE Systems, Warton, for RAFO

Serial	Type (code/other identity)	Owner/operator, location or fate	Notes
ZB129	BAE Systems Hawk Mk.166	BAE Systems, Warton, for RAFO	
ZB130	BAE Systems Hawk Mk.166	BAE Systems, Warton, for RAFO	
ZB131	BAE Systems Hawk Mk.166	BAE Systems, Warton, for RAFO	
ZB132	BAE Systems Hawk Mk.166	BAE Systems, Warton, for RAFO	
ZB133	BAE Systems Hawk Mk.166	BAE Systems, Warton, for RAFO	
ZB500	WS Lynx 800 (G-LYNX/ZA500)	The Helicopter Museum, Weston-super-Mare	
ZB506	WS61 Sea King Mk 4X	Privately owned, Horsham	
ZB507	WS61 Sea King HC4 [F]	*Currently not known*	
ZB601	BAe Harrier T4 (fuselage)	Privately owned, Selby, N Yorks	
ZB603	BAe Harrier T8 [T03/DD]	SFDO, RNAS Culdrose	
ZB604	BAe Harrier T8 [722]	FAA Museum, stored Cobham Hall, RNAS Yeovilton	
ZB615	SEPECAT Jaguar T2A	DSAE No 1 SoTT, Cosford	
ZB625	WS Gazelle HT3	MoD/AFD/QinetiQ, Boscombe Down	
ZB627	WS Gazelle HT3 (G-CBSK) [A]	Privately owned, Hurstbourne Tarrant, Hants	
ZB646	WS Gazelle HT2 (G-CBGZ) [59/CU]	Privately owned, Knebworth	
ZB647	WS Gazelle HT2 (G-CBSF) [40]	Privately owned, Hurstbourne Tarrant, Hants	
ZB665	WS Gazelle AH1	AAC No 665 Sqn/5 Regt, Aldergrove	
ZB667	WS Gazelle AH1	AAC, Middle Wallop	
ZB668	WS Gazelle AH1 (TAD 015)	DSAE SAAE, Lyneham	
ZB669	WS Gazelle AH1	AAC No 665 Sqn/5 Regt, Aldergrove	
ZB670	WS Gazelle AH1	AAC Dishforth, on display	
ZB671	WS Gazelle AH1	AAC No 667 Sqn/7 Regt, Middle Wallop	
ZB672	WS Gazelle AH1	Army Training Regiment, Winchester	
ZB673	WS Gazelle AH1 [P]	Privately owned, Stapleford Tawney	
ZB674	WS Gazelle AH1	AAC No 665 Sqn/5 Regt, Aldergrove	
ZB677	WS Gazelle AH1 [5B]	AAC No 29 Flt, BATUS, Suffield, Canada	
ZB678	WS Gazelle AH1	AAC No 665 Sqn/5 Regt, Aldergrove	
ZB679	WS Gazelle AH1	AAC 7 Regt Conversion Flt, Middle Wallop	
ZB682	WS Gazelle AH1 (G-CIEX)	*To Hungary, 2016*	
ZB683	WS Gazelle AH1	AAC No 665 Sqn/5 Regt, Aldergrove	
ZB684	WS Gazelle AH1	RAF JADTEU, Brize Norton, instructional use	
ZB686	WS Gazelle AH1 <ff>	The Helicopter Museum, Weston-super-Mare	
ZB689	WS Gazelle AH1	AAC No 665 Sqn/5 Regt, Aldergrove	
ZB690	WS Gazelle AH1	MoD AM&SU, stored Shawbury	
ZB691	WS Gazelle AH1 [S]	AAC No 667 Sqn/7 Regt, Middle Wallop	
ZB692	WS Gazelle AH1	AAC No 667 Sqn/7 Regt, Middle Wallop	
ZB693	WS Gazelle AH1	AAC No 667 Sqn/7 Regt, Middle Wallop	
ZD230	BAC Super VC10 K4 (G-ASGA) <ff>	Privately owned, Crondall, Hants	
ZD240	BAC Super VC10 K4 (G-ASGL) <ff>	Privately owned, Crondall, Hants	
ZD241	BAC Super VC10 K4 (G-ASGM) [N]	Privately owned, Bruntingthorpe	
ZD242	BAC Super VC10 K4 (G-ASGP) <ff>	JARTS, Boscombe Down	
ZD249	WS Lynx HAS3S <rf>	Delta Force, stored Upminster	
ZD250	WS Lynx HAS3S [636]	RAF Henlow, instructional use	
ZD251	WS Lynx HAS3S	Privately owned, Hixon, Staffs	
ZD252	WS Lynx HMA8SRU [312/VL]	AAC MPSU, Middle Wallop	
ZD254	WS Lynx HAS3S [305]	DSAE RNAES, *HMS Sultan*, Gosport	
ZD255	WS Lynx HAS3GMS [635]	Bawtry Paintball Park, S Yorks	
ZD257	WS Lynx HMA8SRU [302/VL]	AAC MPSU, Middle Wallop	
ZD258	WS Lynx HMA8SRU [365]	Privately owned, Bentwaters	
ZD259	WS Lynx HMA8SRU [474/RM]	RN, stored St Athan	
ZD260	WS Lynx HMA8SRU [313/VL]	RN, stored St Athan	
ZD261	WS Lynx HMA8SRU [314]	RN, stored St Athan	
ZD262	WS Lynx HMA8SRU [316]	RN, stored St Athan	
ZD263	WS Lynx HAS3S [632]	Bawtry Paintball Park, S Yorks	
ZD264	WS Lynx HAS3GMS [407] (fuselage)	Privately owned, Hixon, Staffs	
ZD265	WS Lynx HMA8SRU [302]	AAC Middle Wallop, GI use	
ZD266	WS Lynx HMA8SRU [673]	*Currently not known*	
ZD267	WS Lynx HMA8 (comp XZ672) [LST-2]	RN ETS, Yeovilton, GI use	
ZD268	WS Lynx HMA8SRU [366/YB]	RN, stored St Athan	
ZD273	WS Lynx AH7 [E]	Territorial Army, Bury St Edmunds, Suffolk	
ZD274	WS Lynx AH7 [M]	AAC, stored Middle Wallop	

Notes	Serial	Type (code/other identity)	Owner/operator, location or fate
	ZD276	WS Lynx AH7	Mayhem Paintball, Abridge, Essex
	ZD277	WS Lynx AH7 <ff>	Sold to The Netherlands, 2016
	ZD278	WS Lynx AH7 [F]	Delta Force, stored Upminster
	ZD279	WS Lynx AH7 <ff>	Privately owned, Hixon, Staffs
	ZD280	WS Lynx AH7	AAC MPSU, Middle Wallop
	ZD281	WS Lynx AH7 [K]	MoD/Vector Aerospace, Fleetlands, GI use
	ZD283	WS Lynx AH7 <ff>	Privately owned,
	ZD284	WS Lynx AH7 [K]	Privately owned, Corley Moor, Warks
	ZD285	WS Lynx AH7	QinetiQ Boscombe Down, Apprentice School
	ZD318	BAe Harrier GR7A	Harrier Heritage Centre, RAF Wittering
	ZD353	BAe Harrier GR5 (fuselage)	Privately owned, Bentwaters
	ZD412	BAe Harrier GR5 (fuselage)	Privately owned, Sproughton
	ZD433	BAe Harrier GR9A [45A]	FAA Museum, stored Cobham Hall, RNAS Yeovilton
	ZD461	BAe Harrier GR9A [51A]	IWM London, Lambeth
	ZD462	BAe Harrier GR7 (9302M) [52]	Privately owned, Malmesbury, Glos
	ZD465	BAe Harrier GR9 [55]	DSAE AESS, HMS Sultan, Gosport
	ZD469	BAe Harrier GR7A	RAF Wittering, on display
	ZD476	WS61 Sea King HC4 [WZ]	Privately owned, Colsterworth, Leics
	ZD477	WS61 Sea King HC4 [E]	Privately owned, Bruntingthorpe
	ZD478	WS61 Sea King HC4 [J]	Privately owned, Hixon, Staffs
	ZD479	WS61 Sea King HC4 [WQ]	DSAE, stored HMS Sultan, Gosport
	ZD480	WS61 Sea King HC4 [J]	Vector Aerospace, Fleetlands, on display
	ZD559	WS Lynx AH5X	MoD, Boscombe Down Apprentice School
	ZD560	WS Lynx AH7	QinetiQ, Boscombe Down (wfu)
	ZD565	WS Lynx HMA8SRU [404/IR]	Delta Force, stored Upminster
	ZD566	WS Lynx HMA8SRU [305]	Privately owned, Bentwaters
	ZD574	B-V Chinook HC4 (N37077) [DB]	RAF No 18 Sqn/No 27 Sqn, Odiham
	ZD575	B-V Chinook HC4 (N37078) [DC]	RAF No 18 Sqn/No 27 Sqn, Odiham
	ZD578	BAe Sea Harrier FA2 [000,122]	RNAS Yeovilton, at main gate
	ZD579	BAe Sea Harrier FA2 [79/DD]	SFDO, RNAS Culdrose
	ZD581	BAe Sea Harrier FA2 [124]	RN, Predannack Fire School
	ZD582	BAe Sea Harrier FA2 [002/N]	Privately owned, Banbury, Oxon
	ZD607	BAe Sea Harrier FA2	DSDA, Arncott, Oxon, preserved
	ZD610	BAe Sea Harrier FA2 [714,002/N]	Bristol Aerospace Centre, Filton
	ZD611	BAe Sea Harrier FA2	SFDO, RNAS Culdrose, preserved
	ZD612	BAe Sea Harrier FA2 [724]	Privately owned, Topsham, Devon
	ZD613	BAe Sea Harrier FA2 [127/R]	Privately owned, Cross Green, Leeds
	ZD614	BAe Sea Harrier FA2	Privately owned, Lymington, Hants
	ZD620	BAe 125 CC3	Bournemouth Aviation Museum
	ZD621	BAe 125 CC3	RAF Northolt, on display
	ZD625	WS61 Sea King HC4 [P]	Mini Moos Farm, Edmondsley, Durham
	ZD626	WS61 Sea King HC4 (fuselage)	Vector Aerospace, Fleetlands (dumped)
	ZD627	WS61 Sea King HC4 <ff>	Privately owned, Bruntingthorpe
	ZD630	WS61 Sea King HAS6 [012/L]	DSAE RNAESS, HMS Sultan, Gosport
	ZD631	WS61 Sea King HAS6 [66] (fuselage)	Privately owned, St Agnes, Cornwall
	ZD634	WS61 Sea King HAS6 [503]	DSAE AESS, HMS Sultan, Gosport
	ZD636	WS61 Sea King ASaC7 [182/CU]	DSAE, stored HMS Sultan, Gosport
	ZD637	WS61 Sea King HAS6 [700/PW]	DSAE RNAESS, HMS Sultan, Gosport
	ZD667	BAe Harrier GR3 (9201M) [U]	Bentwaters Cold War Museum
	ZD703	BAe 125 CC3	Privately owned, Biggin Hill
	ZD704	BAe 125 CC3	MoD DFTDC, Manston
	ZD707	Panavia Tornado GR4 [077]	Scrapped at Leeming, 2016
	ZD709	Panavia Tornado GR4 [078]	Scrapped at Leeming, 2017
	ZD710	Panavia Tornado GR1 <ff>	Privately owned, Hawarden
	ZD711	Panavia Tornado GR4 [079]	RAF No 15(R) Sqn, Lossiemouth
	ZD713	Panavia Tornado GR4 [081]	RAF No 15(R) Sqn, Lossiemouth
	ZD715	Panavia Tornado GR4 [083]	RAF Cosford, GI use
	ZD716	Panavia Tornado GR4 [084]	RAF CMU, Marham
	ZD739	Panavia Tornado GR4 [087]	RAF No 15(R) Sqn, Lossiemouth
	ZD740	Panavia Tornado GR4 [088]	Scrapped at Leeming, 2016
	ZD741	Panavia Tornado GR4 [LS-F] $	RAF No 15(R) Sqn, Lossiemouth
	ZD742	Panavia Tornado GR4 [090]	RAF Leeming, RTP

Serial	Type (code/other identity)	Owner/operator, location or fate	Notes
ZD744	Panavia Tornado GR4 [092]	RAF CMU, Marham	
ZD745	Panavia Tornado GR4 [093]	*Scrapped at Leeming, 2016*	
ZD747	Panavia Tornado GR4 [095]	*Scrapped at Leeming, 2017*	
ZD748	Panavia Tornado GR4 [096] $	*Scrapped at Leeming, 2016*	
ZD749	Panavia Tornado GR4 [097]	*Scrapped at Leeming, 2016*	
ZD788	Panavia Tornado GR4 $	*Scrapped at Leeming, 2016*	
ZD790	Panavia Tornado GR4 [099]	*Scrapped at Leeming, 2017*	
ZD792	Panavia Tornado GR4 [100]	RAF CMU, Marham	
ZD793	Panavia Tornado GR4 [101]	DSAE No 1 SoTT, Cosford	
ZD842	Panavia Tornado GR4 [105]	*Scrapped at Leeming, 2016*	
ZD843	Panavia Tornado GR4	*Scrapped at Leeming, 2016*	
ZD848	Panavia Tornado GR4 [109]	RAF No 15(R) Sqn, Lossiemouth	
ZD849	Panavia Tornado GR4 [110]	RAF No 15(R) Sqn, Lossiemouth	
ZD851	Panavia Tornado GR4 [112]	RAF Leeming, RTP	
ZD890	Panavia Tornado GR4 [113]	RAF Marham Wing	
ZD899	Panavia Tornado F2	Gr Manchester Fire & Rescue Training Centre, Bury	
ZD902	Panavia Tornado F2A(TIARA)	Privately owned, Church Fenton	
ZD906	Panavia Tornado F2 (comp ZE294) <ff>	RAF Leuchars, BDRT	
ZD932	Panavia Tornado F2 (comp ZE255) (9308M) (fuselage)	Privately owned, Thorpe Wood, N Yorks	
ZD936	Panavia Tornado F2 (comp ZE251) <ff>	Boscombe Down Aviation Collection, Old Sarum	
ZD938	Panavia Tornado F2 (comp ZE295) <ff>	South Yorkshire Aircraft Museum, Doncaster	
ZD939	Panavia Tornado F2 (comp ZE292) <ff>	DSAE No 1 SoTT, Cosford, instructional use	
ZD948	Lockheed TriStar KC1 (G-BFCA/N304CS)	Privately owned, Bruntingthorpe	
ZD951	Lockheed TriStar K1 (G-BFCD/N309CS) $	Privately owned, Bruntingthorpe	
ZD980	B-V Chinook HC4 (N37082) [DD]	RAF No 18 Sqn/No 27 Sqn, Odiham	
ZD981	B-V Chinook HC4 (N37083)	RAF No 28(R) Sqn, Benson	
ZD982	B-V Chinook HC4 (N37085) [DF]	RAF No 18 Sqn/No 27 Sqn, Odiham	
ZD983	B-V Chinook HC4 (N37086) [DG]	RAF No 18 Sqn/No 27 Sqn, Odiham	
ZD984	B-V Chinook HC4 (N37088) [DH]	RAF No 18 Sqn/No 27 Sqn, Odiham	
ZD990	BAe Harrier T8 [T90/DD]	SFDO, RNAS Culdrose	
ZD992	BAe Harrier T8 [724]	Privately owned, Knutsford, Cheshire	
ZE114	Panavia Tornado IDS (RSAF 703)	BAE Systems, Warton	
ZE116	Panavia Tornado GR4A [116]	*Scrapped at Leeming*	
ZE119	Panavia Tornado IDS (RSAF 760)	BAE Systems, Warton	
ZE165	Panavia Tornado F3 [GE]	MoD DFTDC, Manston	
ZE168	Panavia Tornado F3 <ff>	Privately owned, Thorpe Wood, N Yorks	
ZE204	Panavia Tornado F3 [FC]	MoD DFTDC, Manston	
ZE256	Panavia Tornado F3 [DZ] (wears ZE343 on port side)	Privately owned, Thorpe Wood, N Yorks	
ZE340	Panavia Tornado F3 (ZE758/9298M) [GO]	DSAE No 1 SoTT, Cosford	
ZE342	Panavia Tornado F3 [HP]	Rolls Royce, RAF Leeming	
ZE350	McD F-4J(UK) Phantom (9080M) <ff>	Privately owned, Tunbridge Wells	
ZE352	McD F-4J(UK) Phantom (9086M) <ff>	Privately owned, Hooton Park	
ZE360	McD F-4J(UK) Phantom (9059M) [O]	MoD DFTDC, Manston	
ZE368	WS61 Sea King HAR3 [R]	Mini Moos Farm, Edmondsley, Durham	
ZE369	WS61 Sea King HAR3 [S]	*Currently not known*	
ZE370	WS61 Sea King HAR3 [T]	DSAE, stored *HMS Sultan*, Gosport	
ZE375	WS Lynx AH9A	Privately owned, Bentwaters	
ZE376	WS Lynx AH9A	AAC No 667 Sqn/7 Regt, Middle Wallop	
ZE378	WS Lynx AH7	AAC MPSU, Middle Wallop	
ZE379	WS Lynx AH7 <ff>	QinetiQ, Boscombe Down	
ZE380	WS Lynx AH9A	AAC No 657 Sqn, Odiham	
ZE381	WS Lynx AH7	DSAE SAAE, Lyneham	
ZE395	BAe 125 CC3	Privately owned, Dunsfold	
ZE396	BAe 125 CC3	Privately owned, Bentwaters	
ZE410	Agusta A109A (AE-334)	Museum of Army Flying, stored Middle Wallop	
ZE412	Agusta A109A	Army, Middle Wallop (for display at Credenhill)	
ZE413	Agusta A109A	Perth Technical College	
ZE416	Agusta A109E Power Elite (G-ESLH)	MoD/ETPS, Boscombe Down	
ZE418	WS61 Sea King ASaC7 [186]	DSAE, stored *HMS Sultan*, Gosport	

Notes	Serial	Type (code/other identity)	Owner/operator, location or fate
	ZE420	WS61 Sea King ASaC7 [189]	RN No 849 NAS, Culdrose
	ZE422	WS61 Sea King ASaC7 [192]	RN No 849 NAS, Culdrose
	ZE425	WS61 Sea King HC4 [WR]	*Currently not known*
	ZE426	WS61 Sea King HC4 [WX]	DSAE RNAESS, *HMS Sultan*, Gosport
	ZE427	WS61 Sea King HC4 [K]	DSAE, stored *HMS Sultan*, Gosport
	ZE428	WS61 Sea King HC4 [H]	*Currently not known*
	ZE432	BAC 1-11/479FU (DQ-FBV) <ff>	Bournemouth Aviation Museum
	ZE449	SA330L Puma HC1 (9017M/PA-12)	Army Whittington Barracks, Lichfield, on display
	ZE477	WS Lynx 3	The Helicopter Museum, Weston-super-Mare
	ZE495	Grob G103 Viking T1 (BGA3000) [VA]	RAF, stored Little Rissington
	ZE496	Grob G103 Viking T1 (BGA3001) [VB]	MoD/Southern Sailplanes, Membury
	ZE498	Grob G103 Viking T1 (BGA3003) [VC]	RAF, stored Little Rissington
	ZE499	Grob G103 Viking T1 (BGA3004) [VD]	RAF, stored Little Rissington
	ZE502	Grob G103 Viking T1 (BGA3007) [VF]	RAF ACCGS/No 643 VGS, Syerston
	ZE503	Grob G103 Viking T1 (BGA3008) [VG]	MoD/MADG, Cambridge (spares use)
	ZE504	Grob G103 Viking T1 (BGA3009) [VH]	RAF ACCGS/No 643 VGS, Syerston
	ZE520	Grob G103 Viking T1 (BGA3010) [VJ]	MoD/MADG, Cambridge
	ZE521	Grob G103 Viking T1 (BGA3011) [VK]	MoD/Southern Sailplanes, Membury
	ZE522	Grob G103 Viking T1 (BGA3012) [VL]	RAF, stored Abingdon
	ZE524	Grob G103 Viking T1 (BGA3014) [VM]	RAF, stored Little Rissington
	ZE526	Grob G103 Viking T1 (BGA3016) [VN]	RAF CGMF, stored Syerston
	ZE527	Grob G103 Viking T1 (BGA3017) [VP]	RAF, stored Little Rissington
	ZE528	Grob G103 Viking T1 (BGA3018) [VQ]	MoD/Southern Sailplanes, Membury
	ZE529	Grob G103 Viking T1 (BGA3019) (comp ZE655) [VR]	RAF, stored Little Rissington
	ZE530	Grob G103 Viking T1 (BGA3020) [VS]	RAF, stored Little Rissington
	ZE531	Grob G103 Viking T1 (BGA3021) [VT]	RAF, stored Little Rissington
	ZE532	Grob G103 Viking T1 (BGA3022) [VU]	RAF CGMF, stored Syerston
	ZE533	Grob G103 Viking T1 (BGA3023) [VV]	MoD/MADG, Cambridge
	ZE550	Grob G103 Viking T1 (BGA3025) [VX]	MoD/MADG, Cambridge (spares use)
	ZE551	Grob G103 Viking T1 (BGA3026) [VY]	RAF, stored Little Rissington
	ZE552	Grob G103 Viking T1 (BGA3027) [VZ]	RAF CGMF, stored Syerston
	ZE553	Grob G103 Viking T1 (BGA3028) [WA]	MoD/Southern Sailplanes, Membury
	ZE554	Grob G103 Viking T1 (BGA3029) [WB]	RAF, stored Kenley
	ZE555	Grob G103 Viking T1 (BGA3030) [WC]	RAF ACCGS/No 643 VGS, Syerston
	ZE556	Grob G103 Viking T1 (BGA3031) <ff>	RAF CGMF, stored Syerston
	ZE557	Grob G103 Viking T1 (BGA3032) [WE]	RAF CGMF, Syerston
	ZE558	Grob G103 Viking T1 (BGA3033) [WF]	RAF, stored Little Rissington
	ZE559	Grob G103 Viking T1 (BGA3034) [WG]	RAF CGMF, Syerston
	ZE560	Grob G103 Viking T1 (BGA3035) [WH]	RAF, stored Little Rissington
	ZE561	Grob G103 Viking T1 (BGA3036) [WJ]	MoD/Southern Sailplanes, Membury
	ZE562	Grob G103 Viking T1 (BGA3037) [WK]	RAF, stored Little Rissington
	ZE563	Grob G103 Viking T1 (BGA3038) [WL]	RAF CGMF, Syerston
	ZE564	Grob G103 Viking T1 (BGA3039) [WN]	RAF, stored Upavon
	ZE584	Grob G103 Viking T1 (BGA3040) [WP]	RAF, stored Little Rissington
	ZE585	Grob G103 Viking T1 (BGA3041) [WQ]	RAF, stored Little Rissington
	ZE586	Grob G103 Viking T1 (BGA3042) [WR]	MoD/Southern Sailplanes, Membury
	ZE587	Grob G103 Viking T1 (BGA3043) [WS]	RAF, stored Little Rissington
	ZE590	Grob G103 Viking T1 (BGA3046) [WT]	MoD/Southern Sailplanes, Membury
	ZE591	Grob G103 Viking T1 (BGA3047) [WU]	RAF CGMF, stored Syerston
	ZE592	Grob G103 Viking T1 (BGA3048) <ff>	RAFGSA, stored Halton
	ZE593	Grob G103 Viking T1 (BGA3049) [WW]	RAF, stored Kenley
	ZE594	Grob G103 Viking T1 (BGA3050) [WX]	RAF, stored Little Rissington
	ZE595	Grob G103 Viking T1 (BGA3051) [WY]	RAF, stored Little Rissington
	ZE600	Grob G103 Viking T1 (BGA3052) [WZ]	RAF, stored Kenley
	ZE601	Grob G103 Viking T1 (BGA3053) [XA]	RAF, stored Little Rissington
	ZE602	Grob G103 Viking T1 (BGA3054) [XB]	MoD/MADG, Cambridge
	ZE603	Grob G103 Viking T1 (BGA3055) [XC]	RAF, stored Little Rissington
	ZE604	Grob G103 Viking T1 (BGA3056) [XD]	RAF, stored Little Rissington
	ZE605	Grob G103 Viking T1 (BGA3057) [XE]	RAF ACCGS/No 643 VGS, Syerston
	ZE606	Grob G103 Viking T1 (BGA3058) [XF]	RAF CGMF, Syerston
	ZE607	Grob G103 Viking T1 (BGA3059) [XG]	RAF, stored Little Rissington

Serial	Type (code/other identity)	Owner/operator, location or fate	Notes
ZE608	Grob G103 Viking T1 (BGA3060) [XH]	RAF CGMF, Syerston	
ZE609	Grob G103 Viking T1 (BGA3061) [XJ]	MoD/Southern Sailplanes, Membury	
ZE610	Grob G103 Viking T1 (BGA3062) [XK]	RAF, stored Little Rissington	
ZE611	Grob G103 Viking T1 (BGA3063) [XL]	RAF, stored Little Rissington	
ZE613	Grob G103 Viking T1 (BGA3065) [XM]	RAF, stored Little Rissington	
ZE614	Grob G103 Viking T1 (BGA3066) [XN]	RAF, stored Little Rissington	
ZE625	Grob G103 Viking T1 (BGA3067) [XP]	RAF ACCGS/No 643 VGS, Syerston	
ZE626	Grob G103 Viking T1 (BGA3068) [XQ]	MoD/Southern Sailplanes, Membury	
ZE627	Grob G103 Viking T1 (BGA3069) [XR]	RAF, stored Little Rissington	
ZE628	Grob G103 Viking T1 (BGA3070) [XS]	RAF CGMF, stored Syerston	
ZE629	Grob G103 Viking T1 (BGA3071) [XT]	RAF, stored Little Rissington	
ZE630	Grob G103 Viking T1 (BGA3072) [XU]	RAF ACCGS/No 643 VGS, Syerston	
ZE631	Grob G103 Viking T1 (BGA3073) [XV]	RAF, stored Syerston	
ZE632	Grob G103 Viking T1 (BGA3074) [XW]	RAF, stored Little Rissington	
ZE633	Grob G103 Viking T1 (BGA3075) [XX]	RAF CGMF, Syerston	
ZE636	Grob G103 Viking T1 (BGA3078) [XZ]	RAF, stored Little Rissington	
ZE637	Grob G103 Viking T1 (BGA3079) [YA]	RAF, stored Little Rissington	
ZE650	Grob G103 Viking T1 (BGA3080) [YB]	RAF ACCGS/No 643 VGS, Syerston	
ZE651	Grob G103 Viking T1 (BGA3081) [YC]	RAF CGMF, Syerston	
ZE652	Grob G103 Viking T1 (BGA3082) [YD]	RAF CGMF, stored Syerston	
ZE653	Grob G103 Viking T1 (BGA3083) [YE]	RAF, stored Little Rissington	
ZE656	Grob G103 Viking T1 (BGA3086) [YH]	RAF, stored Kenley	
ZE657	Grob G103 Viking T1 (BGA3087) [YJ]	RAF, stored Little Rissington	
ZE658	Grob G103 Viking T1 (BGA3088) [YK]	RAF CGMF, stored Syerston	
ZE677	Grob G103 Viking T1 (BGA3090) [YM]	RAF, stored Kenley	
ZE678	Grob G103 Viking T1 (BGA3091) [YN]	RAF ACCGS/No 643 VGS, Syerston	
ZE679	Grob G103 Viking T1 (BGA3092) [YP]	RAF, stored Little Rissington	
ZE680	Grob G103 Viking T1 (BGA3093) [YQ]	RAF CGMF, Syerston	
ZE681	Grob G103 Viking T1 (BGA3094) <ff>	Currently not known	
ZE682	Grob G103 Viking T1 (BGA3095) [YS]	RAF ACCGS/No 643 VGS, Syerston	
ZE683	Grob G103 Viking T1 (BGA3096) [YT]	RAF, stored Little Rissington	
ZE684	Grob G103 Viking T1 (BGA3097) [YU]	RAF, stored Little Rissington	
ZE685	Grob G103 Viking T1 (BGA3098) [YV]	MoD/Southern Sailplanes, Membury	
ZE686	Grob G103 Viking T1 (BGA3099) <ff>	RAF Museum, Hendon	
ZE690	BAe Sea Harrier FA2 [90/DD]	SFDO, RNAS Culdrose	
ZE691	BAe Sea Harrier FA2 [710]	Classic Autos, Winsford, Cheshire	
ZE692	BAe Sea Harrier FA2 [92/DD]	SFDO, RNAS Culdrose	
ZE694	BAe Sea Harrier FA2 [004]	Midland Air Museum, Coventry	
ZE697	BAe Sea Harrier FA2 [006]	Privately owned, Binbrook	
ZE698	BAe Sea Harrier FA2 [001]	Privately owned, Charlwood	
ZE700	BAe 146 CC2 (G-6-021) $	RAF No 32(The Royal) Sqn, Northolt	
ZE701	BAe 146 CC2 (G-6-029)	RAF No 32(The Royal) Sqn, Northolt	
ZE704	Lockheed TriStar C2 (N508PA/N507CS)	Privately owned, Bruntingthorpe	
ZE705	Lockheed TriStar C2 (N509PA/N703CS)	Privately owned, Bruntingthorpe	
ZE707	BAe 146 C3 (OO-TAZ)	RAF No 32(The Royal) Sqn, Northolt	
ZE708	BAe 146 C3 (OO-TAY)	RAF No 32(The Royal) Sqn, Northolt	
ZE760	Panavia Tornado F3 (MM7206) [AP]	RAF Coningsby, on display	
ZE887	Panavia Tornado F3 [GF] $	RAF Museum, Hendon	
ZE934	Panavia Tornado F3 [TA]	National Museum of Flight, E Fortune	
ZE936	Panavia Tornado F3 <ff>	Privately owned, Church Fenton	
ZE965	Panavia Tornado F3 <ff>	Privately owned, Church Fenton	
ZE966	Panavia Tornado F3 [VT]	Tornado Heritage Centre, Hawarden	
ZE967	Panavia Tornado F3 [UT]	RAF Leuchars, at main gate	
ZF115	WS61 Sea King HC4 [R,WV]	DSAE, stored HMS Sultan, Gosport	
ZF116	WS61 Sea King HC4 [WP]	DSAE, stored HMS Sultan, Gosport	
ZF117	WS61 Sea King HC4 [X]	DSAE, stored HMS Sultan, Gosport	
ZF118	WS61 Sea King HC4 [O]	School of Maritime Survival HMS Raleigh, Plymouth	
ZF119	WS61 Sea King HC4 [WY]	DSAE, stored HMS Sultan, Gosport	
ZF120	WS61 Sea King HC4 [Z]	Privately owned, Colsterworth, Leics	
ZF121	WS61 Sea King HC4 [T]	Mini Moos Farm, Edmondsley, Durham	
ZF122	WS61 Sea King HC4 [V]	Privately owned, Colsterworth, Leics	

Notes	Serial	Type (code/other identity)	Owner/operator, location or fate
	ZF135	Shorts Tucano T1 [135]	RAF No 1 FTS, Linton-on-Ouse
	ZF137	Shorts Tucano T1 [137]	RAF, stored Linton-on-Ouse
	ZF139	Shorts Tucano T1 [139]	RAF No 1 FTS, Linton-on-Ouse
	ZF140	Shorts Tucano T1 [140] $	RAF No 1 FTS/72(R) Sqn, Linton-on-Ouse
	ZF142	Shorts Tucano T1 [142]	RAF No 1 FTS, Linton-on-Ouse
	ZF143	Shorts Tucano T1 [143]	RAF, stored Linton-on-Ouse
	ZF144	Shorts Tucano T1 [144]	RAF No 1 FTS, Linton-on-Ouse
	ZF145	Shorts Tucano T1 [145]	RAF No 1 FTS, Linton-on-Ouse
	ZF160	Shorts Tucano T1 [160]	Privately owned, Bentwaters
	ZF161	Shorts Tucano T1 [161]	*Sold to the USA, July 2016*
	ZF163	Shorts Tucano T1 [163]	RAF AM&SU, stored Shawbury
	ZF166	Shorts Tucano T1 [166]	Privately owned, Bentwaters
	ZF167	Shorts Tucano T1 (fuselage)	Ulster Aviation Society, Long Kesh
	ZF169	Shorts Tucano T1 [169]	RAF, stored Linton-on-Ouse
	ZF170	Shorts Tucano T1 [MP-A]	RAF, stored Linton-on-Ouse
	ZF171	Shorts Tucano T1 [171]	RAF No 1 FTS, Linton-on-Ouse
	ZF172	Shorts Tucano T1 [172]	RAF No 1 FTS, Linton-on-Ouse
	ZF202	Shorts Tucano T1 [202]	RAF Linton-on-Ouse, on display
	ZF203	Shorts Tucano T1 [203]	*Sold to the USA, July 2016*
	ZF204	Shorts Tucano T1 [204]	RAF No 1 FTS, Linton-on-Ouse
	ZF205	Shorts Tucano T1 [205]	RAF No 1 FTS/72(R) Sqn, Linton-on-Ouse
	ZF210	Shorts Tucano T1 [210]	RAF, stored Linton-on-Ouse
	ZF211	Shorts Tucano T1 [211]	Privately owned, Bentwaters
	ZF212	Shorts Tucano T1 [212]	*Sold to the USA, July 2016*
	ZF239	Shorts Tucano T1 [239]	RAF No 1 FTS, Linton-on-Ouse
	ZF240	Shorts Tucano T1 [240]	RAF No 1 FTS, Linton-on-Ouse
	ZF242	Shorts Tucano T1 [242]	*Sold to the USA, July 2016*
	ZF243	Shorts Tucano T1 [243]	RAF No 1 FTS, Linton-on-Ouse
	ZF244	Shorts Tucano T1 [244] $	RAF No 1 FTS/72(R) Sqn, Linton-on-Ouse
	ZF263	Shorts Tucano T1 [263]	RAF AM&SU, stored Shawbury
	ZF264	Shorts Tucano T1 [264]	RAF No 1 FTS, Linton-on-Ouse
	ZF268	Shorts Tucano T1 [268]	RAF AM&SU, stored Shawbury
	ZF269	Shorts Tucano T1 [269]	RAF No 1 FTS, Linton-on-Ouse
	ZF286	Shorts Tucano T1 [286]	RAF AM&SU, stored Shawbury
	ZF287	Shorts Tucano T1 [287]	RAF No 1 FTS, Linton-on-Ouse
	ZF288	Shorts Tucano T1 [288]	RAF AM&SU, stored Shawbury
	ZF289	Shorts Tucano T1 [289]	RAF No 1 FTS, Linton-on-Ouse
	ZF290	Shorts Tucano T1 [290]	RAF, stored Linton-on-Ouse
	ZF291	Shorts Tucano T1 [291]	RAF No 1 FTS, Linton-on-Ouse
	ZF292	Shorts Tucano T1 [292]	RAF, stored Linton-on-Ouse
	ZF293	Shorts Tucano T1 [293]	RAF No 1 FTS/72(R) Sqn, Linton-on-Ouse
	ZF294	Shorts Tucano T1 [294]	RAF, stored Linton-on-Ouse
	ZF295	Shorts Tucano T1 [295] $	RAF, stored Linton-on-Ouse
	ZF315	Shorts Tucano T1 [315]	RAF AM&SU, stored Shawbury
	ZF317	Shorts Tucano T1 [317]	RAF No 1 FTS, Linton-on-Ouse
	ZF318	Shorts Tucano T1 [318] $	RAF AM&SU, stored Shawbury
	ZF319	Shorts Tucano T1 [319]	RAF, stored Linton-on-Ouse
	ZF338	Shorts Tucano T1 [338]	RAF No 1 FTS, Linton-on-Ouse
	ZF339	Shorts Tucano T1 [339]	RAF No 1 FTS/72(R) Sqn, Linton-on-Ouse
	ZF341	Shorts Tucano T1 [341]	RAF, stored Linton-on-Ouse
	ZF342	Shorts Tucano T1 [342]	RAF No 1 FTS, Linton-on-Ouse
	ZF343	Shorts Tucano T1 [343]	RAF No 1 FTS/72(R) Sqn, Linton-on-Ouse
	ZF345	Shorts Tucano T1 [345]	*Sold to the USA, July 2016*
	ZF347	Shorts Tucano T1 [347]	RAF No 1 FTS, Linton-on-Ouse
	ZF348	Shorts Tucano T1 [348]	RAF, stored Linton-on-Ouse
	ZF349	Shorts Tucano T1 [349] (fuselage)	RN No 1710 NAS, Portsmouth Dockyard (wreck)
	ZF350	Shorts Tucano T1 [350]	RAF AM&SU, stored Shawbury
	ZF355	WS Lynx HAS3S(ICE) (XZ238) [633]	Privately owned
	ZF372	Shorts Tucano T1 [372]	RAF AM&SU, stored Shawbury
	ZF374	Shorts Tucano T1 [374]	RAF No 1 FTS, Linton-on-Ouse
	ZF376	Shorts Tucano T1 [376]	RAF AM&SU, stored Shawbury
	ZF377	Shorts Tucano T1 [377]	RAF No 1 FTS, Linton-on-Ouse

Serial	Type (code/other identity)	Owner/operator, location or fate	Notes
ZF378	Shorts Tucano T1 [378] $	RAF No 1 FTS, Linton-on-Ouse	
ZF379	Shorts Tucano T1 [379]	RAF, stored Linton-on-Ouse	
ZF380	Shorts Tucano T1 [380]	Privately owned, Bentwaters	
ZF405	Shorts Tucano T1 [405]	RAF AM&SU, stored Shawbury	
ZF406	Shorts Tucano T1 [406]	RAF, stored Linton-on-Ouse	
ZF407	Shorts Tucano T1 [407]	RAF No 1 FTS, Linton-on-Ouse	
ZF408	Shorts Tucano T1 [408]	RAF AM&SU, stored Shawbury	
ZF410	Shorts Tucano T1 [410]	*Sold to the USA, July 2016*	
ZF412	Shorts Tucano T1 [412]	Privately owned, Bentwaters	
ZF414	Shorts Tucano T1 [414]	RAF AM&SU, stored Shawbury	
ZF416	Shorts Tucano T1 [416]	RAF AM&SU, stored Shawbury	
ZF417	Shorts Tucano T1 [417]	RAF No 1 FTS, Linton-on-Ouse	
ZF418	Shorts Tucano T1 [418]	RAF AM&SU, stored Shawbury	
ZF446	Shorts Tucano T1 [446]	RAF AM&SU, stored Shawbury	
ZF447	Shorts Tucano T1 [447]	*Sold to the USA, July 2016*	
ZF448	Shorts Tucano T1 [448]	RAF, stored Linton-on-Ouse	
ZF449	Shorts Tucano T1 [449]	RAF AM&SU, stored Shawbury	
ZF483	Shorts Tucano T1 [483]	*Sold to the USA, July 2016*	
ZF484	Shorts Tucano T1 [484]	*Sold to the USA, July 2016*	
ZF485	Shorts Tucano T1 (G-BULU) [485]	RAF No 1 FTS, Linton-on-Ouse	
ZF486	Shorts Tucano T1 [486]	RAF AM&SU, stored Shawbury	
ZF487	Shorts Tucano T1 [487]	RAF AM&SU, stored Shawbury	
ZF488	Shorts Tucano T1 [488]	RAF AM&SU, stored Shawbury	
ZF489	Shorts Tucano T1 [489]	RAF No 1 FTS, Linton-on-Ouse	
ZF490	Shorts Tucano T1 [490]	RAF AM&SU, stored Shawbury	
ZF491	Shorts Tucano T1 [491]	RAF No 1 FTS, Linton-on-Ouse	
ZF492	Shorts Tucano T1 [492]	RAF AM&SU, stored Shawbury	
ZF510	Shorts Tucano T1 [510]	MoD/AFD/QinetiQ, Boscombe Down	
ZF511	Shorts Tucano T1 [511]	MoD/AFD/QinetiQ, Boscombe Down	
ZF512	Shorts Tucano T1 [512]	RAF No 1 FTS/*72(R) Sqn*, Linton-on-Ouse	
ZF513	Shorts Tucano T1 [513]	RAF AM&SU, stored Shawbury	
ZF514	Shorts Tucano T1 [514]	*Sold to the USA, July 2016*	
ZF515	Shorts Tucano T1 [515]	RAF No 1 FTS, Linton-on-Ouse	
ZF516	Shorts Tucano T1 [516]	Privately owned, Bentwaters	
ZF534	BAe EAP	RAF Museum, Cosford	
ZF537	WS Lynx AH9A	AAC No 657 Sqn, Odiham	
ZF538	WS Lynx AH9A	AAC No 657 Sqn, Odiham	
ZF539	WS Lynx AH9A	AAC MPSU, Middle Wallop	
ZF557	WS Lynx HMA8SRU [426/PD]	RN No 815 NAS, *Portland* Flt, Yeovilton	
ZF558	WS Lynx HMA8SRU [336/WK]	RN No 815 NAS, *Wave Knight* Flt, Yeovilton	
ZF560	WS Lynx HMA8SRU [456]	RN, stored St Athan	
ZF562	WS Lynx HMA8SRU [353/MB]	RN No 815 NAS, *Mounts Bay* Flt, Yeovilton	
ZF563	WS Lynx HMA8SRU [312/VL]	RN No 815 NAS, MI Flt, Yeovilton	
ZF573	PBN 2T Islander CC2 (G-SRAY)	RAF Northolt Station Flight	
ZF579	BAC Lightning F53	Gatwick Aviation Museum, Charlwood	
ZF580	BAC Lightning F53	Cornwall Aviation Heritage Centre, Newquay	
ZF581	BAC Lightning F53	Bentwaters Cold War Museum	
ZF582	BAC Lightning F53 <ff>	Bournemouth Aviation Museum	
ZF583	BAC Lightning F53	Solway Aviation Society, Carlisle	
ZF584	BAC Lightning F53	Dumfries & Galloway Avn Mus, Dumfries	
ZF587	BAC Lightning F53 <ff>	Lashenden Air Warfare Museum, Headcorn	
ZF587	BAC Lightning F53 <rf>	Privately owned, Stowmarket, Suffolk	
ZF588	BAC Lightning F53 [L]	East Midlands Airport Aeropark	
ZF589	BAC Lightning F53 <ff>	Gatwick Aviation Museum, stored Charlwood	
ZF590	BAC Lightning F53 <ff>	Privately owned, stored Bruntingthorpe	
ZF595	BAC Lightning T55 (fuselage)	Privately owned, Binbrook	
ZF596	BAC Lightning T55 <ff>	Lakes Lightnings, Spark Bridge, Cumbria	
ZF622	Piper PA-31 Navajo Chieftain 350 (N3548Y)	QinetiQ, Boscombe Down, wfu	
ZF641	EHI-101 [PP1]	SFDO, RNAS Culdrose	
ZF649	EHI-101 Merlin (A2714) [PP5]	DSAE AESS, *HMS Sultan*, Gosport	
ZG101	EHI-101 (mock-up) [GB]	Leonardo, Yeovil	

Notes	Serial	Type (code/other identity)	Owner/operator, location or fate
	ZG347	Northrop Chukar D2	Davidstow Airfield & Cornwall At War Museum
	ZG477	BAe Harrier GR9 $	RAF Museum, Cosford
	ZG478	BAe Harrier GR9 (fuselage)	Privately owned, Sproughton
	ZG509	BAe Harrier GR7 [80]	Privately owned, Sproughton
	ZG631	Northrop Chukar D2	Farnborough Air Sciences Trust, Farnborough
	ZG705	Panavia Tornado GR4A [118]	RAF CMU, stored Marham
	ZG707	Panavia Tornado GR4A [119]	RAF No 15(R) Sqn, Lossiemouth
	ZG714	Panavia Tornado GR4A [124]	RAF Leeming, RTP
	ZG729	Panavia Tornado GR4A [127]	Scrapped at Leeming, 2016
	ZG750	Panavia Tornado GR4 [128]	RAF No 31 Sqn, Marham
	ZG752	Panavia Tornado GR4 [129]	RAF No 15(R) Sqn, Lossiemouth
	ZG771	Panavia Tornado GR4 $	RAF No 9 Sqn, Marham
	ZG773	Panavia Tornado GR4	MoD/BAE Systems, Warton
	ZG775	Panavia Tornado GR4 [EB-Z]	RAF TASF(S), Marham
	ZG777	Panavia Tornado GR4 [135]	RAF No 12 Sqn, Marham
	ZG779	Panavia Tornado GR4 [136]	RAF No 31 Sqn, Marham
	ZG791	Panavia Tornado GR4 [137]	RAF No 12 Sqn, Marham
	ZG816	WS61 Sea King HAS6 [014/L]	DSAE, stored HMS Sultan, Gosport
	ZG817	WS61 Sea King HAS6 [702/PW]	DSAE AESS, HMS Sultan, Gosport
	ZG818	WS61 Sea King HAS6 [707/PW]	DSAE AESS, HMS Sultan, Gosport
	ZG819	WS61 Sea King HAS6 [265/N]	DSAE AESS, HMS Sultan, Gosport
	ZG821	WS61 Sea King HC4 [G]	MoD/Vector Aerospace, Fleetlands
	ZG822	WS61 Sea King HC4 [WS]	Privately owned, Bruntingthorpe
	ZG844	PBN 2T Islander AL1 (G-BLNE)	AAC AM&SU, stored Shawbury
	ZG845	PBN 2T Islander AL1 (G-BLNT)	AAC No 651 Sqn/5 Regt, Aldergrove
	ZG846	PBN 2T Islander AL1 (G-BLNU)	AAC No 651 Sqn/5 Regt, Aldergrove
	ZG847	PBN 2T Islander AL1 (G-BLNV)	AAC AM&SU, stored Shawbury
	ZG848	PBN 2T Islander AL1 (G-BLNY)	AAC No 651 Sqn/5 Regt, Aldergrove
	ZG875	WS61 Sea King HAS6 [013] <ff>	Privately owned, Market Drayton, Shrops
	ZG875	WS61 Sea King HAS6 <rf>	Mayhem Paintball, Aybridge, Essex
	ZG884	WS Lynx AH9A	Privately owned, Bentwaters
	ZG885	WS Lynx AH9A	AAC No 657 Sqn, Odiham
	ZG886	WS Lynx AH9A	Privately owned, Bentwaters
	ZG887	WS Lynx AH9A	AAC MPSU, stored Middle Wallop
	ZG888	WS Lynx AH9A	AAC MPSU, Middle Wallop
	ZG889	WS Lynx AH9A	Privately owned, Bentwaters
	ZG914	WS Lynx AH9A	AAC MPSU, Middle Wallop
	ZG915	WS Lynx AH9A	AAC MPSU, Middle Wallop
	ZG916	WS Lynx AH9A	AAC MPSU, Middle Wallop
	ZG917	WS Lynx AH9A	AAC No 657 Sqn, Odiham
	ZG918	WS Lynx AH9A	AAC No 657 Sqn, Odiham
	ZG919	WS Lynx AH9A	AAC MPSU, Middle Wallop
	ZG920	WS Lynx AH9A	AAC MPSU, Middle Wallop
	ZG921	WS Lynx AH9A	AAC No 657 Sqn, Odiham
	ZG922	WS Lynx AH9	Privately owned, Staverton, instructional use
	ZG923	WS Lynx AH9A	AAC No 657 Sqn, Odiham
	ZG969	Pilatus PC-9 (HB-HQE)	Currently not known
	ZG989	PBN 2T Islander ASTOR (G-DLRA)	AAC AM&SU, stored Shawbury
	ZG993	PBN 2T Islander AL1 (G-BOMD)	Museum of Army Flying, stored Middle Wallop
	ZG994	PBN 2T Islander AL1 (G-BPLN) (fuselage)	Britten-Norman, stored Bembridge
	ZG995	PBN 2T Defender AL1 (G-SURV)	AAC No 651 Sqn/5 Regt, Aldergrove
	ZG996	PBN 2T Defender AL2 (G-BWPR)	AAC No 651 Sqn/5 Regt, Aldergrove
	ZG997	PBN 2T Defender AL2 (G-BWPV)	AAC No 651 Sqn/5 Regt, Aldergrove
	ZG998	PBN 2T Defender AL1 (G-BWPX)	AAC No 651 Sqn/5 Regt, Aldergrove
	ZH001	PBN 2T Defender AL2 (G-CEIO)	AAC No 651 Sqn/5 Regt, Aldergrove
	ZH002	PBN 2T Defender AL2 (G-CEIP)	AAC No 651 Sqn/5 Regt, Aldergrove
	ZH003	PBN 2T Defender AL2 (G-CEIR)	AAC No 651 Sqn/5 Regt, Aldergrove
	ZH004	PBN 2T Defender T3 (G-BWPO)	AAC No 651 Sqn/5 Regt, Aldergrove
	ZH005	PBN 2T Defender AL2 (G-CGVB)	AAC No 651 Sqn/5 Regt, Aldergrove
	ZH101	Boeing E-3D Sentry AEW1 [01]	RAF No 8 Sqn/No 54(R) Sqn, Waddington
	ZH102	Boeing E-3D Sentry AEW1 [02]	RAF No 8 Sqn/No 54(R) Sqn, Waddington
	ZH103	Boeing E-3D Sentry AEW1 [03]	RAF No 8 Sqn/No 54(R) Sqn, Waddington

Serial	Type (code/other identity)	Owner/operator, location or fate	Notes
ZH104	Boeing E-3D Sentry AEW1 [04]	RAF No 8 Sqn/No 54(R) Sqn, Waddington	
ZH105	Boeing E-3D Sentry AEW1 [05]	RAF, stored Waddington	
ZH106	Boeing E-3D Sentry AEW1 [06]	RAF No 8 Sqn/No 54(R) Sqn, Waddington	
ZH107	Boeing E-3D Sentry AEW1 [07] $	RAF No 8 Sqn/No 54(R) Sqn, Waddington	
ZH115	Grob G109B Vigilant T1 [TA]	RAF, stored Little Rissington	
ZH116	Grob G109B Vigilant T1 [TB]	RAF, stored Watton	
ZH117	Grob G109B Vigilant T1 [TC]	RAF, stored Little Rissington	
ZH118	Grob G109B Vigilant T1 [TD]	RAF, stored Watton	
ZH119	Grob G109B Vigilant T1 [TE]	RAF/MADG, Cambridge	
ZH120	Grob G109B Vigilant T1 [TF]	RAF, stored Little Rissington	
ZH121	Grob G109B Vigilant T1 [TG]	RAF CGMF, Syerston	
ZH122	Grob G109B Vigilant T1 [TH]	RAF, stored Little Rissington	
ZH123	Grob G109B Vigilant T1 [TJ]	RAF No 645 VGS, Topcliffe	
ZH124	Grob G109B Vigilant T1 [TK]	RAF, stored Woodvale	
ZH125	Grob G109B Vigilant T1 [TL]	RAF, stored Syerston	
ZH126	Grob G109B Vigilant T1 (D-KGRA) [TM]	RAF, stored Abingdon	
ZH127	Grob G109B Vigilant T1 (D-KEEC) [TN]	RAF CGMF, Syerston	
ZH128	Grob G109B Vigilant T1 [TP]	RAF CGMF, Syerston	
ZH129	Grob G109B Vigilant T1 [TQ]	RAF CGMF, Syerston	
ZH139	BAe Harrier GR7 <R> (BAPC 191/ZD472)	Currently not known	
ZH144	Grob G109B Vigilant T1 [TR]	Grob Aircraft, Tussenhausen, Germany (for disposal)	
ZH145	Grob G109B Vigilant T1 [TS]	RAF, stored Little Rissington	
ZH146	Grob G109B Vigilant T1 [TT]	RAF, stored Linton-on-Ouse	
ZH147	Grob G109B Vigilant T1 [TU]	RAF, stored Little Rissington	
ZH148	Grob G109B Vigilant T1 [TV]	RAF CGMF, stored Syerston	
ZH184	Grob G109B Vigilant T1 [TW]	RAF, stored Ternhill	
ZH185	Grob G109B Vigilant T1 [TX]	RAF, stored Cosford	
ZH186	Grob G109B Vigilant T1 [TY]	RAF ACCGS/No 644 VGS, Syerston	
ZH187	Grob G109B Vigilant T1 [TZ]	RAF CGMF, stored Syerston	
ZH188	Grob G109B Vigilant T1 [UA]	RAF CGMF, stored Syerston	
ZH189	Grob G109B Vigilant T1 [UB]	RAF, stored St Athan	
ZH190	Grob G109B Vigilant T1 [UC]	RAF, stored Little Rissington	
ZH191	Grob G109B Vigilant T1 [UD]	RAF, stored Abingdon	
ZH192	Grob G109B Vigilant T1 [UE]	RAF, stored Cosford	
ZH193	Grob G109B Vigilant T1 [UF]	RAF, stored Woodvale	
ZH194	Grob G109B Vigilant T1 [UG]	RAF, stored Cosford	
ZH195	Grob G109B Vigilant T1 [UH]	RAF, stored Little Rissington	
ZH196	Grob G109B Vigilant T1 [UJ]	RAF, stored Watton	
ZH197	Grob G109B Vigilant T1 [UK]	RAF CGMF, Syerston	
ZH200	BAe Hawk 200	Loughborough University	
ZH205	Grob G109B Vigilant T1 [UL]	RAF, stored Linton-on-Ouse	
ZH206	Grob G109B Vigilant T1 [UM]	RAF ACCGS/No 644 VGS, Syerston	
ZH207	Grob G109B Vigilant T1 [UN]	RAF No 645 VGS, Topcliffe	
ZH208	Grob G109B Vigilant T1 [UP]	RAF, stored Little Rissington	
ZH209	Grob G109B Vigilant T1 [UQ]	RAF, stored Little Rissington	
ZH211	Grob G109B Vigilant T1 [UR]	RAF, stored St Athan	
ZH247	Grob G109B Vigilant T1 [US]	RAF, stored Henlow	
ZH248	Grob G109B Vigilant T1 [UT]	RAF CGMF, stored Syerston	
ZH249	Grob G109B Vigilant T1 [UU]	RAF CGMF, Syerston	
ZH257	B-V CH-47C Chinook (9217M) (fuselage)	RAF Odiham, BDRT	
ZH263	Grob G109B Vigilant T1 [UV]	RAF, stored Henlow	
ZH264	Grob G109B Vigilant T1 [UW]	RAF, stored Little Rissington	
ZH265	Grob G109B Vigilant T1 [UX]	RAF, stored Little Rissington	
ZH266	Grob G109B Vigilant T1 [UY]	RAF, stored Little Rissington	
ZH267	Grob G109B Vigilant T1 [UZ]	RAF, stored Little Rissington	
ZH268	Grob G109B Vigilant T1 [SA]	RAF, stored Little Rissington	
ZH269	Grob G109B Vigilant T1 [SB]	RAF, stored Little Rissington	
ZH270	Grob G109B Vigilant T1 [SC]	RAF, stored Henlow	
ZH271	Grob G109B Vigilant T1 [SD]	RAF ACCGS/No 644 VGS, Syerston	
ZH278	Grob G109B Vigilant T1 (D-KAIS) [SF]	RAF, stored Little Rissington	
ZH279	Grob G109B Vigilant T1 (D-KNPS) [SG]	RAF CGMF, stored Syerston	
ZH536	PBN 2T Islander CC2 (G-BSAH)	RAF Northolt Station Flight	

Notes	Serial	Type (code/other identity)	Owner/operator, location or fate
	ZH537	PBN 2T Islander CC2 (G-SELX)	RAF Northolt Station Flight
	ZH544	WS61 Sea King HAR3A	DSAE, stored *HMS Sultan*, Gosport
	ZH545	WS61 Sea King HAR3A [Z]	DSAE, stored *HMS Sultan*, Gosport
	ZH552	Panavia Tornado F3	RAF Leeming, at main gate
	ZH553	Panavia Tornado F3 [RT]	MoD DFTDC, Manston
	ZH588	Eurofighter Typhoon (DA2)	RAF Museum, Hendon
	ZH590	Eurofighter Typhoon (DA4)	IWM Duxford
	ZH654	BAe Harrier T10 <ff>	*Currently not known*
	ZH655	BAe Harrier T10 <ff>	Privately owned, Bentwaters
	ZH658	BAe Harrier T10 (fuselage)	Privately owned, Sproughton
	ZH763	BAC 1-11/539GL (G-BGKE)	Cornwall Aviation Heritage Centre, Newquay
	ZH775	B-V Chinook HC4 (N7424J) [HB]	RAF No 18 Sqn/No 27 Sqn, Odiham
	ZH776	B-V Chinook HC6A (N7424L) [HC]	MoD/AFD/QinetiQ, Boscombe Down (conversion)
	ZH777	B-V Chinook HC4 (N7424M) $	RAF No 28(R) Sqn, Benson
	ZH796	BAe Sea Harrier FA2 [001/L]	DSAE No 1 SoTT, stored Cosford
	ZH797	BAe Sea Harrier FA2 [97/DD]	SFDO, RNAS Culdrose
	ZH798	BAe Sea Harrier FA2 [98/DD]	SFDO, RNAS Culdrose
	ZH799	BAe Sea Harrier FA2 [730]	Privately owned, Tunbridge Wells
	ZH800	BAe Sea Harrier FA2 (ZH801) [123]	RNAS Yeovilton, stored
	ZH801	BAe Sea Harrier FA2 (ZH800) [001]	RNAS Yeovilton, stored
	ZH802	BAe Sea Harrier FA2 [02/DD]	SFDO, RNAS Culdrose
	ZH803	BAe Sea Harrier FA2 [03/DD]	SFDO, RNAS Culdrose
	ZH804	BAe Sea Harrier FA2 [003/L]	RN, stored Culdrose
	ZH806	BAe Sea Harrier FA2 [007]	Privately owned, Bentwaters
	ZH807	BAe Sea Harrier FA2 <ff>	Privately owned, Thorpe Wood, N Yorks
	ZH810	BAe Sea Harrier FA2 [125]	Privately owned, Sproughton
	ZH811	BAe Sea Harrier FA2 [002/L]	RN, stored Culdrose
	ZH812	BAe Sea Harrier FA2 [005/L]	Privately owned, Bentwaters
	ZH813	BAe Sea Harrier FA2 [13/DD]	SFDO, RNAS Culdrose
	ZH814	Bell 212HP AH1 (G-BGMH) [X]	AAC No 7 Flt, Brunei
	ZH815	Bell 212HP AH1 (G-BGCZ) [Y]	AAC No 7 Flt, Brunei
	ZH816	Bell 212HP AH1 (G-BGMG)	AAC No 7 Flt, Brunei
	ZH821	EHI-101 Merlin HM1	RN AM&SU, stored Shawbury
	ZH822	EHI-101 Merlin HM1	RN AM&SU, stored Shawbury
	ZH823	EHI-101 Merlin HM1	RN AM&SU, stored Shawbury
	ZH824	EHI-101 Merlin HM2 [83]	RN No 824 NAS, Culdrose
	ZH825	EHI-101 Merlin HM1 [583]	RN AM&SU, stored Shawbury
	ZH826	EHI-101 Merlin HM2 [65]	RN No 814 NAS, Culdrose
	ZH827	EHI-101 Merlin HM2	RN No 820 NAS, Culdrose
	ZH828	EHI-101 Merlin HM2 [88/CU]	RN No 824 NAS, Culdrose
	ZH829	EHI-101 Merlin HM2 [NL]	MoD/AFD/QinetiQ, Boscombe Down
	ZH830	EHI-101 Merlin HM1	QinetiQ, stored Boscombe Down
	ZH831	EHI-101 Merlin HM2	MoD/Leonardo, Yeovil
	ZH832	EHI-101 Merlin HM2 [81]	RN No 824 NAS, Culdrose
	ZH833	EHI-101 Merlin HM2 [82]	RN No 824 NAS, Culdrose
	ZH834	EHI-101 Merlin HM2 [87]	MoD/AFD/QinetiQ, Boscombe Down
	ZH835	EHI-101 Merlin HM2	RN No 820 NAS, Culdrose
	ZH836	EHI-101 Merlin HM2 [70]	RN No 829 NAS, Culdrose
	ZH837	EHI-101 Merlin HM2	RN MDMF, Culdrose
	ZH838	EHI-101 Merlin HM1 [70]	QinetiQ, stored Boscombe Down
	ZH839	EHI-101 Merlin HM2	RN No 814 NAS, Culdrose
	ZH840	EHI-101 Merlin HM2	RN No 820 NAS, Culdrose
	ZH841	EHI-101 Merlin HM2 [501]	RN No 829 NAS, Culdrose
	ZH842	EHI-101 Merlin HM2 [86]	RN MDMF, Culdrose
	ZH843	EHI-101 Merlin HM2	RN No 829 NAS, Culdrose
	ZH845	EHI-101 Merlin HM2 [81]	MoD/AFD/QinetiQ, Boscombe Down
	ZH846	EHI-101 Merlin HM2 [80]	RN No 820 NAS, Culdrose
	ZH847	EHI-101 Merlin HM2 [67/CU]	RN No 820 NAS, Culdrose
	ZH848	EHI-101 Merlin HM1	QinetiQ, stored Boscombe Down
	ZH849	EHI-101 Merlin HM1 [67]	QinetiQ, stored Boscombe Down
	ZH850	EHI-101 Merlin HM2 [67]	RN MDMF, Culdrose
	ZH851	EHI-101 Merlin HM2 [84]	RN No 824 NAS, Culdrose

Serial	Type (code/other identity)	Owner/operator, location or fate	Notes
ZH852	EHI-101 Merlin HM1(mod)	QinetiQ, stored Boscombe Down	
ZH853	EHI-101 Merlin HM2 [87]	RN No 824 NAS, Culdrose	
ZH854	EHI-101 Merlin HM2	RN No 829 NAS, Culdrose	
ZH855	EHI-101 Merlin HM1 [68]	QinetiQ, stored Boscombe Down	
ZH856	EHI-101 Merlin HM2 [13]	RN MDMF, Culdrose	
ZH857	EHI-101 Merlin HM2 [86]	RN No 824 NAS, Culdrose	
ZH858	EHI-101 Merlin HM1 [17]	QinetiQ, stored Boscombe Down	
ZH860	EHI-101 Merlin HM2 [66]	RN No 820 NAS, Culdrose	
ZH861	EHI-101 Merlin HM2	RN No 829 NAS, Culdrose	
ZH862	EHI-101 Merlin HM2 [85]	RN No 824 NAS, Culdrose	
ZH863	EHI-101 Merlin HM1	RN stored, QinetiQ Boscombe Down	
ZH864	EHI-101 Merlin HM2 [66]	RN MDMF, Culdrose	
ZH865	Lockheed C-130J-30 Hercules C4 (N130JA) [865]	RAF No 24 Sqn/No 30 Sqn/No 47 Sqn, Brize Norton	
ZH866	Lockheed C-130J-30 Hercules C6 (N130JE) [866] $	MoD/AFD/QinetiQ, Boscombe Down	
ZH867	Lockheed C-130J-30 Hercules C4 (N130JJ) [867]	RAF No 24 Sqn/No 30 Sqn/No 47 Sqn, Brize Norton	
ZH868	Lockheed C-130J-30 Hercules C4 (N130JN) [868]	RAF No 24 Sqn/No 30 Sqn/No 47 Sqn, Brize Norton	
ZH869	Lockheed C-130J-30 Hercules C4 (N130JV) [869]	RAF No 24 Sqn/No 30 Sqn/No 47 Sqn, Brize Norton	
ZH870	Lockheed C-130J-30 Hercules C4 (N78235) [870]	RAF No 24 Sqn/No 30 Sqn/No 47 Sqn, Brize Norton	
ZH871	Lockheed C-130J-30 Hercules C4 (N73238) [871]	RAF No 24 Sqn/No 30 Sqn/No 47 Sqn, Brize Norton	
ZH872	Lockheed C-130J-30 Hercules C4 (N4249Y) [872]	RAF No 24 Sqn/No 30 Sqn/No 47 Sqn, Brize Norton	
ZH873	Lockheed C-130J-30 Hercules C4 (N4242N) [873]	RAF No 24 Sqn/No 30 Sqn/No 47 Sqn, Brize Norton	
ZH874	Lockheed C-130J-30 Hercules C4 (N41030) [874]	RAF No 24 Sqn/No 30 Sqn/No 47 Sqn, Brize Norton	
ZH875	Lockheed C-130J-30 Hercules C4 (N4099R) [875]	RAF No 24 Sqn/No 30 Sqn/No 47 Sqn, Brize Norton	
ZH877	Lockheed C-130J-30 Hercules C4 (N4081M) [877]	RAF No 24 Sqn/No 30 Sqn/No 47 Sqn, Brize Norton	
ZH878	Lockheed C-130J-30 Hercules C4 (N73232) [878]	RAF No 24 Sqn/No 30 Sqn/No 47 Sqn, Brize Norton	
ZH879	Lockheed C-130J-30 Hercules C4 (N4080M) [879]	RAF No 24 Sqn/No 30 Sqn/No 47 Sqn, Brize Norton	
ZH880	Lockheed C-130J Hercules C5 (N73238) [880] $	MoD/MADG, Cambridge (wfu)	
ZH881	Lockheed C-130J Hercules C5 (N4081M) [881]	MoD/MADG, Cambridge (wfu)	
ZH882	Lockheed C-130J Hercules C5 (N4099R) [882]	MoD/MADG, Cambridge	
ZH883	Lockheed C-130J Hercules C5 (N4242N) [883] $	MoD/MADG, Cambridge	
ZH884	Lockheed C-130J Hercules C5 (N4249Y) [884]	MoD/MADG, Cambridge (wfu)	
ZH885	Lockheed C-130J Hercules C5 (N41030) [885]	RAF No 24 Sqn/No 30 Sqn/No 47 Sqn, Brize Norton	
ZH886	Lockheed C-130J Hercules C5 (N73235) [886]	MoD/MADG, Cambridge (wfu)	
ZH887	Lockheed C-130J Hercules C5 (N4187W) [887]	RAF No 24 Sqn/No 30 Sqn/No 47 Sqn, Brize Norton	
ZH888	Lockheed C-130J Hercules C5 (N4187) [888]	RAF No 1312 Flt, Mount Pleasant, FI	
ZH889	Lockheed C-130J Hercules C5 (N4099R) [889]	RAF No 24 Sqn/No 30 Sqn/No 47 Sqn, Brize Norton	
ZH890	Grob G109B Vigilant T1 [SE]	MoD/MADG, Cambridge	
ZH891	B-V Chinook HC4 (N20075) [HF]	MoD/AFD/QinetiQ, Boscombe Down	
ZH892	B-V Chinook HC6A (N2019V) [HG]	MoD/AFD/QinetiQ, Boscombe Down (conversion)	
ZH893	B-V Chinook HC6A (N2025L) [HH]	MoD/AFD/QinetiQ, Boscombe Down (conversion)	
ZH894	B-V Chinook HC6A (N2026E) [HI]	MoD/AFD/QinetiQ, Boscombe Down (conversion)	
ZH895	B-V Chinook HC6A (N2034K) [HJ] $	MoD/AFD/QinetiQ, Boscombe Down	
ZH896	B-V Chinook HC6A (N2038G) [HK]	MoD/AFD/QinetiQ, Boscombe Down (conversion)	
ZH897	B-V Chinook HC5 (N2045G)	MoD/Vector Aerospace, Fleetlands	
ZH898	B-V Chinook HC5 (N2057Q)	MoD/Vector Aerospace, Fleetlands (conversion)	
ZH899	B-V Chinook HC5 (N2057R)	MoD/Vector Aerospace, Fleetlands	
ZH900	B-V Chinook HC5 (N2060H)	MoD/Vector Aerospace, Fleetlands	
ZH901	B-V Chinook HC5 (N2060M)	MoD/Vector Aerospace, Fleetlands (conversion)	
ZH902	B-V Chinook HC5 (N2064W)	MoD/Vector Aerospace, Fleetlands	
ZH903	B-V Chinook HC5 (N20671) [HR]	MoD/Vector Aerospace, Fleetlands (conversion)	
ZH904	B-V Chinook HC5 (N2083K)	MoD/Vector Aerospace, Fleetlands (conversion)	
ZJ100	BAe Hawk 102D	BAE Systems National Training Academy, Humberside	
ZJ117	EHI-101 Merlin HC3 [A]	QinetiQ, stored Boscombe Down	
ZJ118	EHI-101 Merlin HC3i [B]	RN No 846 NAS, Yeovilton	
ZJ119	EHI-101 Merlin HC3 [C]	RN MDMF, Culdrose	
ZJ120	EHI-101 Merlin HC4 [D]	MoD/Leonardo, Yeovil (conversion)	
ZJ121	EHI-101 Merlin HC4 [E]	MoD/Leonardo, Yeovil (conversion)	
ZJ122	EHI-101 Merlin HC4 [F]	MoD/Leonardo, Yeovil	
ZJ123	EHI-101 Merlin HC3 [G]	RN MDMF, Culdrose	
ZJ124	EHI-101 Merlin HC3 [H]	RN No 845 NAS, Yeovilton	
ZJ125	EHI-101 Merlin HC3 [J]	RN No 845 NAS, Yeovilton	

Notes	Serial	Type (code/other identity)	Owner/operator, location or fate
	ZJ126	EHI-101 Merlin HC3i [K]	RN MDMF, Culdrose
	ZJ127	EHI-101 Merlin HC4 [L]	MoD/Leonardo, Yeovil
	ZJ128	EHI-101 Merlin HC3 [M]	RN MDMF, Culdrose
	ZJ129	EHI-101 Merlin HC4 [N]	MoD/Leonardo, Yeovil (conversion)
	ZJ130	EHI-101 Merlin HC3i [O]	RN No 846 NAS, Yeovilton
	ZJ131	EHI-101 Merlin HC3 [P]	RN No 845 NAS, Yeovilton
	ZJ132	EHI-101 Merlin HC3i [Q]	RN No 846 NAS, Yeovilton
	ZJ133	EHI-101 Merlin HC3 [R]	QinetiQ, stored Boscombe Down
	ZJ134	EHI-101 Merlin HC3 [S]	RN No 845 NAS, Yeovilton
	ZJ135	EHI-101 Merlin HC3i [T]	RN No 846 NAS, Yeovilton
	ZJ136	EHI-101 Merlin HC3i [U]	RN No 846 NAS, Yeovilton
	ZJ137	EHI-101 Merlin HC3i [W]	RN No 846 NAS, Yeovilton
	ZJ138	EHI-101 Merlin HC3 [X]	QinetiQ, stored Boscombe Down
	ZJ164	AS365N-2 Dauphin 2 (G-BTLC)	RN/Bond Helicopters, Newquay
	ZJ165	AS365N-2 Dauphin 2 (G-NTOO)	RN/Bond Helicopters, Newquay
	ZJ166	WAH-64 Apache AH1 (N9219G)	AAC, stored Wattisham
	ZJ167	WAH-64 Apache AH1 (N3266B)	AAC, stored Wattisham
	ZJ168	WAH-64 Apache AH1 (N3123T)	AAC, stored Wattisham
	ZJ169	WAH-64 Apache AH1 (N3114H)	AAC, stored Wattisham
	ZJ170	WAH-64 Apache AH1 (N3065U)	AAC, stored Wattisham
	ZJ171	WAH-64 Apache AH1 (N3266T)	AAC, stored Wattisham
	ZJ172	WAH-64 Apache AH1	AAC, stored Wattisham
	ZJ173	WAH-64 Apache AH1 (N3266W)	AAC, stored Wattisham
	ZJ174	WAH-64 Apache AH1	AAC, stored Wattisham
	ZJ175	WAH-64 Apache AH1 (N3218V)	AAC, stored Wattisham
	ZJ176	WAH-64 Apache AH1	AAC, stored Wattisham
	ZJ178	WAH-64 Apache AH1	AAC No 3 Regt, Wattisham
	ZJ179	WAH-64 Apache AH1	AAC No 3 Regt, Wattisham
	ZJ180	WAH-64 Apache AH1	AAC No 673 Sqn/7 Regt, Middle Wallop
	ZJ181	WAH-64 Apache AH1	AAC No 3 Regt, Wattisham
	ZJ182	WAH-64 Apache AH1	AAC No 4 Regt, Wattisham
	ZJ183	WAH-64 Apache AH1	AAC No 3 Regt, Wattisham
	ZJ184	WAH-64 Apache AH1	AAC No 3 Regt, Wattisham
	ZJ185	WAH-64 Apache AH1	AAC No 3 Regt, Wattisham
	ZJ186	WAH-64 Apache AH1	AAC No 3 Regt, Wattisham
	ZJ187	WAH-64 Apache AH1	AAC No 673 Sqn/7 Regt, Middle Wallop
	ZJ188	WAH-64 Apache AH1	AAC No 673 Sqn/7 Regt, Middle Wallop
	ZJ189	WAH-64 Apache AH1	AAC No 4 Regt, Wattisham
	ZJ190	WAH-64 Apache AH1	AAC No 4 Regt, Wattisham
	ZJ191	WAH-64 Apache AH1	MoD/Leonardo, Yeovil
	ZJ192	WAH-64 Apache AH1	AAC No 3 Regt, Wattisham
	ZJ193	WAH-64 Apache AH1	AAC No 3 Regt, Wattisham
	ZJ194	WAH-64 Apache AH1	AAC No 3 Regt, Wattisham
	ZJ195	WAH-64 Apache AH1	AAC No 673 Sqn/7 Regt, Middle Wallop
	ZJ196	WAH-64 Apache AH1	AAC No 3 Regt, Wattisham
	ZJ197	WAH-64 Apache AH1	AAC No 3 Regt, Wattisham
	ZJ198	WAH-64 Apache AH1	AAC No 4 Regt, Wattisham
	ZJ199	WAH-64 Apache AH1	AAC No 673 Sqn/7 Regt, Middle Wallop
	ZJ200	WAH-64 Apache AH1	AAC No 3 Regt, Wattisham
	ZJ202	WAH-64 Apache AH1	AAC, stored Wattisham
	ZJ203	WAH-64 Apache AH1	AAC No 3 Regt, Wattisham
	ZJ204	WAH-64 Apache AH1	AAC No 3 Regt, Wattisham
	ZJ205	WAH-64 Apache AH1	AAC No 4 Regt, Wattisham
	ZJ206	WAH-64 Apache AH1	AAC, stored Wattisham
	ZJ207	WAH-64 Apache AH1	AAC No 3 Regt, Wattisham
	ZJ208	WAH-64 Apache AH1	AAC No 4 Regt, Wattisham
	ZJ209	WAH-64 Apache AH1	AAC No 673 Sqn/7 Regt, Middle Wallop
	ZJ210	WAH-64 Apache AH1	AAC No 4 Regt, Wattisham
	ZJ211	WAH-64 Apache AH1	AAC No 3 Regt, Wattisham
	ZJ212	WAH-64 Apache AH1	AAC, stored Wattisham
	ZJ213	WAH-64 Apache AH1	AAC No 673 Sqn/7 Regt, Middle Wallop
	ZJ214	WAH-64 Apache AH1	AAC, stored Wattisham

Serial	Type (code/other identity)	Owner/operator, location or fate	Notes
ZJ215	WAH-64 Apache AH1	AAC No 4 Regt, Wattisham	
ZJ216	WAH-64 Apache AH1	AAC No 673 Sqn/7 Regt, Middle Wallop	
ZJ217	WAH-64 Apache AH1	AAC No 673 Sqn/7 Regt, Middle Wallop	
ZJ218	WAH-64 Apache AH1	AAC No 4 Regt, Wattisham	
ZJ219	WAH-64 Apache AH1	AAC, stored Wattisham	
ZJ220	WAH-64 Apache AH1	AAC No 3 Regt, Wattisham	
ZJ221	WAH-64 Apache AH1	AAC No 3 Regt, Wattisham	
ZJ222	WAH-64 Apache AH1	AAC No 4 Regt, Wattisham	
ZJ223	WAH-64 Apache AH1	AAC No 4 Regt, Wattisham	
ZJ224	WAH-64 Apache AH1	AAC No 3 Regt, Wattisham	
ZJ225	WAH-64 Apache AH1	AAC No 3 Regt, Wattisham	
ZJ226	WAH-64 Apache AH1	AAC No 4 Regt, Wattisham	
ZJ227	WAH-64 Apache AH1	AAC No 3 Regt, Wattisham	
ZJ228	WAH-64 Apache AH1	AAC No 3 Regt, Wattisham	
ZJ229	WAH-64 Apache AH1	AAC No 3 Regt, Wattisham	
ZJ230	WAH-64 Apache AH1	AAC No 3 Regt, Wattisham	
ZJ231	WAH-64 Apache AH1	AAC No 673 Sqn/7 Regt, Middle Wallop	
ZJ232	WAH-64 Apache AH1	AAC No 673 Sqn/7 Regt, Middle Wallop	
ZJ233	WAH-64 Apache AH1	AAC No 3 Regt, Wattisham	
ZJ234	Bell 412EP Griffin HT1 (G-BWZR) [S]	DHFS No 202(R) Sqn, RAF Valley	
ZJ235	Bell 412EP Griffin HT1 (G-BXBF) [I]	DHFS No 60(R) Sqn, RAF Shawbury	
ZJ236	Bell 412EP Griffin HT1 (G-BXBE) [X]	DHFS No 60(R) Sqn, RAF Shawbury	
ZJ237	Bell 412EP Griffin HT1 (G-BXFF) [T]	DHFS No 60(R) Sqn, RAF Shawbury	
ZJ238	Bell 412EP Griffin HT1 (G-BXHC) [Y]	DHFS No 60(R) Sqn, RAF Shawbury	
ZJ239	Bell 412EP Griffin HT1 (G-BXFH) [R]	DHFS No 202(R) Sqn, RAF Valley	
ZJ240	Bell 412EP Griffin HT1 (G-BXIR) [U]	DHFS No 60(R) Sqn, RAF Shawbury	
ZJ241	Bell 412EP Griffin HT1 (G-BXIS) [L]	*Crashed 9 August 2016, Yr Aran*	
ZJ242	Bell 412EP Griffin HT1 (G-BXDK) [E]	DHFS No 202(R) Sqn, RAF Valley	
ZJ243	AS350BA Squirrel HT2 (G-BWZS) [43]	DHFS, RAF Shawbury	
ZJ244	AS350BA Squirrel HT2 (G-BXMD) [44]	School of Army Aviation/No 670 Sqn, Middle Wallop	
ZJ245	AS350BA Squirrel HT2 (G-BXME) [45]	School of Army Aviation/No 670 Sqn, Middle Wallop	
ZJ246	AS350BA Squirrel HT2 (G-BXMJ) [46]	School of Army Aviation/No 670 Sqn, Middle Wallop	
ZJ248	AS350BA Squirrel HT2 (G-BXNE) [48]	School of Army Aviation/No 670 Sqn, Middle Wallop	
ZJ249	AS350BA Squirrel HT2 (G-BXNJ) [49]	School of Army Aviation/No 670 Sqn, Middle Wallop	
ZJ250	AS350BA Squirrel HT2 (G-BXNY) [50]	School of Army Aviation/No 670 Sqn, Middle Wallop	
ZJ251	AS350BA Squirrel HT2 (G-BXOG) [51]	DHFS, RAF Shawbury	
ZJ252	AS350BA Squirrel HT2 (G-BXOK) [52]	School of Army Aviation/No 670 Sqn, Middle Wallop	
ZJ253	AS350BA Squirrel HT2 (G-BXPG) [53]	School of Army Aviation/No 670 Sqn, Middle Wallop	
ZJ254	AS350BA Squirrel HT2 (G-BXPJ) [54]	School of Army Aviation/No 670 Sqn, Middle Wallop	
ZJ255	AS350BB Squirrel HT1 (G-BXAG) [55]	DHFS, RAF Shawbury	
ZJ256	AS350BB Squirrel HT1 (G-BXCE) [56]	DHFS, RAF Shawbury	
ZJ257	AS350BB Squirrel HT1 (G-BXDJ) [57]	DHFS, RAF Shawbury	
ZJ260	AS350BB Squirrel HT1 (G-BXGB) [60]	DHFS, RAF Shawbury	
ZJ261	AS350BB Squirrel HT1 (G-BXGJ) [61]	DHFS, RAF Shawbury	
ZJ262	AS350BB Squirrel HT1 (G-BXHB) [62]	DHFS, RAF Shawbury	
ZJ264	AS350BB Squirrel HT1 (G-BXHW) [64]	DHFS, RAF Shawbury	
ZJ265	AS350BB Squirrel HT1 (G-BXHX) [65]	DHFS, RAF Shawbury	
ZJ266	AS350BB Squirrel HT1 (G-BXIL) [66]	DHFS, RAF Shawbury	
ZJ267	AS350BB Squirrel HT1 (G-BXIP) [67]	DHFS, RAF Shawbury	
ZJ268	AS350BB Squirrel HT1 (G-BXJE) [68]	DHFS, RAF Shawbury	
ZJ269	AS350BB Squirrel HT1 (G-BXJN) [69]	DHFS, RAF Shawbury	
ZJ270	AS350BB Squirrel HT1 (G-BXJR) [70]	DHFS, RAF Shawbury	
ZJ271	AS350BB Squirrel HT1 (G-BXKE) [71]	DHFS, RAF Shawbury	
ZJ272	AS350BB Squirrel HT1 (G-BXKN) [72]	DHFS, RAF Shawbury	
ZJ273	AS350BB Squirrel HT1 (G-BXKP) [73]	DHFS, RAF Shawbury	
ZJ274	AS350BB Squirrel HT1 (G-BXKR) [74]	DHFS, RAF Shawbury	
ZJ275	AS350BB Squirrel HT1 (G-BXLB) [75]	DHFS, RAF Shawbury	
ZJ276	AS350BB Squirrel HT1 (G-BXLE) [76]	DHFS, RAF Shawbury	
ZJ277	AS350BB Squirrel HT1 (G-BXLH) [77]	DHFS, RAF Shawbury	
ZJ278	AS350BB Squirrel HT1 (G-BXMB) [78]	DHFS, RAF Shawbury	
ZJ279	AS350BB Squirrel HT1 (G-BXMC) [79]	DHFS, RAF Shawbury	
ZJ280	AS350BB Squirrel HT1 (G-BXMI) [80]	DHFS, RAF Shawbury	

Notes	Serial	Type (code/other identity)	Owner/operator, location or fate
	ZJ369	GEC Phoenix RPAS	Defence Academy of the UK, Shrivenham
	ZJ385	GEC Phoenix RPAS	Muckleburgh Collection, Weybourne, Norfolk
	ZJ392	GEC Phoenix RPAS	Privately owned, Holt Heath, Worcs
	ZJ449	GEC Phoenix RPAS	REME Museum, Lyneham
	ZJ452	GEC Phoenix RPAS	Science Museum, stored Wroughton
	ZJ469	GEC Phoenix RPAS	Army, Larkhill, on display
	ZJ489	GAF Jindivik 104AL (A92-808)	*Scrapped at Caernarfon, 2016*
	ZJ493	GAF Jindivik 104AL (A92-814)	RAF Museum Reserve Collection, Stafford
	ZJ496	GAF Jindivik 104AL (A92-901)	Farnborough Air Sciences Trust, Farnborough
	ZJ515	BAE Systems Nimrod MRA4 (XV258) <ff>	Cranfield University, instructional use
	ZJ620	AgustaWestland Merlin Simulator	RN No 824 NAS, Culdrose
	ZJ621	AgustaWestland Merlin Simulator	RN No 824 NAS, Culdrose
	ZJ622	AgustaWestland Merlin Simulator	RN No 824 NAS, Culdrose
	ZJ623	AgustaWestland Merlin Simulator	RN No 824 NAS, Culdrose
	ZJ624	AgustaWestland Merlin Simulator	RN No 824 NAS, Culdrose
	ZJ625	AgustaWestland Merlin Simulator	RN No 824 NAS, Culdrose
	ZJ626	AgustaWestland Merlin Simulator	RN No 824 NAS, Culdrose
	ZJ645	D-BD Alpha Jet (98+62) [45]	MoD/AFD/QinetiQ, Boscombe Down
	ZJ646	D-BD Alpha Jet (98+55) [46]	MoD/AFD/QinetiQ, Boscombe Down
	ZJ647	D-BD Alpha Jet (98+71) [47]	MoD/AFD/QinetiQ, Boscombe Down
	ZJ648	D-BD Alpha Jet (98+09) [48]	MoD/QinetiQ Boscombe Down, spares use
	ZJ649	D-BD Alpha Jet (98+73) [49]	MoD/ETPS, Boscombe Down
	ZJ650	D-BD Alpha Jet (98+35)	MoD/QinetiQ, stored Boscombe Down
	ZJ651	D-BD Alpha Jet (41+42) [51]	MoD/ETPS, Boscombe Down
	ZJ652	D-BD Alpha Jet (41+09)	MoD/QinetiQ Boscombe Down, spares use
	ZJ653	D-BD Alpha Jet (40+22)	MoD/QinetiQ Boscombe Down, spares use
	ZJ654	D-BD Alpha Jet (41+02)	MoD/QinetiQ Boscombe Down, spares use
	ZJ655	D-BD Alpha Jet (41+19)	MoD/QinetiQ Boscombe Down, spares use
	ZJ656	D-BD Alpha Jet (41+40)	MoD/QinetiQ Boscombe Down, spares use
	ZJ690	Bombardier Sentinel R1 (C-GJRG)	RAF No 5 Sqn, Waddington
	ZJ691	Bombardier Sentinel R1 (C-FZVM)	RAF No 5 Sqn, Waddington
	ZJ692	Bombardier Sentinel R1 (C-FZWW)	RAF No 5 Sqn, Waddington
	ZJ693	Bombardier Sentinel R1 (C-FZXC)	RAF No 5 Sqn, Waddington
	ZJ694	Bombardier Sentinel R1 (C-FZYL)	RAF No 5 Sqn, Waddington
	ZJ699	Eurofighter Typhoon (PT001)	MoD/BAE Systems, Warton
	ZJ700	Eurofighter Typhoon (PS002)	MoD/BAE Systems, Warton
	ZJ703	Bell 412EP Griffin HAR2 (G-CBST) [Spades,3]	RAF No 84 Sqn, Akrotiri
	ZJ704	Bell 412EP Griffin HAR2 (G-CBWT) [Clubs,4]	RAF No 84 Sqn, Akrotiri
	ZJ705	Bell 412EP Griffin HAR2 (G-CBXL) [Hearts,5]	MoD/ETPS, Boscombe Down
	ZJ706	Bell 412EP Griffin HAR2 (G-CBYR) [Diamonds,6]	RAF No 84 Sqn, Akrotiri
	ZJ707	Bell 412EP Griffin HT1 (G-CBUB) [O]	DHFS No 60(R) Sqn, RAF Shawbury
	ZJ708	Bell 412EP Griffin HT1 (G-CBVP) [K]	DHFS No 202(R) Sqn, RAF Valley
	ZJ780	AS365N-3 Dauphin AH1 (G-CEXT)	AAC No 658 Sqn, Credenhill
	ZJ781	AS365N-3 Dauphin AH1 (G-CEXU)	AAC No 658 Sqn, Credenhill
	ZJ782	AS365N-3 Dauphin AH1 (G-CEXV)	AAC No 658 Sqn, Credenhill
	ZJ783	AS365N-3 Dauphin AH1 (G-CEXW)	AAC No 658 Sqn, Credenhill
	ZJ785	AS365N-3 Dauphin AH1 (G-CFFW)	AAC No 658 Sqn, Credenhill
	ZJ787	AS365N-3 Dauphin AH1 (G-CHNJ)	AAC No 658 Sqn, Credenhill
	ZJ800	Eurofighter Typhoon T3 [BC]	RAF No 29(R) Sqn, Coningsby
	ZJ801	Eurofighter Typhoon T3 [BJ]	RAF No 29(R) Sqn, Coningsby
	ZJ802	Eurofighter Typhoon T3 [DW]	RAF No 11 Sqn, Coningsby
	ZJ803	Eurofighter Typhoon T3 [BA]	RAF No 29(R) Sqn, Coningsby
	ZJ804	Eurofighter Typhoon T3 [BM]	RAF No 29(R) Sqn, Coningsby
	ZJ805	Eurofighter Typhoon T3 [BD]	RAF No 29(R) Sqn, Coningsby
	ZJ806	Eurofighter Typhoon T3 [BE]	RAF No 29(R) Sqn, Coningsby
	ZJ807	Eurofighter Typhoon T3 [BF]	RAF No 29(R) Sqn, Coningsby
	ZJ808	Eurofighter Typhoon T3 [BP]	RAF No 29(R) Sqn, Coningsby
	ZJ809	Eurofighter Typhoon T3 [FZ]	RAF No 1 Sqn, Lossiemouth
	ZJ810	Eurofighter Typhoon T3 [BI]	RAF No 29(R) Sqn, Coningsby
	ZJ811	Eurofighter Typhoon T3 [W]	RAF No 2 Sqn, Lossiemouth
	ZJ812	Eurofighter Typhoon T3 [BK]	RAF No 29(R) Sqn, Coningsby
	ZJ813	Eurofighter Typhoon T3 [BL]	RAF Coningsby, GI use

Serial	Type (code/other identity)	Owner/operator, location or fate	Notes
ZJ814	Eurofighter Typhoon T3 [814]	RAF No 29(R) Sqn, Coningsby	
ZJ815	Eurofighter Typhoon T3 [EB-H]	RAF Coningsby, RTP	
ZJ910	Eurofighter Typhoon FGR4 [DO]	RAF AM&SU, stored Shawbury	
ZJ911	Eurofighter Typhoon FGR4 [QO-Z]	RAF AM&SU, stored Shawbury	
ZJ912	Eurofighter Typhoon FGR4 [DR]	RAF No 11 Sqn, Coningsby	
ZJ913	Eurofighter Typhoon FGR4 [II]	RAF No 2 Sqn, Lossiemouth	
ZJ914	Eurofighter Typhoon FGR4 [DZ]	RAF No 3 Sqn, Coningsby	
ZJ915	Eurofighter Typhoon FGR4 [F]	RAF No 1435 Flt, Mount Pleasant, FI	
ZJ916	Eurofighter Typhoon FGR4 [S]	RAF No 2 Sqn, Lossiemouth	
ZJ917	Eurofighter Typhoon FGR4 [DG]	RAF No 11 Sqn, Coningsby	
ZJ918	Eurofighter Typhoon FGR4	RAF No 3 Sqn, Coningsby	
ZJ919	Eurofighter Typhoon FGR4 [DC]	RAF No 1 Sqn, Lossiemouth	
ZJ920	Eurofighter Typhoon FGR4 [R]	RAF No 3 Sqn, Coningsby	
ZJ921	Eurofighter Typhoon FGR4 [E]	RAF No 3 Sqn, Coningsby	
ZJ922	Eurofighter Typhoon FGR4 [QO-C]	MoD/BAE Systems, Warton	
ZJ923	Eurofighter Typhoon FGR4	RAF No 11 Sqn, Coningsby	
ZJ924	Eurofighter Typhoon FGR4 [II]	RAF TMU, Coningsby	
ZJ925	Eurofighter Typhoon FGR4 [DXI] $	RAF AM&SU, stored Shawbury	
ZJ926	Eurofighter Typhoon FGR4 [H]	RAF No 1435 Flt, Mount Pleasant, FI	
ZJ927	Eurofighter Typhoon FGR4	RAF No 29(R) Sqn, Coningsby	
ZJ928	Eurofighter Typhoon FGR4 [FQ]	RAF No 3 Sqn, Coningsby	
ZJ929	Eurofighter Typhoon FGR4 [DL]	RAF No 11 Sqn, Coningsby	
ZJ930	Eurofighter Typhoon FGR4	RAF No 29(R) Sqn, Coningsby	
ZJ931	Eurofighter Typhoon FGR4 [DA]	RAF No 1 Sqn, Lossiemouth	
ZJ932	Eurofighter Typhoon FGR4 [DB]	RAF AM&SU, stored Shawbury	
ZJ933	Eurofighter Typhoon FGR4 [C]	RAF No 1435 Flt, Mount Pleasant, FI	
ZJ934	Eurofighter Typhoon FGR4 [U]	RAF No 2 Sqn, Lossiemouth	
ZJ935	Eurofighter Typhoon FGR4 [DJ]	RAF TMU, Coningsby	
ZJ936	Eurofighter Typhoon FGR4 [QO-C]	RAF AM&SU, stored Shawbury	
ZJ937	Eurofighter Typhoon FGR4 [DT]	RAF Coningsby, WLT	
ZJ938	Eurofighter Typhoon FGR4	MoD/BAE Systems, Warton	
ZJ939	Eurofighter Typhoon FGR4 [DN]	RAF No 3 Sqn, Coningsby	
ZJ940	Eurofighter Typhoon FGR4 [DJ666]	RAF, stored Coningsby	
ZJ941	Eurofighter Typhoon FGR4 [D]	RAF No 1435 Flt, Mount Pleasant, FI	
ZJ942	Eurofighter Typhoon FGR4 [DH]	RAF No 11 Sqn, Coningsby	
ZJ943	Eurofighter Typhoon FGR4 (fuselage)	RAF AM&SU, stored Shawbury (wreck)	
ZJ944	Eurofighter Typhoon FGR4	RAF, stored Coningsby	
ZJ945	Eurofighter Typhoon FGR4	RAF, stored Coningsby	
ZJ946	Eurofighter Typhoon FGR4	RAF TMU, Coningsby	
ZJ947	Eurofighter Typhoon FGR4 [EB-L]	RAF No 2 Sqn, Lossiemouth	
ZJ948	Eurofighter Typhoon FGR4	RAF, stored Coningsby	
ZJ949	Eurofighter Typhoon FGR4	RAF No 2 Sqn, Lossiemouth	
ZJ950	Eurofighter Typhoon FGR4	RAF No 1 Sqn, Lossiemouth	
ZJ951	BAE Systems Hawk 120D	MoD/BAE Systems, stored Warton	
ZJ954	SA330H Puma HC2 (SAAF 144)	RAF No 28(R) Sqn, Benson	
ZJ955	SA330H Puma HC2 (SAAF 148) [P] $	RAF No 28(R) Sqn/No 33 Sqn/No 230 Sqn, Benson	
ZJ956	SA330H Puma HC2 (SAAF 172/F-ZWCC)	RAF No 28(R) Sqn/No 33 Sqn/No 230 Sqn, Benson	
ZJ957	SA330H Puma HC2 (SAAF 169)	RAF No 28(R) Sqn/No 33 Sqn/No 230 Sqn, Benson	
ZJ960	Grob G109B Vigilant T1 (D-KSMU) [SH]	RAF, stored Syerston	
ZJ961	Grob G109B Vigilant T1 (D-KLCW) [SJ]	RAF, stored Little Rissington	
ZJ962	Grob G109B Vigilant T1 (D-KBEU) [SK]	RAF, stored St Athan	
ZJ963	Grob G109B Vigilant T1 (D-KMSN) [SL]	RAF, stored Watton	
ZJ967	Grob G109B Vigilant T1 (G-DEWS) [SM]	RAF CGMF, Syerston	
ZJ968	Grob G109B Vigilant T1 (N109BT) [SN]	RAF, stored Woodvale	
ZJ969	Bell 212HP AH1 (G-BGLJ) [K]	AAC JHC/No 7 Regt, Middle Wallop	
ZJ990	EHI-101 Merlin HC3A (M-501) [AA]	RN No 845 NAS, Yeovilton	
ZJ992	EHI-101 Merlin HC3A (M-503) [AB]	RN No 845 NAS, Yeovilton	
ZJ994	EHI-101 Merlin HC3A (M-505) [AC]	RN No 845 NAS, Yeovilton	
ZJ995	EHI-101 Merlin HC3A (M-506) [AD]	RN MDMF, Culdrose	
ZJ998	EHI-101 Merlin HC3A (M-509) [AE]	RN No 845 NAS, Yeovilton	
ZK001	EHI-101 Merlin HC3A (M-511) [AF]	RN, stored Culdrose	
ZK005	Grob G109B Vigilant T1 (OH-797) [SP]	RAF, stored Little Rissington	

Notes	Serial	Type (code/other identity)	Owner/operator, location or fate
	ZK010	BAE Systems Hawk T2 [A]	RAF No 4 FTS/4(R) Sqn, Valley
	ZK011	BAE Systems Hawk T2 [B]	RAF No 4 FTS/4(R) Sqn, Valley
	ZK012	BAE Systems Hawk T2 [C]	RAF No 4 FTS/4(R) Sqn, Valley
	ZK013	BAE Systems Hawk T2 [D]	RAF No 4 FTS/4(R) Sqn, Valley
	ZK014	BAE Systems Hawk T2 [E]	RAF No 4 FTS/4(R) Sqn, Valley
	ZK015	BAE Systems Hawk T2 [F]	RAF No 4 FTS/4(R) Sqn, Valley
	ZK016	BAE Systems Hawk T2 [G]	RAF No 4 FTS/4(R) Sqn, Valley
	ZK017	BAE Systems Hawk T2 [H]	RAF No 4 FTS/4(R) Sqn, Valley
	ZK018	BAE Systems Hawk T2 [I] $	RAF HSF, stored Valley
	ZK019	BAE Systems Hawk T2 [J]	RAF No 4 FTS/4(R) Sqn, Valley
	ZK020	BAE Systems Hawk T2 [K] $	RAF No 4 FTS/4(R) Sqn, Valley
	ZK021	BAE Systems Hawk T2 [L]	RAF No 4 FTS/4(R) Sqn, Valley
	ZK022	BAE Systems Hawk T2 [M]	RAF No 4 FTS/4(R) Sqn, Valley
	ZK023	BAE Systems Hawk T2 [N]	RAF No 4 FTS/4(R) Sqn, Valley
	ZK024	BAE Systems Hawk T2 [O]	RAF No 4 FTS/4(R) Sqn, Valley
	ZK025	BAE Systems Hawk T2 [P]	RAF No 4 FTS/4(R) Sqn, Valley
	ZK026	BAE Systems Hawk T2 [Q]	RAF No 4 FTS/4(R) Sqn, Valley
	ZK027	BAE Systems Hawk T2 [R]	RAF No 4 FTS/4(R) Sqn, Valley
	ZK028	BAE Systems Hawk T2 [S]	RAF No 4 FTS/4(R) Sqn, Valley
	ZK029	BAE Systems Hawk T2 [T]	RAF No 4 FTS/4(R) Sqn, Valley
	ZK030	BAE Systems Hawk T2 [U]	RAF No 4 FTS/4(R) Sqn, Valley
	ZK031	BAE Systems Hawk T2 [V]	RAF No 4 FTS/4(R) Sqn, Valley
	ZK032	BAE Systems Hawk T2 [W]	RAF No 4 FTS/4(R) Sqn, Valley
	ZK033	BAE Systems Hawk T2 [X]	RAF No 4 FTS/4(R) Sqn, Valley
	ZK034	BAE Systems Hawk T2 [Y]	RAF No 4 FTS/4(R) Sqn, Valley
	ZK035	BAE Systems Hawk T2 [Z]	RAF No 4 FTS/4(R) Sqn, Valley
	ZK036	BAE Systems Hawk T2 [AA]	RAF No 4 FTS/4(R) Sqn, Valley
	ZK037	BAE Systems Hawk T2 [AB]	RAF No 4 FTS/4(R) Sqn, Valley
	ZK067	Bell 212HP AH3 (G-BFER) [B]	AAC No 7 Flt, Brunei
	ZK114	M2370 RPAS	QinetiQ
	ZK150*	Lockheed Martin Desert Hawk 3 RPAS	Army 47 Regt Royal Artillery, Thorney Island
	ZK150	Lockheed Martin Desert Hawk 3 RPAS (ZK150/617)	Imperial War Museum, Lambeth
	ZK155*	Honeywell T-Hawk RPAS	Army 32 Regt Royal Artillery, Larkhill
	ZK192	AgustaWestland Super Lynx Mk.140	Leonardo, Yeovil, for Algeria as LC-32
	ZK195	AgustaWestland Super Lynx Mk.140	Leonardo, Yeovil, for Algeria as LC-35
	ZK196	AgustaWestland Super Lynx Mk.140	*To Algeria as LC-36, 15 August 2016*
	ZK205	Grob G109B Vigilant T1 (D-KBRU) [SS]	RAF, stored Little Rissington
	ZK210	BAE Systems Mantis RPAS	MoD/BAE Systems, Warton
	ZK300	Eurofighter Typhoon FGR4 [H]	RAF No 2 Sqn, Lossiemouth
	ZK301	Eurofighter Typhoon FGR4 [EW]	RAF TMU, Coningsby
	ZK302	Eurofighter Typhoon FGR4 [EC]	RAF TMU, Coningsby
	ZK303	Eurofighter Typhoon T3 [AX]	MoD/BAE Systems, Warton
	ZK304	Eurofighter Typhoon FGR4 [FM]	RAF TMU, Coningsby
	ZK305	Eurofighter Typhoon FGR4 [EE]	RAF TMU, Coningsby
	ZK306	Eurofighter Typhoon FGR4 [ED]	RAF No 6 Sqn, Lossiemouth
	ZK307	Eurofighter Typhoon FGR4 [O]	RAF No 3 Sqn, Coningsby
	ZK308	Eurofighter Typhoon FGR4 [BW]	RAF No 2 Sqn, Lossiemouth
	ZK309	Eurofighter Typhoon FGR4 [QO-P]	RAF No 1 Sqn, Lossiemouth
	ZK310	Eurofighter Typhoon FGR4	RAF No 11 Sqn, Coningsby
	ZK311	Eurofighter Typhoon FGR4 [N]	RAF No 2 Sqn, Lossiemouth
	ZK312	Eurofighter Typhoon FGR4 [EM]	RAF No 6 Sqn, Lossiemouth
	ZK313	Eurofighter Typhoon FGR4 [W]	RAF No 3 Sqn, Coningsby
	ZK314	Eurofighter Typhoon FGR4 [EO]	RAF No 6 Sqn, Lossiemouth
	ZK315	Eurofighter Typhoon FGR4 $	RAF AWC/FJWOEU/No 41(R) Sqn, Coningsby
	ZK316	Eurofighter Typhoon FGR4 [FA]	RAF No 6 Sqn, Lossiemouth
	ZK317	Eurofighter Typhoon FGR4 [317]	RAF No 6 Sqn, Lossiemouth
	ZK318	Eurofighter Typhoon FGR4 [FG]	RAF No 6 Sqn, Lossiemouth
	ZK319	Eurofighter Typhoon FGR4	RAF No 2 Sqn, Lossiemouth
	ZK320	Eurofighter Typhoon FGR4 [320]	RAF No 6 Sqn, Lossiemouth
	ZK321	Eurofighter Typhoon FGR4 [EG]	RAF No 6 Sqn, Lossiemouth
	ZK322	Eurofighter Typhoon FGR4 [GS]	RAF TMU, Coningsby
	ZK323	Eurofighter Typhoon FGR4 [C]	RAF No 2 Sqn, Lossiemouth

Serial	Type (code/other identity)	Owner/operator, location or fate	Notes
ZK324	Eurofighter Typhoon FGR4 [EI]	RAF No 6 Sqn, Lossiemouth	
ZK325	Eurofighter Typhoon FGR4 [325]	RAF No 3 Sqn, Coningsby	
ZK326	Eurofighter Typhoon FGR4 [FB]	RAF, stored Coningsby	
ZK327	Eurofighter Typhoon FGR4 [FR]	RAF No 1 Sqn, Lossiemouth	
ZK328	Eurofighter Typhoon FGR4 [EB]	RAF TMU, Coningsby	
ZK329	Eurofighter Typhoon FGR4 [FH]	RAF TMU, Coningsby	
ZK330	Eurofighter Typhoon FGR4 [330]	RAF No 11 Sqn, Coningsby	
ZK331	Eurofighter Typhoon FGR4 [BT]	RAF No 29(R) Sqn, Coningsby	
ZK332	Eurofighter Typhoon FGR4 [EB-J]	RAF No 1 Sqn, Lossiemouth	
ZK333	Eurofighter Typhoon FGR4	RAF No 6 Sqn, Lossiemouth	
ZK334	Eurofighter Typhoon FGR4 [A]	RAF No 1 Sqn, Lossiemouth	
ZK335	Eurofighter Typhoon FGR4 [EB-G]	RAF AWC/FJWOEU/No 41(R) Sqn, Coningsby	
ZK336	Eurofighter Typhoon FGR4 [FD]	RAF No 1 Sqn, Lossiemouth	
ZK337	Eurofighter Typhoon FGR4 [FP]	RAF No 1 Sqn, Lossiemouth	
ZK338	Eurofighter Typhoon FGR4 [FF]	RAF No 2 Sqn, Lossiemouth	
ZK339	Eurofighter Typhoon FGR4 [EB-E]	RAF AWC/FJWOEU/No 41(R) Sqn, Coningsby	
ZK340	Eurofighter Typhoon FGR4 [340]	RAF No 11 Sqn, Coningsby	
ZK341	Eurofighter Typhoon FGR4 [EG]	RAF TMU, Coningsby	
ZK342	Eurofighter Typhoon FGR4 [EA] $	RAF No 2 Sqn, Lossiemouth	
ZK343	Eurofighter Typhoon FGR4 [X]	RAF No 2 Sqn, Lossiemouth	
ZK344	Eurofighter Typhoon FGR4	RAF No 6 Sqn, Lossiemouth	
ZK345	Eurofighter Typhoon FGR4 [EP]	RAF No 6 Sqn, Lossiemouth	
ZK346	Eurofighter Typhoon FGR4 [ER]	RAF No 3 Sqn, Coningsby	
ZK347	Eurofighter Typhoon FGR4 [347]	RAF No 6 Sqn, Lossiemouth	
ZK348	Eurofighter Typhoon FGR4 [FN]	RAF No 6 Sqn, Lossiemouth	
ZK349	Eurofighter Typhoon FGR4 [GN-A] $	RAF TMU, Coningsby	
ZK350	Eurofighter Typhoon FGR4	MoD/BAE Systems, Warton	
ZK351	Eurofighter Typhoon FGR4 [BU]	RAF No 6 Sqn, Lossiemouth	
ZK352	Eurofighter Typhoon FGR4 [BV]	RAF No 29(R) Sqn, Coningsby	
ZK353	Eurofighter Typhoon FGR4 [BQ]	RAF No 3 Sqn, Coningsby	
ZK354	Eurofighter Typhoon FGR4 [BY]	RAF No 29(R) Sqn, Coningsby	
ZK355	Eurofighter Typhoon FGR4	MoD/BAE Systems, Warton	
ZK356	Eurofighter Typhoon FGR4	MoD/BAE Systems, Warton	
ZK357	Eurofighter Typhoon FGR4	MoD/BAE Systems, Warton	
ZK358	Eurofighter Typhoon FGR4	MoD/BAE Systems, Warton	
ZK359	Eurofighter Typhoon FGR4	MoD/BAE Systems, Warton	
ZK360	Eurofighter Typhoon FGR4	MoD/BAE Systems, Warton	
ZK361	Eurofighter Typhoon FGR4	MoD/BAE Systems, Warton	
ZK362	Eurofighter Typhoon FGR4	MoD/BAE Systems, Warton	
ZK363	Eurofighter Typhoon FGR4	MoD/BAE Systems, Warton	
ZK364	Eurofighter Typhoon FGR4	MoD/BAE Systems, Warton	
ZK365	Eurofighter Typhoon FGR4 [EB-L]	RAF AWC/FJWOEU/No 41(R) Sqn, Coningsby	
ZK366	Eurofighter Typhoon FGR4	MoD/BAE Systems, Warton	
ZK367	Eurofighter Typhoon FGR4 [EB-R]	RAF AWC/FJWOEU/No 41(R) Sqn, Coningsby	
ZK368	Eurofighter Typhoon FGR4 [368]	RAF No 2 Sqn, Lossiemouth	
ZK369	Eurofighter Typhoon FGR4	RAF No 6 Sqn, Lossiemouth	
ZK370	Eurofighter Typhoon FGR4	MoD/BAE Systems, Warton	
ZK371	Eurofighter Typhoon FGR4	MoD/BAE Systems, Warton	
ZK372	Eurofighter Typhoon FGR4 [BB]	RAF No 1 Sqn, Lossiemouth	
ZK373	Eurofighter Typhoon FGR4	RAF No 29(R) Sqn, Coningsby	
ZK374	Eurofighter Typhoon FGR4	MoD/BAE Systems, Warton	
ZK375	Eurofighter Typhoon FGR4	MoD/BAE Systems, Warton	
ZK376	Eurofighter Typhoon FGR4	RAF TMU, Coningsby	
ZK377	Eurofighter Typhoon FGR4	MoD/BAE Systems, Warton	
ZK378	Eurofighter Typhoon FGR4	MoD/BAE Systems, Warton	
ZK379	Eurofighter Typhoon T3 [EB-B]	RAF AWC/FJWOEU/No 41(R) Sqn, Coningsby	
ZK380	Eurofighter Typhoon T3 [T]	RAF TMU, Coningsby	
ZK381	Eurofighter Typhoon T3	RAF No 29(R) Sqn, Coningsby	
ZK382	Eurofighter Typhoon T3 [BG]	RAF No 29(R) Sqn, Coningsby	
ZK383	Eurofighter Typhoon T3 [FY]	RAF No 29(R) Sqn, Coningsby	
ZK395	Eurofighter Typhoon	*To R Saudi AF as 1024, 14 March 2016*	
ZK424	Eurofighter Typhoon FGR4	DE&S/BAE Systems, Warton	

Notes	Serial	Type (code/other identity)	Owner/operator, location or fate
	ZK425	Eurofighter Typhoon FGR4	DE&S/BAE Systems, Warton
	ZK426	Eurofighter Typhoon FGR4	DE&S/BAE Systems, Warton
	ZK427	Eurofighter Typhoon FGR4	DE&S/BAE Systems, Warton
	ZK451	Beech King Air B200 (G-RAFK) [K]	SERCO/RAF No 3 FTS/45(R) Sqn, Cranwell
	ZK452	Beech King Air B200 (G-RAFL) [L]	SERCO/RAF No 3 FTS/45(R) Sqn, Cranwell
	ZK455	Beech King Air B200 (G-RAFO) [O]	SERCO/RAF No 3 FTS/45(R) Sqn, Cranwell
	ZK456	Beech King Air B200 (G-RAFP) [P]	SERCO/RAF No 3 FTS/45(R) Sqn, Cranwell
	ZK458	Hawker Beechcraft King Air B200GT (G-RAFD) [D]	SERCO/RAF No 3 FTS/45(R) Sqn, Cranwell
	ZK459	Hawker Beechcraft King Air B200GT (G-RAFX) [X]	SERCO/RAF No 3 FTS/45(R) Sqn, Cranwell
	ZK460	Hawker Beechcraft King Air B200GT (G-RAFU) [U] $	SERCO/RAF No 3 FTS/45(R) Sqn, Cranwell
	ZK531	BAe Hawk T53 (LL-5306)	BAE Systems Aircraft Maintenance Academy, Humberside
	ZK532	BAe Hawk T53 (LL-5315)	MoD/BAE Systems, Warton
	ZK533	BAe Hawk T53 (LL-5317)	BAE Systems Aircraft Maintenance Academy, Humberside
	ZK534	BAe Hawk T53 (LL-5319)	Privately owned, Bentwaters
	ZK535	BAe Hawk T53 (LL-5320)	BAE Systems Aircraft Maintenance Academy, Humberside
	ZK550	Boeing Chinook HC6 (N701UK)	RAF No 7 Sqn, Odiham
	ZK551	Boeing Chinook HC6 (N702UK)	RAF No 7 Sqn, Odiham
	ZK552	Boeing Chinook HC6 (N703UK)	MoD/Vector Aerospace, Fleetlands
	ZK553	Boeing Chinook HC6 (N700UK)	MoD/Vector Aerospace, Fleetlands
	ZK554	Boeing Chinook HC6 (N705UK)	MoD/Vector Aerospace, Fleetlands
	ZK555	Boeing Chinook HC6 (N706UK)	RAF No 7 Sqn, Odiham
	ZK556	Boeing Chinook HC6 (N707UK)	RAF No 7 Sqn, Odiham
	ZK557	Boeing Chinook HC6 (N708UK)	RAF No 7 Sqn, Odiham
	ZK558	Boeing Chinook HC6 (N709UK)	RAF No 7 Sqn, Odiham
	ZK559	Boeing Chinook HC6 (N710UK)	RAF No 7 Sqn, Odiham
	ZK560	Boeing Chinook HC6 (N711UK)	RAF No 7 Sqn, Odiham
	ZK561	Boeing Chinook HC6 (N712UK)	RAF No 7 Sqn, Odiham
	ZK562	Boeing Chinook HC6 (N713UK)	RAF No 7 Sqn, Odiham
	ZK563	Boeing Chinook HC6 (N714UK)	RAF No 7 Sqn, Odiham
	ZK610	Eurofighter Typhoon	*To R Saudi AF as 8011, 14 March 2016*
	ZK611	Eurofighter Typhoon	*To R Saudi AF as 8012, 17 May 2016*
	ZK612	Eurofighter Typhoon	*To R Saudi AF as 8013, 20 July 2016*
	ZK613	Eurofighter Typhoon	*To R Saudi AF as 8014, 17 May 2016*
	ZK614	Eurofighter Typhoon	*To R Saudi AF as 8015, 20 July 2016*
	ZK615	Eurofighter Typhoon	*To R Saudi AF as 8016, 25 July 2016*
	ZK616	Eurofighter Typhoon	*To R Saudi AF as 8017, 20 October 2016*
	ZK617	Eurofighter Typhoon	*To R Saudi AF as 8018, 20 October 2016*
	ZK618	Eurofighter Typhoon	*To R Saudi AF as 8019, 13 December 2016*
	ZK619	Eurofighter Typhoon	*To R Saudi AF as 8020, 13 December 2016*
	ZK620	Eurofighter Typhoon	BAE Systems, for R Saudi AF as 8021
	ZK621	Eurofighter Typhoon	BAE Systems, for R Saudi AF as 8022
	ZK622	Eurofighter Typhoon	BAE Systems, for R Saudi AF as 8023
	ZK623	Eurofighter Typhoon	BAE Systems, for R Saudi AF as 8024
	ZK848	McD F-4F Phantom II (38+48)	For Hawker Hunter Aviation
	ZM135	Lockheed Martin F-35B Lightning II (168315/BK-1)	RAF No 17(R) Sqn, Edwards AFB, California
	ZM136	Lockheed Martin F-35B Lightning II (168316/BK-2)	RAF No 17(R) Sqn, Edwards AFB, California
	ZM137	Lockheed Martin F-35B Lightning II (168737/BK-3)	RAF/VMFAT-501, MCAS Beaufort, South Carolina
	ZM138	Lockheed Martin F-35B Lightning II (169170/BK-4)	RAF No 17(R) Sqn, Edwards AFB, California
	ZM139	Lockheed Martin F-35B Lightning II (169298/BK-5)	RAF No 617 Sqn, MCAS Beaufort, South Carolina
	ZM140	Lockheed Martin F-35B Lightning II (169300/BK-6)	RAF No 617 Sqn, MCAS Beaufort, South Carolina
	ZM141	Lockheed Martin F-35B Lightning II (169301/BK-7)	RAF No 617 Sqn, MCAS Beaufort, South Carolina
	ZM142	Lockheed Martin F-35B Lightning II (169302/BK-8)	RAF No 617 Sqn, MCAS Beaufort, South Carolina
	ZM143	Lockheed Martin F-35B Lightning II (BK-9)	LMTAS, Fort Worth, USA, for RAF/RN
	ZM144	Lockheed Martin F-35B Lightning II (BK-10)	LMTAS, Fort Worth, USA, for RAF/RN
	ZM145	Lockheed Martin F-35B Lightning II (BK-11)	LMTAS, Fort Worth, USA, for RAF/RN
	ZM146	Lockheed Martin F-35B Lightning II (BK-12)	LMTAS, Fort Worth, USA, for RAF/RN
	ZM147	Lockheed Martin F-35B Lightning II (BK-13)	LMTAS, Fort Worth, USA, for RAF/RN

Serial	Type (code/other identity)	Owner/operator, location or fate	Notes
ZM148	Lockheed Martin F-35B Lightning II (BK-14)	LMTAS, Fort Worth, USA, for RAF/RN	
ZM149	Lockheed Martin F-35B Lightning II (BK-15)	LMTAS, Fort Worth, USA, for RAF/RN	
ZM150	Lockheed Martin F-35B Lightning II (BK-16)	LMTAS, Fort Worth, USA, for RAF/RN	
ZM151	Lockheed Martin F-35B Lightning II (BK-17)	LMTAS, Fort Worth, USA, for RAF/RN	
ZM152	Lockheed Martin F-35B Lightning II (BK-18)	LMTAS, Fort Worth, USA, for RAF/RN	
ZM153	Lockheed Martin F-35B Lightning II	Reservation for RAF/RN	
ZM154	Lockheed Martin F-35B Lightning II	Reservation for RAF/RN	
ZM155	Lockheed Martin F-35B Lightning II	Reservation for RAF/RN	
ZM156	Lockheed Martin F-35B Lightning II	Reservation for RAF/RN	
ZM157	Lockheed Martin F-35B Lightning II	Reservation for RAF/RN	
ZM158	Lockheed Martin F-35B Lightning II	Reservation for RAF/RN	
ZM159	Lockheed Martin F-35B Lightning II	Reservation for RAF/RN	
ZM160	Lockheed Martin F-35B Lightning II	Reservation for RAF/RN	
ZM161	Lockheed Martin F-35B Lightning II	Reservation for RAF/RN	
ZM162	Lockheed Martin F-35B Lightning II	Reservation for RAF/RN	
ZM163	Lockheed Martin F-35B Lightning II	Reservation for RAF/RN	
ZM164	Lockheed Martin F-35B Lightning II	Reservation for RAF/RN	
ZM165	Lockheed Martin F-35B Lightning II	Reservation for RAF/RN	
ZM166	Lockheed Martin F-35B Lightning II	Reservation for RAF/RN	
ZM167	Lockheed Martin F-35B Lightning II	Reservation for RAF/RN	
ZM168	Lockheed Martin F-35B Lightning II	Reservation for RAF/RN	
ZM169	Lockheed Martin F-35B Lightning II	Reservation for RAF/RN	
ZM170	Lockheed Martin F-35B Lightning II	Reservation for RAF/RN	
ZM171	Lockheed Martin F-35B Lightning II	Reservation for RAF/RN	
ZM172	Lockheed Martin F-35B Lightning II	Reservation for RAF/RN	
ZM173	Lockheed Martin F-35B Lightning II	Reservation for RAF/RN	
ZM174	Lockheed Martin F-35B Lightning II	Reservation for RAF/RN	
ZM175	Lockheed Martin F-35B Lightning II	Reservation for RAF/RN	
ZM176	Lockheed Martin F-35B Lightning II	Reservation for RAF/RN	
ZM177	Lockheed Martin F-35B Lightning II	Reservation for RAF/RN	
ZM178	Lockheed Martin F-35B Lightning II	Reservation for RAF/RN	
ZM179	Lockheed Martin F-35B Lightning II	Reservation for RAF/RN	
ZM180	Lockheed Martin F-35B Lightning II	Reservation for RAF/RN	
ZM181	Lockheed Martin F-35B Lightning II	Reservation for RAF/RN	
ZM182	Lockheed Martin F-35B Lightning II	Reservation for RAF/RN	
ZM183	Lockheed Martin F-35B Lightning II	Reservation for RAF/RN	
ZM184	Lockheed Martin F-35B Lightning II	Reservation for RAF/RN	
ZM185	Lockheed Martin F-35B Lightning II	Reservation for RAF/RN	
ZM186	Lockheed Martin F-35B Lightning II	Reservation for RAF/RN	
ZM187	Lockheed Martin F-35B Lightning II	Reservation for RAF/RN	
ZM188	Lockheed Martin F-35B Lightning II	Reservation for RAF/RN	
ZM189	Lockheed Martin F-35B Lightning II	Reservation for RAF/RN	
ZM190	Lockheed Martin F-35B Lightning II	Reservation for RAF/RN	
ZM191	Lockheed Martin F-35B Lightning II	Reservation for RAF/RN	
ZM192	Lockheed Martin F-35B Lightning II	Reservation for RAF/RN	
ZM193	Lockheed Martin F-35B Lightning II	Reservation for RAF/RN	
ZM194	Lockheed Martin F-35B Lightning II	Reservation for RAF/RN	
ZM195	Lockheed Martin F-35B Lightning II	Reservation for RAF/RN	
ZM196	Lockheed Martin F-35B Lightning II	Reservation for RAF/RN	
ZM197	Lockheed Martin F-35B Lightning II	Reservation for RAF/RN	
ZM198	Lockheed Martin F-35B Lightning II	Reservation for RAF/RN	
ZM199	Lockheed Martin F-35B Lightning II	Reservation for RAF/RN	
ZM200	Lockheed Martin F-35B Lightning II	Reservation for RAF/RN	
ZM300	Grob G120TP-A Prefect T1 (D-ETPJ/G-MFTS)	RAF No 3 FTS, Cranwell	
ZM301	Grob G120TP-A Prefect T1 (D-EGUX/G-MEFT)	RAF No 3 FTS, Cranwell	
ZM302	Grob G120TP-A Prefect T1	For RAF	
ZM303	Grob G120TP-A Prefect T1	For RAF	
ZM304	Grob G120TP-A Prefect T1	For RAF	
ZM305	Grob G120TP-A Prefect T1	For RAF	
ZM306	Grob G120TP-A Prefect T1	For RAF	
ZM307	Grob G120TP-A Prefect T1	For RAF	
ZM308	Grob G120TP-A Prefect T1	For RAF	

Notes	Serial	Type (code/other identity)	Owner/operator, location or fate
	ZM309	Grob G120TP-A Prefect T1	For RAF
	ZM310	Grob G120TP-A Prefect T1	For RAF
	ZM311	Grob G120TP-A Prefect T1	For RAF
	ZM312	Grob G120TP-A Prefect T1	For RAF
	ZM313	Grob G120TP-A Prefect T1	For RAF
	ZM314	Grob G120TP-A Prefect T1	For RAF
	ZM315	Grob G120TP-A Prefect T1	For RAF
	ZM316	Grob G120TP-A Prefect T1	For RAF
	ZM317	Grob G120TP-A Prefect T1	For RAF
	ZM318	Grob G120TP-A Prefect T1	For RAF
	ZM319	Grob G120TP-A Prefect T1	For RAF
	ZM320	Grob G120TP-A Prefect T1	For RAF
	ZM321	Grob G120TP-A Prefect T1	For RAF
	ZM322	Grob G120TP-A Prefect T1	For RAF
	ZM323	Beechcraft T-6C Texan II	For RAF
	ZM324	Beechcraft T-6C Texan II	For RAF
	ZM325	Beechcraft T-6C Texan II	For RAF
	ZM326	Beechcraft T-6C Texan II	For RAF
	ZM327	Beechcraft T-6C Texan II	For RAF
	ZM328	Beechcraft T-6C Texan II	For RAF
	ZM329	Beechcraft T-6C Texan II	For RAF
	ZM330	Beechcraft T-6C Texan II	For RAF
	ZM331	Beechcraft T-6C Texan II	For RAF
	ZM332	Beechcraft T-6C Texan II	For RAF
	ZM333	Embraer EMB-500 Phenom 100	Embraer, for RAF
	ZM334	Embraer EMB-500 Phenom 100 (PR-PHK)	Embraer, for RAF
	ZM335	Embraer EMB-500 Phenom 100	For RAF
	ZM336	Embraer EMB-500 Phenom 100	For RAF
	ZM337	Embraer EMB-500 Phenom 100	For RAF
	ZM398	Airbus A400M Atlas Full Flight Simulator	RAF Brize Norton
	ZM399	Airbus A400M Atlas Full Flight Simulator	RAF Brize Norton
	ZM400	Airbus A400M Atlas C1 (A4M015/EC-405)	RAF No 24 Sqn/No 70 Sqn, Brize Norton
	ZM401	Airbus A400M Atlas C1 (A4M016/EC-406)	RAF No 24 Sqn/No 70 Sqn, Brize Norton
	ZM402	Airbus A400M Atlas C1 (A4M017/EC-407)	RAF No 24 Sqn/No 70 Sqn, Brize Norton
	ZM403	Airbus A400M Atlas C1 (A4M020)	RAF No 24 Sqn/No 70 Sqn, Brize Norton
	ZM404	Airbus A400M Atlas C1 (A4M021/EC-401)	RAF No 24 Sqn/No 70 Sqn, Brize Norton
	ZM405	Airbus A400M Atlas C1 (A4M024)	RAF No 24 Sqn/No 70 Sqn, Brize Norton
	ZM406	Airbus A400M Atlas C1 (A4M025/EC-405) $	RAF No 24 Sqn/No 70 Sqn, Brize Norton
	ZM407	Airbus A400M Atlas C1 (A4M026)	RAF No 24 Sqn/No 70 Sqn, Brize Norton
	ZM408	Airbus A400M Atlas C1 (A4M027)	RAF No 24 Sqn/No 70 Sqn, Brize Norton
	ZM409	Airbus A400M Atlas C1 (A4M034) $	RAF No 24 Sqn/No 70 Sqn, Brize Norton
	ZM410	Airbus A400M Atlas C1 (A4M038)	RAF No 24 Sqn/No 70 Sqn, Brize Norton
	ZM411	Airbus A400M Atlas C1 (A4M039)	RAF No 24 Sqn/No 70 Sqn, Brize Norton
	ZM412	Airbus A400M Atlas C1 (A4M042)	RAF No 24 Sqn/No 70 Sqn, Brize Norton
	ZM413	Airbus A400M Atlas C1 (A4M045)	RAF No 24 Sqn/No 70 Sqn, Brize Norton
	ZM414	Airbus A400M Atlas C1 (A4M047)	RAF No 24 Sqn/No 70 Sqn, Brize Norton
	ZM415	Airbus A400M Atlas C1 (A4M052)	Airbus Defence & Space, Seville, for RAF
	ZM416	Airbus A400M Atlas C1 (A4M058)	Airbus Defence & Space, Seville, for RAF
	ZM417	Airbus A400M Atlas C1	Airbus Defence & Space, Seville, for RAF
	ZM418	Airbus A400M Atlas C1	Reservation for RAF
	ZM419	Airbus A400M Atlas C1	Reservation for RAF
	ZM420	Airbus A400M Atlas C1	Reservation for RAF
	ZM421	Airbus A400M Atlas C1	Reservation for RAF
	ZM500	Airbus H145 Jupiter HT1 [00] (D-HADT/G-CJIV)	Airbus Helicopters, Kidlington
	ZM501	Airbus H145 Jupiter HT1 [01] (D-HADM/G-CJIZ/ G-CKGE)	Airbus Helicopters, Kidlington
	ZM502	Airbus H145 Jupiter HT1	Airbus Helicopters, for RAF
	ZM503	Airbus H145 Jupiter HT1	Reservation for MoD
	ZM504	Airbus H135 Juno HT1 [04] (D-HECZ/G-CJJG)	Airbus Helicopters, Donauwörth, for MoD
	ZM505	Airbus H135 Juno HT1 [05] (D-HECV/G-CJIW)	Airbus Helicopters, Kidlington
	ZM506	Airbus H135 Juno HT1 [06] (D-HECW/G-CJIY)	Airbus Helicopters, Kidlington
	ZM507	Airbus H135 Juno HT1	For MoD
	ZM508	Airbus H135 Juno HT1	For MoD

Serial	Type (code/other identity)	Owner/operator, location or fate	Notes
ZM509	Airbus H135 Juno HT1	For MoD	
ZM510	Airbus H135 Juno HT1	For MoD	
ZM511	Airbus H135 Juno HT1	For MoD	
ZM512	Airbus H135 Juno HT1	For MoD	
ZM513	Airbus H135 Juno HT1	For MoD	
ZM514	Airbus H135 Juno HT1	For MoD	
ZM515	Airbus H135 Juno HT1	For MoD	
ZM516	Airbus H135 Juno HT1	For MoD	
ZM517	Airbus H135 Juno HT1	For MoD	
ZM518	Airbus H135 Juno HT1	For MoD	
ZM519	Airbus H135 Juno HT1	For MoD	
ZM520	Airbus H135 Juno HT1	For MoD	
ZM521	Airbus H135 Juno HT1	For MoD	
ZM522	Airbus H135 Juno HT1	For MoD	
ZM523	Airbus H135 Juno HT1	For MoD	
ZM524	Airbus H135 Juno HT1	For MoD	
ZM525	Airbus H135 Juno HT1	For MoD	
ZM526	Airbus H135 Juno HT1	For MoD	
ZM527	Airbus H135 Juno HT1	For MoD	
ZM528	Airbus H135 Juno HT1	For MoD	
ZM529	Airbus H135 Juno HT1	For MoD	
ZM530	Airbus H135 Juno HT1	For MoD	
ZM531	Airbus H135 Juno HT1	For MoD	
ZM532	Airbus H135 Juno HT1	For MoD	
ZM533	Airbus H135 Juno HT1	Reservation for MoD	
ZM534	Airbus H135 Juno HT1	Reservation for MoD	
ZP801	Boeing P-8A Poseidon	For RAF	
ZP802	Boeing P-8A Poseidon	For RAF	
ZP803	Boeing P-8A Poseidon	For RAF	
ZP804	Boeing P-8A Poseidon	For RAF	
ZP805	Boeing P-8A Poseidon	For RAF	
ZP806	Boeing P-8A Poseidon	For RAF	
ZP807	Boeing P-8A Poseidon	For RAF	
ZP808	Boeing P-8A Poseidon	For RAF	
ZP809	Boeing P-8A Poseidon	For RAF	
ZP810	Boeing P-8A Poseidon	Reservation for RAF	
ZP811	Boeing P-8A Poseidon	Reservation for RAF	
ZP812	Boeing P-8A Poseidon	Reservation for RAF	
ZP813	Boeing P-8A Poseidon	Reservation for RAF	
ZP814	Boeing P-8A Poseidon	Reservation for RAF	
ZP815	Boeing P-8A Poseidon	Reservation for RAF	
ZR283	AgustaWestland AW139 (G-FBHA)	DHFS No 202(R) Sqn, Valley	
ZR322	Agusta A109E Power Elite (G-CDVC)	*Sold as G-CDVC, 12 April 2016*	
ZR324	Agusta A109E Power (G-EMHB)	DHFS, RAF Shawbury	
ZR325	Agusta A109E Power (G-BZEI)	DHFS, RAF Shawbury	
ZR339	AgustaWestland AW101 Mk.641 (ZW-4302)	Leonardo, Yeovil	
ZR342	AgustaWestland AW101 Mk.641 (ZW-4305)	Leonardo, Yeovil	
ZR343	AgustaWestland AW101 Mk.641 (ZW-4306) [01]	*To Indonesia as H-1001, 19 January 2017*	
ZR346	AgustaWestland AW101 Mk.641 (ZW-4309)	Leonardo, Yeovil	
ZR347	AgustaWestland AW101 Mk.641 (ZW-4310)	Leonardo, Yeovil, for Azerbaijan as 4K-Ai010	
ZR348	AgustaWestland AW101 Mk.641 (ZW-4311)	Leonardo, Yeovil	
ZR349	AgustaWestland AW101 Mk.641 (ZW-4312)	Leonardo, Yeovil	
ZR353	AgustaWestland AW101 Mk.611	*To the Italian AF as MM81865, 2016*	
ZR355	AgustaWestland AW101 Mk.611 [15-04]	*To the Italian AF as MM81867, 2016*	
ZR356	AgustaWestland AW101 Mk.611 [15-05]	Leonardo, Yeovil, for It AF as MM81868	
ZR357	AgustaWestland AW101 Mk.611 [15-06]	Leonardo, Yeovil, for It AF as MM81869	
ZR401	Eurofighter Typhoon	BAE Systems, for RAFO	
ZR402	Eurofighter Typhoon	BAE Systems, for RAFO	
ZR403	Eurofighter Typhoon	BAE Systems, for RAFO	
ZR404	Eurofighter Typhoon	BAE Systems, for RAFO	

Notes	Serial	Type (code/other identity)	Owner/operator, location or fate
	ZR405	Eurofighter Typhoon	BAE Systems, for RAFO
	ZR406	Eurofighter Typhoon	BAE Systems, for RAFO
	ZR407	Eurofighter Typhoon	BAE Systems, for RAFO
	ZR408	Eurofighter Typhoon	BAE Systems, for RAFO
	ZR409	Eurofighter Typhoon	BAE Systems, for RAFO
	ZR410	Eurofighter Typhoon T	BAE Systems, for RAFO
	ZR411	Eurofighter Typhoon T	BAE Systems, for RAFO
	ZR412	Eurofighter Typhoon T	BAE Systems, for RAFO
	ZS782	WS WG25 Sharpeye	The Helicopter Museum, Weston-super-Mare
	ZT800	WS Super Lynx Mk 300	Yeovil College, instructional use
	ZZ100	AgustaWestland AW101 Mk.612	Leonardo, Yeovil, for Norway as 0262
	ZZ101	AgustaWestland AW101 Mk.612	Leonardo, Yeovil, for Norway as 0264
	ZZ102	AgustaWestland AW101 Mk.612	Leonardo, Yeovil, for Norway as 0265
	ZZ103	AgustaWestland AW101 Mk.612	Leonardo, Yeovil, for Norway as 0268
	ZZ104	AgustaWestland AW101 Mk.612	Leonardo, Yeovil, for Norway as 0270
	ZZ105	AgustaWestland AW101 Mk.612	Leonardo, Yeovil, for Norway as 0273
	ZZ106	AgustaWestland AW101 Mk.612	Leonardo, Yeovil, for Norway as 0275
	ZZ107	AgustaWestland AW101 Mk.612	Leonardo, Yeovil, for Norway as 0276
	ZZ108	AgustaWestland AW101 Mk.612	Leonardo, Yeovil, for Norway as 0277
	ZZ109	AgustaWestland AW101 Mk.612	Leonardo, Yeovil, for Norway as 0278
	ZZ110	AgustaWestland AW101 Mk.612	Leonardo, Yeovil, for Norway as 0279
	ZZ111	AgustaWestland AW101 Mk.612	Leonardo, Yeovil, for Norway as 0280
	ZZ112	AgustaWestland AW101 Mk.612	Leonardo, Yeovil, for Norway as 0281
	ZZ113	AgustaWestland AW101 Mk.612	Leonardo, Yeovil, for Norway as 0282
	ZZ114	AgustaWestland AW101 Mk.612	Leonardo, Yeovil, for Norway as 0283
	ZZ115	AgustaWestland AW101 Mk.612	Leonardo, Yeovil, for Norway as 0284
	ZZ171	Boeing C-17A Globemaster III (00-201/N171UK)	RAF No 99 Sqn, Brize Norton
	ZZ172	Boeing C-17A Globemaster III (00-202/N172UK)	RAF No 99 Sqn, Brize Norton
	ZZ173	Boeing C-17A Globemaster III (00-203/N173UK)	RAF No 99 Sqn, Brize Norton
	ZZ174	Boeing C-17A Globemaster III (00-204/N174UK)	RAF No 99 Sqn, Brize Norton
	ZZ175	Boeing C-17A Globemaster III (06-0205/N9500Z)	RAF No 99 Sqn, Brize Norton
	ZZ176	Boeing C-17A Globemaster III (08-0206/N9500B) $	RAF No 99 Sqn, Brize Norton
	ZZ177	Boeing C-17A Globemaster III (09-8207/N9500B)	RAF No 99 Sqn, Brize Norton
	ZZ178	Boeing C-17A Globemaster III (12-0208/N9500N)	RAF No 99 Sqn, Brize Norton
	ZZ190	Hawker Hunter F58 (J-4066/G-HHAE)	HHA, Scampton
	ZZ191	Hawker Hunter F58 (J-4058/G-HHAD)	HHA, Scampton
	ZZ192	Grob G109B Vigilant T1 (D-KLVI) [SQ]	RAF, stored Syerston
	ZZ193	Grob G109B Vigilant T1 (D-KBLO) [SR]	RAF, stored Little Rissington
	ZZ194	Hawker Hunter F58 (J-4021/G-HHAC)	HHA, Scampton
	ZZ201	General Atomics Reaper RPAS (07-0111)	RAF No 13 Sqn/No 39 Sqn, Creech AFB, Nevada, USA
	ZZ202	General Atomics Reaper RPAS (07-0117)	RAF No 13 Sqn/No 39 Sqn, Creech AFB, Nevada, USA
	ZZ203	General Atomics Reaper RPAS (08-0113)	RAF No 13 Sqn/No 39 Sqn, Creech AFB, Nevada, USA
	ZZ204	General Atomics Reaper RPAS (10-0157)	RAF No 13 Sqn/No 39 Sqn, Creech AFB, Nevada, USA
	ZZ205	General Atomics Reaper RPAS (10-0162)	RAF No 13 Sqn/No 39 Sqn, Creech AFB, Nevada, USA
	ZZ206	General Atomics Reaper RPAS (12-0707)	RAF No 13 Sqn/No 39 Sqn, Creech AFB, Nevada, USA
	ZZ207	General Atomics Reaper RPAS (12-0708)	RAF No 13 Sqn/No 39 Sqn, Creech AFB, Nevada, USA
	ZZ208	General Atomics Reaper RPAS (12-0709)	RAF No 13 Sqn/No 39 Sqn, Creech AFB, Nevada, USA
	ZZ209	General Atomics Reaper RPAS (12-0710)	RAF No 13 Sqn/No 39 Sqn, Creech AFB, Nevada, USA
	ZZ210	General Atomics Reaper RPAS (12-0711)	RAF No 13 Sqn/No 39 Sqn, Creech AFB, Nevada, USA
	ZZ211	General Atomics Reaper RPAS	General Atomics, for RAF
	ZZ212	General Atomics Reaper RPAS	General Atomics, for RAF
	ZZ213	General Atomics Reaper RPAS	General Atomics, for RAF
	ZZ250	BAE Systems Taranis RPAS	BAE Systems, Warton
	ZZ251	BAE Systems HERTI RPAS	BAE Systems, Warton
	ZZ252	BAE Systems HERTI RPAS	BAE Systems, Woomera, Australia
	ZZ253	BAE Systems HERTI RPAS	BAE Systems, Woomera, Australia
	ZZ254	BAE Systems HERTI RPAS	BAE Systems, Warton
	ZZ330	Airbus A330 Voyager KC2 (MRTT017/EC-337/G-VYGA)	RAF No 10 Sqn/No 101 Sqn, Brize Norton

Serial	Type (code/other identity)	Owner/operator, location or fate	Notes
ZZ331	Airbus A330 Voyager KC2 (MRTT018/EC-331/G-VYGB)	RAF No 10 Sqn/No 101 Sqn, Brize Norton	
ZZ332	Airbus A330 Voyager KC3 (MRTT019/EC-330/G-VYGC)	RAF No 10 Sqn/No 101 Sqn, Brize Norton	
ZZ333	Airbus A330 Voyager KC3 (MRTT020/EC-337/G-VYGD)	RAF No 10 Sqn/No 101 Sqn, Brize Norton	
ZZ334	Airbus A330 Voyager KC3 (MRTT016/EC-335/G-VYGE)	RAF No 1312 Flt, Mount Pleasant, FI	
ZZ335	Airbus A330 Voyager KC3 (MRTT021/EC-338/G-VYGF)	RAF No 10 Sqn/No 101 Sqn, Brize Norton	
ZZ336	Airbus A330 Voyager KC3 (MRTT022/EC-333/G-VYGG)	RAF No 10 Sqn/No 101 Sqn, Brize Norton	
ZZ337	Airbus A330 Voyager KC3 (MRTT023/EC-336/G-VYGH)	RAF No 10 Sqn/No 101 Sqn, Brize Norton	
ZZ338	Airbus A330 Voyager KC3 (MRTT024/EC-331/G-VYGI)	RAF No 10 Sqn/No 101 Sqn, Brize Norton	
ZZ339	Airbus A330-243 (MRTT025/EC-333/G-VYGJ)	Airtanker Ltd, Brize Norton [flies as G-VYGJ]	
ZZ340	Airbus A330-243 (MRTT026/EC-330/G-VYGK)	Airtanker Ltd/Thomas Cook Airlines, Manchester [flies as G-VYGK]	
ZZ341	Airbus A330-243 (MRTT027/EC-336/G-VYGL)	Airtanker Ltd, Brize Norton [flies as G-VYGL]	
ZZ342	Airbus A330-243 (MRTT028/EC-332/G-VYGM)	Airtanker Ltd/Thomas Cook Airlines, Manchester [flies as G-VYGM]	
ZZ343	Airbus A330 Voyager KC2 (MRTT029/EC-331/G-VYGN)	RAF No 10 Sqn/No 101 Sqn, Brize Norton	
ZZ375	AgustaWestland AW159 Wildcat HMA2	RN No 825 NAS, Yeovilton	
ZZ376	AgustaWestland AW159 Wildcat HMA2	RN No 825 NAS, Yeovilton	
ZZ377	AgustaWestland AW159 Wildcat HMA2	RN WST, Yeovilton	
ZZ378	AgustaWestland AW159 Wildcat HMA2	RN No 825 NAS, Yeovilton	
ZZ379	AgustaWestland AW159 Wildcat HMA2	RN WST, Yeovilton	
ZZ380	AgustaWestland AW159 Wildcat HMA2	RN No 815 NAS, Yeovilton	
ZZ381	AgustaWestland AW159 Wildcat HMA2	RN No 815 NAS, Yeovilton	
ZZ382	AgustaWestland AW159 Wildcat AH1	MoD/Leonardo, Yeovil	
ZZ383	AgustaWestland AW159 Wildcat AH1	RM No 847 NAS, Yeovilton	
ZZ384	AgustaWestland AW159 Wildcat AH1	AAC No 1 Regiment, Yeovilton	
ZZ385	AgustaWestland AW159 Wildcat AH1	AAC WST, Yeovilton	
ZZ386	AgustaWestland AW159 Wildcat AH1	AAC WST, Yeovilton	
ZZ387	AgustaWestland AW159 Wildcat AH1	AAC No 1 Regiment, Yeovilton	
ZZ388	AgustaWestland AW159 Wildcat AH1	AAC WCM, Yeovilton	
ZZ389	AgustaWestland AW159 Wildcat AH1	RM No 847 NAS, Yeovilton	
ZZ390	AgustaWestland AW159 Wildcat AH1	AAC No 1 Regiment, Yeovilton	
ZZ391	AgustaWestland AW159 Wildcat AH1	AAC No 1 Regiment, Yeovilton	
ZZ392	AgustaWestland AW159 Wildcat AH1	RM No 847 NAS, Yeovilton	
ZZ393	AgustaWestland AW159 Wildcat AH1	AAC WST, Yeovilton	
ZZ394	AgustaWestland AW159 Wildcat AH1	RM No 847 NAS, Yeovilton	
ZZ395	AgustaWestland AW159 Wildcat AH1	RM No 847 NAS, Yeovilton	
ZZ396	AgustaWestland AW159 Wildcat HMA2	RN No 825 NAS, Yeovilton	
ZZ397	AgustaWestland AW159 Wildcat HMA2	RM No 825 NAS, Yeovilton	
ZZ398	AgustaWestland AW159 Wildcat AH1	RM No 847 NAS, Yeovilton	
ZZ399	AgustaWestland AW159 Wildcat AH1	MoD/Leonardo, stored Yeovil	
ZZ400	AgustaWestland AW159 Wildcat (TI01)	DSAE SAAE, Lyneham	
ZZ401	AgustaWestland AW159 Wildcat (TI02)	RNAS Yeovilton, instructional use	
ZZ402	AgustaWestland AW159 Wildcat (TI03)	DSAE HMS Sultan, stored Gosport	
ZZ403	AgustaWestland AW159 Wildcat AH1	AAC No 1 Regiment, Yeovilton	
ZZ404	AgustaWestland AW159 Wildcat AH1	AAC No 1 Regiment, Yeovilton	
ZZ405	AgustaWestland AW159 Wildcat AH1	MoD/Leonardo, stored Yeovil	
ZZ406	AgustaWestland AW159 Wildcat AH1	AAC WST, Yeovilton	
ZZ407	AgustaWestland AW159 Wildcat AH1	RM No 847 NAS, Yeovilton	
ZZ408	AgustaWestland AW159 Wildcat AH1	AAC No 1 Regiment, Yeovilton	
ZZ409	AgustaWestland AW159 Wildcat AH1	AAC WST, Yeovilton	
ZZ410	AgustaWestland AW159 Wildcat AH1	RM No 847 NAS, Yeovilton	
ZZ413	AgustaWestland AW159 Wildcat HMA2	RN No 825 NAS, Yeovilton	
ZZ414	AgustaWestland AW159 Wildcat HMA2	RN No 815 NAS, Yeovilton	

Notes	Serial	Type (code/other identity)	Owner/operator, location or fate
	ZZ415	AgustaWestland AW159 Wildcat HMA2	MoD/Leonardo, Yeovil
	ZZ416	Hawker Beechcraft Shadow R1 (G-JENC)	RAF No 14 Sqn, Waddington
	ZZ417	Hawker Beechcraft Shadow R1 (G-NICY)	RAF No 14 Sqn, Waddington
	ZZ418	Hawker Beechcraft Shadow R1 (G-JIMG)	RAF No 14 Sqn, Waddington
	ZZ419	Hawker Beechcraft Shadow R1 (G-OTCS)	RAF No 14 Sqn, Waddington
	ZZ500	Hawker Beechcraft Avenger T1 (G-MFTA)	RN No 750 NAS, Culdrose
	ZZ501	Hawker Beechcraft Avenger T1 (G-MFTB)	RN No 750 NAS, Culdrose
	ZZ502	Hawker Beechcraft Avenger T1 (G-MFTC)	RN No 750 NAS, Culdrose
	ZZ503	Hawker Beechcraft Avenger T1 (G-MFTD)	RN No 750 NAS, Culdrose
	ZZ504	Hawker Beechcraft Shadow R1 (G-CGUM)	RAF No 14 Sqn, Waddington
	ZZ510	AgustaWestland AW159 Wildcat AH1	AAC WST, Yeovilton
	ZZ511	AgustaWestland AW159 Wildcat AH1	AAC WCM, Yeovilton
	ZZ512	AgustaWestland AW159 Wildcat AH1	RM No 847 NAS, Yeovilton
	ZZ513	AgustaWestland AW159 Wildcat HMA2	RN No 825 NAS, Yeovilton
	ZZ514	AgustaWestland AW159 Wildcat HMA2	RN No 825 NAS, Yeovilton
	ZZ515	AgustaWestland AW159 Wildcat HMA2	RN No 815 NAS, Yeovilton
	ZZ516	AgustaWestland AW159 Wildcat HMA2	RN No 815 NAS, Yeovilton
	ZZ517	AgustaWestland AW159 Wildcat HMA2	RN No 815 NAS, Yeovilton
	ZZ518	AgustaWestland AW159 Wildcat HMA2	RN No 825 NAS, Yeovilton
	ZZ519	AgustaWestland AW159 Wildcat HMA2	RN No 825 NAS, Yeovilton
	ZZ520	AgustaWestland AW159 Wildcat AH1	AAC No 1 Regiment, Yeovilton
	ZZ521	AgustaWestland AW159 Wildcat AH1	RM No 847 NAS, Yeovilton
	ZZ522	AgustaWestland AW159 Wildcat HMA2	RN No 825 NAS, Yeovilton
	ZZ523	AgustaWestland AW159 Wildcat AH1	AAC WCM, Yeovilton
	ZZ524	AgustaWestland AW159 Wildcat AH1	AAC No 1 Regiment, Yeovilton
	ZZ525	AgustaWestland AW159 Wildcat AH1	AAC No 1 Regiment, Yeovilton
	ZZ526	AgustaWestland AW159 Wildcat AH1	AAC No 1 Regiment, Yeovilton
	ZZ527	AgustaWestland AW159 Wildcat AH1	AAC No 1 Regiment, Yeovilton
	ZZ528	AgustaWestland AW159 Wildcat HMA2	RN No 815 NAS, Yeovilton
	ZZ529	AgustaWestland AW159 Wildcat HMA2	RN No 815 NAS, Yeovilton
	ZZ530	AgustaWestland AW159 Wildcat HMA2	RN No 825 NAS, Yeovilton
	ZZ531	AgustaWestland AW159 Wildcat HMA2	RN No 825 NAS, Yeovilton
	ZZ532	AgustaWestland AW159 Wildcat HMA2	RN No 815 NAS, Yeovilton
	ZZ533	AgustaWestland AW159 Wildcat HMA2	RN No 815 NAS, Yeovilton
	ZZ534	AgustaWestland AW159 Wildcat HMA2	RN No 825 NAS, Yeovilton
	ZZ535	AgustaWestland AW159 Wildcat HMA2	RN No 825 NAS, Yeovilton
	ZZ541	AgustaWestland AW159 Mk.210	*To RoK Navy as 15-0601, June 2016*
	ZZ542	AgustaWestland AW159 Mk.210	*To RoK Navy as 15-0602, June 2016*
	ZZ543	AgustaWestland AW159 Mk.210	*To RoK Navy as 15-0603, June 2016*
	ZZ544	AgustaWestland AW159 Mk.210	*To RoK Navy as 15-0605, June 2016*
	ZZ545	AgustaWestland AW159 Mk.210	*To RoK Navy as 16-0606, 22 November 2016*
	ZZ546	AgustaWestland AW159 Mk.210	*To RoK Navy as 16-0607, 22 November 2016*
	ZZ547	AgustaWestland AW159 Mk.210	*To RoK Navy as 16-0608, 23 November 2016*
	ZZ548	AgustaWestland AW159 Mk.210	*To RoK Navy as 16-0609, 23 November 2016*
	ZZ664	Boeing RC-135W (64-14833) $	RAF No 51 Sqn, Waddington
	ZZ665	Boeing RC-135W (64-14838)	RAF No 51 Sqn, Waddington
	ZZ666	Boeing RC-135W (64-14830)	Boeing, for RAF

Serial	Type (code/other identity)	Owner/operator, location or fate	Notes
G-BVRJ	BAe RJ.70ER	MoD/ETPS, Boscombe Down	
G-BYUA	Grob G.115E Tutor T1	VT Aerospace/No 16(R) Sqn/No 57(R) Sqn, Cranwell	
G-BYUB	Grob G.115E Tutor T1	VT Aerospace/No 16(R) Sqn/No 57(R) Sqn, Cranwell	
G-BYUC	Grob G.115E Tutor T1	VT Aerospace/No 16(R) Sqn/No 57(R) Sqn, Cranwell	
G-BYUD	Grob G.115E Tutor T1	VT Aerospace/No 16(R) Sqn/No 57(R) Sqn, Cranwell	
G-BYUE	Grob G.115E Tutor T1	VT Aerospace/Cambridge UAS/East Midlands Universities AS/University of London AS/No 115(R) Sqn, Wittering	
G-BYUF	Grob G.115E Tutor T1	VT Aerospace/University of Birmingham AS, Cosford	
G-BYUG	Grob G.115E Tutor T1	VT Aerospace/No 16(R) Sqn/No 57(R) Sqn, Cranwell	
G-BYUH	Grob G.115E Tutor T1	VT Aerospace/No 1 EFTS/676 Sqn, Middle Wallop	
G-BYUI	Grob G.115E Tutor T1	VT Aerospace/Southampton UAS, Boscombe Down	
G-BYUJ	Grob G.115E Tutor T1	VT Aerospace/East of Scotland UAS, Leuchars	
G-BYUK	Grob G.115E Tutor T1	VT Aerospace/Cambridge UAS/East Midlands Universities AS/University of London AS/No 115(R) Sqn, Wittering	
G-BYUL	Grob G.115E Tutor T1	VT Aerospace/Liverpool UAS/Manchester and Salford Universities AS, Woodvale	
G-BYUM	Grob G.115E Tutor T1	VT Aerospace/Cambridge UAS/East Midlands Universities AS/University of London AS/No 115(R) Sqn, Wittering	
G-BYUN	Grob G.115E Tutor T1	VT Aerospace/No 16(R) Sqn/No 57(R) Sqn, Cranwell	
G-BYUO	Grob G.115E Tutor T1	VT Aerospace/Cambridge UAS/East Midlands Universities AS/University of London AS/No 115(R) Sqn, Wittering	
G-BYUP	Grob G.115E Tutor T1	VT Aerospace/Cambridge UAS/East Midlands Universities AS/University of London AS/No 115(R) Sqn, Wittering	
G-BYUR	Grob G.115E Tutor T1	VT Aerospace/East of Scotland UAS, Leuchars	
G-BYUS	Grob G.115E Tutor T1	VT Aerospace/No 16(R) Sqn/No 57(R) Sqn, Cranwell	
G-BYUU	Grob G.115E Tutor T1	VT Aerospace/Cambridge UAS/East Midlands Universities AS/University of London AS/No 115(R) Sqn, Wittering	
G-BYUV	Grob G.115E Tutor T1	VT Aerospace/Bristol UAS, Boscombe Down	
G-BYUW	Grob G.115E Tutor T1	VT Aerospace/No 16(R) Sqn/No 57(R) Sqn, Cranwell	
G-BYUX	Grob G.115E Tutor T1	VT Aerospace/No 16(R) Sqn/No 57(R) Sqn, Cranwell	
G-BYUY	Grob G.115E Tutor T1	VT Aerospace/Cambridge UAS/East Midlands Universities AS/University of London AS/No 115(R) Sqn, Wittering	
G-BYUZ	Grob G.115E Tutor T1	VT Aerospace/No 16(R) Sqn/No 57(R) Sqn, Cranwell	
G-BYVA	Grob G.115E Tutor T1	VT Aerospace/Bristol UAS, Boscombe Down	
G-BYVB	Grob G.115E Tutor T1	VT Aerospace/University of Wales AS, St Athan	
G-BYVC	Grob G.115E Tutor T1	VT Aerospace/Cambridge UAS/East Midlands Universities AS/University of London AS/No 115(R) Sqn, Wittering	
G-BYVD	Grob G.115E Tutor T1	VT Aerospace/Southampton UAS, Boscombe Down	
G-BYVE	Grob G.115E Tutor T1	VT Aerospace/Cambridge UAS/East Midlands Universities AS/University of London AS/No 115(R) Sqn, Wittering	
G-BYVF	Grob G.115E Tutor T1	VT Aerospace/RN No 727 NAS, Yeovilton	
G-BYVG	Grob G.115E Tutor T1	VT Aerospace/Cambridge UAS/East Midlands Universities AS/University of London AS/No 115(R) Sqn, Wittering	
G-BYVH	Grob G.115E Tutor T1	VT Aerospace/No 16(R) Sqn/No 57(R) Sqn, Cranwell	
G-BYVI	Grob G.115E Tutor T1	VT Aerospace/Cambridge UAS/East Midlands Universities AS/University of London AS/No 115(R) Sqn, Wittering	
G-BYVJ	Grob G.115E Tutor T1	VT Aerospace/Yorkshire Universities AS, Linton-on-Ouse	
G-BYVK	Grob G.115E Tutor T1	VT Aerospace/RN No 727 NAS, Yeovilton	
G-BYVL	Grob G.115E Tutor T1	VT Aerospace/University of Birmingham AS, Cosford	
G-BYVM	Grob G.115E Tutor T1	VT Aerospace/No 16(R) Sqn/No 57(R) Sqn, Cranwell	
G-BYVO	Grob G.115E Tutor T1	VT Aerospace/No 16(R) Sqn/No 57(R) Sqn, Cranwell	
G-BYVP	Grob G.115E Tutor T1	VT Aerospace/Cambridge UAS/East Midlands Universities AS/University of London AS/No 115(R) Sqn, Wittering	
G-BYVR	Grob G.115E Tutor T1	VT Aerospace/Cambridge UAS/East Midlands Universities AS/University of London AS/No 115(R) Sqn, Wittering	
G-BYVS	Grob G.115E Tutor T1	VT Aerospace/University of Wales AS, St Athan	
G-BYVT	Grob G.115E Tutor T1	VT Aerospace/No 16(R) Sqn/No 57(R) Sqn, Cranwell	
G-BYVU	Grob G.115E Tutor T1	VT Aerospace/No 1 EFTS/676 Sqn, Middle Wallop	

Notes	Serial	Type (code/other identity)	Owner/operator, location or fate
	G-BYVV	Grob G.115E Tutor T1	VT Aerospace/Northumbrian Universities AS, Leeming
	G-BYVW	Grob G.115E Tutor T1	VT Aerospace/University of Wales AS, St Athan
	G-BYVX	Grob G.115E Tutor T1	VT Aerospace/Yorkshire Universities AS, Linton-on-Ouse
	G-BYVY	Grob G.115E Tutor T1	VT Aerospace/Southampton UAS, Boscombe Down
	G-BYVZ	Grob G.115E Tutor T1	VT Aerospace/No 16(R) Sqn/No 57(R) Sqn, Cranwell
	G-BYWA	Grob G.115E Tutor T1	VT Aerospace/Yorkshire Universities AS, Linton-on-Ouse
	G-BYWB	Grob G.115E Tutor T1	VT Aerospace/No 16(R) Sqn/No 57(R) Sqn, Cranwell
	G-BYWC	Grob G.115E Tutor T1	VT Aerospace/Bristol UAS, Boscombe Down
	G-BYWD	Grob G.115E Tutor T1	VT Aerospace/University of Birmingham AS, Cosford
	G-BYWE	Grob G.115E Tutor T1	VT Aerospace/Liverpool UAS/Manchester and Salford Universities AS, Woodvale
	G-BYWF	Grob G.115E Tutor T1	VT Aerospace/Cambridge UAS/East Midlands Universities AS/University of London AS/No 115(R) Sqn, Wittering
	G-BYWG	Grob G.115E Tutor T1	VT Aerospace/University of Birmingham AS, Cosford
	G-BYWH	Grob G.115E Tutor T1	VT Aerospace/Cambridge UAS/East Midlands Universities AS/University of London AS/No 115(R) Sqn, Wittering
	G-BYWI	Grob G.115E Tutor T1	VT Aerospace/No 16(R) Sqn/No 57(R) Sqn, Cranwell
	G-BYWJ	Grob G.115E Tutor T1	VT Aerospace/No 16(R) Sqn/No 57(R) Sqn, Cranwell
	G-BYWK	Grob G.115E Tutor T1	VT Aerospace/Northumbrian Universities AS, Leeming
	G-BYWL	Grob G.115E Tutor T1	VT Aerospace/Southampton UAS, Boscombe Down
	G-BYWM	Grob G.115E Tutor T1	VT Aerospace/RN No 727 NAS, Yeovilton
	G-BYWN	Grob G.115E Tutor T1	VT Aerospace/No 16(R) Sqn/No 57(R) Sqn, Cranwell
	G-BYWO	Grob G.115E Tutor T1	VT Aerospace/Cambridge UAS/East Midlands Universities AS/University of London AS/No 115(R) Sqn, Wittering
	G-BYWP	Grob G.115E Tutor T1	VT Aerospace/No 16(R) Sqn/No 57(R) Sqn, Cranwell
	G-BYWR	Grob G.115E Tutor T1	VT Aerospace/No 16(R) Sqn/No 57(R) Sqn, Cranwell
	G-BYWS	Grob G.115E Tutor T1	VT Aerospace/No 16(R) Sqn/No 57(R) Sqn, Cranwell
	G-BYWT	Grob G.115E Tutor T1	VT Aerospace/Cambridge UAS/East Midlands Universities AS/University of London AS/No 115(R) Sqn, Wittering
	G-BYWU	Grob G.115E Tutor T1	VT Aerospace/University of Birmingham AS, Cosford
	G-BYWV	Grob G.115E Tutor T1	VT Aerospace/Yorkshire Universities AS, Linton-on-Ouse
	G-BYWW	Grob G.115E Tutor T1	VT Aerospace/Southampton UAS, Boscombe Down
	G-BYWX	Grob G.115E Tutor T1	VT Aerospace/Cambridge UAS/East Midlands Universities AS/University of London AS/No 115(R) Sqn, Wittering
	G-BYWY	Grob G.115E Tutor T1	VT Aerospace/Oxford UAS, Benson
	G-BYWZ	Grob G.115E Tutor T1	VT Aerospace/Cambridge UAS/East Midlands Universities AS/University of London AS/No 115(R) Sqn, Wittering
	G-BYXA	Grob G.115E Tutor T1	VT Aerospace/University of Birmingham AS, Cosford
	G-BYXB	Grob G.115E Tutor T1	VT Aerospace/No 16(R) Sqn/No 57(R) Sqn, Cranwell
	G-BYXC	Grob G.115E Tutor T1	VT Aerospace/Cambridge UAS/East Midlands Universities AS/University of London AS/No 115(R) Sqn, Wittering
	G-BYXD	Grob G.115E Tutor T1	VT Aerospace/Southampton UAS, Boscombe Down
	G-BYXE	Grob G.115E Tutor T1	VT Aerospace/Cambridge UAS/East Midlands Universities AS/University of London AS/No 115(R) Sqn, Wittering
	G-BYXF	Grob G.115E Tutor T1	VT Aerospace/No 1 EFTS/676 Sqn, Middle Wallop
	G-BYXG	Grob G.115E Tutor T1	VT Aerospace/No 16(R) Sqn/No 57(R) Sqn, Cranwell
	G-BYXH	Grob G.115E Tutor T1	VT Aerospace/Cambridge UAS/East Midlands Universities AS/University of London AS/No 115(R) Sqn, Wittering
	G-BYXI	Grob G.115E Tutor T1	VT Aerospace/No 1 EFTS/676 Sqn, Middle Wallop
	G-BYXJ	Grob G.115E Tutor T1	VT Aerospace/No 1 EFTS/676 Sqn, Middle Wallop
	G-BYXK	Grob G.115E Tutor T1	VT Aerospace/RN No 727 NAS, Yeovilton
	G-BYXL	Grob G.115E Tutor T1	VT Aerospace/East of Scotland UAS, Leuchars
	G-BYXM	Grob G.115E Tutor T1 $	VT Aerospace/No 16(R) Sqn/No 57(R) Sqn, Cranwell
	G-BYXN	Grob G.115E Tutor T1	VT Aerospace/Cambridge UAS/East Midlands Universities AS/University of London AS/No 115(R) Sqn, Wittering
	G-BYXO	Grob G.115E Tutor T1	VT Aerospace/No 16(R) Sqn/No 57(R) Sqn, Cranwell
	G-BYXP	Grob G.115E Tutor T1	VT Aerospace/Cambridge UAS/East Midlands Universities AS/University of London AS/No 115(R) Sqn, Wittering

Serial	Type (code/other identity)	Owner/operator, location or fate	Notes
G-BYXS	Grob G.115E Tutor T1	VT Aerospace/RN No 727 NAS, Yeovilton	
G-BYXT	Grob G.115E Tutor T1	VT Aerospace/Yorkshire Universities AS, Linton-on-Ouse	
G-BYXX	Grob G.115E Tutor T1	VT Aerospace/East of Scotland UAS, Leuchars	
G-BYXY	Grob G.115E Tutor T1	VT Aerospace/No 16(R) Sqn/No 57(R) Sqn, Cranwell	
G-BYXZ	Grob G.115E Tutor T1	VT Aerospace/No 16(R) Sqn/No 57(R) Sqn, Cranwell	
G-BYYA	Grob G.115E Tutor T1	VT Aerospace/Northumbrian Universities AS, Leeming	
G-BYYB	Grob G.115E Tutor T1	VT Aerospace/No 16(R) Sqn/No 57(R) Sqn, Cranwell	
G-CEYO	AS350BB Squirrel HT3 [00]	DHFS stored, RAF Shawbury	
G-CGKA	Grob G.115E Tutor T1EA	*To Finnish Air Force as GO-1, November 2016*	
G-CGKB	Grob G.115E Tutor T1EA	VT Aerospace/No 3 FTS/45(R) Sqn, D Flt, Cranwell	
G-CGKC	Grob G.115E Tutor T1EA	VT Aerospace/No 3 FTS/45(R) Sqn, D Flt, Cranwell	
G-CGKD	Grob G.115E Tutor T1EA	VT Aerospace/Oxford UAS, Benson	
G-CGKE	Grob G.115E Tutor T1EA	VT Aerospace/No 3 FTS/45(R) Sqn, D Flt, Cranwell	
G-CGKF	Grob G.115E Tutor T1EA	VT Aerospace/Universities of Glasgow & Strathclyde AS, Glasgow	
G-CGKG	Grob G.115E Tutor T1EA	VT Aerospace/Oxford UAS, Benson	
G-CGKH	Grob G.115E Tutor T1EA	VT Aerospace/Oxford UAS, Benson	
G-CGKI	Grob G.115E Tutor T1EA	VT Aerospace/No 3 FTS/45(R) Sqn, D Flt, Cranwell	
G-CGKJ	Grob G.115E Tutor T1EA	VT Aerospace/Oxford UAS, Benson	
G-CGKK	Grob G.115E Tutor T1EA	VT Aerospace/Oxford UAS, Benson	
G-CGKL	Grob G.115E Tutor T1EA	VT Aerospace/No 3 FTS/45(R) Sqn, D Flt, Cranwell	
G-CGKM	Grob G.115E Tutor T1EA	VT Aerospace/Universities of Glasgow & Strathclyde AS, Glasgow	
G-CGKN	Grob G.115E Tutor T1EA	VT Aerospace/Oxford UAS, Benson	
G-CGKO	Grob G.115E Tutor T1EA	VT Aerospace/Liverpool UAS/Manchester and Salford Universities AS, Woodvale	
G-CGKP	Grob G.115E Tutor T1EA	VT Aerospace/Oxford UAS, Benson	
G-CGKR	Grob G.115E Tutor T1EA	VT Aerospace/No 3 FTS/45(R) Sqn, D Flt, Cranwell	
G-CGKS	Grob G.115E Tutor T1EA	VT Aerospace/Universities of Glasgow & Strathclyde AS, Glasgow	
G-CGKT	Grob G.115E Tutor T1EA	VT Aerospace/Oxford UAS, Benson	
G-CGKU	Grob G.115E Tutor T1EA	VT Aerospace/Liverpool UAS/Manchester and Salford Universities AS, Woodvale	
G-CGKV	Grob G.115E Tutor T1EA	VT Aerospace/University of Birmingham AS, Cosford	
G-CGKW	Grob G.115E Tutor T1EA	VT Aerospace/No 3 FTS/45(R) Sqn, D Flt, Cranwell	
G-CGKX	Grob G.115E Tutor T1EA	VT Aerospace/Liverpool UAS/Manchester and Salford Universities AS, Woodvale	
G-DOIT	AS350BB Squirrel HT3 [99]	DHFS stored, RAF Shawbury	
G-FFRA	Dassault Falcon 20DC (N902FR)	Cobham Leasing Ltd, Bournemouth	
G-FRAD	Dassault Falcon 20E (9M-BDK)	Cobham Leasing Ltd, Bournemouth	
G-FRAF	Dassault Falcon 20E (N911FR)	Cobham Leasing Ltd, Bournemouth	
G-FRAH	Dassault Falcon 20DC (N900FR)	Cobham Leasing Ltd, Durham/Tees Valley	
G-FRAI	Dassault Falcon 20E (N901FR)	Cobham Leasing Ltd, Bournemouth	
G-FRAJ	Dassault Falcon 20E (N903FR)	Cobham Leasing Ltd, Bournemouth	
G-FRAK	Dassault Falcon 20DC (N905FR)	Cobham Leasing Ltd, Durham/Tees Valley	
G-FRAL	Dassault Falcon 20DC (N904FR)	Cobham Leasing Ltd, Durham/Tees Valley	
G-FRAO	Dassault Falcon 20DC (N906FR)	Cobham Leasing Ltd, Bournemouth	
G-FRAP	Dassault Falcon 20DC (N908FR)	Cobham Leasing Ltd, Bournemouth	
G-FRAR	Dassault Falcon 20DC (N909FR)	Cobham Leasing Ltd, Bournemouth	
G-FRAS	Dassault Falcon 20C (117501)	Cobham Leasing Ltd, Bournemouth	
G-FRAT	Dassault Falcon 20C (117502)	Cobham Leasing Ltd, Bournemouth	
G-FRAU	Dassault Falcon 20C (117504)	Cobham Leasing Ltd, Bournemouth	
G-FRAW	Dassault Falcon 20ECM (117507)	Cobham Leasing Ltd, Bournemouth	
G-LBSB	Hawker Beechcraft Super King Air 350C	RAF No 14 Sqn, Waddington	
G-LTPA	Diamond DA.42M-NG Twin Star	*To QQ103, 3 August 2016*	

1764M/K4972	7491M/WT569	7839M/WV781	8019M/WZ869
2015M/K5600	7496M/WT612	7841M/WV783	8021M/XL824
2292M/K8203	7499M/WT555	7851M/WZ706	8027M/XM555
2361M/K6035	7510M/WT694	7854M/XM191	8032M/XH837
3118M/H5199/(BK892)	7525M/WT619	7855M/XK416	8034M/*XL554*/(XL703)
3858M/X7688	7530M/WT648	7859M/XP283	8041M/XF690
4354M/BL614	7532M/WT651	7861M/*XL738*/(XM565)	8043M/XF836
4552M/T5298	7533M/WT680	7862M/XR246	8046M/XL770
4887M/JN768	7544M/WN904	7863M/*XP248*	8049M/WE168
5377M/EP120	7548M/PS915	7864M/XP244	8050M/XG329
5405M/LF738	7556M/WK584	7865M/TX226	8052M/WH166
5466M/*BN230*/(LF751)	7564M/XE982	7866M/XH278	8054AM/XM410
5690M/MK356	7570M/XD674	7868M/WZ736	8054BM/XM417
5718M/BM597	7582M/WP190	7869M/WK935	8055BM/XM402
5758M/DG202	7583M/WP185	7872M/*WZ826*/(XD826)	8055BM/XM404
6457M/ML427	7602M/WE600	7881M/WD413	8056M/XG337
6490M/LA255	7605M/WS692	7882M/XD525	8057M/XR243
6640M/RM694	7606M/*XF688*/ (WV562)	7883M/XT150	8063M/WT536
6850M/TE184	7607M/TJ138	7887M/XD375	8070M/EP120
6946M/RW388	7615M/WV679	7891M/XM693	8072M/PK624
6948M/DE673	7616M/WW388	7894M/XD818	8073M/TB252
6960M/MT847	7618M/WW442	7895M/WF784	8075M/RW382
7008M/EE549	7622M/WV606	7898M/XP854	8078M/XM351
7014M/N6720	7631M/VX185	7900M/WA576	8080M/XM480
7015M/NL985	7641M/XA634	7906M/WH132	8081M/XM468
7035M/*K2567*/(DE306)	7645M/WD293	7917M/WA591	8082M/XM409
7060M/VF301	7648M/XF785	7930M/WH301	8086M/TB752
7090M/EE531	7673M/WV332	7931M/RD253	8092M/WK654
7118M/LA198	7689M/*WW421*/(WW450)	7932M/WZ744	8094M/WT520
7119M/LA226	7696M/WV493	7933M/XR220	8097M/XN492
7150M/PK683	7698M/WV499	7937M/WS843	8101M/WH984
7154M/WB188	7704M/TW536	7938M/XH903	8102M/WT486
7174M/*VX272*	7705M/WL505	7939M/XD596	8103M/WR985
7175M/VV106	7706M/WB584	7940M/XL764	8106M/WR982
7200M/VT812	7709M/WT933	7955M/XH767	8114M/WL798
7241M/TE311/*(MK178)*	7711M/PS915	7957M/XF545	8117M/WR974
7243M/TE462	7712M/WK281	7960M/WS726	8118M/WZ549
7245M/RW382	7715M/XK724	7961M/WS739	8119M/WR971
7246M/TD248	7716M/WS776	7964M/WS760	8121M/XM474
7256M/TB752	7718M/WA577	7965M/WS792	8124M/WZ572
7257M/TB252	7719M/WK277	7967M/WS788	8128M/WH775
7279M/TB752	7726M/XM373	7969M/WS840	8130M/WH798
7281M/TB252	7741M/VZ477	7971M/XK699	8131M/WT507
7288M/PK724	7750M/*WK864*/(WL168)	7973M/WS807	8140M/XJ571
7293M/*TB675*/(RW393)	7751M/WL131	7979M/XM529	8142M/XJ560
7323M/VV217	7755M/WG760	7980M/XM561	8147M/XR526
7325M/R5868	7759M/PK664	7982M/XH892	8151M/WV795
7326M/VN485	7761M/XH318	7983M/XD506	8153M/WV903
7362M/475081/(VP546)	7762M/XE670	7984M/XN597	8154M/WV908
7416M/WN907	7764M/XH318	7986M/WG777	8155M/WV797
7421M/WT660	7770M/*XF506*/(WT746)	7988M/XL149	8156M/XE339
7422M/WT684	7793M/XG523	7990M/XD452	8158M/XE369
7428M/WK198	7798M/XH783	7997M/XG452	8162M/WM913
7432M/WZ724	7806M/TA639	7998M/*XM515*/(XD515)	8164M/*WN105*/(WF299)
7438M/*18671*/(WP905)	7809M/XA699	8005M/WG768	8165M/WH791
7443M/WX853	7816M/WG763	8009M/XG518	8169M/WH364
7458M/WX905	7817M/TX214	8010M/XG547	8173M/XN685
7464M/XA564	7825M/WK991	8012M/WS562	8176M/WH791
7470M/XA553	7827M/XA917	8017M/XL762	8177M/WM224
7473M/XE946	7829M/XH992	8018M/XN344	8179M/XN928

8183M/*XN972*/(XN962)	8394M/WG422	8538M/XN781	8703M/VW453
8184M/WT520	8395M/WF408	8545M/XN726	8706M/XF383
8186M/WR977	8396M/XK740	8546M/XN728	8708M/XF509
8187M/WH791	8399M/WH539	8548M/WT507	8709M/XG209
8189M/*WD615* (WD646)	8401M/XP686	8549M/WT534	8710M/XG274
8190M/XJ918	8406M/XP831	8554M/TG511	8711M/XG290
8192M/XR658	8407M/XP585	8561M/XS100	8713M/XG225
8198M/WT339	8408M/XS186	8563M/*XX822*/(XW563)	8718M/XX396
8203M/XD377	8409M/XS209	8565M/*WT720*/(E-408)	8719M/XT257
8205M/XN819	8410M/XR662	8566M/XV279	8721M/XP354
8206M/WG419	8413M/XM192	8573M/XM708	8724M/XW923
8208M/WG303	8414M/XM173	8575M/XP542	8726M/XP299
8209M/WG418	8417M/XM144	8576M/XP502	8727M/XR486
8210M/WG471	8422M/XM169	8578M/XR534	8728M/WT532
8211M/WK570	8427M/XM172	8581M/WJ775	8729M/XJ815
8213M/WK626	8429M/XH592	8582M/XE874	8732M/XJ729
8215M/WP869	8434M/XM411	8583M/BAPC 94	8733M/XL318
8216M/WP927	8436M/XN554	8585M/XE670	8736M/XF375
8218M/WB645	8437M/WG362	8586M/XE643	8739M/XH170
8229M/XM355	8439M/WZ846	8588M/XR681	8740M/WE173
8230M/XM362	8440M/WD935	8589M/XR700	8741M/XW329
8234M/XN458	8442M/XP411	8590M/XM191	8743M/WD790
8235M/XN549	8452M/XK885	8591M/XA813	8746M/XH171
8236M/XP573	8453M/XP745	8595M/XH278	8749M/XH537
8237M/XS179	8458M/XP672	8598M/WP270	8751M/XT255
8238M/XS180	8459M/XR650	8600M/XX761	8753M/WL795
8338M/XS180	8460M/XP680	8602M/*PF179*/(XR541)	8762M/WH740
8342M/WP848	8462M/XX477	8604M/XS104	8764M/XP344
8344M/WH960	8463M/XP355	8606M/XP530	8768M/A-522
8350M/WH840	8464M/XJ758	8608M/XP540	8769M/A-528
8352M/XN632	8465M/W1048	8610M/XL502	8770M/XL623
8355M/KN645	8466M/L-866	8611M/WF128	8771M/XM602
8357M/WK576	8467M/WP912	8620M/XP534	8772M/WR960
8359M/WF825	8468M/MM5701/(BT474)	8621M/XR538	8778M/XM598
8361M/WB670	8469M/100503	8624M/*XR991*/(XS102)	8779M/XM607
8362M/WG477	8470M/584219	8627M/XP558	8780M/WK102
8364M/WG464	8471M/701152	8628M/XJ380	8781M/WE982
8365M/XK421	8472M/120227/(VN679)	8630M/WG362	8782M/XH136
8366M/XG454	8473M/WP190	8631M/XR574	8783M/XW272
8367M/XG474	8474M/494083	8633M/3W-17/MK732	8785M/XS642
8368M/XF926	8475M/360043/(PJ876)	8634M/WP314	8789M/XK970
8369M/WE139	8476M/24	8640M/XR977	8791M/XP329
8370M/N1671	8477M/4101/(DG200)	8642M/XR537	8792M/XP345
8371M/XA847	8478M/10639	8645M/XD163	8793M/XP346
8372M/K8042	8479M/730301	8648M/XK526	8794M/XP398
8373M/P2617	8481M/191614	8653M/XS120	8796M/XK943
8375M/NX611	8482M/112372/(VK893)	8655M/XN126	8799M/WV787
8376M/RF398	8483M/420430	8656M/XP405	8800M/XG226
8377M/R9125	8484M/5439	8657M/VZ634	8805M/XV722
8378M/*T9707*	8485M/997	8661M/XJ727	8807M/XL587
8379M/DG590	8486M/BAPC 99	8662M/XR458	8810M/XJ825
8380M/Z7197	8487M/J-1172	8666M/XE793	8816M/XX734
8382M/VR930	8488M/WL627	8671M/XJ435	8818M/XK527
8383M/K9942	8491M/WJ880	8672M/XP351	8820M/VP952
8384M/X4590	8493M/XR571	8673M/XD165	8821M/XX115
8385M/N5912	8494M/XP557	8676M/XL577	8822M/VP957
8386M/NV778	8501M/XP640	8679M/XF526	8828M/XS587
8387M/T6296	8502M/XP686	8680M/XF527	8830M/*N-294*/(XF515)
8388M/XL993	8508M/XS218	8681M/XG164	8831M/XG160
8389M/VX573	8509M/XT141	8682M/XP404	8832M/*XG168*/(XG172)
8390M/SL542	8514M/XS176	8693M/WH863	8833M/XL569
8392M/SL674	8535M/XN776	8702M/XG196	8834M/*XL571*

8836M/XL592	8946M/XZ389	9067M/XV586	9179M/XW309
8838M/*34037*/(429356)	8947M/XX726	9070M/XV581	9180M/XW311
8839M/XG194	8949M/XX743	9072M/XW768	9181M/XW358
8841M/XE606	8951M/XX727	9073M/XW924	9185M/XZ987
8853M/XT277	8953M/XX959	9075M/XV752	9187M/XW405
8855M/XT284	8954M/XZ384	9076M/XV808	9188M/XW364
8857M/XW544	8955M/XX110	9078M/XV753	9191M/XW416
8858M/XW541	8957M/XN582	9079M/XZ130	9194M/XW420
8863M/XG154	8961M/XS925	9080M/ZE350	9195M/XW330
8867M/XK532	8967M/XV263	9086M/ZE352	9196M/XW370
8868M/WH775	8969M/XR753	9087M/XX753	9197M/*XX530*/(XX637)
8869M/WH957	8972M/XR754	9090M/XW353	9198M/XS641
8870M/WH964	8973M/XS922	9091M/XW434	9199M/XW290
8871M/WJ565	8974M/XM473	9092M/XH669	9201M/ZD667
8873M/XR453	8975M/XW917	9093M/WK124	9203M/*3066*
8874M/XE597	8976M/XZ630	9095M/XW547	9205M/*E449*
8875M/XE624	8978M/XX837	9096M/WV322	9206M/F6314
8876M/*VM791*/(XA312)	8984M/XN551	9098M/XV406	9207M/8417/18
8880M/XF435	8985M/WK127	9103M/XV411	9208M/F938
8881M/XG254	8986M/XV261	9110M/XX736	9210M/MF628
8883M/XX946	8987M/XM358	9111M/XW421	9211M/733682
8884M/VX275	8990M/XM419	9115M/XV863	9212M/*KL216*/(45-49295)
8885M/XW922	8995M/XM425	9117M/XV161	9213M/N5182
8886M/XA243	8996M/XM414	9119M/XW303	9215M/XL164
8888M/XA231	8997M/XX669	9120M/XW419	9216M/XL190
8889M/XN239	8998M/XT864	9122M/XZ997	9217M/ZH257
8890M/WT532	9002M/XW763	9123M/XT773	9218M/XL563
8895M/XX746	9003M/XZ390	9125M/XW410	9219M/XZ971
8896M/XX821	9004M/XZ370	9127M/XW432	9221M/XZ966
8897M/XX969	9005M/XZ374	9130M/XW327	9222M/XZ968
8898M/XX119	9006M/XX967	9131M/*DD931*	9224M/XL568
8899M/XX756	9007M/XX968	9132M/XX977	9225M/XX885
8900M/XZ368	9008M/XX140	9133M/*413573*	9226M/XV865
8901M/XZ383	9009M/XX763	9134M/XT288	9227M/XB812
8902M/XZ739	9010M/XX764	9136M/XT891	9229M/ZA678
8903M/XX747	9011M/XM412	9137M/XN579	9233M/XZ431
8905M/XX975	9012M/XN494	9139M/XV863	9234M/XV864
8906M/XX976	9014M/XN584	9140M/XZ287	9236M/WV318
8907M/XZ371	9015M/XW320	9141M/XV118	9237M/XF445
8908M/XZ382	9017M/ZE449	9143M/XN589	9238M/ZA717
8909M/XV784	9019M/XX824	9145M/XV863	9239M/7198/18
8910M/XL160	9020M/XX825	9146M/XW299	9241M/XS639
8911M/XH673	9021M/XX826	9148M/XW436	9242M/XH672
8918M/XX109	9022M/XX958	9149M/XW375	9246M/XS714
8919M/XT486	9026M/XP629	9150M/*FX760*	9248M/WB627
8920M/XT469	9027M/XP556	9151M/XT907	9249M/WV396
8921M/XT466	9032M/XR673	9152M/XV424	9251M/XX744
8922M/XT467	9033M/XS181	9153M/XW360	9252M/XX722
8923M/XX819	9036M/XM350	9154M/XW321	9254M/XX965
8924M/XP701	9038M/XV810	9155M/WL679	9255M/XZ375
8925M/XP706	9039M/XN586	9162M/XZ991	9257M/XX962
8931M/XV779	9040M/XZ138	9163M/XV415	9258M/XW265
8932M/XR718	9041M/XW763	9166M/XW323	9259M/XS710
8934M/XR749	9042M/XL954	9167M/XV744	9260M/XS734
8935M/XR713	9044M/XS177	9168M/XZ132	9261M/*W2068*
8937M/XX751	9047M/XW409	9169M/XW547	9262M/XZ358
8938M/WV746	9048M/XM403	9170M/XZ994	9263M/XW267
8941M/XT456	9049M/XW404	9172M/XW304	9264M/XS735
8942M/XN185	9052M/WJ717	9173M/XW418	9265M/WK585
8943M/XE799	9056M/XS488	9174M/XZ131	9266M/XZ119
8944M/WZ791	9059M/ZE360	9175M/P1344	9267M/XW269
8945M/XX818	9066M/XV582	9176M/XW430	9268M/XR529

9269M/XT914	9288M/XX520	9311M/ZA475	9330M/ZB684
9270M/XZ145	9289M/XX665	9312M/ZA474	9331M/XW852
9272M/XS486	9290M/XX626	9314M/ZA320	9332M/XZ935
9273M/XS726	9292M/XW892	9315M/ZA319	9335M/ZA375
9274M/XS738	9293M/XX830	9316M/ZA399	9336M/ZA407
9275M/XS729	9294M/XX655	9317M/ZA450	9337M/ZA774
9276M/XS733	9295M/XV497	9318M/ZA360	9338M/ZA325
9277M/XT601	9298M/ZE340	9319M/XR516	9339M/ZA323
9278M/XS643	9299M/XW870	9320M/XX153	9340M/XX745
9279M/XT681	9300M/XX431	9321M/XZ367	9341M/ZA357
9281M/XZ146	9301M/XZ941	9322M/ZB686	9342M/XR498
9283M/XZ322	9302M/ZD462	9323M/XV643	9343M/XR506
9284M/ZA267	9303M/XV709	9324M/XV659	9344M/XV706
9285M/XR806	9306M/XX979	9326M/XV653	
9286M/XT905	9308M/ZD932	9328M/ZD607	
9287M/WP962	9310M/ZA355	9329M/ZD578	

'ZH800'/123 is actually Sea Harrier FA2 ZH801 and is preserved at RNAS Yeovilton where one can also find Sea Harrier FA2 ZH800 painted as 'ZH801'!

ZH851 is a Merlin HMA2 currently operating with 824 NAS at RNAS Culdrose in Cornwall. With the retirement of the Sea King and the completion of the conversion of the Merlin HMA1 fleet to HMA2 status, these are very much the backbone of Navy helicopter operations around the World.

SHIPS' NUMERIC CODE — DECK LETTERS ANALYSIS

	0	1	2	3	4	5	6	7	8	9
30	LA									
32		FV								
33							WK	CB		
35			MB							
36						AY	YB			
37			NL			SM				
40					IR					
41						MM				
42			SU			KT	PD	SB		
44					MR					
45		DA	DT	DM	DF	DN	DU			
46			WM							
47					RM					

RN CODE – SQUADRON – BASE – AIRCRAFT CROSS-CHECK

Deck/Base Code Numbers	Letters	Unit	Location	Aircraft Type(s)
010 — 015	CU	820 NAS	Culdrose	Merlin HM2
180 — 190	CU	849 NAS	Culdrose	Sea King ASaC7
264 — 274	CU	814 NAS	Culdrose	Merlin HM2
310 — 314	VL	815 NAS	Yeovilton	Lynx HMA8
336 — 426	*	815 NAS	Yeovilton	Lynx HMA8
500 — 515	CU	829 NAS	Culdrose	Merlin HM2
580 — 588	CU	824 NAS	Culdrose	Merlin HM2

*See foregoing separate ships' Deck Letters Analysis
Note that only the 'last two' digits of the Code are worn by some aircraft types, especially helicopters.

Code	Deck Letters	Vessel Name and Pennant No.	Vessel Type and Unit
—	AB	HMS *Albion* (L14)	Assault
—	AS	RFA *Argus* (A135)	Aviation Training ship
365	AY	HMS *Argyll* (F231)	Type 23 (815 NAS/211 Flt)
—	BK	HMS *Bulwark* (L15)	Assault
—	BV	RFA *Black Rover* (A273)	Fleet tanker
337	CB	RFA *Cardigan Bay* (L3009)	Landing ship(815 NAS/229 Flt)
—	CU	RNAS Culdrose (HMS *Seahawk*)	
451	DA	HMS *Daring* (D32)	Type 45 (815 NAS/200 Flt)
454	DF	HMS *Defender* (D36)	Type 45 (815 NAS)
—	DG	RFA *Diligence* (A132)	Maintenance
453	DM	HMS *Diamond* (D34)	Type 45 (815 NAS/208 Flt)
455	DN	HMS *Dragon* (D35)	Type 45 (815 NAS/219 Flt/226/Flt)
452	DT	HMS *Dauntless* (D33)	Type 45 (815 NAS)
456	DU	HMS *Duncan* (D37)	Type 45 (815 NAS)
—	FA	RFA *Fort Austin* (A386)	Support ship
—	FE	RFA *Fort Rosalie* (A385)	Support ship
321	FV	RFA *Fort Victoria* (A387)	Auxiliary Oiler
—	GV	RFA *Gold Rover* (A271)	Fleet tanker
404	IR	HMS *Iron Duke* (F234)	Type 23 (815 NAS/207 Flt)
425	KT	HMS *Kent* (F78)	Type 23 (815 NAS)
300	LA	HMS *Lancaster* (F229)	Type 23 (829 NAS/202 Flt)
353	MB	RFA *Mounts Bay* (L3008)	Landing ship (815 NAS/229 Flt)
415	MM	HMS *Monmouth* (F235)	Type 23 (829 NAS/215 Flt)
444	MR	HMS *Montrose* (F236)	Type 23 (815 NAS/214 Flt)
372	NL	HMS *Northumberland* (F238)	Type 23 (829 NAS)
—	O	HMS *Ocean* (L12)	Helicopter carrier
—	P	HMS *Prince of Wales* (R09)	Aircraft carrier
—	Q	HMS *Queen Elizabeth* (R08)	Aircraft carrier
426	PD	HMS *Portland* (F79)	Type 23 (815 NAS/210 Flt)
474	RM	HMS *Richmond* (F239)	Type 23 (815 NAS/206 Flt)
427	SB	HMS *St Albans* (F83)	Type 23 (829 NAS)
375	SM	HMS *Somerset* (F82)	Type 23 (815 NAS/203 Flt)
422	SU	HMS *Sutherland* (F81)	Type 23 (829 NAS)
—	VL	RNAS Yeovilton (HMS *Heron*)	
336	WK	RFA *Wave Knight* (A389)	Fleet tanker (815 NAS)
462	WM	HMS *Westminster* (F237)	Type 23 (829 NAS/234 Flt)
YB	RFA *Lyme Bay* (L3007)	Landing ship	
—	—	HMS *Protector* (A173)	Ice patrol
—	—	RFA *Wave Ruler* (A390)	Fleet tanker

ZD257/302-VL is one of just eight Lynx HMA8SRUs left in operation with 815 NAS, based at RNAS Yeovilton in Somerset.

This table gives brief details of the markings worn by aircraft of RAF squadrons. While this may help to identify the operator of a particular machine, it may not always give the true picture. For example, from time to time aircraft are loaned to other units while others wear squadron marks but are actually operated on a pool basis. Squadron badges are usually located on the front fuselage.

Squadron	Type(s) operated	Base(s)	Distinguishing marks & other comments
No 1 Sqn	Typhoon T3/FGR4	RAF Lossiemouth	Badge (on tail): A red 1 with yellow wings on a white background, flanked in red. Roundel is flanked by two white chevrons, edged in red. Aircraft are coded F*.
No 2 Sqn	Typhoon T3/FGR4	RAF Lossiemouth	Badge: A wake knot on a white circular background flanked on either side by black and white triangles. Tail fin has a black stripe with white triangles and the badge repeated on it.
No 3 Sqn	Typhoon T3/FGR4	RAF Coningsby	Badge: A blue cockatrice on a white circular background flanked by two green bars edged with yellow. Tail fin as a green stripe edged with yellow. Aircraft are coded QO-*
No 4(R) Sqn	Hawk T2	RAF Valley	Badge (on nose): A yellow lightning flash on a red background with IV superimposed. Aircraft carry a yellow lightning flash on a red and black background on the tail and this is repeated in bars either side of the roundel on the fuselage. Part of No 4 FTS.
No 5 Sqn	Sentinel R1	RAF Waddington	Badge (on tail): A green maple leaf on a white circle over a red horizontal band.
No 6 Sqn	Typhoon T3/FGR4	RAF Lossiemouth	Badge (on tail): A red, winged can opener on a blue shield, edged in red. The roundel is flanked by a red zigzag on a blue background. Aircraft are coded E*.
No 7 Sqn	Chinook HC6	RAF Odiham	Badge (on tail): A blue badge containing the seven stars of Ursa Major ('The Plough') in yellow.
No 8 Sqn	Sentry AEW1	RAF Waddington	Badge (on tail): A grey, sheathed, Arabian dagger. Aircraft pooled with No 54(R) Sqn.
No 9 Sqn	Tornado GR4/GR4A	RAF Marham	Badge: A green bat on a black circular background, flanked by yellow and green horizontal stripes. The green bat also appears on the tail, edged in yellow.
No 10 Sqn	Voyager KC2/KC3	RAF Brize Norton	No markings worn.
No 11 Sqn	Typhoon T3/FGR4	RAF Coningsby	Badge (on tail): Two eagles in flight on a white shield. The roundel is flanked by yellow and black triangles. Aircraft are coded D*
No 12 Sqn	Tornado GR4/GR4A	RAF Marham	Roundel is superimposed on a green chevron. Tail fin has a black and white horizontal stripe with the squadron badge, a fox's head on a white circle, in the middle.
No 13 Sqn	Reaper	RAF Waddington	No markings worn.
No 14 Sqn	Shadow R1	RAF Waddington	No markings worn.
No 15(R) Sqn	Tornado GR4/GR4A	RAF Lossiemouth	Roman numerals XV appear in white on the tail. [To disband, 31 March 2017]

Squadron	Type(s) operated	Base(s)	Distinguishing marks & other comments
No 16(R) Sqn	Tutor T1	RAF Cranwell	No markings carried. Aircraft pooled with No 57(R) Sqn. Part of No 1 EFTS.
No 17(R) Test & Evaluation Sqn	Lightning II	Edwards AFB, USA	No markings worn
No 18 Sqn	Chinook HC4/HC5	RAF Odiham	Badge (on tail): A red winged horse on a black circle. Aircraft pooled with No 27 Sqn.
No 24 Sqn	Hercules C4/C5/Atlas C1	RAF Brize Norton	No squadron markings carried. Aircraft pooled with No 30 Sqn, No 47 Sqn and No 70 Sqn.
No 27 Sqn	Chinook HC4/HC5	RAF Odiham	Badge (on tail): A dark green elephant on a green circle, flanked by green and dark green stripes. Aircraft pooled with No 18 Sqn.
No 28(R) Sqn	Chinook HC4/Puma HC2	RAF Benson	Badge: A winged horse above two white crosses on a red shield.
No 29(R) Sqn	Typhoon T3/FGR4	RAF Coningsby	Badge (on tail): An eagle in flight, preying on a buzzard, with three red Xs across the top. The roundel is flanked by two white bars outlined by a red line, each containing three red Xs. Aircraft are coded B*.
No 30 Sqn	Hercules C4/C5	RAF Brize Norton	No squadron markings carried. Aircraft pooled with No 24 Sqn and No 47 Sqn.
No 31 Sqn	Tornado GR4/GR4A	RAF Marham	Badge: A gold, five-pointed star on a yellow circle flanked by yellow and green checks. The star is repeated on the tail.
No 32(The Royal) Sqn	BAe 146 CC2/146 C3/Agusta 109	RAF Northolt	No squadron markings carried but aircraft carry a distinctive livery with a red stripe, edged in blue along the middle of the fuselage and a red tail.
No 33 Sqn	Puma HC2	RAF Benson	Badge: A stag's head.
No 39 Sqn	Predator/Reaper	Nellis AFB Creech AFB	No markings worn
No 41(R) Test & Evaluation Sqn [FJWOEU]	Tornado GR4/Typhoon T3/FGR4	RAF Coningsby	Badge: A red, double armed cross on the tail with a gold crown above. White and red horizontal bars flanking the roundel on the fuselage. Aircraft are coded EB-*.
No 45(R) Sqn	Super King Air 200/200GT/Tutor T1EA	RAF Cranwell	The King Airs carry a dark blue stripe on the tail superimposed with red diamonds. Part of No 3 FTS.
No 47 Sqn	Hercules C4/C5	RAF Brize Norton	No squadron markings usually carried. Aircraft pooled with No 24 Sqn and No 30 Sqn.
No 51 Sqn	Airseeker R1	RAF Waddington	Badge (on tail): A red goose in flight.
No 54(R) Sqn [ISTAR OCU]	Sentry AEW1	RAF Waddington	Based aircraft as required.
No 56(R) Sqn [ISTAR Test & Evaluation Sqn]	Shadow R1/Sentry AEW1/Sentinel R1	RAF Waddington	Based aircraft as required.

Squadron	Type(s) operated	Base(s)	Distinguishing marks & other comments
No 57(R) Sqn	Tutor T1	RAF Cranwell	No markings carried. Aircraft pooled with No 16(R) Sqn. Part of No 1 EFTS.
No 60(R) Sqn	Griffin HT1	RAF Shawbury [DHFS] & RAF Valley [SARTU]	No squadron markings usually carried.
No 70 Sqn Fixed Wing Air Mobility OCU	Atlas C1	RAF Brize Norton	No squadron markings usually carried. Aircraft pooled with No 24 Sqn.
No 72(R) Sqn	Tucano T1	RAF Linton-on-Ouse	Badge: A black swift in flight on a red disk, flanked by blue bars edged with red. The blue bars edged with red also flank the roundel on the fuselage; part of No 1 FTS
No 84 Sqn	Griffin HAR2	RAF Akrotiri	Badge (on tail): A scorpion on a playing card symbol (diamonds, clubs etc.). Aircraft carry a vertical light blue stripe through the roundel on the fuselage.
No 99 Sqn	Globemaster III	RAF Brize Norton	Badge (on tail): A black puma leaping.
No 100 Sqn	Hawk T1A	RAF Leeming	Badge (on tail): A skull in front of two bones crossed. Aircraft are usually coded C*. Incorporates the Joint Forward Air Control Training and Standards Unit (JFACTSU)
No 101 Sqn	Voyager KC2/KC3	RAF Brize Norton	No markings worn.
No 115(R) Sqn	Tutor T1	Wittering	No markings carried. Part of the CFS.
No 202(R) Sqn	Griffin HT1/AW139	RAF Valley	Badge: A mallard alighting on a white circle.
No 206(R) Sqn [HAT&ES]	Hercules C4/C5/C6	RAF Brize Norton/ Boscombe Down	No squadron markings usually carried.
No 230 Sqn	Puma HC2	RAF Benson	Badge: A tiger in front of a palm tree on a black pentagon.
No 617 Sqn	Lightning II	MCAS Beaufort, USA	No markings worn
No 1310 Flt	Chinook HC4	Mount Pleasant, FI	No markings worn
No 1312 Flt	Hercules C5/ Voyager KC2/KC3	Mount Pleasant, FI	Badge (on tail): A red Maltese cross on a white circle, flanked by red and white horizontal bars.
No 1435 Flt	Typhoon FGR4	Mount Pleasant, FI	Badge (on tail): A red Maltese cross on a white circle, flanked by red and white horizontal bars.

UNIVERSITY AIR SQUADRONS/AIR EXPERIENCE FLIGHTS*

As from 7 September 2015 all UAS flights and AEFs are commanded and managed by No 6 FTS RAF. Some UAS aircraft carry squadron badges and markings, usually on the tail. Squadron crests all consist of a white circle surrounded by a blue circle, topped with a red crown and having a yellow scroll beneath. Each differs by the motto on the scroll, the UAS name running around the blue circle & by the contents at the centre and it is the latter which are described below.
* All AEFs come under the administration of local UASs and these are listed here.

UAS	Base	Marks
Bristol UAS/ No 3 AEF	Boscombe Down	A sailing ship on water.
Cambridge UAS/ No 5 AEF	Wittering	A heraldic lion in front of a red badge. Aircraft pooled with University of London AS.
East Midlands Universities AS/ No 7 AEF	Wittering	A yellow quiver, full of arrows.
East of Scotland UAS/ No 12 AEF	RAF Leuchars	An open book in front of a white diagonal cross edged in blue.
Liverpool UAS	RAF Woodvale	A bird atop an open book, holding a branch in its beak. Aircraft pooled with Manchester and Salford Universities AS
Manchester and Salford Universities AS/ No 10 AEF	RAF Woodvale	A bird of prey with a green snake in its beak. Aircraft pooled with Liverpool UAS
Northern Ireland Universities AS/ No 14 AEF	JHFS Aldergrove	(Currently not known)
Northumbrian Universities AS/ No 11 AEF	RAF Leeming	A white cross on a blue background.
Oxford UAS/ No 6 AEF	RAF Benson	An open book in front of crossed swords.
Southampton UAS/ No 2 AEF	Boscombe Down	A red stag in front of a stone pillar.
Universities of Glasgow and Strathclyde AS/ No 4 AEF	Glasgow	A bird of prey in flight, holding a branch in its beak, in front of an upright sword.
University of Birmingham AS/ No 8 AEF	DCAE Cosford	A blue griffon with two heads.
University of London AS	Wittering	A globe superimposed over an open book. Aircraft pooled with Cambridge UAS.
University of Wales AS/ No 1 AEF	MoD St Athan	A red Welsh dragon in front of an open book, clasping a sword. Some aircraft have the dragon in front of white and green squares.
Yorkshire Universities AS/ No 9 AEF	RAF Linton-on-Ouse	An open book in front of a Yorkshire rose with leaves.

This table gives brief details of the markings worn by aircraft of FAA squadrons. Squadron badges, when worn, are usually located on the front fuselage. All FAA squadron badges comprise a crown atop a circle edged in gold braid and so the badge details below list only what appears in the circular part.

Squadron	Type(s) operated	Base(s)	Distinguishing marks & other comments
No 700X NAS	Scan Eagle RM1	RNAS Culdrose	Badge: No markings carried.
No 727 NAS	Tutor T1	RNAS Yeovilton	Badge: The head of Britannia wearing a gold helmet on a background of blue and white waves.
No 736 NAS	Hawk T1A	RNAS Culdrose & RNAS Yeovilton	A white lightning bolt on the tail.
No 750 NAS	Avenger T1	RNAS Culdrose	Badge: A Greek runner bearing a torch & sword on a background of blue and white waves.
No 814 NAS	Merlin HM2	RNAS Culdrose	Badge: A winged tiger mask on a background of dark blue and white waves.
No 815 NAS	Lynx HMA8/ Wildcat HMA2	RNAS Yeovilton	Badge: A winged, gold harpoon on a background of blue and white waves.
No 820 NAS	Merlin HM2	RNAS Culdrose	Badge: A flying fish on a background of blue and white waves.
No 824 NAS	Merlin HM2	RNAS Culdrose	Badge: A heron on a background of blue and white waves.
No 825 NAS	Wildcat HMA2	RNAS Yeovilton	Badge: An eagle over a Maltese cross.
No 829 NAS	Merlin HM2	RNAS Culdrose	Badge: A kingfisher hovering on a background of blue and white waves.
No 845 NAS	Merlin HC3i	RNAS Yeovilton	Badge: A dragonfly on a background of blue and white waves.
No 846 NAS	Merlin HC3/HC3A	RNAS Yeovilton	Badge: A swordsman riding a winged horse whilst attacking a serpent on a background of blue and white waves.
No 847 NAS	Wildcat AH1	RNAS Yeovilton	Badge (not currently worn): A gold sea lion on a blue background.
No 849 NAS	Sea King ASaC7	RNAS Culdrose	Badge: A winged streak of lightning with an eye in front on a background of blue and white waves.

This section lists the codes worn by some UK military aircraft and, alongside, the Registration of the aircraft currently wearing this code. It should be pointed out that in some cases more than one aircraft wears the same code but the aircraft listed is the one believed to be in service with the unit concerned at the time of going to press. This list will be updated regularly and those with Internet access can download the latest version via the 'Military Aircraft Markings' Web Site, www.militaryaircraftmarkings.co.uk.

Code	Serial	Code	Serial	Code	Serial	Code	Serial
ROYAL AIR FORCE		X	ZK459	340	ZK340	EC	ZK302
BAE Hawk T1/T2				347	ZK347	ED	ZK306
95-Y	XX318	**Bell 412EP Griffin HT1**		814	ZJ814	EE	ZK305
A	ZK010	E	ZJ242	A	ZK334	EG	ZK321
B	ZK011	I	ZJ235	C	ZK935/1435 Flt &	EI	ZK324
C	ZK012	K	ZJ708		ZK323/2 Sqn	EJ	ZJ946
D	ZK013	O	ZJ707	D	ZJ941/1435 Flt	EM	ZK312
E	ZK014	R	ZJ239	E	ZJ921	EO	ZK314
F	ZK015	S	ZJ234	F	ZJ915	EP	ZK345
G	ZK016	T	ZJ237	H	ZJ926/1435 Flt &	ER	ZK346
H	ZK017	U	ZJ240		ZK300/2 Sqn	EW	ZK301
I	ZK018	X	ZJ236	I	ZJ924	FA	ZK316
J	ZK019	Y	ZJ238	N	ZK311	FB	ZK334
K	ZK020			O	ZK307	FD	ZK336
L	ZK021	**B-V Chinook**		R	ZJ920	FF	ZK338
M	ZK022	W	ZA712	S	ZJ916	FG	ZK318
N	ZK023	AA	ZA670	T	ZK380	FH	ZK329
O	ZK024	AB	ZA671	U	ZJ934	FL	ZK310
P	ZK025	AD	ZA674	W	ZJ811 & ZK313	FM	ZK304
Q	ZK026	AE	ZA675	X	ZK343	FN	ZK348
R	ZK027	AF	ZA677	AX	ZK303	FP	ZK337
S	ZK028	AG	ZA679	BA	ZJ803	FQ	ZJ928
T	ZK029	AH	ZA680	BB	ZK372	FR	ZK327
U	ZK030	AI	ZA681	BC	ZJ800	FY	ZK383
V	ZK031	AJ	ZA682	BD	ZJ805	FZ	ZJ809
W	ZK032	AL	ZA684	BE	ZJ806	GS	ZK322
X	ZK033	AN	ZA705	BF	ZJ807	EB-A	ZJ946
Y	ZK034	AO	ZA707	BG	ZK382	EB-B	ZK379
Z	ZK035	AP	ZA708	BI	ZJ810	EB-E	ZK339
AA	ZK036	AR	ZA710	BJ	ZJ801	EB-G	ZK335
AB	ZK037	AV	ZA714	BK	ZJ812	EB-L	ZJ947 & ZK365
CA	XX246	AW	ZA720	BL	ZJ813	EB-R	ZK367
CB	XX345	BN	ZA718	BM	ZJ804	GN-A	ZK349
CC	XX191	DB	ZD574	BP	ZJ808	II	ZJ913
CD	XX332	DC	ZD575	BQ	ZK353	QO-B	ZJ811
CE	XX258	DD	ZD980	BR	ZK320	QO-P	ZK309
CF	XX203	DF	ZD982	BT	ZK331		
CH	XX346	DG	ZD983	BU	ZK351	**Panavia Tornado GR4**	
CJ	XX329	DH	ZD984	BV	ZK352	003	ZA369
CK	XX285	HB	ZH775	BW	ZK308	004	ZA370
CL	XX255	HC	ZH776	BY	ZK354	015	ZA406
CM	XX230	HF	ZH891	DA	ZJ931	019	ZA447
CN	XX284	HG	ZH892	DC	ZJ919	020	ZA449
CO	XX200	HH	ZH893	DG	ZJ917	022	ZA453
CP	XX265	HI	ZH894	DH	ZJ942	024	ZA458
CR	XX189	HJ	ZH895	DJ	ZJ935	025	ZA459
		HK	ZH896	DL	ZJ929	027	ZA462
Beech King Air 200		HR	ZH903	DN	ZJ939	028	ZA463
D	ZK458			DR	ZJ912	029	ZA469
K	ZK451	**Eurofighter Typhoon**		DT	ZJ937	031	ZA472
L	ZK452	317	ZK317	DW	ZJ802	032	ZA473
O	ZK455	320	ZK320	DZ	ZJ914	035	ZA542
P	ZK456	325	ZK325	EA	ZK342	036	ZA543
U	ZK460	330	ZK330	EB	ZK328	038	ZA546

Code	Serial	Code	Serial	Code	Serial	Code	Serial
040	ZA548	129	ZG752	87	ZH853	**WS Lynx**	
041	ZA549	135	ZG777	88	ZH828	310	XZ691
042	ZA550	136	ZG779	501	ZH841	311	XZ731
045	ZA553	137	ZG791	A	ZJ117	312	ZF563
046	ZA554	EB-Q	ZA560	B	ZJ118	314	XZ689
047	ZA556	EB-X	ZA607	C	ZJ119	336	ZF558
049	ZA559	EB-Z	ZG775	D	ZJ120	353	ZF562
054	ZA585	LS-F	ZD741	E	ZJ121	426	ZF557
055	ZA587			F	ZJ122		
056	ZA588	**Shorts Tucano T1**		G	ZJ123	**WS61 Sea King**	
058	ZA591	MP-A	ZF170	H	ZJ124	181	XV697
060	ZA594			J	ZJ125	183	XV671
063	ZA597	**ROYAL NAVY**		K	ZJ126	185	XV656
066	ZA601	**BAE Hawk T1**		L	ZJ127	188	XV714
073	ZA611	840	XX240	M	ZJ128	189	ZE420
074	ZA612	842	XX205	N	ZJ129	190	XV664
075	ZA613	849	XX316	O	ZJ130	191	ZA126
076	ZA614			P	ZJ131	192	ZE422
079	ZD711	**EHI-101 Merlin**		Q	ZJ132		
081	ZD713	13	ZH856	R	ZJ133	**ARMY AIR CORPS**	
084	ZD716	65	ZH826	S	ZJ134	**Bell 212**	
087	ZD739	66	ZH860	T	ZJ135	B	ZK067
092	ZD744	67	ZH847	U	ZJ136	K	ZJ969
100	ZD792	70	ZH836	W	ZJ137	X	ZH814
101	ZD793	80	ZH846	X	ZJ138	Y	ZH815
109	ZD848	81	ZH832	AA	ZJ990		
110	ZD849	82	ZH833	AB	ZJ992	**WS Gazelle AH1**	
113	ZD890	83	ZH824	AC	ZJ994	M	XZ345
118	ZG705	84	ZH851	AD	ZJ995	S	ZB691
119	ZG707	85	ZH862	AE	ZJ998		
128	ZG750	86	ZH857	AF	ZK001		

As its markings show, ZK310/FL is a Typhoon FGR4 operated by No 1 Squadron RAF at Lossiemouth, seen here at the Royal International Air Tattoo at Fairford.

Some *historic, classic and warbird* aircraft carry the markings of overseas air arms and can be seen in the UK, mainly preserved in museums and collections or taking part in air shows.

Serial	Type (code/other identity)	Owner/operator, location or fate	Notes
AFGHANISTAN			
-	Hawker Afghan Hind (K4672/BAPC 82)	RAF Museum Reserve Collection, Stafford	
ARGENTINA			
-	Bell UH-1H Iroquois (AE-406/*998-8888*) [Z]	RAF Valley, instructional use	
0729	Beech T-34C Turbo Mentor	FAA Museum, stored Cobham Hall, RNAS Yeovilton	
0767	Aermacchi MB339AA	South Yorkshire Aircraft Museum, Doncaster	
A-515	FMA IA58 Pucará (ZD485)	RAF Museum, stored Cosford	
A-517	FMA IA58 Pucará (G-BLRP)	Privately owned, Channel Islands	
A-522	FMA IA58 Pucará (8768M)	FAA Museum, at NE Aircraft Museum, Usworth	
A-528	FMA IA58 Pucará (8769M)	Norfolk & Suffolk Avn Museum, Flixton	
A-533	FMA IA58 Pucará (ZD486) <ff>	Privately owned, Cheltenham	
A-549	FMA IA58 Pucará (ZD487)	IWM Duxford	
AE-331	Agusta A109A (ZE411)	FAA Museum, stored Cobham Hall, RNAS Yeovilton	
AE-409	Bell UH-1H Iroquois [656]	Museum of Army Flying, Middle Wallop	
AE-422	Bell UH-1H Iroquois	FAA Museum, stored Cobham Hall, RNAS Yeovilton	
AUSTRALIA			
369	Hawker Fury ISS (F-AZXL) [D]	Privately owned, Cannes, France	
A2-4	Supermarine Seagull V (VH-ALB)	RAF Museum, Hendon	
A11-301	Auster J/5G (G-ARKG) [931-NW]	Privately owned, Spanhoe	
A16-199	Lockheed Hudson IIIA (G-BEOX) [SF-R]	RAF Museum, Hendon	
A17-48	DH82A Tiger Moth (G-BPHR)	Privately owned, Wanborough, Wilts	
A17-376	DH82A Tiger Moth (T6830/G-ANJI) [376]	Privately owned, Gloucester	
A19-144	Bristol 156 Beaufighter Xlc (JM135/A8-324)	The Fighter Collection, Duxford	
A92-255	GAF Jindivik 102	DPA/QinetiQ, Boscombe Down, apprentice use	
A92-664	GAF Jindivik 103A	Boscombe Down Aviation Collection, Old Sarum	
A92-708	GAF Jindivik 103BL	Bristol Aero Collection, stored Filton	
A92-740	GAF Jindivik 103BL	*Scrapped at Caernarfon, 2016*	
A92-908	GAF Jindivik 104AL (ZJ503)	Privately owned, Llanbedr	
N16-114	WS61 Sea King Mk.50A	Privately owned, Horsham	
N16-125	WS61 Sea King Mk.50A	Privately owned, Horsham	
N16-238	WS61 Sea King Mk.50A	Privately owned, Horsham	
N16-239	WS61 Sea King Mk.50A	Privately owned, Horsham	
N16-918	WS61 Sea King Mk.50B	Privately owned, Horsham	
WH589	Hawker Fury ISS (F-AZXJ) [115-NW]	Privately owned, Dijon, France	
BELGIUM			
A-41	SA318C Alouette II	The Helicopter Museum, Weston-super-Mare	
FT-36	Lockheed T-33A Shooting Star	Dumfries & Galloway Avn Mus, Dumfries	
H-01	Agusta A109HO	*Scrapped at Cotswold Airport, 2016*	
H-02	Agusta A109HO	Privately owned, Cotswold Airport	
H-05	Agusta A109HO	Privately owned, Cotswold Airport	
H-50	Noorduyn AT-16 Harvard IIB (OO-DAF)	Privately owned, Brasschaat, Belgium	
IF-68	Hawker Hunter F6 <ff>	Privately owned, Kings Lynn	
L-44	Piper L-18C Super Cub (OO-SPQ)	Royal Aéro Para Club de Spa, Belgium	
l -47	Piper L-18C Super Cub (OO-SPG)	Aeroclub Brasschaat VZW, Brasschaat, Belgium	
OL-L49	Piper L-18C Super Cub (L-156/OO-LGB)	Aeroclub Brasschaat VZW, Brasschaat, Belgium	
V-4	SNCAN Stampe SV-4B (OO-EIR)	Antwerp Stampe Centre, Antwerp-Deurne, Belgium	

Notes	Serial	Type (code/other identity)	Owner/operator, location or fate
	V-18	SNCAN Stampe SV-4B (OO-GWD)	Antwerp Stampe Centre, Antwerp-Deurne, Belgium
	V-29	SNCAN Stampe SV-4B (OO-GWB)	Antwerp Stampe Centre, Antwerp-Deurne, Belgium
	V-66	SNCAN Stampe SV-4C (OO-GWA)	Antwerp Stampe Centre, Antwerp-Deurne, Belgium

BRAZIL

| | 1317 | Embraer T-27 Tucano | Shorts, Belfast (engine test bed) |

BURKINA FASO

| | BF8431 | SIAI-Marchetti SF.260 (G-NRRA) [31] | Privately owned, Lydd |

CANADA

	-	Lockheed T-33A Shooting Star (17473)	Midland Air Museum, Coventry
	595	CCF T-6J Harvard IV (20306/G-CJWE) [310]	Privately owned, Sywell
	622	Piasecki HUP-3 Retriever (51-16622/N6699D)	The Helicopter Museum, Weston-super-Mare
	920	VS Stranraer (CF-BXO) [Q-N]	RAF Museum, Hendon
	3091	NA81 Harvard II (3019/G-CPPM)	Beech Restorations, Bruntingthorpe
	3349	NA64 Yale (G-BYNF)	Privately owned, Duxford
	5084	DH82C Tiger Moth (G-FCTK)	Privately owned, Hailsham
	9041	Bristol 149 Bolingbroke IV <ff>	Manx Aviation Museum, Ronaldsway
	9048	Bristol 149 Bolingbroke IV	Bristol Aero Collection, Filton
	9754	Consolidated PBY-5A Catalina (VP-BPS) [P]	*Scrapped, 2014*
	9893	Bristol 149 Bolingbroke IVT	IWM Duxford, stored
	9940	Bristol 149 Bolingbroke IVT	National Museum of Flight, E Fortune
	15252	Fairchild PT-19A Cornell (comp 15195)	RAF Museum Reserve Collection, Stafford
	16693	Auster J/1N Alpha (G-BLPG) [693]	Privately owned, Darley Moor, Derbys
	18393	Avro Canada CF-100 Canuck 4B (G-BCYK)	IWM Duxford
	18671	DHC1 Chipmunk 22 (WP905/7438M/G-BNZC) [671]	The Shuttleworth Collection, Old Warden
	20249	Noorduyn AT-16 Harvard IIB (PH-KLU) [XS-249]	Privately owned, Texel, The Netherlands
	20310	CCF T-6J Texan (G-BSBG) [310]	*Repainted in US marks as 28562, August 2016*
	21417	Canadair CT-133 Silver Star	Yorkshire Air Museum, Elvington
	23140	Canadair CL-13A Sabre 5 [AX] <rf>	Midland Air Museum, Coventry
	23380	Canadair CL-13B Sabre 6 <rf>	Privately owned, Haverigg
	KN448	Douglas Dakota IV <ff>	Science Museum, South Kensington

CHILE

| | H-225 | Aérospatiale SA330H Puma | Ultimate Activity, Faygate |

CHINA

	68 r	Nanchang CJ-6A Chujiao (2751219/G-BVVG)	Privately owned, White Waltham
	61367	Nanchang CJ-6A Chujiao (4532009/G-CGHB) [37]	Privately owned, Redhill
	61762	Nanchang CJ-6A Chujiao (4532008/G-CGFS) [72]	*Sold to France, 2013*

CZECH REPUBLIC

	3677	Letov S-103 (MiG-15bisSB) (613677)	National Museum of Flight, E Fortune
	3794	Letov S-102 (MiG-15) (623794)	Norfolk & Suffolk Avn Museum, Flixton
		(starboard side only, painted in Polish marks as 1972 on port side)	
	9147	Mil Mi-4	The Helicopter Museum, Weston-super-Mare

DENMARK

	A-011	SAAB A-35XD Draken	Privately owned, Westhoughton, Lancs
	AR-107	SAAB S-35XD Draken	Newark Air Museum, Winthorpe
	E-419	Hawker Hunter F51 (G-9-441)	North-East Aircraft Museum, Usworth
	E-420	Hawker Hunter F51 (G-9-442) <ff>	Privately owned, Walton-on-Thames
	E-421	Hawker Hunter F51 (G-9-443)	Brooklands Museum, Weybridge
	E-424	Hawker Hunter F51 (G-9-445)	South Yorkshire Aircraft Museum, Doncaster
	ET-272	Hawker Hunter T53 <ff>	Norfolk & Suffolk Avn Museum, Flixton
	K-682	Douglas C-47A Skytrain (OY-BPB)	Foreningen For Flyvende Mus, Vaerløse, Denmark

Serial	Type (code/other identity)	Owner/operator, location or fate	Notes
L-866	Consolidated PBY-6A Catalina (8466M)	RAF Museum, Cosford	
P-129	DHC-1 Chipmunk 22 (OY-ATO)	Privately owned, Roskilde, Denmark	
P-139	DHC-1 Chipmunk 22 (OY-AVF)	Privately owned, Roskilde, Denmark	
R-756	Lockheed F-104G Starfighter	Midland Air Museum, Coventry	
S-881	Sikorsky S-55C	The Helicopter Museum, Weston-super-Mare	
S-882	Sikorsky S-55C	Skirmish Paintball, Portishead	
S-886	Sikorsky S-55C	Hamburger Hill Paintball, Marksbury, Somerset	
S-887	Sikorsky S-55C	The Helicopter Museum, Weston-super-Mare	

ECUADOR

FAE 259	BAC Strikemaster Mk.80A (G-UPPI) [T59]	*Crashed Witheridge, Devon, 26 April 2009*	

EGYPT

356	Heliopolis Gomhouria Mk 6	*Scrapped*	
764	Mikoyan MiG-21SPS <ff>	Privately owned, Northampton	
773	WS61 Sea King Mk.47 (WA.823)	RNAS Yeovilton Fire Section	
774	WS61 Sea King Mk.47 (WA.822)	*Currently not known*	
775	WS61 Sea King Mk.47 (WA.824)	*Currently not known*	
776	WS61 Sea King Mk.47 (WA.825) <ff>	Mayhem Paintball, Aybridge, Essex	
0446	Mikoyan MiG-21UM <ff>	*Currently not known*	
7907	Sukhoi Su-7 <ff>	Robertsbridge Aviation Society, Mayfield	

FINLAND

GA-43	Gloster Gamecock II (G-CGYF)	Privately owned, Dursley, Glos	
GN-101	Folland Gnat F1 (XK741)	Midland Air Museum, Coventry	
SZ-12	Focke-Wulf Fw44J Stieglitz (D-EXWO)	Privately owned, Bienenfarm, Germany	
VI-3	Valtion Viima 2 (OO-EBL)	Privately owned, Brasschaat, Belgium	

FRANCE

1/4513	Spad XIII <R> (G-BFYO/*S3398*)	American Air Museum, Duxford	
7	Nord NC854 (G-NORD)	Privately owned, English Bicknor, Glos	
37	Nord 3400 (G-ZARA) [MAB]	Privately owned, Swanton Morley	
54	SNCAN NC856A Norvigie (G-CGWR) [AOM]	Privately owned, Spanhoe	
67	SNCAN 1101 Noralpha (F-GMCY) [CY]	Privately owned, la Ferté-Alais, France	
70	Dassault Mystère IVA	Midland Air Museum, Coventry	
78	Nord 3202B-1 (G-BIZK)	Privately owned, Norfolk	
79	Dassault Mystère IVA [2-EG]	Norfolk & Suffolk Avn Museum, Flixton	
82	Curtiss H75-C1 Hawk (G-CCVH) [X-881]	The Fighter Collection, Duxford	
82	NA T-28D Fennec (F-AZKG)	Privately owned, Strasbourg, France	
83	Dassault Mystère IVA [8-MS]	Newark Air Museum, Winthorpe	
83	Morane-Saulnier MS733 Alcyon (F-AZKS)	Privately owned, Montlucon, France	
84	Dassault Mystère IVA [8-NF]	Lashenden Air Warfare Museum, Headcorn	
85	Dassault Mystère IVA [8-MV]	Cold War Jets Collection, Bruntingthorpe	
104	MH1521M Broussard (F-GHFG) [307-FG]	Privately owned, Montceau-les-Mines, France	
105	Nord N2501F Noratlas (F-AZVM) [62-SI]	Le Noratlas de Provence, Marseilles, France	
106	MH1521M Broussard (F-GKJT) [33-JT]	Privately owned, Montceau-les-Mines, France	
108	MH1521M Broussard (F-BNEX) [50S9]	Privately owned, Lelystad, The Netherlands	
108	SO1221 Djinn (FR108) [CDL]	The Helicopter Museum, Weston-super-Mare	
121	Dassault Mystère IVA [8-MY]	City of Norwich Aviation Museum	
128	Morane-Saulnier MS733 Alcyon (F-BMMY)	Privately owned, St Cyr, France	
143	Morane-Saulnier MS733 Alcyon (G-MSAL)	Privately owned, Spanhoe	
146	Dassault Mystère IVA [8-MC]	North-East Aircraft Museum, Usworth	
154	MH1521M Broussard (F-GKRO) [315-SM]	Privately owned, Damyns Hall, Essex	
156	SNCAN Stampe SV-4B (G-NIFE)	Privately owned, Gloucester	
158	Dassault MD312 Flamant (F-AZGE) [12-XA]	Privately owned, Albert, France	
160	Dassault MD312 Flamant (F-AZDR) [V]	Privately owned, Alençon, France	
189	Dassault MD312 Flamant (F-AZVG) [G]	Ailes Anciennes de Corbas, Lyon, France	
208	MH1521C1 Broussard (G-YYYY) [IR]	Privately owned, Eggesford	
226	Dassault MD312 Flamant (F-AZES) [319-CG]	Privately owned, Montbeliard, France	
237	Dassault MD312 Flamant (F-AZFE) [319-DM]	Privately owned, Alençon, France	
255	MH1521M Broussard (G-CIGH) [5-ML]	Privately owned, Breighton	

Notes	Serial	Type (code/other identity)	Owner/operator, location or fate
	260	Dassault MD311 Flamant (F-AZKT) [316-KT]	Privately owned, Albert, France
	261	MH1521M Broussard (F-GIBN) [30-QA]	Privately owned, Walldürn, Germany
	276	Dassault MD311 Flamant (F-AZER)	Privately owned, Alençon, France
	282	Dassault MD311 Flamant (F-AZFX) [316-KY]	*Withdrawn from use and preserved at Bordeaux*
	290	Dewoitine D27 (F-AZJD)	Les Casques de Cuir, la Ferté-Alais, France
	316	MH1521M Broussard (F-GGKR) [315-SN]	Privately owned, Lognes, France
	318	Dassault Mystère IVA [8-NY]	Dumfries & Galloway Avn Mus, Dumfries
	319	Dassault Mystère IVA [8-ND]	Rebel Air Museum, Andrewsfield
319	Grumman TBM-3E Avenger (HB-RDG) [4F.6]	*Repainted in US marks as 53319 by 2016*
	351	Morane-Saulnier MS317 (G-MOSA) [HY22]	Privately owned, Barton
	354	Morane-Saulnier MS315E-D2 (G-BZNK)	Privately owned, Wickenby
	538	Dassault Mirage IIIE [3-QH]	Yorkshire Air Museum, Elvington
	569	Fouga CM170R Magister [F-AZZP]	Privately owned, Le Havre, France
	24541	Cessna L-19E Bird Dog (G-JDOG) [BMG]	Privately owned, Cotswold Airport
	42157	NA F-100D Super Sabre [11-ML]	North-East Aircraft Museum, stored Usworth
	54439	Lockheed T-33A Shooting Star (55-4439) [WI]	North-East Aircraft Museum, Usworth
	63938	NA F-100F Super Sabre [11-EZ]	Lashenden Air Warfare Museum, Headcorn
	125716	Douglas AD-4N Skyraider (F-AZFN) [22-DG]	Privately owned, Mélun, France
	127002	Douglas AD-4NA Skyraider (F-AZHK) [20-LN]	Privately owned, Avignon, France
	517692	NA T-28S Fennec (G-TROY) [142]	Privately owned, Duxford
	18-5395	Piper L-18C Super Cub (52-2436/G-CUBJ) [CDG]	Privately owned, Old Warden
	51-7545	NA T-28S Fennec (N14113)	*To France, 17 January 2017*
C850	Salmson 2A2 <R>	Barton Aviation Heritage Society, Barton
FR41	Piasecki H-21C	The Helicopter Museum, Weston-super-Mare
MS824	Morane-Saulnier Type N <R> (G-AWBU)	Privately owned, Stow Maries
N856	SNCAN NC856 (G-CDWE)	Privately owned, Wickenby
N1977	Nieuport Scout 17/23 <R> (*N1723*/G-BWMJ) [8]	Privately owned, Stow Maries
XC	Piper L-4J Grasshopper (44-80513/G-BSYO)	Privately owned, Postling, Kent
	GERMANY		
	-	Fieseler Fi103R-IV (V-1) (BAPC 91)	Lashenden Air Warfare Museum, Headcorn
	-	Fokker Dr1 Dreidekker <R> (BAPC 88)	FAA Museum, stored Cobham Hall, RNAS Yeovilton
	-	Messerschmitt Bf109 <R> (*6357*/BAPC 74) [6]	Kent Battle of Britain Museum, Hawkinge
	-	Messerschmitt Bf109 <R> [<-]	Battle of Britain Experience, Canterbury
Black 1	Hispano HA 1.112M1L Buchón (C.4K-31/G-AWHE)	Spitfire Ltd, Humberside
Green 1	Messerschmitt Bf109G <R> (BAPC 240)	Yorkshire Air Museum, Elvington
White 1	Focke-Wulf Fw190 <R> (G-WULF)	Privately owned, Halfpenny Green
Black 2	Hispano HA 1.112M1L Buchón (C.4K-102/G-AWHK)	Historic Flying Ltd, Duxford
3	SNCAN 1101 Noralpha (G-BAYV) (fuselage)	Privately owned, Newquay
Yellow 3	Messerschmitt Bf109G-10 (D-FDME)	Messerschmitt Stiftung, Manching, Germany
Black 6	Messerschmitt Bf109G-2/Trop (10639/8478M/G-USTV)	RAF Museum, Cosford
Red 7	Messerschmitt Bf109G-4 (D-FWME)	Messerschmitt Stiftung, Manching, Germany
Yellow 7	Hispano HA 1.112M1L Buchón (C.4K-99/N90604)	Privately owned, Sywell
Red 8	Focke-Wulf Fw190 <R> (G-WULF)	*Repainted as White 1, October 2015*
White 9	Focke-Wulf Fw190 <R> (G-CCFW)	Privately owned, Oaksey Park
Yellow 10	Hispano HA 1.112M1L Buchón (C.4K-102/G-AWHK)	*Repainted as Black 2 by May 2016*
Red 11	Hispano HA 1.112K1L Buchón (C.4K-112/N1109G)	Privately owned, Sywell
Yellow 12	Messerschmitt Bf109G-2(13605/G-JIMP)	Privately owned, Knutsford
White 14	Messerschmitt Bf109 <R> (BAPC 67)	Kent Battle of Britain Museum, Hawkinge
White 14	Messerschmitt Bf109E-4 (G-CIPB)	Privately owned, Biggin Hill
Yellow 14	Nord 1002 (G-ETME)	Privately owned, White Waltham
33/15	Fokker EIII <R> (G-CHAW)	Privately owned, Membury
87	Heinkel He111 <R> <ff>	Privately owned, East Kirkby
105/15	Fokker EIII <R> (G-UDET)	Privately owned, Horsham
139	SNCAN 1101 Noralpha (G-BSMD)	*Sold to Italy, 2014*
152/17	Fokker Dr1 Dreidekker <R> (F-AZPQ)	Les Casques de Cuir, la Ferté-Alais, France
152/17	Fokker Dr1 Dreidekker <R> (G-BVGZ)	Privately owned, Breighton
157/18	Fokker D.VIII <R> (BAPC 239)	Norfolk & Suffolk Air Museum, Flixton
210/16	Fokker EIII (BAPC 56)	Science Museum, South Kensington
403/17	Fokker Dr1 Dreidekker <R> (G-CDXR)	Privately owned, Popham

Serial	Type (code/other identity)	Owner/operator, location or fate	Notes
416/15	Fokker EIII <R> (G-GSAL)	Privately owned, Aston Down	
422/15	Fokker EIII <R> (G-AVJO)	Privately owned, Stow Maries	
422/15	Fokker EIII <R> (G-FOKR)	Privately owned, Eshott	
425/17	Fokker Dr1 Dreidekker <R> (BAPC 133)	Kent Battle of Britain Museum, Hawkinge	
477/17	Fokker Dr1 Dreidekker <R> (G-FOKK)	Privately owned, Sywell	
556/17	Fokker Dr1 Dreidekker <R> (G-CFHY)	Privately owned, Tibenham	
626/8	Fokker DVII <R> (N6268)	Privately owned, Booker	
764	Mikoyan MiG-21SPS <ff>	Privately owned, Norfolk	
959	Mikoyan MiG-21SPS	Midland Air Museum, Coventry	
1160	Dornier Do17Z-2	Michael Beetham Conservation Centre, Cosford	
1190	Messerschmitt Bf109E-3 [White 4]	IWM Duxford	
1480	Messerschmitt Bf109 <R> (BAPC 66) [6]	Kent Battle of Britain Museum, Hawkinge	
1801/18	Bowers Fly Baby 1A (G-BNPV)	Privately owned, Chessington	
1803/18	Bowers Fly Baby 1A (G-BUYU)	Privately owned, Chessington	
1983	Messerschmitt Bf109E-3 (G-EMIL)	Privately owned, Colchester	
2100	Focke-Wulf Fw189A-1 (G-BZKY) [V7+1H]	Sold as N189FW, January 2008	
3579	Messerschmitt Bf109E-7 (G-CIPB) [14+]	Privately owned, Biggin Hill	
4101	Messerschmitt Bf109E-3 (DG200/8477M) [Black 12]	RAF Museum, Hendon	
4477	CASA 1.131E Jungmann (G-RETA) [GD+EG]	The Shuttleworth Collection, Old Warden	
7198/18	LVG CVI (G-AANJ/9239M)	Michael Beetham Conservation Centre, Cosford	
8417/18	Fokker DVII (9207M)	RAF Museum, Hendon	
12802	Antonov An-2T (D-FOFM)	Historische Flugzeuge, Grossenhain, Germany	
100143	Focke-Achgelis Fa330A-1 Bachstelze	IWM Duxford	
100502	Focke-Achgelis Fa330A-1 Bachstelze	Privately owned, Millom	
100503	Focke-Achgelis Fa330A-1 Bachstelze (8469M)	RAF Museum, Cosford	
100509	Focke-Achgelis Fa330A-1 Bachstelze	Science Museum, stored Wroughton	
100545	Focke-Achgelis Fa330A-1 Bachstelze	FAA Museum, RNAS Yeovilton	
100549	Focke-Achgelis Fa330A-1 Bachstelze	Lashenden Air Warfare Museum, Headcorn	
112372	Messerschmitt Me262A-2a (VK893/8482M) [Yellow 4]	RAF Museum, Hendon	
120227	Heinkel He162A-2 Salamander (VN679/8472M) [Red 2]	RAF Museum, Hendon	
120235	Heinkel He162A-1 Salamander (AM.68) [Yellow 6]	IWM Duxford	
191316	Messerschmitt Me163B Komet	Science Museum, South Kensington	
191454	Messerschmitt Me163B Komet <R> (BAPC 271)	The Shuttleworth Collection, Old Warden	
191461	Messerschmitt Me163B Komet (191614/8481M) [Yellow 14]	RAF Museum, Cosford	
191659	Messerschmitt Me163B Komet (8480M) [Yellow 15]	National Museum of Flight, E Fortune	
280020	Flettner Fl282/B-V20 Kolibri (frame only)	Midland Air Museum, Coventry	
360043	Junkers Ju88R-1 (PJ876/8475M) [D5+EV]	RAF Museum, Cosford	
420430	Messerschmitt Me410A-1/U2 (AM.72/8483M) [3U+CC]	RAF Museum, Cosford	
475081	Fieseler Fi156C-7 Storch (VP546/AM.101/7362M) [GM+AK]	RAF Museum, Cosford	
494083	Junkers Ju87D-3 (8474M) [RI+JK]	RAF Museum, Hendon	
502074	Heliopolis Gomhouria Mk 6 (158/G-CGEV) [CG+EV]	Privately owned, Breighton	
584219	Focke-Wulf Fw190F-8/U1 (AM.29/8470M) [Black 38]	RAF Museum, Hendon	
701152	Heinkel He111H-23 (8471M) [NT+SL]	RAF Museum, Hendon	
730301	Messerschmitt Bf110G-4 (AM.34/8479M) [D5+RL]	RAF Museum, Hendon	
733682	Focke-Wulf Fw190A-8/R7 (AM.75/9211M)	RAF Museum, Cosford	
980554	Flug Werk FW190A-8/N (D-FWMW)	Meier Motors, Bremgarten, Germany	
2+1	Focke-Wulf Fw190 <R> (G-SYFW) [7334]	Privately owned, Empingham, Rutland	
17+TF	CASA 1.133C Jungmeister (G-BZTJ)	Sold to Sweden, August 2016	
22+35	Lockheed F-104G Starfighter	Privately owned, Bruntingthorpe	
23.02	Albatros B.II <R> (D-EKGH)	Sold to New Zealand	
28+08	Aero L-39ZO Albatros (142/28+04)	Pinewood Studios, Bucks	
2E+RA	Fieseler Fi-156C-3 Storch (F-AZRA)	Amicale J-B Salis, la Ferté-Alais, France	
4+1	Focke-Wulf Fw190 <R> (G-BSLX)	Privately owned, Norwich	
6G+ED	Slepcev Storch (G-BZOB) [5447]	Privately owned, Breighton	
37+86	McD F-4F Phantom II <ff>	Privately owned, Bruntingthorpe	
37+89	McD F-4F Phantom II	HHA, Scampton (spares)	
58+89	Dornier Do28D-2 Skyservant (D-ICDY)	Privately owned, Uetersen, Germany	

Notes	Serial	Type (code/other identity)	Owner/operator, location or fate
	80+39	MBB Bo.105M	*To Germany, 2015*
	80+40	MBB Bo.105M	*To Germany, 2015*
	80+55	MBB Bo.105M	Lufthansa Resource Technical Training, Cotswold Airport
	80+77	MBB Bo.105M	Lufthansa Resource Technical Training, Cotswold Airport
	81+00	MBB Bo.105M (D-HZYR)	The Helicopter Museum, Weston-super-Mare
	96+26	Mil Mi-24D (421)	The Helicopter Museum, Weston-super-Mare
	98+14	Sukhoi Su-22M-4	HHA, stored Scampton
	99+18	NA OV-10B Bronco (G-ONAA)	Bronco Demo Team, Wevelgem, Belgium
	99+26	NA OV-10B Bronco (G-BZGL)	Bronco Demo Team, Wevelgem, Belgium
	AZ+JU	CASA 3.52L (F-AZJU)	Amicale J-B Salis, la Ferté-Alais, France
	BB+103	Canadair CL-13B Sabre 6 (1730/JB+114)	Privately owned, Bruntingthorpe
	BF+070	CCF T-6J Texan (G-CHYN)	Privately owned, Cotswold Airport
	BG+KM	Nord 1002 Pingouin (G-ASTG)	Privately owned, Peterborough
	BU+CC	CASA 1.131E Jungmann (G-BUCC)	Privately owned, Sandown
	CX+HI	CASA 1.131E Jungmann (E.3B-379/G-CDJU)	Privately owned, Sleap
	D5397/17	Albatros DVA <R> (G-BFXL)	*Sold as N482UT, December 2012*
	D7343/17	Albatros DVA <R> (ZK-TVD)	RAF Museum, Hendon
	DM+BK	Morane-Saulnier MS505 (G-BPHZ)	Aero Vintage, Westfield, E Sussex
	E37/15	Fokker EIII <R> (G-CGJF)	Privately owned, Herts
	ES+BH	Messerschmitt Bf108B-2 (D-ESBH)	Messerschmitt Stiftung, Manching, Germany
	FI+S	Morane-Saulnier MS505 (G-BIRW)	National Museum of Flight, E Fortune
	FM+BB	Messerschmitt Bf109G-6 (D-FMBB)	Messerschmitt Stiftung, Manching, Germany
	GM+AI	Fieseler Fi156A Storch (2088/G-STCH)	*Sold to Norway, 2016*
	KB+GB	CASA 1.131E Jungmann (G-BHSL)	Privately owned, Oaksey Park
	LG+01	CASA 1.133L Jungmeister (ES.1-16/G-CIJV)	Privately owned, Sleap
	LG+03	Bücker Bü133C Jungmeister (G-AEZX)	Privately owned, Milden
	NJ+C11	Nord 1002 (G-ATBG)	Privately owned, Duxford
	NM+AA	CASA 1.131E Jungmann 1000 (G-BZJV)	Privately owned, Sleap
	NQ+NR	Klemm KI35D (D-EQXD)	Quax Flieger, Paderborn, Germany
	NV+KG	Focke-Wulf Fw44J Stieglitz (D-ENAY)	Quax Flieger, Paderborn, Germany
	S4-A07	CASA 1.131E Jungmann (G-BWHP)	Privately owned, Yarcombe, Devon
	S5+B06	CASA 1.131E Jungmann 2000 (G-BSFB)	*Repainted as G-WJCM, 2012*
	TP+WX	Heliopolis Gomhouria Mk 6 (G-TPWX)	Privately owned, Swanborough
	GHANA		
	G360	PBN 2T Islander (G-BRSR)	Privately owned, Biggin Hill
	G361	PBN 2T Islander (G-BRPB)	Privately owned, Biggin Hill
	G362	PBN 2T Islander (G-BRPC)	Privately owned, Biggin Hill
	G363	PBN 2T Islander (G-BRSV)	Privately owned, Biggin Hill
	GREECE		
	52-6541	Republic F-84F Thunderflash [541]	North-East Aircraft Museum, Usworth
	63-8418	Northrop F-5A <ff>	*Scrapped*
	HONG KONG		
	HKG-5	SA128 Bulldog (G-BULL)	Privately owned, Cotswold Airport
	HKG-6	SA128 Bulldog (G-BPCL)	Privately owned, North Weald
	HKG-11	Slingsby T.67M Firefly 200 (G-BYRY)	Privately owned, Wellesbourne Mountford
	HKG-13	Slingsby T.67M Firefly 200 (G-BXKW)	Privately owned, St Ghislain, Belgium
	HUNGARY		
	125	Aero L-39ZO Albatros (831125/G-JMGP)	Privately owned, France
	335	Mil Mi-24D (3532461715415)	Privately owned, Dunsfold
	501	Mikoyan MiG-21PF	IWM Duxford
	503	Mikoyan MiG-21SMT (G-BRAM)	RAF Museum, Cosford
	INDIA		
	E296	Hindustan Gnat F1 (G-SLYR)	Privately owned, North Weald
	Q497	EE Canberra T4 (WE191) <ff>	Privately owned, Stoneykirk, D&G

Serial	Type (code/other identity)	Owner/operator, location or fate	Notes
HA561	Hawker Tempest II (MW743)	Privately owned, stored Wickenby	
KN397	Douglas C-47B Skytrain (G-AMSV)	Privately owned, Coventry	
INDONESIA			
LL-5313	BAe Hawk T53	BAE Systems, Brough, on display	
IRAQ			
333	DH115 Vampire T55 <ff>	South Yorkshire Aircraft Mus'm, stored Doncaster	
ITALY			
MM5701	Fiat CR42 (BT474/8468M) [13-95]	RAF Museum, Hendon	
MM53211	Fiat G46-1B (MM52799) [ZI-4]	Privately owned, Shipdham	
MM53692	CCF T-6G Texan	RAeS Medway Branch, Rochester	
MM53774	Fiat G59-4B (I-MRSV) [181]	Privately owned, Parma, Italy	
MM54099	NA T-6G Texan (G-BRBC) [RR-56]	Privately owned, Chigwell	
MM54532	SIAI-Marchetti SF.260AM (G-ITAF) [70-42]	Privately owned, Leicester	
MM80270	Agusta-Bell AB204B (MM80279)	London Motor Museum, Hayes	
MM80927	Agusta-Bell AB206A-1 JetRanger [CC-49]	The Helicopter Museum, Weston-super-Mare	
MM81205	Agusta A109A-2 SEM [GF-128]	The Helicopter Museum, Weston-super-Mare	
MM54-2372	Piper L-21B Super Cub	Privately owned, Foxhall Heath, Suffolk	
JAPAN			
-	Kawasaki Ki100-1B (16336/8476M/BAPC 83)	RAF Museum, Cosford	
-	Mitsubishi A6M5-52 Zero (196) [CI-05] <ff>	IWM Duxford	
-	Yokosuka MXY 7 Ohka II (BAPC 159)	IWM Duxford, stored	
997	Yokosuka MXY 7 Ohka II (8485M/BAPC 98)	Museum of Science & Industry, Manchester	
3443	NA T-6 Texan Zero (F-AZRO)	Privately owned, St Rambert d'Albon, France	
5439	Mitsubishi Ki46-III (8484M/BAPC 84)	RAF Museum, Cosford	
15-1585	Yokosuka MXY 7 Ohka II (BAPC 58)	Science Museum, at FAA Museum, RNAS Yeovilton	
I-13	Yokosuka MXY 7 Ohka II (8486M/BAPC 99)	RAF Museum, Cosford	
Y2-176	Mitsubishi A6M3-2 Zero (3685) [76]	IWM London, Lambeth	
JORDAN			
408	SA125 Bulldog (G-BDIN)	*Currently not known*	
KENYA			
115	Dornier Do28D-2 Skyservant	Privately owned, stored Hibaldstow	
117	Dornier Do28D-2 Skyservant	Privately owned, stored Hibaldstow	
MYANMAR			
UB441	VS361 Spitfire IX (ML119/G-SDNI)	Privately owned, Sandown	
THE NETHERLANDS			
16-218	Consolidated PBY-5A Catalina (2459/PH-PBY)	Neptune Association, Lelystad, The Netherlands	
174	Fokker S-11 Instructor (E-31/G-BEPV) [K]	Privately owned, Spanhoe	
179	Fokker S-11 Instructor (PH-ACG) [K]	Privately owned, Lelystad, The Netherlands	
197	Fokker S-11 Instructor (PH-GRY) [K]	KLu Historic Flt, Gilze-Rijen, The Netherlands	
204	Lockheed SP-2H Neptune [V]	RAF Museum, Cosford	
A-57	DH82A Tiger Moth (PH-TYG)	KLu Historic Flt, Gilze-Rijen, The Netherlands	
B-64	Noorduyn AT-16 Harvard IIB (PH-LSK)	KLu Historic Flt, Gilze-Rijen, The Netherlands	
B-71	Noorduyn AT-16 Harvard IIB (PH-MLM)	KLu Historic Flt, Gilze-Rijen, The Netherlands	
B-118	Noorduyn AT-16 Harvard IIB (PH-IIB)	KLu Historic Flt, Gilze-Rijen, The Netherlands	
B-182	Noorduyn AT-16 Harvard IIB (PH-TBR)	KLu Historic Flt, Gilze-Rijen, The Netherlands	
E-14	Fokker S-11 Instructor (PH-AFS)	Privately owned, Lelystad, The Netherlands	
E-15	Fokker S-11 Instructor (G-BIYU)	Privately owned, RAF Topcliffe	
E-20	Fokker S-11 Instructor (PH-GRB)	Privately owned, Gilze-Rijen, The Netherlands	
E-27	Fokker S-11 Instructor (PH-HOL)	Privately owned, Lelystad, The Netherlands	
E-29	Fokker S-11 Instructor (PH-HOK)	Privately owned, Lelystad, The Netherlands	

Notes	Serial	Type (code/other identity)	Owner/operator, location or fate
	E-32	Fokker S-11 Instructor (PH-HOI)	Privately owned, Gilze-Rijen, The Netherlands
	E-39	Fokker S-11 Instructor (PH-HOG)	Privately owned, Lelystad, The Netherlands
	G-29	Beech D18S (PH-KHV)	KLu Historic Flt, Gilze-Rijen, The Netherlands
MH424		VS361 Spitfire LFIXC (MJ271/H-53/G-IRTY)	Privately owned, Duxford
	MK732	VS361 Spitfire LFIXC (8633M/PH-OUQ) [3W-17]	KLu Historic Flt, Gilze-Rijen, The Netherlands
	N-202	Hawker Hunter F6 [10] <ff>	Privately owned, Stockport
	N-250	Hawker Hunter F6 (G-9-185) <ff>	IWM Duxford
N-294		Hawker Hunter F6A (XF515/G-KAXF)	Stichting Hawker Hunter Foundation, Leeuwarden, The Netherlands
	N-302	Hawker Hunter T7 (ET-273/G-9-431) <ff>	South Yorkshire Aircraft Museum, Doncaster
	N-315	Hawker Hunter T7 (comp XM121)	Privately owned, Netherley, Aberdeenshire
N-321		Hawker Hunter T8C (G-BWGL)	Stichting Hawker Hunter Foundation, Leeuwarden, The Netherlands
N5-149		NA B-25J Mitchell (44-29507/*HD346*/PH-XXV) [232511]	KLu Historic Flt, Gilze-Rijen, The Netherlands
	R-18	Auster III (PH-NGK)	KLu Historic Flt, Gilze-Rijen, The Netherlands
	R-55	Piper L-18C Super Cub (52-2466/G-BLMI)	Privately owned, Antwerp, Belgium
	R-109	Piper L-21B Super Cub (54-2337/PH-GAZ)	KLu Historic Flt, Gilze-Rijen, The Netherlands
	R-122	Piper L-21B Super Cub (54-2412/PH-PPW)	KLu Historic Flt, Gilze-Rijen, The Netherlands
	R-124	Piper L-21B Super Cub (54-2414/PH-APA)	Privately owned, Eindhoven, The Netherlands
	R-137	Piper L-21B Super Cub (54-2427/PH-PSC)	Privately owned, Gilze-Rijen, The Netherlands
	R-151	Piper L-21B Super Cub (54-2441/G-BIYR)	Privately owned, Yarcombe, Devon
	R-156	Piper L-21B Super Cub (54-2446/G-ROVE)	Privately owned, Headcorn
	R-167	Piper L-21B Super Cub (54-2457/G-LION)	Privately owned, Turweston, Bucks
R-170		Piper L-21B Super Cub (52-6222/PH-ENJ)	Privately owned, Midden Zealand, The Netherlands
	R-177	Piper L-21B Super Cub (54-2467/PH-KNR)	KLu Historic Flt, Gilze-Rijen, The Netherlands
	R-181	Piper L-21B Super Cub (54-2471/PH-GAU)	Privately owned, Gilze-Rijen, The Netherlands
	R-213	Piper L-21A Super Cub (51-15682/PH-RED)	Privately owned, Seppe, The Netherlands
R-345		Piper L-4J Grasshopper (PH-UCS)	Privately owned, Hilversum, The Netherlands
	S-9	DHC2 L-20A Beaver (55-4585/PH-DHC)	KLu Historic Flt, Gilze-Rijen, The Netherlands
NEW ZEALAND			
	NZ3909	WS Wasp HAS1 (XT782/G-KANZ)	Privately owned, Thruxton
NORTH KOREA			
	-	WSK Lim-2 (MiG-15) (01420/G-BMZF)	FAA Museum, RNAS Yeovilton
NORTH VIETNAM			
	1211	WSK Lim-5 (MiG-17F) (G-MIGG)	Privately owned, North Weald
NORWAY			
145		DH82A Tiger Moth II (DE248/LN-BDM)	Privately owned, Kjeller, Norway
163		Fairchild PT-19A Cornell (42-83641/LN-BIF)	Privately owned, Kjeller, Norway
171		DH82A Tiger Moth II (T6168/LN-KAY)	Privately owned, Kjeller, Norway
599		Canadair CT-133AUP Silver Star Mk.3 (133599/NX865SA)	Norwegian AF Historical Sqn, Ørland, Norway
	848	Piper L-18C Super Cub (LN-ACL) [FA-N]	Privately owned, Norway
	56321	SAAB S91B Safir (G-BKPY)	Newark Air Museum, Winthorpe
PX-K		DH100 Vampire FB6 (LN-DHY)	Norwegian AF Historical Sqn, Rygge, Norway
PX-M		DH115 Vampire T55 (LN-DHZ)	Norwegian AF Historical Sqn, Rygge, Norway
OMAN			
417		BAC Strikemaster Mk.80A (G-RSAF)	Privately owned, Hawarden
	425	BAC Strikemaster Mk.82A (G-SOAF)	Privately owned, Hawarden
	801	Hawker Hunter T66B <ff>	Privately owned, St Athan
	801	Hawker Hunter T66B <rf>	Privately owned, Hawarden
	853	Hawker Hunter FR10 (XF426)	RAF Museum, Hendon

F5459 is a 1983 vintage replica SE5A (G-INNY), based at Temple Bruer in Lincolnshire.

Spitfire IIA P7350 is the oldest Spitfire operated by the Battle of Britain Memorial Flight, based at RAF Coningsby. She is currently painted as Spitfire N3162/EB-G of No 41 Squadron, the aircraft flown by the top-scoring Battle of Britain fighter ace Eric Lock when he destroyed 3 enemy aircraft in a single sortie on 5 September 1940.

The Royal Navy Historic Flight's Blackburn-built Swordfish, W5856 (G-BMGC) is the oldest surviving Fairey Swordfish in the world. She first flew on 21 October 1941.

Tiger Moth NM138/41 (G-ANEW) was built by Morris Motors at Cowley in 1943 and delivered to the RAF Aston Down on the 31 January 1944. Nowadays she is one of a fleet of five Tiger Moths owned by Tiger Moth Training at Henstridge, who offer everything from flying experiences for those who don't want to obtain a licence through to aerobatics and formation flying.

TZ164 is an Isaacs Spitfire, based at Hampstead Norreys in Berkshire.

Chipmunk T10 WD390/68 is registered as G-BWNK and in 2016 moved to be a resident at Compton Abbas in Dorset, where it is seen here.

Following the Shoreham crash in 2015, Hawker Hunters have become very rare on the air show scene. T7 XL565/Y is not airworthy but can be seen doing fast runs down the runway at its Bruntingthorpe base.

The Lightning Preservation Group has two of these beautiful machines which do fast runs regularly. Here F6 XR728/JS streams its parachute after another magnificent display on the Bruntingthorpe runway.

XT787 is a Wasp HAS1, registered as G-KAXT and operating from a base in Hampshire. Sadly it was involved in a forced landing in 2016, sustaining some damage but hopefully it will return to the air soon.

XW544/O is a Buccaneer S2B belonging to the Buccaneer Preservation Group. It is one of several which can be seen flexing its wings and engines down the Bruntingthorpe runway throughout the year.

2015 saw No 4 FTS at RAF Valley retire its Hawk T1s, making these machines far rarer in UK skies. This one, T1A XX200/CO, wears the distinctive skull and crossbones of No 100 Squadron at RAF Leeming.

XX342 is a Hawk T1 belonging to the Empire Test Pilots School at Boscombe Down and is believed to be the last active Hawk wearing the distinctive 'raspberry ripple' markings.

By the end of 2016 Lynx HMA8SRU XZ689 was the oldest of the remaining eight Lynx still in operation with the Navy's 815 NAS. Seen here at its Yeovilton base, it is interesting to compare it with its successor, the Wildcat HMA2, behind.

ZB627/A is a former RAF Gazelle HT3, now flying as G-CBSK. Named 'Ginger' and operated by the Gazelle Squadron Display Team based at Hurstbourne Tarrant in Hampshire, it is one of several of the type, all in different markings, flown by the Team.

ZF485 is a Shorts Tucano T1 based at Linton-on-Ouse in Yorkshire with No 1 FTS. With its successor, the T-6C Texan, now on order, this is a type which will not be seen in UK skies for much longer and indeed a significant number of the fleet have either been sold or put into storage already.

ZG771 is a Tornado GR4, wearing special markings to celebrate the centenary of operations at its RAF Marham base.

ZJ118/B is a Merlin HC3i, one of seven operated by 846 NAS at RNAS Yeovilton. With the transfer of the RAF's Merlin HC3 fleet to the Royal Navy completed in 2016, seven were converted to an interim configuration with folding rotor heads, including this one. Eventually the fleet will consist solely of the grey-painted HC4 variant, the first of which flew late in 2016.

ZJ268/68 is a Squirrel HT1, one of a large number operated by the Defence Helicopter Flying School at RAF Shawbury.

ZJ651/51 is one of a small fleet of Alpha Jets operated by QinetiQ from its Boscombe Down base.

ZK027/R is a Hawk T2 in the markings of No 4(R) Squadron RAF, part of No 4 Flying Training School at RAF Valley. With the retirement of its Hawk T1s in 2016, the T2 is the sole type now operated by 4 FTS.

ZK315 is a Typhoon FGR4 operated by 41(R) Squadron at RAF Coningsby. It wears special markings for the squadron's centenary, with the words 'Seek' and 'Destroy' on its canards.

The small bumps on the rear fuselage forward of the tail reveal this to be a Tranche 3 Typhoon FGR4, designed to take Conformal Fuel Tanks. ZK356 is the second Tranche 3 machine for the RAF and was flown superbly with a full weapons load by a BAE Systems test pilot at the Royal International Air Tattoo at Fairford.

ZM137 is the first Lightning II for the RAF to be seen flying in UK skies. Seen here in the hover, notice the open jet intake on the upper fuselage and the rotated jet nozzle under the rear fuselage.

ZZ384 is a Wildcat AH1, seen operating from its Yeovilton base. Deliveries of this type were almost complete by the end of 2016 and in due course it will be operated by 1 Regiment and 9 Regiment of the Army Air Corps.

ZZ409 is a Wildcat AH1, seen in Army markings operating from Yeovilton. Some Wildcats have been operated by 847 NAS of the Royal Marines but they also wore Army titles. In the case of this machine, by the end of 2016 is was back at Yeovil with Leonardo for modifications.

ZZ514 is a Wildcat HMA2, one of 28 operated by the Royal Navy from Yeovilton. Unlike the Lynx, these don't appear to be likely to be wearing squadron codes or even markings but at the time of this photo this one was being operated by 815 NAS.

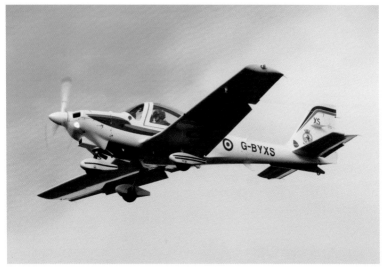

G-BYXS is a Tutor T1 of 727 NAS, RNAS Yeovilton, as evidenced by the badge on the tail. At the end of 2016 it was announced that 28 of these will be sold to Finland and this has also led to a few fleet changes but 'XS remained based with the same unit throughout the year.

85/8-MV is an ex French Air Force Dassault Mystere IVA which is now one of the gate guards at Bruntingthorpe.

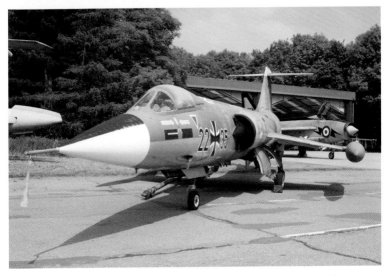

22+35 is a Lockheed F-104G Starfighter, preserved at Bruntingthorpe and looking very much at home with two Cold War cousins for company.

This anonymous nose at Bruntingthorpe is from ex Luftwaffe F-4F Phantom II 37+86, which still wears red 'R' the badge of JG 71 'Richthofen' on the air intake. Clearly it is now used for storing footballs!

L-29 Delfin 53 (66654) is kept in taxiable condition at Bruntingthorpe.

18 red is a Polish-built WSK SBLim-2 (MiG-15UTI) which belongs to the Norwegian Air Force Historical Squadron. It wears its civil identity, N104CJ on the tail and rear fuselage.

252 is one of two Airtech CN.235MPA Persuaders operated by the Irish Air Corps from Baldonnel.

A41-213 is one of eight Globemaster IIIs operated by the Royal Australian Air Force from it base at Amberley, Queensland.

Belgian Sea King Mk.48 RS05 still wears special markings to celebrate 25 years of Belgian Sea King operations, an event celebrated way back in 2001.

069 is a Pilatus PC-9M belonging to the Croatian Air Force's 'Krija Oluje' aerobatic team based at Zadar. The team made its UK debut at the Royal International Air Tattoo in July 2016.

Rafale C 142 is seen here wearing the code 4-GU of Escadron de Transformation Rafale 03.004 'Aquitaine', of the French Air Force, based at Saint Dizier.

Mirage 2000N 353/125-AM of the French Air Force Escadron de Chasse 02.004 'La Fayette' wore these special markings in 2016 and is seen here at the Royal International Air Tattoo at Fairford where it was one half of the magnificent 'Ramex Delta' team. Sadly on this very day the team did its last UK show before retirement - their precision flying of these magnificent aircraft will be greatly missed.

30+29 is a Luftwaffe Eurofighter EF.2000GS of the Luftwaffe's TLG 74 'Molders', based at Neuburg. It wears special NATO Tiger Meet 2016 markings.

2016 saw the 60th anniversary of the Luftwaffe and to celebrate this EF.2000GS 30+68 of TLG 74 'Molders', based at Neuburg was painted in this striking colour scheme.

These spectacular markings were applied to the Hellenic Air Force's solo F-16C-52 display ship, operated by 343 Mira. Named 'Zeus' the serial is 523.

505 is one of two short fuselage C-130J Hercules II operated by the Royal Air Force of Oman's 16 Squadron at Musannah.

As it says on the tail, 051 is a PZL-130TC-II Orlik, in this case being operated by the Polish Air Force's 'Team Orlik', based at Radom.

J-3090 is a F-5E Tiger II of the Swiss Air Force's 'Patrouille Suisse' aerobatic team and these aircraft are slowly disappearing from the Swiss inventory. This particular display at RIAT 2016 was grounded by low cloud, leading to the unique situation of the team displaying on the runway with its commentator coming up with a very amusing variation on his normal speech!

09-(4)181/FF is a Lockheed Martin F-22A Raptor of the USAF's 1st Fighter Wing, based at Langley AFB, Virginia.

(12-)0064 is a Bell-Boeing CV-22B Osprey of the USAF's 7th Special Operations Squadron, part of the 352nd Special Operations Wing, based at RAF Mildenhall in Suffolk.

Virtually all of the USAF's C-5 Galaxy fleet is now in the form of the C-5M Super Galaxy variant which, to many, sounds a lot less impressive but which undoubtedly has a much better performance and reliability. C-5M 87-0045 belongs to the 436th Airlift Wing, based at Dover, Delaware.

59-1458 is a KC-135R Stratotanker of the 166th Air Refueling Squadron, belonging to the Ohio Air National Guard's 121st Air Refueling Wing, based at Rickenbacker ANGB and wears a slightly non-standard colour scheme.

Serial	Type (code/other identity)	Owner/operator, location or fate	Notes
XF688	Percival P56 Provost T1 (WV562/7606M)	Michael Beetham Conservation Centre, Cosford	
XL554	SAL Pioneer CC1 (XL703/8034M)	Michael Beetham Conservation Centre, Cosford	
POLAND			
05	WSK SM-2 (Mi-2) (S2-03006)	The Helicopter Museum, Weston-super-Mare	
309	WSK SBLim-2A (MiG-15UTI) <ff>	R Scottish Mus'm of Flight, stored Granton	
458	Mikoyan MiG-23ML (04 red/024003607)	Newark Air Museum, Winthorpe	
618	Mil Mi-8P (10618)	The Helicopter Museum, Weston-super-Mare	
1018	WSK-PZL Mielec TS-11 Iskra (1H-1018/G-ISKA)	Cold War Jets Collection, Bruntingthorpe	
1120	WSK Lim-2 (MiG-15bis)	RAF Museum, Cosford	
1706	WSK-PZL Mielec TS-11 Iskra (1H-0408)	Midland Air Museum, Coventry	
1972	Letov S-102 (MiG-15) (623794)	Norfolk & Suffolk Avn Museum, Flixton	
	(port side only, painted in Czech marks as 3794 on starboard side)		
PORTUGAL			
85	Isaacs Fury II (G-BTPZ)	*Cancelled as not built*	
1350	OGMA/DHC1 Chipmunk T20 (G-CGAO)	Privately owned, Spanhoe	
1365	OGMA/DHC1 Chipmunk T20 (G-DHPM)	Privately owned, Sywell	
1367	OGMA/DHC1 Chipmunk T20 (G-UANO)	Privately owned, Sherburn-in-Elmet	
1372	OGMA/DHC1 Chipmunk T20 (HB-TUM)	Privately owned, Switzerland	
1373	OGMA/DHC1 Chipmunk T20 (G-CBJG)	Privately owned, Winwick, Cambs	
1375	OGMA/DHC1 Chipmunk T20 (F-AZJV)	Privately owned, Valenciennes, France	
1377	DHC1 Chipmunk Mk.22 (G-BARS)	Privately owned, Yeovilton	
1741	CCF T-6J Texan (G-HRVD)	Privately owned, Bruntingthorpe	
1747	CCF T-6J Texan (20385/G-BGPB)	The Aircraft Restoration Co, Duxford	
1765	CCF T-6J Texan (G-CHYN)	*Repainted in German marks as BF+070, 2016*	
3303	MH1521M Broussard (G-CBGL)	Privately owned, Rochester	
QATAR			
QA10	Hawker Hunter FGA78	Yorkshire Air Museum, Elvington	
QA12	Hawker Hunter FGA78 <ff>	Privately owned, New Inn, Torfaen	
QP30	WS Lynx Mk.28 (G-BFDV/TAD013)	*Currently not known*	
QP31	WS Lynx Mk.28	Vector Aerospace Fleetlands Apprentice School	
QP32	WS Lynx Mk.28 (TD 016) [A]	DSAE SAAE, Lyneham	
ROMANIA			
29	LET L-29 Delfin	Privately owned, Pocklington	
42	LET L-29 Delfin <ff>	Privately owned, Catshill, Worcs	
42	LET L-29 Delfin <rf>	Privately owned, Hinstock, Shrops	
47	LET L-29 Delfin <ff>	Top Gun Flight Simulator Centre, Stalybridge	
53	LET L-29 Delfin [66654]	Privately owned, Bruntingthorpe	
RUSSIA (& FORMER SOVIET UNION)			
-	Mil Mi-24D (3532464505029)	Midland Air Museum, Coventry	
00 w	Yakovlev Yak-3M (0470202/G-OLEG)	Privately owned, Goodwood	
1 w	SPP Yak C-11 (171314/G-BZMY)	Privately owned, Booker	
01 y	Yakovlev Yak-52 (9311709/G-YKSZ)	Privately owned, White Waltham	
03 bl	Yakovlev Yak-55M (910103/RA-01274)	Privately owned, Halfpenny Green	
03 w	Yakovlev Yak-18A (1160403/G-CEIB)	Privately owned, Breighton	
5 w	Yakovlev Yak-3UA (0470204/D-FYGJ)	Privately owned, Bremgarten, Germany	
06 y	Yakovlev Yak-9UM (HB-RYA)	Flying Fighter Association, Bex, Switzerland	
07 y	WSK SM-1 (Mi-1) (Polish AF 2007)	The Helicopter Museum, Weston-super-Mare	
07 y	Yakovlev Yak-18M (G-BMJY)	Privately owned, Membury, Bucks	
07 r	Yakovlev Yak-52 (9011107/G-HYAK)	*Sold as RA-3585K, December 2009*	
09 y	Yakovlev Yak-52 (9411809/G-BVMU)	*Sold as LN-AIA, March 2015*	
9 w	SPP Yak C-11 (1701139/G-OYAK)	Privately owned, Little Gransden	
10 r	Yakovlev Yak-50 (801810/G-BTZB)	Privately owned, Lee-on-Solent	
10 r	Yakovlev Yak-50 (877610/G-YAKE)	Privately owned, Henstridge	
11 y	SPP Yak C-11 (G-YCII)	Privately owned, Henstridge	

121

Notes	Serial	Type (code/other identity)	Owner/operator, location or fate
	12 r	LET L-29 Delfin (194555/ES-YLM/G-DELF)	Privately owned, St Athan
	15 w	SPP Yak C-11 (170103/D-FYAK)	Classic Aviation Company, Hannover, Germany
	18 r	LET L-29 Delfin (591771/YL-PAF)	Privately owned, Hawarden
	18 r	WSK SBLim-2 (MiG-15UTI) (1A01004/N104CJ)	Norwegian AF Historical Sqn, Rygge, Norway
	20 r	Yakovlev Yak-50 (812003/G-YAAK)	Privately owned, Henstridge
	20 w	Lavochkin La-11	The Fighter Collection, Duxford
	21 w	Yakovlev Yak-3UA (0470203/G-CDBJ)	Privately owned, Folkestone
	21 w	Yakovlev Yak-9UM (0470403/D-FENK)	Privately owned, Magdeburg, Germany
	23 y	Bell P-39Q Airacobra (44-2911)	Privately owned, Sussex
	23 r	Mikoyan MiG-27D (83712515040)	Privately owned, Hawarden
	26 bl	Yakovlev Yak-52 (9111306/G-BVXK)	Privately owned, White Waltham
	27 w	Yakovlev Yak-3UTI-PW (9/04623/F-AZIM)	Privately owned, la Ferté-Alais, France
	27 r	Yakovlev Yak-52 (9111307/G-YAKX)	Privately owned, Popham
	28 w	Polikarpov Po-2 (0094/G-BSSY)	The Shuttleworth Collection, Old Warden
	33 r	Yakovlev Yak-50 (853206/G-YAKZ)	Privately owned, Henstridge
	33 w	Yakovlev Yak-52 (899915/G-YAKH)	Privately owned, White Waltham
	35 r	Sukhoi Su-17M-3 (25102)	Privately owned, Hawarden
	36 w	LET/Yak C-11 (171101/G-KYAK)	Privately owned, North Weald
	36 r	Yakovlev Yak-52 (9111604/G-IUII)	Privately owned, Gloucester
	43 bl	Yakovlev Yak-52 (877601/G-BWSV)	Privately owned, North Weald
	48 bl	Yakovlev Yak-52 (9111413/G-CBSN)	Sold as RA-3480K, January 2008
	49 r	Yakovlev Yak-50 (822305/G-YAKU)	Privately owned, Henstridge
	50 gy	Yakovlev Yak-52 (9111415/G-CBRW)	Meier Motors, Bremgarten, Germany
	51 r	LET L-29 Delfin (893019/G-BZNT)	Privately owned, St Athan
	51 r	LET L-29S Delfin (491273/YL-PAG)	Privately owned, Breighton
	51 y	Yakovlev Yak-50 (812004/G-BWYK)	Privately owned, West Meon, Hants
	52 w	Yakovlev Yak C-11 (171312/G-BTZE)	Privately owned, Booker
	52 w	Yakovlev Yak-52 (9111311/G-YAKV)	Sold as ZK-YIK, December 2015
	52 w	Yakovlev Yak-52 (9612001/G-CCJK)	Privately owned, White Waltham
	52 y	Yakovlev Yak-52 (878202/G-BWVR)	Privately owned, Eshott
	54 r	Sukhoi Su-17M (69004)	Privately owned, Hawarden
	55 y	Yakovlev Yak-52 (9111505/G-BVOK)	Sold as LN-HAD, February 2014
	61 r	Yakovlev Yak-50 (842710/G-YAKM)	Privately owned, Henstridge
	66 r	Yakovlev Yak-52 (855905/G-YAKN)	Privately owned, Henstridge
	67 r	Yakovlev Yak-52 (822013/G-CBSL)	Privately owned, Tollerton
	69 y	Yakovlev Yak-52 (888712/G-CCSU)	Sold as SP-YSU, September 2015
	71 r	Mikoyan MiG-27K (61912507006)	Newark Air Museum, Winthorpe
	74 w	Yakovlev Yak-52 (877404/G-OUGH) [JA-74, IV-62]	Privately owned, Swansea
	93 w	Yakovlev Yak-50 (853001/G-JYAK) [R]	Privately owned, North Weald
	100 bl	Yakovlev Yak-52 (866904/G-YAKI)	Privately owned, Popham
	100 w	Yakovlev Yak-3M (0470107/G-CGXG)	Privately owned, Bentwaters
	139 y	Yakovlev Yak-52 (833810/G-BWOD)	Privately owned, Sywell
	526 bk	Mikoyan MiG-29 (2960725887) <ff>	Fenland & West Norfolk Aviation Museum, Wisbech
	1342	Yakovlev Yak-1 (G-BTZD)	Privately owned, Westfield, Sussex
	1870710	Ilyushin Il-2 (G-BZVW)	Privately owned, Wickenby
	1878576	Ilyushin Il-2 (G-BZVX)	Privately owned, Wickenby
	(PT879)	VS361 Spitfire FIX (G-BYDE)	Repainted in UK markings, 2016
	(RK858)	VS361 Spitfire LFIX (G-CGJE)	The Fighter Collection, Duxford
	(SM639)	VS361 Spitfire LFIX	Privately owned, Catfield

SAUDI ARABIA

Notes	Serial	Type (code/other identity)	Owner/operator, location or fate
	1104	BAC Strikemaster Mk.80 (G-SMAS)	Sold as N702MF, October 2016
	1112	BAC Strikemaster Mk.80 (G-FLYY)	Repainted as G-FLYY
	1115	BAC Strikemaster Mk.80A	Global Aviation, Humberside
	1120	BAC Strikemaster Mk.80A (G-RSAF)	Repainted in Omani marks as 417, February 2016
	1129	BAC Strikemaster Mk.80A	Global Aviation, Humberside
	1133	BAC Strikemaster Mk.80A (G-BESY)	IWM Duxford
	53-686	BAC Lightning F53 (G-AWON/ZF592)	City of Norwich Aviation Museum
	55-713	BAC Lightning T55 (ZF598) [C]	Midland Air Museum, Coventry

Serial	Type (code/other identity)	Owner/operator, location or fate	Notes
SINGAPORE			
311	BAC Strikemaster Mk.84 (G-MXPH)	Privately owned, North Weald	
323	BAC Strikemaster Mk.81 (N21419)	Privately owned, stored Hawarden	
SOUTH AFRICA			
91	Westland Wasp HAS1 (pod)	Privately owned, Oaksey Park	
92	Westland Wasp HAS1 (G-BYCX)	Privately owned, Thruxton	
6130	Lockheed Ventura II (AJ469)	RAF Museum, stored Cosford	
7429	NA AT-6D Harvard III (D-FASS)	Privately owned, Aachen, Germany	
SOUTH ARABIA			
104	BAC Jet Provost T52A (G-PROV)	Privately owned, North Weald	
SOUTH VIETNAM			
24550	Cessna L-19E Bird Dog (G-PDOG) [GP]	Privately owned, Fenland	
SPAIN			
B.2I-27	CASA 2.111B (He111H-16) (B.2I-103)	IWM Duxford, stored	
E.3B-143	CASA 1.131E Jungmann (G-JUNG)	Privately owned, White Waltham	
E.3B-153	CASA 1.131E Jungmann (G-BPTS) [781-75]	Privately owned, Egginton	
E.3B-350	CASA 1.131E Jungmann (G-BHPL) [05-97]	Privately owned, Henstridge	
(E.3B+79)	CASA 1.131E Jungmann (G-CDJU) [72-36]	Repainted as CX+HI, April 2016	
E.3B-494	CASA 1.131E Jungmann (G-CDLC) [81-47]	Privately owned, Chiseldon	
E.3B-521	CASA 1.131E Jungmann [781-3]	RAF Museum Reserve Collection, Stafford	
E.3B-599	CASA 1.131E Jungmann (G-CGTX) [31]	Privately owned, Archerfield, Lothian	
E.18-2	Piper PA-31P Navajo 425 [42-71]	High Harthay Outdoor Pursuits, Huntingdon	
EM-01	DH60G Moth (G-AAOR)	Repainted as G-AAOR	
ES.1-4	Bücker Bü133C Jungmeister (G-BUTX)	Repainted as G-BUTX	
SRI LANKA			
CT180	Nanchang CJ-6A Chujiao (2632016/G-BXZB)	Privately owned, White Waltham	
SWEDEN			
-	Thulin A/Bleriot XI (SE-XMC)	Privately owned, Loberod, Sweden	
087	CFM 01 Tummelisa <R> (SE-XIL)	Privately owned, Loberod, Sweden	
2542	Fiat CR42 (G-CBLS)	The Fighter Collection, Duxford	
5033	Klemm Kl35D (SE-BPT) [78]	Privately owned, Barkaby, Sweden	
5060	Klemm Kl35D (SE-BPU) [174]	Privately owned, Barkaby, Sweden	
05108	DH60 Moth	Privately owned, Langham	
17239	SAAB B 17A (SE-BYH) [7-J]	Flygvapenmuseum, Linköping, Sweden	
28693	DH100 Vampire FB6 (J-1184/LN-VMP) [9-G]	Stored at Halmstad, Sweden	
29640	SAAB J 29F [20-08]	Midland Air Museum, Coventry	
29670	SAAB J 29F (SE-DXB) [10-R]	Swedish Air Force Historic Flt, Såtenäs, Sweden	
32028	SAAB 32A Lansen (G-BMSG) <ff>	Privately owned, Willenhall, Staffs	
35075	SAAB J 35A Draken [40]	Dumfries & Galloway Aviation Museum	
35515	SAAB J 35F Draken [49]	Airborne Systems, Llangeinor	
35810	SAAB Sk 35C Draken (SE-DXP) [810]	Swedish Air Force Historic Flt, Såtenäs, Sweden	
37098	SAAB AJSF 37 Viggen (SE-DXN) [52]	Swedish Air Force Historic Flt, Såtenäs, Sweden	
37918	SAAB AJSH 37 Viggen [57]	Newark Air Museum, Winthorpe	
60140	SAAB Sk 60E (SE-DXG) [140-5]	Swedish Air Force Historic Flt, Såtenäs, Sweden	
91130	SAAB S91A Safir (SE-BNN) [10-30]	Privately owned, Barkaby, Sweden	
SWITZERLAND			
-	DH112 Venom FB54 (J-1758/N203DM)	Grove Technology Park, Wantage, Oxon	
A-10	CASA 1.131E Jungmann (G-BECW)	Privately owned, Rochester	
A-44	CASA 1.131E Jungmann 2000 (G-CIUE)	Privately owned, Breighton	
A-57	CASA 1.131E Jungmann (G-BECT)	Privately owned, Goodwood	
A-125	Pilatus P2-05 (G-BLKZ) (fuselage)	Privately owned, Newquay	

Notes	Serial	Type (code/other identity)	Owner/operator, location or fate
	A-701	Junkers Ju52/3m (HB-HOS)	*Repainted as HB-HOS*
	A-702	Junkers Ju52/3m (HB-HOT)	*Repainted as HB-HOT*
	A-703	Junkers Ju52/3m (HB-HOP)	*Repainted as HB-HOP*
	A-806	Pilatus P3-03 (G-BTLL)	Privately owned, Guist, Norfolk
	A-815	Pilatus P3-03 (HB-RCQ)	Privately owned, Locarno, Switzerland
	A-818	Pilatus P3-03 (HB-RCH)	Privately owned, Ambri, Switzerland
	A-829	Pilatus P3-03 (HB-RCJ)	Privately owned, Altenrhein, Switzerland
	A-873	Pilatus P3-03 (HB-RCL)	Privately owned, Locarno, Switzerland
	C-552	EKW C-3605 (G-DORN)	Privately owned, Little Gransden (dismantled)
	C-558	EKW C-3605 (G-CCYZ)	Privately owned, Wickenby
	J-143	F+W D-3801 (MS406) (HB-RCF)	Privately owned, Bex, Switzerland
	J-1008	DH100 Vampire FB6	de Havilland Aircraft Museum, London Colney
	J-1169	DH100 Vampire FB6	Privately owned, Henley-on-Thames
	J-1172	DH100 Vampire FB6 (8487M)	RAF Museum Reserve Collection, Stafford
	J-1605	DH112 Venom FB50 (G-BLID)	Gatwick Aviation Museum, Charlwood, Surrey
	J-1629	DH112 Venom FB50	Privately owned, Shropshire
	J-1632	DH112 Venom FB50 (G-VNOM) <ff>	Privately owned, Cantley, Norfolk
	J-1649	DH112 Venom FB50 <ff>	Cornwall Aviation Heritage Centre, Newquay
	J-1704	DH112 Venom FB54	RAF Museum, stored Cosford
	J-1712	DH112 Venom FB54 <ff>	Privately owned, Connah's Quay, Flintshire
	J-4015	Hawker Hunter F58 (J-4040/HB-RVS)	Privately owned, St Stephan, Switzerland
	J-4064	Hawker Hunter F58 (HB-RVQ)	Fliegermuseum Altenrhein, Switzerland
	J-4083	Hawker Hunter F58 (G-EGHH)	Privately owned, St Athan
	J-4086	Hawker Hunter F58 (HB-RVU)	Privately owned, Altenrhein, Switzerland
	J-4110	Hawker Hunter F58A (XF318/G-CJWL)	HHA Ltd, Scampton
	J-4201	Hawker Hunter T68 (HB-RVR)	Amici dell'Hunter, Sion, Switzerland
	J-4205	Hawker Hunter T68 (HB-RVP)	Fliegermuseum Altenrhein, Switzerland
	J-4206	Hawker Hunter T68 (HB-RVV)	Fliegermuseum Altenrhein, Switzerland
	U-80	Bücker Bü133D Jungmeister (G-BUKK)	Privately owned, Kirdford, W Sussex
	U-95	Bücker Bü133C Jungmeister (G-BVGP)	Privately owned, Turweston
	U-99	Bücker Bü133C Jungmeister (G-AXMT)	Privately owned, Italy
	U-1215	DH115 Vampire T11 (XE998)	Solent Sky, Southampton
	U-1229	DH115 Vampire T55 (G-HATD)	Aviation Heritage Ltd, Coventry
	V-54	SE3130 Alouette II (G-BVSD)	Privately owned, Glos
	UNITED ARAB EMIRATES		
	DU-103	Bell 206B JetRanger II	Privately owned, Coney Park, Leeds
	USA		
	-	Noorduyn AT-16 Harvard IIB (KLu B-168)	American Air Museum, Duxford
	001	Ryan ST-3KR Recruit (G-BYPY)	Privately owned, Goodwood
	07	Boeing-Stearman PT-17 Kaydet (N62658)	Privately owned, Hurstbourne Tarrant, Hants
	14	Boeing-Stearman A75N-1 Kaydet (3486/G-ISDN)	Privately owned, Oaksey Park
	23	Fairchild PT-23 (N49272)	Privately owned, Sleap
	26	Boeing-Stearman A75N-1 Kaydet (G-BAVO)	Privately owned, Enstone
	27	NA SNJ-7 Texan (90678/G-BRVG)	Privately owned, Rochester
	31	Boeing-Stearman A75N-1 Kaydet (42-16338/G-KAYD)	Privately owned, Enstone
	43	Noorduyn AT-16 Harvard IIB (43-13064/G-AZSC) [SC]	Privately owned, Goodwood
	44	Boeing-Stearman D75N-1 Kaydet (42-15852/G-RJAH)	Privately owned, Duxford
	72	NA SNJ-5 Texan (42-85897/N6972C/G-DHHF) [JF]	Privately owned, Compton Abbas
	85	WAR P-47 Thunderbolt <R> (G-BTBI)	Privately owned, Perth
	104	Boeing-Stearman PT-13D Kaydet (42-16931/N4712V) [W]	Privately owned, Hardwick, Norfolk
	107	Boeing-Stearman PT-17 Kaydet (42-16107/N62658)	Privately owned, Hurstbourne Tarrant, Hants
	112	Boeing-Stearman PT-13D Kaydet (42-17397/G-BSWC)	Privately owned, Gloucester
	131	Boeing-Stearman PT-17 Kaydet (38254/N74677)	Privately owned, Enstone
	164	Boeing-Stearman PT-13B Kaydet (41-0823/N60320)	Privately owned, Fenland
	317	Boeing-Stearman PT-18 Kaydet (41-61042/G-CIJN)	Privately owned, Goodwood
	379	Boeing-Stearman PT-13D Kaydet (42-14865/G-ILLE)	Privately owned, Hohenems, Austria
	399	Boeing-Stearman N2S-5 Kaydet (38495/N67193)	Privately owned, Gelnhausen, Germany
	441	Boeing-Stearman N2S-4 Kaydet (30010/G-BTFG)	Privately owned, Postling, Kent
	443	Boeing-Stearman E75 Kaydet (N43YP) [6018]	Privately owned, Bicester

Serial	Type (code/other identity)	Owner/operator, location or fate	Notes
466	Boeing-Stearman PT-13A Kaydet (37-0089/G-PTBA)	Privately owned, Gloucester	
540	Piper L-4H Grasshopper (43-29877/G-BCNX)	Privately owned, Monewden	
560	Bell UH-1H Iroquois (73-22077/G-HUEY)	Privately owned, North Weald	
578	Boeing-Stearman N2S-5 Kaydet (N1364V)	Privately owned, North Weald	
586	Boeing-Stearman N2S-3 Kaydet (07874/N74650)	Privately owned, Seppe, The Netherlands	
628	Beech D17S (44-67761/N18V)	Privately owned, stored East Garston, Bucks	
669	Boeing-Stearman A75N-1 Kaydet (37869/G-CCXA)	Privately owned, Old Buckenham	
671	Boeing-Stearman PT-13D Kaydet (61181/G-CGPY)	Privately owned, Gloucester	
699	Boeing-Stearman N2S-3 Kaydet (38233/G-CCXB)	Privately owned, Goodwood	
716	Boeing-Stearman PT-13D Kaydet (42-17553/N1731B)	Privately owned, Compton Abbas	
718	Boeing-Stearman PT-13D Kaydet (42-17555/N5345N)	Privately owned, Tibenham	
744	Boeing-Stearman A75N-1 Kaydet (42-16532/OO-USN)	Privately owned, Wevelgem, Belgium	
805	Boeing-Stearman PT-17 Kaydet (42-17642/N3922B)	Privately owned, Tibenham	
854	Ryan PT-22 Recruit (41-20854/G-BTBH)	Privately owned, Goodwood	
855	Ryan PT-22 Recruit (41-15510/N56421)	Privately owned, Sleap	
897	Aeronca 11AC Chief (G-BJEV) [E]	Privately owned, English Bicknor, Glos	
985	Boeing-Stearman PT-13D Kaydet (42-16930/OO-OPS)	Privately owned, Antwerp, Belgium	
1102	Boeing-Stearman N2S-5 Kaydet (43449/G-AZLE) [102]	Privately owned, Tongham	
1164	Beech D18S (G-BKGL)	Privately owned,	
3072	NA T-6G Texan (49-3072/G-TEXN) [72]	Privately owned, Goodwood	
3397	Boeing-Stearman N2S-3 Kaydet (G-OBEE) [174]	Privately owned, Old Buckenham	
3403	Boeing-Stearman N2S-3 Kaydet (N75TQ) [180]	Privately owned, Tibenham	
3583	Piper L-4B Grasshopper (45-0583/G-FINT) [44-D]	Privately owned, Eggesford	
3681	Piper L-4J Grasshopper (44-80248/G-AXGP)	Privately owned, Bentwaters	
4406	Naval Aircraft Factory N3N-3 (G-ONAF) [12]	Privately owned, Sandown	
6136	Boeing-Stearman A75N-1 Kaydet(44-16136/G-BRUJ) [205]	Privately owned, Liverpool	
6771	Republic F-84F Thunderstreak (BAF FU-6)	RAF Museum, stored Cosford	
7797	Aeronca L-16A Grasshopper (47-0797/G-BFAF)	Privately owned, Finmere	
8242	NA F-86A Sabre (48-0242) [FU-242]	Midland Air Museum, Coventry	
01532	Northrop F-5E Tiger II <R> (BAPC 336)	RAF Alconbury on display	
02538	Fairchild PT-19B (N33870)	Privately owned, Mendlesham, Suffolk	
07539	Boeing-Stearman N2S-3 Kaydet (N63590) [143]	Privately owned, North Weald	
14286	Lockheed T-33A Shooting Star (51-4286)	IWM, stored Duxford	
O-14419	Lockheed T-33A Shooting Star (51-4419)	Midland Air Museum, Coventry	
14863	NA AT-6D Harvard III (41-33908/G-BGOR)	Privately owned, Rednal	
15372	Piper L-18C Super Cub (51-15372/N123SA) [372-A]	Privately owned, Crowfield	
15979	Hughes OH-6A Cayuse (69-15979)	RAF Mildenhall, instructional use	
15990	Bell AH-1F Hueycobra (70-15990)	Museum of Army Flying, Middle Wallop	
16011	Hughes OH-6A Cayuse (69-16011/G-OHGA)	Privately owned, Wesham, Lancs	
16037	Piper J-3C-65 Cub (G-BSFD)	Privately owned, Sleap	
16171	NA F-86D Sabre (51-6171)	North-East Aircraft Museum, Usworth	
16445	Bell AH-1F Hueycobra (69-16445)	Defence Academy of the UK, Shrivenham	
16506	Hughes OH-6A Cayuse (67-16506)	The Helicopter Museum, Weston-super-Mare	
16544	NA AT-6A Texan (41-16544/N13FY) [FY]	Privately owned, Hilversum, The Netherlands	
16579	Bell OH-1H Iroquois (66-16579)	The Helicopter Museum, Weston-super-Mare	
16718	Lockheed T-33A Shooting Star (51-6718)	City of Norwich Aviation Museum	
17962	Lockheed SR-71A Blackbird (61-7962)	American Air Museum, Duxford	
18263	Boeing-Stearman PT-17 Kaydet (41-8263/N38940) [822]	Privately owned, Tibenham	
19252	Lockheed T-33A Shooting Star (51-9252)	Tangmere Military Aviation Museum	
21509	Bell UH-1H Iroquois (72-21509/G-UHIH)	Privately owned, Wesham, Lancs	
21605	Bell UH-1H Iroquois (72-21605)	American Air Museum, Duxford	
24538	Kaman HH-43F Huskie (62-4535)	Midland Air Museum, Coventry	
24568	Cessna L-19E Bird Dog (LN-WNO)	Army Aviation Norway, Kjeller, Norway	
24582	Cessna L-19E Bird Dog (G-VDOG)	Privately owned, Dundee	
28521	CCF T-6J Texan(52-8521/G-TVIJ) [TA-521]	Privately owned, Woodchurch, Kent	
28562	CCF T-6J Texan (52-8562/20310/G-BSBG) [TA-562]	Privately owned, Tatenhill	
30274	Piper AE-1 Cub Cruiser (N203SA)	Privately owned, Nangis, France	
30861	NA TB-25J Mitchell (44-30861/N9089Z)	Privately owned, Booker	
31145	Piper L-4B Grasshopper (43-1145/G-BBLH) [26-G]	Privately owned, Biggin Hill	
31430	Piper L-4B Grasshopper (43-1430/G-BHVV)	Privately owned, Perranporth	
31952	Aeronca O-58B Defender (G-BRPR)	Privately owned, Belchamp Water	

Notes	Serial	Type (code/other identity)	Owner/operator, location or fate
	34037	NA TB-25N Mitchell (44-29366/N9115Z/8838M)	RAF Museum, Hendon
	34064	NA B-25J Mitchell (44-31171/N7614C) [8U]	American Air Museum, Duxford
	36922	Titan T-51 Mustang (G-CMPC) [WD-Y]	Privately owned, Benwick, Cambs
	37414	McD F-4C Phantom II (63-7414)	Midland Air Museum, stored Coventry
	39624	Wag Aero Sport Trainer (EI-GMH) [39-D]	Privately owned, Abbeyshrule, Eire
	41386	Thomas-Morse S4 Scout <R> (G-MJTD)	Privately owned, Lutterworth
	42165	NA F-100D Super Sabre (54-2165) [VM]	IWM, stored Duxford
	42196	NA F-100D Super Sabre (54-2196)	Norfolk & Suffolk Avn Museum, Flixton
	43517	Boeing-Stearman N2S-5 Kaydet (G-NZSS) [227]	Privately owned, Woodchurch, Kent
	46214	Grumman TBM-3E Avenger (69327/CF-KCG) [X-3]	IWM, Duxford
	51970	NA AT-6D Texan (41-33888/G-TXAN) [V-970]	Privately owned, Rottweil, Germany
	53319	Grumman TBM-3E Avenger (HB-RDG) [19]	Privately owned, Lausanne, Switzerland
	54433	Lockheed T-33A Shooting Star (55-4433) [TR-433]	Norfolk & Suffolk Avn Museum, Flixton
	54884	Piper L-4J Grasshopper (45-4884/N61787) [57-D]	Privately owned, Sywell
	55771	Boeing-Stearman N2S-4 Kaydet (N68427) [427]	Privately owned, Bodmin
	56498	Douglas C-54Q Skymaster (N44914)	Privately owned, stored North Weald
	60312	McD F-101F Voodoo (56-0312)	Midland Air Museum, Coventry
	60344	Ryan Navion (N4956C)	Privately owned, Earls Colne
	60689	Boeing B-52D Stratofortress (56-0689)	American Air Museum, Duxford
	63000	NA F-100D Super Sabre (54-2212) [FW-000]	Scrapped at Molesworth, October 2016
	63319	NA F-100D Super Sabre (54-2269) [FW-319]	RAF Lakenheath, on display
	66692	Lockheed U-2CT (56-6692)	American Air Museum, Duxford
	70270	McD F-101B Voodoo (57-270) (fuselage)	Midland Air Museum, stored Coventry
	80105	Replica SE5a <R> (PH-WWI/G-CCBN) [19]	Privately owned, Thruxton
	82062	DHC U-6A Beaver (58-2062)	Midland Air Museum, Coventry
	85061	NA SNJ-5 Texan (G-CHIA) [7F]	Privately owned, White Waltham
	86690	Grumman FM-2 Wildcat (G-KINL) [F-2]	Privately owned, Duxford
	93542	CCF T-6J Harvard IV (G-BRLV) [LTA-542]	Sold to Norway 18 August 2016
	96995	CV F4U-4 Corsair (OE-EAS) [BR-37]	Flying Bulls, Salzburg, Austria
	111836	NA AT-6C Harvard IIA (41-33262/G-TSIX) [JZ-6]	Privately owned, Gamston
	111989	Cessna L-19A Bird Dog (51-11989/N33600)	Museum of Army Flying, Middle Wallop
	114700	NA T-6G Texan (51-14700/G-TOMC)	Privately owned, Netherthorpe
	115042	NA T-6G Texan (51-15042/G-BGHU) [TA-042]	Privately owned, Postling, Kent
	115227	NA T-6G Texan (51-15227/G-BKRA)	Privately owned, Gloucester
	115302	Piper L-18C Super Cub (51-15302/G-BJTP) [TP]	Privately owned, Defford
	115373	Piper L-18C Super Cub (51-15373/G-AYPM) [A-373]	Privately owned, Leicester
	115684	Piper L-21A Super Cub (51-15684/G-BKVM) [DC]	Privately owned, Strubby
	117415	Canadair CT-133 Silver Star (G-BYOY) [TR-415]	RAF Manston History Museum
	121714	Grumman F8F-2P Bearcat (G-RUMM) [201-B]	The Fighter Collection, Duxford
	123716	CV F4U-5NL Corsair (124541/D-FCOR) [19-WF]	Meier Motors, Bremgarten, Germany
	124143	Douglas AD-4NA Skyraider (F-AZDP) [205-RM]	Amicale J-B Salis, la Ferté-Alais, France
	124485	Boeing B-17G Flying Fortress (44-85784/G-BEDF) [DF-A]	B-17 Preservation Ltd, Duxford
	124724	CV F4U-5NL Corsair (F-AZEG) [22]	Les Casques de Cuir, la Ferté-Alais, France
	126922	Douglas AD-4NA Skyraider (G-RADR) [503-H]	Kennet Aviation, North Weald
	134076	NA AT-6D Texan (41-34671/F-AZSC) [TA076]	Privately owned, Yvetot, France
	138179	NA T-28A Trojan (OE-ESA) [BA]	The Flying Bulls, Salzburg, Austria
	138266	NA T-28B Trojan (HB-RCT) [266-CT]	Jet Alpine Fighter, Sion, Switzerland
	138343	NA T-28B Trojan (N343NA) [212]	Privately owned, Siegerland, Germany
	140547	NA T-28C Trojan (F-AZHN) [IF-28]	Privately owned, Toussus le Noble, France
	140566	NA T-28C Trojan (N556EB) [252]	Privately owned, la Ferté-Alais, France
	146289	NA T-28C Trojan (N99153) [2W]	Norfolk & Suffolk Avn Museum, Flixton
	150225	WS58 Wessex 60 (G-AWOX) [123]	Privately owned, Luisgate
	155454	NA OV-10B Bronco (158300/99+24/F-AZKM) [26]	Privately owned, Montelimar, France
	155529	McD F-4J(UK) Phantom II (ZE359) [AJ-114]	American Air Museum, Duxford
	155848	McD F-4S Phantom II [WT-11]	National Museum of Flight, E Fortune
	159233	HS AV-8A Harrier [CG-33]	IWM North, Salford Quays
	162068	McD AV-8B Harrier II <ff>	Privately owned, Thorpe Wood, N Yorks
	162071	McD AV-8B Harrier II (fuselage)	Rolls-Royce, Filton
	162074	McD AV-8B Harrier II <ff>	Privately owned, South Molton, Devon
	162730	McD AV-8B Harrier II <ff>	Privately owned, Liverpool
	162737	McD AV-8B Harrier II (fuselage) [38]	MoD, Boscombe Down

Serial	Type (code/other identity)	Owner/operator, location or fate	Notes
162958	McD AV-8B Harrier II <ff>	QinetiQ, Farnborough	
162964	McD AV-8B Harrier II <ff>	Harrier Heritage Centre, RAF Wittering	
162964	McD AV-8B Harrier II <rf>	Privately owned, Charlwood, Surrey	
163205	McD AV-8B Harrier II (fuselage)	Privately owned, Thorpe Wood, N Yorks	
163423	McD AV-8B Harrier II <ff>	QinetiQ, Boscombe Down	
163423	McD AV-8B Harrier II <rf>	Privately owned, Sproughton	
217786	Boeing-Stearman PT-17 Kaydet (41-8169/CF-EQS) [25]	American Air Museum, Duxford	
224319	Douglas C-47B Skytrain (44-77047/G-AMSN) <ff>	Privately owned, Sussex	
226413	Republic P-47D Thunderbolt (45-49192/N47DD) [ZU-N]	American Air Museum, Duxford	
234539	Fairchild PT-19B Cornell (42-34539/N50429) [63]	Privately owned, Dunkeswell	
236657	Piper L-4A Grasshopper (42-36657/G-BGSJ) [72-D]	Privately owned, Langport	
237123	Waco CG-4A Hadrian <R> (fuselage)	Yorkshire Air Museum, Elvington	
238133	Boeing B-17G Flying Fortress (44-83735/F-BDRS) [C]	American Air Museum, Duxford	
238410	Piper L-4A Grasshopper (42-38410/G-BHPK) [44-A]	Privately owned, Tibenham	
241079	Waco CG-4A Hadrian <R> (BAPC 370)	RAF Museum, stored Cosford	
243809	Waco CG-4A Hadrian (BAPC 185)	Museum of Army Flying, Middle Wallop	
252983	Schweizer TG-3A (42-52983/N66630)	IWM Duxford, stored	
285068	NAA AT-6D Texan (42-85068/G-KAMY)	Kennet Aviation, North Weald/Yeovilton	
298177	Stinson L-5A Sentinel (42-98177/N6438C) [8-R]	Privately owned, Tibenham	
313048	NAA AT-6D Texan (44-81506/G-TDJN)	Privately owned, Gloucester	
314887	Fairchild Argus III (43-14887/G-AJPI)	Privately owned, Eelde, The Netherlands	
315509	Douglas C-47A Skytrain (43-15509/G-BHUB) [W7-S]	American Air Museum, Duxford	
319764	Waco CG-4A Hadrian (237123/BAPC 157) (fuselage)	Yorkshire Air Museum, Elvington	
329282	Piper J-3C-65 Cub (N46779)	Privately owned, Abbots Bromley	
329405	Piper L-4A Grasshopper (43-29405/G-BCOB) [23-A]	Privately owned, Turweston	
329417	Piper L-4A Grasshopper (42-38400/G-BDHK)	Privately owned, English Bicknor, Glos	
329471	Piper L-4H Grasshopper (43-29471/G-BGXA) [44-F]	Privately owned, Martley, Worcs	
329601	Piper L-4H Grasshopper (43-29601/G-AXHR) [44-D]	Privately owned, Nayland	
329707	Piper L-4H Grasshopper (43-29707/G-BFBY) [44-S]	Privately owned, Old Buckenham	
329854	Piper L-4H Grasshopper (43-29854/G-BMKC) [44-R]	Privately owned, Biggin Hill	
329934	Piper L-4H Grasshopper (43-29934/G-BCPH) [72-B]	Privately owned, Garford, Oxon	
330238	Piper L-4H Grasshopper (43-30238/G-LIVH) [24-A]	Privately owned, Yarcombe, Devon	
330244	Piper L-4H Grasshopper (43-30244/G-CGIY) [46-C]	Privately owned, Church Fenton	
330314	Piper L-4H Grasshopper (43-30314/G-BAET)	Privately owned, Winwick, Cambs	
330372	Piper L-4H Grasshopper (43-30372/G-AISX)	Privately owned, Booker	
330426	Piper L-4J Grasshopper (45-4884/N61787) [53-K]	Privately owned, Sywell	
330485	Piper L-4H Grasshopper (43-30485/G-AJES) [44-C]	Privately owned, Shifnal	
379994	Piper J-3L-65 Cub (G-BPUR) [52-J]	Privately owned, Popham	
411622	NA P-51D Mustang (44-74427/F-AZSB) [G4-C]	Privately owned, Melun, France	
411631	NA P-51D Mustang (44-73979/472218) [MX-V]	American Air Museum, Duxford	
413317	NA P-51D Mustang (44-74409/N51RT) [VF-B]	RAF Museum, Hendon	
413357	NA P-51D Mustang <R> [B7-R]	Privately owned, Byfleet, Surrey	
413521	NA P-51D Mustang (44-13521/G-MRLL) [5Q-B]	Sold to Italy, November 2016	
413573	NA P-51D Mustang (43-73415/9133M/N6526D) [B6-V]	RAF Museum, Cosford	
413578	NA P-51D Mustang (44-74923/PH-JAT) [C5-W]	Privately owned, Lelystad, The Netherlands	
413704	NA P-51D Mustang (44-73149/G-BTCD) [B7-H]	The Old Flying Machine Company, Duxford	
413926	Stewart S-51 Mustang (G-CGOI) [E2-S]	Privately owned, Benwick, Cambs	
414419	NA P-51D Mustang (45-15118/G-MSTG) [LH-F]	Crashed at Hardwick, 2 October 2016	
414237	NA P-51D Mustang (44-73656/F-AZXS) [HO-W]	Privately owned, Avignon, France	
414673	Bonsall Replica Mustang (G-BDWM) [LH-I]	Privately owned, Gamston	
414907	Titan T-51 Mustang (G-DHYS) [CY-S]	Privately owned, Pershore	
433915	Consolidated PBV-1A Canso A (RCAF 11005/G-PBYA)	Privately owned, Duxford	
434602	Douglas A-26B Invader (44-34602/LN-IVA) [B]	Nordic Warbirds, Västerås, Sweden	
436021	Piper J-3C-65 Cub (G-BWEZ)	Privately owned, Archerfield, Lothian	
441968	Titan T-51 Mustang (G-FION) [VF-E]	Privately owned, Netherthorpe	
442268	Noorduyn AT-16 Harvard IIB (KF568/LN-TEX) [TA-268]	Privately owned, Kjeller, Norway	
454467	Piper L-4J Grasshopper (45-4467/G-BILI) [44-J]	Privately owned, RAF Halton	
454537	Piper L-4J Grasshopper (45-4537/G-BFDL) [04-J]	Privately owned, Shempston Farm, Lossiemouth	
461748	Boeing B-29A Superfortress (44-61748/G-BHDK) [Y]	American Air Museum, Duxford	
463209	NA P-51D Mustang <R> (BAPC 255) [WZ-S]	American Air Museum, Duxford	

Notes	Serial	Type (code/other identity)	Owner/operator, location or fate
	472035	NA P-51D Mustang (44-72035/G-SIJJ)	*Repainted in US marks as A3-3, April 2016*
	472216	NA P-51D Mustang (44-72216/G-BIXL) [HO-M]	Privately owned, Goodwood
	472218	Titan T-51 Mustang (G-MUZY) [WZ-I]	Privately owned, Tibenham
	472773	NA P-51D Mustang (44-72773/D-FPSI) [QP-M]	Meier Motors, Bremgarten, Germany
	472922	NA TF-51D Mustang (44-72922/PH-VDF) [L2-W]	Privately owned, Antwerp, Belgium
	473871	NA TF-51D Mustang (44-73871/D-FTSI) [TF-871]	Meier Motors, Bremgarten, Germany
	474008	Jurca MJ77 Gnatsum (G-PSIR) [VF-R]	Privately owned, Fishburn
	474425	NA P-51D Mustang (44-74425/PH-PSI) [OC-G]	Privately owned, Lelystad, The Netherlands
	479712	Piper L-4H Grasshopper (44-79826/G-AHIP) [8-R]	Privately owned, Coleford
	479744	Piper L-4H Grasshopper (44-79744/G-BGPD) [49-M]	Privately owned, Marsh, Bucks
	479766	Piper L-4H Grasshopper (44-79766/G-BKHG) [63-D]	Privately owned, Frogland Cross
	479781	Piper L-4H Grasshopper (44-79781/G-AISS)	Privately owned, Insch (under restoration)
	479897	Piper L-4H Grasshopper (44-79897/G-BOXJ) [JD]	Privately owned, Rochester
	480015	Piper L-4H Grasshopper (44-80015/G-AKIB) [44-M]	Privately owned, Perranporth
	480133	Piper L-4J Grasshopper (44-80133/G-BDCD) [44-B]	Privately owned, Slinfold
	480173	Piper L-4J Grasshopper (44-80609/G-RRSR) [57-H]	Privately owned, Shotteswell
	480321	Piper L-4J Grasshopper (44-80321/G-FRAN) [44-H]	Privately owned, Rayne, Essex
	480480	Piper L-4J Grasshopper (44-80480/G-BECN) [44-E]	Privately owned, Rayne, Essex
	480636	Piper L-4J Grasshopper (44-80636/G-AXHP) [58-A]	Privately owned, Spanhoe
	480723	Piper L-4J Grasshopper (44-80723/G-BFZB) [E5-J]	Privately owned, Egginton
	480752	Piper L-4J Grasshopper (44-80752/G-BCXJ) [39-E]	Privately owned, Melksham
	483868	Boeing B-17G Flying Fortress (44-83868/N5237V) [A-N]	RAF Museum, Hendon
	493209	NA T-6G Texan (49-3209/G-DDMV/*41*)	Privately owned, Headcorn
	779465	Hiller UH-12C (N5315V)	Privately owned, Lower Upham, Hants
	2106638	Titan T-51 Mustang (G-CIFD) [E9-R]	Privately owned, Shobdon
	2100882	Douglas C-47A Skytrain (42-100882/N473DC) [3X-P]	Privately owned, East Kirkby
	2100884	Douglas C-47A Skytrain (42-100884/N147DC) [L4-D]	Privately owned, Dunsfold
	2104590	Curtiss P-40M Kittyhawk (43-5802/G-KITT) [44]	Hangar 11 Collection, North Weald
	2105915	Curtiss P-40N Kittyhawk (42-105915/F-AZKU)	France's Flying Warbirds, Melun, France
	03-08003	B-V CH-47F Chinook [DT]	RAF Odiham, at main gate
	3-1923	Aeronca O-58B Defender (43-1923/G-BRHP)	Privately owned, Chiseldon
	18-2001	Piper L-18C Super Cub (52-2401/G-BIZV)	Privately owned, Wicklow, Ireland
	39-139	Beech YC-43 Traveler (N295BS)	Duke of Brabant AF, Eindhoven, The Netherlands
	39-0285	Curtiss P-40B Warhawk	The Fighter Collection, stored Duxford (wreck)
	39-0287	Curtiss P-40B Warhawk	The Fighter Collection, stored Duxford (wreck)
	40-2538	Fairchild PT-19A Cornell (N33870)	Privately owned, Mendlesham
	41-8689	Boeing-Stearman PT-17D Kaydet (G-BIXN) (frame)	Privately owned, Rendcomb
	41-13357	Curtiss P-40C Warhawk (G-CIIO) [160,10AB]	The Fighter Collection, Duxford
	41-19393	Douglas A-20C Havoc (wreck)	WWII Remembrance Museum, Handcross, W Sussex
	41-33275	NA AT-6C Texan (G-BICE) [CE]	Privately owned, Great Oakley, Essex
	42-66841	Lockheed P-38H Lightning [153]	Privately owned, Bentwaters
	42-12417	Noorduyn AT-16 Harvard IIB (KLu. B-163)	Newark Air Museum, Winthorpe
	42-35870	Taylorcraft DCO-65 (G-BWLJ) [129]	Privately owned, Nayland
	42-46703	Stinson AT-19 Reliant (FK877/N69745)	Privately owned, Birmingham
	42-58678	Taylorcraft DF-65 (G-BRIY) [IY]	Privately owned, Carlisle
	42-78044	Aeronca 11AC Chief (G-BRXL)	Privately owned, Andrewsfield
	42-84555	NA AT-6D Harvard III (FAP.1662/G-ELMH) [EP-H]	Privately owned, Hardwick, Norfolk
	42-93510	Douglas C-47A Skytrain [CM] <ff>	Privately owned, Kew
	43-9628	Douglas A-20G Havoc <ff>	Privately owned, Hinckley, Leics
	43-11137	Bell P-63C Kingcobra (wreck)	WWII Remembrance Museum, Handcross, W Sussex
	43-21664	Douglas A-20G Havoc (wreck)	WWII Remembrance Museum, Handcross, W Sussex
	43-29964	Piper L-4H Grasshopper (G-AKRA) [JA]	Privately owned, Cambridge
	43-35943	Beech 3N (G-BKRN) [943]	Beech Restorations, Bruntingthorpe
	43-36140	NA B-25J Mitchell <ff>	WWII Remembrance Museum, Handcross, W Sussex
	44-4315	Bell P-63C Kingcobra	WWII Remembrance Museum, Handcross, W Sussex
	44-4368	Bell P-63C Kingcobra	Privately owned, Surrey

Serial	Type (code/other identity)	Owner/operator, location or fate	Notes
44-13954	NA P-51D Mustang (G-UAKE)	Mustang Restoration Co Ltd, Coventry	
44-14574	NA P-51D Mustang (fuselage)	East Essex Aviation Museum, Clacton	
44-42914	Douglas DC-4 (N31356) <ff>	Privately owned, Burtonwood	
44-51228	Consolidated B-24M Liberator [EC-493]	American Air Museum, Duxford	
44-79609	Piper L-4H Grasshopper (G-BHXY) [PR]	Privately owned, Bealbury, Cornwall	
44-79649	Piper L-4H Grasshopper (G-AIIH)	Privately owned, Stonesfield, Oxon	
44-80594	Piper L-4J Grasshopper (G-BEDJ)	Privately owned, White Waltham	
44-80647	Piper L-4J Grasshopper (D-EGAF)	Privately owned, Donauwörth, Germany	
51-9036	Lockheed T-33A Shooting Star	Newark Air Museum, Winthorpe	
51-15319	Piper L-18C Super Cub (G-FUZZ) [A-319]	Privately owned, Elvington	
51-15555	Piper L-18C Super Cub (G-OSPS)	Privately owned, Andrewsfield	
52-8543	CCF T-6J Texan (G-BUKY) [66]	Privately owned, Dortmund, Germany	
54-005	NA F-100D Super Sabre (54-2163)	Dumfries & Galloway Avn Mus, Dumfries	
54-174	NA F-100D Super Sabre (54-2174) [SM]	Midland Air Museum, Coventry	
54-2223	NA F-100D Super Sabre	Newark Air Museum, Winthorpe	
54-2445	Piper L-21B Super Cub (G-OTAN) [A-445]	Privately owned, Hawarden	
54-2447	Piper L-21B Super Cub (G-SCUB)	Privately owned, Anwick	
55-138354	NA T-28B Trojan (138354/N1328B) [TL-354]	Privately owned, Antwerp, Belgium	
62-428	Republic F-105G Thunderchief (62-4428) [WW]	Scrapped at Molesworth, October 2016	
63-699	McD F-4C Phantom II (63-7699) [CG]	Midland Air Museum, Coventry	
64-17657	Douglas B-26K Counter Invader (N99218) <ff>	WWII Remembrance Museum, Handcross, W Sussex	
65-777	McD F-4C Phantom II (63-7419) [SA]	RAF Lakenheath, on display	
65-10450	Northrop AT-38B Talon <rf>	Scrapped	
66-374	Helio H.295 Super Courier (G-BAGT) [EO]	Privately owned, Spanhoe	
67-120	GD F-111E Aardvark (67-0120) [UH]	American Air Museum, Duxford	
68-0060	GD F-111E Aardvark <ff>	Dumfries & Galloway Avn Mus, Dumfries	
68-8284	Sikorsky MH-53M Pave Low IV	RAF Museum, Cosford	
70-0389	GD F-111E Aardvark (68-0011) [LN]	RAF Lakenheath, on display	
72-1447	GD F-111F Aardvark <ff>	American Air Museum, Duxford	
74-0177	GD F-111F Aardvark [FN]	RAF Museum, Cosford	
76-020	McD F-15A Eagle (76-0020)	American Air Museum, Duxford	
76-124	McD F-15B Eagle (76-0124) [LN]	RAF Lakenheath, instructional use	
77-259	Fairchild A-10A Thunderbolt (77-0259) [AR]	American Air Museum, Duxford	
80-219	Fairchild GA-10A Thunderbolt (80-0219) [AR]	Bentwaters Cold War Museum	
82-23762	B-V CH-47D Chinook <ff>	RAF Odiham, instructional use	
83-24104	B-V CH-47D Chinook [BN] <ff>	RAF Museum, Hendon	
86-180	McD F-15A Eagle (74-0131) [LN]	RAF Lakenheath, on display	
86-01677	B-V CH-47D Chinook	RAF, stored Odiham	
89-00159	B-V CH-47D Chinook	RAF, stored Odiham	
108-1601	Stinson 108-1 Voyager (G-CFGE) [H]	Privately owned, Spanhoe	
146-11042	Wolf W-11 Boredom Fighter (G-BMZX) [7]	Privately owned, Popham	
146-11083	Wolf W-11 Boredom Fighter (G-BNAI) [5]	Privately owned, Haverfordwest	
A3-3	NA P-51D Mustang (44-72035/G-SIJJ)	Hangar 11 Collection, North Weald	
G-57	Piper L-4A Grasshopper (42-36375/G-AKAZ)	Sold to France, May 2016	
X-17	Curtiss P-40F Warhawk (41-19841/G-CGZP)	The Fighter Collection, Duxford	
CY-D	NA TF-51D Mustang (44-84847/G-TFSI)	North Weald Heritage Aviation, North Weald	
CY-G	Titan T-51 Mustang (G-TSIM)	Privately owned, Shobdon	
PA50	Curtiss P-36C Hawk (38-0210/G-CIXJ)	The Fighter Collection, Duxford	

YUGOSLAVIA

30131	Soko P-2 Kraguj [131]	Privately owned, stored Minskip, N Yorks	
30140	Soko P-2 Kraguj (G-RADA) [140]	Privately owned, Linton-on-Ouse	
30146	Soko P-2 Kraguj (G-BSXD) [146]	Privately owned, Linton-on-Ouse	
30149	Soko P-2 Kraguj (G-SOKO) [149]	Privately owned, Fenland	
51109	UTVA-66 (YU-DLG)	Privately owned, Morpeth	

Notes	Serial	Type (code/other identity)	Owner/operator, location or fate
	C7	Avro 631 Cadet (EI-AGO)	IAC Museum, Baldonnel
	34	Miles M14A Magister I (N5392)	National Museum of Ireland, Dublin
	141	Avro 652A Anson C19	IAC Museum, Baldonnel
	164	DHC1 Chipmunk T20	IAC Museum, Baldonnel
	168	DHC1 Chipmunk T20 (EI-HFA)	Irish Historic Flight, Ballyboy
	169	DHC1 Chipmunk 22 (EI-HFB)	Irish Historic Flight, Ballyboy
	170	DHC1 Chipmunk 22 (EI-HFC)	Irish Historic Flight, Ballyboy
	172	DHC1 Chipmunk T20	IAC, stored Baldonnel
	173	DHC1 Chipmunk T20	South East Aviation Enthusiasts, Dromod
	176	DH104 Dove 4 (VP-YKF)	South East Aviation Enthusiasts, Waterford
	183	Percival P56 Provost T51	IAC Museum, Baldonnel
	184	Percival P56 Provost T51	South East Aviation Enthusiasts, Dromod
	187	DH115 Vampire T55 <ff>	South East Aviation Enthusiasts, Dromod
	191	DH115 Vampire T55	IAC Museum, Baldonnel
	192	DH115 Vampire T55 <ff>	South East Aviation Enthusiasts, Dromod
	195	Sud SA316 Alouette III (F-WJDH)	National Museum of Ireland, Dublin
	198	DH115 Vampire T11 (XE977)	National Museum of Ireland, Dublin
	199	DHC1 Chipmunk T22	IAC, stored Baldonnel
	202	Sud SA316 Alouette III	Ulster Aviation Society, Long Kesh
	203	Reims-Cessna FR172H	IAC No 104 Sqn/1 Operations Wing, Baldonnel
	205	Reims-Cessna FR172H	IAC No 104 Sqn/1 Operations Wing, Baldonnel
	206	Reims-Cessna FR172H	IAC No 104 Sqn/1 Operations Wing, Baldonnel
	207	Reims-Cessna FR172H	IAC, stored Waterford
	208	Reims-Cessna FR172H	IAC No 104 Sqn/1 Operations Wing, Baldonnel
	210	Reims-Cessna FR172H	IAC No 104 Sqn/1 Operations Wing, Baldonnel
	215	Fouga CM170R Super Magister	Dublin Institute of Technology
	216	Fouga CM170R Super Magister	IAC Museum, Baldonnel
	218	Fouga CM170R Super Magister	Shannon Aerospace, Shannon Airport
	219	Fouga CM170R Super Magister	IAC Museum, Baldonnel
	220	Fouga CM170R Super Magister	Cork University, instructional use
	221	Fouga CM170R Super Magister [3-KE]	IAC Museum, stored Baldonnel
	231	SIAI SF-260WE Warrior	IAC Museum, Baldonnel
	240	Beech Super King Air 200MR	IAC No 102 Sqn/1 Operations Wing, Baldonnel
	251	Grumman G1159C Gulfstream IV (N17584)	IAC No 102 Sqn/1 Operations Wing, Baldonnel
	252	Airtech CN.235 MPA Persuader	IAC No 101 Sqn/1 Operations Wing, Baldonnel
	253	Airtech CN.235 MPA Persuader	IAC No 101 Sqn/1 Operations Wing, Baldonnel
	254	PBN-2T Defender 4000 (G-BWPN)	IAC No 106 Sqn/1 Operations Wing, Baldonnel
	256	Eurocopter EC135T-1 (G-BZRM)	IAC No 106 Sqn/1 Operations Wing, Baldonnel
	258	Gates Learjet 45 (N5009T)	IAC No 102 Sqn/1 Operations Wing, Baldonnel
	260	Pilatus PC-9M (HB-HQS)	IAC Flying Training School, Baldonnel
	261	Pilatus PC-9M (HB-HQT)	IAC Flying Training School, Baldonnel
	262	Pilatus PC-9M (HB-HQU)	IAC Flying Training School, Baldonnel
	263	Pilatus PC-9M (HB-HQV)	IAC Flying Training School, Baldonnel
	264	Pilatus PC-9M (HB-HQW)	IAC Flying Training School, Baldonnel
	266	Pilatus PC-9M (HB-HQY)	IAC Flying Training School, Baldonnel
	267	Pilatus PC-9M (HB-HQZ)	IAC Flying Training School, Baldonnel
	270	Eurocopter EC135P-2 (D-HECF)	IAC No 302 Sqn/3 Operations Wing, Baldonnel
	271	Eurocopter EC135P-2 (D-HECB)	IAC No 302 Sqn/3 Operations Wing, Baldonnel
	272	Eurocopter EC135T-2 (G-CECT)	IAC No 106 Sqn/1 Operations Wing, Baldonnel
	274	AgustaWestland AW139	IAC No 301 Sqn/3 Operations Wing, Baldonnel
	275	AgustaWestland AW139	IAC No 301 Sqn/3 Operations Wing, Baldonnel
	276	AgustaWestland AW139	IAC No 301 Sqn/3 Operations Wing, Baldonnel
	277	AgustaWestland AW139	IAC No 301 Sqn/3 Operations Wing, Baldonnel
	278	AgustaWestland AW139	IAC No 301 Sqn/3 Operations Wing, Baldonnel
	279	AgustaWestland AW139	IAC No 301 Sqn/3 Operations Wing, Baldonnel
	2..	Pilatus PC-9M	Pilatus, Stans, for IAC

Serial	Type (code/other identity)	Owner/operator, location or fate	Notes

Aircraft included in this section include those likely to be seen visiting UK civil and military airfields on transport flights, exchange visits, exercises and for air shows. It is not a comprehensive list of *all* aircraft operated by the air arms concerned.

ALGERIA
Ministry of Defence

Serial	Type (code/other identity)	Owner/operator, location or fate
7T-VPC	Grumman G.1159C Gulfstream IVSP (1418)	Ministry of Defence, Boufarik
7T-VPG	Gulfstream Aerospace Gulfstream V (617)	Ministry of Defence, Boufarik
7T-VPM	Grumman G.1159C Gulfstream IVSP (1421)	Ministry of Defence, Boufarik
7T-VPP	Airbus A.340-541	Ministry of Defence, Boufarik
7T-VPR	Grumman G.1159C Gulfstream IVSP (1288)	Ministry of Defence, Boufarik
7T-VPS	Grumman G.1159C Gulfstream IVSP (1291)	Ministry of Defence, Boufarik

Force Aérienne Algérienne (FAA)/Al Quwwat al Jawwiya al Jaza'eriya

Serial	Type (code/other identity)	Owner/operator, location or fate
7T-WHA	Lockheed C-130H-30 Hercules (4997)	FAA 2 ETTL, Boufarik
7T-WHB	Lockheed C-130H-30 Hercules (5224)	FAA 2 ETTL, Boufarik
7T-WHD	Lockheed C-130H-30 Hercules (4987)	FAA 2 ETTL, Boufarik
7T-WHE	Lockheed C-130H Hercules (4935)	FAA 2 ETTL, Boufarik
7T-WHF	Lockheed C-130H Hercules (4934)	FAA 2 ETTL, Boufarik
7T-WHI	Lockheed C-130H Hercules (4930)	FAA 2 ETTL, Boufarik
7T-WHJ	Lockheed C-130H Hercules (4928)	FAA 2 ETTL, Boufarik
7T-WHL	Lockheed C-130H-30 Hercules (4989)	FAA 2 ETTL, Boufarik
7T-WHN	Lockheed C-130H-30 Hercules (4894)	FAA 2 ETTL, Boufarik
7T-WHO	Lockheed C-130H-30 Hercules (4897)	FAA 2 ETTL, Boufarik
7T-WHP	Lockheed C-130H-30 Hercules (4921)	FAA 2 ETTL, Boufarik
7T-WHQ	Lockheed C-130H Hercules (4926)	FAA 2 ETTL, Boufarik
7T-WHR	Lockheed C-130H Hercules (4924)	FAA 2 ETTL, Boufarik
7T-WHS	Lockheed C-130H Hercules (4912)	FAA 2 ETTL, Boufarik
7T-WHT	Lockheed C-130H Hercules (4911)	FAA 2 ETTL, Boufarik
7T-WHY	Lockheed C-130H Hercules (4913)	FAA 2 ETTL, Boufarik
7T-WHZ	Lockheed C-130H Hercules (4914)	FAA 2 ETTL, Boufarik
7T-WIA	Ilyushin Il-76MD	FAA 347 ETS, Boufarik
7T-WIB	Ilyushin Il-76MD	FAA 347 ETS, Boufarik
7T-WIC	Ilyushin Il-76MD	FAA 347 ETS, Boufarik
7T-WID	Ilyushin Il-76TD	FAA 347 ETS, Boufarik
7T-WIE	Ilyushin Il-76TD	FAA 347 ETS, Boufarik
7T-WIF	Ilyushin Il-78	FAA 357 ERV, Boufarik
7T-WIG	Ilyushin Il-76TD	FAA 347 ETS, Boufarik
7T-WIL	Ilyushin Il-78	FAA 357 ERV, Boufarik
7T-WIM	Ilyushin Il-76TD	FAA 347 ETS, Boufarik
7T-WIN	Ilyushin Il-78	FAA 357 ERV, Boufarik
7T-WIP	Ilyushin Il-76TD	FAA 347 ETS, Boufarik
7T-WIQ	Ilyushin Il-78	FAA 357 ERV, Boufarik
7T-WIR	Ilyushin Il-76TD	FAA 347 ETS, Boufarik
7T-WIS	Ilyushin Il-78	FAA 357 ERV, Boufarik
7T-WIT	Ilyushin Il-76TD	FAA 347 ETS, Boufarik
7T-WIU	Ilyushin Il-76TD	FAA 347 ETS, Boufarik
7T-WIV	Ilyushin Il-76TD	FAA 347 ETS, Boufarik

ANGOLA

Serial	Type (code/other identity)	Owner/operator, location or fate
D2-ANG	Bombardier Global 5000	Angola Government, Luanda

ARMENIA

Serial	Type (code/other identity)	Owner/operator, location or fate
701	Airbus A.319CJ-132	Armenian Government, Yerevan

AUSTRALIA
Royal Australian Air Force (RAAF)

Serial	Type (code/other identity)	Owner/operator, location or fate
A9-656	Lockheed AP-3C Orion	RAAF 11 Sqn/92 Wing, Edinburgh, NSW
A9-657	Lockheed EAP-3C Orion	RAAF 11 Sqn/92 Wing, Edinburgh, NSW
A9-658	Lockheed AP-3C Orion	RAAF 11 Sqn/92 Wing, Edinburgh, NSW
A9-659	Lockheed AP-3C Orion	RAAF 11 Sqn/92 Wing, Edinburgh, NSW
A9-660	Lockheed EAP-3C Orion	RAAF 11 Sqn/92 Wing, Edinburgh, NSW
A9-661	Lockheed AP-3C Orion	RAAF 11 Sqn/92 Wing, Edinburgh, NSW
A9-662	Lockheed AP-3C Orion	RAAF 11 Sqn/92 Wing, Edinburgh, NSW

Notes	Serial	Type (code/other identity)	Owner/operator, location or fate
	A9-664	Lockheed AP-3C Orion $	RAAF 11 Sqn/92 Wing, Edinburgh, NSW
	A9-665	Lockheed AP-3C Orion	RAAF 11 Sqn/92 Wing, Edinburgh, NSW
	A9-751	Lockheed AP-3C Orion	RAAF 10 Sqn/92 Wing, Edinburgh, NSW
	A9-752	Lockheed AP-3C Orion	RAAF 10 Sqn/92 Wing, Edinburgh, NSW
	A9-753	Lockheed AP-3C Orion	RAAF 10 Sqn/92 Wing, Edinburgh, NSW
	A9-756	Lockheed AP-3C Orion	*Scrapped*
	A9-757	Lockheed AP-3C Orion	RAAF 10 Sqn/92 Wing, Edinburgh, NSW
	A9-759	Lockheed AP-3C Orion	RAAF 10 Sqn/92 Wing, Edinburgh, NSW
	A9-760	Lockheed AP-3C Orion	RAAF 10 Sqn/92 Wing, Edinburgh, NSW
	A30-001	Boeing 737-7ES (E-7A)	RAAF 34 Sqn, Canberra, ACT
	A30-002	Boeing 737-7ES (E-7A)	RAAF 34 Sqn, Canberra, ACT
	A30-003	Boeing 737-7ES (E-7A)	RAAF 34 Sqn, Canberra, ACT
	A30-004	Boeing 737-7ES (E-7A)	RAAF 34 Sqn, Canberra, ACT
	A30-005	Boeing 737-7ES (E-7A)	RAAF 34 Sqn, Canberra, ACT
	A39-006	Airbus A.330-203 MRTT (KC-30A) (VH-EBH)	(on order)
	A36-001	Boeing 737-7DT	RAAF 34 Sqn, Canberra, ACT
	A36-002	Boeing 737-7DF	RAAF 34 Sqn, Canberra, ACT
	A37-001	Canadair CL.604 Challenger	RAAF 34 Sqn, Canberra, ACT
	A37-002	Canadair CL.604 Challenger	RAAF 34 Sqn, Canberra, ACT
	A37-003	Canadair CL.604 Challenger	RAAF 34 Sqn, Canberra, ACT
	A39-001	Airbus A.330-203 MRTT (KC-30A)	RAAF 33 Sqn, Amberley, Queensland
	A39-002	Airbus A.330-203 MRTT (KC-30A)	RAAF 33 Sqn, Amberley, Queensland
	A39-003	Airbus A.330-203 MRTT (KC-30A)	RAAF 33 Sqn, Amberley, Queensland
	A39-004	Airbus A.330-203 MRTT (KC-30A)	RAAF 33 Sqn, Amberley, Queensland
	A39-005	Airbus A.330-203 MRTT (KC-30A)	RAAF 33 Sqn, Amberley, Queensland
	A39-006	Airbus A.330-203 MRTT (KC-30A)	(on order)
	A39-007	Airbus A.330-203 MRTT (KC-30A)	(on order)
	A41-206	Boeing C-17A Globemaster III (06-0206)	RAAF 36 Sqn, Amberley, Queensland
	A41-207	Boeing C-17A Globemaster III (06-0207)	RAAF 36 Sqn, Amberley, Queensland
	A41-208	Boeing C-17A Globemaster III (06-0208)	RAAF 36 Sqn, Amberley, Queensland
	A41-209	Boeing C-17A Globemaster III (06-0209)	RAAF 36 Sqn, Amberley, Queensland
	A41-210	Boeing C-17A Globemaster III (11-0210)	RAAF 36 Sqn, Amberley, Queensland
	A41-211	Boeing C-17A Globemaster III (12-0211)	RAAF 36 Sqn, Amberley, Queensland
	A41-212	Boeing C-17A Globemaster III (14-0001)	RAAF 36 Sqn, Amberley, Queensland
	A41-213	Boeing C-17A Globemaster III (14-0002)	RAAF 36 Sqn, Amberley, Queensland
	A47-001	Boeing P-8A Poseidon	RAAF 11 Sqn/92 Wing, Edinburgh, NSW
	A47-002	Boeing P-8A Poseidon	RAAF (on order)
	A47-003	Boeing P-8A Poseidon	RAAF (on order)
	A47-004	Boeing P-8A Poseidon	RAAF (on order)
	A47-005	Boeing P-8A Poseidon	RAAF (on order)
	A47-006	Boeing P-8A Poseidon	RAAF (on order)
	A47-007	Boeing P-8A Poseidon	RAAF (on order)
	A47-008	Boeing P-8A Poseidon	RAAF (on order)
	A47-009	Boeing P-8A Poseidon	RAAF (on order)
	A47-010	Boeing P-8A Poseidon	RAAF (on order)
	A47-011	Boeing P-8A Poseidon	RAAF (on order)
	A47-012	Boeing P-8A Poseidon	RAAF (on order)
	A97-440	Lockheed C-130J-30 Hercules II	RAAF 37 Sqn, Richmond, NSW
	A97-441	Lockheed C-130J-30 Hercules II	RAAF 37 Sqn, Richmond, NSW
	A97-442	Lockheed C-130J-30 Hercules II	RAAF 37 Sqn, Richmond, NSW
	A97-447	Lockheed C-130J-30 Hercules II	RAAF 37 Sqn, Richmond, NSW
	A97-448	Lockheed C-130J-30 Hercules II	RAAF 37 Sqn, Richmond, NSW
	A97-449	Lockheed C-130J-30 Hercules II	RAAF 37 Sqn, Richmond, NSW
	A97-450	Lockheed C-130J-30 Hercules II	RAAF 37 Sqn, Richmond, NSW
	A97-464	Lockheed C-130J-30 Hercules II	RAAF 37 Sqn, Richmond, NSW
	A97-465	Lockheed C-130J-30 Hercules II	RAAF 37 Sqn, Richmond, NSW
	A97-466	Lockheed C-130J-30 Hercules II	RAAF 37 Sqn, Richmond, NSW
	A97-467	Lockheed C-130J-30 Hercules II	RAAF 37 Sqn, Richmond, NSW
	A97-468	Lockheed C-130J-30 Hercules II	RAAF 37 Sqn, Richmond, NSW

AUSTRIA

Öesterreichische Luftstreitkräfte (OL)

Serial	Type (code/other identity)	Owner/operator, location or fate	Notes
3C-OA	Bell OH-58B Kiowa	OL Mehrzweckhubschrauberstaffel, Tulln	
3C-OB	Bell OH-58B Kiowa	OL Mehrzweckhubschrauberstaffel, Tulln	
3C-OC	Bell OH-58B Kiowa	OL Mehrzweckhubschrauberstaffel, Tulln	
3C-OD	Bell OH-58B Kiowa	OL Mehrzweckhubschrauberstaffel, Tulln	
3C-OE	Bell OH-58B Kiowa	OL Mehrzweckhubschrauberstaffel, Tulln	
3C-OH	Bell OH-58B Kiowa	OL Mehrzweckhubschrauberstaffel, Tulln	
3C-OI	Bell OH-58B Kiowa	OL Mehrzweckhubschrauberstaffel, Tulln	
3C-OJ	Bell OH-58B Kiowa	OL Mehrzweckhubschrauberstaffel, Tulln	
3C-OK	Bell OH-58B Kiowa $	OL Mehrzweckhubschrauberstaffel, Tulln	
3C-OL	Bell OH-58B Kiowa	OL Mehrzweckhubschrauberstaffel, Tulln	
3G-EB	Pilatus PC-6B/B2-H2 Turbo Porter	OL leichte Lufttransportstaffel, Tulln	
3G-ED	Pilatus PC-6B/B2-H2 Turbo Porter	OL leichte Lufttransportstaffel, Tulln	
3G-EE	Pilatus PC-6B/B2-H2 Turbo Porter	OL leichte Lufttransportstaffel, Tulln	
3G-EF	Pilatus PC-6B/B2-H2 Turbo Porter	OL leichte Lufttransportstaffel, Tulln	
3G-EG	Pilatus PC-6B/B2-H2 Turbo Porter	OL leichte Lufttransportstaffel, Tulln	
3G-EH	Pilatus PC-6B/B2-H2 Turbo Porter	OL leichte Lufttransportstaffel, Tulln	
3G-EL	Pilatus PC-6B/B2-H2 Turbo Porter	OL leichte Lufttransportstaffel, Tulln	
3G-EN	Pilatus PC-6B/B2-H4 Turbo Porter $	OL leichte Lufttransportstaffel, Tulln	
3H-FA	Pilatus PC-7 Turbo Trainer	OL Lehrabteilung Fläche, Zeltweg	
3H-FB	Pilatus PC-7 Turbo Trainer	OL Lehrabteilung Fläche, Zeltweg	
3H-FC	Pilatus PC-7 Turbo Trainer $	OL Lehrabteilung Fläche, Zeltweg	
3H-FD	Pilatus PC-7 Turbo Trainer	OL Lehrabteilung Fläche, Zeltweg	
3H-FE	Pilatus PC-7 Turbo Trainer	OL Lehrabteilung Fläche, Zeltweg	
3H-FF	Pilatus PC-7 Turbo Trainer	OL Lehrabteilung Fläche, Zeltweg	
3H-FG	Pilatus PC-7 Turbo Trainer $	OL Lehrabteilung Fläche, Zeltweg	
3H-FH	Pilatus PC-7 Turbo Trainer	OL Lehrabteilung Fläche, Zeltweg	
3H-FJ	Pilatus PC-7 Turbo Trainer	OL Lehrabteilung Fläche, Zeltweg	
3H-FK	Pilatus PC-7 Turbo Trainer	OL Lehrabteilung Fläche, Zeltweg	
3H-FL	Pilatus PC-7 Turbo Trainer	OL Lehrabteilung Fläche, Zeltweg	
3H-FM	Pilatus PC-7 Turbo Trainer	OL Lehrabteilung Fläche, Zeltweg	
3H-FO	Pilatus PC-7 Turbo Trainer	OL Lehrabteilung Fläche, Zeltweg	
5D-HB	Agusta-Bell AB.212	OL 1 Staffel/2 Staffel ITHSSta, Linz	
5D-HC	Agusta-Bell AB.212	OL 1 Staffel/2 Staffel ITHSSta, Linz	
5D-HD	Agusta-Bell AB.212	OL 1 Staffel/2 Staffel ITHSSta, Linz	
5D-HF	Agusta-Bell AB.212	OL 1 Staffel/2 Staffel ITHSSta, Linz	
5D-HG	Agusta-Bell AB.212	OL 1 Staffel/2 Staffel ITHSSta, Linz	
5D-HH	Agusta-Bell AB.212	OL 1 Staffel/2 Staffel ITHSSta, Linz	
5D-HI	Agusta-Bell AB.212	OL 1 Staffel/2 Staffel ITHSSta, Linz	
5D-HJ	Agusta-Bell AB.212	OL 1 Staffel/2 Staffel ITHSSta, Linz	
5D-HK	Agusta-Bell AB.212	OL 1 Staffel/2 Staffel ITHSSta, Linz	
5D-HL	Agusta-Bell AB.212	OL 1 Staffel/2 Staffel ITHSSta, Linz	
5D-HN	Agusta-Bell AB.212	OL 1 Staffel/2 Staffel ITHSSta, Linz	
5D-HO	Agusta-Bell AB.212	OL 1 Staffel/2 Staffel ITHSSta, Linz	
5D-HP	Agusta-Bell AB.212	OL 1 Staffel/2 Staffel ITHSSta, Linz	
5D-HQ	Agusta-Bell AB.212	OL 1 Staffel/2 Staffel ITHSSta, Linz	
5D-HR	Agusta-Bell AB.212	OL 1 Staffel/2 Staffel ITHSSta, Linz	
5D-HS	Agusta-Bell AB.212	OL 1 Staffel/2 Staffel ITHSSta, Linz	
5D-HT	Agusta-Bell AB.212	OL 1 Staffel/2 Staffel ITHSSta, Linz	
5D-HU	Agusta-Bell AB.212	OL 1 Staffel/2 Staffel ITHSSta, Linz	
5D-HV	Agusta-Bell AB.212	OL 1 Staffel/2 Staffel ITHSSta, Linz	
5D-HW	Agusta-Bell AB.212	OL 1 Staffel/2 Staffel ITHSSta, Linz	
5D-HX	Agusta-Bell AB.212	OL 1 Staffel/2 Staffel ITHSSta, Linz	
5D-HY	Bell 212	OL 1 Staffel/2 Staffel ITHSSta, Linz	
5D-HZ	Agusta-Bell AB.212 $	OL 1 Staffel/2 Staffel ITHSSta, Linz	
6M-BA	Sikorsky S-70A	OL mittlere Transporthubschrauberstaffel, Tulln	
6M-BB	Sikorsky S-70A	OL mittlere Transporthubschrauberstaffel, Tulln	
6M-BC	Sikorsky S-70A	OL mittlere Transporthubschrauberstaffel, Tulln	
6M-BD	Sikorsky S-70A	OL mittlere Transporthubschrauberstaffel, Tulln	
6M-BE	Sikorsky S-70A	OL mittlere Transporthubschrauberstaffel, Tulln	
6M-BF	Sikorsky S-70A	OL mittlere Transporthubschrauberstaffel, Tulln	

Notes	Serial	Type (code/other identity)	Owner/operator, location or fate
	6M-BG	Sikorsky S-70A	OL mittlere Transporthubschrauberstaffel, Tulln
	6M-BH	Sikorsky S-70A	OL mittlere Transporthubschrauberstaffel, Tulln
	6M-BI	Sikorsky S-70A	OL mittlere Transporthubschrauberstaffel, Tulln
	7L-WA	Eurofighter EF.2000	OL 1 Staffel/2 Staffel Überwg, Zeltweg
	7L-WB	Eurofighter EF.2000	OL 1 Staffel/2 Staffel Überwg, Zeltweg
	7L-WC	Eurofighter EF.2000 $	OL 1 Staffel/2 Staffel Überwg, Zeltweg
	7L-WD	Eurofighter EF.2000	OL 1 Staffel/2 Staffel Überwg, Zeltweg
	7L-WE	Eurofighter EF.2000	OL 1 Staffel/2 Staffel Überwg, Zeltweg
	7L-WF	Eurofighter EF.2000	OL 1 Staffel/2 Staffel Überwg, Zeltweg
	7L-WG	Eurofighter EF.2000	OL 1 Staffel/2 Staffel Überwg, Zeltweg
	7L-WH	Eurofighter EF.2000	OL 1 Staffel/2 Staffel Überwg, Zeltweg
	7L-WI	Eurofighter EF.2000	OL 1 Staffel/2 Staffel Überwg, Zeltweg
	7L-WJ	Eurofighter EF.2000	OL 1 Staffel/2 Staffel Überwg, Zeltweg
	7L-WK	Eurofighter EF.2000	OL 1 Staffel/2 Staffel Überwg, Zeltweg
	7L-WL	Eurofighter EF.2000	OL 1 Staffel/2 Staffel Überwg, Zeltweg
	7L-WM	Eurofighter EF.2000	OL 1 Staffel/2 Staffel Überwg, Zeltweg
	7L-WN	Eurofighter EF.2000	OL 1 Staffel/2 Staffel Überwg, Zeltweg
	7L-WO	Eurofighter EF.2000	OL 1 Staffel/2 Staffel Überwg, Zeltweg
	8T-CA	Lockheed C-130K Hercules	OL Lufttransportstaffel, Linz
	8T-CB	Lockheed C-130K Hercules	OL Lufttransportstaffel, Linz
	8T-CC	Lockheed C-130K Hercules	OL Lufttransportstaffel, Linz
	YI-09	SAAB 105ÖE [yellow I]	OL Düsentrainerstaffel Überwg, Linz
	YJ-10	SAAB 105ÖE [yellow J]	OL Düsentrainerstaffel Überwg, Linz
	GD-14	SAAB 105ÖE [green D] $	OL Düsentrainerstaffel Überwg, Linz
	GG-17	SAAB 105ÖE [green G]	OL Düsentrainerstaffel Überwg, Linz
	RB-22	SAAB 105ÖE [red B]	OL Düsentrainerstaffel Überwg, Linz
	RC-23	SAAB 105ÖE [red C]	OL Düsentrainerstaffel Überwg, Linz
	RD-24	SAAB 105ÖE [red D]	OL Düsentrainerstaffel Überwg, Linz
	RE-25	SAAB 105ÖE [red E]	OL Düsentrainerstaffel Überwg, Linz
	RF-26	SAAB 105ÖE [red F] $	OL Düsentrainerstaffel Überwg, Linz
	RG-27	SAAB 105ÖE [red G]	OL Düsentrainerstaffel Überwg, Linz
	RH-28	SAAB 105ÖE [red H]	OL Düsentrainerstaffel Überwg, Linz
	RJ-30	SAAB 105ÖE [red J]	OL Düsentrainerstaffel Überwg, Linz
	BA-31	SAAB 105ÖE [blue A]	OL Düsentrainerstaffel Überwg, Linz
	BE-35	SAAB 105ÖE [blue E]	OL, stored Linz
	BF-36	SAAB 105ÖE [blue F]	OL Düsentrainerstaffel Überwg, Linz
	BG-37	SAAB 105ÖE [blue G]	OL Düsentrainerstaffel Überwg, Linz
	BI-39	SAAB 105ÖE [blue I]	OL, stored Linz
	BJ-40	SAAB 105ÖE [blue J]	OL Düsentrainerstaffel Überwg, Linz

AZERBAIJAN

	4K-AI01	Boeing 767-32LER	Azerbaijan Government, Baku
	4K-AI02	Airbus A.319-115LR	Azerbaijan Government, Baku
	4K-AI88	Gulfstream Aerospace G.650	Azerbaijan Government, Baku

BAHRAIN

	A9C-AWL	BAE RJ.100	Bahrain Defence Force
	A9C-BAH	Gulfstream Aerospace G.650	Government of Bahrain
	A9C-BDF	BAE RJ.100	Bahrain Defence Force
	A9C-BG	Grumman G.1159 Gulfstream IITT	Government of Bahrain
	A9C-BHR	Gulfstream Aerospace G.450	Government of Bahrain
	A9C-BRF	Grumman G.1159C Gulfstream IV-SP	Government of Bahrain
	A9C-BRN	Gulfstream Aerospace G.550	Government of Bahrain
	A9C-HAK	Boeing 747SP-Z5	Bahrain Amiri Flt
	A9C-HMH	Boeing 767-4FSER	Bahrain Amiri Flt
	A9C-HMK	Boeing 747-4P8	Bahrain Amiri Flt
	A9C-HWR	BAE RJ.85	Bahrain Defence Force

BELGIUM

Force Aérienne Belge (FAB)/Belgische Luchtmacht: Composante Aérienne Belge/Belgische Luchtcomponent

	AT-01	D-BD Alpha Jet 1B+	FAB 11 Sm (1 Wg), Cazaux, France (ET 02.008)
	AT-02	D-BD Alpha Jet 1B+	FAB 11 Sm (1 Wg), Cazaux, France (ET 02.008)

Serial	Type (code/other identity)	Owner/operator, location or fate	Notes
AT-03	D-BD Alpha Jet 1B+	FAB 11 Sm (1 Wg), Cazaux, France (ET 02.008)	
AT-05	D-BD Alpha Jet 1B+	FAB 11 Sm (1 Wg), Cazaux, France (ET 02.008)	
AT-06	D-BD Alpha Jet 1B+	FAB 11 Sm (1 Wg), Cazaux, France (ET 02.008)	
AT-08	D-BD Alpha Jet 1B+	FAB 11 Sm (1 Wg), Cazaux, France (ET 02.008)	
AT-10	D-BD Alpha Jet 1B+	FAB 11 Sm (1 Wg), Cazaux, France (ET 02.008)	
AT-11	D-BD Alpha Jet 1B+	FAB 11 Sm (1 Wg), Cazaux, France (ET 02.008)	
AT-12	D-BD Alpha Jet 1B+	FAB 11 Sm (1 Wg), Cazaux, France (ET 02.008)	
AT-13	D-BD Alpha Jet 1B+	FAB 11 Sm (1 Wg), Cazaux, France (ET 02.008)	
AT-14	D-BD Alpha Jet 1B+	FAB 11 Sm (1 Wg), Cazaux, France (ET 02.008)	
AT-15	D-BD Alpha Jet 1B+	FAB 11 Sm (1 Wg), Cazaux, France (ET 02.008)	
AT-17	D-BD Alpha Jet 1B+	FAB 11 Sm (1 Wg), Cazaux, France (ET 02.008)	
AT-18	D-BD Alpha Jet 1B+	FAB 11 Sm (1 Wg), Cazaux, France (ET 02.008)	
AT-19	D-BD Alpha Jet 1B+	FAB 11 Sm (1 Wg), Cazaux, France (ET 02.008)	
AT-20	D-BD Alpha Jet 1B+	FAB 11 Sm (1 Wg), Cazaux, France (ET 02.008)	
AT-21	D-BD Alpha Jet 1B+	FAB 11 Sm (1 Wg), Cazaux, France (ET 02.008)	
AT-22	D-BD Alpha Jet 1B+	FAB 11 Sm (1 Wg), Cazaux, France (ET 02.008)	
AT-23	D-BD Alpha Jet 1B+	FAB 11 Sm (1 Wg), Cazaux, France (ET 02.008)	
AT-24	D-BD Alpha Jet 1B+	FAB 11 Sm (1 Wg), Cazaux, France (ET 02.008)	
AT-25	D-BD Alpha Jet 1B+	FAB 11 Sm (1 Wg), Cazaux, France (ET 02.008)	
AT-26	D-BD Alpha Jet 1B+	FAB 11 Sm (1 Wg), Cazaux, France (ET 02.008)	
AT-27	D-BD Alpha Jet 1B+	FAB 11 Sm (1 Wg), Cazaux, France (ET 02.008)	
AT-28	D-BD Alpha Jet 1B+	FAB 11 Sm (1 Wg), Cazaux, France (ET 02.008)	
AT-29	D-BD Alpha Jet 1B+ $	FAB 11 Sm (1 Wg), Cazaux, France (ET 02.008)	
AT-30	D-BD Alpha Jet 1B+	FAB 11 Sm (1 Wg), Cazaux, France (ET 02.008)	
AT-31	D-BD Alpha Jet 1B+	FAB 11 Sm (1 Wg), Cazaux, France (ET 02.008)	
AT-32	D-BD Alpha Jet 1B+ $	FAB 11 Sm (1 Wg), Cazaux, France (ET 02.008)	
AT-33	D-BD Alpha Jet 1B+ $	FAB 11 Sm (1 Wg), Cazaux, France (ET 02.008)	
CD-01	Dassault Falcon 900B	FAB 21 Smaldeel (15 Wg), Brussels/Melsbroek	
CE-01	Embraer ERJ.135LR	FAB 21 Smaldeel (15 Wg), Brussels/Melsbroek	
CE-02	Embraer ERJ.135LR	FAB 21 Smaldeel (15 Wg), Brussels/Melsbroek	
CE-03	Embraer ERJ.145LR $	FAB 21 Smaldeel (15 Wg), Brussels/Melsbroek	
CE-04	Embraer ERJ.145LR $	FAB 21 Smaldeel (15 Wg), Brussels/Melsbroek	
CH-01	Lockheed C-130H Hercules	FAB 20 Smaldeel (15 Wg), Brussels/Melsbroek	
CH-03	Lockheed C-130H Hercules	FAB 20 Smaldeel (15 Wg), Brussels/Melsbroek	
CH-04	Lockheed C-130H Hercules	FAB 20 Smaldeel (15 Wg), Brussels/Melsbroek	
CH-05	Lockheed C-130H Hercules	FAB 20 Smaldeel (15 Wg), Brussels/Melsbroek	
CH-07	Lockheed C-130H Hercules $	FAB 20 Smaldeel (15 Wg), Brussels/Melsbroek	
CH-08	Lockheed C-130H Hercules	FAB 20 Smaldeel (15 Wg), Brussels/Melsbroek	
CH-09	Lockheed C-130H Hercules	FAB 20 Smaldeel (15 Wg), Brussels/Melsbroek	
CH-10	Lockheed C-130H Hercules	FAB 20 Smaldeel (15 Wg), Brussels/Melsbroek	
CH-11	Lockheed C-130H Hercules	FAB 20 Smaldeel (15 Wg), Brussels/Melsbroek	
CH-12	Lockheed C-130H Hercules	FAB 20 Smaldeel (15 Wg), Brussels/Melsbroek	
CH-13	Lockheed C-130H Hercules $	FAB 20 Smaldeel (15 Wg), Brussels/Melsbroek	
CM-02	Dassault Falcon 20-5	*Withdrawn from use, 22 December 2016*	
FA-56	SABCA (GD) F-16A MLU Fighting Falcon	FAB 31 Sm/349 Sm/OCU (10 Wg), Kleine-Brogel	
FA-57	SABCA (GD) F-16A MLU Fighting Falcon	FAB 1 Sm/350 Sm (2 Wg), Florennes	
FA-67	SABCA (GD) F-16A MLU Fighting Falcon	FAB 1 Sm/350 Sm (2 Wg), Florennes	
FA-68	SABCA (GD) F-16A MLU Fighting Falcon $	FAB 1 Sm/350 Sm (2 Wg), Florennes	
FA-69	SABCA (GD) F-16A MLU Fighting Falcon	FAB 1 Sm/350 Sm (2 Wg), Florennes	
FA-70	SABCA (GD) F-16A MLU Fighting Falcon	FAB 31 Sm/349 Sm/OCU (10 Wg), Kleine-Brogel	
FA-71	SABCA (GD) F-16A MLU Fighting Falcon	FAB 1 Sm/350 Sm (2 Wg), Florennes	
FA-72	SABCA (GD) F-16A MLU Fighting Falcon	FAB 1 Sm/350 Sm (2 Wg), Florennes	
FA-77	SABCA (GD) F-16A MLU Fighting Falcon $	FAB 31 Sm/349 Sm/OCU (10 Wg), Kleine-Brogel	
FA-81	SABCA (GD) F-16A MLU Fighting Falcon	FAB 31 Sm/349 Sm/OCU (10 Wg), Kleine-Brogel	
FA-82	SABCA (GD) F-16A MLU Fighting Falcon	FAB 31 Sm/349 Sm/OCU (10 Wg), Kleine-Brogel	
FA-83	SABCA (GD) F-16A MLU Fighting Falcon	FAB 1 Sm/350 Sm (2 Wg), Florennes	
FA-84	SABCA (GD) F-16A MLU Fighting Falcon $	FAB 1 Sm/350 Sm (2 Wg), Florennes	
FA-86	SABCA (GD) F-16A MLU Fighting Falcon	FAB 31 Sm/349 Sm/OCU (10 Wg), Kleine-Brogel	
FA-87	SABCA (GD) F-16A MLU Fighting Falcon	FAB 31 Sm/349 Sm/OCU (10 Wg), Kleine-Brogel	
FA-89	SABCA (GD) F-16A MLU Fighting Falcon	FAB 1 Sm/350 Sm (2 Wg), Florennes	
FA-91	SABCA (GD) F-16A MLU Fighting Falcon	FAB 1 Sm/350 Sm (2 Wg), Florennes	
FA-92	SABCA (GD) F-16A MLU Fighting Falcon	FAB 1 Sm/350 Sm (2 Wg), Florennes	

Notes	Serial	Type (code/other identity)	Owner/operator, location or fate
	FA-94	SABCA(GD) F-16A MLU Fighting Falcon $	FAB 1 Sm/350 Sm (2 Wg), Florennes
	FA-95	SABCA(GD) F-16A MLU Fighting Falcon	FAB 31 Sm/349 Sm/OCU (10 Wg), Kleine-Brogel
	FA-97	SABCA(GD) F-16A MLU Fighting Falcon	FAB 31 Sm/349 Sm/OCU (10 Wg), Kleine-Brogel
	FA-98	SABCA(GD) F-16A MLU Fighting Falcon	FAB 1 Sm/350 Sm (2 Wg), Florennes
	FA-101	SABCA(GD) F-16A MLU Fighting Falcon	FAB 31 Sm/349 Sm/OCU (10 Wg), Kleine-Brogel
	FA-102	SABCA(GD) F-16A MLU Fighting Falcon	FAB 31 Sm/349 Sm/OCU (10 Wg), Kleine-Brogel
	FA-103	SABCA(GD) F-16A MLU Fighting Falcon	FAB 31 Sm/349 Sm/OCU (10 Wg), Kleine-Brogel
	FA-104	SABCA(GD) F-16A MLU Fighting Falcon $	FAB 31 Sm/349 Sm/OCU (10 Wg), Kleine-Brogel
	FA-106	SABCA(GD) F-16A MLU Fighting Falcon $	FAB 31 Sm/349 Sm/OCU (10 Wg), Kleine-Brogel
	FA-107	SABCA(GD) F-16A MLU Fighting Falcon	FAB 31 Sm/349 Sm/OCU (10 Wg), Kleine-Brogel
	FA-109	SABCA(GD) F-16A MLU Fighting Falcon	FAB 31 Sm/349 Sm/OCU (10 Wg), Kleine-Brogel
	FA-110	SABCA(GD) F-16A MLU Fighting Falcon	FAB 31 Sm/349 Sm/OCU (10 Wg), Kleine-Brogel
	FA-114	SABCA(GD) F-16A MLU Fighting Falcon	FAB 31 Sm/349 Sm/OCU (10 Wg), Kleine-Brogel
	FA-116	SABCA(GD) F-16A MLU Fighting Falcon	FAB 1 Sm/350 Sm (2 Wg), Florennes
	FA-117	SABCA(GD) F-16A MLU Fighting Falcon	FAB 1 Sm/350 Sm (2 Wg), Florennes
	FA-118	SABCA(GD) F-16A MLU Fighting Falcon	FAB 31 Sm/349 Sm/OCU (10 Wg), Kleine-Brogel
	FA-119	SABCA(GD) F-16A MLU Fighting Falcon	FAB 31 Sm/349 Sm/OCU (10 Wg), Kleine-Brogel
	FA-121	SABCA(GD) F-16A MLU Fighting Falcon	FAB 1 Sm/350 Sm (2 Wg), Florennes
	FA-123	SABCA(GD) F-16A MLU Fighting Falcon $	FAB 31 Sm/349 Sm/OCU (10 Wg), Kleine-Brogel
	FA-124	SABCA(GD) F-16A MLU Fighting Falcon	FAB 31 Sm/349 Sm/OCU (10 Wg), Kleine-Brogel
	FA-126	SABCA(GD) F-16A MLU Fighting Falcon	FAB 1 Sm/350 Sm (2 Wg), Florennes
	FA-127	SABCA(GD) F-16A MLU Fighting Falcon	FAB 1 Sm/350 Sm (2 Wg), Florennes
	FA-128	SABCA(GD) F-16A MLU Fighting Falcon	FAB 1 Sm/350 Sm (2 Wg), Florennes
	FA-129	SABCA(GD) F-16A MLU Fighting Falcon	FAB 1 Sm/350 Sm (2 Wg), Florennes
	FA-130	SABCA GD) F-16A MLU Fighting Falcon	FAB 31 Sm/349 Sm/OCU (10 Wg), Kleine-Brogel
	FA-131	SABCA(GD) F-16A MLU Fighting Falcon	FAB 1 Sm/350 Sm (2 Wg), Florennes
	FA-132	SABCA(GD) F-16A MLU Fighting Falcon	FAB 1 Sm/350 Sm (2 Wg), Florennes
	FA-133	SABCA(GD) F-16A MLU Fighting Falcon	FAB 1 Sm/350 Sm (2 Wg), Florennes
	FA-134	SABCA(GD) F-16A MLU Fighting Falcon	FAB 31 Sm/349 Sm/OCU (10 Wg), Kleine-Brogel
	FA-135	SABCA(GD) F-16A MLU Fighting Falcon	FAB 1 Sm/350 Sm (2 Wg), Florennes
	FA-136	SABCA(GD) F-16A MLU Fighting Falcon	FAB 31 Sm/349 Sm/OCU (10 Wg), Kleine-Brogel
	FB-12	SABCA(GD) F-16B MLU Fighting Falcon	FAB 1 Sm/350 Sm (2 Wg), Florennes
	FB-14	SABCA(GD) F-16B MLU Fighting Falcon	FAB 31 Sm/349 Sm/OCU (10 Wg), Kleine-Brogel
	FB-15	SABCA(GD) F-16B MLU Fighting Falcon	FAB 31 Sm/349 Sm/OCU (10 Wg), Kleine-Brogel
	FB-17	SABCA(GD) F-16B MLU Fighting Falcon	FAB 31 Sm/349 Sm/OCU (10 Wg), Kleine-Brogel
	FB-18	SABCA(GD) F-16B MLU Fighting Falcon	FAB 31 Sm/349 Sm/OCU (10 Wg), Kleine-Brogel
	FB-20	SABCA(GD) F-16B MLU Fighting Falcon	FAB 31 Sm/349 Sm/OCU (10 Wg), Kleine-Brogel
	FB-21	SABCA(GD) F-16B MLU Fighting Falcon	FAB 1 Sm/350 Sm (2 Wg), Florennes
	FB-22	SABCA(GD) F-16B MLU Fighting Falcon	FAB 1 Sm/350 Sm (2 Wg), Florennes
	FB-23	SABCA(GD) F-16B MLU Fighting Falcon	FAB 31 Sm/349 Sm/OCU (10 Wg), Kleine-Brogel
	FB-24	SABCA(GD) F-16B MLU Fighting Falcon	FAB 31 Sm/349 Sm/OCU (10 Wg), Kleine-Brogel
	G-01	Cessna 182Q Skylane	FAB Federal Police, Brussels/Melsbroek
	G-04	Cessna 182R Skylane	FAB Federal Police, Brussels/Melsbroek
	G-10	MDH MD.902 Explorer	FAB Federal Police, Brussels/Melsbroek
	G-11	MDH MD.902 Explorer	FAB Federal Police, Brussels/Melsbroek
	G-12	MDH MD.902 Explorer	FAB Federal Police, Brussels/Melsbroek
	G-14	MDH MD.520N	FAB Federal Police, Brussels/Melsbroek
	G-15	MDH MD.520N	FAB Federal Police, Brussels/Melsbroek
	G-16	MDH MD.902 Explorer	FAB Federal Police, Brussels/Melsbroek
	H-20	Agusta A109HA	FAB, stored Beauvechain
	H-21	Agusta A109HA	FAB 17 Smaldeel MRH (1 Wg), Beauvechain
	H-22	Agusta A109HA	FAB 17 Smaldeel MRH (1 Wg), Beauvechain
	H-24	Agusta A109HA $	FAB 17 Smaldeel MRH (1 Wg), Beauvechain
	H-25	Agusta A109HA	FAB 17 Smaldeel MRH (1 Wg), Beauvechain
	H-26	Agusta A109HA	FAB 17 Smaldeel MRH (1 Wg), Beauvechain
	H-27	Agusta A109HA	FAB 17 Smaldeel MRH (1 Wg), Beauvechain
	H-28	Agusta A109HA	FAB 17 Smaldeel MRH (1 Wg), Beauvechain
	H-29	Agusta A109HA $	FAB 17 Smaldeel MRH (1 Wg), Beauvechain
	H-30	Agusta A109HA	FAB, stored Beauvechain
	H-31	Agusta A109HA	FAB 17 Smaldeel MRH (1 Wg), Beauvechain
	H-33	Agusta A109HA	FAB, stored Beauvechain
	H-35	Agusta A109HA	FAB 17 Smaldeel MRH (1 Wg), Beauvechain

Serial	Type (code/other identity)	Owner/operator, location or fate	Notes
H-36	Agusta A109HA	FAB 17 Smaldeel MRH (1 Wg), Beauvechain	
H-38	Agusta A109HA	FAB 17 Smaldeel MRH (1 Wg), Beauvechain	
H-39	Agusta A109HA	FAB 17 Smaldeel MRH (1 Wg), Beauvechain	
H-40	Agusta A109HA	FAB 17 Smaldeel MRH/SLV (1 Wg), Beauvechain	
H-41	Agusta A109HA	FAB 17 Smaldeel MRH (1 Wg), Beauvechain	
H-42	Agusta A109HA	FAB SLV (1 Wg), Beauvechain	
H-44	Agusta A109HA	FAB 17 Smaldeel MRH (1 Wg), Beauvechain	
H-45	Agusta A109HA	FAB 17 Smaldeel MRH (1 Wg), Beauvechain	
H-46	Agusta A109HA	FAB 17 Smaldeel MRH (1 Wg), Beauvechain	
LB-01	Piper L-21B Super Cub	FAB Air Cadets, Florennes/Goetsenhoeven/Zoersel	
LB-02	Piper L-21B Super Cub	FAB Air Cadets, Florennes/Goetsenhoeven/Zoersel	
LB-03	Piper L-21B Super Cub	FAB Air Cadets, Florennes/Goetsenhoeven/Zoersel	
LB-05	Piper L-21B Super Cub	FAB Air Cadets, Florennes/Goetsenhoeven/Zoersel	
M-1	Sud SA.316B Alouette III	FAB 40 Smaldeel, Koksijde	
M-2	Sud SA.316B Alouette III	FAB 40 Smaldeel, Koksijde	
M-3	Sud SA.316B Alouette III	FAB 40 Smaldeel, Koksijde	
RN-01	NH Industries NH.90-NFH	FAB 40 Smaldeel (1 Wg), Koksijde	
RN-02	NH Industries NH.90-NFH	FAB 40 Smaldeel (1 Wg), Koksijde	
RN-03	NH Industries NH.90-NFH	FAB 40 Smaldeel (1 Wg), Koksijde	
RN-04	NH Industries NH.90-NFH	FAB 40 Smaldeel (1 Wg), Koksijde	
RN-05	NH Industries NH.90-TTH	FAB 18 Smaldeel MRH (1 Wg), Beauvechain	
RN-06	NH Industries NH.90-TTH	FAB 18 Smaldeel MRH (1 Wg), Beauvechain	
RN-07	NH Industries NH.90-TTH	FAB 18 Smaldeel MRH (1 Wg), Beauvechain	
RN-08	NH Industries NH.90-TTH	FAB 18 Smaldeel MRH (1 Wg), Beauvechain	
RS-02	Westland Sea King Mk.48	FAB 40 Smaldeel (1 Wg), Koksijde	
RS-04	Westland Sea King Mk.48	FAB 40 Smaldeel (1 Wg), Koksijde	
RS-05	Westland Sea King Mk.48 $	FAB 40 Smaldeel (1 Wg), Koksijde	
ST-02	SIAI Marchetti SF260M+	FAB *Red Devils*, CC Air, Beauvechain	
ST-03	SIAI Marchetti SF260M+	FAB *Red Devils*, CC Air, Beauvechain	
ST-04	SIAI Marchetti SF260M+	FAB *Red Devils*, CC Air, Beauvechain	
ST-06	SIAI Marchetti SF260M+	FAB 5 Smaldeel/9 Smaldeel, CC Air, Beauvechain	
ST-12	SIAI Marchetti SF260M+	FAB 5 Smaldeel/9 Smaldeel, CC Air, Beauvechain	
ST-15	SIAI Marchetti SF260M+	FAB *Red Devils*, CC Air, Beauvechain	
ST-16	SIAI Marchetti SF260M+	FAB 5 Smaldeel/9 Smaldeel, CC Air, Beauvechain	
ST-17	SIAI Marchetti SF260M+	FAB 5 Smaldeel/9 Smaldeel, CC Air, Beauvechain	
ST-18	SIAI Marchetti SF260M+	FAB 5 Smaldeel/9 Smaldeel, CC Air, Beauvechain	
ST-19	SIAI Marchetti SF260M+	FAB 5 Smaldeel/9 Smaldeel, CC Air, Beauvechain	
ST-20	SIAI Marchetti SF260M+	FAB 5 Smaldeel/9 Smaldeel, CC Air, Beauvechain	
ST-22	SIAI Marchetti SF260M+	FAB 5 Smaldeel/9 Smaldeel, CC Air, Beauvechain	
ST-23	SIAI Marchetti SF260M+	FAB *Red Devils*, CC Air, Beauvechain	
ST-24	SIAI Marchetti SF260M+	FAB 5 Smaldeel/9 Smaldeel, CC Air, Beauvechain	
ST-25	SIAI Marchetti SF260M+	FAB 5 Smaldeel/9 Smaldeel, CC Air, Beauvechain	
ST-26	SIAI Marchetti SF260M+	FAB 5 Smaldeel/9 Smaldeel, CC Air, Beauvechain	
ST-27	SIAI Marchetti SF260M+	FAB *Red Devils*, CC Air, Beauvechain	
ST-30	SIAI Marchetti SF260M+ $	FAB 5 Smaldeel/9 Smaldeel, CC Beauvechain	
ST-31	SIAI Marchetti SF260M+	FAB *Red Devils*, CC Air, Beauvechain	
ST-32	SIAI Marchetti SF260M+	FAB *Red Devils*, CC Air, Beauvechain	
ST-34	SIAI Marchetti SF260M+	FAB *Red Devils*, CC Air, Beauvechain	

Notes	Serial	Type (code/other identity)	Owner/operator, location or fate
	ST-35	SIAI Marchetti SF260M+	FAB 5 Smaldeel/9 Smaldeel, CC Air, Beauvechain
	ST-36	SIAI Marchetti SF260M+	FAB *Red Devils*, CC Air, Beauvechain
	ST-40	SIAI Marchetti SF260D	FAB 5 Smaldeel/9 Smaldeel, CC Air, Beauvechain
	ST-41	SIAI Marchetti SF260D	FAB *Red Devils*, CC Air, Beauvechain
	ST-42	SIAI Marchetti SF260D	FAB 5 Smaldeel/9 Smaldeel, CC Air, Beauvechain
	ST-43	SIAI Marchetti SF260D	FAB 5 Smaldeel/9 Smaldeel, CC Air, Beauvechain
	ST-44	SIAI Marchetti SF260D	FAB 5 Smaldeel/9 Smaldeel, CC Air, Beauvechain
	ST-45	SIAI Marchetti SF260D	FAB 5 Smaldeel/9 Smaldeel, CC Air, Beauvechain
	ST-46	SIAI Marchetti SF260D	FAB 5 Smaldeel/9 Smaldeel, CC Air, Beauvechain
	ST-47	SIAI Marchetti SF260D	FAB 5 Smaldeel/9 Smaldeel, CC Air, Beauvechain
	ST-48	SIAI Marchetti SF260D	FAB 5 Smaldeel/9 Smaldeel, CC Air, Beauvechain
	CS-TRJ	Airbus A.321-231	FAB 21 Smaldeel (15 Wg), Brussels/Melsbroek

BOTSWANA
Botswana Defence Force (BDF)

Notes	Serial	Type (code/other identity)	Owner/operator, location or fate
	OK1	Bombardier Global Express	BDF VIP Sqn, Sir Seretse Kharma IAP, Gaborone
	OM-1	Lockheed C-130B Hercules	BDF Z10 Sqn, Thebephatshwa
	OM-2	Lockheed C-130B Hercules	BDF Z10 Sqn, Thebephatshwa
	OM-3	Lockheed C-130B Hercules	BDF Z10 Sqn, Thebephatshwa

BRAZIL
Força Aérea Brasileira (FAB)

Notes	Serial	Type (code/other identity)	Owner/operator, location or fate
	2101	Airbus A.319-133CJ (VC-1A)	FAB 1º GT Especial, 1º Esq, Brasilia
	2451	Lockheed C-130E Hercules	*Scrapped at Afonsos, October 2016*
	2454	Lockheed C-130E Hercules	FAB 1º GTT, 1º Esq, Afonsos
	2459	Lockheed SC-130E Hercules	FAB 1º GTT, 1º Esq, Afonsos
	2461	Lockheed KC-130H Hercules	FAB 1º GT, 1º Esq, Galeão
	2462	Lockheed KC-130H Hercules	FAB 1º GT, 1º Esq, Galeão
	2463	Lockheed C-130H Hercules	FAB 1º GT, 1º Esq, Galeão
	2464	Lockheed C-130H Hercules	FAB 1º GT, 1º Esq, Galeão
	2465	Lockheed C-130M Hercules	FAB 1º GT, 1º Esq, Galeão
	2466	Lockheed C-130M Hercules	FAB 1º GT, 1º Esq, Galeão
	2467	Lockheed C-130H Hercules	FAB 1º GT, 1º Esq, Galeão
	2470	Lockheed C-130M Hercules	FAB 1º GT, 1º Esq, Galeão
	2472	Lockheed C-130H Hercules	FAB 1º GT, 1º Esq, Galeão
	2473	Lockheed C-130H Hercules	FAB 1º GT, 1º Esq, Galeão
	2474	Lockheed C-130H Hercules	FAB 1º GT, 1º Esq, Galeão
	2475	Lockheed C-130H Hercules	FAB 1º GT, 1º Esq, Galeão
	2476	Lockheed C-130M Hercules	FAB 1º GTT, 1º Esq, Afonsos
	2479	Lockheed C-130M Hercules	FAB 1º GT, 1º Esq, Galeão
	2550	Embraer VC-99A Legacy	FAB 2º GT Especial, 1º Esq, Brasilia
	2560	Embraer VC-99C Legacy	FAB 2º GT Especial, 1º Esq, Brasilia
	2561	Embraer VC-99C Legacy	FAB 2º GT Especial, 1º Esq, Brasilia
	2580	Embraer VC-99B Legacy	FAB 2º GT Especial, 1º Esq, Brasilia
	2581	Embraer VC-99B Legacy	FAB 2º GT Especial, 1º Esq, Brasilia
	2582	Embraer VC-99B Legacy	FAB 2º GT Especial, 1º Esq, Brasilia
	2583	Embraer VC-99B Legacy	FAB 2º GT Especial, 1º Esq, Brasilia
	2584	Embraer VC-99B Legacy	FAB 2º GT Especial, 1º Esq, Brasilia
	2585	Embraer VC-99B Legacy	FAB 2º GT Especial, 1º Esq, Brasilia
	2586	Embraer VC-99B Legacy	FAB 2º GT Especial, 1º Esq, Brasilia
	2590	Embraer EMB.190-190IGW (VC-2)	FAB 1º GT Especial, 1º Esq, Brasilia
	2591	Embraer EMB.190-190IGW (VC-2)	FAB 1º GT Especial, 1º Esq, Brasilia

Serial	Type (code/other identity)	Owner/operator, location or fate	Notes
2900	Boeing 767-31AER (C-767)	FAB 2° GT, 2° Esq, Galeão	
6700	Embraer E-99	FAB 2° Esq, 6° GAv, Anapolis	
6701	Embraer R-99A	FAB 2° Esq, 6° GAv, Anapolis	
6702	Embraer R-99A	FAB 2° Esq, 6° GAv, Anapolis	
6703	Embraer E-99	FAB 2° Esq, 6° GAv, Anapolis	
6704	Embraer R-99A	FAB 2° Esq, 6° GAv, Anapolis	
6750	Embraer R-99B	FAB 2° Esq, 6° GAv, Anapolis	
6751	Embraer R-99B	FAB 2° Esq, 6° GAv, Anapolis	
6752	Embraer R-99B	FAB 2° Esq, 6° GAv, Anapolis	

BRUNEI

V8-ALI	Boeing 747-430	Brunei Government, Bandar Seri Bergawan	
V8-BKH	Airbus A.340-212	Brunei Government, Bandar Seri Bergawan	
V8-MHB	Boeing 767-27GER	Brunei Government, Bandar Seri Bergawan	

BULGARIA
Bulgarsky Voenno-Vazdushni Sily (BVVS)

020	Pilatus PC.XII/45	BVVS 16 TAP, Sofia/Dobroslavtzi	
055	Antonov An-30	BVVS 16 TAP, Sofia/Dobroslavtzi	
071	Aeritalia C-27J Spartan	BVVS 16 TAB, Sofia/Vrazhdebna	
072	Aeritalia C-27J Spartan	BVVS 16 TAB, Sofia/Vrazhdebna	
073	Aeritalia C-27J Spartan	BVVS 16 TAB, Sofia/Vrazhdebna	
Bulgarian Government			
LZ-AOA	Airbus A.319-112	*Returned to BH Air*	
LZ-AOB	Airbus A.319-112	Bulgarian Government/BH Air, Sofia	
LZ-OOI	Dassault Falcon 2000	Bulgarian Government, Sofia	

BURKINA FASO

XT-BFA	Boeing 727-282	Government of Burkina Faso, Ouagadougou	

CAMEROON

TJ-AAW	Grumman G.1159A Gulfstream III	Government of Cameroon, Yaounde	

CANADA
Royal Canadian Air Force (RCAF)

15001	Airbus CC-150 Polaris (A.310-304) [991]	RCAF 437 Sqn (8 Wing), Trenton	
15002	Airbus CC-150 Polaris (A.310-304F) [992]	RCAF 437 Sqn (8 Wing), Trenton	
15003	Airbus CC-150 Polaris (A.310-304F) [993]	RCAF 437 Sqn (8 Wing), Trenton	
15004	Airbus CC-150 Polaris (A.310-304F) [994]	RCAF 437 Sqn (8 Wing), Trenton	
15005	Airbus CC-150 Polaris (A.310-304F) [995]	RCAF 437 Sqn (8 Wing), Trenton	
130307	Lockheed CC-130E(SAR) Hercules	*To Canada Aviation & Space Museum, April 2016*	
130319	Lockheed CC-130E Hercules	*Withdrawn from use at Trenton*	
130327	Lockheed CC-130E Hercules	*Withdrawn from use at Trenton*	
130332	Lockheed CC-130H(SAR) Hercules	RCAF 413 Sqn (14 Wing), Greenwood	
130334	Lockheed CC-130H(SAR) Hercules	RCAF 413 Sqn (14 Wing), Greenwood	
130335	Lockheed CC-130H Hercules	RCAF 426 Sqn (8 Wing), Trenton	
130336	Lockheed CC-130H Hercules	RCAF 426 Sqn (8 Wing), Trenton	
130337	Lockheed CC-130H Hercules	RCAF 426 Sqn (8 Wing), Trenton	
130338	Lockheed CC-130H(T) Hercules	RCAF 435 Sqn (17 Wing), Winnipeg	
130339	Lockheed CC-130H(T) Hercules	RCAF 435 Sqn (17 Wing), Winnipeg	
130340	Lockheed CC-130H(T) Hercules	RCAF 435 Sqn (17 Wing), Winnipeg	
130341	Lockheed CC-130H(T) Hercules	RCAF 435 Sqn (17 Wing), Winnipeg	
130343	Lockheed CC-130H-30 Hercules	RCAF 426 Sqn (8 Wing), Trenton	
130344	Lockheed CC-130H-30 Hercules	RCAF 426 Sqn (8 Wing), Trenton	
130601	Lockheed CC-130J Hercules II	RCAF 436 Sqn (8 Wing), Trenton	
130602	Lockheed CC-130J Hercules II	RCAF 436 Sqn (8 Wing), Trenton	
130603	Lockheed CC-130J Hercules II	RCAF 436 Sqn (8 Wing), Trenton	
130604	Lockheed CC-130J Hercules II	RCAF 436 Sqn (8 Wing), Trenton	
130605	Lockheed CC-130J Hercules II	RCAF 436 Sqn (8 Wing), Trenton	
130606	Lockheed CC-130J Hercules II	RCAF 436 Sqn (8 Wing), Trenton	
130607	Lockheed CC-130J Hercules II	RCAF 436 Sqn (8 Wing), Trenton	
130608	Lockheed CC-130J Hercules II	RCAF 436 Sqn (8 Wing), Trenton	

Notes	Serial	Type (code/other identity)	Owner/operator, location or fate
	130609	Lockheed CC-130J Hercules II	RCAF 436 Sqn (8 Wing), Trenton
	130610	Lockheed CC-130J Hercules II	RCAF 436 Sqn (8 Wing), Trenton
	130611	Lockheed CC-130J Hercules II	RCAF 436 Sqn (8 Wing), Trenton
	130612	Lockheed CC-130J Hercules II	RCAF 436 Sqn (8 Wing), Trenton
	130613	Lockheed CC-130J Hercules II	RCAF 436 Sqn (8 Wing), Trenton
	130614	Lockheed CC-130J Hercules II	RCAF 436 Sqn (8 Wing), Trenton
	130615	Lockheed CC-130J Hercules II	RCAF 436 Sqn (8 Wing), Trenton
	130616	Lockheed CC-130J Hercules II	RCAF 436 Sqn (8 Wing), Trenton
	130617	Lockheed CC-130J Hercules II	RCAF 436 Sqn (8 Wing), Trenton
	140101	Lockheed CP-140M Aurora	RCAF 404 Sqn/405 Sqn (14 Wing), Greenwood
	140102	Lockheed CP-140 Aurora	RCAF 404 Sqn/405 Sqn (14 Wing), Greenwood
	140103	Lockheed CP-140M Aurora	RCAF 404 Sqn/405 Sqn (14 Wing), Greenwood
	140104	Lockheed CP-140M Aurora	RCAF 404 Sqn/405 Sqn (14 Wing), Greenwood
	140105	Lockheed CP-140M Aurora	RCAF 407 Sqn (19 Wing), Comox
	140106	Lockheed CP-140 Aurora	RCAF 404 Sqn/405 Sqn (14 Wing), Greenwood
	140107	Lockheed CP-140 Aurora	RCAF 407 Sqn (19 Wing), Comox
	140108	Lockheed CP-140M Aurora	RCAF 404 Sqn/405 Sqn (14 Wing), Greenwood
	140109	Lockheed CP-140 Aurora	RCAF 407 Sqn (19 Wing), Comox
	140110	Lockheed CP-140 Aurora	RCAF 404 Sqn/405 Sqn (14 Wing), Greenwood
	140111	Lockheed CP-140M Aurora	RCAF 404 Sqn/405 Sqn (14 Wing), Greenwood
	140112	Lockheed CP-140 Aurora	RCAF 407 Sqn (19 Wing), Comox
	140113	Lockheed CP-140 Aurora	RCAF 407 Sqn (19 Wing), Comox
	140114	Lockheed CP-140M Aurora	RCAF 404 Sqn/405 Sqn (14 Wing), Greenwood
	140115	Lockheed CP-140M Aurora	RCAF 407 Sqn (19 Wing), Comox
	140116	Lockheed CP-140 Aurora	RCAF 404 Sqn/405 Sqn (14 Wing), Greenwood
	140117	Lockheed CP-140M Aurora	RCAF 404 Sqn/405 Sqn (14 Wing), Greenwood
	140118	Lockheed CP-140M Aurora	RCAF 404 Sqn/405 Sqn (14 Wing), Greenwood
	142803	De Havilland Canada CT-142	RCAF 402 Sqn (17 Wing), Winnipeg
	142804	De Havilland Canada CT-142	RCAF 402 Sqn (17 Wing), Winnipeg
	142805	De Havilland Canada CT-142	RCAF 402 Sqn (17 Wing), Winnipeg
	142806	De Havilland Canada CT-142	RCAF 402 Sqn (17 Wing), Winnipeg
	144614	Canadair CC-144B Challenger	RCAF 412 Sqn (8 Wing), Ottawa
	144615	Canadair CC-144B Challenger	RCAF 412 Sqn (8 Wing), Ottawa
	144616	Canadair CC-144B Challenger	*Preserved at the Greenwood Museum, July 2016*
	144617	Canadair CC-144C Challenger	RCAF 412 Sqn (8 Wing), Ottawa
	144618	Canadair CC-144C Challenger	RCAF 412 Sqn (8 Wing), Ottawa
	177701	Boeing CC-177 (C-17A Globemaster III)	RCAF 429 Sqn (8 Wing), Trenton
	177702	Boeing CC-177 (C-17A Globemaster III)	RCAF 429 Sqn (8 Wing), Trenton
	177703	Boeing CC-177 (C-17A Globemaster III)	RCAF 429 Sqn (8 Wing), Trenton
	177704	Boeing CC-177 (C-17A Globemaster III)	RCAF 429 Sqn (8 Wing), Trenton
	177705	Boeing CC-177 (C-17A Globemaster III)	RCAF 429 Sqn (8 Wing), Trenton
	CHAD		
	TT-ABD	Boeing 737-74Q	Chad Government, N'djamena
	CHILE		
	Fuerza Aérea de Chile (FACh)		
	145	Extra EA-300L [5]	FACh *Los Halcones*, Santiago
	146	Extra EA-300L [4]	FACh *Los Halcones*, Santiago
	147	Extra EA-300L [2]	FACh *Los Halcones*, Santiago
	902	Boeing 707-351C	FACh, Grupo de Aviación 10, Santiago
	904	Boeing 707-358C	FACh, Grupo de Aviación 10, Santiago
	911	Grumman G.1159C Gulfstream IV	FACh, Grupo de Aviación 10, Santiago
	912	Grumman G.1159C Gulfstream IV	FACh, Grupo de Aviación 10, Santiago
	921	Boeing 737-58N	FACh, Grupo de Aviación 10, Santiago
	922	Boeing 737-330	FACh, Grupo de Aviación 10, Santiago
	982	Boeing KC-135E Stratotanker	FACh, Grupo de Aviación 10, Santiago
	983	Boeing KC-135E Stratotanker	FACh, Grupo de Aviación 10, Santiago
	985	Boeing 767-3Y0ER	FACh, Grupo de Aviación 10, Santiago
	990	Lockheed KC-130R Hercules	FACh, Grupo de Aviación 10, Santiago
	991	Lockheed C-130H Hercules	FACh, Grupo de Aviación 10, Santiago
	992	Lockheed KC-130R Hercules	FACh, Grupo de Aviación 10, Santiago

Serial	Type (code/other identity)	Owner/operator, location or fate	Notes
995	Lockheed C-130H Hercules	FACh, Grupo de Aviación 10, Santiago	
996	Lockheed C-130H Hercules	FACh, Grupo de Aviación 10, Santiago	
999	Lockheed KC-130R Hercules	FACh, Grupo de Aviación 10, Santiago	
1304	Extra EA-300L [3]	FACh Los Halcones, Santiago	
1325	Extra EA-300L [1]	FACh Los Halcones, Santiago	

COLOMBIA
Fuerza Aérea Colombiana (FAC)

FAC-0001	Boeing 737-74V	FAC Escuadrón de Transporte Especial, Bogotà	

CROATIA
Hrvatske Zračne Snage (HZS)

054	Pilatus PC-9M	HZS 93 Zakroplova Baza, Zadar	
055	Pilatus PC-9M	HZS 93 Zakroplova Baza, Zadar	
056	Pilatus PC-9M	HZS 93 Zakroplova Baza, Zadar	
057	Pilatus PC-9M	HZS 93 Zakroplova Baza, Zadar	
059	Pilatus PC-9M $	HZS 93 Zakroplova Baza, Zadar	
061	Pilatus PC-9M	HZS 93 Zakroplova Baza, Zadar	
062	Pilatus PC-9M	HZS 93 Zakroplova Baza, Zadar	
063	Pilatus PC-9M	HZS 93 Zakroplova Baza, Zadar	
064	Pilatus PC-9M	HZS 93 Zakroplova Baza, Zadar	
066	Pilatus PC-9M	HZS 93 Zakroplova Baza, Zadar	
067	Pilatus PC-9M	HZS 93 Zakroplova Baza, Zadar	
068	Pilatus PC-9M	HZS 93 Zakroplova Baza, Zadar	
069	Pilatus PC-9M	HZS 93 Zakroplova Baza, Zadar	
070	Pilatus PC-9M	HZS 93 Zakroplova Baza, Zadar	

Croatian Government

9A-CRO	Canadair CL.601 Challenger	Croatian Government, Zagreb	
9A-CRT	Canadair CL.601 Challenger	Croatian Government, Zagreb	

CZECH REPUBLIC
Vzdušné Síly Armády (Czech Air Force)

0103	Aero L-39C Albatros	Czech AF CLV, Pardubice	
0106	Aero L-39C Albatros	Czech AF CLV, Pardubice	
0107	Aero L-39C Albatros	Czech AF CLV, Pardubice	
0108	Aero L-39C Albatros	Czech AF CLV, Pardubice	
0113	Aero L-39C Albatros	Czech AF CLV, Pardubice	
0115	Aero L-39C Albatros	Czech AF CLV, Pardubice	
0260	Yakovlev Yak-40	Czech AF 241.dlt/24.zDL, Praha/Kbely	
0441	Aero L-39C Albatros	Czech AF CLV, Pardubice	
0444	Aero L-39C Albatros	Czech AF CLV, Pardubice	
0445	Aero L-39C Albatros	Czech AF CLV, Pardubice	
0452	CASA C-295M	Czech AF 242.tsl/24.zDL, Praha/Kbely	
0453	CASA C-295M	Czech AF 242.tsl/24.zDL, Praha/Kbely	
0454	CASA C-295M	Czech AF 242.tsl/24.zDL, Praha/Kbely	
0455	CASA C-295M	Czech AF 242.tsl/24.zDL, Praha/Kbely	
0458	Evektor EV-55M Outback	Evektor, Kunovice	
0731	LET L-410UVP-E Turbolet	Czech AF CLV, Pardubice	
0803	Mil Mi-17	Czech AF 243.vrl/24.zDL, Praha/Kbely	
0811	Mil Mi-17	Czech AF 243.vrl/24.zDL, Praha/Kbely	
0828	Mil Mi-17	Czech AF 243.vrl/24.zDL, Praha/Kbely	
0832	Mil Mi-17	Czech AF 243.vrl/24.zDL, Praha/Kbely	
0834	Mil Mi-17	Czech AF 243.vrl/24.zDL, Praha/Kbely	
0836	Mil Mi-17	Czech AF CLV, Pardubice	
0837	Mil Mi-17	Czech AF CLV, Pardubice	
0839	Mil Mi-17	Czech AF 243.vrl/24.zDL, Praha/Kbely	
0840	Mil Mi-17	Czech AF 243.vrl/24.zDL, Praha/Kbely	
0848	Mil Mi-17	Czech AF 243.vrl/24.zDL, Praha/Kbely	
0849	Mil Mi-17	Czech AF 243.vrl/24.zDL, Praha/Kbely	
0850	Mil Mi-17	Czech AF 243.vrl/24.zDL, Praha/Kbely	
0928	LET L-410UVP-T Turbolet	Czech AF CLV, Pardubice	
0981	Mil Mi-24V2	Czech AF 221.lbvr/22.zL, Náměšt	

Notes	Serial	Type (code/other identity)	Owner/operator, location or fate
	1257	Yakovlev Yak-40K	Czech AF 241.dlt/24.zDL, Praha/Kbely
	1504	LET L-410UVP Turbolet	Czech AF 242.tsl/24.zDL, Praha/Kbely
	1526	LET L-410FG Turbolet	Czech AF 242.tsl/24.zDL, Praha/Kbely
	2344	Aero L-39ZA Albatros	Czech AF 213.vlt/21.zTL, Cáslav
	2415	Aero L-39ZA Albatros	Czech AF 213.vlt/21.zTL, Cáslav
	2421	Aero L-39ZA Albatros	Czech AF 213.vlt/21.zTL, Cáslav
	2433	Aero L-39ZA Albatros $	Czech AF 213.vlt/21.zTL, Cáslav
	2436	Aero L-39ZA Albatros	Czech AF 213.vlt/21.zTL, Cáslav
	2601	LET L-410UVP-E Turbolet	Czech AF 242.tsl/24.zDL, Praha/Kbely
	2602	LET L-410UVP-E Turbolet	Czech AF 242.tsl/24.zDL, Praha/Kbely
	2626	Aero L-39NG Albatros	Aero, Vodochody
	2801	Airbus A.319CJ-115X	Czech AF 241.dlt/24.zDL, Praha/Kbely
	3085	Airbus A.319CJ-115X	Czech AF 241.dlt/24.zDL, Praha/Kbely
	3361	Mil Mi-35 $	Czech AF 221.lbvr/22.zL, Náměšt
	3362	Mil Mi-35	Czech AF 221.lbvr/22.zL, Náměšt
	3365	Mil Mi-35	Czech AF 221.lbvr/22.zL, Náměšt
	3366	Mil Mi-35 $	Czech AF 221.lbvr/22.zL, Náměšt
	3367	Mil Mi-35	Czech AF 221.lbvr/22.zL, Náměšt
	3368	Mil Mi-35	Czech AF 221.lbvr/22.zL, Náměšt
	3369	Mil Mi-35	Czech AF 221.lbvr/22.zL, Náměšt
	3370	Mil Mi-35 $	Czech AF 221.lbvr/22.zL, Náměšt
	3371	Mil Mi-35	Czech AF 221.lbvr/22.zL, Náměšt
	3903	Aero L-39ZA Albatros	Czech AF 213.vlt/21.zTL, Cáslav
	5015	Aero L-39ZA Albatros	Czech AF 213.vlt/21.zTL, Cáslav
	5017	Aero L-39ZA Albatros	Czech AF 213.vlt/21.zTL, Cáslav
	5019	Aero L-39ZA Albatros	Czech AF 213.vlt/21.zTL, Cáslav
	5105	Canadair CL.601-3A Challenger	Czech AF 241.dlt/24.zDL, Praha/Kbely
	5831	Aero L-159B ALCA	*Withdrawn from use, 2016*
	5832	Aero L-159B ALCA	Czech AF LZO, Praha/Kbely
	6046	Aero L-159T-1 ALCA	Czech AF 213.vlt/21.zTL, Cáslav
	6047	Aero L-159T-1 ALCA	Czech AF 213.vlt/21.zTL, Cáslav
	6048	Aero L-159A ALCA	Czech AF 212.tl/21.zTL, Cáslav
	6049	Aero L-159A ALCA	*Sold to Iraq, 2016*
	6050	Aero L-159A ALCA	Czech AF 212.tl/21.zTL, Cáslav
	6051	Aero L-159A ALCA	Czech AF 212.tl/21.zTL, Cáslav
	6052	Aero L-159A ALCA	Czech AF 212.tl/21.zTL, Cáslav
	6053	Aero L-159A ALCA	Czech AF 212.tl/21.zTL, Cáslav
	6054	Aero L-159A ALCA	Czech AF 212.tl/21.zTL, Cáslav
	6055	Aero L-159A ALCA	*Sold to Iraq, 2016*
	6057	Aero L-159A ALCA	Czech AF 212.tl/21.zTL, Cáslav
	6058	Aero L-159A ALCA	Czech AF 212.tl/21.zTL, Cáslav
	6059	Aero L-159A ALCA	Czech AF 212.tl/21.zTL, Cáslav
	6060	Aero L-159A ALCA	Czech AF 212.tl/21.zTL, Cáslav
	6062	Aero L-159A ALCA	Czech AF 212.tl/21.zTL, Cáslav
	6063	Aero L-159A ALCA	Czech AF 212.tl/21.zTL, Cáslav
	6064	Aero L-159A ALCA	Czech AF 212.tl/21.zTL, Cáslav
	6066	Aero L-159A ALCA $	Czech AF 212.tl/21.zTL, Cáslav
	6069	Aero L-159B ALCA	Czech AF 212.tl/21.zTL, Cáslav
	6070	Aero L-159A ALCA	Czech AF 212.tl/21.zTL, Cáslav
	6073	Aero L-159T-2X ALCA	Aero, Vodochody
	6075	Aero L-159T-1 ALCA	Czech AF 213.vlt/21.zTL, Cáslav
	6078	Aero L-159T-1 ALCA	Czech AF 213.vlt/21.zTL, Cáslav
	6079	Aero L-159T-1 ALCA	Czech AF 213.vlt/21.zTL, Cáslav
	7353	Mil Mi-24V $	Czech AF 221.lbvr/22.zL, Náměšt
	7354	Mil Mi-24V	Czech AF 221.lbvr/22.zL, Náměšt
	7355	Mil Mi-24V	Czech AF 221.lbvr/22.zL, Náměšt
	7356	Mil Mi-24V	Czech AF 221.lbvr/22.zL, Náměšt
	7357	Mil Mi-24V	Czech AF 221.lbvr/22.zL, Náměšt
	7360	Mil Mi-24V	Czech AF 221.lbvr/22.zL, Náměšt
	9234	SAAB JAS 39C Gripen	Czech AF 211.tl/21.zTL, Cáslav
	9235	SAAB JAS 39C Gripen $	Czech AF 211.tl/21.zTL, Cáslav
	9236	SAAB JAS 39C Gripen $	Czech AF 211.tl/21.zTL, Cáslav

Serial	Type (code/other identity)	Owner/operator, location or fate	Notes
9237	SAAB JAS 39C Gripen	Czech AF 211.tl/21.zTL, Cáslav	
9238	SAAB JAS 39C Gripen S	Czech AF 211.tl/21.zTL, Cáslav	
9239	SAAB JAS 39C Gripen	Czech AF 211.tl/21.zTL, Cáslav	
9240	SAAB JAS 39C Gripen $	Czech AF 211.tl/21.zTL, Cáslav	
9241	SAAB JAS 39C Gripen	Czech AF 211.tl/21.zTL, Cáslav	
9242	SAAB JAS 39C Gripen	Czech AF 211.tl/21.zTL, Cáslav	
9243	SAAB JAS 39C Gripen	Czech AF 211.tl/21.zTL, Cáslav	
9244	SAAB JAS 39C Gripen	Czech AF 211.tl/21.zTL, Cáslav	
9245	SAAB JAS 39C Gripen	Czech AF 211.tl/21.zTL, Cáslav	
9767	Mil Mi-171Sh	Czech AF 221.lbvr & 222.vrlt/22.zVrL, Námĕšt	
9774	Mil Mi-171Sh	Czech AF 221.lbvr & 222.vrlt/22.zVrL, Námĕšt	
9781	Mil Mi-171Sh	Czech AF 221.lbvr & 222.vrlt/22.zVrL, Námĕšt	
9799	Mil Mi-171Sh	Czech AF 221.lbvr & 222.vrlt/22.zVrL, Námĕšt	
9806	Mil Mi-171Sh	Czech AF 221.lbvr & 222.vrlt/22.zVrL, Námĕšt	
9813	Mil Mi-171Sh	Czech AF 221.lbvr & 222.vrlt/22.zVrL, Námĕšt	
9819	SAAB JAS 39D Gripen $	Czech AF 211.tl/21.zTL, Cáslav	
9820	SAAB JAS 39D Gripen $	Czech AF 211.tl/21.zTL, Cáslav	
9825	Mil Mi-171Sh	Czech AF 221.lbvr & 222.vrlt/22.zVrL, Námĕšt	
9837	Mil Mi-171Sh	Czech AF 221.lbvr & 222.vrlt/22.zVrL, Námĕšt	
9844	Mil Mi-171Sh	Czech AF 221.lbvr & 222.vrlt/22.zVrL, Námĕšt	
9868	Mil Mi-171Sh	Czech AF 221.lbvr & 222.vrlt/22.zVrL, Námĕšt	
9873	Mil Mi-171Sh	Czech AF 221.lbvr & 222.vrlt/22.zVrL, Námĕšt	
9887	Mil Mi-171Sh	Czech AF 221.lbvr & 222.vrlt/22.zVrL, Námĕšt	
9892	Mil Mi-171Sh	Czech AF 221.lbvr & 222.vrlt/22.zVrL, Námĕšt	
9904	Mil Mi-171Sh	Czech AF 221.lbvr & 222.vrlt/22.zVrL, Námĕšt	
9915	Mil Mi-171Sh	Czech AF 221.lbvr & 222.vrlt/22.zVrL, Námĕšt	
9926	Mil Mi-171Sh	Czech AF 221.lbvr & 222.vrlt/22.zVrL, Námĕšt	

DENMARK

Kongelige Danske Flyvevåben (KDF)

Serial	Type (code/other identity)	Owner/operator, location or fate	Notes
B-536	Lockheed C-130J-30 Hercules II	KDF Eskadrille 721, Aalborg	
B-537	Lockheed C-130J-30 Hercules II	KDF Eskadrille 721, Aalborg	
B-538	Lockheed C-130J-30 Hercules II	KDF Eskadrille 721, Aalborg	
B-583	Lockheed C-130J-30 Hercules II	KDF Eskadrille 721, Aalborg	
C-080	Canadair CL.604 Challenger	KDF Eskadrille 721, Aalborg	
C-168	Canadair CL.604 Challenger $	KDF Eskadrille 721, Aalborg	
C-172	Canadair CL.604 Challenger	KDF Eskadrille 721, Aalborg	
C-215	Canadair CL.604 Challenger	KDF Eskadrille 721, Aalborg	
E-004	SABCA (GD) F-16A MLU Fighting Falcon	KDF Eskadrille 727, Skrydstrup	
E-005	SABCA (GD) F-16A MLU Fighting Falcon	KDF Eskadrille 727, Skrydstrup	
E-006	SABCA (GD) F-16A MLU Fighting Falcon	KDF Eskadrille 730, Skrydstrup	
E-007	SABCA (GD) F-16A MLU Fighting Falcon	KDF Eskadrille 727, Skrydstrup	
E-008	SABCA (GD) F-16A MLU Fighting Falcon $	KDF Eskadrille 727, Skrydstrup	
E-011	GD F-16A MLU Fighting Falcon	KDF Eskadrille 727, Skrydstrup	
E-016	SABCA (GD) F-16A MLU Fighting Falcon	KDF Eskadrille 727, Skrydstrup	
E-017	SABCA (GD) F-16A MLU Fighting Falcon	KDF Eskadrille 727, Skrydstrup	
E-018	SABCA (GD) F-16A MLU Fighting Falcon	KDF Eskadrille 730, Skrydstrup	
E-024	GD F-16A MLU Fighting Falcon	KDF Eskadrille 727, Skrydstrup	
E-074	GD F-16A MLU Fighting Falcon	KDF Eskadrille 730, Skrydstrup	
E-075	GD F-16A MLU Fighting Falcon	KDF Eskadrille 727, Skrydstrup	
E-107	GD F-16A MLU Fighting Falcon	KDF Eskadrille 727, Skrydstrup	
E-189	SABCA (GD) F-16A MLU Fighting Falcon	KDF Eskadrille 730, Skrydstrup	
E-190	SABCA (GD) F-16A MLU Fighting Falcon	KDF Eskadrille 730, Skrydstrup	
E-191	SABCA (GD) F-16A MLU Fighting Falcon	KDF Eskadrille 730, Skrydstrup	
E-194	SABCA (GD) F-16A MLU Fighting Falcon $	KDF Eskadrille 730, Skrydstrup	
E-596	SABCA (GD) F-16A MLU Fighting Falcon	KDF Eskadrille 730, Skrydstrup	
E-597	SABCA (GD) F-16A MLU Fighting Falcon	KDF Eskadrille 730, Skrydstrup	
E-598	SABCA (GD) F-16A MLU Fighting Falcon	KDF Eskadrille 727, Skrydstrup	
E-599	SABCA (GD) F-16A MLU Fighting Falcon	KDF, stored Skrydstrup	
E-600	SABCA (GD) F-16A MLU Fighting Falcon	KDF Eskadrille 730, Skrydstrup	
E-601	SABCA (GD) F-16A MLU Fighting Falcon	KDF Eskadrille 730, Skrydstrup	
E-602	SABCA (GD) F-16A MLU Fighting Falcon	KDF Eskadrille 730, Skrydstrup	

Notes	Serial	Type (code/other identity)	Owner/operator, location or fate
	E-603	SABCA (GD) F-16A MLU Fighting Falcon	KDF Eskadrille 730, Skrydstrup
	E-604	SABCA (GD) F-16A MLU Fighting Falcon	KDF Eskadrille 727, Skrydstrup
	E-605	SABCA (GD) F-16A MLU Fighting Falcon	KDF Eskadrille 730, Skrydstrup
	E-606	SABCA (GD) F-16A MLU Fighting Falcon	KDF Eskadrille 730, Skrydstrup
	E-607	SABCA (GD) F-16A MLU Fighting Falcon	KDF Eskadrille 727, Skrydstrup
	E-608	SABCA (GD) F-16A MLU Fighting Falcon	KDF Eskadrille 727, Skrydstrup
	E-609	SABCA (GD) F-16A MLU Fighting Falcon	KDF Eskadrille 727, Skrydstrup
	E-610	SABCA (GD) F-16A MLU Fighting Falcon	KDF Eskadrille 730, Skrydstrup
	E-611	SABCA (GD) F-16A MLU Fighting Falcon	KDF Eskadrille 727, Skrydstrup
	ET-022	Fokker (GD) F-16B MLU Fighting Falcon	KDF Eskadrille 730, Skrydstrup
	ET-197	Fokker (GD) F-16B MLU Fighting Falcon	KDF Eskadrille 727, Skrydstrup
	ET-198	Fokker (GD) F-16B MLU Fighting Falcon	KDF Eskadrille 730, Skrydstrup
	ET-199	Fokker (GD) F-16B MLU Fighting Falcon	KDF Eskadrille 730, Skrydstrup
	ET-207	SABCA (GD) F-16B MLU Fighting Falcon	KDF Eskadrille 727, Skrydstrup
	ET-208	SABCA (GD) F-16B MLU Fighting Falcon	KDF Eskadrille 730, Skrydstrup
	ET-210	SABCA (GD) F-16B MLU Fighting Falcon	KDF Eskadrille 727/730, Skrydstrup
	ET-612	SABCA (GD) F-16B MLU Fighting Falcon	KDF Eskadrille 727, Skrydstrup
	ET-613	SABCA (GD) F-16B MLU Fighting Falcon	KDF Eskadrille 727, Skrydstrup
	ET-614	SABCA (GD) F-16B MLU Fighting Falcon	KDF Eskadrille 727, Skrydstrup
	ET-615	SABCA (GD) F-16B MLU Fighting Falcon	KDF Eskadrille 727, Skrydstrup
	M-502	AgustaWestland EH.101 Mk.512	KDF Eskadrille 722, Karup
	M-504	AgustaWestland EH.101 Mk.512	KDF Eskadrille 722, Karup
	M-507	AgustaWestland EH.101 Mk.512	KDF Eskadrille 722, Karup
	M-508	AgustaWestland EH.101 Mk.512	KDF Eskadrille 722, Karup
	M-510	AgustaWestland EH.101 Mk.512	KDF Eskadrille 722, Karup
	M-512	AgustaWestland EH.101 Mk.512	KDF Eskadrille 722, Karup
	M-513	AgustaWestland EH.101 Mk.512	KDF Eskadrille 722, Karup
	M-514	AgustaWestland EH.101 Mk.512	KDF Eskadrille 722, Karup
	M-515	AgustaWestland EH.101 Mk.512	KDF Eskadrille 722, Karup
	M-516	AgustaWestland EH.101 Mk.512	KDF Eskadrille 722, Karup
	M-517	AgustaWestland EH.101 Mk.512	KDF Eskadrille 722, Karup
	M-518	AgustaWestland EH.101 Mk.512	KDF Eskadrille 722, Karup
	M-519	AgustaWestland EH.101 Mk.512	KDF Eskadrille 722, Karup
	M-520	AgustaWestland EH.101 Mk.512	KDF Eskadrille 722, Karup
	N-971	Sikorsky MH-60R Sea Hawk	KDF Eskadrille 723, Karup
	N-972	Sikorsky MH-60R Sea Hawk	KDF Eskadrille 723, Karup
	N-973	Sikorsky MH-60R Sea Hawk	KDF Eskadrille 723, Karup
	N-974	Sikorsky MH-60R Sea Hawk	KDF Eskadrille 723, Karup (on order)
	N-975	Sikorsky MH-60R Sea Hawk	KDF Eskadrille 723, Karup (on order)
	N-976	Sikorsky MH-60R Sea Hawk	KDF Eskadrille 723, Karup (on order)
	N-977	Sikorsky MH-60R Sea Hawk	KDF Eskadrille 723, Karup (on order)
	N-978	Sikorsky MH-60R Sea Hawk	KDF Eskadrille 723, Karup (on order)
	N-979	Sikorsky MH-60R Sea Hawk	KDF Eskadrille 723, Karup (on order)
	P-090	Aérospatiale AS.550C-2 Fennec	KDF Eskadrille 724, Karup
	P-234	Aérospatiale AS.550C-2 Fennec	KDF Eskadrille 724, Karup
	P-254	Aérospatiale AS.550C-2 Fennec	KDF Eskadrille 724, Karup
	P-275	Aérospatiale AS.550C-2 Fennec	KDF Eskadrille 724, Karup
	P-276	Aérospatiale AS.550C-2 Fennec	KDF Eskadrille 724, Karup
	P-287	Aérospatiale AS.550C-2 Fennec	KDF Eskadrille 724, Karup
	P-288	Aérospatiale AS.550C-2 Fennec	KDF Eskadrille 724, Karup
	P-319	Aérospatiale AS.550C-2 Fennec	KDF Eskadrille 724, Karup
	P-320	Aérospatiale AS.550C-2 Fennec	KDF Eskadrille 724, Karup
	P-339	Aérospatiale AS.550C-2 Fennec	KDF Eskadrille 724, Karup
	P-352	Aérospatiale AS.550C-2 Fennec	KDF Eskadrille 724, Karup
	P-369	Aérospatiale AS.550C-2 Fennec	KDF Eskadrille 724, Karup
	S-134	Westland Lynx Mk.90B	KDF Eskadrille 723, Karup
	S-142	Westland Lynx Mk.90B	KDF Eskadrille 723, Karup
	S-170	Westland Lynx Mk.90B	KDF Eskadrille 723, Karup
	S-175	Westland Lynx Mk.90B	KDF Eskadrille 723, Karup
	S-181	Westland Lynx Mk.90B	KDF Eskadrille 723, Karup
	S-191	Westland Lynx Mk.90B	KDF Eskadrille 723, Karup
	S-256	Westland Lynx Mk.90B	KDF Eskadrille 723, Karup

Serial	Type (code/other identity)	Owner/operator, location or fate	Notes
T-401	SAAB T-17 Supporter	KDF Flyveskolen, Karup	
T-402	SAAB T-17 Supporter	KDF Flyveskolen, Karup	
T-403	SAAB T-17 Supporter	KDF Flyveskolen, Karup	
T-404	SAAB T-17 Supporter	KDF Flyveskolen, Karup	
T-405	SAAB T-17 Supporter	KDF Skrydstrup Station Flight	
T-407	SAAB T-17 Supporter	KDF Eskadrille 721, Aalborg	
T-409	SAAB T-17 Supporter	KDF Aalborg Station Flight	
T-410	SAAB T-17 Supporter	KDF Flyveskolen, Karup	
T-411	SAAB T-17 Supporter	KDF Skrydstrup Station Flight	
T-412	SAAB T-17 Supporter	KDF Flyveskolen, Karup	
T-413	SAAB T-17 Supporter	KDF Flyveskolen, Karup	
T-414	SAAB T-17 Supporter	KDF Eskadrille 721, Aalborg	
T-415	SAAB T-17 Supporter	KDF Flyveskolen, Karup	
T-417	SAAB T-17 Supporter	KDF Flyveskolen, Karup	
T-418	SAAB T-17 Supporter	KDF Skrydstrup Station Flight	
T-419	SAAB T-17 Supporter	KDF Flyveskolen, Karup	
T-420	SAAB T-17 Supporter	KDF Flyveskolen, Karup	
T-421	SAAB T-17 Supporter	KDF Flyveskolen, Karup	
T-423	SAAB T-17 Supporter	KDF Flyveskolen, Karup	
T-425	SAAB T-17 Supporter	KDF Flyveskolen, Karup	
T-426	SAAB T-17 Supporter	KDF Flyveskolen, Karup	
T-427	SAAB T-17 Supporter	KDF Flyveskolen, Karup	
T-428	SAAB T-17 Supporter	KDF Flyveskolen, Karup	
T-429	SAAB T-17 Supporter	KDF Flyveskolen, Karup	
T-430	SAAB T-17 Supporter	KDF Flyveskolen, Karup	
T-431	SAAB T-17 Supporter	KDF Eskadrille 721, Aalborg	
T-432	SAAB T-17 Supporter	KDF Skrydstrup Station Flight	

ECUADOR
Fuerza Aérea Ecuatoriana (FAE)

Serial	Type (code/other identity)	Owner/operator, location or fate	Notes
FAE-051	Embraer ERJ.135 Legacy 600	FAE Escuadrón de Transporte 1114, Quito	
FAE-052	Dassault Falcon 7X	FAE Escuadrón de Transporte 1114, Quito	

EGYPT
Al Quwwat al-Jawwiya il Misriya (Egyptian Air Force)

Serial	Type (code/other identity)	Owner/operator, location or fate	Notes
1271	Lockheed C-130H Hercules (SU-BAB)	Egyptian AF 16 Sqn, Cairo West	
1273	Lockheed C-130H Hercules (SU-BAD)	Egyptian AF 16 Sqn, Cairo West	
1274	Lockheed C-130H Hercules (SU-BAE)	Egyptian AF 16 Sqn, Cairo West	
1275	Lockheed C-130H Hercules (SU-BAF)	Egyptian AF 16 Sqn, Cairo West	
1277	Lockheed C-130H Hercules (SU-BAI)	Egyptian AF 16 Sqn, Cairo West	
1278	Lockheed C-130H Hercules (SU-BAJ)	Egyptian AF 16 Sqn, Cairo West	
1279	Lockheed C-130H Hercules (SU-BAK)	Egyptian AF 16 Sqn, Cairo West	
1280	Lockheed C-130H Hercules (SU-BAL)	Egyptian AF 16 Sqn, Cairo West	
1281	Lockheed C-130H Hercules (SU-BAM)	Egyptian AF 16 Sqn, Cairo West	
1282	Lockheed C-130H Hercules (SU-BAN)	Egyptian AF 16 Sqn, Cairo West	
1283	Lockheed C-130H Hercules (SU-BAP)	Egyptian AF 16 Sqn, Cairo West	
1284	Lockheed C-130H Hercules (SU-BAQ)	Egyptian AF 16 Sqn, Cairo West	
1285	Lockheed C-130H Hercules (SU-BAR)	Egyptian AF 16 Sqn, Cairo West	
1286	Lockheed C-130H Hercules (SU-BAS)	Egyptian AF 16 Sqn, Cairo West	
1287	Lockheed C-130H Hercules (SU-BAT)	Egyptian AF 16 Sqn, Cairo West	
1288	Lockheed C-130H Hercules (SU-BAU)	Egyptian AF 16 Sqn, Cairo West	
1289	Lockheed C-130H Hercules (SU-BAV)	Egyptian AF 16 Sqn, Cairo West	
1290	Lockheed C-130H Hercules (SU-BEW)	Egyptian AF 16 Sqn, Cairo West	
1291	Lockheed C-130H Hercules (SU-BEX)	Egyptian AF 16 Sqn, Cairo West	
1292	Lockheed C-130H Hercules (SU-BEY)	Egyptian AF 16 Sqn, Cairo West	
1293	Lockheed C-130H-30 Hercules (SU-BKS)	Egyptian AF 16 Sqn, Cairo West	
1294	Lockheed C-130H-30 Hercules (SU-BKT)	Egyptian AF 16 Sqn, Cairo West	
1295	Lockheed C-130H-30 Hercules (SU-BKU)	Egyptian AF 16 Sqn, Cairo West	
1296	Lockheed C-130H Hercules (SU-BPJ)	Egyptian AF 16 Sqn, Cairo West	
1297	Lockheed C-130H Hercules (SU-BPK)	Egyptian AF 16 Sqn, Cairo West	
1298	Lockheed C-130H Hercules (SU-BPL)	Egyptian AF 16 Sqn, Cairo West	
....	Lockheed C-130J Hercules II	Egyptian AF (on order)	

Notes	Serial	Type (code/other identity)	Owner/operator, location or fate
	....	Lockheed C-130J Hercules II	Egyptian AF (on order)
Egyptian Government			
	SU-BGM	Grumman G.1159C Gulfstream IV	*Withdrawn from use, 2016*
	SU-BGU	Grumman G.1159A Gulfstream III	*Withdrawn from use, 2016*
	SU-BGV	Grumman G.1159A Gulfstream III	Egyptian AF/Government, Cairo
	SU-BNC	Grumman G.1159C Gulfstream IV	Egyptian AF/Government, Cairo
	SU-BND	Grumman G.1159C Gulfstream IV	Egyptian AF/Government, Cairo
	SU-BNO	Grumman G.1159C Gulfstream IV-SP	Egyptian AF/Government, Cairo
	SU-BNP	Grumman G.1159C Gulfstream IV-SP	Egyptian AF/Government, Cairo
	SU-BPE	Gulfstream Aerospace G.400	Egyptian AF/Government, Cairo
	SU-BPF	Gulfstream Aerospace G.400	Egyptian AF/Government, Cairo
	SU-BRF	Cessna 680 Citation Sovereign	Egyptian Government, Cairo
	SU-BRG	Cessna 680 Citation Sovereign	Egyptian Government, Cairo
	SU-GGG	Airbus A.340-211	Egyptian Government, Cairo
ESTONIA			
Estonian Air Force			
	10	Aero L-39C Albatros	Estonian AF Fixed Wing Squadron, Ämari
	11	Aero L-39C Albatros	Estonian AF Fixed Wing Squadron, Ämari
	20 y	WSK-PZL An-2T	Estonian AF Fixed Wing Squadron, Ämari
	40 y	WSK-PZL An-2T	Estonian AF Fixed Wing Squadron, Ämari
	41 y	Antonov An-2	Estonian AF Fixed Wing Squadron, Ämari
FINLAND			
Suomen Ilmavoimat (Finnish Air Force) & Suomen Maavoimat (Finnish Army)			
	CC-1	CASA C-295M	Ilmavoimat TukiLLv, Jyväskylä/Tikkakoski
	CC-2	CASA C-295M	Ilmavoimat TukiLLv, Jyväskylä/Tikkakoski
	CC-3	CASA C-295M	Ilmavoimat TukiLLv, Jyväskylä/Tikkakoski
	FF-1	Fokker F.27-100 Friendship	Ilmavoimat TukiLLv, Jyväskylä/Tikkakoski
	HN-401	McDonnell Douglas F-18C Hornet	Ilmavoimat HavLLv 31, Kuopio/Rissala
	HN-402	McDonnell Douglas F-18C Hornet	Ilmavoimat HavLLv 31, Kuopio/Rissala
	HN-403	McDonnell Douglas F-18C Hornet	Ilmavoimat HavLLv 31, Kuopio/Rissala
	HN-404	McDonnell Douglas F-18C Hornet	Ilmavoimat HavLLv 31, Kuopio/Rissala
	HN-405	McDonnell Douglas F-18C Hornet	Ilmavoimat HavLLv 31, Kuopio/Rissala
	HN-406	McDonnell Douglas F-18C Hornet	Ilmavoimat HavLLv 31, Kuopio/Rissala
	HN-407	McDonnell Douglas F-18C Hornet	Ilmavoimat HavLLv 31, Kuopio/Rissala
	HN-408	McDonnell Douglas F-18C Hornet	Ilmavoimat HavLLv 31, Kuopio/Rissala
	HN-409	McDonnell Douglas F-18C Hornet	Ilmavoimat HavLLv 11, Roveniemi
	HN-410	McDonnell Douglas F-18C Hornet	Ilmavoimat IlmaStk, Tampere/Pirkkala
	HN-411	McDonnell Douglas F-18C Hornet	Ilmavoimat HavLLv 11, Roveniemi
	HN-412	McDonnell Douglas F-18C Hornet	Ilmavoimat HavLLv 11, Roveniemi
	HN-414	McDonnell Douglas F-18C Hornet	Ilmavoimat HavLLv 31, Kuopio/Rissala
	HN-415	McDonnell Douglas F-18C Hornet	Ilmavoimat HavLLv 11, Roveniemi
	HN-416	McDonnell Douglas F-18C Hornet	Ilmavoimat
	HN-417	McDonnell Douglas F-18C Hornet	Ilmavoimat HavLLv 31, Kuopio/Rissala
	HN-418	McDonnell Douglas F-18C Hornet	Ilmavoimat HavLLv 31, Kuopio/Rissala
	HN-419	McDonnell Douglas F-18C Hornet	Ilmavoimat HavLLv 11, Roveniemi
	HN-420	McDonnell Douglas F-18C Hornet	Ilmavoimat HavLLv 31, Kuopio/Rissala
	HN-421	McDonnell Douglas F-18C Hornet	Ilmavoimat HavLLv 11, Roveniemi
	HN-422	McDonnell Douglas F-18C Hornet	Ilmavoimat HavLLv 11, Roveniemi
	HN-423	McDonnell Douglas F-18C Hornet	Ilmavoimat HavLLv 31, Kuopio/Rissala
	HN-424	McDonnell Douglas F-18C Hornet	Ilmavoimat HavLLv 11, Roveniemi
	HN-425	McDonnell Douglas F-18C Hornet	Ilmavoimat HavLLv 31, Kuopio/Rissala
	HN-426	McDonnell Douglas F-18C Hornet	Ilmavoimat HavLLv 31, Kuopio/Rissala
	HN-427	McDonnell Douglas F-18C Hornet	Ilmavoimat HavLLv 11, Roveniemi
	HN-428	McDonnell Douglas F-18C Hornet	Ilmavoimat HavLLv 11, Roveniemi
	HN-429	McDonnell Douglas F-18C Hornet	Ilmavoimat HavLLv 11, Roveniemi
	HN-431	McDonnell Douglas F-18C Hornet	Ilmavoimat HavLLv 31, Kuopio/Rissala
	HN-432	McDonnell Douglas F-18C Hornet	Ilmavoimat HavLLv 31, Kuopio/Rissala
	HN-433	McDonnell Douglas F-18C Hornet	Ilmavoimat HavLLv 31, Kuopio/Rissala
	HN-434	McDonnell Douglas F-18C Hornet	Ilmavoimat HavLLv 31, Kuopio/Rissala
	HN-435	McDonnell Douglas F-18C Hornet	Ilmavoimat

Serial	Type (code/other identity)	Owner/operator, location or fate	Notes
HN-436	McDonnell Douglas F-18C Hornet	Ilmavoimat HavLLv 31, Kuopio/Rissala	
HN-437	McDonnell Douglas F-18C Hornet	Ilmavoimat HavLLv 31, Kuopio/Rissala	
HN-438	McDonnell Douglas F-18C Hornet	Ilmavoimat HavLLv 31, Kuopio/Rissala	
HN-439	McDonnell Douglas F-18C Hornet	Ilmavoimat HavLLv 31, Kuopio/Rissala	
HN-440	McDonnell Douglas F-18C Hornet	Ilmavoimat HavLLv 31, Kuopio/Rissala	
HN-441	McDonnell Douglas F-18C Hornet	Ilmavoimat HavLLv 11, Roveniemi	
HN-442	McDonnell Douglas F-18C Hornet	Ilmavoimat HavLLv 11, Roveniemi	
HN-443	McDonnell Douglas F-18C Hornet	Ilmavoimat HavLLv 31, Kuopio/Rissala	
HN-444	McDonnell Douglas F-18C Hornet	Ilmavoimat HavLLv 11, Roveniemi	
HN-445	McDonnell Douglas F-18C Hornet	Ilmavoimat HavLLv 11, Roveniemi	
HN-446	McDonnell Douglas F-18C Hornet	Ilmavoimat HavLLv 11, Roveniemi	
HN-447	McDonnell Douglas F-18C Hornet	Ilmavoimat HavLLv 31, Kuopio/Rissala	
HN-448	McDonnell Douglas F-18C Hornet	Ilmavoimat HavLLv 31, Kuopio/Rissala	
HN-449	McDonnell Douglas F-18C Hornet	Ilmavoimat HavLLv 31, Kuopio/Rissala	
HN-450	McDonnell Douglas F-18C Hornet	Ilmavoimat HavLLv 11, Roveniemi	
HN-451	McDonnell Douglas F-18C Hornet	Ilmavoimat HavLLv 31, Kuopio/Rissala	
HN-452	McDonnell Douglas F-18C Hornet	Ilmavoimat	
HN-453	McDonnell Douglas F-18C Hornet	Ilmavoimat HavLLv 31, Kuopio/Rissala	
HN-454	McDonnell Douglas F-18C Hornet	Ilmavoimat HavLLv 11, Roveniemi	
HN-455	McDonnell Douglas F-18C Hornet	Ilmavoimat HavLLv 31, Kuopio/Rissala	
HN-456	McDonnell Douglas F-18C Hornet	Ilmavoimat HavLLv 31, Kuopio/Rissala	
HN-457	McDonnell Douglas F-18C Hornet	Ilmavoimat HavLLv 31, Kuopio/Rissala	
HN-461	McDonnell Douglas F-18D Hornet	Ilmavoimat HavLLv 31, Kuopio/Rissala	
HN-462	McDonnell Douglas F-18D Hornet	Ilmavoimat IlmaStk, Tampere/Pirkkala	
HN-463	McDonnell Douglas F-18D Hornet	Ilmavoimat HavLLv 11, Roveniemi	
HN-464	McDonnell Douglas F-18D Hornet	Ilmavoimat HavLLv 11, Roveniemi	
HN-465	McDonnell Douglas F-18D Hornet	Ilmavoimat	
HN-466	McDonnell Douglas F-18D Hornet	Ilmavoimat IlmaStk, Tampere/Pirkkala	
HN-467	McDonnell Douglas F-18D Hornet	Ilmavoimat HavLLv 31, Kuopio/Rissala	
HW-307	BAe Hawk 51	Ilmavoimat TukiLLv, Jyväskylä/Tikkakoski	
HW-320	BAe Hawk 51	Ilmavoimat, stored Halli (for upgrade)	
HW-321	BAe Hawk 51	Ilmavoimat, stored Halli (for upgrade)	
HW-327	BAe Hawk 51	Ilmavoimat TukiLLv, Jyväskylä/Tikkakoski	
HW-330	BAe Hawk 51	Ilmavoimat, stored Halli (for upgrade)	
HW-333	BAe Hawk 51	Ilmavoimat TukiLLv, Jyväskylä/Tikkakoski	
HW-334	BAe Hawk 51	Ilmavoimat TukiLLv, Jyväskylä/Tikkakoski	
HW-336	BAe Hawk 51	Ilmavoimat, stored Halli (for upgrade)	
HW-338	BAe Hawk 51	Ilmavoimat TukiLLv, Jyväskylä/Tikkakoski	
HW-339	BAe Hawk 51	Ilmavoimat, stored Halli (for upgrade)	
HW-340	BAe Hawk 51	Ilmavoimat TukiLLv, Jyväskylä/Tikkakoski	
HW-341	BAe Hawk 51	Ilmavoimat TukiLLv, Jyväskylä/Tikkakoski	
HW-343	BAe Hawk 51	Ilmavoimat TukiLLv, Jyväskylä/Tikkakoski	
HW-344	BAe Hawk 51	Ilmavoimat, stored Halli (for upgrade)	
HW-345	BAe Hawk 51	Ilmavoimat TukiLLv, Jyväskylä/Tikkakoski	
HW-348	BAe Hawk 51	Ilmavoimat, stored Halli (for upgrade)	
HW-349	BAe Hawk 51	Ilmavoimat, stored Halli (for upgrade)	
HW-350	BAe Hawk 51	Ilmavoimat, stored Halli (for upgrade)	
HW-351	BAe Hawk 51A	Ilmavoimat TukiLLv, Jyväskylä/Tikkakoski	
HW-352	BAe Hawk 51A	Ilmavoimat TukiLLv, Jyväskylä/Tikkakoski	
HW-353	BAe Hawk 51A	Ilmavoimat TukiLLv, Jyväskylä/Tikkakoski	
HW-354	BAe Hawk 51A	Ilmavoimat TukiLLv, Jyväskylä/Tikkakoski	
HW-355	BAe Hawk 51A	Ilmavoimat TukiLLv, Jyväskylä/Tikkakoski	
HW-356	BAe Hawk 51A	Ilmavoimat TukiLLv, Jyväskylä/Tikkakoski	
HW-357	BAe Hawk 51A	Ilmavoimat TukiLLv, Jyväskylä/Tikkakoski	
HW-360	BAe Hawk 66	Ilmavoimat TukiLLv, Jyväskylä/Tikkakoski	
HW-361	BAe Hawk 66	Ilmavoimat TukiLLv, Jyväskylä/Tikkakoski	
HW-362	BAe Hawk 66	Ilmavoimat TukiLLv, Jyväskylä/Tikkakoski	
HW-363	BAe Hawk 66	Ilmavoimat TukiLLv, Jyväskylä/Tikkakoski	
HW-364	BAe Hawk 66	Ilmavoimat TukiLLv, Jyväskylä/Tikkakoski	
HW-365	BAe Hawk 66	Ilmavoimat TukiLLv, Jyväskylä/Tikkakoski	
HW-366	BAe Hawk 66	Ilmavoimat TukiLLv, Jyväskylä/Tikkakoski	
HW-367	BAe Hawk 66	Ilmavoimat TukiLLv, Jyväskylä/Tikkakoski	

Notes	Serial	Type (code/other identity)	Owner/operator, location or fate
	HW-368	BAe Hawk 66	Ilmavoimat TukiLLv, Jyväskylä/Tikkakoski
	HW-370	BAe Hawk 66	Ilmavoimat TukiLLv, Jyväskylä/Tikkakoski
	HW-371	BAe Hawk 66	Ilmavoimat TukiLLv, Jyväskylä/Tikkakoski
	HW-373	BAe Hawk 66	Ilmavoimat TukiLLv, Jyväskylä/Tikkakoski
	HW-374	BAe Hawk 66	Ilmavoimat TukiLLv, Jyväskylä/Tikkakoski
	HW-375	BAe Hawk 66	Ilmavoimat TukiLLv, Jyväskylä/Tikkakoski
	HW-376	BAe Hawk 66	Ilmavoimat TukiLLv, Jyväskylä/Tikkakoski
	HW-377	BAe Hawk 66	Ilmavoimat TukiLLv, Jyväskylä/Tikkakoski
	LJ-1	Gates Learjet 35A	Ilmavoimat TukiLLv (Det.), Kuopio/Rissala
	LJ-2	Gates Learjet 35A	Ilmavoimat TukiLLv, Jyväskylä/Tikkakoski
	LJ-3	Gates Learjet 35A	Ilmavoimat TukiLLv, Jyväskylä/Tikkakoski
	NH-202	NH Industries NH.90-TTH	Maavoimat 1.HK/HekoP, Utti
	NH-203	NH Industries NH.90-TTH	Maavoimat 1.HK/HekoP, Utti
	NH-204	NH Industries NH.90-TTH	Maavoimat 1.HK/HekoP, Utti
	NH-205	NH Industries NH.90-TTH	Maavoimat 1.HK/HekoP, Utti
	NH-206	NH Industries NH.90-TTH	Maavoimat 1.HK/HekoP, Utti
	NH-207	NH Industries NH.90-TTH	Maavoimat 1.HK/HekoP, Utti
	NH-208	NH Industries NH.90-TTH	Maavoimat 1.HK/HekoP, Utti
	NH-209	NH Industries NH.90-TTH	Maavoimat 1.HK/HekoP, Utti
	NH-210	NH Industries NH.90-TTH	Maavoimat 1.HK/HekoP, Utti
	NH-211	NH Industries NH.90-TTH	Maavoimat 1.HK/HekoP, Utti
	NH-212	NH Industries NH.90-TTH	Maavoimat 1.HK/HekoP, Utti
	NH-213	NH Industries NH.90-TTH	Maavoimat 1.HK/HekoP, Utti
	NH-214	NH Industries NH.90-TTH	Maavoimat 1.HK/HekoP, Utti
	NH-215	NH Industries NH.90-TTH	Maavoimat 1.HK/HekoP, Utti
	NH-216	NH Industries NH.90-TTH	Maavoimat 1.HK/HekoP, Utti
	NH-217	NH Industries NH.90-TTH	Maavoimat 1.HK/HekoP, Utti
	NH-218	NH Industries NH.90-TTH	Maavoimat 1.HK/HekoP, Utti
	NH-219	NH Industries NH.90-TTH	Maavoimat 1.HK/HekoP, Utti
	NH-220	NH Industries NH.90-TTH	Maavoimat 1.HK/HekoP, Utti
	NH-221	NH Industries NH.90-TTH	Maavoimat 1.HK/HekoP, Utti
	PI-01	Pilatus PC-12/47E	Ilmavoimat TukiLLv, Jyväskylä/Tikkakoski
	PI-02	Pilatus PC-12/47E	Ilmavoimat TukiLLv, Jyväskylä/Tikkakoski
	PI-03	Pilatus PC-12/47E	Ilmavoimat TukiLLv, Jyväskylä/Tikkakoski
	PI-04	Pilatus PC-12/47E	Ilmavoimat TukiLLv, Jyväskylä/Tikkakoski
	PI-05	Pilatus PC-12/47E	Ilmavoimat TukiLLv, Jyväskylä/Tikkakoski
	PI-06	Pilatus PC-12/47E	Ilmavoimat TukiLLv, Jyväskylä/Tikkakoski

FRANCE

NB: Due to the way in which French military aircraft serials are issued, this section is sorted by type

Armée de l'Air (AA)

	418	Airbus A.310-304 (F-RADC)	AA ET 03.060 *Esterel*, Paris/Charles de Gaulle
	421	Airbus A.310-304 (F-RADA)	AA ET 03.060 *Esterel*, Paris/Charles de Gaulle
	422	Airbus A.310-304 (F-RADB)	AA ET 03.060 *Esterel*, Paris/Charles de Gaulle
	240	Airbus A.330-223 (F-RARF)	AA ET 00.060, Evreux
	1735	Airbus A.330-243 MRTT Phénix	AA GRV 02.093 *Bretagne*, Istres (on order)
	1...	Airbus A.330-243 MRTT Phénix	AA GRV 02.093 *Bretagne*, Istres (on order)
	1...	Airbus A.330-243 MRTT Phénix	AA GRV 02.093 *Bretagne*, Istres (on order)
	1...	Airbus A.330-243 MRTT Phénix	AA GRV 02.093 *Bretagne*, Istres (on order)
	1...	Airbus A.330-243 MRTT Phénix	AA GRV 02.093 *Bretagne*, Istres (on order)
	1...	Airbus A.330-243 MRTT Phénix	AA GRV 02.093 *Bretagne*, Istres (on order)
	1...	Airbus A.330-243 MRTT Phénix	AA GRV 02.093 *Bretagne*, Istres (on order)
	1...	Airbus A.330-243 MRTT Phénix	AA GRV 02.093 *Bretagne*, Istres (on order)
	1...	Airbus A.330-243 MRTT Phénix	AA GRV 02.093 *Bretagne*, Istres (on order)
	1...	Airbus A.330-243 MRTT Phénix	AA GRV 02.093 *Bretagne*, Istres (on order)
	1...	Airbus A.330-243 MRTT Phénix	AA GRV 02.093 *Bretagne*, Istres (on order)
	075	Airbus A.340-212 (F-RAJA)	AA ET 03.060 *Esterel*, Paris/Charles de Gaulle
	081	Airbus A.340-212 (F-RAJB)	AA ET 03.060 *Esterel*, Paris/Charles de Gaulle
	0007	Airbus Military A.400M (F-RBAA)	AA ET 01.061 *Touraine*, Orléans
	0008	Airbus Military A.400M (F-RBAB)	AA ET 01.061 *Touraine*, Orléans
	0010	Airbus Military A.400M (F-RBAC)	AA ET 01.061 *Touraine*, Orléans

Serial	Type (code/other identity)	Owner/operator, location or fate	Notes
0011	Airbus Military A.400M (F-RBAD)	AA ET 01.061 *Touraine*, Orléans	
0012	Airbus Military A.400M (F-RBAE)	AA ET 01.061 *Touraine*, Orléans	
0014	Airbus Military A.400M (F-RBAF)	AA ET 01.061 *Touraine*, Orléans	
0019	Airbus Military A.400M (F-RBAG)	AA ET 01.061 *Touraine*, Orléans	
0031	Airbus Military A.400M (F-RBAH)	AA ET 01.061 *Touraine*, Orléans	
0033	Airbus Military A.400M (F-RBAI)	AA ET 01.061 *Touraine*, Orléans)	
0037	Airbus Military A.400M (F-RBAJ)	AA (on order)	
0053	Airbus Military A.400M (F-RBAK)	AA (on order)	
0063	Airbus Military A.400M (F-RBAL)	AA (on order)	
0...	Airbus Military A.400M (F-RBAM)	AA (on order)	
045	Airtech CN-235M-200 [62-IB]	AA ET 01.062 *Vercours*, Evreux	
065	Airtech CN-235M-200 [52-IC]	AA ET 00.052 *La Tontouta*, Nouméa	
066	Airtech CN-235M-200 [52-ID]	AA ET 00.052 *La Tontouta*, Nouméa	
071	Airtech CN-235M-200 [62-IE]	AA ET 01.062 *Vercours*, Evreux	
072	Airtech CN-235M-200 [62-IF]	AA ET 01.062 *Vercours*, Evreux	
105	Airtech CN-235M-200 [52-IG]	AA ET 00.052 *La Tontouta*, Nouméa	
107	Airtech CN-235M-200 [52-IH]	AA ET 00.052 *La Tontouta*, Nouméa	
111	Airtech CN-235M-200 [62-II]	AA ET 01.062 *Vercours*, Evreux	
114	Airtech CN-235M-200 [62-IJ]	AA ET 01.062 *Vercours*, Evreux	
123	Airtech CN-235M-200 [62-IM]	AA ET 01.062 *Vercours*, Evreux	
128	Airtech CN-235M-200 [62-IK]	AA ET 01.062 *Vercours*, Evreux	
129	Airtech CN-235M-200 [62-IL]	AA ET 01.062 *Vercours*, Evreux	
137	Airtech CN-235M-200 [62-IN]	AA ET 01.062 *Vercours*, Evreux	
141	Airtech CN-235M-200 [62-IO]	AA ET 00.058 *Antilles*, Fort-de-France	
152	Airtech CN-235M-200 [62-IP]	AA ET 01.062 *Vercours*, Evreux	
156	Airtech CN-235M-200 [62-IQ]	AA ET 01.062 *Vercours*, Evreux	
158	Airtech CN-235M-200 [62-IR]	AA ET 01.062 *Vercours*, Evreux	
160	Airtech CN-235M-200 [62-IS]	AA ET 01.062 *Vercours*, Evreux	
165	Airtech CN-235M-200 [62-IT]	AA ET 01.062 *Vercours*, Evreux	
193	Airtech CN-235M-300 [62-HA]	AA ET 03.062 *Ventoux*, Evreux	
194	Airtech CN-235M-300 [62-HB]	AA ET 03.062 *Ventoux*, Evreux	
195	Airtech CN-235M-300 [62-HC]	AA ET 03.062 *Ventoux*, Evreux	
196	Airtech CN-235M-300 [62-HD]	AA ET 03.062 *Ventoux*, Evreux	
197	Airtech CN-235M-300 [62-HE]	AA ET 03.062 *Ventoux*, Evreux	
198	Airtech CN-235M-300 [62-HF]	AA ET 03.062 *Ventoux*, Evreux	
199	Airtech CN-235M-300 [62-HG]	AA ET 03.062 *Ventoux*, Evreux	
200	Airtech CN-235M-300 [62-HH]	AA ET 03.062 *Ventoux*, Evreux	
470	Boeing C-135FR Stratotanker [93-CA]	AA GRV 02.093 *Bretagne*, Istres	
471	Boeing C-135FR Stratotanker [93-CB]	AA GRV 02.093 *Bretagne*, Istres	
472	Boeing C-135FR Stratotanker [93-CC]	AA GRV 02.093 *Bretagne*, Istres	
474	Boeing C-135FR Stratotanker [93-CE]	AA GRV 02.093 *Bretagne*, Istres	
475	Boeing C-135FR Stratotanker [31-CF]	AA GRV 02.093 *Bretagne*, Istres	
497	Boeing C-135FR Stratotanker [93-CM] $	AA GRV 02.093 *Bretagne*, Istres	
525	Boeing C-135FR Stratotanker [93-CN]	AA GRV 02.093 *Bretagne*, Istres	
574	Boeing KC-135RG Stratotanker [31-CP] $	AA GRV 02.093 *Bretagne*, Istres	
735	Boeing C-135FR Stratotanker [93-CG]	AA GRV 02.093 *Bretagne*, Istres	
736	Boeing C-135FR Stratotanker [93-CH]	AA GRV 02.093 *Bretagne*, Istres	
737	Boeing C-135FR Stratotanker [31-CI]	AA GRV 02.093 *Bretagne*, Istres	
738	Boeing C-135FR Stratotanker [93-CJ]	AA GRV 02.093 *Bretagne*, Istres	
739	Boeing C-135FR Stratotanker [93-CK]	AA GRV 02.093 *Bretagne*, Istres	
740	Boeing C-135FR Stratotanker [93-CL]	AA GRV 02.093 *Bretagne*, Istres	
201	Boeing E-3F Sentry [36-CA]	AA EDCA 00.036, Avord	
202	Boeing E-3F Sentry [36-CB]	AA EDCA 00.036, Avord	
203	Boeing E-3F Sentry [36-CC]	AA EDCA 00.036, Avord	
204	Boeing E-3F Sentry [36-CD] $	AA EDCA 00.036, Avord	
377	CASA 212-300 Aviocar (F-ZAEA)	AA DGA EV, Cazaux & Istres	
378	CASA 212-300 Aviocar [MP]	AA DGA EV, Cazaux & Istres	
386	CASA 212-300 Aviocar [MQ]	AA DGA EV, Cazaux & Istres	
569	Cessna 310R [CS]	*Withdrawn from use, 2016*	
820	Cessna 310Q [CL]	AA DGA EV, Cazaux & Istres	
981	Cessna 310Q [BF]	AA DGA EV, Cazaux & Istres	
E4	D-BD Alpha Jet E	AA DGA EV, Cazaux & Istres	

Notes	Serial	Type (code/other identity)	Owner/operator, location or fate
	E7	D-BD Alpha Jet E [705-TU]	AA EAC 00.314, Tours
	E8	D-BD Alpha Jet E	AA DGA EV, Cazaux & Istres
	E11	D-BD Alpha Jet E [705-UB]	AA EAC 00.314, Tours
	E12	D-BD Alpha Jet E	AA DGA EV, Cazaux & Istres
	E13	D-BD Alpha Jet E [8-MM]	AA EE 03.008 Côte d'Or, Cazaux
	E17	D-BD Alpha Jet E [705-AA]	AA, stored Châteaudun
	E18	D-BD Alpha Jet E [118-AK]	AA CEAM/ECE 01.030 Côte d'Argent, Mont-de-Marsan
	E20	D-BD Alpha Jet E [705-MS]	AA EAC 00.314, Tours
	E22	D-BD Alpha Jet E [120-LS]	AA EE 03.008 Côte d'Or, Cazaux
	E25	D-BD Alpha Jet E [705-TJ]	AA EAC 00.314, Tours
	E26	D-BD Alpha Jet E [102-ND]	AA EE 03.008 Côte d'Or, Cazaux
	E28	D-BD Alpha Jet E [705-AB]	AA EAC 00.314, Tours
	E29	D-BD Alpha Jet E [102-NB]	AA EE 03.008 Côte d'Or, Cazaux
	E30	D-BD Alpha Jet E [705-MD]	AA EAC 00.314, Tours
	E31	D-BD Alpha Jet E [705-RK]	AA EAC 00.314, Tours
	E32	D-BD Alpha Jet E [102-FI]	AA EE 03.008 Côte d'Or, Cazaux
	E33	D-BD Alpha Jet E [120-FJ]	AA ETO 01.008 Saintonge, Cazaux
	E35	D-BD Alpha Jet E [705-MA]	AA EAC 00.314, Tours
	E37	D-BD Alpha Jet E [705-NL]	AA EAC 00.314, Tours
	E38	D-BD Alpha Jet E $	AA ETO 01.008 Saintonge, Cazaux
	E41	D-BD Alpha Jet E [8-RA]	AA EE 03.008 Côte d'Or, Cazaux
	E42	D-BD Alpha Jet E [705-TA]	AA EAC 00.314, Tours
	E44	D-BD Alpha Jet E [F-UHRE]	AA Patrouille de France, Salon de Provence
	E45	D-BD Alpha Jet E [F-TETF,1]	AA Patrouille de France, Salon de Provence
	E46	D-BD Alpha Jet E [F-UHRF,2]	AA Patrouille de France, Salon de Provence
	E48	D-BD Alpha Jet E [705-MH]	AA EAC 00.314, Tours
	E51	D-BD Alpha Jet E [705-AD]	AA EAC 00.314, Tours
	E53	D-BD Alpha Jet E [102-LI]	AA EE 03.008 Côte d'Or, Cazaux
	E58	D-BD Alpha Jet E [705-TK]	AA EAC 00.314, Tours
	E60	D-BD Alpha Jet E	AA EPNER, Istres
	E67	D-BD Alpha Jet E [705-TB]	AA EAC 00.314, Tours
	E68	D-BD Alpha Jet E [F-TEMO,8]	AA Patrouille de France, Salon de Provence
	E72	D-BD Alpha Jet E [705-LA]	AA EAC 00.314, Tours
	E73	D-BD Alpha Jet E [F-TENE]	AA Patrouille de France, Salon de Provence
	E74	D-BD Alpha Jet E	AA
	E76	D-BD Alpha Jet E [102-RJ]	AA EE 03.008 Côte d'Or, Cazaux
	E79	D-BD Alpha Jet E [F-TENA,5]	AA Patrouille de France, Salon de Provence
	E80	D-BD Alpha Jet E	AA DGA EV, Cazaux & Istres
	E81	D-BD Alpha Jet E [8-FO]	AA ETO 01.008 Saintonge, Cazaux
	E82	D-BD Alpha Jet E [120-LW]	AA ETO 01.008 Saintonge, Cazaux
	E83	D-BD Alpha Jet E [705-TZ]	AA EAC 00.314, Tours
	E85	D-BD Alpha Jet E [F-UGFF]	AA Patrouille de France, Salon de Provence
	E86	D-BD Alpha Jet E [102-FB]	AA EE 03.008 Côte d'Or, Cazaux
	E87	D-BD Alpha Jet E [705-LC]	AA EAC 00.314, Tours
	E88	D-BD Alpha Jet E [F-TELL]	AA Patrouille de France, Salon de Provence
	E89	D-BD Alpha Jet E [120-LX]	AA ETO 01.008 Saintonge, Cazaux
	E90	D-BD Alpha Jet E [120-TH]	AA ETO 01.008 Saintonge, Cazaux
	E93	D-BD Alpha Jet E [120-TX]	AA ETO 01.008 Saintonge, Cazaux
	E94	D-BD Alpha Jet E [F-TERH]	AA Patrouille de France, Salon de Provence
	E95	D-BD Alpha Jet E [F-TERQ]	AA Patrouille de France, Salon de Provence
	E97	D-BD Alpha Jet E [102-MB]	AA EE 03.008 Côte d'Or, Cazaux
	E98	D-BD Alpha Jet E [705-MF]	AA EAC 00.314, Tours
	E99	D-BD Alpha Jet E [120-AH]	AA ETO 01.008 Saintonge, Cazaux
	E100	D-BD Alpha Jet E $	AA EPNER, Istres
	E101	D-BD Alpha Jet E [120-TT]	AA ETO 01.008 Saintonge, Cazaux
	E102	D-BD Alpha Jet E [120-LM]	AA ETO 01.008 Saintonge, Cazaux
	E104	D-BD Alpha Jet E [705-TG]	AA EAC 00.314, Tours
	E105	D-BD Alpha Jet E [8-FM]	AA EE 03.008 Côte d'Or, Cazaux
	E106	D-BD Alpha Jet E	Preserved at Châteaudun
	E108	D-BD Alpha Jet E [8-AF]	AA ETO 01.008 Saintonge, Cazaux
	E109	D-BD Alpha Jet E [120-AG]	AA ETO 01.008 Saintonge, Cazaux

Serial	Type (code/other identity)	Owner/operator, location or fate	Notes
E110	D-BD Alpha Jet E [705-AH]	AA EAC 00.314, Tours	
E112	D-BD Alpha Jet E [30-AO]	AA CEAM/ECE 01.030 Côte d'Argent, Mont-de-Marsan	
E113	D-BD Alpha Jet E [F-TETD,4]	AA Patrouille de France, Salon de Provence	
E114	D-BD Alpha Jet E [F-TERR,0]	AA Patrouille de France, Salon de Provence	
E115	D-BD Alpha Jet E [705-MR]	AA CEAM/ECE 01.030 Côte d'Argent, Mont-de-Marsan	
E116	D-BD Alpha Jet E [8-FN]	AA ETO 01.008 Saintonge, Cazaux	
E117	D-BD Alpha Jet E [102-AI]	AA EE 03.008 Côte d'Or, Cazaux	
E118	D-BD Alpha Jet E [8-LN]	AA ETO 01.008 Saintonge, Cazaux	
E119	D-BD Alpha Jet E [F-UGFE,3]	AA Patrouille de France, Salon de Provence	
E120	D-BD Alpha Jet E [705-LG]	AA EAC 00.314, Tours	
E121	D-BD Alpha Jet E [705-LE]	Withdrawn from use, June 2016	
E123	D-BD Alpha Jet E [705-RM]	AA EAC 00.314, Tours	
E124	D-BD Alpha Jet E [120-RN]	AA ETO 01.008 Saintonge, Cazaux	
E125	D-BD Alpha Jet E [705-LK]	AA EAC 00.314, Tours	
E127	D-BD Alpha Jet E [F-UGFK,6]	AA Patrouille de France, Salon de Provence	
E128	D-BD Alpha Jet E [705-TM]	AA EAC 00.314, Tours	
E129	D-BD Alpha Jet E [705-LP]	AA EAC 00.314, Tours	
E130	D-BD Alpha Jet E [F-TERP]	AA Patrouille de France, Salon de Provence	
E131	D-BD Alpha Jet E [120-RO]	AA ETO 01.008 Saintonge, Cazaux	
E134	D-BD Alpha Jet E	AA	
E135	D-BD Alpha Jet E [102-RX]	AA EE 03.008 Côte d'Or, Cazaux	
E136	D-BD Alpha Jet E [8-RP]	AA EE 03.008 Côte d'Or, Cazaux	
E137	D-BD Alpha Jet E [705-LJ]	AA EAC 00.314, Tours	
E138	D-BD Alpha Jet E [8-RQ]	AA EE 03.008 Côte d'Or, Cazaux	
E139	D-BD Alpha Jet E [F-UGFC]	AA Patrouille de France, Salon de Provence	
E140	D-BD Alpha Jet E [102-FA]	AA EE 03.008 Côte d'Or, Cazaux	
E141	D-BD Alpha Jet E [705-NF]	AA EAC 00.314, Tours	
E142	D-BD Alpha Jet E [120-LO]	AA ETO 01.008 Saintonge, Cazaux	
E143	D-BD Alpha Jet E	AA	
E144	D-BD Alpha Jet E [8-AK]	AA ETO 01.008 Saintonge, Cazaux	
E145	D-BD Alpha Jet E	AA	
E146	D-BD Alpha Jet E [F-UHRR,9]	AA Patrouille de France, Salon de Provence	
E147	D-BD Alpha Jet E [118-LT]	AA CEAM/ECE 01.030 Côte d'Argent, Mont-de-Marsan	
E148	D-BD Alpha Jet E [705-LU]	AA EAC 00.314, Tours	
E149	D-BD Alpha Jet E [705-RS]	AA EAC 00.314, Tours	
E151	D-BD Alpha Jet E [8-FD]	AA EE 03.008 Côte d'Or, Cazaux	
E152	D-BD Alpha Jet E [F-UHRT,7]	AA Patrouille de France, Salon de Provence	
E153	D-BD Alpha Jet E [705-RU]	AA EAC 00.314, Tours	
E154	D-BD Alpha Jet E [120-AL]	AA ETO 01.008 Saintonge, Cazaux	
E156	D-BD Alpha Jet E [30-TI]	AA CEAM/ECE 01.030 Côte d'Argent, Mont-de-Marsan	
E157	D-BD Alpha Jet E [120-UC]	AA ETO 02.008 Nice, Cazaux	
E158	D-BD Alpha Jet E [F-TERF]	AA Patrouille de France, Salon de Provence	
E160	D-BD Alpha Jet E [120-UH]	AA ETO 01.008 Saintonge, Cazaux	
E162	D-BD Alpha Jet E [F-TERJ]	AA Patrouille de France, Salon de Provence	
E163	D-BD Alpha Jet E [705-RB]	AA EAC 00.314, Tours	
E164	D-BD Alpha Jet E [120-RV]	AA ETO 01.008 Saintonge, Cazaux	
E165	D-BD Alpha Jet E [102-RE]	AA EE 03.008 Côte d'Or, Cazaux	
E166	D-BD Alpha Jet E [F-UHRW]	AA Patrouille de France, Salon de Provence	
E167	D-BD Alpha Jet E [705-MN]	AA EAC 00.314, Tours	
E168	D-BD Alpha Jet E [102-FP]	AA EE 03.008 Côte d'Or, Cazaux	
E169	D-BD Alpha Jet E [30-RX]	AA CEAM/ECE 01.030 Côte d'Argent, Mont-de-Marsan	
E170	D-BD Alpha Jet E [705-RY]	AA EAC 00.314, Tours	
E171	D-BD Alpha Jet E [705-RZ]	AA EAC 00.314, Tours	
E173	D-BD Alpha Jet E [F-UHMA] $	AA EAC 00.314, Tours	
E176	D-BD Alpha Jet E [120-MB]	AA ETO 01.008 Saintonge, Cazaux	
68	Dassault Falcon 7X (F-RAFA)	AA ET 00.060, Villacoublay	

Notes	Serial	Type (code/other identity)	Owner/operator, location or fate
	86	Dassault Falcon 7X (F-RAFB)	AA ET 00.060, Villacoublay
	79	Dassault Falcon 20C [CT]	AA DGA EV, Cazaux & Istres
	104	Dassault Falcon 20C [CW]	AA DGA EV, Cazaux & Istres
	138	Dassault Falcon 20C [CR]	AA, stored Cazaux
	252	Dassault Falcon 20E [CA]	AA DGA EV, Cazaux & Istres
	288	Dassault Falcon 20E [CV]	AA DGA EV, Cazaux & Istres
	342	Dassault Falcon 20F [CU]	AA DGA EV, Cazaux & Istres
	375	Dassault Falcon 20F [CZ]	AA DGA EV, Cazaux & Istres
	02	Dassault Falcon 900 (F-RAFP)	AA ET 00.060, Villacoublay
	004	Dassault Falcon 900 (F-RAFQ)	AA ET 00.060, Villacoublay
	...	Dassault Falcon 900	(on order)
	...	Dassault Falcon 900	(on order)
	...	Dassault Falcon 900	(on order)
	231	Dassault Falcon 2000LX (F-RAFC)	AA ET 00.060, Villacoublay
	237	Dassault Falcon 2000LX (F-RAFD)	AA ET 00.060, Villacoublay
	501	Dassault Mirage 2000B (BX1)	AA DGA EV, Cazaux & Istres
	523	Dassault Mirage 2000B [115-KJ]	AA EC 02.005 *Ile de France*, Orange
	524	Dassault Mirage 2000B [115-OA]	AA EC 02.005 *Ile de France*, Orange
	525	Dassault Mirage 2000B [115-AM]	AA EC 02.005 *Ile de France*, Orange
	527	Dassault Mirage 2000B [115-OR]	AA EC 02.005 *Ile de France*, Orange
	528	Dassault Mirage 2000B [115-KS]	AA EC 02.005 *Ile de France*, Orange
	529	Dassault Mirage 2000B [115-OC]	AA EC 02.005 *Ile de France*, Orange
	530	Dassault Mirage 2000B [115-OL]	AA EC 02.005 *Ile de France*, Orange
	01	Dassault Mirage 2000-5F	AA DGA EV, Istres
	2	Dassault Mirage 2000C	AA DGA EV, Istres
	38	Dassault Mirage 2000-5F [116-EI]	AA GC 01.002 *Cigognes*, Luxeuil
	40	Dassault Mirage 2000-5F [2-EX]	AA GC 01.002 *Cigognes*, Luxeuil
	41	Dassault Mirage 2000-5F [2-FZ]	AA GC 01.002 *Cigognes*, Luxeuil
	42	Dassault Mirage 2000-5F [2-EY]	AA GC 01.002 *Cigognes*, Luxeuil
	43	Dassault Mirage 2000-5F [2-EJ]	AA GC 01.002 *Cigognes*, Luxeuil
	44	Dassault Mirage 2000-5F [2-EQ]	AA GC 01.002 *Cigognes*, Luxeuil
	45	Dassault Mirage 2000-5F [2-EF]	AA GC 01.002 *Cigognes*, Luxeuil
	46	Dassault Mirage 2000-5F [2-EN]	AA GC 01.002 *Cigognes*, Luxeuil
	47	Dassault Mirage 2000-5F [2-EP]	AA GC 01.002 *Cigognes*, Luxeuil
	48	Dassault Mirage 2000-5F [2-EW]	AA GC 01.002 *Cigognes*, Luxeuil
	49	Dassault Mirage 2000-5F [116-EA]	AA GC 01.002 *Cigognes*, Luxeuil
	51	Dassault Mirage 2000-5F [30-AS]	AA CEAM/ECE 01.030 *Côte d'Argent*, Mont-de-Marsan
	52	Dassault Mirage 2000-5F [2-EH]	AA GC 01.002 *Cigognes*, Luxeuil
	54	Dassault Mirage 2000-5F [2-EZ]	AA GC 01.002 *Cigognes*, Luxeuil
	55	Dassault Mirage 2000-5F [2-EU]	AA GC 01.002 *Cigognes*, Luxeuil
	56	Dassault Mirage 2000-5F [2-EG]	AA GC 01.002 *Cigognes*, Luxeuil
	57	Dassault Mirage 2000-5F [2-ET]	AA GC 01.002 *Cigognes*, Luxeuil
	58	Dassault Mirage 2000-5F [188-EL]	AA EC 03.011 *Corse*, Djibouti
	59	Dassault Mirage 2000-5F [2-EV]	AA GC 01.002 *Cigognes*, Luxeuil
	61	Dassault Mirage 2000-5F [116-ME]	AA GC 01.002 *Cigognes*, Luxeuil
	62	Dassault Mirage 2000-5F [2-ED]	AA GC 01.002 *Cigognes*, Luxeuil
	63	Dassault Mirage 2000-5F [2-EM]	AA GC 01.002 *Cigognes*, Luxeuil
	64	Dassault Mirage 2000C	AA DGA EV, Istres
	65	Dassault Mirage 2000-5F [2-MG]	AA GC 01.002 *Cigognes*, Luxeuil
	66	Dassault Mirage 2000-5F [2-EO]	AA GC 01.002 *Cigognes*, Luxeuil
	67	Dassault Mirage 2000-5F [2-MH]	AA GC 01.002 *Cigognes*, Luxeuil
	71	Dassault Mirage 2000-5F [116-EE]	AA GC 01.002 *Cigognes*, Luxeuil
	74	Dassault Mirage 2000-5F [116-MK]	AA GC 01.002 *Cigognes*, Luxeuil
	77	Dassault Mirage 2000-5F [118-AX]	AA CEAM/ECE 01.030 *Côte d'Argent*, Mont-de-Marsan
	78	Dassault Mirage 2000-5F [116-EC]	AA GC 01.002 *Cigognes*, Luxeuil
	82	Dassault Mirage 2000C [115-YL]	AA EC 02.005 *Ile de France*, Orange
	83	Dassault Mirage 2000C [115-YC]	AA EC 02.005 *Ile de France*, Orange
	85	Dassault Mirage 2000C [115-LK]	AA EC 02.005 *Ile de France*, Orange
	88	Dassault Mirage 2000C [115-KV]	AA EC 02.005 *Ile de France*, Orange
	93	Dassault Mirage 2000C [115-YA]	AA EC 02.005 *Ile de France*, Orange

Serial	Type (code/other identity)	Owner/operator, location or fate	Notes
94	Dassault Mirage 2000C [115-KB]	AA EC 02.005 *Ile de France*, Orange	
96	Dassault Mirage 2000C [115-KI]	AA EC 02.005 *Ile de France*, Orange	
99	Dassault Mirage 2000C [115-YB]	AA EC 02.005 *Ile de France*, Orange	
100	Dassault Mirage 2000C [115-YF]	AA EC 02.005 *Ile de France*, Orange	
101	Dassault Mirage 2000C [115-KE] $	AA EC 02.005 *Ile de France*, Orange	
102	Dassault Mirage 2000C [115-KR]	AA EC 02.005 *Ile de France*, Orange	
104	Dassault Mirage 2000C [115-KG]	AA EC 02.005 *Ile de France*, Orange	
105	Dassault Mirage 2000C [115-LJ]	AA EC 02.005 *Ile de France*, Orange	
106	Dassault Mirage 2000C [115-KL]	AA EC 02.005 *Ile de France*, Orange	
107	Dassault Mirage 2000C [115-YD]	AA EC 02.005 *Ile de France*, Orange	
108	Dassault Mirage 2000C [115-LC]	AA EC 02.005 *Ile de France*, Orange	
109	Dassault Mirage 2000C [115-YH]	AA EC 02.005 *Ile de France*, Orange	
111	Dassault Mirage 2000C [115-KF]	AA EC 02.005 *Ile de France*, Orange	
113	Dassault Mirage 2000C [115-YO]	AA EC 02.005 *Ile de France*, Orange	
115	Dassault Mirage 2000C [115-YM]	AA EC 02.005 *Ile de France*, Orange	
117	Dassault Mirage 2000C [115-LD]	AA EC 02.005 *Ile de France*, Orange	
118	Dassault Mirage 2000C [115-YG]	AA EC 02.005 *Ile de France*, Orange	
120	Dassault Mirage 2000C [115-KC]	AA EC 02.005 *Ile de France*, Orange	
121	Dassault Mirage 2000C [115-KN]	AA EC 02.005 *Ile de France*, Orange	
122	Dassault Mirage 2000C [115-YE]	AA EC 02.005 *Ile de France*, Orange	
123	Dassault Mirage 2000C [115-KD]	AA EC 02.005 *Ile de France*, Orange	
124	Dassault Mirage 2000C [115-YT]	AA EC 02.005 *Ile de France*, Orange	
601	Dassault Mirage 2000D [133-JG]	AA EC 01.003 *Navarre*, Nancy	
602	Dassault Mirage 2000D [3-XJ]	AA EC 03.003 *Ardennes*, Nancy	
603	Dassault Mirage 2000D [3-XL]	AA EC 03.003 *Ardennes*, Nancy	
604	Dassault Mirage 2000D [30-IP]	AA CEAM/ECE 01.030 *Côte d'Argent*, Mont-de-Marsan	
605	Dassault Mirage 2000D [133-LF]	AA EC 02.003 *Champagne*, Nancy	
606	Dassault Mirage 2000D [133-JC]	AA EC 02.003 *Champagne*, Nancy	
607	Dassault Mirage 2000D	AA DGA EV, Istres	
609	Dassault Mirage 2000D [118-IF]	AA CEAM/ECE 01.030 *Côte d'Argent*, Mont-de-Marsan	
610	Dassault Mirage 2000D [133-XX]	AA EC 03.003 *Ardennes*, Nancy	
611	Dassault Mirage 2000D [3-JP]	AA EC 02.003 *Champagne*, Nancy	
613	Dassault Mirage 2000D [133-MO]	AA EC 03.003 *Ardennes*, Nancy	
614	Dassault Mirage 2000D [133-JU]	AA EC 02.003 *Champagne*, Nancy	
615	Dassault Mirage 2000D [3-JY]	AA EC 02.003 *Champagne*, Nancy	
616	Dassault Mirage 2000D [118-XH]	AA CEAM/ECE 01.030 *Côte d'Argent*, Mont-de-Marsan	
617	Dassault Mirage 2000D [3-IS]	AA EC 01.003 *Navarre*, Nancy	
618	Dassault Mirage 2000D [133-XC]	AA EC 03.003 *Ardennes*, Nancy	
620	Dassault Mirage 2000D [3-IU]	AA EC 01.003 *Navarre*, Nancy	
622	Dassault Mirage 2000D [3-IL]	AA EC 01.003 *Navarre*, Nancy	
623	Dassault Mirage 2000D [133-MP]	AA EC 02.003 *Champagne*, Nancy	
624	Dassault Mirage 2000D [3-IT] $	AA EC 02.003 *Ardennes*, Nancy	
625	Dassault Mirage 2000D [3-XG]	AA EC 03.003 *Ardennes*, Nancy	
626	Dassault Mirage 2000D [133-IC]	AA EC 01.003 *Navarre*, Nancy	
627	Dassault Mirage 2000D [30-JO]	AA CEAM/ECE 01.030 *Côte d'Argent*, Mont-de-Marsan	
628	Dassault Mirage 2000D [133-JL]	AA EC 02.003 *Champagne*, Nancy	
629	Dassault Mirage 2000D [3-XO]	AA EC 03.003 *Ardennes*, Nancy	
630	Dassault Mirage 2000D [3-XD] $	AA EC 03.003 *Ardennes*, Nancy	
631	Dassault Mirage 2000D [133-IH]	AA EC 01.003 *Navarre*, Nancy	
632	Dassault Mirage 2000D [133-XE]	AA EC 01.003 *Navarre*, Nancy	
634	Dassault Mirage 2000D [133-JE]	AA EC 01.003 *Navarre*, Nancy	
635	Dassault Mirage 2000D [133-AS]	AA EC 01.003 *Navarre*, Nancy	
636	Dassault Mirage 2000D [133-JV]	AA EC 02.003 *Champagne*, Nancy	
637	Dassault Mirage 2000D [3-XQ]	AA EC 03.003 *Ardennes*, Nancy	
638	Dassault Mirage 2000D [3-IJ]	AA EC 03.003 *Ardennes*, Nancy	
639	Dassault Mirage 2000D [3-JJ]	AA EC 02.003 *Champagne*, Nancy	
640	Dassault Mirage 2000D [3-IN]	AA EC 01.003 *Navarre*, Nancy	
641	Dassault Mirage 2000D [133-JW]	AA EC 02.003 *Champagne*, Nancy	

Notes	Serial	Type (code/other identity)	Owner/operator, location or fate
	642	Dassault Mirage 2000D [30-IE]	AA CEAM/ECE 01.030 *Côte d'Argent*, Mont-de-Marsan
	643	Dassault Mirage 2000D [3-JD]	AA EC 02.003 *Champagne*, Nancy
	644	Dassault Mirage 2000D	AA DGA EV, Istres
	645	Dassault Mirage 2000D [133-XP]	AA EC 03.003 *Ardennes*, Nancy
	646	Dassault Mirage 2000D [3-MQ]	AA EC 01.003 *Navarre*, Nancy
	647	Dassault Mirage 2000D [133-IO]	AA EC 01.003 *Navarre*, Nancy
	648	Dassault Mirage 2000D [3-XT] $	AA EC 03.003 *Ardennes*, Nancy
	649	Dassault Mirage 2000D [3-XY]	AA EC 03.003 *Ardennes*, Nancy
	650	Dassault Mirage 2000D [3-IA]	AA EC 01.003 *Navarre*, Nancy
	652	Dassault Mirage 2000D [3-XN] $	AA EC 03.003 *Ardennes*, Nancy
	653	Dassault Mirage 2000D [3-AU]	AA ETD 04.003 *Argonne*, Nancy
	654	Dassault Mirage 2000D [3-ID]	AA EC 01.003 *Navarre*, Nancy
	655	Dassault Mirage 2000D [133-LH]	AA EC 01.003 *Navarre*, Nancy
	657	Dassault Mirage 2000D [3-JM]	AA EC 03.003 *Ardennes*, Nancy
	658	Dassault Mirage 2000D [3-JN]	AA EC 02.003 *Champagne*, Nancy
	659	Dassault Mirage 2000D [133-XR]	AA EC 03.003 *Ardennes*, Nancy
	660	Dassault Mirage 2000D [3-JF]	AA ETD 04.003 *Argonne*, Nancy
	661	Dassault Mirage 2000D [133-XI]	AA EC 03.003 *Ardennes*, Nancy
	662	Dassault Mirage 2000D [3-XA]	AA EC 03.003 *Ardennes*, Nancy
	664	Dassault Mirage 2000D [133-IW]	AA EC 01.003 *Navarre*, Nancy
	666	Dassault Mirage 2000D [133-IQ]	AA EC 01.003 *Navarre*, Nancy
	667	Dassault Mirage 2000D [133-JZ]	AA EC 02.003 *Champagne*, Nancy
	668	Dassault Mirage 2000D [133-IG]	AA EC 03.003 *Ardennes*, Nancy
	669	Dassault Mirage 2000D [133-AL]	AA ETD 04.003 *Argonne*, Nancy
	670	Dassault Mirage 2000D [133-XF]	AA EC 03.003 *Ardennes*, Nancy
	671	Dassault Mirage 2000D [3-XK]	AA EC 03.003 *Ardennes*, Nancy
	672	Dassault Mirage 2000D [3-XV]	AA EC 03.003 *Ardennes*, Nancy
	673	Dassault Mirage 2000D	AA DGA EV, Istres
	674	Dassault Mirage 2000D [30-IR]	AA CEAM/ECE 01.030 *Côte d'Argent*, Mont-de-Marsan
	675	Dassault Mirage 2000D [3-JI] $	AA EC 01.003 *Navarre*, Nancy
	676	Dassault Mirage 2000D $	AA DGA EV, Istres
	677	Dassault Mirage 2000D [133-JT]	AA EC 02.003 *Champagne*, Nancy
	678	Dassault Mirage 2000D [133-JB]	AA EC 02.003 *Champagne*, Nancy
	679	Dassault Mirage 2000D [3-JX]	AA EC 01.003 *Navarre*, Nancy
	680	Dassault Mirage 2000D [3-XM]	AA EC 03.003 *Ardennes*, Nancy
	681	Dassault Mirage 2000D [133-AG]	AA EC 01.003 *Navarre*, Nancy
	682	Dassault Mirage 2000D [133-JR]	AA EC 02.003 *Champagne*, Nancy
	683	Dassault Mirage 2000D [3-IV]	AA EC 01.003 *Navarre*, Nancy
	684	Dassault Mirage 2000D	AA
	685	Dassault Mirage 2000D [133-XZ]	AA EC 01.003 *Navarre*, Nancy
	686	Dassault Mirage 2000D [133-JH]	AA EC 02.003 *Champagne*, Nancy
	D02	Dassault Mirage 2000D	AA DGA EV, Istres
	301	Dassault Mirage 2000N	AA DGA EV, Istres
	306	Dassault Mirage 2000N [116-BL]	AA EC 02.004 *La Fayette*, Istres
	316	Dassault Mirage 2000N [116-AU] $	AA EC 02.004 *La Fayette*, Istres
	319	Dassault Mirage 2000N	AA
	333	Dassault Mirage 2000N	AA
	334	Dassault Mirage 2000N	AA DGA EV, Istres
	335	Dassault Mirage 2000N [125-CI]	AA EC 02.004 *La Fayette*, Istres
	338	Dassault Mirage 2000N [125-CG]	AA EC 02.004 *La Fayette*, Istres
	340	Dassault Mirage 2000N [125-AA]	AA EC 02.004 *La Fayette*, Istres
	342	Dassault Mirage 2000N [125-BA]	AA EC 02.004 *La Fayette*, Istres
	345	Dassault Mirage 2000N [125-BU]	AA EC 02.004 *La Fayette*, Istres
	348	Dassault Mirage 2000N [125-AL]	AA EC 02.004 *La Fayette*, Istres
	350	Dassault Mirage 2000N [125-AJ]	AA EC 02.004 *La Fayette*, Istres
	351	Dassault Mirage 2000N [125-AQ]	AA EC 02.004 *La Fayette*, Istres
	353	Dassault Mirage 2000N [125-AM] $	*Preserved at St Dizier, 2016*
	354	Dassault Mirage 2000N [125-BJ]	AA EC 02.004 *La Fayette*, Istres
	355	Dassault Mirage 2000N [125-AE]	AA EC 02.004 *La Fayette*, Istres
	356	Dassault Mirage 2000N [125-BX]	AA EC 02.004 *La Fayette*, Istres

Serial	Type (code/other identity)	Owner/operator, location or fate	Notes
357	Dassault Mirage 2000N [125-CO]	AA EC 02.004 *La Fayette*, Istres	
358	Dassault Mirage 2000N [125-BQ]	AA EC 02.004 *La Fayette*, Istres	
359	Dassault Mirage 2000N [125-AK] $	AA EC 02.004 *La Fayette*, Istres	
360	Dassault Mirage 2000N [125-CB]	AA EC 02.004 *La Fayette*, Istres	
361	Dassault Mirage 2000N [125-CK]	AA EC 02.004 *La Fayette*, Istres	
362	Dassault Mirage 2000N [125-CU]	AA EC 02.004 *La Fayette*, Istres	
364	Dassault Mirage 2000N [125-BB]	AA EC 02.004 *La Fayette*, Istres	
365	Dassault Mirage 2000N [125-AI]	AA EC 02.004 *La Fayette*, Istres	
366	Dassault Mirage 2000N [125-BC]	AA EC 02.004 *La Fayette*, Istres	
367	Dassault Mirage 2000N [125-AW]	AA EC 02.004 *La Fayette*, Istres	
368	Dassault Mirage 2000N [125-AR]	AA EC 02.004 *La Fayette*, Istres	
369	Dassault Mirage 2000N [125-AG]	AA EC 02.004 *La Fayette*, Istres	
370	Dassault Mirage 2000N [125-CQ]	AA EC 02.004 *La Fayette*, Istres	
371	Dassault Mirage 2000N [125-BD]	AA EC 02.004 *La Fayette*, Istres	
372	Dassault Mirage 2000N [125-CM]	AA EC 02.004 *La Fayette*, Istres	
373	Dassault Mirage 2000N [125-CF]	AA EC 02.004 *La Fayette*, Istres	
374	Dassault Mirage 2000N [125-BS]	AA EC 02.004 *La Fayette*, Istres	
375	Dassault Mirage 2000N [125-CL]	AA EC 02.004 *La Fayette*, Istres	
301	Dassault Rafale B	AA DGA EV, Istres	
302	Dassault Rafale B	AA DGA EV, Istres	
303	Dassault Rafale B [4-EA]	AA ETR 03.004 *Aquitaine*, St Dizier	
304	Dassault Rafale B [4-EB]	AA ETR 03.004 *Aquitaine*, St Dizier	
305	Dassault Rafale B [30-EC]	AA CEAM/ECE 01.030 *Côte d'Argent*, Mont-de-Marsan	
306	Dassault Rafale B [30-IB]	AA CEAM/ECE 01.030 *Côte d'Argent*, Mont-de-Marsan	
307	Dassault Rafale B [30-IA]	AA CEAM/ECE 01.030 *Côte d'Argent*, Mont-de-Marsan	
308	Dassault Rafale B [30-HA]	AA CEAM/ECE 01.030 *Côte d'Argent*, Mont-de-Marsan	
309	Dassault Rafale B [113-HB]	AA EC 03.030 *Lorraine*, St Dizier	
310	Dassault Rafale B [4-HC]	AA ETR 03.004 *Aquitaine*, St Dizier	
311	Dassault Rafale B [113-HD]	AA EC 01.004 *Gascogne*, St Dizier	
312	Dassault Rafale B [4-HF]	AA EC 01.004 *Gascogne*, St Dizier	
313	Dassault Rafale B [4-HI]	AA ETR 03.004 *Aquitaine*, St Dizier	
314	Dassault Rafale B [4-HP]	AA EC 01.004 *Gascogne*, St Dizier	
315	Dassault Rafale B [4-HK]	AA EC 01.004 *Gascogne*, St Dizier	
317	Dassault Rafale B [4-HO]	AA ETR 03.004 *Aquitaine*, St Dizier	
318	Dassault Rafale B [30-HM]	AA EC 02.030 *Normandie-Niémen*, Mont-de-Marsan	
319	Dassault Rafale B [4-HN]	AA EC 01.004 *Gascogne*, St Dizier	
320	Dassault Rafale B [4-HV]	AA EC 01.004 *Gascogne*, St Dizier	
321	Dassault Rafale B [4-HQ]	AA EC 03.030 *Lorraine*, St Dizier	
322	Dassault Rafale B [4-HU]	AA EC 01.004 *Gascogne*, St Dizier	
323	Dassault Rafale B [30-HT]	AA CEAM/ECE 01.030 *Côte d'Argent*, Mont-de-Marsan	
324	Dassault Rafale B [30-HW]	AA CEAM/ECE 01.030 *Côte d'Argent*, Mont-de-Marsan	
325	Dassault Rafale B [7-HX]	AA EC 03.030 *Lorraine*, St Dizier	
326	Dassault Rafale B [113-HY]	AA EC 01.004 *Gascogne*, St Dizier	
327	Dassault Rafale B [4-HZ]	AA ETR 03.004 *Aquitaine*, St Dizier	
328	Dassault Rafale B [4-IC]	AA EC 01.004 *Gascogne*, St Dizier	
329	Dassault Rafale B [4-ID]	AA ETR 03.004 *Aquitaine*, St Dizier	
330	Dassault Rafale B [4-IE]	AA EC 01.004 *Gascogne*, St Dizier	
331	Dassault Rafale B [30-IF]	AA EC 02.030 *Normandie-Niémen*, Mont-de-Marsan	
332	Dassault Rafale B [4-IG]	AA EC 01.004 *Gascogne*, St Dizier	
333	Dassault Rafale B [30-IH]	AA CEAM/ECE 01.030 *Côte d'Argent*, Mont-de-Marsan	
334	Dassault Rafale B [30-II]	AA CEAM/ECE 01.030 *Côte d'Argent*, Mont-de-Marsan	
335	Dassault Rafale B [4-IJ]	AA EC 01.004 *Gascogne*, St Dizier	

Notes	Serial	Type (code/other identity)	Owner/operator, location or fate
	336	Dassault Rafale B [4-IK] $	AA EC 01.004 *Gascogne*, St Dizier
	337	Dassault Rafale B [4-IL]	AA EC 01.004 *Gascogne*, St Dizier
	338	Dassault Rafale B [113-IO]	AA EC 01.004 *Gascogne*, St Dizier
	339	Dassault Rafale B [4-FF]	AA ETR 03.004 *Aquitaine*, St Dizier
	340	Dassault Rafale B [4-FG]	AA EC 01.004 *Gascogne*, St Dizier
	341	Dassault Rafale B [4-FH]	AA EC 01.004 *Gascogne*, St Dizier
	342	Dassault Rafale B [4-FI]	AA EC 01.004 *Gascogne*, St Dizier
	343	Dassault Rafale B [4-FJ]	AA EC 01.004 *Gascogne*, St Dizier
	344	Dassault Rafale B [4-FK]	AA EC 01.004 *Gascogne*, St Dizier
	345	Dassault Rafale B [4-FL]	AA EC 01.004 *Gascogne*, St Dizier
	346	Dassault Rafale B [4-FM]	AA ETR 03.004 *Aquitaine*, St Dizier
	347	Dassault Rafale B [4-FN]	AA ETR 03.004 *Aquitaine*, St Dizier
	348	Dassault Rafale B [4-FO]	AA ETR 03.004 *Aquitaine*, St Dizier
	349	Dassault Rafale B [4-FP]	AA ETR 03.004 *Aquitaine*, St Dizier
	350	Dassault Rafale B [113-FQ]	AA ETR 03.004 *Aquitaine*, St Dizier
	351	Dassault Rafale B [4-FR]	AA EC 02.004 *La Fayette*, St Dizier
	352	Dassault Rafale B [4-FS]	AA ETR 03.004 *Aquitaine*, St Dizier
	353	Dassault Rafale B [4-FT]	AA ETR 03.004 *Aquitaine*, St Dizier
	354	Dassault Rafale B [4-FU]	AA EC 02.004 *La Fayette*, St Dizier)
	355	Dassault Rafale B	AA (on order)
	356	Dassault Rafale B	AA (on order)
	357	Dassault Rafale B	AA (on order)
	358	Dassault Rafale B	AA (on order)
	101	Dassault Rafale C	AA DGA EV, Istres
	102	Dassault Rafale C [30-EF]	AA CEAM/ECE 01.030 *Côte d'Argent*, Mont-de-Marsan
	103	Dassault Rafale C [104-HR]	AA EC 01.007 *Provence*, Al Dhafra, UAE
	104	Dassault Rafale C [113-HH] $	AA EC 03.030 *Lorraine*, St Dizier
	105	Dassault Rafale C [30-HE]	AA EC 03.030 *Lorraine*, St Dizier
	106	Dassault Rafale C [113-HG]	AA EC 03.030 *Lorraine*, St Dizier
	107	Dassault Rafale C [113-HJ] $	AA EC 03.030 *Lorraine*, St Dizier
	108	Dassault Rafale C [113-HS]	AA EC 03.030 *Lorraine*, St Dizier
	109	Dassault Rafale C [30-IM]	AA EC 02.030 *Normandie-Niémen*, Mont-de-Marsan
	110	Dassault Rafale C [30-IN]	AA EC 03.030 *Lorraine*, St Dizier
	111	Dassault Rafale C [118-IP]	AA EC 02.030 *Normandie-Niémen*, Mont-de-Marsan
	112	Dassault Rafale C [30-IQ]	AA EC 02.030 *Normandie-Niémen*, Mont-de-Marsan
	113	Dassault Rafale C [30-IR]	AA EC 02.030 *Normandie-Niémen*, Mont-de-Marsan
	114	Dassault Rafale C [30-IS]	AA EC 02.030 *Normandie-Niémen*, Mont-de-Marsan
	115	Dassault Rafale C [30-IT]	AA EC 03.030 *Lorraine*, St Dizier
	116	Dassault Rafale C [30-IU]	AA EC 02.030 *Normandie-Niémen*, Mont-de-Marsan
	117	Dassault Rafale C [113-IV]	AA EC 03.030 *Lorraine*, St Dizier
	118	Dassault Rafale C [30-IW]	AA EC 02.030 *Normandie-Niémen*, Mont-de-Marsan
	119	Dassault Rafale C [30-IX]	AA EC 03.030 *Lorraine*, St Dizier
	120	Dassault Rafale C [4-IY]	AA EC 03.030 *Lorraine*, St Dizier
	121	Dassault Rafale C [113-IZ]	AA EC 01.004 *Gascogne*, St Dizier
	122	Dassault Rafale C [30-GA]	AA EC 02.030 *Normandie-Niémen*, Mont-de-Marsan
	123	Dassault Rafale C [30-GB]	AA EC 02.030 *Normandie-Niémen*, Mont-de-Marsan
	124	Dassault Rafale C [4-GC]	AA EC 03.030 *Lorraine*, St Dizier
	125	Dassault Rafale C [30-GD]	AA EC 02.030 *Normandie-Niémen*, Mont-de-Marsan
	126	Dassault Rafale C [30-GE]	AA EC 02.030 *Normandie-Niémen*, Mont-de-Marsan

Serial	Type (code/other identity)	Owner/operator, location or fate	Notes
127	Dassault Rafale C [30-GF]	AA EC 02.030 *Normandie-Niémen*, Mont-de-Marsan	
128	Dassault Rafale C [104-GG]	AA EC 01.007 *Provence*, Al Dhafra, UAE	
129	Dassault Rafale C [118-GH]	AA EC 02.030 *Normandie-Niémen*, Mont-de-Marsan	
130	Dassault Rafale C [104-GI]	AA EC 01.007 *Provence*, Al Dhafra, UAE	
131	Dassault Rafale C [30-GJ]	AA EC 02.030 *Normandie-Niémen*, Mont-de-Marsan	
132	Dassault Rafale C [30-GK]	AA EC 02.030 *Normandie-Niémen*, Mont-de-Marsa	
133	Dassault Rafale C [4-GL]	AN ETR 03.004 *Aquitaine*, St Dizier	
134	Dassault Rafale C [104-GM]	AA EC 01.007 *Provence*, Al Dhafra, UAE	
135	Dassault Rafale C [113-GN]	AA ETR 03.004 *Aquitaine*, St Dizier	
136	Dassault Rafale C [104-GO]	AA EC 01.007 *Provence*, Al Dhafra, UAE	
137	Dassault Rafale C [104-GP]	AA EC 01.007 *Provence*, Al Dhafra, UAE	
138	Dassault Rafale C [30-GQ]	AA EC 02.030 *Normandie-Niémen*, Mont-de-Marsan	
139	Dassault Rafale C [30-GR]	AA EC 02.030 *Normandie-Niémen*, Mont-de-Marsan	
140	Dassault Rafale C [30-GS]	AA EC 02.030 *Normandie-Niémen*, Mont-de-Marsan	
141	Dassault Rafale C [30-GT]	AA EC 02.030 *Normandie-Niémen*, Mont-de-Marsan	
142	Dassault Rafale C [4-GU]	AA ETR 03.004 *Aquitaine*, St Dizier	
143	Dassault Rafale C [30-GV]	AA EC 03.030 *Lorraine*, St Dizier	
144	Dassault Rafale C [30-GW]	AA EC 03.030 *Lorraine*, St Dizier	
145	Dassault Rafale C [30-GX]	AA EC 03.030 *Lorraine*, St Dizier	
146	Dassault Rafale C [104-GY]	AA EC 01.007 *Provence*, Al Dhafra, UAE	
147	Dassault Rafale C [30-GZ]	AA EC 02.030 *Normandie-Niémen*, Mont-de-Marsan	
148	Dassault Rafale C [30-VA]	AA EC 02.030 *Normandie-Niémen*, Mont-de-Marsan	
149	Dassault Rafale C	AA (on order)	
150	Dassault Rafale C	AA (on order)	
151	Dassault Rafale C	AA (on order)	
152	Dassault Rafale C	AA (on order)	
153	Dassault Rafale C	AA (on order)	
154	Dassault Rafale C	AA (on order)	
155	Dassault Rafale C	AA (on order)	
156	Dassault Rafale C	AA (on order)	
157	Dassault Rafale C	AA (on order)	
158	Dassault Rafale C	AA (on order)	
159	Dassault Rafale C	AA (on order)	
160	Dassault Rafale C	AA (on order)	
292	DHC-6 Twin Otter 200 [F-RACC]	AA GAM 00.056 *Vaucluse*, Evreux	
298	DHC-6 Twin Otter 200 [F-RACD]	AA GAM 00.056 *Vaucluse*, Evreux	
300	DHC-6 Twin Otter 200 [F-RACE]	AA GAM 00.056 *Vaucluse*, Evreux	
730	DHC-6 Twin Otter 300 [F-RACA]	AA ET 03.061 *Poitou*, Orléans	
745	DHC-6 Twin Otter 300 [CV]	AA ET 03.061 *Poitou*, Orléans	
054	Embraer EMB.121AA Xingu [YX]	AA EAT 00.319 *Capitaine Dartigues*, Avord	
064	Embraer EMB.121AA Xingu [YY]	AA EAT 00.319 *Capitaine Dartigues*, Avord	
066	Embraer EMB.121AN Xingu [ZA]	AA EAT 00.319 *Capitaine Dartigues*, Avord	
072	Embraer EMB.121AA Xingu [YA]	AA EAT 00.319 *Capitaine Dartigues*, Avord	
075	Embraer EMB.121AA Xingu [YC]	AA EAT 00.319 *Capitaine Dartigues*, Avord	
078	Embraer EMB.121AA Xingu [YE]	AA EAT 00.319 *Capitaine Dartigues*, Avord	
082	Embraer EMB.121AA Xingu [YG] $	AA EAT 00.319 *Capitaine Dartigues*, Avord	
083	Embraer EMB.121AN Xingu [ZE]	AA EAT 00.319 *Capitaine Dartigues*, Avord	
084	Embraer EMB.121AA Xingu [YH]	AA EAT 00.319 *Capitaine Dartigues*, Avord	
086	Embraer EMB.121AA Xingu [YI]	AA EAT 00.319 *Capitaine Dartigues*, Avord	
089	Embraer EMB.121AA Xingu [YJ]	AA EAT 00.319 *Capitaine Dartigues*, Avord	
090	Embraer EMB.121AN Xingu [ZF]	AA EAT 00.319 *Capitaine Dartigues*, Avord	
091	Embraer EMB.121AA Xingu [YK]	AA EAT 00.319 *Capitaine Dartigues*, Avord	

Notes	Serial	Type (code/other identity)	Owner/operator, location or fate
	092	Embraer EMB.121AA Xingu [YL]	AA EAT 00.319 *Capitaine Dartigues*, Avord
	096	Embraer EMB.121AA Xingu [YN]	AA EAT 00.319 *Capitaine Dartigues*, Avord
	098	Embraer EMB.121AA Xingu [YO]	AA EAT 00.319 *Capitaine Dartigues*, Avord
	099	Embraer EMB.121AA Xingu [YP]	AA EAT 00.319 *Capitaine Dartigues*, Avord
	102	Embraer EMB.121AA Xingu [YS]	AA EAT 00.319 *Capitaine Dartigues*, Avord
	103	Embraer EMB.121AA Xingu [YT]	AA EAT 00.319 *Capitaine Dartigues*, Avord
	105	Embraer EMB.121AA Xingu [YU]	AA EAT 00.319 *Capitaine Dartigues*, Avord
	107	Embraer EMB.121AA Xingu [YV]	AA EAT 00.319 *Capitaine Dartigues*, Avord
	108	Embraer EMB.121AA Xingu [YW]	AA EAT 00.319 *Capitaine Dartigues*, Avord
	2014	Eurocopter AS.332C Super Puma [PN]	*Withdrawn from use, 2016*
	2093	Eurocopter AS.332C Super Puma [PP]	*Withdrawn from use, 2016*
	2233	Eurocopter AS.332L-1 Super Puma [FY]	AA GAM 00.056 *Vaucluse*, Evreux
	2235	Eurocopter AS.332L-1 Super Puma [FZ]	AA EH 03.067 *Parisis*, Villacoublay
	2244	Eurocopter AS.332L-1 Super Puma [PM]	AA EH 01.044 *Solenzara*, Solenzara
	2377	Eurocopter AS.332L-1 Super Puma [FU]	AA EH 03.067 *Parisis*, Villacoublay
	2461	Eurocopter EC.725AP Cougar [SA]	AA EH 01.067 *Pyrénées*, Cazaux
	2549	Eurocopter EC.725AP Cougar [SB]	AA EH 01.067 *Pyrénées*, Cazaux
	2552	Eurocopter EC.725AP Cougar [SE]	AA EH 01.067 *Pyrénées*, Cazaux
	2619	Eurocopter EC.725AP Cougar [SC]	AA EH 05.067 *Alpilles*, Aix-en-Provence
	2626	Eurocopter EC.725AP Cougar [SD]	AA EH 01.067 *Pyrénées*, Cazaux
	2741	Eurocopter EC.225LP Super Puma 2+ [SY]	AA EH 01.067 *Pyrénées*, Cazaux
	2752	Eurocopter EC.225LP Super Puma 2+ [SZ]	AA EH 01.067 *Pyrénées*, Cazaux
	2770	Eurocopter EC.725R-2 Cougar [SG]	AA EH 01.067 *Pyrénées*, Cazaux
	2772	Eurocopter EC.725R-2 Cougar [SH]	AA EH 01.067 *Pyrénées*, Cazaux
	2778	Eurocopter EC.725R-2 Cougar [SI]	AA EH 01.067 *Pyrénées*, Cazaux
	2789	Eurocopter EC.725R-2 Cougar [SJ]	AA EH 01.067 *Pyrénées*, Cazaux
	2802	Eurocopter EC.725R-2 Cougar [SK]	AA EH 01.067 *Pyrénées*, Cazaux
	5361	Eurocopter AS.555AN Fennec [UT]	AA ET 00.068 *Antilles-Guyane*, Cayenne
	5382	Eurocopter AS.555AN Fennec [UV]	AA EH 05.067 *Alpilles*, Orange
	5386	Eurocopter AS.555AN Fennec [UX]	AA EH 03.067 *Parisis*, Villacoublay
	5387	Eurocopter AS.555AN Fennec [UY]	AA EH 05.067 *Alpilles*, Orange
	5390	Eurocopter AS.555AN Fennec [UZ]	AA EH 03.067 *Parisis*, Villacoublay
	5391	Eurocopter AS.555AN Fennec [VA]	AA EH 05.067 *Alpilles*, Orange
	5392	Eurocopter AS.555AN Fennec [VB]	AA EH 05.067 *Alpilles*, Orange
	5393	Eurocopter AS.555AN Fennec [VC]	AA EH 05.067 *Alpilles*, Orange
	5396	Eurocopter AS.555AN Fennec [VD]	AA EH 05.067 *Alpilles*, Orange
	5397	Eurocopter AS.555AN Fennec [VE]	AA ET 00.068 *Antilles-Guyane*, Cayenne
	5398	Eurocopter AS.555AN Fennec [VF]	AA EH 03.067 *Parisis*, Villacoublay
	5399	Eurocopter AS.555AN Fennec [VG] $	AA
	5400	Eurocopter AS.555AN Fennec [VH]	AA EH 05.067 *Alpilles*, Orange
	5412	Eurocopter AS.555AN Fennec [VI]	AA EH 05.067 *Alpilles*, Orange
	5427	Eurocopter AS.555AN Fennec [VJ]	AA EH 03.067 *Parisis*, Villacoublay
	5430	Eurocopter AS.555AN Fennec [VL]	AA EH 03.067 *Parisis*, Villacoublay
	5431	Eurocopter AS.555AN Fennec [VM] $	AA EH 03.067 *Parisis*, Villacoublay
	5440	Eurocopter AS.555AN Fennec [VN]	AA, stored Creil
	5441	Eurocopter AS.555AN Fennec [VO]	AA EH 03.067 *Parisis*, Villacoublay
	5444	Eurocopter AS.555AN Fennec [VP]	AA EH 03.067 *Parisis*, Villacoublay
	5445	Eurocopter AS.555AN Fennec [VQ]	AA EH 05.067 *Alpilles*, Orange
	5448	Eurocopter AS.555AN Fennec [VR]	AA EH 03.067 *Parisis*, Villacoublay
	5452	Eurocopter AS.555AN Fennec [VS]	AA EH 05.067 *Alpilles*, Orange
	5455	Eurocopter AS.555AN Fennec [VT]	AA EH 03.067 *Parisis*, Villacoublay
	5457	Eurocopter AS.555AN Fennec [VU]	AA ET 00.068 *Antilles-Guyane*, Cayenne
	5458	Eurocopter AS.555AN Fennec [VV]	AA EH 05.067 *Alpilles*, Orange
	5466	Eurocopter AS.555AN Fennec [VW]	AA ET 00.068 *Antilles-Guyane*, Cayenne
	5468	Eurocopter AS.555AN Fennec [VX]	AA EH 03.067 *Parisis*, Villacoublay
	5490	Eurocopter AS.555AN Fennec [VY]	AA EH 05.067 *Alpilles*, Orange
	5506	Eurocopter AS.555AN Fennec [WA]	AA EH 05.067 *Alpilles*, Orange
	5509	Eurocopter AS.555AN Fennec [WB]	AA EH 05.067 *Alpilles*, Orange
	5511	Eurocopter AS.555AN Fennec [WC]	AA EH 03.067 *Parisis*, Villacoublay
	5516	Eurocopter AS.555AN Fennec [WD]	AA EH 03.067 *Parisis*, Villacoublay
	5520	Eurocopter AS.555AN Fennec [WE]	AA EH 03.067 *Parisis*, Villacoublay
	5523	Eurocopter AS.555AN Fennec [WF]	AA EH 05.067 *Alpilles*, Orange

Serial	Type (code/other identity)	Owner/operator, location or fate	Notes
5526	Eurocopter AS.555AN Fennec [WG]	AA EH 03.067 *Parisis*, Villacoublay	
5530	Eurocopter AS.555AN Fennec [WH]	AA EH 05.067 *Alpilles*, Orange	
5532	Eurocopter AS.555AN Fennec [WI]	AA EH 05.067 *Alpilles*, Orange	
5534	Eurocopter AS.555AN Fennec [WJ]	AA EH 05.067 *Alpilles*, Orange	
5536	Eurocopter AS.555AN Fennec [WK]	AA EH 03.067 *Parisis*, Villacoublay	
5559	Eurocopter AS.555AN Fennec [WL]	AA EH 05.067 *Alpilles*, Orange	
03	Extra EA-330LC [F-TGCH]	AA EVAA, Salon de Provence	
04	Extra EA-330SC [F-TGCI]	AA EVAA, Salon de Provence	
05	Extra EA-330SC [F-TGCJ]	AA EVAA, Salon de Provence	
290	Fokker 100 [F-ZAFT]	AA DGA EV, Istres	
...	Fokker 100	AA DGA EV, Istres (on order)	
4588	Lockheed C-130H Hercules [61-PM]	AA ET 02.061 *Franche-Comté*, Orléans	
4589	Lockheed C-130H Hercules [61-PN]	AA ET 02.061 *Franche-Comté*, Orléans	
5114	Lockheed C-130H Hercules [61-PA]	AA ET 02.061 *Franche-Comté*, Orléans	
5116	Lockheed C-130H Hercules [61-PB]	AA ET 02.061 *Franche-Comté*, Orléans	
5119	Lockheed C-130H Hercules [61-PC]	AA ET 02.061 *Franche-Comté*, Orléans	
5140	Lockheed C-130H Hercules [61-PD]	AA ET 02.061 *Franche-Comté*, Orléans	
5142	Lockheed C-130H-30 Hercules [61-PE]	AA ET 02.061 *Franche-Comté*, Orléans	
5144	Lockheed C-130H-30 Hercules [61-PF] $	AA ET 02.061 *Franche-Comté*, Orléans	
5150	Lockheed C-130H-30 Hercules [61-PG]	AA ET 02.061 *Franche-Comté*, Orléans	
5151	Lockheed C-130H-30 Hercules [61-PH]	AA ET 02.061 *Franche-Comté*, Orléans	
5152	Lockheed C-130H-30 Hercules [61-PI]	AA ET 02.061 *Franche-Comté*, Orléans	
5153	Lockheed C-130H-30 Hercules [61-PJ]	AA ET 02.061 *Franche-Comté*, Orléans	
5226	Lockheed C-130H-30 Hercules [61-PK]	AA ET 02.061 *Franche-Comté*, Orléans	
5227	Lockheed C-130H-30 Hercules [61-PL]	AA ET 02.061 *Franche-Comté*, Orléans	
....	Lockheed C-130J Hercules II	AA (on order)	
....	Lockheed C-130J Hercules II	AA (on order)	
....	Lockheed KC-130J Hercules II	AA (on order)	
....	Lockheed KC-130J Hercules II	AA (on order)	
...	Pilatus PC-21	AA (on order)	
...	Pilatus PC-21	AA (on order)	
...	Pilatus PC-21	AA (on order)	
...	Pilatus PC-21	AA (on order)	
...	Pilatus PC-21	AA (on order)	
...	Pilatus PC-21	AA (on order)	
...	Pilatus PC-21	AA (on order)	
...	Pilatus PC-21	AA (on order)	
...	Pilatus PC-21	AA (on order)	
...	Pilatus PC-21	AA (on order)	
...	Pilatus PC-21	AA (on order)	
...	Pilatus PC-21	AA (on order)	
...	Pilatus PC-21	AA (on order)	
...	Pilatus PC-21	AA (on order)	
...	Pilatus PC-21	AA (on order)	
...	Pilatus PC-21	AA (on order)	
...	Pilatus PC-21	AA (on order)	
7	SOCATA TB-30 Epsilon [315-UF]	AA EPAA 00.315, Cognac	
26	SOCATA TB-30 Epsilon [315-UY]	AA EPAA 00.315, Cognac	
27	SOCATA TB-30 Epsilon [315-UZ]	AA EPAA 00.315, Cognac	
30	SOCATA TB-30 Epsilon [315-VC]	AA EPAA 00.315, Cognac	
64	SOCATA TB-30 Epsilon [315-WG]	AA EPAA 00.315, Cognac	
65	SOCATA TB-30 Epsilon [315-WH]	AA EPAA 00.315, Cognac	
66	SOCATA TB-30 Epsilon [315-WI]	AA EPAA 00.315, Cognac	
67	SOCATA TB-30 Epsilon [315-WJ]	AA EPAA 00.315, Cognac	
69	SOCATA TB-30 Epsilon [F-SEWL]	AA *Cartouche Dorée* (EPAA 00.315), Cognac	
73	SOCATA TB-30 Epsilon [315-WP]	AA EPAA 00.315, Cognac	
74	SOCATA TB-30 Epsilon [315-WQ]	*Withdrawn from use*	
78	SOCATA TB-30 Epsilon [315-WU]	AA EPAA 00.315, Cognac	
82	SOCATA TB-30 Epsilon [315-WY]	AA EPAA 00.315, Cognac	
83	SOCATA TB-30 Epsilon [315-WZ]	AA EPAA 00.315, Cognac	
84	SOCATA TB-30 Epsilon [315-XA]	AA EPAA 00.315, Cognac	
90	SOCATA TB-30 Epsilon [F-SEXG]	AA *Cartouche Dorée* (EPAA 00.315), Cognac	

Notes	Serial	Type (code/other identity)	Owner/operator, location or fate
	91	SOCATA TB-30 Epsilon [315-XH]	AA EPAA 00.315, Cognac
	92	SOCATA TB-30 Epsilon [315-XI]	AA EPAA 00.315, Cognac
	95	SOCATA TB-30 Epsilon [315-XL]	AA EPAA 00.315, Cognac
	96	SOCATA TB-30 Epsilon [315-XM]	AA EPAA 00.315, Cognac
	97	SOCATA TB-30 Epsilon [315-XN]	AA EPAA 00.315, Cognac
	99	SOCATA TB-30 Epsilon [F-SEXP]	AA *Cartouche Dorée* (EPAA 00.315), Cognac
	101	SOCATA TB-30 Epsilon [315-XR]	AA EPAA 00.315, Cognac
	102	SOCATA TB-30 Epsilon [F-SEXS,2]	AA *Cartouche Dorée* (EPAA 00.315), Cognac
	103	SOCATA TB-30 Epsilon [315-XT]	AA EPAA 00.315, Cognac
	104	SOCATA TB-30 Epsilon [315-XU]	AA EPAA 00.315, Cognac
	113	SOCATA TB-30 Epsilon [F-SEYD]	AA *Cartouche Dorée* (EPAA 00.315), Cognac
	116	SOCATA TB-30 Epsilon [F-SEYG]	AA *Cartouche Dorée* (EPAA 00.315), Cognac
	117	SOCATA TB-30 Epsilon [315-YH]	AA EPAA 00.315, Cognac
	118	SOCATA TB-30 Epsilon [315-YI]	AA EPAA 00.315, Cognac
	121	SOCATA TB-30 Epsilon [315-YL]	AA EPAA 00.315, Cognac
	127	SOCATA TB-30 Epsilon [315-YR]	AA EPAA 00.315, Cognac
	131	SOCATA TB-30 Epsilon [315-YV]	AA EPAA 00.315, Cognac
	133	SOCATA TB-30 Epsilon [315-YX]	AA EPAA 00.315, Cognac
	136	SOCATA TB-30 Epsilon [315-ZA]	AA EPAA 00.315, Cognac
	141	SOCATA TB-30 Epsilon [F-SEZF]	AA *Cartouche Dorée* (EPAA 00.315), Cognac
	142	SOCATA TB-30 Epsilon [315-ZG]	AA EPAA 00.315, Cognac
	144	SOCATA TB-30 Epsilon [315-ZI]	AA EPAA 00.315, Cognac
	146	SOCATA TB-30 Epsilon [315-ZK]	AA EPAA 00.315, Cognac
	149	SOCATA TB-30 Epsilon [315-ZM]	AA EPAA 00.315, Cognac
	150	SOCATA TB-30 Epsilon [315-ZN]	AA EPAA 00.315, Cognac
	33	SOCATA TBM 700A [XA]	AA ET 00.043 *Médoc*, Bordeaux
	35	SOCATA TBM 700A [BW]	AA DGA EV, Cazaux & Istres
	77	SOCATA TBM 700A [XD]	AA ET 00.043 *Médoc*, Bordeaux
	78	SOCATA TBM 700A [XE]	AA CEAM, Mont-de-Marsan
	80	SOCATA TBM 700A [BY]	AA DGA EV, Cazaux & Istres
	93	SOCATA TBM 700A [XL]	AA ET 00.041 *Verdun*, Villacoublay
	94	SOCATA TBM 700A [BZ]	AA DGA EV, Cazaux & Istres
	95	SOCATA TBM 700A [XH]	AA CEAM, Mont-de-Marsan
	103	SOCATA TBM 700A [XI]	AA ET 00.041 *Verdun*, Villacoublay
	104	SOCATA TBM 700A [XJ]	AA EdC 00.070, Châteaudun
	105	SOCATA TBM 700A [XK]	AA ET 00.043 *Médoc*, Bordeaux
	106	SOCATA TBM 700A [BX]	AA DGA EV, Cazaux & Istres
	110	SOCATA TBM 700A [XP]	AA ET 00.041 *Verdun*, Villacoublay
	111	SOCATA TBM 700A [XM]	AA ET 00.041 *Verdun*, Villacoublay
	115	SOCATA TBM 700A [BQ]	AA DGA EV, Cazaux & Istres
	117	SOCATA TBM 700A [XN]	AA ET 00.043 *Médoc*, Bordeaux
	125	SOCATA TBM 700A [XO]	AA EdC 00.070, Châteaudun
	131	SOCATA TBM 700A [XQ]	AA ET 00.041 *Verdun*, Villacoublay
	146	SOCATA TBM 700A [XR]	AA ET 00.041 *Verdun*, Villacoublay
	147	SOCATA TBM 700A [XS]	AA ET 00.041 *Verdun*, Villacoublay
	R87	Transall C-160R [61-ZE]	AA ET 00.064, Evreux
	R89	Transall C-160R [61-ZG] $	AA ET 00.064, Evreux
	R90	Transall C-160R [61-ZH]	AA ET 00.064, Evreux
	R91	Transall C-160R [61-ZI]	AA ET 00.064, Evreux
	R93	Transall C-160R [61-ZK]	AA ET 00.064, Evreux
	R94	Transall C-160R [61-ZL]	AA ET 00.064, Evreux
	R96	Transall C-160R [61-ZN]	AA ET 00.064, Evreux
	R97	Transall C-160R [61-ZA]	AA ET 00.064, Evreux
	R158	Transall C-160R [61-ZX]	AA, Evreux (wfu)
	R160	Transall C-160R [61-ZZ]	AA ET 00.064, Evreux
	R201	Transall C-160R [64-GA]	AA ET 01.064 *Bearn*, Evreux
	R202	Transall C-160R [64-GB]	AA ET 02.064 *Anjou*, Evreux
	R203	Transall C-160R [64-GC] $	AA ET 01.064 *Bearn*, Evreux
	R204	Transall C-160R [64-GD]	AA ET 02.064 *Anjou*, Evreux
	R206	Transall C-160R [64-GF]	AA ET 02.064 *Anjou*, Evreux
	R208	Transall C-160R [64-GH] $	AA ET 02.064 *Anjou*, Evreux
	R210	Transall C-160R [64-GJ]	AA ET 02.064 *Anjou*, Evreux

Serial	Type (code/other identity)	Owner/operator, location or fate	Notes
R212	Transall C-160R [64-GL]	AA ET 02.064 *Anjou*, Evreux	
R213	Transall C-160R [64-GM]	AA ET 01.064 *Bearn*, Evreux	
R214	Transall C-160R [64-GN]	AA ET 02.064 *Anjou*, Evreux	
F216	Transall C-160NG GABRIEL [GT]	AA EEA 00.054 *Dunkerque*, Evreux	
R217	Transall C-160R [64-GQ]	AA ET 01.064 *Bearn*, Evreux	
R218	Transall C-160R [64-GR]	AA ET 02.064 *Anjou*, Evreux	
F221	Transall C-160NG GABRIEL [GS] $	AA EEA 00.054 *Dunkerque*, Evreux	
R223	Transall C-160R [64-GW]	AA ET 01.064 *Bearn*, Evreux	
R224	Transall C-160R [64-GX]	AA ET 02.064 *Anjou*, Evreux	
R225	Transall C-160R [64-GY]	AA ET 01.064 *Bearn*, Evreux	
R226	Transall C-160R [64-GZ]	AA ET 02.064 *Anjou*, Evreux	
Aéronautique Navale/Marine (AN)			
2	Dassault-Breguet Atlantique 2	AN 21 Flottille, Lorient/Lann Bihoué	
3	Dassault-Breguet Atlantique 2	AN 23 Flottille, Lorient/Lann Bihoué	
4	Dassault-Breguet Atlantique 2	AN 23 Flottille, Lorient/Lann Bihoué	
5	Dassault-Breguet Atlantique 2	AN 21 Flottille, Lorient/Lann Bihoué	
9	Dassault-Breguet Atlantique 2	AN 23 Flottille, Lorient/Lann Bihoué	
12	Dassault-Breguet Atlantique 2	AN 21 Flottille, Lorient/Lann Bihoué	
13	Dassault-Breguet Atlantique 2	AN 21 Flottille, Lorient/Lann Bihoué	
14	Dassault-Breguet Atlantique 2	AN 23 Flottille, Lorient/Lann Bihoué	
16	Dassault-Breguet Atlantique 2	AN 21 Flottille, Lorient/Lann Bihoué	
17	Dassault-Breguet Atlantique 2 $	AN 21 Flottille, Lorient/Lann Bihoué	
18	Dassault-Breguet Atlantique 2	AN 21 Flottille, Lorient/Lann Bihoué	
19	Dassault-Breguet Atlantique 2	AN 23 Flottille, Lorient/Lann Bihoué	
20	Dassault-Breguet Atlantique 2	AN 23 Flottille, Lorient/Lann Bihoué	
21	Dassault-Breguet Atlantique 2	AN 21 Flottille, Lorient/Lann Bihoué	
22	Dassault-Breguet Atlantique 2	AN 21 Flottille, Lorient/Lann Bihoué	
23	Dassault-Breguet Atlantique 2	AN 21 Flottille, Lorient/Lann Bihoué	
24	Dassault-Breguet Atlantique 2	AN 21 Flottille, Lorient/Lann Bihoué	
26	Dassault-Breguet Atlantique 2	AN 21 Flottille, Lorient/Lann Bihoué	
27	Dassault-Breguet Atlantique 2	AN 21 Flottille, Lorient/Lann Bihoué	
32	Dassault Falcon 10(MER)	AN 57 Escadrille, Landivisiau	
101	Dassault Falcon 10(MER)	AN 57 Escadrille, Landivisiau	
129	Dassault Falcon 10(MER)	AN 57 Escadrille, Landivisiau	
133	Dassault Falcon 10(MER)	AN 57 Escadrille, Landivisiau	
143	Dassault Falcon 10(MER)	AN 57 Escadrille, Landivisiau	
185	Dassault Falcon 10(MER) $	AN 57 Escadrille, Landivisiau	
48	Dassault Falcon 20G Guardian	AN 25 Flottille, Papeete & Tontouta	
65	Dassault Falcon 20G Guardian	AN 25 Flottille, Papeete & Tontouta	
72	Dassault Falcon 20G Guardian	AN 25 Flottille, Papeete & Tontouta	
77	Dassault Falcon 20G Guardian	AN 25 Flottille, Papeete & Tontouta	
80	Dassault Falcon 20G Guardian	AN 25 Flottille, Papeete & Tontouta	
5	Dassault Falcon 50MS SURMAR	AN 24 Flottille, Lorient/Lann Bihoué	
7	Dassault Falcon 50MI SURMAR	AN 24 Flottille, Lorient/Lann Bihoué	
27	Dassault Falcon 50MS SURMAR	AN 24 Flottille, Lorient/Lann Bihoué	
30	Dassault Falcon 50MI SURMAR	AN 24 Flottille, Lorient/Lann Bihoué	
34	Dassault Falcon 50MS SURMAR	AN 24 Flottille, Lorient/Lann Bihoué	
36	Dassault Falcon 50MI SURMAR	AN 24 Flottille, Lorient/Lann Bihoué	
78	Dassault Falcon 50MS SURMAR	AN 24 Flottille, Lorient/Lann Bihoué	
132	Dassault Falcon 50MI SURMAR	AN 24 Flottille, Lorient/Lann Bihoué	
6	Dassault Rafale M	AN 11 Flottille, Landivisiau	
7	Dassault Rafale M	AMD-BA, Istres	
9	Dassault Rafale M	AN 12 Flottille, Landivisiau	
10	Dassault Rafale M	AN 12 Flottille, Landivisiau	
11	Dassault Rafale M	AN 12 Flottille, Landivisiau	
12	Dassault Rafale M	AN ETR 03.004 *Aquitaine*, St Dizier	
13	Dassault Rafale M	AN 11 Flottille, Landivisiau	
14	Dassault Rafale M	AN 11 Flottille, Landivisiau	
15	Dassault Rafale M	AN 12 Flottille, Landivisiau	
16	Dassault Rafale M	AN 12 Flottille, Landivisiau	
17	Dassault Rafale M	AN 12 Flottille, Landivisiau	
19	Dassault Rafale M $	AN 12 Flottille, Landivisiau	

Notes	Serial	Type (code/other identity)	Owner/operator, location or fate
	20	Dassault Rafale M	AN 17 Flottille, Landivisiau
	21	Dassault Rafale M	AN 12 Flottille, Landivisiau
	23	Dassault Rafale M	AN 12 Flottille, Landivisiau
	26	Dassault Rafale M	AN 12 Flottille, Landivisiau
	27	Dassault Rafale M $	AN ETR 03.004 *Aquitaine*, St Dizier
	28	Dassault Rafale M	AN ETR 03.004 *Aquitaine*, St Dizier
	29	Dassault Rafale M	AN 12 Flottille, Landivisiau
	30	Dassault Rafale M	AN 12 Flottille, Landivisiau
	31	Dassault Rafale M	AN 11 Flottille, Landivisiau
	32	Dassault Rafale M	AN 11 Flottille, Landivisiau
	33	Dassault Rafale M	AN 11 Flottille, Landivisiau
	34	Dassault Rafale M	AN ETR 03.004 *Aquitaine*, St Dizier
	35	Dassault Rafale M	AN 12 Flottille, Landivisiau
	36	Dassault Rafale M	AN 11 Flottille, Landivisiau
	37	Dassault Rafale M	AN 11 Flottille, Landivisiau
	38	Dassault Rafale M	AN 12 Flottille, Landivisiau
	39	Dassault Rafale M	AN 11 Flottille, Landivisiau
	40	Dassault Rafale M	AN 11 Flottille, Landivisiau
	41	Dassault Rafale M	AN (on order)
	42	Dassault Rafale M	AN 11 Flottille, Landivisiau
	43	Dassault Rafale M	AN 11 Flottille, Landivisiau
	44	Dassault Rafale M	AN (on order)
	45	Dassault Rafale M	AN 12 Flottille, Landivisiau
	46	Dassault Rafale M	AN 17 Flottille, Landivisiau
	47	Dassault Rafale M	AN (on order)
	48	Dassault Rafale M	AN (on order)
	49	Dassault Rafale M	AN (on order)
	50	Dassault Rafale M	AN (on order)
	M01	Dassault Rafale M	AN DGA EV, Istres
	M02	Dassault Rafale M	AN DGA EV, Istres
	1	Dassault Super Etendard	*Withdrawn from use, July 2016*
	2	Dassault Super Etendard	*Withdrawn from use, July 2016*
	8	Dassault Super Etendard	*Withdrawn from use, July 2016*
	10	Dassault Super Etendard	*Withdrawn from use, July 2016*
	12	Dassault Super Etendard	*Withdrawn from use, July 2016*
	17	Dassault Super Etendard	*Withdrawn from use, July 2016*
	19	Dassault Super Etendard	*Withdrawn from use, July 2016*
	31	Dassault Super Etendard	*Withdrawn from use, July 2016*
	32	Dassault Super Etendard	*Withdrawn from use, July 2016*
	33	Dassault Super Etendard	*Withdrawn from use, July 2016*
	35	Dassault Super Etendard	*Withdrawn from use, July 2016*
	41	Dassault Super Etendard	*Withdrawn from use, July 2016*
	43	Dassault Super Etendard	*Withdrawn from use, July 2016*
	44	Dassault Super Etendard	*Withdrawn from use, July 2016*
	46	Dassault Super Etendard	*Withdrawn from use, July 2016*
	51	Dassault Super Etendard	*Withdrawn from use, July 2016*
	52	Dassault Super Etendard	*Withdrawn from use, July 2016*
	65	Dassault Super Etendard	*Withdrawn from use, July 2016*
	69	Dassault Super Etendard	*Withdrawn from use, July 2016*
	65	Embraer EMB.121AN Xingu	AN 28 Flottille, Hyères
	67	Embraer EMB.121AN Xingu $	AN 28 Flottille, Hyères
	68	Embraer EMB.121AN Xingu	AN 28 Flottille, Hyères
	69	Embraer EMB.121AN Xingu	AN 28 Flottille, Hyères
	71	Embraer EMB.121AN Xingu	AN 28 Flottille, Hyères
	74	Embraer EMB.121AN Xingu $	AN 28 Flottille, Hyères
	77	Embraer EMB.121AN Xingu	AN 28 Flottille, Hyères
	81	Embraer EMB.121AN Xingu	AN 24 Flottille, Lorient/Lann Bihoué
	85	Embraer EMB.121AN Xingu	AN 24 Flottille, Lorient/Lann Bihoué
	87	Embraer EMB.121AN Xingu	AN 28 Flottille, Hyères
	17	Eurocopter AS.365N Dauphin	AN 35 Flottille, Hyères
	19	Eurocopter AS.365N Dauphin	AN 35 Flottille, Le Touquet
	24	Eurocopter AS.365N Dauphin	AN 35 Flottille, Hyères

Serial	Type (code/other identity)	Owner/operator, location or fate	Notes
57	Eurocopter AS.365N Dauphin	AN 35 Flottille, Hyères	
81	Eurocopter AS.365N Dauphin	AN 35 Flottille, Hyères	
91	Eurocopter AS.365N Dauphin	AN 35 Flottille, Hyères	
157	Eurocopter AS.365N Dauphin	AN 35 Flottille, Hyères	
313	Eurocopter SA.365F-1 Dauphin II	AN 35 Flottille, Hyères	
318	Eurocopter SA.365F-1 Dauphin II	AN 35 Flottille, Hyères	
322	Eurocopter SA.365F-1 Dauphin II	AN 35 Flottille, Hyères	
355	Eurocopter AS.565MA Panther	AN 36 Flottille, Hyères	
362	Eurocopter AS.565MA Panther	AN 36 Flottille, Hyères	
403	Eurocopter AS.565MA Panther	AN 36 Flottille, Hyères	
436	Eurocopter AS.565MA Panther	AN 36 Flottille, Hyères	
452	Eurocopter AS.565MA Panther	AN 36 Flottille, Hyères	
453	Eurocopter AS.565MA Panther	AN 36 Flottille, Hyères	
466	Eurocopter AS.565MA Panther	AN 36 Flottille, Hyères	
482	Eurocopter AS.565MA Panther	AN 36 Flottille, Hyères	
486	Eurocopter AS.565MA Panther	AN 36 Flottille, Hyères	
488	Eurocopter AS.565MA Panther	AN 36 Flottille, Hyères	
503	Eurocopter AS.565MA Panther	AN 36 Flottille, Hyères	
505	Eurocopter AS.565MA Panther	AN 36 Flottille, Hyères	
506	Eurocopter AS.565MA Panther	AN 36 Flottille, Hyères	
507	Eurocopter AS.565MA Panther $	AN 36 Flottille, Hyères	
511	Eurocopter AS.565MA Panther	AN 36 Flottille, Hyères	
519	Eurocopter AS.565MA Panther	AN 36 Flottille, Hyères	
522	Eurocopter AS.565MA Panther $	AN 36 Flottille, Hyères	
524	Eurocopter AS.565MA Panther	AN 36 Flottille, Hyères	
542	Eurocopter AS.565MA Panther	AN 36 Flottille, Hyères	
6872	Eurocopter AS.365N-3 Dauphin	AN 35 Flottille, Tahiti	
6928	Eurocopter AS.365N-3 Dauphin	AN 35 Flottille, Tahiti	
2741	Eurocopter EC.225LP Super Puma 2+	*Transferred to l'Armée de l'Air, June 2016*	
2752	Eurocopter EC.225LP Super Puma 2+	*Transferred to l'Armée de l'Air, June 2016*	
1	NH Industries NH.90-NFH Caïman (F-ZWTO)	AN 33 Flottille, Lanvéoc/Poulmic	
2	NH Industries NH.90-NFH Caïman	AN CEPA/10 Escadrille, Hyères	
3	NH Industries NH.90-NFH Caïman	AN 31 Flottille, Hyères	
4	NH Industries NH.90-NFH Caïman	AN 33 Flottille, Lanvéoc/Poulmic	
5	NH Industries NH.90-NFH Caïman	AN 33 Flottille, Lanvéoc/Poulmic	
6	NH Industries NH.90-NFH Caïman	AN 33 Flottille, Lanvéoc/Poulmic	
7	NH Industries NH.90-NFH Caïman	AN 33 Flottille, Lanvéoc/Poulmic	
8	NH Industries NH.90-NFH Caïman	AN 31 Flottille, Hyères	
9	NH Industries NH.90-NFH Caïman	AN 31 Flottille, Hyères	
10	NH Industries NH.90-NFH Caïman	AN 31 Flottille, Hyères	
11	NH Industries NH.90-NFH Caïman	AN 33 Flottille, Lanvéoc/Poulmic	
12	NH Industries NH.90-NFH Caïman	AN 31 Flottille, Hyères	
13	NH Industries NH.90-NFH Caïman	AN 31 Flottille, Hyères	
14	NH Industries NH.90-NFH Caïman	AN 33 Flottille, Lanvéoc/Poulmic	
15	NH Industries NH.90-NFH Caïman	AN CEPA/10 Escadrille, Hyères	
16	NH Industries NH.90-NFH Caïman	AN 31 Flottille, Hyères	
17	NH Industries NH.90-NFH Caïman	AN (on order)	
18	NH Industries NH.90-NFH Caïman	AN (on order)	
19	NH Industries NH.90-NFH Caïman	AN (on order)	
20	NH Industries NH.90-NFH Caïman	AN (on order)	
21	NH Industries NH.90-NFH Caïman	AN (on order)	
22	NH Industries NH.90-NFH Caïman	AN (on order)	
23	NH Industries NH.90-NFH Caïman	AN (on order)	
24	NH Industries NH.90-NFH Caïman	AN (on order)	
25	NH Industries NH.90-NFH Caïman	AN (on order)	
26	NH Industries NH.90-NFH Caïman	AN (on order)	
27	NH Industries NH.90-NFH Caïman	AN (on order)	
1	Northrop Grumman E-2C Hawkeye (165455)	AN 4 Flottille, Lorient/Lann Bihoué	
2	Northrop Grumman E-2C Hawkeye (165456)	AN 4 Flottille, Lorient/Lann Bihoué	
3	Northrop Grumman E-2C Hawkeye (166417)	AN 4 Flottille, Lorient/Lann Bihoué	
4	Northrop Grumman E-2C Hawkeye	AN (on order)	
13	Sud Aviation SE.3160 Alouette III	AN 35 Flottille, Hyères	

Notes	Serial	Type (code/other identity)	Owner/operator, location or fate
	14	Sud Aviation SE.3160 Alouette III	AN 22 Escadrille/ESHE, Lanvéoc/Poulmic
	41	Sud Aviation SE.3160 Alouette III	AN 35 Flottille, Hyères
	100	Sud Aviation SA.319B Alouette III	AN 22 Escadrille/ESHE, Lanvéoc/Poulmic
	114	Sud Aviation SA.319B Alouette III	AN 22 Escadrille/ESHE, Lanvéoc/Poulmic
	161	Sud Aviation SA.319B Alouette III	AN 22 Escadrille/ESHE, Lanvéoc/Poulmic
	237	Sud Aviation SA.319B Alouette III	AN 35 Flottille, Hyères
	244	Sud Aviation SE.3160 Alouette III	AN 22 Escadrille/ESHE, Lanvéoc/Poulmic
	245	Sud Aviation SE.3160 Alouette III	AN 22 Escadrille/ESHE, Lanvéoc/Poulmic
	262	Sud Aviation SA.319B Alouette III	AN 22 Escadrille/ESHE, Lanvéoc/Poulmic
	268	Sud Aviation SA.319B Alouette III	AN 22 Escadrille/ESHE, Lanvéoc/Poulmic
	279	Sud Aviation SE.3160 Alouette III	AN 22 Escadrille/ESHE, Lanvéoc/Poulmic
	302	Sud Aviation SA.319B Alouette III	AN 22 Escadrille/ESHE, Lanvéoc/Poulmic
	303	Sud Aviation SA.319B Alouette III	AN 22 Escadrille/ESHE, Lanvéoc/Poulmic
	309	Sud Aviation SA.319B Alouette III	AN 22 Escadrille/ESHE, Lanvéoc/Poulmic
	314	Sud Aviation SA.319B Alouette III	AN 22 Escadrille/ESHE, Lanvéoc/Poulmic
	347	Sud Aviation SA.319B Alouette III	AN 22 Escadrille/ESHE, Lanvéoc/Poulmic
	358	Sud Aviation SA.319B Alouette III	AN 22 Escadrille/ESHE, Lanvéoc/Poulmic
	731	Sud Aviation SA.316B Alouette III	AN 22 Escadrille/ESHE, Lanvéoc/Poulmic
	806	Sud Aviation SA.316B Alouette III	AN 22 Escadrille/ESHE, Lanvéoc/Poulmic
	809	Sud Aviation SA.316B Alouette III	AN 22 Escadrille/ESHE, Lanvéoc/Poulmic
	997	Sud Aviation SA.319B Alouette III	AN 22 Escadrille/ESHE, Lanvéoc/Poulmic
	260	Westland Lynx HAS2(FN)	AN 34 Flottille, Lanvéoc/Poulmic
	263	Westland Lynx HAS2(FN)	AN 34 Flottille, Lanvéoc/Poulmic
	264	Westland Lynx HAS2(FN)	AN 34 Flottille, Lanvéoc/Poulmic
	265	Westland Lynx HAS2(FN)	AN 34 Flottille, Lanvéoc/Poulmic
	267	Westland Lynx HAS2(FN)	AN 34 Flottille, Lanvéoc/Poulmic
	270	Westland Lynx HAS2(FN)	AN 34 Flottille, Lanvéoc/Poulmic
	271	Westland Lynx HAS2(FN)	AN 34 Flottille, Lanvéoc/Poulmic
	272	Westland Lynx HAS2(FN) $	AN 34 Flottille, Lanvéoc/Poulmic
	273	Westland Lynx HAS2(FN)	AN 34 Flottille, Lanvéoc/Poulmic
	621	Westland Lynx HAS2(FN)	AN 34 Flottille, Lanvéoc/Poulmic
	623	Westland Lynx HAS2(FN)	AN 34 Flottille, Lanvéoc/Poulmic
	624	Westland Lynx HAS2(FN)	AN 34 Flottille, Lanvéoc/Poulmic
	625	Westland Lynx HAS2(FN)	AN 34 Flottille, Lanvéoc/Poulmic
	627	Westland Lynx HAS2(FN)	AN 34 Flottille, Lanvéoc/Poulmic
	801	Westland Lynx HAS4(FN)	AN 34 Flottille, Lanvéoc/Poulmic
	802	Westland Lynx HAS4(FN)	AN 34 Flottille, Lanvéoc/Poulmic
	804	Westland Lynx HAS4(FN)	AN 34 Flottille, Lanvéoc/Poulmic
	806	Westland Lynx HAS4(FN)	AN 34 Flottille, Lanvéoc/Poulmic
	807	Westland Lynx HAS4(FN)	AN 34 Flottille, Lanvéoc/Poulmic
	808	Westland Lynx HAS4(FN)	AN 34 Flottille, Lanvéoc/Poulmic
	810	Westland Lynx HAS4(FN)	AN 34 Flottille, Lanvéoc/Poulmic
	811	Westland Lynx HAS4(FN)	AN 34 Flottille, Lanvéoc/Poulmic
	813	Westland Lynx HAS4(FN)	AN 34 Flottille, Lanvéoc/Poulmic
	814	Westland Lynx HAS4(FN)	AN 34 Flottille, Lanvéoc/Poulmic
	Aviation Legére de l'Armée de Terre (ALAT)		
	1005	Aérospatiale SA.330Ba Puma [DCA]	ALAT ESAM, Bourges
	1006	Aérospatiale SA.330Ba Puma [DAA]	ALAT
	1020	Aérospatiale SA.330Ba Puma [DAB]	ALAT 5 RHC, Pau
	1036	Aérospatiale SA.330Ba Puma [DAC]	ALAT 3 RHC, Etain
	1037	Aérospatiale SA.330Ba Puma [DAD]	ALAT 5 RHC, Pau
	1049	Aérospatiale SA.330Ba Puma [DAE]	ALAT 5 RHC, Pau
	1052	Aérospatiale SA.330Ba Puma [DCB]	ALAT EALAT, Le Luc
	1055	Aérospatiale SA.330Ba Puma [DAF]	ALAT GIH, Cazaux
	1056	Aérospatiale SA.330Ba Puma [DCC]	ALAT GAM/STAT, Valence
	1057	Aérospatiale SA.330Ba Puma [DCD]	ALAT EALAT, Le Luc
	1069	Aérospatiale SA.330Ba Puma [DAG]	ALAT 1 RHC, Phalsbourg
	1071	Aérospatiale SA.330Ba Puma [DCE]	ALAT EALAT, Le Luc
	1073	Aérospatiale SA.330Ba Puma [DCF]	ALAT EALAT, Le Luc
	1078	Aérospatiale SA.330Ba Puma [DAH]	ALAT 3 RHC, Etain
	1092	Aérospatiale SA.330Ba Puma [DAI]	ALAT 1 RHC, Phalsbourg
	1093	Aérospatiale SA.330Ba Puma [DCG]	ALAT 3 RHC, Etain

Serial	Type (code/other identity)	Owner/operator, location or fate	Notes
1100	Aérospatiale SA.330Ba Puma [DAJ]	ALAT 3 RHC, Etain	
1102	Aérospatiale SA.330Ba Puma [DAK]	ALAT	
1107	Aérospatiale SA.330Ba Puma [DAL]	ALAT 1 RHC, Phalsbourg	
1109	Aérospatiale SA.330Ba Puma [DAM]	ALAT 5 RHC, Pau	
1114	Aérospatiale SA.330Ba Puma [DCH]	ALAT 3 RHC, Etain	
1122	Aérospatiale SA.330Ba Puma [DCI]	ALAT 5 RHC, Pau	
1123	Aérospatiale SA.330Ba Puma [DCJ]	ALAT 5 RHC, Pau	
1128	Aérospatiale SA.330Ba Puma [DAN]	ALAT 1 RHC, Phalsbourg	
1130	Aérospatiale SA.330Ba Puma [DCK]	ALAT 5 RHC, Pau	
1135	Aérospatiale SA.330Ba Puma [DCL]	ALAT 1 RHC, Phalsbourg	
1136	Aérospatiale SA.330Ba Puma [DCM]	ALAT 1 RHC, Phalsbourg	
1142	Aérospatiale SA.330Ba Puma [DCN]	ALAT EALAT, Le Luc	
1143	Aérospatiale SA.330Ba Puma [DAO]	ALAT 1 RHC, Phalsbourg	
1145	Aérospatiale SA.330Ba Puma [DCO]	ALAT 3 RHC, Etain	
1149	Aérospatiale SA.330Ba Puma [DAP]	ALAT 5 RHC, Pau	
1150	Aérospatiale SA.330Ba Puma [DCP]	ALAT 3 RHC, Etain	
1155	Aérospatiale SA.330Ba Puma [DCQ]	ALAT 4 RHFS, Pau	
1156	Aérospatiale SA.330Ba Puma [DAQ]	ALAT 1 RHC, Phalsbourg	
1163	Aérospatiale SA.330Ba Puma [DCR]	ALAT EALAT, Le Luc	
1164	Aérospatiale SA.330Ba Puma [DCS]	ALAT 1 RHC, Phalsbourg	
1165	Aérospatiale SA.330Ba Puma [DCT]	ALAT 1 RHC, Phalsbourg	
1171	Aérospatiale SA.330Ba Puma [DCU]	ALAT 1 RHC, Phalsbourg	
1172	Aérospatiale SA.330Ba Puma [DCV]	ALAT EALAT, Le Luc	
1173	Aérospatiale SA.330Ba Puma [DAR]	ALAT 3 RHC, Etain	
1176	Aérospatiale SA.330Ba Puma [DAS]	ALAT 3 RHC, Etain	
1177	Aérospatiale SA.330Ba Puma [DCW]	ALAT 3 RHC, Etain	
1179	Aérospatiale SA.330Ba Puma [DCX]	ALAT	
1182	Aérospatiale SA.330Ba Puma [DCY]	ALAT 1 RHC, Phalsbourg	
1186	Aérospatiale SA.330Ba Puma [DCZ]	ALAT 5 RHC, Pau	
1189	Aérospatiale SA.330Ba Puma [DAT]	ALAT 3 RHC, Etain	
1190	Aérospatiale SA.330Ba Puma [DDA]	ALAT 1 RHC, Phalsbourg	
1192	Aérospatiale SA.330Ba Puma [DDB]	ALAT 1 RHC, Phalsbourg	
1196	Aérospatiale SA.330Ba Puma [DDC]	ALAT EALAT, Le Luc	
1197	Aérospatiale SA.330Ba Puma [DAU]	ALAT 5 RHC, Pau	
1198	Aérospatiale SA.330Ba Puma [DDD]	ALAT 1 RHC, Phalsbourg	
1204	Aérospatiale SA.330Ba Puma [DAV]	ALAT 3 RHC, Etain	
1206	Aérospatiale SA.330Ba Puma [DDE]	ALAT 3 RHC, Etain	
1211	Aérospatiale SA.330Ba Puma [DAW]	ALAT	
1213	Aérospatiale SA.330Ba Puma [DDF]	ALAT 1 RHC, Phalsbourg	
1214	Aérospatiale SA.330Ba Puma [DAX]	ALAT 3 RHC, Etain	
1217	Aérospatiale SA.330Ba Puma [DAY]	ALAT	
1219	Aérospatiale SA.330Ba Puma [DAZ]	ALAT 3 RHC, Etain	
1222	Aérospatiale SA.330Ba Puma [DDG]	ALAT 1 RHC, Phalsbourg	
1223	Aérospatiale SA.330Ba Puma [DDH]	ALAT EALAT, Le Luc	
1228	Aérospatiale SA.330Ba Puma [DDI]	*Withdrawn from use, 2016*	
1229	Aérospatiale SA.330Ba Puma [DDJ]	ALAT EALAT, Le Luc	
1231	Aérospatiale SA.330Ba Puma [DDK]	ALAT 5 RHC, Pau	
1232	Aérospatiale SA.330Ba Puma [DBA]	ALAT 5 RHC, Pau	
1235	Aérospatiale SA.330Ba Puma [DDL]	ALAT 5 RHC, Pau	
1236	Aérospatiale SA.330Ba Puma [DDM]	ALAT EALAT, Le Luc	
1239	Aérospatiale SA.330Ba Puma [DDN]	ALAT 5 RHC, Pau	
1243	Aérospatiale SA.330Ba Puma [DBB]	ALAT 5 RHC, Pau	
1244	Aérospatiale SA.330Ba Puma [DDO]	ALAT 5 RHC, Pau	
1248	Aérospatiale SA.330Ba Puma [DBC]	ALAT 3 RHC, Etain	
1252	Aérospatiale SA.330Ba Puma [DDP]	ALAT EALAT, Le Luc	
1255	Aérospatiale SA.330Ba Puma [DDQ]	ALAT 1 RHC, Phalsbourg	
1256	Aérospatiale SA.330Ba Puma [DDR]	ALAT GAM/STAT, Valence	
1260	Aérospatiale SA.330Ba Puma [DDS]	ALAT EALAT, Le Luc	
1262	Aérospatiale SA.330Ba Puma [DBD]	ALAT 5 RHC, Pau	
1269	Aérospatiale SA.330Ba Puma [DDT]	ALAT 5 RHC, Pau	
1277	Aérospatiale SA.330Ba Puma [DBE]	ALAT 1 RHC, Phalsbourg	
1411	Aérospatiale SA.330Ba Puma [DDU]	ALAT 3 RHC, Etain	

Notes	Serial	Type (code/other identity)	Owner/operator, location or fate
	1417	Aérospatiale SA.330Ba Puma [DBF]	ALAT
	1419	Aérospatiale SA.330Ba Puma [DDV]	ALAT 1 RHC, Phalsbourg
	1438	Aérospatiale SA.330Ba Puma [DBG]	ALAT GAM/STAT, Valence
	1447	Aérospatiale SA.330Ba Puma [DDW]	ALAT 3 RHC, Etain
	1451	Aérospatiale SA.330Ba Puma [DBH]	ALAT 1 RHC, Phalsbourg
	1507	Aérospatiale SA.330Ba Puma [DBI]	ALAT EALAT, Le Luc
	1510	Aérospatiale SA.330Ba Puma [DBJ]	ALAT 3 RHC, Etain
	1512	Aérospatiale SA.330Ba Puma [DBK]	ALAT
	1519	Aérospatiale SA.330Ba Puma [DBL]	ALAT 3 RHC, Etain
	1617	Aérospatiale SA.330Ba Puma [DBM]	ALAT 1 RHC, Phalsbourg
	1632	Aérospatiale SA.330Ba Puma [DBN]	ALAT 5 RHC, Pau
	1634	Aérospatiale SA.330Ba Puma [DBO]	ALAT 3 RHC, Etain
	1654	Aérospatiale SA.330Ba Puma [DBP]	ALAT 5 RHC, Pau
	1662	Aérospatiale SA.330Ba Puma [DDX]	ALAT EALAT, Le Luc
	1663	Aérospatiale SA.330Ba Puma [DBQ]	ALAT 4 RHFS, Pau
	5682	Aérospatiale SA.330Ba Puma [DBR]	ALAT 4 RHFS, Pau
	1732	Aérospatiale SA.342M Gazelle [GJA]	ALAT EALAT, Le Luc
	3458	Aérospatiale SA.342M Gazelle [GNA]	ALAT EALAT, Le Luc
	3459	Aérospatiale SA.342M Gazelle [GAA]	ALAT 1 RHC, Phalsbourg
	3476	Aérospatiale SA.342M Gazelle [GAB]	ALAT 4 RHFS, Pau
	3477	Aérospatiale SA.342M Gazelle [GJB]	ALAT 1 RHC, Phalsbourg
	3511	Aérospatiale SA.342M Gazelle [GJC]	ALAT EALAT, Le Luc
	3512	Aérospatiale SA.342M Gazelle [GAC]	ALAT 1 RHC, Phalsbourg
	3513	Aérospatiale SA.342M Gazelle [GNB]	ALAT 1 RHC, Phalsbourg
	3529	Aérospatiale SA.342M Gazelle [GJD]	ALAT EALAT, Le Luc
	3530	Aérospatiale SA.342M Gazelle [GAD]	ALAT 4 RHFS, Pau
	3546	Aérospatiale SA.342M Gazelle [GJF]	ALAT EALAT, Le Luc
	3548	Aérospatiale SA.342M Gazelle [GAE]	ALAT 1 RHC, Phalsbourg
	3549	Aérospatiale SA.342M Gazelle [GNC]	ALAT EALAT, Le Luc
	3567	Aérospatiale SA.342M Gazelle [GMA]	ALAT EALAT, Le Luc
	3615	Aérospatiale SA.342M Gazelle [GJH]	ALAT 1 RHC, Phalsbourg
	3617	Aérospatiale SA.342M Gazelle [GND]	ALAT GAM/STAT, Valence
	3664	Aérospatiale SA.342M Gazelle [GAF]	ALAT 1 RHC, Phalsbourg
	3848	Aérospatiale SA.342M Gazelle [GAG]	ALAT 5 RHC, Pau
	3849	Aérospatiale SA.342M Gazelle [GAH]	ALAT 5 RHC, Pau
	3850	Aérospatiale SA.342M Gazelle [GAI]	ALAT 3 RHC, Etain
	3851	Aérospatiale SA.342M Gazelle [GJI]	ALAT EALAT, Le Luc
	3852	Aérospatiale SA.342M Gazelle [GNE]	ALAT 1 RHC, Phalsbourg
	3853	Aérospatiale SA.342M Gazelle [GNF]	ALAT EALAT, Le Luc
	3855	Aérospatiale SA.342M Gazelle [GJJ]	ALAT EALAT, Le Luc
	3856	Aérospatiale SA.342M Gazelle [GAJ]	ALAT 5 RHC, Pau
	3857	Aérospatiale SA.342M Gazelle [GJK]	ALAT EALAT, Le Luc
	3858	Aérospatiale SA.342M Gazelle [GNG]	ALAT
	3859	Aérospatiale SA.342M Gazelle [GAK]	ALAT 5 RHC, Pau
	3862	Aérospatiale SA.342M Gazelle [GAL] $	ALAT 1 RHC, Phalsbourg
	3863	Aérospatiale SA.342M Gazelle [GAM]	ALAT 3 RHC, Etain
	3864	Aérospatiale SA.342M Gazelle [GJL]	ALAT
	3865	Aérospatiale SA.342M Gazelle [GAN]	ALAT EALAT, Le Luc
	3866	Aérospatiale SA.342M Gazelle [GNI]	ALAT 1 RHC, Phalsbourg
	3867	Aérospatiale SA.342M Gazelle [GJM]	ALAT EALAT, Le Luc
	3868	Aérospatiale SA.342M Gazelle [GAO]	ALAT 1 RHC, Phalsbourg
	3870	Aérospatiale SA.342M Gazelle [GME]	ALAT
	3896	Aérospatiale SA.342M Gazelle [GNJ]	ALAT
	3911	Aérospatiale SA.342M Gazelle [GAP]	ALAT 1 RHC, Phalsbourg
	3921	Aérospatiale SA.342M Gazelle [GAQ]	ALAT EALAT, Le Luc
	3929	Aérospatiale SA.342M Gazelle [GJN]	ALAT EALAT, Le Luc
	3930	Aérospatiale SA.342M Gazelle [GMF]	ALAT
	3938	Aérospatiale SA.342M Gazelle [GAR]	ALAT EALAT, Le Luc
	3939	Aérospatiale SA.342M Gazelle [GMG]	ALAT
	3947	Aérospatiale SA.342M Gazelle [GAS]	ALAT 5 RHC, Pau
	3948	Aérospatiale SA.342M Gazelle [GAT]	ALAT 1 RHC, Phalsbourg
	3956	Aérospatiale SA.342M Gazelle [GNK]	ALAT

Serial	Type (code/other identity)	Owner/operator, location or fate	Notes
3957	Aérospatiale SA.342M Gazelle [GAU]	ALAT 5 RHC, Pau	
3964	Aérospatiale SA.342M Gazelle [GAV]	ALAT 3 RHC, Etain	
3965	Aérospatiale SA.342M Gazelle [GJO]	ALAT EALAT, Le Luc	
3992	Aérospatiale SA.342M Gazelle [GNM]	ALAT EALAT, Le Luc	
3996	Aérospatiale SA.342M Gazelle [GAW]	ALAT 5 RHC, Pau	
4008	Aérospatiale SA.342M Gazelle [GNN]	ALAT	
4014	Aérospatiale SA.342M Gazelle [GJP]	ALAT GAM/STAT, Valence	
4018	Aérospatiale SA.342M Gazelle [GAX]	ALAT 3 RHC, Etain	
4019	Aérospatiale SA.342M Gazelle [GAY]	ALAT 3 RHC, Etain	
4020	Aérospatiale SA.342M Gazelle [GAZ]	ALAT 1 RHC, Phalsbourg	
4022	Aérospatiale SA.342M Gazelle [GJQ]	ALAT EALAT, Le Luc	
4023	Aérospatiale SA.342M Gazelle [GMH]	ALAT ESAM, Bourges	
4026	Aérospatiale SA.342M Gazelle [GBA]	ALAT 1 RHC, Phalsbourg	
4032	Aérospatiale SA.342M Gazelle [GNO]	ALAT EALAT, Le Luc	
4034	Aérospatiale SA.342M Gazelle [GBB]	ALAT 1 RHC, Phalsbourg	
4038	Aérospatiale SA.342M Gazelle [GJR]	ALAT EALAT, Le Luc	
4039	Aérospatiale SA.342M Gazelle [GBC]	ALAT 1 RHC, Phalsbourg	
4042	Aérospatiale SA.342M Gazelle [GMB]	ALAT EALAT, Le Luc	
4047	Aérospatiale SA.342M Gazelle [GJS]	ALAT EALAT, Le Luc	
4048	Aérospatiale SA.342M Gazelle [GBD]	ALAT EALAT, Le Luc	
4049	Aérospatiale SA.342M Gazelle [GNP]	ALAT EALAT, Le Luc	
4053	Aérospatiale SA.342M Gazelle [GBE]	ALAT 1 RHC, Phalsbourg	
4059	Aérospatiale SA.342M Gazelle [GBF]	ALAT 1 RHC, Phalsbourg	
4060	Aérospatiale SA.342M Gazelle [GNQ]	ALAT EALAT, Le Luc	
4061	Aérospatiale SA.342M Gazelle [GBG]	ALAT GAM/STAT, Valence	
4065	Aérospatiale SA.342M Gazelle [GNR]	ALAT EALAT, Le Luc	
4066	Aérospatiale SA.342M Gazelle [GBH]	ALAT 3 RHC, Etain	
4067	Aérospatiale SA.342M Gazelle [GJU]	ALAT EALAT, Le Luc	
4071	Aérospatiale SA.342M Gazelle [GNS]	ALAT EHADT, Etain	
4072	Aérospatiale SA.342M Gazelle [GBI]	ALAT 3 RHC, Etain	
4078	Aérospatiale SA.342M Gazelle [GJV]	ALAT EALAT, Le Luc	
4079	Aérospatiale SA.342M Gazelle [GMC]	ALAT EALAT, Le Luc	
4083	Aérospatiale SA.342M Gazelle [GNT]	ALAT EALAT, Le Luc	
4084	Aérospatiale SA.342M Gazelle [GBJ]	ALAT 3 RHC, Etain	
4095	Aérospatiale SA.342M Gazelle [GBL]	ALAT 5 RHC, Pau	
4096	Aérospatiale SA.342M Gazelle [GNU]	ALAT EALAT, Le Luc	
4102	Aérospatiale SA.342M Gazelle [GJW]	ALAT EALAT, Le Luc	
4103	Aérospatiale SA.342M Gazelle [GJX]	ALAT EALAT, Le Luc	
4108	Aérospatiale SA.342M Gazelle [GBM]	ALAT GAM/STAT, Valence	
4109	Aérospatiale SA.342M Gazelle [GBN]	ALAT 5 RHC, Pau	
4114	Aérospatiale SA.342M Gazelle [GBO]	ALAT EALAT, Le Luc	
4115	Aérospatiale SA.342M Gazelle [GBP]	ALAT 5 RHC, Pau	
4118	Aérospatiale SA.342M Gazelle [GNV]	ALAT EALAT, Le Luc	
4119	Aérospatiale SA.342M Gazelle [GBQ]	ALAT 5 RHC, Pau	
4120	Aérospatiale SA.342M Gazelle [GBR]	ALAT EALAT, Le Luc	
4123	Aérospatiale SA.342M Gazelle [GJY]	ALAT EALAT, Le Luc	
4124	Aérospatiale SA.342M Gazelle [GBS]	ALAT 1 RHC, Phalsbourg	
4135	Aérospatiale SA.342M Gazelle [GNW]	ALAT	
4136	Aérospatiale SA.342M Gazelle [GBT]	ALAT 1 RHC, Phalsbourg	
4140	Aérospatiale SA.342M Gazelle [GBU]	ALAT 1 RHC, Phalsbourg	
4141	Aérospatiale SA.342M Gazelle [GBV]	ALAT	
4142	Aérospatiale SA.342M Gazelle [GBW]	ALAT 5 RHC, Pau	
4143	Aérospatiale SA.342M Gazelle [GNX]	ALAT EALAT, Le Luc	
4144	Aérospatiale SA.342M Gazelle [GBX]	ALAT 1 RHC, Phalsbourg	
4145	Aérospatiale SA.342M Gazelle [GBY]	ALAT 1 RHC, Phalsbourg	
4146	Aérospatiale SA.342M Gazelle [GNY]	ALAT EALAT, Le Luc	
4151	Aérospatiale SA.342M Gazelle [GBZ]	ALAT 3 RHC, Etain	
4155	Aérospatiale SA.342M Gazelle [GCA]	ALAT 3 RHC, Etain	
4159	Aérospatiale SA.342M Gazelle [GNZ]	ALAT EALAT, Le Luc	
4160	Aérospatiale SA.342M Gazelle [GCC]	ALAT 1 RHC, Phalsbourg	
4161	Aérospatiale SA.342M Gazelle [GCD]	ALAT 1 RHC, Phalsbourg	
4162	Aérospatiale SA.342M Gazelle [GCE]	ALAT 5 RHC, Pau	

Notes	Serial	Type (code/other identity)	Owner/operator, location or fate
	4164	Aérospatiale SA.342M Gazelle [GCF]	ALAT 5 RHC, Pau
	4166	Aérospatiale SA.342M Gazelle [GJZ]	ALAT EALAT, Le Luc
	4168	Aérospatiale SA.342M Gazelle [GCG]	ALAT 5 RHC, Pau
	4171	Aérospatiale SA.342M Gazelle [GMI]	ALAT EALAT, Le Luc
	4172	Aérospatiale SA.342M Gazelle [GCH]	ALAT 5 RHC, Pau
	4175	Aérospatiale SA.342M Gazelle [GCI]	ALAT 4 RHFS, Pau
	4176	Aérospatiale SA.342M Gazelle [GKA]	ALAT EALAT, Le Luc
	4177	Aérospatiale SA.342M Gazelle [GKB]	ALAT 1 RHC, Phalsbourg
	4178	Aérospatiale SA.342M Gazelle [GOA]	ALAT EALAT, Le Luc
	4179	Aérospatiale SA.342M Gazelle [GCJ]	ALAT 3 RHC, Etain
	4180	Aérospatiale SA.342M Gazelle [GCK]	ALAT GAM/STAT, Valence
	4181	Aérospatiale SA.342M Gazelle [GCL]	ALAT 3 RHC, Etain
	4182	Aérospatiale SA.342M Gazelle [GKC]	ALAT EALAT, Le Luc
	4183	Aérospatiale SA.342M Gazelle [GOB]	ALAT EALAT, Le Luc
	4184	Aérospatiale SA.342M Gazelle [GOC]	ALAT 1 RHC, Phalsbourg
	4185	Aérospatiale SA.342M Gazelle [GKD]	ALAT 3 RHC, Etain
	4186	Aérospatiale SA.342M Gazelle [GCM]	ALAT 1 RHC, Phalsbourg
	4187	Aérospatiale SA.342M Gazelle [GKE]	ALAT EALAT, Le Luc
	4189	Aérospatiale SA.342M Gazelle [GCN]	ALAT 4 RHFS, Pau
	4190	Aérospatiale SA.342M Gazelle [GMJ]	ALAT EALAT, Le Luc
	4191	Aérospatiale SA.342M Gazelle [GCO]	ALAT 4 RHFS, Pau
	4192	Aérospatiale SA.342M Gazelle [GOD]	ALAT
	4194	Aérospatiale SA.342M Gazelle [GMD]	ALAT EALAT, Le Luc
	4195	Aérospatiale SA.342M Gazelle [GCP]	ALAT 3 RHC, Etain
	4198	Aérospatiale SA.342M Gazelle [GCQ]	ALAT 3 RHC, Etain
	4201	Aérospatiale SA.342M Gazelle [GMK]	ALAT EALAT, Le Luc
	4205	Aérospatiale SA.342L-1 Gazelle [GEA]	ALAT EALAT, Le Luc
	4206	Aérospatiale SA.342L-1 Gazelle [GEB]	ALAT EALAT, Le Luc
	4207	Aérospatiale SA.342L-1, Gazelle [GEC]	ALAT 3 RHC, Etain
	4208	Aérospatiale SA.342L-1 Gazelle [GED]	ALAT GAM/STAT, Valence
	4209	Aérospatiale SA.342L-1 Gazelle [GEE]	ALAT EALAT, Le Luc
	4210	Aérospatiale SA.342L-1 Gazelle [GEF]	ALAT 1 RHC, Phalsbourg
	4211	Aérospatiale SA.342L-1 Gazelle [GEG]	ALAT 5 RHC, Pau
	4212	Aérospatiale SA.342L-1 Gazelle [GEH]	ALAT ESAM, Bourges
	4214	Aérospatiale SA.342L-1 Gazelle [GEI]	ALAT EALAT, Le Luc
	4215	Aérospatiale SA.342L-1 Gazelle [GEJ]	ALAT 5 RHC, Pau
	4216	Aérospatiale SA.342L-1 Gazelle [GEK]	ALAT GAM/STAT, Valence
	4217	Aérospatiale SA.342L-1 Gazelle [GEL]	ALAT 1 RHC, Phalsbourg
	4218	Aérospatiale SA.342L-1 Gazelle [GEM]	ALAT 1 RHC, Phalsbourg
	4219	Aérospatiale SA.342L-1 Gazelle [GEN]	ALAT 4 RHFS, Pau
	4220	Aérospatiale SA.342L-1 Gazelle [GEO]	ALAT 1 RHC, Phalsbourg
	4221	Aérospatiale SA.342L-1 Gazelle [GEP]	ALAT EALAT, Le Luc
	4222	Aérospatiale SA.342L-1 Gazelle [GEQ]	ALAT EALAT, Le Luc
	4223	Aérospatiale SA.342L-1 Gazelle [GER]	ALAT 3 RHC, Etain
	4224	Aérospatiale SA.342L-1 Gazelle [GES]	ALAT 1 RHC, Phalsbourg
	4225	Aérospatiale SA.342L-1 Gazelle [GET]	ALAT GAM/STAT, Valence
	4226	Aérospatiale SA.342L-1 Gazelle [GEU]	ALAT GAM/STAT, Valence
	4227	Aérospatiale SA.342L-1 Gazelle [GEV]	ALAT 1 RHC, Phalsbourg
	4228	Aérospatiale SA.342L-1 Gazelle [GEW]	ALAT 1 RHC, Phalsbourg
	4229	Aérospatiale SA.342L-1 Gazelle [GEX]	ALAT 4 RHFS, Pau
	4230	Aérospatiale SA.342L-1 Gazelle [GEY]	ALAT GAM/STAT, Valence
	4231	Aérospatiale SA.342L-1 Gazelle [GEZ]	ALAT 5 RHC, Pau
	4232	Aérospatiale SA.342L-1 Gazelle [GFA]	ALAT EALAT, Le Luc
	4233	Aérospatiale SA.342L-1 Gazelle [GFB]	ALAT 3 RHC, Etain
	4234	Aérospatiale SA.342L-1 Gazelle [GFC]	ALAT
	2252	Aérospatiale AS.532UL Cougar [CGA]	ALAT GAM/STAT, Valence
	2266	Aérospatiale AS.532UL Cougar [CGB]	ALAT 5 RHC, Pau
	2267	Aérospatiale AS.532UL Cougar [CGC]	ALAT 4 RHFS, Pau
	2271	Aérospatiale AS.532UL Cougar [CGD]	ALAT 4 RHFS, Pau
	2272	Aérospatiale AS.532UL Cougar [CGE]	ALAT GAM/STAT, Valence
	2273	Aérospatiale AS.532UL Cougar [CGF]	ALAT 1 RHC, Phalsbourg
	2282	Aérospatiale AS.532UL Cougar [CGG]	ALAT

Serial	Type (code/other identity)	Owner/operator, location or fate	Notes
2285	Aérospatiale AS.532UL Cougar [CGH]	ALAT	
2290	Aérospatiale AS.532UL Cougar [CGI]	ALAT 4 RHFS, Pau	
2293	Aérospatiale AS.532UL Cougar [CGJ]	ALAT 4 RHFS, Pau	
2299	Aérospatiale AS.532UL Cougar [CGK]	ALAT 4 RHFS, Pau	
2300	Aérospatiale AS.532UL Cougar [CGL]	ALAT 1 RHC, Phalsbourg	
2301	Aérospatiale AS.532UL Cougar [CGM]	ALAT 1 RHC, Phalsbourg	
2303	Aérospatiale AS.532UL Cougar [CGN]	ALAT 1 RHC, Phalsbourg	
2316	Aérospatiale AS.532UL Cougar [CGO]	ALAT 4 RHFS, Pau	
2323	Aérospatiale AS.532UL Cougar [CGQ]	ALAT 4 RHFS, Pau	
2324	Aérospatiale AS.532UL Cougar [CGR]	ALAT 4 RHFS, Pau	
2325	Aérospatiale AS.532UL Cougar [CGS]	ALAT	
2327	Aérospatiale AS.532UL Cougar [CGT]	ALAT	
2331	Aérospatiale AS.532UL Cougar [CGU]	ALAT	
2336	Aérospatiale AS.532UL Cougar [CGV]	ALAT 4 RHFS, Pau	
2342	Aérospatiale AS.532UL Cougar [CHA]	ALAT	
2369	Aérospatiale AS.532UL Cougar [CHB]	ALAT	
2375	Aérospatiale AS.532UL Cougar [CHC]	ALAT	
2443	Aérospatiale AS.532UL Cougar [CGW]	ALAT	
2446	Aérospatiale AS.532UL Cougar [CGX]	ALAT 1 RHC, Phalsbourg	
2001	Eurocopter EC.665 Tigre HAP [BHH]	ALAT EFA, Le Luc	
2002	Eurocopter EC.665 Tigre HAP [BHI]	ALAT EFA, Le Luc	
2003	Eurocopter EC.665 Tigre HAP [BHJ]	ALAT 5 RHC, Pau	
2004	Eurocopter EC.665 Tigre HAP [BHK]	ALAT EFA, Le Luc	
2006	Eurocopter EC.665 Tigre HAP [BHL]	ALAT EFA, Le Luc	
2009	Eurocopter EC.665 Tigre HAP [BHB]	ALAT EFA, Le Luc	
2010	Eurocopter EC.665 Tigre HAP [BHA]	ALAT EFA, Le Luc	
2011	Eurocopter EC.665 Tigre HAP [BHM]	ALAT 5 RHC, Pau	
2012	Eurocopter EC.665 Tigre HAP [BHT]	ALAT GAM/STAT, Valence	
2013	Eurocopter EC.665 Tigre HAP [BHC]	ALAT GAM/STAT, Valence	
2015	Eurocopter EC.665 Tigre HAP [BHD]	ALAT 5 RHC, Pau	
2016	Eurocopter EC.665 Tigre HAP [BIA]	Airbus Helicopters, Marseille	
2018	Eurocopter EC.665 Tigre HAP [BHE]	ALAT 5 RHC, Pau	
2019	Eurocopter EC.665 Tigre HAP [BHF]	ALAT 5 RHC, Pau	
2021	Eurocopter EC.665 Tigre HAP [BHN] $	ALAT EFA, Le Luc	
2022	Eurocopter EC.665 Tigre HAP [BHG]	ALAT 5 RHC, Pau	
2023	Eurocopter EC.665 Tigre HAP [BHP]	ALAT 5 RHC, Pau	
2024	Eurocopter EC.665 Tigre HAP [BHO]	ALAT 5 RHC, Pau	
2025	Eurocopter EC.665 Tigre HAP [BHQ]	ALAT 5 RHC, Pau	
2026	Eurocopter EC.665 Tigre HAP [BHR]	ALAT GAM/STAT, Valence	
2027	Eurocopter EC.665 Tigre HAP [BHS]	ALAT 5 RHC, Pau	
2028	Eurocopter EC.665 Tigre HAP [BHU]	ALAT 5 RHC, Pau	
2029	Eurocopter EC.665 Tigre HAP [BHV]	ALAT 5 RHC, Pau	
2030	Eurocopter EC.665 Tigre HAP [BHW]	ALAT	
2031	Eurocopter EC.665 Tigre HAP [BHX]	ALAT EFA, Le Luc	
2032	Eurocopter EC.665 Tigre HAP [BHY]	Withdrawn from use	
2033	Eurocopter EC.665 Tigre HAP [BHZ]	ALAT 5 RHC, Pau	
2034	Eurocopter EC.665 Tigre HAP [BIB]	ALAT EFA, Le Luc	
2035	Eurocopter EC.665 Tigre HAP [BIC]	ALAT 4 RHFS, Pau	
2036	Eurocopter EC.665 Tigre HAP [BID]	Withdrawn from use	
2037	Eurocopter EC.665 Tigre HAP [BIE]	ALAT 5 RHC, Pau	
2038	Eurocopter EC.665 Tigre HAP	Airbus Helicopters, Marseille	
2039	Eurocopter EC.665 Tigre HAP [BIG]	ALAT	
2040	Eurocopter EC.665 Tigre HAP [BIH]	ALAT 5 RHC, Pau	
2041	Eurocopter EC.665 Tigre HAP [BII]	ALAT	
2042	Eurocopter EC.665 Tigre HAP [BIJ]	ALAT 5 RHC, Pau	
2043	Eurocopter EC.665 Tigre HAP [BIK]	ALAT 5 RHC, Pau	
2044	Eurocopter EC.665 Tigre HAP [BIL]	ALAT GAM/STAT, Valence	
2045	Eurocopter EC.665 Tigre HAP [BIM]	ALAT EFA, Le Luc	
2046	Eurocopter EC.665 Tigre HAP [BIN]	ALAT EFA, Le Luc	
2047	Eurocopter EC.665 Tigre HAP [BIO]	ALAT (on order)	
2048	Eurocopter EC.665 Tigre HAP [BIP]	ALAT (on order)	
2049	Eurocopter EC.665 Tigre HAP [BIQ]	ALAT (on order)	

Notes	Serial	Type (code/other identity)	Owner/operator, location or fate
	2050	Eurocopter EC.665 Tigre HAP [BIR]	ALAT (on order)
	2051	Eurocopter EC.665 Tigre HAP [BIS]	ALAT (on order)
	2052	Eurocopter EC.665 Tigre HAP [BIT]	ALAT (on order)
	6001	Eurocopter EC.665 Tigre HAD [BJA]	ALAT GAM/STAT, Valence
	6002	Eurocopter EC.665 Tigre HAD [BJB]	ALAT EFA, Le Luc
	6003	Eurocopter EC.665 Tigre HAD [BJC]	ALAT EFA, Le Luc
	6004	Eurocopter EC.665 Tigre HAD [BJD]	ALAT EFA, Le Luc
	6005	Eurocopter EC.665 Tigre HAD [BJE]	ALAT EFA, Le Luc
	6006	Eurocopter EC.665 Tigre HAD [BJF]	ALAT 1 RHC, Phalsbourg
	6007	Eurocopter EC.665 Tigre HAD [BJG]	ALAT 1 RHC, Phalsbourg
	6008	Eurocopter EC.665 Tigre HAD [BJH]	ALAT (on order)
	6009	Eurocopter EC.665 Tigre HAD [BJI]	ALAT (on order)
	6010	Eurocopter EC.665 Tigre HAD [BJJ]	ALAT (on order)
	6011	Eurocopter EC.665 Tigre HAD [BJK]	ALAT (on order)
	6012	Eurocopter EC.665 Tigre HAD [BJL]	ALAT (on order)
	6013	Eurocopter EC.665 Tigre HAD [BJM]	ALAT (on order)
	6014	Eurocopter EC.665 Tigre HAD [BJN]	ALAT (on order)
	6015	Eurocopter EC.665 Tigre HAD [BJO]	ALAT
	6016	Eurocopter EC.665 Tigre HAD [BJP]	ALAT (on order)
	6017	Eurocopter EC.665 Tigre HAD [BJQ]	ALAT (on order)
	6018	Eurocopter EC.665 Tigre HAD [BJR]	ALAT (on order)
	6019	Eurocopter EC.665 Tigre HAD [BJS]	ALAT (on order)
	6020	Eurocopter EC.665 Tigre HAD [BJT]	ALAT (on order)
	6021	Eurocopter EC.665 Tigre HAD [BJU]	ALAT (on order)
	6022	Eurocopter EC.665 Tigre HAD	ALAT (on order)
	6023	Eurocopter EC.665 Tigre HAD	ALAT (on order)
	6024	Eurocopter EC.665 Tigre HAD	ALAT (on order)
	6025	Eurocopter EC.665 Tigre HAD	ALAT (on order)
	6026	Eurocopter EC.665 Tigre HAD	ALAT (on order)
	6027	Eurocopter EC.665 Tigre HAD	ALAT (on order)
	6028	Eurocopter EC.665 Tigre HAD	ALAT (on order)
	6029	Eurocopter EC.665 Tigre HAD	ALAT (on order)
	6030	Eurocopter EC.665 Tigre HAD	ALAT (on order)
	6031	Eurocopter EC.665 Tigre HAD	ALAT (on order)
	2611	Eurocopter EC.725AP Caracal [CAA]	ALAT 4 RHFS, Pau
	2628	Eurocopter EC.725AP Caracal [CAB]	ALAT GIH, Cazaux
	2630	Eurocopter EC.725AP Caracal [CAC]	ALAT 4 RHFS, Pau
	2631	Eurocopter EC.725AP Caracal [CAD]	ALAT 4 RHFS, Pau
	2633	Eurocopter EC.725AP Caracal [CAE]	ALAT 4 RHFS, Pau
	2638	Eurocopter EC.725AP Caracal [CAF]	ALAT GIH, Cazaux
	2640	Eurocopter EC.725AP Caracal [CAG]	ALAT GIH, Cazaux
	2642	Eurocopter EC.725AP Caracal [CAH]	ALAT GIH, Cazaux
	1239	NH Industries NH.90-TTH [EAA]	ALAT CFIA NH.90, Le Luc
	1256	NH Industries NH.90-TTH [EAB]	ALAT GAM/STAT, Valence
	1271	NH Industries NH.90-TTH [EAC]	ALAT CFIA NH.90, Le Luc
	1273	NH Industries NH.90-TTH [EAD]	ALAT 1 RHC, Phalsbourg
	1290	NH Industries NH.90-TTH [EAE]	ALAT CFIA NH.90, Le Luc
	1291	NH Industries NH.90-TTH [EAF]	ALAT CFIA NH.90, Le Luc
	1292	NH Industries NH.90-TTH [EAG]	ALAT 1 RHC, Phalsbourg
	1293	NH Industries NH.90-TTH [EAH]	ALAT CFIA NH.90, Le Luc
	1294	NH Industries NH.90-TTH [EAI]	ALAT 1 RHC, Phalsbourg
	1295	NH Industries NH.90-TTH [EAJ]	ALAT 1 RHC, Phalsbourg
	1306	NH Industries NH.90-TTH [EAK]	ALAT
	1307	NH Industries NH.90-TTH [EAL]	ALAT 1 RHC, Phalsbourg
	1308	NH Industries NH.90-TTH [EAM]	ALAT (on order)
	1309	NH Industries NH.90-TTH [EAN]	ALAT (on order)
	1310	NH Industries NH.90-TTH [EAO]	ALAT 1 RHC, Phalsbourg
	1311	NH Industries NH.90-TTH [EAP]	ALAT 1 RHC, Phalsbourg
	1312	NH Industries NH.90-TTH [EAQ]	ALAT 1 RHC, Phalsbourg
	1313	NH Industries NH.90-TTH [EAR]	ALAT (on order)
	1332	NH Industries NH.90-TTH [EAS]	ALAT (on order)
	1333	NH Industries NH.90-TTH [EAT]	ALAT (on order)

Serial	Type (code/other identity)	Owner/operator, location or fate	Notes
887	Pilatus PC-6B/B2-H4 Turbo Porter [MCA]	ALAT 1 GSALAT, Montauban	
888	Pilatus PC-6B/B2-H4 Turbo Porter [MCB]	ALAT 1 GSALAT, Montauban	
889	Pilatus PC-6B/B2-H4 Turbo Porter [MCC]	ALAT 1 GSALAT, Montauban	
890	Pilatus PC-6B/B2-H4 Turbo Porter [MCD]	ALAT 1 GSALAT, Montauban	
891	Pilatus PC-6B/B2-H4 Turbo Porter [MCE]	ALAT 1 GSALAT, Montauban	
99	SOCATA TBM 700A [ABO]	ALAT EAAT, Rennes	
100	SOCATA TBM 700A [ABP]	ALAT EAAT, Rennes	
136	SOCATA TBM 700A [ABR]	ALAT EAAT, Rennes	
139	SOCATA TBM 700A [ABS]	ALAT EAAT, Rennes	
156	SOCATA TBM 700B [ABT]	ALAT EAAT, Rennes	
159	SOCATA TBM 700B [ABU]	ALAT EAAT, Rennes	
160	SOCATA TBM 700B [ABV]	ALAT EAAT, Rennes	

French Government

Serial	Type (code/other identity)	Owner/operator, location or fate	Notes
JBA	Eurocopter EC.145C-1 (9008)	Gendarmerie	
JBB	Eurocopter EC.145C-1 (9014)	*Crashed 20 May 2016, Cauterets, France*	
JBC	Eurocopter EC.145C-1 (9018)	Gendarmerie	
JBD	Eurocopter EC.145C-1 (9019)	Gendarmerie	
JBE	Eurocopter EC.145C-1 (9025)	Gendarmerie	
JBF	Eurocopter EC.145C-2 (9035)	Gendarmerie	
JBG	Eurocopter EC.145C-2 (9036)	Gendarmerie	
JBH	Eurocopter EC.145C-2 (9037)	Gendarmerie	
JBI	Eurocopter EC.145C-2 (9127)	Gendarmerie	
JBJ	Eurocopter EC.145C-2 (9140)	Gendarmerie	
JBK	Eurocopter EC.145C-2 (9162)	Gendarmerie	
JBM	Eurocopter EC.145C-2 (9113)	Gendarmerie	
JBN	Eurocopter EC.145C-2 (9173)	Gendarmerie	
JBO	Eurocopter EC.145C-2 (9124)	Gendarmerie	
JBR	Eurocopter EC.145C-2 (9169)	Gendarmerie	
JBT	Eurocopter EC.145C-2 (9173)	Gendarmerie	
JCA	Aérospatiale AS.350BA Ecureuil (1028)	Gendarmerie, St Nazaire	
JCB	Aérospatiale AS.350BA Ecureuil (1574)	Gendarmerie, Bayonne	
JCD	Aérospatiale AS.350BA Ecureuil (1576)	Gendarmerie, Hyères	
JCE	Aérospatiale AS.350B-2 Ecureuil (1812)	Gendarmerie, Saint-Denis, Réunion	
JCF	Aérospatiale AS.350B-2 Ecureuil (1691)	Gendarmerie, Mayotte	
JCI	Aérospatiale AS.350B-2 Ecureuil (2222)	Gendarmerie, Pointe-à-Pitre	
JCK	Aérospatiale AS.350B-2 Ecureuil (1953)	Gendarmerie, Egletons	
JCL	Aérospatiale AS.350B-2 Ecureuil (1811)	Gendarmerie, Fort-de-France	
JCM	Aérospatiale AS.350BA Ecureuil (1952)	Gendarmerie, Rennes	
JCN	Aérospatiale AS.350BA Ecureuil (2044)	Gendarmerie, Bordeaux	
JCO	Aérospatiale AS.350BA Ecureuil (1917)	Gendarmerie, Metz	
JCP	Aérospatiale AS.350BA Ecureuil (2045)	Gendarmerie, stored Orléans	
JCQ	Aérospatiale AS.350BA Ecureuil (2057)	Gendarmerie, Dijon	
JCR	Aérospatiale AS.350BA Ecureuil (2088)	Gendarmerie, stored Orléans	
JCS	Aérospatiale AS.350B-2 Ecureuil (1575)	Gendarmerie, Cayenne	
JCT	Aérospatiale AS.350BA Ecureuil (2104)	Gendarmerie, Amiens	
JCU	Aérospatiale AS.350BA Ecureuil (2117)	Gendarmerie, Orléans	
JCV	Aérospatiale AS.350BA Ecureuil (2118)	Gendarmerie, Orléans	
JCW	Aérospatiale AS.350BA Ecureuil (2218)	Gendarmerie, Cazaux	
JCX	Aérospatiale AS.350BA Ecureuil (2219)	Gendarmerie, Tours	
JCY	Aérospatiale AS.350BA Ecureuil (2221)	Gendarmerie, Limoges	
JCZ	Aérospatiale AS.350BA Ecureuil (1467) $	Gendarmerie, Lyon	
JDA	Eurocopter EC.135T-2 (0642)	Gendarmerie	
JDB	Eurocopter EC.135T-2 (0654)	Gendarmerie	
JDC	Eurocopter EC.135T-2 (0717)	Gendarmerie, Lyon	
JDD	Eurocopter EC.135T-2 (0727)	Gendarmerie	
JDE	Eurocopter EC.135T-2 (0747)	Gendarmerie	
JDF	Eurocopter EC.135T-2 (0757)	Gendarmerie	
JDG	Eurocopter EC.135T-2 (0772)	Gendarmerie	
JDH	Eurocopter EC.135T-2 (0787)	Gendarmerie	
JDI	Eurocopter EC.135T-2 (0797)	Gendarmerie	
JDJ	Eurocopter EC.135T-2 (0806)	Gendarmerie	
JDK	Eurocopter EC.135T-2 (0857)	Gendarmerie, Toulouse/Francazal	

Notes	Serial	Type (code/other identity)	Owner/operator, location or fate
	JDL	Eurocopter EC.135T-2 (0867)	Gendarmerie
	JDM	Eurocopter EC.135T-2 (1055)	Gendarmerie
	JDN	Eurocopter EC.135T-2 (1058)	Gendarmerie
	JDO	Eurocopter EC.135T-2 (1086)	Gendarmerie, Bordeaux/Merignac
	JEB	Aérospatiale AS.350B Ecureuil (1692)	*Withdrawn from use*
	JEC	Aérospatiale AS.350B Ecureuil (1810)	*Scrapped*
	JED	Aérospatiale AS.350B-2 Ecureuil (2096)	Gendarmerie, St Nazaire
	JEE	Aérospatiale AS.350B-2 Ecureuil (2423)	Gendarmerie, Nouméa
	JEF	Aérospatiale AS.350B-2 Ecureuil (2225)	Gendarmerie, Nouméa
	F-ZBAA	Conair Turbo Firecat [22]	Sécurité Civile, Nimes/Garons
	F-ZBAB	Cessna F.406 Caravan II (0025)	Douanes Françaises, stored Bordeaux/Merignac
	F-ZBAD	Aérospatiale AS.355F-2 Twin Ecureuil	Douanes Françaises
	F-ZBAP	Conair Turbo Firecat [12]	Sécurité Civile, Nimes/Garons
	F-ZBAZ	Conair Turbo Firecat [01]	Sécurité Civile, Nimes/Garons
	F-ZBBB	Cessna F.406 Caravan II (0039)	Douanes Françaises, stored Bordeaux/Merignac
	F-ZBBN	Aérospatiale AS.350B Ecureuil	Sécurité Civile
	F-ZBCE	Cessna F.406 Caravan II (0042)	Douanes Françaises
	F-ZBCF	Cessna F.406 Caravan II (0077)	Douanes Françaises
	F-ZBCG	Cessna F.406 Caravan II (0066)	Douanes Françaises
	F-ZBCH	Cessna F.406 Caravan II (0075)	Douanes Françaises
	F-ZBCI	Cessna F.406 Caravan II (0070)	Douanes Françaises
	F-ZBCJ	Cessna F.406 Caravan II (0074)	Douanes Françaises
	F-ZBCZ	Conair Turbo Firecat [23]	Sécurité Civile, Nimes/Garons
	F-ZBEA	Aérospatiale AS.350B Ecureuil	Sécurité Civile
	F-ZBEF	Aérospatiale AS.355F-1 Twin Ecureuil	Douanes Françaises
	F-ZBEG	Canadair CL-415 [39]	Sécurité Civile, Nimes/Garons
	F-ZBEH	Conair Turbo Firecat [20]	Sécurité Civile, Nimes/Garons
	F-ZBEK	Aérospatiale AS.355F-1 Twin Ecureuil	Douanes Françaises
	F-ZBEL	Aérospatiale AS.355F-1 Twin Ecureuil	Douanes Françaises
	F-ZBEP	Cessna F.406 Caravan II (0006)	Douanes Françaises
	F-ZBES	Cessna F.406 Caravan II (0017)	Douanes Françaises
	F-ZBET	Conair Turbo Firecat [15]	Sécurité Civile, Nimes/Garons
	F-ZBEU	Canadair CL-415 [42]	Sécurité Civile, Nimes/Garons
	F-ZBEW	Conair Turbo Firecat [11] $	Sécurité Civile, Nimes/Garons
	F-ZBEY	Conair Turbo Firecat [07]	Sécurité Civile, Nimes/Garons
	F-ZBFC	Aérospatiale AS.350B-1 Ecureuil	Sécurité Civile
	F-ZBFD	Aérospatiale AS.350B-1 Ecureuil	Sécurité Civile
	F-ZBFJ	Beech Super King Air B200 [98]	Sécurité Civile, Nimes/Garons
	F-ZBFK	Beech Super King Air B200 [96]	Sécurité Civile, Nimes/Garons
	F-ZBFN	Canadair CL-415 [33]	Sécurité Civile, Nimes/Garons
	F-ZBFP	Canadair CL-415 [31]	Sécurité Civile, Nimes/Garons
	F-ZBFS	Canadair CL-415 [32] $	Sécurité Civile, Nimes/Garons
	F-ZBFV	Canadair CL-415 [37]	Sécurité Civile, Nimes/Garons
	F-ZBFW	Canadair CL-415 [38]	Sécurité Civile, Nimes/Garons
	F-ZBFX	Canadair CL-415 [34]	Sécurité Civile, Nimes/Garons
	F-ZBFY	Canadair CL-415 [35]	Sécurité Civile, Nimes/Garons
	F-ZBGA	Cessna F.406 Caravan II (0086)	Douanes Françaises
	F-ZBGD	Cessna F.406 Caravan II (0090)	Douanes Françaises
	F-ZBGE	Cessna F.406 Caravan II (0061)	Douanes Françaises
	F-ZBGF	Eurocopter EC.135T-2	Douanes Françaises
	F-ZBGG	Eurocopter EC.135T-2	Douanes Françaises
	F-ZBGH	Eurocopter EC.135T-2	Douanes Françaises
	F-ZBGI	Eurocopter EC.135T-2	Douanes Françaises
	F-ZBGJ	Eurocopter EC.135T-2	Douanes Françaises
	F-ZBGK	Hawker Beechcraft King Air B350ER (FL-682)	Douanes Francaises
	F-ZBGL	Hawker Beechcraft King Air B350ER (FL-746)	Douanes Francaises
	F-ZBGM	Hawker Beechcraft King Air B350ER (FL-752)	Douanes Francaises
	F-ZBGN	Hawker Beechcraft King Air B350ER (FL-781)	Douanes Francaises
	F-ZBGO	Hawker Beechcraft King Air B350ER (FL-800)	Douanes Francaises
	F-ZBGP	Hawker Beechcraft King Air B350ER (FL-802)	Douanes Francaises
	F-ZBGQ	Hawker Beechcraft King Air B350ER (FL-777)	Douanes Francaises
	F-ZBGR	Hawker Beechcraft King Air B350ER	Douanes Francaises (on order)

Serial	Type (code/other identity)	Owner/operator, location or fate	Notes
F-ZBMA	Conair Turbo Firecat [24]	Sécurité Civile, Nimes/Garons	
F-ZBMB	Beech Super King Air B200 [97]	Sécurité Civile, Nimes/Garons	
F-ZBMC	De Havilland Canada DHC-8Q-402MR [73] $	Sécurité Civile, Nimes/Garons	
F-ZBMD	De Havilland Canada DHC-8Q-402MR [74]	Sécurité Civile, Nimes/Garons	
F-ZBME	Canadair CL-415 [44]	Sécurité Civile, Nimes/Garons	
F-ZBMF	Canadair CL-415 [45]	Sécurité Civile, Nimes/Garons	
F-ZBMG	Canadair CL-415 [48]	Sécurité Civile, Nimes/Garons	
F-ZBPA	Eurocopter EC.145C-1	Sécurité Civile, Le Havre/Octeville	
F-ZBPD	Eurocopter EC.145C-1	Sécurité Civile, Nimes/Garons	
F-ZBPE	Eurocopter EC.145C-1	Sécurité Civile, Lyon/Bron	
F-ZBPF	Eurocopter EC.145C-1	Sécurité Civile, Montpellier	
F-ZBPG	Eurocopter EC.145C-1	Sécurité Civile, Ajaccio	
F-ZBPH	Eurocopter EC.145C-1	Sécurité Civile, Bordeaux/Merignac	
F-ZBPI	Eurocopter EC.145C-1	Sécurité Civile, Quimper	
F-ZBPJ	Eurocopter EC.145C-1	Sécurité Civile, Perpignan	
F-ZBPK	Eurocopter EC.145C-1	Sécurité Civile, Nimes/Garons	
F-ZBPM	Eurocopter EC.145C-1	Sécurité Civile, Bordeaux/Merignac	
F-ZBPN	Eurocopter EC.145C-1	Sécurité Civile, Granville	
F-ZBPO	Eurocopter EC.145C-1	Sécurité Civile, Paris/Issy-les-Molineaux	
F-ZBPP	Eurocopter EC.145C-2	Sécurité Civile, Besancon	
F-ZBPQ	Eurocopter EC.145C-2	Sécurité Civile, Quimper	
F-ZBPS	Eurocopter EC.145C-2	Sécurité Civile, Ajaccio	
F-ZBPT	Eurocopter EC.145C-2	Sécurité Civile, Clermont-Ferrand	
F-ZBPU	Eurocopter EC.145C-2	Sécurité Civile, Nimes/Garons	
F-ZBPV	Eurocopter EC.145C-2	Sécurité Civile, Le Luc	
F-ZBPW	Eurocopter EC.145C-2	Sécurité Civile, Le Touquet	
F-ZBPX	Eurocopter EC.145C-2	Sécurité Civile, Paris/Issy-les-Molineaux	
F-ZBPY	Eurocopter EC.145C-2	Sécurité Civile, Montpellier	
F-ZBPZ	Eurocopter EC.145C-2	Sécurité Civile, Annecy	
F-ZBQA	Eurocopter EC.145C-2	Sécurité Civile, Grenoble/Le Versoud	
F-ZBQB	Eurocopter EC.145C-2	Sécurité Civile, Bastia	
F-ZBQC	Eurocopter EC.145C-2	Sécurité Civile, Strasbourg/Entzheim	
F-ZBQD	Eurocopter EC.145C-2	Sécurité Civile, Nimes/Garons	
F-ZBQE	Eurocopter EC.145C-2	Sécurité Civile, Marseille	
F-ZBQF	Eurocopter EC.145C-2	Sécurité Civile, Perpignan	
F-ZBQG	Eurocopter EC.145C-2	Sécurité Civile, Annecy	
F-ZBQH	Eurocopter EC.145C-2	Sécurité Civile, Fort de France, Martinique	
F-ZBQI	Eurocopter EC.145C-2	Sécurité Civile, Lorient	
F-ZBQJ	Eurocopter EC.145C-2	Sécurité Civile, Le Raizet, Guadeloupe	
F-ZBQK	Eurocopter EC.145C-2	Sécurité Civile, Versoud	
F-ZBQL	Eurocopter EC.145C-2	Sécurité Civile, La Rochelle	

Civil operated aircraft in military use

Serial	Type (code/other identity)	Owner/operator, location or fate	Notes
F-GJDB	Dassault Falcon 20C	AVDEF, Nimes/Garons	
F-GPAA	Dassault Falcon 20ECM	AVDEF, Nimes/Garons	
F-GPAD	Dassault Falcon 20E	AVDEF, Nimes/Garons	
F-GUKA	Grob G120A-F	CATS/EPAA 00.315, Cognac	
F-GUKB	Grob G120A-F	CATS/EPAA 00.315, Cognac	
F-GUKC	Grob G120A-F	CATS/EPAA 00.315, Cognac	
F-GUKD	Grob G120A-F	CATS/EPAA 00.315, Cognac	
F-GUKE	Grob G120A-F	CATS/EPAA 00.315, Cognac	
F-GUKF	Grob G120A-F	CATS/EPAA 00.315, Cognac	
F-GUKG	Grob G120A-F	CATS/EPAA 00.315, Cognac	
F-GUKH	Grob G120A-F	CATS/EPAA 00.315, Cognac	
F-GUKI	Grob G120A-F	CATS/EPAA 00.315, Cognac	
F-GUKJ	Grob G120A-F	CATS/EPAA 00.315, Cognac	
F-GUKK	Grob G120A-F	CATS/EPAA 00.315, Cognac	
F-GUKL	Grob G120A-F	CATS/EPAA 00.315, Cognac	
F-GUKM	Grob G120A-F	CATS/EPAA 00.315, Cognac	
F-GUKN	Grob G120A-F	CATS/EPAA 00.315, Cognac	
F-GUKO	Grob G120A-F	CATS/EPAA 00.315, Cognac	
F-GUKP	Grob G120A-F	CATS/EPAA 00.315, Cognac	

Notes	Serial	Type (code/other identity)	Owner/operator, location or fate
	F-GUKR	Grob G120A-F	CATS/EPAA 00.315, Cognac
	F-GUKS	Grob G120A-F	CATS/EPAA 00.315, Cognac
	F-HAVD	BAE Jetstream 41	AVDEF, Nimes/Garons
	F-HAVF	BAE Jetstream 41	AVDEF, Nimes/Garons
	F-HGDU	Cirrus SR.20	CATS/CFAMI 05.312, Salon de Provence
	F-HKCA	Cirrus SR.22	CATS/CFAMI 05.312, Salon de Provence
	F-HKCB	Cirrus SR.20	CATS/CFAMI 05.312, Salon de Provence
	F-HKCD	Cirrus SR.20	CATS/CFAMI 05.312, Salon de Provence
	F-HKCE	Cirrus SR.20	CATS/CFAMI 05.312, Salon de Provence
	F-HKCF	Cirrus SR.22	CATS/CFAMI 05.312, Salon de Provence
	F-HKCG	Cirrus SR.20	CATS/CFAMI 05.312, Salon de Provence
	F-HKCH	Cirrus SR.20	CATS/CFAMI 05.312, Salon de Provence
	F-HKCI	Cirrus SR.22	CATS/CFAMI 05.312, Salon de Provence
	F-HKCJ	Cirrus SR.20	CATS/CFAMI 05.312, Salon de Provence
	F-HKCK	Cirrus SR.20	CATS/CFAMI 05.312, Salon de Provence
	F-HKCL	Cirrus SR.22	CATS/CFAMI 05.312, Salon de Provence
	F-HKCN	Cirrus SR.20	CATS/CFAMI 05.312, Salon de Provence
	F-HKCO	Cirrus SR.22	CATS/CFAMI 05.312, Salon de Provence
	F-HKCP	Cirrus SR.20	CATS/CFAMI 05.312, Salon de Provence
	F-HKCQ	Cirrus SR.20	CATS/CFAMI 05.312, Salon de Provence
	F-HKCR	Cirrus SR.22	CATS/CFAMI 05.312, Salon de Provence
	F-HKCS	Cirrus SR.22	CATS/CFAMI 05.312, Salon de Provence
	F-HKCT	Cirrus SR.20	CATS/CFAMI 05.312, Salon de Provence
	F-HKCU	Cirrus SR.20	CATS/CFAMI 05.312, Salon de Provence
	F-HKCV	Cirrus SR.20	CATS/CFAMI 05.312, Salon de Provence
	F-HKCX	Cirrus SR.20	CATS/CFAMI 05.312, Salon de Provence

GABON

	Serial	Type	Owner/operator
	TR-KGM	Gulfstream Aerospace G.650ER	Gabonese Government, Libreville
	TR-KPR	Boeing 777-236	Gabonese Government, Libreville
	TR-KSP	Grumman G.1159C Gulfstream IVSP	Gabonese Government, Libreville
	TR-LEX	Dassault Falcon 900EX	Gabonese Government, Libreville

GERMANY

Please note that German serials do not officially include the '+' part in them but aircraft wearing German markings are often painted with a cross in the middle, which is why it is included here.

Luftwaffe, Marineflieger & Heeresfliegertruppe (Heer)

	Serial	Type	Owner/operator
	10+23	Airbus A.310-304	Luftwaffe 1/FBS, Köln-Bonn
	10+24	Airbus A.310-304/MRTT	Luftwaffe 1/FBS, Köln-Bonn
	10+25	Airbus A.310-304/MRTT	Luftwaffe 1/FBS, Köln-Bonn
	10+26	Airbus A.310-304/MRTT	Luftwaffe 1/FBS, Köln-Bonn
	10+27	Airbus A.310-304/MRTT	Luftwaffe 1/FBS, Köln-Bonn
	14+01	Bombardier Global 5000	Luftwaffe 3/FBS, Köln-Bonn
	14+02	Bombardier Global 5000	Luftwaffe 3/FBS, Köln-Bonn
	14+03	Bombardier Global 5000	Luftwaffe 3/FBS, Köln-Bonn
	14+04	Bombardier Global 5000	Luftwaffe 3/FBS, Köln-Bonn
	15+01	Airbus A.319CJ-115X	Luftwaffe 3/FBS, Köln-Bonn
	15+02	Airbus A.319CJ-115X	Luftwaffe 3/FBS, Köln-Bonn
	16+01	Airbus A.340-313X	Luftwaffe 3/FBS, Köln-Bonn
	16+02	Airbus A.340-313X	Luftwaffe 3/FBS, Köln-Bonn
	30+01	Eurofighter EF.2000GT	Luftwaffe TLG 73 *Steinhoff*, Laage
	30+02	Eurofighter EF.2000GT	Luftwaffe TLG 74 *Molders*, Neuburg/Donau
	30+03	Eurofighter EF.2000GT	Luftwaffe TLG 74 *Molders*, Neuburg/Donau
	30+04	Eurofighter EF.2000GT	Luftwaffe TLG 31 *Boelcke*, Nörvenich
	30+05	Eurofighter EF.2000GT	Luftwaffe TLG 31 *Boelcke*, Nörvenich
	30+06	Eurofighter EF.2000GS	Luftwaffe TLG 74 *Molders*, Neuburg/Donau
	30+07	Eurofighter EF.2000GS	Luftwaffe TLG 74 *Molders*, Neuburg/Donau
	30+09	Eurofighter EF.2000GS	Luftwaffe TLG 31 *Boelcke*, Nörvenich
	30+10	Eurofighter EF.2000GT	Luftwaffe TLG 74 *Molders*, Neuburg/Donau
	30+11	Eurofighter EF.2000GS	Luftwaffe TLG 74 *Molders*, Neuburg/Donau
	30+12	Eurofighter EF.2000GS	Luftwaffe TLG 74 *Molders*, Neuburg/Donau
	30+14	Eurofighter EF.2000GT	Luftwaffe TLG 74 *Molders*, Neuburg/Donau

Serial	Type (code/other identity)	Owner/operator, location or fate	Notes
30+15	Eurofighter EF.2000GS	Luftwaffe TLG 74 *Molders*, Neuburg/Donau	
30+17	Eurofighter EF.2000GT	Luftwaffe TLG 73 *Steinhoff*, Laage	
30+20	Eurofighter EF.2000GT	Luftwaffe TLG 73 *Steinhoff*, Laage	
30+22	Eurofighter EF.2000GS	Luftwaffe TLG 74 *Boelcke*, Nörvenich	
30+23	Eurofighter EF.2000GS	Luftwaffe TLG 74 *Molders*, Neuburg/Donau	
30+24	Eurofighter EF.2000GT	Luftwaffe TLG 31 *Boelcke*, Nörvenich	
30+25	Eurofighter EF.2000GS	Luftwaffe TLG 74 *Molders*, Neuburg/Donau	
30+26	Eurofighter EF.2000GS	Luftwaffe TLG 74 *Molders*, Neuburg/Donau	
30+27	Eurofighter EF.2000GT	Luftwaffe TLG 73 *Steinhoff*, Laage	
30+28	Eurofighter EF.2000GS	Luftwaffe TLG 74 *Molders*, Neuburg/Donau	
30+29	Eurofighter EF.2000GS $	Luftwaffe TLG 74 *Molders*, Neuburg/Donau	
30+30	Eurofighter EF.2000GS	Luftwaffe TLG 74 *Molders*, Neuburg/Donau	
30+31	Eurofighter EF.2000GT	Luftwaffe TLG 31 *Boelcke*, Nörvenich	
30+32	Eurofighter EF.2000GS	Luftwaffe TLG 74 *Molders*, Neuburg/Donau	
30+33	Eurofighter EF.2000GS	Luftwaffe TLG 74 *Molders*, Neuburg/Donau	
30+35	Eurofighter EF.2000GT	Luftwaffe TLG 73 *Steinhoff*, Laage	
30+38	Eurofighter EF.2000GT	Luftwaffe TLG 73 *Steinhoff*, Laage	
30+39	Eurofighter EF.2000GS	Luftwaffe TLG 74 *Molders*, Neuburg/Donau	
30+40	Eurofighter EF.2000GS	Luftwaffe TLG 74 *Molders*, Neuburg/Donau	
30+42	Eurofighter EF.2000GT	Luftwaffe TLG 74 *Molders*, Neuburg/Donau	
30+45	Eurofighter EF.2000GS $	Luftwaffe TLG 73 *Steinhoff*, Laage	
30+46	Eurofighter EF.2000GS	Luftwaffe TLG 73 *Steinhoff*, Laage	
30+47	Eurofighter EF.2000GS	Luftwaffe TLG 71 *Richthofen*, Wittmund	
30+48	Eurofighter EF.2000GS $	Luftwaffe TLG 73 *Steinhoff*, Laage	
30+49	Eurofighter EF.2000GS	Luftwaffe TLG 73 *Steinhoff*, Laage	
30+50	Eurofighter EF.2000GS	Luftwaffe TLG 73 *Steinhoff*, Laage	
30+51	Eurofighter EF.2000GS	Luftwaffe TLG 73 *Steinhoff*, Laage	
30+52	Eurofighter EF.2000GS	Luftwaffe TLG 73 *Steinhoff*, Laage	
30+53	Eurofighter EF.2000GS	Luftwaffe TLG 31 *Boelcke*, Nörvenich	
30+54	Eurofighter EF.2000GT	Luftwaffe TLG 73 *Steinhoff*, Laage	
30+55	Eurofighter EF.2000GS	Luftwaffe TLG 73 *Steinhoff*, Laage	
30+56	Eurofighter EF.2000GS	Luftwaffe TLG 73 *Steinhoff*, Laage	
30+57	Eurofighter EF.2000GS	Luftwaffe TLG 31 *Boelcke*, Nörvenich	
30+58	Eurofighter EF.2000GS	Luftwaffe TLG 31 *Boelcke*, Nörvenich	
30+59	Eurofighter EF.2000GT	Luftwaffe TLG 73 *Steinhoff*, Laage	
30+60	Eurofighter EF.2000GS	Luftwaffe TLG 73 *Steinhoff*, Laage	
30+61	Eurofighter EF.2000GS	Luftwaffe TLG 74 *Molders*, Neuburg/Donau	
30+62	Eurofighter EF.2000GS	Luftwaffe TLG 74 *Molders*, Neuburg/Donau	
30+63	Eurofighter EF.2000GS	Luftwaffe TLG 74 *Molders*, Neuburg/Donau	
30+64	Eurofighter EF.2000GS	Luftwaffe TLG 73 *Steinhoff*, Laage	
30+65	Eurofighter EF.2000GS	Luftwaffe TLG 31 *Boelcke*, Nörvenich	
30+66	Eurofighter EF.2000GS	Luftwaffe TLG 71 *Richthofen*, Wittmund	
30+67	Eurofighter EF.2000GT	Luftwaffe TLG 73 *Steinhoff*, Laage	
30+68	Eurofighter EF.2000GS $	Luftwaffe TLG 74 *Molders*, Neuburg/Donau	
30+69	Eurofighter EF.2000GS	Luftwaffe TLG 74 *Molders*, Neuburg/Donau	
30+70	Eurofighter EF.2000GS	Luftwaffe TLG 73 *Steinhoff*, Laage	
30+71	Eurofighter EF.2000GT	Luftwaffe TLG 73 *Steinhoff*, Laage	
30+72	Eurofighter EF.2000GS	Luftwaffe TLG 74 *Molders*, Neuburg/Donau	
30+73	Eurofighter EF.2000GS	Luftwaffe TLG 73 *Steinhoff*, Laage	
30+74	Eurofighter EF.2000GS	Luftwaffe TLG 74 *Molders*, Neuburg/Donau	
30+75	Eurofighter EF.2000GS $	Luftwaffe TLG 71 *Richthofen*, Wittmund	
30+76	Eurofighter EF.2000GS	Luftwaffe TLG 74 *Molders*, Neuburg/Donau	
30+77	Eurofighter EF.2000GT	Luftwaffe TLG 73 *Steinhoff*, Laage	
30+78	Eurofighter EF.2000GS	Luftwaffe TLG 71 *Richthofen*, Wittmund	
30+79	Eurofighter EF.2000GS	Luftwaffe TLG 73 *Steinhoff*, Laage	
30+80	Eurofighter EF.2000GS	Luftwaffe TLG 74 *Molders*, Neuburg/Donau	
30+81	Eurofighter EF.2000GS	Luftwaffe TLG 73 *Steinhoff*, Laage	
30+82	Eurofighter EF.2000GS	Luftwaffe TLG 31 *Boelcke*, Nörvenich	
30+83	Eurofighter EF.2000GS	Luftwaffe TLG 31 *Boelcke*, Nörvenich	
30+84	Eurofighter EF.2000GT	Luftwaffe TLG 31 *Boelcke*, Nörvenich	
30+85	Eurofighter EF.2000GS	Luftwaffe TLG 71 *Richthofen*, Wittmund	
30+86	Eurofighter EF.2000GS	Luftwaffe TLG 71 *Richthofen*, Wittmund	

Notes	Serial	Type (code/other identity)	Owner/operator, location or fate
	30+87	Eurofighter EF.2000GS $	Luftwaffe TLG 71 *Richthofen*, Wittmund
	30+88	Eurofighter EF.2000GS	Luftwaffe TLG 74 *Molders*, Neuburg/Donau
	30+89	Eurofighter EF.2000GS	Luftwaffe TLG 71 *Richthofen*, Wittmund
	30+90	Eurofighter EF.2000GS $	Luftwaffe TLG 71 *Richthofen*, Wittmund
	30+91	Eurofighter EF.2000GS	Luftwaffe TLG 31 *Boelcke*, Nörvenich
	30+92	Eurofighter EF.2000GS	Luftwaffe TLG 73 *Steinhoff*, Laage
	30+93	Eurofighter EF.2000GS	Luftwaffe TLG 74 *Molders*, Neuburg/Donau
	30+94	Eurofighter EF.2000GS	Luftwaffe TLG 74 *Molders*, Neuburg/Donau
	30+95	Eurofighter EF.2000GT	Luftwaffe TLG 74 *Molders*, Neuburg/Donau
	30+96	Eurofighter EF.2000GS	Luftwaffe TLG 31 *Boelcke*, Nörvenich
	30+97	Eurofighter EF.2000GS	Luftwaffe TLG 31 *Boelcke*, Nörvenich
	30+98	Eurofighter EF.2000GS	Luftwaffe TLG 31 *Boelcke*, Nörvenich
	30+99	Eurofighter EF.2000GT	Luftwaffe TLG 73 *Steinhoff*, Laage
	31+00	Eurofighter EF.2000GS $	Luftwaffe TLG 31 *Boelcke*, Nörvenich
	31+01	Eurofighter EF.2000GS	Luftwaffe TLG 71 *Richthofen*, Wittmund
	31+02	Eurofighter EF.2000GS	Luftwaffe TLG 71 *Richthofen*, Wittmund
	31+03	Eurofighter EF.2000GT	EADS, Manching
	31+04	Eurofighter EF.2000GS	Luftwaffe TLG 71 *Richthofen*, Wittmund
	31+05	Eurofighter EF.2000GS	Luftwaffe TLG 31 *Boelcke*, Nörvenich
	31+06	Eurofighter EF.2000GS $	Luftwaffe TLG 31 *Boelcke*, Nörvenich
	31+07	Eurofighter EF.2000GS	Luftwaffe TLG 71 *Richthofen*, Wittmund
	31+08	Eurofighter EF.2000GS	Luftwaffe TLG 31 *Boelcke*, Nörvenich
	31+09	Eurofighter EF.2000GS	Luftwaffe TLG 31 *Boelcke*, Nörvenich
	31+10	Eurofighter EF.2000GS	Luftwaffe TLG 31 *Boelcke*, Nörvenich
	31+11	Eurofighter EF.2000GS	Luftwaffe TLG 74 *Molders*, Neuburg/Donau
	31+12	Eurofighter EF.2000GS	Luftwaffe TLG 31 *Boelcke*, Nörvenich
	31+13	Eurofighter EF.2000GT	Luftwaffe TLG 73 *Steinhoff*, Laage
	31+14	Eurofighter EF.2000GS	Luftwaffe TAubZLwSüd, Kaufbeuren
	31+15	Eurofighter EF.2000GS	Luftwaffe TAubZLwSüd, Kaufbeuren
	31+16	Eurofighter EF.2000GS	Luftwaffe TLG 73 *Steinhoff*, Laage
	31+17	Eurofighter EF.2000GS	Luftwaffe TLG 73 *Steinhoff*, Laage
	31+18	Eurofighter EF.2000GS	Luftwaffe TLG 73 *Steinhoff*, Laage
	31+19	Eurofighter EF.2000GS	Luftwaffe TLG 73 *Steinhoff*, Laage
	31+20	Eurofighter EF.2000GS	Luftwaffe TLG 73 *Steinhoff*, Laage
	31+21	Eurofighter EF.2000GS	Luftwaffe TLG 73 *Steinhoff*, Laage
	31+22	Eurofighter EF.2000GS	Luftwaffe TLG 73 *Steinhoff*, Laage
	31+24	Eurofighter EF.2000GT	Luftwaffe
	31+25	Eurofighter EF.2000GT	Luftwaffe TLG 31 *Boelcke*, Nörvenich
	31+26	Eurofighter EF.2000GT	Luftwaffe
	31+27	Eurofighter EF.2000GT	Luftwaffe
	31+28	Eurofighter EF.2000GT	Luftwaffe
	31+29	Eurofighter EF.2000GS	Luftwaffe TLG 31 *Boelcke*, Nörvenich
	31+30	Eurofighter EF.2000GS	Luftwaffe TLG 31 *Boelcke*, Nörvenich
	31+31	Eurofighter EF.2000GS $	Luftwaffe TLG 31 *Boelcke*, Nörvenich
	31+32	Eurofighter EF.2000GS $	Luftwaffe TLG 31 *Boelcke*, Nörvenich
	31+33	Eurofighter EF.2000GS	Luftwaffe TLG 31 *Boelcke*, Nörvenich
	31+34	Eurofighter EF.2000GS	Luftwaffe TLG 31 *Boelcke*, Nörvenich
	31+35	Eurofighter EF.2000GS	Luftwaffe TLG 31 *Boelcke*, Nörvenich
	31+36	Eurofighter EF.2000GS	Luftwaffe TLG 31 *Boelcke*, Nörvenich
	31+37	Eurofighter EF.2000GS	Luftwaffe TLG 31 *Boelcke*, Nörvenich
	31+38	Eurofighter EF.2000GS	Luftwaffe TLG 31 *Boelcke*, Nörvenich
	31+39	Eurofighter EF.2000GS	Luftwaffe (on order)
	31+40	Eurofighter EF.2000GS	Luftwaffe TLG 31 *Boelcke*, Nörvenich
	31+41	Eurofighter EF.2000GS	Luftwaffe (on order)
	31+42	Eurofighter EF.2000GS	Luftwaffe (on order)
	31+43	Eurofighter EF.2000GS	Luftwaffe (on order)
	31+44	Eurofighter EF.2000GS	Luftwaffe (on order)
	31+45	Eurofighter EF.2000GS $	Luftwaffe (on order)
	31+46	Eurofighter EF.2000GS	Luftwaffe (on order)
	31+47	Eurofighter EF.2000GS	Luftwaffe (on order)
	31+48	Eurofighter EF.2000GS	Luftwaffe (on order)
	31+49	Eurofighter EF.2000GS	Luftwaffe (on order)

Serial	Type (code/other identity)	Owner/operator, location or fate	Notes
31+50	Eurofighter EF.2000GS	Luftwaffe (on order)	
31+51	Eurofighter EF.2000GS	Luftwaffe (on order)	
31+52	Eurofighter EF.2000GS	Luftwaffe (on order)	
31+53	Eurofighter EF.2000GS	Luftwaffe (on order)	
43+01	Panavia Tornado IDS(T) $	Luftwaffe TLG 33, Büchel	
43+07	Panavia Tornado IDS(T)	Luftwaffe TLG 51 Immelmann, Schleswig/Jagel	
43+10	Panavia Tornado IDS(T)	Luftwaffe TLG 33, Büchel	
43+25	Panavia Tornado IDS	Luftwaffe TLG 33, Büchel	
43+29	Panavia Tornado IDS(T)	Luftwaffe GAFFTC, Holloman AFB, USA	
43+32	Panavia Tornado IDS	Scrapped	
43+34	Panavia Tornado IDS	Luftwaffe TAubZLwSüd, Kaufbeuren	
43+38	Panavia Tornado IDS	Luftwaffe TLG 33, Büchel	
43+42	Panavia Tornado IDS(T)	Luftwaffe GAFFTC, Holloman AFB, USA	
43+45	Panavia Tornado IDS(T)	Luftwaffe TLG 51 Immelmann, Schleswig/Jagel	
43+46	Panavia Tornado IDS	Luftwaffe TLG 33, Büchel	
43+48	Panavia Tornado IDS	Luftwaffe TLG 33, Büchel	
43+50	Panavia Tornado IDS	Luftwaffe TLG 33, Büchel	
43+52	Panavia Tornado IDS	Luftwaffe TLG 33, Büchel	
43+54	Panavia Tornado IDS	Luftwaffe TAubZLwSüd, Kaufbeuren	
43+59	Panavia Tornado IDS	Luftwaffe TAubZLwSüd, Kaufbeuren	
43+92	Panavia Tornado IDS(T)	Luftwaffe GAFFTC, Holloman AFB, USA	
43+94	Panavia Tornado IDS(T)	Luftwaffe GAFFTC, Holloman AFB, USA	
43+97	Panavia Tornado IDS(T)	Luftwaffe TLG 51 Immelmann, Schleswig/Jagel	
43+98	Panavia Tornado IDS	Luftwaffe TLG 33, Büchel	
44+06	Panavia Tornado IDS	Luftwaffe GAFFTC, Holloman AFB, USA	
44+16	Panavia Tornado IDS(T)	Luftwaffe TLG 51 Immelmann, Schleswig/Jagel	
44+17	Panavia Tornado IDS	Luftwaffe TLG 51 Immelmann, Schleswig/Jagel	
44+21	Panavia Tornado IDS	Luftwaffe TLG 51 Immelmann, Schleswig/Jagel	
44+23	Panavia Tornado IDS	Luftwaffe TLG 33, Büchel	
44+29	Panavia Tornado IDS	Luftwaffe GAFFTC, Holloman AFB, USA	
44+30	Panavia Tornado IDS	Luftwaffe GAFFTC, Holloman AFB, USA	
44+33	Panavia Tornado IDS	Luftwaffe TLG 33, Büchel	
44+34	Panavia Tornado IDS	Luftwaffe GAFFTC, Holloman AFB, USA	
44+58	Panavia Tornado IDS	Luftwaffe TLG 33, Büchel	
44+61	Panavia Tornado IDS $	Luftwaffe TLG 33, Büchel	
44+64	Panavia Tornado IDS	Luftwaffe TLG 33, Büchel	
44+65	Panavia Tornado IDS	Luftwaffe TLG 33, Büchel	
44+69	Panavia Tornado IDS	Luftwaffe TLG 51 Immelmann, Schleswig/Jagel	
44+70	Panavia Tornado IDS	Luftwaffe TLG 33, Büchel	
44+72	Panavia Tornado IDS(T)	Luftwaffe TLG 33, Büchel	
44+73	Panavia Tornado IDS(T)	Luftwaffe WTD 61, Ingolstadt	
44+75	Panavia Tornado IDS(T)	Luftwaffe TLG 51 Immelmann, Schleswig/Jagel	
44+78	Panavia Tornado IDS	Luftwaffe TLG 33, Büchel	
44+79	Panavia Tornado IDS	Luftwaffe TLG 33, Büchel	
44+90	Panavia Tornado IDS	Luftwaffe TLG 51 Immelmann, Schleswig/Jagel	
45+00	Panavia Tornado IDS	Luftwaffe GAFFTC, Holloman AFB, USA	
45+08	Panavia Tornado IDS	Luftwaffe GAFFTC, Holloman AFB, USA	
45+09	Panavia Tornado IDS	Luftwaffe TLG 33, Büchel	
45+13	Panavia Tornado IDS(T)	Luftwaffe GAFFTC, Holloman AFB, USA	
45+14	Panavia Tornado IDS(T)	Luftwaffe GAFFTC, Holloman AFB, USA	
45+16	Panavia Tornado IDS(T)	Luftwaffe GAFFTC, Holloman AFB, USA	
45+19	Panavia Tornado IDS	Luftwaffe TLG 33, Büchel	
45+20	Panavia Tornado IDS	Luftwaffe TLG 33, Büchel	
45+22	Panavia Tornado IDS	Luftwaffe TLG 51 Immelmann, Schleswig/Jagel	
45+23	Panavia Tornado IDS	Luftwaffe TLG 33, Büchel	
45+28	Panavia Tornado IDS	Luftwaffe TLG 33, Büchel	
45+35	Panavia Tornado IDS	Luftwaffe TLG 33, Büchel	
45+39	Panavia Tornado IDS	Luftwaffe TLG 33, Büchel	
45+50	Panavia Tornado IDS	Luftwaffe TLG 51 Immelmann, Schleswig/Jagel	
45+53	Panavia Tornado IDS	Luftwaffe TAubZLwSüd, Kaufbeuren	
45+54	Panavia Tornado IDS	Luftwaffe GAFFTC, Holloman AFB, USA	
45+57	Panavia Tornado IDS	Luftwaffe TLG 33, Büchel	

Notes	Serial	Type (code/other identity)	Owner/operator, location or fate
	45+59	Panavia Tornado IDS	Luftwaffe TLG 33, Büchel
	45+60	Panavia Tornado IDS(T)	Luftwaffe TLG 51 *Immelmann*, Schleswig/Jagel
	45+61	Panavia Tornado IDS(T)	Luftwaffe TLG 51 *Immelmann*, Schleswig/Jagel
	45+64	Panavia Tornado IDS	Luftwaffe TLG 33, Büchel
	45+66	Panavia Tornado IDS	Luftwaffe TLG 33, Büchel
	45+67	Panavia Tornado IDS	Luftwaffe TLG 33, Büchel
	45+68	Panavia Tornado IDS	Luftwaffe TLG 33, Büchel
	45+69	Panavia Tornado IDS	Luftwaffe GAFFTC, Holloman AFB, USA
	45+70	Panavia Tornado IDS(T)	Luftwaffe TLG 51 *Immelmann*, Schleswig/Jagel
	45+71	Panavia Tornado IDS	Luftwaffe TLG 33, Büchel
	45+72	Panavia Tornado IDS	Luftwaffe
	45+74	Panavia Tornado IDS	Luftwaffe TAubZLwSüd, Kaufbeuren
	45+76	Panavia Tornado IDS	Luftwaffe TLG 33, Büchel
	45+77	Panavia Tornado IDS(T)	Luftwaffe TLG 51 *Immelmann*, Schleswig/Jagel
	45+84	Panavia Tornado IDS	Luftwaffe TLG 33, Büchel
	45+85	Panavia Tornado IDS	Luftwaffe TLG 33, Büchel
	45+88	Panavia Tornado IDS	Luftwaffe TLG 33, Büchel
	45+90	Panavia Tornado IDS	Luftwaffe TLG 33, Büchel
	45+92	Panavia Tornado IDS	Luftwaffe TLG 33, Büchel
	45+93	Panavia Tornado IDS	Luftwaffe TLG 33, Büchel
	45+94	Panavia Tornado IDS	Luftwaffe TLG 33, Büchel
	46+00	Panavia Tornado IDS(T)	Luftwaffe GAFFTC, Holloman AFB, USA
	46+02	Panavia Tornado IDS	Luftwaffe TLG 33, Büchel
	46+05	Panavia Tornado IDS(T)	Luftwaffe GAFFTC, Holloman AFB, USA
	46+07	Panavia Tornado IDS(T)	Luftwaffe TLG 33, Büchel
	46+09	Panavia Tornado IDS(T)	Luftwaffe GAFFTC, Holloman AFB, USA
	46+10	Panavia Tornado IDS	Luftwaffe TLG 33, Büchel
	46+11	Panavia Tornado IDS	Luftwaffe TLG 33, Büchel
	46+15	Panavia Tornado IDS	Luftwaffe TLG 33, Büchel
	46+18	Panavia Tornado IDS	Luftwaffe TLG 33, Büchel
	46+20	Panavia Tornado IDS	Luftwaffe TLG 51 *Immelmann*, Schleswig/Jagel
	46+21	Panavia Tornado IDS	Luftwaffe TLG 33, Büchel
	46+22	Panavia Tornado IDS	Luftwaffe TLG 33, Büchel
	46+23	Panavia Tornado ECR	Luftwaffe TLG 51 *Immelmann*, Schleswig/Jagel
	46+24	Panavia Tornado ECR	Luftwaffe TLG 51 *Immelmann*, Schleswig/Jagel
	46+25	Panavia Tornado ECR	Luftwaffe TLG 51 *Immelmann*, Schleswig/Jagel
	46+26	Panavia Tornado ECR	Luftwaffe
	46+28	Panavia Tornado ECR $	Luftwaffe TLG 51 *Immelmann*, Schleswig/Jagel
	46+29	Panavia Tornado ECR	Luftwaffe
	46+30	Panavia Tornado ECR	Luftwaffe
	46+32	Panavia Tornado ECR	Luftwaffe TLG 51 *Immelmann*, Schleswig/Jagel
	46+33	Panavia Tornado ECR	Luftwaffe
	46+34	Panavia Tornado ECR	Luftwaffe
	46+35	Panavia Tornado ECR	Luftwaffe TLG 51 *Immelmann*, Schleswig/Jagel
	46+36	Panavia Tornado ECR	Luftwaffe TLG 51 *Immelmann*, Schleswig/Jagel
	46+37	Panavia Tornado ECR	Luftwaffe
	46+38	Panavia Tornado ECR	Luftwaffe WTD 61, Ingolstadt
	46+39	Panavia Tornado ECR	Luftwaffe TAubZLwSüd, Kaufbeuren
	46+40	Panavia Tornado ECR	Luftwaffe TLG 51 *Immelmann*, Schleswig/Jagel
	46+41	Panavia Tornado ECR	Luftwaffe
	46+43	Panavia Tornado ECR	Luftwaffe
	46+44	Panavia Tornado ECR	Luftwaffe TLG 51 *Immelmann*, Schleswig/Jagel
	46+45	Panavia Tornado ECR	Luftwaffe TLG 51 *Immelmann*, Schleswig/Jagel
	46+46	Panavia Tornado ECR	Luftwaffe TLG 51 *Immelmann*, Schleswig/Jagel
	46+48	Panavia Tornado ECR	Luftwaffe TLG 51 *Immelmann*, Schleswig/Jagel
	46+49	Panavia Tornado ECR	Luftwaffe TLG 51 *Immelmann*, Schleswig/Jagel
	46+50	Panavia Tornado ECR	Luftwaffe TLG 51 *Immelmann*, Schleswig/Jagel
	46+51	Panavia Tornado ECR	Luftwaffe TLG 51 *Immelmann*, Schleswig/Jagel
	46+52	Panavia Tornado ECR	Luftwaffe TLG 51 *Immelmann*, Schleswig/Jagel
	46+53	Panavia Tornado ECR	Luftwaffe
	46+54	Panavia Tornado ECR	Luftwaffe TLG 51 *Immelmann*, Schleswig/Jagel
	46+55	Panavia Tornado ECR	Luftwaffe TLG 51 *Immelmann*, Schleswig/Jagel

Serial	Type (code/other identity)	Owner/operator, location or fate	Notes
46+56	Panavia Tornado ECR	Luftwaffe TLG 51 *Immelmann*, Schleswig/Jagel	
46+57	Panavia Tornado ECR $	Luftwaffe TLG 51 *Immelmann*, Schleswig/Jagel	
50+08	Transall C-160D	Luftwaffe LTG 61 (1.LwDiv), Landsberg	
50+09	Transall C-160D	Luftwaffe LTG 61 (1.LwDiv), Landsberg	
50+10	Transall C-160D	Luftwaffe	
50+17	Transall C-160D	Luftwaffe LTG 63 (4.LwDiv), Hohn	
50+29	Transall C-160D	Luftwaffe	
50+33	Transall C-160D	Luftwaffe LTG 63 (4.LwDiv), Hohn	
50+34	Transall C-160D	Luftwaffe LTG 63 (4.LwDiv), Hohn	
50+36	Transall C-160D	Luftwaffe LTG 63 (4.LwDiv), Hohn	
50+38	Transall C-160D	Luftwaffe LTG 63 (4.LwDiv), Hohn	
50+40	Transall C-160D	Luftwaffe LTG 63 (4.LwDiv), Hohn	
50+41	Transall C-160D $	Luftwaffe LTG 63 (4.LwDiv), Hohn	
50+42	Transall C-160D	Luftwaffe LTG 63 (4.LwDiv), Hohn	
50+44	Transall C-160D	Luftwaffe LTG 61 (1.LwDiv), Landsberg	
50+45	Transall C-160D	Luftwaffe LTG 61 (1.LwDiv), Landsberg	
50+46	Transall C-160D	Luftwaffe	
50+47	Transall C-160D	Luftwaffe LTG 61 (1.LwDiv), Landsberg	
50+48	Transall C-160D $	Luftwaffe LTG 61 (1.LwDiv), Landsberg	
50+49	Transall C-160D	Luftwaffe LTG 63 (4.LwDiv), Hohn	
50+51	Transall C-160D	Luftwaffe LTG 61 (1.LwDiv), Landsberg	
50+53	Transall C-160D	Luftwaffe LTG 61 (1.LwDiv), Landsberg	
50+54	Transall C-160D	Luftwaffe LTG 63 (4.LwDiv), Hohn	
50+55	Transall C-160D	Luftwaffe LTG 63 (4.LwDiv), Hohn	
50+57	Transall C-160D	Luftwaffe LTG 63 (4.LwDiv), Hohn	
50+58	Transall C-160D	Luftwaffe LTG 63 (4.LwDiv), Hohn	
50+59	Transall C-160D	Luftwaffe LTG 63 (4.LwDiv), Hohn	
50+61	Transall C-160D	Luftwaffe LTG 63 (4.LwDiv), Hohn	
50+64	Transall C-160D	Luftwaffe LTG 61 (1.LwDiv), Landsberg	
50+65	Transall C-160D $	Luftwaffe LTG 61 (1.LwDiv), Landsberg	
50+66	Transall C-160D	Luftwaffe LTG 61 (1.LwDiv), Landsberg	
50+67	Transall C-160D	Luftwaffe LTG 61 (1.LwDiv), Landsberg	
50+69	Transall C-160D	Luftwaffe LTG 63 (4.LwDiv), Hohn	
50+70	Transall C-160D	Luftwaffe	
50+71	Transall C-160D	Luftwaffe LTG 63 (4.LwDiv), Hohn	
50+72	Transall C-160D	Luftwaffe LTG 61 (1.LwDiv), Landsberg	
50+73	Transall C-160D	Luftwaffe LTG 61 (1.LwDiv), Landsberg	
50+74	Transall C-160D	Luftwaffe LTG 61 (1.LwDiv), Landsberg	
50+75	Transall C-160D	Luftwaffe LTG 63 (4.LwDiv), Hohn	
50+76	Transall C-160D	Luftwaffe LTG 63 (4.LwDiv), Hohn	
50+77	Transall C-160D	Luftwaffe LTG 63 (4.LwDiv), Hohn	
50+78	Transall C-160D	Luftwaffe LTG 63 (4.LwDiv), Hohn	
50+79	Transall C-160D	Luftwaffe LTG 63 (4.LwDiv), Hohn	
50+81	Transall C-160D	Luftwaffe LTG 61 (1.LwDiv), Landsberg	
50+82	Transall C-160D $	Luftwaffe LTG 63 (4.LwDiv), Hohn	
50+83	Transall C-160D	Luftwaffe LTG 61 (1.LwDiv), Landsberg	
50+84	Transall C-160D	Luftwaffe LTG 61 (1.LwDiv), Landsberg	
50+86	Transall C-160D	Luftwaffe WTD 61, Ingolstadt	
50+87	Transall C-160D	Luftwaffe LTG 63 (4.LwDiv), Hohn	
50+88	Transall C-160D	Luftwaffe LTG 61 (1.LwDiv), Landsberg	
50+89	Transall C-160D	Luftwaffe	
50+90	Transall C-160D	*Scrapped at Landsberg, 2015*	
50+91	Transall C-160D	Luftwaffe	
50+92	Transall C-160D	Luftwaffe LTG 61 (1.LwDiv), Landsberg	
50+93	Transall C-160D $	Luftwaffe LTG 63 (4.LwDiv), Hohn	
50+95	Transall C-160D $	*Preserved at Eindhoven, The Netherlands, 2016*	
50+96	Transall C-160D	Luftwaffe LTG 61 (1.LwDiv), Landsberg	
50+97	Transall C-160D	Luftwaffe LTG 63 (4.LwDiv), Hohn	
51+01	Transall C-160D	Luftwaffe LTG 63 (4.LwDiv), Hohn	
51+03	Transall C-160D	Luftwaffe LTG 63 (4.LwDiv), Hohn	
51+04	Transall C-160D	Luftwaffe LTG 63 (4.LwDiv), Hohn	
51+05	Transall C-160D	Luftwaffe LTG 63 (4.LwDiv), Hohn	

Notes	Serial	Type (code/other identity)	Owner/operator, location or fate
	51+06	Transall C-160D	Luftwaffe LTG 63 (4.LwDiv), Hohn
	51+08	Transall C-160D	Luftwaffe WTD 61, Ingolstadt
	51+09	Transall C-160D	*Withdrawn from use, December 2016*
	51+10	Transall C-160D	Luftwaffe LTG 61 (1.LwDiv), Landsberg
	51+12	Transall C-160D	Luftwaffe LTG 63 (4.LwDiv), Hohn
	51+13	Transall C-160D	Luftwaffe LTG 61 (1.LwDiv), Landsberg
	51+14	Transall C-160D	Luftwaffe LTG 63 (4.LwDiv), Hohn
	51+15	Transall C-160D	Luftwaffe LTG 61 (1.LwDiv), Landsberg
	54+01	Airbus Military A.400M	Luftwaffe LTG 62, Wunstorf
	54+02	Airbus Military A.400M	Luftwaffe LTG 62, Wunstorf
	54+03	Airbus Military A.400M $	Luftwaffe LTG 62, Wunstorf
	54+04	Airbus Military A.400M	Luftwaffe LTG 62, Wunstorf
	54+05	Airbus Military A.400M	Luftwaffe LTG 62, Wunstorf
	54+06	Airbus Military A.400M	Luftwaffe LTG 62, Wunstorf
	54+07	Airbus Military A.400M	Luftwaffe LTG 62, Wunstorf
	54+08	Airbus Military A.400M	Luftwaffe LTG 62, Wunstorf
	54+09	Airbus Military A.400M	Airbus Military, Seville
	54+10	Airbus Military A.400M	Airbus Military, Seville
	54+11	Airbus Military A.400M	Airbus Military, Seville
	54+12	Airbus Military A.400M	Airbus Military, Seville
	54+13	Airbus Military A.400M	Luftwaffe (on order)
	54+14	Airbus Military A.400M	Luftwaffe (on order)
	54+15	Airbus Military A.400M	Luftwaffe (on order)
	54+16	Airbus Military A.400M	Luftwaffe (on order)
	54+17	Airbus Military A.400M	Luftwaffe (on order)
	54+18	Airbus Military A.400M	Luftwaffe (on order)
	54+19	Airbus Military A.400M	Luftwaffe (on order)
	54+20	Airbus Military A.400M	Luftwaffe (on order)
	57+04	Dornier Do.228LM	Marineflieger MFG 3, Nordholz
	57+05	Dornier Do.228NG	Marineflieger MFG 3, Nordholz
	60+01	Lockheed P-3C CUP Orion $	Marineflieger MFG 3, Nordholz
	60+02	Lockheed P-3C CUP Orion	Marineflieger MFG 3, Nordholz
	60+03	Lockheed P-3C CUP Orion	Marineflieger MFG 3, Nordholz
	60+04	Lockheed P-3C CUP Orion	Marineflieger MFG 3, Nordholz
	60+05	Lockheed P-3C CUP Orion $	Marineflieger MFG 3, Nordholz
	60+06	Lockheed P-3C CUP Orion	Marineflieger MFG 3, Nordholz
	60+07	Lockheed P-3C CUP Orion	Marineflieger MFG 3, Nordholz
	60+08	Lockheed P-3C CUP Orion	Marineflieger MFG 3, Nordholz
	74+01	Eurocopter EC.665 Tiger UHT	Luftwaffe WTD 61, Ingolstadt
	74+02	Eurocopter EC.665 Tiger UHT	Heer KHR 36, Fritzlar
	74+03	Eurocopter EC.665 Tiger UHT	Luftwaffe TsLw 3, Fassberg
	74+05	Eurocopter EC.665 Tiger UHT	Heer IntHubschrAusbZ, Le Luc, France
	74+06	Eurocopter EC.665 Tiger UHT	Heer KHR 36, Fritzlar
	74+07	Eurocopter EC.665 Tiger UHT	Heer IntHubschrAusbZ, Le Luc, France
	74+08	Eurocopter EC.665 Tiger UHT	Luftwaffe TsLw 3, Fassberg
	74+09	Eurocopter EC.665 Tiger UHT	Heer IntHubschrAusbZ, Le Luc, France
	74+10	Eurocopter EC.665 Tiger UHT	Heer KHR 36, Fritzlar
	74+11	Eurocopter EC.665 Tiger UHT	Heer IntHubschrAusbZ, Le Luc, France
	74+13	Eurocopter EC.665 Tiger UHT	Heer IntHubschrAusbZ, Le Luc, France
	74+14	Eurocopter EC.665 Tiger UHT	Heer IntHubschrAusbZ, Le Luc, France
	74+15	Eurocopter EC.665 Tiger UHT	Heer IntHubschrAusbZ, Le Luc, France
	74+16	Eurocopter EC.665 Tiger UHT	Heer KHR 36, Fritzlar
	74+17	Eurocopter EC.665 Tiger UHT	Heer KHR 36, Fritzlar
	74+18	Eurocopter EC.665 Tiger UHT	Heer KHR 36, Fritzlar
	74+19	Eurocopter EC.665 Tiger UHT	Heer KHR 36, Fritzlar
	74+20	Eurocopter EC.665 Tiger UHT	Heer KHR 36, Fritzlar
	74+21	Eurocopter EC.665 Tiger UHT	Heer KHR 36, Fritzlar
	74+22	Eurocopter EC.665 Tiger UHT	Heer KHR 36, Fritzlar
	74+23	Eurocopter EC.665 Tiger UHT	Heer KHR 36, Fritzlar
	74+24	Eurocopter EC.665 Tiger UHT	Heer KHR 36, Fritzlar
	74+25	Eurocopter EC.665 Tiger UHT	Heer KHR 36, Fritzlar
	74+26	Eurocopter EC.665 Tiger UHT	Heer KHR 36, Fritzlar

Serial	Type (code/other identity)	Owner/operator, location or fate	Notes
74+28	Eurocopter EC.665 Tiger UHT	Heer KHR 36, Fritzlar	
74+29	Eurocopter EC.665 Tiger UHT	Heer KHR 36, Fritzlar	
74+30	Eurocopter EC.665 Tiger UHT	Heer KHR 36, Fritzlar	
74+31	Eurocopter EC.665 Tiger UHT	Heer KHR 36, Fritzlar	
74+32	Eurocopter EC.665 Tiger UHT	Heer KHR 36, Fritzlar	
74+34	Eurocopter EC.665 Tiger UHT	Heer KHR 36, Fritzlar	
74+35	Eurocopter EC.665 Tiger UHT	Heer KHR 36, Fritzlar	
74+36	Eurocopter EC.665 Tiger UHT	Heer KHR 36, Fritzlar	
74+37	Eurocopter EC.665 Tiger UHT	Heer IntHubschrAusbZ, Le Luc, France	
74+38	Eurocopter EC.665 Tiger UHT	Heer KHR 36, Fritzlar	
74+39	Eurocopter EC.665 Tiger UHT	Airbus Helicopters, Donauwörth	
74+40	Eurocopter EC.665 Tiger UHT	Heer KHR 36, Fritzlar	
74+41	Eurocopter EC.665 Tiger UHT	Airbus Helicopters, Donauwörth	
74+42	Eurocopter EC.665 Tiger UHT	Heer KHR 36, Fritzlar	
74+43	Eurocopter EC.665 Tiger UHT	Airbus Helicopters, Donauwörth	
74+44	Eurocopter EC.665 Tiger UHT	Airbus Helicopters, Donauwörth	
74+45	Eurocopter EC.665 Tiger UHT	Heer KHR 36, Fritzlar	
74+46	Eurocopter EC.665 Tiger UHT	Heer KHR 36, Fritzlar	
74+47	Eurocopter EC.665 Tiger UHT	Heer KHR 36, Fritzlar	
74+48	Eurocopter EC.665 Tiger UHT	Heer (on order)	
74+49	Eurocopter EC.665 Tiger UHT	Heer (on order)	
74+50	Eurocopter EC.665 Tiger UHT	Heer KHR 36, Fritzlar	
74+51	Eurocopter EC.665 Tiger UHT	Heer IntHubschrAusbZ, Le Luc, France	
74+52	Eurocopter EC.665 Tiger UHT	Heer (on order)	
74+53	Eurocopter EC.665 Tiger UHT	Heer KHR 36, Fritzlar	
74+54	Eurocopter EC.665 Tiger UHT	Heer KHR 36, Fritzlar	
74+55	Eurocopter EC.665 Tiger UHT	Heer (on order)	
74+56	Eurocopter EC.665 Tiger UHT	Heer (on order)	
74+57	Eurocopter EC.665 Tiger UHT	Heer (on order)	
74+58	Eurocopter EC.665 Tiger UHT	Heer (on order)	
74+59	Eurocopter EC.665 Tiger UHT	Heer (on order)	
74+61	Eurocopter EC.665 Tiger UHT	Heer KHR 36, Fritzlar	
74+62	Eurocopter EC.665 Tiger UHT	Airbus Helicopters, Donauwörth	
74+63	Eurocopter EC.665 Tiger UHT	Heer (on order)	
74+64	Eurocopter EC.665 Tiger UHT	Heer (on order)	
74+65	Eurocopter EC.665 Tiger UHT	Heer (on order)	
76+01	Airbus Helicopters H.145M	Heer IntHubschrAusbZ, Bückeburg	
76+02	Airbus Helicopters H.145M	Heer IntHubschrAusbZ, Bückeburg	
76+03	Airbus Helicopters H.145M	Luftwaffe HSG 64, Laupheim	
76+04	Airbus Helicopters H.145M	Luftwaffe HSG 64, Laupheim	
76+05	Airbus Helicopters H.145M	Luftwaffe HSG 64, Laupheim	
76+06	Airbus Helicopters H.145M	Luftwaffe HSG 64, Laupheim	
76+07	Airbus Helicopters H.145M	Luftwaffe HSG 64, Laupheim	
76+08	Airbus Helicopters H.145M	Luftwaffe (on order)	
76+09	Airbus Helicopters H.145M	Luftwaffe (on order)	
76+10	Airbus Helicopters H.145M	Luftwaffe (on order)	
76+11	Airbus Helicopters H.145M	Luftwaffe HSG 64, Laupheim	
76+12	Airbus Helicopters H.145M	Luftwaffe (on order)	
76+13	Airbus Helicopters H.145M	Luftwaffe (on order)	
76+14	Airbus Helicopters H.145M	Luftwaffe (on order)	
76+15	Airbus Helicopters H.145M	Luftwaffe (on order)	
78+01	NH Industries NH.90-TTH	Heer IntHubschrAusbZ, Bückeburg	
78+02	NH Industries NH.90-TTH	Heer IntHubschrAusbZ, Bückeburg	
78+03	NH Industries NH.90-TTH	Heer IntHubschrAusbZ, Bückeburg	
78+04	NH Industries NH.90-TTH	Luftwaffe TsLw 3, Fassberg	
78+05	NH Industries NH.90-TTH	Luftwaffe TsLw 3, Fassberg	
78+06	NH Industries NH.90-TTH	Heer IntHubschrAusbZ, Bückeburg	
78+07	NH Industries NH.90-TTH	Heer IntHubschrAusbZ, Bückeburg	
78+08	NH Industries NH.90-TTH	Heer IntHubschrAusbZ, Bückeburg	
78+09	NH Industries NH.90-TTH	Heer IntHubschrAusbZ, Bückeburg	
78+10	NH Industries NH.90-TTH	Heer IntHubschrAusbZ, Bückeburg	
78+11	NH Industries NH.90-TTH	Heer THR 10, Fassberg	

Notes	Serial	Type (code/other identity)	Owner/operator, location or fate
	78+12	NH Industries NH.90-TTH	Heer THR 10, Fassberg
	78+13	NH Industries NH.90-TTH	Heer THR 10, Fassberg
	78+14	NH Industries NH.90-TTH	Heer THR 10, Fassberg
	78+15	NH Industries NH.90-TTH	Heer THR 10, Fassberg
	78+16	NH Industries NH.90-TTH	Airbus Helicopters, Donauwörth
	78+17	NH Industries NH.90-TTH	Heer IntHubschrAusbZ, Bückeburg
	78+18	NH Industries NH.90-TTH	Heer THR 10, Fassberg
	78+19	NH Industries NH.90-TTH	Heer IntHubschrAusbZ, Bückeburg
	78+20	NH Industries NH.90-TTH	Heer IntHubschrAusbZ, Bückeburg
	78+21	NH Industries NH.90-TTH	Heer IntHubschrAusbZ, Bückeburg
	78+22	NH Industries NH.90-TTH	Heer IntHubschrAusbZ, Bückeburg
	78+23	NH Industries NH.90-TTH	Heer THR 10, Fassberg
	78+24	NH Industries NH.90-TTH	Airbus Helicopters, Donauwörth
	78+25	NH Industries NH.90-TTH	Heer THR 10, Fassberg
	78+26	NH Industries NH.90-TTH	Heer IntHubschrAusbZ, Bückeburg
	78+27	NH Industries NH.90-TTH	Heer IntHubschrAusbZ, Bückeburg
	78+28	NH Industries NH.90-TTH	Heer THR 10, Fassberg
	78+29	NH Industries NH.90-TTH	Heer IntHubschrAusbZ, Bückeburg
	78+30	NH Industries NH.90-TTH	Heer IntHubschrAusbZ, Bückeburg
	78+31	NH Industries NH.90-TTH	Heer THR 10, Fassberg
	78+32	NH Industries NH.90-TTH	Heer IntHubschrAusbZ, Bückeburg
	78+33	NH Industries NH.90-TTH	Heer (on order)
	78+34	NH Industries NH.90-TTH	Heer IntHubschrAusbZ, Bückeburg
	78+35	NH Industries NH.90-TTH	Heer (on order)
	78+36	NH Industries NH.90-TTH	Heer (on order)
	78+37	NH Industries NH.90-TTH	Heer (on order)
	78+38	NH Industries NH.90-TTH	Heer (on order)
	78+39	NH Industries NH.90-TTH	Heer (on order)
	78+40	NH Industries NH.90-TTH	Heer (on order)
	78+41	NH Industries NH.90-TTH	Heer (on order)
	78+42	NH Industries NH.90-TTH	Heer (on order)
	78+43	NH Industries NH.90-TTH	Heer (on order)
	78+44	NH Industries NH.90-TTH	Heer (on order)
	78+45	NH Industries NH.90-TTH	Heer (on order)
	78+46	NH Industries NH.90-TTH	Heer (on order)
	78+47	NH Industries NH.90-TTH	Heer (on order)
	78+48	NH Industries NH.90-TTH	Heer (on order)
	78+49	NH Industries NH.90-TTH	Heer (on order)
	78+50	NH Industries NH.90-TTH	Heer (on order)
	79+01	NH Industries NH.90-TTH	Heer IntHubschrAusbZ, Bückeburg
	79+02	NH Industries NH.90-TTH	Heer IntHubschrAusbZ, Bückeburg
	79+03	NH Industries NH.90-TTH	Heer THR 10, Fassberg
	79+04	NH Industries NH.90-TTH	Heer THR 10, Fassberg
	79+05	NH Industries NH.90-TTH	Heer THR 10, Fassberg
	79+06	NH Industries NH.90-TTH	Heer IntHubschrAusbZ, Bückeburg
	79+07	NH Industries NH.90-TTH	Heer IntHubschrAusbZ, Bückeburg
	79+09	NH Industries NH.90-TTH	Heer IntHubschrAusbZ, Bückeburg
	79+10	NH Industries NH.90-TTH	Heer
	79+24	NH Industries NH.90-TTH	Heer THR 10, Fassberg
	79+25	NH Industries NH.90-TTH	Heer
	79+26	NH Industries NH.90-TTH	Luftwaffe TsLw 3, Fassberg
	79+27	NH Industries NH.90-TTH	Heer (on order)
	79+28	NH Industries NH.90-TTH	Heer (on order)
	79+29	NH Industries NH.90-TTH	Heer (on order)
	79+30	NH Industries NH.90-TTH	Heer (on order)
	79+52	NH Industries NH.90-NFH Sea Lion	Marineflieger (on order)
	79+53	NH Industries NH.90-NFH Sea Lion	Marineflieger (on order)
	79+54	NH Industries NH.90-NFH Sea Lion	Marineflieger (on order)
	79+55	NH Industries NH.90-NFH Sea Lion	Marineflieger (on order)
	79+56	NH Industries NH.90-NFH Sea Lion	Marineflieger (on order)
	79+57	NH Industries NH.90-NFH Sea Lion	Marineflieger (on order)
	79+58	NH Industries NH.90-NFH Sea Lion	Marineflieger (on order)

Serial	Type (code/other identity)	Owner/operator, location or fate	Notes
79+59	NH Industries NH.90-NFH Sea Lion	Marineflieger (on order)	
79+60	NH Industries NH.90-NFH Sea Lion	Marineflieger (on order)	
79+61	NH Industries NH.90-NFH Sea Lion	Marineflieger (on order)	
79+62	NH Industries NH.90-NFH Sea Lion	Marineflieger (on order)	
79+63	NH Industries NH.90-NFH Sea Lion	Marineflieger (on order)	
79+64	NH Industries NH.90-NFH Sea Lion	Marineflieger (on order)	
79+65	NH Industries NH.90-NFH Sea Lion	Marineflieger (on order)	
79+66	NH Industries NH.90-NFH Sea Lion	Marineflieger (on order)	
79+67	NH Industries NH.90-NFH Sea Lion	Marineflieger (on order)	
79+68	NH Industries NH.90-NFH Sea Lion	Marineflieger (on order)	
82+01	Eurocopter AS.532U-2 Cougar	Luftwaffe 3/FBS, Berlin-Tegel	
82+02	Eurocopter AS.532U-2 Cougar	Luftwaffe 3/FBS, Berlin-Tegel	
82+03	Eurocopter AS.532U-2 Cougar	Luftwaffe 3/FBS, Berlin-Tegel	
82+51	Eurocopter EC.135P-1	Heer IntHubschrAusbZ, Bückeburg	
82+52	Eurocopter EC.135P-1	Heer IntHubschrAusbZ, Bückeburg	
82+53	Eurocopter EC.135P-1	Heer IntHubschrAusbZ, Bückeburg	
82+54	Eurocopter EC.135P-1	Heer IntHubschrAusbZ, Bückeburg	
82+55	Eurocopter EC.135P-1	Heer IntHubschrAusbZ, Bückeburg	
82+56	Eurocopter EC.135P-1	Heer IntHubschrAusbZ, Bückeburg	
82+57	Eurocopter EC.135P-1	Heer IntHubschrAusbZ, Bückeburg	
82+59	Eurocopter EC.135P-1	Heer IntHubschrAusbZ, Bückeburg	
82+60	Eurocopter EC.135P-1	Heer IntHubschrAusbZ, Bückeburg	
82+61	Eurocopter EC.135P-1	Heer IntHubschrAusbZ, Bückeburg	
82+62	Eurocopter EC.135P-1	Heer IntHubschrAusbZ, Bückeburg	
82+63	Eurocopter EC.135P-1	Heer IntHubschrAusbZ, Bückeburg	
82+64	Eurocopter EC.135P-1	Heer IntHubschrAusbZ, Bückeburg	
82+65	Eurocopter EC.135P-1	Heer IntHubschrAusbZ, Bückeburg	
83+02	Westland Sea Lynx Mk88A	Marineflieger MFG 5, Nordholz	
83+03	Westland Sea Lynx Mk88A	Marineflieger MFG 5, Nordholz	
83+04	Westland Sea Lynx Mk88A	Marineflieger MFG 5, Nordholz	
83+05	Westland Sea Lynx Mk88A	Marineflieger MFG 5, Nordholz	
83+06	Westland Sea Lynx Mk88A	Marineflieger MFG 5, Nordholz	
83+07	Westland Sea Lynx Mk88A	Luftwaffe WTD 61, Ingolstadt	
83+09	Westland Sea Lynx Mk88A	Marineflieger MFG 5, Nordholz	
83+10	Westland Sea Lynx Mk88A	Marineflieger MFG 5, Nordholz	
83+11	Westland Sea Lynx Mk88A $	Marineflieger MFG 5, Nordholz	
83+12	Westland Sea Lynx Mk88A	Marineflieger MFG 5, Nordholz	
83+13	Westland Sea Lynx Mk88A	Marineflieger MFG 5, Nordholz	
83+15	Westland Sea Lynx Mk88A	Marineflieger MFG 5, Nordholz	
83+17	Westland Sea Lynx Mk88A	Marineflieger MFG 5, Nordholz	
83+18	Westland Sea Lynx Mk88A	Marineflieger MFG 5, Nordholz	
83+19	Westland Sea Lynx Mk88A	Marineflieger MFG 5, Nordholz	
83+20	Westland Sea Lynx Mk88A $	Marineflieger MFG 5, Nordholz	
83+21	Westland Sea Lynx Mk88A	Marineflieger MFG 5, Nordholz	
83+22	Westland Sea Lynx Mk88A	Marineflieger MFG 5, Nordholz	
83+23	Westland Sea Lynx Mk88A	Marineflieger MFG 5, Nordholz	
83+24	Westland Sea Lynx Mk88A	Marineflieger MFG 5, Nordholz	
83+25	Westland Sea Lynx Mk88A	Marineflieger MFG 5, Nordholz	
84+05	Sikorsky/VFW CH-53G	Luftwaffe HSG 64, Laupheim & Rheine-Bentlage	
84+09	Sikorsky/VFW CH-53G	Luftwaffe TsLw 3, Fassberg	
84+10	Sikorsky/VFW CH-53G	Luftwaffe TsLw 3, Fassberg	
84+12	Sikorsky/VFW CH-53G	Luftwaffe HSG 64, Laupheim & Rheine-Bentlage	
84+13	Sikorsky/VFW CH-53GA	Luftwaffe HSG 64, Laupheim & Rheine-Bentlage	
84+14	Sikorsky/VFW CH-53GE	Luftwaffe HSG 64, Laupheim & Rheine-Bentlage	
84+15	Sikorsky/VFW CH-53GS	Luftwaffe HSG 64, Laupheim & Rheine-Bentlage	
84+16	Sikorsky/VFW CH-53G	Luftwaffe	
84+18	Sikorsky/VFW CH-53G	Luftwaffe HSG 64, Laupheim & Rheine-Bentlage	
84+19	Sikorsky/VFW CH-53G	Luftwaffe TsLw 3, Fassberg	
84+24	Sikorsky/VFW CH-53GA	Luftwaffe HSG 64, Laupheim & Rheine-Bentlage	
84+25	Sikorsky/VFW CH-53GS	Luftwaffe HSG 64, Laupheim & Rheine-Bentlage	
84+26	Sikorsky/VFW CH-53GE	Luftwaffe WTD 61, Ingolstadt	
84+27	Sikorsky/VFW CH-53G	Luftwaffe	

Notes	Serial	Type (code/other identity)	Owner/operator, location or fate
	84+28	Sikorsky/VFW CH-53G	Luftwaffe HSG 64, Laupheim & Rheine-Bentlage
	84+29	Sikorsky/VFW CH-53G	Luftwaffe HSG 64, Laupheim & Rheine-Bentlage
	84+30	Sikorsky/VFW CH-53GS	Luftwaffe HSG 64, Laupheim & Rheine-Bentlage
	84+31	Sikorsky/VFW CH-53GA	Luftwaffe HSG 64, Laupheim & Rheine-Bentlage
	84+32	Sikorsky/VFW CH-53G	Luftwaffe HSG 64, Laupheim & Rheine-Bentlage
	84+33	Sikorsky/VFW CH-53GA	Luftwaffe HSG 64, Laupheim & Rheine-Bentlage
	84+34	Sikorsky/VFW CH-53G	Luftwaffe HSG 64, Laupheim & Rheine-Bentlage
	84+35	Sikorsky/VFW CH-53G	Luftwaffe HSG 64, Laupheim & Rheine-Bentlage
	84+37	Sikorsky/VFW CH-53GA	Luftwaffe HSG 64, Laupheim & Rheine-Bentlage
	84+38	Sikorsky/VFW CH-53G	Luftwaffe HSG 64, Laupheim & Rheine-Bentlage
	84+39	Sikorsky/VFW CH-53GA	Luftwaffe HSG 64, Laupheim & Rheine-Bentlage
	84+40	Sikorsky/VFW CH-53G	Luftwaffe HSG 64, Laupheim & Rheine-Bentlage
	84+42	Sikorsky/VFW CH-53GS	Luftwaffe HSG 64, Laupheim & Rheine-Bentlage
	84+43	Sikorsky/VFW CH-53G	Luftwaffe HSG 64, Laupheim & Rheine-Bentlage
	84+44	Sikorsky/VFW CH-53G	Luftwaffe HSG 64, Laupheim & Rheine-Bentlage
	84+45	Sikorsky/VFW CH-53GS	Luftwaffe HSG 64, Laupheim & Rheine-Bentlage
	84+46	Sikorsky/VFW CH-53G	Luftwaffe HSG 64, Laupheim & Rheine-Bentlage
	84+47	Sikorsky/VFW CH-53GA	Luftwaffe HSG 64, Laupheim & Rheine-Bentlage
	84+48	Sikorsky/VFW CH-53G	Luftwaffe HSG 64, Laupheim & Rheine-Bentlage
	84+49	Sikorsky/VFW CH-53GA	Luftwaffe HSG 64, Laupheim & Rheine-Bentlage
	84+50	Sikorsky/VFW CH-53GA	Luftwaffe HSG 64, Laupheim & Rheine-Bentlage
	84+51	Sikorsky/VFW CH-53GS	Luftwaffe HSG 64, Laupheim & Rheine-Bentlage
	84+52	Sikorsky/VFW CH-53GS	Luftwaffe HSG 64, Laupheim & Rheine-Bentlage
	84+53	Sikorsky/VFW CH-53GE	Luftwaffe HSG 64, Laupheim & Rheine-Bentlage
	84+54	Sikorsky/VFW CH-53G	Luftwaffe HSG 64, Laupheim & Rheine-Bentlage
	84+55	Sikorsky/VFW CH-53G	Airbus Helicopters, Donauwörth
	84+57	Sikorsky/VFW CH-53G	Luftwaffe HSG 64, Laupheim & Rheine-Bentlage
	84+58	Sikorsky/VFW CH-53G	Luftwaffe HSG 64, Laupheim & Rheine-Bentlage
	84+59	Sikorsky/VFW CH-53GS	Luftwaffe HSG 64, Laupheim & Rheine-Bentlage
	84+60	Sikorsky/VFW CH-53G	Luftwaffe HSG 64, Laupheim & Rheine-Bentlage
	84+62	Sikorsky/VFW CH-53GS	Luftwaffe HSG 64, Laupheim & Rheine-Bentlage
	84+63	Sikorsky/VFW CH-53G	Luftwaffe HSG 64, Laupheim & Rheine-Bentlage
	84+64	Sikorsky/VFW CH-53GS	Luftwaffe HSG 64, Laupheim & Rheine-Bentlage
	84+65	Sikorsky/VFW CH-53G	Luftwaffe HSG 64, Laupheim & Rheine-Bentlage
	84+66	Sikorsky/VFW CH-53GS	Luftwaffe HSG 64, Laupheim & Rheine-Bentlage
	84+67	Sikorsky/VFW CH-53GS	Luftwaffe HSG 64, Laupheim & Rheine-Bentlage
	84+68	Sikorsky/VFW CH-53GS	Luftwaffe HSG 64, Laupheim & Rheine-Bentlage
	84+70	Sikorsky/VFW CH-53GA	Luftwaffe TsLw 3, Fassberg
	84+71	Sikorsky/VFW CH-53G	Luftwaffe HSG 64, Laupheim & Rheine-Bentlage
	84+72	Sikorsky/VFW CH-53G	Luftwaffe HSG 64, Laupheim & Rheine-Bentlage
	84+73	Sikorsky/VFW CH-53GS	Luftwaffe HSG 64, Laupheim & Rheine-Bentlage
	84+74	Sikorsky/VFW CH-53G	Luftwaffe HSG 64, Laupheim & Rheine-Bentlage
	84+75	Sikorsky/VFW CH-53G	Luftwaffe HSG 64, Laupheim & Rheine-Bentlage
	84+76	Sikorsky/VFW CH-53G	Luftwaffe HSG 64, Laupheim & Rheine-Bentlage
	84+77	Sikorsky/VFW CH-53G	Luftwaffe HSG 64, Laupheim & Rheine-Bentlage
	84+78	Sikorsky/VFW CH-53GS	Luftwaffe TsLw 3, Fassberg
	84+79	Sikorsky/VFW CH-53GS	Luftwaffe HSG 64, Laupheim & Rheine-Bentlage
	84+80	Sikorsky/VFW CH-53G	Luftwaffe HSG 64, Laupheim & Rheine-Bentlage
	84+82	Sikorsky/VFW CH-53GE	Luftwaffe HSG 64, Laupheim & Rheine-Bentlage
	84+83	Sikorsky/VFW CH-53G	Luftwaffe TsLw 3, Fassberg
	84+84	Sikorsky/VFW CH-53G	Luftwaffe HSG 64, Laupheim & Rheine-Bentlage
	84+85	Sikorsky/VFW CH-53GS	Luftwaffe HSG 64, Laupheim & Rheine-Bentlage
	84+86	Sikorsky/VFW CH-53GA	Airbus Helicopters, Donauwörth
	84+87	Sikorsky/VFW CH-53GS	Luftwaffe HSG 64, Laupheim & Rheine-Bentlage
	84+88	Sikorsky/VFW CH-53G	Luftwaffe HSG 64, Laupheim & Rheine-Bentlage
	84+89	Sikorsky/VFW CH-53GA	Luftwaffe HSG 64, Laupheim & Rheine-Bentlage
	84+90	Sikorsky/VFW CH-53G	Luftwaffe HSG 64, Laupheim & Rheine-Bentlage
	84+91	Sikorsky/VFW CH-53GS	Luftwaffe HSG 64, Laupheim & Rheine-Bentlage
	84+92	Sikorsky/VFW CH-53GS	Luftwaffe HSG 64, Laupheim & Rheine-Bentlage
	84+94	Sikorsky/VFW CH-53G	Luftwaffe WTD 61, Ingolstadt
	84+95	Sikorsky/VFW CH-53GA	Luftwaffe HSG 64, Laupheim & Rheine-Bentlage
	84+96	Sikorsky/VFW CH-53GE	Luftwaffe HSG 64, Laupheim & Rheine-Bentlage

Serial	Type (code/other identity)	Owner/operator, location or fate	Notes
84+97	Sikorsky/VFW CH-53G	Luftwaffe HSG 64, Laupheim & Rheine-Bentlage	
84+98	Sikorsky/VFW CH-53GS	Luftwaffe HSG 64, Laupheim & Rheine-Bentlage	
84+99	Sikorsky/VFW CH-53GA	Luftwaffe	
85+00	Sikorsky/VFW CH-53GS	Luftwaffe HSG 64, Laupheim & Rheine-Bentlage	
85+01	Sikorsky/VFW CH-53GS	Luftwaffe HSG 64, Laupheim & Rheine-Bentlage	
85+02	Sikorsky/VFW CH-53G	Luftwaffe HSG 64, Laupheim & Rheine-Bentlage	
85+03	Sikorsky/VFW CH-53G	Luftwaffe HSG 64, Laupheim & Rheine-Bentlage	
85+04	Sikorsky/VFW CH-53GA	Luftwaffe HSG 64, Laupheim & Rheine-Bentlage	
85+05	Sikorsky/VFW CH-53GS	Luftwaffe HSG 64, Laupheim & Rheine-Bentlage	
85+06	Sikorsky/VFW CH-53GA	Luftwaffe HSG 64, Laupheim & Rheine-Bentlage	
85+07	Sikorsky/VFW CH-53GS	Luftwaffe HSG 64, Laupheim & Rheine-Bentlage	
85+08	Sikorsky/VFW CH-53G	Luftwaffe HSG 64, Laupheim & Rheine-Bentlage	
85+10	Sikorsky/VFW CH-53GS	Luftwaffe HSG 64, Laupheim & Rheine-Bentlage	
85+11	Sikorsky/VFW CH-53G	Luftwaffe HSG 64, Laupheim & Rheine-Bentlage	
85+12	Sikorsky/VFW CH-53GS	Luftwaffe HSG 64, Laupheim & Rheine-Bentlage	
86+07	MBB Bo.105P	*Withdrawn from use*	
86+11	MBB Bo.105P1M	*Withdrawn from use, 2016*	
86+15	MBB Bo.105P1M	*Withdrawn from use, December 2016*	
86+16	MBB Bo.105P1	*Withdrawn from use, 2016*	
86+18	MBB Bo.105P1	*Withdrawn from use*	
86+21	MBB Bo.105P1M	*Withdrawn from use, December 2016*	
86+22	MBB Bo.105P1	*Withdrawn from use, 2016*	
86+24	MBB Bo.105P1M	*Withdrawn from use, 2016*	
86+25	MBB Bo.105P1M	*Withdrawn from use, 2016*	
86+27	MBB Bo.105P1	*Withdrawn from use*	
86+29	MBB Bo.105P1M	*Withdrawn from use, December 2016*	
86+30	MBB Bo.105P1	*Withdrawn from use, 2016*	
86+33	MBB Bo.105P1M	*Withdrawn from use, December 2016*	
86+34	MBB Bo.105P1M	*Withdrawn from use, December 2016*	
86+39	MBB Bo.105P1M	*Withdrawn from use, 2016*	
86+40	MBB Bo.105P1M	*Withdrawn from use, 2016*	
86+44	MBB Bo.105P1M	*Withdrawn from use, December 2016*	
86+45	MBB Bo.105P1	*Withdrawn from use, 2016*	
86+47	MBB Bo.105P1M	*Withdrawn from use, December 2016*	
86+48	MBB Bo.105P1M	*Withdrawn from use*	
86+55	MBB Bo.105P1M	*Withdrawn from use*	
86+56	MBB Bo.105P1	*Withdrawn from use, December 2016*	
86+59	MBB Bo.105P1M	*Withdrawn from use, December 2016*	
86+60	MBB Bo.105P1	*Withdrawn from use*	
86+62	MBB Bo.105P1M	*Withdrawn from use*	
86+66	MBB Bo.105P1	*Withdrawn from use, 2016*	
86+70	MBB Bo.105P1M $	*Withdrawn from use*	
86+77	MBB Bo.105P1M	*Withdrawn from use*	
86+78	MBB Bo.105P1M	*Withdrawn from use, 2016*	
86+79	MBB Bo.105P1M	*Withdrawn from use*	
86+83	MBB Bo.105P1	*Withdrawn from use*	
86+87	MBB Bo.105P1M	*Withdrawn from use, 2016*	
86+90	MBB Bo.105P1	*Withdrawn from use, 2016*	
86+95	MBB Bo.105P1M	*Withdrawn from use, December 2016*	
86+99	MBB Bo.105P1	*Withdrawn from use*	
87+02	MBB Bo.105P1	*Withdrawn from use*	
87+04	MBB Bo.105P1M	*Withdrawn from use*	
87+11	MBB Bo.105P1M	*Withdrawn from use, 2016*	
87+12	MBB Bo.105P1M	*Withdrawn from use*	
87+15	MBB Bo.105P	*Withdrawn from use*	
87+16	MBB Bo.105P1M	*Withdrawn from use, December 2016*	
87+25	MBB Bo.105P1	*Withdrawn from use*	
87+26	MBB Bo.105P1M	*Withdrawn from use, December 2016*	
87+39	MBB Bo.105P1M	*Withdrawn from use*	
87+41	MBB Bo.105P1M	*Withdrawn from use*	
87+52	MBB Bo.105P1M	*Withdrawn from use, 2016*	
87+56	MBB Bo.105P1M	*Withdrawn from use, 2016*	

Notes	Serial	Type (code/other identity)	Owner/operator, location or fate
	87+61	MBB Bo.105P1M	*Withdrawn from use*
	87+62	MBB Bo.105P1	*Withdrawn from use, December 2016*
	87+66	MBB Bo.105P1M	*Withdrawn from use, December 2016*
	87+71	MBB Bo.105P1	*Withdrawn from use*
	87+73	MBB Bo.105P1M	*Withdrawn from use, December 2016*
	87+76	MBB Bo.105P1M	*Withdrawn from use, 2016*
	87+78	MBB Bo.105P1M	*Withdrawn from use, December 2016*
	87+81	MBB Bo.105P1	*Withdrawn from use*
	87+85	MBB Bo.105P1M	*Withdrawn from use, 2016*
	87+87	MBB Bo.105P1M	*Withdrawn from use, December 2016*
	88+04	MBB Bo.105P1	*Withdrawn from use*
	89+50	Westland Sea King HAS41	Marineflieger MFG 5, Nordholz
	89+51	Westland Sea King HAS41	Marineflieger MFG 5, Nordholz
	89+52	Westland Sea King HAS41	Marineflieger MFG 5, Nordholz
	89+53	Westland Sea King HAS41	Marineflieger MFG 5, Nordholz
	89+54	Westland Sea King HAS41	Marineflieger MFG 5, Nordholz
	89+55	Westland Sea King HAS41 $	Marineflieger MFG 5, Nordholz
	89+56	Westland Sea King HAS41	Marineflieger MFG 5, Nordholz
	89+57	Westland Sea King HAS41	Marineflieger MFG 5, Nordholz
	89+58	Westland Sea King HAS41 $	Marineflieger MFG 5, Nordholz
	89+60	Westland Sea King HAS41	Marineflieger MFG 5, Nordholz
	89+61	Westland Sea King HAS41	Marineflieger MFG 5, Nordholz
	89+62	Westland Sea King HAS41	Marineflieger MFG 5, Nordholz
	89+63	Westland Sea King HAS41	Marineflieger MFG 5, Nordholz
	89+64	Westland Sea King HAS41 $	Marineflieger MFG 5, Nordholz
	89+65	Westland Sea King HAS41	Marineflieger MFG 5, Nordholz
	89+66	Westland Sea King HAS41	Marineflieger MFG 5, Nordholz
	89+67	Westland Sea King HAS41	Marineflieger MFG 5, Nordholz
	89+68	Westland Sea King HAS41	Marineflieger MFG 5, Nordholz
	89+69	Westland Sea King HAS41	Marineflieger MFG 5, Nordholz
	89+70	Westland Sea King HAS41	Marineflieger MFG 5, Nordholz
	89+71	Westland Sea King HAS41	Marineflieger MFG 5, Nordholz
	98+03	Eurofighter EF.2000(T) (IPA3)	Luftwaffe WTD 61, Ingolstadt
	98+07	Eurofighter EF.2000 (IPA7)	Luftwaffe WTD 61, Ingolstadt
	98+08	Eurofighter EF.2000GT (IPA8)	Airbus Defence & Space, Manching
	98+16	Eurocopter EC.665 Tiger UHT	Luftwaffe TsLw 3, Fassberg
	98+18	Eurocopter EC.665 Tiger UHT	Airbus Helicopters, Donauwörth
	98+50	NH Industries NH.90-TTH	Airbus Helicopters, Donauwörth
	98+51	NH Industries NH.90-NFH Sea Lion	Airbus Helicopters, Donauwörth
	98+59	Panavia Tornado IDS(T)	Luftwaffe WTD 61, Ingolstadt
	98+60	Panavia Tornado IDS	Luftwaffe WTD 61, Ingolstadt
	98+77	Panavia Tornado IDS $	Luftwaffe WTD 61, Ingolstadt
	98+79	Panavia Tornado ECR	Luftwaffe WTD 61, Ingolstadt
	98+90	NH Industries NH.90-TTH	Airbus Helicopters, Donauwörth
	99+01	Northrop Grumman RQ-4E Euro Hawk	Luftwaffe WTD 61, Manching
	Civil operated aircraft in military use		
	D-HCDL	Eurocopter EC.135P-2+	Marineflieger MFG 5, Nordholz
	D-HDDL	Eurocopter EC.135P-2+	Marineflieger MFG 5, Nordholz
	GHANA		
	9G-EXE	Dassault Falcon 900EASy	Ghana Air Force VIP Flight, Accra
	GREECE		
	Elliniki Polemiki Aeroporía/Hellenic Air Force (HAF)		
	001	Lockheed Martin F-16C-52 Fighting Falcon	HAF 335 Mira/116 PM, Áraxos
	002	Lockheed Martin F-16C-52 Fighting Falcon	HAF 335 Mira/116 PM, Áraxos
	003	Lockheed Martin F-16C-52 Fighting Falcon	HAF 335 Mira/116 PM, Áraxos
	004	Lockheed Martin F-16C-52 Fighting Falcon	HAF 335 Mira/116 PM, Áraxos
	005	Lockheed Martin F-16C-52 Fighting Falcon $	HAF 335 Mira/116 PM, Áraxos
	006	Lockheed Martin F-16C-52 Fighting Falcon	HAF 335 Mira/116 PM, Áraxos
	007	Lockheed Martin F-16C-52 Fighting Falcon	HAF 335 Mira/116 PM, Áraxos
	008	Lockheed Martin F-16C-52 Fighting Falcon	HAF 335 Mira/116 PM, Áraxos

Serial	Type (code/other identity)	Owner/operator, location or fate	Notes
009	Lockheed Martin F-16C-52 Fighting Falcon	HAF 335 Mira/116 PM, Áraxos	
010	Lockheed Martin F-16C-52 Fighting Falcon	HAF 335 Mira/116 PM, Áraxos	
011	Lockheed Martin F-16C-52 Fighting Falcon	HAF 335 Mira/116 PM, Áraxos	
012	Lockheed Martin F-16C-52 Fighting Falcon	HAF 335 Mira/116 PM, Áraxos	
013	Lockheed Martin F-16C-52 Fighting Falcon	HAF 335 Mira/116 PM, Áraxos	
014	Lockheed Martin F-16C-52 Fighting Falcon	HAF 335 Mira/116 PM, Áraxos	
015	Lockheed Martin F-16C-52 Fighting Falcon	HAF 335 Mira/116 PM, Áraxos	
016	Lockheed Martin F-16C-52 Fighting Falcon	HAF 335 Mira/116 PM, Áraxos	
017	Lockheed Martin F-16C-52 Fighting Falcon	HAF 335 Mira/116 PM, Áraxos	
018	Lockheed Martin F-16C-52 Fighting Falcon	HAF 335 Mira/116 PM, Áraxos	
019	Lockheed Martin F-16C-52 Fighting Falcon	HAF 335 Mira/116 PM, Áraxos	
020	Lockheed Martin F-16C-52 Fighting Falcon	HAF 335 Mira/116 PM, Áraxos	
021	Lockheed Martin F-16D-52 Fighting Falcon	HAF 335 Mira/116 PM, Áraxos	
022	Lockheed Martin F-16D-52 Fighting Falcon	HAF 335 Mira/116 PM, Áraxos	
023	Lockheed Martin F-16D-52 Fighting Falcon	HAF 335 Mira/116 PM, Áraxos	
024	Lockheed Martin F-16D-52 Fighting Falcon	HAF 335 Mira/116 PM, Áraxos	
025	Lockheed Martin F-16D-52 Fighting Falcon	HAF 335 Mira/116 PM, Áraxos	
026	Lockheed Martin F-16D-52 Fighting Falcon	HAF 335 Mira/116 PM, Áraxos	
027	Lockheed Martin F-16D-52 Fighting Falcon	HAF 335 Mira/116 PM, Áraxos	
028	Lockheed Martin F-16D-52 Fighting Falcon	HAF 335 Mira/116 PM, Áraxos	
029	Lockheed Martin F-16D-52 Fighting Falcon	HAF 335 Mira/116 PM, Áraxos	
030	Lockheed Martin F-16D-52 Fighting Falcon	HAF 335 Mira/116 PM, Áraxos	
045	Lockheed Martin F-16C-50 Fighting Falcon	HAF 347 Mira/111 PM, Nea Ankhialos	
046	Lockheed Martin F-16C-50 Fighting Falcon	HAF 341 Mira/111 PM, Nea Ankhialos	
047	Lockheed Martin F-16C-50 Fighting Falcon	HAF 347 Mira/111 PM, Nea Ankhialos	
048	Lockheed Martin F-16C-50 Fighting Falcon	HAF 341 Mira/111 PM, Nea Ankhialos	
049	Lockheed Martin F-16C-50 Fighting Falcon	HAF 347 Mira/111 PM, Nea Ankhialos	
050	Lockheed Martin F-16C-50 Fighting Falcon	HAF 341 Mira/111 PM, Nea Ankhialos	
051	Lockheed Martin F-16C-50 Fighting Falcon	HAF 347 Mira/111 PM, Nea Ankhialos	
052	Lockheed Martin F-16C-50 Fighting Falcon	HAF 341 Mira/111 PM, Nea Ankhialos	
053	Lockheed Martin F-16C-50 Fighting Falcon	HAF 347 Mira/111 PM, Nea Ankhialos	
054	Lockheed Martin F-16C-50 Fighting Falcon	HAF 341 Mira/111 PM, Nea Ankhialos	
055	Lockheed Martin F-16C-50 Fighting Falcon	HAF 347 Mira/111 PM, Nea Ankhialos	
056	Lockheed Martin F-16C-50 Fighting Falcon	HAF 341 Mira/111 PM, Nea Ankhialos	
057	Lockheed Martin F-16C-50 Fighting Falcon	HAF 347 Mira/111 PM, Nea Ankhialos	
058	Lockheed Martin F-16C-50 Fighting Falcon	HAF 341 Mira/111 PM, Nea Ankhialos	
060	Lockheed Martin F-16C-50 Fighting Falcon	HAF 347 Mira/111 PM, Nea Ankhialos	
061	Lockheed Martin F-16C-50 Fighting Falcon	HAF 347 Mira/111 PM, Nea Ankhialos	
062	Lockheed Martin F-16C-50 Fighting Falcon $	HAF 341 Mira/111 PM, Nea Ankhialos	
063	Lockheed Martin F-16C-50 Fighting Falcon	HAF 347 Mira/111 PM, Nea Ankhialos	
064	Lockheed Martin F-16C-50 Fighting Falcon	HAF 341 Mira/111 PM, Nea Ankhialos	
065	Lockheed Martin F-16C-50 Fighting Falcon	HAF 347 Mira/111 PM, Nea Ankhialos	
066	Lockheed Martin F-16C-50 Fighting Falcon	HAF 341 Mira/111 PM, Nea Ankhialos	
067	Lockheed Martin F-16C-50 Fighting Falcon	HAF 347 Mira/111 PM, Nea Ankhialos	
068	Lockheed Martin F-16C-50 Fighting Falcon	HAF 341 Mira/111 PM, Nea Ankhialos	
069	Lockheed Martin F-16C-50 Fighting Falcon	HAF 347 Mira/111 PM, Nea Ankhialos	
070	Lockheed Martin F-16C-50 Fighting Falcon	HAF 341 Mira/111 PM, Nea Ankhialos	
071	Lockheed Martin F-16C-50 Fighting Falcon	HAF 347 Mira/111 PM, Nea Ankhialos	
072	Lockheed Martin F-16C-50 Fighting Falcon	HAF 341 Mira/111 PM, Nea Ankhialos	
073	Lockheed Martin F-16C-50 Fighting Falcon	HAF 347 Mira/111 PM, Nea Ankhialos	
074	Lockheed Martin F-16C-50 Fighting Falcon	HAF 341 Mira/111 PM, Nea Ankhialos	
075	Lockheed Martin F-16C-50 Fighting Falcon	HAF 347 Mira/111 PM, Nea Ankhialos	
076	Lockheed Martin F-16C-50 Fighting Falcon $	HAF 341 Mira/111 PM, Nea Ankhialos	
077	Lockheed Martin F-16D-50 Fighting Falcon	HAF 341 Mira/111 PM, Nea Ankhialos	
078	Lockheed Martin F-16D-50 Fighting Falcon	HAF 347 Mira/111 PM, Nea Ankhialos	
079	Lockheed Martin F-16D-50 Fighting Falcon	HAF 347 Mira/111 PM, Nea Ankhialos	
080	Lockheed Martin F-16D-50 Fighting Falcon	HAF 341 Mira/111 PM, Nea Ankhialos	
081	Lockheed Martin F-16D-50 Fighting Falcon	HAF 347 Mira/111 PM, Nea Ankhialos	
082	Lockheed Martin F-16D-50 Fighting Falcon	HAF 341 Mira/111 PM, Nea Ankhialos	
083	Lockheed Martin F-16D-50 Fighting Falcon	HAF 347 Mira/111 PM, Nea Ankhialos	
110	Lockheed Martin F-16C-30 Fighting Falcon	HAF 330 Mira/111 PM, Nea Ankhialos	
111	Lockheed Martin F-16C-30 Fighting Falcon	HAF 330 Mira/111 PM, Nea Ankhialos	

Notes	Serial	Type (code/other identity)	Owner/operator, location or fate
	112	Lockheed Martin F-16C-30 Fighting Falcon	HAF
	113	Lockheed Martin F-16C-30 Fighting Falcon	HAF 330 Mira/111 PM, Nea Ankhialos
	114	Lockheed Martin F-16C-30 Fighting Falcon	HAF 330 Mira/111 PM, Nea Ankhialos
	115	Lockheed Martin F-16C-30 Fighting Falcon	HAF 330 Mira/111 PM, Nea Ankhialos
	116	Lockheed Martin F-16C-30 Fighting Falcon	HAF 330 Mira/111 PM, Nea Ankhialos
	117	Lockheed Martin F-16C-30 Fighting Falcon	HAF 330 Mira/111 PM, Nea Ankhialos
	118	Lockheed Martin F-16C-30 Fighting Falcon	HAF
	119	Lockheed Martin F-16C-30 Fighting Falcon	HAF 330 Mira/111 PM, Nea Ankhialos
	120	Lockheed Martin F-16C-30 Fighting Falcon	HAF
	121	Lockheed Martin F-16C-30 Fighting Falcon	HAF 341 Mira/111 PM, Nea Ankhialos
	122	Lockheed Martin F-16C-30 Fighting Falcon	HAF 330 Mira/111 PM, Nea Ankhialos
	124	Lockheed Martin F-16C-30 Fighting Falcon	HAF
	125	Lockheed Martin F-16C-30 Fighting Falcon	HAF 330 Mira/111 PM, Nea Ankhialos
	126	Lockheed Martin F-16C-30 Fighting Falcon	HAF 330 Mira/111 PM, Nea Ankhialos
	127	Lockheed Martin F-16C-30 Fighting Falcon	HAF 330 Mira/111 PM, Nea Ankhialos
	128	Lockheed Martin F-16C-30 Fighting Falcon	HAF 330 Mira/111 PM, Nea Ankhialos
	129	Lockheed Martin F-16C-30 Fighting Falcon	HAF 330 Mira/111 PM, Nea Ankhialos
	130	Lockheed Martin F-16C-30 Fighting Falcon	HAF 330 Mira/111 PM, Nea Ankhialos
	132	Lockheed Martin F-16C-30 Fighting Falcon	HAF
	133	Lockheed Martin F-16C-30 Fighting Falcon	HAF 330 Mira/111 PM, Nea Ankhialos
	134	Lockheed Martin F-16C-30 Fighting Falcon	HAF 330 Mira/111 PM, Nea Ankhialos
	136	Lockheed Martin F-16C-30 Fighting Falcon	HAF 330 Mira/111 PM, Nea Ankhialos
	138	Lockheed Martin F-16C-30 Fighting Falcon	HAF
	139	Lockheed Martin F-16C-30 Fighting Falcon	HAF 330 Mira/111 PM, Nea Ankhialos
	140	Lockheed Martin F-16C-30 Fighting Falcon	HAF 330 Mira/111 PM, Nea Ankhialos
	141	Lockheed Martin F-16C-30 Fighting Falcon	HAF 330 Mira/111 PM, Nea Ankhialos
	143	Lockheed Martin F-16C-30 Fighting Falcon	HAF 330 Mira/111 PM, Nea Ankhialos
	144	Lockheed Martin F-16D-30 Fighting Falcon	HAF 330 Mira/111 PM, Nea Ankhialos
	145	Lockheed Martin F-16D-30 Fighting Falcon	HAF 330 Mira/111 PM, Nea Ankhialos
	146	Lockheed Martin F-16D-30 Fighting Falcon	HAF
	147	Lockheed Martin F-16D-30 Fighting Falcon	HAF 330 Mira/111 PM, Nea Ankhialos
	148	Lockheed Martin F-16D-30 Fighting Falcon	HAF 330 Mira/111 PM, Nea Ankhialos
	149	Lockheed Martin F-16D-30 Fighting Falcon	HAF 330 Mira/111 PM, Nea Ankhialos
	201	Dassault Mirage 2000-BG	HAF 332 MAPK/114 PM, Tanagra
	202	Dassault Mirage 2000-BG	HAF 332 MAPK/114 PM, Tanagra
	210	Dassault Mirage 2000-EG	HAF 332 MAPK/114 PM, Tanagra
	212	Dassault Mirage 2000-EG	HAF 332 MAPK/114 PM, Tanagra
	213	Dassault Mirage 2000-EG	HAF 332 MAPK/114 PM, Tanagra
	215	Dassault Mirage 2000-EG	HAF 332 MAPK/114 PM, Tanagra
	216	Dassault Mirage 2000-EG	HAF 332 MAPK/114 PM, Tanagra
	217	Dassault Mirage 2000-EG	HAF 332 MAPK/114 PM, Tanagra
	218	Dassault Mirage 2000-EG	HAF 332 MAPK/114 PM, Tanagra
	219	Dassault Mirage 2000-EG	HAF 332 MAPK/114 PM, Tanagra
	220	Dassault Mirage 2000-EG	HAF 332 MAPK/114 PM, Tanagra
	221	Dassault Mirage 2000-EG	HAF 332 MAPK/114 PM, Tanagra
	226	Dassault Mirage 2000-EG	HAF 332 MAPK/114 PM, Tanagra
	231	Dassault Mirage 2000-EG	HAF 332 MAPK/114 PM, Tanagra
	232	Dassault Mirage 2000-EG	HAF 332 MAPK/114 PM, Tanagra
	233	Dassault Mirage 2000-EG	HAF 332 MAPK/114 PM, Tanagra
	237	Dassault Mirage 2000-EG	HAF 332 MAPK/114 PM, Tanagra
	239	Dassault Mirage 2000-EG $	HAF 332 MAPK/114 PM, Tanagra
	241	Dassault Mirage 2000-EG	HAF 332 MAPK/114 PM, Tanagra
	242	Dassault Mirage 2000-EG	HAF 332 MAPK/114 PM, Tanagra
	374	Embraer ERJ.145H AEW&C	HAF 380 Mira/112 PM, Elefsis
	500	Lockheed Martin F-16C-52 Fighting Falcon	HAF 343 Mira/115 PM, Souda
	501	Lockheed Martin F-16C-52 Fighting Falcon	HAF 337 Mira/110 PM, Larissa
	502	Lockheed Martin F-16C-52 Fighting Falcon	HAF 337 Mira/110 PM, Larissa
	503	Lockheed Martin F-16C-52 Fighting Falcon	HAF 343 Mira/115 PM, Souda
	504	Lockheed Martin F-16C-52 Fighting Falcon	HAF 343 Mira/115 PM, Souda
	505	Dassault Mirage 2000-5BG	HAF 331 MAPK/114 PM, Tanagra
	505	Lockheed Martin F-16C-52 Fighting Falcon $	HAF 343 Mira/115 PM, Souda
	506	Dassault Mirage 2000-5BG	HAF 331 MAPK/114 PM, Tanagra

Serial	Type (code/other identity)	Owner/operator, location or fate	Notes
506	Lockheed Martin F-16C-52 Fighting Falcon	HAF 340 Mira/115 PM, Souda	
507	Dassault Mirage 2000-5BG	HAF 331 MAPK/114 PM, Tanagra	
507	Lockheed Martin F-16C-52 Fighting Falcon	HAF 337 Mira/110 PM, Larissa	
508	Dassault Mirage 2000-5BG	HAF 331 MAPK/114 PM, Tanagra	
508	Lockheed Martin F-16C-52 Fighting Falcon	HAF 337 Mira/110 PM, Larissa	
509	Dassault Mirage 2000-5BG	HAF 331 MAPK/114 PM, Tanagra	
509	Lockheed Martin F-16C-52 Fighting Falcon	HAF 343 Mira/115 PM, Souda	
510	Lockheed Martin F-16C-52 Fighting Falcon	HAF 343 Mira/115 PM, Souda	
511	Dassault Mirage 2000-5BG	HAF 331 MAPK/114 PM, Tanagra	
511	Lockheed Martin F-16C-52 Fighting Falcon	HAF 343 Mira/115 PM, Souda	
512	Lockheed Martin F-16C-52 Fighting Falcon	*Destroyed by fire, 2 November 2016, Souda*	
513	Lockheed Martin F-16C-52 Fighting Falcon	HAF 343 Mira/115 PM, Souda	
514	Dassault Mirage 2000-5BG	HAF 331 MAPK/114 PM, Tanagra	
515	Lockheed Martin F-16C-52 Fighting Falcon	HAF 343 Mira/115 PM, Souda	
517	Lockheed Martin F-16C-52 Fighting Falcon	HAF 337 Mira/110 PM, Larissa	
518	Lockheed Martin F-16C-52 Fighting Falcon	HAF 340 Mira/115 PM, Souda	
519	Lockheed Martin F-16C-52 Fighting Falcon	HAF 340 Mira/115 PM, Souda	
520	Lockheed Martin F-16C-52 Fighting Falcon	HAF 343 Mira/115 PM, Souda	
521	Lockheed Martin F-16C-52 Fighting Falcon	HAF 340 Mira/115 PM, Souda	
523	Lockheed Martin F-16C-52 Fighting Falcon $	HAF 340 Mira/115 PM, Souda	
524	Lockheed Martin F-16C-52 Fighting Falcon	HAF 337 Mira/110 PM, Larissa	
525	Lockheed Martin F-16C-52 Fighting Falcon	HAF 340 Mira/115 PM, Souda	
526	Lockheed Martin F-16C-52 Fighting Falcon	HAF 343 Mira/115 PM, Souda	
527	Dassault Mirage 2000-5BG	HAF 331 MAPK/114 PM, Tanagra	
527	Lockheed Martin F-16C-52 Fighting Falcon	HAF 343 Mira/115 PM, Souda	
528	Lockheed Martin F-16C-52 Fighting Falcon	HAF 337 Mira/110 PM, Larissa	
529	Lockheed Martin F-16C-52 Fighting Falcon	HAF 343 Mira/115 PM, Souda	
530	Dassault Mirage 2000-5BG	HAF 331 MAPK/114 PM, Tanagra	
530	Lockheed Martin F-16C-52 Fighting Falcon	HAF 337 Mira/110 PM, Larissa	
531	Lockheed Martin F-16C-52 Fighting Falcon	HAF 337 Mira/110 PM, Larissa	
532	Lockheed Martin F-16C-52 Fighting Falcon	HAF 337 Mira/110 PM, Larissa	
533	Lockheed Martin F-16C-52 Fighting Falcon	HAF 340 Mira/115 PM, Souda	
534	Dassault Mirage 2000-5BG	HAF 331 MAPK/114 PM, Tanagra	
534	Lockheed Martin F-16C-52 Fighting Falcon	HAF 340 Mira/115 PM, Souda	
535	Dassault Mirage 2000-5BG	HAF 331 MAPK/114 PM, Tanagra	
535	Lockheed Martin F-16C-52 Fighting Falcon	HAF 340 Mira/115 PM, Souda	
536	Dassault Mirage 2000-5BG	HAF 331 MAPK/114 PM, Tanagra	
536	Lockheed Martin F-16C-52 Fighting Falcon	HAF 340 Mira/115 PM, Souda	
537	Lockheed Martin F-16C-52 Fighting Falcon	HAF 340 Mira/115 PM, Souda	
538	Lockheed Martin F-16C-52 Fighting Falcon	HAF 340 Mira/115 PM, Souda	
539	Lockheed Martin F-16C-52 Fighting Falcon	HAF 337 Mira/110 PM, Larissa	
540	Dassault Mirage 2000-5BG	HAF 331 MAPK/114 PM, Tanagra	
543	Dassault Mirage 2000-5BG	HAF 331 MAPK/114 PM, Tanagra	
545	Dassault Mirage 2000-5BG	HAF 331 MAPK/114 PM, Tanagra	
546	Dassault Mirage 2000-5BG	HAF 331 MAPK/114 PM, Tanagra	
547	Dassault Mirage 2000-5BG	HAF 331 MAPK/114 PM, Tanagra	
548	Dassault Mirage 2000-5BG	HAF 331 MAPK/114 PM, Tanagra	
549	Dassault Mirage 2000-5BG	HAF 331 MAPK/114 PM, Tanagra	
550	Dassault Mirage 2000-5BG	HAF 331 MAPK/114 PM, Tanagra	
551	Dassault Mirage 2000-5BG	HAF 331 MAPK/114 PM, Tanagra	
552	Dassault Mirage 2000-5BG	HAF 331 MAPK/114 PM, Tanagra	
553	Dassault Mirage 2000-5BG	HAF 331 MAPK/114 PM, Tanagra	
554	Dassault Mirage 2000-5BG	HAF 331 MAPK/114 PM, Tanagra	
555	Dassault Mirage 2000-5BG	HAF 331 MAPK/114 PM, Tanagra	
600	Lockheed Martin F-16D-52 Fighting Falcon	HAF 337 Mira/110 PM, Larissa	
601	Lockheed Martin F-16D-52 Fighting Falcon	HAF 340 Mira/115 PM, Souda	
602	Lockheed Martin F-16D-52 Fighting Falcon	HAF 340 Mira/115 PM, Souda	
603	Lockheed Martin F-16D-52 Fighting Falcon	HAF 340 Mira/115 PM, Souda	
605	Lockheed Martin F-16D-52 Fighting Falcon	HAF 340 Mira/115 PM, Souda	
606	Lockheed Martin F-16D-52 Fighting Falcon	HAF 337 Mira/110 PM, Larissa	
607	Lockheed Martin F-16D-52 Fighting Falcon	HAF 343 Mira/115 PM, Souda	
608	Lockheed Martin F-16D-52 Fighting Falcon	HAF 340 Mira/115 PM, Souda	

Notes	Serial	Type (code/other identity)	Owner/operator, location or fate
	609	Lockheed Martin F-16D-52 Fighting Falcon	HAF 337 Mira/110 PM, Larissa
	610	Lockheed Martin F-16D-52 Fighting Falcon	HAF 340 Mira/115 PM, Souda
	611	Lockheed Martin F-16D-52 Fighting Falcon	HAF 337 Mira/110 PM, Larissa
	612	Lockheed Martin F-16D-52 Fighting Falcon	HAF 337 Mira/110 PM, Larissa
	613	Lockheed Martin F-16D-52 Fighting Falcon	HAF 343 Mira/115 PM, Souda
	615	Lockheed Martin F-16D-52 Fighting Falcon	HAF 343 Mira/115 PM, Souda
	616	Lockheed Martin F-16D-52 Fighting Falcon	HAF 343 Mira/115 PM, Souda
	617	Lockheed Martin F-16D-52 Fighting Falcon	HAF 343 Mira/115 PM, Souda
	618	Lockheed Martin F-16D-52 Fighting Falcon	HAF 343 Mira/115 PM, Souda
	619	Lockheed Martin F-16D-52 Fighting Falcon $	HAF 337 Mira/110 PM, Larissa
	671	Embraer ERJ.145H AEW&C	HAF 380 Mira/112 PM, Elefsís
	678	Gulfstream Aerospace Gulfstream V	HAF 352 MMYP/112 PM, Elefsís
	729	Embraer ERJ.145H AEW&C	HAF 380 Mira/112 PM, Elefsís
	741	Lockheed C-130H Hercules (ECM)	HAF 356 MTM/112 PM, Elefsís
	742	Lockheed C-130H Hercules	HAF 356 MTM/112 PM, Elefsís
	743	Lockheed C-130H Hercules	HAF 356 MTM/112 PM, Elefsís
	744	Lockheed C-130H Hercules	HAF 356 MTM/112 PM, Elefsís
	745	Lockheed C-130H Hercules $	HAF 356 MTM/112 PM, Elefsís
	746	Lockheed C-130H Hercules	HAF 356 MTM/112 PM, Elefsís
	747	Lockheed C-130H Hercules (ECM)	HAF 356 MTM/112 PM, Elefsís
	749	Lockheed C-130H Hercules	HAF 356 MTM/112 PM, Elefsís
	751	Lockheed C-130H Hercules	HAF 356 MTM/112 PM, Elefsís
	752	Lockheed C-130H Hercules $	HAF 356 MTM/112 PM, Elefsís
	757	Embraer ERJ.145H AEW&C	HAF 380 Mira/112 PM, Elefsís
	4117	Aeritalia C-27J Spartan	HAF 354 Mira, Elefsís
	4118	Aeritalia C-27J Spartan	HAF 354 Mira, Elefsís
	4120	Aeritalia C-27J Spartan	HAF 354 Mira, Elefsís
	4121	Aeritalia C-27J Spartan	HAF 354 Mira, Elefsís
	4122	Aeritalia C-27J Spartan	HAF 354 Mira, Elefsís
	4123	Aeritalia C-27J Spartan	HAF 354 Mira, Elefsís
	4124	Aeritalia C-27J Spartan	HAF 354 Mira, Elefsís
	4125	Aeritalia C-27J Spartan	HAF 354 Mira, Elefsís
	135L-484	Embraer ERJ.135BJ Legacy	HAF 352 MMYP/112 PM, Elefsís
	145-209	Embraer ERJ.135LR	HAF 352 MMYP/112 PM, Elefsís

HONDURAS
Fuerza Aérea Hondureña (FAH)/Honduran Air Force

	FAH-001	Embraer ERJ.135BJ Legacy 600	FAH, Tegucigalpa

HUNGARY
Magyar Légierö/Hungarian Air Force

	01	Boeing C-17A Globemaster III (08-0001)	Hungarian AF SAC, Heavy Airlift Wing, Pápa
	02	Boeing C-17A Globemaster III (08-0002)	Hungarian AF SAC, Heavy Airlift Wing, Pápa
	03	Boeing C-17A Globemaster III (08-0003)	Hungarian AF SAC, Heavy Airlift Wing, Pápa
	30	SAAB 39C Gripen	Hungarian AF 59 Sz.D.REB, Kecskemét
	31	SAAB 39C Gripen	Hungarian AF 59 Sz.D.REB, Kecskemét
	32	SAAB 39C Gripen	Hungarian AF 59 Sz.D.REB, Kecskemét
	33	SAAB 39C Gripen	Hungarian AF 59 Sz.D.REB, Kecskemét
	34	SAAB 39C Gripen	Hungarian AF 59 Sz.D.REB, Kecskemét
	35	SAAB 39C Gripen	Hungarian AF 59 Sz.D.REB, Kecskemét
	36	SAAB 39C Gripen	Hungarian AF 59 Sz.D.REB, Kecskemét
	37	SAAB 39C Gripen	Hungarian AF 59 Sz.D.REB, Kecskemét
	38	SAAB 39C Gripen	Hungarian AF 59 Sz.D.REB, Kecskemét
	39	SAAB 39C Gripen	Hungarian AF 59 Sz.D.REB, Kecskemét
	40	SAAB 39C Gripen $	Hungarian AF 59 Sz.D.REB, Kecskemét
	41	SAAB 39C Gripen	Hungarian AF 59 Sz.D.REB, Kecskemét
	43	SAAB 39D Gripen	Hungarian AF 59 Sz.D.REB, Kecskemét
	44	SAAB 39D Gripen (39842)	Hungarian AF 59 Sz.D.REB, Kecskemét
	110	Antonov An-26	Hungarian AF 59 Sz.D.REB, Kecskemét
	405	Antonov An-26	Hungarian AF 59 Sz.D.REB, Kecskemét
	406	Antonov An-26	Hungarian AF 59 Sz.D.REB, Kecskemét
	407	Antonov An-26	Hungarian AF 59 Sz.D.REB, Kecskemét

Serial	Type (code/other identity)	Owner/operator, location or fate	Notes
603	Antonov An-26	Hungarian AF 59 Sz.D.REB, Kecskemét	

INDIA
Bharatiya Vayu Sena/Indian Air Force (IAF)

CB-8001	Boeing C-17A Globemaster III	IAF 81 Sqn, Hindon AB	
CB-8002	Boeing C-17A Globemaster III	IAF 81 Sqn, Hindon AB	
CB-8003	Boeing C-17A Globemaster III	IAF 81 Sqn, Hindon AB	
CB-8004	Boeing C-17A Globemaster III	IAF 81 Sqn, Hindon AB	
CB-8005	Boeing C-17A Globemaster III	IAF 81 Sqn, Hindon AB	
CB-8006	Boeing C-17A Globemaster III	IAF 81 Sqn, Hindon AB	
CB-8007	Boeing C-17A Globemaster III	IAF 81 Sqn, Hindon AB	
CB-8008	Boeing C-17A Globemaster III	IAF 81 Sqn, Hindon AB	
CB-8009	Boeing C-17A Globemaster III	IAF 81 Sqn, Hindon AB	
CB-8010	Boeing C-17A Globemaster III	IAF 81 Sqn, Hindon AB	
KC-3801	Lockheed C-130J-30 Hercules II	IAF 77 Sqn, Hindon AB/87 Sqn, Arjan Singh AB	
KC-3802	Lockheed C-130J-30 Hercules II	IAF 77 Sqn, Hindon AB/87 Sqn, Arjan Singh AB	
KC-3804	Lockheed C-130J-30 Hercules II	IAF 77 Sqn, Hindon AB/87 Sqn, Arjan Singh AB	
KC-3805	Lockheed C-130J-30 Hercules II	IAF 77 Sqn, Hindon AB/87 Sqn, Arjan Singh AB	
KC-3806	Lockheed C-130J-30 Hercules II	IAF 77 Sqn, Hindon AB/87 Sqn, Arjan Singh AB	
KC-3807	Lockheed C-130J-30 Hercules II	(on order)	
KC-3808	Lockheed C-130J-30 Hercules II	(on order)	
KC-3809	Lockheed C-130J-30 Hercules II	(on order)	
KC-3810	Lockheed C-130J-30 Hercules II	(on order)	
KC-3811	Lockheed C-130J-30 Hercules II	(on order)	
KC-3812	Lockheed C-130J-30 Hercules II	(on order)	
KC-3813	Lockheed C-130J-30 Hercules II	(on order)	

INDONESIA
Indonesian Government

A-001	Boeing 737-8U3	Government of Indonesia, Jakarta	

ISRAEL
Heyl ha'Avir/Israeli Air Force

102	Lockheed C-130H Karnaf	Israeli AF 131 Sqn, Nevatim	
140	Boeing KC-707 Re'em	Israeli AF 120 Sqn, Nevatim	
208	Lockheed C-130E Karnaf	Israeli AF 131 Sqn, Nevatim	
248	Boeing KC-707 Re'em	Israeli AF 120 Sqn, Nevatim	
250	Boeing KC-707 Re'em	Israeli AF 120 Sqn, Nevatim	
260	Boeing KC-707 Re'em	Israeli AF 120 Sqn, Nevatim	
264	Boeing KC-707 Re'em	Israeli AF 120 Sqn, Nevatim	
272	Boeing KC-707 Re'em	Israeli AF 120 Sqn, Nevatim	
275	Boeing KC-707 Re'em	Israeli AF 120 Sqn, Nevatim	
290	Boeing KC-707 Re'em	Israeli AF 120 Sqn, Nevatim	
295	Boeing VC-707 Re'em	Israeli AF 120 Sqn, Nevatim	
305	Lockheed C-130E Karnaf	Israeli AF 131 Sqn, Nevatim	
309	Lockheed C-130E Karnaf	Israeli AF 131 Sqn, Nevatim	
310	Lockheed C-130E Karnaf	Israeli AF 131 Sqn, Nevatim	
314	Lockheed C-130E Karnaf	Israeli AF 131 Sqn, Nevatim	
316	Lockheed C-130E Karnaf	Israeli AF 131 Sqn, Nevatim	
318	Lockheed C-130E Karnaf	Israeli AF 131 Sqn, Nevatim	
420	Lockheed KC-130H Karnaf	Israeli AF 131 Sqn, Nevatim	
427	Lockheed C-130H Karnaf	Israeli AF 131 Sqn, Nevatim	
428	Lockheed C-130H Karnaf	Israeli AF 131 Sqn, Nevatim	
435	Lockheed C-130H Karnaf	Israeli AF 131 Sqn, Nevatim	
436	Lockheed C-130H Karnaf	Israeli AF 131 Sqn, Nevatim	
522	Lockheed KC-130H Karnaf	Israeli AF 131 Sqn, Nevatim	
545	Lockheed KC-130H Karnaf	Israeli AF 131 Sqn, Nevatim	
661	Lockheed C-130J-30 Shimshon	Israeli AF 103 Sqn, Nevatim	
662	Lockheed C-130J-30 Shimshon	Israeli AF 103 Sqn, Nevatim	
663	Lockheed C-130J-30 Shimshon	(on order)	
664	Lockheed C-130J-30 Shimshon	(on order)	
665	Lockheed C-130J-30 Shimshon	Israeli AF 103 Sqn, Nevatim	

Notes	Serial	Type (code/other identity)	Owner/operator, location or fate
	667	Lockheed C-130J-30 Shimshon	Israeli AF 103 Sqn, Nevatim
	668	Lockheed C-130J-30 Shimshon	(on order)

ITALY:

Aeronautica Militare Italiana (AMI), Aviazione dell'Esercito, Guardia di Finanza (GdiF) & Marina Militare Italiana (MMI)

Notes	Serial	Type (code/other identity)	Owner/operator, location or fate
	MMX602	Eurofighter F-2000A Typhoon [RS-01]	Alenia, stored Torino/Caselle
	MMX603	Eurofighter F-2000A Typhoon [RMV-01]	*Preserved at Cameri*
	MMX614	Eurofighter TF-2000A Typhoon	Alenia, Torino/Caselle
	CPX616	Aermacchi M-346 Master	Aermacchi, Venegono
	CPX619	Aermacchi M-345HET [1]	Aermacchi, Venegono
	CPX622	Aermacchi M-346A Master	Aermacchi, Venegono
	MM7003	Panavia A-200C Tornado (IDS (MLU))	*Scrapped at Cameri*
	MM7004	Panavia A-200C Tornado (IDS (MLU)) [6-55]	AMI GEA 6° Stormo, Ghedi
	MM7006	Panavia A-200C Tornado (IDS (MLU)) [6-31] $	AMI GEA 6° Stormo, Ghedi
	MM7007	Panavia A-200A Tornado (IDS) [6-01] $	AMI GEA 6° Stormo, Ghedi
	MM7008	Panavia A-200C Tornado (IDS (MLU)) [50-53]	AMI GEA 6° Stormo, Ghedi
	MM7013	Panavia A-200C Tornado (IDS (MLU)) [6-75]	AMI GEA 6° Stormo, Ghedi
	MM7014	Panavia A-200C Tornado (IDS (MLU)) [6-13]	AMI GEA 6° Stormo, Ghedi
	MM7015	Panavia A-200C Tornado (IDS (MLU)) [6-32]	AMI GEA 6° Stormo, Ghedi
	MM7019	Panavia EA-200B Tornado (ECR) [50-05]	AMI GEA 6° Stormo, Ghedi
	MM7020	Panavia EA-200B Tornado (ECR) [50-41]	AMI GEA 6° Stormo, Ghedi
	MM7021	Panavia EA-200B Tornado (ECR) [6-20]	AMI GEA 6° Stormo, Ghedi
	MM7023	Panavia A-200A Tornado (IDS) [6-63]	AMI GEA 6° Stormo, Ghedi
	MM7024	Panavia A-200C Tornado (IDS (MLU)) [6-50]	AMI GEA 6° Stormo, Ghedi
	MM7025	Panavia A-200A Tornado (IDS) [6-05]	AMI GEA 6° Stormo, Ghedi
	MM7026	Panavia A-200C Tornado (IDS (MLU)) [6-35]	AMI GEA 6° Stormo, Ghedi
	MM7029	Panavia A-200A Tornado (IDS) [6-22]	AMI GEA 6° Stormo, Ghedi
	CSX7030	Panavia EA-200C Tornado (ECR (MLU))	Leonardo, Turin
	MM7034	Panavia EA-200B Tornado (ECR)	AMI, stored Gioia del Colle
	MM7035	Panavia A-200C Tornado (IDS (MLU)) [6-27]	AMI GEA 6° Stormo, Ghedi
	MM7036	Panavia EA-200B Tornado (ECR) [6-06]	AMI GEA 6° Stormo, Ghedi
	MM7037	Panavia A-200A Tornado (IDS) [6-16]	AMI GEA 6° Stormo, Ghedi
	MM7038	Panavia A-200C Tornado (IDS (MLU)) [6-37]	AMI GEA 6° Stormo, Ghedi
	MM7039	Panavia EA-200C Tornado (ECR (MLU)) [6-33]	AMI GEA 6° Stormo, Ghedi
	MM7040	Panavia A-200A Tornado (IDS) [6-21]	AMI GEA 6° Stormo, Ghedi
	CSX7041	Panavia A-200C Tornado (IDS (MLU)) [RS-01] $	AMI RSV, Pratica di Mare
	MM7042	Panavia A-200A Tornado (IDS)	*Scrapped*
	MM7043	Panavia A-200A Tornado (IDS) [6-25]	AMI GEA 6° Stormo, Ghedi
	MM7044	Panavia A-200C Tornado (IDS (MLU)) [6-76]	AMI GEA 6° Stormo, Ghedi
	MM7047	Panavia EA-200C Tornado (ECR (MLU)) [50-43]	AMI GEA 6° Stormo, Ghedi
	MM7048	Panavia A-200C Tornado (IDS (MLU))	*Withdrawn from use, 2016*
	MM7051	Panavia EA-200B Tornado (ECR) [6-72]	AMI GEA 6° Stormo, Ghedi
	MM7052	Panavia EA-200C Tornado (ECR (MLU)) [50-02]	AMI GEA 6° Stormo, Ghedi
	MM7053	Panavia EA-200B Tornado (ECR) [50-07]	AMI GEA 6° Stormo, Ghedi
	MM7054	Panavia EA-200C Tornado (ECR (MLU)) [50-40] $	AMI GEA 6° Stormo, Ghedi
	MM7055	Panavia A-200A Tornado (IDS) [50-42]	AMI GEA 6° Stormo, Ghedi
	MM7056	Panavia A-200A Tornado (IDS)	AMI GEA 6° Stormo, Ghedi
	MM7057	Panavia A-200A Tornado (IDS) [6-04]	AMI GEA 6° Stormo, Ghedi
	MM7058	Panavia A-200C Tornado (IDS (MLU)) [6-11]	AMI GEA 6° Stormo, Ghedi
	MM7059	Panavia A-200A Tornado (IDS) [6-66]	AMI GEA 6° Stormo, Ghedi
	MM7062	Panavia EA-200C Tornado (ECR (MLU)) [50-44]	AMI GEA 6° Stormo, Ghedi
	MM7063	Panavia A-200C Tornado (IDS (MLU)) [6-26]	AMI GEA 6° Stormo, Ghedi
	MM7065	Panavia A-200C Tornado (IDS (MLU)) [50-56]	*Withdrawn from use at Cameri, 2015*
	MM7066	Panavia A-200A Tornado (IDS) [50-03]	AMI GEA 6° Stormo, Ghedi
	MM7067	Panavia EA-200C Tornado (ECR (MLU))	AMI GEA 6° Stormo, Ghedi
	MM7068	Panavia EA-200B Tornado (ECR) [6-67]	AMI GEA 6° Stormo, Ghedi
	MM7070	Panavia EA-200C Tornado (ECR (MLU)) [6-71]	AMI GEA 6° Stormo, Ghedi
	MM7071	Panavia A-200C Tornado (IDS (MLU)) [6-12]	AMI GEA 6° Stormo, Ghedi
	MM7072	Panavia A-200C Tornado (IDS (MLU)) [6-30]	AMI GEA 6° Stormo, Ghedi
	MM7073	Panavia EA-200B Tornado (ECR) [6-34]	AMI GEA 6° Stormo, Ghedi
	MM7075	Panavia A-200A Tornado (IDS) [6-07]	AMI GEA 6° Stormo, Ghedi

Serial	Type (code/other identity)	Owner/operator, location or fate	Notes
CMX7079	Panavia EA-200B Tornado (ECR)	Alenia, Torino/Caselle	
MM7081	Panavia EA-200C Tornado (ECR (MLU)) [6-57]	AMI GEA 6° Stormo, Ghedi	
MM7082	Panavia EA-200C Tornado (ECR (MLU)) [6-62]	AMI GEA 6° Stormo, Ghedi	
MM7083	Panavia A-200A Tornado (IDS)	AMI GEA 6° Stormo, Ghedi	
MM7084	Panavia EA-200C Tornado (ECR (MLU)) [50-52]	AMI GEA 6° Stormo, Ghedi	
CMX7085	Panavia A-200A Tornado (IDS) [36-50]	Alenia, Torino/Caselle	
MM7086	Panavia A-200A Tornado (IDS) [6-60]	AMI GEA 6° Stormo, Ghedi	
MM7088	Panavia A-200A Tornado (IDS) [6-10]	AMI GEA 6° Stormo, Ghedi	
MM7126	Aeritalia-EMB A-11B (AMX-ACOL) [51-61]	AMI GEA 51° Stormo, Istrana	
MM7129	Aeritalia-EMB A-11B (AMX-ACOL) [32-15]	AMI, stored Amendola	
MM7147	Aeritalia-EMB A-11A (AMX) [32-01] $	Withdrawn from use, 2015	
MM7148	Aeritalia-EMB A-11B (AMX-ACOL)	AMI, stored Amendola	
MM7149	Aeritalia-EMB A-11B (AMX-ACOL) [51-26]	AMI GEA 51° Stormo, Istrana	
MM7151	Aeritalia-EMB A-11B (AMX-ACOL) [51-51]	AMI GEA 51° Stormo, Istrana	
MM7159	Aeritalia-EMB A-11A (AMX) [51-10] $	AMI GEA 51° Stormo, Istrana	
MM7160	Aeritalia-EMB A-11B (AMX-ACOL)	AMI, stored Amendola	
MM7161	Aeritalia-EMB A-11B (AMX-ACOL) [51-37]	AMI GEA 51° Stormo, Istrana	
MM7162	Aeritalia-EMB A-11B (AMX-ACOL) [51-33]	AMI GEA 51° Stormo, Istrana	
MM7163	Aeritalia-EMB A-11B (AMX-ACOL) [51-72]	AMI GEA 51° Stormo, Istrana	
MM7164	Aeritalia-EMB A-11B (AMX-ACOL) [51-40]	AMI GEA 51° Stormo, Istrana	
MM7165	Aeritalia-EMB A-11B (AMX-ACOL) [32-16]	AMI, stored Amendola	
MM7166	Aeritalia-EMB A-11B (AMX-ACOL) [51-32]	AMI GEA 51° Stormo, Istrana	
MM7167	Aeritalia-EMB A-11B (AMX-ACOL) [51-56]	AMI GEA 51° Stormo, Istrana	
MM7168	Aeritalia-EMB A-11B (AMX-ACOL) [51-55]	AMI GEA 51° Stormo, Istrana	
MM7169	Aeritalia-EMB A-11B (AMX-ACOL) [51-66]	AMI GEA 51° Stormo, Istrana	
MM7170	Aeritalia-EMB A-11B (AMX-ACOL) [51-30]	AMI GEA 51° Stormo, Istrana	
MM7171	Aeritalia-EMB A-11B (AMX-ACOL) [51-52]	AMI GEA 51° Stormo, Istrana	
MM7172	Aeritalia-EMB A-11B (AMX-ACOL)	AMI GEA 51° Stormo, Istrana	
MM7173	Aeritalia-EMB A-11B (AMX-ACOL) [51-63]	AMI GEA 51° Stormo, Istrana	
MM7174	Aeritalia-EMB A-11B (AMX-ACOL) [51-60]	AMI GEA 51° Stormo, Istrana	
MM7175	Aeritalia-EMB A-11A (AMX) [51-45]	AMI GEA 51° Stormo, Istrana	
MM7176	Aeritalia-EMB A-11B (AMX-ACOL)	AMI GEA 51° Stormo, Istrana	
MM7177	Aeritalia-EMB A-11B (AMX-ACOL) [51-42]	AMI GEA 51° Stormo, Istrana	
MM7178	Aeritalia-EMB A-11B (AMX-ACOL) [51-43]	AMI GEA 51° Stormo, Istrana	
MM7179	Aeritalia-EMB A-11B (AMX-ACOL) [51-64]	AMI GEA 51° Stormo, Istrana	
MM7180	Aeritalia-EMB A-11B (AMX-ACOL) [51-53]	Alenia, Torino/Caselle	
MM7182	Aeritalia-EMB A-11B (AMX-ACOL) [51-62]	AMI GEA 51° Stormo, Istrana	
MM7183	Aeritalia-EMB A-11B (AMX-ACOL) [51-41]	AMI GEA 51° Stormo, Istrana	
MM7184	Aeritalia-EMB A-11B (AMX-ACOL) [51-65]	AMI GEA 51° Stormo, Istrana	
MM7185	Aeritalia-EMB A-11B (AMX-ACOL) [51-36]	AMI GEA 51° Stormo, Istrana	
MM7186	Aeritalia-EMB A-11B (AMX-ACOL) [51-50]	AMI GEA 51° Stormo, Istrana	
MM7189	Aeritalia-EMB A-11B (AMX-ACOL) [51-71]	AMI GEA 51° Stormo, Istrana	
MM7190	Aeritalia-EMB A-11B (AMX-ACOL) [51-57]	AMI GEA 51° Stormo, Istrana	
MM7191	Aeritalia-EMB A-11B (AMX-ACOL) [51-34]	AMI GEA 51° Stormo, Istrana	
MM7192	Aeritalia-EMB A-11B (AMX-ACOL) [51-70]	AMI GEA 51° Stormo, Istrana	
MM7194	Aeritalia-EMB A-11B (AMX-ACOL) [51-67]	AMI GEA 51° Stormo, Istrana	
CSX7195	Aeritalia-EMB A-11A (AMX)	Withdrawn from use, 2016	
MM7196	Aeritalia-EMB A-11A (AMX) [51-35]	AMI GEA 51° Stormo, Istrana	
MM7197	Aeritalia-EMB A-11B (AMX-ACOL) [51-46]	AMI GEA 51° Stormo, Istrana	
MM7198	Aeritalia-EMB A-11B (AMX-ACOL) [51-44] $	AMI GEA 51° Stormo, Istrana	
MM7199	McDonnell Douglas AV-8B Harrier II+ [1-03]	MMI Gruppo Aerei Imbarcarti, Taranto/Grottaglie	
MM7200	McDonnell Douglas AV-8B Harrier II+ [1-04]	MMI Gruppo Aerei Imbarcarti, Taranto/Grottaglie	
MM7201	McDonnell Douglas AV-8B Harrier II+ [1-05]	MMI Gruppo Aerei Imbarcarti, Taranto/Grottaglie	
MM7212	McDonnell Douglas AV-8B Harrier II+ [1-06]	MMI Gruppo Aerei Imbarcarti, Taranto/Grottaglie	
MM7213	McDonnell Douglas AV-8B Harrier II+ [1-07]	MMI Gruppo Aerei Imbarcarti, Taranto/Grottaglie	
MM7214	McDonnell Douglas AV-8B Harrier II+ [1-08]	MMI Gruppo Aerei Imbarcarti, Taranto/Grottaglie	
MM7215	McDonnell Douglas AV-8B Harrier II+ [1-09]	MMI Gruppo Aerei Imbarcarti, Taranto/Grottaglie	
MM7217	McDonnell Douglas AV-8B Harrier II+ [1-11]	Alenia Gruppo Aerei Imbarcarti, Taranto/Grottaglie	
MM7218	McDonnell Douglas AV-8B Harrier II+ [1-12]	MMI Gruppo Aerei Imbarcarti, Taranto/Grottaglie	
MM7219	McDonnell Douglas AV-8B Harrier II+ [1-13]	MMI Gruppo Aerei Imbarcarti, Taranto/Grottaglie	
MM7220	McDonnell Douglas AV-8B Harrier II+ [1-14]	MMI Gruppo Aerei Imbarcarti, Taranto/Grottaglie	
MM7222	McDonnell Douglas AV-8B Harrier II+ [1-16]	MMI Gruppo Aerei Imbarcarti, Taranto/Grottaglie	

Notes	Serial	Type (code/other identity)	Owner/operator, location or fate
	MM7223	McDonnell Douglas AV-8B Harrier II+ [1-18]	MMI Gruppo Aerei Imbarcati, Taranto/Grottaglie
	MM7224	McDonnell Douglas AV-8B Harrier II+ [1-19] $	MMI Gruppo Aerei Imbarcati, Taranto/Grottaglie
	MM7235	Eurofighter F-2000A Typhoon [4-13]	AMI 904° GEA, Grosseto
	MM7270	Eurofighter F-2000A Typhoon [4-1]	AMI 904° GEA, Grosseto
	MM7271	Eurofighter F-2000A Typhoon [4-15]	AMI 904° GEA, Grosseto
	MM7272	Eurofighter F-2000A Typhoon [36-14]	AMI 936° GEA, Gioia del Colle
	MM7273	Eurofighter F-2000A Typhoon [4-10]	AMI 904° GEA, Grosseto
	MM7274	Eurofighter F-2000A Typhoon [4-4]	AMI 904° GEA, Grosseto
	MM7275	Eurofighter F-2000A Typhoon [36-11]	AMI 936° GEA, Gioia del Colle
	MM7276	Eurofighter F-2000A Typhoon [36-05]	AMI 936° GEA, Gioia del Colle
	MM7277	Eurofighter F-2000A Typhoon [4-40]	AMI 904° GEA, Grosseto
	MM7278	Eurofighter F-2000A Typhoon [RS-23]	AMI RSV, Pratica di Mare
	MM7279	Eurofighter F-2000A Typhoon [4-20]	AMI 904° GEA, Grosseto
	MM7280	Eurofighter F-2000A Typhoon [36-30]	AMI 936° GEA, Gioia del Colle
	MM7281	Eurofighter F-2000A Typhoon [4-14]	AMI 904° GEA, Grosseto
	MM7282	Eurofighter F-2000A Typhoon [36-15]	AMI 936° GEA, Gioia del Colle
	MM7284	Eurofighter F-2000A Typhoon [36-10]	AMI 936° GEA, Gioia del Colle
	MM7285	Eurofighter F-2000A Typhoon [36-07]	AMI 936° GEA, Gioia del Colle
	MM7286	Eurofighter F-2000A Typhoon [36-02]	AMI 936° GEA, Gioia del Colle
	MM7287	Eurofighter F-2000A Typhoon [4-3]	AMI 904° GEA, Grosseto
	MM7288	Eurofighter F-2000A Typhoon [36-42]	AMI 936° GEA, Gioia del Colle
	MM7289	Eurofighter F-2000A Typhoon [4-5]	AMI 904° GEA, Grosseto
	MM7290	Eurofighter F-2000A Typhoon [4-7]	AMI 904° GEA, Grosseto
	MM7291	Eurofighter F-2000A Typhoon [4-11]	AMI 904° GEA, Grosseto
	MM7292	Eurofighter F-2000A Typhoon [36-21]	AMI 936° GEA, Gioia del Colle
	MM7293	Eurofighter F-2000A Typhoon [36-33]	AMI 936° GEA, Gioia del Colle
	MM7294	Eurofighter F-2000A Typhoon [4-52]	AMI 904° GEA, Grosseto
	MM7295	Eurofighter F-2000A Typhoon [4-51]	AMI 904° GEA, Grosseto
	MM7296	Eurofighter F-2000A Typhoon [36-22]	AMI 936° GEA, Gioia del Colle
	MM7297	Eurofighter F-2000A Typhoon [36-23]	AMI 936° GEA, Gioia del Colle
	MM7298	Eurofighter F-2000A Typhoon [36-24]	AMI 936° GEA, Gioia del Colle
	MM7299	Eurofighter F-2000A Typhoon [4-41]	AMI 904° GEA, Grosseto
	MM7300	Eurofighter F-2000A Typhoon [4-44]	AMI 904° GEA, Grosseto
	MM7301	Eurofighter F-2000A Typhoon [4-53]	AMI 904° GEA, Grosseto
	MM7302	Eurofighter F-2000A Typhoon [36-25]	AMI 936° GEA, Gioia del Colle
	MM7303	Eurofighter F-2000A Typhoon [4-2]	AMI 904° GEA, Grosseto
	MM7304	Eurofighter F-2000A Typhoon [4-21]	AMI 904° GEA, Grosseto
	CSX7305	Eurofighter F-2000A Typhoon	AMI RSV, Pratica di Mare
	MM7306	Eurofighter F-2000A Typhoon [4-50]	AMI 904° GEA, Grosseto
	MM7307	Eurofighter F-2000A Typhoon [37-01]	AMI 18° Gruppo/37° Stormo, Trapani/Birgi
	MM7308	Eurofighter F-2000A Typhoon [36-31]	AMI 936° GEA, Gioia del Colle
	MM7309	Eurofighter F-2000A Typhoon [37-03]	AMI 18° Gruppo/37° Stormo, Trapani/Birgi
	MM7310	Eurofighter F-2000A Typhoon [36-32]	AMI 936° GEA, Gioia del Colle
	MM7311	Eurofighter F-2000A Typhoon [37-10]	AMI 18° Gruppo/37° Stormo, Trapani/Birgi
	MM7312	Eurofighter F-2000A Typhoon [36-34]	AMI 936° GEA, Gioia del Colle
	MM7313	Eurofighter F-2000A Typhoon [36-35]	AMI 936° GEA, Gioia del Colle
	MM7314	Eurofighter F-2000A Typhoon [36-37]	AMI 936° GEA, Gioia del Colle
	MM7315	Eurofighter F-2000A Typhoon [36-46]	AMI 936° GEA, Gioia del Colle
	MM7316	Eurofighter F-2000A Typhoon [37-07]	AMI 18° Gruppo/37° Stormo, Trapani/Birgi
	MM7317	Eurofighter F-2000A Typhoon [4-43]	AMI 904° GEA, Grosseto
	MM7318	Eurofighter F-2000A Typhoon [37-04]	AMI 18° Gruppo/37° Stormo, Trapani/Birgi
	MM7319	Eurofighter F-2000A Typhoon [36-45]	AMI 936° GEA, Gioia del Colle
	MM7320	Eurofighter F-2000A Typhoon [4-45]	AMI 904° GEA, Grosseto
	MM7321	Eurofighter F-2000A Typhoon [37-12]	AMI 18° Gruppo/37° Stormo, Trapani/Birgi
	MM7322	Eurofighter F-2000A Typhoon [36-40]	AMI 936° GEA, Gioia del Colle
	MM7323	Eurofighter F-2000A Typhoon [4-6]	AMI 904° GEA, Grosseto
	MM7324	Eurofighter F-2000A Typhoon [36-41]	AMI 936° GEA, Gioia del Colle
	MM7325	Eurofighter F-2000A Typhoon [37-20]	AMI 18° Gruppo/37° Stormo, Trapani/Birgi
	MM7326	Eurofighter F-2000A Typhoon [4-46] $	AMI 904° GEA, Grosseto
	MM7327	Eurofighter F-2000A Typhoon [4-47]	AMI 904° GEA, Grosseto
	MM7328	Eurofighter F-2000A Typhoon [37-14]	AMI 18° Gruppo/37° Stormo, Trapani/Birgi
	MM7329	Eurofighter F-2000A Typhoon [37-15]	AMI 18° Gruppo/37° Stormo, Trapani/Birgi

Serial	Type (code/other identity)	Owner/operator, location or fate	Notes
MM7330	Eurofighter F-2000A Typhoon [37-21]	AMI 18° Gruppo/37° Stormo, Trapani/Birgi	
MM7331	Eurofighter F-2000A Typhoon [37-16]	AMI 18° Gruppo/37° Stormo, Trapani/Birgi	
MM7332	Lockheed Martin F-35A Lightning II [32-01]	AMI 62nd FS/56th FW, Luke AFB, AZ, USA	
MM7333	Lockheed Martin F-35A Lightning II [32-02]	AMI 62nd FS/56th FW, Luke AFB, AZ, USA	
MM7334	Lockheed Martin F-35A Lightning II [32-03]	AMI 62nd FS/56th FW, Luke AFB, AZ, USA	
MM7335	Lockheed Martin F-35A Lightning II [32-04]	AMI 62nd FS/56th FW, Luke AFB, AZ, USA	
MM7336	Lockheed Martin F-35A Lightning II [32-05]	AMI 13° Gruppo/32° Stormo, Cameri	
MM7337	Lockheed Martin F-35A Lightning II [32-13]	AMI 13° Gruppo/32° Stormo, Cameri	
MM7338	Eurofighter F-2000A Typhoon [4-60]	AMI 904° GEA, Grosseto	
MM7339	Eurofighter F-2000A Typhoon [4-61]	AMI 904° GEA, Grosseto	
MM7340	Eurofighter F-2000A Typhoon [4-9]	AMI 904° GEA, Grosseto	
MM7341	Eurofighter F-2000A Typhoon [36-50]	AMI 936° GEA, Gioia del Colle	
MM7342	Eurofighter F-2000A Typhoon	AMI (on order)	
MM7343	Eurofighter F-2000A Typhoon [36-52]	AMI 936° GEA, Gioia del Colle	
MM7344	Eurofighter F-2000A Typhoon	AMI (on order)	
MM7345	Eurofighter F-2000A Typhoon	AMI (on order)	
CSX7346	Eurofighter F-2000A Typhoon	Leonardo, Turin	
CSX7347	Eurofighter F-2000A Typhoon	Leonardo, Turin	
MM7348	Eurofighter F-2000A Typhoon	AMI (on order)	
MM7349	Eurofighter F-2000A Typhoon	AMI (on order)	
MM7350	Eurofighter F-2000A Typhoon	AMI (on order)	
MM7351	Eurofighter F-2000A Typhoon	AMI (on order)	
MM7352	Eurofighter F-2000A Typhoon	AMI (on order)	
MM7353	Eurofighter F-2000A Typhoon	AMI (on order)	
MM7354	Eurofighter F-2000A Typhoon	AMI (on order)	
MM7355	Eurofighter F-2000A Typhoon	AMI (on order)	
MM7356	Eurofighter F-2000A Typhoon	AMI (on order)	
MM7357	Lockheed Martin F-35A Lightning II [32-07]	AMI FACO, Cameri	
MM7358	Lockheed Martin F-35A Lightning II	AMI FACO, Cameri	
MM40115	Breguet P-1150A (Br.1150) Atlantic [41-77] $	AMI 88° Gruppo/41° Stormo, Catania	
MM40118	Breguet P-1150A (Br.1150) Atlantic [41-03]	AMI 88° Gruppo/41° Stormo, Catania	
MM40122	Breguet P-1150A (Br.1150) Atlantic [41-07]	AMI 88° Gruppo/41° Stormo, Catania	
MM40125	Breguet P-1150A (Br.1150) Atlantic [41-12]	AMI 88° Gruppo/41° Stormo, Catania	
MM54443	Aermacchi T-339A (MB339A) [61-50]	*Preserved at Gallarate*	
MM54446	Aermacchi T-339A (MB339A(MLU)) [61-01]	*Withdrawn from use at Lecce, 2015*	
MM54452	Aermacchi T-339A (MB339A)	*Crashed*	
CSX54453	Aermacchi T-339A (MB339A(MLU)) [RS-11]	*Withdrawn from use at Lecce, 2015*	
MM54456	Aermacchi T-339A (MB339A) [61-10]	AMI, stored Lecce	
MM54457	Aermacchi T-339A (MB339A(MLU)) [61-11]	AMI 61° Stormo, Lecce	
MM54458	Aermacchi T-339A (MB339A(MLU)) [61-12]	AMI 61° Stormo, Lecce	
MM54465	Aermacchi T-339A (MB339A(MLU)) [61-21]	AMI 61° Stormo, Lecce	
MM54467	Aermacchi T-339A (MB339A) [61-23]	*Crashed 16 June 1994, Melpignano*	
MM54468	Aermacchi T-339A (MB339A(MLU)) [61-24]	AMI 61° Stormo, Lecce	
MM54473	Aermacchi AT-339A (MB339PAN)	AMI *Frecce Tricolori* (313° Gruppo), Rivolto	
MM54475	Aermacchi AT-339A (MB339PAN)	*Withdrawn from use at Lecce, 2015*	
MM54477	Aermacchi AT-339A (MB339PAN)	AMI *Frecce Tricolori* (313° Gruppo), Rivolto	
MM54479	Aermacchi AT-339A (MB339PAN)	AMI 632ª SC/32° Stormo, Amendola	
MM54480	Aermacchi AT-339A (MB339PAN)	AMI *Frecce Tricolori* (313° Gruppo), Rivolto	
MM54482	Aermacchi AT-339A (MB339PAN)	AMI *Frecce Tricolori* (313° Gruppo), Rivolto	
MM54487	Aermacchi AT-339A (MB339PAN)	AMI *Frecce Tricolori* (313° Gruppo), Rivolto	
MM54488	Aermacchi T-339A (MB339A(MLU)) [61-32]	AMI 61° Stormo, Lecce	
MM54492	Aermacchi T-339A (MB339A(MLU)) [61-36]	AMI 61° Stormo, Lecce	
MM54493	Aermacchi T-339A (MB339A(MLU)) [61-37]	AMI 61° Stormo, Lecce	
MM54496	Aermacchi T-339A (MB339A(MLU)) [61-42]	AMI 61° Stormo, Lecce	
MM54499	Aermacchi T-339A (MB339A(MLU)) [61-45]	AMI 61° Stormo, Lecce	
MM54500	Aermacchi AT-339A (MB339PAN) [8]	AMI *Frecce Tricolori* (313° Gruppo), Rivolto	
MM54504	Aermacchi T-339A (MB339A(MLU)) [61-52]	AMI 61° Stormo, Lecce	
MM54505	Aermacchi AT-339A (MB339PAN) [5]	AMI *Frecce Tricolori* (313° Gruppo), Rivolto	
MM54507	Aermacchi T-339A (MB339A(MLU)) [61-55]	AMI 61° Stormo, Lecce	
MM54509	Aermacchi T-339A (MB339A(MLU)) [61-57]	AMI 61° Stormo, Lecce	
MM54510	Aermacchi AT-339A (MB339PAN) [12]	AMI *Frecce Tricolori* (313° Gruppo), Rivolto	
MM54511	Aermacchi T-339A (MB339A(MLU)) [61-61]	AMI 61° Stormo, Lecce	

Notes	Serial	Type (code/other identity)	Owner/operator, location or fate
	MM54512	Aermacchi T-339A (MB339A(MLU)) [61-62]	AMI 61° Stormo, Lecce
	MM54514	Aermacchi AT-339A (MB339PAN) [0]	AMI *Frecce Tricolori* (313° Gruppo), Rivolto
	MM54515	Aermacchi T-339A (MB339A(MLU)) [61-65]	AMI 61° Stormo, Lecce
	MM54516	Aermacchi T-339A (MB339A(MLU)) [61-66]	AMI 61° Stormo, Lecce
	MM54517	Aermacchi AT-339A (MB339PAN) [2]	AMI *Frecce Tricolori* (313° Gruppo), Rivolto
	MM54518	Aermacchi AT-339A (MB339PAN) [5]	AMI *Frecce Tricolori* (313° Gruppo), Rivolto
	MM54533	Aermacchi T-339A (MB339A(MLU)) [61-72]	AMI 61° Stormo, Lecce
	MM54534	Aermacchi AT-339A (MB339PAN) [6]	AMI *Frecce Tricolori* (313° Gruppo), Rivolto
	MM54535	Aermacchi T-339A (MB339A(MLU)) [61-74]	AMI 61° Stormo, Lecce
	MM54536	Aermacchi T-339A (MB339A)	*Withdrawn from use at Lecce, 2015*
	MM54537	Aermacchi T-339A (MB339A)	*Crashed 12 December 1988, Rivolto*
	MM54538	Aermacchi AT-339A (MB339PAN) [1]	AMI *Frecce Tricolori* (313° Gruppo), Rivolto
	MM54539	Aermacchi AT-339A (MB339PAN) [11]	AMI *Frecce Tricolori* (313° Gruppo), Rivolto
	MM54542	Aermacchi AT-339A (MB339PAN)	AMI *Frecce Tricolori* (313° Gruppo), Rivolto
	CSX54544	Aermacchi FT-339 (MB339CD)	*Withdrawn from use at Lecce, 2015*
	MM54547	Aermacchi AT-339A (MB339PAN)	AMI *Frecce Tricolori* (313° Gruppo), Rivolto
	MM54548	Aermacchi T-339A (MB339A(MLU)) [61-106]	AMI 61° Stormo, Lecce
	MM54549	Aermacchi T-339A (MB339A(MLU)) [61-107]	AMI 61° Stormo, Lecce
	MM54551	Aermacchi AT-339A (MB339PAN) [1]	AMI *Frecce Tricolori* (313° Gruppo), Rivolto
	MM55002	Panavia TA-200A Tornado (IDS Trainer) [6-52] $	AMI GEA 6° Stormo, Ghedi
	MM55003	Panavia TA-200A Tornado (IDS Trainer)	AMI
	MM55004	Panavia TA-200A Tornado (IDS Trainer) [6-53]	AMI GEA 6° Stormo, Ghedi
	MM55006	Panavia TA-200C Tornado (IDS Trainer (MLU)) [6-15]	AMI GEA 6° Stormo, Ghedi
	MM55007	Panavia TA-200A Tornado (IDS Trainer) [6-51]	AMI GEA 6° Stormo, Ghedi
	MM55008	Panavia TA-200A Tornado (IDS Trainer) [6-45]	AMI GEA 6° Stormo, Ghedi
	MM55009	Panavia TA-200A Tornado (IDS Trainer) [6-44]	AMI GEA 6° Stormo, Ghedi
	MM55010	Panavia TA-200A Tornado (IDS Trainer) [6-42]	AMI GEA 6° Stormo, Ghedi
	MM55029	Aeritalia-EMB TA-11A (AMX-T) [32-50] $]	AMI GEA 51° Stormo, Istrana
	MM55030	Aeritalia-EMB TA-11A (AMX-T) [32-41]	AMI GEA 51° Stormo, Istrana
	MM55032	McDonnell Douglas TAV-8B Harrier II+ [1-01]	MMI Gruppo Aerei Imbarcarti, Taranto/Grottaglie
	MM55033	McDonnell Douglas TAV-8B Harrier II+ [1-02]	MMI, stored Taranto/Grottaglie
	CSX55034	Aeritalia-EMB TA-11B (AMX-T-ACOL) [RS-18]	AMI RSV, Pratica di Mare
	MM55036	Aeritalia-EMB TA-11A (AMX-T) [32-51]	AMI GEA 51° Stormo, Istrana
	MM55037	Aeritalia-EMB TA-11A (AMX-T) [51-80]	AMI GEA 51° Stormo, Istrana
	MM55042	Aeritalia-EMB TA-11A (AMX-T) [32-56]	AMI GEA 51° Stormo, Istrana
	MM55043	Aeritalia-EMB TA-11A (AMX-T) [51-21]	AMI GEA 51° Stormo, Istrana
	MM55044	Aeritalia-EMB TA-11A (AMX-T) [51-82]	AMI GEA 51° Stormo, Istrana
	MM55046	Aeritalia-EMB TA-11A (AMX-T) [32-47]	AMI GEA 51° Stormo, Istrana
	MM55047	Aeritalia-EMB TA-11A (AMX-T) [32-53]	AMI GEA 51° Stormo, Istrana
	MM55049	Aeritalia-EMB TA-11A (AMX-T) [51-83]	AMI GEA 51° Stormo, Istrana
	MM55051	Aeritalia-EMB TA-11A (AMX-T) [51-84]	AMI GEA 51° Stormo, Istrana
	MM55052	Aermacchi AT-339A (MB339PAN) [4]	AMI *Frecce Tricolori* (313° Gruppo), Rivolto
	MM55053	Aermacchi AT-339A (MB339PAN) [7]	AMI *Frecce Tricolori* (313° Gruppo), Rivolto
	MM55054	Aermacchi AT-339A (MB339PAN) [9]	AMI *Frecce Tricolori* (313° Gruppo), Rivolto
	MM55055	Aermacchi AT-339A (MB339PAN)	AMI *Frecce Tricolori* (313° Gruppo), Rivolto
	MM55058	Aermacchi AT-339A (MB339PAN) [3]	AMI *Frecce Tricolori* (313° Gruppo), Rivolto
	MM55059	Aermacchi AT-339A (MB339PAN)	AMI *Frecce Tricolori* (313° Gruppo), Rivolto
	MM55062	Aermacchi FT-339 (MB339CD) [61-126]	AMI 61° Stormo, Lecce
	MM55063	Aermacchi FT-339 (MB339CD) [61-127]	AMI 61° Stormo, Lecce
	MM55064	Aermacchi FT-339 (MB339CD) [61-130]	AMI 61° Stormo, Lecce
	MM55065	Aermacchi FT-339 (MB339CD) [61-131]	AMI 61° Stormo, Lecce
	MM55066	Aermacchi FT-339 (MB339CD) [61-132]	AMI 61° Stormo, Lecce
	MM55067	Aermacchi FT-339 (MB339CD) [61-133]	AMI 61° Stormo, Lecce
	MM55068	Aermacchi FT-339 (MB339CD) [RS-33]	AMI RSV, Pratica di Mare
	MM55069	Aermacchi FT-339 (MB339CD) [61-135]	AMI 61° Stormo, Lecce
	MM55070	Aermacchi FT-339 (MB339CD) [61-136]	AMI 61° Stormo, Lecce
	MM55072	Aermacchi FT-339 (MB339CD) [61-140]	AMI 61° Stormo, Lecce
	MM55073	Aermacchi FT-339 (MB339CD) [61-141]	AMI 61° Stormo, Lecce
	MM55074	Aermacchi FT-339 (MB339CD) [36-06]	AMI 12° Gruppo/36° Stormo, Gioia del Colle
	MM55075	Aermacchi FT-339 (MB339CD) [61-143]	AMI 61° Stormo, Lecce
	MM55076	Aermacchi FT-339 (MB339CD) [61-144]	AMI 61° Stormo, Lecce
	MM55077	Aermacchi FT-339 (MB339CD) [61-145]	AMI 61° Stormo, Lecce

Serial	Type (code/other identity)	Owner/operator, location or fate	Notes
MM55078	Aermacchi FT-339 (MB339CD) [61-146]	AMI 61° Stormo, Lecce	
MM55079	Aermacchi FT-339 (MB339CD) [61-147]	AMI 61° Stormo, Lecce	
MM55080	Aermacchi FT-339 (MB339CD) [61-150]	AMI 61° Stormo, Lecce	
MM55081	Aermacchi FT-339 (MB339CD) [61-151]	AMI 61° Stormo, Lecce	
MM55082	Aermacchi FT-339 (MB339CD) [61-152]	AMI 61° Stormo, Lecce	
MM55084	Aermacchi FT-339 (MB339CD) [61-154]	AMI 61° Stormo, Lecce	
MM55085	Aermacchi FT-339 (MB339CD) [61-155]	AMI 61° Stormo, Lecce	
MM55086	Aermacchi FT-339 (MB339CD) [61-156]	AMI 61° Stormo, Lecce	
MM55087	Aermacchi FT-339 (MB339CD) [61-167]	AMI 61° Stormo, Lecce	
MM55088	Aermacchi FT-339 (MB339CD) [61-160]	AMI 61° Stormo, Lecce	
MM55089	Aermacchi FT-339 (MB339CD) [32-161]	AMI 632ª SC/32° Stormo, Amendola	
MM55090	Aermacchi FT-339 (MB339CD) [61-162]	AMI 61° Stormo, Lecce	
MM55091	Aermacchi FT-339 (MB339CD) [RS-32]	AMI RSV, Pratica di Mare	
MM55092	Eurofighter TF-2000A Typhoon [36-62]	AMI 936° GEA, Gioia del Colle	
MM55093	Eurofighter TF-2000A Typhoon [4-31]	AMI 904° GEA, Grosseto	
MM55094	Eurofighter TF-2000A Typhoon [36-60]	AMI 936° GEA, Gioia del Colle	
MM55095	Eurofighter TF-2000A Typhoon [4-23]	AMI 904° GEA, Grosseto	
MM55096	Eurofighter TF-2000A Typhoon [4-30]	AMI 904° GEA, Grosseto	
MM55097	Eurofighter TF-2000A Typhoon [36-61]	AMI 936° GEA, Gioia del Colle	
MM55128	Eurofighter TF-2000A Typhoon [4-26]	AMI 904° GEA, Grosseto	
MM55129	Eurofighter TF-2000A Typhoon [4-32]	AMI 904° GEA, Grosseto	
MM55130	Eurofighter TF-2000A Typhoon [4-33]	AMI 904° GEA, Grosseto	
MM55131	Eurofighter TF-2000A Typhoon [37-30]	AMI 18° Gruppo/37° Stormo, Trapani/Birgi	
MM55132	Eurofighter TF-2000A Typhoon	AMI 18° Gruppo/37° Stormo, Trapani/Birgi	
MM55133	Eurofighter TF-2000A Typhoon	AMI 18° Gruppo/37° Stormo, Trapani/Birgi	
MM55144	Aermacchi T-346A Master [61-02]	AMI 61° Stormo, Lecce	
MM55145	Aermacchi T-346A Master [61-03]	AMI 61° Stormo, Lecce	
CSX55152	Aermacchi M-346FT	Leonardo, Turin	
MM55153	Aermacchi T-346A Master [61-05]	AMI 61° Stormo, Lecce	
MM55154	Aermacchi T-346A Master [61-01]	AMI 61° Stormo, Lecce	
MM55155	Aermacchi T-346A Master [61-04]	AMI 61° Stormo, Lecce	
CSX55168	Eurofighter TF-2000A Typhoon	Leonardo, Turin	
MM55213	Aermacchi T-346A Master [61-06]	AMI 61° Stormo, Lecce	
MM55214	Aermacchi T-346A Master [61-07]	AMI 61° Stormo, Lecce	
MM55215	Aermacchi T-346A Master [61-10]	AMI 61° Stormo, Lecce	
MM55216	Aermacchi T-346A Master [61-12]	AMI 61° Stormo, Lecce	
MM55217	Aermacchi T-346A Master [61-13]	AMI 61° Stormo, Lecce	
MM55218	Aermacchi T-346A Master [61-14]	AMI 61° Stormo, Lecce	
MM55219	Aermacchi T-346A Master	AMI (on order)	
MM55220	Aermacchi T-346A Master	AMI (on order)	
MM55221	Aermacchi T-346A Master	AMI (on order)	
MM55222	Aermacchi T-346A Master	AMI (on order)	
MM55223	Aermacchi T-346A Master	AMI (on order)	
MM55224	Aermacchi T-346A Master	AMI (on order)	
MM62026	Dassault VC-50A (Falcon 50)	AMI 93° Gruppo/31° Stormo, Roma-Ciampino	
MM62029	Dassault VC-50A (Falcon 50)	AMI 93° Gruppo/31° Stormo, Roma-Ciampino	
CSX62127	Aeritalia MC-27J Pretorian	Alenia, Turin	
MM62156	Dornier UC-228 (Do.228-212) [E.I.101]	Esercito 28° Gruppo Squadroni, Viterbo	
MM62157	Dornier UC-228 (Do.228-212) [E.I.102]	Esercito 28° Gruppo Squadroni, Viterbo	
MM62158	Dornier UC-228 (Do.228-212) [E.I.103]	Esercito 28° Gruppo Squadroni, Viterbo	
MM62159	Piaggio VC-180A (P-180AM) Avanti	AMI RSV, Pratica di Mare	
MM62160	Piaggio RC-180A (P-180RM) Avanti	AMI 71° Gruppo/14° Stormo, Pratica di Mare	
MM62161	Piaggio VC-180A (P-180AM) Avanti	AMI RSV, Pratica di Mare	
MM62162	Piaggio RC-180A (P-180RM) Avanti	AMI 71° Gruppo/14° Stormo, Pratica di Mare	
MM62163	Piaggio RC-180A (P-180RM) Avanti	AMI 71° Gruppo/14° Stormo, Pratica di Mare	
MM62164	Piaggio RC-180A (P-180RM) Avanti	AMI 71° Gruppo/14° Stormo, Pratica di Mare	
MM62165	Aérospatiale P-42A (ATR.42-400MP) [GF-13]	GdiF GEA, Pratica di Mare	
MM62166	Aérospatiale P-42A (ATR.42-400MP) [GF-14]	GdiF GEA, Pratica di Mare	
MM62167	Piaggio VC-180A (P-180AM) Avanti	Esercito 28° Gruppo Sqd Det, Roma/Ciampino	
MM62168	Piaggio VC-180A (P-180AM) Avanti	Esercito 28° Gruppo Sqd Det, Roma/Ciampino	
MM62169	Piaggio VC-180A (P-180AM) Avanti	Esercito 28° Gruppo Sqd Det, Roma/Ciampino	
MM62170	Aérospatiale P-42A (ATR.42-400MP) [10-01]	Guardia Costiera 3° Nucleo, Pescara	

Notes	Serial	Type (code/other identity)	Owner/operator, location or fate
	MM62171	Dassault VC-900A (Falcon 900EX) $	AMI 93° Gruppo/31° Stormo, Roma-Ciampino
	MM62172	Dassault VC-900A (Falcon 900EX)	AMI 93° Gruppo/31° Stormo, Roma-Ciampino
	MM62174	Airbus VC-319A (A.319CJ-115X)	AMI 306° Gruppo/31° Stormo, Roma-Ciampino
	MM62175	Lockheed C-130J Hercules II [46-40]	AMI 46ª Brigata Aerea, Pisa
	MM62177	Lockheed C-130J Hercules II [46-42]	AMI 46ª Brigata Aerea, Pisa
	MM62178	Lockheed C-130J Hercules II [46-43]	AMI 46ª Brigata Aerea, Pisa
	MM62179	Lockheed C-130J Hercules II [46-44]	AMI 46ª Brigata Aerea, Pisa
	MM62180	Lockheed C-130J Hercules II [46-45]	AMI 46ª Brigata Aerea, Pisa
	MM62181	Lockheed C-130J Hercules II [46-46]	AMI 46ª Brigata Aerea, Pisa
	MM62182	Lockheed C-130J Hercules II [46-47]	AMI, stored Pisa
	MM62183	Lockheed KC-130J Hercules II [46-48]	AMI, stored Pisa
	MM62184	Lockheed KC-130J Hercules II [46-49]	AMI, stored Pisa
	MM62185	Lockheed C-130J Hercules II [46-50]	AMI 46ª Brigata Aerea, Pisa
	MM62186	Lockheed C-130J Hercules II [46-51]	AMI 46ª Brigata Aerea, Pisa
	MM62187	Lockheed C-130J-30 Hercules II [46-53]	AMI 46ª Brigata Aerea, Pisa
	MM62188	Lockheed C-130J-30 Hercules II [46-54]	AMI 46ª Brigata Aerea, Pisa
	MM62189	Lockheed C-130J-30 Hercules II [46-55]	AMI 46ª Brigata Aerea, Pisa
	MM62190	Lockheed C-130J-30 Hercules II [46-56]	AMI 46ª Brigata Aerea, Pisa
	MM62191	Lockheed C-130J-30 Hercules II [46-57]	AMI 46ª Brigata Aerea, Pisa
	MM62192	Lockheed C-130J-30 Hercules II [46-58]	AMI, stored Pisa
	MM62193	Lockheed C-130J-30 Hercules II [46-59]	AMI 46ª Brigata Aerea, Pisa
	MM62194	Lockheed C-130J-30 Hercules II [46-60]	AMI 46ª Brigata Aerea, Pisa
	MM62195	Lockheed C-130J-30 Hercules II [46-61]	AMI 46ª Brigata Aerea, Pisa
	MM62196	Lockheed C-130J-30 Hercules II [46-62]	AMI 46ª Brigata Aerea, Pisa
	MM62199	Piaggio VC-180A (P-180AM) Avanti	AMI CAE Multicrew, Pratica di Mare
	MM62200	Piaggio VC-180A (P-180AM) Avanti	AMI 71° Gruppo/14° Stormo, Pratica di Mare
	MM62201	Piaggio VC-180A (P-180AM) Avanti	AMI CAE Multicrew, Pratica di Mare
	MM62202	Piaggio VC-180A (P-180AM) Avanti	AMI 71° Gruppo/14° Stormo, Pratica di Mare
	MM62203	Piaggio VC-180A (P-180AM) Avanti	AMI CAE Multicrew, Pratica di Mare
	MM62204	Piaggio VC-180A (P-180AM) Avanti	AMI 71° Gruppo/14° Stormo, Pratica di Mare
	MM62205	Piaggio VC-180A (P-180AM) Avanti	AMI CAE Multicrew, Pratica di Mare
	MM62206	Piaggio VC-180A (P-180AM) Avanti	AMI CAE Multicrew, Pratica di Mare
	MM62207	Piaggio VC-180A (P-180AM) Avanti	AMI CAE Multicrew, Pratica di Mare
	MM62208	Aérospatiale P-42A (ATR.42-400MP) [10-02]	Guardia Costiera 2° Nucleo, Catania
	MM62209	Airbus VC-319A (A.319CJ-115X)	AMI 306° Gruppo/31° Stormo, Roma-Ciampino
	MM62210	Dassault VC-900A (Falcon 900EX)	AMI 93° Gruppo/31° Stormo, Roma-Ciampino
	MM62211	Piaggio VC-180A (P-180AM) Avanti [9-02]	MMI 9ª Brigata Aerea, Pratica di Mare
	MM62212	Piaggio VC-180A (P-180AM) Avanti [9-01]	MMI 9ª Brigata Aerea, Pratica di Mare
	MM62213	Piaggio VC-180A (P-180AM) Avanti [9-03]	MMI 9ª Brigata Aerea, Pratica di Mare
	MM62214	Aeritalia C-27J Spartan [46-84]	AMI, stored Pisa
	MM62215	Aeritalia C-27J Spartan [46-80]	AMI 98° Gruppo/46ª Brigata Aerea, Pisa
	MM62217	Aeritalia C-27J Spartan [46-81]	AMI, stored Pisa
	MM62218	Aeritalia C-27J Spartan [46-82]	AMI 98° Gruppo/46ª Brigata Aerea, Pisa
	CSX62219	Aeritalia C-27J Spartan [RS-50]	AMI RSV, Pratica di Mare
	MM62220	Aeritalia MC-27J Pretorian [46-83]	AMI 98° Gruppo/46ª Brigata Aerea, Pisa
	MM62221	Aeritalia EC-27J JEDI [46-85]	AMI 98° Gruppo/46ª Brigata Aerea, Pisa
	MM62222	Aeritalia C-27J Spartan [46-86]	AMI 98° Gruppo/46ª Brigata Aerea, Pisa
	MM62223	Aeritalia C-27J Spartan [46-88]	AMI 98° Gruppo/46ª Brigata Aerea, Pisa
	MM62224	Aeritalia EC-27J JEDI [46-89]	AMI 98° Gruppo/46ª Brigata Aerea, Pisa
	MM62225	Aeritalia C-27J Spartan [46-90]	AMI 98° Gruppo/46ª Brigata Aerea, Pisa
	MM62226	Boeing KC-767A (767-2EYER) [14-01] $	AMI 8° Gruppo/14° Stormo, Pratica di Mare
	MM62227	Boeing KC-767A (767-2EYER) [14-02]	AMI 8° Gruppo/14° Stormo, Pratica di Mare
	MM62228	Boeing KC-767A (767-2EYER) [14-03]	AMI 8° Gruppo/14° Stormo, Pratica di Mare
	MM62229	Boeing KC-767A (767-2EYER) [14-04]	AMI 8° Gruppo/14° Stormo, Pratica di Mare
	MM62230	Aérospatiale P-42A (ATR.42-400MP) [GF-15]	GdiF GEA, Pratica di Mare
	MM62243	Airbus VC-319A (A.319CJ-115X)	AMI 306° Gruppo/31° Stormo, Roma-Ciampino
	MM62244	Dassault VC-900B (Falcon 900EX EASy)	AMI 93° Gruppo/31° Stormo, Roma-Ciampino
	MM62245	Dassault VC-900B (Falcon 900EX EASy)	AMI 93° Gruppo/31° Stormo, Roma-Ciampino
	MM62248	Piaggio VC-180A (P-180AM) Avanti [GF-18]	GdiF GEA, Pratica di Mare
	MM62249	Piaggio VC-180B (P-180AM) Avanti II [GF-19]	GdiF GEA, Pratica di Mare
	MM62250	Aeritalia C-27J Spartan [46-91]	AMI 98° Gruppo/46ª Brigata Aerea, Pisa
	MM62251	Aérospatiale P-42A (ATR.42-400MP) [GF-16]	GdiF GEA, Pratica di Mare

Serial	Type (code/other identity)	Owner/operator, location or fate	Notes
MM62270	Aérospatiale P-42B (ATR.42-500MP) [10-03]	Guardia Costiera 2° Nucleo, Catania	
CSX62279	Aérospatiale P-72A (ATR.72-600MP)	Alenia	
CSX62280	Aérospatiale P-72A (ATR.72-600MP)	Alenia	
MM62281	Aérospatiale P-72A (ATR.72-600MP) [41-04]	AMI 88° Gruppo/41° Stormo, Catania	
CSX62282	Aérospatiale P-72A (ATR.72-600MP)	(on order)	
MM62286	Piaggio VC-180A (P-180AM) Avanti	AMI 93° Gruppo/31° Stormo, Roma-Ciampino	
MM62287	Piaggio VC-180A (P-180AM) Avanti	AMI 93° Gruppo/31° Stormo, Roma-Ciampino	
MM62293	Gulfstream Aerospace E-550A (N849GA) [14-11]	AMI 71° Gruppo/14° Stormo, Pratica di Mare	
MM62294	Gulfstream Aerospace E-550A (N554GA) [14-12]	AMI (on order)	
MM62298	Aérospatiale P-72A (ATR.72-600MP) [41-03]	AMI (on order)	
MM81480	AgustaWestland SH-101A (EH-101 Mk110 ASW) [2-01]	MMI 3° Grupelicot, Catania	
MM81481	AgustaWestland SH-101A (EH-101 Mk110 ASW) [2-02]	MMI 3° Grupelicot, Catania	
MM81482	AgustaWestland SH-101A (EH-101 Mk110 ASW) [2-03]	MMI 3° Grupelicot, Catania	
MM81483	AgustaWestland SH-101A (EH-101 Mk110 ASW) [2-04]	MMI 3° Grupelicot, Catania	
MM81484	AgustaWestland SH-101A (EH-101 Mk110 ASW) [2-05]	MMI 3° Grupelicot, Catania	
MM81485	AgustaWestland SH-101A (EH-101 Mk110 ASW) [2-06]	MMI 3° Grupelicot, Catania	
MM81486	AgustaWestland SH-101A (EH-101 Mk110 ASW) [2-07]	MMI 3° Grupelicot, Catania	
MM81487	AgustaWestland SH-101A (EH-101 Mk110 ASW) [2-08]	MMI 3° Grupelicot, Catania	
MM81488	AgustaWestland EH-101A (EH-101 Mk112 AEW) [2-09]	MMI 1° Grupelicot, La Spezia/Luni	
MM81489	AgustaWestland EH-101A (EH-101 Mk112 AEW) [2-10]	MMI 3° Grupelicot, Catania	
MM81490	AgustaWestland EH-101A (EH-101 Mk112 AEW) [2-11]	MMI 3° Grupelicot, Catania	
MM81491	AgustaWestland EH-101A (EH-101 Mk112 AEW) [2-12]	MMI 1° Grupelicot, La Spezia/Luni	
MM81492	AgustaWestland UH-101A (EH-101 Mk410 UTY) [2-13]	MMI 1° Grupelicot, La Spezia/Luni	
MM81493	AgustaWestland UH-101A (EH-101 Mk410 UTY) [2-14]	MMI 1° Grupelicot, La Spezia/Luni	
MM81494	AgustaWestland UH-101A (EH-101 Mk410 UTY) [2-15]	MMI 1° Grupelicot, La Spezia/Luni	
MM81495	AgustaWestland UH-101A (EH-101 Mk410 UTY) [2-16]	MMI 1° Grupelicot, La Spezia/Luni	
MM81633	AgustaWestland UH-101A (EH-101 Mk410 UTY) [2-18]	MMI 1° Grupelicot, La Spezia/Luni	
MM81634	AgustaWestland UH-101A (EH-101 Mk410 UTY) [2-19]	MMI 1° Grupelicot, La Spezia/Luni	
MM81635	AgustaWestland UH-101A (EH-101 Mk410 UTY) [2-20]	MMI 1° Grupelicot, La Spezia/Luni	
MM81636	AgustaWestland UH-101A (EH-101 Mk410 UTY) [2-21]	MMI 1° Grupelicot, La Spezia/Luni	
MM81719	AgustaWestland SH-101A (EH-101 Mk110 ASW) [2-22]	MMI 1° Grupelicot, La Spezia/Luni	
MM81726	AgustaWestland SH-101A (EH-101 Mk110 ASW) [2-23]	MMI 1° Grupelicot, La Spezia/Luni	
MM81796	AgustaWestland HH-139A [15-40]	AMI 83° Gruppo SAR/15° Stormo, Cervia	
MM81797	AgustaWestland HH-139A [15-41]	AMI 84° Centro SAR/15° Stormo, Gioia del Colle	
MM81798	AgustaWestland HH-139A [15-42]	AMI 83° Gruppo SAR/15° Stormo, Cervia	
MM81799	AgustaWestland HH-139A [15-43]	AMI 81° Centro/15° Stormo, Cervia	
MM81800	AgustaWestland HH-139A [15-44]	AMI 82° Centro SAR/15° Stormo, Trapani/Birgi	
MM81801	AgustaWestland HH-139A [15-45]	AMI 85° Centro SAR/15° Stormo, Gioia del Colle	
MM81802	AgustaWestland HH-139A [15-46]	AMI 85° Centro SAR/15° Stormo, Gioia del Colle	
MM81803	AgustaWestland HH-139A [15-47]	AMI 81° Centro/15° Stormo, Cervia	
MM81804	AgustaWestland HH-139A [15-48]	AMI 85° Centro SAR/15° Stormo, Gioia del Colle	
MM81805	AgustaWestland HH-139A [15-49]	AMI 82° Centro SAR/15° Stormo, Trapani/Birgi	
MM81806	AgustaWestland VH-139A	AMI 93° Gruppo/31° Stormo, Roma-Ciampino	
MM81807	AgustaWestland VH-139A	AMI 93° Gruppo/31° Stormo, Roma-Ciampino	
MM81811	AgustaWestland VH-139A	AMI 93° Gruppo/31° Stormo, Roma-Ciampino	
MM81812	AgustaWestland VH-139A	AMI 93° Gruppo/31° Stormo, Roma-Ciampino	
MM81822	AgustaWestland HH-139A [15-50]	AMI 85° Centro SAR/15° Stormo, Gioia del Colle	
MM81823	AgustaWestland HH-139A [15-51]	AMI 81° Centro/15° Stormo, Cervia	
MM81824	AgustaWestland HH-139A [15-52]	AMI 85° Centro SAR/15° Stormo, Gioia del Colle	
CSX81848	AgustaWestland AW149 [1-49]	Leonardo	
MM81864	AgustaWestland HH-101A Caesar [15-01]	AMI 85° Centro SAR/15° Stormo, Pratica di Mare	
MM81865	AgustaWestland HH-101A Caesar [15-02]	AMI 81° Centro/15° Stormo, Cervia	
MM81866	AgustaWestland HH-101A Caesar [15-03]	AMI 85° Centro SAR/15° Stormo, Pratica di Mare	
MM81867	AgustaWestland HH-101A Caesar [15-04]	AMI 81° Centro/15° Stormo, Cervia	
MM81868	AgustaWestland HH-101A Caesar [15-05]	AMI (on order)	
MM81869	AgustaWestland HH-101A Caesar [15-06]	AMI (on order)	
CSX81890	AgustaWestland AW149	Leonardo	
MM81...	AgustaWestland HH-101A Caesar	AMI (on order)	
MM81...	AgustaWestland HH-101A Caesar	AMI (on order)	
MM81...	AgustaWestland HH-101A Caesar	AMI (on order)	
MM81...	AgustaWestland HH-101A Caesar	AMI (on order)	
MM81...	AgustaWestland HH-101A Caesar	AMI (on order)	

Notes	Serial	Type (code/other identity)	Owner/operator, location or fate
	MM81...	AgustaWestland HH-101A Caesar	AMI (on order)
	Italian Government		
	I-CAEX	Dassault Falcon 900	Italian Government/Soc. CAI, Roma/Ciampino
	I-DIES	Dassault Falcon 900	Italian Government/Soc. CAI, Roma/Ciampino
	I-TALY	Airbus A.340-541 (A6-EHA)	AMI 306° Gruppo/31° Stormo, Roma-Ciampino
	IVORY COAST		
	TU-VAD	Grumman G.1159C Gulfstream IV	Ivory Coast Government, Abidjan
	TU-VAE	Gulfstream Aerospace G.550	Ivory Coast Government, Abidjan
	TU-VAF	Grumman G.1159A Gulfstream III	Ivory Coast Government, Abidjan
	TU-VAO	Boeing 727-2Y4	Sold as N621AZ, December 2016
	TU-VAS	Airbus A.319CJ-133	Ivory Coast Government, Abidjan
	JAPAN		
	Japan Air Self Defence Force (JASDF)		
	07-3604	Boeing KC-767J	JASDF 404th Hikotai, Nagoya
	20-1101	Boeing 747-47C	JASDF 701st Flight Sqn, Chitose
	20-1102	Boeing 747-47C	JASDF 701st Flight Sqn, Chitose
	87-3601	Boeing KC-767J	JASDF 404th Hikotai, Nagoya
	87-3602	Boeing KC-767J	JASDF 404th Hikotai, Nagoya
	97-3603	Boeing KC-767J	JASDF 404th Hikotai, Nagoya
	..-....	Boeing 777-3SB(ER) (N509BJ)	JASDF, on order
	..-....	Boeing 777-3SB(ER) (N511BJ)	JASDF, on order
	JORDAN		
	Al Quwwat al Jawwiya al Malakiya al Urduniya/Jordanian Air Force		
	344	Lockheed C-130H Hercules	Jordanian AF 3 Sqn, Amman/Marka
	345	Lockheed C-130H Hercules $	Jordanian AF 3 Sqn, Amman/Marka
	346	Lockheed C-130H Hercules	Jordanian AF 3 Sqn, Amman/Marka
	347	Lockheed C-130H Hercules	Jordanian AF 3 Sqn, Amman/Marka
	360	Ilyushin Il-76MF (JY-JIC)	Jordanian AF 3 Sqn, Amman/Marka
	361	Ilyushin Il-76MF (JY-JID)	Jordanian AF 3 Sqn, Amman/Marka
	JY-RFA	Extra EA-300LP	Jordanian AF Royal Jordanian Falcons, Amman
	JY-RFB	Extra EA-300LP	Jordanian AF Royal Jordanian Falcons, Amman
	JY-RFC	Extra EA-300LP	Jordanian AF Royal Jordanian Falcons, Amman
	JY-RFD	Extra EA-300LP	Jordanian AF Royal Jordanian Falcons, Amman
	JY-RFE	Extra EA-300LP	Jordanian AF Royal Jordanian Falcons, Amman
	Jordanian Government		
	VQ-BCE	Gulfstream Aerospace G.450	Sold as N451WW
	VQ-BDD	Airbus A.318-112	Jordanian Government, Amman
	VQ-BMZ	Gulfstream Aerospace G.650	Jordanian Government, Amman
	VQ-BNZ	Gulfstream Aerospace G.650ER	Jordanian Government, Amman
	KAZAKHSTAN		
	01 r	CASA C-295M	Kazakstan ADF 18th Air Transport Sqn, Almaty
	02 r	CASA C-295M	Kazakstan ADF 18th Air Transport Sqn, Almaty
	03 r	CASA C-295M	Kazakstan ADF 18th Air Transport Sqn, Almaty
	04 r	CASA C-295M	Kazakstan ADF 18th Air Transport Sqn, Almaty
	05 r	CASA C-295M	Kazakstan ADF 18th Air Transport Sqn, Almaty
	07 r	Antonov An-72	Kazakstan ADF 18th Air Transport Sqn, Almaty
	08 r	Antonov An-72	Kazakstan ADF 18th Air Transport Sqn, Almaty
	UP-A3001	Airbus A.330-223	Government of Kazakhstan, Almaty
	UP-B5701	Boeing 757-2M6	Government of Kazakhstan, Almaty
	UP-T5401	Tupolev Tu-154M	Government of Kazakhstan, Almaty
	KENYA		
	KAF 308	Fokker 70ER	Kenyan Government, Nairobi
	KUWAIT		
	Al Quwwat al Jawwiya al Kuwaitiya/Kuwaiti Air Force		
	KAF 323	Lockheed L100-30 Hercules	Kuwaiti AF 41 Sqn, Kuwait International

Serial	Type (code/other identity)	Owner/operator, location or fate	Notes
KAF 324	Lockheed L100-30 Hercules	Kuwaiti AF 41 Sqn, Kuwait International	
KAF 325	Lockheed L100-30 Hercules	Kuwaiti AF 41 Sqn, Kuwait International	
KAF 326	Lockheed KC-130J Hercules II	Kuwaiti AF 41 Sqn, Kuwait International	
KAF 327	Lockheed KC-130J Hercules II	Kuwaiti AF 41 Sqn, Kuwait International	
KAF 328	Lockheed KC-130J Hercules II	Kuwaiti AF 41 Sqn, Kuwait International	
KAF 342	Boeing C-17A Globemaster III (13-0001)	Kuwaiti AF 41 Sqn, Kuwait International	
KAF 343	Boeing C-17A Globemaster III (13-0002)	Kuwaiti AF 41 Sqn, Kuwait International	

Kuwaiti Government

9K-ADE	Boeing 747-469	*Returned to Kuwait Airways*	
9K-AHI	Airbus A.300C4-620	*Withdrawn from use*	
9K-AJD	Gulfstream Aerospace Gulfstream V	*Withdrawn from use, April 2016*	
9K-AJE	Gulfstream Aerospace Gulfstream V	*Withdrawn from use, April 2016*	
9K-AJF	Gulfstream Aerospace Gulfstream V	*Withdrawn from use, April 2016*	
9K-AKD	Airbus A.320-212	Kuwaiti Government, Safat	
9K-ALD	Airbus A.310-308	*Withdrawn from use*	
9K-GAA	Boeing 747-8JK	Kuwaiti Government, Safat	
9K-GBA	Airbus A.340-542	Kuwaiti Government, Safat	
9K-GBB	Airbus A.340-542	Kuwaiti Government, Safat	
9K-GCC	Boeing 737-9BQER	Kuwaiti Government, Safat	
9K-GEA	Airbus A.319CJ-115X	Kuwaiti Government, Safat	
9K-GFA	Gulfstream Aerospace G.550	Kuwaiti Government, Safat	
9K-GGA	Gulfstream Aerospace G.650	Kuwaiti Government, Safat	
9K-GGB	Gulfstream Aerospace G.650	Kuwaiti Government, Safat	
9K-GGC	Gulfstream Aerospace G.650	Kuwaiti Government, Safat	
9K-GGD	Gulfstream Aerospace G.650	Kuwaiti Government, Safat	

KYRGYZSTAN

EX-00001	Tupolev Tu-154M	Government of Kyrgyzstan, Bishkek	

LITHUANIA
Karines Oro Pajegos (KOP)

01	LET 410UVP Turbolet	KOP Transporto Esk, Siauliai/Zokniai	
02	Mil Mi-8T	KOP Sraigtasparniu Esk, Panevezys/Pajuostis	
03	Antonov An-26RV	KOP Transporto Esk, Siauliai/Zokniai	
04	Antonov An-26RV	KOP Transporto Esk, Siauliai/Zokniai	
05	Antonov An-26RV	KOP Transporto Esk, Siauliai/Zokniai	
06	Aeritalia C-27J Spartan	KOP Transporto Esk, Siauliai/Zokniai	
07	Aeritalia C-27J Spartan	KOP Transporto Esk, Siauliai/Zokniai	
08	Aeritalia C-27J Spartan	KOP Transporto Esk, Siauliai/Zokniai	
09	Mil Mi-8T	KOP Sraigtasparniu Esk, Panevezys/Pajuostis	
10	Mil Mi-8T	KOP Sraigtasparniu Esk, Panevezys/Pajuostis	
11	Mil Mi-8PS	KOP Sraigtasparniu Esk, Panevezys/Pajuostis	
21	Mil Mi-8MTV-1	KOP Sraigtasparniu Esk, Panevezys/Pajuostis	
22	Mil Mi-8MTV-1	KOP Sraigtasparniu Esk, Panevezys/Pajuostis	
28	Mil Mi-8T	KOP Sraigtasparniu Esk, Panevezys/Pajuostis	

LUXEMBOURG
NATO

LX-N90442	Boeing E-3A Sentry	NATO NAEW&CF, Geilenkirchen, Germany	
LX-N90443	Boeing E-3A Sentry $	NATO NAEW&CF, Geilenkirchen, Germany $	
LX-N90444	Boeing E-3A Sentry	NATO NAEW&CF, Geilenkirchen, Germany	
LX-N90445	Boeing E-3A Sentry	NATO NAEW&CF, Geilenkirchen, Germany	
LX-N90446	Boeing E-3A Sentry	NATO NAEW&CF, Geilenkirchen, Germany	
LX-N90447	Boeing E-3A Sentry	NATO NAEW&CF, Geilenkirchen, Germany	
LX-N90448	Boeing E-3A Sentry	NATO NAEW&CF, Geilenkirchen, Germany	
LX-N90450	Boeing E-3A Sentry	NATO NAEW&CF, Geilenkirchen, Germany	
LX-N90451	Boeing E-3A Sentry	NATO NAEW&CF, Geilenkirchen, Germany	
LX-N90452	Boeing E-3A Sentry	NATO NAEW&CF, Geilenkirchen, Germany	
LX-N90453	Boeing E-3A Sentry	Boeing, Renton, USA (on upgrade)	
LX-N90454	Boeing E-3A Sentry	Airbus, Manching, Germany (on upgrade)	
LX-N90455	Boeing E-3A Sentry	NATO NAEW&CF, Geilenkirchen, Germany	
LX-N90456	Boeing E-3A Sentry	NATO NAEW&CF, Geilenkirchen, Germany	

Notes	Serial	Type (code/other identity)	Owner/operator, location or fate
	LX-N90458	Boeing E-3A Sentry	NATO NAEW&CF, Geilenkirchen, Germany
	LX-N90459	Boeing E-3A Sentry	NATO NAEW&CF, Geilenkirchen, Germany
	OO-TFA	Boeing 757-28A	NATO, Geilenkirchen, Germany

MACEDONIA

	Z3-MKD	Bombardier Lear 60	Macedonian Government, Skopje

MALAYSIA
Tentera Udara Diraja Malaysia/Royal Malaysian Air Force (RMAF)

	M30-01	Lockheed C-130T Hercules	RMAF 20 Sqn, Subang
	M30-02	Lockheed C-130H Hercules	RMAF 20 Sqn, Subang
	M30-03	Lockheed C-130H Hercules	RMAF 14 Sqn, Labuan
	M30-04	Lockheed C-130H-30 Hercules	RMAF 20 Sqn, Subang
	M30-05	Lockheed C-130H-30 Hercules	RMAF 14 Sqn, Labuan
	M30-06	Lockheed C-130H-30 Hercules	RMAF 14 Sqn, Labuan
	M30-07	Lockheed C-130T Hercules	RMAF 20 Sqn, Subang
	M30-08	Lockheed C-130H(MP) Hercules	RMAF 20 Sqn, Subang
	M30-09	Lockheed C-130H(MP) Hercules	RMAF 20 Sqn, Subang
	M30-10	Lockheed C-130H-30 Hercules	RMAF 20 Sqn, Subang
	M30-11	Lockheed C-130H-30 Hercules	RMAF 20 Sqn, Subang
	M30-12	Lockheed C-130H-30 Hercules	RMAF 20 Sqn, Subang
	M30-14	Lockheed C-130H-30 Hercules	RMAF 14 Sqn, Labuan
	M30-15	Lockheed C-130H-30 Hercules	RMAF 20 Sqn, Subang
	M30-16	Lockheed C-130H-30 Hercules	RMAF 20 Sqn, Subang
	M37-01	Dassault Falcon 900	RMAF 2 Sqn, Simpang
	M48-02	Bombardier BD.700-1A10 Global Express	RMAF 2 Sqn, Simpang
	M53–01	Boeing 737-7H6	RMAF 2 Sqn, Simpang
	M54-01	Airbus Military A.400M	RMAF 22 Sqn, Subang
	M54-02	Airbus Military A.400M	RMAF 22 Sqn, Subang
	M54-03	Airbus Military A.400M	RMAF 22 Sqn, Subang
	M54-04	Airbus Military A.400M	RMAF (on order)
	9M-NAA	Airbus A.319CJ-115X	RMAF, Subang
	9M-NAB	Airbus A.320CJ-214 (M37-07)	RMAF, Subang

MALTA

	9H-AFK	Bombardier Learjet 60	Government of Malta, Luqa

MEXICO
Fuerza Aérea Mexicana (FAM)/Mexican Air Force

	TP-01	Boeing 787-8 (XC-MEX)	FAM 8° Grupo Aéreo, Mexico City
	TP-02	Boeing 757-225 (XC-UJM)	FAM 8° Grupo Aéreo, Mexico City

Armada de Mexico/Mexican Navy

	ANX-1207	Gulfstream Aerospace G.550	Armada PRIESCAERTRANS, Mexico City
	XC-LMF	Gulfstream Aerospace G.450	Armada PRIESCAERTRANS, Mexico City

MOROCCO
Al Quwwat al Jawwiya al Malakiya Marakishiya/Force Aérienne Royaume Marocaine/Royal Moroccan Air Force (RMAF) & Moroccan Government

	CN-ABP	CAP-232 (28) [6]	RMAF *Marche Verte*, Marrakech/Ménara
	CN-ABQ	CAP-232 (29) [5]	RMAF *Marche Verte*, Marrakech/Ménara
	CN-ABR	CAP-232 (31) [2]	RMAF *Marche Verte*, Marrakech/Ménara
	CN-ABS	CAP-232 (36)	RMAF *Marche Verte*, Marrakech/Ménara
	CN-ABT	CAP-232 (37) [1]	RMAF *Marche Verte*, Marrakech/Ménara
	CN-ABU	CAP-232 (41) [3]	RMAF *Marche Verte*, Marrakech/Ménara
	CN-ABV	CAP-232 (42) [4]	RMAF *Marche Verte*, Marrakech/Ménara
	CN-ABW	CAP-232 (43)	RMAF *Marche Verte*, Marrakech/Ménara
	CN-ABX	CAP-232 (44) [7]	RMAF *Marche Verte*, Marrakech/Ménara
	CN-AMA	Airtech CN.235M-100 (023)	RMAF Escadrille de Transport 3, Kenitra
	CN-AMB	Airtech CN.235M-100 (024)	RMAF Escadrille de Transport 3, Kenitra
	CN-AMC	Airtech CN.235M-100 (025)	RMAF Escadrille de Transport 3, Kenitra
	CN-AMD	Airtech CN.235M-100 (026)	RMAF Escadrille de Transport 3, Kenitra

Serial	Type (code/other identity)	Owner/operator, location or fate	Notes
CN-AME	Airtech CN.235M-100 (027)	RMAF Escadrille de Transport 3, Kenitra	
CN-AMF	Airtech CN.235M-100 (028)	RMAF Escadrille de Transport 3, Kenitra	
CNA-MG	Airtech CN.235M-100 (031)	RMAF Escadrille de Transport 3, Kenitra	
CN-AMJ	Cessna 560XLS Citation Excel	Government of Morocco, Rabat	
CN-AMK	Cessna 560XLS Citation Excel	Government of Morocco, Rabat	
CN-AMN	Aeritalia C-27J Spartan	RMAF Escadrille de Transport 3, Kenitra	
CN-AMO	Aeritalia C-27J Spartan	RMAF Escadrille de Transport 3, Kenitra	
CN-AMP	Aeritalia C-27J Spartan	RMAF Escadrille de Transport 3, Kenitra	
CN-AMQ	Aeritalia C-27J Spartan	RMAF Escadrille de Transport 3, Kenitra	
CN-AMS	Gulfstream Aerospace G.550	Government of Morocco, Rabat	
CN-ANL	Grumman G.1159 Gulfstream IITT	Government of Morocco, Rabat	
CN-ANO	Dassault Falcon 50	Government of Morocco, Rabat	
CN-ANU	Grumman G.1159A Gulfstream III	Government of Morocco, Rabat	
CNA-NV	Cessna 560 Citation V	Government of Morocco, Rabat	
CNA-NW	Cessna 560 Citation V	Government of Morocco, Rabat	
CN-AOA	Lockheed C-130H Hercules (4535)	RMAF Escadrille de Transport 3, Kenitra	
CNA-OC	Lockheed C-130H Hercules (4551)	RMAF Escadrille de Transport 3, Kenitra	
CNA-OD	Lockheed C-130H Hercules (4575)	RMAF Escadrille de Transport 3, Kenitra	
CN-AOE	Lockheed C-130H Hercules (4581)	RMAF Escadrille de Transport 3, Kenitra	
CNA-OF	Lockheed C-130H Hercules (4583)	RMAF Escadrille de Transport 3, Kenitra	
CN-AOG	Lockheed C-130H Hercules (4713)	RMAF Escadrille de Transport 3, Kenitra	
CN-AOI	Lockheed C-130H Hercules (4733)	RMAF Escadrille de Transport 3, Kenitra	
CNA-OJ	Lockheed C-130H Hercules (4738)	RMAF Escadrille de Transport 3, Kenitra	
CNA-OK	Lockheed C-130H Hercules (4739)	RMAF Escadrille de Transport 3, Kenitra	
CN-AOL	Lockheed C-130H Hercules (4742)	RMAF Escadrille de Transport 3, Kenitra	
CN-AOM	Lockheed C-130H Hercules (4875)	RMAF Escadrille de Transport 3, Kenitra	
CN-AON	Lockheed C-130H Hercules (4876)	RMAF Escadrille de Transport 3, Kenitra	
CNA-OO	Lockheed C-130H Hercules (4877)	RMAF Escadrille de Transport 3, Kenitra	
CN-AOP	Lockheed C-130H Hercules (4888)	RMAF Escadrille de Transport 3, Kenitra	
CN-AOR	Lockheed KC-130H Hercules (4907)	RMAF Escadrille de Transport 3, Kenitra	
CNA-OS	Lockheed KC-130H Hercules (4909)	RMAF Escadrille de Transport 3, Kenitra	
CN-MBH	Boeing 747-48E	Government of Morocco, Rabat	
CN-MVI	Boeing 737-8KB	Government of Morocco, Rabat	
NAMIBIA			
V5-GON	Dassault Falcon 7X	Government of Namibia, Eros	
V5-NAM	Dassault Falcon 900B	Government of Namibia, Eros	
NETHERLANDS			
Koninklijke Luchtmacht (KLu)			
D-101	Boeing-Vertol CH-47D Chinook	KLu 298 Sqn, Gilze-Rijen	
D-102	Boeing-Vertol CH-47D Chinook	KLu 298 Sqn, Gilze-Rijen	
D-103	Boeing-Vertol CH-47D Chinook	KLu 298 Sqn, Gilze-Rijen	
D-106	Boeing-Vertol CH-47D Chinook	KLu 298 Sqn, Gilze-Rijen	
D-661	Boeing-Vertol CH-47D Chinook	KLu 298 Sqn, Gilze-Rijen	
D-662	Boeing-Vertol CH-47D Chinook	KLu 298 Sqn, Gilze-Rijen	
D-663	Boeing-Vertol CH-47D Chinook	KLu 298 Sqn, Gilze-Rijen	
D-664	Boeing-Vertol CH-47D Chinook	KLu 298 Sqn, Gilze-Rijen	
D-665	Boeing-Vertol CH-47D Chinook	KLu 298 Sqn, Gilze-Rijen	
D-666	Boeing-Vertol CH-47D Chinook	KLu 298 Sqn, Gilze-Rijen	
D-667	Boeing-Vertol CH-47D Chinook	KLu 298 Sqn, Gilze-Rijen	
D-890	Boeing-Vertol CH-47F Chinook	KLu 298 Sqn, Gilze-Rijen	
D-891	Boeing-Vertol CH-47F Chinook	KLu 302 Sqn, Fort Hood, Texas, USA	
D-892	Boeing-Vertol CH-47F Chinook	KLu 298 Sqn, Gilze-Rijen	
D-893	Boeing-Vertol CH-47F Chinook	KLu 302 Sqn, Fort Hood, Texas, USA	
D-894	Boeing-Vertol CH-47F Chinook	KLu 302 Sqn, Fort Hood, Texas, USA	
D-895	Boeing-Vertol CH-47F Chinook	KLu 302 Sqn, Fort Hood, Texas, USA	
F-001	Lockheed Martin F-35A Lightning II [OT]	KLu 323 Sqn, Edwards AFB California, USA	
F-002	Lockheed Martin F-35A Lightning II [OT]	KLu 323 Sqn, Edwards AFB California, USA	
G-273	Lockheed C-130H-30 Hercules	KLu 336 Sqn, Eindhoven	
G-275	Lockheed C-130H-30 Hercules	KLu 336 Sqn, Eindhoven	
G-781	Lockheed C-130H Hercules	KLu 336 Sqn, Eindhoven	

Notes	Serial	Type (code/other identity)	Owner/operator, location or fate
	G-988	Lockheed C-130H Hercules	KLu 336 Sqn, Eindhoven
	J-001	Fokker (GD) F-16AM Fighting Falcon	KLu 312 Sqn, Volkel
	J-002	Fokker (GD) F-16AM Fighting Falcon $	KLu 322 Sqn, Leeuwarden
	J-003	Fokker (GD) F-16AM Fighting Falcon	KLu 313 Sqn, Volkel
	J-004	Fokker (GD) F-16AM Fighting Falcon [AZ]	KLu 148th FS/162th FW, Tucson IAP, Arizona, USA
	J-005	Fokker (GD) F-16AM Fighting Falcon	KLu 313 Sqn, Volkel
	J-006	Fokker (GD) F-16AM Fighting Falcon $	KLu 322 Sqn, Leeuwarden
	J-008	Fokker (GD) F-16AM Fighting Falcon $	KLu 313 Sqn, Volkel
	J-009	Fokker (GD) F-16AM Fighting Falcon	KLu 322 Sqn, Leeuwarden
	J-010	Fokker (GD) F-16AM Fighting Falcon [AZ]	KLu 148th FS/162th FW, Tucson IAP, Arizona, USA
	J-011	Fokker (GD) F-16AM Fighting Falcon	KLu 312 Sqn/313 Sqn, Volkel
	J-013	Fokker (GD) F-16AM Fighting Falcon	KLu 312 Sqn/313 Sqn, Volkel
	J-014	Fokker (GD) F-16AM Fighting Falcon	KLu 313 Sqn, Volkel
	J-015	Fokker (GD) F-16AM Fighting Falcon	KLu 322 Sqn, Leeuwarden
	J-016	Fokker (GD) F-16AM Fighting Falcon	KLu 312 Sqn, Volkel
	J-017	Fokker (GD) F-16AM Fighting Falcon	KLu 322 Sqn, Leeuwarden
	J-018	Fokker (GD) F-16AM Fighting Falcon [AZ]	KLu 148th FS/162th FW, Tucson IAP, Arizona, USA
	J-019	Fokker (GD) F-16AM Fighting Falcon [AZ]	KLu 148th FS/162th FW, Tucson IAP, Arizona, USA
	J-020	Fokker (GD) F-16AM Fighting Falcon	KLu 312 Sqn, Volkel
	J-021	Fokker (GD) F-16AM Fighting Falcon	KLu 322 Sqn, Leeuwarden
	J-055	Fokker (GD) F-16AM Fighting Falcon	KLu 313 Sqn, Volkel
	J-057	Fokker (GD) F-16AM Fighting Falcon	KLu, stored Volkel
	J-060	Fokker (GD) F-16AM Fighting Falcon	KLu 322 Sqn, Leeuwarden
	J-061	Fokker (GD) F-16AM Fighting Falcon	KLu 322 Sqn, Leeuwarden
	J-062	Fokker (GD) F-16AM Fighting Falcon	KLu 313 Sqn, Volkel
	J-063	Fokker (GD) F-16AM Fighting Falcon	KLu 313 Sqn, Volkel
	J-064	Fokker (GD) F-16BM Fighting Falcon [AZ]	KLu 148th FS/162th FW, Tucson IAP, Arizona, USA
	J-065	Fokker (GD) F-16BM Fighting Falcon	KLu 322 Sqn, Leeuwarden
	J-066	Fokker (GD) F-16BM Fighting Falcon	KLu Test Flt, Leeuwarden
	J-067	Fokker (GD) F-16BM Fighting Falcon [AZ]	KLu 148th FS/162th FW, Tucson IAP, Arizona, USA
	J-135	Fokker (GD) F-16AM Fighting Falcon	KLu 322 Sqn, Leeuwarden
	J-136	Fokker (GD) F-16AM Fighting Falcon	KLu 312 Sqn, Volkel
	J-142	Fokker (GD) F-16AM Fighting Falcon	KLu 322 Sqn, Leeuwarden
	J-144	Fokker (GD) F-16AM Fighting Falcon	KLu 312 Sqn/313 Sqn, Volkel
	J-145	Fokker (GD) F-16AM Fighting Falcon	KLu, stored Volkel
	J-146	Fokker (GD) F-16AM Fighting Falcon	KLu 322 Sqn, Leeuwarden
	J-193	Fokker (GD) F-16AM Fighting Falcon	KLu, stored Volkel
	J-196	Fokker (GD) F-16AM Fighting Falcon $	KLu 313 Sqn, Volkel
	J-197	Fokker (GD) F-16AM Fighting Falcon	KLu 312 Sqn/313 Sqn, Volkel
	J-199	Fokker (GD) F-16AM Fighting Falcon	KLu, stored Volkel
	J-201	Fokker (GD) F-16AM Fighting Falcon	KLu 322 Sqn, Leeuwarden
	J-202	Fokker (GD) F-16AM Fighting Falcon	KLu, stored Volkel
	J-208	Fokker (GD) F-16BM Fighting Falcon	KLu, stored Volkel
	J-209	Fokker (GD) F-16BM Fighting Falcon [AZ]	KLu 148th FS/162th FW, Tucson IAP, Arizona, USA
	J-210	Fokker (GD) F-16BM Fighting Falcon [AZ]	KLu 148th FS/162th FW, Tucson IAP, Arizona, USA
	J-362	Fokker (GD) F-16AM Fighting Falcon	KLu 322 Sqn, Leeuwarden
	J-366	Fokker (GD) F-16AM Fighting Falcon [AZ]	KLu 148th FS/162th FW, Tucson IAP, Arizona, USA
	J-367	Fokker (GD) F-16AM Fighting Falcon	KLu 322 Sqn, Leeuwarden
	J-368	Fokker (GD) F-16BM Fighting Falcon	KLu, stored Volkel
	J-369	Fokker (GD) F-16BM Fighting Falcon [AZ]	KLu 148th FS/162th FW, Tucson IAP, Arizona, USA
	J-508	Fokker (GD) F-16AM Fighting Falcon	KLu 313 Sqn, Volkel
	J-509	Fokker (GD) F-16AM Fighting Falcon	KLu 322 Sqn, Leeuwarden

Serial	Type (code/other identity)	Owner/operator, location or fate	Notes
J-510	Fokker (GD) F-16AM Fighting Falcon	KLu, stored Volkel	
J-511	Fokker (GD) F-16AM Fighting Falcon	KLu 322 Sqn, Leeuwarden	
J-512	Fokker (GD) F-16AM Fighting Falcon	KLu 313 Sqn, Volkel	
J-513	Fokker (GD) F-16AM Fighting Falcon	KLu 323 Sqn, Volkel	
J-514	Fokker (GD) F-16AM Fighting Falcon	KLu 313 Sqn, Volkel	
J-515	Fokker (GD) F-16AM Fighting Falcon	KLu 312 Sqn/313 Sqn, Volkel	
J-516	Fokker (GD) F-16AM Fighting Falcon	KLu 322 Sqn, Leeuwarden	
J-616	Fokker (GD) F-16AM Fighting Falcon	KLu 312 Sqn, Volkel	
J-623	Fokker (GD) F-16AM Fighting Falcon	KLu, stored Volkel	
J-624	Fokker (GD) F-16AM Fighting Falcon	KLu 322 Sqn, Leeuwarden	
J-628	Fokker (GD) F-16AM Fighting Falcon	KLu 322 Sqn, Leeuwarden	
J-630	Fokker (GD) F-16AM Fighting Falcon	KLu 312 Sqn/313 Sqn, Volkel	
J-631	Fokker (GD) F-16AM Fighting Falcon $	KLu 322 Sqn, Leeuwarden	
J-632	Fokker (GD) F-16AM Fighting Falcon	KLu 322 Sqn, Leeuwarden	
J-635	Fokker (GD) F-16AM Fighting Falcon	KLu 312 Sqn, Volkel	
J-637	Fokker (GD) F-16AM Fighting Falcon	KLu 312 Sqn, Volkel	
J-638	Fokker (GD) F-16AM Fighting Falcon	KLu 313 Sqn, Volkel	
J-641	Fokker (GD) F-16AM Fighting Falcon	KLu 312 Sqn, Volkel	
J-642	Fokker (GD) F-16AM Fighting Falcon	KLu 322 Sqn, Leeuwarden	
J-643	Fokker (GD) F-16AM Fighting Falcon	KLu 313 Sqn, Volkel	
J-644	Fokker (GD) F-16AM Fighting Falcon	KLu 312 Sqn/313 Sqn, Volkel	
J-646	Fokker (GD) F-16AM Fighting Falcon	KLu 312 Sqn, Volkel	
J-647	Fokker (GD) F-16AM Fighting Falcon	KLu, stored Volkel	
J-866	Fokker (GD) F-16AM Fighting Falcon	KLu 312 Sqn, Volkel	
J-868	Fokker (GD) F-16AM Fighting Falcon	KLu, stored Volkel	
J-870	Fokker (GD) F-16AM Fighting Falcon	KLu, stored Volkel	
J-871	Fokker (GD) F-16AM Fighting Falcon	KLu 322 Sqn, Leeuwarden	
J-872	Fokker (GD) F-16AM Fighting Falcon	KLu, stored Volkel	
J-873	Fokker (GD) F-16AM Fighting Falcon	KLu, stored Volkel	
J-877	Fokker (GD) F-16AM Fighting Falcon	KLu Leeuwarden, WLT	
J-879	Fokker (GD) F-16AM Fighting Falcon	KLu 322 Sqn, Leeuwarden	
J-881	Fokker (GD) F-16AM Fighting Falcon	KLu 322 Sqn, Leeuwarden	
J-882	Fokker (GD) F-16BM Fighting Falcon	KLu 322 Sqn, Leeuwarden	
L-01	Pilatus PC-7 Turbo Trainer	Pilatus, Stans, Switzerland (upgrade)	
L-02	Pilatus PC-7 Turbo Trainer $	KLu 131 EMVO Sqn, Woensdrecht	
L-03	Pilatus PC-7 Turbo Trainer	KLu 131 EMVO Sqn, Woensdrecht	
L-04	Pilatus PC-7 Turbo Trainer	KLu 131 EMVO Sqn, Woensdrecht	
L-05	Pilatus PC-7 Turbo Trainer	KLu 131 EMVO Sqn, Woensdrecht	
L-06	Pilatus PC-7 Turbo Trainer	KLu 131 EMVO Sqn, Woensdrecht	
L-07	Pilatus PC-7 Turbo Trainer	KLu 131 EMVO Sqn, Woensdrecht	
L-08	Pilatus PC-7 Turbo Trainer	KLu 131 EMVO Sqn, Woensdrecht	
L-09	Pilatus PC-7 Turbo Trainer	KLu 131 EMVO Sqn, Woensdrecht	
L-10	Pilatus PC-7 Turbo Trainer	KLu 131 EMVO Sqn, Woensdrecht	
L-11	Pilatus PC-7 Turbo Trainer	KLu 131 EMVO Sqn, Woensdrecht	
L-12	Pilatus PC-7 Turbo Trainer	KLu 131 EMVO Sqn, Woensdrecht	
L-13	Pilatus PC-7 Turbo Trainer	KLu 131 EMVO Sqn, Woensdrecht	
N-088	NH Industries NH.90-NFH	KLu 860 Sqn, De Kooij	
N-102	NH Industries NH.90-NFH	KLu 860 Sqn, De Kooij	
N-110	NH Industries NH.90-NFH	KLu 860 Sqn, De Kooij	
N-164	NH Industries NH.90-NFH	KLu 860 Sqn, De Kooij	
N-175	NH Industries NH.90-NFH	KLu 860 Sqn, De Kooij	
N-195	NH Industries NH.90-NFH	KLu 860 Sqn, De Kooij	
N-227	NH Industries NH.90-NFH	KLu 860 Sqn, De Kooij	
N-228	NH Industries NH.90-NFH	KLu 860 Sqn, De Kooij	
N-233	NH Industries NH.90-NFH	KLu 860 Sqn, De Kooij	
N-234	NH Industries NH.90-NFH	KLu 860 Sqn, De Kooij	
N-258	NH Industries NH.90-NFH	KLu 860 Sqn, De Kooij	
N-277	NH Industries NH.90-NFH	KLu 860 Sqn, De Kooij	
N-316	NH Industries NH.90-NFH	KLu 860 Sqn, De Kooij	
N-317	NH Industries NH.90-NFH	KLu 860 Sqn, De Kooij	
N-318	NH Industries NH.90-NFH	KLu 860 Sqn, De Kooij	
N-319	NH Industries NH.90-NFH	KLu 860 Sqn, De Kooij	

Notes	Serial	Type (code/other identity)	Owner/operator, location or fate
	N-324	NH Industries NH.90-NFH	KLu 860 Sqn, De Kooij
	N-325	NH Industries NH.90-NFH	KLu 860 Sqn, De Kooij
	N-326	NH Industries NH.90-NFH	KLu 860 Sqn, De Kooij
	N-327	NH Industries NH.90-NFH	KLu 860 Sqn, De Kooij
	Q-01	MDH AH-64D Apache Longbow	KLu 301 Sqn, Gilze-Rijen
	Q-02	MDH AH-64D Apache Longbow	KLu 302 Sqn, Fort Hood, Texas, USA
	Q-03	MDH AH-64D Apache Longbow	KLu 302 Sqn, Fort Hood, Texas, USA
	Q-04	MDH AH-64D Apache Longbow	KLu 301 Sqn, Gilze-Rijen
	Q-05	MDH AH-64D Apache Longbow	KLu 301 Sqn, Gilze-Rijen
	Q-06	MDH AH-64D Apache Longbow	KLu 302 Sqn, Fort Hood, Texas, USA
	Q-07	MDH AH-64D Apache Longbow	KLu 302 Sqn, Fort Hood, Texas, USA
	Q-08	MDH AH-64D Apache Longbow	KLu 301 Sqn, Gilze-Rijen
	Q-09	MDH AH-64D Apache Longbow	KLu 301 Sqn, Gilze-Rijen
	Q-10	MDH AH-64D Apache Longbow	KLu 301 Sqn, Gilze-Rijen
	Q-11	MDH AH-64D Apache Longbow	KLu 302 Sqn, Fort Hood, Texas, USA
	Q-12	MDH AH-64D Apache Longbow	KLu 302 Sqn, Fort Hood, Texas, USA
	Q-13	MDH AH-64D Apache Longbow	KLu 301 Sqn, Gilze-Rijen
	Q-14	MDH AH-64D Apache Longbow	KLu 301 Sqn, Gilze-Rijen
	Q-16	MDH AH-64D Apache Longbow	KLu 301 Sqn, Gilze-Rijen
	Q-17	MDH AH-64D Apache Longbow	KLu 301 Sqn, Gilze-Rijen
	Q-18	MDH AH-64D Apache Longbow	KLu 301 Sqn, Gilze-Rijen
	Q-19	MDH AH-64D Apache Longbow	KLu 301 Sqn, Gilze-Rijen
	Q-21	MDH AH-64D Apache Longbow	KLu 301 Sqn, Gilze-Rijen
	Q-22	MDH AH-64D Apache Longbow	KLu 301 Sqn, Gilze-Rijen
	Q-23	MDH AH-64D Apache Longbow	KLu 301 Sqn, Gilze-Rijen
	Q-24	MDH AH-64D Apache Longbow	KLu 301 Sqn, Gilze-Rijen
	Q-25	MDH AH-64D Apache Longbow	KLu 301 Sqn, Gilze-Rijen
	Q-26	MDH AH-64D Apache Longbow	KLu 301 Sqn, Gilze-Rijen
	Q-27	MDH AH-64D Apache Longbow	KLu 302 Sqn, Fort Hood, Texas, USA
	Q-28	MDH AH-64D Apache Longbow	KLu 302 Sqn, Fort Hood, Texas, USA
	Q-29	MDH AH-64D Apache Longbow	KLu 301 Sqn, Gilze-Rijen
	Q-30	MDH AH-64D Apache Longbow	KLu 301 Sqn, Gilze-Rijen
	S-419	Eurocopter AS.532U-2 Cougar	KLu 300 Sqn, Gilze-Rijen
	S-440	Eurocopter AS.532U-2 Cougar	KLu 300 Sqn, Gilze-Rijen
	S-441	Eurocopter AS.532U-2 Cougar	KLu 300 Sqn, Gilze-Rijen
	S-442	Eurocopter AS.532U-2 Cougar	KLu 300 Sqn, Gilze-Rijen
	S-444	Eurocopter AS.532U-2 Cougar	KLu 300 Sqn, Gilze-Rijen
	S-445	Eurocopter AS.532U-2 Cougar	KLu 300 Sqn, Gilze-Rijen
	S-447	Eurocopter AS.532U-2 Cougar	KLu 300 Sqn, Gilze-Rijen
	S-453	Eurocopter AS.532U-2 Cougar	KLu 300 Sqn, Gilze-Rijen
	S-454	Eurocopter AS.532U-2 Cougar	KLu 300 Sqn, Gilze-Rijen
	S-456	Eurocopter AS.532U-2 Cougar	KLu 300 Sqn, Gilze-Rijen
	S-457	Eurocopter AS.532U-2 Cougar	KLu, Woensdrecht (wfu)
	S-458	Eurocopter AS.532U-2 Cougar	KLu 300 Sqn, Gilze-Rijen
	S-459	Eurocopter AS.532U-2 Cougar	KLu 300 Sqn, Gilze-Rijen
	T-235	McDonnell Douglas KDC-10	KLu 334 Sqn, Eindhoven
	T-264	McDonnell Douglas KDC-10	KLu 334 Sqn, Eindhoven
	V-11	Grumman G.1159C Gulfstream IV	KLu 334 Sqn, Eindhoven
	Kustwacht & Netherlands Government		
	PH-CGC	Dornier Do.228-212	Kustwacht, Amsterdam/Schiphol
	PH-CGN	Dornier Do.228-212	Kustwacht, Amsterdam/Schiphol
	PH-KBX	Fokker 70	Dutch Royal Flight, Amsterdam/Schiphol
	NEW ZEALAND		
	Royal New Zealand Air Force (RNZAF)		
	NZ4201	Lockheed P-3K2 Orion	RNZAF 5 Sqn, Whenuapai
	NZ4202	Lockheed P-3K2 Orion	RNZAF 5 Sqn, Whenuapai
	NZ4203	Lockheed P-3K2 Orion	RNZAF 5 Sqn, Whenuapai
	NZ4204	Lockheed P-3K2 Orion	RNZAF 5 Sqn, Whenuapai
	NZ4205	Lockheed P-3K2 Orion	RNZAF 5 Sqn, Whenuapai
	NZ4206	Lockheed P-3K2 Orion	RNZAF 5 Sqn, Whenuapai
	NZ7001	Lockheed C-130H(NZ) Hercules $	RNZAF 40 Sqn, Whenuapai

Serial	Type (code/other identity)	Owner/operator, location or fate	Notes
NZ7002	Lockheed C-130H(NZ) Hercules	RNZAF 40 Sqn, Whenuapai	
NZ7003	Lockheed C-130H(NZ) Hercules	RNZAF 40 Sqn, Whenuapai	
NZ7004	Lockheed C-130H(NZ) Hercules	RNZAF 40 Sqn, Whenuapai	
NZ7005	Lockheed C-130H Hercules	RNZAF 40 Sqn, Whenuapai	
NZ7571	Boeing 757-2K2	RNZAF 40 Sqn, Whenuapai	
NZ7572	Boeing 757-2K2	RNZAF 40 Sqn, Whenuapai	

NIGER

5U-BAG	Boeing 737-2N9C	Government of Niger, Niamey	
5U-GRN	Boeing 737-75U	Government of Niger, Niamey	

NIGERIA

Nigerian Air Force (NAF)

NAF-910	Lockheed C-130H Hercules	NAF 88 MAG, Lagos	
NAF-912	Lockheed C-130H Hercules	NAF 88 MAG, Lagos	
NAF-913	Lockheed C-130H Hercules	NAF 88 MAG, Lagos	
NAF-917	Lockheed C-130H-30 Hercules	NAF 88 MAG, Lagos	
NAF-918	Lockheed C-130H-30 Hercules	NAF 88 MAG, Lagos	
NAF-961	Dassault Falcon 900	NAF, Abuja	

Nigerian Government

5N-FGS	Gulfstream Aerospace Gulfstream V	Federal Government of Nigeria, Abuja	
5N-FGT	Boeing 737-7N6 [001]	Federal Government of Nigeria, Abuja	
5N-FGU	Dassault Falcon 7X	Federal Government of Nigeria, Abuja	
5N-FGV	Dassault Falcon 7X	Federal Government of Nigeria, Abuja	
5N-FGW	Gulfstream Aerospace G.550	Federal Government of Nigeria, Abuja	
5N-FGX	Hawker 4000 Horizon	Federal Government of Nigeria, Abuja	

NORWAY

Luftforsvaret/Royal Norwegian Air Force (RNoAF)

013	NH Industries NH.90-NFH	RNoAF (on order)	
027	NH Industries NH.90-NFH	RNoAF (on order)	
041	Dassault Falcon 20 ECM	RNoAF 717 Skv, Gardermoen	
049	NH Industries NH.90-NFH	RNoAF 337 Skv, Bardufoss	
053	Dassault Falcon 20 ECM	RNoAF 717 Skv, Gardermoen	
057	NH Industries NH.90-NFH	RNoAF 337 Skv, Bardufoss	
058	NH Industries NH.90-NFH	RNoAF 337 Skv, Bardufoss	
060	Westland Sea King Mk.43	RNoAF 330 Skv Bodø/Banak/Ørland & Sola	
062	Westland Sea King Mk.43	RNoAF 330 Skv Bodø/Banak/Ørland & Sola	
066	Westland Sea King Mk.43	RNoAF 330 Skv Bodø/Banak/Ørland & Sola	
069	Westland Sea King Mk.43	RNoAF 330 Skv Bodø/Banak/Ørland & Sola	
070	Westland Sea King Mk.43	RNoAF 330 Skv Bodø/Banak/Ørland & Sola	
071	Westland Sea King Mk.43B	RNoAF 330 Skv Bodø/Banak/Ørland & Sola	
072	Westland Sea King Mk.43	RNoAF 330 Skv Bodø/Banak/Ørland & Sola	
073	Westland Sea King Mk.43	RNoAF 330 Skv Bodø/Banak/Ørland & Sola	
074	Westland Sea King Mk.43	RNoAF 330 Skv Bodø/Banak/Ørland & Sola	
087	NH Industries NH.90-NFH	RNoAF 337 Skv, Bardufoss	
0125	Dassault Falcon 20 ECM	RNoAF 717 Skv, Gardermoen	
139	Bell 412HP	RNoAF 339 Skv, Bardufoss	
140	Bell 412HP	RNoAF 339 Skv, Bardufoss	
141	Bell 412HP	RNoAF 339 Skv, Bardufoss	
142	Bell 412HP	RNoAF 339 Skv, Bardufoss	
143	Bell 412HP	RNoAF 339 Skv, Bardufoss	
144	Bell 412HP	RNoAF 339 Skv, Bardufoss	
145	Bell 412HP	RNoAF 339 Skv, Bardufoss	
146	Bell 412HP	RNoAF 339 Skv, Bardufoss	
147	Bell 412HP	RNoAF 339 Skv, Bardufoss	
148	Bell 412HP	RNoAF 339 Skv, Bardufoss	
149	Bell 412HP	RNoAF 339 Skv, Bardufoss	
161	Bell 412HP	RNoAF 339 Skv, Bardufoss	
162	Bell 412HP	RNoAF 339 Skv, Bardufoss	
163	Bell 412HP	RNoAF 339 Skv, Bardufoss	
164	Bell 412HP	RNoAF 339 Skv, Bardufoss	

Notes	Serial	Type (code/other identity)	Owner/operator, location or fate
	165	Bell 412HP	RNoAF 339 Skv, Bardufoss
	166	Bell 412HP	RNoAF 339 Skv, Bardufoss
	167	Bell 412HP	RNoAF 339 Skv, Bardufoss
	171	NH Industries NH.90-NFH	RNoAF 337 Skv, Bardufoss
	189	Westland Sea King Mk.43A	RNoAF 330 Skv Bodø/Banak/Ørland & Sola
	194	Bell 412SP	RNoAF 339 Skv, Bardufoss
	217	NH Industries NH.90-NFH	RNoAF (on order)
	0262	AgustaWestland AW101 Mk612	RNoAF (on order)
	0264	AgustaWestland AW101 Mk612	RNoAF (on order)
	0265	AgustaWestland AW101 Mk612	RNoAF (on order)
	0268	AgustaWestland AW101 Mk612	RNoAF (on order)
	0270	AgustaWestland AW101 Mk612	RNoAF (on order)
	272	Fokker (GD) F-16A MLU Fighting Falcon $	RNoAF FLO 331 Skv, Bodø/338 Skv, Ørland
	273	Fokker (GD) F-16A MLU Fighting Falcon	RNoAF FLO 331 Skv, Bodø/338 Skv, Ørland
	0273	AgustaWestland AW101 Mk612	RNoAF (on order)
	275	Fokker (GD) F-16A MLU Fighting Falcon	RNoAF FLO 331 Skv, Bodø/338 Skv, Ørland
	0275	AgustaWestland AW101 Mk612	RNoAF (on order)
	276	Fokker (GD) F-16A MLU Fighting Falcon	RNoAF FLO 331 Skv, Bodø/338 Skv, Ørland
	0276	AgustaWestland AW101 Mk612	RNoAF (on order)
	277	Fokker (GD) F-16A MLU Fighting Falcon	RNoAF FLO 331 Skv, Bodø/338 Skv, Ørland
	0277	AgustaWestland AW101 Mk612	RNoAF (on order)
	0278	AgustaWestland AW101 Mk612	RNoAF (on order)
	279	Fokker (GD) F-16A MLU Fighting Falcon	RNoAF FLO 331 Skv, Bodø/338 Skv, Ørland
	0279	AgustaWestland AW101 Mk612	RNoAF (on order)
	0280	AgustaWestland AW101 Mk612	RNoAF (on order)
	281	Fokker (GD) F-16A MLU Fighting Falcon	RNoAF FLO 331 Skv, Bodø/338 Skv, Ørland
	0281	AgustaWestland AW101 Mk612	RNoAF (on order)
	282	Fokker (GD) F-16A MLU Fighting Falcon	RNoAF FLO 331 Skv, Bodø/338 Skv, Ørland
	0282	AgustaWestland AW101 Mk612	RNoAF (on order)
	0283	AgustaWestland AW101 Mk612	RNoAF (on order)
	284	Fokker (GD) F-16A MLU Fighting Falcon	RNoAF FLO 331 Skv, Bodø/338 Skv, Ørland
	0284	AgustaWestland AW101 Mk612	RNoAF (on order)
	285	Fokker (GD) F-16A MLU Fighting Falcon	RNoAF FLO 331 Skv, Bodø/338 Skv, Ørland
	286	Fokker (GD) F-16A MLU Fighting Falcon	RNoAF FLO 331 Skv, Bodø/338 Skv, Ørland
	288	Fokker (GD) F-16A MLU Fighting Falcon	RNoAF FLO 331 Skv, Bodø/338 Skv, Ørland
	289	Fokker (GD) F-16A MLU Fighting Falcon	RNoAF FLO 331 Skv, Bodø/338 Skv, Ørland
	291	Fokker (GD) F-16A MLU Fighting Falcon	RNoAF FLO 331 Skv, Bodø/338 Skv, Ørland
	292	Fokker (GD) F-16A MLU Fighting Falcon	RNoAF FLO 331 Skv, Bodø/338 Skv, Ørland
	293	Fokker (GD) F-16A MLU Fighting Falcon	RNoAF FLO 331 Skv, Bodø/338 Skv, Ørland
	295	Fokker (GD) F-16A MLU Fighting Falcon	RNoAF FLO 331 Skv, Bodø/338 Skv, Ørland
	297	Fokker (GD) F-16A MLU Fighting Falcon	RNoAF FLO 331 Skv, Bodø/338 Skv, Ørland
	298	Fokker (GD) F-16A MLU Fighting Falcon $	RNoAF FLO 331 Skv, Bodø/338 Skv, Ørland
	299	Fokker (GD) F-16A MLU Fighting Falcon	RNoAF FLO 331 Skv, Bodø/338 Skv, Ørland
	302	Fokker (GD) F-16B MLU Fighting Falcon	RNoAF FLO 331 Skv, Bodø/338 Skv, Ørland
	304	Fokker (GD) F-16B MLU Fighting Falcon	RNoAF FLO 331 Skv, Bodø/338 Skv, Ørland
	305	Fokker (GD) F-16B MLU Fighting Falcon	RNoAF FLO 331 Skv, Bodø/338 Skv, Ørland
	306	Fokker (GD) F-16B MLU Fighting Falcon	RNoAF FLO 331 Skv, Bodø/338 Skv, Ørland
	322	Westland Sea King Mk.43B	RNoAF 330 Skv Bodø/Banak/Ørland & Sola
	329	Westland Sea King Mk.43B	RNoAF 330 Skv Bodø/Banak/Ørland & Sola
	330	Westland Sea King Mk.43B	RNoAF 330 Skv Bodø/Banak/Ørland & Sola
	658	Fokker (GD) F-16A MLU Fighting Falcon	RNoAF FLO 331 Skv, Bodø/338 Skv, Ørland
	659	Fokker (GD) F-16A MLU Fighting Falcon	RNoAF FLO 331 Skv, Bodø/338 Skv, Ørland
	660	Fokker (GD) F-16A MLU Fighting Falcon	RNoAF FLO 331 Skv, Bodø/338 Skv, Ørland
	661	Fokker (GD) F-16A MLU Fighting Falcon	RNoAF FLO 331 Skv, Bodø/338 Skv, Ørland
	662	Fokker (GD) F-16A MLU Fighting Falcon	RNoAF FLO 331 Skv, Bodø/338 Skv, Ørland
	663	Fokker (GD) F-16A MLU Fighting Falcon	RNoAF FLO 331 Skv, Bodø/338 Skv, Ørland
	664	Fokker (GD) F-16A MLU Fighting Falcon $	RNoAF FLO 331 Skv, Bodø/338 Skv, Ørland
	665	Fokker (GD) F-16A MLU Fighting Falcon	RNoAF FLO 331 Skv, Bodø/338 Skv, Ørland
	666	Fokker (GD) F-16A MLU Fighting Falcon	RNoAF/USAF 416th FTS/412th TW, Edwards AFB, USA
	667	Fokker (GD) F-16A MLU Fighting Falcon	RNoAF FLO 331 Skv, Bodø/338 Skv, Ørland
	668	Fokker (GD) F-16A MLU Fighting Falcon	RNoAF FLO 331 Skv, Bodø/338 Skv, Ørland

Serial	Type (code/other identity)	Owner/operator, location or fate	Notes
670	Fokker (GD) F-16A MLU Fighting Falcon	RNoAF FLO 331 Skv, Bodø/338 Skv, Ørland	
671	Fokker (GD) F-16A MLU Fighting Falcon $	RNoAF FLO 331 Skv, Bodø/338 Skv, Ørland	
672	Fokker (GD) F-16A MLU Fighting Falcon	RNoAF FLO 331 Skv, Bodø/338 Skv, Ørland	
673	Fokker (GD) F-16A MLU Fighting Falcon	RNoAF FLO 331 Skv, Bodø/338 Skv, Ørland	
674	Fokker (GD) F-16A MLU Fighting Falcon	RNoAF FLO 331 Skv, Bodø/338 Skv, Ørland	
675	Fokker (GD) F-16A MLU Fighting Falcon	RNoAF FLO 331 Skv, Bodø/338 Skv, Ørland	
677	Fokker (GD) F-16A MLU Fighting Falcon	RNoAF FLO 331 Skv, Bodø/338 Skv, Ørland	
678	Fokker (GD) F-16A MLU Fighting Falcon	RNoAF FLO 331 Skv, Bodø/338 Skv, Ørland	
680	Fokker (GD) F-16A MLU Fighting Falcon	RNoAF FLO 331 Skv, Bodø/338 Skv, Ørland	
681	Fokker (GD) F-16A MLU Fighting Falcon	RNoAF FLO 331 Skv, Bodø/338 Skv, Ørland	
682	Fokker (GD) F-16A MLU Fighting Falcon	RNoAF FLO 331 Skv, Bodø/338 Skv, Ørland	
683	Fokker (GD) F-16A MLU Fighting Falcon	RNoAF FLO 331 Skv, Bodø/338 Skv, Ørland	
686	Fokker (GD) F-16A MLU Fighting Falcon $	RNoAF FLO 331 Skv, Bodø/338 Skv, Ørland	
687	Fokker (GD) F-16A MLU Fighting Falcon	RNoAF FLO 331 Skv, Bodø/338 Skv, Ørland	
688	Fokker (GD) F-16A MLU Fighting Falcon	RNoAF FLO 331 Skv, Bodø/338 Skv, Ørland	
689	Fokker (GD) F-16B MLU Fighting Falcon	RNoAF FLO 331 Skv, Bodø/338 Skv, Ørland	
690	Fokker (GD) F-16B MLU Fighting Falcon	RNoAF FLO 331 Skv, Bodø/338 Skv, Ørland	
691	Fokker (GD) F-16B MLU Fighting Falcon	RNoAF FLO 331 Skv, Bodø/338 Skv, Ørland	
692	Fokker (GD) F-16B MLU Fighting Falcon $	RNoAF FLO 331 Skv, Bodø/338 Skv, Ørland	
693	Fokker (GD) F-16B MLU Fighting Falcon	RNoAF FLO 331 Skv, Bodø/338 Skv, Ørland	
711	GD F-16B MLU Fighting Falcon	RNoAF FLO 331 Skv, Bodø/338 Skv, Ørland	
1216	NH Industries NH.90-NFH (ASW)	RNoAF 337 Skv, Bardufoss	
3296	Lockheed P-3C UIP Orion	RNoAF 333 Skv, Andøya	
3297	Lockheed P-3C UIP Orion	RNoAF 333 Skv, Andøya	
3298	Lockheed P-3C UIP Orion	RNoAF 333 Skv, Andøya	
3299	Lockheed P-3C UIP Orion	RNoAF 333 Skv, Andøya	
4576	Lockheed P-3N Orion	RNoAF 333 Skv, Andøya	
5087	Lockheed Martin F-35A Lightning II	RNoAF 62nd FS/56th FW, Luke AFB, AZ, USA	
5088	Lockheed Martin F-35A Lightning II	RNoAF 62nd FS/56th FW, Luke AFB, AZ, USA	
5110	Lockheed Martin F-35A Lightning II	RNoAF 62nd FS/56th FW, Luke AFB, AZ, USA	
5111	Lockheed Martin F-35A Lightning II	RNoAF 62nd FS/56th FW, Luke AFB, AZ, USA	
5601	Lockheed C-130J-30 Hercules II	RNoAF 335 Skv, Gardermoen	
5607	Lockheed C-130J-30 Hercules II	RNoAF 335 Skv, Gardermoen	
5629	Lockheed C-130J-30 Hercules II	RNoAF 335 Skv, Gardermoen	
5699	Lockheed C-130J-30 Hercules II	RNoAF 335 Skv, Gardermoen	
6603	Lockheed P-3N Orion	RNoAF 333 Skv, Andøya	
...	NH Industries NH.90-NFH	RNoAF (on order)	
...	NH Industries NH.90-NFH	RNoAF (on order)	
...	NH Industries NH.90-NFH	RNoAF (on order)	
...	NH Industries NH.90-NFH	RNoAF (on order)	

OMAN
Royal Air Force of Oman (RAFO)

Serial	Type (code/other identity)	Owner/operator, location or fate	Notes
501	Lockheed C-130H Hercules	RAFO 16 Sqn, Al Musana	
502	Lockheed C-130H Hercules	RAFO 16 Sqn, Al Musana	
503	Lockheed C-130H Hercules	RAFO 16 Sqn, Al Musana	
505	Lockheed C-130J Hercules II	RAFO 16 Sqn, Al Musana	
506	Lockheed C-130J Hercules II	RAFO 16 Sqn, Al Musana	
507	Lockheed C-130J-30 Hercules II	RAFO (on order)	
508	Lockheed C-130J-30 Hercules II	RAFO (on order)	
525	Lockheed C-130J-30 Hercules II	RAFO Royal Flt, Seeb	
554	Airbus A.320-214X	RAFO 4 Sqn, Seeb	
555	Airbus A.320-214X	RAFO 4 Sqn, Seeb	
556	Airbus A.320-214X	RAFO 4 Sqn, Seeb	
557	Grumman G.1159C Gulfstream IV	RAFO 4 Sqn, Seeb	
558	Grumman G.1159C Gulfstream IV	RAFO 4 Sqn, Seeb	
901	CASA C-295M	RAFO 5 Sqn, Salalah	
902	CASA C-295M	RAFO 5 Sqn, Salalah	
903	CASA C-295M	RAFO 5 Sqn, Salalah	
904	CASA C-295M	RAFO 5 Sqn, Salalah	
905	CASA C-295M	RAFO (on order)	
906	CASA C-295M	RAFO (on order)	

Notes	Serial	Type (code/other identity)	Owner/operator, location or fate
	907	CASA C-295M	RAFO (on order)
	908	CASA C-295M	RAFO (on order)
	909	CASA C-295M	RAFO (on order)
	910	CASA C-295MPA Persuader	RAFO 2 Sqn, Al Musana
	911	CASA C-295MPA Persuader	RAFO 2 Sqn, Al Musana
	912	CASA C-295MPA Persuader	RAFO 2 Sqn, Al Musana
	913	CASA C-295MPA Persuader	RAFO 2 Sqn, Al Musana
	914	CASA C-295MPA Persuader	RAFO (on order)
	915	CASA C-295MPA Persuader	RAFO (on order)
	916	CASA C-295MPA Persuader	RAFO (on order)
	Omani Government		
	A4O-AA	Airbus A.320-233	Government of Oman, Seeb
	A4O-AJ	Airbus A.319-115CJ	Government of Oman, Seeb
	A4O-AD	Gulfstream Aerospace G.550	Government of Oman, Seeb
	A4O-AE	Gulfstream Aerospace G.550	Government of Oman, Seeb
	A4O-SO	Boeing 747SP-27	Government of Oman, Seeb
	A4O-HMS	Boeing 747-8H0	Government of Oman, Seeb
	A4O-OMN	Boeing 747-430	Government of Oman, Seeb
	PAKISTAN		
	Pakistan Air Force (PAF)/Pakistani Army		
	4270	Gulfstream Aerospace G.450	Pakistani Army, Rawalpindi
	EYE77	Bombardier Challenger 605	Pakistani Army, Rawalpindi
	J-754	Cessna 560 Citation VI	PAF 12 VIP Communications Sqn, Islamabad
	J-755	Gulfstream Aerospace G.1159C Gulfstream IV-SP	PAF 12 VIP Communications Sqn, Islamabad
	J-756	Gulfstream Aerospace G.450	PAF 12 VIP Communications Sqn, Islamabad
	POLAND		
	Sily Powietrzne (SP)/Polish Air Force & Lotnictwo Marynarki Wojennej (LMW)/Polish Navy		
	011	CASA C-295M	SP 13.eltr/8.BLTr, Kraków/Balice
	012	CASA C-295M $	SP 13.eltr/8.BLTr, Kraków/Balice
	013	CASA C-295M	SP 13.eltr/8.BLTr, Kraków/Balice
	014	CASA C-295M	SP 13.eltr/8.BLTr, Kraków/Balice
	015	CASA C-295M	SP 13.eltr/8.BLTr, Kraków/Balice
	15	Mikoyan MiG-29UB $	SP 1.elt/23.BLT, Minsk/Mazowiecki
	016	CASA C-295M	SP 13.eltr/8.BLTr, Kraków/Balice
	016	PZL 130TC-I Orlik	SP 2.OSzL/42.BLSz, Radom
	017	CASA C-295M	SP 13.eltr/8.BLTr, Kraków/Balice
	018	CASA C-295M	SP 13.eltr/8.BLTr, Kraków/Balice
	020	CASA C-295M	SP 13.eltr/8.BLTr, Kraków/Balice
	021	CASA C-295M	SP 13.eltr/8.BLTr, Kraków/Balice
	022	CASA C-295M	SP 13.eltr/8.BLTr, Kraków/Balice
	023	CASA C-295M	SP 13.eltr/8.BLTr, Kraków/Balice
	024	CASA C-295M	SP 13.eltr/8.BLTr, Kraków/Balice
	025	CASA C-295M	SP 13.eltr/8.BLTr, Kraków/Balice
	026	CASA C-295M	SP 13.eltr/8.BLTr, Kraków/Balice
	027	CASA C-295M	SP 13.eltr/8.BLTr, Kraków/Balice
	28	Mikoyan MiG-29UB	SP 1.elt/23.BLT, Minsk/Mazowiecki
	030	PZL 130TC-II Orlik	SP 2.OSzL/42.BLSz, Radom
	031	PZL 130TC-II Orlik	SP 2.OSzL/42.BLSz, Radom
	032	PZL 130TC-II Orlik	SP 2.OSzL/42.BLSz, Radom
	037	PZL 130TC-II Orlik	SP 2.OSzL/42.BLSz, Radom
	38	Mikoyan MiG-29A	SP 1.elt/23.BLT, Minsk/Mazowiecki
	038	PZL 130TC-II Orlik	SP 2.OSzL/42.BLSz, Radom
	40	Mikoyan MiG-29A	SP 1.elt/23.BLT, Minsk/Mazowiecki
	040	PZL 130TC-II Orlik	SP 2.OSzL/42.BLSz, Radom
	041	PZL 130TC-II Orlik	SP 2.OSzL/42.BLSz, Radom
	42	Mikoyan MiG-29UB	SP 1.elt/23.BLT, Minsk/Mazowiecki
	042	PZL 130TC-II Orlik	SP 2.OSzL/42.BLSz, Radom
	043	PZL 130TC-II Orlik	SP 2.OSzL/42.BLSz, Radom
	045	PZL 130TC-I Orlik	SP 2.OSzL/42.BLSz, Radom
	047	PZL 130TC-II Orlik	SP 2.OSzL/42.BLSz, Radom

Serial	Type (code/other identity)	Owner/operator, location or fate	Notes
048	PZL 130TC-II Orlik	SP 2.OSzL/42.BLSz, Radom	
049	PZL 130TC-I Orlik	SP 2.OSzL/42.BLSz, Radom	
050	PZL 130TC-II Orlik	SP 2.OSzL/42.BLSz, Radom	
051	PZL 130TC-II Orlik	SP 2.OSzL/42.BLSz, Radom	
052	PZL 130TC-II Orlik	SP 2.OSzL/42.BLSz, Radom	
54	Mikoyan MiG-29A	SP 1.elt/23.BLT, Minsk/Mazowiecki	
56	Mikoyan MiG-29A	SP 1.elt/23.BLT, Minsk/Mazowiecki	
59	Mikoyan MiG-29A	SP 1.elt/23.BLT, Minsk/Mazowiecki	
64	Mikoyan MiG-29UB	SP	
65	Mikoyan MiG-29A	SP 41.elt/22.BLT, Malbork	
66	Mikoyan MiG-29A	SP 41.elt/22.BLT, Malbork	
67	Mikoyan MiG-29A	SP 41.elt/22.BLT, Malbork	
70	Mikoyan MiG-29A	SP 41.elt/22.BLT, Malbork	
83	Mikoyan MiG-29A	SP 1.elt/23.BLT, Minsk/Mazowiecki	
89	Mikoyan MiG-29A	SP 1.elt/23.BLT, Minsk/Mazowiecki	
92	Mikoyan MiG-29A	SP 41.elt/22.BLT, Malbork	
105	Mikoyan MiG-29A	SP 1.elt/23.BLT, Minsk/Mazowiecki	
108	Mikoyan MiG-29A	SP 1.elt/23.BLT, Minsk/Mazowiecki	
111	Mikoyan MiG-29A	SP 1.elt/23.BLT, Minsk/Mazowiecki	
114	Mikoyan MiG-29A	SP 1.elt/23.BLT, Minsk/Mazowiecki	
115	Mikoyan MiG-29A	SP 1.elt/23.BLT, Minsk/Mazowiecki	
0204	PZL M28B-TD Bryza	SP 1.OSzL/41.BLSz, Deblin	
0205	PZL M28B-TD Bryza	SP 1.OSzL/41.BLSz, Deblin	
0206	PZL M28B-TD Bryza	SP 14.eltr/33.BLTr, Powidz	
0207	PZL M28B-TD Bryza	SP 13.eltr/8.BLTr, Kraków/Balice	
0208	PZL M28B-TD Bryza	SP 14.eltr/33.BLTr, Powidz	
0209	PZL M28B-TD Bryza	SP 14.eltr/33.BLTr, Powidz	
0210	PZL M28B-TD Bryza	SP 14.eltr/33.BLTr, Powidz	
0211	PZL M28B-TD Bryza	SP 14.eltr/33.BLTr, Powidz	
0212	PZL M28B-TD Bryza	SP 13.eltr/8.BLTr, Kraków/Balice	
0213	PZL M28B/PT Bryza	SP 13.eltr/8.BLTr, Kraków/Balice	
0214	PZL M28B/PT Bryza	SP 13.eltr/8.BLTr, Kraków/Balice	
0215	PZL M28B/PT Bryza	SP 13.eltr/8.BLTr, Kraków/Balice	
0216	PZL M28B/PT Bryza	SP 13.eltr/8.BLTr, Kraków/Balice	
0217	PZL M28B/PT Bryza	SP 13.eltr/8.BLTr, Kraków/Balice	
0218	PZL M28B/PT Bryza	SP 13.eltr/8.BLTr, Kraków/Balice	
0219	PZL M28B/PT Bryza	SP 13.eltr/8.BLTr, Kraków/Balice	
0220	PZL M28B/PT Bryza	SP 13.eltr/8.BLTr, Kraków/Balice	
0221	PZL M28B/PT Bryza	SP 13.eltr/8.BLTr, Kraków/Balice	
0222	PZL M28B/PT Bryza	SP 13.eltr/8.BLTr, Kraków/Balice	
0223	PZL M28B/PT Bryza	SP 13.eltr/8.BLTr, Kraków/Balice	
0224	PZL M28B/PT Bryza	SP 13.eltr/8.BLTr, Kraków/Balice	
0225	PZL M28B/PT Bryza	SP 13.eltr/8.BLTr, Kraków/Balice	
305	Sukhoi Su-22UM-3K	SP 8.elt/21.BLT, Swidwin	
308	Sukhoi Su-22UM-3K	SP 40.elt/21.BLT, Swidwin	
310	Sukhoi Su-22UM-3K	SP 40.elt/21.BLT, Swidwin	
0404	PZL M28B-1E Bryza	LMW 30.el/44.BLMW, Cewice/Siemirowice	
0405	PZL M28B-1E Bryza	LMW 30.el/44.BLMW, Cewice/Siemirowice	
508	Sukhoi Su-22UM-3K	SP 8.elt/21.BLT, Swidwin	
509	Sukhoi Su-22UM-3K	SP 40.elt/21.BLT, Swidwin	
707	Sukhoi Su-22UM-3K	SP 8.elt/21.BLT, Swidwin	
0723	PZL M28B-TD Bryza	LMW 28.el/43.BLMW, Gydnia/Babie Doly	
0810	PZL M28B-1RM Bryza	LMW 30.el/44.BLMW, Cewice/Siemirowice	
1001	Mil Mi-14PL	LMW 29.el/44.BLMW, Darlowo	
1002	Mil Mi-14PL	LMW 29.el/44.BLMW, Darlowo	
1003	Mil Mi-14PL	LMW 29.el/44.BLMW, Darlowo	
1003	PZL M28B-TD Bryza	LMW 28.el/43.BLMW, Gydnia/Babie Doly	
1005	Mil Mi-14PL	LMW 29.el/44.BLMW, Darlowo	
1006	PZL M28B-1R Bryza	LMW 30.el/44.BLMW, Cewice/Siemirowice	
1007	Mil Mi-14PL	LMW 29.el/44.BLMW, Darlowo	
1008	Mil Mi-14PL	LMW 29.el/44.BLMW, Darlowo	
1008	PZL M28B-1R Bryza	LMW 30.el/44.BLMW, Cewice/Siemirowice	

Notes	Serial	Type (code/other identity)	Owner/operator, location or fate
	1009	Mil Mi-14PL	LMW 29.el/44.BLMW, Darlowo
	1010	Mil Mi-14PL	LMW 29.el/44.BLMW, Darlowo
	1011	Mil Mi-14PL	LMW 29.el/44.BLMW, Darlowo
	1012	Mil Mi-14PL/R	LMW 29.el/44.BLMW, Darlowo
	1017	PZL M28B-1R Bryza $	LMW 30.el/44.BLMW, Cewice/Siemirowice
	1022	PZL M28B-1R Bryza	LMW 30.el/44.BLMW, Cewice/Siemirowice
	1114	PZL M28B-1R Bryza	LMW 30.el/44.BLMW, Cewice/Siemirowice
	1115	PZL M28B-1R Bryza	LMW 30.el/44.BLMW, Cewice/Siemirowice
	1116	PZL M28B-1R Bryza	LMW 30.el/44.BLMW, Cewice/Siemirowice
	1117	PZL M28B-1 Bryza	LMW 28.el/43.BLMW, Gydnia/Babie Doly
	1118	PZL M28B-1 Bryza	LMW 28.el/43.BLMW, Gydnia/Babie Doly
	1501	Lockheed C-130E Hercules	SP 14.eltr/33.BLTr, Powidz
	1502	Lockheed C-130E Hercules	SP 14.eltr/33.BLTr, Powidz
	1503	Lockheed C-130E Hercules	SP 14.eltr/33.BLTr, Powidz
	1504	Lockheed C-130E Hercules	SP 14.eltr/33.BLTr, Powidz
	1505	Lockheed C-130E Hercules	SP 14.eltr/33.BLTr, Powidz
	3201	Sukhoi Su-22M-4	SP 8.elt/21.BLT, Swidwin
	3304	Sukhoi Su-22M-4	SP 8.elt/21.BLT, Swidwin
	3612	Sukhoi Su-22M-4	SP 40.elt/21.BLT, Swidwin
	3713	Sukhoi Su-22M-4 $	SP 40.elt/21.BLT, Swidwin
	3715	Sukhoi Su-22M-4	SP 40.elt/21.BLT, Swidwin
	3816	Sukhoi Su-22M-4	SP 40.elt/21.BLT, Swidwin
	3817	Sukhoi Su-22M-4	SP 40.elt/21.BLT, Swidwin
	3819	Sukhoi Su-22M-4	SP 8.elt/21.BLT, Swidwin
	3920	Sukhoi Su-22M-4	SP 40.elt/21.BLT, Swidwin
	4040	Lockheed Martin F-16C-52 Fighting Falcon	SP/USAF 416th FTS/412th TW, Edwards AFB, USA
	4041	Lockheed Martin F-16C-52 Fighting Falcon	SP 6.elt/31.BLT, Poznan/Krzesiny
	4042	Lockheed Martin F-16C-52 Fighting Falcon	SP 3.elt/31.BLT, Poznan/Krzesiny
	4043	Lockheed Martin F-16C-52 Fighting Falcon	SP 3.elt/31.BLT, Poznan/Krzesiny
	4044	Lockheed Martin F-16C-52 Fighting Falcon	SP 3.elt/31.BLT, Poznan/Krzesiny
	4045	Lockheed Martin F-16C-52 Fighting Falcon	SP 3.elt/31.BLT, Poznan/Krzesiny
	4046	Lockheed Martin F-16C-52 Fighting Falcon	SP 3.elt/31.BLT, Poznan/Krzesiny
	4047	Lockheed Martin F-16C-52 Fighting Falcon	SP 3.elt/31.BLT, Poznan/Krzesiny
	4048	Lockheed Martin F-16C-52 Fighting Falcon	SP 3.elt/31.BLT, Poznan/Krzesiny
	4049	Lockheed Martin F-16C-52 Fighting Falcon	SP 3.elt/31.BLT, Poznan/Krzesiny
	4050	Lockheed Martin F-16C-52 Fighting Falcon	SP 3.elt/31.BLT, Poznan/Krzesiny
	4051	Lockheed Martin F-16C-52 Fighting Falcon	SP 3.elt/31.BLT, Poznan/Krzesiny
	4052	Lockheed Martin F-16C-52 Fighting Falcon $	SP 6.elt/31.BLT, Poznan/Krzesiny
	4053	Lockheed Martin F-16C-52 Fighting Falcon	SP 6.elt/31.BLT, Poznan/Krzesiny
	4054	Lockheed Martin F-16C-52 Fighting Falcon	SP 6.elt/31.BLT, Poznan/Krzesiny
	4055	Lockheed Martin F-16C-52 Fighting Falcon $	SP 6.elt/31.BLT, Poznan/Krzesiny
	4056	Lockheed Martin F-16C-52 Fighting Falcon $	SP 6.elt/31.BLT, Poznan/Krzesiny
	4057	Lockheed Martin F-16C-52 Fighting Falcon	SP 6.elt/31.BLT, Poznan/Krzesiny
	4058	Lockheed Martin F-16C-52 Fighting Falcon	SP 6.elt/31.BLT, Poznan/Krzesiny
	4059	Lockheed Martin F-16C-52 Fighting Falcon	SP 6.elt/31.BLT, Poznan/Krzesiny
	4060	Lockheed Martin F-16C-52 Fighting Falcon	SP 6.elt/31.BLT, Poznan/Krzesiny
	4061	Lockheed Martin F-16C-52 Fighting Falcon	SP 6.elt/31.BLT, Poznan/Krzesiny
	4062	Lockheed Martin F-16C-52 Fighting Falcon $	SP 6.elt/31.BLT, Poznan/Krzesiny
	4063	Lockheed Martin F-16C-52 Fighting Falcon	SP 10.elt/32.BLT, Lask
	4064	Lockheed Martin F-16C-52 Fighting Falcon	SP 10.elt/32.BLT, Lask
	4065	Lockheed Martin F-16C-52 Fighting Falcon	SP 10.elt/32.BLT, Lask
	4066	Lockheed Martin F-16C-52 Fighting Falcon	SP 10.elt/32.BLT, Lask
	4067	Lockheed Martin F-16C-52 Fighting Falcon	SP 10.elt/32.BLT, Lask
	4068	Lockheed Martin F-16C-52 Fighting Falcon	SP 10.elt/32.BLT, Lask
	4069	Lockheed Martin F-16C-52 Fighting Falcon	SP 10.elt/32.BLT, Lask
	4070	Lockheed Martin F-16C-52 Fighting Falcon	SP 10.elt/32.BLT, Lask
	4071	Lockheed Martin F-16C-52 Fighting Falcon	SP 10.elt/32.BLT, Lask
	4072	Lockheed Martin F-16C-52 Fighting Falcon	SP 10.elt/32.BLT, Lask
	4073	Lockheed Martin F-16C-52 Fighting Falcon	SP 10.elt/32.BLT, Lask
	4074	Lockheed Martin F-16C-52 Fighting Falcon	SP 10.elt/32.BLT, Lask
	4075	Lockheed Martin F-16C-52 Fighting Falcon	SP 10.elt/32.BLT, Lask

Serial	Type (code/other identity)	Owner/operator, location or fate	Notes
4076	Lockheed Martin F-16D-52 Fighting Falcon	SP 3.elt/31.BLT, Poznan/Krzesiny	
4077	Lockheed Martin F-16D-52 Fighting Falcon	SP 3.elt/31.BLT, Poznan/Krzesiny	
4078	Lockheed Martin F-16D-52 Fighting Falcon	SP 3.elt/31.BLT, Poznan/Krzesiny	
4079	Lockheed Martin F-16D-52 Fighting Falcon	SP 3.elt/31.BLT, Poznan/Krzesiny	
4080	Lockheed Martin F-16D-52 Fighting Falcon	SP 3.elt/31.BLT, Poznan/Krzesiny	
4081	Lockheed Martin F-16D-52 Fighting Falcon	SP 3.elt/31.BLT, Poznan/Krzesiny	
4082	Lockheed Martin F-16D-52 Fighting Falcon $	SP 6.elt/31.BLT, Poznan/Krzesiny	
4083	Lockheed Martin F-16D-52 Fighting Falcon $	SP 6.elt/31.BLT, Poznan/Krzesiny	
4084	Lockheed Martin F-16D-52 Fighting Falcon $	SP 6.elt/31.BLT, Poznan/Krzesiny	
4085	Lockheed Martin F-16D-52 Fighting Falcon	SP 10.elt/32.BLT, Lask	
4086	Lockheed Martin F-16D-52 Fighting Falcon	SP 10.elt/32.BLT, Lask	
4087	Lockheed Martin F-16D-52 Fighting Falcon	SP 10.elt/32.BLT, Lask	
4101	Mikoyan MiG-29A	SP 41.elt/22.BLT, Malbork	
4103	Mikoyan MiG-29A	SP 41.elt/22.BLT, Malbork	
4104	Mikoyan MiG-29A	SP 41.elt/22.BLT, Malbork	
4105	Mikoyan MiG-29A	SP 1.elt/23.BLT, Minsk/Mazowiecki	
4110	Mikoyan MiG-29UB	SP 41.elt/22.BLT, Malbork	
4113	Mikoyan MiG-29A	SP 41.elt/22.BLT, Malbork	
4116	Mikoyan MiG-29A	SP 41.elt/22.BLT, Malbork	
4120	Mikoyan MiG-29A	SP 41.elt/22.BLT, Malbork	
4121	Mikoyan MiG-29A	SP 41.elt/22.BLT, Malbork	
4122	Mikoyan MiG-29A	SP 41.elt/22.BLT, Malbork	
4123	Mikoyan MiG-29UB	SP 41.elt/22.BLT, Malbork	
7411	Sukhoi Su-22M-4	SP 40.elt/21.BLT, Swidwin	
7412	Sukhoi Su-22M-4	SP 8.elt/21.BLT, Swidwin	
7701	Aermacchi M-346 Master (CSX55209)	SP 1.OSzL/41.BLSz, Deblin	
7702	Aermacchi M-346 Master (CSX55210)	SP 1.OSzL/41.BLSz, Deblin	
7703	Aermacchi M-346 Master (CSX55211)	SP 1.OSzL/41.BLSz, Deblin	
7704	Aermacchi M-346 Master	SP (on order)	
7705	Aermacchi M-346 Master	SP (on order)	
7706	Aermacchi M-346 Master	SP (on order)	
7707	Aermacchi M-346 Master	SP (on order)	
7708	Aermacchi M-346 Master	SP (on order)	
8101	Sukhoi Su-22M-4	SP 40.elt/21.BLT, Swidwin	
8102	Sukhoi Su-22M-4	SP 8.elt/21.BLT, Swidwin	
8103	Sukhoi Su-22M-4	SP 8.elt/21.BLT, Swidwin	
8205	Sukhoi Su-22M-4	SP 40.elt/21.BLT, Swidwin	
8308	Sukhoi Su-22M-4 $	SP 8.elt/21.BLT, Swidwin	
8309	Sukhoi Su-22M-4	SP 40.elt/21.BLT, Swidwin	
8310	Sukhoi Su-22M-4	SP 40.elt/21.BLT, Swidwin	
8715	Sukhoi Su-22M-4	SP 40.elt/21.BLT, Swidwin	
8816	Sukhoi Su-22M-4	SP 40.elt/21.BLT, Swidwin	
8818	Sukhoi Su-22M-4 $	SP 8.elt/21.BLT, Swidwin	
8919	Sukhoi Su-22M-4 $	SP 8.elt/21.BLT, Swidwin	
8920	Sukhoi Su-22M-4	SP 40.elt/21.BLT, Swidwin	
9102	Sukhoi Su-22M-4 $	SP 40.elt/21.BLT, Swidwin	
9615	Sukhoi Su-22M-4	SP 8.elt/21.BLT, Swidwin	
9616	Sukhoi Su-22M-4	SP 40.elt/21.BLT, Swidwin	
...	Gulfstream Aerospace G.550	SP (on order)	
...	Gulfstream Aerospace G.550	SP (on order)	
Straz Graniczna (Polish Border Guard)			
SN-50YG	PZL M28-05 Skytruck	Straz Graniczna, Gdansk/Rebiechowo	
SN-60YG	PZL M28-05 Skytruck	Straz Graniczna, Gdansk/Rebiechowo	
Polish Government			
SP-LIG	Embraer EMB.175-200LR	Polish Government, Warszawa	
SP-LIH	Embraer EMB.175-200LR	Polish Government, Warszawa	
PORTUGAL			
Força Aérea Portuguesa (FAP)/Marinha			
11401	Aérospatiale TB-30 Epsilon	FAP Esq 101, Sintra	
11402	Aérospatiale TB-30 Epsilon	FAP Esq 101, Sintra	
11403	Aérospatiale TB-30 Epsilon	FAP Esq 101, Sintra	

Notes	Serial	Type (code/other identity)	Owner/operator, location or fate
	11404	Aérospatiale TB-30 Epsilon	FAP Esq 101, Sintra
	11405	Aérospatiale TB-30 Epsilon $	FAP Esq 101, Sintra
	11406	Aérospatiale TB-30 Epsilon	FAP Esq 101, Sintra
	11407	Aérospatiale TB-30 Epsilon	FAP Esq 101, Sintra
	11409	Aérospatiale TB-30 Epsilon	FAP Esq 101, Sintra
	11410	Aérospatiale TB-30 Epsilon $	FAP Esq 101, Sintra
	11411	Aérospatiale TB-30 Epsilon	FAP Esq 101, Sintra
	11413	Aérospatiale TB-30 Epsilon	FAP Esq 101, Sintra
	11414	Aérospatiale TB-30 Epsilon	FAP Esq 101, Sintra
	11415	Aérospatiale TB-30 Epsilon	FAP Esq 101, Sintra
	11416	Aérospatiale TB-30 Epsilon $	FAP Esq 101, Sintra
	11417	Aérospatiale TB-30 Epsilon	FAP Esq 101, Sintra
	11418	Aérospatiale TB-30 Epsilon	FAP Esq 101, Sintra
	14807	Lockheed P-3C CUP+ Orion	FAP Esq 601, Beja
	14808	Lockheed P-3C CUP+ Orion $	FAP Esq 601, Beja
	14809	Lockheed P-3C CUP+ Orion	FAP Esq 601, Beja
	14810	Lockheed P-3C CUP+ Orion	FAP, stored Beja
	14811	Lockheed P-3C CUP+ Orion	FAP Esq 601, Beja
	15101	Lockheed Martin F-16A MLU Fighting Falcon	FAP Esq 201/Esq 301, Monte Real
	15102	Lockheed Martin F-16A MLU Fighting Falcon	FAP Esq 201/Esq 301, Monte Real
	15103	Lockheed Martin F-16A MLU Fighting Falcon	FAP Esq 201/Esq 301, Monte Real
	15104	Lockheed Martin F-16A MLU Fighting Falcon	FAP Esq 201/Esq 301, Monte Real
	15105	Lockheed Martin F-16A MLU Fighting Falcon	FAP Esq 201/Esq 301, Monte Real
	15106	Lockheed Martin F-16A MLU Fighting Falcon $	FAP Esq 201/Esq 301, Monte Real
	15107	Lockheed Martin F-16A MLU Fighting Falcon	FAP Esq 201/Esq 301, Monte Real
	15108	Lockheed Martin F-16A MLU Fighting Falcon	FAP Esq 201/Esq 301, Monte Real
	15109	Lockheed Martin F-16A MLU Fighting Falcon	FAP Esq 201/Esq 301, Monte Real
	15110	Lockheed Martin F-16A MLU Fighting Falcon	FAP Esq 201/Esq 301, Monte Real
	15112	Lockheed Martin F-16A MLU Fighting Falcon	FAP Esq 201/Esq 301, Monte Real
	15113	Lockheed Martin F-16A MLU Fighting Falcon	FAP Esq 201/Esq 301, Monte Real
	15114	Lockheed Martin F-16A MLU Fighting Falcon	FAP Esq 201/Esq 301, Monte Real
	15115	Lockheed Martin F-16A MLU Fighting Falcon	FAP Esq 201/Esq 301, Monte Real
	15116	Lockheed Martin F-16A MLU Fighting Falcon	FAP Esq 201/Esq 301, Monte Real
	15117	Lockheed Martin F-16A MLU Fighting Falcon	FAP Esq 201/Esq 301, Monte Real
	15118	Lockheed Martin F-16B MLU Fighting Falcon	FAP Esq 201/Esq 301, Monte Real
	15119	Lockheed Martin F-16B MLU Fighting Falcon	FAP Esq 201/Esq 301, Monte Real
	15120	Lockheed Martin F-16B MLU Fighting Falcon	FAP Esq 201/Esq 301, Monte Real
	15121	Lockheed Martin F-16A MLU Fighting Falcon	*To Romania, September 2016*
	15122	Lockheed Martin F-16A MLU Fighting Falcon	FAP Esq 201/Esq 301, Monte Real
	15123	Lockheed Martin F-16A MLU Fighting Falcon	*To Romania, September 2016*
	15124	Lockheed Martin F-16A MLU Fighting Falcon	*To Romania, September 2016*
	15125	Lockheed Martin F-16A MLU Fighting Falcon	*To Romania, September 2016*
	15126	Lockheed Martin F-16A MLU Fighting Falcon	*To Romania, December 2016*
	15127	Lockheed Martin F-16A MLU Fighting Falcon	*To Romania, December 2016*
	15128	Lockheed Martin F-16A MLU Fighting Falcon	*Sold to Romania*
	15129	Lockheed Martin F-16A MLU Fighting Falcon	*Sold to Romania*
	15130	Lockheed Martin F-16A MLU Fighting Falcon	*To Romania, September 2016*
	15131	Lockheed Martin F-16A MLU Fighting Falcon	FAP Esq 201/Esq 301, Monte Real
	15132	Lockheed Martin F-16A MLU Fighting Falcon	FAP Esq 201/Esq 301, Monte Real
	15133	Lockheed Martin F-16A MLU Fighting Falcon	FAP Esq 201/Esq 301, Monte Real
	15134	Lockheed Martin F-16A MLU Fighting Falcon	FAP Esq 201/Esq 301, Monte Real
	15135	Lockheed Martin F-16A MLU Fighting Falcon	FAP Esq 201/Esq 301, Monte Real
	15136	Lockheed Martin F-16A MLU Fighting Falcon	FAP Esq 201/Esq 301, Monte Real
	15137	Lockheed Martin F-16B MLU Fighting Falcon	*To Romania, September 2016*
	15138	Lockheed Martin F-16A MLU Fighting Falcon	*To Romania, December 2016*
	15139	Lockheed Martin F-16B MLU Fighting Falcon	*Sold to Romania*
	15141	Lockheed Martin F-16A MLU Fighting Falcon	FAP Esq 201/Esq 301, Monte Real
	15202	D-BD Alpha Jet A	FAP *Asas de Portugal*, Beja
	15206	D-BD Alpha Jet A	FAP *Asas de Portugal*, Beja
	15208	D-BD Alpha Jet A	FAP *Asas de Portugal*, Beja
	15211	D-BD Alpha Jet A $	FAP Esq 103, Beja
	15220	D-BD Alpha Jet A	FAP *Asas de Portugal*, Beja

Serial	Type (code/other identity)	Owner/operator, location or fate	Notes
15226	D-BD Alpha Jet A	FAP Esq 103, Beja	
15227	D-BD Alpha Jet A	FAP *Asas de Portugal*, Beja	
15230	D-BD Alpha Jet A	FAP Esq 103, Beja	
15236	D-BD Alpha Jet A	FAP Esq 103, Beja	
15250	D-BD Alpha Jet A	FAP Esq 103, Beja	
16701	CASA C-295M	FAP Esq 502, Lisbon/Montijo & Lajes	
16702	CASA C-295M	FAP Esq 502, Lisbon/Montijo & Lajes	
16703	CASA C-295M	FAP Esq 502, Lisbon/Montijo & Lajes	
16704	CASA C-295M	FAP Esq 502, Lisbon/Montijo & Lajes	
16705	CASA C-295M $	FAP Esq 502, Lisbon/Montijo & Lajes	
16706	CASA C-295M	FAP Esq 502, Lisbon/Montijo & Lajes	
16707	CASA C-295M	FAP Esq 502, Lisbon/Montijo & Lajes	
16708	CASA C-295MPA	FAP Esq 502, Lisbon/Montijo & Lajes	
16709	CASA C-295MPA	FAP Esq 502, Lisbon/Montijo & Lajes	
16710	CASA C-295MPA	FAP Esq 502, Lisbon/Montijo & Lajes	
16711	CASA C-295MPA	FAP Esq 502, Lisbon/Montijo & Lajes	
16712	CASA C-295MPA	FAP Esq 502, Lisbon/Montijo & Lajes	
16801	Lockheed C-130H-30 Hercules	FAP Esq 501, Lisbon/Montijo	
16802	Lockheed C-130H-30 Hercules	FAP Esq 501, Lisbon/Montijo	
16803	Lockheed C-130H Hercules $	FAP Esq 501, Lisbon/Montijo	
16804	Lockheed C-130H Hercules	*Crashed Lisbon/Montijo, 11 July 2016*	
16805	Lockheed C-130H Hercules	FAP Esq 501, Lisbon/Montijo	
16806	Lockheed C-130H-30 Hercules	FAP Esq 501, Lisbon/Montijo	
17401	Dassault Falcon 50	FAP Esq 504, Lisbon/Montijo	
17402	Dassault Falcon 50	FAP Esq 504, Lisbon/Montijo	
17403	Dassault Falcon 50	FAP Esq 504, Lisbon/Montijo	
19201	Westland Super Lynx Mk.95	Marinha Esq de Helicopteros, Lisbon/Montijo	
19202	Westland Super Lynx Mk.95	Marinha Esq de Helicopteros, Lisbon/Montijo	
19203	Westland Super Lynx Mk.95	Marinha Esq de Helicopteros, Lisbon/Montijo	
19204	Westland Super Lynx Mk.95	Marinha Esq de Helicopteros, Lisbon/Montijo	
19205	Westland Super Lynx Mk.95	Marinha Esq de Helicopteros, Lisbon/Montijo	
19601	EHI EH-101 Mk.514	FAP Esq 751, Lisbon/Montijo	
19602	EHI EH-101 Mk.514	FAP Esq 751, Lisbon/Montijo	
19603	EHI EH-101 Mk.514	FAP Esq 751, Lisbon/Montijo	
19604	EHI EH-101 Mk.514	FAP Esq 751, Lisbon/Montijo	
19605	EHI EH-101 Mk.514	FAP Esq 751, Lisbon/Montijo	
19606	EHI EH-101 Mk.514	FAP Esq 751, Lisbon/Montijo	
19607	EHI EH-101 Mk.515	FAP Esq 751, Lisbon/Montijo	
19608	EHI EH-101 Mk.515	FAP Esq 751, Lisbon/Montijo	
19609	EHI EH-101 Mk.516	FAP Esq 751, Lisbon/Montijo	
19610	EHI EH-101 Mk.516	FAP Esq 751, Lisbon/Montijo	
19611	EHI EH-101 Mk.516	FAP Esq 751, Lisbon/Montijo	
19612	EHI EH-101 Mk.516	FAP Esq 751, Lisbon/Montijo	

QATAR
Qatar Emiri Air Force (QEAF)

211	Lockheed C-130J-30 Hercules II (08-0211) [MAH]	QEAF 12 Transport Sqn, Al-Udeid	
212	Lockheed C-130J-30 Hercules II (08-0212) [MAI]	QEAF 12 Transport Sqn, Al-Udeid	
213	Lockheed C-130J-30 Hercules II (08-0213) [MAJ]	QEAF 12 Transport Sqn, Al-Udeid	
214	Lockheed C-130J-30 Hercules II (08-0214) [MAK]	QEAF 12 Transport Sqn, Al-Udeid	
MAA	Boeing C-17A Globemaster III (08-0201)	QEAF 12 Transport Sqn, Al-Udeid	
MAB	Boeing C-17A Globemaster III (08-0202)	QEAF 12 Transport Sqn, Al-Udeid	
MAC	Boeing C-17A Globemaster III (10-0203)	QEAF 12 Transport Sqn, Al-Udeid	
MAE	Boeing C-17A Globemaster III (10-0204)	QEAF 12 Transport Sqn, Al-Udeid	
MAM	Boeing C-17A Globemaster III (14-0005)	QEAF (on order)	
MAN	Boeing C-17A Globemaster III (14-0006)	QEAF (on order)	
MAO	Boeing C-17A Globemaster III (14-0009)	QEAF (on order)	
MAP	Boeing C-17A Globemaster III (14-0010)	QEAF (on order)	

Qatari Government

A7-AAG	Airbus A.320-232	Qatari Amiri Flight, Doha	
A7-AAH	Airbus A.340-313X	Qatari Amiri Flight, Doha	
A7-AAM	Bombardier Global Express	Qatari Amiri Flight/Qatar Airways, Doha	

Notes	Serial	Type (code/other identity)	Owner/operator, location or fate
	A7-AFE	Airbus A.310-308	Qatari Amiri Flight, Doha
	A7-HBJ	Boeing 747-8KB	Qatari Amiri Flight, Doha
	A7-HHE	Boeing 747-8KJ	Qatari Amiri Flight, Doha
	A7-HHH	Airbus A.340-541	Qatari Amiri Flight, Doha
	A7-HHJ	Airbus A.319CJ-133	Qatari Amiri Flight, Doha
	A7-HHK	Airbus A.340-211	Qatari Amiri Flight, Doha
	A7-HHM	Airbus A.330-203	Qatari Amiri Flight, Doha
	A7-HJJ	Airbus A.330-202	Qatari Amiri Flight, Doha
	A7-HSJ	Airbus A.320-232	Qatari Amiri Flight, Doha
	A7-MBK	Airbus A.320-232CJ	Qatari Amiri Flight, Doha
	A7-MED	Airbus A.319CJ-133	Qatari Amiri Flight, Doha
	A7-MHH	Airbus A.319CJ-115	Qatari Amiri Flight, Doha

ROMANIA
Fortele Aeriene Romania (FAR)

	2701	Alenia C-27J Spartan	FAR Escadrilla 902, Bucharest/Otopeni
	2702	Alenia C-27J Spartan	FAR Escadrilla 902, Bucharest/Otopeni
	2703	Alenia C-27J Spartan	FAR Escadrilla 902, Bucharest/Otopeni
	2704	Alenia C-27J Spartan	FAR Escadrilla 902, Bucharest/Otopeni
	2705	Alenia C-27J Spartan	FAR Escadrilla 902, Bucharest/Otopeni
	2706	Alenia C-27J Spartan	FAR Escadrilla 902, Bucharest/Otopeni
	2707	Alenia C-27J Spartan	FAR Escadrilla 902, Bucharest/Otopeni
	5930	Lockheed C-130B Hercules	FAR Escadrilla 901, Bucharest/Otopeni
	6166	Lockheed C-130H Hercules	FAR Escadrilla 901, Bucharest/Otopeni
	6191	Lockheed C-130H Hercules	FAR Escadrilla 901, Bucharest/Otopeni

RUSSIA
Voenno-Vozdushniye Sily Rossioki Federatsii (VVS) (Russian Air Force)/Russian Government

	595 w	Sukhoi Su-27P(LL) (36911037511)	VVS, Gromov Research Institute, Zhukhovsky
	597 w	Sukhoi Su-30LL (79371010102)	VVS, Gromov Research Institute, Zhukhovsky
	598 w	Sukhoi Su-27P(LL) (36911037820)	VVS, Gromov Research Institute, Zhukhovsky
	RA-26226	Antonov An-30	VVS (Open Skies), Moscow/Kubinka
	RA-30078	Antonov An-30	VVS (Open Skies), Moscow/Kubinka
	RA-64057	Tupolev Tu-204-300	Rossiya Special Flight Det, Moscow/Vnukovo
	RA-64058	Tupolev Tu-204-300	Rossiya Special Flight Det, Moscow/Vnukovo
	RA-64504	Tupolev Tu-214	Rossiya Special Flight Det, Moscow/Vnukovo
	RA-64505	Tupolev Tu-214	Rossiya Special Flight Det, Moscow/Vnukovo
	RA-64506	Tupolev Tu-214	Rossiya Special Flight Det, Moscow/Vnukovo
	RA-64515	Tupolev Tu-214SR	Rossiya Special Flight Det, Moscow/Vnukovo
	RA-64516	Tupolev Tu-214SR	Rossiya Special Flight Det, Moscow/Vnukovo
	RA-64517	Tupolev Tu-214SR	Rossiya Special Flight Det, Moscow/Vnukovo
	RA-64520	Tupolev Tu-214PU	Rossiya Special Flight Det, Moscow/Vnukovo
	RA-64521	Tupolev Tu-214	Rossiya Special Flight Det, Ulyanovsk
	RA-64522	Tupolev Tu-214SUS	Rossiya Special Flight Det, Moscow/Vnukovo
	RA-64524	Tupolev Tu-214SUS	Rossiya Special Flight Det, Moscow/Vnukovo
	RA-65904	Tupolev Tu-134AK-3	Rossiya Special Flight Det, Moscow/Vnukovo
	RA-82011	Antonov An-124	VVS 224th Transport Regiment, Seshcha/Bryansk
	RA-82021	Antonov An-124	VVS 224th Transport Regiment, Seshcha/Bryansk
	RA-82023	Antonov An-124	VVS 224th Transport Regiment, Seshcha/Bryansk
	RA-82025	Antonov An-124	VVS 224th Transport Regiment, Seshcha/Bryansk
	RA-82028	Antonov An-124	VVS 224th Transport Regiment, Seshcha/Bryansk
	RA-82030	Antonov An-124	VVS 224th Transport Regiment, Seshcha/Bryansk
	RA-82032	Antonov An-124	VVS 224th Transport Regiment, Seshcha/Bryansk
	RA-82035	Antonov An-124	VVS 224th Transport Regiment, Seshcha/Bryansk
	RA-82036	Antonov An-124	VVS 224th Transport Regiment, Seshcha/Bryansk
	RA-82038	Antonov An-124	VVS 224th Transport Regiment, Seshcha/Bryansk
	RA-82039	Antonov An-124	VVS 224th Transport Regiment, Seshcha/Bryansk
	RA-82040	Antonov An-124	VVS 224th Transport Regiment, Seshcha/Bryansk
	RA-82041	Antonov An-124	VVS 224th Transport Regiment, Seshcha/Bryansk
	RA-85041	Tupolev Tu-154M	VVS 6991 AvB, Chalovskiy
	RA-85155	Tupolev Tu-154M	VVS 8 oae, Chalovskiy
	RA-85629	Tupolev Tu-154M	Rossiya Special Flight Det, Moscow/Vnukovo

Serial	Type (code/other identity)	Owner/operator, location or fate	Notes
RA-85631	Tupolev Tu-154M	Rossiya Special Flight Det, Moscow/Vnukovo	
RA-85659	Tupolev Tu-154M	Rossiya Special Flight Det, Moscow/Vnukovo	
RA-85686	Tupolev Tu-154M	Rossiya Special Flight Det, Moscow/Vnukovo	
RA-85843	Tupolev Tu-154M	Rossiya Special Flight Det, Moscow/Vnukovo	
RA-86466	Ilyushin Il-62M	Rossiya Special Flight Det, Moscow/Vnukovo	
RA-86467	Ilyushin Il-62M	Rossiya Special Flight Det, Moscow/Vnukovo	
RA-86468	Ilyushin Il-62M	Rossiya Special Flight Det, Moscow/Vnukovo	
RA-86536	Ilyushin Il-62M	Rossiya Special Flight Det, Moscow/Vnukovo	
RA-86540	Ilyushin Il-62M	Rossiya Special Flight Det, Moscow/Vnukovo	
RA-86559	Ilyushin Il-62M	Rossiya Special Flight Det, Moscow/Vnukovo	
RA-86561	Ilyushin Il-62M	Rossiya Special Flight Det, Moscow/Vnukovo	
RA-86710	Ilyushin Il-62M	Rossiya Special Flight Det, Moscow/Vnukovo	
RA-86712	Ilyushin Il-62M	Rossiya Special Flight Det, Moscow/Vnukovo	
RA-96012	Ilyushin Il-96-300PU	Rossiya Special Flight Det, Moscow/Vnukovo	
RA-96016	Ilyushin Il-96-300PU	Rossiya Special Flight Det, Moscow/Vnukovo	
RA-96017	Ilyushin Il-96-300S	Rossiya Special Flight Det, Moscow/Vnukovo	
RA-96018	Ilyushin Il-96-300	Rossiya Special Flight Det, Moscow/Vnukovo	
RA-96019	Ilyushin Il-96-300	Rossiya Special Flight Det, Moscow/Vnukovo	
RA-96020	Ilyushin Il-96-300PU	Rossiya Special Flight Det, Moscow/Vnukovo	
RA-96021	Ilyushin Il-96-300PU	Rossiya Special Flight Det, Moscow/Vnukovo	
RA-96102	Ilyushin Il-96-400T	Rossiya Special Flight Det, Moscow/Vnukovo	
RA-96104	Ilyushin Il-96-400T	Rossiya Special Flight Det, Moscow/Vnukovo	
RF-64519	Tupolev Tu-214ON	VVS (Open Skies), Moscow/Kubinka	
RF-85655	Tupolev Tu-154M-LK1	VVS (Open Skies), Moscow/Kubinka	

SAUDI ARABIA

Al Quwwat al Jawwiya as Sa'udiya/Royal Saudi Air Force (RSAF) & Saudi Government

111	Lockheed VC-130H Hercules	RSAF 1 Sqn, Riyadh	
112	Lockheed VC-130H Hercules	RSAF 1 Sqn, Riyadh	
464	Lockheed C-130H Hercules	RSAF 4 Sqn, Jeddah	
465	Lockheed C-130H Hercules	RSAF 4 Sqn, Jeddah	
466	Lockheed C-130H Hercules	RSAF 4 Sqn, Jeddah	
467	Lockheed C-130H Hercules	RSAF 4 Sqn, Jeddah	
468	Lockheed C-130H Hercules	RSAF 4 Sqn, Jeddah	
472	Lockheed C-130H Hercules	RSAF 4 Sqn, Jeddah	
473	Lockheed C-130H Hercules	RSAF 4 Sqn, Jeddah	
474	Lockheed C-130H Hercules	RSAF 4 Sqn, Jeddah	
475	Lockheed C-130H Hercules	RSAF 4 Sqn, Jeddah	
477	Lockheed C-130H Hercules	RSAF 4 Sqn, Jeddah	
478	Lockheed C-130H Hercules	RSAF 4 Sqn, Jeddah	
482	Lockheed C-130H Hercules	RSAF 4 Sqn, Jeddah	
483	Lockheed C-130H Hercules	RSAF 4 Sqn, Jeddah	
484	Lockheed C-130H Hercules	RSAF 4 Sqn, Jeddah	
485	Lockheed C-130H Hercules	RSAF 4 Sqn, Jeddah	
486	Lockheed C-130H Hercules	RSAF 4 Sqn, Jeddah	
1601	Lockheed C-130H Hercules	RSAF 4 Sqn, Jeddah	
1602	Lockheed C-130H Hercules	RSAF 16 Sqn, Jeddah	
1604	Lockheed C-130H Hercules	RSAF 16 Sqn, Jeddah	
1605	Lockheed C-130H Hercules	RSAF 16 Sqn, Jeddah	
1615	Lockheed C-130H Hercules	RSAF 16 Sqn, Jeddah	
1622	Lockheed C-130H-30 Hercules	RSAF 16 Sqn, Jeddah	
1623	Lockheed C-130H Hercules	RSAF 16 Sqn, Jeddah	
1624	Lockheed C-130H Hercules	RSAF 16 Sqn, Jeddah	
1625	Lockheed C-130H Hercules	RSAF 16 Sqn, Jeddah	
1626	Lockheed C-130H Hercules	RSAF 16 Sqn, Jeddah	
1627	Lockheed C-130H Hercules	RSAF 16 Sqn, Jeddah	
1628	Lockheed C-130H Hercules	RSAF 16 Sqn, Jeddah	
1629	Lockheed C-130H Hercules	RSAF 16 Sqn, Jeddah	
1630	Lockheed C-130H-30 Hercules	RSAF 16 Sqn, Jeddah	
1631	Lockheed C-130H-30 Hercules	RSAF 16 Sqn, Jeddah	
1632	Lockheed L.100-30 Hercules	RSAF 16 Sqn, Jeddah	
1801	Boeing E-3A Sentry	RSAF 18 Sqn, Al Kharj	

Notes	Serial	Type (code/other identity)	Owner/operator, location or fate
	1802	Boeing E-3A Sentry	RSAF 18 Sqn, Al Kharj
	1803	Boeing E-3A Sentry	RSAF 18 Sqn, Al Kharj
	1804	Boeing E-3A Sentry	RSAF 18 Sqn, Al Kharj
	1805	Boeing E-3A Sentry	RSAF 18 Sqn, Al Kharj
	1901	Boeing RE-3A Sentry	RSAF 19 Sqn, Al Kharj
	1902	Boeing RE-3A Sentry	RSAF 19 Sqn, Al Kharj
	2301	Boeing KE-3A Sentry (1811)	RSAF 23 Sqn, Al Kharj
	2302	Boeing KE-3A Sentry (1812)	RSAF 23 Sqn, Al Kharj
	2303	Boeing KE-3A Sentry (1813)	RSAF 23 Sqn, Al Kharj
	2304	Boeing KE-3A Sentry (1814)	RSAF 23 Sqn, Al Kharj
	2305	Boeing KE-3A Sentry (1815)	RSAF 23 Sqn, Al Kharj
	2306	Boeing KE-3A Sentry (1816)	RSAF 23 Sqn, Al Kharj
	2307	Boeing KE-3A Sentry (1818)	RSAF 23 Sqn, Al Kharj
	2401	Airbus A.330-203 MRTT	RSAF 24 Sqn, Al Kharj
	2402	Airbus A.330-203 MRTT	RSAF 24 Sqn, Al Kharj
	2403	Airbus A.330-203 MRTT	RSAF 24 Sqn, Al Kharj
	2404	Airbus A.330-203 MRTT	RSAF 24 Sqn, Al Kharj
	2405	Airbus A.330-203 MRTT	RSAF 24 Sqn, Al Kharj
	2406	Airbus A.330-203 MRTT	RSAF 24 Sqn, Al Kharj
	3201	Lockheed KC-130H Hercules	RSAF 32 Sqn, Al Kharj
	3202	Lockheed KC-130H Hercules	RSAF 32 Sqn, Al Kharj
	3203	Lockheed KC-130H Hercules	RSAF 32 Sqn, Al Kharj
	3204	Lockheed KC-130H Hercules	RSAF 32 Sqn, Al Kharj
	3205	Lockheed KC-130H Hercules	RSAF 32 Sqn, Al Kharj
	3206	Lockheed KC-130H Hercules	RSAF 32 Sqn, Al Kharj
	3207	Lockheed KC-130H Hercules	RSAF 32 Sqn, Al Kharj
	3208	Lockheed KC-130J Hercules II	RSAF 32 Sqn, Al Kharj
	3209	Lockheed KC-130J Hercules II	RSAF 32 Sqn, Al Kharj
	8805	BAe Hawk 65A	RSAF 88 Sqn, *Saudi Hawks*, Tabuk
	8806	BAe Hawk 65A	RSAF 88 Sqn, *Saudi Hawks*, Tabuk
	8807	BAe Hawk 65	RSAF 88 Sqn, *Saudi Hawks*, Tabuk
	8808	BAe Hawk 65	RSAF 88 Sqn, *Saudi Hawks*, Tabuk
	8810	BAe Hawk 65	RSAF 88 Sqn, *Saudi Hawks*, Tabuk
	8811	BAe Hawk 65A	RSAF 88 Sqn, *Saudi Hawks*, Tabuk
	8812	BAe Hawk 65A	RSAF 88 Sqn, *Saudi Hawks*, Tabuk
	8813	BAe Hawk 65	RSAF 88 Sqn, *Saudi Hawks*, Tabuk
	8814	BAe Hawk 65	RSAF 88 Sqn, *Saudi Hawks*, Tabuk
	8816	BAe Hawk 65	RSAF 88 Sqn, *Saudi Hawks*, Tabuk
	8818	BAe Hawk 65A	RSAF 88 Sqn, *Saudi Hawks*, Tabuk
	8820	BAe Hawk 65	RSAF 88 Sqn, *Saudi Hawks*, Tabuk
	HZ-101	Boeing 737-7DP	RSAF 1 Sqn, Riyadh
	HZ-102	Boeing 737-8DP	RSAF 1 Sqn, Riyadh
	HZ-103	Grumman G.1159C Gulfstream IV	RSAF 1 Sqn, Riyadh
	HZ-105	BAe 125-800	RSAF 1 Sqn, Riyadh
	HZ-109	BAe 125-800B	RSAF 1 Sqn, Riyadh
	HZ-110	BAe 125-800B	RSAF 1 Sqn, Riyadh
	HZ-117	Lockheed L.100-30 Hercules	RSAF 1 Sqn, Riyadh
	HZ-128	Lockheed L.100-30 Hercules	RSAF 1 Sqn, Riyadh
	HZ-129	Lockheed L.100-30 Hercules	RSAF 1 Sqn, Riyadh
	HZ-130	BAe 125-800B	RSAF 1 Sqn, Riyadh
	HZ-132	Lockheed L.100-30 Hercules	RSAF 1 Sqn, Riyadh
	HZ-133	Cessna 550 Citation II	RSAF 1 Sqn, Riyadh
	HZ-134	Cessna 550 Citation II	RSAF 1 Sqn, Riyadh
	HZ-135	Cessna 550 Citation II	RSAF 1 Sqn, Riyadh
	HZ-136	Cessna 550 Citation II	RSAF 1 Sqn, Riyadh
	HZ-AFN	Grumman G.1159A Gulfstream III	Saudi Special Flight Services, Jeddah
	HZ-AFR	Grumman G.1159A Gulfstream III	Saudi Special Flight Services, Jeddah
	HZ-AFT	Dassault Falcon 900	Saudi Special Flight Services, Jeddah
	HZ-AFU	Grumman G.1159C Gulfstream IV	Saudi Special Flight Services, Jeddah
	HZ-AFV	Grumman G.1159C Gulfstream IV	Saudi Special Flight Services, Jeddah
	HZ-AFW	Grumman G.1159C Gulfstream IV	Saudi Special Flight Services, Jeddah
	HZ-AFX	Grumman G.1159C Gulfstream IV	Saudi Special Flight Services, Jeddah

Serial	Type (code/other identity)	Owner/operator, location or fate	Notes
HZ-AFY	Grumman G.1159C Gulfstream IV	Saudi Special Flight Services, Jeddah	
HZ-AFZ	Dassault Falcon 900	Saudi Special Flight Services, Jeddah	
HZ-AIF	Boeing 747SP-68	Saudi Royal Flight, Jeddah	
HZ-AIJ	Boeing 747SP-68	Saudi Royal Flight, Jeddah	
HZ-HM1	Boeing 747-468	Saudi Royal Flight, Jeddah	
HZ-HM1A	Boeing 747-3G1	Saudi Royal Flight, Jeddah	
HZ-HM1B	Boeing 747SP-68	Saudi Royal Flight, Jeddah	
HZ-HM1C	Boeing 747SP-68	Saudi Royal Flight, Jeddah	
HZ-HMED	Boeing 757-23A	Saudi Royal Flight, Riyadh	
HZ-HMS2	Airbus A.340-213X	RSAF, Riyadh	
HZ-MFL	Grumman G.1159C Gulfstream IV	Saudi Special Flight Services, Jeddah	
HZ-MS1A	Bombardier Lear 60	Saudi Armed Forces Medical Services, Riyadh	
HZ-MS1B	Bombardier Lear 60	Saudi Armed Forces Medical Services, Riyadh	
HZ-MS02	Lockheed C-130H Hercules	Saudi Armed Forces Medical Services, Riyadh	
HZ-MS4	Grumman G.1159C Gulfstream IV-SP	Saudi Armed Forces Medical Services, Riyadh	
HZ-MS4A	Gulfstream Aerospace G.450	Saudi Armed Forces Medical Services, Riyadh	
HZ-MS4B	Gulfstream Aerospace G.450	Saudi Armed Forces Medical Services, Riyadh	
HZ-MS4C	Gulfstream Aerospace G.450	Saudi Armed Forces Medical Services, Riyadh	
HZ-MS5A	Gulfstream Aerospace Gulfstream V	Saudi Armed Forces Medical Services, Riyadh	
HZ-MS5B	Gulfstream Aerospace Gulfstream V	Saudi Armed Forces Medical Services, Riyadh	
HZ-MS06	Lockheed L.100-30 Hercules	Saudi Armed Forces Medical Services, Riyadh	
HZ-MS07	Lockheed C-130H Hercules	Saudi Armed Forces Medical Services, Riyadh	
HZ-MS09	Lockheed L.100-30 Hercules	Saudi Armed Forces Medical Services, Riyadh	

SENEGAL

6V-ONE	Airbus A.319CJ-115X	Government of Senegal, Dakar	

SERBIA

YU-BNA	Dassault Falcon 50	Government of Serbia, Belgrade	

SINGAPORE
Republic of Singapore Air Force (RSAF)

720	Lockheed KC-130B Hercules	RSAF 122 Sqn, Paya Labar	
721	Lockheed KC-130B Hercules	RSAF 122 Sqn, Paya Labar	
724	Lockheed KC-130B Hercules	RSAF 122 Sqn, Paya Labar	
725	Lockheed KC-130B Hercules	RSAF 122 Sqn, Paya Labar	
730	Lockheed C-130H Hercules	RSAF 122 Sqn, Paya Labar	
731	Lockheed KC-130H Hercules	RSAF 122 Sqn, Paya Labar	
732	Lockheed C-130H Hercules	RSAF 122 Sqn, Paya Labar	
733	Lockheed C-130H Hercules	RSAF 122 Sqn, Paya Labar	
734	Lockheed KC-130H Hercules	RSAF 122 Sqn, Paya Labar	
735	Lockheed C-130H Hercules	RSAF 122 Sqn, Paya Labar	
750	Boeing KC-135R Stratotanker	RSAF 112 Sqn, Changi	
751	Boeing KC-135R Stratotanker	RSAF 112 Sqn, Changi	
752	Boeing KC-135R Stratotanker	RSAF 112 Sqn, Changi	
753	Boeing KC-135R Stratotanker	RSAF 112 Sqn, Changi	
...	Airbus A.330-203 MRTT	RSAF 112 Sqn, Changi (on order)	
...	Airbus A.330-203 MRTT	RSAF 112 Sqn, Changi (on order)	
...	Airbus A.330-203 MRTT	RSAF 112 Sqn, Changi (on order)	
...	Airbus A.330-203 MRTT	RSAF 112 Sqn, Changi (on order)	
...	Airbus A.330-203 MRTT	RSAF 112 Sqn, Changi (on order)	

SLOVAKIA
Slovenské Vojensko Letectvo (SVL)

0619	Mikoyan MiG-29AS	SVL 1.Blt/Zmiešané Letecké Kridlo, Sliač	
0807	Mil Mi-17	SVL 2.Dvlt/Vrtulnikové Letecké Kridlo, Prešov	
0808	Mil Mi-17	SVL 2.Dvlt/Vrtulnikové Letecké Kridlo, Prešov	
0820	Mil Mi-17	SVL 2.Dvlt/Vrtulnikové Letecké Kridlo, Prešov	
0821	Mil Mi-17	SVL 2.Dvlt/Vrtulnikové Letecké Kridlo, Prešov	
0823	Mil Mi-17M	SVL 2.Dvlt/Vrtulnikové Letecké Kridlo, Prešov	
0824	Mil Mi-17	SVL 2.Dvlt/Vrtulnikové Letecké Kridlo, Prešov	
0826	Mil Mi-17	SVL 2.Dvlt/Vrtulnikové Letecké Kridlo, Prešov	

Notes	Serial	Type (code/other identity)	Owner/operator, location or fate
	0841	Mil Mi-17	SVL 2.Dvlt/Vrtulnikové Letcecké Kridlo, Prešov
	0844	Mil Mi-17	SVL 2.Dvlt/Vrtulnikové Letcecké Kridlo, Prešov
	0845	Mil Mi-17	SVL 2.Dvlt/Vrtulnikové Letcecké Kridlo, Prešov
	0846	Mil Mi-17	SVL 2.Dvlt/Vrtulnikové Letcecké Kridlo, Prešov
	0847	Mil Mi-17	SVL 2.Dvlt/Vrtulnikové Letcecké Kridlo, Prešov
	0921	Mikoyan MiG-29AS	SVL 1.Blt/Zmiešané Letecké Kridlo, Sliač
	1133	LET L-410T Turbolet	SVL 2 Dopravná Roj/Dopravniho Kridlo, Malacky
	1303	Mikoyan MiG-29UBS $	SVL 1.Blt/Zmiešané Letecké Kridlo, Sliač
	1521	LET L-410FG Turbolet	SVL 2 Dopravná Roj/Dopravniho Kridlo, Malacky
	2123	Mikoyan MiG-29AS	SVL 1.Blt/Zmiešané Letecké Kridlo, Sliač
	2311	LET L-410UVP Turbolet	SVL 2 Dopravná Roj/Dopravniho Kridlo, Malacky
	2421	LET L-410UVP Turbolet	SVL 2 Dopravná Roj/Dopravniho Kridlo, Malacky
	2506	Antonov An-26	*Withdrawn from use, 5 March 2016*
	2718	LET L-401UVP-E Turbolet	SVL 2 Dopravná Roj/Dopravniho Kridlo, Malacky
	2721	LET L-401UVP-E Turbolet	SVL 2 Dopravná Roj/Dopravniho Kridlo, Malacky
	2818	LET L-401UVP-20 Turbolet	SVL 2 Dopravná Roj/Dopravniho Kridlo, Malacky
	2901	LET L-401UVP-20 Turbolet	SVL 2 Dopravná Roj/Dopravniho Kridlo, Malacky
	3208	Antonov An-26	SVL 1 Dopravná Roj/Dopravniho Kridlo, Malacky
	3709	Mikoyan MiG-29AS	SVL 1.Blt/Zmiešané Letecké Kridlo, Sliač
	3911	Mikoyan MiG-29AS	SVL 1.Blt/Zmiešané Letecké Kridlo, Sliač
	4701	Aero L-39ZAM Albatros	SVL 2.vlt/Zmiešané Letecké Kridlo, Sliač
	4703	Aero L-39ZAM Albatros	SVL 2.vlt/Zmiešané Letecké Kridlo, Sliač
	4707	Aero L-39ZAM Albatros	SVL 2.vlt/Zmiešané Letecké Kridlo, Sliač
	4711	Aero L-39ZAM Albatros	SVL 2.vlt/Zmiešané Letecké Kridlo, Sliač
	5252	Aero L-39CM Albatros	SVL 2.vlt/Zmiešané Letecké Kridlo, Sliač
	5253	Aero L-39CM Albatros	SVL 2.vlt/Zmiešané Letecké Kridlo, Sliač
	5301	Aero L-39CM Albatros $	SVL 2.vlt/Zmiešané Letecké Kridlo, Sliač
	5302	Aero L-39CM Albatros	SVL 2.vlt/Zmiešané Letecké Kridlo, Sliač
	5304	Mikoyan MiG-29UBS $	SVL 1.Blt/Zmiešané Letecké Kridlo, Sliač
	6124	Mikoyan MiG-29AS	SVL 1.Blt/Zmiešané Letecké Kridlo, Sliač
	6526	Mikoyan MiG-29AS	SVL 1.Blt/Zmiešané Letecké Kridlo, Sliač
	6627	Mikoyan MiG-29AS	SVL 1.Blt/Zmiešané Letecké Kridlo, Sliač
	6728	Mikoyan MiG-29AS	SVL 1.Blt/Zmiešané Letecké Kridlo, Sliač
	Slovak Government		
	OM-BYA	Airbus A.319-115	Slovak Government, Bratislava/Ivanka
	OM-BYB	Fokker 100	Slovak Government, Bratislava/Ivanka
	OM-BYC	Fokker 100	Slovak Government, Bratislava/Ivanka
	OM-BYE	Yakovlev Yak-40	Slovak Government, Bratislava/Ivanka
	OM-BYL	Yakovlev Yak-40	Slovak Government, Bratislava/Ivanka
	OM-BYO	Tupolev Tu-154M	Slovak Government, Bratislava/Ivanka

SLOVENIA
Slovenska Vojska (SV)/Slovenian Armed Forces

Notes	Serial	Type (code/other identity)	Owner/operator, location or fate
	L1-01	Dassault Falcon 2000EX	Government of Slovenia, Ljubljana
	L4-01	LET 410UVP-E Turbolet	SV 107.Letalska Baza, Cerklje ob Krki
	L9-61	Pilatus PC-9M	SV Letalska Šola, Cerklje ob Krki
	L9-62	Pilatus PC-9M	SV Letalska Šola, Cerklje ob Krki
	L9-63	Pilatus PC-9M	SV Letalska Šola, Cerklje ob Krki
	L9-64	Pilatus PC-9M	SV Letalska Šola, Cerklje ob Krki
	L9-65	Pilatus PC-9M	SV Letalska Šola, Cerklje ob Krki
	L9-66	Pilatus PC-9M	SV Letalska Šola, Cerklje ob Krki
	L9-67	Pilatus PC-9M	SV Letalska Šola, Cerklje ob Krki
	L9-68	Pilatus PC-9M	SV Letalska Šola, Cerklje ob Krki
	L9-69	Pilatus PC-9M	SV Letalska Šola, Cerklje ob Krki

SOUTH AFRICA
Suid Afrikaanse Lugmag/South African Air Force (SAAF)

Notes	Serial	Type (code/other identity)	Owner/operator, location or fate
	401	Lockheed C-130B Hercules	SAAF 28 Sqn, Waterkloof
	402	Lockheed C-130BZ Hercules	SAAF 28 Sqn, Waterkloof
	403	Lockheed C-130B Hercules	SAAF 28 Sqn, Waterkloof
	404	Lockheed C-130B Hercules	SAAF 28 Sqn, Waterkloof
	405	Lockheed C-130BZ Hercules	SAAF 28 Sqn, Waterkloof

Serial	Type (code/other identity)	Owner/operator, location or fate	Notes
406	Lockheed C-130BZ Hercules	SAAF 28 Sqn, Waterkloof	
ZS-NAN	Dassault Falcon 900	SAAF 21 Sqn, Waterkloof	
ZS-RSA	Boeing 737-7ED	SAAF 21 Sqn, Waterkloof	

SOUTH KOREA
Han Guk Gong Gun/Republic of Korea Air Force

10001	Boeing 747-4B5	RoKAF 296 Sqn/35 Combined Group, Seoul AB	

SPAIN
Arma Aérea de l'Armada Española, Ejército del Aire (EdA)/Spanish Air Force & Guardia Civil

Serial	Type (code/other identity)	Owner/operator, location or fate	Notes
CE.15-01	McDonnell Douglas EF-18BM Hornet [15-70] $	EdA 151 Esc/152 Esc/153 Esc/Ala 15, Zaragoza	
CE.15-2	McDonnell Douglas EF-18BM Hornet [15-71]	EdA 151 Esc/152 Esc/153 Esc/Ala 15, Zaragoza	
CE.15-03	McDonnell Douglas EF-18BM Hornet [15-72]	EdA 151 Esc/152 Esc/153 Esc/Ala 15, Zaragoza	
CE.15-04	McDonnell Douglas EF-18BM Hornet [15-73]	EdA 151 Esc/152 Esc/153 Esc/Ala 15, Zaragoza	
CE.15-5	McDonnell Douglas EF-18BM Hornet [15-74]	EdA 151 Esc/152 Esc/153 Esc/Ala 15, Zaragoza	
CE.15-06	McDonnell Douglas EF-18BM Hornet [15-75]	EdA 151 Esc/152 Esc/153 Esc/Ala 15, Zaragoza	
CE.15-07	McDonnell Douglas EF-18BM Hornet [15-76]	EdA 151 Esc/152 Esc/153 Esc/Ala 15, Zaragoza	
CE.15-08	McDonnell Douglas EF-18BM Hornet [12-71]	EdA 121 Esc/122 Esc/Ala 12, Madrid/Torrejón	
CE.15-09	McDonnell Douglas EF-18BM Hornet [15-77]	EdA 151 Esc/152 Esc/153 Esc/Ala 15, Zaragoza	
CE.15-10	McDonnell Douglas EF-18BM Hornet [12-73] $	EdA 121 Esc/122 Esc/Ala 12, Madrid/Torrejón	
CE.15-11	McDonnell Douglas EF-18BM Hornet [12-74]	EdA 121 Esc/122 Esc/Ala 12, Madrid/Torrejón	
CE.15-12	McDonnell Douglas EF-18BM Hornet [12-75]	EdA 121 Esc/122 Esc/Ala 12, Madrid/Torrejón	
C.15-13	McDonnell Douglas EF-18M Hornet [12-01]	EdA 121 Esc/122 Esc/Ala 12, Madrid/Torrejón	
C.15-14	McDonnell Douglas EF-18M Hornet [15-01] $	EdA 151 Esc/152 Esc/153 Esc/Ala 15, Zaragoza	
C.15-15	McDonnell Douglas EF-18M Hornet [15-02]	EdA 151 Esc/152 Esc/153 Esc/Ala 15, Zaragoza	
C.15-16	McDonnell Douglas EF-18M Hornet [15-03]	EdA 151 Esc/152 Esc/153 Esc/Ala 15, Zaragoza	
C.15-18	McDonnell Douglas EF-18M Hornet [15-05]	EdA 151 Esc/152 Esc/153 Esc/Ala 15, Zaragoza	
C.15-20	McDonnell Douglas EF-18M Hornet [15-07]	EdA 151 Esc/152 Esc/153 Esc/Ala 15, Zaragoza	
C.15-21	McDonnell Douglas EF-18M Hornet [15-08]	EdA 151 Esc/152 Esc/153 Esc/Ala 15, Zaragoza	
C.15-22	McDonnell Douglas EF-18M Hornet [15-09]	EdA 151 Esc/152 Esc/153 Esc/Ala 15, Zaragoza	
C.15-23	McDonnell Douglas EF-18M Hornet [15-10]	EdA 151 Esc/152 Esc/153 Esc/Ala 15, Zaragoza	
C.15-24	McDonnell Douglas EF-18M Hornet [15-11]	EdA 151 Esc/152 Esc/153 Esc/Ala 15, Zaragoza	
C.15-25	McDonnell Douglas EF-18M Hornet [15-12]	EdA 151 Esc/152 Esc/153 Esc/Ala 15, Zaragoza	
C.15-26	McDonnell Douglas EF-18M Hornet [15-13] $	EdA 151 Esc/152 Esc/153 Esc/Ala 15, Zaragoza	
C.15-27	McDonnell Douglas EF-18M Hornet [15-14]	EdA 151 Esc/152 Esc/153 Esc/Ala 15, Zaragoza	
C.15-28	McDonnell Douglas EF-18M Hornet [15-15]	EdA 151 Esc/152 Esc/153 Esc/Ala 15, Zaragoza	
C.15-29	McDonnell Douglas EF-18M Hornet [15-16]	EdA 151 Esc/152 Esc/153 Esc/Ala 15, Zaragoza	
C.15-30	McDonnell Douglas EF-18M Hornet [15-17]	EdA 151 Esc/152 Esc/153 Esc/Ala 15, Zaragoza	
C.15-31	McDonnell Douglas EF-18M Hornet [15-18]	EdA 151 Esc/152 Esc/153 Esc/Ala 15, Zaragoza	
C.15-32	McDonnell Douglas EF-18M Hornet [15-19]	EdA 151 Esc/152 Esc/153 Esc/Ala 15, Zaragoza	
C.15-33	McDonnell Douglas EF-18M Hornet [15-20]	EdA 151 Esc/152 Esc/153 Esc/Ala 15, Zaragoza	
C.15-34	McDonnell Douglas EF-18M Hornet [12-50] $	EdA 121 Esc/122 Esc/Ala 12, Madrid/Torrejón	
C.15-35	McDonnell Douglas EF-18M Hornet [15-22]	EdA 151 Esc/152 Esc/153 Esc/Ala 15, Zaragoza	
C.15-36	McDonnell Douglas EF-18M Hornet [15-23]	EdA 151 Esc/152 Esc/153 Esc/Ala 15, Zaragoza	
C.15-37	McDonnell Douglas EF-18M Hornet [15-24]	EdA 151 Esc/152 Esc/153 Esc/Ala 15, Zaragoza	
C.15-38	McDonnell Douglas EF-18M Hornet [15-25]	EdA 151 Esc/152 Esc/153 Esc/Ala 15, Zaragoza	
C.15-39	McDonnell Douglas EF-18M Hornet [15-26]	EdA 151 Esc/152 Esc/153 Esc/Ala 15, Zaragoza	
C.15-40	McDonnell Douglas EF-18M Hornet [15-27]	EdA 151 Esc/152 Esc/153 Esc/Ala 15, Zaragoza	
C.15-41	McDonnell Douglas EF-18M Hornet [15-28] $	EdA 151 Esc/152 Esc/153 Esc/Ala 15, Zaragoza	
C.15-43	McDonnell Douglas EF-18M Hornet [15-30]	EdA 151 Esc/152 Esc/153 Esc/Ala 15, Zaragoza	
C.15-44	McDonnell Douglas EF-18M Hornet [12-02]	EdA 121 Esc/122 Esc/Ala 12, Madrid/Torrejón	
C.15-45	McDonnell Douglas EF-18M Hornet [12-03]	EdA 121 Esc/122 Esc/Ala 12, Madrid/Torrejón	
C.15-46	McDonnell Douglas EF-18M Hornet [12-04]	EdA 121 Esc/122 Esc/Ala 12, Madrid/Torrejón	
C.15-47	McDonnell Douglas EF-18M Hornet [15-31]	EdA 151 Esc/152 Esc/153 Esc/Ala 15, Zaragoza	
C.15-48	McDonnell Douglas EF-18M Hornet [12-06]	EdA 121 Esc/122 Esc/Ala 12, Madrid/Torrejón	
C.15-49	McDonnell Douglas EF-18M Hornet [12-07]	EdA 121 Esc/122 Esc/Ala 12, Madrid/Torrejón	
C.15-50	McDonnell Douglas EF-18M Hornet [12-08]	EdA 121 Esc/122 Esc/Ala 12, Madrid/Torrejón	
C.15-51	McDonnell Douglas EF-18M Hornet [12-09]	EdA 121 Esc/122 Esc/Ala 12, Madrid/Torrejón	
C.15-52	McDonnell Douglas EF-18M Hornet [12-10]	EdA 121 Esc/122 Esc/Ala 12, Madrid/Torrejón	
C.15-53	McDonnell Douglas EF-18M Hornet [12-11]	EdA 121 Esc/122 Esc/Ala 12, Madrid/Torrejón	
C.15-54	McDonnell Douglas EF-18M Hornet [12-12]	EdA 121 Esc/122 Esc/Ala 12, Madrid/Torrejón	

Notes	Serial	Type (code/other identity)	Owner/operator, location or fate
	C.15-55	McDonnell Douglas EF-18M Hornet [12-13]	EdA 121 Esc/122 Esc/Ala 12, Madrid/Torrejón
	C.15-56	McDonnell Douglas EF-18M Hornet [12-14]	EdA 121 Esc/122 Esc/Ala 12, Madrid/Torrejón
	C.15-57	McDonnell Douglas EF-18M Hornet [12-15]	EdA 121 Esc/122 Esc/Ala 12, Madrid/Torrejón
	C.15-59	McDonnell Douglas EF-18M Hornet [12-17]	EdA 121 Esc/122 Esc/Ala 12, Madrid/Torrejón
	C.15-60	McDonnell Douglas EF-18M Hornet [12-18]	EdA 121 Esc/122 Esc/Ala 12, Madrid/Torrejón
	C.15-61	McDonnell Douglas EF-18M Hornet [12-19]	EdA 121 Esc/122 Esc/Ala 12, Madrid/Torrejón
	C.15-62	McDonnell Douglas EF-18M Hornet [12-20]	EdA 121 Esc/122 Esc/Ala 12, Madrid/Torrejón
	C.15-64	McDonnell Douglas EF-18M Hornet [15-34]	EdA 151 Esc/152 Esc/153 Esc/Ala 15, Zaragoza
	C.15-65	McDonnell Douglas EF-18M Hornet [12-23]	EdA 121 Esc/122 Esc/Ala 12, Madrid/Torrejón
	C.15-66	McDonnell Douglas EF-18M Hornet [12-24]	EdA 121 Esc/122 Esc/Ala 12, Madrid/Torrejón
	C.15-67	McDonnell Douglas EF-18M Hornet [15-33]	EdA 151 Esc/152 Esc/153 Esc/Ala 15, Zaragoza
	C.15-68	McDonnell Douglas EF-18M Hornet [12-26] $	EdA 121 Esc/122 Esc/Ala 12, Madrid/Torrejón
	C.15-69	McDonnell Douglas EF-18M Hornet [12-27]	EdA 121 Esc/122 Esc/Ala 12, Madrid/Torrejón
	C.15-70	McDonnell Douglas EF-18M Hornet [12-28]	EdA 121 Esc/122 Esc/Ala 12, Madrid/Torrejón
	C.15-72	McDonnell Douglas EF-18M Hornet [12-30]	EdA 121 Esc/122 Esc/Ala 12, Madrid/Torrejón
	C.15-73	McDonnell Douglas F/A-18A+ Hornet [46-01] $	EdA 462 Esc/Ala 46, Gran Canaria
	C.15-75	McDonnell Douglas F/A-18A+ Hornet [46-03]	EdA 462 Esc/Ala 46, Gran Canaria
	C.15-77	McDonnell Douglas F/A-18A+ Hornet [46-05]	EdA 462 Esc/Ala 46, Gran Canaria
	C.15-79	McDonnell Douglas F/A-18A+ Hornet [46-07]	EdA 462 Esc/Ala 46, Gran Canaria
	C.15-80	McDonnell Douglas F/A-18A+ Hornet [46-08]	EdA 462 Esc/Ala 46, Gran Canaria
	C.15-81	McDonnell Douglas F/A-18A+ Hornet [46-09]	EdA 462 Esc/Ala 46, Gran Canaria
	C.15-82	McDonnell Douglas F/A-18A+ Hornet [46-10]	EdA 462 Esc/Ala 46, Gran Canaria
	C.15-83	McDonnell Douglas F/A-18A+ Hornet [46-11]	EdA 462 Esc/Ala 46, Gran Canaria
	C.15-84	McDonnell Douglas F/A-18A+ Hornet [46-12]	EdA 462 Esc/Ala 46, Gran Canaria
	C.15-85	McDonnell Douglas F/A-18A+ Hornet [46-13]	EdA 462 Esc/Ala 46, Gran Canaria
	C.15-86	McDonnell Douglas F/A-18A+ Hornet [46-14]	EdA 462 Esc/Ala 46, Gran Canaria
	C.15-87	McDonnell Douglas F/A-18A+ Hornet [46-15]	EdA 462 Esc/Ala 46, Gran Canaria
	C.15-88	McDonnell Douglas F/A-18A+ Hornet [46-16] $	EdA 462 Esc/Ala 46, Gran Canaria
	C.15-89	McDonnell Douglas F/A-18A+ Hornet [46-17]	EdA 462 Esc/Ala 46, Gran Canaria
	C.15-90	McDonnell Douglas F/A-18A+ Hornet [46-18]	EdA 462 Esc/Ala 46, Gran Canaria
	C.15-92	McDonnell Douglas F/A-18A+ Hornet [46-20]	EdA 462 Esc/Ala 46, Gran Canaria
	C.15-93	McDonnell Douglas F/A-18A+ Hornet [46-21]	EdA 462 Esc/Ala 46, Gran Canaria
	C.15-94	McDonnell Douglas F/A-18A+ Hornet [46-22]	EdA 462 Esc/Ala 46, Gran Canaria
	C.15-95	McDonnell Douglas F/A-18A+ Hornet [46-23]	EdA 462 Esc/Ala 46, Gran Canaria
	C.15-96	McDonnell Douglas F/A-18A+ Hornet [46-24]	EdA 462 Esc/Ala 46, Gran Canaria
	CE.16-01	Eurofighter EF.2000(T) Tifón [11-70]	EdA 111 Esc/113 Esc/Ala 11, Sevilla/Morón
	CE.16-02	Eurofighter EF.2000(T) Tifón [11-71]	EdA 111 Esc/113 Esc/Ala 11, Sevilla/Morón
	CE.16-03	Eurofighter EF.2000(T) Tifón [11-72]	EdA 111 Esc/113 Esc/Ala 11, Sevilla/Morón
	CE.16-04	Eurofighter EF.2000(T) Tifón [11-73]	EdA 111 Esc/113 Esc/Ala 11, Sevilla/Morón
	CE.16-05	Eurofighter EF.2000(T) Tifón [11-74]	EdA 111 Esc/113 Esc/Ala 11, Sevilla/Morón
	CE.16-06	Eurofighter EF.2000(T) Tifón [11-75]	EdA 111 Esc/113 Esc/Ala 11, Sevilla/Morón
	CE.16-07	Eurofighter EF.2000(T) Tifón [11-76]	EdA 111 Esc/113 Esc/Ala 11, Sevilla/Morón
	CE.16-09	Eurofighter EF.2000(T) Tifón [11-78]	EdA 111 Esc/113 Esc/Ala 11, Sevilla/Morón
	CE.16-10	Eurofighter EF.2000(T) Tifón [11-79]	EdA 111 Esc/113 Esc/Ala 11, Sevilla/Morón
	CE.16-11	Eurofighter EF.2000(T) Tifón [14-70]	EdA 142 Esc/Ala 14, Albacete/Los Llanos
	CE.16-12	Eurofighter EF.2000(T) Tifón (CE.16-10000) [14-71]	EdA 142 Esc/Ala 14, Albacete/Los Llanos
	CE.16-13	Eurofighter EF.2000(T) Tifón (10005) [11-80]	EdA 111 Esc/113 Esc/Ala 11, Sevilla/Morón
	CE.16-14	Eurofighter EF.2000(T) Tifón (10015) [11-81]	EdA 111 Esc/113 Esc/Ala 11, Sevilla/Morón
	C.16-20	Eurofighter EF.2000 Tifón [11-91]	EdA 111 Esc/113 Esc/Ala 11, Sevilla/Morón
	C.16-21	Eurofighter EF.2000 Tifón [11-01]	EdA 111 Esc/113 Esc/Ala 11, Sevilla/Morón
	C.16-22	Eurofighter EF.2000 Tifón [11-02]	EdA 111 Esc/113 Esc/Ala 11, Sevilla/Morón
	C.16-23	Eurofighter EF.2000 Tifón [11-03]	EdA 111 Esc/113 Esc/Ala 11, Sevilla/Morón
	C.16-24	Eurofighter EF.2000 Tifón [11-04]	EdA 111 Esc/113 Esc/Ala 11, Sevilla/Morón
	C.16-25	Eurofighter EF.2000 Tifón [11-05]	EdA 111 Esc/113 Esc/Ala 11, Sevilla/Morón
	C.16-26	Eurofighter EF.2000 Tifón [11-06]	EdA 111 Esc/113 Esc/Ala 11, Sevilla/Morón
	C.16-27	Eurofighter EF.2000 Tifón [11-07]	EdA 111 Esc/113 Esc/Ala 11, Sevilla/Morón
	C.16-28	Eurofighter EF.2000 Tifón [11-08]	EdA 111 Esc/113 Esc/Ala 11, Sevilla/Morón
	C.16-29	Eurofighter EF.2000 Tifón [11-09]	EdA 111 Esc/113 Esc/Ala 11, Sevilla/Morón
	C.16-30	Eurofighter EF.2000 Tifón [11-10]	EdA 111 Esc/113 Esc/Ala 11, Sevilla/Morón
	C.16-31	Eurofighter EF.2000 Tifón [14-01]	EdA 142 Esc/Ala 14, Albacete/Los Llanos
	C.16-32	Eurofighter EF.2000 Tifón [11-11]	EdA 111 Esc/113 Esc/Ala 11, Sevilla/Morón
	C.16-33	Eurofighter EF.2000 Tifón [11-12]	EdA 111 Esc/113 Esc/Ala 11, Sevilla/Morón

Serial	Type (code/other identity)	Owner/operator, location or fate	Notes
C.16-35	Eurofighter EF.2000 Tifón [14-02]	EdA 142 Esc/Ala 14, Albacete/Los Llanos	
C.16-36	Eurofighter EF.2000 Tifón [14-03]	EdA 142 Esc/Ala 14, Albacete/Los Llanos	
C.16-37	Eurofighter EF.2000 Tifón [14-04]	EdA 142 Esc/Ala 14, Albacete/Los Llanos	
C.16-38	Eurofighter EF.2000 Tifón [14-05]	EdA 142 Esc/Ala 14, Albacete/Los Llanos	
C.16-39	Eurofighter EF.2000 Tifón [14-06] $	EdA 142 Esc/Ala 14, Albacete/Los Llanos	
C.16-40	Eurofighter EF.2000 Tifón [11-14]	EdA 111 Esc/113 Esc/Ala 11, Sevilla/Morón	
C.16-41	Eurofighter EF.2000 Tifón [14-07]	EdA 142 Esc/Ala 14, Albacete/Los Llanos	
C.16-42	Eurofighter EF.2000 Tifón [14-08] $	EdA 142 Esc/Ala 14, Albacete/Los Llanos	
C.16-43	Eurofighter EF.2000 Tifón [11-15]	EdA 111 Esc/113 Esc/Ala 11, Sevilla/Morón	
C.16-44	Eurofighter EF.2000 Tifón [14-09]	EdA 142 Esc/Ala 14, Albacete/Los Llanos	
C.16-45	Eurofighter EF.2000 Tifón [14-10]	EdA 142 Esc/Ala 14, Albacete/Los Llanos	
C.16-46	Eurofighter EF.2000 Tifón [11-16]	EdA 111 Esc/113 Esc/Ala 11, Sevilla/Morón	
C.16-47	Eurofighter EF.2000 Tifón [14-11]	EdA 142 Esc/Ala 14, Albacete/Los Llanos	
C.16-48	Eurofighter EF.2000 Tifón [14-12]	EdA 142 Esc/Ala 14, Albacete/Los Llanos	
C.16-49	Eurofighter EF.2000 Tifón [14-13]	EdA 142 Esc/Ala 14, Albacete/Los Llanos	
C.16-50	Eurofighter EF.2000 Tifón [14-14]	EdA 142 Esc/Ala 14, Albacete/Los Llanos	
C.16-51	Eurofighter EF.2000 Tifón [11-17]	EdA 111 Esc/113 Esc/Ala 11, Sevilla/Morón	
C.16-52	Eurofighter EF.2000 Tifón (C.16-10001) [11-18]	EdA 111 Esc/113 Esc/Ala 11, Sevilla/Morón	
C.16-53	Eurofighter EF.2000 Tifón (C.16-10002) [11-19]	EdA 111 Esc/113 Esc/Ala 11, Sevilla/Morón	
C.16-54	Eurofighter EF.2000 Tifón (C.16-10003) [11-20]	EdA 111 Esc/113 Esc/Ala 11, Sevilla/Morón	
C.16-55	Eurofighter EF.2000 Tifón (C.16-10004) [14-15]	EdA 142 Esc/Ala 14, Albacete/Los Llanos	
C.16-56	Eurofighter EF.2000 Tifón (10007)	EdA 142 Esc/Ala 14, Albacete/Los Llanos	
C.16-57	Eurofighter EF.2000 Tifón (10012)	EdA, stored Albacete/Los Llanos	
C.16-58	Eurofighter EF.2000 Tifón (10019)	EdA, stored Albacete/Los Llanos	
C.16-59	Eurofighter EF.2000 Tifón (10020)	EdA, stored Albacete/Los Llanos	
C.16-60	Eurofighter EF.2000 Tifón (10040)	EdA, stored Albacete/Los Llanos	
C.16-61	Eurofighter EF.2000 Tifón (10046)	EdA, stored Albacete/Los Llanos	
C.16-62	Eurofighter EF.2000 Tifón (10047)	EdA	
C.16-63	Eurofighter EF.2000 Tifón (10048) [11-28]	EdA 111 Esc/113 Esc/Ala 11, Sevilla/Morón	
C.16-64	Eurofighter EF.2000 Tifón (10053)	EdA	
C.16-65	Eurofighter EF.2000 Tifón (10054)	EdA, stored Albacete/Los Llanos	
C.16-66	Eurofighter EF.2000 Tifón (10064)	EdA	
C.16-67	Eurofighter EF.2000 Tifón	EdA (on order)	
C.16-68	Eurofighter EF.2000 Tifón (10091)	EdA (on order)	
C.16-69	Eurofighter EF.2000 Tifón	EdA (on order)	
C.16-70	Eurofighter EF.2000 Tifón	EdA (on order)	
C.16-71	Eurofighter EF.2000 Tifón	EdA (on order)	
C.16-72	Eurofighter EF.2000 Tifón	EdA (on order)	
C.16-73	Eurofighter EF.2000 Tifón	EdA (on order)	
D.4-01	Airtech CN.235M-100(MPA) [T.19B-12]	EdA 801 Esc/Ala 49, Palma/Son San Juan	
D.4-02	Airtech CN.235M-100(MPA) [T.19B-09]	EdA 801 Esc/Ala 49, Palma/Son San Juan	
D.4-03	Airtech CN.235M-100(MPA) [T.19B-10]	EdA 801 Esc/Ala 49, Palma/Son San Juan	
D.4-04	Airtech CN.235M-100(MPA) [T.19B-08]	EdA 802 Esc/Ala 46, Gran Canaria	
D.4-05	Airtech CN.235M-100(MPA) [T.19B-06]	EdA 801 Esc/Ala 49, Palma/Son San Juan	
D.4-06	Airtech CN.235M-100(MPA) [T.19B-05]	EdA 801 Esc/Ala 49, Palma/Son San Juan	
D.4-07	Airtech CN.235M-100(MPA) [T.19B-15]	EdA 803 Esc/Ala 48, Madrid/Getafe	
D.4-08	Airtech CN.235M-100(MPA) [T.19B-14]	EdA 802 Esc/Ala 46, Gran Canaria	
E.25-05	CASA 101EB Aviojet [79-05]	EdA 793 Esc/794 Esc/AGA, Murcia/San Javier	
E.25-06	CASA 101EB Aviojet [79-06,2]	EdA Patrulla Aguila/AGA, Murcia/San Javier	
E.25-08	CASA 101EB Aviojet [79-08]	EdA 793 Esc/794 Esc/AGA, Murcia/San Javier	
E.25-09	CASA 101EB Aviojet [79-09]	EdA 793 Esc/794 Esc/AGA, Murcia/San Javier	
E.25-10	CASA 101EB Aviojet [79-20]	EdA 793 Esc/794 Esc/AGA, Murcia/San Javier	
E.25-11	CASA 101EB Aviojet [79-11]	EdA 793 Esc/794 Esc/AGA, Murcia/San Javier	
E.25-12	CASA 101EB Aviojet [79-12]	EdA 793 Esc/794 Esc/AGA, Murcia/San Javier	
E.25-13	CASA 101EB Aviojet [79-13]	EdA 793 Esc/794 Esc/AGA, Murcia/San Javier	
E.25-14	CASA 101EB Aviojet [79-14]	EdA 793 Esc/794 Esc/AGA, Murcia/San Javier	
E.25-15	CASA 101EB Aviojet [79-15,1]	EdA Patrulla Aguila/AGA, Murcia/San Javier	
E.25-16	CASA 101EB Aviojet [79-16]	EdA 793 Esc/794 Esc/AGA, Murcia/San Javier	
E.25-17	CASA 101EB Aviojet [74-40]	EdA 741 Esc/GEM, Salamanca/Matacán	
E.25-18	CASA 101EB Aviojet [74-42] $	EdA 741 Esc/GEM, Salamanca/Matacán	
E.25-19	CASA 101EB Aviojet [79-19]	EdA 793 Esc/794 Esc/AGA, Murcia/San Javier	
E.25-20	CASA 101EB Aviojet [79-20]	EdA 793 Esc/794 Esc/AGA, Murcia/San Javier	

Notes	Serial	Type (code/other identity)	Owner/operator, location or fate
	E.25-21	CASA 101EB Aviojet [79-21]	EdA 793 Esc/794 Esc/AGA, Murcia/San Javier
	E.25-22	CASA 101EB Aviojet [79-22,6]	EdA *Patrulla Aguila*/AGA, Murcia/San Javier
	E.25-23	CASA 101EB Aviojet [79-23,5]	EdA *Patrulla Aguila*/AGA, Murcia/San Javier
	E.25-24	CASA 101EB Aviojet [79-24]	EdA 793 Esc/794 Esc/AGA, Murcia/San Javier
	E.25-25	CASA 101EB Aviojet [79-25]	EdA 793 Esc/794 Esc/AGA, Murcia/San Javier
	E.25-26	CASA 101EB Aviojet [79-26]	EdA 793 Esc/794 Esc/AGA, Murcia/San Javier
	E.25-27	CASA 101EB Aviojet [79-27]	EdA 793 Esc/794 Esc/AGA, Murcia/San Javier
	E.25-28	CASA 101EB Aviojet [79-28]	EdA 793 Esc/794 Esc/AGA, Murcia/San Javier
	E.25-29	CASA 101EB Aviojet [74-45]	EdA 741 Esc/GEM, Salamanca/Matacán
	E.25-31	CASA 101EB Aviojet [79-31]	EdA 793 Esc/794 Esc/AGA, Murcia/San Javier
	E.25-33	CASA 101EB Aviojet [74-02]	EdA 741 Esc/GEM, Salamanca/Matacán
	E.25-34	CASA 101EB Aviojet [74-44]	EdA 741 Esc/GEM, Salamanca/Matacán
	E.25-35	CASA 101EB Aviojet [54-20] $	EdA 541 Esc/CLAEX/Grupo 54, Madrid/Torrejón
	E.25-37	CASA 101EB Aviojet [79-37]	EdA 793 Esc/794 Esc/AGA, Murcia/San Javier
	E.25-38	CASA 101EB Aviojet [79-38]	EdA 793 Esc/794 Esc/AGA, Murcia/San Javier
	E.25-40	CASA 101EB Aviojet [79-40,3]	EdA *Patrulla Aguila*/AGA, Murcia/San Javier
	E.25-41	CASA 101EB Aviojet [74-41]	EdA 741 Esc/GEM, Salamanca/Matacán
	E.25-43	CASA 101EB Aviojet [74-43]	EdA 741 Esc/GEM, Salamanca/Matacán
	E.25-44	CASA 101EB Aviojet [79-44]	EdA 793 Esc/794 Esc/AGA, Murcia/San Javier
	E.25-45	CASA 101EB Aviojet [79-45]	*Preserved at Torrejón, October 2016*
	E.25-46	CASA 101EB Aviojet [79-46]	EdA 793 Esc/794 Esc/AGA, Murcia/San Javier
	E.25-50	CASA 101EB Aviojet [79-33]	EdA 793 Esc/794 Esc/AGA, Murcia/San Javier
	E.25-51	CASA 101EB Aviojet [74-07]	EdA 741 Esc/GEM, Salamanca/Matacán
	E.25-52	CASA 101EB Aviojet [79-34]	EdA 793 Esc/794 Esc/AGA, Murcia/San Javier
	E.25-53	CASA 101EB Aviojet [74-09]	EdA 741 Esc/GEM, Salamanca/Matacán
	E.25-54	CASA 101EB Aviojet [79-35]	EdA 793 Esc/794 Esc/AGA, Murcia/San Javier
	E.25-55	CASA 101EB Aviojet [54-21]	EdA 541 Esc/CLAEX/Grupo 54, Madrid/Torrejón
	E.25-56	CASA 101EB Aviojet [74-11]	EdA 741 Esc/GEM, Salamanca/Matacán
	E.25-57	CASA 101EB Aviojet [74-12]	EdA 741 Esc/GEM, Salamanca/Matacán
	E.25-59	CASA 101EB Aviojet [74-13]	EdA 741 Esc/GEM, Salamanca/Matacán
	E.25-61	CASA 101EB Aviojet [54-22]	EdA 541 Esc/CLAEX/Grupo 54, Madrid/Torrejón
	E.25-62	CASA 101EB Aviojet [79-17]	EdA 793 Esc/794 Esc/AGA, Murcia/San Javier
	E.25-63	CASA 101EB Aviojet [74-17]	EdA 741 Esc/GEM, Salamanca/Matacán
	E.25-65	CASA 101EB Aviojet [79-95]	EdA 793 Esc/794 Esc/AGA, Murcia/San Javier
	E.25-66	CASA 101EB Aviojet [74-20]	EdA 741 Esc/GEM, Salamanca/Matacán
	E.25-67	CASA 101EB Aviojet [74-21]	EdA 741 Esc/GEM, Salamanca/Matacán
	E.25-68	CASA 101EB Aviojet [74-22]	EdA 741 Esc/GEM, Salamanca/Matacán
	E.25-69	CASA 101EB Aviojet [79-97,7]	EdA *Patrulla Aguila*/AGA, Murcia/San Javier
	E.25-71	CASA 101EB Aviojet [74-25]	EdA 741 Esc/GEM, Salamanca/Matacán
	E.25-72	CASA 101EB Aviojet [74-26]	EdA 741 Esc/GEM, Salamanca/Matacán
	E.25-73	CASA 101EB Aviojet [79-98]	EdA 793 Esc/794 Esc/AGA, Murcia/San Javier
	E.25-74	CASA 101EB Aviojet [74-28]	EdA 741 Esc/GEM, Salamanca/Matacán
	E.25-76	CASA 101EB Aviojet [74-30]	EdA 741 Esc/GEM, Salamanca/Matacán
	E.25-78	CASA 101EB Aviojet [79-02]	EdA 793 Esc/794 Esc/AGA, Murcia/San Javier
	E.25-79	CASA 101EB Aviojet [79-39]	EdA 793 Esc/794 Esc/AGA, Murcia/San Javier
	E.25-80	CASA 101EB Aviojet [79-03]	EdA 793 Esc/794 Esc/AGA, Murcia/San Javier
	E.25-81	CASA 101EB Aviojet [74-34]	EdA 741 Esc/GEM, Salamanca/Matacán
	E.25-83	CASA 101EB Aviojet [74-35]	EdA 741 Esc/GEM, Salamanca/Matacán
	E.25-84	CASA 101EB Aviojet [79-04]	EdA 793 Esc/794 Esc/AGA, Murcia/San Javier
	E.25-86	CASA 101EB Aviojet [79-32,8]	EdA *Patrulla Aguila*/AGA, Murcia/San Javier
	E.25-87	CASA 101EB Aviojet [79-29]	EdA 793 Esc/794 Esc/AGA, Murcia/San Javier
	E.25-88	CASA 101EB Aviojet [74-39]	EdA 741 Esc/GEM, Salamanca/Matacán
	HS.23-01	Sikorsky SH-60B Seahawk [01-1001]	Armada 10 Esc, Rota
	HS.23-02	Sikorsky SH-60B Seahawk [01-1002]	Armada 10 Esc, Rota
	HS.23-03	Sikorsky SH-60B Seahawk [01-1003]	Armada 10 Esc, Rota
	HS.23-04	Sikorsky SH-60B Seahawk [01-1004]	Armada 10 Esc, Rota
	HS.23-05	Sikorsky SH-60B Seahawk [01-1005]	Armada 10 Esc, Rota
	HS.23-06	Sikorsky SH-60B Seahawk [01-1006]	Armada 10 Esc, Rota
	HS.23-07	Sikorsky SH-60B Seahawk [01-1007]	Armada 10 Esc, Rota
	HS.23-08	Sikorsky SH-60B Seahawk [01-1008]	Armada 10 Esc, Rota
	HS.23-09	Sikorsky SH-60B Seahawk [01-1009]	Armada 10 Esc, Rota
	HS.23-10	Sikorsky SH-60B Seahawk [01-1010]	Armada 10 Esc, Rota

Serial	Type (code/other identity)	Owner/operator, location or fate	Notes
HS.23-11	Sikorsky SH-60B Seahawk [01-1011]	Armada 10 Esc, Rota	
HS.23-12	Sikorsky SH-60B Seahawk [01-1012]	Armada 10 Esc, Rota	
HS.25-1	Eurocopter EC.120B Colibri [78-20]	EdA Patrulla Aspa/Ala 78, Granada/Armilla	
HS.25-2	Eurocopter EC.120B Colibri [78-21]	EdA Patrulla Aspa/Ala 78, Granada/Armilla	
HS.25-3	Eurocopter EC.120B Colibri [78-22]	EdA Patrulla Aspa/Ala 78, Granada/Armilla	
HS.25-4	Eurocopter EC.120B Colibri [78-23]	EdA Patrulla Aspa/Ala 78, Granada/Armilla	
HS.25-5	Eurocopter EC.120B Colibri [78-24]	EdA Patrulla Aspa/Ala 78, Granada/Armilla	
HS.25-6	Eurocopter EC.120B Colibri [78-25]	EdA Patrulla Aspa/Ala 78, Granada/Armilla	
HS.25-7	Eurocopter EC.120B Colibri [78-26]	EdA Patrulla Aspa/Ala 78, Granada/Armilla	
HS.25-8	Eurocopter EC.120B Colibri [78-27]	EdA Patrulla Aspa/Ala 78, Granada/Armilla	
HS.25-9	Eurocopter EC.120B Colibri [78-28]	EdA Patrulla Aspa/Ala 78, Granada/Armilla	
HS.25-10	Eurocopter EC.120B Colibri [78-29]	EdA 782 Esc/Ala 78, Granada/Armilla	
HS.25-11	Eurocopter EC.120B Colibri [78-30]	EdA 782 Esc/Ala 78, Granada/Armilla	
HS.25-12	Eurocopter EC.120B Colibri [78-31]	EdA Patrulla Aspa/Ala 78, Granada/Armilla	
HS.25-13	Eurocopter EC.120B Colibri [78-32]	EdA Patrulla Aspa/Ala 78, Granada/Armilla	
HS.25-14	Eurocopter EC.120B Colibri [78-33]	EdA Patrulla Aspa/Ala 78, Granada/Armilla	
HS.25-15	Eurocopter EC.120B Colibri [78-34]	EdA Patrulla Aspa/Ala 78, Granada/Armilla	
P.3A-01	Lockheed P-3A Orion [22-21]	EdA 221 Esc/Grupo 22, Sevilla/Morón	
P.3M-08	Lockheed P-3M Orion [22-31]	EdA 221 Esc/Grupo 22, Sevilla/Morón	
P.3M-09	Lockheed P-3M Orion [22-32]	EdA 221 Esc/Grupo 22, Sevilla/Morón	
P.3M-12	Lockheed P-3M Orion [22-35]	EdA 221 Esc/Grupo 22, Sevilla/Morón	
TL.10-01	Lockheed C-130H-30 Hercules [31-01]	EdA 311 Esc/312 Esc/Ala 31, Zaragoza	
T.10-03	Lockheed C-130H Hercules [31-03]	EdA 311 Esc/312 Esc/Ala 31, Zaragoza	
T.10-04	Lockheed C-130H Hercules [31-04]	EdA, stored Sevilla/Morón	
TK.10-05	Lockheed KC-130H Hercules [31-50]	EdA 311 Esc/312 Esc/Ala 31, Zaragoza	
TK.10-06	Lockheed KC-130H Hercules [31-51]	EdA 311 Esc/312 Esc/Ala 31, Zaragoza	
TK.10-07	Lockheed KC-130H Hercules [31-52]	EdA 311 Esc/312 Esc/Ala 31, Zaragoza	
T.10-08	Lockheed C-130H Hercules [31-05]	EdA 311 Esc/312 Esc/Ala 31, Zaragoza	
T.10-09	Lockheed C-130H Hercules [31-06]	EdA 311 Esc/312 Esc/Ala 31, Zaragoza	
T.10-10	Lockheed C-130H Hercules [31-07]	EdA 311 Esc/312 Esc/Ala 31, Zaragoza	
TK.10-11	Lockheed KC-130H Hercules [31-53]	EdA 311 Esc/312 Esc/Ala 31, Zaragoza	
TK.10-12	Lockheed KC-130H Hercules [31-54]	EdA 311 Esc/312 Esc/Ala 31, Zaragoza	
TM.11-2	Dassault Falcon 20D [47-22]	EdA 472 Esc/Grupo Mixto 47, Madrid/Torrejón	
TM.11-3	Dassault Falcon 20D [47-23]	EdA 472 Esc/Grupo Mixto 47, Madrid/Torrejón	
TM.11-4	Dassault Falcon 20E [47-24]	EdA 472 Esc/Grupo Mixto 47, Madrid/Torrejón	
T.12B-13	CASA 212A Aviocar [72-01]	EdA 721 Esc/Ala 72, Murcia/Alcantarilla	
T.12B-49	CASA 212A Aviocar [72-07]	EdA 721 Esc/Ala 72, Murcia/Alcantarilla	
T.12B-55	CASA 212A Aviocar [72-08]	EdA 721 Esc/Ala 72, Murcia/Alcantarilla	
T.12B-62	CASA 212A Aviocar [72-18]	EdA 721 Esc/Ala 72, Murcia/Alcantarilla	
T.12B-63	CASA 212A Aviocar [72-14]	EdA 721 Esc/Ala 72, Murcia/Alcantarilla	
T.12B-65	CASA 212A Aviocar [72-11]	EdA 721 Esc/Ala 72, Murcia/Alcantarilla	
T.12B-66	CASA 212A Aviocar [72-09]	Withdrawn from use at Cuatro Vientos, 2015	
T.12B-67	CASA 212A Aviocar [72-12]	EdA 721 Esc/Ala 72, Murcia/Alcantarilla	
T.12B-69	CASA 212A Aviocar [72-15]	Withdrawn from use at Cuatro Vientos, 2015	
T.12B-70	CASA 212A Aviocar [72-17]	EdA 721 Esc/Ala 72, Murcia/Alcantarilla	
T.12B-71	CASA 212A Aviocar [72-10]	EdA 721 Esc/Ala 72, Murcia/Alcantarilla	
TM.12D-72	CASA 212-200ECM Aviocar [47-12]	EdA 472 Esc/Grupo Mixto 47, Madrid/Torrejón	
T.12D-75	CASA 212-200 Aviocar [47-14]	EdA 472 Esc/Grupo Mixto 47, Madrid/Torrejón	
TR.12D-76	CASA 212-200 Aviocar [72-21]	EdA 721 Esc/Ala 72, Murcia/Alcantarilla	
TR.12D-77	CASA 212-200 Aviocar [72-22]	EdA 721 Esc/Ala 72, Murcia/Alcantarilla	
TR.12D-79	CASA 212-200 Aviocar [72-23]	EdA 721 Esc/Ala 72, Murcia/Alcantarilla	
TR.12D-81	CASA 212-200 Aviocar [72-24]	EdA 721 Esc/Ala 72, Murcia/Alcantarilla	
T.17-2	Boeing 707-331B [47-02]	Withdrawn from use, 12 March 2015	
T.17-3	Boeing 707-368C [47-03]	Withdrawn from use, 27 September 2016	
T.18-1	Dassault Falcon 900 [45-40]	EdA 451 Esc/Grupo 45, Madrid/Torrejón	
T.18-2	Dassault Falcon 900 [45-41]	EdA 451 Esc/Grupo 45, Madrid/Torrejón	
T.18-3	Dassault Falcon 900B [45-42]	EdA 451 Esc/Grupo 45, Madrid/Torrejón	
T.18-4	Dassault Falcon 900B [45-43]	EdA 451 Esc/Grupo 45, Madrid/Torrejón	
T.18-5	Dassault Falcon 900B [45-44]	EdA 451 Esc/Grupo 45, Madrid/Torrejón	
T.19A-01	Airtech CN.235M-10 [403-01]	EdA 403 Esc, Madrid/Getafe	
T.19A-02	Airtech CN.235M-10 [403-02]	EdA 403 Esc, Madrid/Getafe	
T.19B-07	Airtech CN.235M-100 [74-07]	EdA 744 Esc/GEM, Salamanca/Matacán	

Notes	Serial	Type (code/other identity)	Owner/operator, location or fate
	T.19B-11	Airtech CN.235M-100 [74-11]	EdA 744 Esc/GEM, Salamanca/Matacán
	T.19B-13	Airtech CN.235M-100 [74-31]	EdA 744 Esc/GEM, Salamanca/Matacán
	T.19B-16	Airtech CN.235M-100 [74-34]	EdA 744 Esc/GEM, Salamanca/Matacán
	T.19B-17	Airtech CN.235M-100 [74-17]	EdA 744 Esc/GEM, Salamanca/Matacán
	T.19B-18	Airtech CN.235M-100 [74-36]	EdA 744 Esc/GEM, Salamanca/Matacán
	T.19B-19	Airtech CN.235M-100 [74-19]	EdA 744 Esc/GEM, Salamanca/Matacán
	T.19B-20	Airtech CN.235M-100 [74-38]	EdA 744 Esc/GEM, Salamanca/Matacán
	T.19B-21	Airtech CN.235M VIGMA [09-501]	Guardia Civil Servicio Aéreo, Gran Canaria
	T.19B-22	Airtech CN.235M VIGMA [09-502]	Guardia Civil Servicio Aéreo, Gran Canaria
	TR.20-01	Cessna 560 Citation VI [403-11]	EdA 403 Esc, Madrid/Getafe
	TR.20-02	Cessna 560 Citation VI [403-12]	EdA 403 Esc, Madrid/Getafe
	TR.20-03	Cessna 560 Citation VI [403-21]	EdA 403 Esc, Madrid/Getafe
	T.21-01	CASA C-295M [35-39]	EdA 353 Esc/Ala 35, Madrid/Getafe
	T.21-02	CASA C-295M [35-40]	EdA 353 Esc/Ala 35, Madrid/Getafe
	T.21-03	CASA C-295M [35-41]	EdA 353 Esc/Ala 35, Madrid/Getafe
	T.21-04	CASA C-295M [35-42]	EdA 353 Esc/Ala 35, Madrid/Getafe
	T.21-05	CASA C-295M [35-43]	EdA 353 Esc/Ala 35, Madrid/Getafe
	T.21-06	CASA C-295M [35-44]	EdA 353 Esc/Ala 35, Madrid/Getafe
	T.21-07	CASA C-295M [35-45]	EdA 353 Esc/Ala 35, Madrid/Getafe
	T.21-08	CASA C-295M [35-46]	EdA 353 Esc/Ala 35, Madrid/Getafe
	T.21-09	CASA C-295M [35-47]	EdA 353 Esc/Ala 35, Madrid/Getafe
	T.21-10	CASA C-295M [35-48]	EdA 353 Esc/Ala 35, Madrid/Getafe
	T.21-11	CASA C-295M [35-49]	EdA 353 Esc/Ala 35, Madrid/Getafe
	T.21-12	CASA C-295M [35-50]	EdA 353 Esc/Ala 35, Madrid/Getafe
	T.21-13	CASA C-295M [35-51]	EdA 353 Esc/Ala 35, Madrid/Getafe
	T.22-1	Airbus A.310-304 [45-50]	EdA 451 Esc/Grupo 45, Madrid/Torrejón
	T.22-2	Airbus A.310-304 [45-51]	EdA 451 Esc/Grupo 45, Madrid/Torrejón
	T.23-01	Airbus Military A.400M (10074) [31-21]	EdA 311 Esc/312 Esc/Ala 31, Zaragoza
	TK.23-02	Airbus Military A.400M (10075)	EdA (on order)
	TK.23-03	Airbus Military A.400M (10076)	EdA (on order)
	T.23-04	Airbus Military A.400M	EdA (on order)
	T.23-05	Airbus Military A.400M	EdA (on order)
	U.20-1	Cessna 550 Citation II [01-405]	Armada 4 Esc, Rota
	U.20-2	Cessna 550 Citation II [01-406]	Armada 4 Esc, Rota
	U.20-3	Cessna 550 Citation II [01-407]	Armada 4 Esc, Rota
	U.21-01	Cessna 650 Citation VII [01-408]	Armada 4 Esc, Rota
	VA.1A-15	McDonnell Douglas EAV-8B Harrier II [01-903]	Armada 9 Esc, Rota
	VA.1A-19	McDonnell Douglas EAV-8B Harrier II [01-907]	Armada 9 Esc, Rota
	VA.1A-20	McDonnell Douglas EAV-8B Harrier II [01-909]	Armada 9 Esc, Rota
	VA.1A-22	McDonnell Douglas EAV-8B Harrier II [01-911]	Armada 9 Esc, Rota
	VA.1B-24	McDonnell Douglas EAV-8B+ Harrier II [01-914]	Armada 9 Esc, Rota
	VA.1B-25	McDonnell Douglas EAV-8B+ Harrier II [01-915]	Armada 9 Esc, Rota
	VA.1B-26	McDonnell Douglas EAV-8B+ Harrier II [01-916]	Armada 9 Esc, Rota
	VA.1B-27	McDonnell Douglas EAV-8B+ Harrier II [01-917]	Armada 9 Esc, Rota
	VA.1B-28	McDonnell Douglas EAV-8B+ Harrier II [01-918]	Armada 9 Esc, Rota
	VA.1B-29	McDonnell Douglas EAV-8B+ Harrier II [01-919]	Armada 9 Esc, Rota
	VA.1B-30	McDonnell Douglas EAV-8B+ Harrier II [01-920]	Armada 9 Esc, Rota
	VA.1B-35	McDonnell Douglas EAV-8B+ Harrier II [01-923]	Armada 9 Esc, Rota
	VA.1B-36	McDonnell Douglas EAV-8B+ Harrier II [01-924]	Armada 9 Esc, Rota
	VA.1B-37	McDonnell Douglas EAV-8B+ Harrier II [01-925]	Armada 9 Esc, Rota
	VA.1B-38	McDonnell Douglas EAV-8B+ Harrier II [01-926]	Armada 9 Esc, Rota
	VA.1B-39	McDonnell Douglas EAV-8B+ Harrier II [01-927]	Armada 9 Esc, Rota
	VA.1B-33	McDonnell Douglas TAV-8B Harrier II [01-922]	Armada 9 Esc, Rota

SUDAN

	ST-PSA	Dassault Falcon 900B	Sudanese Government, Khartoum
	ST-PSR	Dassault Falcon 50	Sudanese Government, Khartoum

SWEDEN

Försvarsmakten/Swedish Armed Forces: Försvarsmaktens Helikopterflottilj (Hkpflj)/Armed Forces Helicopter Wing & Svenska Flygvapnet/Swedish Air Force

	39-6	SAAB JAS 39C Gripen [6]	SAAB, Linköping/Malmen

Serial	Type (code/other identity)	Owner/operator, location or fate	Notes
39-7	SAAB JAS 39NG Gripen	SAAB, Linköping/Malmen	
39-8	SAAB JAS 39E Gripen	SAAB, Linköping/Malmen	
39208	SAAB JAS 39C Gripen [208]	Flygvapnet Flottiljer 17, Ronneby/Kallinge	
39209	SAAB JAS 39C Gripen [209]	Flygvapnet Flottiljer 7, Såtenäs	
39210	SAAB JAS 39C Gripen [210]	Flygvapnet Flottiljer 17, Ronneby/Kallinge	
39211	SAAB JAS 39C Gripen [211]	Flygvapnet Flottiljer 7, Såtenäs	
39212	SAAB JAS 39C Gripen [212]	Flygvapnet Flottiljer 17, Ronneby/Kallinge	
39213	SAAB JAS 39C Gripen [213]	Flygvapnet Flottiljer 7, Såtenäs	
39214	SAAB JAS 39C Gripen [214]	Flygvapnet Flottiljer 7, Såtenäs	
39215	SAAB JAS 39C Gripen [215]	Flygvapnet Flottiljer 7, Såtenäs	
39216	SAAB JAS 39C Gripen [216]	Flygvapnet Flottiljer 17, Ronneby/Kallinge	
39217	SAAB JAS 39C Gripen [217]	Flygvapnet Flottiljer 7, Såtenäs	
39218	SAAB JAS 39C Gripen [218]	Flygvapnet Flottiljer 21, Luleå/Kallax	
39219	SAAB JAS 39C Gripen [219]	Flygvapnet Flottiljer 21, Luleå/Kallax	
39220	SAAB JAS 39C Gripen [220]	Flygvapnet Flottiljer 7, Såtenäs	
39221	SAAB JAS 39C Gripen [221]	Flygvapnet Flottiljer 17, Ronneby/Kallinge	
39222	SAAB JAS 39C Gripen [222]	Flygvapnet Flottiljer 17, Ronneby/Kallinge	
39223	SAAB JAS 39C Gripen [223]	Flygvapnet Flottiljer 21, Luleå/Kallax	
39224	SAAB JAS 39C Gripen [224]	Flygvapnet Flottiljer 17, Ronneby/Kallinge	
39225	SAAB JAS 39C Gripen [225]	Flygvapnet Flottiljer 7, Såtenäs	
39226	SAAB JAS 39C Gripen [226]	Flygvapnet Flottiljer 7, Såtenäs	
39227	SAAB JAS 39C Gripen [227]	Flygvapnet Flottiljer 7, Såtenäs	
39228	SAAB JAS 39C Gripen [228]	Flygvapnet Flottiljer 17, Ronneby/Kallinge	
39229	SAAB JAS 39C Gripen [229]	Flygvapnet Flottiljer 21, Luleå/Kallax	
39230	SAAB JAS 39C Gripen [230]	Flygvapnet Flottiljer 17, Ronneby/Kallinge	
39231	SAAB JAS 39C Gripen [231]	Flygvapnet Flottiljer 7, Såtenäs	
39232	SAAB JAS 39C Gripen [232]	Flygvapnet Flottiljer 21, Luleå/Kallax	
39233	SAAB JAS 39C Gripen [233]	Flygvapnet Flottiljer 21, Luleå/Kallax	
39246	SAAB JAS 39C Gripen [246]	Flygvapnet Flottiljer 21, Luleå/Kallax	
39247	SAAB JAS 39C Gripen [247]	Flygvapnet Flottiljer 17, Ronneby/Kallinge	
39248	SAAB JAS 39C Gripen [248]	Flygvapnet Flottiljer 21, Luleå/Kallax	
39249	SAAB JAS 39C Gripen [249]	Flygvapnet Flottiljer 17, Ronneby/Kallinge	
39250	SAAB JAS 39C Gripen [250]	Flygvapnet FC, Linköping/Malmen	
39251	SAAB JAS 39C Gripen [251]	Flygvapnet FC, Linköping/Malmen	
39252	SAAB JAS 39C Gripen [252]	Flygvapnet Flottiljer 17, Ronneby/Kallinge	
39253	SAAB JAS 39C Gripen [253]	Flygvapnet Flottiljer 7, Såtenäs	
39254	SAAB JAS 39C Gripen [254]	Flygvapnet Flottiljer 17, Ronneby/Kallinge	
39255	SAAB JAS 39C Gripen [255]	Flygvapnet Flottiljer 7, Såtenäs	
39256	SAAB JAS 39C Gripen [256]	Flygvapnet Flottiljer 17, Ronneby/Kallinge	
39257	SAAB JAS 39C Gripen [257]	Flygvapnet Flottiljer 21, Luleå/Kallax	
39258	SAAB JAS 39C Gripen [258]	Flygvapnet Flottiljer 21, Luleå/Kallax	
39260	SAAB JAS 39C Gripen [260]	Flygvapnet Flottiljer 21, Luleå/Kallax	
39261	SAAB JAS 39C Gripen [261]	Flygvapnet Flottiljer 17, Ronneby/Kallinge	
39262	SAAB JAS 39C Gripen [262]	Flygvapnet Flottiljer 17, Ronneby/Kallinge	
39263	SAAB JAS 39C Gripen [263]	Flygvapnet Flottiljer 21, Luleå/Kallax	
39264	SAAB JAS 39C Gripen [264]	Flygvapnet Flottiljer 17, Ronneby/Kallinge	
39265	SAAB JAS 39C Gripen [265]	Flygvapnet Flottiljer 21, Luleå/Kallax	
39266	SAAB JAS 39C Gripen [266]	Flygvapnet Flottiljer 7, Såtenäs	
39267	SAAB JAS 39C Gripen [267]	Flygvapnet Flottiljer 21, Luleå/Kallax	
39268	SAAB JAS 39C Gripen [268]	Flygvapnet Flottiljer 7, Såtenäs	
39269	SAAB JAS 39C Gripen [269]	Flygvapnet Flottiljer 17, Ronneby/Kallinge	
39270	SAAB JAS 39C Gripen [270]	Flygvapnet Flottiljer 7, Såtenäs	
39271	SAAB JAS 39C Gripen [271]	Flygvapnet Flottiljer 17, Ronneby/Kallinge	
39272	SAAB JAS 39C Gripen [272]	Flygvapnet Flottiljer 7, Såtenäs	
39273	SAAB JAS 39C Gripen [273]	Flygvapnet Flottiljer 17, Ronneby/Kallinge	
39274	SAAB JAS 39C Gripen [274]	Flygvapnet Flottiljer 21, Luleå/Kallax	
39275	SAAB JAS 39C Gripen [275]	Flygvapnet Flottiljer 7, Såtenäs	
39276	SAAB JAS 39C Gripen [276]	Flygvapnet Flottiljer 21, Luleå/Kallax	
39277	SAAB JAS 39C Gripen [277]	Flygvapnet Flottiljer 7, Såtenäs	
39278	SAAB JAS 39C Gripen [278]	Flygvapnet Flottiljer 17, Ronneby/Kallinge	
39279	SAAB JAS 39C Gripen [279]	Flygvapnet Flottiljer 21, Luleå/Kallax	
39280	SAAB JAS 39C Gripen [280]	Flygvapnet Flottiljer 21, Luleå/Kallax	

Notes	Serial	Type (code/other identity)	Owner/operator, location or fate
	39281	SAAB JAS 39C Gripen [281]	Flygvapnet Flottiljer 17, Ronneby/Kallinge
	39282	SAAB JAS 39C Gripen [282]	Flygvapnet Flottiljer 17, Ronneby/Kallinge
	39283	SAAB JAS 39C Gripen [283]	Flygvapnet Flottiljer 21, Luleå/Kallax
	39284	SAAB JAS 39C Gripen [284]	Flygvapnet Flottiljer 17, Ronneby/Kallinge
	39285	SAAB JAS 39C Gripen [285]	Flygvapnet Flottiljer 21, Luleå/Kallax
	39286	SAAB JAS 39C Gripen [286]	Flygvapnet Flottiljer 21, Luleå/Kallax
	39287	SAAB JAS 39C Gripen [287]	Flygvapnet Flottiljer 17, Ronneby/Kallinge
	39288	SAAB JAS 39C Gripen [288]	Flygvapnet Flottiljer 21, Luleå/Kallax
	39289	SAAB JAS 39C Gripen [289]	Flygvapnet Flottiljer 17, Ronneby/Kallinge
	39290	SAAB JAS 39C Gripen [290]	Flygvapnet Flottiljer 21, Luleå/Kallax
	39291	SAAB JAS 39C Gripen [291]	Flygvapnet Flottiljer 21, Luleå/Kallax
	39292	SAAB JAS 39C Gripen [292]	Flygvapnet Flottiljer 17, Ronneby/Kallinge
	39293	SAAB JAS 39C Gripen [293]	Flygvapnet Flottiljer 7, Såtenäs
	39294	SAAB JAS 39C Gripen [294]	Flygvapnet Flottiljer 17, Ronneby/Kallinge
	39815	SAAB JAS 39D Gripen [815]	Flygvapnet Flottiljer 7, Såtenäs
	39816	SAAB JAS 39D Gripen [816]	Flygvapnet Flottiljer 7, Såtenäs
	39817	SAAB JAS 39D Gripen [817]	Flygvapnet Flottiljer 21, Luleå/Kallax
	39818	SAAB JAS 39D Gripen	Flygvapnet (on order)
	39821	SAAB JAS 39D Gripen [821]	Flygvapnet Flottiljer 7, Såtenäs
	39822	SAAB JAS 39D Gripen [822]	Flygvapnet Flottiljer 21, Luleå/Kallax
	39823	SAAB JAS 39D Gripen [823]	Flygvapnet Flottiljer 21, Luleå/Kallax
	39824	SAAB JAS 39D Gripen [824]	Flygvapnet Flottiljer 21, Luleå/Kallax
	39825	SAAB JAS 39D Gripen [825]	Flygvapnet Flottiljer 7, Såtenäs
	39826	SAAB JAS 39D Gripen [826]	Flygvapnet Flottiljer 17, Ronneby/Kallinge
	39827	SAAB JAS 39D Gripen [827]	Flygvapnet Flottiljer 7, Såtenäs
	39829	SAAB JAS 39D Gripen [829]	Flygvapnet Flottiljer 17, Ronneby/Kallinge
	39830	SAAB JAS 39D Gripen [830]	Flygvapnet Flottiljer 7, Såtenäs
	39831	SAAB JAS 39D Gripen [831]	Flygvapnet Flottiljer 17, Ronneby/Kallinge
	39832	SAAB JAS 39D Gripen [832]	SAAB, Linköping/Malmen
	39833	SAAB JAS 39D Gripen [833]	Flygvapnet Flottiljer 21, Luleå/Kallax
	39834	SAAB JAS 39D Gripen [834]	Flygvapnet Flottiljer 7, Såtenäs
	39835	SAAB JAS 39D Gripen [835]	Flygvapnet Flottiljer 7, Såtenäs
	39836	SAAB JAS 39D Gripen [836]	Flygvapnet Flottiljer 17, Ronneby/Kallinge
	39837	SAAB JAS 39D Gripen [837]	Flygvapnet Flottiljer 21, Luleå/Kallax
	39838	SAAB JAS 39D Gripen	Flygvapnet (on order)
	39839	SAAB JAS 39D Gripen [839]	Flygvapnet Flottiljer 7, Såtenäs
	39840	SAAB JAS 39D Gripen [840]	Flygvapnet Flottiljer 17, Ronneby/Kallinge
	39841	SAAB JAS 39D Gripen [841]	Flygvapnet Flottiljer 7, Såtenäs
	39842	SAAB JAS 39D Gripen [842]	*To Hungary as 44, 2016*
	84004	Lockheed C-130H Hercules (Tp.84) [844]	Flygvapnet TSFE, Såtenäs
	84005	Lockheed C-130H Hercules (Tp.84) [845]	Flygvapnet TSFE, Såtenäs
	84006	Lockheed C-130H Hercules (Tp.84) [846]	Flygvapnet TSFE, Såtenäs
	84007	Lockheed C-130H Hercules (Tp.84) [847]	Flygvapnet TSFE, Såtenäs
	84008	Lockheed C-130H Hercules (Tp.84) [848]	Flygvapnet TSFE, Såtenäs
	86001	Rockwell Sabreliner-40 (Tp.86) [861]	Flygvapnet FC, Linköping/Malmen
	100001	SAAB SF.340 (OS.100) [001]	Flygvapnet TSFE, Linköping/Malmen
	100003	SAAB SF.340AEW&C (S.100D Argus) [003]	Flygvapnet TSFE, Linköping/Malmen
	100004	SAAB SF.340AEW&C (S.100D Argus) [004]	Flygvapnet TSFE, Linköping/Malmen
	100008	SAAB SF.340 (Tp.100C) [008]	Flygvapnet TSFE, Linköping/Malmen
	102001	Grumman G.1159C Gulfstream IV (Tp.102A) [021]	Flygvapnet TSFE, Linköping/Malmen
	102002	Grumman G.1159C Gulfstream IV (S.102B Korpen)[022]	Flygvapnet TSFE, Linköping/Malmen
	102003	Grumman G.1159C Gulfstream IV (S.102B Korpen)[023]	Flygvapnet TSFE, Linköping/Malmen
	102004	Grumman G.1159C Gulfstream IV-SP (Tp.102C) [024]	Flygvapnet TSFE, Linköping/Malmen
	102005	Gulfstream Aerospace G.550 (Tp.102D) [025]	Flygvapnet TSFE, Linköping/Malmen
	141041	NH Industries NH.90-TTH (Hkp.14A) [41]	Airbus Helicopters, Marignane, France
	141046	NH Industries NH.90-TTH (Hkp.14A) [46]	Hkpflj 1.HkpSkv, Luleå/Kallax
	141047	NH Industries NH.90-TTH (Hkp.14A) [47]	Hkpflj 1.HkpSkv, Luleå/Kallax
	142042	NH Industries NH.90-TTH (Hkp.14B) [42]	Hkpflj 3.HkpSkv, Ronneby/Kallinge
	142043	NH Industries NH.90-TTH (Hkp.14B) [43]	Hkpflj 3.HkpSkv, Ronneby/Kallinge
	142044	NH Industries NH.90-TTH (Hkp.14B) [44]	Hkpflj 3.HkpSkv, Ronneby/Kallinge
	142045	NH Industries NH.90-TTH (Hkp.14B) [45]	Hkpflj 3.HkpSkv, Ronneby/Kallinge
	144048	NH Industries NH.90-TTH (Hkp.14D) [48]	Hkpflj 3.HkpSkv, Ronneby/Kallinge

Serial	Type (code/other identity)	Owner/operator, location or fate	Notes
144049	NH Industries NH.90-TTH (Hkp.14D) [49]	Hkpflj 1.HkpSkv, Luleå/Kallax	
144050	NH Industries NH.90-TTH (Hkp.14D) [50]	Hkpflj 1.HkpSkv, Luleå/Kallax	
144051	NH Industries NH.90-TTH (Hkp.14D) [51]	Hkpflj 1.HkpSkv, Luleå/Kallax	
144052	NH Industries NH.90-TTH (Hkp.14D) [52]	Hkpflj 1.HkpSkv, Luleå/Kallax	
144053	NH Industries NH.90-TTH (Hkp.14D) [53]	Hkpflj 1.HkpSkv, Luleå/Kallax	
144054	NH Industries NH.90-TTH (Hkp.14D) [54]	Hkpflj 3.HkpSkv, Ronneby/Kallinge	
146055	NH Industries NH.90-SAR (Hkp.14F) [55]	Hkpflj (on order)	
146056	NH Industries NH.90-SAR (Hkp.14F) [56]	Hkpflj 3.HkpSkv, Ronneby/Kallinge	
146057	NH Industries NH.90-SAR (Hkp.14F) [57]	Hkpflj (on order)	
146058	NH Industries NH.90-SAR (Hkp.14F) [58]	Hkpflj (on order)	
146059	NH Industries NH.90-SAR (Hkp.14F) [59]	Hkpflj (on order)	
151751	Agusta A109LUH Power (Hkp.15A) [21]	Hkpflj 2.HkpSkv, Linköping/Malmen	
151752	Agusta A109LUH Power (Hkp.15A) [22]	Hkpflj 2.HkpSkv, Linköping/Malmen	
151753	Agusta A109LUH Power (Hkp.15A) [23]	Hkpflj 2.HkpSkv, Linköping/Malmen	
151754	Agusta A109LUH Power (Hkp.15A) [24]	Hkpflj 2.HkpSkv, Linköping/Malmen	
151755	Agusta A109LUH Power (Hkp.15A) [25]	Hkpflj 2.HkpSkv, Linköping/Malmen	
151756	Agusta A109LUH Power (Hkp.15A) [26]	Hkpflj 2.HkpSkv, Linköping/Malmen	
151757	Agusta A109LUH Power (Hkp.15A) [27]	Hkpflj 2.HkpSkv, Linköping/Malmen	
151758	Agusta A109LUH Power (Hkp.15A) [28]	Hkpflj 2.HkpSkv, Linköping/Malmen	
151759	Agusta A109LUH Power (Hkp.15A) [29]	Hkpflj 2.HkpSkv, Linköping/Malmen	
152760	Agusta A109LUH Power (Hkp.15B) [30]	Hkpflj 3.HkpSkv, Ronneby/Kallinge	
151761	Agusta A109LUH Power (Hkp.15A) [31]	Hkpflj 2.HkpSkv, Linköping/Malmen	
151762	Agusta A109LUH Power (Hkp.15A) [32]	Hkpflj 2.HkpSkv, Linköping/Malmen	
152763	Agusta A109LUH Power (Hkp.15B) [33]	Hkpflj 3.HkpSkv, Ronneby/Kallinge	
151764	Agusta A109LUH Power (Hkp.15A) [34]	Hkpflj 2.HkpSkv, Linköping/Malmen	
152765	Agusta A109LUH Power (Hkp.15B) [35]	Hkpflj 3.HkpSkv, Ronneby/Kallinge	
152766	Agusta A109LUH Power (Hkp.15B) [36]	Hkpflj 3.HkpSkv, Ronneby/Kallinge	
152767	Agusta A109LUH Power (Hkp.15B) [37]	Hkpflj 3.HkpSkv, Ronneby/Kallinge	
152768	Agusta A109LUH Power (Hkp.15B) [38]	Hkpflj 3.HkpSkv, Ronneby/Kallinge	
152769	Agusta A109LUH Power (Hkp.15B) [39]	Hkpflj 3.HkpSkv, Ronneby/Kallinge	
152770	Agusta A109LUH Power (Hkp.15B) [40]	Hkpflj 3.HkpSkv, Ronneby/Kallinge	
161226	Sikorsky UH-60M Black Hawk (Hkp.16A) [01]	Hkpflj 2.HkpSkv, Linköping/Malmen	
161227	Sikorsky UH-60M Black Hawk (Hkp.16A) [02]	Hkpflj 2.HkpSkv, Linköping/Malmen	
161228	Sikorsky UH-60M Black Hawk (Hkp.16A) [03]	Hkpflj 2.HkpSkv, Linköping/Malmen	
161229	Sikorsky UH-60M Black Hawk (Hkp.16A) [04]	Hkpflj 2.HkpSkv, Linköping/Malmen	
161230	Sikorsky UH-60M Black Hawk (Hkp.16A) [05]	Hkpflj 2.HkpSkv, Linköping/Malmen	
161231	Sikorsky UH-60M Black Hawk (Hkp.16A) [06]	Hkpflj 2.HkpSkv, Linköping/Malmen	
161232	Sikorsky UH-60M Black Hawk (Hkp.16A) [07]	Hkpflj 2.HkpSkv, Linköping/Malmen	
161233	Sikorsky UH-60M Black Hawk (Hkp.16A) [08]	Hkpflj 2.HkpSkv, Linköping/Malmen	
161234	Sikorsky UH-60M Black Hawk (Hkp.16A) [09]	Hkpflj 2.HkpSkv, Linköping/Malmen	
161235	Sikorsky UH-60M Black Hawk (Hkp.16A) [10]	Hkpflj 2.HkpSkv, Linköping/Malmen	
161236	Sikorsky UH-60M Black Hawk (Hkp.16A) [11]	Hkpflj 2.HkpSkv, Linköping/Malmen	
161237	Sikorsky UH-60M Black Hawk (Hkp.16A) [12]	Hkpflj 2.HkpSkv, Linköping/Malmen	
161238	Sikorsky UH-60M Black Hawk (Hkp.16A) [13]	Hkpflj 2.HkpSkv, Linköping/Malmen	
161239	Sikorsky UH-60M Black Hawk (Hkp.16A) [14]	Hkpflj 2.HkpSkv, Linköping/Malmen	
161240	Sikorsky UH-60M Black Hawk (Hkp.16A) [15]	Hkpflj 2.HkpSkv, Linköping/Malmen	

Kustbevakning/Swedish Coast Guard

Serial	Type (code/other identity)	Owner/operator, location or fate	Notes
SE-MAA	Bombardier DHC-8Q-311 [501]	Kustbevakning, Nykoping	
SE-MAB	Bombardier DHC-8Q-311 [502]	Kustbevakning, Nykoping	
SE-MAC	Bombardier DHC-8Q-311 [503]	Kustbevakning, Nykoping	

SWITZERLAND

Schweizer Luftwaffe/Swiss Air Force

(Most aircraft are pooled centrally. Some carry unit badges but these rarely indicate actual operators.)

Serial	Type (code/other identity)	Owner/operator, location or fate	Notes
A-101	Pilatus PC-21	Swiss AF Pilotenschule, Emmen	
A-102	Pilatus PC-21	Swiss AF Pilotenschule, Emmen	
A-103	Pilatus PC-21	Swiss AF Pilotenschule, Emmen	
A-104	Pilatus PC-21	Swiss AF Pilotenschule, Emmen	
A-105	Pilatus PC-21	Swiss AF Pilotenschule, Emmen	
A-106	Pilatus PC-21	Swiss AF Pilotenschule, Emmen	
A-107	Pilatus PC-21	Swiss AF Pilotenschule, Emmen	
A-108	Pilatus PC-21	Swiss AF Pilotenschule, Emmen	

Notes	Serial	Type (code/other identity)	Owner/operator, location or fate
	A-912	Pilatus NCPC-7 Turbo Trainer	Swiss AF Instrumentenflugstaffel 14, Emmen
	A-913	Pilatus NCPC-7 Turbo Trainer	Swiss AF Instrumentenflugstaffel 14, Emmen
	A-914	Pilatus NCPC-7 Turbo Trainer	Swiss AF Instrumentenflugstaffel 14, Emmen
	A-915	Pilatus NCPC-7 Turbo Trainer	Swiss AF Instrumentenflugstaffel 14, Emmen
	A-916	Pilatus NCPC-7 Turbo Trainer	Swiss AF Instrumentenflugstaffel 14, Emmen
	A-917	Pilatus NCPC-7 Turbo Trainer	Swiss AF Instrumentenflugstaffel 14, Emmen
	A-918	Pilatus NCPC-7 Turbo Trainer	Swiss AF Instrumentenflugstaffel 14, Emmen
	A-919	Pilatus NCPC-7 Turbo Trainer	Swiss AF Instrumentenflugstaffel 14, Emmen
	A-922	Pilatus NCPC-7 Turbo Trainer	Swiss AF Instrumentenflugstaffel 14, Emmen
	A-923	Pilatus NCPC-7 Turbo Trainer	Swiss AF Instrumentenflugstaffel 14, Emmen
	A-924	Pilatus NCPC-7 Turbo Trainer	Swiss AF Instrumentenflugstaffel 14, Emmen
	A-925	Pilatus NCPC-7 Turbo Trainer	Swiss AF Instrumentenflugstaffel 14, Emmen
	A-926	Pilatus NCPC-7 Turbo Trainer	Swiss AF Instrumentenflugstaffel 14, Emmen
	A-927	Pilatus NCPC-7 Turbo Trainer	Swiss AF Instrumentenflugstaffel 14, Emmen
	A-928	Pilatus NCPC-7 Turbo Trainer	Swiss AF Instrumentenflugstaffel 14, Emmen
	A-929	Pilatus NCPC-7 Turbo Trainer	Swiss AF Instrumentenflugstaffel 14, Emmen
	A-930	Pilatus NCPC-7 Turbo Trainer	Swiss AF Instrumentenflugstaffel 14, Emmen
	A-931	Pilatus NCPC-7 Turbo Trainer	Swiss AF Instrumentenflugstaffel 14, Emmen
	A-932	Pilatus NCPC-7 Turbo Trainer	Swiss AF Instrumentenflugstaffel 14, Emmen
	A-933	Pilatus NCPC-7 Turbo Trainer	Swiss AF Instrumentenflugstaffel 14, Emmen
	A-934	Pilatus NCPC-7 Turbo Trainer	Swiss AF Instrumentenflugstaffel 14, Emmen
	A-935	Pilatus NCPC-7 Turbo Trainer	Swiss AF Instrumentenflugstaffel 14, Emmen
	A-936	Pilatus NCPC-7 Turbo Trainer	Swiss AF Instrumentenflugstaffel 14, Emmen
	A-937	Pilatus NCPC-7 Turbo Trainer	Swiss AF Instrumentenflugstaffel 14, Emmen
	A-938	Pilatus NCPC-7 Turbo Trainer	Swiss AF Instrumentenflugstaffel 14, Emmen
	A-939	Pilatus NCPC-7 Turbo Trainer	Swiss AF Instrumentenflugstaffel 14, Emmen
	A-940	Pilatus NCPC-7 Turbo Trainer	Swiss AF Instrumentenflugstaffel 14, Emmen
	A-941	Pilatus NCPC-7 Turbo Trainer	Swiss AF Instrumentenflugstaffel 14, Emmen
	C-401	Pilatus PC-9	*Withdrawn from use at Emmen, 2016*
	C-402	Pilatus PC-9	*Withdrawn from use at Emmen, 2016*
	C-403	Pilatus PC-9	*Withdrawn from use at Emmen, 2016*
	C-405	Pilatus PC-9	Swiss AF Zielflugstaffel 12, Emmen
	C-406	Pilatus PC-9	Swiss AF Zielflugstaffel 12, Emmen
	C-407	Pilatus PC-9	Swiss AF Zielflugstaffel 12, Emmen
	C-408	Pilatus PC-9	Swiss AF Zielflugstaffel 12, Emmen
	C-409	Pilatus PC-9	Swiss AF Zielflugstaffel 12, Emmen
	C-410	Pilatus PC-9	Swiss AF Zielflugstaffel 12, Emmen
	C-411	Pilatus PC-9	Swiss AF Zielflugstaffel 12, Emmen
	C-412	Pilatus PC-9	Swiss AF Zielflugstaffel 12, Emmen
	J-3005	Northrop F-5E Tiger II	Swiss AF FlSt 8, Meiringen/FlSt 6 & 19, Payerne
	J-3015	Northrop F-5E Tiger II	Swiss AF FlSt 8, Meiringen/FlSt 6 & 19, Payerne
	J-3030	Northrop F-5E Tiger II	Swiss AF FlSt 8, Meiringen/FlSt 6 & 19, Payerne
	J-3033	Northrop F-5E Tiger II	Swiss AF FlSt 8, Meiringen/FlSt 6 & 19, Payerne
	J-3036	Northrop F-5E Tiger II $	Swiss AF, stored Sion
	J-3038	Northrop F-5E Tiger II $	Swiss AF FlSt 8, Meiringen/FlSt 6 & 19, Payerne
	J-3041	Northrop F-5E Tiger II	Swiss AF, stored Sion
	J-3044	Northrop F-5E Tiger II	Swiss AF, stored Emmen
	J-3056	Northrop F-5E Tiger II	Swiss AF, stored Emmen
	J-3057	Northrop F-5E Tiger II	*Preserved at Payerne, 2016*
	J-3062	Northrop F-5E Tiger II	Swiss AF, stored Sion
	J-3063	Northrop F-5E Tiger II	Swiss AF FlSt 8, Meiringen/FlSt 6 & 19, Payerne
	J-3065	Northrop F-5E Tiger II	Swiss AF FlSt 8, Meiringen/FlSt 6 & 19, Payerne
	J-3067	Northrop F-5E Tiger II	Swiss AF FlSt 8, Meiringen/FlSt 6 & 19, Payerne
	J-3068	Northrop F-5E Tiger II	Swiss AF FlSt 8, Meiringen/FlSt 6 & 19, Payerne
	J-3069	Northrop F-5E Tiger II	Swiss AF FlSt 8, Meiringen/FlSt 6 & 19, Payerne
	J-3070	Northrop F-5E Tiger II	Swiss AF FlSt 8, Meiringen/FlSt 6 & 19, Payerne
	J-3072	Northrop F-5E Tiger II	Swiss AF FlSt 8, Meiringen/FlSt 6 & 19, Payerne
	J-3073	Northrop F-5E Tiger II	Swiss AF, stored Emmen
	J-3074	Northrop F-5E Tiger II	Swiss AF FlSt 8, Meiringen/FlSt 6 & 19, Payerne
	J-3076	Northrop F-5E Tiger II	Swiss AF FlSt 8, Meiringen/FlSt 6 & 19, Payerne
	J-3077	Northrop F-5E Tiger II	Swiss AF FlSt 8, Meiringen/FlSt 6 & 19, Payerne
	J-3079	Northrop F-5E Tiger II	Swiss AF, stored Sion

Serial	Type (code/other identity)	Owner/operator, location or fate	Notes
J-3080	Northrop F-5E Tiger II	RUAG, Emmen	
J-3081	Northrop F-5E Tiger II	Swiss AF *Patrouille Suisse*, Emmen	
J-3082	Northrop F-5E Tiger II	Swiss AF *Patrouille Suisse*, Emmen	
J-3083	Northrop F-5E Tiger II	Swiss AF *Patrouille Suisse*, Emmen	
J-3084	Northrop F-5E Tiger II	Swiss AF *Patrouille Suisse*, Emmen	
J-3085	Northrop F-5E Tiger II	Swiss AF *Patrouille Suisse*, Emmen	
J-3086	Northrop F-5E Tiger II	*Crashed Leeuwarden, 9 June 2016*	
J-3087	Northrop F-5E Tiger II	Swiss AF *Patrouille Suisse*, Emmen	
J-3088	Northrop F-5E Tiger II	Swiss AF *Patrouille Suisse*, Emmen	
J-3089	Northrop F-5E Tiger II	Swiss AF *Patrouille Suisse*, Emmen	
J-3090	Northrop F-5E Tiger II	Swiss AF *Patrouille Suisse*, Emmen	
J-3091	Northrop F-5E Tiger II	Swiss AF *Patrouille Suisse*, Emmen	
J-3092	Northrop F-5E Tiger II	Swiss AF FlSt 8, Meiringen/FlSt 6 & 19, Payerne	
J-3093	Northrop F-5E Tiger II	Swiss AF FlSt 8, Meiringen/FlSt 6 & 19, Payerne	
J-3094	Northrop F-5E Tiger II	Swiss AF, stored Emmen	
J-3095	Northrop F-5E Tiger II	Swiss AF FlSt 8, Meiringen/FlSt 6 & 19, Payerne	
J-3097	Northrop F-5E Tiger II	Swiss AF FlSt 8, Meiringen/FlSt 6 & 19, Payerne	
J-3201	Northrop F-5F Tiger II	Swiss AF, stored Emmen	
J-3202	Northrop F-5F Tiger II	Swiss AF, stored Dübendorf	
J-3203	Northrop F-5F Tiger II	Swiss AF FlSt 8, Meiringen/FlSt 6 & 19, Payerne	
J-3204	Northrop F-5F Tiger II	Swiss AF FlSt 8, Meiringen/FlSt 6 & 19, Payerne	
J-3206	Northrop F-5F Tiger II	Swiss AF, stored Emmen	
J-3210	Northrop F-5F Tiger II	Swiss AF FlSt 8, Meiringen/FlSt 6 & 19, Payerne	
J-3211	Northrop F-5F Tiger II	Swiss AF FlSt 8, Meiringen/FlSt 6 & 19, Payerne	
J-3212	Northrop F-5F Tiger II	Swiss AF FlSt 8, Meiringen/FlSt 6 & 19, Payerne	
J-5001	McDonnell Douglas F/A-18C Hornet	Swiss AF FlSt 11, Meiringen/FlSt 17 & 18 Payerne	
J-5002	McDonnell Douglas F/A-18C Hornet	Swiss AF FlSt 11, Meiringen/FlSt 17 & 18 Payerne	
J-5003	McDonnell Douglas F/A-18C Hornet	Swiss AF FlSt 11, Meiringen/FlSt 17 & 18 Payerne	
J-5004	McDonnell Douglas F/A-18C Hornet	Swiss AF FlSt 11, Meiringen/FlSt 17 & 18 Payerne	
J-5005	McDonnell Douglas F/A-18C Hornet	Swiss AF FlSt 11, Meiringen/FlSt 17 & 18 Payerne	
J-5006	McDonnell Douglas F/A-18C Hornet	Swiss AF FlSt 11, Meiringen/FlSt 17 & 18 Payerne	
J-5007	McDonnell Douglas F/A-18C Hornet	Swiss AF FlSt 11, Meiringen/FlSt 17 & 18 Payerne	
J-5008	McDonnell Douglas F/A-18C Hornet	Swiss AF FlSt 11, Meiringen/FlSt 17 & 18 Payerne	
J-5009	McDonnell Douglas F/A-18C Hornet	Swiss AF FlSt 11, Meiringen/FlSt 17 & 18 Payerne	
J-5010	McDonnell Douglas F/A-18C Hornet	Swiss AF FlSt 11, Meiringen/FlSt 17 & 18 Payerne	
J-5011	McDonnell Douglas F/A-18C Hornet $	Swiss AF FlSt 11, Meiringen/FlSt 17 & 18 Payerne	
J-5012	McDonnell Douglas F/A-18C Hornet	Swiss AF FlSt 11, Meiringen/FlSt 17 & 18 Payerne	
J-5013	McDonnell Douglas F/A-18C Hornet	Swiss AF FlSt 11, Meiringen/FlSt 17 & 18 Payerne	
J-5014	McDonnell Douglas F/A-18C Hornet $	Swiss AF FlSt 11, Meiringen/FlSt 17 & 18 Payerne	
J-5015	McDonnell Douglas F/A-18C Hornet	Swiss AF FlSt 11, Meiringen/FlSt 17 & 18 Payerne	
J-5016	McDonnell Douglas F/A-18C Hornet	Swiss AF FlSt 11, Meiringen/FlSt 17 & 18 Payerne	
J-5017	McDonnell Douglas F/A-18C Hornet $	Swiss AF FlSt 11, Meiringen/FlSt 17 & 18 Payerne	
J-5018	McDonnell Douglas F/A-18C Hornet $	Swiss AF FlSt 11, Meiringen/FlSt 17 & 18 Payerne	
J-5019	McDonnell Douglas F/A-18C Hornet	Swiss AF FlSt 11, Meiringen/FlSt 17 & 18 Payerne	
J-5020	McDonnell Douglas F/A-18C Hornet	Swiss AF FlSt 11, Meiringen/FlSt 17 & 18 Payerne	
J-5021	McDonnell Douglas F/A-18C Hornet	Swiss AF FlSt 11, Meiringen/FlSt 17 & 18 Payerne	
J-5022	McDonnell Douglas F/A-18C Hornet	*Crashed Susten Pass, 29 August 2016*	
J-5023	McDonnell Douglas F/A-18C Hornet	Swiss AF FlSt 11, Meiringen/FlSt 17 & 18 Payerne	
J-5024	McDonnell Douglas F/A-18C Hornet	Swiss AF FlSt 11, Meiringen/FlSt 17 & 18 Payerne	
J-5025	McDonnell Douglas F/A-18C Hornet	Swiss AF FlSt 11, Meiringen/FlSt 17 & 18 Payerne	
J-5026	McDonnell Douglas F/A-18C Hornet	Swiss AF FlSt 11, Meiringen/FlSt 17 & 18 Payerne	
J-5232	McDonnell Douglas F/A-18D Hornet	Swiss AF FlSt 11, Meiringen/FlSt 17 & 18 Payerne	
J-5233	McDonnell Douglas F/A-18D Hornet	Swiss AF FlSt 11, Meiringen/FlSt 17 & 18 Payerne	
J-5234	McDonnell Douglas F/A-18D Hornet	Swiss AF FlSt 11, Meiringen/FlSt 17 & 18 Payerne	
J-5236	McDonnell Douglas F/A-18D Hornet	Swiss AF FlSt 11, Meiringen/FlSt 17 & 18 Payerne	
J-5238	McDonnell Douglas F/A-18D Hornet	Swiss AF FlSt 11, Meiringen/FlSt 17 & 18 Payerne	
R-711	Aurora Flight Services Centaur OPA	Armasuisse, Emmen	
T-311	Aérospatiale AS.332M-1 Super Puma (TH 89)	Swiss AF LtSt 6 & 8, Alpnach/ LtSt 3 & 4, Dübendorf/LtSt 1 & 5, Payerne	
T-312	Aérospatiale AS.332M-1 Super Puma (TH 89)	Swiss AF LtSt 6 & 8, Alpnach/ LtSt 3 & 4, Dübendorf/LtSt 1 & 5, Payerne	

Notes	Serial	Type (code/other identity)	Owner/operator, location or fate
	T-313	Aérospatiale AS.332M-1 Super Puma (TH 89)	Swiss AF LtSt 6 & 8, Alpnach/ LtSt 3 & 4, Dübendorf/LtSt 1 & 5, Payerne
	T-314	Aérospatiale AS.332M-1 Super Puma (TH 89)	Swiss AF LtSt 6 & 8, Alpnach/ LtSt 3 & 4, Dübendorf/LtSt 1 & 5, Payerne
	T-315	Aérospatiale AS.332M-1 Super Puma (TH 89)	Swiss AF LtSt 6 & 8, Alpnach/ LtSt 3 & 4, Dübendorf/LtSt 1 & 5, Payerne
	T-316	Aérospatiale AS.332M-1 Super Puma (TH 89) $	Swiss AF LtSt 6 & 8, Alpnach/ LtSt 3 & 4, Dübendorf/LtSt 1 & 5, Payerne
	T-317	Aérospatiale AS.332M-1 Super Puma (TH 89)	Swiss AF LtSt 6 & 8, Alpnach/ LtSt 3 & 4, Dübendorf/LtSt 1 & 5, Payerne
	T-318	Aérospatiale AS.332M-1 Super Puma (TH 89)	Swiss AF LtSt 6 & 8, Alpnach/ LtSt 3 & 4, Dübendorf/LtSt 1 & 5, Payerne
	T-319	Aérospatiale AS.332M-1 Super Puma (TH 89)	Swiss AF LtSt 6 & 8, Alpnach/ LtSt 3 & 4, Dübendorf/LtSt 1 & 5, Payerne
	T-320	Aérospatiale AS.332M-1 Super Puma (TH 89)	Swiss AF LtSt 6 & 8, Alpnach/ LtSt 3 & 4, Dübendorf/LtSt 1 & 5, Payerne
	T-321	Aérospatiale AS.332M-1 Super Puma (TH 89)	Swiss AF LtSt 6 & 8, Alpnach/ LtSt 3 & 4, Dübendorf/LtSt 1 & 5, Payerne
	T-322	Aérospatiale AS.332M-1 Super Puma (TH 89)	Swiss AF LtSt 6 & 8, Alpnach/ LtSt 3 & 4, Dübendorf/LtSt 1 & 5, Payerne
	T-323	Aérospatiale AS.332M-1 Super Puma (TH 89)	Swiss AF LtSt 6 & 8, Alpnach/ LtSt 3 & 4, Dübendorf/LtSt 1 & 5, Payerne
	T-324	Aérospatiale AS.332M-1 Super Puma (TH 89)	Swiss AF LtSt 6 & 8, Alpnach/ LtSt 3 & 4, Dübendorf/LtSt 1 & 5, Payerne
	T-325	Aérospatiale AS.332M-1 Super Puma (TH 89)	Swiss AF LtSt 6 & 8, Alpnach/ LtSt 3 & 4, Dübendorf/LtSt 1 & 5, Payerne
	T-331	Aérospatiale AS.532UL Super Puma (TH 98)	Swiss AF LtSt 6 & 8, Alpnach/ LtSt 3 & 4, Dübendorf/LtSt 1 & 5, Payerne
	T-332	Aérospatiale AS.532UL Super Puma (TH 98)	Swiss AF LtSt 6 & 8, Alpnach/ LtSt 3 & 4, Dübendorf/LtSt 1 & 5, Payerne
	T-333	Aérospatiale AS.532UL Super Puma (TH 98)	Swiss AF LtSt 6 & 8, Alpnach/ LtSt 3 & 4, Dübendorf/LtSt 1 & 5, Payerne
	T-334	Aérospatiale AS.532UL Super Puma (TH 98)	Swiss AF LtSt 6 & 8, Alpnach/ LtSt 3 & 4, Dübendorf/LtSt 1 & 5, Payerne
	T-335	Aérospatiale AS.532UL Super Puma (TH 98)	Swiss AF LtSt 6 & 8, Alpnach/ LtSt 3 & 4, Dübendorf/LtSt 1 & 5, Payerne
	T-336	Aérospatiale AS.532UL Super Puma (TH 98)	Swiss AF LtSt 6 & 8, Alpnach/ LtSt 3 & 4, Dübendorf/LtSt 1 & 5, Payerne
	T-337	Aérospatiale AS.532UL Super Puma (TH 98)	Swiss AF LtSt 6 & 8, Alpnach/ LtSt 3 & 4, Dübendorf/LtSt 1 & 5, Payerne
	T-338	Aérospatiale AS.532UL Super Puma (TH 98)	*Crashed Gotthard Pass, 28 September 2016*
	T-339	Aérospatiale AS.532UL Super Puma (TH 98)	Swiss AF LtSt 6 & 8, Alpnach/ LtSt 3 & 4, Dübendorf/LtSt 1 & 5, Payerne
	T-340	Aérospatiale AS.532UL Super Puma (TH 98)	Swiss AF LtSt 6 & 8, Alpnach/ LtSt 3 & 4, Dübendorf/LtSt 1 & 5, Payerne
	T-342	Aérospatiale AS.532UL Super Puma (TH 98)	Swiss AF LtSt 6 & 8, Alpnach/ LtSt 3 & 4, Dübendorf/LtSt 1 & 5, Payerne
	T-351	Eurocopter EC.135P-2	Swiss AF LTDB, Dübendorf
	T-352	Eurocopter EC.135P-2	Swiss AF LTDB, Dübendorf
	T-353	Eurocopter EC.635P-2	Swiss AF LtSt 6 & 8, Alpnach/ LtSt 3 & 4, Dübendorf/LtSt 1 & 5, Payerne
	T-354	Eurocopter EC.635P-2	Swiss AF LtSt 6 & 8, Alpnach/ LtSt 3 & 4, Dübendorf/LtSt 1 & 5, Payerne
	T-355	Eurocopter EC.635P-2	Swiss AF LtSt 6 & 8, Alpnach/ LtSt 3 & 4, Dübendorf/LtSt 1 & 5, Payerne
	T-356	Eurocopter EC.635P-2	Swiss AF LtSt 6 & 8, Alpnach/ LtSt 3 & 4, Dübendorf/LtSt 1 & 5, Payerne
	T-357	Eurocopter EC.635P-2	Swiss AF LtSt 6 & 8, Alpnach/ LtSt 3 & 4, Dübendorf/LtSt 1 & 5, Payerne
	T-358	Eurocopter EC.635P-2	Swiss AF LtSt 6 & 8, Alpnach/ LtSt 3 & 4, Dübendorf/LtSt 1 & 5, Payerne

Serial	Type (code/other identity)	Owner/operator, location or fate	Notes
T-359	Eurocopter EC.635P-2	Swiss AF LtSt 6 & 8, Alpnach/ LtSt 3 & 4, Dübendorf/LtSt 1 & 5, Payerne	
T-360	Eurocopter EC.635P-2	Swiss AF LtSt 6 & 8, Alpnach/ LtSt 3 & 4, Dübendorf/LtSt 1 & 5, Payerne	
T-361	Eurocopter EC.635P-2	Swiss AF LtSt 6 & 8, Alpnach/ LtSt 3 & 4, Dübendorf/LtSt 1 & 5, Payerne	
T-362	Eurocopter EC.635P-2	Swiss AF LtSt 6 & 8, Alpnach/ LtSt 3 & 4, Dübendorf/LtSt 1 & 5, Payerne	
T-363	Eurocopter EC.635P-2	Swiss AF LtSt 6 & 8, Alpnach/ LtSt 3 & 4, Dübendorf/LtSt 1 & 5, Payerne	
T-364	Eurocopter EC.635P-2	Swiss AF LtSt 6 & 8, Alpnach/ LtSt 3 & 4, Dübendorf/LtSt 1 & 5, Payerne	
T-365	Eurocopter EC.635P-2	Swiss AF LtSt 6 & 8, Alpnach/ LtSt 3 & 4, Dübendorf/LtSt 1 & 5, Payerne	
T-366	Eurocopter EC.635P-2	Swiss AF LtSt 6 & 8, Alpnach/ LtSt 3 & 4, Dübendorf/LtSt 1 & 5, Payerne	
T-367	Eurocopter EC.635P-2	Swiss AF LtSt 6 & 8, Alpnach/ LtSt 3 & 4, Dübendorf/LtSt 1 & 5, Payerne	
T-368	Eurocopter EC.635P-2	Swiss AF LtSt 6 & 8, Alpnach/ LtSt 3 & 4, Dübendorf/LtSt 1 & 5, Payerne	
T-369	Eurocopter EC.635P-2	Swiss AF LtSt 6 & 8, Alpnach/ LtSt 3 & 4, Dübendorf/LtSt 1 & 5, Payerne	
T-370	Eurocopter EC.635P-2	Swiss AF LtSt 6 & 8, Alpnach/ LtSt 3 & 4, Dübendorf/LtSt 1 & 5, Payerne	
T-721	Beech King Air 350C	Swiss AF LTDB, Dübendorf	
T-729	Beech 1900D	Swiss AF LTDB, Dübendorf	
T-784	Cessna 560XL Citation Excel	Swiss AF LTDB, Dübendorf	
T-785	Dassault Falcon 900EX EASy II	Swiss AF LTDB, Bern/Belp	
V-612	Pilatus PC.6B/B2-H2 Turbo Porter	Swiss AF LtSt 7, Emmen	
V-613	Pilatus PC.6B/B2-H2 Turbo Porter	Swiss AF LtSt 7, Emmen	
V-614	Pilatus PC.6B/B2-H2 Turbo Porter	Swiss AF LtSt 7, Emmen	
V-616	Pilatus PC.6B/B2-H2 Turbo Porter	Swiss AF LtSt 7, Emmen	
V-617	Pilatus PC.6B/B2-H2 Turbo Porter	Swiss AF LtSt 7, Emmen	
V-618	Pilatus PC.6B/B2-H2 Turbo Porter	Swiss AF LtSt 7, Emmen	
V-619	Pilatus PC.6B/B2-H2 Turbo Porter	Swiss AF LtSt 7, Emmen	
V-620	Pilatus PC.6B/B2-H2 Turbo Porter	Swiss AF LtSt 7, Emmen	
V-622	Pilatus PC.6B/B2-H2 Turbo Porter $	Swiss AF LtSt 7, Emmen	
V-623	Pilatus PC.6B/B2-H2 Turbo Porter	Swiss AF LtSt 7, Emmen	
V-631	Pilatus PC.6B/B2-H2 Turbo Porter	Swiss AF LtSt 7, Emmen	
V-632	Pilatus PC.6B/B2-H2 Turbo Porter	Swiss AF LtSt 7, Emmen	
V-633	Pilatus PC.6B/B2-H2 Turbo Porter	Swiss AF LtSt 7, Emmen	
V-634	Pilatus PC.6B/B2-H2 Turbo Porter	Swiss AF LtSt 7, Emmen	
V-635	Pilatus PC.6B/B2-H2 Turbo Porter	Swiss AF LtSt 7, Emmen	

Swiss Government

| HB-FOG | Pilatus PC-12/45 | Armasuisse, Emmen | |

SYRIA

| YK-ASC | Dassault Falcon 900 | Government of Syria, Damascus | |

TANZANIA

| 5H-ONE | Gulfstream Aerospace G.550 | Tanzanian Government, Dar-es-Salaam | |

THAILAND

HS-CMV	Boeing 737-4Z6 [11-111, 90401]	Royal Flight, Bangkok	
HS-HRH	Boeing 737-448 [99-999, 90409]	Royal Flight, Bangkok	
HS-TYQ	Airbus A.310-324 (B.L13-1/34) [60201]	Withdrawn from use at Bangkok, 31 March 2016	
HS-TYR	Airbus A.319CJ-133 (B.L15-1/47) [60202]	Royal Thai AF 6 Wing, Don Muang	
HS-TYS	Boeing 737-8Z6 (L11Kh2-1/50) [55-555]	Royal Flight, Bangkok	
HS-TYT	Airbus A.320CJ-214 (L15K-1/58) [60203]	Royal Thai AF 6 Wing, Don Muang	
HS-TYU	Boeing 737-8Z6 (L11Kh2-2/59) [60205]	Royal Thai AF 6 Wing, Don Muang	
HS-TYV	Airbus A.340-541 (L19-1/59) [60204]	Royal Thai AF 6 Wing, Don Muang	
L18-1/59	Sukhoi SSJ100-95LR Superjet [60317]	Royal Thai AF 6 Wing, Don Muang	

Notes	Serial	Type (code/other identity)	Owner/operator, location or fate
	L18-2/59	Sukhoi SSJ100-95LR Superjet [60318]	Royal Thai AF 6 Wing, Don Muang
	L18-3/59	Sukhoi SSJ100-95LR Superjet [60318]	Royal Thai AF (on order)
	TUNISIA		
	Tunisian Air Force/Al Quwwat al-Jawwiya al-Jamahiriyah At'Tunisia & Tunisian Government		
	Z21012	Lockheed C-130H Hercules (TS-MTB)	Tunisian AF 21 Sqn, Bizerte/Sidi Ahmed
	Z21121	Lockheed C-130J-30 Hercules II (TS-MTK)	Tunisian AF 21 Sqn, Bizerte/Sidi Ahmed
	Z21122	Lockheed C-130J-30 Hercules II (TS-MTL)	Tunisian AF 21 Sqn, Bizerte/Sidi Ahmed
	TS-IOO	Boeing 737-7HJ	Government of Tunisia, Tunis
	TURKEY		
	Please note: Following the failed coup in July 2016, a number of bases will be closed and aircraft dispersed to other squadrons.		
	Türk Hava Kuvvetleri (THK)/Turkish Air Force & Turkish Government		
	004	Cessna 650 Citation VII	THK 212 Filo/11 HUAÜK, Ankara/Etimesgut
	3004	Canadair NF-5A-2000 Freedom Fighter	THK 134 Filo, *Turkish Stars*/3 AJEÜ, Konya
	3023	Canadair NF-5A-2000 Freedom Fighter	THK 134 Filo, *Turkish Stars*/3 AJEÜ, Konya
	3025	Canadair NF-5A-2000 Freedom Fighter	THK 134 Filo, *Turkish Stars*/3 AJEÜ, Konya
	3027	Canadair NF-5A-2000 Freedom Fighter	THK 134 Filo, *Turkish Stars*/3 AJEÜ, Konya
	3032	Canadair NF-5A-2000 Freedom Fighter	THK 134 Filo, *Turkish Stars*/3 AJEÜ, Konya
	3036	Canadair NF-5A-2000 Freedom Fighter	THK 134 Filo, *Turkish Stars*/3 AJEÜ, Konya
	3039	Canadair NF-5A-2000 Freedom Fighter	THK 134 Filo, *Turkish Stars*/3 AJEÜ, Konya
	3046	Canadair NF-5A-2000 Freedom Fighter [7]	THK 134 Filo, *Turkish Stars*/3 AJEÜ, Konya
	3048	Canadair NF-5A-2000 Freedom Fighter [5]	THK 134 Filo, *Turkish Stars*/3 AJEÜ, Konya
	3049	Canadair NF-5A-2000 Freedom Fighter [6]	THK 134 Filo, *Turkish Stars*/3 AJEÜ, Konya
	3052	Canadair NF-5A-2000 Freedom Fighter [2]	THK 134 Filo, *Turkish Stars*/3 AJEÜ, Konya
	3058	Canadair NF-5A-2000 Freedom Fighter [3]	THK 134 Filo, *Turkish Stars*/3 AJEÜ, Konya
	3066	Canadair NF-5A-2000 Freedom Fighter	THK 134 Filo, *Turkish Stars*/3 AJEÜ, Konya
	3072	Canadair NF-5A-2000 Freedom Fighter	THK 134 Filo, *Turkish Stars*/3 AJEÜ, Konya
	4005	Canadair NF-5B-2000 Freedom Fighter	THK 134 Filo, *Turkish Stars*/3 AJEÜ, Konya
	4009	Canadair NF-5B-2000 Freedom Fighter	THK 134 Filo, *Turkish Stars*/3 AJEÜ, Konya
	4013	Canadair NF-5B-2000 Freedom Fighter	THK 134 Filo, *Turkish Stars*/3 AJEÜ, Konya
	4020	Canadair NF-5B-2000 Freedom Fighter	THK 134 Filo, *Turkish Stars*/3 AJEÜ, Konya
	4021	Canadair NF-5B-2000 Freedom Fighter	THK 134 Filo, *Turkish Stars*/3 AJEÜ, Konya
	57-2609	Boeing KC-135R Stratotanker	THK 101 Filo/10 TÜK, Incirlik
	58-0110	Boeing KC-135R Stratotanker	THK 101 Filo/10 TÜK, Incirlik
	60-0325	Boeing KC-135R Stratotanker	THK 101 Filo/10 TÜK, Incirlik
	60-0326	Boeing KC-135R Stratotanker	THK 101 Filo/10 TÜK, Incirlik
	62-3539	Boeing KC-135R Stratotanker	THK 101 Filo/10 TÜK, Incirlik
	62-3563	Boeing KC-135R Stratotanker	THK 101 Filo/10 TÜK, Incirlik
	62-3567	Boeing KC-135R Stratotanker	THK 101 Filo/10 TÜK, Incirlik
	63-3186	Lockheed C-130E Hercules (63-13186)	THK 222 Filo/12 HUAÜ, Erkilet
	63-13187	Lockheed C-130E Hercules	THK 222 Filo/12 HUAÜ, Erkilet
	63-3188	Lockheed C-130E Hercules (63-13188)	THK 222 Filo/12 HUAÜ, Erkilet
	63-13189	Lockheed C-130E Hercules $	THK 222 Filo/12 HUAÜ, Erkilet
	65-0451	Lockheed C-130E Hercules	THK 222 Filo/12 HUAÜ, Erkilet
	67-0455	Lockheed C-130E Hercules	THK 222 Filo/12 HUAÜ, Erkilet
	68-020	Transall C-160D	THK 221 Filo/12 HUAÜ, Erkilet
	68-023	Transall C-160D	THK 221 Filo/12 HUAÜ, Erkilet
	68-01606	Lockheed C-130E Hercules	THK 222 Filo/12 HUAÜ, Erkilet
	68-01608	Lockheed C-130E Hercules	THK 222 Filo/12 HUAÜ, Erkilet
	68-01609	Lockheed C-130E Hercules	THK 222 Filo/12 HUAÜ, Erkilet
	69-019	Transall C-160D	THK 221 Filo/12 HUAÜ, Erkilet
	69-021	Transall C-160D	THK 221 Filo/12 HUAÜ, Erkilet
	69-024	Transall C-160D	THK 221 Filo/12 HUAÜ, Erkilet
	69-026	Transall C-160D	THK 221 Filo/12 HUAÜ, Erkilet
	69-027	Transall C-160D	THK 221 Filo/12 HUAÜ, Erkilet
	69-029	Transall C-160D	THK 221 Filo/12 HUAÜ, Erkilet
	69-031	Transall C-160D	THK 221 Filo/12 HUAÜ, Erkilet
	69-032	Transall C-160D	THK 221 Filo/12 HUAÜ, Erkilet
	69-033	Transall C-160D $	THK 221 Filo/12 HUAÜ, Erkilet
	69-034	Transall C-160D	THK 221 Filo/12 HUAÜ, Erkilet

Serial	Type (code/other identity)	Owner/operator, location or fate	Notes
69-036	Transall C-160D	THK 221 Filo/12 HUAÜ, Erkilet	
69-040	Transall C-160D $	THK 221 Filo/12 HUAÜ, Erkilet	
70-01610	Lockheed C-130E Hercules	THK 222 Filo/12 HUAÜ, Erkilet	
70-1947	Lockheed C-130E Hercules	THK 222 Filo/12 HUAÜ, Erkilet	
71-01468	Lockheed C-130E Hercules	THK 222 Filo/12 HUAÜ, Erkilet	
73-0991	Lockheed C-130E Hercules $	THK 222 Filo/12 HUAÜ, Erkilet	
86-0066	TUSAS (GD) F-16C-30 Fighting Falcon	THK 132 Filo/3 AJEÜ, Konya	
86-0068	TUSAS (GD) F-16C-30 Fighting Falcon	THK 132 Filo/3 AJEÜ, Konya	
86-0069	TUSAS (GD) F-16C-30 Fighting Falcon	THK 132 Filo/3 AJEÜ, Konya	
86-0070	TUSAS (GD) F-16C-30 Fighting Falcon	THK 152 Filo/5 AJÜ, Merzifon	
86-0071	TUSAS (GD) F-16C-30 Fighting Falcon	THK 152 Filo/5 AJÜ, Merzifon	
86-0072	TUSAS (GD) F-16C-30 Fighting Falcon	THK 152 Filo/5 AJÜ, Merzifon	
86-0192	TUSAS (GD) F-16D-30 Fighting Falcon	THK 132 Filo/3 AJEÜ, Konya	
86-0193	TUSAS (GD) F-16D-30 Fighting Falcon	THK 132 Filo/3 AJEÜ, Konya	
86-0194	TUSAS (GD) F-16D-30 Fighting Falcon	THK 132 Filo/3 AJEÜ, Konya	
86-0195	TUSAS (GD) F-16D-30 Fighting Falcon	THK 132 Filo/3 AJEÜ, Konya	
86-0196	TUSAS (GD) F-16D-30 Fighting Falcon	THK 132 Filo/3 AJEÜ, Konya	
87-0002	TUSAS (GD) F-16D-30 Fighting Falcon	THK 113 Filo/1 AJÜ, Eskisehir	
87-0003	TUSAS (GD) F-16D-30 Fighting Falcon	THK 401 Filo/1 AJÜ, Eskisehir	
87-0009	TUSAS (GD) F-16C-30 Fighting Falcon	THK 113 Filo/1 AJÜ, Eskisehir	
87-0010	TUSAS (GD) F-16C-30 Fighting Falcon	THK 132 Filo/3 AJEÜ, Konya	
87-0011	TUSAS (GD) F-16C-30 Fighting Falcon	THK 132 Filo/3 AJEÜ, Konya	
87-0013	TUSAS (GD) F-16C-30 Fighting Falcon	THK 152 Filo/5 AJÜ, Merzifon	
87-0014	TUSAS (GD) F-16C-30 Fighting Falcon	THK 113 Filo/1 AJÜ, Eskisehir	
87-0015	TUSAS (GD) F-16C-30 Fighting Falcon	THK 113 Filo/1 AJÜ, Eskisehir	
87-0016	TUSAS (GD) F-16C-30 Fighting Falcon	THK 132 Filo/3 AJEÜ, Konya	
87-0017	TUSAS (GD) F-16C-30 Fighting Falcon	THK 152 Filo/5 AJÜ, Merzifon	
87-0018	TUSAS (GD) F-16C-30 Fighting Falcon	THK 152 Filo/5 AJÜ, Merzifon	
87-0019	TUSAS (GD) F-16C-30 Fighting Falcon	THK 132 Filo/3 AJEÜ, Konya	
87-0020	TUSAS (GD) F-16C-30 Fighting Falcon	THK 152 Filo/5 AJÜ, Merzifon	
87-0021	TUSAS (GD) F-16C-30 Fighting Falcon	THK 132 Filo/3 AJEÜ, Konya	
88-0013	TUSAS (GD) F-16D-30 Fighting Falcon	THK 152 Filo/5 AJÜ, Merzifon	
88-0014	TUSAS (GD) F-16D-40 Fighting Falcon	THK 192 Filo/9 AJÜ, Balikesir	
88-0015	TUSAS (GD) F-16D-40 Fighting Falcon	THK 191 Filo/9 AJÜ, Balikesir	
88-0019	TUSAS (GD) F-16C-30 Fighting Falcon	THK 132 Filo/3 AJEÜ, Konya	
88-0020	TUSAS (GD) F-16C-30 Fighting Falcon	THK 132 Filo/3 AJEÜ, Konya	
88-0021	TUSAS (GD) F-16C-30 Fighting Falcon	THK 152 Filo/5 AJÜ, Merzifon	
88-0024	TUSAS (GD) F-16C-30 Fighting Falcon	THK 152 Filo/5 AJÜ, Merzifon	
88-0025	TUSAS (GD) F-16C-30 Fighting Falcon	THK 152 Filo/5 AJÜ, Merzifon	
88-0026	TUSAS (GD) F-16C-30 Fighting Falcon	THK 152 Filo/5 AJÜ, Merzifon	
88-0027	TUSAS (GD) F-16C-30 Fighting Falcon	THK 152 Filo/5 AJÜ, Merzifon	
88-0028	TUSAS (GD) F-16C-30 Fighting Falcon	THK 191 Filo/9 AJÜ, Balikesir	
88-0029	TUSAS (GD) F-16C-30 Fighting Falcon $	THK 132 Filo/3 AJEÜ, Konya	
88-0030	TUSAS (GD) F-16C-30 Fighting Falcon	THK 152 Filo/5 AJÜ, Merzifon	
88-0031	TUSAS (GD) F-16C-30 Fighting Falcon	THK 401 Filo/1 AJÜ, Eskisehir	
88-0032	TUSAS (GD) F-16C-30 Fighting Falcon $	THK 132 Filo/3 AJEÜ, Konya	
88-0033	TUSAS (GD) F-16C-40 Fighting Falcon	THK 152 Filo/5 AJÜ, Merzifon	
88-0034	TUSAS (GD) F-16C-40 Fighting Falcon	THK 191 Filo/9 AJÜ, Balikesir	
88-0035	TUSAS (GD) F-16C-40 Fighting Falcon	THK 152 Filo/5 AJÜ, Merzifon	
88-0036	TUSAS (GD) F-16C-40 Fighting Falcon	THK 191 Filo/9 AJÜ, Balikesir	
88-0037	TUSAS (GD) F-16C-40 Fighting Falcon	THK 182 Filo/8 AJÜ, Diyarbakir	
89-0022	TUSAS (GD) F-16C-40 Fighting Falcon	THK	
89-0023	TUSAS (GD) F-16C-40 Fighting Falcon	THK 192 Filo/9 AJÜ, Balikesir	
89-0024	TUSAS (GD) F-16C-40 Fighting Falcon	THK 192 Filo/9 AJÜ, Balikesir	
89-0025	TUSAS (GD) F-16C-40 Fighting Falcon	THK 191 Filo/9 AJÜ, Balikesir	
89-0026	TUSAS (GD) F-16C-40 Fighting Falcon	THK	
89-0027	TUSAS (GD) F-16C-40 Fighting Falcon	THK	
89-0028	TUSAS (GD) F-16C-40 Fighting Falcon	THK	
89-0030	TUSAS (GD) F-16C-40 Fighting Falcon	THK	
89-0031	TUSAS (GD) F-16C-40 Fighting Falcon	THK	
89-0034	TUSAS (GD) F-16C-40 Fighting Falcon	THK	
89-0035	TUSAS (GD) F-16C-40 Fighting Falcon	THK 152 Filo/5 AJÜ, Merzifon	

Notes	Serial	Type (code/other identity)	Owner/operator, location or fate
	89-0036	TUSAS (GD) F-16C-40 Fighting Falcon	THK
	89-0037	TUSAS (GD) F-16C-40 Fighting Falcon	THK
	89-0038	TUSAS (GD) F-16C-40 Fighting Falcon	THK
	89-0039	TUSAS (GD) F-16C-40 Fighting Falcon	THK 152 Filo/5 AJÜ, Merzifon
	89-0040	TUSAS (GD) F-16C-40 Fighting Falcon	THK 192 Filo/9 AJÜ, Balikesir
	89-0041	TUSAS (GD) F-16C-40 Fighting Falcon	THK 152 Filo/5 AJÜ, Merzifon
	89-0042	TUSAS (GD) F-16D-40 Fighting Falcon	THK 191 Filo/9 AJÜ, Balikesir
	89-0043	TUSAS (GD) F-16D-40 Fighting Falcon	THK 192 Filo/9 AJÜ, Balikesir
	89-0044	TUSAS (GD) F-16D-40 Fighting Falcon	THK 132 Filo/3 AJEÜ, Konya
	89-0045	TUSAS (GD) F-16D-40 Fighting Falcon	THK 152 Filo/5 AJÜ, Merzifon
	90-0004	TUSAS (GD) F-16C-40 Fighting Falcon	THK 152 Filo/5 AJÜ, Merzifon
	90-0005	TUSAS (GD) F-16C-40 Fighting Falcon	THK 191 Filo/9 AJÜ, Balikesir
	90-0006	TUSAS (GD) F-16C-40 Fighting Falcon	THK 182 Filo/8 AJÜ, Diyarbakir
	90-0007	TUSAS (GD) F-16C-40 Fighting Falcon	THK
	90-0008	TUSAS (GD) F-16C-40 Fighting Falcon	THK
	90-0009	TUSAS (GD) F-16C-40 Fighting Falcon	THK
	90-0010	TUSAS (GD) F-16C-40 Fighting Falcon	THK
	90-0011	TUSAS (GD) F-16C-40 Fighting Falcon $	THK
	90-0012	TUSAS (GD) F-16C-40 Fighting Falcon	THK 191 Filo/9 AJÜ, Balikesir
	90-0013	TUSAS (GD) F-16C-40 Fighting Falcon	THK 182 Filo/8 AJÜ, Diyarbakir
	90-0014	TUSAS (GD) F-16C-40 Fighting Falcon $	THK
	90-0016	TUSAS (GD) F-16C-40 Fighting Falcon	THK 182 Filo/8 AJÜ, Diyarbakir
	90-0017	TUSAS (GD) F-16C-40 Fighting Falcon	THK 191 Filo/9 AJÜ, Balikesir
	90-0018	TUSAS (GD) F-16C-40 Fighting Falcon	THK 191 Filo/9 AJÜ, Balikesir
	90-0019	TUSAS (GD) F-16C-40 Fighting Falcon	THK
	90-0020	TUSAS (GD) F-16C-40 Fighting Falcon	THK
	90-0021	TUSAS (GD) F-16C-40 Fighting Falcon	THK
	90-0022	TUSAS (GD) F-16D-40 Fighting Falcon	THK 182 Filo/8 AJÜ, Diyarbakir
	90-0023	TUSAS (GD) F-16D-40 Fighting Falcon	THK 152 Filo/5 AJÜ, Merzifon
	90-0024	TUSAS (GD) F-16D-40 Fighting Falcon	THK 182 Filo/8 AJÜ, Diyarbakir
	91-003	Grumman G.1159C Gulfstream IV	THK 212 Filo/11 HUAÜK, Ankara/Etimesgut
	91-0001	TUSAS (GD) F-16C-40 Fighting Falcon	THK
	91-0002	TUSAS (GD) F-16C-40 Fighting Falcon	THK 401 Filo/1 AJÜ, Eskisehir
	91-0003	TUSAS (GD) F-16C-40 Fighting Falcon	THK 182 Filo/8 AJÜ, Diyarbakir
	91-0004	TUSAS (GD) F-16C-40 Fighting Falcon	THK
	91-0005	TUSAS (GD) F-16C-40 Fighting Falcon	THK 182 Filo/8 AJÜ, Diyarbakir
	91-0006	TUSAS (GD) F-16C-40 Fighting Falcon	THK
	91-0007	TUSAS (GD) F-16C-40 Fighting Falcon	THK
	91-0008	TUSAS (GD) F-16C-40 Fighting Falcon	THK 192 Filo/9 AJÜ, Balikesir
	91-0010	TUSAS (GD) F-16C-40 Fighting Falcon	THK
	91-0011	TUSAS (GD) F-16C-40 Fighting Falcon $	THK
	91-0012	TUSAS (GD) F-16C-40 Fighting Falcon	THK
	91-0013	TUSAS (GD) F-16C-40 Fighting Falcon	THK 192 Filo/9 AJÜ, Balikesir
	91-0014	TUSAS (GD) F-16C-40 Fighting Falcon	THK
	91-0015	TUSAS (GD) F-16C-40 Fighting Falcon	THK 401 Filo/1 AJÜ, Eskisehir
	91-0016	TUSAS (GD) F-16C-40 Fighting Falcon	THK 182 Filo/8 AJÜ, Diyarbakir
	91-0017	TUSAS (GD) F-16C-40 Fighting Falcon	THK 182 Filo/8 AJÜ, Diyarbakir
	91-0018	TUSAS (GD) F-16C-40 Fighting Falcon	THK 191 Filo/9 AJÜ, Balikesir
	91-0020	TUSAS (GD) F-16C-40 Fighting Falcon	THK
	91-0022	TUSAS (GD) F-16D-40 Fighting Falcon	THK 191 Filo/9 AJÜ, Balikesir
	91-0024	TUSAS (GD) F-16D-40 Fighting Falcon	THK
	92-0001	TUSAS (GD) F-16C-40 Fighting Falcon	THK 182 Filo/8 AJÜ, Diyarbakir
	92-0002	TUSAS (GD) F-16C-40 Fighting Falcon	THK 182 Filo/8 AJÜ, Diyarbakir
	92-0003	TUSAS (GD) F-16C-40 Fighting Falcon	THK 191 Filo/9 AJÜ, Balikesir
	92-0004	TUSAS (GD) F-16C-40 Fighting Falcon	THK
	92-0005	TUSAS (GD) F-16C-40 Fighting Falcon	THK 192 Filo/9 AJÜ, Balikesir
	92-0006	TUSAS (GD) F-16C-40 Fighting Falcon	THK 182 Filo/8 AJÜ, Diyarbakir
	92-0007	TUSAS (GD) F-16C-40 Fighting Falcon	THK 192 Filo/9 AJÜ, Balikesir
	92-0008	TUSAS (GD) F-16C-40 Fighting Falcon	THK 152 Filo/5 AJÜ, Merzifon
	92-0009	TUSAS (GD) F-16C-40 Fighting Falcon	THK 191 Filo/9 AJÜ, Balikesir
	92-0010	TUSAS (GD) F-16C-40 Fighting Falcon	THK 191 Filo/9 AJÜ, Balikesir
	92-0011	TUSAS (GD) F-16C-40 Fighting Falcon	THK 182 Filo/8 AJÜ, Diyarbakir

Serial	Type (code/other identity)	Owner/operator, location or fate	Notes
92-0012	TUSAS (GD) F-16C-40 Fighting Falcon	THK 182 Filo/8 AJÜ, Diyarbakir	
92-0013	TUSAS (GD) F-16C-40 Fighting Falcon	THK	
92-0014	TUSAS (GD) F-16C-40 Fighting Falcon $	THK 192 Filo/9 AJÜ, Balikesir	
92-0015	TUSAS (GD) F-16C-40 Fighting Falcon	THK	
92-0016	TUSAS (GD) F-16C-40 Fighting Falcon	THK	
92-0017	TUSAS (GD) F-16C-40 Fighting Falcon	THK 152 Filo/5 AJÜ, Merzifon	
92-0018	TUSAS (GD) F-16C-40 Fighting Falcon	THK	
92-0019	TUSAS (GD) F-16C-40 Fighting Falcon	THK 181 Filo/8 AJÜ, Diyarbakir	
92-0020	TUSAS (GD) F-16C-40 Fighting Falcon	THK 181 Filo/8 AJÜ, Diyarbakir	
92-0021	TUSAS (GD) F-16C-40 Fighting Falcon	THK 191 Filo/9 AJÜ, Balikesir	
92-0022	TUSAS (GD) F-16D-40 Fighting Falcon	THK	
92-0023	TUSAS (GD) F-16D-40 Fighting Falcon	THK	
92-0024	TUSAS (GD) F-16D-40 Fighting Falcon	THK 191 Filo/9 AJÜ, Balikesir	
93-005	Cessna 650 Citation VII	THK 212 Filo/11 HUAÜK, Ankara/Etimesgut	
93-0001	TUSAS (GD) F-16C-40 Fighting Falcon	THK 401 Filo/1 AJÜ, Eskisehir	
93-0003	TUSAS (GD) F-16C-40 Fighting Falcon	THK 192 Filo/9 AJÜ, Balikesir	
93-0004	TUSAS (GD) F-16C-40 Fighting Falcon	THK 181 Filo/8 AJÜ, Diyarbakir	
93-0005	TUSAS (GD) F-16C-40 Fighting Falcon	THK 181 Filo/8 AJÜ, Diyarbakir	
93-0006	TUSAS (GD) F-16C-40 Fighting Falcon	THK 181 Filo/8 AJÜ, Diyarbakir	
93-0007	TUSAS (GD) F-16C-40 Fighting Falcon	THK 182 Filo/8 AJÜ, Diyarbakir	
93-0008	TUSAS (GD) F-16C-40 Fighting Falcon	THK 181 Filo/8 AJÜ, Diyarbakir	
93-0009	TUSAS (GD) F-16C-40 Fighting Falcon	THK 182 Filo/8 AJÜ, Diyarbakir	
93-0010	TUSAS (GD) F-16C-40 Fighting Falcon	THK 132 Filo/3 AJEÜ, Konya	
93-0011	TUSAS (GD) F-16C-40 Fighting Falcon	THK 181 Filo/8 AJÜ, Diyarbakir	
93-0012	TUSAS (GD) F-16C-40 Fighting Falcon	THK 181 Filo/8 AJÜ, Diyarbakir	
93-0013	TUSAS (GD) F-16C-40 Fighting Falcon	THK 181 Filo/8 AJÜ, Diyarbakir	
93-0658	TUSAS (GD) F-16C-50 Fighting Falcon	THK 132 Filo/3 AJEÜ, Konya	
93-0659	TUSAS (GD) F-16C-50 Fighting Falcon	THK 191 Filo/9 AJÜ, Balikesir	
93-0660	TUSAS (GD) F-16C-50 Fighting Falcon	THK 152 Filo/5 AJÜ, Merzifon	
93-0661	TUSAS (GD) F-16C-50 Fighting Falcon	THK 132 Filo/3 AJEÜ, Konya	
93-0663	TUSAS (GD) F-16C-50 Fighting Falcon	THK 401 Filo/1 AJÜ, Eskisehir	
93-0664	TUSAS (GD) F-16C-50 Fighting Falcon	THK 132 Filo/3 AJEÜ, Konya	
93-0665	TUSAS (GD) F-16C-50 Fighting Falcon	THK 191 Filo/9 AJÜ, Balikesir	
93-0667	TUSAS (GD) F-16C-50 Fighting Falcon	THK 151 Filo/5 AJÜ, Merzifon	
93-0668	TUSAS (GD) F-16C-50 Fighting Falcon	THK	
93-0669	TUSAS (GD) F-16C-50 Fighting Falcon	THK 151 Filo/5 AJÜ, Merzifon	
93-0670	TUSAS (GD) F-16C-50 Fighting Falcon	THK 191 Filo/9 AJÜ, Balikesir	
93-0671	TUSAS (GD) F-16C-50 Fighting Falcon	THK	
93-0672	TUSAS (GD) F-16C-50 Fighting Falcon	THK 132 Filo/3 AJEÜ, Konya	
93-0673	TUSAS (GD) F-16C-50 Fighting Falcon	THK 132 Filo/3 AJEÜ, Konya	
93-0674	TUSAS (GD) F-16C-50 Fighting Falcon	THK 132 Filo/3 AJEÜ, Konya	
93-0675	TUSAS (GD) F-16C-50 Fighting Falcon	THK 191 Filo/9 AJÜ, Balikesir	
93-0676	TUSAS (GD) F-16C-50 Fighting Falcon	THK 192 Filo/9 AJÜ, Balikesir	
93-0677	TUSAS (GD) F-16C-50 Fighting Falcon $	THK 192 Filo/9 AJÜ, Balikesir	
93-0678	TUSAS (GD) F-16C-50 Fighting Falcon	THK 152 Filo/5 AJÜ, Merzifon	
93-0679	TUSAS (GD) F-16C-50 Fighting Falcon	THK 192 Filo/9 AJÜ, Balikesir	
93-0680	TUSAS (GD) F-16C-50 Fighting Falcon $	THK 192 Filo/9 AJÜ, Balikesir	
93-0681	TUSAS (GD) F-16C-50 Fighting Falcon	THK 192 Filo/9 AJÜ, Balikesir	
93-0682	TUSAS (GD) F-16C-50 Fighting Falcon $	THK 192 Filo/9 AJÜ, Balikesir	
93-0683	TUSAS (GD) F-16C-50 Fighting Falcon	THK 192 Filo/9 AJÜ, Balikesir	
93-0684	TUSAS (GD) F-16C-50 Fighting Falcon	THK	
93-0685	TUSAS (GD) F-16C-50 Fighting Falcon	THK	
93-0687	TUSAS (GD) F-16C-50 Fighting Falcon	THK 132 Filo/3 AJEÜ, Konya	
93-0688	TUSAS (GD) F-16C-50 Fighting Falcon	THK 151 Filo/5 AJÜ, Merzifon	
93-0689	TUSAS (GD) F-16C-50 Fighting Falcon	THK 192 Filo/9 AJÜ, Balikesir	
93-0690	TUSAS (GD) F-16C-50 Fighting Falcon	THK 141 Filo/4 AJÜ, Akinci	
93-0691	TUSAS (GD) F-16D-50 Fighting Falcon $	THK 192 Filo/9 AJÜ, Balikesir	
93-0692	TUSAS (GD) F-16D-50 Fighting Falcon	THK 151 Filo/5 AJÜ, Merzifon	
93-0693	TUSAS (GD) F-16D-50 Fighting Falcon	THK 152 Filo/5 AJÜ, Merzifon	
93-0694	TUSAS (GD) F-16D-50 Fighting Falcon	THK 151 Filo/5 AJÜ, Merzifon	
93-0695	TUSAS (GD) F-16D-50 Fighting Falcon	THK 141 Filo/4 AJÜ, Akinci	
93-0696	TUSAS (GD) F-16D-50 Fighting Falcon $	THK 151 Filo/5 AJÜ, Merzifon	

Notes	Serial	Type (code/other identity)	Owner/operator, location or fate
	94-0071	TUSAS (GD) F-16C-50 Fighting Falcon	THK 192 Filo/9 AJÜ, Balikesir
	94-0072	TUSAS (GD) F-16C-50 Fighting Falcon	THK 151 Filo/5 AJÜ, Merzifon
	94-0073	TUSAS (GD) F-16C-50 Fighting Falcon	THK 151 Filo/5 AJÜ, Merzifon
	94-0074	TUSAS (GD) F-16C-50 Fighting Falcon	THK 191 Filo/9 AJÜ, Balikesir
	94-0075	TUSAS (GD) F-16C-50 Fighting Falcon	THK 151 Filo/5 AJÜ, Merzifon
	94-0076	TUSAS (GD) F-16C-50 Fighting Falcon	THK 151 Filo/5 AJÜ, Merzifon
	94-0077	TUSAS (GD) F-16C-50 Fighting Falcon	THK 141 Filo/4 AJÜ, Akinci
	94-0078	TUSAS (GD) F-16C-50 Fighting Falcon	THK 151 Filo/5 AJÜ, Merzifon
	94-0079	TUSAS (GD) F-16C-50 Fighting Falcon	THK 191 Filo/9 AJÜ, Balikesir
	94-0080	TUSAS (GD) F-16C-50 Fighting Falcon	THK 191 Filo/9 AJÜ, Balikesir
	94-0082	TUSAS (GD) F-16C-50 Fighting Falcon	THK 151 Filo/5 AJÜ, Merzifon
	94-0083	TUSAS (GD) F-16C-50 Fighting Falcon	THK 151 Filo/5 AJÜ, Merzifon
	94-0084	TUSAS (GD) F-16C-50 Fighting Falcon	THK 141 Filo/4 AJÜ, Akinci
	94-0085	TUSAS (GD) F-16C-50 Fighting Falcon	THK 191 Filo/9 AJÜ, Balikesir
	94-0086	TUSAS (GD) F-16C-50 Fighting Falcon	THK 191 Filo/9 AJÜ, Balikesir
	94-0088	TUSAS (GD) F-16C-50 Fighting Falcon	THK 151 Filo/5 AJÜ, Merzifon
	94-0089	TUSAS (GD) F-16C-50 Fighting Falcon	THK 152 Filo/5 AJÜ, Merzifon
	94-0090	TUSAS (GD) F-16C-50 Fighting Falcon $	THK 192 Filo/9 AJÜ, Balikesir
	94-0091	TUSAS (GD) F-16C-50 Fighting Falcon	THK 132 Filo/3 AJEÜ, Konya
	94-0092	TUSAS (GD) F-16C-50 Fighting Falcon	THK 132 Filo/3 AJEÜ, Konya
	94-0093	TUSAS (GD) F-16C-50 Fighting Falcon	THK 141 Filo/4 AJÜ, Akinci
	94-0094	TUSAS (GD) F-16C-50 Fighting Falcon	THK 141 Filo/4 AJÜ, Akinci
	94-0095	TUSAS (GD) F-16C-50 Fighting Falcon	THK 192 Filo/9 AJÜ, Balikesir
	94-0096	TUSAS (GD) F-16C-50 Fighting Falcon	THK 141 Filo/4 AJÜ, Akinci
	94-0105	TUSAS (GD) F-16D-50 Fighting Falcon	THK 141 Filo/4 AJÜ, Akinci
	94-0106	TUSAS (GD) F-16D-50 Fighting Falcon	THK 401 Filo/1 AJÜ, Eskisehir
	94-0108	TUSAS (GD) F-16D-50 Fighting Falcon	THK 191 Filo/9 AJÜ, Balikesir
	94-0109	TUSAS (GD) F-16D-50 Fighting Falcon	THK 132 Filo/3 AJEÜ, Konya
	94-0110	TUSAS (GD) F-16D-50 Fighting Falcon	THK 401 Filo/1 AJÜ, Eskisehir
	94-1557	TUSAS (GD) F-16D-50 Fighting Falcon	THK 152 Filo/5 AJÜ, Merzifon
	94-1558	TUSAS (GD) F-16D-50 Fighting Falcon	THK 132 Filo/3 AJEÜ, Konya
	94-1559	TUSAS (GD) F-16D-50 Fighting Falcon	THK 152 Filo/5 AJÜ, Merzifon
	94-1560	TUSAS (GD) F-16D-50 Fighting Falcon	THK 192 Filo/9 AJÜ, Balikesir
	94-1561	TUSAS (GD) F-16D-50 Fighting Falcon	THK 192 Filo/9 AJÜ, Balikesir
	94-1562	TUSAS (GD) F-16D-50 Fighting Falcon	THK 192 Filo/9 AJÜ, Balikesir
	94-1563	TUSAS (GD) F-16D-50 Fighting Falcon	THK 192 Filo/9 AJÜ, Balikesir
	94-1564	TUSAS (GD) F-16D-50 Fighting Falcon	THK 192 Filo/9 AJÜ, Balikesir
	07-1001	TUSAS (GD) F-16C-50 Fighting Falcon	THK
	07-1002	TUSAS (GD) F-16C-50 Fighting Falcon	THK 181 Filo/8 AJÜ, Diyarbakir
	07-1003	TUSAS (GD) F-16C-50 Fighting Falcon	THK 181 Filo/8 AJÜ, Diyarbakir
	07-1004	TUSAS (GD) F-16C-50 Fighting Falcon	THK
	07-1005	TUSAS (GD) F-16C-50 Fighting Falcon	THK 181 Filo/8 AJÜ, Diyarbakir
	07-1006	TUSAS (GD) F-16C-50 Fighting Falcon	THK 181 Filo/8 AJÜ, Diyarbakir
	07-1007	TUSAS (GD) F-16C-50 Fighting Falcon	THK
	07-1008	TUSAS (GD) F-16C-50 Fighting Falcon	THK
	07-1009	TUSAS (GD) F-16C-50 Fighting Falcon	THK 152 Filo/5 AJÜ, Merzifon
	07-1010	TUSAS (GD) F-16C-50 Fighting Falcon	THK 152 Filo/5 AJÜ, Merzifon
	07-1011	TUSAS (GD) F-16C-50 Fighting Falcon	THK
	07-1012	TUSAS (GD) F-16C-50 Fighting Falcon	THK
	07-1013	TUSAS (GD) F-16C-50 Fighting Falcon	THK 181 Filo/8 AJÜ, Diyarbakir
	07-1014	TUSAS (GD) F-16C-50 Fighting Falcon	THK
	07-1015	TUSAS (GD) F-16D-50 Fighting Falcon	THK
	07-1016	TUSAS (GD) F-16D-50 Fighting Falcon	THK
	07-1017	TUSAS (GD) F-16D-50 Fighting Falcon	THK 181 Filo/8 AJÜ, Diyarbakir
	07-1018	TUSAS (GD) F-16D-50 Fighting Falcon	THK 181 Filo/8 AJÜ, Diyarbakir
	07-1019	TUSAS (GD) F-16D-50 Fighting Falcon	THK
	07-1020	TUSAS (GD) F-16D-50 Fighting Falcon	THK 181 Filo/8 AJÜ, Diyarbakir
	07-1021	TUSAS (GD) F-16D-50 Fighting Falcon	THK 181 Filo/8 AJÜ, Diyarbakir
	07-1022	TUSAS (GD) F-16D-50 Fighting Falcon	THK
	07-1023	TUSAS (GD) F-16D-50 Fighting Falcon	THK 152 Filo/5 AJÜ, Merzifon
	07-1024	TUSAS (GD) F-16D-50 Fighting Falcon	THK 152 Filo/5 AJÜ, Merzifon
	07-1025	TUSAS (GD) F-16D-50 Fighting Falcon	THK 181 Filo/8 AJÜ, Diyarbakir

Serial	Type (code/other identity)	Owner/operator, location or fate	Notes
07-1026	TUSAS (GD) F-16D-50 Fighting Falcon	THK 152 Filo/5 AJÜ, Merzifon	
07-1027	TUSAS (GD) F-16D-50 Fighting Falcon	THK	
07-1028	TUSAS (GD) F-16D-50 Fighting Falcon	THK	
07-1029	TUSAS (GD) F-16D-50 Fighting Falcon	THK	
07-1030	TUSAS (GD) F-16D-50 Fighting Falcon	THK	
09-001	Gulfstream Aerospace G.550	THK 212 Filo/11 HUAÜK, Ankara/Etimesgut	
13-001	Boeing 737-7FS AEW&C (E-7T)	THK 131 Filo/3 AJEÜ, Konya	
13-002	Boeing 737-7FS AEW&C (E-7T)	THK 131 Filo/3 AJEÜ, Konya	
13-003	Boeing 737-7FS AEW&C (E-7T)	THK 131 Filo/3 AJEÜ, Konya	
13-0009	Airbus Military A.400M	THK 221 Filo/12 HUAÜ, Erkilet	
13-004	Boeing 737-7FS AEW&C (E-7T)	THK 131 Filo/3 AJEÜ, Konya	
14-0013	Airbus Military A.400M	THK 221 Filo/12 HUAÜ, Erkilet	
14-0028	Airbus Military A.400M	THK 221 Filo/12 HUAÜ, Erkilet	
15-0051	Airbus Military A.400M	THK (on order)	
1.-....	Airbus Military A.400M	THK (on order)	
1.-....	Airbus Military A.400M	THK (on order)	
1.-....	Airbus Military A.400M	THK (on order)	
1.-....	Airbus Military A.400M	THK (on order)	
1.-....	Airbus Military A.400M	THK (on order)	
TC-ANA	Airbus A.319CJ-115X	Turkish Government, Istanbul/Ataturk	
TC-ATA	Gulfstream Aerospace G.550	*Re-registered as TC-GVA, 2016*	
TC-CBK	Gulfstream Aerospace G.550	THK 212 Filo/11 HUAÜK, Ankara/Etimesgut	
TC-DAP	Gulfstream Aerospace G.550	Turkish Government, Ankara	
TC-GAP	Gulfstream Aerospace G.450	*Re-registered as TC-GVB, 2016*	
TC-GVA	Gulfstream Aerospace G.550 (TC-ATA)	Turkish Government, Ankara	
TC-GVB	Gulfstream Aerospace G.450 (TC-GAP)	Turkish Government, Ankara	
TC-IST	Airbus A.319CJ-133	Turkish Government, Istanbul/Ataturk	
TC-TUR	Airbus A.330-243	Turkish Government, Istanbul/Ataturk	

TURKMENISTAN

EZ-A010	Boeing 757-23A	Government of Turkmenistan, Ashkhabad	
EZ-A777	Boeing 777-22KLR	Government of Turkmenistan, Ashkhabad	
EZ-B021	BAe 1000B	Government of Turkmenistan, Ashkhabad	

UGANDA

5X-UGF	Gulfstream Aerospace G.550	Government of Uganda, Entebbe	

UKRAINE
Ukrainian Air Force

81 y	Antonov An-30	Ukrainian AF 15 Tr AB, Kiev/Boryspil	
76321	Ilyushin Il-76MD	Ukrainian AF 25 Tr AB, Melitopol	
76322	Ilyushin Il-76MD	Ukrainian AF 25 Tr AB, Melitopol	
76323	Ilyushin Il-76MD	Ukrainian AF 25 Tr AB, Melitopol	
76413	Ilyushin Il-76MD	Ukrainian AF 25 Tr AB, Melitopol	
76423	Ilyushin Il-76MD	Ukrainian AF 25 Tr AB, Melitopol	
76531	Ilyushin Il-76MD	Ukrainian AF 25 Tr AB, Melitopol	
76559	Ilyushin Il-76MD	Ukrainian AF 25 Tr AB, Melitopol	
76564	Ilyushin Il-76MD	Ukrainian AF 25 Tr AB, Melitopol	
76566	Ilyushin Il-76MD	Ukrainian AF 25 Tr AB, Melitopol	
76585	Ilyushin Il-76MD	Ukrainian AF 25 Tr AB, Melitopol	
76631	Ilyushin Il-76MD	Ukrainian AF 25 Tr AB, Melitopol	
76637	Ilyushin Il-76MD	Ukrainian AF 25 Tr AB, Melitopol	
76645	Ilyushin Il-76MD	Ukrainian AF 25 Tr AB, Melitopol	
76647	Ilyushin Il-76MD	Ukrainian AF 25 Tr AB, Melitopol	
76654	Ilyushin Il-76MD	Ukrainian AF 25 Tr AB, Melitopol	
76660	Ilyushin Il-76MD	Ukrainian AF 25 Tr AB, Melitopol	
76661	Ilyushin Il-76MD	Ukrainian AF 25 Tr AB, Melitopol	
76680	Ilyushin Il-76MD	Ukrainian AF 25 Tr AB, Melitopol	
76683	Ilyushin Il-76MD	Ukrainian AF 25 Tr AB, Melitopol	
76697	Ilyushin Il-76MD	Ukrainian AF 25 Tr AB, Melitopol	
76698	Ilyushin Il-76MD	Ukrainian AF 25 Tr AB, Melitopol	
76699	Ilyushin Il-76MD	Ukrainian AF 25 Tr AB, Melitopol	

Notes	Serial	Type (code/other identity)	Owner/operator, location or fate
	76732	Ilyushin Il-76MD	Ukrainian AF 25 Tr AB, Melitopol
	78820	Ilyushin Il-76MD	Ukrainian AF 25 Tr AB, Melitopol
	86915	Ilyushin Il-76MD	Ukrainian AF 25 Tr AB, Melitopol
	86922	Ilyushin Il-76MD	Ukrainian AF 25 Tr AB, Melitopol
	Government of Ukraine		
	UR-86527	Ilyushin Il-62M	Government of Ukraine, Kiev/Boryspil
	UR-86528	Ilyushin Il-62M	Government of Ukraine, Kiev/Boryspil
	UR-ABA	Airbus A.319CJ-115X	Government of Ukraine, Kiev/Boryspil
	UNITED ARAB EMIRATES		
	United Arab Emirates Air Force (UAEAF)		
	312	Lockheed C-130H-30 Hercules	UAEAF 4 Sqn/Transport Wing, Abu Dhabi/ Bateen
	430	Aermacchi MB339NAT	UAEAF *Al Fursan*, Al Ain
	431	Aermacchi MB339NAT	UAEAF *Al Fursan*, Al Ain
	432	Aermacchi MB339NAT	UAEAF *Al Fursan*, Al Ain
	433	Aermacchi MB339NAT	UAEAF *Al Fursan*, Al Ain
	434	Aermacchi MB339NAT	UAEAF *Al Fursan*, Al Ain
	435	Aermacchi MB339NAT	UAEAF *Al Fursan*, Al Ain
	436	Aermacchi MB339NAT	UAEAF *Al Fursan*, Al Ain
	437	Aermacchi MB339NAT	UAEAF *Al Fursan*, Al Ain
	438	Aermacchi MB339NAT	UAEAF *Al Fursan*, Al Ain
	439	Aermacchi MB339NAT	UAEAF *Al Fursan*, Al Ain
	440	Aermacchi MB339NAT	UAEAF *Al Fursan*, Al Ain
	441	Aermacchi MB339NAT	UAEAF *Al Fursan*, Al Ain
	442	Aermacchi MB339NAT	UAEAF *Al Fursan*, Al Ain
	1211	Lockheed C-130H Hercules	UAEAF 4 Sqn/Transport Wing, Abu Dhabi/ Bateen
	1212	Lockheed C-130H Hercules	UAEAF 4 Sqn/Transport Wing, Abu Dhabi/ Bateen
	1213	Lockheed C-130H Hercules	UAEAF 4 Sqn/Transport Wing, Abu Dhabi/ Bateen
	1214	Lockheed C-130H Hercules	UAEAF 4 Sqn/Transport Wing, Abu Dhabi/ Bateen
	1215	Lockheed L.100-30 Hercules	UAEAF 4 Sqn/Transport Wing, Abu Dhabi/ Bateen
	1216	Lockheed L.100-30 Hercules	UAEAF 4 Sqn/Transport Wing, Abu Dhabi/ Bateen
	1217	Lockheed L.100-30 Hercules	UAEAF 4 Sqn/Transport Wing, Abu Dhabi/ Bateen
	1223	Boeing C-17A Globemaster III (10-0401)	UAEAF Heavy Transport Sqn, Abu Dhabi/Bateen
	1224	Boeing C-17A Globemaster III (10-0402)	UAEAF Heavy Transport Sqn, Abu Dhabi/Bateen
	1225	Boeing C-17A Globemaster III (10-0403)	UAEAF Heavy Transport Sqn, Abu Dhabi/Bateen
	1226	Boeing C-17A Globemaster III (10-0404)	UAEAF Heavy Transport Sqn, Abu Dhabi/Bateen
	1227	Boeing C-17A Globemaster III (10-0405)	UAEAF Heavy Transport Sqn, Abu Dhabi/Bateen
	1228	Boeing C-17A Globemaster III (10-0406)	UAEAF Heavy Transport Sqn, Abu Dhabi/Bateen
	1229	Boeing C-17A Globemaster III (14-0007)	UAEAF Heavy Transport Sqn, Abu Dhabi/Bateen
	1230	Boeing C-17A Globemaster III (14-0008)	UAEAF Heavy Transport Sqn, Abu Dhabi/Bateen
	1300	Airbus A.330-243 MRTT	UAEAF MRTT Sqn, Al Ain
	1301	Airbus A.330-243 MRTT	UAEAF MRTT Sqn, Al Ain
	1302	Airbus A.330-243 MRTT	UAEAF MRTT Sqn, Al Ain
	1303	Airbus A.330-243 MRTT	UAEAF (on order)
	UAE Government		
	A6-ALN	Boeing 777-2ANER	Amiri Flight, Abu Dhabi
	A6-AUH	Boeing 737-8EX	Amiri Flight, Abu Dhabi
	A6-COM	Boeing 747-433	Dubai Air Wing
	A6-DFR	Boeing 737-7BC	Amiri Flight, Abu Dhabi
	A6-DLM	Airbus A.320-232	Amiri Flight, Abu Dhabi
	A6-GGP	Boeing 747-412F	Dubai Air Wing
	A6-HEH	Boeing 737-8AJ	Dubai Air Wing
	A6-HHH	Gulfstream Aerospace G.400	Dubai Air Wing
	A6-HMS	Airbus A.320-232	Dubai Air Wing

Serial	Type (code/other identity)	Owner/operator, location or fate	Notes
A6-HRM	Boeing 747-422	Dubai Air Wing	
A6-HRS	Boeing 737-7F0	Dubai Air Wing	
A6-MMM	Boeing 747-422	Dubai Air Wing	
A6-MRM	Boeing 737-8EC	Dubai Air Wing	
A6-MRS	Boeing 737-8EO	Dubai Air Wing	
A6-PFA	Boeing 747-8Z5	Amiri Flight, Abu Dhabi	
A6-PFC	Boeing 787-8	Amiri Flight, Abu Dhabi	
A6-RJ1	BAE RJ.85	Dubai Air Wing	
A6-RJ2	BAE RJ.85	Dubai Air Wing	
A6-SHJ	Airbus A.320CJ-232X	Ruler of Sharjah Air Wing	
A6-SIL	Boeing 777-35RER	Amiri Flight, Abu Dhabi	
A6-UAE	Boeing 747-48E	*Sold as CN-MBH, December 2015*	
A6-YAS	Boeing 747-4F6	Amiri Flight, Abu Dhabi	
DU-140	AgustaWestland AW.139	Dubai Air Wing, Fairoaks, UK (Summer)	
DU-142	AgustaWestland AW.139	Dubai Air Wing, Fairoaks, UK (Summer)	

4056 is a F-16C-52 of the Polish Air Force's 31.BLT, based at Poznan/Krzesiny. It wears these subtle but impressive tiger markings.

C.16-55/14-15 is a Eurofighter Tifon of the Spanish Air Force's Ala 15 at Albacete. From serial Tifon CE.16-12 onwards Spanish military aircraft have also been allocated inventory numbers, starting at 10000 and these are worn (or not, as in this case) in a number of different formats on the tail, usually below the serial. C.16-55 has inventory number 10004, for the record.

This section lists the codes worn by some overseas air forces and, alongside, the serial of the aircraft currently wearing this code. This list will be updated occasionally and those with Internet access can download the latest version via the 'Military Aircraft Markings' Web Site, www.militaryaircraftmarkings.co.uk and via the MAM2009 Yahoo! Group.

FRANCE
FRENCH AIR FORCE
D-BD Alpha Jet

Code	Serial	Code	Serial	Code	Serial	Code	Serial
0 [PDF]	E114	120-UC	E157	F-UHRE	E44	3-XV	672
1 [PDF]	E45	120-UH	E160	F-UHRF	E46	3-XY	649
2 [PDF]	E46	705-AB	E28	F-UHRR	E146	30-AS	51
3 [PDF]	E119	705-AD	E51	F-UHRT	E152	30-IE	642
5 [PDF]	E79	705-AH	E110	F-UHRW	E166	30-IP	604
6 [PDF]	E127	705-FK	E127			30-IR	674
9 [PDF]	E146	705-LA	E72	**Dassault Mirage 2000**		30-JO	627
8-AF	E108	705-LC	E87	2-ED	62	115-AM	525
8-AK	E144	705-LG	E120	2-EF	45	115-KB	94
8-FD	E151	705-LJ	E137	2-EG	56	115-KC	120
8-FM	E105	705-LK	E125	2-EJ	43	115-KD	123
8-FN	E116	705-LP	E129	2-EH	52	115-KE	101
8-FO	E81	705-LU	E148	2-EM	63	115-KF	111
8-LN	E118	705-MA	E35	2-EN	46	115-KG	104
8-MM	E13	705-MD	E30	2-EO	66	115-KI	96
8-RA	E41	705-MF	E98	2-EP	47	115-KJ	523
8-RP	E136	705-MH	E48	2-EQ	44	115-KL	106
8-RQ	E138	705-MN	E167	2-ET	57	115-KN	121
30-AO	E112	705-MR	E115	2-EU	55	115-KR	102
30-RX	E169	705-MS	E20	2-EV	59	115-KS	528
30-TI	E156	705-NF	E141	2-EW	48	115-KV	88
102-AI	E117	705-NL	E37	2-EX	40	115-LB	87
102-FA	E140	705-NP	E155	2-EY	42	115-LC	108
102-FB	E86	705-RB	E163	2-EZ	54	115-LD	117
102-FI	E32	705-RK	E31	2-FZ	41	115-LE	79
102-FP	E168	705-RM	E123	2-MG	65	115-LJ	105
102-LI	E53	705-RS	E149	2-MH	67	115-LK	85
102-MB	E97	705-RT	E152	3-AU	653	115-OA	524
102-NA	E79	705-RU	E153	3-IA	650	115-OC	529
102-NB	E29	705-RW	E166	3-ID	654	115-OL	530
102-ND	E26	705-RY	E170	3-IJ	638	115-OR	527
102-RE	E165	705-RZ	E171	3-IL	622	115-YA	93
102-RJ	E76	705-TA	E42	3-IN	640	115-YB	99
102-RX	E135	705-TB	E67	3-IS	617	115-YC	85
118-AK	E18	705-TG	E104	3-IT	624	115-YD	107
118-FE	E119	705-TJ	E25	3-IU	620	115-YE	122
118-LT	E147	705-TK	E58	3-IV	683	115-YF	100
118-TD	E113	705-TM	E128	3-JD	643	115-YG	118
120-AG	E109	705-TU	E7	3-JF	660	115-YH	109
120-AH	E99	705-TZ	E83	3-JI	675	115-YL	82
120-AL	E154	705-UB	E11	3-JJ	639	115-YM	115
120-FJ	E33	F-TELL	E88	3-JM	657	115-YO	113
120-FM	E105	F-TEMO	E68	3-JN	658	115-YT	124
120-LM	E102	F-TENE	E73	3-JP	611	116-AU	316
120-LO	E142	F-TERD	E121	3-JX	679	116-BL	306
120-LS	E22	F-TERF	E158	3-JY	615	116-EA	49
120-LW	E82	F-TERH	E94	3-MQ	646	116-EC	78
120-LX	E89	F-TERI	E117	3-XA	662	116-EE	71
120-MB	E176	F-TERJ	E162	3-XD	630	116-EI	38
120-RN	E124	F-TERK	E31	3-XG	625	116-ER	68
120-RO	E131	F-TERN	E46	3-XJ	602	116-ME	61
120-RV	E164	F-TERP	E130	3-XK	671	116-MK	74
120-TH	E90	F-TERQ	E95	3-XL	603	118-AX	77
120-TT	E101	F-TERR	E114	3-XM	680	118-EB	76
120-TX	E93	F-TETF	E45	3-XN	652	118-IF	609
		F-UGFC	E139	3-XO	629	118-JK	612
		F-UGFE	E119	3-XQ	637	118-KQ	112
		F-UHMA	E173	3-XT	648	118-XH	616

125-AA	340		**Dassault Rafale**			30-IA	307		DAS	1176
125-AE	355		4-EA	303		30-IB	306		DAT	1189
125-AI	365		4-EB	304		30-IF	331		DAU	1197
125-AL	348		4-FF	339		30-IH	333		DAV	1204
125-AK	359		4-FG	340		30-II	334		DAW	1211
125-AQ	351		4-FH	341		30-IM	109		DAX	1214
125-AR	368		4-FI	342		30-IN	110		DAY	1217
125-BA	342		4-FJ	343		30-IQ	112		DAZ	1219
125-BB	364		4-FK	344		30-IR	113		DBA	1232
125-BC	366		4-FL	345		30-IS	114		DBB	1243
125-BD	371		4-FM	346		30-IT	115		DBC	1248
125-BJ	354		4-FN	347		30-IU	116		DBD	1262
125-BQ	358		4-FO	348		30-IW	118		DBE	1277
125-BS	374		4-FP	349		30-IX	119		DBF	1417
125-BU	345		4-FR	351		30-VA	148		DBG	1438
125-BX	356		4-FS	352		104-GG	128		DBH	1451
125-CB	360		4-FT	353		104-GI	130		DBI	1507
125-CF	373		4-FU	354		104-GM	134		DBJ	1510
125-CG	338		4-GL	133		104-GO	136		DBK	1512
125-CI	335		4-GU	142		104-GP	137		DBL	1519
125-CL	375		4-HC	310		104-GY	146		DBM	1617
125-CM	372		4-HF	312		104-HR	103		DBN	1632
125-CO	357		4-HI	313		113-FQ	350		DBO	1634
125-CQ	370		4-HK	315		113-GC	124		DBP	1654
125-CU	362		4-HN	319		113-GN	135		DBQ	1663
133-AG	681		4-HO	317		113-HB	309		DBR	5682
133-AL	669		4-HP	314		113-HD	311		DCA	1005
133-AS	635		4 HQ	321		113-HG	106		DCB	1052
133-IC	626		4-HU	322		113-HH	104		DCC	1056
133-IG	668		4-HV	320		113-HJ	107		DCD	1057
133-IH	631		4-HZ	327		113-HS	108		DCE	1071
133-IO	647		4-IC	328		113-HY	326		DCF	1073
133-IQ	666		4-ID	329		113-IO	338		DCG	1093
133-IW	664		4-IE	330		113-IV	117		DCH	1114
133-JB	678		4-IG	332		113-IZ	121		DCI	1122
133-JC	606		4-IJ	335		118-FQ	350		DCJ	1122
133-JE	634		4-IK	336		118-FR	351		DCK	1130
133-JG	601		4-IL	337		118-GH	129		DCL	1135
133-JH	686		4-IY	120		118-GP	137		DCM	1136
133-JL	628		7-HX	325		118-IP	111		DCN	1142
133-JR	682		30-EC	305		118-IR	113		DCO	1145
133-JT	677		30-EF	102					DCP	1150
133-JU	614		30-GA	122		**FRENCH ARMY**			DCQ	1155
133-JV	636		30-GB	123		**SA.330 Puma**			DCR	1163
133-JW	641		30-GD	125		DAA	1006		DCS	1164
133-JZ	667		30-GE	126		DAB	1020		DCT	1165
133-LF	605		30-GF	127		DAC	1036		DCU	1171
133-LH	655		30-GJ	131		DAD	1037		DCV	1172
133-MO	613		30-GK	132		DAE	1049		DCW	1177
133-MP	623		30-GQ	138		DAF	1055		DCX	1179
133-XC	618		30-GR	139		DAG	1069		DCY	1182
133-XE	632		30-GS	140		DAH	1078		DCZ	1186
133-XF	670		30-GT	141		DAI	1092		DDA	1190
133-XI	661		30-GV	143		DAJ	1100		DDB	1192
133-XP	645		30-GW	144		DAK	1102		DDC	1196
133-XR	659		30-GX	145		DAL	1107		DDD	1198
133-XX	610		30-GZ	147		DAM	1109		DDE	1206
133-XZ	685		30-HA	308		DAN	1128		DDF	1213
188-EL	58		30-HE	105		DAO	1143		DDG	1222
188-XJ	602		30-HM	318		DAP	1149		DDH	1223
188-YR	91		30-HT	323		DAQ	1156		DDI	1228
			30-HW	324		DAR	1173		DDJ	1229

DDK	1231	GBV	4141	GJO	3965	CAF	2638
DDL	1235	GBW	4142	GJP	4014	CAG	2640
DDM	1236	GBX	4144	GJQ	4022	CAH	2642
DDN	1239	GBY	4145	GJR	4038	CGA	2252
DDO	1244	GBZ	4151	GJS	4047	CGB	2266
DDP	1252	GCA	4155	GJU	4067	CGC	2267
DDQ	1255	GCC	4160	GJV	4078	CGD	2271
DDR	1256	GCD	4161	GJW	4102	CGE	2272
DDS	1260	GCE	4162	GJX	4103	CGF	2273
DDT	1269	GCF	4164	GJY	4123	CGG	2282
DDU	1411	GCG	4168	GJZ	4166	CGH	2285
DDV	1419	GCH	4172	GKA	4176	CGI	2290
DDW	1447	GCI	4175	GKB	4177	CGJ	2292
DDX	1662	GCJ	4179	GKC	4182	CGK	2299
		GCK	4180	GKD	4185	CGL	2300
SA.342 Gazelle		GCL	4181	GKE	4187	CGM	2301
GAA	3459	GCM	4186	GMA	3567	CGN	2303
GAB	3476	GCN	4189	GMB	4042	CGO	2316
GAC	3512	GCO	4191	GMC	4079	CGQ	2323
GAD	3530	GCP	4195	GMD	4194	CGR	2324
GAE	3548	GCQ	4198	GME	3870	CGS	2325
GAF	3664	GEA	4204	GMF	3930	CGT	2327
GAG	3848	GEB	4206	GMG	3939	CGU	2331
GAH	3849	GEC	4207	GMH	4023	CGV	2336
GAI	3850	GED	4208	GMI	4171	CGW	2443
GAJ	3856	GEE	4209	GMJ	4190	CGX	2446
GAK	3859	GEF	4210	GMK	4201	CHA	2342
GAL	3862	GEG	4211	GNA	3458	CHB	2369
GAM	3863	GEH	4212	GNB	3513	CHC	2375
GAN	3865	GEI	4214	GNC	3549		
GAO	3868	GEJ	4215	GND	3617	**EC.665 Tigre**	
GAP	3911	GEK	4216	GNE	3852	BHA	2010
GAQ	3921	GEL	4217	GNF	3853	BHB	2009
GAR	3938	GEM	4218	GNG	3858	BHC	2013
GAS	3947	GEN	4219	GNI	3866	BHD	2015
GAT	3948	GEO	4220	GNJ	3896	BHE	2018
GAU	3957	GEP	4221	GNK	3956	BHF	2019
GAV	3964	GEQ	4222	GNM	3992	BHG	2022
GAW	3996	GER	4223	GNN	4008	BHH	2001
GAX	4018	GES	4224	GNO	4032	BHI	2002
GAY	4019	GET	4225	GNP	4049	BHJ	2003
GAZ	4020	GEU	4226	GNQ	4060	BHK	2004
GBA	4026	GEV	4227	GNR	4065	BHL	2006
GBB	4034	GEW	4228	GNS	4071	BHM	2011
GBC	4039	GEX	4229	GNT	4083	BHN	2021
GBD	4048	GEY	4230	GNU	4096	BHO	2024
GBE	4053	GEZ	4231	GNV	4118	BHP	2023
GBF	4059	GFA	4231	GNW	4135	BHQ	2025
GBG	4061	GFB	4233	GNX	4143	BHR	2026
GBH	4066	GFC	4234	GNY	4146	BHS	2027
GBI	4072	GJA	1732	GNZ	4159	BHT	2012
GBJ	4084	GJB	3477	GOA	4178	BHU	2028
GBL	4095	GJC	3511	GOB	4183	BHV	2029
GBM	4108	GJD	3529	GOC	4184	BHW	2030
GBN	4109	GJF	3546	GOD	4192	BHX	2031
GBO	4114	GJH	3615			BHX	
GBP	4115	GJI	3851	**AS.532UL/EC.725AP Cougar**		BHZ	2033
GBQ	4119	GJJ	3855	CAA	2611	BIA	2016
GBR	4120	GJK	3857	CAB	2628	BIB	2034
GBS	4124	GJL	3864	CAC	2630	BIC	2035
GBT	4136	GJM	3867	CAD	2631	BIE	2037
GBU	4140	GJN	3929	CAE	2633	BIG	2039

Code	Serial
BIH	2040
BII	2041
BIJ	2042
BIK	2043
BIL	2044
BIM	2045
BIN	2046
BIO	2047
BIP	2048
BIQ	2049
BIR	2050
BIS	2051
BIT	2052
BJA	6001
BJB	6002
BJC	6003
BJD	6004
BJE	6005
BJF	6006
BJG	6007
BJH	6008
BJI	6009
BJJ	6010
BJK	6011
BJL	6012
BJM	6013
BJN	6014
BJO	6015
BJP	6016
BJQ	6017
BJR	6018
BJS	6019
BJT	6020
BJU	6021

NH.90-TTH

Code	Serial
EAA	1239
EAB	1256
EAC	1271
EAD	1273
EAF	1291
EAG	1292
EAH	1293
EAI	1294
EAJ	1295
EAK	1306
EAL	1307
EAM	1308
EAN	1309
EAO	1310
EAP	1311
EAQ	1312
EAR	1313
EAS	1332
EAT	1333

ITALY
Aeritalia-EMB AMX

Code	Serial
32-41	MM55030
32-47	MM55046
32-50	MM55029
32-51	MM55036
32-53	MM55047
32-56	MM55042
51-10	MM7159
51-21	MM55043
51-26	MM7149
51-30	MM7170
51-32	MM7166
51-33	MM7162
51-34	MM7191
51-35	MM7196
51-36	MM7185
51-37	MM7161
51-40	MM7164
51-41	MM7183
51-42	MM7177
51-43	MM7178
51-44	MM7198
51-45	MM7175
51-46	MM7197
51-50	MM7186
51-51	MM7151
51-52	MM7171
51-53	MM7180
51-55	MM7168
51-56	MM7167
51-57	MM7190
51-60	MM7174
51-61	MM7126
51-62	MM7182
51-63	MM7173
51-64	MM7179
51-65	MM7184
51-66	MM7169
51-67	MM7194
51-70	MM7192
51-71	MM7189
51-72	MM7163
51-80	MM55037
51-82	MM55044
51-83	MM55049
51-84	MM55051
RS-14	MM7177
RS-18	MM55034

Aermacchi MB339

Code	Serial
1 [FT]	MM54551
2 [FT]	MM54517
3 [FT]	MM55058
4 [FT]	MM55052
5 [FT]	MM54505
6 [FT]	MM54534
7 [FT]	MM55053
8 [FT]	MM54500
9 [FT]	MM55054
10 [FT]	MM54500
11 [FT]	MM54539
12 [FT]	MM54510
32-161	MM55089
36-06	MM55074
61-11	MM54457
61-12	MM54458
61-15	MM55054
61-20	MM55055
61-21	MM54465
61-24	MM54468
61-26	MM55059
61-32	MM54488
61-36	MM54492
61-37	MM54493
61-42	MM54496
61-45	MM54499
61-52	MM54504
61-55	MM54507
61-57	MM54509
61-60	MM54510
61-61	MM54511
61-62	MM54512
61-64	MM54514
61-65	MM54515
61-66	MM54516
61-70	MM54518
61-72	MM54533
61-74	MM54535
61-106	MM54548
61-107	MM54549
61-126	MM55062
61-127	MM55063
61-130	MM55064
61-131	MM55065
61-132	MM55066
61-133	MM55067
61-135	MM55069
61-136	MM55070
61-140	MM55072
61-141	MM55073
61-143	MM55075
61-144	MM55076
61-145	MM55077
61-146	MM55078
61-147	MM55079
61-150	MM55080
61-151	MM55081
61-152	MM55082
61-154	MM55084
61-155	MM55085
61-156	MM55086
61-157	MM55087
61-160	MM55088
61-162	MM55090
RS-32	MM55091
RS-33	MM55068

Aermacchi T-346A Master

Code	Serial
61-01	MM55154
61-02	MM55144
61-03	MM55145
61-04	MM55155
61-05	MM55153
61-06	MM55213
61-07	MM55214
61-10	MM55215
61-12	MM55216
61-13	MM55217
61-14	MM55218

Eurofighter Typhoon

Code	Serial
4-1	MM7270
4-2	MM7303
4-3	MM7287
4-4	MM7274
4-5	MM7289
4-6	MM7323
4-7	MM7290
4-9	MM7340
4-11	MM7291
4-13	MM7235
4-14	MM7281
4-15	MM7271
4-20	MM7279
4-21	MM7304
4-23	MM55095
4-26	MM55128
4-30	MM55096
4-31	MM55093
4-32	MM55129
4-33	MM55130
4-40	MM7277
4-41	MM7299
4-44	MM7300
4-45	MM7320
4-46	MM7326
4-47	MM7327
4-50	MM7306
4-51	MM7295
4-52	MM7294
4-53	MM7301
4-60	MM7338
4-61	MM7339
36-02	MM7286
36-05	MM7276
36-07	MM7285
36-11	MM7275
36-14	MM7272
36-15	MM7282
36-21	MM7292
36-22	MM7296
36-23	MM7297
36-24	MM7298
36-25	MM7302
36-26	MM7294
36-30	MM7280
36-31	MM7308
36-32	MM7310
36-33	MM7293
36-34	MM7312
36-35	MM7313
36-37	MM7314
36-40	MM7322
36-41	MM7324
36-42	MM7288
36-45	MM7319
36-46	MM7315
36-50	MM7341
36-52	MM7343
36-60	MM55094
36-61	MM55097
36-62	MM55092

Code	Serial	Code	Serial	Code	Serial	Code	Serial
37-01	MM7307	6-63	MM7023	79-14	E.25-14	11-16	C.16-46
37-03	MM7309	6-66	MM7059	79-15	E.25-15	11-17	C.16-51
37-04	MM7318	6-67	MM7068	79-16	E.25-16	11-18	C.16-52
37-07	MM7316	6-71	MM7070	79-17	E.25-62	11-19	C.16-53
37-10	MM7311	6-72	MM7051	79-20	E.25-20	11-20	C.16-54
37-12	MM7321	6-75	MM7013	79-21	E.25-21	11-28	C.16-63
37-14	MM7328	6-76	MM7044	79-22	E.25-22	11-70	CE.16-01
37-15	MM7329	36-50	CSX7085	79-23	E.25-23	11-71	CE.16-02
37-16	MM7331	50-01	MM7021	79-24	E.25-24	11-72	CE.16-03
37-20	MM7325	50-02	MM7052	79-25	E.25-25	11-73	CE.16-04
37-21	MM7330	50-03	MM7066	79-27	E.25-27	11-74	CE.16-05
37-30	MM55131	50-04	MM7030	79-28	E.25-28	11-75	CE.16-06
RMV-01	MMX603	50-05	MM7019	79-29	E.25-87	11-76	CE.16-07
RS-01	MMX602	50-07	MM7053	79-31	E.25-31	11-78	CE.16-09
RS-23	MM7278	50-40	MM7054	79-32	E.25-86	11-79	CE.16-10
		50-42	MM7055	79-33	E.25-50	11-80	CE.16-13
Lockheed Martin F-35A		50-43	MM7047	79-34	E.25-52	11-81	CE.16-14
Lightning II		50-44	MM7062	79-35	E.25-54	11-91	C.16-20
32-01	MM7332	50-52	MM7084	79-37	E.25-37	14-01	C.16-31
32-02	MM7333	50-53	MM7008	79-38	E.25-38	14-02	C.16-35
32-03	MM7334	50-57	MM7067	79-39	E.25-79	14-03	C.16-36
32-04	MM7335	RS-01	CSX7041	79-40	E.25-40	14-04	C.16-37
32-05	MM7336	RS-05	CSX7047	79-44	E.25-44	14-05	C.16-38
32-07	MM7357			79-46	E.25-46	14-06	C.16-39
32-13	MM7337	**SPAIN**		79-49	E.25-49	14-07	C.16-41
		CASA 101EB Aviojet		79-95	E.25-65	14-08	C.16-42
Panavia Tornado		54-20	E.25-35	79-97	E.25-69	14-09	C.16-44
6-01	MM7007	54-21	E.25-55	79-98	E.25-73	14-10	C.16-45
6-04	MM7057	54-22	E.25-61			14-11	C.16-47
6-05	MM7025	74-02	E.25-33	**CASA 212 Aviocar**		14-12	C.16-48
6-06	MM7036	74-07	E.25-51	47-12	TM.12D-72	14-13	C.16-49
6-07	MM7075	74-09	E.25-53	47-14	T.12D-75	14-14	C.16-50
6-10	MM7088	74-11	E.25-56	72-01	T.12B-13	14-15	C.16-55
6-11	MM7058	74-12	E.25-57	72-07	T.12B-49	14-70	CE.16-11
6-12	MM7071	74-13	E.25-59	72-08	T.12B-55	14-71	CE.16-12
6-13	MM7014	74-17	E.25-63	72-09	T.12B-66		
6-15	MM55006	74-20	E.25-66	72-11	T.12B-65		
6-16	MM7037	74-21	E.25-67	72-12	T.12B-67		
6-20	MM7021	74-22	E.25-68	72-14	T.12B-63		
6-21	MM7040	74-25	E.25-71	72-15	T.12B-69		
6-22	MM7029	74-26	E.25-72	72-17	T.12B-70		
6-25	MM7043	74-28	E.25-74	72-18	T.12B-62		
6-26	MM7063	74-30	E.25-76	72-21	TR.12D-76		
6-27	MM7035	74-34	E.25-81	72-22	TR.12D-77		
6-30	MM7072	74-35	E.25-83	72-23	TR.12D-79		
6-31	MM7006	74-39	E.25-88	72-24	TR.12D-81		
6-32	MM7015	74-40	E.25-17				
6-33	MM7039	74-41	E.25-41	**Eurofighter Tifón**			
6-34	MM7073	74-42	E.25-18	11-01	C.16-21		
6-35	MM7026	74-43	E.25-43	11-02	C.16-22		
6-37	MM7038	74-44	E.25-34	11-03	C.16-23		
6-42	MM55010	74-45	E.25-29	11-04	C.16-24		
6-44	MM55009	79-02	E.25-78	11-05	C.16-25		
6-45	MM55008	79-03	E.25-80	11-06	C.16-26		
6-50	MM7024	79-04	E.25-84	11-07	C.16-27		
6-51	MM55007	79-05	E.25-05	11-08	C.16-28		
6-52	MM55001	79-06	E.25-06	11-09	C.16-29		
6-53	MM55004	79-08	E.25-08	11-10	C.16-30		
6-55	MM7004	79-09	E.25-09	11-11	C.16-32		
6-57	MM7081	79-11	E.25-11	11-12	C.16-33		
6-60	MM7086	79-12	E.25-12	11-14	C.16-40		
6-62	MM7082	79-13	E.25-13	11-15	C.16-43		

US MILITARY AIRCRAFT MARKINGS

All USAF and US Army aircraft have been allocated a fiscal year (FY) number since 1921. Individual aircraft are given a serial according to the fiscal year in which they are ordered. The numbers commence at 0001 and are prefixed with the year of allocation. For example F-15C Eagle 84-0001 was the first aircraft ordered in 1984. The fiscal year (FY) serial is carried on the technical data block which is usually stencilled on the left-hand side of the aircraft just below the cockpit. The number displayed on the fin is a corruption of the FY serial. Most tactical aircraft carry the fiscal year in small figures followed by the last three or four digits of the serial in large figures. Large transport and tanker aircraft such as C-130s and KC-135s sometimes display a five-figure number commencing with the last digit of the appropriate fiscal year and four figures of the production number. An example of this is Boeing KC-135R Stratotanker 58-0128 which displays 80128 on its fin.

US Army serials have been allocated in a similar way to USAF serials although in recent years an additional zero has been added so that all US Army serials now have the two-figure fiscal year part followed by five digits. This means that, for example C-20E 70140 is officially 87-00140 although as yet this has not led to any alterations to serials painted on aircraft.

USN and USMC serials follow a straightforward numerical sequence which commenced, for the present series, with the allocation of 00001 to an SB2C Helldiver by the Bureau of Aeronautics in 1940. Numbers in the 168000 series are presently being issued. They are usually carried in full on the rear fuselage of the aircraft.

US Coast Guard serials began with the allocation of the serial 1 to a Loening OL-5 in 1927.

UK-BASED USAF AIRCRAFT

The following aircraft are normally based in the UK. They are listed in numerical order of type with individual aircraft in serial number order, as depicted on the aircraft. The number in brackets is either the alternative presentation of the five-figure number commencing with the last digit of the fiscal year, or the fiscal year where a five-figure serial is presented on the aircraft. Where it is possible to identify the allocation of aircraft to individual squadrons by means of colours carried on fin or cockpit edge, this is also provided.

Notes	Serial	Type (code/other identity)	Owner/operator, location or fate
	McDonnell Douglas F-15C Eagle/F-15D Eagle/F-15E Strike Eagle		
	LN: 48th FW, RAF Lakenheath: 492nd FS *blue*/white, 493rd FS *black/yellow* & 494th FS *red*/white		
	00-3000	McD F-15E Strike Eagle [LN] *r*	USAF 494th FS/48th FW, Lakenheath
	00-3001	McD F-15E Strike Eagle [LN] *r*	USAF 494th FS/48th FW, Lakenheath
	00-3002	McD F-15E Strike Eagle [LN] *r*	USAF 494th FS/48th FW, Lakenheath
	00-3003	McD F-15E Strike Eagle [LN] *r*	USAF 494th FS/48th FW, Lakenheath
	00-3004	McD F-15E Strike Eagle [LN] *r*	USAF 494th FS/48th FW, Lakenheath
	01-2000	McD F-15E Strike Eagle [LN] *r*	USAF 494th FS/48th FW, Lakenheath
	01-2001	McD F-15E Strike Eagle [LN] *r*	USAF 494th FS/48th FW, Lakenheath
	01-2002	McD F-15E Strike Eagle [LN] *r*	USAF 494th FS/48th FW, Lakenheath
	01-2003	McD F-15E Strike Eagle [LN] *r*	USAF 494th FS/48th FW, Lakenheath
	01-2004	McD F-15E Strike Eagle [LN] *r*	USAF 494th FS/48th FW, Lakenheath
	84-0001	McD F-15C Eagle [LN] *y*	USAF 493rd FS/48th FW, Lakenheath
	84-0010	McD F-15C Eagle [LN] *y*	USAF 493rd FS/48th FW, Lakenheath
	84-0015	McD F-15C Eagle [LN] *y*	USAF 493rd FS/48th FW, Lakenheath
	84-0019	McD F-15C Eagle [LN] *y*	USAF 493rd FS/48th FW, Lakenheath
	84-0027	McD F-15C Eagle [LN] *y* [493 FS]	USAF 493rd FS/48th FW, Lakenheath
	84-0044	McD F-15D Eagle [LN] *y*	USAF 493rd FS/48th FW, Lakenheath
	84-0046	McD F-15D Eagle [LN] *y*	USAF 493rd FS/48th FW, Lakenheath
	86-0154	McD F-15C Eagle [LN] *y*	USAF 493rd FS/48th FW, Lakenheath
	86-0156	McD F-15C Eagle [LN] *y*	USAF 493rd FS/48th FW, Lakenheath
	86-0159	McD F-15C Eagle [LN] *y*	USAF 493rd FS/48th FW, Lakenheath
	86-0160	McD F-15C Eagle [LN] *y*	USAF 493rd FS/48th FW, Lakenheath
	86-0163	McD F-15C Eagle [LN] *y*	USAF 493rd FS/48th FW, Lakenheath
	86-0164	McD F-15C Eagle [LN] *y*	USAF 493rd FS/48th FW, Lakenheath
	86-0165	McD F-15C Eagle [LN] *y*	USAF 493rd FS/48th FW, Lakenheath
	86-0166	McD F-15C Eagle [LN] *y*	USAF 493rd FS/48th FW, Lakenheath
	86-0171	McD F-15C Eagle [LN] *y*	USAF 493rd FS/48th FW, Lakenheath
	86-0172	McD F-15C Eagle [LN] *y*	USAF 493rd FS/48th FW, Lakenheath
	86-0174	McD F-15C Eagle [LN] *y*	USAF 493rd FS/48th FW, Lakenheath
	86-0175	McD F-15C Eagle [LN] *y*	USAF 493rd FS/48th FW, Lakenheath
	86-0176	McD F-15C Eagle [LN] *y*	USAF 493rd FS/48th FW, Lakenheath
	86-0178	McD F-15C Eagle [LN] *y*	USAF 493rd FS/48th FW, Lakenheath
	91-0301	McD F-15E Strike Eagle [LN] *bl*	USAF 492nd FS/48th FW, Lakenheath
	91-0302	McD F-15E Strike Eagle [LN] *bl*	USAF 492nd FS/48th FW, Lakenheath
	91-0303	McD F-15E Strike Eagle [LN] *bl*	USAF 492nd FS/48th FW, Lakenheath

Notes	Serial	Type (code/other identity)	Owner/operator, location or fate
	91-0306	McD F-15E Strike Eagle [LN] *bl*	USAF 492nd FS/48th FW, Lakenheath
	91-0307	McD F-15E Strike Eagle [LN] *bl*	USAF 492nd FS/48th FW, Lakenheath
	91-0308	McD F-15E Strike Eagle [LN] *bl*	USAF 492nd FS/48th FW, Lakenheath
	91-0309	McD F-15E Strike Eagle [LN] *r*	USAF 494th FS/48th FW, Lakenheath
	91-0310	McD F-15E Strike Eagle [LN] *r*	USAF 494th FS/48th FW, Lakenheath
	91-0311	McD F-15E Strike Eagle [LN] *m* [48 FW]	USAF 494th FS/48th FW, Lakenheath
	91-0312	McD F-15E Strike Eagle [LN] *bl*	USAF 492nd FS/48th FW, Lakenheath
	91-0313	McD F-15E Strike Eagle [LN] *r*	USAF 494th FS/48th FW, Lakenheath
	91-0314	McD F-15E Strike Eagle [LN] *r*	USAF 494th FS/48th FW, Lakenheath
	91-0315	McD F-15E Strike Eagle [LN] *bl*	USAF 492nd FS/48th FW, Lakenheath
	91-0316	McD F-15E Strike Eagle [LN] *bl*	USAF 492nd FS/48th FW, Lakenheath
	91-0317	McD F-15E Strike Eagle [LN] *bl*	USAF 492nd FS/48th FW, Lakenheath
	91-0318	McD F-15E Strike Eagle [LN] *m* [48 OG]	USAF 494th FS/48th FW, Lakenheath
	91-0320	McD F-15E Strike Eagle [LN] *r* [494 FS]	USAF 494th FS/48th FW, Lakenheath
	91-0321	McD F-15E Strike Eagle [LN] *bl*	USAF 492nd FS/48th FW, Lakenheath
	91-0324	McD F-15E Strike Eagle [LN] *r*	USAF 494th FS/48th FW, Lakenheath
	91-0326	McD F-15E Strike Eagle [LN] *r*	USAF 494th FS/48th FW, Lakenheath
	91-0327	McD F-15E Strike Eagle [LN] *bl*	USAF 492nd FS/48th FW, Lakenheath
	91-0329	McD F-15E Strike Eagle [LN] *r*	USAF 494th FS/48th FW, Lakenheath
	91-0331	McD F-15E Strike Eagle [LN] *bl*	USAF 492nd FS/48th FW, Lakenheath
	91-0332	McD F-15E Strike Eagle [LN] *bl*	USAF 492nd FS/48th FW, Lakenheath
	91-0334	McD F-15E Strike Eagle [LN] *r*	USAF 494th FS/48th FW, Lakenheath
	91-0335	McD F-15E Strike Eagle [LN] *r*	USAF 494th FS/48th FW, Lakenheath
	91-0602	McD F-15E Strike Eagle [LN] *r*	USAF 494th FS/48th FW, Lakenheath
	91-0603	McD F-15E Strike Eagle [LN] *r*	USAF 494th FS/48th FW, Lakenheath
	91-0604	McD F-15E Strike Eagle [LN] *r*	USAF 494th FS/48th FW, Lakenheath
	91-0605	McD F-15E Strike Eagle [LN] *bl*	USAF 492nd FS/48th FW, Lakenheath
	92-0364	McD F-15E Strike Eagle [LN] *r*	USAF 494th FS/48th FW, Lakenheath
	96-0201	McD F-15E Strike Eagle [LN] *r*	USAF 494th FS/48th FW, Lakenheath
	96-0202	McD F-15E Strike Eagle [LN] *bl*	USAF 492nd FS/48th FW, Lakenheath
	96-0204	McD F-15E Strike Eagle [LN] *r*	USAF 494th FS/48th FW, Lakenheath
	96-0205	McD F-15E Strike Eagle [LN] *bl*	USAF 492nd FS/48th FW, Lakenheath
	97-0218	McD F-15E Strike Eagle [LN] *bl*	USAF 492nd FS/48th FW, Lakenheath
	97-0219	McD F-15E Strike Eagle [LN] *bl*	USAF 492nd FS/48th FW, Lakenheath
	97-0220	McD F-15E Strike Eagle [LN] *bl*	USAF 492nd FS/48th FW, Lakenheath
	97-0221	McD F-15E Strike Eagle [LN] *bl* [492 FS]	USAF 492nd FS/48th FW, Lakenheath
	97-0222	McD F-15E Strike Eagle [LN] *bl*	USAF 492nd FS/48th FW, Lakenheath
	98-0131	McD F-15E Strike Eagle [LN] *bl*	USAF 492nd FS/48th FW, Lakenheath
	98-0132	McD F-15E Strike Eagle [LN] *r*	USAF 494th FS/48th FW, Lakenheath
	98-0133	McD F-15E Strike Eagle [LN] *bl*	USAF 492nd FS/48th FW, Lakenheath
	98-0134	McD F-15E Strike Eagle [LN] *bl*	USAF 492nd FS/48th FW, Lakenheath
	98-0135	McD F-15E Strike Eagle [LN] *bl*	USAF 492nd FS/48th FW, Lakenheath

Bell-Boeing CV-22B Osprey

Notes	Serial	Type (code/other identity)	Owner/operator, location or fate
	0033	Bell-Boeing CV-22B Osprey (07-0033)	*Returned to the USA, January 2016*
	0050	Bell-Boeing CV-22B Osprey (08-0050)	USAF 7th SOS/352nd SOW, Mildenhall
	0051	Bell-Boeing CV-22B Osprey (08-0051)	USAF 7th SOS/352nd SOW, Mildenhall
	0057	Bell-Boeing CV-22B Osprey (11-0057)	USAF 7th SOS/352nd SOW, Mildenhall
	0058	Bell-Boeing CV-22B Osprey (11-0058)	USAF 7th SOS/352nd SOW, Mildenhall
	0061	Bell-Boeing CV-22B Osprey (11-0061)	USAF 7th SOS/352nd SOW, Mildenhall
	0062	Bell-Boeing CV-22B Osprey (12-0062)	*Returned to the USA, January 2016*
	0063	Bell-Boeing CV-22B Osprey (12-0063)	USAF 7th SOS/352nd SOW, Mildenhall
	0064	Bell-Boeing CV-22B Osprey (12-0064)	USAF 7th SOS/352nd SOW, Mildenhall

Sikorsky HH-60G Pave Hawk

Notes	Serial	Type (code/other identity)	Owner/operator, location or fate
	26205	Sikorsky HH-60G Pave Hawk (89-26205) [LN]	USAF 56th RQS/48th FW, RAF Lakenheath
	26206	Sikorsky HH-60G Pave Hawk (89-26206) [LN]	USAF 56th RQS/48th FW, RAF Lakenheath
	26208	Sikorsky HH-60G Pave Hawk (89-26208) [LN]	USAF 56th RQS/48th FW, RAF Lakenheath
	26212	Sikorsky HH-60G Pave Hawk (89-26212) [LN]	USAF 56th RQS/48th FW, RAF Lakenheath
	26353	Sikorsky HH-60G Pave Hawk (91-26353) [LN]	USAF 56th RQS/48th FW, RAF Lakenheath

Serial	Type (code/other identity)	Owner/operator, location or fate	Notes
Lockheed MC-130J Commando II			
05714	Lockheed MC-130J Commando II (10-5714)	USAF 67th SOS/352nd SOW, RAF Mildenhall	
15731	Lockheed MC-130J Commando II (11-5731)	USAF 67th SOS/352nd SOW, RAF Mildenhall	
15733	Lockheed MC-130J Commando II (11-5733)	USAF 67th SOS/352nd SOW, RAF Mildenhall	
15737	Lockheed MC-130J Commando II (11-5737)	USAF 67th SOS/352nd SOW, RAF Mildenhall	
25757	Lockheed MC-130J Commando II (12-5757)	USAF 67th SOS/352nd SOW, RAF Mildenhall	
25759	Lockheed MC-130J Commando II (12-5759)	USAF 67th SOS/352nd SOW, RAF Mildenhall	
25760	Lockheed MC-130J Commando II (12-5760)	USAF 67th SOS/352nd SOW, RAF Mildenhall	
35778	Lockheed MC-130J Commando II (13-5778)	USAF 67th SOS/352nd SOW, RAF Mildenhall	
35786	Lockheed MC-130J Commando II (13-5786)	USAF 67th SOS/352nd SOW, RAF Mildenhall	
Boeing KC-135R Stratotanker/Boeing KC-135T Stratotanker			
00324	Boeing KC-135R Stratotanker (60-0324) [D] *r/w/bl*	USAF 351st ARS/100th ARW, RAF Mildenhall	
10267	Boeing KC-135R Stratotanker (61-0267) [D] *r/w/bl*	USAF 351st ARS/100th ARW, RAF Mildenhall	
10299	Boeing KC-135R Stratotanker (61-0299) [D] *r/w/bl*	USAF 351st ARS/100th ARW, RAF Mildenhall	
10321	Boeing KC-135R Stratotanker (61-0321) [D] *r/w/bl*	USAF 351st ARS/100th ARW, RAF Mildenhall	
23559	Boeing KC-135R Stratotanker (62-3559) [D] *r/w/bl*	USAF 351st ARS/100th ARW, RAF Mildenhall	
23565	Boeing KC-135R Stratotanker (62-3565) [D] *r/w/bl*	*Returned to the USA, 18 March 2016*	
37999	Boeing KC-135R Stratotanker (63-7999) [D] *r/w/bl*	USAF 351st ARS/100th ARW, RAF Mildenhall	
38021	Boeing KC-135R Stratotanker (63-8021) [D] *r/w/bl*	USAF 351st ARS/100th ARW, RAF Mildenhall	
38027	Boeing KC-135R Stratotanker (63-8027) [D] *r/w/bl*	*Returned to the USA, 14 October 2016*	
38871	Boeing KC-135R Stratotanker (63-8871) [D] *r/w/bl*	USAF 351st ARS/100th ARW, RAF Mildenhall	
38884	Boeing KC-135R Stratotanker (63-8884) [D] *r/w/bl*	USAF 351st ARS/100th ARW, RAF Mildenhall	
72605	Boeing KC-135R Stratotanker (57-2605) [D] *r/w/bl*	USAF 351st ARS/100th ARW, RAF Mildenhall	
80069	Boeing KC-135T Stratotanker (58-0069) [D] *r/w/bl*	USAF 351st ARS/100th ARW, RAF Mildenhall	
80094	Boeing KC-135T Stratotanker (58-0094) [D] *r/w/bl*	USAF 351st ARS/100th ARW, RAF Mildenhall	
80100	Boeing KC-135R Stratotanker (58-0100) [D] *r/w/bl*	USAF 351st ARS/100th ARW, RAF Mildenhall	
80118	Boeing KC-135R Stratotanker (58-0118) [D] *r/w/bl*	USAF 351st ARS/100th ARW, RAF Mildenhall	
91464	Boeing KC-135T Stratotanker (59-1464) [D] *r/w/bl*	*Returned to the USA, 21 July 2016*	
91471	Boeing KC-135R Stratotanker (59-1471) [D] *r/w/bl*	USAF 351st ARS/100th ARW, RAF Mildenhall	
91492	Boeing KC-135R Stratotanker (59-1492) [D] *r/w/bl*	*Returned to the USA, 19 February 2016*	
91513	Boeing KC-135T Stratotanker (59-1513) [D] *r/w/bl*	*Returned to the USA, 31 August 2016*	

60-0037/MT is a B-52H Stratofortress of the USAF's 23rd Bomb Squadron 'Barons', part of the 5th Bomb Wing based at Minot AFB in North Dakota, a machine now well over 50 years old and still in service.

These aircraft are normally based in Western Europe with the USAFE. They are shown in numerical order of type designation, with individual aircraft in serial number order as carried on the aircraft. Fiscal year (FY) details are also provided if necessary. The unit allocation and operating bases are given for most aircraft.

Notes	Serial	Type (code/other identity)	Owner/operator, location or fate
	Beech C-12 Super King Air		
	30497	Beech C-12D Super King Air (83-0497)	USAF US Embassy Flight, Taszár, Hungary
	60160	Beech C-12C Super King Air (76-0160)	*Returned to the USA*
	63239	Beech C-12C Super King Air (76-3239)	USAF US Embassy Flight, Taszár, Hungary
	Lockheed (GD) F-16CM/F-16DM Fighting Falcon		
	87-0350	Lockheed (GD) F-16CM-40 Fighting Falcon [AV] *gn/y*	USAF 555th FS/31st FW, Aviano, Italy
	87-0351	Lockheed (GD) F-16CM-40 Fighting Falcon [AV] *gn/y*	USAF 555th FS/31st FW, Aviano, Italy
	87-0355	Lockheed (GD) F-16CM-40 Fighting Falcon [AV] *pr/w*	USAF 510th FS/31st FW, Aviano, Italy
	87-0359	Lockheed (GD) F-16CM-40 Fighting Falcon [AV] *gn/y*	USAF 555th FS/31st FW, Aviano, Italy
	88-0413	Lockheed (GD) F-16CM-40 Fighting Falcon [AV] *pr/w*	USAF 510th FS/31st FW, Aviano, Italy
	88-0425	Lockheed (GD) F-16CM-40 Fighting Falcon [AV] *gn/y*	USAF 555th FS/31st FW, Aviano, Italy
	88-0435	Lockheed (GD) F-16CM-40 Fighting Falcon [AV] *gn/y*	USAF 555th FS/31st FW, Aviano, Italy
	88-0443	Lockheed (GD) F-16CM-40 Fighting Falcon [AV] *pr/w*	USAF 510th FS/31st FW, Aviano, Italy
	88-0444	Lockheed (GD) F-16CM-40 Fighting Falcon [AV] *pr/w*	USAF 510th FS/31st FW, Aviano, Italy
	88-0446	Lockheed (GD) F-16CM-40 Fighting Falcon [AV] *gn/y*	USAF 555th FS/31st FW, Aviano, Italy
	88-0491	Lockheed (GD) F-16CM-40 Fighting Falcon [AV] *pr/w*	USAF 510th FS/31st FW, Aviano, Italy
	88-0516	Lockheed (GD) F-16CM-40 Fighting Falcon [AV] *pr/w*	USAF 510th FS/31st FW, Aviano, Italy
	88-0525	Lockheed (GD) F-16CM-40 Fighting Falcon [AV] *pr/w*	USAF 510th FS/31st FW, Aviano, Italy
	88-0526	Lockheed (GD) F-16CM-40 Fighting Falcon [AV] *gn/y*	USAF 555th FS/31st FW, Aviano, Italy
	88-0532	Lockheed (GD) F-16CM-40 Fighting Falcon [AV] *gn/y*	USAF 555th FS/31st FW, Aviano, Italy
	88-0535	Lockheed (GD) F-16CM-40 Fighting Falcon [AV] *gn/y*	USAF 555th FS/31st FW, Aviano, Italy
	88-0541	Lockheed (GD) F-16CM-40 Fighting Falcon [AV] *pr/w*	USAF 510th FS/31st FW, Aviano, Italy
	89-2001	Lockheed (GD) F-16CM-40 Fighting Falcon [AV] *m* [31 FW]	USAF 31st FW, Aviano, Italy
	89-2008	Lockheed (GD) F-16CM-40 Fighting Falcon [AV] *pr/w*	USAF 510th FS/31st FW, Aviano, Italy
	89-2009	Lockheed (GD) F-16CM-40 Fighting Falcon [AV] *pr/w*	USAF 510th FS/31st FW, Aviano, Italy
	89-2011	Lockheed (GD) F-16CM-40 Fighting Falcon [AV] *pr/w*	USAF 510th FS/31st FW, Aviano, Italy
	89-2016	Lockheed (GD) F-16CM-40 Fighting Falcon [AV] *gn/y*	USAF 555th FS/31st FW, Aviano, Italy
	89-2018	Lockheed (GD) F-16CM-40 Fighting Falcon [AV] *gn/y*	USAF 555th FS/31st FW, Aviano, Italy
	89-2023	Lockheed (GD) F-16CM-40 Fighting Falcon [AV] *gn/y*	USAF 555th FS/31st FW, Aviano, Italy
	89-2024	Lockheed (GD) F-16CM-40 Fighting Falcon [AV] *gn/y*	USAF 555th FS/31st FW, Aviano, Italy
	89-2026	Lockheed (GD) F-16CM-40 Fighting Falcon [AV] *pr/w*	USAF 510th FS/31st FW, Aviano, Italy
	89-2029	Lockheed (GD) F-16CM-40 Fighting Falcon [AV] *pr/w*	USAF 510th FS/31st FW, Aviano, Italy
	89-2030	Lockheed (GD) F-16CM-40 Fighting Falcon [AV] *pr/w* [510 FS]	USAF 510th FS/31st FW, Aviano, Italy
	89-2035	Lockheed (GD) F-16CM-40 Fighting Falcon [AV] *gn/y* [555 FS]	USAF 555th FS/31st FW, Aviano, Italy
	89-2038	Lockheed (GD) F-16CM-40 Fighting Falcon [AV] *pr/w*	USAF 510th FS/31st FW, Aviano, Italy
	89-2039	Lockheed (GD) F-16CM-40 Fighting Falcon [AV] *gn/y*	USAF 555th FS/31st FW, Aviano, Italy
	89-2041	Lockheed (GD) F-16CM-40 Fighting Falcon [AV] *gn/y*	USAF 555th FS/31st FW, Aviano, Italy
	89-2044	Lockheed (GD) F-16CM-40 Fighting Falcon [AV] *gn/y*	USAF 555th FS/31st FW, Aviano, Italy
	89-2046	Lockheed (GD) F-16CM-40 Fighting Falcon [AV] *pr/w*	USAF 510th FS/31st FW, Aviano, Italy
	89-2047	Lockheed (GD) F-16CM-40 Fighting Falcon [AV] *pr/w*	USAF 510th FS/31st FW, Aviano, Italy
	89-2049	Lockheed (GD) F-16CM-40 Fighting Falcon [AV] *pr/w* [USAFE]	USAF 510th FS/31st FW, Aviano, Italy
	89-2057	Lockheed (GD) F-16CM-40 Fighting Falcon [AV] *pr/w*	USAF 510th FS/31st FW, Aviano, Italy
	89-2068	Lockheed (GD) F-16CM-40 Fighting Falcon [AV] *gn/y*	USAF 555th FS/31st FW, Aviano, Italy
	89-2096	Lockheed (GD) F-16CM-40 Fighting Falcon [AV] *pr/w*	USAF 510th FS/31st FW, Aviano, Italy
	89-2102	Lockheed (GD) F-16CM-40 Fighting Falcon [AV] *pr/w*	USAF 510th FS/31st FW, Aviano, Italy
	89-2118	Lockheed (GD) F-16CM-40 Fighting Falcon [AV] *gn/y*	USAF 555th FS/31st FW, Aviano, Italy
	89-2137	Lockheed (GD) F-16CM-40 Fighting Falcon [AV] *pr/w* [31 OG]	USAF 510th FS/31st FW, Aviano, Italy
	89-2152	Lockheed (GD) F-16CM-40 Fighting Falcon [AV] *gn/y*	USAF 555th FS/31st FW, Aviano, Italy
	89-2178	Lockheed (GD) F-16DM-40 Fighting Falcon [AV] *gn/y*	USAF 555th FS/31st FW, Aviano, Italy
	90-0709	Lockheed (GD) F-16CM-40 Fighting Falcon [AV] *pr/w*	USAF 510th FS/31st FW, Aviano, Italy
	90-0772	Lockheed (GD) F-16CM-40 Fighting Falcon [AV] *gn/y*	USAF 555th FS/31st FW, Aviano, Italy
	90-0773	Lockheed (GD) F-16CM-40 Fighting Falcon [AV] *gn/y*	USAF 555th FS/31st FW, Aviano, Italy

Serial	Type (code/other identity)	Owner/operator, location or fate	Notes
90-0777	Lockheed (GD) F-16DM-40 Fighting Falcon [AV] *pr/w*	USAF 510th FS/31st FW, Aviano, Italy	
90-0795	Lockheed (GD) F-16DM-40 Fighting Falcon [AV] *gn/y*	USAF 555th FS/31st FW, Aviano, Italy	
90-0796	Lockheed (GD) F-16DM-40 Fighting Falcon [AV] *gn/y*	USAF 555th FS/31st FW, Aviano, Italy	
90-0800	Lockheed (GD) F-16DM-40 Fighting Falcon [AV] *gn/y*	USAF 555th FS/31st FW, Aviano, Italy	
90-0813	Lockheed (GD) F-16CM-50 Fighting Falcon [SP] *r*	USAF 480th FS/52nd FW, Spangdahlem, Germany	
90-0818	Lockheed (GD) F-16CM-50 Fighting Falcon [SP] *r*	USAF 480th FS/52nd FW, Spangdahlem, Germany	
90-0827	Lockheed (GD) F-16CM-50 Fighting Falcon [SP] *r*	USAF 480th FS/52nd FW, Spangdahlem, Germany	
90-0829	Lockheed (GD) F-16CM-50 Fighting Falcon [SP] *r* [52 OG]	USAF 480th FS/52nd FW, Spangdahlem, Germany	
90-0833	Lockheed (GD) F-16CM-50 Fighting Falcon [SP] *r*	USAF 480th FS/52nd FW, Spangdahlem, Germany	
91-0338	Lockheed (GD) F-16CM-50 Fighting Falcon [SP] *r*	USAF 480th FS/52nd FW, Spangdahlem, Germany	
91-0340	Lockheed (GD) F-16CM-50 Fighting Falcon [SP] *r*	USAF 480th FS/52nd FW, Spangdahlem, Germany	
91-0342	Lockheed (GD) F-16CM-50 Fighting Falcon [SP] *r*	USAF 480th FS/52nd FW, Spangdahlem, Germany	
91-0343	Lockheed (GD) F-16CM-50 Fighting Falcon [SP] *r*	USAF 480th FS/52nd FW, Spangdahlem, Germany	
91-0344	Lockheed (GD) F-16CM-50 Fighting Falcon [SP] *r*	USAF 480th FS/52nd FW, Spangdahlem, Germany	
91-0351	Lockheed (GD) F-16CM-50 Fighting Falcon [SP] *r*	USAF 480th FS/52nd FW, Spangdahlem, Germany	
91-0352	Lockheed (GD) F-16CM-50 Fighting Falcon [SP] *m* [52 FW]	USAF 480th FS/52nd FW, Spangdahlem, Germany	
91-0358	Lockheed (GD) F-16CM-50 Fighting Falcon [SP] *r*	USAF 480th FS/52nd FW, Spangdahlem, Germany	
91-0360	Lockheed (GD) F-16CM-50 Fighting Falcon [SP] *r*	USAF 480th FS/52nd FW, Spangdahlem, Germany	
91-0361	Lockheed (GD) F-16CM-50 Fighting Falcon [SP] *r*	USAF 480th FS/52nd FW, Spangdahlem, Germany	
91-0368	Lockheed (GD) F-16CM-50 Fighting Falcon [SP]	USAF 480th FS/52nd FW, Spangdahlem, Germany	
91-0402	Lockheed (GD) F-16CM-50 Fighting Falcon [SP] *r*	USAF 480th FS/52nd FW, Spangdahlem, Germany	
91-0403	Lockheed (GD) F-16CM-50 Fighting Falcon [SP] *r*	USAF 480th FS/52nd FW, Spangdahlem, Germany	
91-0407	Lockheed (GD) F-16CM-50 Fighting Falcon [SP] *r*	USAF 480th FS/52nd FW, Spangdahlem, Germany	
91-0412	Lockheed (GD) F-16CM-50 Fighting Falcon [SP] *r*	USAF 480th FS/52nd FW, Spangdahlem, Germany	
91-0416	Lockheed (GD) F-16CM-50 Fighting Falcon [SP] *r*	USAF 480th FS/52nd FW, Spangdahlem, Germany	
91-0417	Lockheed (GD) F-16CM-50 Fighting Falcon [SP] *r*	USAF 480th FS/52nd FW, Spangdahlem, Germany	
91-0418	Lockheed (GD) F-16CM-50 Fighting Falcon [SP] *r*	USAF 480th FS/52nd FW, Spangdahlem, Germany	
91-0472	Lockheed (GD) F-16DM-50 Fighting Falcon [SP]	USAF 480th FS/52nd FW, Spangdahlem, Germany	
91-0481	Lockheed (GD) F-16DM-50 Fighting Falcon [SP] *r*	USAF 480th FS/52nd FW, Spangdahlem, Germany	
92-3918	Lockheed (GD) F-16CM-50 Fighting Falcon [SP] *r*	USAF 480th FS/52nd FW, Spangdahlem, Germany	
96-0080	Lockheed (GD) F-16CM-50 Fighting Falcon [SP] *r*	USAF 480th FS/52nd FW, Spangdahlem, Germany	
96-0083	Lockheed (GD) F-16CM-50 Fighting Falcon [SP] *r*	USAF 480th FS/52nd FW, Spangdahlem, Germany	

Notes	Serial	Type (code/other identity)	Owner/operator, location or fate
	Grumman C-20H Gulfstream IV		
	00300	Grumman C-20H Gulfstream IV (90-0300)	USAF 76th AS/86th AW, Ramstein, Germany
	20375	Grumman C-20H Gulfstream IV (92-0375)	USAF 76th AS/86th AW, Ramstein, Germany
	Gates C-21A		
	40083	Gates C-21A (84-0083)	USAF 76th AS/86th AW, Ramstein, Germany
	40085	Gates C-21A (84-0085)	USAF 76th AS/86th AW, Ramstein, Germany
	40087	Gates C-21A (84-0087)	USAF 76th AS/86th AW, Ramstein, Germany
	40096	Gates C-21A (84-0096)	USAF 76th AS/86th AW, Ramstein, Germany
	40126	Gates C-21A (84-0126)	USAF 76th AS/86th AW, Ramstein, Germany
	Gulfstream Aerospace C-37A Gulfstream V		
	10076	Gulfstream Aerospace C-37A Gulfstream V (01-0076)	USAF 309th AS/86th AW, Chièvres, Belgium
	90402	Gulfstream Aerospace C-37A Gulfstream V (99-0402)	USAF 309th AS/86th AW, Chièvres, Belgium
	Boeing C-40B		
	20042	Boeing C-40B (02-0042)	USAF 76th AS/86th AW, Ramstein, Germany
	Lockheed C-130J-30 Hercules II		
	43142	Lockheed C-130J-30 Hercules II (04-3142)[RS] *bl/w*	USAF 37th AS/86th AW, Ramstein, Germany
	68610	Lockheed C-130J-30 Hercules II (06-8610)[RS] *bl/w*	USAF 37th AS/86th AW, Ramstein, Germany
	68611	Lockheed C-130J-30 Hercules II (06-8611)[RS] *bl/w*	USAF 37th AS/86th AW, Ramstein, Germany
	68612	Lockheed C-130J-30 Hercules II (06-8612)[RS] *bl/w*	USAF 37th AS/86th AW, Ramstein, Germany
	78608	Lockheed C-130J-30 Hercules II (07-8608)[RS] *bl/w*	USAF 37th AS/86th AW, Ramstein, Germany
	78609	Lockheed C-130J-30 Hercules II (07-8609)[RS] *bl/w*	USAF 37th AS/86th AW, Ramstein, Germany
	78613	Lockheed C-130J-30 Hercules II (07-8613)[RS] *bl/w*	USAF 37th AS/86th AW, Ramstein, Germany
	78614	Lockheed C-130J-30 Hercules II (07-8614)[RS] *bl/w*	USAF 37th AS/86th AW, Ramstein, Germany
	88601	Lockheed C-130J-30 Hercules II (08-8601)[RS] *bl/w* [86 AW]	USAF 37th AS/86th AW, Ramstein, Germany
	88602	Lockheed C-130J-30 Hercules II (08-8602)[RS] *bl/w* [86 OG]	USAF 37th AS/86th AW, Ramstein, Germany
	88603	Lockheed C-130J-30 Hercules II (08-8603)[RS] *bl/w* [37 AS]	USAF 37th AS/86th AW, Ramstein, Germany
	88604	Lockheed C-130J-30 Hercules II (08-8604)[RS] *bl/w*	USAF 37th AS/86th AW, Ramstein, Germany
	88605	Lockheed C-130J-30 Hercules II (08-8605)[RS] *bl/w*	USAF 37th AS/86th AW, Ramstein, Germany
	88607	Lockheed C-130J-30 Hercules II (08-8607)[RS] *bl/w*	USAF 37th AS/86th AW, Ramstein, Germany

C-130H 90-1798 belongs to the USAF's 180th Airlift Squadron, part of the 139th Airlift Wing, Missouri Air National Guard, based at St. Joseph-Rosecrans Memorial Airport. In recent years the squadron markings of these machines have been toned down somewhat to the black and grey depicted here.

EUROPEAN-BASED US NAVY AIRCRAFT

Serial	Type (code/other identity)	Owner/operator, location or fate	Notes
Fairchild C-26D			
900528	Fairchild C-26D	USN NAF Sigonella, Italy	
900530	Fairchild C-26D	USN NAF Sigonella, Italy	
900531	Fairchild C-26D	USN NAF Naples, Italy	
910502	Fairchild C-26D	USN NAF Naples, Italy	

EUROPEAN-BASED US ARMY AIRCRAFT

Serial	Type (code/other identity)	Owner/operator, location or fate
Beech C-12 Huron		
40156	Beech C-12U-3 Huron (84-00156)	US Army E/1-214th AVN, Wiesbaden, Germany
40157	Beech C-12U-3 Huron (84-00157)	US Army E/1-214th AVN, Wiesbaden, Germany
40160	Beech C-12U-3 Huron (84-00160)	US Army E/1-214th AVN, Wiesbaden, Germany
40162	Beech C-12U-3 Huron (84-00162)	US Army E/1-214th AVN, Wiesbaden, Germany
40165	Beech C-12U-3 Huron (84-00165)	US Army E/1-214th AVN, Wiesbaden, Germany
40173	Beech C-12U-3 Huron (84-00173)	US Army E/1-214th AVN, Wiesbaden, Germany
Cessna UC-35A Citation V		
50123	Cessna UC-35A Citation V (95-00123)	US Army E/1-214th AVN, Wiesbaden, Germany
70102	Cessna UC-35A Citation V (97-00102)	US Army E/1-214th AVN, Wiesbaden, Germany
70105	Cessna UC-35A Citation V (97-00105)	US Army E/1-214th AVN, Wiesbaden, Germany
90102	Cessna UC-35A Citation V (99-00102)	US Army E/1-214th AVN, Wiesbaden, Germany
Boeing-Vertol CH-47F Chinook		
13-08132	Boeing-Vertol CH-47F Chinook	US Army H/1-214th AVN, Ansbach, Germany
13-08133	Boeing-Vertol CH-47F Chinook	US Army H/1-214th AVN, Ansbach, Germany
13-08134	Boeing-Vertol CH-47F Chinook	US Army H/1-214th AVN, Ansbach, Germany
13-08135	Boeing-Vertol CH-47F Chinook	US Army H/1-214th AVN, Ansbach, Germany
13-08432	Boeing-Vertol CH-47F Chinook	US Army H/1-214th AVN, Ansbach, Germany
13-08434	Boeing-Vertol CH-47F Chinook	US Army H/1-214th AVN, Ansbach, Germany
13-08435	Boeing-Vertol CH-47F Chinook	US Army H/1-214th AVN, Ansbach, Germany
13-08436	Boeing-Vertol CH-47F Chinook	US Army H/1-214th AVN, Ansbach, Germany
13-08437	Boeing-Vertol CH-47F Chinook	US Army H/1-214th AVN, Ansbach, Germany
Sikorsky H-60 Black Hawk		
23936	Sikorsky UH-60A+ Black Hawk (84-23936)	US Army C/1-214th AVN, Grafenwöhr, Germany
24397	Sikorsky UH-60A+ Black Hawk (85-24397)	US Army C/1-214th AVN, Grafenwöhr, Germany
24437	Sikorsky UH-60A+ Black Hawk (85-24437)	US Army C/1-214th AVN, Grafenwöhr, Germany
24446	Sikorsky UH-60A+ Black Hawk (85-24446)	US Army C/1-214th AVN, Grafenwöhr, Germany
24538	Sikorsky UH-60A Black Hawk (86-24538)	US Army A/1-214th AVN, Wiesbaden, Germany
24583	Sikorsky UH-60A Black Hawk (87-24583)	US Army A/1-214th AVN, Wiesbaden, Germany

Notes	Serial	Type (code/other identity)	Owner/operator, location or fate
	24584	Sikorsky UH-60A Black Hawk (87-24584)	US Army A/1-214th AVN, Wiesbaden, Germany
	24589	Sikorsky UH-60A Black Hawk (87-24589)	US Army A/1-214th AVN, Wiesbaden, Germany
	24614	Sikorsky UH-60A+ Black Hawk (87-24614)	US Army C/1-214th AVN, Grafenwöhr, Germany
	24642	Sikorsky UH-60A Black Hawk (87-24642)	US Army A/1-214th AVN, Wiesbaden, Germany
	24643	Sikorsky UH-60A Black Hawk (87-24643)	US Army A/1-214th AVN, Wiesbaden, Germany
	26004	Sikorsky UH-60A+ Black Hawk (87-26004)	US Army C/1-214th AVN, Grafenwöhr, Germany
	26027	Sikorsky UH-60A Black Hawk (88-26027)	US Army A/1-214th AVN, Wiesbaden, Germany
	26071	Sikorsky UH-60A Black Hawk (88-26071)	US Army A/1-214th AVN, Wiesbaden, Germany
	26142	Sikorsky UH-60A Black Hawk (89-26142)	US Army A/1-214th AVN, Wiesbaden, Germany
	26163	Sikorsky UH-60A+ Black Hawk (89-26163)	US Army C/1-214th AVN, Grafenwöhr, Germany
	26165	Sikorsky UH-60A Black Hawk (89-26165)	US Army A/1-214th AVN, Wiesbaden, Germany

MDH AH-64D Apache

Notes	Serial	Type (code/other identity)	Owner/operator, location or fate
	05316	MDH AH-64D Apache (02-05316)	US Army 1-3rd AVN, Ansbach, Germany
	05321	MDH AH-64D Apache (02-05321)	US Army 1-3rd AVN, Ansbach, Germany
	05327	MDH AH-64D Apache (02-05327)	US Army 1-3rd AVN, Ansbach, Germany
	05381	MDH AH-64D Apache (03-05381)	US Army 1-3rd AVN, Ansbach, Germany
	05384	MDH AH-64D Apache (03-05384)	US Army 1-3rd AVN, Ansbach, Germany
	05419	MDH AH-64D Apache (04-05419)	US Army 1-3rd AVN, Ansbach, Germany
	05426	MDH AH-64D Apache (04-05426)	US Army 1-3rd AVN, Ansbach, Germany
	05429	MDH AH-64D Apache (04-05429)	US Army 1-3rd AVN, Ansbach, Germany
	05431	MDH AH-64D Apache (04-05431)	US Army 1-3rd AVN, Ansbach, Germany
	05437	MDH AH-64D Apache (04-05437)	US Army 1-3rd AVN, Ansbach, Germany
	05439	MDH AH-64D Apache (04-05439)	US Army 1-3rd AVN, Ansbach, Germany
	05444	MDH AH-64D Apache (04-05444)	US Army 1-3rd AVN, Ansbach, Germany
	05453	MDH AH-64D Apache (04-05453)	US Army 1-3rd AVN, Ansbach, Germany
	05467	MDH AH-64D Apache (04-05467)	US Army 1-3rd AVN, Ansbach, Germany
	05535	MDH AH-64D Apache (07-05535)	US Army 1-3rd AVN, Ansbach, Germany
	05543	MDH AH-64D Apache (08-05543)	US Army 1-3rd AVN, Ansbach, Germany
	05550	MDH AH-64D Apache (08-05550)	US Army 1-3rd AVN, Ansbach, Germany
	05580	MDH AH-64D Apache (09-05580)	US Army 1-3rd AVN, Ansbach, Germany
	05581	MDH AH-64D Apache (09-05581)	US Army 1-3rd AVN, Ansbach, Germany
	05587	MDH AH-64D Apache (09-05587)	US Army 1-3rd AVN, Ansbach, Germany
	05589	MDH AH-64D Apache (09-05589)	US Army 1-3rd AVN, Ansbach, Germany
	05620	MDH AH-64D Apache (10-05620)	US Army 1-3rd AVN, Ansbach, Germany
	07010	MDH AH-64D Apache (05-07010)	US Army 1-3rd AVN, Ansbach, Germany
	07014	MDH AH-64D Apache (06-07014)	US Army 1-3rd AVN, Ansbach, Germany

Eurocopter UH-72A Lakota

Notes	Serial	Type (code/other identity)	Owner/operator, location or fate
	72029	Eurocopter UH-72A Lakota (07-72029)	US Army JMRC, Hohenfels
	72097	Eurocopter UH-72A Lakota (09-72097)	US Army JMRC, Hohenfels
	72098	Eurocopter UH-72A Lakota (09-72098)	US Army JMRC, Hohenfels
	72100	Eurocopter UH-72A Lakota (09-72100)	US Army JMRC, Hohenfels
	72105	Eurocopter UH-72A Lakota (09-72105)	US Army JMRC, Hohenfels
	72106	Eurocopter UH-72A Lakota (09-72106)	US Army JMRC, Hohenfels
	72107	Eurocopter UH-72A Lakota (09-72107)	US Army JMRC, Hohenfels
	72108	Eurocopter UH-72A Lakota (09-72108)	US Army JMRC, Hohenfels

The following aircraft are normally based in the USA but are likely to be seen visiting the UK from time to time. The presentation is in numerical order of the type, commencing with the B-1B and concluding with the C-135. The aircraft are listed in numerical progression by the serial actually carried externally. Fiscal year information is provided, together with details of mark variations and in some cases operating units. Where base-code letter information is carried on the aircrafts' tails, this is detailed with the squadron/base data; for example the 7th Wing's B-1B 60105 carries the letters DY on its tail, thus identifying the Wing's home base as Dyess AFB, Texas.

Serial	Type (code/other identity)	Owner/operator, location or fate
Rockwell B-1B Lancer		
50059	Rockwell B-1B Lancer (85-0059) [DY] bk/w $	USAF 9th BS/7th BW, Dyess AFB, TX
50060	Rockwell B-1B Lancer (85-0060) [EL] bk/r	USAF 34th BS/28th BW, Ellsworth AFB, SD
50061	Rockwell B-1B Lancer (85-0061) [DY] bl/w	USAF 28th BS/7th BW, Dyess AFB, TX
50064	Rockwell B-1B Lancer (85-0064) [DY] bl/w	USAF 28th BS/7th BW, Dyess AFB, TX
50066	Rockwell B-1B Lancer (85-0066) [EL] bk/y $	USAF 37th BS/28th BW, Ellsworth AFB, SD
50068	Rockwell B-1B Lancer (85-0068) [ED]	USAF 419th FLTS/412th TW, Edwards AFB
50069	Rockwell B-1B Lancer (85-0069) [EL] bk/w	USAF 28th BW, Ellsworth AFB, SD
50072	Rockwell B-1B Lancer (85-0072) [EL] bk/r	USAF 34th BS/28th BW, Ellsworth AFB, SD
50073	Rockwell B-1B Lancer (85-0073) [DY] bk/w [7 OG]	USAF 9th BS/7th BW, Dyess AFB, TX
50074	Rockwell B-1B Lancer (85-0074) [DY] bk/w	USAF 9th BS/7th BW, Dyess AFB, TX
50075	Rockwell B-1B Lancer (85-0075) [ED]	USAF 419th FLTS/412th TW, Edwards AFB
50077	Rockwell B-1B Lancer (85-0077) [WA] y/bk [77 WPS]	USAF 77th WPS/57th Wg, Dyess AFB, TX
50079	Rockwell B-1B Lancer (85-0079) [EL] bk/r	USAF 34th BS/28th BW, Ellsworth AFB, SD
50080	Rockwell B-1B Lancer (85-0080) [DY] bk/w	USAF 9th BS/7th BW, Dyess AFB, TX
50081	Rockwell B-1B Lancer (85-0081) [EL] bk/r	USAF 34th BS/28th BW, Ellsworth AFB, SD
50084	Rockwell B-1B Lancer (85-0084) [EL] bk/r	USAF 34th BS/28th BW, Ellsworth AFB, SD
50085	Rockwell B-1B Lancer (85-0085) [EL] bk/y	USAF 37th BS/28th BW, Ellsworth AFB, SD
50087	Rockwell B-1B Lancer (85-0087) [DY] bk/w	USAF 98th BS/7th BW, Dyess AFB, TX
50088	Rockwell B-1B Lancer (85-0088) [DY] bl/w	USAF 28th BS/7th BW, Dyess AFB, TX
50089	Rockwell B-1B Lancer (85-0089) [DY] r/y [489 BG]	USAF 28th BS/7th BW, Dyess AFB, TX
50090	Rockwell B-1B Lancer (85-0090) [DY] bl/w	USAF 28th BS/7th BW, Dyess AFB, TX
60094	Rockwell B-1B Lancer (86-0094) [EL] bk/y $	USAF 37th BS/28th BW, Ellsworth AFB, SD
60095	Rockwell B-1B Lancer (86-0095) [EL] bk/r	USAF 34th BS/28th BW, Ellsworth AFB, SD
60097	Rockwell B-1B Lancer (86-0097) [EL] bk/y	USAF 37th BS/28th BW, Ellsworth AFB, SD
60098	Rockwell B-1B Lancer (86-0098) [DY] bk/w	USAF 9th BS/7th BW, Dyess AFB, TX
60099	Rockwell B-1B Lancer (86-0099) [EL] bk/y $	USAF 37th BS/28th BW, Ellsworth AFB, SD
60101	Rockwell B-1B Lancer (86-0101) [DY] bl/w	USAF 28th BS/7th BW, Dyess AFB, TX
60102	Rockwell B-1B Lancer (86-0102) [EL] bk/y	USAF 37th BS/28th BW, Ellsworth AFB, SD
60103	Rockwell B-1B Lancer (86-0103) [DY] bl/w	USAF 28th BS/7th BW, Dyess AFB, TX
60104	Rockwell B-1B Lancer (86-0104) [EL] bk/y	USAF 37th BS/28th BW, Ellsworth AFB, SD
60105	Rockwell B-1B Lancer (86-0105) [DY] bl/w	USAF 28th BS/7th BW, Dyess AFB, TX
60107	Rockwell B-1B Lancer (86-0107) [DY] bk/w	USAF 9th BS/7th BW, Dyess AFB, TX
60108	Rockwell B-1B Lancer (86-0108) [EL] bk/y	USAF 37th BS/28th BW, Ellsworth AFB, SD
60109	Rockwell B-1B Lancer (86-0109) [DY] bl/w	USAF 289th BS/7th BW, Dyess AFB, TX
60110	Rockwell B-1B Lancer (86-0110) [DY] bl/w	USAF 28th BS/7th BW, Dyess AFB, TX
60111	Rockwell B-1B Lancer (86-0111) [EL] bk/r	USAF 34th BS/28th BW, Ellsworth AFB, SD
60112	Rockwell B-1B Lancer (86-0112) [DY] bl/w	USAF 28th BS/7th BW, Dyess AFB, TX
60113	Rockwell B-1B Lancer (86-0113) [EL] bk/y	USAF 37th BS/28th BW, Ellsworth AFB, SD
60115	Rockwell B-1B Lancer (86-0115) [EL] bk/r	USAF 34th BS/28th BW, Ellsworth AFB, SD
60117	Rockwell B-1B Lancer (86-0117) [DY] bk/w	USAF 9th BS/7th BW, Dyess AFB, TX
60118	Rockwell B-1B Lancer (86-0118) [EL] bk/y	USAF 37th BS/28th BW, Ellsworth AFB, SD
60119	Rockwell B-1B Lancer (86-0119) [DY] bl/w	USAF 28th BS/7th BW, Dyess AFB, TX
60120	Rockwell B-1B Lancer (86-0120) [OT] bk/gy	USAF 337th TES/53rd Wg, Dyess AFB, TX
60121	Rockwell B-1B Lancer (86-0121) [EL] bk/y	USAF 37th BS/28th BW, Ellsworth AFB, SD
60122	Rockwell B-1B Lancer (86-0122) [OT] bk/gy [337 TES]	USAF 337th TES/53rd Wg, Dyess AFB, TX
60123	Rockwell B-1B Lancer (86-0123) [DY] bl/w	USAF 28th BS/7th BW, Dyess AFB, TX
60124	Rockwell B-1B Lancer (86-0124) [DY] bl/w	USAF 28th BS/7th BW, Dyess AFB, TX
60125	Rockwell B-1B Lancer (86-0125) [DY] bk/w	USAF 9th BS/7th BW, Dyess AFB, TX
60126	Rockwell B-1B Lancer (86-0126) [DY] bl/w	USAF 28th BS/7th BW, Dyess AFB, TX
60127	Rockwell B-1B Lancer (86-0127) [DY] bk/w	USAF 9th BS/7th BW, Dyess AFB, TX
60129	Rockwell B-1B Lancer (86-0129) [EL] bk/y	USAF 37th BS/28th BW, Ellsworth AFB, SD
60132	Rockwell B-1B Lancer (86-0132) [DY] bl/w	USAF 28th BS/7th BW, Dyess AFB, TX

Notes	Serial	Type (code/other identity)	Owner/operator, location or fate
	60133	Rockwell B-1B Lancer (86-0133) [DY] *bl/w*	USAF 28th BS/7th BW, Dyess AFB, TX
	60134	Rockwell B-1B Lancer (86-0134) [EL] *bk/r*	USAF 34th BS/28th BW, Ellsworth AFB, SD
	60135	Rockwell B-1B Lancer (86-0135) [DY] *bl/w*	USAF 28th BS/7th BW, Dyess AFB, TX
	60136	Rockwell B-1B Lancer (86-0136) [DY] *bl/w*	USAF 28th BS/7th BW, Dyess AFB, TX
	60138	Rockwell B-1B Lancer (86-0138) [DY] *y/bk*	USAF 7th BW, Dyess AFB, TX
	60139	Rockwell B-1B Lancer (86-0139) [EL] *bl/y* [34 BS]	USAF 34th BS/28th BW, Ellsworth AFB, SD
	60140	Rockwell B-1B Lancer (86-0140) [DY] *bl/w*	USAF 28th BS/7th BW, Dyess AFB, TX
		Northrop B-2 Spirit	
		(Names are given where known. Each begins *Spirit of ... *)	
	00040	Northrop B-2 Spirit (90-0040) [WM] *Alaska*	USAF 509th BW, Whiteman AFB, MO
	00041	Northrop B-2 Spirit (90-0041) [WM] *Hawaii*	USAF 509th BW, Whiteman AFB, MO
	20700	Northrop B-2 Spirit (92-0700) [WM] *Florida*	USAF 509th BW, Whiteman AFB, MO
	21066	Northrop B-2 Spirit (82-1066) [WM] *America*	USAF 509th BW, Whiteman AFB, MO
	21067	Northrop B-2 Spirit (82-1067) [WM] *Arizona*	USAF 509th BW, Whiteman AFB, MO
	21068	Northrop B-2 Spirit (82-1068) [WM] *New York*	USAF 509th BW, Whiteman AFB, MO
	21069	Northrop B-2 Spirit (82-1069) [WM] *Indiana*	USAF 509th BW, Whiteman AFB, MO
	21070	Northrop B-2 Spirit (82-1070) [WM] *Ohio*	USAF 509th BW, Whiteman AFB, MO
	21071	Northrop B-2 Spirit (82-1071) [WM] *Mississippi*	USAF 509th BW, Whiteman AFB, MO
	31085	Northrop B-2 Spirit (93-1085) [ED] *Oklahoma*	USAF 419th FLTS/412th TW, Edwards AFB,CA
	31086	Northrop B-2 Spirit (93-1086) [WM] *Kitty Hawk*	USAF 509th BW, Whiteman AFB, MO
	31087	Northrop B-2 Spirit (93-1087) [WM] *Pennsylvania*	USAF 509th BW, Whiteman AFB, MO
	31088	Northrop B-2 Spirit (93-1088) [WM] *Louisiana*	USAF 509th BW, Whiteman AFB, MO
	80328	Northrop B-2 Spirit (88-0328) [WM] *Texas*	USAF 509th BW, Whiteman AFB, MO
	80329	Northrop B-2 Spirit (88-0329) [WM] *Missouri*	USAF 509th BW, Whiteman AFB, MO
	80330	Northrop B-2 Spirit (88-0330) [WM] *California*	USAF 509th BW, Whiteman AFB, MO
	80331	Northrop B-2 Spirit (88-0331) [WM] *South Carolina*	USAF 509th BW, Whiteman AFB, MO
	80332	Northrop B-2 Spirit (88-0332) [WM] *Washington*	USAF 509th BW, Whiteman AFB, MO
	90128	Northrop B-2 Spirit (89-0128) [WM] *Nebraska*	USAF 509th BW, Whiteman AFB, MO
	90129	Northrop B-2 Spirit (89-0129) [WM] *Georgia*	USAF 509th BW, Whiteman AFB, MO
		Lockheed U-2	
	68-10329	Lockheed U-2S [BB]	USAF 9th RW, Beale AFB, CA
	68-10331	Lockheed U-2S [BB]	USAF 9th RW, Beale AFB, CA
	68-10336	Lockheed U-2S [BB]	USAF 9th RW, Beale AFB, CA
	68-10337	Lockheed U-2S [BB] [9 OG]	USAF 9th RW, Beale AFB, CA
	80-1064	Lockheed TU-2S [BB]	USAF 9th RW, Beale AFB, CA
	80-1065	Lockheed TU-2S [BB]	USAF 9th RW, Beale AFB, CA
	80-1066	Lockheed U-2S [BB]	USAF 9th RW, Beale AFB, CA
	80-1067	Lockheed U-2S [BB]	USAF 9th RW, Beale AFB, CA
	80-1068	Lockheed TU-2S [BB]	*Crashed Sutter, CA, 20 September 2016*
	80-1069	Lockheed U-2S [BB]	USAF 9th RW, Beale AFB, CA
	80-1070	Lockheed U-2S	USAF WR-ALC, Robins AFB, GA
	80-1071	Lockheed U-2S [BB]	USAF 9th RW, Beale AFB, CA
	80-1073	Lockheed U-2S [BB]	USAF 9th RW, Beale AFB, CA
	80-1074	Lockheed U-2S [BB]	USAF 9th RW, Beale AFB, CA
	80-1076	Lockheed U-2S [BB]	USAF 9th RW, Beale AFB, CA
	80-1077	Lockheed U-2S [BB]	USAF 9th RW, Beale AFB, CA
	80-1078	Lockheed TU-2S [BB]	USAF 9th RW, Beale AFB, CA
	80-1079	Lockheed U-2S [BB]	USAF 9th RW, Beale AFB, CA
	80-1080	Lockheed U-2S [BB]	USAF 9th RW, Beale AFB, CA
	80-1081	Lockheed U-2S [BB]	USAF 9th RW, Beale AFB, CA
	80-1083	Lockheed U-2S [BB]	USAF 9th RW, Beale AFB, CA
	80-1084	Lockheed U-2S [BB]	USAF 9th RW, Beale AFB, CA
	80-1085	Lockheed U-2S [BB]	USAF 9th RW, Beale AFB, CA
	80-1086	Lockheed U-2S [BB]	USAF 9th RW, Beale AFB, CA
	80-1087	Lockheed U-2S [BB]	USAF 9th RW, Beale AFB, CA
	80-1089	Lockheed U-2S [BB]	USAF 9th RW, Beale AFB, CA
	80-1090	Lockheed U-2S [BB]	USAF 9th RW, Beale AFB, CA
	80-1091	Lockheed TU-2S [BB]	USAF 9th RW, Beale AFB, CA
	80-1092	Lockheed U-2S [BB]	USAF 9th RW, Beale AFB, CA
	80-1093	Lockheed U-2S [BB]	USAF 9th RW, Beale AFB, CA

Serial	Type (code/other identity)	Owner/operator, location or fate	Notes
80-1094	Lockheed U-2S [BB]	USAF 9th RW, Beale AFB, CA	
80-1096	Lockheed U-2S [BB]	USAF 9th RW, Beale AFB, CA	
80-1099	Lockheed U-2S [BB]	USAF 9th RW, Beale AFB, CA	

Boeing E-3 Sentry

Serial	Type (code/other identity)	Owner/operator, location or fate	Notes
00137	Boeing E-3B(mod) Sentry (80-0137) [OK] w	USAF 552nd ACW, Tinker AFB, OK	
00138	Boeing E-3G Sentry (80-0138) [OK] w	USAF 552nd ACW, Tinker AFB, OK	
00139	Boeing E-3C Sentry (80-0139) [OK] w	USAF 552nd ACW, Tinker AFB, OK	
10004	Boeing E-3C Sentry (81-0004) [OK] w	USAF 552nd ACW, Tinker AFB, OK	
10005	Boeing E-3G Sentry (81-0005) [OK] w	USAF 552nd ACW, Tinker AFB, OK	
11407	Boeing E-3B Sentry (71-1407) [ZZ] or	USAF 961st ACS/18th Wg, Kadena AB, Japan	
11408	Boeing E-3B Sentry (71-1408) [ZZ] or	USAF 961st ACS/18th Wg, Kadena AB, Japan	
20006	Boeing E-3C Sentry (82-0006) [OK]	USAF 552nd ACW, Tinker AFB, OK	
20007	Boeing E-3G Sentry (82-0007)	Boeing, Seattle, WA	
30009	Boeing E-3C Sentry (83-0009) [OK]	USAF 552nd ACW, Tinker AFB, OK	
31675	Boeing E-3B Sentry (73-1675) [ZZ] or	USAF 961st ACS/18th Wg, Kadena AB, Japan	
50556	Boeing E-3B Sentry (75-0556) [OK] w	USAF 552nd ACW, Tinker AFB, OK	
50557	Boeing E-3B Sentry (75-0557) [OK] r	USAF 552nd ACW, Tinker AFB, OK	
50558	Boeing E-3B Sentry (75-0558) [OK]	USAF 552nd ACW, Tinker AFB, OK	
50559	Boeing E-3B Sentry (75-0559) [OK] r	USAF 552nd ACW, Tinker AFB, OK	
50560	Boeing E-3B Sentry (75-0560) [OK] gn	USAF 552nd ACW, Tinker AFB, OK	
61604	Boeing E-3G Sentry (76-1604) [OK] w	USAF 552nd ACW, Tinker AFB, OK	
61605	Boeing E-3B Sentry (76-1605) [OK] w	USAF 552nd ACW, Tinker AFB, OK	
61606	Boeing E-3B Sentry (76-1606) [OK] w	USAF 552nd ACW, Tinker AFB, OK	
61607	Boeing E-3G Sentry (76-1607) [OK] w	USAF 552nd ACW, Tinker AFB, OK	
70351	Boeing E-3G Sentry (77-0351) [OK] w	USAF 552nd ACW, Tinker AFB, OK	
70352	Boeing E-3B Sentry (77-0352) [OK] w	USAF 552nd ACW, Tinker AFB, OK	
70353	Boeing E-3B Sentry (77-0353) [OK] r	USAF 552nd ACW, Tinker AFB, OK	
70355	Boeing E-3B Sentry (77-0355) [OK] w	USAF 552nd ACW, Tinker AFB, OK	
70356	Boeing E-3B Sentry (77-0356) [OK] w	USAF 552nd ACW, Tinker AFB, OK	
80576	Boeing E-3G Sentry (78-0576) [OK] w	USAF 552nd ACW, Tinker AFB, OK	
80577	Boeing E-3B Sentry (78-0577) [OK] w	USAF 552nd ACW, Tinker AFB, OK	
80578	Boeing E-3B Sentry (78-0578) [OK] w	USAF 552nd ACW, Tinker AFB, OK	
90001	Boeing E-3G Sentry (79-0001) [OK] w	USAF 552nd ACW, Tinker AFB, OK	
90002	Boeing E-3B Sentry (79-0002) [OK] w	USAF 552nd ACW, Tinker AFB, OK	
90003	Boeing E-3B Sentry (79-0003) [OK] m	USAF 552nd ACW, Tinker AFB, OK	

Boeing E-4B

Serial	Type (code/other identity)	Owner/operator, location or fate	Notes
31676	Boeing E-4B (73-1676)	USAF 1st ACCS/595th CACG, Offutt AFB, NE	
31677	Boeing E-4B (73-1677)	USAF 1st ACCS/595th CACG, Offutt AFB, NE	
40787	Boeing E-4B (74-0787)	USAF 1st ACCS/595th CACG, Offutt AFB, NE	
50125	Boeing E-4B (75-0125)	USAF 1st ACCS/595th CACG, Offutt AFB, NE	

Lockheed C-5 Galaxy/C-5M Super Galaxy

Serial	Type (code/other identity)	Owner/operator, location or fate	Notes
00448	Lockheed C-5A Galaxy (70-0448) bl/r	USAF 337th AS/439th AW, Westover ARB, MA	
00451	Lockheed C-5A Galaxy (70-0451) bl/r	USAF 337th AS/439th AW, Westover ARB, MA	
00456	Lockheed C-5A Galaxy (70-0456) bl/r	To AMARG, March 2017	
00461	Lockheed C-5A Galaxy (70-0461) bl/r	USAF 337th AS/439th AW, Westover ARB, MA	
31285	Lockheed C-5M Super Galaxy (83-1285) bl/y	USAF 9th AS/436th AW, Dover AFB, DE	
40060	Lockheed C-5M Super Galaxy (84-0060) w/bk	USAF 22nd AS/60th AMW, Travis AFB, CA	
40061	Lockheed C-5M Super Galaxy (84-0061) bl/y	USAF 9th AS/436th AW, Dover AFB, DE	
40062	Lockheed C-5M Super Galaxy (84-0062) w/bk	USAF 22nd AS/60th AMW, Travis AFB, CA	
50001	Lockheed C-5M Super Galaxy (85-0001) bl/y	USAF 9th AS/436th AW, Dover AFB, DE	
50002	Lockheed C-5M Super Galaxy (85-0002) bl/y	USAF 9th AS/436th AW, Dover AFB, DE	
50003	Lockheed C-5M Super Galaxy (85-0003) bl/y	USAF 9th AS/436th AW, Dover AFB, DE	
50004	Lockheed C-5M Super Galaxy (85-0004) bl/y	USAF 9th AS/436th AW, Dover AFB, DE	
50005	Lockheed C-5M Super Galaxy (85-0005) bl/y	USAF 9th AS/436th AW, Dover AFB, DE	
50006	Lockheed C-5M Super Galaxy (85-0006)	USAF 68th AS/433rd AW Kelly AFB, TX	
50007	Lockheed C-5M Super Galaxy (85-0007) bl/y	USAF 9th AS/436th AW, Dover AFB, DE	
50008	Lockheed C-5M Super Galaxy (85-0008) bl/y	USAF 9th AS/436th AW, Dover AFB, DE	
50009	Lockheed C-5M Super Galaxy (85-0009)	USAF 68th AS/433rd AW Kelly AFB, TX	
50010	Lockheed C-5M Super Galaxy (85-0010) w/bk	USAF 22nd AS/60th AMW, Travis AFB, CA	

Notes	Serial	Type (code/other identity)	Owner/operator, location or fate
	60011	Lockheed C-5M Super Galaxy (86-0011) *w/bk*	USAF 22nd AS/60th AMW, Travis AFB, CA
	60012	Lockheed C-5M Super Galaxy (86-0012)	LMTAS, Marietta, GA
	60013	Lockheed C-5M Super Galaxy (86-0013) *bl/y*	USAF 9th AS/436th AW, Dover AFB, DE
	60014	Lockheed C-5M Super Galaxy (86-0014)	LMTAS, Marietta, GA
	60015	Lockheed C-5M Super Galaxy (86-0015) *w/bk*	USAF 22nd AS/60th AMW, Travis AFB, CA
	60016	Lockheed C-5M Super Galaxy (86-0016) *w/bk*	USAF 22nd AS/60th AMW, Travis AFB, CA
	60017	Lockheed C-5M Super Galaxy (86-0017) *bl/y*	USAF 9th AS/436th AW, Dover AFB, DE
	60018	Lockheed C-5M Super Galaxy (86-0018)	LMTAS, Marietta, GA
	60019	Lockheed C-5M Super Galaxy (86-0019)	USAF 68th AS/433rd AW Kelly AFB, TX
	60020	Lockheed C-5M Super Galaxy (86-0020) *bl/y*	USAF 9th AS/436th AW, Dover AFB, DE
	60021	Lockheed C-5M Super Galaxy (86-0021)	LMTAS, Marietta, GA
	60022	Lockheed C-5M Super Galaxy (86-0022) *w/bk*	USAF 22nd AS/60th AMW, Travis AFB, CA
	60023	Lockheed C-5M Super Galaxy (86-0023)	USAF 68th AS/433rd AW Kelly AFB, TX
	60024	Lockheed C-5M Super Galaxy (86-0024) *w/bk*	USAF 22nd AS/60th AMW, Travis AFB, CA
	60025	Lockheed C-5M Super Galaxy (86-0025) *bl/y*	USAF 9th AS/436th AW, Dover AFB, DE
	60026	Lockheed C-5M Super Galaxy (86-0026) *w/bk*	USAF 22nd AS/60th AMW, Travis AFB, CA
	70027	Lockheed C-5M Super Galaxy (87-0027)	USAF 68th AS/433rd AW Kelly AFB, TX
	70028	Lockheed C-5M Super Galaxy (87-0028) *w/bk*	USAF 22nd AS/60th AMW, Travis AFB, CA
	70029	Lockheed C-5M Super Galaxy (87-0029) *w/bk*	USAF 22nd AS/60th AMW, Travis AFB, CA
	70030	Lockheed C-5M Super Galaxy (87-0030) *w/bk*	USAF 22nd AS/60th AMW, Travis AFB, CA
	70031	Lockheed C-5M Super Galaxy (87-0031)	LMTAS, Marietta, GA
	70032	Lockheed C-5M Super Galaxy (87-0032) *w/bk*	USAF 22nd AS/60th AMW, Travis AFB, CA
	70033	Lockheed C-5M Super Galaxy (87-0033)	LMTAS, Marietta, GA
	70034	Lockheed C-5M Super Galaxy (87-0034) *w/bk*	USAF 22nd AS/60th AMW, Travis AFB, CA
	70035	Lockheed C-5M Super Galaxy (87-0035) *bl/y*	USAF 9th AS/436th AW, Dover AFB, DE
	70036	Lockheed C-5M Super Galaxy (87-0036) *bl/y*	USAF 9th AS/436th AW, Dover AFB, DE
	70037	Lockheed C-5M Super Galaxy (87-0037)	LMTAS, Marietta, GA
	70038	Lockheed C-5M Super Galaxy (87-0038)	USAF 68th AS/433rd AW Kelly AFB, TX
	70039	Lockheed C-5M Super Galaxy (87-0039)	LMTAS, Marietta, GA
	70040	Lockheed C-5M Super Galaxy (87-0040) *bl/y*	USAF 9th AS/436th AW, Dover AFB, DE
	70041	Lockheed C-5M Super Galaxy (87-0041)	LMTAS, Marietta, GA
	70042	Lockheed C-5M Super Galaxy (87-0042) *w/bk*	USAF 22nd AS/60th AMW, Travis AFB, CA
	70043	Lockheed C-5M Super Galaxy (87-0043)	LMTAS, Marietta, GA
	70044	Lockheed C-5M Super Galaxy (87-0044) *w/bk*	USAF 22nd AS/60th AMW, Travis AFB, CA
	70045	Lockheed C-5M Super Galaxy (87-0045) *bl/y*	USAF 9th AS/436th AW, Dover AFB, DE
	80213	Lockheed C-5M Super Galaxy (68-0213) *w/bk*	USAF 22nd AS/60th AMW, Travis AFB, CA
	80216	Lockheed C-5M Super Galaxy (68-0216)	LMTAS, Marietta, GA
	90020	Lockheed C-5A Galaxy (69-0020) *bl/r*	USAF 337th AS/439th AW, Westover ARB, MA
	90024	Lockheed C-5M Super Galaxy (69-0024) *bl/y*	USAF 9th AS/436th AW, Dover AFB, DE
	Boeing E-8C J-STARS		
	02000	Boeing E-8C J-STARS (00-2000) [WR]	USAF 116th ACW, Robins AFB, GA
	12005	Boeing E-8C J-STARS (01-2005) [WR]	USAF 116th ACW, Robins AFB, GA
	29111	Boeing E-8C J-STARS (02-9111) [WR]	USAF 116th ACW, Robins AFB, GA
	23289	Boeing E-8C J-STARS (02-3289) [WR] *m*	USAF 116th ACW, Robins AFB, GA
	23290	Boeing E-8C J-STARS (02-3290) [WR] *bk*	USAF 16th ACCS/116th ACW, Robins AFB, GA
	31097	Boeing E-8C J-STARS (93-1097) [GA] *r*	USAF 128th ACCS/116th ACW GA ANG, Robins AFB
	40284	Boeing E-8C J-STARS (94-0284) [GA] *r*	USAF 128th ACCS/116th ACW GA ANG, Robins AFB
	40285	Boeing E-8C J-STARS (94-0285) [WR] *bk*	USAF 16th ACCS/116th ACW, Robins AFB, GA
	50121	Boeing E-8C J-STARS (95-0121) [GA] *r*	USAF 128th ACCS/116th ACW GA ANG, Robins AFB
	50122	Boeing E-8C J-STARS (95-0122) [GA] *r*	USAF 128th ACCS/116th ACW GA ANG, Robins AFB
	60042	Boeing E-8C J-STARS (96-0042) [WR] *bk*	USAF 16th ACCS/116th ACW, Robins AFB, GA
	60043	Boeing E-8C J-STARS (96-0043) [GA] *r*	USAF 128th ACCS/116th ACW GA ANG, Robins AFB
	70100	Boeing E-8C J-STARS (97-0100) [GA] *r*	USAF 128th ACCS/116th ACW GA ANG, Robins AFB
	70200	Boeing E-8C J-STARS (97-0200) [WR] *bk*	USAF 16th ACCS/116th ACW, Robins AFB, GA

Serial	Type (code/other identity)	Owner/operator, location or fate	Notes
70201	Boeing E-8C J-STARS (97-0201) [GA] *r*	USAF 128th ACCS/116th ACW GA ANG, Robins AFB	
90006	Boeing E-8C J-STARS (99-0006) [WR] *gn*	USAF 16th ACCS/116th ACW, Robins AFB, GA	

McDonnell Douglas KC-10A Extender

Serial	Type (code/other identity)	Owner/operator, location or fate	Notes
20191	McDonnell Douglas KC-10A Extender (82-0191) *w/bk*	USAF 60th AMW, Travis AFB, CA	
20192	McDonnell Douglas KC-10A Extender (82-0192) *w/bk*	USAF 60th AMW, Travis AFB, CA	
20193	McDonnell Douglas KC-10A Extender (82-0193) *w/bk*	USAF 60th AMW, Travis AFB, CA	
30075	McDonnell Douglas KC-10A Extender (83-0075) *w/bk*	USAF 60th AMW, Travis AFB, CA	
30076	McDonnell Douglas KC-10A Extender (83-0076) *w/bk*	USAF 60th AMW, Travis AFB, CA	
30077	McDonnell Douglas KC-10A Extender (83-0077) *w/bk*	USAF 60th AMW, Travis AFB, CA	
30078	McDonnell Douglas KC-10A Extender (83-0078) *w/bk*	USAF 60th AMW, Travis AFB, CA	
30079	McDonnell Douglas KC-10A Extender (83-0079) *bl*	USAF 305th AMW, McGuire AFB, NJ	
30080	McDonnell Douglas KC-10A Extender (83-0080) *w/bk*	USAF 60th AMW, Travis AFB, CA	
30081	McDonnell Douglas KC-10A Extender (83-0081) *bl*	USAF 305th AMW, McGuire AFB, NJ	
30082	McDonnell Douglas KC-10A Extender (83-0082) *bl*	USAF 305th AMW, McGuire AFB, NJ	
40185	McDonnell Douglas KC-10A Extender (84-0185) *w/bk*	USAF 60th AMW, Travis AFB, CA	
40186	McDonnell Douglas KC-10A Extender (84-0186) *bl*	USAF 305th AMW, McGuire AFB, NJ	
40187	McDonnell Douglas KC-10A Extender (84-0187) *w/bk*	USAF 60th AMW, Travis AFB, CA	
40188	McDonnell Douglas KC-10A Extender (84-0188) *bl*	USAF 305th AMW, McGuire AFB, NJ	
40189	McDonnell Douglas KC-10A Extender (84-0189) *bl*	USAF 305th AMW, McGuire AFB, NJ	
40190	McDonnell Douglas KC-10A Extender (84-0190) *bl*	USAF 305th AMW, McGuire AFB, NJ	
40191	McDonnell Douglas KC-10A Extender (84-0191) *w/bk*	USAF 60th AMW, Travis AFB, CA	
40192	McDonnell Douglas KC-10A Extender (84-0192) *bl*	USAF 305th AMW, McGuire AFB, NJ	
50027	McDonnell Douglas KC-10A Extender (85-0027) *bl*	USAF 305th AMW, McGuire AFB, NJ	
50028	McDonnell Douglas KC-10A Extender (85-0028) *bl*	USAF 305th AMW, McGuire AFB, NJ	
50029	McDonnell Douglas KC-10A Extender (85-0029) *w/bk*	USAF 60th AMW, Travis AFB, CA	
50030	McDonnell Douglas KC-10A Extender (85-0030) *bl*	USAF 305th AMW, McGuire AFB, NJ	
50031	McDonnell Douglas KC-10A Extender (85-0031) *bl*	USAF 305th AMW, McGuire AFB, NJ	
50032	McDonnell Douglas KC-10A Extender (85-0032) *bl*	USAF 305th AMW, McGuire AFB, NJ	
50033	McDonnell Douglas KC-10A Extender (85-0033) *w/bk*	USAF 60th AMW, Travis AFB, CA	
50034	McDonnell Douglas KC-10A Extender (85-0034) *bl*	USAF 305th AMW, McGuire AFB, NJ	
60027	McDonnell Douglas KC-10A Extender (86-0027) *bl*	USAF 305th AMW, McGuire AFB, NJ	
60028	McDonnell Douglas KC-10A Extender (86-0028) *bl*	USAF 305th AMW, McGuire AFB, NJ	
60029	McDonnell Douglas KC-10A Extender (86-0029) *w/bk*	USAF 60th AMW, Travis AFB, CA	
60030	McDonnell Douglas KC-10A Extender (86-0030) *bl*	USAF 305th AMW, McGuire AFB, NJ	
60031	McDonnell Douglas KC-10A Extender (86-0031) *w/bk*	USAF 60th AMW, Travis AFB, CA	
60032	McDonnell Douglas KC-10A Extender (86-0032) *bl*	USAF 305th AMW, McGuire AFB, NJ	
60033	McDonnell Douglas KC-10A Extender (86-0033) *w/bk*	USAF 60th AMW, Travis AFB, CA	
60034	McDonnell Douglas KC-10A Extender (86-0034) *w/bk*	USAF 60th AMW, Travis AFB, CA	
60035	McDonnell Douglas KC-10A Extender (86-0035) *bl*	USAF 305th AMW, McGuire AFB, NJ	
60036	McDonnell Douglas KC-10A Extender (86-0036) *bl*	USAF 305th AMW, McGuire AFB, NJ	
60037	McDonnell Douglas KC-10A Extender (86-0037) *w/bk*	USAF 60th AMW, Travis AFB, CA	
60038	McDonnell Douglas KC-10A Extender (86-0038) *w/bk*	USAF 60th AMW, Travis AFB, CA	
70117	McDonnell Douglas KC-10A Extender (87-0117) *w/bk*	USAF 60th AMW, Travis AFB, CA	
70118	McDonnell Douglas KC-10A Extender (87-0118) *bl*	USAF 305th AMW, McGuire AFB, NJ	
70119	McDonnell Douglas KC-10A Extender (87-0119) *w/bk*	USAF 60th AMW, Travis AFB, CA	
70120	McDonnell Douglas KC-10A Extender (87-0120) *bl*	USAF 305th AMW, McGuire AFB, NJ	
70121	McDonnell Douglas KC-10A Extender (87-0121) *bl*	USAF 305th AMW, McGuire AFB, NJ	
70122	McDonnell Douglas KC-10A Extender (87-0122) *bl*	USAF 305th AMW, McGuire AFB, NJ	
70123	McDonnell Douglas KC-10A Extender (87-0123) *w/bk*	USAF 60th AMW, Travis AFB, CA	
70124	McDonnell Douglas KC-10A Extender (87-0124) *bl*	USAF 305th AMW, McGuire AFB, NJ	
90433	McDonnell Douglas KC-10A Extender (79-0433) *bl*	USAF 305th AMW, McGuire AFB, NJ	
90434	McDonnell Douglas KC-10A Extender (79-0434) *bl*	USAF 305th AMW, McGuire AFB, NJ	
91710	McDonnell Douglas KC-10A Extender (79-1710) *bl*	USAF 305th AMW, McGuire AFB, NJ	
91711	McDonnell Douglas KC-10A Extender (79-1711) *bl*	USAF 305th AMW, McGuire AFB, NJ	
91712	McDonnell Douglas KC-10A Extender (79-1712) *bl*	USAF 305th AMW, McGuire AFB, NJ	
91713	McDonnell Douglas KC-10A Extender (79-1713) *w/bk*	USAF 60th AMW, Travis AFB, CA	
91946	McDonnell Douglas KC-10A Extender (79-1946) *w/bk*	USAF 60th AMW, Travis AFB, CA	
91947	McDonnell Douglas KC-10A Extender (79-1947) *bl*	USAF 305th AMW, McGuire AFB, NJ	
91948	McDonnell Douglas KC-10A Extender (79-1948) *w/bk*	USAF 60th AMW, Travis AFB, CA	
91949	McDonnell Douglas KC-10A Extender (79-1949) *bl*	USAF 305th AMW, McGuire AFB, NJ	

Notes	Serial	Type (code/other identity)	Owner/operator, location or fate
	91950	McDonnell Douglas KC-10A Extender (79-1950) *w/bk*	USAF 60th AMW, Travis AFB, CA
	91951	McDonnell Douglas KC-10A Extender (79-1951) *w/bk*	USAF 60th AMW, Travis AFB, CA

Bombardier E-11A Global Express

	19001	Bombardier E-11A Global Express (11-9001)	USAF 430th EECS/653rd ELSW, Hanscom MA
	19355	Bombardier E-11A Global Express (11-9355)	USAF 430th EECS/653rd ELSW, Hanscom MA
	19358	Bombardier E-11A Global Express (11-9358)	USAF 430th EECS/653rd ELSW, Hanscom MA
	29506	Bombardier E-11A Global Express (12-9506)	USAF 430th EECS/653rd ELSW, Hanscom MA

Boeing C-17A Globemaster III

	00171	Boeing C-17A Globemaster III (00-0171) [AK] *w/bk*	USAF 517th AS/3rd Wg, Elmendorf AFB, AK
	00172	Boeing C-17A Globemaster III (00-0172) *r/y*	USAF 58th AS/97th AMW, Altus AFB, OK
	00174	Boeing C-17A Globemaster III (00-0174) [AK] *w/bk*	USAF 517th AS/3rd Wg, Elmendorf AFB, AK
	00175	Boeing C-17A Globemaster III (00-0175) *r/y*	USAF 58th AS/97th AMW, Altus AFB, OK
	00176	Boeing C-17A Globemaster III (00-0176) *r/w*	USAF 155th AS/164th AW, Memphis, TN ANG
	00177	Boeing C-17A Globemaster III (00-0177) *bl*	USAF 137th AS/105th AW, Stewart AFB, NY ANG
	00178	Boeing C-17A Globemaster III (00-0178) *r/w*	USAF 89th AS/445th AW AFRC, Wright-Patterson AFB, OH
	00179	Boeing C-17A Globemaster III (00-0179) *r/y*	USAF 58th AS/97th AMW, Altus AFB, OK
	00180	Boeing C-17A Globemaster III (00-0180) *gn*	USAF 62nd AW, McChord AFB, WA
	00181	Boeing C-17A Globemaster III (00-0181) *r/w*	USAF 167th AS/167th AW, Martinsburg, WV ANG
	00182	Boeing C-17A Globemaster III (00-0182) *r/w*	USAF 167th AS/167th AW, Martinsburg, WV ANG
	00183	Boeing C-17A Globemaster III (00-0183) *gn*	USAF 62nd AW, McChord AFB, WA
	00184	Boeing C-17A Globemaster III (00-0184) *gn*	USAF 62nd AW, McChord AFB, WA
	00185	Boeing C-17A Globemaster III (00-0185) [AK] *w/bk*	USAF 517th AS/3rd Wg, Elmendorf AFB, AK
	00213	Boeing C-17A Globemaster III (10-0213) *y/bl*	USAF 437th AW, Charleston AFB, SC
	00214	Boeing C-17A Globemaster III (10-0214) *y/bl*	USAF 437th AW, Charleston AFB, SC
	00215	Boeing C-17A Globemaster III (10-0215) *y/bl*	USAF 437th AW, Charleston AFB, SC
	00216	Boeing C-17A Globemaster III (10-0216) *gn*	USAF 62nd AW, McChord AFB, WA
	00217	Boeing C-17A Globemaster III (10-0217) *gn*	USAF 62nd AW, McChord AFB, WA
	00218	Boeing C-17A Globemaster III (10-0218) *gn*	USAF 62nd AW, McChord AFB, WA
	00219	Boeing C-17A Globemaster III (10-0219) *gn*	USAF 62nd AW, McChord AFB, WA
	00220	Boeing C-17A Globemaster III (10-0220) *gn*	USAF 62nd AW, McChord AFB, WA
	00221	Boeing C-17A Globemaster III (10-0221) *y/bl*	USAF 437th AW, Charleston AFB, SC
	00222	Boeing C-17A Globemaster III (10-0222) *y/bl*	USAF 437th AW, Charleston AFB, SC
	00223	Boeing C-17A Globemaster III (10-0223) *y/bl*	USAF 437th AW, Charleston AFB, SC
	00532	Boeing C-17A Globemaster III (90-0532) *gn*	USAF 62nd AW, McChord AFB, WA
	00533	Boeing C-17A Globemaster III (90-0533) [HH] *r/y*	USAF 535th AS/15th Wg, Hickam AFB, HI
	00534	Boeing C-17A Globemaster III (90-0534) *y/bl*	USAF 437th AW, Charleston AFB, SC
	00535	Boeing C-17A Globemaster III (90-0535) *r/w*	USAF 89th AS/445th AW AFRC, Wright-Patterson AFB, OH
	10186	Boeing C-17A Globemaster III (01-0186) *bl/y*	USAF 3rd AS/436th AW, Dover AFB, DE
	10187	Boeing C-17A Globemaster III (01-0187) *gn*	USAF 62nd AW, McChord AFB, WA
	10188	Boeing C-17A Globemaster III (01-0188) *bl*	USAF 137th AS/105th AW, Stewart AFB, NY ANG
	10189	Boeing C-17A Globemaster III (01-0189) *r/w*	USAF 155th AS/164th AW, Memphis, TN ANG
	10190	Boeing C-17A Globemaster III (01-0190) *r/y*	USAF 58th AS/97th AMW, Altus AFB, OK
	10191	Boeing C-17A Globemaster III (01-0191) *bl/y*	USAF 3rd AS/436th AW, Dover AFB, DE
	10192	Boeing C-17A Globemaster III (01-0192) *bl*	USAF 137th AS/105th AW, Stewart AFB, NY ANG
	10193	Boeing C-17A Globemaster III (01-0193) *y/bl*	USAF 437th AW, Charleston AFB, SC
	10194	Boeing C-17A Globemaster III (01-0194) *r/w*	USAF 89th AS/445th AW AFRC, Wright-Patterson AFB, OH
	10195	Boeing C-17A Globemaster III (01-0195) *r/y*	USAF 58th AS/97th AMW, Altus AFB, OK
	10196	Boeing C-17A Globemaster III (01-0196) *r/w*	USAF 167th AS/167th AW, Martinsburg, WV ANG
	10197	Boeing C-17A Globemaster III (01-0197) *y/bl*	USAF 437th AW, Charleston AFB, SC
	21098	Boeing C-17A Globemaster III (02-1098) *bl*	USAF 6th AS/305th AMW, McGuire AFB, NJ
	21099	Boeing C-17A Globemaster III (02-1099) *r/y*	USAF 58th AS/97th AMW, Altus AFB, OK
	21100	Boeing C-17A Globemaster III (02-1100) *r/w*	USAF 155th AS/164th AW, Memphis, TN ANG
	21101	Boeing C-17A Globemaster III (02-1101) *y/bl*	USAF 437th AW, Charleston AFB, SC
	21102	Boeing C-17A Globemaster III (02-1102) *r/y*	USAF 58th AS/97th AMW, Altus AFB, OK
	21103	Boeing C-17A Globemaster III (02-1103) *gn*	USAF 62nd AW, McChord AFB, WA

Serial	Type (code/other identity)	Owner/operator, location or fate	Notes
21104	Boeing C-17A Globemaster III (02-1104) r/y	USAF 58th AS/97th AMW, Altus AFB, OK	
21105	Boeing C-17A Globemaster III (02-1105) gn	USAF 62nd AW, McChord AFB, WA	
21106	Boeing C-17A Globemaster III (02-1106) gn	USAF 62nd AW, McChord AFB, WA	
21107	Boeing C-17A Globemaster III (02-1107) gn	USAF 62nd AW, McChord AFB, WA	
21108	Boeing C-17A Globemaster III (02-1108) gn	USAF 62nd AW, McChord AFB, WA	
21109	Boeing C-17A Globemaster III (02-1109) gn	USAF 62nd AW, McChord AFB, WA	
21110	Boeing C-17A Globemaster III (02-1110) r/w	USAF 155th AS/164th AW, Memphis, TN ANG	
21111	Boeing C-17A Globemaster III (02-1111) gn	USAF 62nd AW, McChord AFB, WA	
21112	Boeing C-17A Globemaster III (02-1112) bl/gd	USAF 183rd AS/172nd AW, Jackson Int'l Airport, MS ANG	
23291	Boeing C-17A Globemaster III (92-3291) r/w	USAF 155th AS/164th AW, Memphis, TN ANG	
23292	Boeing C-17A Globemaster III (92-3292) y/bl	USAF 437th AW, Charleston AFB, SC	
23293	Boeing C-17A Globemaster III (92-3293) y/bl	USAF 437th AW, Charleston AFB, SC	
23294	Boeing C-17A Globemaster III (92-3294)	USAF 62nd AW, McChord AFB, WA	
30599	Boeing C-17A Globemaster III (93-0599) [AK] w/bk	USAF 517th AS/3rd Wg, Elmendorf AFB, AK	
30600	Boeing C-17A Globemaster III (93-0600) r/w	USAF 155th AS/164th AW, Memphis, TN ANG	
30601	Boeing C-17A Globemaster III (93-0601) gn	USAF 62nd AW, McChord AFB, WA	
30602	Boeing C-17A Globemaster III (93-0602) y/bl	USAF 437th AW, Charleston AFB, SC	
30603	Boeing C-17A Globemaster III (93-0603) r/w	USAF 89th AS/445th AW AFRC, Wright-Patterson AFB, OH	
30604	Boeing C-17A Globemaster III (93-0604) r/w	USAF 89th AS/445th AW AFRC, Wright-Patterson AFB, OH	
33113	Boeing C-17A Globemaster III (03-3113) bl/gd	USAF 183rd AS/172nd AW, Jackson Int'l Airport, MS ANG	
33114	Boeing C-17A Globemaster III (03-3114) bl/gd	USAF 183rd AS/172nd AW, Jackson Int'l Airport, MS ANG	
33115	Boeing C-17A Globemaster III (03-3115) bl/gd	USAF 183rd AS/172nd AW, Jackson Int'l Airport, MS ANG	
33116	Boeing C-17A Globemaster III (03-3116) bl/gd	USAF 183rd AS/172nd AW, Jackson Int'l Airport, MS ANG	
33117	Boeing C-17A Globemaster III (03-3117) bl/gd	USAF 183rd AS/172nd AW, Jackson Int'l Airport, MS ANG	
33118	Boeing C-17A Globemaster III (03-3118) bl/gd	USAF 183rd AS/172nd AW, Jackson Int'l Airport, MS ANG	
33119	Boeing C-17A Globemaster III (03-3119) bl/gd	USAF 183rd AS/172nd AW, Jackson Int'l Airport, MS ANG	
33120	Boeing C-17A Globemaster III (03-3120) gn	USAF 62nd AW, McChord AFB, WA	
33121	Boeing C-17A Globemaster III (03-3121) [ED]	USAF 418th FLTS/412th TW, Edwards AFB, CA	
33122	Boeing C-17A Globemaster III (03-3122) y/bl	USAF 437th AW, Charleston AFB, SC	
33123	Boeing C-17A Globemaster III (03-3123) r/w	USAF 167th AS/167th AW, Martinsburg, WV ANG	
33124	Boeing C-17A Globemaster III (03-3124) y/bl	USAF 437th AW, Charleston AFB, SC	
33125	Boeing C-17A Globemaster III (03-3125) bl	USAF 6th AS/305th AMW, McGuire AFB, NJ	
33126	Boeing C-17A Globemaster III (03-3126) bl	USAF 6th AS/305th AMW, McGuire AFB, NJ	
33127	Boeing C-17A Globemaster III (03-3127) gn	USAF 62nd AW, McChord AFB, WA	
40065	Boeing C-17A Globemaster III (94-0065) r/w	USAF 155th AS/164th AW, Memphis, TN ANG	
40066	Boeing C-17A Globemaster III (94-0066) gn	USAF 62nd AW, McChord AFB, WA	
40067	Boeing C-17A Globemaster III (94-0067) bl	USAF 137th AS/105th AW, Stewart AFB, NY ANG	
40068	Boeing C-17A Globemaster III (94-0068) or/y	USAF 729th AS/452nd AMW AFRC, March ARB, CA	
40069	Boeing C-17A Globemaster III (94-0069) r/w	USAF 167th AS/167th AW, Martinsburg, WV ANG	
40070	Boeing C-17A Globemaster III (94-0070) r/w	USAF 167th AS/167th AW, Martinsburg, WV ANG	
44128	Boeing C-17A Globemaster III (04-4128) bl	USAF 6th AS/305th AMW, McGuire AFB, NJ	
44129	Boeing C-17A Globemaster III (04-4129) r/y	USAF 58th AS/97th AMW, Altus AFB, OK	
44130	Boeing C-17A Globemaster III (04-4130) bl	USAF 6th AS/305th AMW, McGuire AFB, NJ	
44131	Boeing C-17A Globemaster III (04-4131) bl	USAF 6th AS/305th AMW, McGuire AFB, NJ	
44132	Boeing C-17A Globemaster III (04-4132) bl	USAF 6th AS/305th AMW, McGuire AFB, NJ	
44133	Boeing C-17A Globemaster III (04-4133) bl	USAF 6th AS/305th AMW, McGuire AFB, NJ	
44134	Boeing C-17A Globemaster III (04-4134) bl	USAF 6th AS/305th AMW, McGuire AFB, NJ	
44135	Boeing C-17A Globemaster III (04-4135) y/bl	USAF 437th AW, Charleston AFB, SC	
44136	Boeing C-17A Globemaster III (04-4136) bl	USAF 6th AS/305th AMW, McGuire AFB, NJ	

Notes	Serial	Type (code/other identity)	Owner/operator, location or fate
	44137	Boeing C-17A Globemaster III (04-4137) *bl*	USAF 6th AS/305th AMW, McGuire AFB, NJ
	44138	Boeing C-17A Globemaster III (04-4138) *or/y*	USAF 729th AS/452nd AMW AFRC, March ARB, CA
	50102	Boeing C-17A Globemaster III (95-0102) *y/bl*	USAF 437th AW, Charleston AFB, SC
	50103	Boeing C-17A Globemaster III (95-0103) *gn*	USAF 62nd AW, McChord AFB, WA
	50104	Boeing C-17A Globemaster III (95-0104) *r/w*	USAF 155th AS/164th AW, Memphis, TN ANG
	50105	Boeing C-17A Globemaster III (95-0105) *bl*	USAF 137th AS/105th AW, Stewart AFB, NY ANG
	50106	Boeing C-17A Globemaster III (95-0106) *gn*	USAF 62nd AW, McChord AFB, WA
	50107	Boeing C-17A Globemaster III (95-0107) *y/bl*	USAF 437th AW, Charleston AFB, SC
	55139	Boeing C-17A Globemaster III (05-5139) *or/y*	USAF 729th AS/452nd AMW AFRC, March ARB, CA
	55140	Boeing C-17A Globemaster III (05-5140) *or/y*	USAF 729th AS/452nd AMW AFRC, March ARB, CA
	55141	Boeing C-17A Globemaster III (05-5141) *or/y*	USAF 729th AS/452nd AMW AFRC, March ARB, CA
	55142	Boeing C-17A Globemaster III (05-5142) *or/y*	USAF 729th AS/452nd AMW AFRC, March ARB, CA
	55143	Boeing C-17A Globemaster III (05-5143) *r/w*	USAF 89th AS/445th AW AFRC, Wright-Patterson AFB, OH
	55144	Boeing C-17A Globemaster III (05-5144) *or/y*	USAF 729th AS/452nd AMW AFRC, March ARB, CA
	55145	Boeing C-17A Globemaster III (05-5145) *or/y*	USAF 729th AS/452nd AMW AFRC, March ARB, CA
	55146	Boeing C-17A Globemaster III (05-5146) [HH] *r/y*	USAF 535th AS/15th Wg, Hickam AFB, HI
	55147	Boeing C-17A Globemaster III (05-5147) [HH] *r/y*	USAF 535th AS/15th Wg, Hickam AFB, HI
	55148	Boeing C-17A Globemaster III (05-5148) [HH] *r/y*	USAF 535th AS/15th Wg, Hickam AFB, HI
	55149	Boeing C-17A Globemaster III (05-5149) [HH] *r/y*	USAF 535th AS/15th Wg, Hickam AFB, HI
	55150	Boeing C-17A Globemaster III (05-5150) [HH] *r/y*	USAF 535th AS/15th Wg, Hickam AFB, HI
	55151	Boeing C-17A Globemaster III (05-5151) [HH] *r/y*	USAF 535th AS/15th Wg, Hickam AFB, HI
	55152	Boeing C-17A Globemaster III (05-5152) [HH] *r/y*	USAF 535th AS/15th Wg, Hickam AFB, HI
	55153	Boeing C-17A Globemaster III (05-5153) [HH] *r/y]*	USAF 535th AS/15th Wg, Hickam AFB, HI
	60001	Boeing C-17A Globemaster III (96-0001) *gn*	USAF 62nd AW, McChord AFB, WA
	60002	Boeing C-17A Globemaster III (96-0002) *y/bl*	USAF 437th AW, Charleston AFB, SC
	60003	Boeing C-17A Globemaster III (96-0003) *gn*	USAF 62nd AW, McChord AFB, WA
	60004	Boeing C-17A Globemaster III (96-0004) *gn*	USAF 62nd AW, McChord AFB, WA
	60005	Boeing C-17A Globemaster III (96-0005) *bl*	USAF 137th AS/105th AW, Stewart AFB, NY ANG
	60006	Boeing C-17A Globemaster III (96-0006) *r/w*	USAF 167th AS/167th AW, Martinsburg, WV ANG
	60007	Boeing C-17A Globemaster III (96-0007) *bl/gd*	USAF 183rd AS/172nd AW, Jackson Int'l Airport, MS ANG
	60008	Boeing C-17A Globemaster III (96-0008) *r/y*	USAF 58th AS/97th AMW, Altus AFB, OK
	66154	Boeing C-17A Globemaster III (06-6154) *w/bk*	USAF 21st AS/60th AMW, Travis AFB, CA
	66155	Boeing C-17A Globemaster III (06-6155) *w/bk*	USAF 21st AS/60th AMW, Travis AFB, CA
	66156	Boeing C-17A Globemaster III (06-6156) *w/bk*	USAF 21st AS/60th AMW, Travis AFB, CA
	66157	Boeing C-17A Globemaster III (06-6157) *w/bk*	USAF 21st AS/60th AMW, Travis AFB, CA
	66158	Boeing C-17A Globemaster III (06-6158) *w/bk*	USAF 21st AS/60th AMW, Travis AFB, CA
	66159	Boeing C-17A Globemaster III (06-6159) *w/bk*	USAF 21st AS/60th AMW, Travis AFB, CA
	66160	Boeing C-17A Globemaster III (06-6160) *w/bk*	USAF 21st AS/60th AMW, Travis AFB, CA
	66161	Boeing C-17A Globemaster III (06-6161) *w/bk*	USAF 21st AS/60th AMW, Travis AFB, CA
	66162	Boeing C-17A Globemaster III (06-6162) *w/bk*	USAF 21st AS/60th AMW, Travis AFB, CA
	66163	Boeing C-17A Globemaster III (06-6163) *w/bk*	USAF 21st AS/60th AMW, Travis AFB, CA
	66164	Boeing C-17A Globemaster III (06-6164) *w/bk*	USAF 21st AS/60th AMW, Travis AFB, CA
	66165	Boeing C-17A Globemaster III (06-6165) *bl/y*	USAF 3rd AS/436th AW, Dover AFB, DE
	66166	Boeing C-17A Globemaster III (06-6166) *bl/y*	USAF 3rd AS/436th AW, Dover AFB, DE
	66167	Boeing C-17A Globemaster III (06-6167) *bl/y*	USAF 3rd AS/436th AW, Dover AFB, DE
	66168	Boeing C-17A Globemaster III (06-6168) *bl/y*	USAF 3rd AS/436th AW, Dover AFB, DE
	70041	Boeing C-17A Globemaster III (97-0041) *y/bl*	USAF 437th AW, Charleston AFB, SC
	70042	Boeing C-17A Globemaster III (97-0042) *r/w*	USAF 155th AS/164th AW, Memphis, TN ANG
	70043	Boeing C-17A Globemaster III (97-0043) *or/y*	USAF 729th AS/452nd AMW AFRC, March ARB, CA

Serial	Type (code/other identity)	Owner/operator, location or fate	Notes
70044	Boeing C-17A Globemaster III (97-0044) *r/w*	USAF 89th AS/445th AW AFRC, Wright-Patterson AFB, OH	
70045	Boeing C-17A Globemaster III (97-0045) *bl*	USAF 137th AS/105th AW, Stewart AFB, NY ANG	
70046	Boeing C-17A Globemaster III (97-0046) *y/bl*	USAF 437th AW, Charleston AFB, SC	
70047	Boeing C-17A Globemaster III (97-0047) *y/bl*	USAF 437th AW, Charleston AFB, SC	
70048	Boeing C-17A Globemaster III (97-0048) *r/w*	USAF 89th AS/445th AW AFRC, Wright-Patterson AFB, OH	
77169	Boeing C-17A Globemaster III (07-7169) *bl/y*	USAF 3rd AS/436th AW, Dover AFB, DE	
77170	Boeing C-17A Globemaster III (07-7170) *bl/y*	USAF 3rd AS/436th AW, Dover AFB, DE	
77171	Boeing C-17A Globemaster III (07-7171) *bl*	USAF 6th AS/305th AMW, McGuire AFB, NJ	
77172	Boeing C-17A Globemaster III (07-7172) *w/bk*	USAF 21st AS/60th AMW, Travis AFB, CA	
77173	Boeing C-17A Globemaster III (07-7173) *bl/y*	USAF 3rd AS/436th AW, Dover AFB, DE	
77174	Boeing C-17A Globemaster III (07-7174) *bl/y*	USAF 3rd AS/436th AW, Dover AFB, DE	
77175	Boeing C-17A Globemaster III (07-7175) *bl/y*	USAF 3rd AS/436th AW, Dover AFB, DE	
77176	Boeing C-17A Globemaster III (07-7176) *bl/y*	USAF 3rd AS/436th AW, Dover AFB, DE	
77177	Boeing C-17A Globemaster III (07-7177) *bl/y*	USAF 3rd AS/436th AW, Dover AFB, DE	
77178	Boeing C-17A Globemaster III (07-7178) *bl*	USAF 6th AS/305th AMW, McGuire AFB, NJ	
77179	Boeing C-17A Globemaster III (07-7179) *w/bk*	USAF 21st AS/60th AMW, Travis AFB, CA	
77180	Boeing C-17A Globemaster III (07-7180) *y/bl*	USAF 437th AW, Charleston AFB, SC	
77181	Boeing C-17A Globemaster III (07-7181) *y/bl*	USAF 437th AW, Charleston AFB, SC	
77182	Boeing C-17A Globemaster III (07-7182) *y/bl*	USAF 437th AW, Charleston AFB, SC	
77183	Boeing C-17A Globemaster III (07-7183) *y/bl*	USAF 437th AW, Charleston AFB, SC	
77184	Boeing C-17A Globemaster III (07-7184) *y/bl*	USAF 437th AW, Charleston AFB, SC	
77185	Boeing C-17A Globemaster III (07-7185) *y/bl*	USAF 437th AW, Charleston AFB, SC	
77186	Boeing C-17A Globemaster III (07-7186) *y/bl*	USAF 437th AW, Charleston AFB, SC	
77187	Boeing C-17A Globemaster III (07-7187) *y/bl*	USAF 437th AW, Charleston AFB, SC	
77188	Boeing C-17A Globemaster III (07-7188) *y/bl*	USAF 437th AW, Charleston AFB, SC	
77189	Boeing C-17A Globemaster III (07-7189) *y/bl*	USAF 437th AW, Charleston AFB, SC	
80049	Boeing C-17A Globemaster III (98-0049) *r/y*	USAF 58th AS/97th AMW, Altus AFB, OK	
80050	Boeing C-17A Globemaster III (98-0050) *r/y*	USAF 58th AS/97th AMW, Altus AFB, OK	
80051	Boeing C-17A Globemaster III (98-0051) [AK] *w/bk*	USAF 517th AS/3rd Wg, Elmendorf AFB, AK	
80052	Boeing C-17A Globemaster III (98-0052) *gn*	USAF 62nd aW, McChord AFB, WA	
80053	Boeing C-17A Globemaster III (98-0053) *gn*	USAF 62nd AW, McChord AFB, WA	
80054	Boeing C-17A Globemaster III (98-0054) *y/bl*	USAF 437th AW, Charleston AFB, SC	
80055	Boeing C-17A Globemaster III (98-0055) *r/y $*	USAF 58th AS/97th AMW, Altus AFB, OK	
80056	Boeing C-17A Globemaster III (98-0056) [AK] *w/bk*	USAF 517th AS/3rd Wg, Elmendorf AFB, AK	
80057	Boeing C-17A Globemaster III (98-0057) *bl*	USAF 137th AS/105th AW, Stewart AFB, NY ANG	
80265	Boeing C-17A Globemaster III (88-0265) *gn*	USAF 62nd AW, McChord AFB, WA	
80266	Boeing C-17A Globemaster III (88-0266) *y/bl*	USAF 437th AW, Charleston AFB, SC	
88190	Boeing C-17A Globemaster III (08-8190) *y/bl*	USAF 437th AW, Charleston AFB, SC	
88191	Boeing C-17A Globemaster III (08-8191) *y/bl*	USAF 437th AW, Charleston AFB, SC	
88192	Boeing C-17A Globemaster III (08-8192) *gn*	USAF 62nd AW, McChord AFB, WA	
88193	Boeing C-17A Globemaster III (08-8193) *gn*	USAF 62nd AW, McChord AFB, WA	
88194	Boeing C-17A Globemaster III (08-8194) *gn*	USAF 62nd AW, McChord AFB, WA	
88195	Boeing C-17A Globemaster III (08-8195) *gn*	USAF 62nd AW, McChord AFB, WA	
88196	Boeing C-17A Globemaster III (08-8196) *gn*	USAF 62nd AW, McChord AFB, WA	
88197	Boeing C-17A Globemaster III (08-8197) *gn*	USAF 62nd AW, McChord AFB, WA	
88198	Boeing C-17A Globemaster III (08-8198) *y/bl*	USAF 437th AW, Charleston AFB, SC	
88199	Boeing C-17A Globemaster III (08-8199) *gn*	USAF 62nd AW, McChord AFB, WA	
88200	Boeing C-17A Globemaster III (08-8200) *gn*	USAF 62nd AW, McChord AFB, WA	
88201	Boeing C-17A Globemaster III (08-8201) *gn*	USAF 62nd AW, McChord AFB, WA	
88202	Boeing C-17A Globemaster III (08-8202) *gn*	USAF 62nd AW, McChord AFB, WA	
88203	Boeing C-17A Globemaster III (08-8203) *gn*	USAF 62nd AW, McChord AFB, WA	
88204	Boeing C-17A Globemaster III (08-8204) *y/bl*	USAF 437th AW, Charleston AFB, SC	
90058	Boeing C-17A Globemaster III (99-0058) *gn*	USAF 62nd AW, McChord AFB, WA	
90059	Boeing C-17A Globemaster III (99-0059) *gn*	USAF 62nd AW, McChord AFB, WA	
90060	Boeing C-17A Globemaster III (99-0060) *gn*	USAF 62nd AW, McChord AFB, WA	
90061	Boeing C-17A Globemaster III (99-0061) *r/y*	USAF 58th AS/97th AMW, Altus AFB, OK	
90062	Boeing C-17A Globemaster III (99-0062) *y/bl*	USAF 437th AW, Charleston AFB, SC	
90063	Boeing C-17A Globemaster III (99-0063) *r/y*	USAF 58th AS/97th AMW, Altus AFB, OK	
90064	Boeing C-17A Globemaster III (99-0064) *r/y*	USAF 58th AS/97th AMW, Altus AFB, OK	

US-BASED USAF AIRCRAFT

Notes	Serial	Type (code/other identity)	Owner/operator, location or fate
	90165	Boeing C-17A Globemaster III (99-0165) *r/w*	USAF 89th AS/445th AW AFRC, Wright-Patterson AFB, OH
	90166	Boeing C-17A Globemaster III (99-0166) *gn*	USAF 62nd AW, McChord AFB, WA
	90167	Boeing C-17A Globemaster III (99-0167) [AK] *w/bk*	USAF 517th AS/3rd Wg, Elmendorf AFB, AK
	90168	Boeing C-17A Globemaster III (99-0168) [AK] *w/bk*	USAF 517th AS/3rd Wg, Elmendorf AFB, AK
	90169	Boeing C-17A Globemaster III (99-0169) *y/bl*	USAF 437th AW, Charleston AFB, SC
	90170	Boeing C-17A Globemaster III (99-0170) [AK] *w/bk*	USAF 517th AS/3rd Wg, Elmendorf AFB, AK
	91189	Boeing C-17A Globemaster III (89-1189) *y/bl*	USAF 437th AW, Charleston AFB, SC
	91190	Boeing C-17A Globemaster III (89-1190) *r/w*	USAF 167th AS/167th AW, Martinsburg, WV ANG
	91191	Boeing C-17A Globemaster III (89-1191) *bl*	USAF 137th AS/105th AW, Stewart AFB, NY ANG
	91192	Boeing C-17A Globemaster III (89-1192) *y/bl*	USAF 437th AW, Charleston AFB, SC
	99205	Boeing C-17A Globemaster III (09-9205) *y/bl*	USAF 437th AW, Charleston AFB, SC
	99206	Boeing C-17A Globemaster III (09-9206) *y/bl*	USAF 437th AW, Charleston AFB, SC
	99207	Boeing C-17A Globemaster III (09-9207) *y/bl*	USAF 437th AW, Charleston AFB, SC
	99208	Boeing C-17A Globemaster III (09-9208) *y/bl*	USAF 437th AW, Charleston AFB, SC
	99209	Boeing C-17A Globemaster III (09-9209) *gn*	USAF 62nd AW, McChord AFB, WA
	99210	Boeing C-17A Globemaster III (09-9210) *gn*	USAF 62nd AW, McChord AFB, WA
	99211	Boeing C-17A Globemaster III (09-9211) *gn*	USAF 62nd AW, McChord AFB, WA
	99212	Boeing C-17A Globemaster III (09-9212) *y/bl*	USAF 437th AW, Charleston AFB, SC

Grumman C-20 Gulfstream III/IV

	10108	Grumman C-20F Gulfstream IV (91-0108)	US Army OSAC/PAT, Andrews AFB, MD
	60201	Grumman C-20B Gulfstream III (86-0201)	USAF 99th AS/89th AW, Andrews AFB, MD
	60203	Grumman C-20B Gulfstream III (86-0203)	USAF 99th AS/89th AW, Andrews AFB, MD
	60204	Grumman C-20B Gulfstream III (86-0204)	USAF 99th AS/89th AW, Andrews AFB, MD
	60206	Grumman C-20B Gulfstream III (86-0206)	USAF 99th AS/89th AW, Andrews AFB, MD

Lockheed Martin F-22A Raptor

	00-4012	Lockheed Martin F-22A Raptor [TY]	USAF 43rd FS/325th FW, Tyndall AFB, FL
	00-4015	Lockheed Martin F-22A Raptor [TY]	USAF 43rd FS/325th FW, Tyndall AFB, FL
	00-4016	Lockheed Martin F-22A Raptor [TY]	USAF 43rd FS/325th FW, Tyndall AFB, FL
	00-4017	Lockheed Martin F-22A Raptor [TY]	USAF 43rd FS/325th FW, Tyndall AFB, FL
	01-4018	Lockheed Martin F-22A Raptor [TY]	USAF 43rd FS/325th FW, Tyndall AFB, FL
	01-4019	Lockheed Martin F-22A Raptor [TY]	USAF 43rd FS/325th FW, Tyndall AFB, FL
	01-4020	Lockheed Martin F-22A Raptor [TY]	USAF 43rd FS/325th FW, Tyndall AFB, FL
	01-4021	Lockheed Martin F-22A Raptor [TY]	USAF 43rd FS/325th FW, Tyndall AFB, FL
	01-4022	Lockheed Martin F-22A Raptor [TY]	USAF 43rd FS/325th FW, Tyndall AFB, FL
	01-4023	Lockheed Martin F-22A Raptor [TY]	USAF 43rd FS/325th FW, Tyndall AFB, FL
	01-4024	Lockheed Martin F-22A Raptor [TY]	USAF 43rd FS/325th FW, Tyndall AFB, FL
	01-4025	Lockheed Martin F-22A Raptor [TY]	USAF 43rd FS/325th FW, Tyndall AFB, FL
	01-4026	Lockheed Martin F-22A Raptor [TY]	USAF 43rd FS/325th FW, Tyndall AFB, FL
	01-4027	Lockheed Martin F-22A Raptor [TY]	USAF 43rd FS/325th FW, Tyndall AFB, FL
	02-4028	Lockheed Martin F-22A Raptor [TY]	USAF 43rd FS/325th FW, Tyndall AFB, FL
	02-4029	Lockheed Martin F-22A Raptor [TY]	USAF 43rd FS/325th FW, Tyndall AFB, FL
	02-4030	Lockheed Martin F-22A Raptor [TY]	USAF 43rd FS/325th FW, Tyndall AFB, FL
	02-4031	Lockheed Martin F-22A Raptor [TY]	USAF 43rd FS/325th FW, Tyndall AFB, FL
	02-4032	Lockheed Martin F-22A Raptor [TY]	USAF 43rd FS/325th FW, Tyndall AFB, FL
	02-4033	Lockheed Martin F-22A Raptor [TY]	USAF 43rd FS/325th FW, Tyndall AFB, FL
	02-4034	Lockheed Martin F-22A Raptor [TY]	USAF 43rd FS/325th FW, Tyndall AFB, FL
	02-4035	Lockheed Martin F-22A Raptor [TY] [325 OG]	USAF 43rd FS/325th FW, Tyndall AFB, FL
	02-4036	Lockheed Martin F-22A Raptor [TY]	USAF 43rd FS/325th FW, Tyndall AFB, FL
	02-4037	Lockheed Martin F-22A Raptor	USAF
	02-4038	Lockheed Martin F-22A Raptor [TY]	USAF 43rd FS/325th FW, Tyndall AFB, FL
	02-4039	Lockheed Martin F-22A Raptor [TY]	USAF 43rd FS/325th FW, Tyndall AFB, FL
	02-4040	Lockheed Martin F-22A Raptor [TY] [325 FW]	USAF 43rd FS/325th FW, Tyndall AFB, FL
	03-4041	Lockheed Martin F-22A Raptor [TY]	USAF 43rd FS/325th FW, Tyndall AFB, FL
	03-4042	Lockheed Martin F-22A Raptor [TY]	USAF 43rd FS/325th FW, Tyndall AFB, FL
	03-4043	Lockheed Martin F-22A Raptor [TY] [43 FS]	USAF 43rd FS/325th FW, Tyndall AFB, FL
	03-4044	Lockheed Martin F-22A Raptor [TY]	USAF 43rd FS/325th FW, Tyndall AFB, FL
	03-4045	Lockheed Martin F-22A Raptor [HH]	USAF 199th FS/154th Wg, Hickam AFB, HI ANG
	03-4046	Lockheed Martin F-22A Raptor [HH]	USAF 199th FS/154th Wg, Hickam AFB, HI ANG
	03-4047	Lockheed Martin F-22A Raptor [HH]	USAF 199th FS/154th Wg, Hickam AFB, HI ANG

Serial	Type (code/other identity)	Owner/operator, location or fate	Notes
03-4048	Lockheed Martin F-22A Raptor [HH]	USAF 199th FS/154th Wg, Hickam AFB, HI ANG	
03-4049	Lockheed Martin F-22A Raptor [HH]	USAF 199th FS/154th Wg, Hickam AFB, HI ANG	
03-4050	Lockheed Martin F-22A Raptor [HH]	USAF 199th FS/154th Wg, Hickam AFB, HI ANG	
03-4051	Lockheed Martin F-22A Raptor [HH]	USAF 199th FS/154th Wg, Hickam AFB, HI ANG	
03-4052	Lockheed Martin F-22A Raptor [HH]	USAF 199th FS/154th Wg, Hickam AFB, HI ANG	
03-4053	Lockheed Martin F-22A Raptor [HH]	USAF 199th FS/154th Wg, Hickam AFB, HI ANG	
03-4054	Lockheed Martin F-22A Raptor [HH] [154 Wg]	USAF 199th FS/154th Wg, Hickam AFB, HI ANG	
03-4055	Lockheed Martin F-22A Raptor [HH]	USAF 199th FS/154th Wg, Hickam AFB, HI ANG	
03-4056	Lockheed Martin F-22A Raptor [HH]	USAF 199th FS/154th Wg, Hickam AFB, HI ANG	
03-4057	Lockheed Martin F-22A Raptor [HH]	USAF 199th FS/154th Wg, Hickam AFB, HI ANG	
03-4058	Lockheed Martin F-22A Raptor [HH]	USAF 199th FS/154th Wg, Hickam AFB, HI ANG	
03-4059	Lockheed Martin F-22A Raptor [HH]	USAF 199th FS/154th Wg, Hickam AFB, HI ANG	
03-4060	Lockheed Martin F-22A Raptor [HH]	USAF 199th FS/154th Wg, Hickam AFB, HI ANG	
03-4061	Lockheed Martin F-22A Raptor [HH]	USAF 199th FS/154th Wg, Hickam AFB, HI ANG	
04-4062	Lockheed Martin F-22A Raptor [HH]	USAF 199th FS/154th Wg, Hickam AFB, HI ANG	
04-4063	Lockheed Martin F-22A Raptor [HH]	USAF 199th FS/154th Wg, Hickam AFB, HI ANG	
04-4064	Lockheed Martin F-22A Raptor [HH]	USAF 199th FS/154th Wg, Hickam AFB, HI ANG	
04-4065	Lockheed Martin F-22A Raptor [FF]	USAF 94th FS/1st FW, Langley AFB, VA	
04-4066	Lockheed Martin F-22A Raptor [OT]	USAF 422nd TES/53rd Wg, Nellis AFB, NV	
04-4067	Lockheed Martin F-22A Raptor [FF]	USAF 94th FS/1st FW, Langley AFB, VA	
04-4068	Lockheed Martin F-22A Raptor [OT]	USAF 422nd TES/53rd Wg, Nellis AFB, NV	
04-4069	Lockheed Martin F-22A Raptor [OT]	USAF 422nd TES/53rd Wg, Nellis AFB, NV	
04-4070	Lockheed Martin F-22A Raptor [FF]	USAF 94th FS/1st FW, Langley AFB, VA	
04-4071	Lockheed Martin F-22A Raptor [WA]	USAF 433rd WPS/57th Wg, Nellis AFB, NV	
04-4072	Lockheed Martin F-22A Raptor [TY]	USAF 95th FS/325th FW, Tyndall AFB, FL	
04-4073	Lockheed Martin F-22A Raptor [FF]	USAF 27th FS/1st FW, Langley AFB, VA	
04-4074	Lockheed Martin F-22A Raptor [AK]	USAF 90th FS/3rd Wg, Elmendorf AFB, AK	
04-4075	Lockheed Martin F-22A Raptor [AK]	USAF 90th FS/3rd Wg, Elmendorf AFB, AK	
04-4076	Lockheed Martin F-22A Raptor [TY]	USAF 95th FS/325th FW, Tyndall AFB, FL	
04-4077	Lockheed Martin F-22A Raptor [AK]	USAF 525th FS/3rd Wg, Elmendorf AFB, AK	
04-4078	Lockheed Martin F-22A Raptor [TY]	USAF 95th FS/325th FW, Tyndall AFB, FL	
04-4079	Lockheed Martin F-22A Raptor [TY]	USAF 95th FS/325th FW, Tyndall AFB, FL	
04-4080	Lockheed Martin F-22A Raptor [TY]	USAF 95th FS/325th FW, Tyndall AFB, FL	
04-4082	Lockheed Martin F-22A Raptor [FF] [149 FS]	USAF 149th FS/192nd FW/1st FW, Langley AFB, VA ANG	
04-4083	Lockheed Martin F-22A Raptor [TY] [301 FS]	USAF 301st FS/44th FG AFRES/325th FW, Tyndall AFB, FL	
05-4081	Lockheed Martin F-22A Raptor (04-4081) [TY]	USAF 95th FS/325th FW, Tyndall AFB, FL	
05-4084	Lockheed Martin F-22A Raptor [TY]	USAF 95th FS/325th FW, Tyndall AFB, FL	
05-4085	Lockheed Martin F-22A Raptor [FF]	USAF 94th FS/1st FW, Langley AFB, VA	
05-4086	Lockheed Martin F-22A Raptor [TY]	USAF 95th FS/325th FW, Tyndall AFB, FL	
05-4087	Lockheed Martin F-22A Raptor [AK]	USAF 90th FS/3rd Wg, Elmendorf AFB, AK	
05-4088	Lockheed Martin F-22A Raptor [TY]	USAF 95th FS/325th FW, Tyndall AFB, FL	
05-4089	Lockheed Martin F-22A Raptor [TY]	USAF 95th FS/325th FW, Tyndall AFB, FL	
05-4090	Lockheed Martin F-22A Raptor [AK]	USAF 90th FS/3rd Wg, Elmendorf AFB, AK	
05-4091	Lockheed Martin F-22A Raptor [TY]	USAF 95th FS/325th FW, Tyndall AFB, FL	
05-4092	Lockheed Martin F-22A Raptor [AK]	USAF 525th FS/3rd Wg, Elmendorf AFB, AK	
05-4093	Lockheed Martin F-22A Raptor [TY]	USAF 95th FS/325th FW, Tyndall AFB, FL	
05-4094	Lockheed Martin F-22A Raptor [TY]	USAF 95th FS/325th FW, Tyndall AFB, FL	
05-4095	Lockheed Martin F-22A Raptor [TY] [95 FS]	USAF 95th FS/325th FW, Tyndall AFB, FL	
05-4096	Lockheed Martin F-22A Raptor [WA]	USAF 433rd WPS/57th Wg, Nellis AFB, NV	
05-4097	Lockheed Martin F-22A Raptor [TY]	USAF 95th FS/325th FW, Tyndall AFB, FL	
05-4098	Lockheed Martin F-22A Raptor [TY]	USAF 95th FS/325th FW, Tyndall AFB, FL	
05-4099	Lockheed Martin F-22A Raptor [TY]	USAF 95th FS/325th FW, Tyndall AFB, FL	
05-4100	Lockheed Martin F-22A Raptor [TY]	USAF 95th FS/325th FW, Tyndall AFB, FL	
05-4101	Lockheed Martin F-22A Raptor [TY]	USAF 95th FS/325th FW, Tyndall AFB, FL	
05-4102	Lockheed Martin F-22A Raptor [AK] [302 FS]	USAF 302nd FS/477th FG AFRES/3rd Wg, Elmendorf AFB, AK	
05-4103	Lockheed Martin F-22A Raptor [AK] [3 Wg]	USAF 90th FS/3rd Wg, Elmendorf AFB, AK	
05-4104	Lockheed Martin F-22A Raptor [TY]	USAF 95th FS/325th FW, Tyndall AFB, FL	
05-4105	Lockheed Martin F-22A Raptor [TY] [95 FS]	USAF 95th FS/325th FW, Tyndall AFB, FL	

Notes	Serial	Type (code/other identity)	Owner/operator, location or fate
	05-4106	Lockheed Martin F-22A Raptor [TY]	USAF 95th FS/325th FW, Tyndall AFB, FL
	05-4107	Lockheed Martin F-22A Raptor [TY]	USAF 95th FS/325th FW, Tyndall AFB, FL
	06-4108	Lockheed Martin F-22A Raptor [AK]	USAF 525th FS/3rd Wg, Elmendorf AFB, AK
	06-4109	Lockheed Martin F-22A Raptor [WA]	USAF 433rd WPS/57th Wg, Nellis AFB, NV
	06-4110	Lockheed Martin F-22A Raptor [AK] [11 AF]	USAF 525th FS/3rd Wg, Elmendorf AFB, AK
	06-4111	Lockheed Martin F-22A Raptor [OT]	USAF 422nd TES/53rd Wg, Nellis AFB, NV
	06-4112	Lockheed Martin F-22A Raptor [AK]	USAF 525th FS/3rd Wg, Elmendorf AFB, AK
	06-4113	Lockheed Martin F-22A Raptor [AK] [3 OG]	USAF 525th FS/3rd Wg, Elmendorf AFB, AK
	06-4114	Lockheed Martin F-22A Raptor [AK]	USAF 525th FS/3rd Wg, Elmendorf AFB, AK
	06-4115	Lockheed Martin F-22A Raptor [AK] [525 FS]	USAF 525th FS/3rd Wg, Elmendorf AFB, AK
	06-4116	Lockheed Martin F-22A Raptor [WA] [433 WPS]	USAF 433rd WPS/57th Wg, Nellis AFB, NV
	06-4117	Lockheed Martin F-22A Raptor [AK]	USAF 525th FS/3rd Wg, Elmendorf AFB, AK
	06-4118	Lockheed Martin F-22A Raptor [AK]	USAF 525th FS/3rd Wg, Elmendorf AFB, AK
	06-4119	Lockheed Martin F-22A Raptor [AK]	USAF 525th FS/3rd Wg, Elmendorf AFB, AK
	06-4120	Lockheed Martin F-22A Raptor [OT]	USAF 422nd TES/53rd Wg, Nellis AFB, NV
	06-4121	Lockheed Martin F-22A Raptor [AK]	USAF 525th FS/3rd Wg, Elmendorf AFB, AK
	06-4122	Lockheed Martin F-22A Raptor [AK]	USAF 525th FS/3rd Wg, Elmendorf AFB, AK
	06-4123	Lockheed Martin F-22A Raptor [AK]	USAF 525th FS/3rd Wg, Elmendorf AFB, AK
	06-4124	Lockheed Martin F-22A Raptor [OT]	USAF 422nd TES/53rd Wg, Nellis AFB, NV
	06-4126	Lockheed Martin F-22A Raptor [AK]	USAF 525th FS/3rd Wg, Elmendorf AFB, AK
	06-4127	Lockheed Martin F-22A Raptor [AK]	USAF 525th FS/3rd Wg, Elmendorf AFB, AK
	06-4128	Lockheed Martin F-22A Raptor [OT]	USAF 422nd TES/53rd Wg, Nellis AFB, NV
	06-4129	Lockheed Martin F-22A Raptor [AK]	USAF 525th FS/3rd Wg, Elmendorf AFB, AK
	06-4130	Lockheed Martin F-22A Raptor [AK]	USAF 525th FS/3rd Wg, Elmendorf AFB, AK
	07-4131	Lockheed Martin F-22A Raptor [AK]	USAF 525th FS/3rd Wg, Elmendorf AFB, AK
	07-4132	Lockheed Martin F-22A Raptor [ED] [411 FLTS]	USAF 411th FLTS/412th TW, Edwards AFB, CA
	07-4133	Lockheed Martin F-22A Raptor [AK]	USAF 525th FS/3rd Wg, Elmendorf AFB, AK
	07-4134	Lockheed Martin F-22A Raptor [AK]	USAF 525th FS/3rd Wg, Elmendorf AFB, AK
	07-4135	Lockheed Martin F-22A Raptor [AK]	USAF 90th FS/3rd Wg, Elmendorf AFB, AK
	07-4136	Lockheed Martin F-22A Raptor [AK]	USAF 90th FS/3rd Wg, Elmendorf AFB, AK
	07-4137	Lockheed Martin F-22A Raptor [AK]	USAF 90th FS/3rd Wg, Elmendorf AFB, AK
	07-4138	Lockheed Martin F-22A Raptor [AK]	USAF 90th FS/3rd Wg, Elmendorf AFB, AK
	07-4139	Lockheed Martin F-22A Raptor [AK]	USAF 90th FS/3rd Wg, Elmendorf AFB, AK
	07-4140	Lockheed Martin F-22A Raptor [AK]	USAF 90th FS/3rd Wg, Elmendorf AFB, AK
	07-4141	Lockheed Martin F-22A Raptor [AK]	USAF 90th FS/3rd Wg, Elmendorf AFB, AK
	07-4142	Lockheed Martin F-22A Raptor [AK]	USAF 90th FS/3rd Wg, Elmendorf AFB, AK
	07-4143	Lockheed Martin F-22A Raptor [AK]	USAF 90th FS/3rd Wg, Elmendorf AFB, AK
	07-4144	Lockheed Martin F-22A Raptor [AK]	USAF 90th FS/3rd Wg, Elmendorf AFB, AK
	07-4145	Lockheed Martin F-22A Raptor [AK]	USAF 90th FS/3rd Wg, Elmendorf AFB, AK
	07-4146	Lockheed Martin F-22A Raptor [AK]	USAF 90th FS/3rd Wg, Elmendorf AFB, AK
	07-4147	Lockheed Martin F-22A Raptor [AK]	USAF 90th FS/3rd Wg, Elmendorf AFB, AK
	07-4148	Lockheed Martin F-22A Raptor [AK]	USAF 90th FS/3rd Wg, Elmendorf AFB, AK
	07-4149	Lockheed Martin F-22A Raptor [AK]	USAF 90th FS/3rd Wg, Elmendorf AFB, AK
	07-4150	Lockheed Martin F-22A Raptor [AK]	USAF 90th FS/3rd Wg, Elmendorf AFB, AK
	07-4151	Lockheed Martin F-22A Raptor [AK]	USAF 90th FS/3rd Wg, Elmendorf AFB, AK
	08-4152	Lockheed Martin F-22A Raptor [FF]	USAF 94th FS/1st FW, Langley AFB, VA
	08-4153	Lockheed Martin F-22A Raptor [FF]	USAF 27th FS/1st FW, Langley AFB, VA
	08-4154	Lockheed Martin F-22A Raptor [FF]	USAF 94th FS/1st FW, Langley AFB, VA
	08-4155	Lockheed Martin F-22A Raptor [FF]	USAF 27th FS/1st FW, Langley AFB, VA
	08-4156	Lockheed Martin F-22A Raptor [FF]	USAF 94th FS/1st FW, Langley AFB, VA
	08-4157	Lockheed Martin F-22A Raptor [FF]	USAF 27th FS/1st FW, Langley AFB, VA
	08-4158	Lockheed Martin F-22A Raptor [FF]	USAF 94th FS/1st FW, Langley AFB, VA
	08-4159	Lockheed Martin F-22A Raptor [FF]	USAF 27th FS/1st FW, Langley AFB, VA
	08-4160	Lockheed Martin F-22A Raptor [FF]	USAF 94th FS/1st FW, Langley AFB, VA
	08-4161	Lockheed Martin F-22A Raptor [FF]	USAF 27th FS/1st FW, Langley AFB, VA
	08-4162	Lockheed Martin F-22A Raptor [FF] [1 FW]	USAF 94th FS/1st FW, Langley AFB, VA
	08-4163	Lockheed Martin F-22A Raptor [FF]	USAF 27th FS/1st FW, Langley AFB, VA
	08-4164	Lockheed Martin F-22A Raptor [FF]	USAF 94th FS/1st FW, Langley AFB, VA
	08-4165	Lockheed Martin F-22A Raptor [FF]	USAF 27th FS/1st FW, Langley AFB, VA
	08-4166	Lockheed Martin F-22A Raptor [FF]	USAF 94th FS/1st FW, Langley AFB, VA
	08-4167	Lockheed Martin F-22A Raptor [FF]	USAF 27th FS/1st FW, Langley AFB, VA
	08-4168	Lockheed Martin F-22A Raptor [FF]	USAF 94th FS/1st FW, Langley AFB, VA

Serial	Type (code/other identity)	Owner/operator, location or fate	Notes
08-4169	Lockheed Martin F-22A Raptor [FF]	USAF 94th FS/1st FW, Langley AFB, VA	
08-4170	Lockheed Martin F-22A Raptor [FF]	USAF 27th FS/1st FW, Langley AFB, VA	
08-4171	Lockheed Martin F-22A Raptor [FF]	USAF 27th FS/1st FW, Langley AFB, VA	
09-4172	Lockheed Martin F-22A Raptor [FF] [27 FS]	USAF 27th FS/1st FW, Langley AFB, VA	
09-4173	Lockheed Martin F-22A Raptor [FF]	USAF 27th FS/1st FW, Langley AFB, VA	
09-4174	Lockheed Martin F-22A Raptor [FF]	USAF 27th FS/1st FW, Langley AFB, VA	
09-4175	Lockheed Martin F-22A Raptor [FF]	USAF 94th FS/1st FW, Langley AFB, VA	
09-4176	Lockheed Martin F-22A Raptor [FF]	USAF 27th FS/1st FW, Langley AFB, VA	
09-4177	Lockheed Martin F-22A Raptor [FF]	USAF 94th FS/1st FW, Langley AFB, VA	
09-4178	Lockheed Martin F-22A Raptor [FF]	USAF 27th FS/1st FW, Langley AFB, VA	
09-4179	Lockheed Martin F-22A Raptor [FF]	USAF 94th FS/1st FW, Langley AFB, VA	
09-4180	Lockheed Martin F-22A Raptor [FF]	USAF 27th FS/1st FW, Langley AFB, VA	
09-4181	Lockheed Martin F-22A Raptor [FF]	USAF 94th FS/1st FW, Langley AFB, VA	
09-4182	Lockheed Martin F-22A Raptor [FF]	USAF 27th FS/1st FW, Langley AFB, VA	
09-4183	Lockheed Martin F-22A Raptor [FF]	USAF 94th FS/1st FW, Langley AFB, VA	
09-4184	Lockheed Martin F-22A Raptor [FF]	USAF 27th FS/1st FW, Langley AFB, VA	
09-4185	Lockheed Martin F-22A Raptor [FF] [1 OG]	USAF 27th FS/1st FW, Langley AFB, VA	
09-4186	Lockheed Martin F-22A Raptor [FF]	USAF 27th FS/1st FW, Langley AFB, VA	
09-4187	Lockheed Martin F-22A Raptor [FF]	USAF 94th FS/1st FW, Langley AFB, VA	
09-4188	Lockheed Martin F-22A Raptor [OT]	USAF 422nd TES/53rd Wg, Nellis AFB, NV	
09-4189	Lockheed Martin F-22A Raptor [FF]	USAF 27th FS/1st FW, Langley AFB, VA	
09-4190	Lockheed Martin F-22A Raptor [AK]	USAF 90th FS/3rd Wg, Elmendorf AFB, AK	
09-4191	Lockheed Martin F-22A Raptor [FF]	USAF 94th FS/1st FW, Langley AFB, VA	
10-4192	Lockheed Martin F-22A Raptor [FF] [192 FW]	USAF 149th FS/192nd FW/1st FW, Langley AFB, VA ANG	
10-4193	Lockheed Martin F-22A Raptor [AK] [3 Wg]	USAF 525th FS/3rd Wg, Elmendorf AFB, AK	
10-4194	Lockheed Martin F-22A Raptor [FF] [94 FS]	USAF 94th FS/1st FW, Langley AFB, VA	
10-4195	Lockheed Martin F-22A Raptor [AK] [525 FS]	USAF 525th FS/3rd Wg, Elmendorf AFB, AK	
91-4004	Lockheed Martin F-22A Raptor [ED]	USAF 411th FLTS/412th TW, Edwards AFB, CA	
91-4006	Lockheed Martin F-22A Raptor	USAF	
91-4007	Lockheed Martin F-22A Raptor [ED] [412 TW]	USAF 411th FLTS/412th TW, Edwards AFB, CA	
91-4009	Lockheed Martin F-22A Raptor [ED]	USAF 411th FLTS/412th TW, Edwards AFB, CA	
99-4010	Lockheed Martin F-22A Raptor [OT] [422 TES]	USAF 422nd TES/53rd Wg, Nellis AFB, NV	
99-4011	Lockheed Martin F-22A Raptor [WA]	USAF 433rd WPS/57th Wg, Nellis AFB, NV	

Boeing VC-25A

28000	Boeing VC-25A (82-8000)	USAF PAS/89th AW, Andrews AFB, MD	
29000	Boeing VC-25A (92-9000)	USAF PAS/89th AW, Andrews AFB, MD	

Pilatus U-28A

10415	Pilatus U-28A (N415PB/01-0415)	USAF 318th SOS/27th SOW, Cannon AFB, NM	
40688	Pilatus U-28A (N707KH/04-0688)	USAF 318th SOS/27th SOW, Cannon AFB, NM	
50409	Pilatus U-28A (N922RG/05-0409)	USAF 319th SOS/1st SOW, Hurlburt Field, FL	
50419	Pilatus U-28A (N419WA/05-0419)	USAF 319th SOS/1st SOW, Hurlburt Field, FL	
50424	Pilatus U-28A (N424PB/05-0424)	USAF 318th SOS/27th SOW, Cannon AFB, NM	
50446	Pilatus U-28A (N131JN/05-0446)	USAF 318th SOS/27th SOW, Cannon AFB, NM	
50447	Pilatus U-28A (N447PC/05-0447)	USAF 319th SOS/1st SOW, Hurlburt Field, FL	
50482	Pilatus U-28A (N482WA/05-0482)	USAF 319th SOS/1st SOW, Hurlburt Field, FL	
50556	Pilatus U-28A (N556HL/05-0556)	USAF 319th SOS/1st SOW, Hurlburt Field, FL	
50573	Pilatus U-28A (N666GT/05-0573)	USAF 319th SOS/1st SOW, Hurlburt Field, FL	
50597	Pilatus U-28A (N597CH/05-0597)	USAF 318th SOS/27th SOW, Cannon AFB, NM	
60692	Pilatus U-28A (N692BC/06-0692)	USAF 318th SOS/27th SOW, Cannon AFB, NM	
60740	Pilatus U-28A (N740AF/06-0740)	USAF 318th SOS/27th SOW, Cannon AFB, NM	
70488	Pilatus U-28A (N56EZ/07-0488)	USAF 319th SOS/1st SOW, Hurlburt Field, FL	
70691	Pilatus U-28A (N691PC/07-0691)	USAF 319th SOS/1st SOW, Hurlburt Field, FL	
70711	Pilatus U-28A (N711PN/07-0711)	USAF 319th SOS/1st SOW, Hurlburt Field, FL	
70712	Pilatus U-28A (N609TW/07-0712)	USAF 319th SOS/1st SOW, Hurlburt Field, FL	
70777	Pilatus U-28A (N72DZ/07-0777)	USAF 318th SOS/27th SOW, Cannon AFB, NM	
70779	Pilatus U-28A (N779PC/07-0779)	USAF 319th SOS/1st SOW, Hurlburt Field, FL	
70793	Pilatus U-28A (N96MV/07-0793)	USAF 319th SOS/1st SOW, Hurlburt Field, FL	
70808	Pilatus U-28A (N531MP/07-0808)	USAF 318th SOS/27th SOW, Cannon AFB, NM	
70821	Pilatus U-28A (N821PE/07-0821)	USAF 319th SOS/1st SOW, Hurlburt Field, FL	

Notes	Serial	Type (code/other identity)	Owner/operator, location or fate
	70829	Pilatus U-28A (N829PE/07-0829)	USAF 319th SOS/1st SOW, Hurlburt Field, FL
	70838	Pilatus U-28A (N838PE/07-0838)	USAF 319th SOS/1st SOW, Hurlburt Field, FL
	70840	Pilatus U-28A (N840PE/07-0840)	USAF 319th SOS/1st SOW, Hurlburt Field, FL
	80519	Pilatus U-28A (N519PC/08-0519)	USAF 319th SOS/1st SOW, Hurlburt Field, FL
	80581	Pilatus U-28A (N581PC/08-0581)	USAF 319th SOS/1st SOW, Hurlburt Field, FL
	80646	Pilatus U-28A (N875RJ/08-0646)	USAF 319th SOS/1st SOW, Hurlburt Field, FL
	80718	Pilatus U-28A (N824BK/08-0718)	USAF 319th SOS/1st SOW, Hurlburt Field, FL
	80724	Pilatus U-28A (N624TS/08-0724)	USAF 319th SOS/1st SOW, Hurlburt Field, FL
	80790	Pilatus U-28A (N757ED/08-0790)	USAF 319th SOS/1st SOW, Hurlburt Field, FL
	80809	Pilatus U-28A (N36EG/08-0809)	USAF 319th SOS/1st SOW, Hurlburt Field, FL
	80822	Pilatus U-28A (N822BM/08-0822)	USAF 319th SOS/1st SOW, Hurlburt Field, FL
	80835	Pilatus U-28A (N100MS/08-0835)	USAF 318th SOS/27th SOW, Cannon AFB, NM
	80850	Pilatus U-28A (N850CB/08-0850)	USAF 319th SOS/1st SOW, Hurlburt Field, FL

Boeing C-32

	09001	Boeing C-32B (00-9001)	USAF 150th SOS/108th Wg, McGuire AFB, NJ
	24452	Boeing C-32B (02-4452)	USAF 150th SOS/108th Wg, McGuire AFB, NJ
	25001	Boeing C-32B (02-5001)	USAF 486th FLTS/46th TW, Eglin AFB, FL
	80001	Boeing C-32A (98-0001)	USAF 1st AS/89th AW, Andrews AFB, MD
	80002	Boeing C-32A (98-0002)	USAF 1st AS/89th AW, Andrews AFB, MD
	86006	Boeing C-32B (98-6006)	USAF 486th FLTS/46th TW, Eglin AFB, FL
	90003	Boeing C-32A (99-0003)	USAF 1st AS/89th AW, Andrews AFB, MD
	90004	Boeing C-32A (99-0004)	USAF 1st AS/89th AW, Andrews AFB, MD
	90015	Boeing C-32A (09-0015)	USAF 1st AS/89th AW, Andrews AFB, MD
	90016	Boeing C-32A (09-0016)	USAF 1st AS/89th AW, Andrews AFB, MD
	90017	Boeing C-32A (09-0017)	USAF 1st AS/89th AW, Andrews AFB, MD
	96143	Boeing C-32B (99-6143)	USAF 486th FLTS/46th TW, Eglin AFB, FL

Gulfstream Aerospace C-37 Gulfstream V

	1778	Gulfstream Aerospace C-37A Gulfstream V (04-01778)	US Army OSAC/PAT, Andrews AFB, MD
	1863	Gulfstream Aerospace C-37A Gulfstream V (02-01863)	US Army OSAC/PAT, Andrews AFB, MD
	1944	Gulfstream Aerospace C-37A Gulfstream V (97-01944)	US Army OSAC/PAT, Andrews AFB, MD
	10028	Gulfstream Aerospace C-37A Gulfstream V (01-0028)	USAF 310th AS/6th AMW, MacDill AFB, FL
	10029	Gulfstream Aerospace C-37A Gulfstream V (01-0029)	USAF 310th AS/6th AMW, MacDill AFB, FL
	10030	Gulfstream Aerospace C-37A Gulfstream V (01-0030)	USAF 310th AS/6th AMW, MacDill AFB, FL
	10065	Gulfstream Aerospace C-37A Gulfstream V (01-0065)	USAF 65th AS/15th Wg, Hickam AFB, HI
	10550	Gulfstream Aerospace C-37B Gulfstream V (11-0550)	USAF 99th AS/89th AW, Andrews AFB, MD
	60500	Gulfstream Aerospace C-37B Gulfstream V (06-0500)	USAF 99th AS/89th AW, Andrews AFB, MD
	70400	Gulfstream Aerospace C-37A Gulfstream V (97-0400)	USAF 99th AS/89th AW, Andrews AFB, MD
	70401	Gulfstream Aerospace C-37A Gulfstream V (97-0401)	USAF 99th AS/89th AW, Andrews AFB, MD
	90404	Gulfstream Aerospace C-37A Gulfstream V (99-0404)	USAF 99th AS/89th AW, Andrews AFB, MD
	90525	Gulfstream Aerospace C-37B Gulfstream V (09-0525)	USAF 99th AS/89th AW, Andrews AFB, MD

Boeing C-40

	10015	Boeing C-40B (N378BJ/01-0015)	USAF 65th AS/15th Wg, Hickam AFB, HI
	10040	Boeing C-40B (N371BJ/01-0040)	USAF 1st AS/89th AW, Andrews AFB, MD
	10041	Boeing C-40B (N374BC/01-0041)	USAF 1st AS/89th AW, Andrews AFB, MD
	20201	Boeing C-40C (N752BC/02-0201)	USAF 201st AS/113th FW DC ANG, Andrews AFB, MD
	20202	Boeing C-40C (N754BC/02-0202)	USAF 201st AS/113th FW DC ANG, Andrews AFB, MD
	20203	Boeing C-40C (N236BA/02-0203)	USAF 201st AS/113th FW DC ANG, Andrews AFB, MD
	50730	Boeing C-40C (N365BJ/05-0730)	USAF 73rd AS/932nd AW AFRC, Scott AFB, IL
	50932	Boeing C-40C (N366BJ/05-0932)	USAF 73rd AS/932nd AW AFRC, Scott AFB, IL
	54613	Boeing C-40C (N368BJ/05-4613)	USAF 73rd AS/932nd AW AFRC, Scott AFB, IL
	90540	Boeing C-40C (N736JS/09-0540)	USAF 73rd AS/932nd AW AFRC, Scott AFB, IL

Boeing 767-2C/KC-46A Pegasus

	46001	Boeing 767-2LKC (N461FT/11-46001)	USAF 418th FLTS, 412th TW, Edwards AFB, CA
	46002	Boeing KC-46A Pegasus (N462KC/11-46002)	Boeing, Everett, for USAF
	46003	Boeing 767-2LKC (N463FT/11-46003)	Boeing, Everett, for USAF

Serial	Type (code/other identity)	Owner/operator, location or fate	Notes
46004	Boeing KC-46A Pegasus (N464KC/11-46004)	Boeing, Everett, for USAF	
46005	Boeing KC-46A Pegasus (N842BA/16-46005)	Boeing, Everett, for USAF	
46006	Boeing 767-2LKC (N884BA/16-46006)	Boeing, Everett, for USAF	
46007	Boeing KC-46A Pegasus (16-46007)	USAF (on order)	
46008	Boeing KC-46A Pegasus (16-46008)	USAF (on order)	
46009	Boeing KC-46A Pegasus (16-46009)	USAF (on order)	
46010	Boeing KC-46A Pegasus (16-46010)	USAF (on order)	
46011	Boeing KC-46A Pegasus (16-46011)	USAF (on order)	
46012	Boeing KC-46A Pegasus (16-46012)	USAF (on order)	
46013	Boeing KC-46A Pegasus (1.-46013)	USAF (on order)	
46014	Boeing KC-46A Pegasus (1.-46014)	USAF (on order)	
46015	Boeing KC-46A Pegasus (1.-46015)	USAF (on order)	
46016	Boeing KC-46A Pegasus (1.-46016)	USAF (on order)	
46017	Boeing KC-46A Pegasus (1.-46017)	USAF (on order)	
46018	Boeing KC-46A Pegasus (1.-46018)	USAF (on order)	
46019	Boeing KC-46A Pegasus (1.-46019)	USAF (on order)	
46020	Boeing KC-46A Pegasus (1.-46020)	USAF (on order)	
46021	Boeing KC-46A Pegasus (1.-46021)	USAF (on order)	
46022	Boeing KC-46A Pegasus (1.-46022)	USAF (on order)	
46023	Boeing KC-46A Pegasus (1.-46023)	USAF (on order)	
46024	Boeing KC-46A Pegasus (1.-46024)	USAF (on order)	
46025	Boeing KC-46A Pegasus (1.-46025)	USAF (on order)	
46026	Boeing KC-46A Pegasus (1.-46026)	USAF (on order)	
46027	Boeing KC-46A Pegasus (1.-46027)	USAF (on order)	
46028	Boeing KC-46A Pegasus (1.-46028)	USAF (on order)	
46029	Boeing KC-46A Pegasus (1.-46029)	USAF (on order)	
46030	Boeing KC-46A Pegasus (1.-46030)	USAF (on order)	
46031	Boeing KC-46A Pegasus (1.-46031)	USAF (on order)	
46032	Boeing KC-46A Pegasus (1.-46032)	USAF (on order)	
46033	Boeing KC-46A Pegasus (1.-46033)	USAF (on order)	
46034	Boeing KC-46A Pegasus (1.-46034)	USAF (on order)	

Boeing B-52H Stratofortress

Serial	Type (code/other identity)	Owner/operator, location or fate	Notes
00001	Boeing B-52H Stratofortress (60-0001) [LA] *r*	USAF 96th BS/2nd BW, Barksdale AFB, LA	
00002	Boeing B-52H Stratofortress (60-0002) [LA] *gn* $	USAF 96th BS/2nd BW, Barksdale AFB, LA	
00003	Boeing B-52H Stratofortress (60-0003) [BD] *or/bl*	USAF 93rd BS/307th BW AFRC, Barksdale AFB, LA	
00004	Boeing B-52H Stratofortress (60-0004) [MT] *r/y*	USAF 23rd BS/5th BW, Minot AFB, ND	
00005	Boeing B-52H Stratofortress (60-0005) [MT] *r/y* $	USAF 23rd BS/5th BW, Minot AFB, ND	
00007	Boeing B-52H Stratofortress (60-0007) [MT] *r/y*	USAF 23rd BS/5th BW, Minot AFB, ND	
00008	Boeing B-52H Stratofortress (60-0008) [LA] *bl* [8th AF]	USAF 20th BS/2nd BW, Barksdale AFB, LA	
00009	Boeing B-52H Stratofortress (60-0009) [MT] *y/bk* $	USAF 69th BS/5th BW, Minot AFB, ND	
00011	Boeing B-52H Stratofortress (60-0011) [BD] *or/bl* [11 BS]	USAF 93rd BS/307th BW AFRC, Barksdale AFB, LA	
00012	Boeing B-52H Stratofortress (60-0012) [MT] *y/bk*	USAF 69th BS/5th BW, Minot AFB, ND	
00013	Boeing B-52H Stratofortress (60-0013) [LA] *bl*	USAF 20th BS/2nd BW, Barksdale AFB, LA	
00015	Boeing B-52H Stratofortress (60-0015) [BD] *or/bl*	USAF 93rd BS/307th BW AFRC, Barksdale AFB, LA	
00017	Boeing B-52H Stratofortress (60-0017) [MT] *y/bk*	USAF 69th BS/5th BW, Minot AFB, ND	
00018	Boeing B-52H Stratofortress (60-0018) [MT] *y/bk*	USAF 69th BS/5th BW, Minot AFB, ND	
00021	Boeing B-52H Stratofortress (60-0021) [LA] *r*	USAF 96th BS/2nd BW, Barksdale AFB, LA	
00022	Boeing B-52H Stratofortress (60-0022) [LA] *r*	USAF 96th BS/2nd BW, Barksdale AFB, LA	
00023	Boeing B-52H Stratofortress (60-0023) [BD] *or/bl*	USAF 93rd BS/307th BW AFRC, Barksdale AFB, LA	
00024	Boeing B-52H Stratofortress (60-0024) [LA] *bl*	USAF 20th BS/2nd BW, Barksdale AFB, LA	
00025	Boeing B-52H Stratofortress (60-0025) [LA] *bl*	USAF 20th BS/2nd BW, Barksdale AFB, LA	
00026	Boeing B-52H Stratofortress (60-0026) [MT] *r/y*	USAF 23rd BS/5th BW, Minot AFB, ND	
00028	Boeing B-52H Stratofortress (60-0028) [LA] *r*	USAF 96th BS/2nd BW, Barksdale AFB, LA	
00029	Boeing B-52H Stratofortress (60-0029) [MT] *r/y*	USAF 23rd BS/5th BW, Minot AFB, ND	
00031	Boeing B-52H Stratofortress (60-0031) [OT] *y/w*	USAF 49th TES/53rd TEG, Barksdale AFB, LA	
00032	Boeing B-52H Stratofortress (60-0032) [LA] *r*	USAF 96th BS/2nd BW, Barksdale AFB, LA	

Notes	Serial	Type (code/other identity)	Owner/operator, location or fate
	00033	Boeing B-52H Stratofortress (60-0033) [MT] r/y	USAF 23rd BS/5th BW, Minot AFB, ND
	00035	Boeing B-52H Stratofortress (60-0035) [BD] or/bl	USAF 93rd BS/307th BW AFRC, Barksdale AFB, LA
	00036	Boeing B-52H Stratofortress (60-0036) [ED]	USAF 419th FLTS/412th TW, Edwards AFB, CA
	00037	Boeing B-52H Stratofortress (60-0037) [MT] r/y	USAF 23rd BS/5th BW, Minot AFB, ND
	00038	Boeing B-52H Stratofortress (60-0038) [BD] or/bl	USAF 93rd BS/307th BW AFRC, Barksdale AFB, LA
	00041	Boeing B-52H Stratofortress (60-0041) [BD] or/bl	USAF 93rd BS/307th BW AFRC, Barksdale AFB, LA
	00042	Boeing B-52H Stratofortress (60-0042) [BD] or/bl	USAF 93rd BS/307th BW AFRC, Barksdale AFB, LA
	00044	Boeing B-52H Stratofortress (60-0044) [MT] r/y	USAF 23rd BS/5th BW, Minot AFB, ND
	00045	Boeing B-52H Stratofortress (60-0045) [BD] or/bl	USAF 93rd BS/307th BW AFRC, Barksdale AFB, LA
	00047	Boeing B-52H Stratofortress (60-0047) [MT] y/bk	Crashed 19 May 2016, Guam
	00048	Boeing B-52H Stratofortress (60-0048) [LA] bl	USAF 20th BS/2nd BW, Barksdale AFB, LA
	00050	Boeing B-52H Stratofortress (60-0050) [ED]	USAF 419th FLTS/412th TW, Edwards AFB, CA
	00051	Boeing B-52H Stratofortress (60-0051) [BD] or/bl	USAF 93rd BS/307th BW AFRC, Barksdale AFB, LA
	00052	Boeing B-52H Stratofortress (60-0052) [LA] r	USAF 96th BS/2nd BW, Barksdale AFB, LA
	00054	Boeing B-52H Stratofortress (60-0054) [LA] bl	USAF 20th BS/2nd BW, Barksdale AFB, LA
	00055	Boeing B-52H Stratofortress (60-0055) [MT] r/y	USAF 23rd BS/5th BW, Minot AFB, ND
	00056	Boeing B-52H Stratofortress (60-0056) [MT] r/y	USAF 23rd BS/5th BW, Minot AFB, ND
	00057	Boeing B-52H Stratofortress (60-0057) [BD] or/bl $	USAF 93rd BS/307th BW AFRC, Barksdale AFB, LA
	00058	Boeing B-52H Stratofortress (60-0058) [LA] bl	USAF 20th BS/2nd BW, Barksdale AFB, LA
	00059	Boeing B-52H Stratofortress (60-0059) [LA] r [96 BS]	USAF 96th BS/2nd BW, Barksdale AFB, LA
	00060	Boeing B-52H Stratofortress (60-0060) [MT] r/y	USAF 23rd BS/5th BW, Minot AFB, ND
	00061	Boeing B-52H Stratofortress (60-0061) [BD] or/bl [307 BW]	USAF 93rd BS/307th BW AFRC, Barksdale AFB, LA
	00062	Boeing B-52H Stratofortress (60-0062) [LA] r	USAF 96th BS/2nd BW, Barksdale AFB, LA
	10001	Boeing B-52H Stratofortress (61-0001) [MT] y/bk	USAF 69th BS/5th BW, Minot AFB, ND
	10002	Boeing B-52H Stratofortress (61-0002) [LA] bl	USAF 20th BS/2nd BW, Barksdale AFB, LA
	10003	Boeing B-52H Stratofortress (61-0003) [BD] or/bl	USAF 93rd BS/307th BW AFRC, Barksdale AFB, LA
	10004	Boeing B-52H Stratofortress (61-0004) [LA] bl	USAF 20th BS/2nd BW, Barksdale AFB, LA
	10006	Boeing B-52H Stratofortress (61-0006) [LA] r	USAF 96th BS/2nd BW, Barksdale AFB, LA
	10007	Boeing B-52H Stratofortress (61-0007) [MT] y/bk	USAF 69th BS/5th BW, Minot AFB, ND
	10008	Boeing B-52H Stratofortress (61-0008) [BD] or/bl	USAF 93rd BS/307th BW AFRC, Barksdale AFB, LA
	10010	Boeing B-52H Stratofortress (61-0010) [LA] bl [434 BS]	USAF 20th BS/2nd BW, Barksdale AFB, LA
	10011	Boeing B-52H Stratofortress (61-0011) [BD] or/bl	USAF 93rd BS/307th BW AFRC, Barksdale AFB, LA
	10012	Boeing B-52H Stratofortress (61-0012) [LA] r	USAF 96th BS/2nd BW, Barksdale AFB, LA
	10013	Boeing B-52H Stratofortress (61-0013) [LA] bl	USAF 20th BS/2nd BW, Barksdale AFB, LA
	10014	Boeing B-52H Stratofortress (61-0014) [MT] y/bk	USAF 69th BS/5th BW, Minot AFB, ND
	10015	Boeing B-52H Stratofortress (61-0015) [LA] r	USAF 96th BS/2nd BW, Barksdale AFB, LA
	10016	Boeing B-52H Stratofortress (61-0016) [LA] r	USAF 96th BS/2nd BW, Barksdale AFB, LA
	10017	Boeing B-52H Stratofortress (61-0017) [BD] or/bl	USAF 93rd BS/307th BW AFRC, Barksdale AFB, LA
	10018	Boeing B-52H Stratofortress (61-0018) [MT] y/bk	USAF 69th BS/5th BW, Minot AFB, ND
	10019	Boeing B-52H Stratofortress (61-0019) [LA] r	USAF 96th BS/2nd BW, Barksdale AFB, LA
	10020	Boeing B-52H Stratofortress (61-0020) [LA] bl [20 BS]	USAF 20th BS/2nd BW, Barksdale AFB, LA
	10021	Boeing B-52H Stratofortress (61-0021) [BD] or/bl	USAF 93rd BS/307th BW AFRC, Barksdale AFB, LA
	10028	Boeing B-52H Stratofortress (61-0028) [OT] y/w [49 TES]	USAF 49th TES/53rd TEG, Barksdale AFB, LA

Serial	Type (code/other identity)	Owner/operator, location or fate	Notes
10029	Boeing B-52H Stratofortress (61-0029) [BD] or/bl [93 BS]	USAF 93rd BS/307th BW AFRC, Barksdale AFB, LA	
10031	Boeing B-52H Stratofortress (61-0031) [BD] or/bl	USAF 93rd BS/307th BW AFRC, Barksdale AFB, LA	
10032	Boeing B-52H Stratofortress (61-0032) [MT] r/y	USAF 23rd BS/5th BW, Minot AFB, ND	
10034	Boeing B-52H Stratofortress (61-0034) [MT] r/y	USAF 23rd BS/5th BW, Minot AFB, ND	
10035	Boeing B-52H Stratofortress (61-0035) [MT] r/y	USAF 23rd BS/5th BW, Minot AFB, ND	
10036	Boeing B-52H Stratofortress (61-0036) [LA] r	USAF 96th BS/2nd BW, Barksdale AFB, LA	
10038	Boeing B-52H Stratofortress (61-0038) [BD] or/bl	USAF 93rd BS/307th BW AFRC, Barksdale AFB, LA	
10039	Boeing B-52H Stratofortress (61-0039) [MT] y/bky	USAF 69th BS/5th BW, Minot AFB, ND	
10040	Boeing B-52H Stratofortress (61-0040) [MT] r/y	USAF 23rd BS/5th BW, Minot AFB, ND	

Lockheed C-130

Serial	Type (code/other identity)	Owner/operator, location or fate	Notes
00162	Lockheed MC-130H Combat Talon II (90-0162)	USAF 1st SOS/353rd SOG, Kadena AB, Japan	
00164	Lockheed AC-130U Spooky (90-0164)	USAF 4th SOS/1st SOW, Hurlburt Field, FL	
00165	Lockheed AC-130U Spooky (90-0165)	USAF 4th SOS/1st SOW, Hurlburt Field, FL	
00166	Lockheed AC-130U Spooky (90-0166)	USAF 4th SOS/1st SOW, Hurlburt Field, FL	
00167	Lockheed AC-130U Spooky (90-0167)	USAF 4th SOS/1st SOW, Hurlburt Field, FL	
00322	Lockheed C-130H Hercules (80-0322) y/bk	USAF 118th AS/103rd AW, Bradley ANGB, CT ANG	
00323	Lockheed C-130H Hercules (80-0323)	To AMARG, June 2016	
00324	Lockheed C-130H Hercules (80-0324)	USAF 186th AS/120th AW, Great Falls, MT ANG	
00326	Lockheed C-130H Hercules (80-0326) y/bk	USAF 118th AS/103rd AW, Bradley ANGB, CT ANG	
00332	Lockheed C-130H Hercules (80-0332)	To AMARG, May 2016	
01057	Lockheed C-130H Hercules (90-1057) bl	USAF 142nd AS/166th AW, New Castle County, DE ANG	
01058	Lockheed AC-130W Stinger II (90-1058)	USAF 16th SOS/27th SOW, Cannon AFB, NM	
01791	Lockheed C-130H Hercules (90-1791)	USAF 180th AS/139th AW, Rosencrans Memorial, MO ANG	
01792	Lockheed C-130H Hercules (90-1792)	USAF 180th AS/139th AW, Rosencrans Memorial, MO ANG	
01793	Lockheed C-130H Hercules (90-1793)	USAF 180th AS/139th AW, Rosencrans Memorial, MO ANG	
01794	Lockheed C-130H Hercules (90-1794)	USAF 180th AS/139th AW, Rosencrans Memorial, MO ANG	
01795	Lockheed C-130H Hercules (90-1795)	USAF 180th AS/139th AW, Rosencrans Memorial, MO ANG	
01796	Lockheed C-130H Hercules (90-1796)	USAF 180th AS/139th AW, Rosencrans Memorial, MO ANG	
01797	Lockheed C-130H Hercules (90-1797)	USAF 180th AS/139th AW, Rosencrans Memorial, MO ANG	
01798	Lockheed C-130H Hercules (90-1798)	USAF 180th AS/139th AW, Rosencrans Memorial, MO ANG	
01934	Lockheed EC-130J Commando Solo III (00-1934)	USAF 193rd SOS/193rd SOW, Harrisburg, PA ANG	
02103	Lockheed HC-130N Combat King (90-2103)	USAF 211th RQS/176th Wg, Elmendorf AFB, AK ANG	
05700	Lockheed C-130J-30 Hercules II (10-5700) r	USAF 39th AS/317th AG, Dyess AFB, TX	
05701	Lockheed C-130J-30 Hercules II (10-5701) r	USAF 39th AS/317th AG, Dyess AFB, TX	
05714	Lockheed MC-130J Commando II (10-5714)	USAF 67th SOS/352nd SOG, RAF Mildenhall, UK	
05716	Lockheed HC-130J Combat King II (10-5716) [FT]	USAF 79th RQS/563rd RQG, Davis-Monthan AFB, AZ	
05717	Lockheed HC-130J Combat King II (10-5717) [FT]	USAF 79th RQS/563rd RQG, Davis-Monthan AFB, AZ	
05728	Lockheed C-130J-30 Hercules II (10-5728) y	USAF 48th AS/314th AW, Little Rock AFB, AR	
05771	Lockheed C-130J-30 Hercules II (10-5771) w/bk	USAF 61st AS/19th AW Little Rock AFB, AR	
09107	Lockheed C-130H Hercules (90-9107) bl/r	USAF 757th AS/910th AW AFRC, Youngstown ARS, OH	

Notes	Serial	Type (code/other identity)	Owner/operator, location or fate
	09108	Lockheed C-130H Hercules (90-9108) bl/r	USAF 757th AS/910th AW AFRC, Youngstown ARS, OH
	10626	Lockheed C-130H Hercules (81-0626) r	USAF 164th AS/179th AW, Mansfield, OH ANG
	10627	Lockheed C-130H Hercules (81-0627) r	USAF 154th TS/189th AW, Little Rock, AR ANG
	10628	Lockheed C-130H Hercules (81-0628) r	USAF 154th TS/189th AW, Little Rock, AR ANG
	10629	Lockheed C-130H Hercules (81-0629) r	USAF 164th AS/179th AW, Mansfield, OH ANG
	10630	Lockheed C-130H Hercules (81-0630) r	USAF 164th AS/179th AW, Mansfield, OH ANG
	10631	Lockheed C-130H Hercules (81-0631) r	USAF 154th TS/189th AW, Little Rock, AR ANG
	11231	Lockheed C-130H Hercules (91-1231)	USAF 165th AS/123rd AW, Standiford Field, KY ANG
	11232	Lockheed C-130H Hercules (91-1232)	USAF 165th AS/123rd AW, Standiford Field, KY ANG
	11233	Lockheed C-130H Hercules (91-1233)	USAF 165th AS/123rd AW, Standiford Field, KY ANG
	11234	Lockheed C-130H Hercules (91-1234)	USAF 165th AS/123rd AW, Standiford Field, KY ANG
	11235	Lockheed C-130H Hercules (91-1235)	USAF 165th AS/123rd AW, Standiford Field, KY ANG
	11236	Lockheed C-130H Hercules (91-1236)	USAF 165th AS/123rd AW, Standiford Field, KY ANG
	11237	Lockheed C-130H Hercules (91-1237)	USAF 165th AS/123rd AW, Standiford Field, KY ANG
	11238	Lockheed C-130H Hercules (91-1238)	USAF 165th AS/123rd AW, Standiford Field, KY ANG
	11239	Lockheed C-130H Hercules (91-1239) r	USAF 154th TS/189th AW, Little Rock, AR ANG
	11461	Lockheed C-130J-30 Hercules II (01-1461) gn	USAF 115th AS/146th AW, Channel Island ANGS, CA ANG
	11462	Lockheed C-130J-30 Hercules II (01-1462) gn	USAF 115th AS/146th AW, Channel Island ANGS, CA ANG
	11651	Lockheed C-130H Hercules (91-1651) r	USAF 154th TS/189th AW, Little Rock, AR ANG
	11652	Lockheed C-130H Hercules (91-1652)	USAF 180th AS/139th AW, Rosencrans Memorial, MO ANG
	11653	Lockheed C-130H Hercules (91-1653)	USAF 180th AS/139th AW, Rosencrans Memorial, MO ANG
	11935	Lockheed EC-130J Commando Solo III (01-1935)	USAF 193rd SOS/193rd SOW, Harrisburg, PA ANG
	14852	Lockheed HC-130P Combat King (64-14852)	USAF 39th RQS/920th RQW AFRC, Patrick AFB, FL
	14859	Lockheed EC-130H Compass Call (64-14859)	To AMARG, June 2016
	14861	Lockheed C-130H Hercules (64-14861)	To AMARG, June 2016
	14862	Lockheed EC-130H Compass Call (64-14862)	USAF 43rd ECS/55th ECG, Davis-Monthan AFB, AZ
	14866	Lockheed C-130H Hercules (64-14866)	USAF 198th AS/156th AW, San Juan, PR ANG
	15719	Lockheed HC-130J Combat King II (11-5719) [FT]	USAF 79th RQS/563rd RQG, Davis-Monthan AFB, AZ
	15725	Lockheed HC-130J Combat King II (11-5725) [FT]	USAF 71st RQS/347th RG, Moody AFB, GA
	15727	Lockheed HC-130J Combat King II (11-5727) [FT]	USAF 71st RQS/347th RG, Moody AFB, GA
	15729	Lockheed AC-130J Ghostrider (11-5729)	USAF 1st SOG Det.2, Hurlburt Field, FL
	15731	Lockheed MC-130J Commando II (11-5731)	USAF 67th SOS/352nd SOG, RAF Mildenhall, UK
	15732	Lockheed C-130J-30 Hercules II (11-5732) y	USAF 48th AS/314th AW, Little Rock AFB, AR
	15733	Lockheed MC-130J Commando II (11-5733)	USAF 67th SOS/352nd SOG, RAF Mildenhall, UK
	15734	Lockheed C-130J-30 Hercules II (11-5734) [YJ] r	USAF 36th AS/374th AW, Yokota AB, Japan
	15735	Lockheed MC-130J Commando II (11-5735)	USAF 522nd SOS/27th SOW, Cannon AFB, NM
	15736	Lockheed C-130J-30 Hercules II (11-5736) w/bk	USAF 61st AS/19th AW Little Rock AFB, AR
	15737	Lockheed MC-130J Commando II (11-5737)	USAF 67th SOS/352nd SOG, RAF Mildenhall, UK
	15738	Lockheed C-130J-30 Hercules II (11-5738) w/bk	USAF 61st AS/19th AW Little Rock AFB, AR
	15740	Lockheed C-130J-30 Hercules II (11-5740) w/bk	USAF 61st AS/19th AW Little Rock AFB, AR
	15745	Lockheed C-130J-30 Hercules II (11-5745) w/bk	USAF 41st AS/19th AW Little Rock AFB, AR
	15748	Lockheed C-130J-30 Hercules II (11-5748) w/bk	USAF 61st AS/19th AW Little Rock AFB, AR
	15752	Lockheed C-130J-30 Hercules II (11-5752) w/bk	USAF 61st AS/19th AW Little Rock AFB, AR
	15765	Lockheed HC-130J Combat King II (11-5765) [FT]	USAF 71st RQS/347th RG, Moody AFB, GA
	19141	Lockheed C-130H Hercules (91-9141) bl/y	USAF 328th AS/914th AW AFRC, Niagara Falls, NY

Serial	Type (code/other identity)	Owner/operator, location or fate	Notes
19142	Lockheed C-130H Hercules (91-9142) bl/y	USAF 328th AS/914th AW AFRC, Niagara Falls, NY	
19143	Lockheed C-130H Hercules (91-9143) bl/y	USAF 328th AS/914th AW AFRC, Niagara Falls, NY	
19144	Lockheed C-130H Hercules (91-9144) bl/y	USAF 328th AS/914th AW AFRC, Niagara Falls, NY	
20054	Lockheed C-130H Hercules (82-0054) r	USAF 164th AS/179th AW, Mansfield, OH ANG	
20055	Lockheed C-130H Hercules (82-0055) r	USAF 164th AS/179th AW, Mansfield, OH ANG	
20056	Lockheed C-130H Hercules (82-0056) r	USAF 164th AS/179th AW, Mansfield, OH ANG	
20057	Lockheed C-130H Hercules (82-0057) bk/y	USAF 144th AS/176th CW, Elmendorf AFB, AK ANG	
20059	Lockheed C-130H Hercules (82-0059) bk/y	USAF 144th AS/176th CW, Elmendorf AFB, AK ANG	
20060	Lockheed C-130H Hercules (82-0060) bk/y	USAF 144th AS/176th CW, Elmendorf AFB, AK ANG	
20061	Lockheed C-130H Hercules (82-0061) bk/y	USAF 144th AS/176th CW, Elmendorf AFB, AK ANG	
20253	Lockheed AC-130U Spooky (92-0253)	USAF 4th SOS/1st SOW, Hurlburt Field, FL	
20314	Lockheed C-130J-30 Hercules II (02-0314) y $	USAF 48th AS/314th AW, Little Rock AFB, AR	
20547	Lockheed C-130H Hercules (92-0547) bl/w	USAF 192nd AS/152nd AW, Reno, NV ANG	
20548	Lockheed C-130H Hercules (92-0548) r/bk	USAF 158th AS/165th AW, Savannah, GA ANG	
20549	Lockheed C-130H Hercules (92-0549) bl/w	USAF 192nd AS/152nd AW, Reno, NV ANG	
20550	Lockheed C-130H Hercules (92-0550) bl	USAF 700th AS/94th AW AFRC, Dobbins ARB, GA	
20551	Lockheed C-130H Hercules (92-0551) bl	USAF 700th AS/94th AW AFRC, Dobbins ARB, GA	
20552	Lockheed C-130H Hercules (92-0552) bl	USAF 700th AS/94th AW AFRC, Dobbins ARB, GA	
20553	Lockheed C-130H Hercules (92-0553) bl	USAF 156th AS/145th AW, Charlotte, NC ANG	
20554	Lockheed C-130H Hercules (92-0554) bl/w	USAF 192nd AS/152nd AW, Reno, NV ANG	
21094	Lockheed LC-130H Hercules (92-1094)	USAF 139th AS/109th AW, Schenectady, NY ANG	
21095	Lockheed LC-130H Hercules (92-1095)	USAF 139th AS/109th AW, Schenectady, NY ANG	
21434	Lockheed C-130J-30 Hercules II (02-1434) r	USAF 143rd AS/143rd AW, Quonset, RI ANG	
21451	Lockheed C-130H Hercules (92-1451) or/bk	USAF 169th AS/182nd AW, Peoria, IL ANG	
21452	Lockheed C-130H Hercules (92-1452) or/bk	USAF 169th AS/182nd AW, Peoria, IL ANG	
21453	Lockheed C-130H-3 Hercules (92-1453) bl	USAF 156th AS/145th AW, Charlotte, NC ANG	
21454	Lockheed C-130H-3 Hercules (92-1454) bl	USAF 156th AS/145th AW, Charlotte, NC ANG	
21463	Lockheed C-130J Hercules II (02-1463) gn	USAF 115th AS/146th AW, Channel Island ANGS, CA ANG	
21464	Lockheed C-130J Hercules II (02-1464) gn	USAF 115th AS/146th AW, Channel Island ANGS, CA ANG	
21531	Lockheed C-130H-3 Hercules (92-1531) y/bk	USAF 187th AS/153rd AW, Cheyenne, WY ANG	
21532	Lockheed C-130H-3 Hercules (92-1532) y/bk	USAF 187th AS/153rd AW, Cheyenne, WY ANG	
21533	Lockheed C-130H-3 Hercules (92-1533) y/bk	USAF 187th AS/153rd AW, Cheyenne, WY ANG	
21534	Lockheed C-130H-3 Hercules (92-1534) y/bk	USAF 187th AS/153rd AW, Cheyenne, WY ANG	
21535	Lockheed C-130H-3 Hercules (92-1535) y/bk	USAF 187th AS/153rd AW, Cheyenne, WY ANG	
21536	Lockheed C-130H-3 Hercules (92-1536) y/bk	USAF 187th AS/153rd AW, Cheyenne, WY ANG	
21537	Lockheed C-130H-3 Hercules (92-1537) y/bk	USAF 187th AS/153rd AW, Cheyenne, WY ANG	
21538	Lockheed C-130H-3 Hercules (92-1538) y/bk	USAF 187th AS/153rd AW, Cheyenne, WY ANG	
22104	Lockheed HC-130N Combat King (92-2104)	USAF 211th RQS/176th Wg, Elmendorf AFB, AK ANG	
23021	Lockheed C-130H Hercules (92-3021)	USAF	
23022	Lockheed C-130H Hercules (92-3022) bl/r	USAF 757th AS/910th AW AFRC, Youngstown ARS, OH	
23023	Lockheed C-130H Hercules (92-3023) bl/r	USAF 757th AS/910th AW AFRC, Youngstown ARS, OH	
23024	Lockheed C-130H Hercules (92-3024) bl/r	USAF 757th AS/910th AW AFRC, Youngstown ARS, OH	
23281	Lockheed C-130H-3 Hercules (92-3281) pr/w	USAF 96th AS/934th AW AFRC, Minneapolis/ St Paul, MN	
23282	Lockheed C-130H-3 Hercules (92-3282) pr/w	USAF 96th AS/934th AW AFRC, Minneapolis/ St Paul, MN	

US-BASED USAF AIRCRAFT

Notes	Serial	Type (code/other identity)	Owner/operator, location or fate
	23283	Lockheed C-130H-3 Hercules (92-3283) *pr/w*	USAF 96th AS/934th AW AFRC, Minneapolis/ St Paul, MN
	23284	Lockheed C-130H-3 Hercules (92-3284) *pr/w*	USAF 96th AS/934th AW AFRC, Minneapolis/ St Paul, MN
	23285	Lockheed C-130H-3 Hercules (92-3285) *pr/w*	USAF 96th AS/934th AW AFRC, Minneapolis/ St Paul, MN
	23286	Lockheed C-130H-3 Hercules (92-3286) *pr/w*	USAF 96th AS/934th AW AFRC, Minneapolis/ St Paul, MN
	23287	Lockheed C-130H-3 Hercules (92-3287) *pr/w*	USAF 96th AS/934th AW AFRC, Minneapolis/ St Paul, MN
	23288	Lockheed C-130H-3 Hercules (92-3288) *pr/w*	USAF 96th AS/934th AW AFRC, Minneapolis/ St Paul, MN
	25753	Lockheed AC-130J Ghostrider (12-5753)	USAF 1st SOG Det.2, Hurlburt Field, FL
	25754	Lockheed AC-130J Ghostrider (12-5754)	LMTAS, Marietta, GA
	25755	Lockheed HC-130J Combat King II (12-5755)	USAF 415th SOS/58th SOW, Kirtland AFB, NM
	25756	Lockheed C-130J-30 Hercules II (12-5756) *w/bk*	USAF 61st AS/19th AW Little Rock AFB, AR
	25757	Lockheed MC-130J Commando II (12-5757)	USAF 67th SOS/352nd SOG, RAF Mildenhall, UK
	25759	Lockheed MC-130J Commando II (12-5759)	USAF 67th SOS/352nd SOG, RAF Mildenhall, UK
	25760	Lockheed MC-130J Commando II (12-5760)	USAF 67th SOS/352nd SOG, RAF Mildenhall, UK
	25761	Lockheed MC-130J Commando II (12-5761)	USAF 17th SOS/353rd SOG, Kadena AB, Japan
	25762	Lockheed MC-130J Commando II (12-5762)	USAF 17th SOS/353rd SOG, Kadena AB, Japan
	25763	Lockheed MC-130J Commando II (12-5763)	USAF 17th SOS/353rd SOG, Kadena AB, Japan
	25768	Lockheed HC-130J Combat King II (12-5768) [FT]	USAF 71st RQS/347th RG, Moody AFB, GA
	25769	Lockheed HC-130J Combat King II (12-5769) [FT]	USAF 71st RQS/347th RG, Moody AFB, GA
	25772	Lockheed AC-130J Ghostrider (12-5772)	USAF 1st SOG Det.2, Hurlburt Field, FL
	25773	Lockheed HC-130J Combat King II (12-5773) [FT]	USAF 71st RQS/347th RG, Moody AFB, GA
	28155	Lockheed C-130J-30 Hercules II (02-8155) *r*	USAF 815th AS/403rd AW AFRC, Keesler AFB, MO
	30486	Lockheed C-130H Hercules (83-0486)	*To AMARG, May 2016*
	30487	Lockheed C-130H Hercules (83-0487)	USAF 139th AS/109th AW, Schenectady, NY ANG
	30488	Lockheed C-130H Hercules (83-0488)	*To AMARG, May 2016*
	30489	Lockheed C-130H Hercules (83-0489)	USAF 139th AS/109th AW, Schenectady, NY ANG
	30490	Lockheed LC-130H Hercules (83-0490)	USAF 139th AS/109th AW, Schenectady, NY ANG
	30491	Lockheed LC-130H Hercules (83-0491)	USAF 139th AS/109th AW, Schenectady, NY ANG
	30492	Lockheed LC-130H Hercules (83-0492)	USAF 139th AS/109th AW, Schenectady, NY ANG
	30493	Lockheed LC-130H Hercules (83-0493)	USAF 139th AS/109th AW, Schenectady, NY ANG
	31036	Lockheed C-130H Hercules (93-1036) *bl*	USAF 700th AS/94th AW AFRC, Dobbins ARB, GA
	31037	Lockheed C-130H Hercules (93-1037) *bl*	USAF 700th AS/94th AW AFRC, Dobbins ARB, GA
	31038	Lockheed C-130H Hercules (93-1038) *bl*	USAF 700th AS/94th AW AFRC, Dobbins ARB, GA
	31039	Lockheed C-130H Hercules (93-1039) *bl*	USAF 700th AS/94th AW AFRC, Dobbins ARB, GA
	31040	Lockheed C-130H Hercules (93-1040) *bl*	USAF 700th AS/94th AW AFRC, Dobbins ARB, GA
	31041	Lockheed C-130H Hercules (93-1041) *bl*	USAF 700th AS/94th AW AFRC, Dobbins ARB, GA
	31096	Lockheed LC-130H Hercules (93-1096)	USAF 139th AS/109th AW, Schenectady, NY ANG

Serial	Type (code/other identity)	Owner/operator, location or fate	Notes
31212	Lockheed MC-130H Combat Talon II (83-1212)	To AMARG, September 2016	
31455	Lockheed C-130H-3 Hercules (93-1455) bl	USAF 156th AS/145th AW, Charlotte, NC ANG	
31456	Lockheed C-130H-3 Hercules (93-1456) bl	USAF 156th AS/145th AW, Charlotte, NC ANG	
31457	Lockheed C-130H-3 Hercules (93-1457) bl	USAF 156th AS/145th AW, Charlotte, NC ANG	
31459	Lockheed C-130H-3 Hercules (93-1459) bl	USAF 156th AS/145th AW, Charlotte, NC ANG	
31561	Lockheed C-130H-3 Hercules (93-1561) bl	USAF 156th AS/145th AW, Charlotte, NC ANG	
31562	Lockheed C-130H-3 Hercules (93-1562) bl	USAF 156th AS/145th AW, Charlotte, NC ANG	
31563	Lockheed C-130H-3 Hercules (93-1563) bl	USAF 156th AS/145th AW, Charlotte, NC ANG	
31580	Lockheed EC-130H Compass Call (73-1580)	USAF 43rd ECS/55th ECG, Davis-Monthan AFB, AZ	
31581	Lockheed EC-130H Compass Call (73-1581) $	USAF 43rd ECS/55th ECG, Davis-Monthan AFB, AZ	
31582	Lockheed C-130H Hercules (73-1582)	Withdrawn from use, 2015	
31583	Lockheed EC-130H Compass Call (73-1583) r	USAF 43rd ECS/55th ECG, Davis-Monthan AFB, AZ	
31584	Lockheed EC-130H Compass Call (73-1584)	USAF 43rd ECS/55th ECG, Davis-Monthan AFB, AZ	
31585	Lockheed EC-130H Compass Call (73-1585)	USAF 43rd ECS/55th ECG, Davis-Monthan AFB, AZ	
31586	Lockheed EC-130H Compass Call (73-1586) bl	USAF 41st ECS/55th ECG, Davis-Monthan AFB, AZ	
31587	Lockheed EC-130H Compass Call (73-1587)	USAF 43rd ECS/55th ECG, Davis-Monthan AFB, AZ	
31588	Lockheed EC-130H Compass Call (73-1588)	USAF 43rd ECS/55th ECG, Davis-Monthan AFB, AZ	
31590	Lockheed EC-130H Compass Call (73-1590)	USAF 43rd ECS/55th ECG, Davis-Monthan AFB, AZ	
31592	Lockheed EC-130H Compass Call (73-1592) bl	USAF 41st ECS/55th ECG, Davis-Monthan AFB, AZ	
31594	Lockheed EC-130H Compass Call (73-1594)	USAF 41st ECS/55th ECG, Davis-Monthan AFB, AZ	
31595	Lockheed EC-130H Compass Call (73-1595)	USAF 43rd ECS/55th ECG, Davis-Monthan AFB, AZ	
31598	Lockheed C-130H Hercules (73-1598)	Withdrawn from use, March 2013	
32041	Lockheed C-130H-3 Hercules (93-2041) or/bk	USAF 169th AS/182nd AW, Peoria, IL ANG	
32042	Lockheed C-130H-3 Hercules (93-2042) or/bk	USAF 169th AS/182nd AW, Peoria, IL ANG	
32105	Lockheed HC-130N Combat King (93-2105)	USAF 211th RQS/176th Wg, Elmendorf AFB, AK ANG	
32106	Lockheed HC-130N Combat King (93-2106)	USAF 211th RQS/176th Wg, Elmendorf AFB, AK ANG	
33300	Lockheed LC-130H Hercules (73-3300)	USAF 139th AS/109th AW, Schenectady, NY ANG	
35770	Lockheed MC-130J Commando II (13-5770)	USAF 522nd SOS/27th SOW, Cannon AFB, NM	
35775	Lockheed MC-130J Commando II (13-5775)	USAF 17th SOS/353rd SOG, Kadena AB, Japan	
35776	Lockheed MC-130J Commando II (13-5776)	USAF 17th SOS/353rd SOG, Kadena AB, Japan	
35777	Lockheed MC-130J Commando II (13-5777)	USAF 17th SOS/353rd SOG, Kadena AB, Japan	
35778	Lockheed MC-130J Commando II (13-5778)	USAF 67th SOS/352nd SOG, RAF Mildenhall, UK	
35782	Lockheed HC-130J Combat King II (13-5782) [FT]	USAF 71st RQS/347th RG, Moody AFB, GA	
35783	Lockheed AC-130J Ghostrider (13-5783)	USAF 1st SOG Det.2, Hurlburt Field, FL	
35784	Lockheed HC-130J Combat King II (13-5784) [FT]	USAF 71st RQS/347th RG, Moody AFB, GA	
35785	Lockheed HC-130J Combat King II (13-5785) [FT]	USAF 71st RQS/347th RG, Moody AFB, GA	
35786	Lockheed MC-130J Commando II (13-5786)	USAF 67th SOS/352nd SOG, RAF Mildenhall, UK	
35790	Lockheed HC-130J Combat King II (13-5790) [FT]	USAF 71st RQS/347th RG, Moody AFB, GA	
37311	Lockheed C-130H-3 Hercules (93-7311) bl/w	USAF 192nd AS/152nd AW, Reno, NV ANG	
37312	Lockheed C-130H-3 Hercules (93-7312) or/bk	USAF 169th AS/182nd AW, Peoria, IL ANG	
37313	Lockheed C-130H-3 Hercules (93-7313) bl/w	USAF 192nd AS/152nd AW, Reno, NV ANG	
37314	Lockheed C-130H-3 Hercules (93-7314) bl/w	USAF 192nd AS/152nd AW, Reno, NV ANG	
38154	Lockheed C-130J-30 Hercules II (03-8154) r	USAF 815th AS/403rd AW AFRC, Keesler AFB, MO	
40204	Lockheed C-130H Hercules (84-0204) r	USAF 154th TS/189th AW, Little Rock, AK ANG	
40205	Lockheed C-130H Hercules (84-0205)	USAF	

Notes	Serial	Type (code/other identity)	Owner/operator, location or fate
	40206	Lockheed C-130H Hercules (84-0206) *bl*	USAF 142nd AS/166th AW, New Castle County, DE ANG
	40207	Lockheed C-130H Hercules (84-0207) *bl*	USAF 142nd AS/166th AW, New Castle County, DE ANG
	40208	Lockheed C-130H Hercules (84-0208) *bl*	USAF 142nd AS/166th AW, New Castle County, DE ANG
	40209	Lockheed C-130H Hercules (84-0209) *bl*	USAF 142nd AS/166th AW, New Castle County, DE ANG
	40210	Lockheed C-130H Hercules (84-0210) *bl*	USAF 142nd AS/166th AW, New Castle County, DE ANG
	40212	Lockheed C-130H Hercules (84-0212) *bl*	USAF 142nd AS/166th AW, New Castle County, DE ANG
	40213	Lockheed C-130H Hercules (84-0213) *bl*	USAF 142nd AS/166th AW, New Castle County, DE ANG
	40476	Lockheed MC-130H Combat Talon II (84-0476)	USAF 15th SOS/1st SOW, Hurlburt Field, FL
	41658	Lockheed C-130H Hercules (74-1658)	*Withdrawn from use, 2015*
	41659	Lockheed C-130H Hercules (74-1659) [YJ] *r*	USAF 36th AS/374th AW, Yokota AB, Japan
	41660	Lockheed C-130H Hercules (74-1660) [YJ] *r*	USAF 36th AS/374th AW, Yokota AB, Japan
	41661	Lockheed C-130H Hercules (74-1661) [YJ] *r*	USAF 36th AS/374th AW, Yokota AB, Japan
	41663	Lockheed C-130H Hercules (74-1663) [YJ] *r* [374 OG]	USAF 36th AS/374th AW, Yokota AB, Japan
	41664	Lockheed C-130H Hercules (74-1664) *y/bk*	USAF 118th AS/103rd AW, Bradley ANGB, CT ANG
	41666	Lockheed C-130H Hercules (74-1666) [YJ] *r* $	USAF 36th AS/374th AW, Yokota AB, Japan
	41667	Lockheed C-130H Hercules (74-1667)	*To AMARG, May 2016*
	41669	Lockheed C-130H Hercules (74-1669) [YJ] *r*	USAF 36th AS/374th AW, Yokota AB, Japan
	41670	Lockheed C-130H Hercules (74-1670)	USAF 186th AS/120th AW, Great Falls, MT ANG
	41671	Lockheed C-130H Hercules (74-1671)	USAF 186th AS/120th AW, Great Falls, MT ANG
	41674	Lockheed C-130H Hercules (74-1674) [YJ] *r*	USAF 36th AS/374th AW, Yokota AB, Japan
	41679	Lockheed C-130H Hercules (74-1679)	USAF 186th AS/120th AW, Great Falls, MT ANG
	41680	Lockheed C-130H Hercules (74-1680) *y/bk*	USAF 118th AS/103rd AW, Bradley ANGB, CT ANG
	41682	Lockheed C-130H Hercules (74-1682) [YJ] *r*	USAF 36th AS/374th AW, Yokota AB, Japan
	41685	Lockheed C-130H Hercules (74-1685) [YJ] *r*	USAF 36th AS/374th AW, Yokota AB, Japan
	41687	Lockheed C-130H Hercules (74-1687) *y/bk*	USAF 118th AS/103rd AW, Bradley ANGB, CT ANG
	41688	Lockheed C-130H Hercules (74-1688)	USAF 186th AS/120th AW, Great Falls, MT ANG
	41691	Lockheed C-130H Hercules (74-1691)	USAF 186th AS/120th AW, Great Falls, MT ANG
	41692	Lockheed C-130H Hercules (74-1692) [YJ] *r*	USAF 36th AS/374th AW, Yokota AB, Japan
	42061	Lockheed C-130H Hercules (74-2061) [YJ] *r*	USAF 36th AS/374th AW, Yokota AB, Japan
	42063	Lockheed C-130H Hercules (74-2063)	*To AMARG, May 2016*
	42065	Lockheed C-130H Hercules (74-2065) [YJ] *r* [374 AW]	USAF 36th AS/374th AW, Yokota AB, Japan
	42067	Lockheed C-130H Hercules (74-2067) [YJ] *r*	USAF 36th AS/374th AW, Yokota AB, Japan
	42069	Lockheed C-130H Hercules (74-2069) *y/bk*	USAF 118th AS/103rd AW, Bradley ANGB, CT ANG
	42131	Lockheed C-130H Hercules (74-2131)	*Withdrawn from use, 2015*
	42132	Lockheed C-130H Hercules (74-2132) [YJ] *r*	USAF 36th AS/374th AW, Yokota AB, Japan
	42134	Lockheed C-130H Hercules (74-2134) *y/bk*	USAF 118th AS/103rd AW, Bradley ANGB, CT ANG
	43142	Lockheed C-130J-30 Hercules II (04-3142) [RS] *bl/w*	USAF 37th AS/86th AW, Ramstein AB, Germany
	43143	Lockheed C-130J-30 Hercules II (04-3143) *w/bk*	USAF 41st AS/19th AW Little Rock AFB, AR
	45787	Lockheed MC-130J Commando II (14-5787)	USAF 15th SOS/1st SOW, Hurlburt Field, FL
	45788	Lockheed C-130J-30 Hercules II (14-5788) *w/bk*	USAF 61st AS/19th AW Little Rock AFB, AR
	45789	Lockheed MC-130J Commando II (14-5789)	USAF 15th SOS/1st SOW, Hurlburt Field, FL
	45791	Lockheed C-130J-30 Hercules II (14-5791) *w/bk*	USAF 61st AS/19th AW Little Rock AFB, AR
	45793	Lockheed MC-130J Commando II (14-5793)	USAF 9th SOS/27th SOW, Cannon AFB, NM
	45795	Lockheed MC-130J Commando II (14-5795)	USAF 9th SOS/27th SOW, Cannon AFB, NM
	45796	Lockheed C-130J-30 Hercules II (14-5796) *w/bk*	USAF 61st AS/19th AW Little Rock AFB, AR
	45797	Lockheed AC-130J Ghostrider (14-5797)	USAF 1st SOG Det.2, Hurlburt Field, FL
	45800	Lockheed MC-130J Commando II (14-5800)	USAF 9th SOS/27th SOW, Cannon AFB, NM

Serial	Type (code/other identity)	Owner/operator, location or fate	Notes
45802	Lockheed C-130J-30 Hercules II (14-5802)	LMTAS, Marietta, GA	
45803	Lockheed MC-130J Commando II (14-5803)	LMTAS, Marietta, GA	
45804	Lockheed C-130J-30 Hercules II (14-5804)	LMTAS, Marietta, GA	
45805	Lockheed MC-130J Commando II (14-5805)	LMTAS, Marietta, GA	
45806	Lockheed MC-130J Commando II (14-5806)	LMTAS, Marietta, GA	
45807	Lockheed C-130J-30 Hercules II (14-5807) [YJ] r [374 AW]	USAF 36th AS/374th AW, Yokota AB, Japan	
45808	Lockheed MC-130J Commando II (14-5808)	LMTAS, Marietta, GA	
45809	Lockheed MC-130J Commando II (14-5809)	LMTAS, Marietta, GA	
45810	Lockheed C-130J-30 Hercules II (14-5810)	LMTAS, Marietta, GA	
46701	Lockheed C-130H-3 Hercules (94-6701) or/bk	USAF 169th AS/182nd AW, Peoria, IL ANG	
46702	Lockheed C-130H-3 Hercules (94-6702) or/bk	USAF 169th AS/182nd AW, Peoria, IL ANG	
46703	Lockheed C-130H-3 Hercules (94-6703) or/bk	USAF 169th AS/182nd AW, Peoria, IL ANG	
46704	Lockheed C-130H-3 Hercules (94-6704) r	USAF 154th TS/189th AW, Little Rock, AR ANG	
46705	Lockheed C-130H-3 Hercules (94-6705) r/bk	USAF 158th AS/165th AW, Savannah, GA ANG	
46706	Lockheed C-130H-3 Hercules (94-6706) r/bk	USAF 158th AS/165th AW, Savannah, GA ANG	
46707	Lockheed C-130H-3 Hercules (94-6707) r/bk	USAF 158th AS/165th AW, Savannah, GA ANG	
46708	Lockheed C-130H-3 Hercules (94-6708) r/bk	USAF 158th AS/165th AW, Savannah, GA ANG	
47310	Lockheed C-130H-3 Hercules (94-7310) pr/w	USAF 731st AS/302nd AW AFRC, Peterson AFB, CO	
47315	Lockheed C-130H-3 Hercules (94-7315) pr/w	USAF 731st AS/302nd AW AFRC, Peterson AFB, CO	
47316	Lockheed C-130H-3 Hercules (94-7316) pr/w	USAF 731st AS/302nd AW AFRC, Peterson AFB, CO	
47317	Lockheed C-130H-3 Hercules (94-7317) pr/w	USAF 731st AS/302nd AW AFRC, Peterson AFB, CO	
47318	Lockheed C-130H-3 Hercules (94-7318) pr/w	USAF 731st AS/302nd AW AFRC, Peterson AFB, CO	
47319	Lockheed C-130H-3 Hercules (94-7319) pr/w	USAF 731st AS/302nd AW AFRC, Peterson AFB, CO	
47320	Lockheed C-130H-3 Hercules (94-7320) pr/w	USAF 731st AS/302nd AW AFRC, Peterson AFB, CO	
47321	Lockheed C-130H-3 Hercules (94-7321) r/bk	USAF 158th AS/165th AW, Savannah, GA ANG	
48151	Lockheed C-130J Hercules II (94-8151) r	USAF 815th AS/403rd AW AFRC, Keesler AFB, MO	
48152	Lockheed C-130J Hercules II (94-8152) r	USAF 815th AS/403rd AW AFRC, Keesler AFB, MO	
48153	Lockheed C-130J-30 Hercules II (04-8153) r	USAF 815th AS/403rd AW AFRC, Keesler AFB, MO	
50011	Lockheed MC-130H Combat Talon II (85-0011)	USAF 15th SOS/1st SOW, Hurlburt Field, FL	
50035	Lockheed C-130H Hercules (85-0035) bl/w	USAF 357th AS/908th AW AFRC, Maxwell AFB, AL	
50036	Lockheed C-130H Hercules (85-0036) bl/w	USAF 357th AS/908th AW AFRC, Maxwell AFB, AL	
50037	Lockheed C-130H Hercules (85-0037) bl/w	USAF 357th AS/908th AW AFRC, Maxwell AFB, AL	
50038	Lockheed C-130H Hercules (85-0038) bl/w	USAF 357th AS/908th AW AFRC, Maxwell AFB, AL	
50039	Lockheed C-130H Hercules (85-0039) bl/w	USAF 357th AS/908th AW AFRC, Maxwell AFB, AL	
50040	Lockheed C-130H Hercules (85-0040) bl/w	USAF 357th AS/908th AW AFRC, Maxwell AFB, AL	
50041	Lockheed C-130H Hercules (85-0041) bl/w	USAF 357th AS/908th AW AFRC, Maxwell AFB, AL	
50042	Lockheed C-130H Hercules (85-0042) bl/w	USAF 357th AS/908th AW AFRC, Maxwell AFB, AL	
50962	Lockheed TC-130H Hercules (65-0962)	To AMARG, July 2016	
50963	Lockheed C-130H Hercules (65-0963)	USAF 198th AS/156th AW, San Juan, PR ANG	
50966	Lockheed C-130H Hercules (65-0966)	USAF 198th AS/156th AW, San Juan, PR ANG	
50967	Lockheed EC-130H Compass Call (65-0967)	L-3 Communications, Waco, TX	

Notes	Serial	Type (code/other identity)	Owner/operator, location or fate
	50968	Lockheed C-130H Hercules (65-0968)	USAF 198th AS/156th AW, San Juan, PR ANG
	50974	Lockheed HC-130P Combat King (65-0974)	USAF 102nd RQS/106th RQW, Suffolk Field, NY ANG
	50978	Lockheed HC-130P Combat King (65-0978)	USAF 102nd RQS/106th RQW, Suffolk Field, NY ANG
	50980	Lockheed WC-130H Hercules (65-0980)	USAF 198th AS/156th AW, San Juan, PR ANG
	50984	Lockheed WC-130H Hercules (65-0984)	USAF 198th AS/156th AW, San Juan, PR ANG
	50985	Lockheed WC-130H Hercules (65-0985)	USAF 198th AS/156th AW, San Juan, PR ANG
	50989	Lockheed EC-130H Compass Call (65-0989) r	USAF 43rd ECS/55th ECG, Davis-Monthan AFB, AZ
	51001	Lockheed C-130H Hercules (95-1001) pr/bk	USAF 109th AS/133rd AW, Minneapolis, MN ANG
	51002	Lockheed C-130H Hercules (95-1002) pr/bk	USAF 109th AS/133rd AW, Minneapolis, MN ANG
	51361	Lockheed C-130H Hercules (85-1361) bl/w	USAF 181st AS/136th AW, NAS Dallas, TX ANG
	51362	Lockheed C-130H Hercules (85-1362) bl/w	USAF 181st AS/136th AW, NAS Dallas, TX ANG
	51363	Lockheed C-130H Hercules (85-1363) bl/w	USAF 181st AS/136th AW, NAS Dallas, TX ANG
	51364	Lockheed C-130H Hercules (85-1364) bl/w	USAF 181st AS/136th AW, NAS Dallas, TX ANG
	51365	Lockheed C-130H Hercules (85-1365) bl/w	USAF 181st AS/136th AW, NAS Dallas, TX ANG
	51366	Lockheed C-130H Hercules (85-1366) bl/w	USAF 181st AS/136th AW, NAS Dallas, TX ANG
	51367	Lockheed C-130H Hercules (85-1367) bl/w	USAF 181st AS/136th AW, NAS Dallas, TX ANG
	51368	Lockheed C-130H Hercules (85-1368) bl/w	USAF 181st AS/136th AW, NAS Dallas, TX ANG
	51435	Lockheed C-130J-30 Hercules II (05-1435) r	USAF 143rd AS/143rd AW, Quonset, RI ANG
	51436	Lockheed C-130J-30 Hercules II (05-1436) r	USAF 143rd AS/143rd AW, Quonset, RI ANG
	51465	Lockheed C-130J-30 Hercules II (05-1465) gn	USAF 115th AS/146th AW, Channel Island ANGS, CA ANG
	51466	Lockheed C-130J-30 Hercules II (05-1466) gn	USAF 115th AS/146th AW, Channel Island ANGS, CA ANG
	53145	Lockheed C-130J-30 Hercules II (05-3145) bk	USAF 41st AS/19th AW Little Rock AFB, AR
	53146	Lockheed C-130J-30 Hercules II (05-3146) y	USAF 48th AS/314th AW, Little Rock AFB, AR
	53147	Lockheed C-130J-30 Hercules II (05-3147) w/bk	USAF 41st AS/19th AW Little Rock AFB, AR
	55814	Lockheed HC-130J Combat King II (15-5814)	LMTAS, Marietta, GA
	55818	Lockheed AC-130J Ghostrider (15-5818)	LMTAS, Marietta, GA
	55821	Lockheed AC-130J Ghostrider (15-5821)	LMTAS, Marietta, GA
	56709	Lockheed C-130H-3 Hercules (95-6709) bl	USAF 156th AS/145th AW, Charlotte, NC ANG
	56710	Lockheed C-130H-3 Hercules (95-6710) pr/y	USAF 130th AS/130th AW, Yeager Int'l, Charleston, WV ANG
	56711	Lockheed C-130H-3 Hercules (95-6711) pr/y	USAF 130th AS/130th AW, Yeager Int'l, Charleston, WV ANG
	56712	Lockheed C-130H-3 Hercules (95-6712) pr/y	USAF 130th AS/130th AW, Yeager Int'l, Charleston, WV ANG
	58152	Lockheed C-130J-30 Hercules II (05-8152) r	USAF 815th AS/403rd AW AFRC, Keesler AFB, MO
	58156	Lockheed C-130J-30 Hercules II (05-8156) r	USAF 815th AS/403rd AW AFRC, Keesler AFB, MO
	58157	Lockheed C-130J-30 Hercules II (05-8157) r	USAF 815th AS/403rd AW AFRC, Keesler AFB, MO
	58158	Lockheed C-130J-30 Hercules II (05-8158) r	USAF 815th AS/403rd AW AFRC, Keesler AFB, MO
	60212	Lockheed MC-130P Combat Shadow (66-0212) bl	USAF 130th RQS/129th RQW, Moffett Field CA ANG
	60216	Lockheed MC-130P Combat Shadow (66-0216) bl	USAF 130th RQS/129th RQW, Moffett Field CA ANG
	60219	Lockheed MC-130P Combat Shadow (66-0219) bl	USAF 130th RQS/129th RQW, Moffett Field CA ANG
	60221	Lockheed HC-130P Combat King (66-0221)	USAF 39th RQS/920th RQW AFRC, Patrick AFB, FL
	60222	Lockheed HC-130P Combat King (66-0222)	USAF 102nd RQS/106th RQW, Suffolk Field, NY ANG
	60223	Lockheed MC-130P Combat Shadow (66-0223) bl	USAF 130th RQS/129th RQW, Moffett Field CA ANG
	60410	Lockheed C-130H Hercules (86-0410)	USAF

Serial	Type (code/other identity)	Owner/operator, location or fate	Notes
60411	Lockheed C-130H Hercules (86-0411)	USAF	
60413	Lockheed C-130H Hercules (86-0413)	USAF	
60414	Lockheed C-130H Hercules (86-0414)	USAF	
60415	Lockheed C-130H Hercules (86-0415) *r*	USAF 154th TS/189th AW, Little Rock, AR ANG	
60418	Lockheed C-130H Hercules (86-0418)	USAF	
60419	Lockheed C-130H Hercules (86-0419)	USAF	
61003	Lockheed C-130H Hercules (96-1003) *pr/bk*	USAF 109th AS/133rd AW, Minneapolis, MN ANG	
61004	Lockheed C-130H Hercules (96-1004) *pr/bk*	USAF 109th AS/133rd AW, Minneapolis, MN ANG	
61005	Lockheed C-130H Hercules (96-1005) *pr/bk*	USAF 109th AS/133rd AW, Minneapolis, MN ANG	
61006	Lockheed C-130H Hercules (96-1006) *pr/bk*	USAF 109th AS/133rd AW, Minneapolis, MN ANG	
61007	Lockheed C-130H Hercules (96-1007) *pr/bk*	USAF 109th AS/133rd AW, Minneapolis, MN ANG	
61008	Lockheed C-130H Hercules (96-1008) *pr/bk*	USAF 109th AS/133rd AW, Minneapolis, MN ANG	
61391	Lockheed C-130H Hercules (86-1391) *r*	USAF 154th TS/189th AW, Little Rock, AR ANG	
61392	Lockheed C-130H Hercules (86-1392)	*To AMARG, July 2016*	
61393	Lockheed C-130H Hercules (86-1393)	*To AMARG, July 2016*	
61394	Lockheed C-130H Hercules (86-1394)	*To AMARG, June 2016*	
61395	Lockheed C-130H Hercules (86-1395) *r*	USAF 154th TS/189th AW, Little Rock, AR ANG	
61396	Lockheed C-130H Hercules (86-1396)	*To AMARG, July 2016*	
61397	Lockheed C-130H Hercules (86-1397)	*To AMARG, July 2016*	
61398	Lockheed C-130H Hercules (86-1398)	*To AMARG, September 2016*	
61437	Lockheed C-130J-30 Hercules II (06-1437) *r*	USAF 143rd AS/143rd AW, Quonset, RI ANG	
61438	Lockheed C-130J-30 Hercules II (06-1438) *r*	USAF 143rd AS/143rd AW, Quonset, RI ANG	
61467	Lockheed C-130J-30 Hercules II (06-1467) *gn*	USAF 115th AS/146th AW, Channel Island ANGS, CA ANG	
61699	Lockheed MC-130H Combat Talon II (86-1699)	USAF 15th SOS/1st SOW, Hurlburt Field, FL	
63171	Lockheed C-130J-30 Hercules II (06-3171) *bl*	USAF 40th AS/317th AG, Dyess AFB, TX	
63301	Lockheed LC-130H Hercules (76-3301)	USAF 139th AS/109th AW, Schenectady, NY ANG	
63302	Lockheed LC-130H Hercules (76-3302)	USAF 139th AS/109th AW, Schenectady, NY ANG	
64631	Lockheed C-130J-30 Hercules II (06-4631) *w/bk*	USAF 41st AS/19th AW Little Rock AFB, AR	
64632	Lockheed C-130J-30 Hercules II (06-4632) *y/bk*	USAF 41st AS/19th AW Little Rock AFB, AR	
64633	Lockheed C-130J-30 Hercules II (06-4633) *y/bk*	USAF 41st AS/19th AW Little Rock AFB, AR	
64634	Lockheed C-130J-30 Hercules II (06-4634) *w/bk*	USAF 41st AS/19th AW Little Rock AFB, AR	
65300	Lockheed WC-130J Hercules II (96-5300)	USAF 53rd WRS/403rd AW AFRC, Keesler AFB, MO	
65301	Lockheed WC-130J Hercules II (96-5301)	USAF 53rd WRS/403rd AW AFRC, Keesler AFB, MO	
65302	Lockheed WC-130J Hercules II (96-5302)	USAF 53rd WRS/403rd AW AFRC, Keesler AFB, MO	
65826	Lockheed AC-130J Ghostrider (16-5826)	LMTAS, Marietta, GA	
65828	Lockheed HC-130J Combat King II (16-5828)	LMTAS, Marietta, GA	
65832	Lockheed AC-130J Ghostrider (16-5832)	LMTAS, Marietta, GA	
65834	Lockheed HC-130J Combat King II (16-5834)	LMTAS, Marietta, GA	
65836	Lockheed AC-130J Ghostrider (16-5836)	LMTAS, Marietta, GA	
65840	Lockheed HC-130J Combat King II (16-5840)	LMTAS, Marietta, GA	
65842	Lockheed AC-130J Ghostrider (16-5842)	LMTAS, Marietta, GA	
65844	Lockheed AC-130J Ghostrider (16-5844)	LMTAS, Marietta, GA	
65846	Lockheed HC-130J Combat King II (16-5846)	LMTAS, Marietta, GA	
67322	Lockheed C-130H-3 Hercules (96-7322) *pr/y*	USAF 130th AS/130th AW, Yeager Int'l, Charleston, WV ANG	
67323	Lockheed C-130H-3 Hercules (96-7323) *pr/w*	USAF 731st AS/302nd AW AFRC, Peterson AFB, CO	
67324	Lockheed C-130H-3 Hercules (96-7324) *pr/y*	USAF 130th AS/130th AW, Yeager Int'l, Charleston, WV ANG	
67325	Lockheed C-130H-3 Hercules (96-7325) *pr/w*	USAF 731st AS/302nd AW AFRC, Peterson AFB, CO	
68153	Lockheed EC-130J Commando Solo III (96-8153)	USAF 193rd SOS/193rd SOW, Harrisburg, PA ANG	
68154	Lockheed EC-130J Commando Solo III (96-8154)	USAF 193rd SOS/193rd SOW, Harrisburg, PA ANG	

Notes	Serial	Type (code/other identity)	Owner/operator, location or fate
	68159	Lockheed C-130J Hercules II (06-8159) *r*	USAF 815th AS/403rd AW AFRC, Keesler AFB, MO
	68610	Lockheed C-130J-30 Hercules II (06-8610) [RS] *bl/w*	USAF 37th AS/86th AW, Ramstein AB, Germany
	68611	Lockheed C-130J-30 Hercules II (06-8611) [RS] *bl/w*	USAF 37th AS/86th AW, Ramstein AB, Germany
	68612	Lockheed C-130J-30 Hercules II (06-8612) [RS] *bl/w*	USAF 37th AS/86th AW, Ramstein AB, Germany
	70023	Lockheed MC-130H Combat Talon II (87-0023)	USAF 15th SOS/1st SOW, Hurlburt Field, FL
	70024	Lockheed MC-130H Combat Talon II (87-0024)	USAF 15th SOS/1st SOW, Hurlburt Field, FL
	70125	Lockheed MC-130H Combat Talon II (87-0125)	USAF 15th SOS/1st SOW, Hurlburt Field, FL
	70126	Lockheed MC-130H Combat Talon II (87-0126)	USAF 15th SOS/1st SOW, Hurlburt Field, FL
	70128	Lockheed AC-130U Spooky (87-0128)	USAF 4th SOS/1st SOW, Hurlburt Field, FL
	71351	Lockheed C-130J Hercules II (97-1351) *y*	USAF 48th AS/314th AW, Little Rock AFB, AR
	71352	Lockheed C-130J Hercules II (97-1352) *y*	USAF 48th AS/314th AW, Little Rock AFB, AR
	71353	Lockheed C-130J Hercules II (97-1353) *y*	USAF 48th AS/314th AW, Little Rock AFB, AR
	71354	Lockheed C-130J Hercules II (97-1354) *y*	USAF 48th AS/314th AW, Little Rock AFB, AR
	71468	Lockheed C-130J-30 Hercules II (07-1468) *gn*	USAF 115th AS/146th AW, Channel Island ANGS, CA ANG
	71931	Lockheed EC-130J Commando Solo III (97-1931)	USAF 193rd SOS/193rd SOW, Harrisburg, PA ANG
	73170	Lockheed C-130J-30 Hercules II (07-3170) *bl*	USAF 40th AS/317th AG, Dyess AFB, TX
	74635	Lockheed C-130J-30 Hercules II (07-4635) *w/bk*	USAF 41st AS/19th AW Little Rock AFB, AR
	74636	Lockheed C-130J-30 Hercules II (07-4636) *w/bk*	USAF 41st AS/19th AW Little Rock AFB, AR
	74637	Lockheed C-130J-30 Hercules II (07-4637) *w/bk*	USAF 41st AS/19th AW Little Rock AFB, AR
	74638	Lockheed C-130J-30 Hercules II (07-4638) *w/bk*	USAF 41st AS/19th AW Little Rock AFB, AR
	74639	Lockheed C-130J-30 Hercules II (07-4639) *w/bk*	USAF 41st AS/19th AW Little Rock AFB, AR
	75303	Lockheed WC-130J Hercules II (97-5303)	USAF 53rd WRS/403rd AW AFRC, Keesler AFB, MO
	75304	Lockheed WC-130J Hercules II (97-5304)	USAF 53rd WRS/403rd AW AFRC, Keesler AFB, MO
	75305	Lockheed WC-130J Hercules II (97-5305)	USAF 53rd WRS/403rd AW AFRC, Keesler AFB, MO
	75306	Lockheed WC-130J Hercules II (97-5306)	USAF 53rd WRS/403rd AW AFRC, Keesler AFB, MO
	76310	Lockheed C-130J-30 Hercules II (07-46310) *w/bk*	USAF 41st AS/19th AW Little Rock AFB, AR
	76311	Lockheed C-130J-30 Hercules II (07-46311) *w/bk*	USAF 41st AS/19th AW Little Rock AFB, AR
	76312	Lockheed C-130J-30 Hercules II (07-46312) *w/bk*	USAF 41st AS/19th AW Little Rock AFB, AR
	78608	Lockheed C-130J-30 Hercules II (07-8608) [RS] *bl/w*	USAF 37th AS/86th AW, Ramstein AB, Germany
	78609	Lockheed C-130J-30 Hercules II (07-8609) [RS] *bl/w*	USAF 37th AS/86th AW, Ramstein AB, Germany
	78613	Lockheed C-130J-30 Hercules II (07-8613) [RS] *bl/w*	USAF 37th AS/86th AW, Ramstein AB, Germany
	78614	Lockheed C-130J-30 Hercules II (07-8614) [RS] *bl/w*	USAF 37th AS/86th AW, Ramstein AB, Germany
	79281	Lockheed C-130H Hercules (87-9281) *bl/y*	USAF 328th AS/914th AW AFRC, Niagara Falls, NY
	79282	Lockheed C-130H Hercules (87-9282) *bl/y*	USAF 328th AS/914th AW AFRC, Niagara Falls, NY
	79283	Lockheed C-130H Hercules (87-9283) *pr/w*	USAF 96th AS/934th AW AFRC, Minneapolis/ St Paul, MN
	79284	Lockheed C-130H Hercules (87-9284)	*To AMARG, 13 June 2016*
	79285	Lockheed C-130H Hercules (87-9285) *bl/y*	USAF 328th AS/914th AW AFRC, Niagara Falls, NY
	79286	Lockheed AC-130W Stinger II (87-9286)	USAF 16th SOS/27th SOW, Cannon AFB, NM
	79287	Lockheed C-130H Hercules (87-9287) *bk/y*	USAF 758th AS/911th AW AFRC, Pittsburgh ARS, PA
	79288	Lockheed AC-130W Stinger II (87-9288)	USAF 16th SOS/27th SOW, Cannon AFB, NM
	80191	Lockheed MC-130H Combat Talon II (88-0191)	USAF 1st SOS/353rd SOG, Kadena AB, Japan
	80193	Lockheed MC-130H Combat Talon II (88-0193)	USAF 15th SOS/1st SOW, Hurlburt Field, FL
	80194	Lockheed MC-130H Combat Talon II (88-0194)	USAF 15th SOS/1st SOW, Hurlburt Field, FL

Serial	Type (code/other identity)	Owner/operator, location or fate	Notes
80195	Lockheed MC-130H Combat Talon II (88-0195)	USAF 15th SOS/1st SOW, Hurlburt Field, FL	
80264	Lockheed MC-130H Combat Talon II (88-0264)	USAF 15th SOS/1st SOW, Hurlburt Field, FL	
80806	Lockheed C-130H Hercules (78-0806)	*To AMARG, April 2016*	
80809	Lockheed C-130H Hercules (78-0809) *r*	USAF 164th AS/179th AW, Mansfield, OH ANG	
80811	Lockheed C-130H Hercules (78-0811)	*To AMARG, September 2016*	
80812	Lockheed C-130H Hercules (78-0812)	*To AMARG, September 2016*	
80813	Lockheed C-130H Hercules (78-0813)	*To AMARG, September 2016*	
81301	Lockheed AC-130W Stinger II (88-1301)	USAF 16th SOS/27th SOW, Cannon AFB, NM	
81302	Lockheed AC-130W Stinger II (88-1302)	USAF 16th SOS/27th SOW, Cannon AFB, NM	
81303	Lockheed AC-130W Stinger II (88-1303)	USAF 16th SOS/27th SOW, Cannon AFB, NM	
81304	Lockheed AC-130W Stinger II (88-1304)	USAF 16th SOS/27th SOW, Cannon AFB, NM	
81305	Lockheed AC-130W Stinger II (88-1305)	USAF 16th SOS/27th SOW, Cannon AFB, NM	
81306	Lockheed AC-130W Stinger II (88-1306)	USAF 16th SOS/27th SOW, Cannon AFB, NM	
81307	Lockheed AC-130W Stinger II (88-1307)	USAF 16th SOS/27th SOW, Cannon AFB, NM	
81308	Lockheed AC-130W Stinger II (88-1308)	USAF 16th SOS/27th SOW, Cannon AFB, NM	
81355	Lockheed C-130J Hercules II (98-1355) *y*	USAF 48th AS/314th AW, Little Rock AFB, AR	
81356	Lockheed C-130J Hercules II (98-1356) *y*	USAF 48th AS/314th AW, Little Rock AFB, AR	
81357	Lockheed C-130J Hercules II (98-1357) *y*	USAF 48th AS/314th AW, Little Rock AFB, AR	
81358	Lockheed C-130J Hercules II (98-1358) *y*	USAF 48th AS/314th AW, Little Rock AFB, AR	
81803	Lockheed MC-130H Combat Talon II (88-1803)	USAF 1st SOS/353rd SOG, Kadena AB, Japan	
81932	Lockheed EC-130J Commando Solo III (98-1932)	USAF 193rd SOS/193rd SOW, Harrisburg, PA ANG	
82101	Lockheed HC-130N Combat King (88-2101)	USAF 102nd RQS/106th RQW, Suffolk Field, NY ANG	
82102	Lockheed HC-130P Combat King (88-2102)	USAF 102nd RQS/106th RQW, Suffolk Field, NY ANG	
83172	Lockheed C-130J-30 Hercules II (08-3172) *bl*	USAF 40th AS/317th AG, Dyess AFB, TX	
83173	Lockheed C-130J-30 Hercules II (08-3173) *bl*	USAF 40th AS/317th AG, Dyess AFB, TX	
83174	Lockheed C-130J-30 Hercules II (08-3174) *bl*	*Crashed 2 October 2015, Jalalabad, Afghanistan*	
83175	Lockheed C-130J-30 Hercules II (08-3175) *bl*	USAF 40th AS/317th AG, Dyess AFB, TX	
83176	Lockheed C-130J-30 Hercules II (08-3176) *bl*	USAF 40th AS/317th AG, Dyess AFB, TX	
83177	Lockheed C-130J-30 Hercules II (08-3177) *bl*	USAF 40th AS/317th AG, Dyess AFB, TX	
83178	Lockheed C-130J-30 Hercules II (08-3178) *bl*	USAF 40th AS/317th AG, Dyess AFB, TX	
83179	Lockheed C-130J-30 Hercules II (08-3179) *bl*	USAF 40th AS/317th AG, Dyess AFB, TX	
84401	Lockheed C-130H Hercules (88-4401)	USAF	
84402	Lockheed C-130H Hercules (88-4402)	USAF	
84403	Lockheed C-130H Hercules (88-4403)	USAF	
84404	Lockheed C-130H Hercules (88-4404)	*To AMARG, 29 June 2016*	
84405	Lockheed C-130H Hercules (88-4405)	USAF	
84406	Lockheed C-130H Hercules (88-4406)	USAF	
84407	Lockheed C-130H Hercules (88-4407)	*To AMARG, August 2016*	
85307	Lockheed WC-130J Hercules II (98-5307)	USAF 53rd WRS/403rd AW AFRC, Keesler AFB, MO	
85308	Lockheed WC-130J Hercules II (98-5308)	USAF 53rd WRS/403rd AW AFRC, Keesler AFB, MO	
85675	Lockheed C-130J-30 Hercules II (08-5675) *bl*	USAF 40th AS/317th AG, Dyess AFB, TX	
85678	Lockheed C-130J-30 Hercules II (08-5678) *bl*	USAF 40th AS/317th AG, Dyess AFB, TX	
85679	Lockheed C-130J-30 Hercules II (08-5679) *bl*	USAF 40th AS/317th AG, Dyess AFB, TX	
85683	Lockheed C-130J-30 Hercules II (08-5683) *r*	USAF 39th AS/317th AG, Dyess AFB, TX	
85684	Lockheed C-130J-30 Hercules II (08-5684) *r*	USAF 39th AS/317th AG, Dyess AFB, TX	
85685	Lockheed C-130J-30 Hercules II (08-5685) *r*	USAF 39th AS/317th AG, Dyess AFB, TX	
85686	Lockheed C-130J-30 Hercules II (08-5686) *r*	USAF 39th AS/317th AG, Dyess AFB, TX	
85691	Lockheed C-130J-30 Hercules II (08-5691) *r*	USAF 39th AS/317th AG, Dyess AFB, TX	
85692	Lockheed C-130J-30 Hercules II (08-5692) *r*	USAF 39th AS/317th AG, Dyess AFB, TX	
85693	Lockheed C-130J-30 Hercules II (08-5693) *r*	USAF 39th AS/317th AG, Dyess AFB, TX	
85697	Lockheed MC-130J Commando II (08-5697)	USAF 522nd SOS/27th SOW, Cannon AFB, NM	
85705	Lockheed C-130J-30 Hercules II (08-5705) *r*	USAF 39th AS/317th AG, Dyess AFB, TX	
85712	Lockheed C-130J-30 Hercules II (08-5712) *r*	USAF 39th AS/317th AG, Dyess AFB, TX	
85715	Lockheed C-130J-30 Hercules II (08-5715) *r*	USAF 39th AS/317th AG, Dyess AFB, TX	
85724	Lockheed C-130J-30 Hercules II (08-5724) *r*	USAF 39th AS/317th AG, Dyess AFB, TX	
85726	Lockheed C-130J-30 Hercules II (08-5726) *r*	USAF 39th AS/317th AG, Dyess AFB, TX	

Notes	Serial	Type (code/other identity)	Owner/operator, location or fate
	86201	Lockheed MC-130J Commando II (08-6201)	USAF 522nd SOS/27th SOW, Cannon AFB, NM
	86202	Lockheed MC-130J Commando II (08-6202)	USAF 522nd SOS/27th SOW, Cannon AFB, NM
	86203	Lockheed MC-130J Commando II (08-6203)	USAF 415th SOS/58th SOW, Kirtland AFB, NM
	86204	Lockheed MC-130J Commando II (08-6204)	USAF 522nd SOS/27th SOW, Cannon AFB, NM
	86205	Lockheed MC-130J Commando II (08-6205)	USAF 415th SOS/58th SOW, Kirtland AFB, NM
	86206	Lockheed MC-130J Commando II (08-6206)	USAF 415th SOS/58th SOW, Kirtland AFB, NM
	88601	Lockheed C-130J-30 Hercules II (08-8601) [RS] bl/w $	USAF 37th AS/86th AW, Ramstein AB, Germany
	88602	Lockheed C-130J-30 Hercules II (08-8602) [RS] bl/w $	USAF 37th AS/86th AW, Ramstein AB, Germany
	88603	Lockheed C-130J-30 Hercules II (08-8603) [RS] bl/w $	USAF 37th AS/86th AW, Ramstein AB, Germany
	88604	Lockheed C-130J-30 Hercules II (08-8604) [RS] bl/w	USAF 37th AS/86th AW, Ramstein AB, Germany
	88605	Lockheed C-130J-30 Hercules II (08-8605) [RS] bl/w	USAF 37th AS/86th AW, Ramstein AB, Germany
	88606	Lockheed C-130J-30 Hercules II (08-8606) y	USAF 48th AS/314th AW, Little Rock AFB, AR
	88607	Lockheed C-130J-30 Hercules II (08-8607) [RS] bl/w	USAF 37th AS/86th AW, Ramstein AB, Germany
	90108	Lockheed HC-130J Combat King II (09-0108) [OT]	USAF 85th TES/53rd Wg, Eglin AFB, FL
	90109	Lockheed HC-130J Combat King II (09-0109)	USAF 415th SOS/58th SOW, Kirtland AFB, NM
	90280	Lockheed MC-130H Combat Talon II (89-0280)	USAF 1st SOS/353rd SOG, Kadena AB, Japan
	90282	Lockheed MC-130H Combat Talon II (89-0282)	USAF 15th SOS/1st SOW, Hurlburt Field, FL
	90283	Lockheed MC-130H Combat Talon II (89-0283)	USAF 1st SOS/353rd SOG, Kadena AB, Japan
	90473	Lockheed C-130H Hercules (79-0473) bl/w	USAF 192nd AS/152nd AW, Reno, NV ANG
	90475	Lockheed C-130H Hercules (79-0475)	USAF 186th AS/120th AW, Great Falls, MT ANG
	90476	Lockheed C-130H Hercules (79-0476)	USAF 186th AS/120th AW, Great Falls, MT ANG
	90477	Lockheed C-130H Hercules (79-0477)	To AMARG, May 2016
	90478	Lockheed C-130H Hercules (79-0478) bl/w	Withdrawn from use, 2016
	90479	Lockheed C-130H Hercules (79-0479) r	USAF 164th AS/179th AW, Mansfield, OH ANG
	90480	Lockheed C-130H Hercules (79-0480) bl/w	USAF 192nd AS/152nd AW, Reno, NV ANG
	90509	Lockheed AC-130U Spooky (89-0509)	USAF 4th SOS/1st SOW, Hurlburt Field, FL
	90510	Lockheed AC-130U Spooky (89-0510)	USAF 4th SOS/1st SOW, Hurlburt Field, FL
	90511	Lockheed AC-130U Spooky (89-0511)	USAF 4th SOS/1st SOW, Hurlburt Field, FL
	90512	Lockheed AC-130U Spooky (89-0512)	USAF 4th SOS/1st SOW, Hurlburt Field, FL
	90513	Lockheed AC-130U Spooky (89-0513)	USAF 4th SOS/1st SOW, Hurlburt Field, FL
	90514	Lockheed AC-130U Spooky (89-0514)	USAF 4th SOS/1st SOW, Hurlburt Field, FL
	91051	Lockheed AC-130W Stinger II (89-1051)	USAF 16th SOS/27th SOW, Cannon AFB, NM
	91052	Lockheed AC-130U Spooky (89-1052)	USAF 4th SOS/1st SOW, Hurlburt Field, FL
	91053	Lockheed AC-130U Spooky (89-1053)	USAF 4th SOS/1st SOW, Hurlburt Field, FL
	91054	Lockheed AC-130U Spooky (89-1054)	USAF 4th SOS/1st SOW, Hurlburt Field, FL
	91055	Lockheed C-130H Hercules (89-1055) bk/y	USAF 758th AS/911th AW AFRC, Pittsburgh ARS, PA
	91056	Lockheed AC-130U Spooky (89-1056)	USAF 4th SOS/1st SOW, Hurlburt Field, FL
	91181	Lockheed C-130H Hercules (89-1181) r/bk	USAF 158th AS/165th AW, Savannah, GA ANG
	91182	Lockheed C-130H Hercules (89-1182) bk/y	USAF 144th AS/176th CW, Elmendorf AFB, AK ANG
	91183	Lockheed C-130H Hercules (89-1183) bk/y	USAF 144th AS/176th CW, Elmendorf AFB, AK ANG
	91184	Lockheed C-130H Hercules (89-1184) bk/y	USAF 144th AS/176th CW, Elmendorf AFB, AK ANG
	91185	Lockheed C-130H Hercules (89-1185) bk/y	USAF 144th AS/176th CW, Elmendorf AFB, AK ANG
	91186	Lockheed C-130H Hercules (89-1186) bl/y	USAF 328th AS/914th AW AFRC, Niagara Falls, NY
	91187	Lockheed C-130H Hercules (89-1187)	USAF
	91188	Lockheed C-130H Hercules (89-1188) bl/w	USAF 357th AS/908th AW AFRC, Maxwell AFB, AL
	91431	Lockheed C-130J-30 Hercules II (99-1431) r	USAF 143rd AS/143rd AW, Quonset, RI ANG
	91432	Lockheed C-130J-30 Hercules II (99-1432) r	USAF 143rd AS/143rd AW, Quonset, RI ANG
	91433	Lockheed C-130J-30 Hercules II (99-1433) r	USAF 143rd AS/143rd AW, Quonset, RI ANG

Serial	Type (code/other identity)	Owner/operator, location or fate	Notes
91933	Lockheed EC-130J Commando Solo III (99-1933)	USAF 193rd SOS/193rd SOW, Harrisburg, PA ANG	
95309	Lockheed WC-130J Hercules II (99-5309)	USAF 53rd WRS/403rd AW AFRC, Keesler AFB, MO	
95706	Lockheed HC-130J Combat King II (09-5706)	USAF 415th SOS/58th SOW, Kirtland AFB, NM	
95707	Lockheed HC-130J Combat King II (09-5707) [FT]	USAF 79th RQS/563rd RQG, Davis-Monthan AFB, AZ	
95708	Lockheed HC-130J Combat King II (09-5708) [FT]	USAF 79th RQS/563rd RQG, Davis-Monthan AFB, AZ	
95709	Lockheed HC-130J Combat King II (09-5709) [FT]	USAF 79th RQS/563rd RQG, Davis-Monthan AFB, AZ	
95711	Lockheed MC-130J Commando II (09-5711)	USAF 522nd SOS/27th SOW, Cannon AFB, NM	
95713	Lockheed MC-130J Commando II (09-5713)	USAF 522nd SOS/27th SOW, Cannon AFB, NM	
95829	Lockheed HC-130N Combat King (69-5829)	USAF 39th RQS/920th RQW AFRC, Patrick AFB, FL	
95830	Lockheed HC-130N Combat King (69-5830)	USAF 39th RQS/920th RQW AFRC, Patrick AFB, FL	
95833	Lockheed HC-130N Combat King (69-5833)	USAF 39th RQS/920th RQW AFRC, Patrick AFB, FL	
96207	Lockheed MC-130J Commando II (09-6207)	USAF 415th SOS/58th SOW, Kirtland AFB, NM	
96208	Lockheed MC-130J Commando II (09-6208)	USAF 522nd SOS/27th SOW, Cannon AFB, NM	
96209	Lockheed MC-130J Commando II (09-6209) [58 SOW]	USAF 415th SOS/58th SOW, Kirtland AFB, NM	
96210	Lockheed MC-130J Commando II (09-6210)	USAF 522nd SOS/27th SOW, Cannon AFB, NM	
99101	Lockheed C-130H Hercules (89-9101)	USAF	
99102	Lockheed C-130H Hercules (89-9102) r/bk	USAF 158th AS/165th AW, Savannah, GA ANG	
99103	Lockheed C-130H Hercules (89-9103) bl/r	USAF 757th AS/910th AW AFRC, Youngstown ARS, OH	
99104	Lockheed C-130H Hercules (89-9104) bl/r	USAF 757th AS/910th AW AFRC, Youngstown ARS, OH	
99105	Lockheed C-130H Hercules (89-9105) bl/r	USAF 757th AS/910th AW AFRC, Youngstown ARS, OH	
99106	Lockheed C-130H Hercules (89-9106) bl/r	USAF 757th AS/910th AW AFRC, Youngstown ARS, OH	

Boeing C-135

00313	Boeing KC-135R Stratotanker (60-0313)	USAF 22nd ARW, McConnell AFB, KS	
00314	Boeing KC-135R Stratotanker (60-0314) r/w	USAF 74th ARS/434th ARW AFRC, Grissom AFB, IN	
00315	Boeing KC-135R Stratotanker (60-0315) w/bl	USAF 126th ARS/128th ARW, Mitchell Field, WI ANG	
00316	Boeing KC-135R Stratotanker (60-0316) bl/bk	USAF 191st ARS/151st ARW, Salt Lake City, UT ANG	
00318	Boeing KC-135R Stratotanker (60-0318) [HH] y/bk	USAF 203rd ARS/15th Wg, Hickam AFB, HI ANG	
00320	Boeing KC-135R Stratotanker (60-0320)	USAF 22nd ARW, McConnell AFB, KS	
00322	Boeing KC-135R Stratotanker (60-0322) bl	USAF 72nd ARS/434th ARW AFRC, Grissom AFB, IN	
00323	Boeing KC-135R Stratotanker (60-0323) [HH] y/bk	USAF 203rd ARS/15th Wg, Hickam AFB, HI ANG	
00324	Boeing KC-135R Stratotanker (60-0324) [D] r/w/bl	USAF 351st ARS/100th ARW, RAF Mildenhall, UK	
00328	Boeing KC-135R Stratotanker (60-0328) [ZZ] or/bk	USAF 909th ARS/18th Wg, Kadena AB, Japan	
00329	Boeing KC-135R Stratotanker (60-0329) [HH] y/bk	USAF 203rd ARS/15th Wg, Hickam AFB, HI ANG	
00331	Boeing KC-135R Stratotanker (60-0331)	USAF 314th ARS/940th ARW, Beale AFB, CA	
00332	Boeing KC-135R Stratotanker (60-0332) [AK] bl/y	USAF 168th ARS/168th ARW, Eielson AFB, AK ANG	
00333	Boeing KC-135R Stratotanker (60-0333)	USAF 92nd ARW, Fairchild AFB, WA	
00334	Boeing KC-135R Stratotanker (60-0334) [AK] bl/y	USAF 168th ARS/168th ARW, Eielson AFB, AK ANG	
00335	Boeing KC-135T Stratotanker (60-0335) y/bl	USAF 91st ARS/6th AMW, MacDill AFB, FL	
00336	Boeing KC-135T Stratotanker (60-0336)	USAF 22nd ARW, McConnell AFB, KS	
00337	Boeing KC-135T Stratotanker (60-0337)	USAF 22nd ARW, McConnell AFB, KS	

Notes	Serial	Type (code/other identity)	Owner/operator, location or fate
	00339	Boeing KC-135T Stratotanker (60-0339)	USAF 92nd ARW, Fairchild AFB, WA
	00341	Boeing KC-135R Stratotanker (60-0341)	USAF 153rd ARS/186th AW, Meridian, MS ANG
	00342	Boeing KC-135T Stratotanker (60-0342)	USAF 92nd ARW, Fairchild AFB, WA
	00343	Boeing KC-135T Stratotanker (60-0343)	USAF 22nd ARW, McConnell AFB, KS
	00344	Boeing KC-135T Stratotanker (60-0344)	USAF 22nd ARW, McConnell AFB, KS
	00345	Boeing KC-135T Stratotanker (60-0345) bk/y	USAF 171st ARS/127th Wg, Selfridge ANGB, MI ANG
	00346	Boeing KC-135T Stratotanker (60-0346) bk/y	USAF 171st ARS/127th Wg, Selfridge ANGB, MI ANG
	00347	Boeing KC-135R Stratotanker (60-0347) r/w	USAF 166th ARS/121st ARW, Rickenbacker ANGB, OH ANG
	00348	Boeing KC-135R Stratotanker (60-0348) y/r	USAF 54th ARS/97th AMW, Altus AFB, OK
	00349	Boeing KC-135R Stratotanker (60-0349) gn/y	USAF 77th ARS/916th ARW AFRC, Seymour Johnson AFB, NC
	00350	Boeing KC-135R Stratotanker (60-0350) [ZZ] or/bk	USAF 909th ARS/18th Wg, Kadena AB, Japan
	00351	Boeing KC-135R Stratotanker (60-0351) [ZZ] or/bk	USAF 909th ARS/18th Wg, Kadena AB, Japan
	00353	Boeing KC-135R Stratotanker (60-0353) y/bl	USAF 91st ARS/6th AMW, MacDill AFB, FL
	00355	Boeing KC-135R Stratotanker (60-0355)	USAF 92nd ARW, Fairchild AFB, WA
	00356	Boeing KC-135R(RT) Stratotanker (60-0356)	USAF 22nd ARW, McConnell AFB, KS
	00357	Boeing KC-135R(RT) Stratotanker (60-0357)	USAF 22nd ARW, McConnell AFB, KS
	00358	Boeing KC-135R Stratotanker (60-0358) w/bl	USAF 108th ARS/126th ARW, Scott AFB, IL ANG
	00359	Boeing KC-135R Stratotanker (60-0359) r/w	USAF 74th ARS/434th ARW AFRC, Grissom AFB, IN
	00360	Boeing KC-135R Stratotanker (60-0360) [ZZ] or/bk	USAF 909th ARS/18th Wg, Kadena AB, Japan
	00362	Boeing KC-135R(RT) Stratotanker (60-0362)	USAF 22nd ARW, McConnell AFB, KS
	00363	Boeing KC-135R Stratotanker (60-0363) bl	USAF 72nd ARS/434th ARW AFRC, Grissom AFB, IN
	00364	Boeing KC-135R Stratotanker (60-0364) r/w	USAF 74th ARS/434th ARW AFRC, Grissom AFB, IN
	00365	Boeing KC-135R Stratotanker (60-0365) bl/y	USAF 117th ARS/190th ARW, Forbes Field, KS ANG
	00366	Boeing KC-135R Stratotanker (60-0366) r	USAF 141st ARS/108th ARW, McGuire AFB, NJ ANG
	00367	Boeing KC-135R Stratotanker (60-0367) r/w	USAF 166th ARS/121st ARW, Rickenbacker ANGB, OH ANG
	10264	Boeing KC-135R Stratotanker (61-0264) r/w	USAF 166th ARS/121st ARW, Rickenbacker ANGB, OH ANG
	10266	Boeing KC-135R Stratotanker (61-0266) bl/y	USAF 117th ARS/190th ARW, Forbes Field, KS ANG
	10267	Boeing KC-135R Stratotanker (61-0267) [D] r/w/bl	USAF 351st ARS/100th ARW, RAF Mildenhall, UK
	10272	Boeing KC-135R Stratotanker (61-0272) r/w	USAF 74th ARS/434th ARW AFRC, Grissom AFB, IN
	10275	Boeing KC-135R Stratotanker (61-0275) bl/bk	USAF 191st ARS/151st ARW, Salt Lake City, UT ANG
	10276	Boeing KC-135R Stratotanker (61-0276) r/w	USAF 173rd ARS/155th ARW, Lincoln, NE ANG
	10277	Boeing KC-135R Stratotanker (61-0277) bl/y	USAF 117th ARS/190th ARW, Forbes Field, KS ANG
	10280	Boeing KC-135R Stratotanker (61-0280) or/y	USAF 336th ARS/452nd AMW AFRC, March ARB, CA
	10284	Boeing KC-135R Stratotanker (61-0284)	USAF 197th ARS/161st ARW, Phoenix, AZ ANG
	10288	Boeing KC-135R Stratotanker (61-0288)	USAF 92nd ARW, Fairchild AFB, WA
	10290	Boeing KC-135R Stratotanker (61-0290) [HH] y/bk	USAF 203rd ARS/15th Wg, Hickam AFB, HI ANG
	10292	Boeing KC-135R Stratotanker (61-0292)	USAF 22nd ARW, McConnell AFB, KS
	10293	Boeing KC-135R(RT) Stratotanker (61-0293)	USAF 22nd ARW, McConnell AFB, KS
	10294	Boeing KC-135R Stratotanker (61-0294) gn/y	USAF 77th ARS/916th ARW AFRC, Seymour Johnson AFB, NC
	10295	Boeing KC-135R Stratotanker (61-0295)	USAF 22nd ARW, McConnell AFB, KS

Serial	Type (code/other identity)	Owner/operator, location or fate	Notes
10298	Boeing KC-135R Stratotanker (61-0298) *w/bl*	USAF 126th ARS/128th ARW, Mitchell Field, WI ANG	
10299	Boeing KC-135R Stratotanker (61-0299) [D] *r/w/bl*	USAF 351st ARS/100th ARW, RAF Mildenhall, UK	
10300	Boeing KC-135R Stratotanker (61-0300) *w/bl*	USAF 108th ARS/126th ARW, Scott AFB, IL ANG	
10305	Boeing KC-135R Stratotanker (61-0305)	USAF 22nd ARW, McConnell AFB, KS	
10307	Boeing KC-135R Stratotanker (61-0307) *y/bk*	USAF 756th ARS/459th ARW AFRC, Andrews AFB, MD	
10308	Boeing NC-135R Stratotanker (61-0308) *y/r*	USAF 54th ARS/97th AMW, Altus AFB, OK	
10309	Boeing KC-135R Stratotanker (61-0309) *w/bl*	USAF 126th ARS/128th ARW, Mitchell Field, WI ANG	
10310	Boeing KC-135R Stratotanker (61-0310) *bl*	USAF 133rd ARS/157th ARW, Pease ANGB, NH ANG	
10311	Boeing KC-135R Stratotanker (61-0311)	USAF 22nd ARW, McConnell AFB, KS	
10313	Boeing KC-135R Stratotanker (61-0313) *gn/y*	USAF 77th ARS/916th ARW AFRC, Seymour Johnson AFB, NC	
10314	Boeing KC-135R Stratotanker (61-0314) *y/bl*	USAF 91st ARS/6th AMW, MacDill AFB, FL	
10315	Boeing KC-135R Stratotanker (61-0315) *y/bl*	USAF 91st ARS/6th AMW, MacDill AFB, FL	
10317	Boeing KC-135R Stratotanker (61-0317) *bl/y*	USAF 117th ARS/190th ARW, Forbes Field, KS ANG	
10318	Boeing KC-135R Stratotanker (61-0318) *w/r*	USAF 106th ARS/117th ARW, Birmingham, AL ANG	
10320	Boeing KC-135R Stratotanker (61-0320) [ED]	USAF 445th FLTS/412th TW, Edwards AFB, CA	
10321	Boeing KC-135R Stratotanker (61-0321) [D] *r/w/bl*	USAF 351st ARS/100th ARW, RAF Mildenhall, UK	
10323	Boeing KC-135R Stratotanker (61-0323)	USAF 314th ARS/940th ARW, Beale AFB, CA	
10324	Boeing KC-135R Stratotanker (61-0324) *or/y*	USAF 336th ARS/452nd AMW AFRC, March ARB, CA	
12662	Boeing RC-135S Cobra Ball (61-2662) [OF] *bk*	USAF 45th RS/55th Wg, Offutt AFB, NE	
12663	Boeing RC-135S Cobra Ball (61-2663) [OF] *bk*	USAF 45th RS/55th Wg, Offutt AFB, NE	
12666	Boeing NC-135W (61-2666)	USAF 645th Materiel Sqn, Greenville, TX	
12667	Boeing WC-135W Constant Phoenix (61-2667) [OF] *bk*	USAF 45th RS/55th Wg, Offutt AFB, NE	
12670	Boeing OC-135B Open Skies (61-2670) [OF] *bk*	USAF 45th RS/55th Wg, Offutt AFB, NE	
12672	Boeing OC-135B Open Skies (61-2672) [OF] *bk*	USAF 45th RS/55th Wg, Offutt AFB, NE	
14828	Boeing KC-135R Stratotanker (64-14828) *bl/bk*	USAF 191st ARS/151st ARW, Salt Lake City, UT ANG	
14829	Boeing KC-135R Stratotanker (64-14829)	USAF 197th ARS/161st ARW, Phoenix, AZ ANG	
14830	Boeing KC-135R Stratotanker (64-14830)	USAF	
14831	Boeing KC-135R Stratotanker (64-14831)	USAF 197th ARS/161st ARW, Phoenix, AZ ANG	
14832	Boeing KC-135R Stratotanker (64-14832) *w/or*	USAF 151st ARS/134th ARW, Knoxville, TN ANG	
14834	Boeing KC-135R Stratotanker (64-14834) *r/w*	USAF 74th ARS/434th ARW AFRC, Grissom AFB, IN	
14835	Boeing KC-135R Stratotanker (64-14835) *or/y*	USAF 336th ARS/452nd AMW AFRC, March ARB, CA	
14836	Boeing KC-135R Stratotanker (64-14836) *bl*	USAF 133rd ARS/157th ARW, Pease ANGB, NH ANG	
14837	Boeing KC-135R Stratotanker (64-14837) *y/bl*	USAF 91st ARS/6th AMW, MacDill AFB, FL	
14839	Boeing KC-135R Stratotanker (64-14839) *w/bl*	USAF 108th ARS/126th ARW, Scott AFB, IL ANG	
14840	Boeing KC-135R Stratotanker (64-14840) *r/w* $	USAF 166th ARS/121st ARW, Rickenbacker ANGB, OH ANG	
14841	Boeing RC-135V Rivet Joint (64-14841) *gn*	USAF 38th RS/55th Wg, Offutt AFB, NE	
14842	Boeing RC-135V Rivet Joint (64-14842) *gn*	USAF 38th RS/55th Wg, Offutt AFB, NE	
14843	Boeing RC-135V Rivet Joint (64-14843) *gn*	USAF 38th RS/55th Wg, Offutt AFB, NE	
14844	Boeing RC-135V Rivet Joint (64-14844) *gn*	USAF 38th RS/55th Wg, Offutt AFB, NE	
14845	Boeing RC-135V Rivet Joint (64-14845) *gn*	USAF 38th RS/55th Wg, Offutt AFB, NE	
14846	Boeing RC-135V Rivet Joint (64-14846) *gn*	USAF 38th RS/55th Wg, Offutt AFB, NE	
14847	Boeing RC-135U Combat Sent (64-14847) [OF] *bk*	USAF 45th RS/55th Wg, Offutt AFB, NE	
14848	Boeing RC-135V Rivet Joint (64-14848) *gn*	USAF 343rd RS/55th Wg, Offutt AFB, NE	
14849	Boeing RC-135U Combat Sent (64-14849) [OF] *bk*	USAF 45th RS/55th Wg, Offutt AFB, NE	

Notes	Serial	Type (code/other identity)	Owner/operator, location or fate
	23498	Boeing KC-135R Stratotanker (62-3498)	USAF 22nd ARW, McConnell AFB, KS
	23499	Boeing KC-135R Stratotanker (62-3499)	USAF 92nd ARW, Fairchild AFB, WA
	23500	Boeing KC-135R Stratotanker (62-3500) *bl*	USAF 133rd ARS/157th ARW, Pease ANGB, NH ANG
	23502	Boeing KC-135R Stratotanker (62-3502) *bl*	USAF 133rd ARS/157th ARW, Pease ANGB, NH ANG
	23503	Boeing KC-135R Stratotanker (62-3503) *bl/y*	USAF 465th ARS/507th ARW AFRC, Tinker AFB, OK
	23505	Boeing KC-135R Stratotanker (62-3505) *y/bl*	USAF 91st ARS/6th AMW, MacDill AFB, FL
	23506	Boeing KC-135R Stratotanker (62-3506) *bl*	USAF 133rd ARS/157th ARW, Pease ANGB, NH ANG
	23507	Boeing KC-135R Stratotanker (62-3507) [ZZ] *or/bk*	USAF 909th ARS/18th Wg, Kadena AB, Japan
	23508	Boeing KC-135R Stratotanker (62-3508) *r*	USAF 141st ARS/108th ARW, McGuire AFB, NJ ANG
	23509	Boeing KC-135R Stratotanker (62-3509) *gn/y*	USAF 77th ARS/916th ARW AFRC, Seymour Johnson AFB, NC
	23510	Boeing KC-135R Stratotanker (62-3510) *r/w*	USAF 74th ARS/434th ARW AFRC, Grissom AFB, IN
	23511	Boeing KC-135R Stratotanker (62-3511) *r/w*	USAF 166th ARS/121st ARW, Rickenbacker ANGB, OH ANG
	23512	Boeing KC-135R Stratotanker (62-3512) *w/bl*	USAF 126th ARS/128th ARW, Mitchell Field, WI ANG
	23513	Boeing KC-135R Stratotanker (62-3513) *w/gn*	USAF 132nd ARS/101st ARW, Bangor, MN ANG
	23514	Boeing KC-135R Stratotanker (62-3514) *r*	USAF 141st ARS/108th ARW, McGuire AFB, NJ ANG
	23515	Boeing KC-135R Stratotanker (62-3515) *bl*	USAF 133rd ARS/157th ARW, Pease ANGB, NH ANG
	23516	Boeing KC-135R Stratotanker (62-3516) $	USAF 197th ARS/161st ARW, Phoenix, AZ ANG
	23517	Boeing KC-135R Stratotanker (62-3517) *y/bl*	USAF 91st ARS/6th AMW, MacDill AFB, FL
	23518	Boeing KC-135R Stratotanker (62-3518) *bl*	USAF 72nd ARS/434th ARW AFRC, Grissom AFB, IN
	23519	Boeing KC-135R Stratotanker (62-3519) *y/bl*	USAF 91st ARS/6th AMW, MacDill AFB, FL
	23521	Boeing KC-135R Stratotanker (62-3521) *bl*	USAF 72nd ARS/434th ARW AFRC, Grissom AFB, IN
	23523	Boeing KC-135R Stratotanker (62-3523)	USAF 22nd ARW, McConnell AFB, KS
	23524	Boeing KC-135R Stratotanker (62-3524) [AK] *bl/y*	USAF 168th ARS/168th ARW, Eielson AFB, AK ANG
	23526	Boeing KC-135R Stratotanker (62-3526) *r/w*	USAF 173rd ARS/155th ARW, Lincoln, NE ANG
	23528	Boeing KC-135R Stratotanker (62-3528) *gn/y*	USAF 77th ARS/916th ARW AFRC, Seymour Johnson AFB, NC
	23529	Boeing KC-135R Stratotanker (62-3529)	USAF 314th ARS/940th ARW, Beale AFB, CA
	23530	Boeing KC-135R Stratotanker (62-3530) *bl*	USAF 72nd ARS/434th ARW AFRC, Grissom AFB, IN
	23531	Boeing KC-135R Stratotanker (62-3531) *r/w*	USAF 166th ARS/121st ARW, Rickenbacker ANGB, OH ANG
	23533	Boeing KC-135R Stratotanker (62-3533) *or/y*	USAF 336th ARS/452nd AMW AFRC, March ARB, CA
	23534	Boeing KC-135R Stratotanker (62-3534)	USAF 22nd ARW, McConnell AFB, KS
	23537	Boeing KC-135R Stratotanker (62-3537) *bl/y*	USAF 465th ARS/507th ARW AFRC, Tinker AFB, OK
	23538	Boeing KC-135R Stratotanker (62-3538) *y/bl*	USAF 91st ARS/6th AMW, MacDill AFB, FL
	23540	Boeing KC-135R Stratotanker (62-3540) *y/r*	USAF 54th ARS/97th AMW, Altus AFB, OK
	23541	Boeing KC-135R Stratotanker (62-3541)	USAF 92nd ARW, Fairchild AFB, WA
	23542	Boeing KC-135R Stratotanker (62-3542) *gn/y*	USAF 77th ARS/916th ARW AFRC, Seymour Johnson AFB, NC
	23543	Boeing KC-135R Stratotanker (62-3543) *y/bk*	USAF 756th ARS/459th ARW AFRC, Andrews AFB, MD
	23544	Boeing KC-135R Stratotanker (62-3544) *r*	USAF 141st ARS/108th ARW, McGuire AFB, NJ ANG
	23545	Boeing KC-135R Stratotanker (62-3545)	USAF 22nd ARW, McConnell AFB, KS

Serial	Type (code/other identity)	Owner/operator, location or fate	Notes
23547	Boeing KC-135R Stratotanker (62-3547) *bl*	USAF 133rd ARS/157th ARW, Pease ANGB, NH ANG	
23549	Boeing KC-135R Stratotanker (62-3549) *y/r*	USAF 54th ARS/97th AMW, Altus AFB, OK	
23550	Boeing KC-135R Stratotanker (62-3550)	USAF 197th ARS/161st ARW, Phoenix, AZ ANG	
23551	Boeing KC-135R Stratotanker (62-3551)	USAF 22nd ARW, McConnell AFB, KS	
23552	Boeing KC-135R Stratotanker (62-3552) [ZZ] *or/bk*	USAF 909th ARS/18th Wg, Kadena AB, Japan	
23553	Boeing KC-135R Stratotanker (62-3553) [ZZ] *or/bk*	USAF 909th ARS/18th Wg, Kadena AB, Japan	
23554	Boeing KC-135R Stratotanker (62-3554)	USAF 22nd ARW, McConnell AFB, KS	
23556	Boeing KC-135R Stratotanker (62-3556) *y/bk*	USAF 756th ARS/459th ARW AFRC, Andrews AFB, MD	
23557	Boeing KC-135R Stratotanker (62-3557)	USAF 328th ARS/914th ARW AFRC, Niagara Falls, NY	
23558	Boeing KC-135R Stratotanker (62-3558) *or/y*	USAF 336th ARS/452nd AMW AFRC, March ARB, CA	
23559	Boeing KC-135R Stratotanker (62-3559) [D] *r/w/bl*	USAF 351st ARS/100th ARW, RAF Mildenhall, UK	
23561	Boeing KC-135R Stratotanker (62-3561) [ZZ] *or/bk*	USAF 909th ARS/18th Wg, Kadena AB, Japan	
23562	Boeing KC-135R Stratotanker (62-3562) [ZZ] *or/bk*	USAF 909th ARS/18th Wg, Kadena AB, Japan	
23564	Boeing KC-135R Stratotanker (62-3564)	USAF 22nd ARW, McConnell AFB, KS	
23565	Boeing KC-135R Stratotanker (62-3565)	USAF 92nd ARW, Fairchild AFB, WA	
23566	Boeing KC-135R Stratotanker (62-3566) *y/bk*	USAF 174th ARS/185th ARW, Sioux City, IA ANG	
23568	Boeing KC-135R Stratotanker (62-3568)	USAF 22nd ARW, McConnell AFB, KS	
23569	Boeing KC-135R Stratotanker (62-3569)	USAF 22nd ARW, McConnell AFB, KS	
23571	Boeing KC-135R Stratotanker (62-3571) [AK] *bl/y*	USAF 168th ARS/168th ARW, Eielson AFB, AK ANG	
23572	Boeing KC-135R Stratotanker (62-3572) *bl/y*	USAF 117th ARS/190th ARW, Forbes Field, KS ANG	
23573	Boeing KC-135R Stratotanker (62-3573) *y/bl*	USAF 91st ARS/6th AMW, MacDill AFB, FL	
23575	Boeing KC-135R Stratotanker (62-3575) *y/bl*	USAF 91st ARS/6th AMW, MacDill AFB, FL	
23576	Boeing KC-135R Stratotanker (62-3576) *bl*	USAF 133rd ARS/157th ARW, Pease ANGB, NH ANG	
23577	Boeing KC-135R Stratotanker (62-3577) *gn/y*	USAF 77th ARS/916th ARW AFRC, Seymour Johnson AFB, NC	
23578	Boeing KC-135R Stratotanker (62-3578) *r*	USAF 141st ARS/108th ARW, McGuire AFB, NJ ANG	
23580	Boeing KC-135R Stratotanker (62-3580) *gn/y*	USAF 77th ARS/916th ARW AFRC, Seymour Johnson AFB, NC	
23582	Boeing WC-135C Constant Phoenix (62-3582) [OF] *bk*	USAF 45th RS/55th Wg, Offutt AFB, NE	
24125	Boeing RC-135W Rivet Joint (62-4125) *gn*	USAF 38th RS/55th Wg, Offutt AFB, NE	
24126	Boeing RC-135W Rivet Joint (62-4126) *gn*	USAF 38th RS/55th Wg, Offutt AFB, NE	
24127	Boeing TC-135W (62-4127) *gn*	USAF 38th RS/55th Wg, Offutt AFB, NE	
24128	Boeing RC-135S Cobra Ball (62-4128) [OF] *bk*	USAF 45th RS/55th Wg, Offutt AFB, NE	
24129	Boeing TC-135W (62-4129) *gn*	USAF 38th RS/55th Wg, Offutt AFB, NE	
24130	Boeing RC-135W Rivet Joint (62-4130) *gn*	USAF 38th RS/55th Wg, Offutt AFB, NE	
24131	Boeing RC-135W Rivet Joint (62-4131) *bl*	USAF 343rd RS/55th Wg, Offutt AFB, NE	
24132	Boeing RC-135W Rivet Joint (62-4132) *gn*	USAF 38th RS/55th Wg, Offutt AFB, NE	
24133	Boeing TC-135W (62-4133) *gn*	USAF 38th RS/55th Wg, Offutt AFB, NE	
24134	Boeing RC-135W Rivet Joint (62-4134) *bl*	USAF 343rd RS/55th Wg, Offutt AFB, NE	
24135	Boeing RC-135W Rivet Joint (62-4135) *gn*	USAF 38th RS/55th Wg, Offutt AFB, NE	
24138	Boeing RC-135W Rivet Joint (62-4138) *bl*	USAF 343rd RS/55th Wg, Offutt AFB, NE	
24139	Boeing RC-135W Rivet Joint (62-4139) *gn*	USAF 38th RS/55th Wg, Offutt AFB, NE	
37976	Boeing KC-135R Stratotanker (63-7976) *y/r*	USAF 54th ARS/97th AMW, Altus AFB, OK	
37977	Boeing KC-135R Stratotanker (63-7977) [ZZ] *or/bk*	USAF 909th ARS/18th Wg, Kadena AB, Japan	
37978	Boeing KC-135R Stratotanker (63-7978)	USAF 22nd ARW, McConnell AFB, KS	
37979	Boeing KC-135R Stratotanker (63-7979) *y/bl*	USAF 91st ARS/6th AMW, MacDill AFB, FL	
37980	Boeing KC-135R Stratotanker (63-7980) [ED]	USAF 418th FLTS/412th TW, Edwards AFB, CA	
37981	Boeing KC-135R Stratotanker (63-7981) *w/bl*	USAF 108th ARS/126th ARW, Scott AFB, IL ANG	
37982	Boeing KC-135R Stratotanker (63-7982)	USAF 92nd ARW, Fairchild AFB, WA	

Notes	Serial	Type (code/other identity)	Owner/operator, location or fate
	37984	Boeing KC-135R Stratotanker (63-7984) w/r	USAF 106th ARS/117th ARW, Birmingham, AL ANG
	37985	Boeing KC-135R Stratotanker (63-7985) bl/y	USAF 465th ARS/507th ARW AFRC, Tinker AFB, OK
	37987	Boeing KC-135R Stratotanker (63-7987)	USAF 22nd ARW, McConnell AFB, KS
	37988	Boeing KC-135R Stratotanker (63-7988) r/w	USAF 173rd ARS/155th ARW, Lincoln, NE ANG
	37991	Boeing KC-135R Stratotanker (63-7991) r/w	USAF 173rd ARS/155th ARW, Lincoln, NE ANG
	37992	Boeing KC-135R Stratotanker (63-7992)	USAF 153rd ARS/186th AW, Meridian, MS ANG
	37993	Boeing KC-135R Stratotanker (63-7993) m	USAF 166th ARS/121st ARW, Rickenbacker ANGB, OH ANG
	37995	Boeing KC-135R Stratotanker (63-7995)	USAF 22nd ARW, McConnell AFB, KS
	37996	Boeing KC-135R Stratotanker (63-7996) bl	USAF 72nd ARS/434th ARW AFRC, Grissom AFB, IN
	37997	Boeing KC-135R Stratotanker (63-7997) [ZZ] or/bk	USAF 909th ARS/18th Wg, Kadena AB, Japan
	37999	Boeing KC-135R Stratotanker (63-7999) [D] r/w/bl	USAF 351st ARS/100th ARW, RAF Mildenhall, UK
	38000	Boeing KC-135R Stratotanker (63-8000)	USAF 92nd ARW, Fairchild AFB, WA
	38002	Boeing KC-135R Stratotanker (63-8002)	USAF 22nd ARW, McConnell AFB, KS
	38003	Boeing KC-135R Stratotanker (63-8003) r	USAF 141st ARS/108th ARW, McGuire AFB, NJ ANG
	38004	Boeing KC-135R Stratotanker (63-8004) bl/y	USAF 117th ARS/190th ARW, Forbes Field, KS ANG
	38006	Boeing KC-135R Stratotanker (63-8006) y/r	USAF 54th ARS/97th AMW, Altus AFB, OK
	38007	Boeing KC-135R Stratotanker (63-8007) w/r	USAF 106th ARS/117th ARW, Birmingham, AL ANG
	38008	Boeing KC-135R Stratotanker (63-8008)	USAF 22nd ARW, McConnell AFB, KS
	38011	Boeing KC-135R Stratotanker (63-8011) y/bl	USAF 91st ARS/6th AMW, MacDill AFB, FL
	38012	Boeing KC-135R Stratotanker (63-8012) bl/y	USAF 465th ARS/507th ARW AFRC, Tinker AFB, OK
	38013	Boeing KC-135R Stratotanker (63-8013) r/w	USAF 166th ARS/121st ARW, Rickenbacker ANGB, OH ANG
	38014	Boeing KC-135R Stratotanker (63-8014) gn/y	USAF 77th ARS/916th ARW AFRC, Seymour Johnson AFB, NC
	38015	Boeing KC-135R Stratotanker (63-8015) [AK] bl/y	USAF 168th ARS/168th ARW, Eielson AFB, AK ANG
	38017	Boeing KC-135R Stratotanker (63-8017) y/bl	USAF 91st ARS/6th AMW, MacDill AFB, FL
	38018	Boeing KC-135R Stratotanker (63-8018) r/w	USAF 173rd ARS/155th ARW, Lincoln, NE ANG
	38019	Boeing KC-135R Stratotanker (63-8019)	USAF 22nd ARW, McConnell AFB, KS
	38020	Boeing KC-135R Stratotanker (63-8020) [ZZ] or/bk [909 ARS]	USAF 909th ARS/18th Wg, Kadena AB, Japan
	38021	Boeing KC-135R Stratotanker (63-8021) [D] r/w/bl	USAF 351st ARS/100th ARW, RAF Mildenhall, UK
	38022	Boeing KC-135R Stratotanker (63-8022) m	USAF 22nd ARW, McConnell AFB, KS
	38023	Boeing KC-135R Stratotanker (63-8023) w/bl	USAF 126th ARS/128th ARW, Mitchell Field, WI ANG
	38024	Boeing KC-135R Stratotanker (63-8024) or/y	USAF 336th ARS/452nd AMW AFRC, March ARB, CA
	38025	Boeing KC-135R Stratotanker (63-8025)	USAF 22nd ARW, McConnell AFB, KS
	38026	Boeing KC-135R Stratotanker (63-8026) bl/bk	USAF 191st ARS/151st ARW, Salt Lake City, UT ANG
	38027	Boeing KC-135R Stratotanker (63-8027)	USAF
	38028	Boeing KC-135R Stratotanker (63-8028) [AK] bl/y	USAF 168th ARS/168th ARW, Eielson AFB, AK ANG
	38029	Boeing KC-135R Stratotanker (63-8029) r	USAF 141st ARS/108th ARW, McGuire AFB, NJ ANG
	38030	Boeing KC-135R Stratotanker (63-8030) [HH] y/bk	USAF 203rd ARS/15th Wg, Hickam AFB, HI ANG
	38031	Boeing KC-135R Stratotanker (63-8031)	USAF 22nd ARW, McConnell AFB, KS
	38032	Boeing KC-135R Stratotanker (63-8032) bl	USAF 72nd ARS/434th ARW AFRC, Grissom AFB, IN
	38033	Boeing KC-135R Stratotanker (63-8033)	USAF 22nd ARW, McConnell AFB, KS
	38034	Boeing KC-135R Stratotanker (63-8034) [ZZ] or/bk	USAF 909th ARS/18th Wg, Kadena AB, Japan

Serial	Type (code/other identity)	Owner/operator, location or fate	Notes
38035	Boeing KC-135R Stratotanker (63-8035) *w/r*	USAF 106th ARS/117th ARW, Birmingham, AL ANG	
38036	Boeing KC-135R Stratotanker (63-8036)	USAF 197th ARS/161st ARW, Phoenix, AZ ANG	
38038	Boeing KC-135R Stratotanker (63-8038) [HH] *y/bk*	USAF 203rd ARS/15th Wg, Hickam AB, HI ANG	
38039	Boeing KC-135R Stratotanker (63-8039) *bl/y*	USAF 465th ARS/507th ARW AFRC, Tinker AFB, OK	
38040	Boeing KC-135R Stratotanker (63-8040) *r*	USAF 141st ARS/108th ARW, McGuire AFB, NJ ANG	
38041	Boeing KC-135R Stratotanker (63-8041) *bl*	USAF 72nd ARS/434th ARW AFRC, Grissom AFB, IN	
38043	Boeing KC-135R Stratotanker (63-8043) [AK] *bl/y*	USAF 168th ARS/168th ARW, Eielson AFB, AK ANG	
38044	Boeing KC-135R Stratotanker (63-8044) *gn/y*	USAF 77th ARS/916th ARW AFRC, Seymour Johnson AFB, NC	
38045	Boeing KC-135R Stratotanker (63-8045)	USAF 92nd ARW, Fairchild AFB, WA	
38871	Boeing KC-135R Stratotanker (63-8871) [D] *r/w/bl*	USAF 351st ARS/100th ARW, RAF Mildenhall, UK	
38872	Boeing KC-135R Stratotanker (63-8872) *w/gn*	USAF 132nd ARS/101st ARW, Bangor, MN ANG	
38873	Boeing KC-135R Stratotanker (63-8873) *w/gn*	USAF 132nd ARS/101st ARW, Bangor, MN ANG	
38874	Boeing KC-135R Stratotanker (63-8874) *y/bl*	USAF 91st ARS/6th AMW, MacDill AFB, FL	
38875	Boeing KC-135R Stratotanker (63-8875) *bl/y*	USAF 117th ARS/190th ARW, Forbes Field, KS ANG	
38876	Boeing KC-135R Stratotanker (63-8876) [AK] *bl/y*	USAF 168th ARS/168th ARW, Eielson AFB, AK ANG	
38878	Boeing KC-135R Stratotanker (63-8878) [ZZ] *or/bk*	USAF 909th ARS/18th Wg, Kadena AB, Japan	
38879	Boeing KC-135R Stratotanker (63-8879)	USAF 314th ARS/940th ARW, Beale AFB, CA	
38880	Boeing KC-135R Stratotanker (63-8880) [HH] *y/bk*	USAF 203rd ARS/15th Wg, Hickam AFB, HI ANG	
38881	Boeing KC-135R Stratotanker (63-8881) *bl/bk*	USAF 191st ARS/151st ARW, Salt Lake City, UT ANG	
38883	Boeing KC-135R Stratotanker (63-8883)	USAF 22nd ARW, McConnell AFB, KS	
38884	Boeing KC-135R Stratotanker (63-8884) [D] *r/w/bl*	USAF 351st ARS/100th ARW, RAF Mildenhall, UK	
38885	Boeing KC-135R Stratotanker (63-8885)	USAF 92nd ARW, Fairchild AFB, WA	
38887	Boeing KC-135R Stratotanker (63-8887) [ZZ] *or/bk*	USAF 909th ARS/18th Wg, Kadena AB, Japan	
38888	Boeing KC-135R Stratotanker (63-8888) *y/r*	USAF 54th ARS/97th AMW, Altus AFB, OK	
39792	Boeing RC-135V Rivet Joint (63-9792) *gn $*	USAF 38th RS/55th Wg, Offutt AFB, NE	
71419	Boeing KC-135R Stratotanker (57-1419) *bl/y*	USAF 117th ARS/190th ARW, Forbes Field, KS ANG	
71427	Boeing KC-135R Stratotanker (57-1427) *bl/y*	USAF 117th ARS/190th ARW, Forbes Field, KS ANG	
71428	Boeing KC-135R Stratotanker (57-1428) *w/or*	USAF 151st ARS/134th ARW, Knoxville, TN ANG	
71430	Boeing KC-135R Stratotanker (57-1430) *bl*	USAF 133rd ARS/157th ARW, Pease ANGB, NH ANG	
71432	Boeing KC-135R Stratotanker (57-1432) *bl/bk*	USAF 191st ARS/151st ARW, Salt Lake City, UT ANG	
71435	Boeing KC-135R Stratotanker (57-1435) *bl/bk*	USAF 191st ARS/151st ARW, Salt Lake City, UT ANG	
71436	Boeing KC-135R Stratotanker (57-1436) *w/or*	USAF 151st ARS/134th ARW, Knoxville, TN ANG	
71437	Boeing KC-135R Stratotanker (57-1437) *gn/y*	USAF 77th ARS/916th ARW AFRC, Seymour Johnson AFB, NC	
71438	Boeing KC-135R Stratotanker (57-1438) *or/y*	USAF 336th ARS/452nd AMW AFRC, March ARB, CA	
71439	Boeing KC-135R Stratotanker (57-1439) *y/bl*	USAF 91st ARS/6th AMW, MacDill AFB, FL	
71440	Boeing KC-135R Stratotanker (57-1440)	USAF 92nd ARW, Fairchild AFB, WA	
71441	Boeing KC-135R Stratotanker (57-1441) *y/bk*	USAF 174th ARS/185th ARW, Sioux City, IA ANG	
71451	Boeing KC-135R Stratotanker (57-1451) *w/or*	USAF 151st ARS/134th ARW, Knoxville, TN ANG	
71453	Boeing KC-135R Stratotanker (57-1453) *y/r*	USAF 54th ARS/97th AMW, Altus AFB, OK	
71454	Boeing KC-135R Stratotanker (57-1454)	USAF 92nd ARW, Fairchild AFB, WA	

Notes	Serial	Type (code/other identity)	Owner/operator, location or fate
	71456	Boeing KC-135R Stratotanker (57-1456) gn/y	USAF 77th ARS/916th ARW AFRC, Seymour Johnson AFB, NC
	71459	Boeing KC-135R Stratotanker (57-1459) or/y	USAF 336th ARS/452nd AMW AFRC, March ARB, CA
	71461	Boeing KC-135R Stratotanker (57-1461) r/w	USAF 173rd ARS/155th ARW, Lincoln, NE ANG
	71462	Boeing KC-135R Stratotanker (57-1462)	USAF 153rd ARS/186th AW, Meridian, MS ANG
	71468	Boeing KC-135R Stratotanker (57-1468) or/y	USAF 336th ARS/452nd AMW AFRC, March ARB, CA
	71469	Boeing KC-135R Stratotanker (57-1469) $	USAF 197th ARS/161st ARW, Phoenix, AZ ANG
	71472	Boeing KC-135R Stratotanker (57-1472) bl	USAF 72nd ARS/434th ARW AFRC, Grissom AFB, IN
	71473	Boeing KC-135R Stratotanker (57-1473) w/r	USAF 106th ARS/117th ARW, Birmingham, AL ANG
	71474	Boeing KC-135R Stratotanker (57-1474) [ZZ] or/bk	USAF 909th ARS/18th Wg, Kadena AB, Japan
	71479	Boeing KC-135R Stratotanker (57-1479) y/bk	USAF 756th ARS/459th ARW AFRC, Andrews AFB, MD
	71483	Boeing KC-135R Stratotanker (57-1483)	USAF 92nd ARW, Fairchild AFB, WA
	71486	Boeing KC-135R Stratotanker (57-1486)	USAF 153rd ARS/186th AW, Meridian, MS ANG
	71487	Boeing KC-135R Stratotanker (57-1487) y/bk	USAF 756th ARS/459th ARW AFRC, Andrews AFB, MD
	71488	Boeing KC-135R Stratotanker (57-1488) y/r	USAF 54th ARS/97th AMW, Altus AFB, OK
	71493	Boeing KC-135R Stratotanker (57-1493) [ZZ] or/bk	USAF 909th ARS/18th Wg, Kadena AB, Japan
	71499	Boeing KC-135R Stratotanker (57-1499) bl/bk	USAF 191st ARS/151st ARW, Salt Lake City, UT ANG
	71502	Boeing KC-135R Stratotanker (57-1502)	USAF 22nd ARW, McConnell AFB, KS
	71506	Boeing KC-135R Stratotanker (57-1506) y/r	USAF 54th ARS/97th AMW, Altus AFB, OK
	71508	Boeing KC-135R Stratotanker (57-1508) [HH] y/bk	USAF 203rd ARS/15th Wg, Hickam AFB, HI ANG
	71512	Boeing KC-135R Stratotanker (57-1512) y/bk	USAF 756th ARS/459th ARW AFRC, Andrews AFB, MD
	71514	Boeing KC-135R Stratotanker (57-1514) w/bl	USAF 126th ARS/128th ARW, Mitchell Field, WI ANG
	72597	Boeing KC-135R Stratotanker (57-2597) w/or	USAF 151st ARS/134th ARW, Knoxville, TN ANG
	72598	Boeing KC-135R Stratotanker (57-2598) or/y	USAF 336th ARS/452nd AMW AFRC, March ARB, CA
	72599	Boeing KC-135R Stratotanker (57-2599) gn/y	USAF 77th ARS/916th ARW AFRC, Seymour Johnson AFB, NC
	72603	Boeing KC-135R Stratotanker (57-2603) or/y	USAF 336th ARS/452nd AMW AFRC, March ARB, CA
	72605	Boeing KC-135R Stratotanker (57-2605) [D] r/w/bl	USAF 351st ARS/100th ARW, RAF Mildenhall, UK
	72606	Boeing KC-135R Stratotanker (57-2606) y/bk	USAF 174th ARS/185th ARW, Sioux City, IA ANG
	80001	Boeing KC-135R Stratotanker (58-0001)	USAF 92nd ARW, Fairchild AFB, WA
	80004	Boeing KC-135R Stratotanker (58-0004) w/r	USAF 106th ARS/117th ARW, Birmingham, AL ANG
	80009	Boeing KC-135R Stratotanker (58-0009) w/bl	USAF 126th ARS/128th ARW, Mitchell Field, WI ANG
	80010	Boeing KC-135R Stratotanker (58-0010) r	USAF 141st ARS/108th ARW, McGuire AFB, NJ ANG
	80011	Boeing KC-135R(RT) Stratotanker (58-0011)	USAF 22nd ARW, McConnell AFB, KS
	80015	Boeing KC-135R Stratotanker (58-0015) bl/y	USAF 465th ARS/507th ARW AFRC, Tinker AFB, OK
	80016	Boeing KC-135R Stratotanker (58-0016)	USAF 92nd ARW, Fairchild AFB, WA
	80018	Boeing KC-135R(RT) Stratotanker (58-0018)	USAF 22nd ARW, McConnell AFB, KS
	80021	Boeing KC-135R Stratotanker (58-0021) w/gn	USAF 132nd ARS/101st ARW, Bangor, MN ANG
	80023	Boeing KC-135R Stratotanker (58-0023) w/bl	USAF 108th ARS/126th ARW, Scott AFB, IL ANG
	80027	Boeing KC-135R Stratotanker (58-0027) bl/bk	USAF 191st ARS/151st ARW, Salt Lake City, UT ANG
	80030	Boeing KC-135R Stratotanker (58-0030) w/gn	USAF 132nd ARS/101st ARW, Bangor, MN ANG
	80034	Boeing KC-135R Stratotanker (58-0034) y/bl	USAF 91st ARS/6th AMW, MacDill AFB, FL
	80035	Boeing KC-135R Stratotanker (58-0035)	USAF 92nd ARW, Fairchild AFB, WA
	80036	Boeing KC-135R Stratotanker (58-0036) y/r	USAF 54th ARS/97th AMW, Altus AFB, OK

Serial	Type (code/other identity)	Owner/operator, location or fate	Notes
80038	Boeing KC-135R Stratotanker (58-0038) *gn/y*	USAF 77th ARS/916th ARW AFRC, Seymour Johnson AFB, NC	
80042	Boeing KC-135T Stratotanker (58-0042)	USAF 22nd ARW, McConnell AFB, KS	
80045	Boeing KC-135T Stratotanker (58-0045)	USAF 171st ARW, Greater Pittsburgh, PA ANG	
80046	Boeing KC-135T Stratotanker (58-0046)	USAF 22nd ARW, McConnell AFB, KS	
80047	Boeing KC-135T Stratotanker (58-0047)	USAF 22nd ARW, McConnell AFB, KS	
80049	Boeing KC-135T Stratotanker (58-0049) *bk/y*	USAF 171st ARS/127th Wg, Selfridge ANGB, MI ANG	
80050	Boeing KC-135T Stratotanker (58-0050)	USAF 92nd ARW, Fairchild AFB, WA	
80051	Boeing KC-135R Stratotanker (58-0051) *bl/y*	USAF 465th ARS/507th ARW AFRC, Tinker AFB, OK	
80052	Boeing KC-135R Stratotanker (58-0052) *or/y*	USAF 336th ARS/452nd AMW AFRC, March ARB, CA	
80054	Boeing KC-135T Stratotanker (58-0054) *y/bk*	USAF 171st ARW, Greater Pittsburgh, PA ANG	
80055	Boeing KC-135T Stratotanker (58-0055) *y/bl*	USAF 91st ARS/6th AMW, MacDill AFB, FL	
80056	Boeing KC-135R Stratotanker (58-0056) [HH] *y/bk*	USAF 203rd ARS/15th Wg, Hickam AFB, HI ANG	
80057	Boeing KC-135R Stratotanker (58-0057) *y/bk*	USAF 174th ARS/185th ARW, Sioux City, IA ANG	
80058	Boeing KC-135R Stratotanker (58-0058) *bl/y*	USAF 465th ARS/507th ARW AFRC, Tinker AFB, OK	
80059	Boeing KC-135R Stratotanker (58-0059) *bl/y*	USAF 117th ARS/190th ARW, Forbes Field, KS ANG	
80060	Boeing KC-135T Stratotanker (58-0060) *y/bk*	USAF 171st ARW, Greater Pittsburgh, PA ANG	
80061	Boeing KC-135T Stratotanker (58-0061)	USAF 22nd ARW, McConnell AFB, KS	
80062	Boeing KC-135T Stratotanker (58-0062) *bk/y*	USAF 171st ARS/127th Wg, Selfridge ANGB, MI ANG	
80063	Boeing KC-135R Stratotanker (58-0063) *bl*	USAF 133rd ARS/157th ARW, Pease ANGB, NH ANG	
80065	Boeing KC-135T Stratotanker (58-0065)	USAF 22nd ARW, McConnell AFB, KS	
80066	Boeing KC-135R Stratotanker (58-0066) *bl*	USAF 133rd ARS/157th ARW, Pease ANGB, NH ANG	
80067	Boeing KC-135R Stratotanker (58-0067) *y/bk*	USAF 174th ARS/185th ARW, Sioux City, IA ANG	
80069	Boeing KC-135T Stratotanker (58-0069) [D] *r/w/bl*	USAF 351st ARS/100th ARW, RAF Mildenhall, UK	
80071	Boeing KC-135T Stratotanker (58-0071)	USAF 22nd ARW, McConnell AFB, KS	
80072	Boeing KC-135T Stratotanker (58-0072) *y/bk*	USAF 171st ARW, Greater Pittsburgh, PA ANG	
80073	Boeing KC-135R Stratotanker (58-0073) *w/r*	USAF 106th ARS/117th ARW, Birmingham, AL ANG	
80074	Boeing KC-135T Stratotanker (58-0074) *y/bk*	USAF 171st ARW, Greater Pittsburgh, PA ANG	
80075	Boeing KC-135R Stratotanker (58-0075) *y/bk*	USAF 756th ARS/459th ARW AFRC, Andrews AFB, MD	
80076	Boeing KC-135R Stratotanker (58-0076) *r/w*	USAF 74th ARS/434th ARW AFRC, Grissom AFB, IN	
80077	Boeing KC-135T Stratotanker (58-0077) *y/bk*	USAF 171st ARW, Greater Pittsburgh, PA ANG	
80079	Boeing KC-135R Stratotanker (58-0079)	USAF 153rd ARS/186th AW, Meridian, MS ANG	
80083	Boeing KC-135R Stratotanker (58-0083) *r/w*	USAF 166th ARS/121st ARW, Rickenbacker ANGB, OH ANG	
80084	Boeing KC-135T Stratotanker (58-0084) *y/bk*	USAF 171st ARW, Greater Pittsburgh, PA ANG	
80085	Boeing KC-135R Stratotanker (58-0085) *or/y*	USAF 336th ARS/452nd AMW AFRC, March ARB, CA	
80086	Boeing KC-135T Stratotanker (58-0086)	USAF 92nd ARW, Fairchild AFB, WA	
80088	Boeing KC-135T Stratotanker (58-0088) *bk/y*	USAF 171st ARS/127th Wg, Selfridge ANGB, MI ANG	
80089	Boeing KC-135T Stratotanker (58-0089) *y/bl*	USAF 91st ARS/6th AMW, MacDill AFB, FL	
80092	Boeing KC-135R Stratotanker (58-0092)	USAF 22nd ARW, McConnell AFB, KS	
80093	Boeing KC-135R Stratotanker (58-0093) [ZZ] *or/bk*	USAF 909th ARS/18th Wg, Kadena AB, Japan	
80094	Boeing KC-135T Stratotanker (58-0094) [D] *r/w/bl*	USAF 351st ARS/100th ARW, RAF Mildenhall, UK	
80095	Boeing KC-135T Stratotanker (58-0095)	USAF 92nd ARW, Fairchild AFB, WA	
80098	Boeing KC-135R Stratotanker (58-0098) *w/gn*	USAF 132nd ARS/101st ARW, Bangor, MN ANG	
80099	Boeing KC-135T Stratotanker (58-0099) *y/bk*	USAF 171st ARW, Greater Pittsburgh, PA ANG	
80100	Boeing KC-135R Stratotanker (58-0100) [D] *r/w/bl*	USAF 351st ARS/100th ARW, RAF Mildenhall, UK	

Notes	Serial	Type (code/other identity)	Owner/operator, location or fate
	80102	Boeing KC-135R Stratotanker (58-0102) *bl/y*	USAF 465th ARS/507th ARW AFRC, Tinker AFB, OK
	80103	Boeing KC-135T Stratotanker (58-0103) *y/bl*	USAF 91st ARS/6th AMW, MacDill AFB, FL
	80104	Boeing KC-135R Stratotanker (58-0104) *w/bl*	USAF 108th ARS/126th ARW, Scott AFB, IL ANG
	80106	Boeing KC-135R Stratotanker (58-0106) *w/r*	USAF 106th ARS/117th ARW, Birmingham, AL ANG
	80107	Boeing KC-135R Stratotanker (58-0107) *w/gn*	USAF 132nd ARS/101st ARW, Bangor, MN ANG
	80109	Boeing KC-135R Stratotanker (58-0109) *y/bk*	USAF 174th ARS/185th ARW, Sioux City, IA ANG
	80112	Boeing KC-135T Stratotanker (58-0112) *y/bk*	USAF 171st ARW, Greater Pittsburgh, PA ANG
	80113	Boeing KC-135T Stratotanker (58-0113) *y/r*	USAF 54th ARS/97th AMW, Altus AFB, OK
	80117	Boeing KC-135T Stratotanker (58-0117) *y/bk*	USAF 171st ARW, Greater Pittsburgh, PA ANG
	80118	Boeing KC-135R Stratotanker (58-0118) [D] *r/w/bl*	USAF 351st ARS/100th ARW, RAF Mildenhall, UK
	80119	Boeing KC-135R Stratotanker (58-0119) *w/or*	USAF 151st ARS/134th ARW, Knoxville, TN ANG
	80120	Boeing KC-135R Stratotanker (58-0120)	USAF 153rd ARS/186th AW, Meridian, MS ANG
	80121	Boeing KC-135R Stratotanker (58-0121) *bl/y*	USAF 465th ARS/507th ARW AFRC, Tinker AFB, OK
	80122	Boeing KC-135R Stratotanker (58-0122) *bl/y*	USAF 117th ARS/190th ARW, Forbes Field, KS ANG
	80123	Boeing KC-135R Stratotanker (58-0123)	USAF 22nd ARW, McConnell AFB, KS
	80124	Boeing KC-135R(RT) Stratotanker (58-0124)	USAF 22nd ARW, McConnell AFB, KS
	80125	Boeing KC-135T Stratotanker (58-0125)	USAF 92nd ARW, Fairchild AFB, WA
	80126	Boeing KC-135R(RT) Stratotanker (58-0126)	USAF 22nd ARW, McConnell AFB, KS
	80128	Boeing KC-135R Stratotanker (58-0128) [ZZ] *or/bk*	USAF 909th ARS/18th Wg, Kadena AB, Japan
	80129	Boeing KC-135T Stratotanker (58-0129) *bk/y*	USAF 171st ARS/127th Wg, Selfridge ANGB, MI ANG
	91444	Boeing KC-135R Stratotanker (59-1444) *r/w*	USAF 166th ARS/121st ARW, Rickenbacker ANGB, OH ANG
	91446	Boeing KC-135R Stratotanker (59-1446) *w/gn*	USAF 132nd ARS/101st ARW, Bangor, MN ANG
	91448	Boeing KC-135R Stratotanker (59-1448)	USAF 153rd ARS/186th AW, Meridian, MS ANG
	91450	Boeing KC-135R Stratotanker (59-1450)	USAF 197th ARS/161st ARW, Phoenix, AZ ANG
	91453	Boeing KC-135R Stratotanker (59-1453)	USAF 153rd ARS/186th AW, Meridian, MS ANG
	91455	Boeing KC-135R Stratotanker (59-1455) [HH] *y/bk*	USAF 203rd ARS/15th Wg, Hickam AFB, HI ANG
	91458	Boeing KC-135R Stratotanker (59-1458) *r/w*	USAF 166th ARS/121st ARW, Rickenbacker ANGB, OH ANG
	91459	Boeing KC-135R Stratotanker (59-1459)	USAF 22nd ARW, McConnell AFB, KS
	91460	Boeing KC-135T Stratotanker (59-1460) *y/bk*	USAF 171st ARW, Greater Pittsburgh, PA ANG
	91461	Boeing KC-135R Stratotanker (59-1461) *w/bl*	USAF 126th ARS/128th ARW, Mitchell Field, WI ANG
	91462	Boeing KC-135T Stratotanker (59-1462) *y/bl*	USAF 91st ARS/6th AMW, MacDill AFB, FL
	91463	Boeing KC-135R Stratotanker (59-1463) *r/w*	USAF 173rd ARS/155th ARW, Lincoln, NE ANG
	91464	Boeing KC-135T Stratotanker (59-1464)	USAF 22nd ARW, McConnell AFB, KS
	91466	Boeing KC-135R Stratotanker (59-1466) *w/bl*	USAF 108th ARS/126th ARW, Scott AFB, IL ANG
	91467	Boeing KC-135T Stratotanker (59-1467) *y/bk*	USAF 171st ARW, Greater Pittsburgh, PA ANG
	91468	Boeing KC-135T Stratotanker (59-1468) *y/bk*	USAF 171st ARW, Greater Pittsburgh, PA ANG
	91469	Boeing KC-135R Stratotanker (59-1469) *y/bk*	USAF 756th ARS/459th ARW AFRC, Andrews AFB, MD
	91470	Boeing KC-135T Stratotanker (59-1470)	USAF 92nd ARW, Fairchild AFB, WA
	91471	Boeing KC-135T Stratotanker (59-1471) [D] *r/w/bl*	USAF 351st ARS/100th ARW, RAF Mildenhall, UK
	91472	Boeing KC-135R Stratotanker (59-1472)	USAF 314th ARS/940th ARW, Beale AFB, CA
	91474	Boeing KC-135T Stratotanker (59-1474) *bk/y*	USAF 171st ARS/127th Wg, Selfridge ANGB, MI ANG
	91475	Boeing KC-135R Stratotanker (59-1475)	USAF 22nd ARW, McConnell AFB, KS
	91476	Boeing KC-135R Stratotanker (59-1476)	USAF 92nd ARW, Fairchild AFB, WA

Serial	Type (code/other identity)	Owner/operator, location or fate	Notes
91478	Boeing KC-135R Stratotanker (59-1478) w/or	USAF 151st ARS/134th ARW, Knoxville, TN ANG	
91480	Boeing KC-135T Stratotanker (59-1480) y/bl	USAF 91st ARS/6th AMW, MacDill AFB, FL	
91482	Boeing KC-135R Stratotanker (59-1482) or/y	USAF 336th ARS/452nd AMW AFRC, March ARB, CA	
91483	Boeing KC-135R Stratotanker (59-1483) r/w	USAF 166th ARS/121st ARW, Rickenbacker ANGB, OH ANG	
91486	Boeing KC-135R Stratotanker (59-1486)	USAF 92nd ARW, Fairchild AFB, WA	
91488	Boeing KC-135R Stratotanker (59-1488) w/gn	USAF 132nd ARS/101st ARW, Bangor, MN ANG	
91490	Boeing KC-135T Stratotanker (59-1490) y/bk	USAF 171st ARW, Greater Pittsburgh, PA ANG	
91492	Boeing KC-135R Stratotanker (59-1492)	USAF 22nd ARW, McConnell AFB, KS	
91495	Boeing KC-135R Stratotanker (59-1495) r/w	USAF 173rd ARS/155th ARW, Lincoln, NE ANG	
91498	Boeing KC-135R Stratotanker (59-1498) w/gn	USAF 132nd ARS/101st ARW, Bangor, MN ANG	
91499	Boeing KC-135R Stratotanker (59-1499) [HH] y/bk	USAF 203rd ARS/15th Wg, Hickam AFB, HI ANG	
91500	Boeing KC-135R Stratotanker (59-1500) w/bl	USAF 108th ARS/126th ARW, Scott AFB, IL ANG	
91501	Boeing KC-135R Stratotanker (59-1501) y/bl	USAF 91st ARS/6th AMW, MacDill AFB, FL	
91502	Boeing KC-135R Stratotanker (59-1502)	USAF 22nd ARW, McConnell AFB, KS	
91504	Boeing KC-135T Stratotanker (59-1504) y/bk	USAF 171st ARW, Greater Pittsburgh, PA ANG	
91505	Boeing KC-135R Stratotanker (59-1505) w/or	USAF 151st ARS/134th ARW, Knoxville, TN ANG	
91506	Boeing KC-135R Stratotanker (59-1506) y/bk	USAF 174th ARS/185th ARW, Sioux City, IA ANG	
91507	Boeing KC-135R Stratotanker (59-1507) bl/y	USAF 117th ARS/190th ARW, Forbes Field, KS ANG	
91508	Boeing KC-135R Stratotanker (59-1508)	USAF 92nd ARW, Fairchild AFB, WA	
91509	Boeing KC-135R Stratotanker (59-1509) w/or	USAF 151st ARS/134th ARW, Knoxville, TN ANG	
91510	Boeing KC-135T Stratotanker (59-1510)y/bl	USAF 91st ARS/6th AMW, MacDill AFB, FL	
91511	Boeing KC-135R Stratotanker (59-1511)	USAF 22nd ARW, McConnell AFB, KS	
91512	Boeing KC-135T Stratotanker (59-1512) bk/y	USAF 171st ARS/127th Wg, Selfridge ANGB, MI ANG	
91513	Boeing KC-135T Stratotanker (59-1513)	USAF	
91515	Boeing KC-135R Stratotanker (59-1515)	USAF 92nd ARW, Fairchild AFB, WA	
91516	Boeing KC-135R Stratotanker (59-1516) w/bl	USAF 126th ARS/128th ARW, Mitchell Field, WI ANG	
91517	Boeing KC-135R Stratotanker (59-1517) w/or	USAF 151st ARS/134th ARW, Knoxville, TN ANG	
91519	Boeing KC-135R Stratotanker (59-1519) y/bk	USAF 174th ARS/185th ARW, Sioux City, IA ANG	
91520	Boeing KC-135T Stratotanker (59-1520)	USAF 92nd ARW, Fairchild AFB, WA	
91521	Boeing KC-135R Stratotanker (59-1521) [AK] bl/y	USAF 168th ARS/168th ARW, Eielson AFB, AK ANG	
91522	Boeing KC-135R Stratotanker (59-1522) w/bl	USAF 108th ARS/126th ARW, Scott AFB, IL ANG	
91523	Boeing KC-135T Stratotanker (59-1523) y/bk	USAF 171st ARW, Greater Pittsburgh, PA ANG	

PZL-Mielec C-145A Combat Coyote

20331	PZL-Mielec C-145A Combat Coyote (N331MF/12-0331)	USAF 6th SOS/919th SOW, Duke Field, FL	
20335	PZL-Mielec C-145A Combat Coyote (N335RH/12-0335)	USAF 6th SOS/919th SOW, Duke Field, FL	
20336	PZL-Mielec C-145A Combat Coyote (N336MJ/12-0336)	USAF 6th SOS/919th SOW, Duke Field, FL	
20337	PZL-Mielec C-145A Combat Coyote (N337GU/12-0337)	USAF 6th SOS/919th SOW, Duke Field, FL	
20338	PZL-Mielec C-145A Combat Coyote (N338CH/12-0338)	USAF 6th SOS/919th SOW, Duke Field, FL	

Dornier C-146A Wolfhound

03026	Dornier C-146A Wolfhound (N929EF/10-3026)	USAF 524th SOS/27th SOW, Cannon AFB, NM	
03068	Dornier C-146A Wolfhound (N565EF/10-3068)	USAF 524th SOS/27th SOW, Cannon AFB, NM	
03077	Dornier C-146A Wolfhound (N577EF/10-3077)	USAF 524th SOS/27th SOW, Cannon AFB, NM	
13016	Dornier C-146A Wolfhound (N941EF/11-3016)	USAF 524th SOS/27th SOW, Cannon AFB, NM	
13031	Dornier C-146A Wolfhound (N975EF/11-3031)	USAF 524th SOS/27th SOW, Cannon AFB, NM	
13075	Dornier C-146A Wolfhound (N953EF/11-3075)	USAF 524th SOS/27th SOW, Cannon AFB, NM	
13097	Dornier C-146A Wolfhound (N307EF/11-3097)	USAF 524th SOS/27th SOW, Cannon AFB, NM	

Notes	Serial	Type (code/other identity)	Owner/operator, location or fate
	13104	Dornier C-146A Wolfhound (N907EF/11-3104)	USAF 524th SOS/27th SOW, Cannon AFB, NM
	23040	Dornier C-146A Wolfhound (N340LS/12-3040)	USAF 524th SOS/27th SOW, Cannon AFB, NM
	23047	Dornier C-146A Wolfhound (N347EF/12-3047)	USAF 524th SOS/27th SOW, Cannon AFB, NM
	23050	Dornier C-146A Wolfhound (N355EF/12-3050)	USAF 524th SOS/27th SOW, Cannon AFB, NM
	23060	Dornier C-146A Wolfhound (N360EF/12-3060)	USAF 524th SOS/27th SOW, Cannon AFB, NM
	23085	Dornier C-146A Wolfhound (N385EF/12-3085)	USAF 49th SOS/919th SOW, Duke Field, FL
	53058	Dornier C-146A Wolfhound (N570EF/95-3058)	USAF 524th SOS/27th SOW, Cannon AFB, NM
	53086	Dornier C-146A Wolfhound (N328ST/15-3086)	USAF 524th SOS/27th SOW, Cannon AFB, NM
	63020	Dornier C-146A Wolfhound (N524AW/16-3020)	USAF 524th SOS/27th SOW, Cannon AFB, NM
	63025	Dornier C-146A Wolfhound (N250BG/16-3025)	USAF 524th SOS/27th SOW, Cannon AFB, NM
	73091	Dornier C-146A Wolfhound (N391EF/97-3091)	USAF 524th SOS/27th SOW, Cannon AFB, NM
	73093	Dornier C-146A Wolfhound (N545EF/97-3093)	USAF 524th SOS/27th SOW, Cannon AFB, NM
	93106	Dornier C-146A Wolfhound (N525EF/99-3106)	USAF 524th SOS/27th SOW, Cannon AFB, NM

Notes	Serial	Type (code/other identity)	Owner/operator, location or fate
	150521	Lockheed NP-3D Orion [521]	USN VX-30, NAS Point Mugu, CA
	153442	Lockheed NP-3D Orion [357]	USN VX-30, NAS Point Mugu, CA
	156507	Lockheed EP-3E ARIES II [507]	*To AMARG, July 2016*
	156510	Lockheed P-3C-IIIR Orion [LL-510]	*To AMARG, July 2016*
	156511	Lockheed EP-3E ARIES II [511]	USN VQ-1, NAS Whidbey Island, WA
	156514	Lockheed EP-3E ARIES II [514]	*To AMARG, April 2016*
	156515	Lockheed P-3C CDU Orion [LL-515]	USN VP-30, NAS Jacksonville, FL
	156517	Lockheed EP-3E ARIES II [517]	USN VQ-1, NAS Whidbey Island, WA
	156528	Lockheed EP-3E ARIES II [528]	USN VQ-1, NAS Whidbey Island, WA
	156529	Lockheed EP-3E ARIES II [529]	USN VQ-1, NAS Whidbey Island, WA
	157316	Lockheed EP-3E ARIES II [316]	USN VQ-1, NAS Whidbey Island, WA
	157318	Lockheed EP-3E ARIES II [318]	USN VQ-1, NAS Whidbey Island, WA
	157325	Lockheed EP-3E ARIES II [325]	USN VQ-1, NAS Whidbey Island, WA
	157326	Lockheed EP-3E ARIES II [326]	USN VQ-1, NAS Whidbey Island, WA
	157331	Lockheed P-3C AIP+ Orion [331]	*To AMARG, May 2016*
	158204	Lockheed NP-3C Orion [RL-204]	*To AMARG, November 2016*
	158210	Lockheed P-3C AIP+ Orion [RC-210]	USN VP-46, NAS Whidbey Island, WA
	158215	Lockheed P-3C AIP Orion [215]	USN VP-1, NAS Whidbey Island, WA
	158222	Lockheed P-3C AIP+ Orion [YD-222]	USN VP-4, MCBH Kaneohe Bay, HI
	158224	Lockheed P-3C AIP+ Orion [YD-224]	USN VP-4, MCBH Kaneohe Bay, HI
	158225	Lockheed P-3C AIP Orion [225]	USN VP-30, NAS Jacksonville, FL
	158227	Lockheed NP-3D Orion [300]	USN VX-30, NAS Point Mugu, CA
	158563	Lockheed P-3C AIP+ Orion [PD-563]	USN VP-9, MCBH Kaneohe Bay, HI
	158564	Lockheed P-3C AIP+ Orion [564]	USN VP-47, MCBH Kaneohe Bay, HI
	158567	Lockheed P-3C AIP+ Orion [PD-567]	USN VP-9, MCBH Kaneohe Bay, HI
	158570	Lockheed P-3C-IIIR Orion [RL-570]	USN VXS-1, Patuxent River, MD
	158571	Lockheed P-3C AIP+ Orion [YB-571]	*To AMARG, March 2016*
	158573	Lockheed P-3C AIP+ Orion [YD-573]	*To AMARG, July 2016*
	158574	Lockheed P-3C-IIIR Orion	USN NASC-FS, Point Mugu, CA
	158912	Lockheed NP-3C Orion [RL-912]	USN VXS-1, Patuxent River, MD
	158914	Lockheed P-3C-IIIR Orion [914]	USN VPU-2, MCBH Kaneohe Bay, HI
	158917	Lockheed P-3C-IIIR Orion [917]	*To AMARG, October 2016*
	158919	Lockheed P-3C AIP Orion [919]	*To AMARG, October 2016*
	158922	Lockheed P-3C AIP Orion [922]	USN VP-9, MCBH Kaneohe Bay, HI
	158926	Lockheed P-3C-IIIR Orion [305]	*To AMARG, December 2016*
	158934	Lockheed P-3C AIP+ Orion [934]	USN VP-40, NAS Whidbey Island, WA
	158935	Lockheed P-3C-IIIR Orion [935]	*To AMARG, June 2016*
	159323	Lockheed P-3C AIP+ Orion [323]	*To AMARG, August 2016*
	159326	Lockheed P-3C AIP+ Orion [326]	USN VP-1, NAS Whidbey Island, WA

Serial	Type (code/other identity)	Owner/operator, location or fate	Notes
159504	Lockheed P-3CSPA Orion	USN VPU-2, MCBH Kaneohe Bay, HI	
159887	Lockheed EP-3E ARIES II [887]	USN VQ-1, NAS Whidbey Island, WA	
159893	Lockheed EP-3E ARIES II [893]	USN VQ-1, NAS Whidbey Island, WA	
159894	Lockheed P-3C AIP+ Orion [894]	USN VP-30, NAS Jacksonville, FL	
160287	Lockheed P-3C AIP+ Orion [YD-287]	USN VP-4, MCBH Kaneohe Bay, HI	
160290	Lockheed P-3CSPA Orion [290]	USN VPU-2, MCBH Kaneohe Bay, HI	
160292	Lockheed P-3CSPA Orion [292]	USN VPU-2, MCBH Kaneohe Bay, HI	
160293	Lockheed P-3C BMUP Orion	USN NASC-FS, Point Mugu, CA	
160610	Lockheed P-3C AIP+ Orion [YD-610]	USN VP-4, MCBH Kaneohe Bay, HI	
160625	Lockheed KC-130R Hercules [625]	*Sold to Chile, May 2016*	
160627	Lockheed KC-130R Hercules [627]	USN VX-20, Patuxent River, MD	
160761	Lockheed P-3C AIP+ Orion [761]	*To AMARG, December 2016*	
160764	Lockheed EP-3E ARIES II [764]	USN VQ-1, NAS Whidbey Island, WA	
160999	Lockheed P-3C-II Orion [999]	*Withdrawn from use, 2015*	
161011	Lockheed P-3C AIP+ Orion [011]	*Scrapped, 2016*	
161012	Lockheed P-3C AIP+ Orion [RD-012]	USN VP-47, MCBH Kaneohe Bay, HI	
161121	Lockheed P-3C BMUP+ Orion [RC-121]	USN VP-46, NAS Whidbey Island, WA	
161122	Lockheed P-3CSPA Orion [226]	USN VPU-2, MCBH Kaneohe Bay, HI	
161124	Lockheed P-3C AIP+ Orion [JA-124]	*To AMARG, July 2016*	
161126	Lockheed P-3C BMUP+ Orion [126]	USN VP-40, NAS Whidbey Island, WA	
161127	Lockheed P-3C BMUP Orion [127]	USN VP-69, NAS Whidbey Island, WA	
161129	Lockheed P-3C BMUP Orion [129]	USN VXS-1, Patuxent River, MD	
161132	Lockheed P-3C BMUP+ Orion [132]	USN VP-46, NAS Whidbey Island, WA	
161333	Lockheed P-3C AIP+ Orion [333]	USN VP-62, NAS Jacksonville, FL	
161337	Lockheed P-3C-II½ Orion [337]	USN VP-47, MCBH Kaneohe Bay, HI	
161339	Lockheed P-3C BMUP Orion [RC-339]	USN VP-46, NAS Whidbey Island, WA	
161404	Lockheed P-3C BMUP+ Orion [YB-404]	USN VP-1, NAS Whidbey Island, WA	
161405	Lockheed P-3C BMUP+ Orion [405]	USN VP-69, NAS Whidbey Island, WA	
161406	Lockheed P-3C AIP+ Orion [PD-406]	USN VP-9, MCBH Kaneohe Bay, HI	
161407	Lockheed P-3C AIP+ Orion [407]	USN VP-47, MCBH Kaneohe Bay, HI	
161408	Lockheed P-3C BMUP+ Orion [408]	USN VP-1, NAS Whidbey Island, WA	
161410	Lockheed EP-3E ARIES II [410]	USN VQ-1, NAS Whidbey Island, WA	
161411	Lockheed P-3C BMUP+ Orion [411]	USN VP-69, NAS Whidbey Island, WA	
161412	Lockheed P-3C BMUP+ Orion [306]	USN VX-30, NAS Point Mugu, CA	
161413	Lockheed P-3C AIP+ Orion [RD-413]	USN VP-47, MCBH Kaneohe Bay, HI	
161414	Lockheed P-3C BMUP+ Orion [RC-414]	USN VP-46, NAS Whidbey Island, WA	
161415	Lockheed P-3C BMUP+ Orion [415]	USN VP-62, NAS Jacksonville, FL	
161529	McDD C-9B Skytrain II	USMC VMR-1, Fort Worth JRB, TX	
161530	McDD C-9B Skytrain II	USMC VMR-1, Fort Worth JRB, TX	
161586	Lockheed P-3C BMUP+ Orion [QE-586]	USN VP-40, NAS Whidbey Island, WA	
161587	Lockheed P-3C BMUP+ Orion [587]	USN VP-1, NAS Whidbey Island, WA	
161588	Lockheed P-3C BMUP+ Orion [588]	USN VP-46, NAS Whidbey Island, WA	
161589	Lockheed P-3C BMUP+ Orion [589]	USN VP-40, NAS Whidbey Island, WA	
161590	Lockheed P-3C BMUP+ Orion [590]	USN VP-30, NAS Jacksonville, FL	
161593	Lockheed P-3C BMUP+ Orion [593]	USN VP-1, NAS Whidbey Island, WA	
161594	Lockheed P-3C AIP+ Orion [594]	USN VP-9, MCBH Kaneohe Bay, HI	
161596	Lockheed P-3C-II½ Orion [596]	USN VP-40, NAS Whidbey Island, WA	
161764	Lockheed P-3C AIP+ Orion [764]	USN VP-40, NAS Whidbey Island, WA	
161766	Lockheed P-3C AIP Orion [RC-766]	USN VP-46, NAS Whidbey Island, WA	
161767	Lockheed P-3C AIP+ Orion [RC-767]	*To AMARG, September 2016*	
162308	Lockheed KC-130T Hercules [308]	USN VX-20, Patuxent River, MD	
162309	Lockheed KC-130T Hercules [406]	USN VX-30, NAS Point Mugu, CA	
162310	Lockheed KC-130T Hercules [309]	USN VX-20, Patuxent River, MD	
162311	Lockheed KC-130T Hercules [QH-405]	USMC VMGR-234, Fort Worth JRB, TX	
162314	Lockheed P-3C AIP+ Orion [RC-314]	*To AMARG, September 2016*	
162315	Lockheed P-3C AIP+ Orion [315]	*To AMARG, September 2016*	
162316	Lockheed P-3C AIP+ Orion [316]	USN VP-62, NAS Jacksonville, FL	
162317	Lockheed P-3C AIP+ Orion [317]	USN VP-30, NAS Jacksonville, FL	
162318	Lockheed P-3C AIP+ Orion [318]	USN VP-1, NAS Whidbey Island, WA	
162770	Lockheed P-3C AIP+ Orion [770]	USN VP-30, NAS Jacksonville, FL	
162771	Lockheed P-3C AIP+ Orion [771]	USN VP-4, MCBH Kaneohe Bay, HI	
162772	Lockheed P-3C AIP+ Orion [772]	USN VP-40, NAS Whidbey Island, WA	

Notes	Serial	Type (code/other identity)	Owner/operator, location or fate
	162773	Lockheed P-3C AIP+ Orion [YD-773]	USN VP-4, MCBH Kaneohe Bay, HI
	162775	Lockheed P-3C AIP+ Orion [RD-775]	USN VP-47, MCBH Kaneohe Bay, HI
	162776	Lockheed P-3C AIP+ Orion [776]	USN VP-40, NAS Whidbey Island, WA
	162777	Lockheed P-3C AIP+ Orion [777]	USN VP-40, NAS Whidbey Island, WA
	162778	Lockheed P-3C AIP+ Orion [PD-778]	USN VP-9, MCBH Kaneohe Bay, HI
	162782	Boeing E-6B Mercury	USN VQ-3/SCW-1, Tinker AFB, OK
	162783	Boeing E-6B Mercury	USN VQ-3/SCW-1, Tinker AFB, OK
	162784	Boeing E-6B Mercury	USN VQ-4/SCW-1, Tinker AFB, OK
	162998	Lockheed P-3C AIP+ Orion [RC-998]	USN VP-46, NAS Whidbey Island, WA
	162999	Lockheed P-3C AIP+ Orion [RC-999]	USN VP-46, NAS Whidbey Island, WA
	163000	Lockheed P-3C AIP+ Orion [000]	USN VP-30, NAS Jacksonville, FL
	163001	Lockheed P-3C AIP+ Orion [001]	USN
	163002	Lockheed P-3C AIP+ Orion [002]	*To AMARG, August 2016*
	163003	Lockheed P-3C AIP+ Orion [PD-003]	*To AMARG, February 2016*
	163004	Lockheed P-3C AIP+ Orion [004]	USN VP-69, NAS Whidbey Island, WA
	163006	Lockheed P-3C AIP Orion [YB-006]	*To AMARG, June 2016*
	163023	Lockheed KC-130T Hercules [404]	USN VX-30, NAS Point Mugu, CA
	163289	Lockheed P-3C AIP+ Orion [289]	*To AMARG, January 2017*
	163290	Lockheed P-3C AIP+ Orion [290]	USN VP-30, NAS Jacksonville, FL
	163291	Lockheed P-3C AIP+ Orion [291]	USN VP-1, NAS Whidbey Island, WA
	163293	Lockheed P-3C AIP+ Orion [293]	USN VP-30, NAS Jacksonville, FL
	163294	Lockheed P-3C AIP+ Orion [303]	USN VX-30, NAS Point Mugu, CA
	163295	Lockheed P-3C AIP+ Orion [295]	USN VP-1, NAS Whidbey Island, WA
	163310	Lockheed KC-130T Hercules [3310]	USN VX-20, Patuxent River, MD
	163311	Lockheed KC-130T Hercules [RU-3311]	USN VR-55, NAS Point Mugu, CA
	163591	Lockheed KC-130T Hercules [RU-591]	USN VR-55, NAS Point Mugu, CA
	163592	Lockheed KC-130T Hercules [NY-592]	USMC VMGR-452, Stewart Field, NY
	163691	Grumman C-20D Gulfstream III	USN VR-1, NAF Washington, MD
	163692	Grumman C-20D Gulfstream III	USN VR-1, NAF Washington, MD
	163918	Boeing E-6B Mercury	USN VQ-3/SCW-1, Tinker AFB, OK
	163919	Boeing E-6B Mercury	USN VQ-3/SCW-1, Tinker AFB, OK
	163920	Boeing E-6B Mercury	USN VQ-3/SCW-1, Tinker AFB, OK
	164105	Lockheed KC-130T Hercules [NY-105]	USMC VMGR-452, Stewart Field, NY
	164106	Lockheed KC-130T Hercules [RU-106]	USN VR-55, NAS Point Mugu, CA
	164180	Lockheed KC-130T Hercules [NY-180]	USMC VMGR-452, Stewart Field, NY
	164181	Lockheed KC-130T Hercules [NY-181]	USMC VMGR-452, Stewart Field, NY
	164386	Boeing E-6B Mercury	USN VQ-4/SCW-1, Tinker AFB, OK
	164387	Boeing E-6B Mercury	USN VQ-3/SCW-1, Tinker AFB, OK
	164388	Boeing E-6B Mercury	USN VQ-4/SCW-1, Tinker AFB, OK
	164404	Boeing E-6B Mercury	USN VQ-4/SCW-1, Tinker AFB, OK
	164405	Boeing E-6B Mercury	USN VQ-4/SCW-1, Tinker AFB, OK
	164406	Boeing E-6B Mercury	USN VQ-3/SCW-1, Tinker AFB, OK
	164407	Boeing E-6B Mercury	USN VQ-4/SCW-1, Tinker AFB, OK
	164408	Boeing E-6B Mercury	USN VQ-4/SCW-1, Tinker AFB, OK
	164409	Boeing E-6B Mercury	USN VQ-4/SCW-1, Tinker AFB, OK
	164410	Boeing E-6B Mercury	USN VQ-4/SCW-1, Tinker AFB, OK
	164441	Lockheed KC-130T Hercules [NY-441]	USMC VMGR-452, Stewart Field, NY
	164442	Lockheed KC-130T Hercules [NY-4442]	USMC VMGR-452, Stewart Field, NY
	164597	Lockheed KC-130T-30 Hercules [RU-597]	USN VR-55, NAS Point Mugu, CA
	164598	Lockheed KC-130T-30 Hercules [RU-598]	USN VR-55, NAS Point Mugu, CA
	164762	Lockheed C-130T Hercules [CW-762]	USN VR-54, NAS New Orleans, LA
	164763	Lockheed C-130T Hercules	USN *Blue Angels*, Pensacola NAS, FL
	164993	Lockheed C-130T Hercules [BD-993]	USN VR-64, NAS Willow Grove, PA
	164994	Lockheed C-130T Hercules [CW-994]	USN VR-54, NAS New Orleans, LA
	164995	Lockheed C-130T Hercules [AX-995]	USN VR-53, NAF Washington, MD
	164996	Lockheed C-130T Hercules [BD-996]	USN VR-64, NAS Willow Grove, PA
	164997	Lockheed C-130T Hercules [AX-997]	USN VR-53, NAF Washington, MD
	164998	Lockheed C-130T Hercules [AX-998]	USN VR-53, NAF Washington, MD
	164999	Lockheed KC-130T Hercules [NY-999]	USMC VMGR-452, Stewart Field, NY
	165000	Lockheed KC-130T Hercules [NY-000]	USMC VMGR-452, Stewart Field, NY
	165093	Grumman C-20G Gulfstream IV	USN VR-51, MCBH Kaneohe Bay, Hawaii
	165094	Grumman C-20G Gulfstream IV	USN VR-51, MCBH Kaneohe Bay, Hawaii

Serial	Type (code/other identity)	Owner/operator, location or fate	Notes
165151	Grumman C-20G Gulfstream IV	USN CFLSW Det., Sigonella, Italy	
165152	Grumman C-20G Gulfstream IV	USN VR-51, MCBH Kaneohe Bay, Hawaii	
165153	Grumman C-20G Gulfstream IV	USMC VMR-Det, MCBH Kaneohe Bay, HI	
165158	Lockheed C-130T Hercules [CW-158]	USN VR-54, NAS New Orleans, LA	
165159	Lockheed C-130T Hercules [CW-159]	USN VR-54, NAS New Orleans, LA	
165160	Lockheed C-130T Hercules [JW-160]	USN VR-62, NAS Jacksonville, FL	
165161	Lockheed C-130T Hercules [BD-161]	USN VR-64, NAS Willow Grove, PA	
165162	Lockheed KC-130T Hercules [NY-162]	USMC VMGR-452, Stewart Field, NY	
165163	Lockheed KC-130T Hercules [NY-163]	USMC VMGR-452, Stewart Field, NY	
165313	Lockheed C-130T Hercules [JW-313]	USN VR-62, NAS Jacksonville, FL	
165314	Lockheed C-130T Hercules [JW-314]	USN VR-62, NAS Jacksonville, FL	
165315	Lockheed KC-130T Hercules [NY-315]	USMC VMGR-452, Stewart Field, NY	
165316	Lockheed KC-130T Hercules [NY-316]	USMC VMGR-452, Stewart Field, NY	
165348	Lockheed C-130T Hercules [JW-5348]	USN VR-62, NAS Jacksonville, FL	
165349	Lockheed C-130T Hercules [JW-349]	USN VR-62, NAS Jacksonville, FL	
165350	Lockheed C-130T Hercules [AX-350]	USN VR-53, NAF Washington, MD	
165351	Lockheed C-130T Hercules [AX-351]	USN VR-53, NAF Washington, MD	
165352	Lockheed KC-130T Hercules [NY-352]	USMC VMGR-452, Stewart Field, NY	
165353	Lockheed KC-130T Hercules [NY-353]	USMC VMGR-452, Stewart Field, NY	
165378	Lockheed C-130T Hercules [RU-378]	USN VR-55, NAS Point Mugu, CA	
165379	Lockheed C-130T Hercules [BD-379]	USN VR-64, NAS Willow Grove, PA	
165735	Lockheed KC-130J Hercules II [QB-735]	USMC VMGR-352, Miramar MCAS, CA	
165736	Lockheed KC-130J Hercules II [QB-736]	USMC VMGR-352, Miramar MCAS, CA	
165737	Lockheed KC-130J Hercules II [QB-737]	USMC VMGR-352, Miramar MCAS, CA	
165738	Lockheed KC-130J Hercules II [BH-738]	USMC VMGR-252, Cherry Point MCAS, NC	
165739	Lockheed KC-130J Hercules II [QH-739]	USMC VMGR-234, Fort Worth JRB, TX	
165740	Cessna UC-35C Citation V [EZ]	USMC MWHS-4, NAS New Orleans, LA	
165741	Cessna UC-35C Citation V [EZ]	USMC MWHS-4, NAS New Orleans, LA	
165809	Lockheed KC-130J Hercules II [BH-809]	USMC VMGR-252, Cherry Point MCAS, NC	
165810	Lockheed KC-130J Hercules II [BH-810]	USMC VMGR-252, Cherry Point MCAS, NC	
165829	Boeing C-40A Clipper [829]	USN VR-58, NAS Jacksonville, FL	
165830	Boeing C-40A Clipper [830]	USN VR-59, Fort Worth JRB, TX	
165831	Boeing C-40A Clipper [831]	USN VR-59, Fort Worth JRB, TX	
165832	Boeing C-40A Clipper [832]	USN VR-61, Fort Worth JRB, TX	
165833	Boeing C-40A Clipper [833]	USN VR-59, Fort Worth JRB, TX	
165834	Boeing C-40A Clipper [834]	USN VR-58, NAS Jacksonville, FL	
165835	Boeing C-40A Clipper [835]	USN VR-57, NAS North Island, CA	
165836	Boeing C-40A Clipper [836]	USN VR-57, NAS North Island, CA	
165939	Cessna UC-35D Citation V	USMC MWHS-1, Futenma MCAS, Japan	
165957	Lockheed KC-130J Hercules II [QD-957] $	USMC VMGR-152, Iwakuni MCAS, Japan	
166374	Cessna UC-35D Citation V	USMC VMR-2, NAF Washington, MD	
166375	Gulfstream Aerospace C-37A Gulfstream V [365]	USN CFLSW Det, MCBH Kaneohe Bay, HI	
166376	Gulfstream Aerospace C-37B Gulfstream V [376]	USN VR-1, NAF Washington, MD	
166377	Gulfstream Aerospace C-37B Gulfstream V [377]	USN VR-1, NAF Washington, MD	
166378	Gulfstream Aerospace C-37B Gulfstream V [378]	USN VR-1, NAF Washington, MD	
166380	Lockheed KC-130J Hercules II [BH-380]	USMC VMGR-252, Cherry Point MCAS, NC	
166381	Lockheed KC-130J Hercules II [381]	USN VX-20, Patuxent River, MD	
166382	Lockheed KC-130J Hercules II [QB-6382]	USMC VMGR-352, Miramar MCAS, CA	
166472	Lockheed KC-130J Hercules II [BH-472]	USMC VMGR-252, Cherry Point MCAS, NC	
166473	Lockheed KC-130J Hercules II [QH-473]	USMC VMGR-234, Fort Worth JRB, TX	
166474	Cessna UC-35D Citation V	USMC VMR-1, Cherry Point MCAS, NC	
166500	Cessna UC-35D Citation V	USMC MAW-4, Miramar MCAS, CA	
166511	Lockheed KC-130J Hercules II [BH-511]	USMC VMGR-252, Cherry Point MCAS, NC	
166512	Lockheed KC-130J Hercules II [QH-512]	USMC VMGR-234, Fort Worth JRB, TX	
166513	Lockheed KC-130J Hercules II [BH-513]	USMC VMGR-252, Cherry Point MCAS, NC	
166514	Lockheed KC-130J Hercules II [BH-514]	USMC VMGR-252, Cherry Point MCAS, NC	
166693	Boeing C-40A Clipper [693]	USN VR-57, NAS North Island, CA	
166694	Boeing C-40A Clipper [694]	USN VR-56, NAS Oceana, VA	
166695	Boeing C-40A Clipper [695]	USN VR-56, NAS Oceana, VA	
166696	Boeing C-40A Clipper [696]	USN VR-56, NAS Oceana, VA	
166712	Cessna UC-35D Citation V	USMC MWHS-1, Futenma MCAS, Japan	
166713	Cessna UC-35D Citation V	USMC MWHS-1, Futenma MCAS, Japan	

Notes	Serial	Type (code/other identity)	Owner/operator, location or fate
	166714	Cessna UC-35D Citation V [VM]	USMC VMR-2, NAF Washington, MD
	166715	Cessna UC-35D Citation V	USMC VMR-1, Cherry Point MCAS, NC
	166762	Lockheed KC-130J Hercules II [QB-762]	USMC VMGR-352, Miramar MCAS, CA
	166763	Lockheed KC-130J Hercules II [QD-763]	USMC VMGR-152, Iwakuni MCAS, Japan
	166764	Lockheed KC-130J Hercules II [BH-764]	USMC VMGR-252, Cherry Point MCAS, NC
	166765	Lockheed KC-130J Hercules II [QB-765]	USMC VMGR-352, Miramar MCAS, CA
	166766	Cessna UC-35D Citation V	USMC MWHS-1, Futenma MCAS, Japan
	166767	Cessna UC-35D Citation V [VM]	USMC VMR-2, NAF Washington, MD
	167108	Lockheed KC-130J Hercules II [QB-108]	USMC VMGR-352, Miramar MCAS, CA
	167109	Lockheed KC-130J Hercules II [QD-109]	USN VX-20, Patuxent River, MD
	167110	Lockheed KC-130J Hercules II [QB-110]	USMC VMGR-352, Miramar MCAS, CA
	167111	Lockheed KC-130J Hercules II [QH-111]	USMC VMGR-234, Fort Worth JRB, TX
	167112	Lockheed KC-130J Hercules II [BH-112]	USMC VMGR-252, Cherry Point MCAS, NC
	167923	Lockheed KC-130J Hercules II [QD-923]	USMC VMGR-152, Iwakuni MCAS, Japan
	167924	Lockheed KC-130J Hercules II [QB-924]	USMC VMGR-352, Miramar MCAS, CA
	167925	Lockheed KC-130J Hercules II [QD-925]	USMC VMGR-152, Iwakuni MCAS, Japan
	167926	Lockheed KC-130J Hercules II [QD-926]	USMC VMGR-152, Iwakuni MCAS, Japan
	167927	Lockheed KC-130J Hercules II [QD-927]	USMC VMGR-152, Iwakuni MCAS, Japan
	167951	Boeing P-8A Poseidon [951]	USN VX-20, Patuxent River, MD
	167952	Boeing P-8A Poseidon [JA-952]	USN VX-1, NAS Patuxent River, MD
	167953	Boeing P-8A Poseidon [953]	USN VX-20, Patuxent River, MD
	167954	Boeing P-8A Poseidon	Boeing, Renton, WA
	167955	Boeing P-8A Poseidon [JA-955]	USN VX-1, NAS Patuxent River, MD
	167956	Boeing P-8A Poseidon [JA-956]	USN VX-1, NAS Patuxent River, MD
	167981	Lockheed KC-130J Hercules II [QD-981]	USMC VMGR-152, Iwakuni MCAS, Japan
	167982	Lockheed KC-130J Hercules II [QD-982]	USMC VMGR-152, Iwakuni MCAS, Japan
	167983	Lockheed KC-130J Hercules II [QD-983]	USMC VMGR-152, Iwakuni MCAS, Japan
	167984	Lockheed KC-130J Hercules II [QB-984]	USMC VMGR-352, Miramar MCAS, CA
	167985	Lockheed KC-130J Hercules II [QB-7985]	USMC VMGR-352, Miramar MCAS, CA
	168065	Lockheed KC-130J Hercules II [QD-065]	USMC VMGR-152, Iwakuni MCAS, Japan
	168066	Lockheed KC-130J Hercules II [QD-066]	USMC VMGR-152, Iwakuni MCAS, Japan
	168067	Lockheed KC-130J Hercules II [QB-067]	USMC VMGR-352, Miramar MCAS, CA
	168068	Lockheed KC-130J Hercules II [QB-068]	USMC VMGR-352, Miramar MCAS, CA
	168069	Lockheed KC-130J Hercules II [BH-069]	USMC VMGR-252, Cherry Point MCAS, NC
	168070	Lockheed KC-130J Hercules II [BH-070]	USMC VMGR-252, Cherry Point MCAS, NC
	168071	Lockheed KC-130J Hercules II [BH-8071]	USMC VMGR-252, Cherry Point MCAS, NC
	168072	Lockheed KC-130J Hercules II [QB-072]	USMC VMGR-352, Miramar MCAS, CA
	168073	Lockheed KC-130J Hercules II [QH-073]	USMC VMGR-234, Fort Worth JRB, TX
	168074	Lockheed KC-130J Hercules II [QD-074]	USMC VMGR-152, Iwakuni MCAS, Japan
	168075	Lockheed KC-130J Hercules II [QD-075]	USMC VMGR-152, Iwakuni MCAS, Japan
	168428	Boeing P-8A Poseidon [LF-428]	USN VP-16, NAS Jacksonville, FL
	168429	Boeing P-8A Poseidon [429]	USN VP-10, NAS Jacksonville, FL
	168430	Boeing P-8A Poseidon [LK-430]	USN VP-26, NAS Jacksonville, FL
	168431	Boeing P-8A Poseidon [LK-431]	USN VP-26, NAS Jacksonville, FL
	168432	Boeing P-8A Poseidon [LF-432]	USN VP-16, NAS Jacksonville, FL
	168433	Boeing P-8A Poseidon [433]	USN VP-10, NAS Jacksonville, FL
	168434	Boeing P-8A Poseidon [LN-434]	USN VP-45, NAS Jacksonville, FL
	168435	Boeing P-8A Poseidon [LA-435]	USN VP-5, NAS Jacksonville, FL
	168436	Boeing P-8A Poseidon [LA-436]	USN VP-5, NAS Jacksonville, FL
	168437	Boeing P-8A Poseidon [LA-437]	USN VP-5, NAS Jacksonville, FL
	168438	Boeing P-8A Poseidon [LA-438]	USN VP-5, NAS Jacksonville, FL
	168439	Boeing P-8A Poseidon [LA-439]	USN VP-5, NAS Jacksonville, FL
	168440	Boeing P-8A Poseidon [440]	USN VP-30, NAS Jacksonville, FL
	168754	Boeing P-8A Poseidon [LL-754]	USN VP-30, NAS Jacksonville, FL
	168755	Boeing P-8A Poseidon [LC-755]	USN VP-8, NAS Jacksonville, FL
	168756	Boeing P-8A Poseidon [756]	USN VP-30, NAS Jacksonville, FL
	168757	Boeing P-8A Poseidon [757]	USN VP-26, NAS Jacksonville, FL
	168758	Boeing P-8A Poseidon [LC-758]	USN VP-8, NAS Jacksonville, FL
	168759	Boeing P-8A Poseidon [LC-759]	USN VP-8, NAS Jacksonville, FL
	168760	Boeing P-8A Poseidon [LC-760]	USN VP-8, NAS Jacksonville, FL
	168761	Boeing P-8A Poseidon [LN-761]	USN VP-45, NAS Jacksonville, FL
	168762	Boeing P-8A Poseidon [LA-762]	USN VP-5, NAS Jacksonville, FL

Serial	Type (code/other identity)	Owner/operator, location or fate	Notes
168763	Boeing P-8A Poseidon [LD-763]	USN VP-10, NAS Jacksonville, FL	
168764	Boeing P-8A Poseidon [LD-764]	USN VP-10, NAS Jacksonville, FL	
168848	Boeing P-8A Poseidon [848]	USN VP-26, NAS Jacksonville, FL	
168849	Boeing P-8A Poseidon [849]	USN VP-10, NAS Jacksonville, FL	
168850	Boeing P-8A Poseidon [850]	USN VP-10, NAS Jacksonville, FL	
168851	Boeing P-8A Poseidon [LC-851]	USN VP-8, NAS Jacksonville, FL	
168852	Boeing P-8A Poseidon [852]	USN VP-45, NAS Jacksonville, FL	
168853	Boeing P-8A Poseidon [853]	USN VP-26, NAS Jacksonville, FL	
168854	Boeing P-8A Poseidon [854]	USN VP-40, NAS Whidbey Island, WA	
168855	Boeing P-8A Poseidon [855]	USN VP-45, NAS Jacksonville, FL	
168856	Boeing P-8A Poseidon [856]	USN VP-30, NAS Jacksonville, FL	
168857	Boeing P-8A Poseidon [LK-857]	USN VP-26, NAS Jacksonville, FL	
168858	Boeing P-8A Poseidon [858]	USN VP-45, NAS Jacksonville, FL	
168859	Boeing P-8A Poseidon [859]	USN VP-45, NAS Jacksonville, FL	
168860	Boeing P-8A Poseidon [860]	USN VP-45, NAS Jacksonville, FL	
168980	Boeing C-40A Clipper [980]	USN VR-61, Fort Worth JRB, TX	
168981	Boeing C-40A Clipper [981]	USN VR-61, Fort Worth JRB, TX	
168996	Boeing P-8A Poseidon [996]	USN VP-30, NAS Jacksonville, FL	
168997	Boeing P-8A Poseidon [997]	USN VP-46, NAS Whidbey Island, WA	
168998	Boeing P-8A Poseidon [998]	USN VP-46, NAS Whidbey Island, WA	
168999	Boeing P-8A Poseidon [999]	USN VP-30, NAS Jacksonville, FL	
169000	Boeing P-8A Poseidon [000]	USN VP-16, NAS Jacksonville, FL	
169001	Boeing P-8A Poseidon [001]	USN VP-30, NAS Jacksonville, FL	
169002	Boeing P-8A Poseidon [002]	USN VP-30, NAS Jacksonville, FL	
169003	Boeing P-8A Poseidon [003]	USN VP-8, NAS Jacksonville, FL	
169004	Boeing P-8A Poseidon [004]	USN VP-30, NAS Jacksonville, FL	
169005	Boeing P-8A Poseidon [LF-005]	USN VP-16, NAS Jacksonville, FL	
169006	Boeing P-8A Poseidon [006]	USN VP-30, NAS Jacksonville, FL	
169007	Boeing P-8A Poseidon [LC-007]	USN VP-8, NAS Jacksonville, FL	
169008	Boeing P-8A Poseidon [008]	USN VP-30, NAS Jacksonville, FL	
169009	Boeing P-8A Poseidon [009]	USN (on order)	
169010	Boeing P-8A Poseidon [010]	USN (on order)	
169011	Boeing P-8A Poseidon [011]	USN (on order)	
169018	Lockheed KC-130J Hercules II [QH-018]	USMC VMGR-234, Fort Worth JRB, TX	
169036	Boeing C-40A Clipper [036]	USN VR-61, Fort Worth JRB, TX	
169225	Lockheed KC-130J Hercules II [BH-225]	USMC VMGR-252, Cherry Point MCAS, NC	
169226	Lockheed KC-130J Hercules II [QB-226]	USMC VMGR-352, Miramar MCAS, CA	
169227	Lockheed KC-130J Hercules II [QD-227]	USMC VMGR-152, Iwakuni MCAS, Japan	
169228	Lockheed KC-130J Hercules II [QH-228]	USMC VMGR-234, Fort Worth JRB, TX	
169229	Lockheed KC-130J Hercules II [QB-229]	USMC VMGR-352, Miramar MCAS, CA	
169324	Boeing P-8A Poseidon [324]	USN (on order)	
169325	Boeing P-8A Poseidon [325]	USN (on order)	
169326	Boeing P-8A Poseidon [326]	USN (on order)	
169327	Boeing P-8A Poseidon [327]	USN (on order)	
169328	Boeing P-8A Poseidon [328]	USN (on order)	
169329	Boeing P-8A Poseidon [329]	USN (on order)	
169330	Boeing P-8A Poseidon [330]	USN (on order)	
169331	Boeing P-8A Poseidon [331]	USN (on order)	
169332	Boeing P-8A Poseidon [332]	USN (on order)	
169...	Boeing P-8A Poseidon	USN (on order)	
169...	Boeing P-8A Poseidon	USN (on order)	
169...	Boeing P-8A Poseidon	USN (on order)	
169...	Boeing P-8A Poseidon	USN (on order)	
169...	Boeing P-8A Poseidon	USN (on order)	
169...	Boeing P-8A Poseidon	USN (on order)	
169...	Boeing P-8A Poseidon	USN (on order)	
169...	Boeing P-8A Poseidon	USN (on order)	
169...	Boeing P-8A Poseidon	USN (on order)	
169...	Boeing P-8A Poseidon	USN (on order)	
169...	Boeing P-8A Poseidon	USN (on order)	
169...	Boeing P-8A Poseidon	USN (on order)	
169...	Boeing C-40A Clipper	USN (on order)	
169...	Boeing C-40A Clipper	USN (on order)	

Notes	Serial	Type (code/other identity)	Owner/operator, location or fate
	01	Gulfstream Aerospace C-37A Gulfstream V	USCG, Washington DC
	02	Gulfstream Aerospace C-37A Gulfstream V	USCG, Washington DC
	1502	Lockheed HC-130H Hercules	*To AMARG, August 2016*
	1503	Lockheed HC-130H Hercules	USCG, USCGS Clearwater, FL
	1701	Lockheed HC-130H Hercules	USCG, USCGS Sacramento, CA
	1702	Lockheed HC-130H Hercules	USCG, USCGS Sacramento, CA
	1703	Lockheed HC-130H Hercules	USCG, USCGS Sacramento, CA
	1704	Lockheed HC-130H Hercules	USCG, USCGS Sacramento, CA
	1706	Lockheed HC-130H Hercules	USCG, USCGS Clearwater, FL
	1707	Lockheed HC-130H Hercules	USCG, USCGS Barbers Point, HI
	1709	Lockheed HC-130H Hercules	USCG, USCGS Sacramento, CA
	1711	Lockheed HC-130H Hercules	USCG, USCGS Clearwater, FL
	1712	Lockheed HC-130H Hercules	USCG, USCGS Kodiak, AK
	1715	Lockheed HC-130H Hercules	USCG, USCGS Clearwater, FL
	1716	Lockheed HC-130H Hercules	USCG, USCGS Barbers Point, HI
	1718	Lockheed HC-130H Hercules	USCG, USCGS Clearwater, FL
	1720	Lockheed HC-130H Hercules	USCG, USCGS Barbers Point, HI
	1790	Lockheed HC-130H Hercules	USCG, USCGS Clearwater, FL
	2001	Lockheed HC-130J Hercules II	USCG, USCGS Elizabeth City, NC
	2002	Lockheed HC-130J Hercules II	USCG, USCGS Elizabeth City, NC
	2003	Lockheed HC-130J Hercules II	USCG, USCGS Elizabeth City, NC
	2004	Lockheed HC-130J Hercules II	USCG, USCGS Elizabeth City, NC
	2005	Lockheed HC-130J Hercules II	USCG, USCGS Elizabeth City, NC
	2006	Lockheed HC-130J Hercules II	USCG, USCGS Elizabeth City, NC
	2007	Lockheed HC-130J Hercules II	USCG, USCGS Elizabeth City, NC
	2008	Lockheed HC-130J Hercules II	USCG, USCGS Elizabeth City, NC
	2009	Lockheed HC-130J Hercules II	USCG, USCGS Elizabeth City, NC
	2010	Lockheed HC-130J Hercules II	USCG (on order)

Boeing P-8A Poseidon 168853 of the US Navy's VP-30, based at Jacksonville, Florida is one of many now in service, slowly replacing the P-3 Orion.

Aircraft in US Government or Military Service with Civil Registrations

Serial	Type (code/other identity)	Owner/operator, location or fate	Notes
N85	Canadair CL.601 Challenger	Federal Aviation Administration, Oklahoma City, OK	
N86	Canadair CL.601 Challenger	Federal Aviation Administration, Oklahoma City, OK	
N87	Canadair CL.601 Challenger	Federal Aviation Administration, Oklahoma City, OK	
N88	Canadair CL.604 Challenger	Federal Aviation Administration, Oklahoma City, OK	
N89	Canadair CL.605 Challenger	Federal Aviation Administration, Oklahoma City, OK	
N90	Canadair CL.605 Challenger	Federal Aviation Administration, Oklahoma City, OK	

The list below is not intended to be a complete list of military aviation sites on the Internet. The sites listed cover Museums, Locations, Air Forces, Companies and Organisations that are mentioned elsewhere in 'Military Aircraft Markings'. Sites listed are in English or contain sufficient English to be reasonably easily understood. Each site address was correct at the time of going to press. Additions are welcome, via the usual address found at the front of the book, or via e-mail to admin@aviation-links.co.uk. An up to date copy of this list is to be found at The 'Military Aircraft Markings' Web Site, http://www.militaryaircraftmarkings.co.uk/.

Name of Site	Web Address All prefixed 'http://'
MILITARY SITES-UK	
No 1 Sqn	www.raf.mod.uk/organisation/1squadron.cfm
No 2 Sqn	www.raf.mod.uk/organisation/2squadron.cfm
No 3 Sqn	www.raf.mod.uk/organisation/3squadron.cfm
No 4(R) Sqn	www.raf.mod.uk/organisation/4squadron.cfm
No 5 Sqn	www.raf.mod.uk/organisation/5squadron.cfm
No 6 Sqn	www.raf.mod.uk/organisation/6squadron.cfm
No 7 Sqn	www.raf.mod.uk/organisation/7squadron.cfm
No 8 Sqn	8squadron.co.uk/
No 9 Sqn	www.raf.mod.uk/organisation/9squadron.cfm
No 10 Sqn	www.raf.mod.uk/organisation/10squadron.cfm
No 11 Sqn	www.raf.mod.uk/organisation/11squadron.cfm
No 14 Sqn	www.raf.mod.uk/organisation/14squadron.cfm
No 15(R) Sqn	www.raf.mod.uk/organisation/15squadron.cfm
No 17(R) Sqn	www.raf.mod.uk/organisation/17squadron.cfm
No 18 Sqn	www.raf.mod.uk/organisation/18squadron.cfm
No 24 Sqn	www.raf.mod.uk/organisation/24squadron.cfm
No 27 Sqn	www.raf.mod.uk/organisation/27squadron.cfm
No 28(R) Sqn	www.raf.mod.uk/organisation/28squadron.cfm
No 29(R) Sqn	www.raf.mod.uk/organisation/29squadron.cfm
No 30 Sqn	www.raf.mod.uk/organisation/30squadron.cfm
No 31 Sqn	www.raf.mod.uk/organisation/31squadron.cfm
No 32(The Royal) Sqn	www.raf.mod.uk/organisation/32squadron.cfm
No 33 Sqn	www.raf.mod.uk/organisation/33squadron.cfm
No 39 Sqn	www.raf.mod.uk/organisation/39squadron.cfm
No 41(R) Sqn	www.raf.mod.uk/organisation/41squadron.cfm
No 45(R) Sqn	www.raf.mod.uk/organisation/45squadron.cfm
No 47 Sqn	www.raf.mod.uk/organisation/47squadron.cfm
No 51 Sqn	www.raf.mod.uk/organisation/51squadron.cfm
No 55(R) Sqn	www.raf.mod.uk/organisation/55squadron.cfm
No 60(R) Sqn	www.raf.mod.uk/organisation/60squadron.cfm
No 72(R) Sqn	www.raf.mod.uk/organisation/72squadron.cfm
No 84 Sqn	www.raf.mod.uk/organisation/84squadron.cfm
No 99 Sqn	www.raf.mod.uk/organisation/99squadron.cfm
No 100 Sqn	www.raf.mod.uk/organisation/100squadron.cfm
No 101 Sqn	www.raf.mod.uk/organisation/101squadron.cfm
No 208(R) Sqn	www.raf.mod.uk/organisation/208squadron.cfm
No 230 Sqn	www.raf.mod.uk/organisation/230squadron.cfm
No 617 Sqn	www.raf.mod.uk/organisation/617squadron.cfm
No 703 NAS	www.royalnavy.mod.uk/our-organisation/the-fighting-arms/fleet-air-arm/support-and-training/703-naval-air-squadronng
No 705 NAS	www.royalnavy.mod.uk/our-organisation/the-fighting-arms/fleet-air-arm/support-and-training/705-naval-air-squadron
No 727 NAS	www.royalnavy.mod.uk/our-organisation/the-fighting-arms/fleet-air-arm/support-and-training/727-naval-air-squadron
No 736 NAS	www.royalnavy.mod.uk/our-organisation/the-fighting-arms/fleet-air-arm/hawk-jets/736-naval-air-squadron
No 750 NAS	www.royalnavy.mod.uk/our-organisation/the-fighting-arms/fleet-air-arm/support-and-training/750-naval-air-squadron
No 809 NAS	www.royalnavy.mod.uk/our-organisation/the-fighting-arms/fleet-air-arm/future-aircraft/809-naval-air-squadron
No 814 NAS	www.royalnavy.mod.uk/our-organisation/the-fighting-arms/fleet-air-arm/helicopter-squadrons/merlin-mk2/814-naval-air-squadron

Name of Site	Web Address All prefixed 'http://')
No 815 NAS	www.royalnavy.mod.uk/our-organisation/the-fighting-arms/fleet-air-arm/helicopter-squadrons/lynx-mk8/815-naval-air-squadron
No 820 NAS	www.royalnavy.mod.uk/our-organisation/the-fighting-arms/fleet-air-arm/helicopter-squadrons/merlin-mk2/820-naval-air-squadron
No 824 NAS	www.royalnavy.mod.uk/our-organisation/the-fighting-arms/fleet-air-arm/helicopter-squadrons/merlin-mk2/824-naval-air-squadron
No 825 NAS	www.royalnavy.mod.uk/our-organisation/the-fighting-arms/fleet-air-arm/helicopter-squadrons/wildcat/825-naval-air-squadron
No 829 NAS	www.royalnavy.mod.uk/our-organisation/the-fighting-arms/fleet-air-arm/helicopter-squadrons/merlin-mk2/829-naval-air-squadron
No 845 NAS	www.royalnavy.mod.uk/our-organisation/the-fighting-arms/fleet-air-arm/helicopter-squadrons/merlin-mk-3/845-naval-air-squadron
No 846 NAS	www.royalnavy.mod.uk/our-organisation/the-fighting-arms/fleet-air-arm/helicopter-squadrons/merlin-mk-3/846-naval-air-squadron
No 847 NAS	www.royalnavy.mod.uk/our-organisation/the-fighting-arms/fleet-air-arm/helicopter-squadrons/wildcat/847-naval-air-squadron
No 849 NAS	www.royalnavy.mod.uk/our-organisation/the-fighting-arms/fleet-air-arm/helicopter-squadrons/sea-king-asac-mk7/849-naval-air-squadron
The Army Air Corps	www.army.mod.uk/aviation/air.aspx
Fleet Air Arm	www.royalnavy.mod.uk/our-organisation/the-fighting-arms/fleet-air-arm
Ministry of Defence	www.mod.uk/
QinetiQ	www.qinetiq.com/
RAF Benson	www.raf.mod.uk/rafbenson/
RAF Brize Norton	www.raf.mod.uk/rafbrizenorton/
RAF Coningsby	www.raf.mod.uk/rafconingsby/
RAF Cosford	www.raf.mod.uk/rafcosford/
RAF Linton-on-Ouse	www.raf.mod.uk/raflintononouse/
RAF Lossiemouth	www.raf.mod.uk/raflossiemouth/
RAF Marham	www.raf.mod.uk/rafmarham/
RAF Northolt	www.raf.mod.uk/rafnortholt/
RAF Odiham	www.raf.mod.uk/rafodiham/
RAF Shawbury	www.raf.mod.uk/rafshawbury/
RAF Valley	www.raf.mod.uk/rafvalley/
RAF Waddington	www.raf.mod.uk/rafwaddington/
RAF Wittering	www.raf.mod.uk/rafwittering/
Red Arrows	www.raf.mod.uk/reds/
Royal Air Force	www.raf.mod.uk/
Royal Air Force Reserves	www.raf.mod.uk/rafreserves/
University Air Squadrons	www.raf.mod.uk/universityairsquadrons/findasquadron/

MILITARY SITES-US

Air Combat Command	www.acc.af.mil/
Air Force Reserve Command	www.afrc.af.mil/
Air National Guard	www.ang.af.mil/
Aviano Air Base	www.aviano.af.mil/
Liberty Wing Home Page (48th FW)	www.lakenheath.af.mil/
NASA	www.nasa.gov/
Mildenhall	www.mildenhall.af.mil/
Ramstein Air Base	www.ramstein.af.mil/
Spangdahlem Air Base	www.spangdahlem.af.mil/
USAF	www.af.mil/
USAF Europe	www.usafe.af.mil/
USAF World Wide Web Sites	www.af.mil/publicwebsites/index.asp
US Army	www.army.mil/
US Marine Corps	www.marines.mil/
US Navy	www.navy.mil/
US Navy Patrol Squadrons (unofficial)	www.vpnavy.com/

MILITARY AVIATION SITES ON THE INTERNET

Name of Site	Web Address All prefixed 'http://'
MILITARY SITES-ELSEWHERE	
Armée de l'Air	www.defense.gouv.fr/air/
Aeronautica Militare	www.aeronautica.difesa.it
Austrian Armed Forces (in German)	www.bmlv.gv.at/
Finnish Defence Force	www.puolustusvoimat.fi/en/
Forca Aerea Portuguesa	www.emfa.pt/
German Marine	www.deutschemarine.de/
Greek Air Force	www.haf.gr/en/
Irish Air Corps	www.military.ie/air-corps
Israeli Defence Forces	www.idf.il/english/
Luftforsvaret	www.mil.no/
Luftwaffe	www.luftwaffe.de/
NATO	www.nato.int/
Royal Australian Air Force	www.airforce.gov.au/
Royal Canadian Air Force	www.airforce.forces.gc.ca/
Royal Danish Air Force (in Danish)	forsvaret.dk/
Royal Netherlands AF	www.defensie.nl/luchtmacht
Royal New Zealand AF	www.airforce.mil.nz/
Singapore Air Force	www.mindef.gov.sg/rsaf/
South African AF Site (unofficial)	www.saairforce.co.za/
Swedish Air Force	www.forsvarsmakten.se/sv/Forband-och-formagor/Flygvapnet/
Turkish Air Force	www.hvkk.tsk.tr/en-us/
AIRCRAFT & AERO ENGINE MANUFACTURERS	
Airbus Defence & Space	airbusdefenceandspace.com/
Airbus Group	www.airbusgroup.com/
BAE Systems	www.baesystems.com/
Beechcraft	www.beechcraft.com/
Bell Helicopter Textron	www.bellhelicopter.textron.com/
Boeing	www.boeing.com/
Bombardier	www.bombardier.com/
Britten-Norman	www.britten-norman.com/
Dassault	www.dassault-aviation.com/
Embraer	www.embraer.com/
General Electric	www.ge.com/
Grob Aircraft AG	grob-aircraft.com/en/
Gulfstream Aerospace	www.gulfstream.com/
Kaman Aerospace	www.kaman.com/
Leonardo	www.leonardocompany.com/
Lockheed Martin	www.lockheedmartin.com/
Rolls-Royce	www.rolls-royce.com/
Sikorsky	www.sikorsky.com/
UK AVIATION MUSEUMS	
Boscombe Down Aviation Collection, Old Sarum	www.boscombedownaviationcollection.co.uk/
Bournemouth Aviation Museum	www.aviation-museum.co.uk/
Brooklands Museum	www.brooklandsmuseum.com/
City of Norwich Aviation Museum	www.cnam.org.uk/
de Havilland Aircraft Museum	www.dehavillandmuseum.co.uk/
Dumfries & Galloway Aviation Museum	www.dumfriesaviationmuseum.com/
Fleet Air Arm Museum	www.fleetairarm.com/
Gatwick Aviation Museum	www.gatwick-aviation-museum.co.uk/
IWM, Duxford	www.iwm.org.uk/visits/iwm-duxford
Imperial War Museum, Duxford (unofficial)	www.axtd59.dsl.pipex.com/
The Jet Age Museum	www.jetagemuseum.org/
Lincs Aviation Heritage Centre	www.lincsaviation.co.uk/
Midland Air Museum	www.midlandairmuseum.co.uk/
Museum of Army Flying	www.armyflying.com/
Museum of Berkshire Aviation	www.museumofberkshireaviation.co.uk/
Museum of Science & Industry, Manchester	www.mosi.org.uk/
National Museum of Flight, East Fortune	www.nms.ac.uk/our_museums/museum_of_flight.aspx
Newark Air Museum	www.newarkairmuseum.org/

Name of Site	Web Address All prefixed 'http://')
North East Aircraft Museum	www.nelsam.org.uk/NEAM/NEAM.htm
RAF Museum, Cosford & Hendon	www.rafmuseum.org.uk/
Science Museum, South Kensington	www.sciencemuseum.org.uk/
South Yorkshire Aircraft Museum	www.southyorkshireaircraftmuseum.org.uk/
Yorkshire Air Museum, Elvington	www.yorkshireairmuseum.org/

AVIATION SOCIETIES

Air Britain	www.air-britain.com/
Air Yorkshire	www.airyorkshire.org.uk/
British Aircraft Preservation Council	www.bapc.org.uk/
LAAS International	www.laasdata.com/
Military Aviation Review	militaryaviationreview.com/
Royal Aeronautical Society	aerosociety.com/
Scramble (Dutch Aviation Society)	www.scramble.nl/
Solent Aviation Society	www.solent-aviation-society.co.uk/
Spitfire Society	www.spitfiresociety.com/
The Aviation Society Manchester	www.tasmanchester.com/
Ulster Aviation Society	www.ulsteraviationsociety.org/
Wolverhampton Aviation Group	www.wolverhamptonaviationgroup.co.uk/

OPERATORS OF HISTORIC AIRCRAFT

The Aircraft Restoration Company	www.arc-duxford.co.uk/
Battle of Britain Memorial Flight	www.raf.mod.uk/bbmf/
The Catalina Society	www.catalina.org.uk/
Hangar 11 Collection	www.hangar11.co.uk/
Horizon Aircraft Services	www.horizonaircraft.co.uk/
Navy Wings	www.navywings.org.uk/
The Fighter Collection	www.fighter-collection.com/
The Real Aeroplane Company	www.realaero.com/
The Shuttleworth Collection	www.shuttleworth.org/

SITES RELATING TO SPECIFIC TYPES OF MILITARY AIRCRAFT

The 655 Maintenance & Preservation Society	www.xm655.com/
B-24 Liberator	www.b24bestweb.com/
C-130 Hercules	www.c-130hercules.net/
EE Canberra	www.bywat.co.uk/
English Electric Lightning – Vertical Reality	www.aviation-picture-hangar.co.uk/Lightning.html
The Eurofighter site	www.eurofighter.com/
The ex FRADU Canberra Site	www.fradu-canberras.co.uk/
The ex FRADU Hunter Site	www.fradu-hunters.co.uk/
F-4 Phantom II Society	www.f4phantom.com/
F-15E.info: Strike Eagle	www.f-15e.info/
F-16: The Complete Reference	www.f-16.net/
The Gripen	www.gripen.com/
Jet Provost Heaven	www.jetprovosts.com
K5083 – Home Page (Hawker Hurricane)	www.k5083.mistral.co.uk/
Lockheed SR-71 Blackbird	www.wvi.com/~lelandh/sr-71~1.htm
The MiG-21 Page	www.topedge.com/panels/aircraft/sites/kraft/mig.htm
P-3 Orion Research Group	www.p3orion.nl/
Thunder & Lightnings (Postwar British Aircraft)	www.thunder-and-lightnings.co.uk/
UK Apache Resource Centre	www.ukapache.com/

Name of Site	Web Address All prefixed 'http://')
MISCELLANEOUS	
Aerodata Software Ltd.	www.aerodata.org/
AeroResource	www.aeroresource.co.uk/
The AirNet Web Site	www.aviation-links.co.uk/
Aviation Databases	www.aviationdatabases.com/
Delta Reflex	www.deltareflex.com/forum
Demobbed – Out of Service British Military Aircraft	demobbed.org.uk/
Euro Demobbed	www.eurodemobbed.org.uk/
Fighter Control	fightercontrol.co.uk/
Freebird Aviation Database	www.freebirddb.com/
Iconic Aircraft	www.iconicaircraft.co.uk/
Joseph F. Baugher's US Military Serials Site	www.joebaugher.com/
The 'Military Aircraft Markings' Web Site	www.militaryaircraftmarkings.co.uk/
Pacific Aviation Database Organisation	www.gfiapac.com/
PlaneBaseNG	www.planebase.biz/
Target Lock Military Aviation E-zine	www.targetlock.org.uk/
Thunder & Lightnings: Airfield Viewing Guides	www.thunder-and-lightnings.co.uk/spotting/
UK Airshow Review	www.airshows.co.uk/
UK Military Aircraft Serials Resource Centre	www.ukserials.com/

Serial	Type	Operator

Serial	Type	Operator

Serial	Type	Operator

Serial	Type	Operator

Serial	Type	Operator

Reg	Type	Owner or Operator

OVERSEAS MILITARY AIRCRAFT MARKINGS

SAUDI ARABIA

HZ-124	Airbus A.340-211	RSAF 1 Sqn, Riyadh

Türk Hava Kuvvetleri (THK)/Turkish Air Force & Turkish Government

4001	Canadair NF-5B-2000 Freedom Fighter [4]	THK 134 Filo, Turkish Stars/3 AJEÜ, Konya
4026	Canadair NF-5B-2000 Freedom Fighter [1]	THK 134 Filo, Turkish Stars/3 AJEÜ, Konya

UAE Government

A6-PFE	Boeing 787-9	Amiri Flight, Abu Dhabi

US-BASED USAF AIRCRAFT

Pilatus U-28A

80700	Pilatus U-28A (N600KP/08-0700)	USAF 319th SOS/1st SOW, Hurlburt Field, FL

BRITISH MILITARY AIRCRAFT MARKINGS

WP266	EoN AP.5 Primary (BAPC 423)	Privately owned, Fishburn

HISTORIC AIRCRAFT IN OVERSEAS MARKINGS

SIERRA LEONE

SL-01	Westland Commando Mk.2C	Privately owned, Dunsfold

USA

210766	Douglas C-47B Skytrain (composite) (K-1) [4U]	Wings Museum, Balcombe, W Sussex